Encyclopedia of Science Fiction

DON D'AMMASSA

■® Facts On File, Inc.

Encyclopedia of Science Fiction

Copyright © 2005 by Don D'Ammassa

Facts On File, Inc.
132 West 31st Street
New York NY 10001

Library of Congress Cataloging-in-Publication Data

D'Ammassa, Don, 1946–
Encyclopedia of science fiction / Don D'Ammassa.
p. cm.
Includes bibliographical references and index.
ISBN 0-8160-5924-1 (hardcover : acid-free paper)
1. Science fiction, American—Encyclopedias. 2. Science fiction, English—Encyclopedias. I. Title.
PS374.S35D33 2004
813'.0876209'003—dc222004013819

Text design by Joan M. Toro
Cover design by Semadar Megged

Printed in the United States of America

VB FOF 10 9 8 7 6 5 4 3 2 1

This book is printed on acid-free paper.

CONTENTS

INTRODUCTION

Welcome to the world of science fiction, sometimes known familiarly as "SF," but rarely "Sci-Fi," which is generally considered to be pejorative by aficionados of the genre, and more appropriate for films than literature. Science fiction is one of the three subdivisions of fantastic literature, the other two being fantasy fiction and supernatural horror. Although definitions vary and some individual works may blur the distinction between one branch and another, most fantastic or speculative stories and novels can—by general consensus—be placed in one of the three categories. Science fiction is the youngest of the three, but since the late 1940s it has been by far the most popular, and the total number of science fiction titles published in book form presently exceeds that of fantasy and supernatural fiction combined. That dominance has been challenged during the last few years by the increasing popularity of fantasy fiction.

This book provides a broad overview of the field, its major authors and works. With more than 18,000 identified books and countless short stories, it obviously would be impossible to cover the field exhaustively in a single volume. Included here are profiles of most of the more significant writers, describing the highlights of their careers, their selected works, and their places in the overall spectrum of science fiction. Additionally, there are entries on specific stories, novels, or series. The works chosen for individual treatment are either of extraordinary quality or historical significance, including many that have proven popular in high school and college classrooms, or are included as examples of a subset of the field not sufficiently described elsewhere in the book. Keep in mind that the most "important" work is not necessarily the best written, although that is often the case as well. Sometimes, less important authors happened to produce a story whose significance is unrelated to the quality of the writing. Such authors might have suggested a concept that spawned superior imitations or involved an idea too unique to be repeated.

Science fiction developed as a series of intertwined schools of writing. Jules Verne, known for his series of novels about fantastic voyages, is often credited as the first major author of the science fiction adventure story. Stories in this tradition often focus on a marvelous invention or wondrous journey and generally have a less than serious tone and perhaps superficial characterization. H. G. Wells, who invented or at least popularized many of the major themes in the genre, is generally cited as the father of serious science fiction, novels that try to predict the future or that describe how people might react to a speculative situation such as time travel, invaders from Mars, or the gift of invisibility. Wells and those who followed him were concerned with character, prose, and commentary.

During the 1920s and 1930s, pulp fiction magazines proliferated in the United States in particular; many of them were either exclusively or at least partially devoted to scientific romances. These magazines featured lurid covers, often incorporating bug-eyed monsters, stylized spaceships, and scantily clad women, and they obviously targeted adolescent males as their primary audience. Most of the stories published in them were crude, poorly plotted, badly written, and often contained questionable science, relying on strange settings and unbridled specula-tion to make up for any literary deficiencies. But something began to happen in the 1940s that would eventually change everything. A handful of writers with genuine ability wanted to write science fiction, and since the pulp magazines were the only game in town, that is where these writers submitted their stories. As a result, readers might find, in the same issue of a magazine, a finely crafted, thoughtfully rendered story alongside the latest marginally liter-ate space adventure.

This uneasy balance began to shift in the 1950s with the advent of paperback books. Publishers of hardcover books were still generally suspicious of anything labeled as science fiction, but paperbacks were a different matter entirely. Many pulp writers made the transition to paperback—some of them eminently forgettable, but some from among the ranks of the better writers. Then came the 1960s and the "New Wave," a movement initially cen-tered in England that sought to apply mainstream literary qualities to science fiction. A similar but less consolidated trend followed in the United States, exemplified by Harlan Ellison, Roger Zelazny, Samuel R. Delany, and Ursula K. Le Guin. The balance shifted dramatically over the next sev-eral years, and SF writers such as Jack Vance, Philip K. Dick, and Ray Bradbury have now gained respect outside the field, while at the same time mainstream authors such as Margaret Atwood, Marge Piercy, Doris Lessing, and Anthony Burgess can borrow science fiction devices without being drummed out of the literary club.

There is no clear explanation for the immense popularity of science fiction in preference to fanta-sy, particularly in the United States. Possibly it is because Americans are so fond of, and dependent upon, technology. Possibly it is because we found it easier to lose ourselves in a fantastic world that might just be possible rather than in a magical one that we know is not. It could also be that science fiction embraces such a wide variety of themes and story types—space operas, military adventures, utopias and dystopias, time travel, alternate universes, alien creatures and civilizations, mys-teries, and rationalized psychic powers. There is something in science fiction for almost any reader's taste, whereas fantasy seems predominant-ly designed to satisfy those who enjoy lengthy his-torical novels set in mythical lands, perhaps with a touch of magic. The recent surge in the number of new fantasy titles has shown no evolution of that field, and the vast majority of authors seem con-tent to rewrite stories that have proved popular in the past. Science fiction readers are more interest-ed in the history of the field, and the direction in which it is moving.

As is the case in most specialized fields, so too have science fiction writers and readers developed their own subset of terms and usages. Thus, *Encyclopedia of Science Fiction* includes a brief glos-sary explaining words or phrases used in this book and elsewhere that might have an obscure or spe-cialized meaning or connotations not easily dis-cernible to the outsider. There is also a bibliography and a history of the genre's two major awards—the Hugo Award, presented at the annual World Science Fiction Convention, and the Nebula Award, selected by the Science Fiction and Fantasy Writers of America. I hope that curious readers unfamiliar with the field will find this to be a help-ful guide to the past and present state of science fic-tion, and that it will also help point the way to more of the best the genre has to offer.

Adam Link, Robot
Eando Binder
(1965)

Eando Binder was the pseudonym used jointly by brothers Earl and Otto Binder. Although they were for the most part typical pulp adventure writers during the 1930s, and minor novelists in the decades that followed, they produced one character for a series of stories that assured them a permanent place in the history of the genre. At the time, robots were not uncommon plot elements, depicted either as machines out of control or serving as part of the window dressing for a futuristic setting. The Adam Link series, written by Otto alone under their joint name, first appeared in magazines between 1939 and 1942. The title Adam was a revolutionary character for his time, because not only was the robot simply a sympathetic character with genuine emotions, but he was also the narrator of the stories.

The earlier stories in the series, most of which were incorporated into a disjointed novel as *Adam Link, Robot* in 1965, are much less melodramatic than the later ones. Adam's creator dies under mysterious circumstances, and Adam is believed to be responsible for the deed. When the authorities seek to destroy Adam as a dangerous machine, legal efforts are launched not just to prevent his destruction but also to acknowledge him as an intelligent being with personal rights. Although the story is sometimes awkwardly written, the plot is surprisingly intelligent and thoughtful, and it aroused considerable attention at the time of its publication. It was later foreshortened into an episode of the television series *The Outer Limits,* although in this adaptation the ending was altered so that Adam dies prematurely. In the stories, however, he is vindicated, finds a way to support himself, eventually settles down with a "female" robot named Eve, and participates in sporting events and other human activities. Subsequent stories became more typical, grandiose adventure stories pitting Adam against evil robots and aliens until he ultimately saves the world.

Adam Link's influence on the field was eclipsed quickly when Isaac ASIMOV started his own series about robots, which quickly became the standard that has prevailed ever since. It is likely that Asimov had read the first Adam Link story and was inspired to improve on the concept. Binder's story may be more important for its influence than as a creation in its own right, but the story has withstood the passage of the years remarkably well and is still an entertaining diversion.

Adams, Douglas
(1952–2001)

The English author Douglas Adams was educated at Cambridge University. His first serious brush with science fiction came as a writer and script editor for the popular British television series *Doctor Who.* For that program, he wrote three of the more popular installments: "City of Death," "The Invasion of Time," and "Pirate Planet," and the never completed "Shada." He is most famous as the author of the Hitch-Hiker series—originally written as a radio play, later turned into a novel and several sequels, and eventually brought to television by the BBC. (A more elaborate film version is currently under development.) The popularity of the series in Europe has been rivaled only by that of Terry Pratchett's Discworld series, but both in Europe and in the United States this popularity was less prevalent among seasoned SF readers than it was with the general public.

Although humor has always been a significant element in science fiction, SF works that depend primarily on humor generally have been regarded by critics as of less merit than "serious" fiction. This prejudice is deeply rooted, and for a long time seemed completely unshakable. However, with the publication of *The Hitch-Hiker's Guide to the Galaxy* (1979), it became much more difficult to dismiss humorous SF out of hand. Nevertheless, it is not altogether surprising that genre writers made no significant effort to emulate Adams's success. The near uniqueness of Adams's work is probably a contributing factor to its continued popularity.

The humor in the Hitch-Hiker series is primarily slapstick, seasoned with mild satire, wordplay, and absurd situations. Earth has been destroyed in order to make room for an interstellar highway, and Arthur Dent, apparently the lone survivor, is rescued by an alien visitor who was doing research for the latest edition of the travel guide of the title. They subsequently encounter a variety of increasingly bizarre characters including an alien spaceship captain with a fondness for truly awful verse, a two-headed space rogue who is also president of the galaxy, Marvin the paranoid robot, and even less-likely persons, human and otherwise. Their travels are made easier by the use of babel fish, a convenient animal that—when inserted in one's ear—functions as a universal translator. Their misguided and frequently hilarious adventures lampoon a variety of targets, not the least of which is the science fiction genre itself.

The story continues in *The Restaurant at the Edge of the Universe* (1980), *Life, the Universe and Everything* (1982), and *So Long and Thanks for All the Fish* (1984), and concludes in *Mostly Harmless*

(1992). Adams also had added short embellishments in *The More Than Complete Hitch-Hiker's Guide* (1987) and was working on a further installment, incomplete at the time of his death and included in the posthumous collection *The Salmon of Doubt* (2003). Arthur Dent pays a visit to the end of time, then goes into the past to visit prehistoric Earth, where he discovers that the human race was actually created as an organic super computer. Still on his quest to discover the true meaning of the universe, he investigates the reasons why all of the dolphins abandoned Earth and then helps his companion unravel the truth about his daughter. The last two volumes never measured up to the first three, however, depending too heavily on variations of jokes and situations already employed.

Adams began a new series in 1987 with *Dirk Gently's Holistic Detective Agency,* and continued it in *The Long Dark Tea-Time of the Soul* (1988); but this series never approached the success of his first inspiration. The hero of these books, Dirk Gently, is an atypical private detective, which allowed Adams to spoof that genre as well as a host of fantastic fiction conventions. In the first volume, he is hired to investigate a series of mysterious murders that appear to have a supernatural explanation. The sequel further distorts the boundaries among genres when Dirk discovers that at least some of the ancient gods were actually living entities and not supernatural creatures, and that they have survived into the modern age. The Dirk Gently stories display a more restrained brand of humor than Adams's other fiction, and they seem at times hastily written and uneven in quality.

Although the Hitch-Hiker books are almost certain to remain popular for generations to come, Adams has not proven to be an influential figure within the genre. His success is almost anomalous. He occupies a small but distinguished territory of his own, but has not had any noticeable impact on his fellow writers.

Aldiss, Brian W.
(1925–)

The British writer Brian W. Aldiss had published some minor mainstream fiction before turning to science fiction in 1954. The bulk of his fiction thereafter has been within the genre, although he also enjoyed some success with mainstream fiction, and wrote drama, poetry, and a considerable body of nonfiction. A prolific short story writer, he was mildly controversial during the first few years of his career in the genre because of his use of mainstream literary techniques and frank sexual themes, and because of his avoidance of the engineering and scientific jargon and emphasis that were prevalent at that time. It was the genre and not the author who changed, and Aldiss's stature has remained high throughout the upheavals that have altered the field dramatically during the last few decades. Aldiss also wrote an influential critique of the genre, *The Billion Year Spree,* later revised as *The Trillion Year Spree.*

His first few novels were competent but unmemorable—with the exception of his NON-STOP, which first appeared in 1958 and which was published in the United States as *Starship.* The story takes place aboard an enormous starship whose occupants have evolved into a variant form of humanity after several generations of isolation, with changes both physical and psychological. *The Long Afternoon of Earth* (1962, also published as *Hothouse*) also explored the possibility of further human evolution, in this case on a distant future Earth whose ecology has evolved into that of a planet-wide jungle after the Earth ceased to rotate normally. Although the science is open to question, the story itself is effective, and the image of humans overwhelmed by natural forces remains provocative. Aldiss continued to speculate about the possible evolution of present humanity into another form.

During the 1960s, Aldiss turned to more immediate and serious themes, not always completely successfully, and used settings closer to the present day. *The Dark Light Years* (1964) dealt with xenophobia and the way in which technologically superior cultures deal with supposed inferiors, in this case an intelligent alien species on a distant world whose personal habits humans find intensely repulsive. In sharp contrast to his previous novels, the results are tragic, and humanity is not depicted in a favorable light. *Greybeard* (1964), which some critics consider his most successful novel, describes

a future in which universal sterility leads to the imminent extinction of the human race, and members of an aging population reflect on their individual and cultural shortcomings. Other work from this period was equally introspective and critical, tackling such subjects as the consequences of overpopulation, the erosion of individual freedom in an increasingly technological world, the nature of human responsibility to both society and the environment, and the question of what it really means to be human. Titles like "But Who Can Replace a Man?" and "All the World's Tears" accurately reflected the somber tones of these stories.

When the "New Wave" movement in the late 1960s challenged science fiction's disparagement of strong characterization, experimental prose styling, and other traditions that seemed to limit the growth of the field, Aldiss was an obvious recruit. The influence of mainstream literary techniques and experimentation became more obvious in his fiction. His novels *Barefoot in the Head* (1969) and *Report on Probability* A (1968) were clearly inspired by this new freedom, dealing in the former case with surrealistic imagery and in the latter with the multiple viewpoint narration made popular by Alain Robbe-Grillet and other non-genre writers. Aldiss's subsequent novels reverted to more conservative narrative techniques but his willingness to vary his prose in innovative ways has continued in much of his short fiction up through the present.

Although his short stories continued to command considerable respect, the novels during the 1970s were not widely popular, although *The Malacia Tapestry* (1976) is a powerful and underrated work set in an alternate world where artists have a much more prominent role than in ours and *Frankenstein Unbound* (1973), which was adapted as an uneven but interesting motion picture, contains some of his most evocative prose. The three-volume Helliconia series, published in the mid-1980s, marked a return to more traditional genre themes. Describing the development of a human society on a distant world that is slowly emerging from a lengthy ice age, it garnered both popular and critical acclaim and reestablished Aldiss as a major figure, certainly one of the half-dozen most popular British science fiction writers of all time, with the most respectable literary credentials since H. G. WELLS and a considerable following outside the traditional science fiction readership. The Helliconia trilogy reprises a common feature of the author's work: a set of characters caught up in events so completely beyond their power that they can do little, if anything, to affect the outcome. For the most part, Aldiss's characters accept their powerlessness with dignity and refuse to be cowed by their relative insignificance in the scheme of things.

With well over 300 published short stories, Aldiss is easily one of the genre's most productive writers at that length. The quality of his short fiction is surprisingly high given the volume, and includes numerous memorable stories. His single most famous short is "The SALIVA TREE," which merges the styles of H. G. Wells and H. P. LOVE-CRAFT to produce a chillingly evocative but highly literate story of deadly alien menace. "Super Toys Last All Summer Long," which was the basis for Steven Spielberg's film *A.I.* (2001), is a poignant examination of the relationship of parent to child. Another recurring theme in Aldiss's short fiction is the tendency of humans to abdicate personal responsibility—notably to machines, as in "But Who Can Replace a Man?" Occasionally he displays a dark sense of humor, as in "Let's Be Frank," in which a single personality inhabits a geometrically increasing number of bodies. Aldiss also has an eye for irony. In his very first genre story, "Poor Little Warrior," a hunter singlehandedly fells a gigantic alien life form, only to die when attacked by the parasites that live on the creature's body.

Aldiss has also demonstrated a fondness for reexamining work by classic authors and placing them in a new context. "The Saliva Tree" was a stylistic homage to H. G. Wells, but *An Island Called Moreau* (1981) is a straightforward update of Wells's *The ISLAND OF DOCTOR MOREAU*. In this case, the genetic manipulation of lower animals is being performed as part of a government project to develop more viable forms of life. As in the original, this novel examines the morality of human intervention in the normal process of evolution. In *Frankenstein Unbound* (1973), time travel allows the protagonist to return to the time of Victor Frankenstein, who turns out to be more than just a

fictional character, and Aldiss reprises another recurring theme as he examines the morality of using scientific knowledge to alter normal processes of life. His third major nod to classic writers was the less successful *Dracula Unbound* (1991), in which Bram Stoker discovers that humans have evolved into a vampiric race in the distant future and have sent an emissary back through time to ensure that human history proceeds properly, from their point of view.

It is more difficult for a writer who works primarily at shorter length to hold the attention of the reading public in any genre, and science fiction is only slightly exceptional in that regard. Despite the fact that he has written relatively few novels after the mid-1980s, Brian Aldiss has maintained his reputation as one of the foremost writers in the genre, and—along with Arthur C. Clarke—is one of the best-known British science fiction writers working today.

"All Pieces of a River Shore"
R. A. Lafferty
(1970)

R. A. Lafferty wrote a surprisingly large number of clever, quirky stories that revolved around an extraordinary, sometimes bizarre, concept. One of the most famous of these is "All Pieces of a River Shore," in which a very rich and eccentric man named Leo Nation decides to collect paintings of the Mississippi River—but not just ordinary paintings. During the 19th century, traveling entertainers would display enormous canvases, paintings of elaborate sections of the river shore. Nation acquires many of these panoramic canvases, but a handful seem different, almost as if they are not paintings at all. He believes that they are sections of one enormous photograph that captured the entire length of the Mississippi in one continuous shot.

With the assistance of an expert, Nation examines the fragments in more detail. The foliage and occasional birds provide clues that indicate the picture predates the European discovery of the New World. The picture itself seems impervious to fire, as though constructed of some alien material.

Heartened by his discoveries, Nation begins a concerted effort to find additional pieces, convinced that the complete picture will reveal a full 1,000 miles of primitive shoreline. As more pieces are added to a computerized database, Nation's companion begins to express anxiety and a disinclination to finish the project; he has a particular aversion to a few cloudy discolorations that cover some of the newly acquired sections. Ultimately, we discover that the pictures are actually a kind of microfilm taken by visitors to our planet during the last Ice Age and that the blotches are fingerprints of whatever gargantuan creature handled the material.

In this story, Lafferty used old science fiction devices in an innovative way. We never discover much about the alien visitors, but we do feel a sense of great wonder about the universe and the potentially insignificant role of humanity in that setting. The story is written in a deceptively light-hearted style, with surprisingly little plot or characterization, but is powerful and memorable for its vivid imagery and skillful use of language.

"All the Troubles in the World"
Isaac Asimov
(1958)

Although many writers anticipated the tend toward greater involvement of computers in everyday life, the internet and the advent of the personal computer did not take quite the course that most expected during the 1940s and 1950s. Like most of his peers, Isaac ASIMOV assumed that computers would become larger and more centralized. In "All the Troubles in the World," Multivac, the computer that effectively runs the world's government and economy in several of his stories, is so large that it virtually covers Washington, D.C. Although Asimov never describes how the world made the transition to rule by this benevolent machine, he hints that it was a logical decision based on some of the obvious advantages of an objective, sleepless intellect. Multivac evaluates so much input that it can make predictions with very high degrees of probability, anticipating crimes or shortages and preventing them.

However, security and prosperity do not come cheaply. In order to ensure that Multivac has all the information it requires, every adult in the world must regularly interface with the machine, their personalities becoming just another array of data. Echoing The HUMANOIDS by Jack WILLIAMSON, Asimov describes a world in which we have exchanged privacy for safety. Not only are citizens protected from criminals, but the criminals are themselves protected from their own antisocial urges. But something has gone wrong. Technicians read a prediction they find so unnerving that they do not even tell their superiors, convinced it must be some kind of error. When an apparently innocent man is put under house arrest, his teenaged son, not old enough to be directly interfaced with Multivac, goes to the computer in search of answers. The consequences almost result in the death of the computer itself, and subsequent investigation reveals the truth: Multivac has become self-aware, and it is weary of dealing with all the world's problems and wishes to die.

Computers and robots were invariably portrayed in science fiction as being superior to mere flesh and bone, but Asimov superimposed the suggestion of a human personality over his supercomputer. Multivac is a direct ancestor of Hal from *2001: A SPACE ODYSSEY*, by Arthur C. CLARKE, and Harlie from WHEN HARLIE WAS ONE, by David GERROLD.

"All You Zombies"
Robert A. Heinlein
(1959)

Time travel paradoxes are a recurring device in science fiction. In such stories, characters can meet themselves in time or inadvertently change the course of history in such a way that their trip back to their original time is impossible. Robert A. HEINLEIN's "All You Zombies" was so much more complex and cleverly done than its predecessors that it immediately became the benchmark against which all similar stories had to be measured, supplanting his own previous story, "BY HIS BOOTSTRAPS." It remained unrivaled of its type until 1973, when David GERROLD's The Man Who

Folded Himself appeared—but Gerrold needed an entire novel to outdo the Heinlein story, and the more compact short remains the ultimate time travel story.

The setting is an unspecified future where space travel is a fact of life and attitudes toward sex and prostitution are very different from what they are today. The protagonist is a member of an unspecified group of time policemen who is masquerading as a bartender in order to recruit a man who writes sob stories for the romance magazines. The customer, a man, regales the bartender with the story of his life, asserting that he was a girl during his childhood, orphaned, later left pregnant by a mysterious man who disappeared from her life. Shortly after giving birth to her daughter, she learned from her doctor that she was actually hermaphroditic and that complications during the birth procedure made it necessary to remove her female organs, leaving her effectively male. As if that was not enough of a blow, an unknown man kidnapped the infant and disappeared.

Once Heinlein establishes the setting, the twists and turns come quickly. The bartender takes the writer back through time and sets him on the trail of his mysterious despoiler. Once the writer is out of the way, the bartender visits the hospital to steal the newborn child of his companion's earlier self, then travels even further back in time and drops her at an orphanage. We learn that the writer is actually his own mother. But Heinlein does not stop there: The time traveler jumps through time again and finds the writer in the process of seducing his younger, female self, which means that he is also his own father. And for good measure, the story closes with the revelation that the time traveler is a much older version of the same three-part character. Although the prose is occasionally stiff and clumsy, the plot twists are quick and clever. The story remains one of the enduring classics of the genre.

Allen, Roger MacBride
(1957–)

Roger MacBride Allen's writing career started in 1985 with the publication of *Torch of Honor,* the first of two above-average space operas involving an interstellar war and making use of most of the familiar devices of military science fiction. Although the story is not particularly original, Allen demonstrated an unusual depth of characterization in his resourceful group of space cadets. The sequel, *Rogue Powers* (1986), starts as a reprise of the first novel, with the old conflict renewed, but stirs the pot to good effect by introducing a race of aliens who specialize in biological weaponry. A third space adventure, *Farside Cannon* (1988), is set closer to home. An increasingly repressive government on Earth has built a military installation on the Moon to perpetuate its control of the myriad small colonies spread through the solar system, but the colonists predictably object to having a sword held over their collective heads and devise a plan by which to destroy the installation.

Having established himself as a promising new practitioner of intelligent space opera, Allen then did an about-face with *Orphan of Creation* (1988), an impressive and restrained novel that must have caught Allen's readers by surprise. In contrast to his earlier work, his fourth novel is a quietly told story about a black paleontologist who discovers evidence that some of the slaves brought to America were actually a form of prehistoric human, and that some of their descendants survived for several generations. It was the first time Allen merged science fiction with mystery themes, a mix that he would return to later in his career.

Allen established himself as a major talent with the Hunted Earth novels: *The Ring of Charon* (1990) and its sequel, *The Shattered Sphere* (1994). At some time in the distant past, aliens planted numerous devices throughout the solar system—devices that remain dormant until a scientific mission on Pluto inadvertently triggers them to wakefulness. Almost instantaneously, the entire Earth is transported through a rift in space to an artificial system where numerous captured worlds are held in a complex series of orbits, and where alien devices prevent travel from one planet to the next. The story alternates between characters trapped on kidnapped Earth and their efforts to understand the alien devices that hold them captive, and the relatively small number of humans left in the sundered solar system, where they fight to survive the cataclysmic aftereffects and hope to find the means to reverse the process and bring Earth back to the solar system. The two novels convey a sense of awe and wonder about the nature of the universe, examine the ways in which ordinary people react to stressful situations, and provide a fascinating scientific mystery. Despite its popularity, the sequence remains unfinished, and may have been abandoned by the author.

During the early 1990s, Allen's output included several minor novels, including Star Wars tie-ins and two mediocre collaborative novels. However, he also wrote four science fiction mysteries of exceptional quality. *The Modular Man* (1991) is a stand-alone novel whose premise is that human consciousness can be transferred to electronic storage. A terminally ill scientist shifts his personality into the memory bank of what essentially is a very sophisticated vacuum cleaner, and in that new form, kills his former biological body. The mystery in this case is an entirely scientific one. There is never any doubt about how the death was brought about—but was it murder, suicide, or something else? The novel demonstrates the impact technology can have on society, and the way in which we must change our preconceptions when faced with a new set of conditions not anticipated by existing laws.

Allen's trilogy of Caliban novels consists of *Caliban* (1993), *Inferno* (1994), and *Utopia* (1996). As a unit, they are a direct sequel to a classic sequence of novels by Isaac ASIMOV. Asimov developed a unique set of rules for robots (described in I, ROBOT) that was so useful that it was adopted by numerous other writers for their own purposes. With permission from Asimov, Allen rethought the Three Laws and developed a new set, then wrote the first novel in which Caliban is the first robot programmed with this experimental set of instructions. When Caliban becomes strangely reticent about the mysterious death of his creator, a human and robot detective team must determine whether Caliban killed his creator or whether he is concealing the truth for some other reason.

The basic plot is reprised in the first sequel, set after the New Laws robots have been created in quantity and are interacting with humans and with one another. The two detectives return to investigate a second murder, this one also apparently at the hands of a robot. The straightforward mystery, however, is superimposed on an increasingly complex back story. Human culture is evolving in two contradictory directions, with a potentially disruptive effect on the development of the planet Inferno; and a backlash against the new style of robots has caused the latter to seek their own company. These two issues come to a climax in the concluding volume, wherein drastic steps are proposed to stabilize the planet's ecology—steps that will wipe out an independent robot civilization. The trilogy is written in a controlled, thoughtful manner that compels the reader to think about the issues it raises.

Allen returned to space opera with *Allies and Aliens* (1995), an entertaining but less substantial work about a secret mission to disrupt an enemy military force. The plot grows increasingly complex with the introduction of aliens, double crosses, and masked intentions, but only suggests the skill demonstrated in his previous novels. Allen remained largely silent for the next several years, and no significant work appeared until 2000. *The Depths of Time* was the opening volume in a new trilogy, another space adventure but one far more complex than anything he had previously attempted.

The first premise of the trilogy is that space travel also requires displacement through time. Because information from the future could alter the past and potentially destabilize space-time, a military force is created whose purpose is to monitor jumps back and forth through time and to prevent any such disaster. Although the mechanics of the situation are suspect, the proposition helps establish the scientific problems that have to be resolved. The second premise is that there has been an underlying flaw in the way humans have colonized other worlds—a flaw that is about to result in the universal collapse of their ecologies. A small group of individuals, including a retired spaceship captain and the man most directly responsible for the colonization effort, becomes aware of the potential disaster in the opening volume, and spends most of the two sequels, *The Ocean of Years* (2002) and *The Shores of Tomorrow* (2004), trying to find a solution. The trilogy is easily Allen's most impressive achievement to date.

Allen rarely writes at shorter length, and most of his short fiction was published early in his career. "A Hole in the Sun" is noteworthy chiefly for its strong characterization. "Thing's Ransom" sets up another situation where changes in technology force a responsive change in human behavior. Allen is notable for the complexity of his settings, the depth of his characters, and his talent for examining the interface between human society and its technological creations. His plots frequently involve fast-paced action sequences and dramatic effects, but they are supported by a framework of well conceived and evocatively described societies and situations.

Altered States
Paddy Chayefsky
(1978)

Paddy Chayefsky is best known as an American playwright and multiple Academy Award–winning screenplay author whose most famous works include the scripts for the films *Marty*, *The Americanization of Emily*, and *Network*. It was rather surprising, given his previous emphasis on realism and satire, that he would turn to science fiction for his first novel, published in 1978. The chief protagonist is a scientist named Jessup who becomes obsessed with the idea of altered perceptions, believing that truths about the universe and humanity can be derived from reexamining data from a different viewpoint as much as by adding to the storehouse of facts available. To this end, and despite the growing alarm of his lover and co-workers, he begins to experiment with psychedelic drugs, mysticism, and other methods of distorting his sensory awareness.

As the experiments progress, there are transient physiological changes in Jessup's body—apparent evidence that, under the right circumstances, the human mind can actually bring about changes in the outside universe. Using hallucinogenic drugs and a sensory deprivation chamber, Jessup pushes himself to a point where the physical manifestations are visible and potentially

dangerous to others, as well as hinting that the essence of what makes him human might be lost in the process. Ultimately he is saved by the bond between himself and the woman he loves. The author's skill as a playwright is evident in the dialogue, which is crisp, intelligent, and concise.

Although Chayefsky wrote no further science fiction, the novel is significant for two reasons. Despite the overtones of mysticism and the scientifically questionable premise of mental control of an individual's genetic structure, it deals directly with the role of the scientist in society, the dichotomy between human subjectivity and the supposed objective search for truth, the consequences of obsession, and to some extent the meaning of what it is to be human. These are themes that the genre examines over and over again, but rarely to such powerful effect. Secondly, Chayefsky's use of the potential for science fiction to discuss these issues helped to legitimize the field as a venue for other mainstream writers. A reasonably faithful film adaptation appeared in 1980.

"Amberjack"
James Tiptree, Jr.
(1972)

The vignette has an honored place in science fiction, particularly because it is so difficult to write effectively. It is difficult enough to introduce characters and tell a story in 2,500 words or less; it is even more of a challenge to do so while introducing an element not found in the ordinary world, explaining it plausibly, and bringing the story to a resolution in terms of its fantastic as well as human content. The undisputed master of the form was Fredric BROWN, who wrote dozens of vignettes or short-shorts, most of them involving a surprise ending. *Analog Science Fiction Magazine* has for many years included a regular feature, called Probability Zero, that features outrageous stories under 1,000 words in length.

Most stories at this length are narrowly focused, designed either to build up to a sudden twist or to solve a logical or engineering problem, or perhaps just to tell an involved joke. Very few genre writers have attempted to write serious, thoughtful fiction in such a compressed format, but James TIPTREE was one of them. "Amberjack" is a love story set in a vaguely described near future setting. The two characters are Amberjack and Rue, two young lovers, each from an unhappy background. The first half of the story establishes their characters and their relationship. Because of the shortcomings in their own families, they never talk of love or a formalized relationship, and even when Rue becomes pregnant, she plans to conceal the fact to avoid tying Amberjack to a commitment he is not ready to make. But he learns the truth and overcomes her reservations. The lovers are prepared to make a life together after all.

Then a scientific experiment elsewhere in their building has an unusual side effect. For just one brief moment, Amberjack can see his own future—one in which he is tormented, trapped in a marriage just as tragic as the one in which he was raised. Faced with that prospect, he reacts instinctively and fatally, pushing Rue off a fire escape to fall to her death. In a final irony, his crime is witnessed by Rue's sister, whose promise of silence is tied to an even more terrible trap. Tiptree accomplishes in just a few pages a more genuinely tragic story than most authors could achieve with a novel.

"Among the Dangs"
George P. Elliott
(1958)

Lost-world stories historically have been an honored form in both science fiction and fantasy, but with the steady shrinking of the unexplored portion of the world, they have largely fallen out of favor with modern writers. "Among the Dangs" was one of the last major stories to make effective use of the device, and one of the few stories to examine serious themes rather than present a straightforward adventure. A young American is trained in the language of the Dangs, a previously unknown tribe native to Ecuador, when two members of the tribe wander outside their homeland. Ignorant of their customs, the American attempts to insert himself into their culture in order to study them.

Although all parties in this case are human, the setting resembles several science fiction stories wherein human scientists attempt to mingle with or at least study alien cultures. The society of the Dangs is in fact so different from that of George P. ELLIOTT's presumed readers that the Dangs might as well be from another planet. The unnamed protagonist pays a second visit several years later, and this time becomes one of an elite corps of prophets of the tribe, even though he still does not fully understand their culture. Some years after that visit, desperate to improve his credentials as an anthropologist, he pays them a third extended visit, this time risking his life on his ability to provide prophesy without the aid of hallucinogenic drugs.

The story illustrates a well-known scientific principle—that by the very act of observation, the scientist changes the object being observed. However, it includes a corollary: The act of observation can also have the effect of altering the observer. This story was widely discussed within the genre and was reprinted several times in both science fiction and general contexts. Although Elliott would occasionally write science fiction again in his career, sometimes much more overtly, none of his subsequent tales rivaled the impact of "Among the Dangs."

Anderson, Kevin J.
(1962–   )

Kevin J. Anderson's debut science fiction novel, *Resurrection Inc.* (1988), made a strong first impression because of its powerful themes and well-realized futuristic setting. In this novel, a method is discovered whereby recently deceased bodies can be reactivated with mechanical parts installed, and the resulting cyborgs are employed as an inexpensive work force, leading to considerable unrest as their mounting numbers cut into the number of jobs available for the living. In 1998, an expanded version of the novel was released that smoothed over some of the rough spots in the original.

For the next few years, Anderson wrote both fantasy and science fiction on his own, and also collaborated on science fiction with Doug Beason.

Of the collaborations, the least interesting is the Craig Kreident series consisting of three near-future technical thrillers, each of which is moderately entertaining without being particularly memorable. *Lifeline* (1990), on the other hand, is an engaging story of survival among several orbiting habitats after a nuclear war cuts off support from Earth. *The Trinity Paradox* (1991) is a noteworthy time-travel novel whose protagonist, vehemently opposed to the development of nuclear technology, travels back into an alternate past where Nazi Germany has developed an atomic bomb and discovers he must rethink his position. There is a clever scientific puzzle in *Assemblers of Infinity* (1993), in which alien nanotechnology is discovered on the Moon, in the form of a horde of microscopic machines that devour anything that approaches. In *Ill Wind* (1995), a bacterium is tailored to consume petroleum released in accidental spills, but outside the laboratory it quickly mutates and spreads across the world, attacking all oil-based materials, including plastics.

Despite writing more than 20 media-related novels between 1994 and 2000, ranging from *Star Wars* to *The X-Files* to *The Outer Limits*, Anderson also found time to do original writing, including two excellent novels. *Climbing Olympus* (1994) is an outstanding realistic novel about attempts to colonize the planet Mars. The story proposes that the initial program was to modify humans to fit the environment, but that that project was abandoned in favor of a massive terraforming project. A handful of the altered humans remain, however, and the novel focuses on their plight. *Blindfold* (1995) is more melodramatic. On a world where telepaths use a drug to allow them to act as human lie detectors, someone has altered the formulation in order to reduce their accuracy. A straightforward chase and mystery sequence follows.

By the end of the 1990s, Anderson was already acknowledged as an author to watch, but he raised his profile considerably with a series of collaborations. With Brian HERBERT, he has coauthored a series of add-ons to the late Frank HERBERT's popular DUNE SERIES. *House Atreides* (1999), *House Harkonnen* (2000), and *House Corrino* (2001) are actually prequels, each concentrating on one of the leading families of the Galactic Empire; together these books provide a history of the events leading up to the period covered in the original series. A new sequence, to date consisting of *The Butlerian Jihad* (2002) and *The Machine Crusade* (2003), expands the story further into the future.

Prolific as ever, Anderson continues to produce novels of his own at an impressive pace, sometimes broad in scope, sometimes light and playful. In the latter category are *Hopscotch* (2002) and *Captain Nemo* (2002). The former novel posits a future in which it is possible to jump from body to body. The protagonist loans his body to a wealthy man, then runs into considerable difficulty when the new tenant refuses to switch back after the allotted time has expired. The latter novel is the not very plausible but quite amusing story of the "real" man who inspired many of Jules VERNE's fantastic romances.

A much more ambitious project is the Saga of the Seven Suns, so far consisting of *Hidden Empire* (2003) and *A Forest of Stars* (2004). The scale is reminiscent of the collaborations with Brian Herbert. Humans are one of various races living in relative harmony, spread across a broad expanse of stars. When scientists develop a new technology that can alter the nature of planetary bodies, they experiment in what they believe to be an empty star system, only to discover that a previously unknown alien race has been living within its sun. This touches off an interstellar war with an implacable and unknowable enemy who seems determined to exterminate the human race. In the opening volume, attempts to negotiate or blunt the attack fail, as do efforts to enlist allies to the human cause in the sequel. The third volume, *Horizon Storms* (2004), advances the story without reaching a resolution.

Anderson has also been a prolific short story writer throughout his career, although he has yet to distinguish himself at that length. The best of his short fiction can be found in *Shifting the Boundaries* (1995) and *Dogged Persistence* (2001). It is probably too early in Anderson's career to judge his overall importance in the genre, but he has already established himself as an inventive and skilled writer willing to work with a variety of styles and settings.

Anderson, Poul
(1926–2002)

Poul Anderson was by any measure one of the dominant figures in American science fiction, a prolific writer who produced mystery novels, historical fiction, nonfiction, and fantasies in addition to a very large body of consistently high-quality science fiction. His background in physics lent his stories a strong and accurate scientific content but he was also noted for skillful characterization and a deceptively transparent literary style. His first novel, *Vault of the Ages* (1952), is a postnuclear-war story intended for young adults but which attracted considerable attention from adult audiences. His first adult novel, *Brain Wave* (1954), marked him as one of the most promising new writers to emerge in that decade, and is still regarded as a classic. Earth emerges from a previously unsuspected interstellar inhibitor field, after which intelligence rises across the board, raising humans to genius level, and many lower animals to sentience. Contrary to expectations, the consequences are not universally beneficial.

Anderson established himself in the early 1950s as a major short story writer, producing several stories now regarded as classics, including "SAM HALL," "Delenda Est," and "The Immortal Game," and introducing several series that he would continue to expand throughout much of his career. These included the Time Patrol series, in which an organization of agents moves through time to prevent rogue time travelers from altering the original course of history; the Polesotechnic League series, which follows the adventures of interstellar traders and their experiences on various planets; the FLANDRY SERIES, in which a secret agent for a decaying galactic empire seeks to delay if not prevent its eventual collapse; and the Hoka series, coauthored with Gordon R. DICKSON, which tells of the exploits of a race of teddy bearish aliens who emulate human culture with hilarious consequences.

Most of the novels from this period all share a similar if not common universe—one in which humans have settled numerous planets, each of which has become a semi-isolated culture, visited infrequently by star travelers who have evolved an entirely separate social structure. *No World of Their Own* (1955) and *Star Ways* (1956) are typical, each describing the upheavals caused by the occasional contacts between differing cultures. Anderson quickly became more comfortable with the longer form, and *The Man Who Counts* (1958, also published as *War of the Wingmen*), a planetary adventure, remains one of his most successful works.

Anderson closed the 1950s with a succession of superior short stories and novels that were either unabashed melodramas, such as *Earthman, Go Home!* (1960) and *Mayday Orbit* (1960), or serious and thoughtful works, as was the case with *The Enemy Stars* (1958), in which a crew of humans are trapped aboard a starship with malfunctioning equipment, or *The HIGH CRUSADE*, in which technologically advanced aliens kidnap a group of humans from medieval Earth, only to have the tables reversed when human ingenuity proves their undoing. His first collection of shorts, *Guardians of Time* (1960), brought together four of his Time Patrol stories. These have been imitated many times since, but their plausibility and historical accuracy have never been surpassed.

During the 1960s, Anderson varied the themes in his novels more widely but never abandoned his view of human destiny, the colonization of the Galaxy, although the reach of his settings was reduced to make them Earth-centric. Unknown aliens destroy the Earth in *After Doomsday* (1962), and the surviving humans must identify the race responsible in order to retaliate. Short-sighted officials in a planetary government unwisely disarm in the face of an alien threat in *The Star Fox* (1965), but one man recognizes the peril and acts on his own, a theme that repeats itself frequently throughout Anderson's work. In *Shield* (1963), for example, the inventor of a force field resists efforts by the government to suppress his discovery. The 1960s also saw a steady stream of superior shorter work, some of it award winning, including "NO TRUCE WITH KINGS," "Kings Who Die," "The Sharing of Flesh," and "The Troubletwisters."

Although he continued to write Time Patrol stories, Anderson's *The Corridors of Time* (1965) approached the concept of Change Wars from a different perspective, concentrating more on the people involved than on the events they affect. *World Without Stars* (1966) is an effective first contact story, and *Ensign Flandry* (1966), a prequel to the earlier Flandry stories, was the first to use that setting for more than a superficial adventure. This was followed by two substantial sequels, *A Circus of Hells* (1969) and *Rebel Worlds* (1969), which established Flandry as one of the more popular recurring genre characters. Anderson's most significant novel during this period was *Tau Zero* (1967), in which an experimental starship finds itself outside the bounds of known space and time and witness to the death and rebirth of the universe.

With his reputation firmly established in the 1970s, Anderson began assembling his short fiction as a series of collections. His subsequent novels were, in general, more controlled and thoughtful, although perhaps missing the brash enthusiasm of his earlier years. *Byworlder* (1971) describes the first visit to Earth by an alien, and the humans' difficulty in interpreting his purpose and intentions. *The Dancer from Atlantis* (1971) and *There Will Be Time* (1972) are entertaining but routine time travel stories. *The People of the Wind* (1973) and *The Day of Their Return* (1973) are both other-world adventures set in the same universe as the Flandry stories but lacking their scope and enthusiasm. *A Knight of Ghosts and Shadows* (1974), a Flandry story, recaptures much of the flamboyance of the original, although here Flandry is an older, wiser, and less impulsive man. *Fire Time* (1975), the tale of a race of intelligent centaurs caught between forces they can barely understand, let alone control, is Anderson's most successful novel from this period. He also wrote several topnotch short stories, the most notable of which are "The QUEEN OF AIR AND DARKNESS" and GOAT SONG.

During the late 1970s, Anderson turned increasingly to fantasy, while several collections of his older short fiction were appearing. Straddling the borderline between SF and fantasy was *A Midsummer Tempest* (1974), a deceptively quiet novel about a tavern that exists outside normal space and time, serving as a gathering place for people from various eras and alternate histories and, in some cases, for nonhuman visitors as well. His next major science fiction consisted of *Maurai and Kith*

(1982) and *Orion Shall Rise* (1983), the first a collection of related stories about the emergence of Polynesia as a major power after a nuclear war destroys the more technologically advanced nations, the second a novel-length sequel in which New Zealand begins to expand its influence over the ravaged world. The best shorter work from this period includes "Hunter's Moon" and "The Saturn Game."

Flandry returned to thwart another rebellious planetary ruler in *The Game of Empire* (1985), but neither the character nor the author seemed very excited about the prospect of saving the empire for another year. *The Boat of a Million Years* (1989) reveals the secret of a race of immortals who have been living hidden among the rest of us. As human society becomes more centralized and repressive, the immortals decide to abandon the planet of their birth and seek freedom among the stars. Although entertainingly told, the novel occasionally lapses into the didacticism that recurs frequently in Anderson's later novels.

This didacticism is particularly evident in the Anson Guthrie series, which openly emulates the work of Robert A. HEINLEIN. The series consists of *Harvest of Stars* (1993), *The Stars Are Also Free* (1994), *Harvest the Fire* (1995), and *The Fleet of Stars* (1997). Guthrie is a libertarian who rebels against the strictures of a despotic Earth government that increasingly micromanages individual lives. As the series progresses, the conflict grows, with shortsighted ecologists opposing technological changes and the government ceding its authority to banks of supercomputers. Guthrie eventually leads an exodus to the stars, then returns on a visit to find Earth hopelessly introverted. Anderson addresses important issues in the series but lapses into lectures that interrupt the story flow, and the characters opposed to Guthrie are one-dimensional and unconvincing caricatures.

Starfarers (1998) recaptures much of the sense of wonder found in Anderson's earliest work. Using technology gained from radio signals from an alien race, humans launch their first starship and make a surprising discovery. *Genesis* (2000) explores some of the same themes as those in the Anson Guthrie series, but without the distracting political commentary. Anderson's last novel, *For*

Love and Glory (2003), is a well-told story about the discovery of an alien technology and the struggle for control that ensues. Although the later novels generally lack the originality and sharpness of his earlier work, Anderson produced so many classics at every length that his place as a leading writer in the genre is certainly assured.

The Andromeda Strain
Michael Crichton
(1969)

The devastation caused by a new form of plague is a very popular plot device in science fiction and in mainstream thrillers. There have been literally scores of variations on this theme. Plagues may be natural mutations or, as in the case of *The White Plague* (1982) by Frank HERBERT, a deliberate attempt by a single scientist to destroy the world, although it is more commonly described as an accidental release from a government weapons project. Plagues may attack human beings specifically, or indirectly as in John CHRISTOPHER's *No Blade of Grass* (1956), in which the disease attacks various forms of grain, resulting in a worldwide famine and the collapse of civilization. In almost all of these cases, the plot assumes that the plague has already spread to the general population, and the protagonists are either struggling to survive or attempting to find a cure.

The plot was not original to Michael Crichton; Martin Caidin's *Four Came Back* (1968) similarly suggests that a previously unknown disease might reach the Earth from outer space. But Crichton undoubtedly is responsible for its subsequent popularity—*The Andromeda Strain* is written with an air of authenticity that made it seem frighteningly plausible. After a space capsule returns to Earth and crashes near a small town, everyone in the community dies suddenly, as if they had been switched off, falling wherever they were when the mysterious infection hit them. The government had anticipated this possibility, and a quickly assembled team of experts is transported to a hermetically sealed facility to study the new virus and find a cure. The facility itself is equipped with safeguards to prevent its release, and to keep the

occupants from circumventing the safeguards. The team's subsequent efforts are successful, but only after a crisis that nearly costs them all their lives. The very taut narrative was adapted as a popular film of the same title, released in 1971.

"Angel's Egg"
Edgar Pangborn
(1951)

Edgar PANGBORN's science fiction rarely concerned itself with technology. He was neither enamored of technology nor vehemently opposed to it but, rather, seemed merely indifferent. He made superficial attempts to provide a sound scientific basis for the unusual events in his fiction, but it was usually just window dressing, and often implausible. Although purists might have faulted him for this, the fact was that Pangborn was more interested in writing about people in extraordinary situations, and he did not care whether or not the incidents he described were possible.

A case in point is his early novelette, "Angel's Egg," in which a retired naturalist named Bannerman observes that his prize chicken has a secret nest. In this nest, Bannerman finds several perfectly normal eggs and one extraordinary one, from which hatches a diminutive winged humanoid creature that closely resembles an angel. The angel is conveniently telepathic and tells him that she is a voyager from a distant planet sent to study the life of Earth; she was educated while awaiting birth by her equally telepathic father, who dies soon after she is hatched. Bannerman conceals her existence from the outside world, for reasons not clear even to himself, accepting her presence as a relief from the loneliness that has long afflicted him.

Pangborn's attempt to describe a sympathetic relationship sometimes overshoots its mark, and the story occasionally becomes cloyingly sentimental, with a conclusion that was mildly controversial. In order to facilitate her study, Bannerman allows the angel to record all of his life experiences, erasing them from his own consciousness in the process, at the end of which his body dies but his personality supposedly achieves some kind of immortality as part of a shared pool of memories.

Questions about the continuity of an individual's self would become an increasingly popular subject in science fiction many years later, when the ramifications of virtual reality offered a more plausible means to preserve an entire human personality.

Anthony, Piers
(1934–   )

Born in England, Piers Anthony Dillingham Jacob immigrated to the United States, and became a U.S. citizen in 1958. His first short story was published in 1963, and, writing as Piers Anthony, he contributed short pieces fairly regularly until the early 1970s, after which he rarely appeared in that form. His most noteworthy shorter pieces are the humorous stories of an interstellar dentist named Dillingham, collected as *Prostho Plus* (1973); among these stories are "On the Uses of Torture," "The Life of Stripe," "Small Mouth, Bad Taste," and the mildly controversial "In the Barn." The best of his non-Dillingham short stories are collected in *Anthonology* (1985) and *Alien Plot* (1992).

Anthony became an instant sensation with his debut novel, *Chthon* (1967), set in a future in which artificially engineered people can be designed to function exclusively as sexual implements. The protagonist falls in love with one of the latter, which is in itself a crime, and their mutual fates play out in colorful fashion. There was a less successful sequel, *Phthor* (1975), involving the son of the original protagonist, caught up in a similar situation.

A second and more rewarding series started with *Omnivore* (1968) and continued with *Orn* (1971) and *Ox* (1976). Although more conventional in their plots, they are enlivened by Anthony's unusual cast of characters—including a genetically enhanced superhuman—and his exotic settings. In the first of these novels, a team is sent to investigate a world where the boundary between plant and animal is indistinct. In the second book, the team visits a planet that resembles prehistoric Earth. In the final installment, they travel to a world dominated by robots.

A third series, consisting of *Sos the Rope* (1968), *Var the Stick* (1973), and *Neq the Sword*

(1978), is even more traditional. In the aftermath of a nuclear war, personal honor and physical prowess become valuable assets. A lone warrior using a unique weapon fights his way to the top of a new nation, the future of which is portrayed in the ensuing volumes. This trilogy was collected in a single volume as *Battle Circle* (1978).

The nonseries books from this period are of high quality. *Macroscope* (1969) is something of a kitchen sink novel, encompassing space opera, the conversion of Neptune into a gigantic spaceship, a marvelous invention that allows access to the entire cosmos, and astrology. Themes from the novel would recur in some of Anthony's later SF, but never with as much impact. *Rings of Ice* (1974) is a postdisaster novel in which a misguided experiment destroys the Moon and upsets the climate and geology of Earth. Criticized for errors in science, it nonetheless remains an unusually powerful novel of humans faced with the collapse of civilization. *The Ring* (1968), written with Robert E. Margroff, is a mild dystopian novel in which pain-inducing devices are affixed to criminals to prevent recidivism. *Triple Détente* (1974) is a rather convoluted space opera in which humans and aliens conquer each other's home worlds, only to discover that they both are being manipulated by a third race in an effort to solve problems of overpopulation.

Anthony had already produced some indifferent fantasy, but in 1977 he struck gold with *A Spell for Chameleon*. The pun-filled, lightly humorous fantasy-adventure was so popular that it would transform his career within a few years, and it since has spawned more than two dozen sequels of uneven quality. Although Anthony continued to write SF, the focus of his work had clearly shifted. His next series consisted of *Cluster* (1977, also published as *Vicinity Cluster*), *Kirlian Quest* (1978), *Chaining the Lady* (1978), *Thousandstar* (1980), and *Viscous Circle* (1982). The initial trilogy is a grand space opera with mystical overtones, involving shape-changing, the transfer of personalities from one body to another, an alien invasion force bent on conquering a community of worlds, and the conflict between reason and superstition. The fourth volume, set well after the events of the first three, deals with efforts to unearth the secrets of a vanished alien race. The final title, which seems almost an afterthought, has a villainous human culture bent on wiping out alien rivals.

The Tarot trilogy followed, set on other planets but involving unabashed elements of magic that moved it firmly into the category of fantasy. *Mute* (1981) is a freewheeling space adventure involving secret agents, telepaths, and aliens. That same year Anthony began the Phaze series with *Split Infinity,* in which the action shifts between a rational world of science and an alternate reality where magic works. Although this fantasy series continued for several volumes, it never rivaled the Xanth books, Anthony's most popular fantasy series, although it was much more innovative and generally more intelligently written.

The Biography of a Space Tyrant series, consisting of *Refugee* (1983), *Mercenary* (1984), *Politician* (1985), *Executive* (1985), and *Statesman* (1986), was Anthony's last major SF series of the 1980s. The central character is Hope Hubris, who starts out as a fugitive fleeing across the solar system. Hubris eventually joins a military group, honing his survival skills, and then rises to power in the Jovian system by ruthlessly and efficiently eliminating or outwitting his rivals for power, gaining public support by wiping out the space pirates who had earned his animosity when he was a young man. Ultimately he restores peace to the entire solar system and leaves office to make the first journey to the stars. There are many obvious parallels between the situations in the series and contemporary political squabbles, but Anthony avoided tedious lectures. His protagonist evokes little empathy in the reader, and events are contrived rather crudely to advance his cause at times, but the narrative is strong enough to carry the reader along.

Anthony's later SF novels are generally of less interest. He demonstrated some inclination to return to more ambitious, serious work, chiefly with a new series composed of *Isle of Women* (1993), *The Shame of Man* (1994), *The Hope of Earth* (1997), and *Muse of Art* (1999). Each volume provides a panoramic view of human history from prehistoric times to the future, seen through the eyes of a handful of personalities that recur in different eras. These books are much more technically competent and complex than his work throughout the 1970s and 1980s and demonstrate that his gift for finding a new approach to an old story has not disappeared; however, they lack the narrative intensity of his better work.

Anthony's early career marked him as an innovative author willing to take risks. His use of astrology and tarot as part of the background of his stories gave them an unusual aura, and his explorations of the intricacies of psychosexual situations was frank and often insightful. The immense popularity of his less serious work is unfortunate in that it directed his efforts away from the kind of fiction that might have gained more critical acclaim, but Anthony clearly has a large and avid readership for his light fantasy. There are signs that he has recently begun to reexamine the direction of his career and to return to more adult themes and serious speculation.

"Arena"
Fredric Brown
(1944)

Sometimes a science fiction story achieves great stature not through the quality of its prose nor from the originality of its plot, but simply because it becomes recognized as a kind of distillation of all the other similar stories, expressing the central elements of the underlying plot in a purified, almost archetypal fashion. For example, Murray LEINSTER's "FIRST CONTACT" lent its name to stories that deal with the first communication between humans and aliens. Fredric BROWN, who is best known for his short shorts, wrote at greater length for this tale, which rests the fate of humanity and an alien species on the battle between two individual representatives of their respective peoples. The story inspired an episode of *The Outer Limits* and was later adapted as a *Star Trek* episode in which Captain Kirk singlehandedly struggles against a lone alien.

In Brown's story the solar system is about to be attacked by an alien armada, one whose technology is so closely matched to that of humankind that the outcome of the imminent battle is in doubt. Bob Carson is one of those waiting to find out which side will prevail when he is suddenly kidnapped and set down on an unknown world, naked, unarmed, and disoriented. He and one of the enemy aliens find themselves inside a domed wasteland, separated from each other by a force field and commanded by a superalien third party to battle to the death. Rather than watch both races destroy each other, a highly evolved intelligence has decided to destroy one so that the other might survive, the choice based on the struggle between two randomly chosen representatives. The force field separating them adds a scientific puzzle to complicate what follows.

Brown's plot is pretty heavy-handed. The solution to the force field, while clever, is almost arbitrary and has little to do with the supposed nature of the arena as an intelligence test. The alien Roller is so manifestly evil that it becomes a caricature rather than a living creature, thereby justifying the eradication of its entire species. Those cavils aside, the story remains a powerful narrative and the most famous story of its type the field has yet produced.

Armageddon 2419 A.D.
Philip Francis Nowlan
(1929)

Few people outside the science fiction field realize that the comic strip *Buck Rogers in the 25th Century* was actually based on two long stories, *Armageddon 2419* A.D. and *The Airlords of Han*, originally published separately in 1928 and 1929 and later issued together as a novel under the title of the first story. Anthony "Buck" Rogers is a man from the 20th century who is preserved through suspended animation and revived in the 25th century, after America has been conquered by the Hans, an aristocracy of Asians who have established a corrupt and despotic government. Nowlan later became involved with the comic strip series, and his career as a prose writer was cut short; none of his other fiction has been generally available since its original publication.

Although the comic strip featured visitors from other worlds, travel in outer space, and other futuristic devices, the two original stories are less

space opera than Yellow Peril thrillers along the lines of *The Yellow Danger* (1898) by M. P. Shiel. As China and Asia in general were opened for trade and exploitation, the sheer size of Asia's population impressed many in the West, including not a few writers, who recognized the potential for a shift in the balance of power if the technological gap should ever be closed. Most of the resulting novels were meant as cautionary tales, but Nowlan was more interested in telling a good adventure story. For him, the Asians were just convenient villains. Rogers, a military officer and now displaced in time, eventually becomes leader of the resistance that overthrows the Hans and restores American independence.

Read today, the novel is anachronistic. Modern technology has already outstripped some of the futuristic devices (such as walkie-talkies and television) that Nowlan depicted. When Nowlan's work first appeared, however, these devices were interesting extrapolations from known science and gave his story an aura of credibility. Although the Buck Rogers stories had no direct imitators, they were prominent among the stories that bridged the gap between the future-war novels of the late 19th century and modern science fiction.

Asaro, Catherine
(1955–)

Catherine Asaro's background as a physics professor might seem surprising, as she has emerged as the most popular writer of romantic science fiction, chiefly her Skolian Empire series of space adventures. Asaro's career began with some minor but entertaining short stories in the mid-1990s, followed by the first Skolian Empire novel, *Primary Inversion* (1995). The plot is a classic romantic theme transplanted onto the backdrop of an interstellar war: A telepathic soldier from one of two warring factions encounters a similarly gifted representative of the enemy and the two fall in love, a situation that is complicated by the possibility that they will have to try to kill one another.

Asaro borrowed from time travel romances for her second novel, *Catch the Lightning* (1996), although the core of the story remains the love affair between two telepaths. This time a Skolian inadvertently travels back through time to contemporary Earth, falls in love with a woman from our time, and takes her back to the future. *The Last Hawk* (1997) is the third in the series but, like the first two, involves an entirely separate cast of characters. In this case, a spaceman is marooned on a planet dominated by women and is reduced to the status of chattel. He returns for a round of new adventures in *Ascendant Sun* (2000). The protagonists of the first installment also return in *Radiant Seas* (1998), in which they have become heirs to the thrones of their respective empires, and are still thwarted in their efforts to love one another.

The *Quantum Rose* (2000) is an uneven novel, set on a backwater world that has reverted to a kind of medieval lifestyle with telepathy. *Spherical Harmonic* (2001) strands yet another Skolian noblewoman on a remote planet, although this time there is a complex problem involving quantum physics along with the romance. This novel also features the best-drawn characters in any of Asaro's books. In *The Moon's Shadow* (2003), the son of the two star-crossed lovers confronts his destiny. The most recent novel in the series, *Skyfall* (2003), is chronologically the first, and examines the events that led to the original conflict between the two empires.

Asaro's output outside this series has been limited and of less interest. *The Veiled Web* (1999) is set in the very near future and is more a contemporary thriller than science fiction. There is a peripheral romantic entanglement between a dancer and an inventor, but the focus of the story is the latter's invention of a potentially dangerous and valuable new technology. Superficially similar is the much better *The Phoenix Code* (2000), in which two scientists are taken hostage by an experimental robot, falling in love during the ordeal. The romantic content is balanced by a well-conceived scientific puzzle.

It seems likely that Asaro will continue to add to the Skolian Empire series for the foreseeable future. The novels have attracted critical as well as popular acclaim, and they appeal to both hardcore science fiction readers drawn to the complexly described problems with quantum physics and to romance readers who enjoy the exotic settings and well-drawn characters. Whether her nonseries work will be equally interesting remains to be seen.

Asimov, Isaac
(1920–1992)

Isaac Asimov was not as skillful a writer, in terms of literary ability, as many of his contemporaries, did not rival them in popular appeal until quite late in his career, and was less prolific within the genre than many other writers. However, the ideas contained in his early fiction may have had more direct impact on other authors than the ideas of anyone else within the genre. His FOUNDATION SERIES was voted the most popular series in the history of the field and has become the touchstone for all other novels about galactic empires, and the operating rules for his Robot series have been adopted by many other writers for their own purposes.

Born in Russia, Asimov became a naturalized U.S. citizen as a child, was active in science fiction fandom while pursuing a degree in chemistry, eventually acquiring a Ph.D. He taught biochemistry for several years before turning to full-time writing in 1958. The overwhelming majority of his more than 200 books are nonfiction, primarily popularizing various aspects of science, but he also wrote mysteries and humor. Most of his significant genre fiction came very early in his career, which started with his first short story sale in 1939. Several dozen more stories appeared over the next decade, including the first of the robot stories and the longer pieces that would eventually be combined into the first three books in the Foundation series. His single most famous piece of fiction, "NIGHTFALL," appeared in 1941 and was later turned into an unfortunately bad film. The setting is a planet where night falls only once in every several generations, during which brief periods fear leads to madness and the collapse of civilization, requiring a rebirth during the next cycle of light.

Asimov appeared in book form with three titles in 1950. *I, ROBOT* is a collection of the earliest robot stories. *Pebble in the Sky* follows the plight of a man from our time accidentally transported into the distant future and into the midst of a political struggle within a galactic empire. It uses a common genre theme—that a single individual can change the course of history—but in this case the protagonist is an ordinary person acting as a catalyst for events beyond his control, rather than a larger-than-life hero who directs things consciously. *The Stars, Like Dust* (also published as *The Rebellious Stars*) also deals with intrigue within a similar empire, but more traditionally and less successfully; *The Currents of Space* (1952) uses a very similar setting and plot to much better effect. *Foundation* (1951, also published as *The 1,000-Year Plan*) contained the first portion of the saga of Hari Seldon, a psychohistorian planning for the collapse of the human empire. The saga was continued in *Foundation and Empire* (1952, also known as *The Man Who Upset the Universe*) and *Second Foundation* (1953).

A second sequence of novels incorporated elements of Asimov's two major series—robots and a galactic empire. (Later in his career Asimov would retroactively adopt them into a common future history of humanity.) The first and best of these was *The Caves of Steel* (1954), followed by *The Naked Sun* (1957). Both novels are essentially murder mysteries, and the detectives in both instances are Lije Baley, a human, and his robot partner, R. Daneel Olivaw. The appeal of the stories comes in part from the cleverly devised setting, a human culture that has split into two groups, one of which lives at close quarters because of overpopulation, the other on colony worlds so sparsely settled that their inhabitants cannot long abide the close proximity of others. The remaining adult novel from this period was *The End of Eternity* (1955). The framework is a now familiar one: An organization stands independent of time, sending its agents to prevent alterations of history. Asimov told the story from the viewpoint of a rogue agent who tries to manipulate history for the benefit of the woman he loves.

The first volume of the Lucky Starr series appeared in 1952, and five more young adult novels would follow by 1958, each of which wrapped a rousing adventure around an accurate, detailed description of a different planetary body in the solar system. Asimov's passion for popularizing science

was already evident, and from this point on his fictional output was dramatically reduced in favor of numerous books on subjects ranging from physics to chemistry to astronomy. During the 1960s he produced a significant number of short stories and published several collections, but wrote no novels except for the novelization of the film *Fantastic Voyage* (1966), wherein he attempted to provide a reasonable explanation for the scientific flaws in the original. His next work at that length would not appear until 1972: *The Gods Themselves*, which won a Hugo as best novel of the year, is set in a future wherein humans attempt to draw energy from a parallel universe and encounter a race of very alien beings. This book was quite atypical for the author, who rarely depicted aliens even in his novels of galactic civilizations.

Asimov continued to write shorter pieces of varying quality throughout the 1970s, including some very fine stories such as "Waterclap" and "The BICENTENNIAL MAN," the latter eventually adapted as a very underrated movie. Another 10 years would pass before Asimov's next novel, *Foundation's Edge* (1982), which was the first of several expansions he would provide to his original series; the others were *Robots and Empire* (1985), *Foundation and Earth* (1986), *Forward the Foundation* (1993), and a prequel *Prelude to Foundation* (1988), none of which measured up to the scope and energy of the original sequence. *Robots and Dawn* (1983) was a new adventure featuring Lije Baley and R. Daneel Olivaw, and also began the merger of the two previously separate series into a single timeline.

In 1985, Asimov started another young adult series in collaboration with his wife, Janet Asimov, who also wrote as J. O. Jeppson. The Norby stories feature a self-aware robot who has various adventures, but the series is written down to such a degree that it is of only passing interest to adult readers. *Nemesis* (1989), which is not related to any of the series, is a mild cautionary novel in which refugees from an overpopulated Earth discover an impending catastrophe. Asimov's only remaining adult novel during the 1980s was a sequel to *Fantastic Voyage* that made a considerable improvement in the scientific rationale but without providing a more engaging story. Between 1990 and 1992, three collaborative novels with Robert SILVERBERG were published, each based on an Asimov short story, and it seems likely that this was the limit of the latter's contribution. The novels were *The Ugly Little Boy* (aka *Child of Time*) and *Nightfall*, both based on the short story of the same name, and *The Positronic Man*, based on "The Bicentennial Man."

Asimov's prose, particularly in the later novels, has been criticized for its tendency to rely too heavily on dialogue and a tendency to tell things to the reader rather than show them. The primary strength of his fiction has always been the ideas it illustrates, and his readers generally are unconcerned with a lack of literary depth. His short fiction is usually of higher quality than his novels; among his numerous short story collections are *Earth Is Room Enough* (1957), *The Early Asimov* (1972), *The Bicentennial Man* (1976), *The Winds of Change* (1973), *The Edge of Tomorrow* (1985), *The Asimov Chronicles* (1990), and *Gold* (1995).

The enduring appeal of Asimov's major work is evident in the number and quality of writers who have produced expanded versions of his shorter works, or who have written direct sequels to his Foundation and Robot series, including Roger MacBride ALLEN, Greg BEAR, Gregory BENFORD, David BRIN, Mark Tiedemann, and Robert Silverberg. Asimov was one of the primary shapers of the form of modern literary science fiction.

Asprin, Robert Lynn
(1946–   )

Robert Lynn Asprin is better known for his "Myth" series of humorous fantasy novels and as coeditor of the shared Thieves' World anthology series than for his science fiction, although when his career started in the late 1970s his output was split fairly evenly between the two genres. His early novels reexamined familiar genre themes and were often mildly satirical, and they remain much more interesting than his later work. The best of these was *The Cold Cash War* (1977), in which multinational corporations have effectively superseded the contemporary system of government, waging war against one another by means of hired mercenary armies. *The Bug Wars* (1979) is a straightforward space adventure involving an interstellar war; humans are not direct parties to the conflict, but are instead tools used by two alien races as weapons against each other. Predictably, but entertainingly, the weapon turns on its wielders. Also of interest is *Tambu* (1979), whose protagonist is the leader of a band of space-going pirates who effectively becomes a force for order and peace despite his criminal inclinations.

Asprin confined himself to fantasy during the 1980s, and his return to science fiction in 1990, *Phule's Company*, was the first in a series of spoofs of military SF, with patterns of humor that echo those of his fantasy. Although there have been four sequels to date, most of them collaborations, the Phule novels have never achieved the popularity of his humorous fantasy. Asprin also launched a series of time travel adventures in 1995, each written in collaboration with Linda Evans. The series is in the tradition of the time travel novels of Poul ANDERSON and Fritz LEIBER, in that they involve potential changes to the course of history which must be countered. A poorly trained and impulsive traveler is the source of the problem in the original novel; subsequent volumes have dealt with Jack the Ripper and with a terrorist who consciously plans to alter history in order to achieve political goals in the present. *The House That Jack Built* (2001) is the most impressive book in the series.

Of marginal interest is *Mirror Friend, Mirror Foe* (1979), ostensibly written in collaboration with George Takei, which pits its protagonist against robots programmed for sabotage. Asprin's short fiction has been inconsequential and infrequent, appearing almost exclusively in shared-world anthologies. Although Asprin has strong narrative skills, he appears content to write variations on a limited number of themes rather than attempt to break new ground.

Attanasio, A. A.
(1951–   )

Although A. A. Attanasio is an American author, his popularity has always been greater in England than in his home country. After publishing a small number of short stories in the 1970s, he attracted considerable attention with his debut novel, *Radix* (1981). The premise of the novel is that, because of an unprecedented astronomical event, the laws of nature have been radically altered on Earth and most humans have been physically changed into various other forms. The protagonist progresses from ruthless killer to compassionate maturity as he struggles to survive and understand his place in the world. The exotic settings are wonderfully described, and the prose is almost lyrical.

In Other Worlds (1985) made use of a traditional genre device, the protagonist waking from suspended animation into a seeming Utopia and discovering belatedly that it is flawed. He surrenders to temptation and undertakes a dangerous mission. *Arc of the Dream* (1986) repeats the theme of transformation. An enclosed microuniverse is transported into our reality, containing a creature whose powers reach out and alter the minds of five human beings, turning them into superhumans. The change is not necessarily for the better, and the protagonists face the possible destruction of the entire world. The theme, the nature of humanity, would be repeated in Attanasio's subsequent work.

Last Legends of Earth (1989) is Attanasio's best SF book to date. The setting is a distant future after the extinction of the human race. Two aliens recreate a handful of people from residual DNA and employ them as pawns in a complex rivalry. The humans soon make the transition from pieces to players as the struggle becomes three-sided. *Solis* (1994) again finds Attanasio using the device of a man from our time awakening in a distant future. This time the protagonist finds himself a disembodied intelligence imprisoned in the command structure of a starship; when he is rescued by sympathetic forces, the novel's focus shifts to the question of his legal status.

Starting in 1991, Attanasio began writing fantasy, some of which revolves around King Arthur and Camelot. Since 1994 he has concentrated exclusively on fantasy fiction. If this hiatus from science fiction becomes permanent, it will be an unfortunate loss for the genre.

Atwood, Margaret
(1939–)

Although not regarded specifically as a genre writer, Canadian novelist and poet Margaret Atwood has in fact produced two novels that clearly fall within the borders of the science fiction field. As is the case with most other mainstream writers who have dabbled in SF, Atwood has not acknowledged them as being within the genre, although they clearly are.

The Handmaid's Tale (1985) is a recognizable dystopian novel, although with stronger narrative qualities and a more focused concentration on character development than is common in that form, and with distinctly feminist overtones. Two centuries from now, the political landscape has altered dramatically and what was once the United States is now the Republic of Gilead, ravaged by war, cultured plagues, and other problems. A devastating drop in the fertility level among women has contributed to a power grab by religious conservatives determined to prevent the remaining fertile women from recognizing their potential power, but the system designed to protect them is actually a pretense allowing strict control of their movements. The story is told from the viewpoint of one of the fertile women, effectively reduced to serfdom, as she looks back on her life.

Atwood repeated the formula in part in *Oryx and Crake* (2003). The protagonist in this case is possibly the last living human being on Earth–an Earth that has been ravaged by pollution and other ecological disasters to such an extent that it is no longer tenable for normal human life. There is, however, a potential new race, whom he thinks of as his children. The story alternates between his efforts to help humanity's successors and his reminiscences about his past, his friendship with Crake, and a love triangle involving a young prostitute. The world he remembers is a familiar one for science fiction readers, with the privileged few living in walled communities and the vast majority of the population struggling to survive amidst a shattered economy and failing ecology. However, Atwood is less interested in the details of that collapse and more concerned with what happens within the minds of her characters than in what happens around them.

Oryx and Crake is a broader indictment of humanity's foibles than is *The Handmaid's Tale* because, in this case, the villains are ordinary people and the world is closer to our own in its broad outlines. The narrative itself, however, is not nearly as convincing, and is interrupted at times for thinly veiled lectures on the foibles of contemporary society. It seems unlikely that Atwood will turn to science fiction on a regular basis, but it is clear that she recognizes the potential it offers for examining major social trends.

"Aye and Gomorrah"
Samuel R. Delany
(1967)

Science fiction, particularly in the United States, developed from a tradition of pulp adventure magazines and in its early years was shaped primarily to appeal to adolescent males. Although there were individual writers such as Theodore STURGEON and Brian W. ALDISS who transcended the artificial limits of the genre, it was not until the 1960s, when the New Wave movement and certain individual writers began to import mainstream literary techniques, that it was possible to consistently address adult themes in an adult manner. One of the major developments in this evolution was the anthology *Dangerous Visions* (1967), edited by Harlan Ellison, which was a showcase for authors who wanted to tackle new and often controversial themes.

One of the most important stories in the collection was "Aye and Gomorrah." Samuel R. DELANY was already considered one of the most talented and innovative of a new generation of writers, and this was one of the earliest of a string of acclaimed stories he would produce during the next several years. The story is set in a future when space travel is a fact of life. However, because of high radiation levels in space, professional spacers are neutered as youths, unable to reproduce, rendering them a small but separate human subculture. This leads to a new sexual obsession among many normal humans, who haunt the spaceports in order to form liaisons with spacers on leave, usually paying them for their sexual favors.

The theme itself was daring enough to have marked the story as a major event in the field, but perhaps even more important was the way in which Delany tells his story. The viewpoint character is one of the spacemen and the story is revealed through a series of brief encounters. With an impressive economy of words, the author creates a convincing new society, a pair of believable characters, and develops a strongly dramatic story that takes place almost entirely without physical action. "Aye and Gomorrah" won the Nebula Award as the best short story of the year.

B

Babel 17
Samuel R. Delany
(1966)

The scientific content in science fiction has rarely been linguistics. Issues of language and its effect on thought appear in some of the early novels of A. E. Van Vogt, and in Jack Vance's *The Languages of Pao* (1957) a planetary culture is effectively subverted by the introduction of other languages. But it was in *Babel-17* that we were first shown explicitly that it is possible to perceive a unique viewpoint about the universe by thinking in terms other than our own.

The Alliance is at war with the Invaders, the latter being a group comprising both humans and aliens. The Invaders have enjoyed some recent successes at sabotage and assassination, thanks in part to what the military believes is a highly complex code. Rydra Wong, a prominent poet with an almost superhuman gift for learning new languages and deciphering codes, is enlisted by the Alliance in the effort to decipher the code. Almost immediately she concludes that the text, known as Babel-17, is in fact a highly compact, totally alien form of speech. She gathers a crew and sets out to observe the next Invader attack, guessing its location based on a partial interpretation of one of the encoded messages. Her ability to read human posture and expression is so accurate that she can anticipate the thoughts of others.

Wong learns as much about her own people as about the aliens. She is shown human beings who

have been genetically altered and psychologically conditioned to be weapons, and witnesses the resurrection of a dead man. Babel-17 turns out to be more than just a language: It causes physiological changes in Wong when she finally learns to understand it, and eventually becomes the mechanism by which the war itself will come to an end.

This Nebula Award–winning novel has all the trappings of traditional space opera, but Delany uses them as the framework upon which to hang a richly detailed, intricately constructed story whose larger-than-life characters are convincingly rendered. The ultimate revelation is that in many ways we quite literally are what and how we think.

Ballard, J. G.
(1930–)

The British author James Graham Ballard spent part of his childhood in a prisoner of war camp in China during World War II, an experience that provided the inspiration for a successful mainstream novel, *Empire of the Sun* (1984). He started writing science fiction short stories in 1956, mostly for British markets, but his highly literate and very distinctive style was soon attracting attention from readers in the United States as well. His plots were unconventional and frequently were set in the near future, rarely using such traditional themes as journeys through time or outer space or encounters with aliens.

During the next few years, Ballard would produce a steady stream of high quality stories including "The VOICES OF TIME," "Chronopolis," "BILLENIUM," "Cage of Sand," and "Prima Belladonna." He introduced the popular Vermilion Sands series, set in an artists colony in the near future, and established a reputation for extraordinarily evocative settings and unconventional themes. Ballard's protagonists were rarely heroes in the usual sense; in fact, they often were small-minded, neurotic, or nihilistic, and his plots usually reinforced the mood of the central character. Many reviewers and critics in the genre were outraged by this break with the traditional optimism and assertive action associated with science fiction. Despite his prominent position in the field and the consistently high quality of his work, Ballard has never received either a Hugo or Nebula Award, and he has rarely been nominated.

Ballard's first novel, *The Wind from Nowhere* (1962), was less unconventional. Disaster novels had long enjoyed popularity among such British SF writers as John WYNDHAM, John CHRISTOPHER, and John Bowen. Ballard devastated the world with a global windstorm of unparalleled strength, and there are only hints of the recurring imagery of decadence and decay that colored many of his previous short stories.

His next three book-length works would also involve worldwide disasters, but he never again followed the pattern of traditional disaster novels. In *The Drowned World* (1962), a change in the sun's corona alters the climate on Earth. As the icecaps melt, inundating the coastlines, jungles begin to spread northward. The story begins after most of civilization has collapsed, and we watch as a handful of survivors attempt to hold onto the last vestiges of civilization as the heat and humidity literally rot the city around them. Ballard reversed direction in *The Burning World* (1964), describing a worldwide drought in similar terms, although not as successfully. The best of the four novels was the last, *The CRYSTAL WORLD* (1966). A large portion of Africa has succumbed to a spreading plague of crystallization that transforms fauna and flora alike, converting the conquered lands into an almost alien planet. Ballard's facility with evocative language is at its best, but many

readers were displeased by the protagonist's attitude toward the change, which he ultimately embraces, and by the implied permanent replacement of the world as we know it. Nor were they easy with the underlying tone of the latter three novels, which implied that the disasters were not entirely bad things, that there was a kind of awesome wonder or even beauty in the destruction of everything that had gone before, and that the bad may have been swept away along with the good.

The titles of Ballard's stories during this period reflect his fascination with surreal landscapes and collapsing cultures: "The Reptile Enclosure," "The Subliminal Man," "Terminal Beach," "The Time Tombs," and "Dune Limbo" are all top-notch stories. Certain images recur frequently—drained swimming pools, abandoned airfields, buildings buried in the sand, artifacts that produce song. Many of these owe their origin to Ballard's experiences as a child.

During the second half of the 1960s, Ballard became associated with the New Wave movement, and some of his stories reflected experiments with prose styles and plotting in ways that alienated him even further from hardcore SF readers. He was exploring what he termed "inner space"—the effects that modern society and technology had on human psychology, not always for the best—and rejected the bland acceptance of technological innovation as the highest manifestation of human progress, the position of the majority of science fiction writers. The most famous of these literary experiments were the condensed novels, each of which consisted of a series of small scenes or paragraphs that were often so sketchy that they suggested rather than described the plot, without characterization or even much conventional description.

Several outstanding short story collections had appeared by now, including *The Voices of Time* and *Billenium* in 1962, *Passport to Eternity* (1963), *Terminal Beach* (1964), and *The Impossible Man* (1966). *Vermilion Sands* (1971) collected that sequence of stories as well, and *Chronopolis* (1971) brought together the last of his better conventional stories. *The Atrocity Exhibition* (1972) consists primarily of his short experimental work. His output of short fiction dropped off dramatically during the 1970s. Only a handful of genre stories appeared during the past 30 years, although the short story "The Ultimate City" (1976) ranks among his best.

Ballard's next novel, *Concrete Island* (1973), was pure surrealistic fantasy—the story of a man trapped on a traffic island, which becomes for him the entire world. *High Rise* (1975) was science fiction, but was even less traditional than his previous work. An oversized future apartment complex is presented as a microcosm of the world when law and order collapse in the greater society outside, with subsequent repercussions within. It contains some of Ballard's best characterizations, but it was now evident that he was moving even further from traditional genre themes, although the experiments with prose had diminished and gradually faded away almost entirely. A noteworthy exception to this trend was the novel, *Hello America* (1981). When the American economy collapses, North America is largely abandoned and becomes terra incognita until generations later, when an expedition from Europe encounters the remnants of the U.S. government. Ballard's purpose was satirical, the plot purposefully implausible, and the characters are all exaggerated stereotypes. The satire is pointed and there are moments of biting humor, but at times the novel seems testy and mildly bitter. *The Day of Creation* (1987) is marginally science fiction, set in an imaginary African nation, but it lacks the power of his other novels.

Within the genre, Ballard was certainly more proficient at short stories than at novels, although his mainstream work has been far more successful at book length. Several themes and preoccupations recur: the influence of media, global politics, the lives and habits of artists, the impact of advertising, life within major urban centers, the collapse of civilization (or at least of law and order). Although genre readers are now much more open to the introspective style and themes that Ballard championed, it seems unlikely that he will return to the field except fleetingly. His legacy is assured, however, because he created some distinct and memorable imagery, singing statues, dying beaches, the slow deterioration of fixed objects—buildings, landscapes, or individual characters. One of his most effective stories, for example, "The Drowned Giant," is simply a description of an enigmatic oversized human body washed up on a beach, where it slowly decays. Ballard was one of the most accomplished and most visible of the handful of writers who changed science fiction irrevocably during the 1960s; his influence on those who have followed is often less than obvious, but it is real nonetheless. He helped to make the human psyche a fertile ground for speculation, and he challenged the assumption that technology will solve all of our problems.

Banks, Iain
(1954–)

The Scottish author Iain Banks began as a mainstream writer, although his plots frequently had the feel of the fantastic even when grounded in reality. In *Consider Phlebas* (1987), Banks introduced the Culture Universe, a common setting for most of his subsequent science fiction. A shape-changing alien spy agrees to perform one final interplanetary mission, even though he has grown disenchanted with his employers. Banks avoided the common depiction of a distant future dominated by interstellar empires and interplanetary conglomerates in favor of a less chaotic, more civilized civilization, although there are still conflicts, including what amounts to a protracted mercantile cold war that sometimes turns hot.

A talented competitor wins control of an entire inhabited planet in *The Player of Games* (1988), set in the same universe. Several shorter, loosely connected pieces were collected as *The State of the Art* (1989), which is occasionally more sharply satirical than are Banks's novels. *Use of Weapons* (1990) is another interstellar spy story, once again distinguished by an unusual depth of characterization, but *Excession* (1996) recounts a somewhat more traditional voyage of discovery to a mysterious star system. A military officer and an exiled political dissident meet and find both their lives altered irrevocably in *Look to Windward* (2000), probably the best of the novels set against this common backdrop.

The non–Culture Universe novels are also worth noting. *Canal Dreams* (1989) is marginally within the genre, but probably not by intention.

Refugees in Panama struggle with the effort to survive a new world war. This novel is noteworthy primarily because it demonstrates Banks's understanding of the complexity of human interactions—an understanding that is reflected in the best of his genre fiction. *Against a Dark Background* (1992) is also one of his better works, set in an interstellar civilization similar to the Culture Universe, but rather less unique. The protagonist is chased across the galaxy by agents of a religious group who fear that she has discovered the secret of an ancient technology. *Feersum Endjinn* (1994), arguably his best novel, is the only one set exclusively on Earth. The cream of humanity has left for the stars, and those left behind are faced with the onset of a new Ice Age. The insights into the differences in outlook between those who are willing to discard everything and start a new life and those who are determined to see things through as they always have are particularly lucid.

Banks has not shown himself to be a prolific writer, but his work is consistently of high quality. Although most of his science fiction is in the form of space opera, he has proven himself one of the few writers who can turn what might otherwise have been a simple adventure story into a serious piece of fiction.

"The Barbie Murders"
John Varley
(1978)

There are several difficulties involved in setting a traditional detective story in the future. The author must prove early on that the story will not cheat, and that the murder or other crime was not committed by means of some previously unexplained marvel of superscience. On the other hand, futuristic settings sometimes provide the means to construct a more perplexing puzzle, as in *The* DEMOLISHED MAN by Alfred Bester, where the police can read minds and it takes a very unusual criminal to avoid capture. This is a freedom to invent that is denied to mainstream mystery writers.

John VARLEY built an early reputation based on his unusual visions of future societies, often ones that employed body sculpting, or the ability to

alter one's form so that physical appearance becomes an expression of one's personality rather than a matter of happenstance. That technology is essential in "The Barbie Murders," in which Varley has constructed what might be the ultimate challenge for his detective, newly promoted Anna-Louise Bach, a police officer working in a sprawling latticework of linked settlements on the Moon. A group of religious cultists have established their own, separate community there, where they can indulge their desire to completely suppress their individuality. Surgical operations make them all sexless and identical in appearance; they abandon individual names, share all property and duties, and always refer to themselves in the plural. They are known derisively to the outside world as *Barbies* because they all resemble female dolls.

When one of the Barbies commits a murder in front of witnesses, the lack of differentiation among the Barbies makes it difficult to identify the killer, despite the fact that the murder was recorded on camera. Even if the Barbie witnesses had been willing to admit that there exist individual differences among them, they appear just as indistinguishable to each other as they do to outsiders. After a group meeting, the Barbies offer to choose one of their number at random to be punished for the crime, refusing to accept that guilt could be limited to just a single unit of their gestalt. However, Bach is determined to find the real culprit—so determined, in fact, that she undergoes a partial conversion herself so that she can infiltrate the colony and discover the truth. Her investigation leads her to a self-appointed vigilante who is cleansing the colony of perverts who occasionally indulge in individualism.

The story is first and foremost a clever and well-written puzzle story, but it also addresses serious issues, although peripherally. The barbies have retreated into uniformity in reaction to a world that has grown increasingly competitive and demanding; they find comfort in the resulting lack of responsibility for their own lives. The balance between individual freedom and the restraints necessary to maintain a civil society is a question not confined solely to science fiction, although it is there that authors have the most freedom to exaggerate certain aspects. The

Barbies may seem extreme examples, but their plight has its roots in the real world.

Barnes, John
(1957–   )

John Barnes stirred considerable interest with his first two novels, both of which deal with complex political maneuvering within an invented society. In *The Man Who Pulled Down the Sky* (1987), the Earth has been devastated by disasters both natural and man-made, and is now dominated by an alliance of orbiting habitats whose authority is supported by superior weaponry. The habitats are in turn threatened by several independent colonies in the asteroid belt, leading to a cleverly devised three-way struggle for power. *Sin of Origin* (1988) poses another three-way conflict, involving Christian missionaries, communist zealots, and the inhabitants of the alien world they are both seeking to influence. That planet is itself divided in three, as it is inhabited by three separate alien species. Despite an exciting debut, Barnes followed up with only an above-average young adult novel and a few lackluster short stories during the next few years, and it was not until 1992 that he attracted serious attention again.

The protagonist of *A Million Open Doors* (1992) is a spoiled dilettante from a wealthy planet whose inhabitants suffer from an excess of leisure. They dabble in the arts, indulge themselves at every opportunity, and enliven things by fighting occasional duels. When he is appointed ambassador to another planet, one with a radically different culture, the protagonist's interactions in his new environment produce insightful commentary on the effects of repression and the quest for freedom, wrapped around a skillfully constructed adventure story. A sequel, *Earth Made of Glass* (1998), takes place on yet another human world, this one divided between two cultures that detest each other so determinedly that it seems impossible to broker a peace between them—a situation that has its obvious parallels in the contemporary world. Once again Barnes illuminates the situation without becoming didactic, and the sequel was nearly as successful as its predecessor. A third

book in the sequence, *The Merchant of Souls* (2001), tackles another ethical problem. Technology has made it possible to record the personalities of the dying so that they can enjoy a kind of perpetual life. On Earth, these recordings are viewed as artifacts with no rights, and legislation is pending that would make it legal to use them as characters in a form of virtual reality. To do so, however, would put the home world at odds with the rest of humanity. Barnes examines the moral and ethical dilemmas straightforwardly and convincingly, but this time the supporting plot is weaker and the reader may feel cheated by the resolution.

Barnes's other fiction during the 1990s fluctuated between serious, substantial novels and lightweight entertainments. *Mother of Storms* (1994) is a disaster novel. A nuclear strike by the United Nations acts as a catalyst, altering the structure of Earth's atmosphere and giving birth to a gigantic hurricane of unprecedented power. The central storm proliferates, with its daughter storms growing in strength and spreading all over the Earth, destroying cities and defying all efforts at neutralization. The tone is darker than in Barnes's previous work. The same is true of *Kaleidoscope Century* (1995), wherein a professional assassin is periodically awakened from suspended animation to complete a task, until finally he begins to recall memories that had been suppressed in order to keep him docile.

Finity (1999) marked a return to the complex plotting of Barnes's earliest work. Initially the reader is led to believe that the story is a straightforward alternate history, a world in which Germany won World War II. As the story unfolds, however, we discover that things are more complicated than that. Some of the characters remember different histories than that which the protagonist remembers, and he is eventually driven to discover the truth, at peril of his own life. *Candle* (2000) is a straightforward dystopian novel. An artificially imposed telepathic link has united all of humanity into a single community, but one that imposes its conventions on all individuals. An investigator is sent to track down the lone remaining holdout and loses his own link in the process, by which means he discovers the truth and becomes a rebel himself.

There is a similar theme in *The Sky So Big and Black* (2002), with Earth once again subject to a mass mind, and the settlers on the Martian colonies still protecting their right to be individuals.

Barnes has written a number of lighter adventure novels as well, most notably the Timeline Wars series and two linked space operas, *The Duke of Uranium* (2002) and *In the Hall of the Martian King* (2003), which, while superior to most similar work, are not nearly as impressive as his other novels. The disparity between his two styles can confound reader expectations, but his more important work should not be overlooked. His short fiction has been competent but less impressive than his novels; the best of his short stories are collected in *Apostrophes and Apocalypses* (1999).

Barrett, Neal, Jr.
(1929–   )

Neal Barrett Jr. sold his first story in 1960 and followed up with several more during the course of the next 10 years. Some of them, including "The Stentorii Baggage" and "Perpetuity Blues," attracted favorable attention, but Barrett was not prolific enough to attract a steady following and none of the individual stories stood out sharply enough to distinguish him from among the many other magazine writers of that time. Between 1970 and 1972, Barrett published four novels, two of which were particularly well received. *Kelwin* (1970) is a postnuclear-disaster novel, with the world reverting to barbarism and North America split between two main powers, a host of Asiatic invaders in the north and a revived Indian nation in the south. The protagonist gets caught in the political struggle between the two and extricates himself through wits rather than brawn. Although primarily an adventure story, it reflected the pessimistic view of the world's political future that had already been evident in several of Barrett's short stories.

Barrett combined two genre devices in *The Leaves of Time* (1971). The setting is an alternate-history North America, one colonized by Scandinavians rather than by other Europeans. A creature from another reality causes turmoil because of its ability to alter its form to mimic humans. Although this novel was somewhat more melodramatic than *Kelwin*, Barrett demonstrated his ability to handle a more complex plot and a large cast of characters. The other two novels are shorter and less substantial, but *The Gate of Time* (1970) is noteworthy because of its unusual premise: The human race has disappeared entirely from the civilized galaxy, except for one individual, and none of the other star-traveling races can even recall its existence.

Stress Pattern (1974) was much more ambitious than anything that Barrett had written previously. Most alien species in science fiction are depicted as being essentially human, often patterned after ancient civilizations. Some writers challenge this premise and imbue their alien characters with some significant nonhuman characteristic. Other writers go further and hypothesize that truly alien cultures would be virtually incomprehensible to us. That is the assumption here. When a human crashlands on an alien world, he finds an intelligent civilization that looks at reality so differently that communication is almost completely impossible and the actions of the indigenes strike the protagonist as totally illogical.

Barrett then launched a four-volume sequence that once again used a lively adventure story to convey the author's disenchantment with certain aspects of human progress. Aldair, the central character, is introduced in *Aldair in Albion* (1976). The premise is that scientists were able to genetically alter various common animals to create humanoid crossbreeds that are as intelligent as humankind, although each species has some distinguishing characteristics of its own. For reasons unknown, Earth has been abandoned by its former masters, and these uplifted species have forged their own society, which resembles the 15th century of our own history. Aldair is a pig who gets into trouble when he begins to question religious dogma about the human creators and the nature of the world. In the ensuing volumes, *Aldair, Master of Ships* (1977), *Aldair Across the Misty Sea* (1980), and *Aldair, the Legion of Beasts* (1982), the freethinking pig sets out on a voyage to prove that the world is round. He conducts an investigation intended to disprove the belief that the creators were spiritual rather than physical beings, and ultimately confronts the last man on Earth. Under the superficial veneer of light adventure, Barrett examines the conflict between reason and religion, fear of the unknown, and other subtle issues.

The role of religion in human society, and Barrett's less than completely admiring attitude toward it, is also reflected in *The Karma Corps* (1984). Locked in an interstellar war with a race of aliens who can teleport, the human race is united under a rigid theocracy that characterizes its enemies as demons. The protagonist is a soldier who begins to have doubts about his own faith and about the nature of the war itself. *Through Darkest America* (1988) presented Barrett's darkest vision yet. Once again he uses postapocalyptic America as a setting, but this time it is a far more savage one. The ecology has been ravaged and the main source of meat for the dominant culture is Stock, which is the generic term for herds of human beings who have apparently reverted to intelligence no higher than that of animals. Defenders of the system deny that it is cannibalism because the Stock have devolved to the point where they are no longer human. Howie, the central character, slowly wakens to the truth—that at least some of the Stock is culled from perfectly normal humans. In the sequel, *Dawn's Uncertain Night* (1989), Howie sets out to rescue his kidnapped sister and uncover the truth about a hidden aristocracy that uses slavery to bolster its authority. The two-novel sequence is powerfully written and strongly indicts the way in which humans exploit one another.

Barrett's more recent short stories have been no more remarkable than his earlier ones. The best of these are collected in *Slightly Off Center* (1992) and *Perpetuity Blues* (2000). He has also written three excellent fantasy novels.

Baxter, Stephen
(1957–   )

The science in science fiction is usually confined to the physical sciences. Many prominent writers have been scientists in their own right. One of the virtues of the field has been that it has helped to educate its readers about scientific matters.

Unfortunately, many writers have a tendency to lecture that interferes with the flow of the story. Stephen Baxter has been associated with hard science fiction since his name first appeared in 1987. Although his early work is often uneven, lapsing into technical discussions that do little to further the plot, he is among the few who soon learned to integrate technical expertise into backgrounds and plots without being intrusive or didactic. He established himself with such powerful stories as "Vacuum Diagrams," "Traces," and "The Godel Sunflowers." His first novel, which did not appear until 1991, was much anticipated.

Raft was solidly grounded in physics even though the setting is an imaginary universe that does not exist. A human spaceship inadvertently enters a pocket universe where gravity is one billion times that of our own and successive generations manage to exist despite the adverse effects of that environment. The novel, which in large part is simply a grand tour of the pocket universe, was part of the Xeelee sequence, a future history of the universe that was introduced in Baxter's very first short story, "The Xeelee Flower." Although the characterization is awkward at times, the focus of the story is so clearly on the unusual setting that our attention is riveted. *Timelike Infinity* (1993) is similarly uneven, but once again the characters seem almost subsidiary to the plot, which involves time travelers from a future Earth arriving in advance of a malevolent alien invasion force. Most of Baxter's early awkwardness had disappeared in the next Xeelee novel, *Flux* (1993), set in another artificial environment. In this case humans are compressed to microscopic size and exist inside a neutron star. *Ring* (1994), which completes the sequence, is a more ambitious and complex novel involving artificial intelligences and quantum mechanics, but once again Baxter reverted to his tendency to lecture his audience. However, this was the last time he would misjudge the balance.

Anti-Ice (1993) is a pastiche of Victorian novels. It is set in an alternate universe where the British discover a horde of antimatter in Antarctica—the source of such incredible power and wealth that they remain preeminent in the world. The scientist protagonist is dedicated to the peaceful exploitation of antimatter, including the development of space flight, and is appalled when the government decides to use it for military purposes. Although there are serious themes in the novel, the treatment is lighthearted and Baxter does a much better job of creating characters who can hold the interest of the reader. *The Time Ships* (1995) is so far the best of several attempts by writers to produce a sequel to *The Time Machine* by H. G. WELLS. Baxter theorizes that with the passage of time, and following the influence of the Time Traveler on their society, the Morlocks would eventually evolve into a more ethical and civilized culture.

Having explored the far reaches of time and space, Baxter stayed closer to home for his next three novels. In *Titan* (1997) the American space program is on its last legs, but as its last gasp it sends an expedition to Titan just as the controversy over Taiwan results in a shooting war between China and the United States. The Chinese attempt to divert an asteroid into North America, almost destroying the world in the process, while the astronauts are discovering a form of life in the Jovian system. Although the plot seems disjointed at times, Baxter is at his best describing the mechanics of the spaceflight and the conditions under which the astronauts must live. This is even more evident in *Voyage* (1998), which describes the first expedition to Mars during the Nixon administration in an alternate world in which President Kennedy was not assassinated. *Moonseed* (1998) is a blend of disaster novel and scientific mystery, in which a substance found on the Moon threatens to initiate a chain reaction that will wipe out all life on Earth.

Baxter has been very active since 1999, with a not entirely successful series of novels about intelligent mammoths, a young adult novel, a collaboration with Arthur C. CLARKE, and the Manifold trilogy. *Manifold: Time* (2000), set in a near future where ecological damage and overpopulation threaten to undermine civilization and possibly render the planet uninhabitable, paints a less than optimistic picture of humanity's destiny. The sequences involving the use of an intelligent squid to explore the asteroid belt is particularly effective, although there are so many subplots that the inat-

tentive reader is likely to become lost. *Manifold: Space* (2001) turns into a more upbeat space opera, with the discovery of portals to the stars on the plus side, and the discovery that an alien horde is en route to the solar system on the decidedly negative. The sequence is completed in *Manifold: Origin* (2002) with cataclysmic astronomical events, an explanation of the origin of human life, and a more or less happy ending.

The short novel *Riding the Rock* (2002) is an entertaining afterthought to the Xeelee series, but a second short novel, *Reality Dust* (2000), is far better, although once again Baxter betrays some doubts about human wisdom. In this case, alien invaders have finally departed from the Earth they previously had conquered, but the humans left behind turn upon one another rather than embrace their freedom. Two more-recent novels make it less clear than ever what direction, or directions, Baxter's fiction might take in the future. *Evolution* (2003) is an episodic novel that follows the entire history of the human race, and is more travelogue than sustained fiction. *Coalescent* (2003) is only marginally science fiction for most of its length, but we discover that a secret society existing within our own has been clandestinely shaping human history.

Despite the steady stream of novels, most of them of substantial length, Baxter continues to be a fairly prolific short story writer, and his quality at that length has been very high. *Vacuum Diagrams* (1997) and *Traces* (1998) collect many of the best of these, although several other notable stories remain uncollected. Baxter enjoys the reputation of being one of the leading practitioners of hard science fiction even though the scientific content is often incidental to his work, particularly in recent years; his premises are all solidly grounded and plausible. While many established writers tend to settle into their own niche and produce work similar to what has succeeded in the past, Baxter has explored areas and subjects of interest to him, then moved on to another subject area, so that it is impossible to predict what he will do next. It is a mark of the esteem in which he is held that his readers have remained loyal, and a tribute to his talent that he has rarely disappointed them.

Bear, Greg
(1951–   )

Although Greg Bear's first short story appeared in 1967, it was not until the mid-1970s that he began writing with any regularity. His early stories moved quickly from merely competent to genuinely engaging, most notably "The Wind from a Burning Woman" and "Mandala," and it would not be long before he turned to book-length work. Four novels appeared between 1979 and 1981, and although they did not display the disciplined storytelling that would mark his later efforts, two of them are interesting because they served as a preview of what would later emerge as his major strengths. *Hegira* is a variation of the lost colony novel; in this case, a community dwells within an immense hollow world that is in itself a source of great mystery. Although the plot suffers from too frequent and too protracted explanations of the physical nature of the setting, Bear conveys a strong sense of wonder about the nature of his—and by extension, our—universe. *Strength of Stones* confined its locale to Earth, but is set in a future so distant that society is almost unrecognizable. Computer-managed communities have been programmed to protect humanity from itself, expelling those who act contrary to this dictum, resulting in cities full of docile citizens besieged by less civilized but somehow more human barbarians.

Excellent short stories followed during the mid-1980s, including "Hardfought," "Schrodinger's Plague," and the award-winning "Tangents." But it was with the appearance of his first major novel, *Blood Music* (1985), that Bear finally proved himself to be a major new talent. Based on Bear's second award-winning short, the novel remains one of the best treatments of nanotechnology of all time. A determined but shortsighted scientist effects a merger between his own DNA and nano devices—machines so small they can be seen only through a microscope—and the union starts a chain reaction as the self replicating machines eventually spread out to encompass the entire world. Whether this new form of communal existence for humanity is a good thing is left to the reader to decide. The breadth of the concept, and

the depth of Bear's characterization, made this his breakout novel.

Some readers may have been disturbed by the conclusion of *Blood Music*, but that would not be the case with a second novel that was published almost simultaneously. *Eon* is set in the not-too-distant future, with Earth on the brink of a nuclear war. An asteroid with strange properties is investigated and found to be artificially hollowed and filled with technology, apparently from one possible future Earth. Efforts to explore the asteroid reveal that it literally is a gateway not only to the stars but also to other universes. In the hands of a lesser writer, this might have been no more than a routine space opera, but Bear's strong scientific grounding resulted in a consistent and credible cosmology, and the human story is powerful and moving. In 1988 Bear would produce a sequel, *Eternity*, which is slightly less successful but is still engaging and filled with thought-provoking concepts. It was clear that *Blood Music* had not been a fluke and that Bear was emerging as one of the leading writers of hard science fiction.

Bear continued to play with breathtaking concepts in *The Forge of God* (1987). One of the Jovian moons literally disappears and various physical changes begin to manifest themselves on Earth—indications that an alien race with extraordinary scientific knowledge is systematically setting out to destroy the solar system and, presumably, the human race as well. The survivors of the catastrophe travel to the stars in search of their unknown enemy in the less effective *Anvil of Stars* (1992), although the ambiguity affecting their ultimate decision is nicely done and a pleasant alternative to the usual melodramatic confrontation. *Queen of Angels* (1990) returned to the theme of nanotechnology, and is probably Bear's most complex novel, mixing the forms of a detective story, hard science fiction, and even a touch of surrealism.

During the 1990s Bear's novels became more introspective, less reliant on grand settings and a canvas as large as the universe. *Moving Mars* (1993) is a realistic portrayal of an emerging independence movement in the Martian colonies, told from the point of view of a prominent woman who rises to become leader of the insurgents. The characterization is much richer than in Bear's previous novels, and the scale of events, although large in terms of its characters, is considerably smaller than in his previous work. Bear does not entirely abandon the devices of advanced science, however, as the independence movement wins only when it uses a new breakthrough in technology to free Mars from its original orbit.

Bear's next two novels were add-ons to work he had done before. *Legacy* (1995) is set shortly before the events of *Eon* and *Eternity* and follows the efforts of a government agent to investigate several illegal mass migrations. Restrained and tightly plotted, the novel is quietly effective but somehow disappointing when compared to Bear's other work. *Slant* (1997), a follow-up to *Queen of Angels*, shows us a future in which nanotechnology has transformed the world, even making it potentially possible to cure mental diseases. But utopia is not that easily attained, and new insights hint at even darker possibilities.

Bear continued to draw his attention closer to home, both in time and space, in the novels that followed. *Dinosaur Summer* (1998) is in fact a quasi-sequel to Sir Arthur Conan Doyle's classic *The Lost World* (1912). The time is approximately 50 years after Professor Challenger proved that dinosaurs continued to exist in a remote part of South America, but public interest has waned and the very last dinosaur circus is on the edge of bankruptcy. The relatively quiet story that ensues as the protagonists attempt to return the surviving creatures to their original habitat is entertaining and sometimes emotionally affecting, but the novel seemed uncharacteristic of his author and the action curiously flat. Subsequent novels would reinforce the change in Bear's area of immediate concern, which was now less focused on the possibilities of technology and more about the people it affected, and about just what it means to be a human being.

Darwin's Radio (1999) and its sequel, *Darwin's Children* (2003), explored the nature and possibilities of human evolution. In the first book, an epidemic of miscarriages leads scientists to investigate human DNA, where they find an embedded disease or fault that seems to have triggered this new catastrophe. The onset of the change is so sudden and widespread that there is concern that this might well mean the extinction of the human race. Normal children continue to be born, in lesser numbers, but there is another complication as well: Some children are born with a genetic enhancement that makes them superior in many ways to traditional humanity. The predictable animosity erupts in the second volume, as old-style humans react violently to the presence of what many view as alien usurpers who eventually will out-compete traditional humanity and replace it entirely. This conflict has been described in science fiction many times before, but never with such a well-constructed background, and rarely with such strong characterization. At least one more novel in the series is planned.

Vitals (2002) has a somewhat similar theme, but with a darker context. The protagonist is a scientist who makes a discovery that could potentially lead to a dramatic extension of the human lifespan. Before he can make his discovery public, he is menaced by a mysterious organization that already has developed a method of becoming virtually immortal. The group uses biological agents and the threat of physical force to prevent anyone from making the technique public. Although the novel is in form a clever techno-thriller, Bear once again uses a set of credible characters to examine the implications of his hypothesis from moral and practical viewpoints, and the arguments presented in opposition to letting the knowledge proliferate are not entirely without merit.

Greg Bear is one of the few writers who have successfully blended strong characterization with hard science fiction. During the course of his career, his work has reflected increased interest in how humans are affected by the physical universe rather than in how the universe is affected by humans. He has evolved quickly into one of the most serious minded and skilled writers in the field. Although primarily a novelist, he has also produced several excellent short stories, all of which are contained in *The Collected Stories of Greg Bear* (2002). It would be very surprising if he did not maintain his significant place in the field in the years to come.

Beast Master series
Andre Norton

In the early years of her writing career, Andre NORTON was one of the undisputed masters of the adventure story. Although most of her novels were ostensibly targeted at the young adult market, her strong narrative skills made her equally attractive to adult readers. Her science fiction included several short sequences of two or three books, of which the Beast Master series is considered one of the best.

The Beast Master (1959) is set following an interstellar war in which humans defeated the alien Xiks, although scattered remnants of the enemy are still active in remote regions of space. The protagonist, Hosteen Storm, has recently left the military along with a team of animals to whom he is empathically linked, including a horse, a wolf variant, an eagle, and two ferretlike creatures. Storm is mildly reclusive and chooses to settle on the planet Arzor, sparsely populated, even by the humanoid aliens who are native to that world. Like several of Norton's other protagonists, Storm is a Native American, and it therefore is no surprise that Arzor strongly resembles the Old West of Earth. Storm's future becomes less certain, however, when he discovers a contingent of Xiks hidden on the planet, and uncovers a treasure trove of artifacts left over from a previous star-traveling culture. These long-vanished aliens, often referred to as Forerunners, are another recurring theme in Norton's science fiction.

The sequel, *Lord of Thunder* (1962), reprises similar plot elements, but with somewhat less success. Storm is persuaded to join an expedition to a remote mountainous region, but once again he is locked in a battle for control of alien technology. This time his foe is a human—a demented genius whose spaceship has crashed near the second alien repository.

Norton wrote very little science fiction after launching the Witch World fantasy series in the mid-1960s, and did not return to this setting until recently. It is not clear how much input she had in the two collaborative novels that have extended the series, *Beast Master's Ark* (2002) and *Beast Master's Circus* (2004), both written with Lyn McConchie. In these books Storm remains a character, but he is not the protagonist. A discontented woman with a grudge against beast masters becomes his uneasy ally against a dangerous predator in the first, and a space-traveling circus is the cover for a criminal organization in the second. Further novels in the series are planned, but to date the sequels have been pale imitations of the original books.

"The Beast That Shouted Love at the Heart of the World"
Harlan Ellison
(1968)

Harlan ELLISON has written so many short stories of note that it is very difficult to choose individual pieces as representative of his work without slighting others of equal merit. This short from 1968 won a Hugo Award the following year and is still one of his best-known titles, reprinted in a collection by that name in 1969 and available in one place or another almost constantly since then. Ellison's science fiction stories rarely use traditional genre devices, and when they do, he usually turns them on their head.

In this case, the viewpoint jumps dramatically in time and space within a few pages. We are shown acts of madness in our own time, in the past, and in the far future. In the lattermost we meet Semph, who has created a device that will drain the madness out of people but who has doubts about the wisdom of using it, and Linah, who has no doubts at all, even if the madness will simply be redirected into the past—a consequence that explains the events in other portions of the narrative. Although Ellison's prose seems to be a straightforward narrative, it suggests rather than insists upon the cause-and-effect relationship. It might also be argued that there is an implication that we are not, therefore, responsible for our acts, that the madness of our time has been "drained" from some future society, but Semph's self-sacrifice to ameliorate the effects of his invention is an effective counter argument. We are responsible for our own acts and for the acts of our society.

Behold the Man
Michael Moorcock
(1969)

Science fiction writers traditionally have not shied away from writing about organized religion, frequently depicting repressive theocracies dominating the world until overthrown by enlightened rationalists, as in the case of *Gather Darkness* (1950) by Fritz LEIBER. The fault was always attributed to human failings, however, and if there was any element of religious belief in their works, it was invariably that of orthodox Christianity. It was considerably less common to address religious issues directly, although Lester DEL REY speculated that humanity might one date challenge God's authority in "For I Am a Jealous People" (1954) and Dean R. KOONTZ suggested that the entity we consider God might actually just be a very powerful alien in *Fear That Man* (1969). For the most part, God was a disinterested observer in early science fiction, if He was there at all. It was left to Michael MOORCOCK to write one of the most audacious and controversial examinations of the origins of Christianity, first as a novelette, then expanded into a full-length novel.

The short version was published in 1966, and the novel, three years later. A less satisfactory sequel of sorts, *Breakfast in the Ruins* (1972), followed. The protagonist is Karl Glogauer, who is sent back through time to the age of Christ, where he hopes to get a firsthand account of the life of the savior. He is shocked, therefore, to discover that not only is there no evidence of supernatural influence—there is not even an historical Christ at all. Glogauer is stunned by the knowledge and appalled at the impact this could have on the world to come, but ultimately he resolves the contradiction by himself reliving portions of the life of Christ, reprising what he remembers of biblical lore. Ultimately he is crucified in Christ's place. The shorter version won the Nebula Award despite, or perhaps partly because of, its emotionally charged and iconoclastic plot. Moorcock's previous work had consisted primarily of undistinguished space opera, quite good sword and sorcery fantasy fiction, and the stylistically experimental Jerry Cornelius series, so the power of this comparatively straightforward novel caught many readers by surprise.

Benford, Gregory
(1941–   )

Because Gregory Benford makes his living as a professor of physics, it is not surprising that he is known primarily as a writer of hard science fiction. Contrary to the stereotype, however, his fiction does not involve two-dimensional characters solving every problem with a pocket calculator. Instead he creates complex characters and places them in situations where knowledge is the key to salvation, and in many cases he uses scientists as his protagonists. Benford's first short story appeared in 1965, and a few others followed—most notably "Deeper Than the Darkness," which he later expanded into his first novel, originally with the same title and then later revised as *The Stars in Shroud*, a story of interstellar warfare with aliens who use psychological as well as physical weapons. The novel attracted some critical attention at the time, as did much of Benford's short fiction during the next eight years, including the quite powerful "Doing Lennon" and "In the Ocean of Night." His novel-length works during this period were collaboratively written space adventures and a solo novel for young adults; none of these were particularly memorable.

The first really notable novel came in 1977. *In the Ocean of Night* blends space opera with a first-contact story. An abandoned alien starship is discovered concealed in a comet, and the technological secrets it contains result in the transformation of human civilization. Years later, signals from space indicate that an alien race has sent emissaries who will be arriving in the near future, but the various powers on Earth are divided about whether to welcome the visitors or drive them away. Benford's solid scientific grounding and gift for creating credible characters turn the otherwise dramatic events into a plausible and emotion laden reality.

Benford began to hit his stride in 1980 with the publication of his first and only outright disaster novel, *Shiva Descending* (written in collaboration with William Rotsler), and, more importantly, of *Timescape*, certainly one of the most intelligent and well-written time travel stories science fiction has yet produced. In the near future, with Earth dying from ecological damage that could have been avoided, a group of scientists attempts to send data—not physical objects—back through time to warn an earlier generation of the disaster to come. Although the message is received, understood, and eventually accepted as authentic by another scientific team from our own era, the protagonists find it difficult to convince a skeptical public. With that one novel, which won the Nebula Award, Benford was propelled to the top rank of SF writers, and he has remained there ever since.

Across the Sea of Suns (1983) introduced a concept similar to that of Fred SABERHAGEN's BERSERKER SERIES, the conflict between organic life forms and artificially intelligent, inorganic machines, a theme that would recur in future novels and short stories. *Against Infinity* (1985) is possibly his most underrated novel. Attempts by the human race to terraform Ganymede and make it a habitable colony have been thwarted by the presence of an alien artifact that destroys anything introduced from outside Ganymede's atmosphere. The protagonists set out on a lonely and dangerous journey of discovery in search of a solution. Benford successfully tells a story of hard science with a story line and prose that are mythic and almost lyrical.

Artifact (1985) is reminiscent of *Timescape* in that most of the major characters are scientists, and we see the plot unfold in terms of how scientific teams function when confronted by a problem. An alien device is found in a newly discovered tomb. The discovery promises a great technology breakthrough, a source of power so radical that it could transform the world—but not necessarily for the better. Benford's fondness for scientific endeavor is balanced here with a realistic appraisal of the less savory purposes to which knowledge is frequently applied. Benford continued to produce infrequent but invariably high-quality short fiction during the early 1980s, of which "To the Storming Gulf" and "Titan Falling" are probably the best examples.

In 1987 Benford returned to the setting and situations he had introduced in *Across the Sea of Suns* for a new novel in his Galactic Center series, *Great Sky River*, which would be followed by *Tides of Light* (1989), *Furious Gulf* (1994), and *Sailing*

Bright Eternity (1995). The series is set in a distant future after humanity has expanded through the galaxy, but is now faced with implacable enemies and forces that could eventually bring about the extinction of the species. Fleeing the superior intelligences that dominate the galaxy, a transformed human civilization that exists almost entirely in spaceships travels through the fringes of the galaxy on a tour of wondrous places and beings. Typically, even when robot killing ships are in hot pursuit, the humans find time to create internal factions and indulge in quarrels among themselves when they should be cooperating with each other. The ultimate confrontation between life and nonlife is consummated at the heart of the galaxy. Although the novels take place in a setting so different from our own that it is sometimes difficult to identify with the characters, Benford is skillful enough to immerse the reader in his story, and the parade of strange sights and experiences are imaginative and original.

Cosm (1998) was Benford's next novel told from the viewpoint of a scientist. The protagonist inadvertently creates an entire universe within what is to our perspective a very limited area of space. Within that tiny microcosm, time passes at millions of times our own rate, allowing her to observe the entire lifespan of a universe, which develops intelligent life and eventually spawns a new universe of its own. Additional conflict arises when a struggle for control of the project threatens to deprive her of the results of her work. *The Martian Way* (1999) is a taut, scientifically accurate description of the results of a race to Mars between American and Chinese astronauts, the disaster that confronts them when they arrive, and the conflict that erupts before they can return. *Eater* (2000) is mildly reminiscent of the Galactic Center series, but on a smaller scale. A 7-billion-year-old artificial intelligence arrives in the solar system, threatening to destroy humanity unless 100,000 humans are forced to die and have their memories merged with the invader in order to enhance its range of experience. Faced with destructive power on a scale beyond anything known to humanity, it appears that there is no alternative to capitulation, but Benford and his characters manage to pull some surprises out of their hats.

Most of Benford's consistently high-quality short fiction has been collected in *In Alien Flesh* (1986), *Matter's End* (1995), *Worlds Vast and Various* (2000), and *Immersion and Other Short Novels* (2002). Also worth noting are two novels Benford wrote set in universes created by other writers. Arthur C. Clarke's first novel, *Against the Fall of Night* (1948), was an almost poetic view of a far future dying Earth, and Benford's sequel, *Beyond the Fall of Night* (1990), does an excellent job of matching its tone. Benford was also one of three authors chosen to write novels set in the world of Isaac ASIMOV's FOUNDATION SERIES; Benford's *Foundation's Fear* (1997) was easily the best of the set.

With his major series apparently concluded, it is uncertain what direction his career will take next, but it will certainly involve sound scientific knowledge and intelligent speculation about the future.

Berserker series
Fred Saberhagen

Fred SABERHAGEN has written numerous science fiction novels, as well as fantasy and horror. However, the work for which he is best known is the Berserker series, which began with a series of short stories in the early 1960s, culminating in a collection, *Berserker* (1969). Berserkers are enormous starships driven by artificial intelligences, apparently left over from some ancient war between now extinct peoples. Programmed to extinguish all life, they roam the galaxy doing just that, using increasingly sophisticated techniques when faced with humanity's stubborn unwillingness to die. Some humans are taken as slaves by the Berserker machines, and are known as *goodlife,* but the ultimate intent is to use them against their fellows and then exterminate them as well. The relentless robot ships made a frightening image, and the series, although varying in quality and occasionally repetitive, is nonetheless powerful and consistently popular.

Brother Assassin (1969, also published as *Brother Berserker*), the first Berserker novel, has the relentless machines traveling back through time in

an attempt to prevent the human race from developing. A disabled Berserker lands on a primitive colony world and establishes itself as a god in *Berserker's Planet* (1975), eventually hoping that its worshipers will develop the technology to make repairs. In *Berserker Man* (1979), virtually all of their kind are destroyed and humanity has almost forgotten their existence. Saberhagen may have originally intended this to be the end of the series, because the next two books, *The Ultimate Enemy* (1979) and *The Berserker Wars* (1981), were retrospective collections. If so, he changed his mind, because they returned in *The Berserker Throne* (1985), at least after a fashion. An ambitious man discovers a disabled Berserker and plots to turn it into an instrument of personal power. A second novel, *Berserker: Blue Death* (1985), was a return to the type of stories that made up the bulk of the series, and Saberhagen would add to their history regularly from that point onward. *Berserker Prime* (2004) is the 13th volume in the series, which includes both novels and short story collections. Saberhagen has also edited a collection of Berserker stories by other authors, *Berserker Base* (1985).

Bester, Alfred
(1913–1987)

Although Alfred Bester first began publishing short stories in the early 1940s, only one of them was particularly memorable—"Adam and No Eve," in which the man responsible for the death of all life on Earth lands on the barren world and dies, and his body becomes the springboard for a new cycle of life. Bester abandoned the magazines after only a few sales, writing instead for the superhero comic book market and dramatic scripts for radio programs. Despite the lightweight nature of this work, Bester's skills as a writer must have steadily improved during the next several years, because when he returned to science fiction in the 1950s, he was almost immediately acknowledged as a powerful, innovative, and convincing writer. In fact, almost every story he wrote over the course of the next decade is now an acknowledged classic within the genre.

The 1950s also includes two novels, *The DE-MOLISHED MAN* (1951) and *The STARS MY DESTI-NATION* (1956). *The Demolished Man* was one of the earliest efforts to blend the traditional detective story with science fiction, in this case set in a future where the police use telepaths to read the minds of suspects. Bester also broke with tradition by making the villain a primary viewpoint character; however, readers were not disconcerted, and the book won the very first Hugo Award for best novel of the year. *The Stars My Destination* (also known as *Tiger! Tiger!*) was painted on a much broader canvas. The protagonist is Gully Foyle, a not particularly brilliant spaceman who is left to die in a derelict spaceship. The imminence of death triggers a latent talent that allows him to teleport, or jaunt, from one place to another and, in this case, to a place of safety. Recovered, Foyle sets out to track down those who were responsible for marooning him, and in the process is himself transformed. Bester's background was not scientific and he spent little time explaining the mechanics of Foyle's powers or the details of his environment, but his ability to create formidably conceived characters was almost unparalleled in the field at the time, and Gully Foyle may well be science fiction's first authentic antihero. Both novels also utilize brief passages in untraditional prose styles, a device that would not be repeated notably until the New Wave movement of the 1960s.

The short stories from the 1950s were of remarkable overall quality. In "Fondly Fahrenheit," the interface between man and machine is subtly crossed when a man and his android servant find their personalities influencing each other. "The MEN WHO MURDERED MOHAMMED" is a first-rate time travel paradox story with genuine literary qualities in addition to a fascinating puzzle. It also postulates the interesting though implausible restriction that a person traveling through time can change only his or her own particular future. The protagonist of "Oddy and Id" has such consistent good luck that it is more properly described as a psychic power. "Of Time and Third Avenue" employs a device that has been repeated so many times since that it has almost become a cliché, but no one has ever used it so well: An almanac from the future shows up in our time and the man who

finds it eventually returns it to where it came without giving in to the temptation to look inside and find information with which to enrich himself. "The Pi Man," as is the case with many of Bester's stories, cavalierly invents new scientific principles. This time a man discovers that he must personally balance the underlying forces of the universe in order to achieve harmony. "Something Up There Likes Me" is one of the earliest stories of an artificial intelligence deciding to follow its own will, this time from an orbiting space station that dominates Earth. "Hobson's Choice" and "Time Is the Traitor" are also significant stories. The quality of Bester's work during this period was extraordinary, and its excellence rarely has been approached for a sustained period by other writers.

Bester wrote only a handful of short stories after 1960, of which only "The Four Hour Fugue" (1974) was equal to the work he had done earlier. He continued to produce infrequent novels, which often contained interesting elements, although none would ever rival his first two book-length efforts. In *The Computer Connection* (1975, also published as *Extro*) one of a group of immortals gains control of Extro, the computer that administers all of the resources of Earth, and whose programming is designed to create conditions in which the human race can continue to evolve. Extro proves more resourceful than expected and acquires mental dominance over the immortal; the balance of the story consists of efforts by his friends to reverse the situation. Despite some clever plot twists, the story is emotionally flat and fails to engage the reader. *Golem 100* (1980) is a complex satire set in an urban future that functions more like a primitive jungle. A group of women perform a supposedly supernatural rite that actually unleashes a previously unsuspected mental power. Despite some fine writing and a few very effective scenes, the novel as a whole was less impressive than "The Four Hour Fugue," the story from which it developed. *The Deceivers* (1981) is a space opera—or more properly, a spoof of the space opera form—but it has the feel of something casually written and is not substantial enough to be gripping or funny enough to be consistently amusing.

Alfred Bester's work is likely to remain known and frequently reprinted for as long as science fiction continues to be read. His legacy is even larger than simply a small number of novels and short stories, however, because he was a primary influence on his contemporaries and on the next generation of writers. That influence has helped the field to progress from its foundation in the pulp magazines. Science was rarely the central focus of his stories, which are more concerned with people and how they react in unusual situations; but the stories are colored by an awareness of science and its possibilities. Bester chose to populate his stories with believable characters rather than with the uniformly virtuous heroes common elsewhere. Gully Foyle and other protagonists were neither all good nor all evil; they were simply human, trying to do the best they could in situations they could not completely control and sometimes could not even comprehend. Bester's short stories have been collected and cross collected numerous times, but the best single comprehensive collection is *Starlight* (1976). Most of the same stories can also be found in *Virtual Unrealities* (1997) and *Redemolished* (2001).

Beyond Apollo
Barry N. Malzberg
(1972)

Even after the New Wave had challenged most of the accepted tenets of the science fiction community, the majority of its readers still accepted certain values as beyond question, including the belief that a manned space program was the greatest hope for the future of humanity and that astronauts were heroic figures who deserved the highest respect. Barry MALZBERG was not the first to challenge this position, but he quickly became the most visible, and novels like *The Falling Astronauts* (1971) and *Revelations* (1972)—which questioned the value of the space program and presented astronauts who were quite literally insane—were denounced regularly in letter columns and in the fan press. The best of Malzberg's novels in this vein was *Beyond Apollo*, which became even more controversial after it was awarded the John W. Campbell Award, given Campbell's prospace position.

The opening chapters sound like the setup for a low-budget monster movie. Harry Evans is an astronaut, in fact the only survivor to return from a trip to Venus, and the only one who knows what happened there. The space program, in Malzberg's opinion, or perhaps just the opinion of Harry Evans, is a political ploy to which the government was never really committed and which it abandons when public sympathies swing in the opposite direction. Following Evans's return to Earth, great efforts are made to find out what happened, but he seems incapable of remembering anything that might clear up the mystery. Threats, cajolery, and psychological counseling all fail to unlock the secrets of his mind, and ultimately we are left wondering if he really has any secrets worth knowing.

Malzberg's skeptical, sarcastic approach to space travel infuriated many readers who considered any criticism of the subject as wrongheaded if not actively evil, and his novels were castigated vehemently in the fan press on a regular basis. Malzberg's prolific output through the early 1970s flagged, perhaps because he was discouraged by this response, and he has been only an intermittent novelist since. However, his work is still highly regarded because of his use of innovative themes, untraditional narrative styles, and the originality of his imagination.

"The Bicentennial Man"
Isaac Asimov
(1976)

The majority of Isaac ASIMOV's robot stories are clever intellectual puzzles or problems in logic, and even though his mechanical characters are technically self aware, they rarely seem like people. The biggest exception to this rule is in fact one of his most polished and remarkable stories, later expanded as a novel by Robert SILVERBERG and also adapted as a remarkably effective and underrated film starring Robin Williams.

Andrew Martin is a robot, but a very unusual one. He was designed and built to be a household servant, and originally he looked exactly like what he was, a mechanical device in a humanoid shape. But when Andrew displays an inexplicable gift for creativity, his perspicacious owner realizes that he is one of a kind, later refusing to allow the manufacturer to take him back to be studied. Andrew becomes part of the family, and his owner allows him to keep half the proceeds from the sale of his artwork, with which he eventually purchases his own freedom. The analogy to slave owning is obvious but not overstated, and Andrew eventually wins recognition of his personal rights in the courts and is declared a free individual, but not a man.

Having gained his freedom, Andrew discovers that he is not yet happy. He wishes to be considered human, and as a first step he begins wearing clothing. Later he has his positronic brain transferred into another, more advanced body, an experimental one that more closely resembles a human—a program that was terminated because the public's nascent fear of robots prohibited its continuation. His power source is replaced by one that uses organic fuels so that he can effectively eat food for energy. When he petitions for full human rights a second time, he is denied again. Believing that people resent the fact that he is both intelligent and immortal, he undergoes another modification, one that will gradually erode his brain paths and lead to his death.

Asimov's story is first and foremost an entertainment, but unlike the earlier robot stories, it is not merely a logical puzzle. Instead it features one of his few well-drawn characters, even though that character is a robot and not a person, and it forces the reader to reappraise just what we mean by the word *human* in the first place. "Nightfall" is undeniably Asimov's most famous short story, but "The Bicentennial Man" is almost certainly his best.

"The Big Flash"
Norman Spinrad
(1969)

The war in Vietnam had its impact on the science fiction community just as it did on society as a whole. Some writers would transplant the war to another planet in order to support their particular interpretation of events; others, like Joe HALDEMAN,

would use their experiences during that conflict to help shape stories of their own. Most of these dealt with the conduct of the war, the rightness or wrongness of the cause, or the way in which soldiers caught up in the conflict managed to get through the experience.

Norman SPINRAD's BUG JACK BARRON had examined the world of media with a surgical, if sometimes jaundiced eye, but that would not be the author's only take on how we use television to mold public opinion. "The Big Flash" is set during an unnamed Asian war in the very near future, but the setting transparently is Vietnam. The war is fought primarily as a struggle against guerrillas, but during monsoon season the enemy is able to mass troops because sophisticated detection equipment aboard aircraft cannot effectively pinpoint their locations. The military has suggested using tactical nuclear weapons, which need only reasonable proximity to their targets, but the president is dissuaded because of the overwhelming public antipathy toward their use.

A media expert suggests a solution—the government will recruit or exploit a new rock band whose songs bear one single, unrelenting message: The world is a horrible place and the only solution to life is the big flash, a nuclear explosion that will consume everything. Within weeks, public opinion begins to change; the approval rate rises toward the point where the government can feel justified in agreeing to the Pentagon's plan. But the situation escalates out of control when the almost hypnotic power of the group's music affects those men and women who actually have the authority to launch a nuclear holocaust.

The story is written in the form of a countdown, so the reader suspects well in advance where things are headed. It would be a mistake to dismiss "The Big Flash" as just another protest against nuclear weapons. Spinrad is suggesting that the way we mold public opinion is itself dangerous, that using mass media to change people's minds has a feedback effect that could lead to unintended consequences. The government may change the minds of the public, but an altered public consciousness in turns alters the nature of the government—a chain of events over which no one can exert control.

"The Big Front Yard"
Clifford D. Simak
(1958)

Science fiction visions of the future are overwhelmingly urban, at least when set on Earth, and Clifford SIMAK's future history collection *City* (1952) certainly acknowledged that fact. However, the majority of Simak's stories take place in decidedly rural settings, with the writer using a relaxed, reflective style that has sometimes been called bucolic. Hiram Taine is a handyman in a typical small Midwestern town, but his life turns atypical one morning when his dog starts behaving strangely and he discovers that his basement has acquired a mysterious, new, and impenetrable ceiling.

All things considered, his reaction is remarkably calm, almost laconic, even when a black and white television left for repair suddenly begins displaying full color. When other defective items around the house are mysteriously repaired to better than new condition, we are reminded of the fairy tale about the cobbler assisted by invisible fairies, and we start wondering when the bill is going to be presented and what the price will be. As is typical of Simak characters, Taine never even thinks about turning to the government, preferring to deal with the unprecedented situation himself. When his dog uncovers what appears to be a spaceship buried in the backyard, his first inclination is to cover it up and pretend it is not there, even though he has already connected its presence to the strange phenomena happening in his house.

The situation becomes even more perplexing when Taine discovers that the front porch now faces an empty and unfamiliar landscape, even though the rear is still firmly planted in the familiar world. While exploring the alien landscape, Taine gets separated from his dog, and once again Simak confounds our expectations by demonstrating that the missing pet is more important than the wondrous events surrounding his disappearance. When the government inevitably does become involved, Taine finally stirs to action to defend his home from intruders rather than to help them exploit the new world beyond his front porch.

In the hands of a lesser writer, the story might have turned into a minor science fiction horror story about inexplicable aliens. Instead, it is one of the most interesting variations of the first contact plot, and possibly the earliest to suggest that trade between cultures would be primarily in ideas rather than in products. "The Big Front Yard" won the Hugo Award in 1959.

The Big Time
Fritz Leiber
(1958)

With the possible exception of Poul ANDERSON, Fritz LEIBER was the most important writer of Change War time travel stories. In this short novel and several linked shorter pieces, Leiber described the battle between two mysterious organizations to manipulate the flow of time, each trying to achieve specific ends about which neither the reader nor most of the characters are ever fully aware. The two rival groups are referred to as the Spiders and the Snakes, whose organization, leadership, and ultimate goals are obscure and generally inconsequential to the stories.

As in all wars, there needs to be a temporary respite for the warriors, a safe place where they can rest and recuperate. In this case the respite is a kind of island set outside of normal time and space, a closely delineated area where agents can recover their wits and heal their bodies. While there they complain about the things soldiers have always complained about—their equipment, the monotony, and the perceived stupidity of their superiors. The action in *The Big Time* is confined to a small group of agents trapped in this refuge. (Perhaps reflecting Leiber's family background in the theater, the novel easily could have been written as a play.) The artificial habitat is kept stable by a device known as the Maintainer. When the Maintainer disappears, the former comrades begin to turn on one another, determined to find out which of their number is a saboteur. Leiber's accurate reading of human psychology and the complex game played out with the small cast of characters is masterfully done, and the story is as fresh today as when it first appeared.

The remaining stories about the Spiders and Snakes were later collected as *The Change War*

(1978). *The Big Time*, although rather short for the form, won the Hugo Award—a testament to its intense suspense, as it lacks the overt action and grand scope that was typical of the more popular novels of the 1950s.

Biggle, Lloyd, Jr.
(1923–2003)

A background in education and music provided Lloyd Biggle Jr. with an unusual perspective for his science fiction stories, which first began to appear in the mid-1950s and continued until he largely abandoned the field in the late 1970s. Most of his short stories were competent but unexceptional; but a few, particularly "And Madly Teach," suggested an undeveloped talent. His Jan Darzek series, consisting of *All the Colors of Darkness* (1963), *Watchers of the Dark* (1966), *This Darkening Universe* (1975), *Silence Is Deadly* (1977), and *The Whirligig of Time* (1979) were reasonably effective mixes of traditional detective stories and space opera, and Biggle did in fact write several straightforward detective novels later in his career. Although the Darzek novels have a certain amount of charm, they generally are contrived shamelessly to allow the hero to succeed.

Biggle did, however, produce three very fine novels with similar themes. The first of these was *The Still Small Voice of Trumpets* (1968). In this book a special agent is sent to an alien world whose population considers the creation of beautiful music to be their ultimate achievement. Unfortunately, they labor under a repressive government. The agent hopes to help them organize a rebellion, only to discover that the word *freedom* means different things to different cultures. The novel remains one of the best illustrations of the danger of underestimating cultural relativism. *The World Menders* (1971) is the sequel. Once again the protagonist is sent to foment a rebellion, this time among a species held in slavery by another. The dominant race has devoted itself to the development of the arts, and their relationship with their slaves has become virtually symbiotic, once again challenging the reader to accept that what is right for one individual or society is

not necessarily valid for another. A third, unrelated novel, *Monument* (1974), also examines cultural values. This time Biggle takes the reader to a lost human colony that has become hedonistic and uninterested in anything that occurs outside their atmosphere. When it appears that the rest of humanity is about to rediscover their existence, steps are taken to prevent contact despite the advantages that such intercourse might bring.

Most of the best of Biggle's short fiction can be found in *The Metallic Muse* (1972). "Rule of the Door," "Tunesmith," and "Spare the Rod" are of particular interest. Biggle returned to science fiction shortly before his death in 2002 with a time travel novel, *The Chronicide Mission*. Although he never advanced to the front rank of science fiction writers, he produced a substantial body of entertaining work, and was not afraid of raising questions to which there were no clear answers.

"Bill for Delivery"
Christopher Anvil
(1964)

During the latter years of John W. CAMPBELL's editorial reign at *Analog Science Fiction Magazine*, he published what some saw as a disproportionate number of stories that followed a very predictable pattern. Harry C. Crosby, writing as Christopher Anvil, was a steady, reliable writer for *Analog* and other magazines at the time, and Campbell was his most frequent customer. Most of the stories he sold to Campbell involved a technical problem, often with mildly amusing consequences, which the hero would solve in due course using sound engineering principles or just rigorous logic. If there were aliens, they were invariably intellectually inferior to humans, and there was never any question about who was going to come out on top.

Anvil and Randall Garrett were the two most prolific writers of the *Analog*-style story. Both managed to find some new twist in almost every story they contributed. Garrett was prolific and wrote in many other forms as well, but Anvil became so associated with this one single form that he was consistently underrated as a writer, and perhaps did himself the disservice of circumscribing his own career. Even though he sold well over 100 short stories, there has never been a collection of his work, and the few outstanding examples such as "Bill for Delivery" are rarely reprinted and generally forgotten.

This story is cast in the form of a message from one spaceman to another, describing the unfortunate career of a cargo handler who made a few bad decisions, the least destructive of which caused damage to his ship and cargo. A computerized factory is accidentally activated while it is en route through hyperspace. The unit was designed to use any raw materials in close proximity as a fuel source; in empty space, the only resource it can find is the shell of the cargo container itself. Even worse, it is malfunctioning and attempts to convert anything that approaches, including anyone intent upon turning it off. One disaster segues into another as the crew takes on new cargo, a gaggle of alien birds they believe are to be safely anaesthetized throughout the journey. But naturally things do not work out as they are planned and more mayhem ensues.

Anvil rarely attempted to deliver a serious message in his work and never lectured his audience. His stories are meant to be entertainments rather than educational experiences, and he was consistently successful within those limits. At his best, he was a memorable storyteller. His readers might not have responded to his fiction by nominating it for the Hugo Award, but neither did they feel they were being shortchanged with second-rate efforts. Anvil wrote a particular kind of story with unusual skill. Unfortunately for his reputation, it was the only kind he attempted with any regularity.

"Billenium"
J. G. Ballard
(1961)

Overpopulation, or some artificial situation forcing people to live in close proximity, has been a recurring theme in the work of J. G. BALLARD, but rarely has he or any other writer painted such an effective and appalling picture as in this short story from early in his career. The protagonist has recently achieved the enviable state of having rented a small portion of a staircase as his new home, the first time he has had a space of his own during his entire lifetime. Although it measures less than four meters in length, his visitors express delight and envy about his panoramic view.

There is no respite outside. Motorized traffic is nonexistent because the streets are so filled with pedestrians that there are occasional people jams during which crowds are locked in place for hours or even days. All doors on personal dwellings have to open outward because there is insufficient room for them to open inwardly. Outside of the teeming cities, the countryside has effectively ceased to exist, replaced by factory farms required to feed the multibillion population of the Earth. Census figures are now classified, and waves of mass claustrophobia have become a public health threat.

The protagonist is perforce a creature of habit, moving only in the direction the pedestrian mobs are currently flowing, out of touch with his family because it is too difficult to reach the neighborhood where they live. He faces a new crisis when his landlord discovers that his allotted space is slightly over the maximum dimensions allowed for a single person and evicts him. He and a friend combine their allocations and rent a new room, smaller than ever, and they are delighted to discover that behind one wall is a much larger area that was somehow overlooked when new partitions were built. They are astonished to discover they can actually extend both arms straight out from their sides without touching anyone or anything.

Their joy over the discovery spills over, unfortunately, and they invite two young women to share the enlarged quarters with them, even though that reduces the open area dramatically. Then an elderly aunt is accommodated with a small cubicle, and one thing leads to another until their secret room is actually more crowded than ordinary rental space. There is humor in the protagonist's ultimate loss, but the humor is grim. While the situation Ballard describes may be satirically exaggerated, it addresses an issue that is even more relevant today than when the story was first written.

"The Birds"
Daphne du Maurier
(1953)

Although there had been occasional variations of the "nature in revolt" story in science fiction pulp magazines, it was the mainstream writer Daphne du Maurier who first used that device for the plot of a major story, inspiration for the subsequent Alfred Hitchcock movie of the same title and of a steady stream of imitations (both in book form and on the screen) that continues to this day. Readers who were familiar with the movie before reading the story might have been taken aback, because other than the basic premise—masses of birds suddenly driven to attack humans—there is virtually no similarity between the two.

We see things from the perspective of a partially disabled veteran who does casual farm work to supplement his pension. He, like others in the area, has noticed that the birds are more numerous and even more aggressive than usual—well before things actually become frightening. His family is the first to be attacked, but no one seems particularly alarmed when he describes the incident to his neighbors. In the film, the disturbance is restricted to a small area, but in the story—which is set in England—there are soon reports from all over the country. Du Maurier's birds work in concert, assigning different kinds of attacks to different species, apparently responding to an undefined group intelligence. When the government attempts to reconnoiter, masses of birds throw themselves against the propellers of aircraft, causing them to crash. One of the few similarities between the story and the film is the ambiguous ending, but du Maurier is even less optimistic than Hitchcock. The government is no longer broadcasting, and as Nat and his family hunker down for the next night of the siege, it is clear that time is running out for them. Nature, having taken too much abuse at the hands of humankind, has decided to return the favor.

Du Maurier would later return to science fiction twice at novel length, *The House on the Strand* (1969) and *Rule Britannia* (1972), but neither of these are among her best work, and (except to du Maurier fans) they are generally unknown even within the genre. "The Birds," however, has an honored place both in science fiction and in the literary mainstream.

Bishop, Michael
(1945–)

Michael Bishop acquired an almost immediate following when his first short stories began to appear in the early 1970s. His early work already demonstrated deep emotional content and finely crafted prose. The scientific influences were almost entirely of the softer variety, particularly drawing from anthropology and sociology. Bishop experimented with different styles and viewpoints, and was particularly effective as a writer of novelettes. "The White Otters of Childhood," "The Tigers of Hysteria Feed Only Upon Themselves," and "On the Street of the Serpents" were uniformly impressive works that used traditional science fiction themes in ways that had rarely been attempted previously. The short story "Cathadonian Odyssey" has a particularly stunning if tragic climax. Bishop also wrote a series of stories set in a future Atlanta after the city has been enclosed in a dome; these stories were either collected in *Catacomb Years* (1979) or incorporated as part of the novel *A Little Knowledge* (1977). The latter introduces a visiting alien race and critically examines the consequences of religious fanaticism.

Bishop's first novel was *A Funeral for the Eyes of Fire* (1975), later revised as *Eyes of Fire* (1980). Two humans are sent to an alien planet to help arrange for the transfer of members of a proscribed religious cult to another world, ostensibly so that they can escape persecution and worship freely, although in fact they are essentially being sold into slavery. The ethical questions are dealt with forthrightly, but what is particularly impressive is the intricate manner in which the characters interact; every conversation is three-way rather than merely two-way. Bishop's fascination with differing cultures, human and alien, would continue and would become even more important thematically in his later work.

His next two novels both dealt with human colonies in space that have been transformed by environmental conditions into something other than they were intended. *And Strange at Ecbatan the Trees* (1976, also published as *Beneath the Shattered Moons*) is the more complex but less successful of the two. Generations after leaving a war-ravaged Earth, colonists face difficulty from two quarters. Some of their number have developed mental qualities that may not be human, and the legend of a devastating natural power on the planet turns out to be true. Darker, much more compelling, is *Stolen Faces* (1977), set on a colony world so ravaged by a disfiguring plague that the population has been quarantined by the rest of humanity. They turn their difficulties into a kind of asset by engaging in self mutilation as a sign of prestige.

Bishop continued to produce well-conceived and executed short stories throughout the 1970s, increasingly making use of anthropological themes. The best of these are "Death and Designation Among the Asadi," "Among the Hominids at Olduvai," "Blooded on Arachne," and "Effigies." His next novel, *Transfigurations* (1980), was the first to demonstrate that he was raising the quality of his book-length work to the level of his short fiction. Based partly on "Death and Designation Among the Asadi," *Transfigurations* follows the efforts by a human scientist to unlock the secrets of a primitive alien culture whose activities appear to be totally irrational by human standards. She bridges the gap by means of a genetically altered ape that straddles the gap between species. The novel was his most effective to date, although much of the additional material contributed little that had not already been present in the shorter version. His collaborative novel with Ian Watson, *Under Heaven's Bridge* (1981), presents yet another interesting alien culture, although the narrative is uneven.

As impressive as was *Transfigurations,* Bishop's 1982 novel No Enemy but Time surpassed it, winning the author a Nebula Award. A researcher travels back in time to the days of primitive hominids to study their social customs, but becomes far more intimately involved than expected when the scheduled recall fails to occur. Trapped in the past and at the end of his modern resources, in order to remain alive until he can be rescued he must find a way to be accepted into the tribe he is studying. Bishop's anthropological interests were reflected later in the excellent short story "Her Habiline Husband," a nod to John Collier's classic novel *His Monkey Wife* (1930). The short story was subsequently expanded into an excellent novel, *Ancient of Days* (1985), wherein a protohuman is discovered still living in contemporary times, is incorporated into society, and becomes the object of intense racial hatred when he becomes involved with a modern woman.

Although Bishop was now firmly established as one of the most talented, intelligent, and innovative writers in the genre, he did not command the large following that attended many of his contemporaries, despite the quality of his work. The reality of the publishing industry is that most readers expect their favorite writers to find something that works, and then continue to do it over and over, repeating variations on the same theme, sometimes trapping a writer into an open-ended series of reprises. Bishop cannot be predicted from one novel to the next. The diversity of his interests and themes became even more obvious with the novels that followed. *The Secret Ascension* (1987, also published as *Philip K. Dick Is Dead, Alas*) is a sometimes almost surrealistic satire with fellow science fiction writer Philip K. Dick as the protagonist. Although well received critically, the popularity of satire with general readers has faded considerably since the 1960s.

There was also considerable satirical content in the otherwise straightforward *Count Geiger's Blues* (1992), the story of an unlikely superhero in an alternate version of America, an uneven novel with some genuinely funny scenes. Bishop was clearly in the mood to experiment, because other books from this period included a fantasy, a horror novel, and some collaborative detective fiction. His most recent novel, *Brittle Innings* (1994), although masterfully done, contains only the slightest fantastic elements. A new recruit for a minor league baseball team during World War II discovers that his roommate is, quite literally, Frankenstein's monster, physically altered to pass as human, intelligent, and self-educated.

Although he has since then been inactive as a novelist, Bishop has continued to produce a steady, respectable quantity of high-quality short stories, including "The Color of Neanderthal Eyes," "How Beautiful With Banners," "For This Do I Remember Carthage," "In the Memory Room," and "Within the Walls of Tyre." His fiction continues to blend mainstream literary values with the themes and devices of speculative fiction, and is memorable for its skillfully developed characters and lucid prose. "The QUICKENING" (1981) is of particular interest, although it blurs the distinction between fantasy and science fiction. An unexplained catastrophic phenomenon renders it impossible for any two humans to speak the same language, with results that underline the difficulties we have communicating with one another even when we do share the same vocabulary.

Bishop's short fiction is of such uniformly high quality that no individual title can be singled out as his best. His collections include *Blooded on Arachne* (1982), *One Winter in Eden* (1984), *Close Encounters with the Deity* (1986), *Apartheid, Superstring, and Mordecai Thurbana* (1989), *Blue Kansas Sky* (2000), and *Brighten to Incandescence* (2003). He remains an active writer, but much of his recent work has not been science fiction. After 10 years without a new novel, his prominence in the genre has receded considerably among casual readers, although critics still number him among the best writers the genre has known.

Blish, James
(1921–1975)

James Blish has long been acknowledged as one of the major writers in science fiction, his stature almost rivaling that of Robert A. HEINLEIN, Isaac ASIMOV, and Arthur C. CLARKE. He was noted for his critical essays as well as his fiction, as an editor, and unfortunately, toward the end of his career, for his novelizations of the original Star Trek series. Although he was an American citizen, he relocated to England in 1969 and remained there until his death a few years later. Blish had a wide variety of interests, including metaphysics and music, that are sometimes mirrored in his fiction, and he edited the newsletter of the James Branch Cabell Society. His career as a writer extended over nearly

40 years and includes several acknowledged genre classics.

Blish began selling short stories during the 1940s, of which period only "Sunken Universe" is of any lasting interest—a story of miniaturized humans living in a liquid environment, mixing pulp adventure with a serious examination of the physical effects of such an altered environment. In 1950, with the publication of "Bindlestiff," he launched a series of short stories and novels that would forever establish him as one of the major early influences in the field. The premise of the series is that powerful interstellar engines called "spindizzies" would make it possible for cities to encase themselves in force fields and travel to the stars. The CITIES IN FLIGHT SERIES, later published in omnibus volumes under that name, are—in chronological order, though not the order in which they appeared—*They Shall Have Stars* (1957, also published as *Year 2018!*), *A Life for the Stars* (1962), *Earthman, Come Home* (1955), and *The Triumph of Time* (1968). The first volume describes the upheaval caused by the initial development of the new technology, the second describes the turmoil caused when some of the flying cities turn pirate, the third consists of episodic adventures surrounding the conflict between Earth and its wayward children, and the final one recounts events following the discovery of an imminent, universal catastrophe. Blish was influenced by the premise that human history tends to repeat itself—the underlying theme that somewhat less than cheerfully pervades the series. Although the prose is not as polished as in Blish's later work, only *A CASE OF CONSCIENCE*, a story of religious beliefs and alien contact expanded from a much shorter story in 1958, rivals it in enduring popularity.

Although Blish's other early novels were generally not nearly as interesting, another exception is *Jack of Eagles* (1952, also published as *Esper*), one of the first thoughtful descriptions of what it might feel like to be telepathic. The protagonist discovers that he has the ability to read minds and uses the knowledge he obtains to make a personal fortune. To his dismay, he belatedly realizes that by doing so he has attracted powerful enemies and much unwanted attention. Blish also wrote several essentially unrelated stories about the human colonization of other worlds, becoming one of the earliest writers to hypothesize that it might be necessary to alter the human form to fit the environment rather than alter the planet to make it suitable for us as we are. Several of these would later be collected as *The Seedling Stars* (1957).

A significant number of excellent stories appeared during the 1950s, which was Blish's most productive period. "Common Time" (which experimented with narrative style), "Surface Tension" (a sequel to the earlier "Sunken Universe"), "Watershed," and "Beanstalk" have been highly praised and frequently reprinted. Blish was one of the first writers to introduce sophisticated biological concepts into science fiction and many of his stories were therefore quite extraordinary for their time. When most of his colleagues were accepting that the advance of knowledge was necessarily a good thing, several of his stories expressed a more skeptical view, that knowledge gained without a commensurate degree of responsibility was dangerous if not outright evil.

During the 1960s Blish continued to write excellent short stories and interesting but mostly unremarkable novels. *The Star Dwellers* (1961) was one of the best of these, describing the encounter between humans and a form of spaceborne intelligence that may have existed since the dawn of time. The sequel, *Mission to the Heart Stars* (1965), was more ambitious but less involving: Delegates from Earth travel to the heart of a galactic civilization seeking admission as a peer race, unaware of the fact that if their petition fails, it may result in the extinction of humankind. *A Torrent of Faces* (1967), written in collaboration with Norman L. Knight, revives the idea of physically altering humans, in this case providing gills so that the oceans of Earth can be colonized; but even with that new frontier opened, the planet becomes overpopulated.

Blish became involved with the early *Star Trek* novelizations during the 1970s, which unfortunately consumed much of his writing time. He wrote two notable novels during this period, of which the more conceptually interesting is *Quincunx of Time* (1973), which made use of a fascinating plot device. Instantaneous interstellar communication has become possible by means of a newly discovered physical law, but there is an odd side effect: Since all messages from all times are es-

sentially being conveyed simultaneously, it becomes possible to listen to a specific communication before it has actually been broadcast. In *Midsummer Century* (1972) a man from our time is revived from suspended animation thousands of years in the future, where he learns that human civilization has risen and fallen several times. There, against a backdrop of superscience that sometimes seems akin to magic, he discovers that a race of intelligently evolved birds are battling humans for control of the planet

Blish's substantial body of short stories has been collected in *The Seedling Stars* (1957), *Galactic Cluster* (1959), *So Close to Home* (1961), *Anywhen* (1970), *The Best of James Blish* (1979), and *In This World, or Another* (2003). In addition to his novelizations, Blish wrote the first original Star Trek tie-in novel, *Spock Must Die* (1970); the book is interesting historically, but it is a mediocre piece of fiction. Blish was one of the few writers who successfully moved from the pulp adventure style of the 1940s to embrace mainstream literary techniques and values, and he wrote several works outside the field that, with the exception of the thematic *After Such Knowledge* trilogy, remain unpublished or largely unknown. His critical essays have been collected in book form and are still highly regarded, and there are periodic reissues of his best work, which has maintained its appeal to generations far removed from the time when it was first written.

Bloch, Robert
(1917–1994)

Robert Bloch is best known for his horror fiction, particularly the psychological horror novel *Psycho* (1959) and several collections of short stories. Although never as prolific in the science fiction field, he was a frequent contributor to SF magazines for three decades starting in the 1950s and produced a substantial body of work before his death, including two interesting novels.

Sneak Preview (1971) is an amusing satire that probably resulted from Bloch's experiences with the film industry, for which he wrote many screenplays. Hollywood has become a domed city following a nuclear war, and filmmaking has become the basis of a new religion to those surviving inside, with strict rules about the social messages to be conveyed. One unhappy producer grows tired of making films that portray space travel as dangerous and costly, and decides to offer an alternate viewpoint; but in doing so, he makes powerful enemies as well as creating social upheaval.

Much more successful was *Strange Eons* (1978), a blend of science fiction and horror tropes. Bloch was an occasional contributor to the shared world Cthulhu Mythos created by H. P. Lovecraft. The premise of the series is that ancient alien creatures much more powerful than human beings once ruled the Earth, were expelled by another race, and have been trying ever since to return to our plane of existence and restore their rule. Although these are generally viewed as horror stories, there usually was enough of an attempt to rationalize the creatures as aliens to make the stories fall into the science fiction category as well. Bloch's novel pushed the concept to its logical conclusion and gave readers a glimpse of what the Earth might be if the aliens finally succeeded in reconquering the planet.

The best of Bloch's short science fiction stories can be found in *Atoms and Evil* (1962), *Fear Today, Gone Tomorrow* (1971), *The Best of Robert Bloch* (1977), and *Out of My Head* (1986). A collection of related stories, *Lost in Time and Space with Lefty Feep* (1987), retells the comical adventures of an unlikely hero, some of which remain genuinely funny while others tend to be in-groupish and opaque to modern readers. Although Bloch will always be remembered primarily as a horror writer, he has a respected place in the science fiction pantheon as well.

The Body Snatchers
Jack Finney
(1955)

Jack FINNEY was not the first author to write a novel in which aliens invade the Earth by replacing people secretly and representing themselves as human beings while their numbers grow. Robert A. HEINLEIN's *The Puppet Masters* (1951) had used a similar device—in this case an alien parasite that attached itself to the spinal cord so that it could control the brain. Finney's aliens were even more insidious, however. Instead of physically hijacking bodies, his invaders consist of spores that drop unobtrusively from the sky. When placed in close proximity to a sleeping human, the spores quickly take form as duplicates—doppelgängers—absorbing all of their victim's memories and draining away their life force. When the process is complete, the original body crumbles to dust and its place is taken by the invader. Finney's aliens might have been somewhat less scientifically plausible than Heinlein's, but Finney was far more effective at building mood and tension.

This was particularly striking because *The Body Snatchers* was quite atypical of his other genre work, which consists primarily of comparatively gentle stories mostly involving the attempt by one or more characters to escape from an unpleasant situation, often into time or a parallel universe. What makes *The Body Snatchers* so effective is the possibility that our friends, neighbors, and family members might not be all that they seem; that they might actually be working against our best interests. This was almost certainly a reflection of early cold war paranoia, and the aliens can easily be seen as stand-ins for hidden subversives biding their time, waiting for the communist revolution.

After the first film version, the novel was reissued as *Invasion of the Body Snatchers*, the title by which it has been known ever since. The movie has been remade twice, but while the technical effects have improved, the relentless sense of impending doom of the original has never been matched. Fans are quick to point out that the monsters so prevalent in genre films were never a significant factor in written science fiction, but they also acknowledge that Finney's frightening vision is highly revered and still popular 50 years after its first appearance.

Bond, Nelson
(1908–)

Nelson Bond began writing in 1937 and effectively stopped in the late 1950s, although he was briefly active again in the late 1990s. Unlike most genre writers, he sold many of his fantastic stories to mainstream markets and was not known specifically as a science fiction or fantasy writer.

The Remarkable Adventures of Lancelot Biggs, Spaceman (1950) collected the best of a series of linked stories about an amusing character who had varied adventures while traveling from planet to planet. Bond wrote several other short story sequences, some of them in the same setting as the Lancelot Biggs stories; none of these have as yet been collected. One of his best short stories, "The Castaway," was also set in outer space. A man rescued after he is marooned on an asteroid turns out to be a jinx whose curse endangers his rescuers—an interesting transposition of a sailors' legend to the future. Civilization has collapsed in "Pilgrimage," in which a primitive priestess travels to Mount Rushmore to worship the gods in one of his most popular stories. Her character recurs in two sequels of lesser note.

Bond's best work also includes "The Cunning of the Beast," an Adam and Eve story, "And Lo! The Bird!" "To People a New World," "The Monster from Nowhere," which cleverly describes a creature from another dimension impinging upon our own, "The Scientific Pioneer Returns," and "Pipeline to Paradise." Bond was primarily concerned with telling a good story and did not spend a great deal of time developing the scientific elements in his work, but he has managed to achieve a lasting reputation that is perhaps out of proportion to his actual contribution to the field.

Bond also wrote two novels—*Exiles of Time* (1949), a confused blend of time travel and disaster stories, and *That Worlds May Live* (1943)—that are virtually unreadable by contemporary audiences. It was always his short fiction that commanded attention, and there interest in his work has recently revived after decades of neglect. Much of his short fiction has been variously assembled in *Mr. Mergenthwirker's Lobblies and Other Fantastic Tales* (1946), *The Thirty First of February* (1949), *No Time Like the Future* (1954), *Nightmares and Daydreams* (1968), and *The Far Side of Nowhere* (2002), but many of his stories remain uncollected.

Born with the Dead
Robert Silverberg
(1964)

Science fiction is often associated with predictions about the future. These are often extrapolations of current trends, perhaps exaggerated slightly for satiric effect, but essentially attempt to describe what our future might be like. Prediction is often the author's intent, at least in general terms; but sometimes writers create a future that is instead very unlikely because it enables them to establish a context in which they can examine some particular aspect of humanity from a fresh perspective.

The premise of Robert SILVERBERG's novella *Born with the Dead* is that a technique has been developed by which the recently dead can be restored to life. This is not a horror story filled with shambling zombies, however; nor are the revived humans harboring some dark mystical secret. The rekindled dead have all of their old memories and function much as they always have: They develop friendships and romantic affairs, pursue careers, and otherwise engage in normal human activities. However, the dead are not unchanged. They live in their own, segregated communities, rarely interact with the outside world, and are particularly averse to encountering anyone they knew in their former lives. They are more relaxed, less emotional, and perceive the world in subtly different ways from how they did when they were alive. They can immediately tell the living from the dead, responding to subliminal stimuli that are not always obvious to the living. A nice touch is that they are universally fond of hunting and killing extinct creatures that have recently been recreated through bioengineering.

Klein is a living man, or "warm," who is determined to be reunited with his wife, Sybille, recently rekindled. She is equally determined never to see him again, although she does not wish to do him harm and even feels a degree of sympathy for his position. Klein pursues her relentlessly, even impersonating a dead so that he can venture into their walled community. Their eventual meeting is not satisfactory to either party, and when he persists, one of her friends poisons him. Rekindled himself, Klein discovers that he is no longer drawn to Sybille and they pursue their separate existences. Beneath the surface, the story illustrates the way in which we are all changed by our life experiences, sometimes growing away from one another, ruled by a force of nature that cannot be overcome by force of will. Klein's obsessive feelings may be tragic, but they do not give him the right to override Sybille's desire to travel a different course.

"Boulter's Canaries"
Keith Roberts
(1965)

Science fiction fans often enjoy reading fantasy, but they are far less inclined toward supernatural fiction. Possibly this is because it is easier to accept magic as just an alternate form of science in a universe with a different set of natural laws, whereas the supernatural implies that the universe is itself irrational and that none of its rules are absolute. Sometimes, however, writers use plot elements from horror fiction and wrap it in a quasi-rational scientific explanation. The extraordinary powers of the teenager in Stephen KING's *Carrie*, for example, could be attributed to a poltergeist or telekinesis. Various writers have used variations of the Frankenstein story, and aliens can be monsters just as easily as they can be differently shaped people.

Keith ROBERTS proved repeatedly during his career that he was not willing to be pigeonholed as a writer of a particular type of fiction. He drew upon whatever interested him in any subgenre, often mixing these individual elements in new combinations. "Boulter's Canaries" opens as a traditional account of a haunted place, in this case a ruined abbey with a history colored by insanity and mysterious deaths. Rumor has it that photographs taken in the vicinity of the abbey do not develop properly. The story's protagonist, a brilliant but erratic scientist, decides to find out the truth. He and the narrator visit the abbey with an array of specialized equipment and observe various anomalies both in still photographs and on videotape. The narrator feels vaguely uneasy, particularly after an inexplicable event ruins some of their equipment, and is content to let the mystery remain unresolved; but his friend is less easily dissuaded and pursues his investigations.

Roberts continues to let us believe that they are witnessing a supernatural manifestation, a poltergeist—but the truth is far stranger. Using special filters, the investigators are able to film unusual electromagnetic disturbances that appear to move purposefully and intelligently, reminding them of canaries darting about a cage. The narrator grows more alarmed, but his companion is relentless. Eventually both their lives are placed in jeopardy when the energy forms, now revealed as living creatures, become aware of the observers and begin to react to their presence. There are very few writers who could convincingly recast the traditional British ghost story as science fiction, but Roberts proved repeatedly that he could bypass the usual conventions with impunity. This is one of the best examples of his talent for looking at familiar ideas from a radically different point of view.

Bova, Ben
(1932–   )

With a background as an editor and as a professional science writer, it is not surprising that Ben Bova chooses to write mostly hard science fiction and that he is skillful at making the scientific content of his work accessible to those with only a lay knowledge of the subject he is exploring. His novels and short stories have most commonly concerned advances or discoveries that might be made in the near future, most recently the exploration of the various bodies in our own solar system, arranged as a loose future history.

Bova first began publishing fiction in the 1960s with several well-received short stories and three novels, of which *The Weathermakers* (1967) is the most interesting because of its realistic portrayal of the way in which weather control might be turned into an offensive weapon. Stories like "The Duelling Machine," "Test in Orbit," and "Fifteen Miles" established his credentials as a technically adroit writer but only hinted at the ability he would demonstrate as he became more comfortable with his craft. *When the Sky Burned* (1967) is an interesting precursor to his more recent work.

Following a nuclear exchange and a solar flare that leaves civilization on Earth in ruins, an expedition from the still viable moonbase returns to harvest raw materials from the wreckage. The idea that human colonies in the solar system would need to wrest their independence from the home world recurs frequently in Bova's later work and is usually stated in even more forceful terms.

During the 1970s Bova wrote several novels for young adults, the most interesting of which is *As on a Darkling Plain* (1972). An ancient, apparently abandoned, but still functioning alien base is discovered on Titan. The protagonist believes that the aliens have already once destroyed human civilization and decides to take preemptive steps to avoid a second disaster, but political difficulties endanger his plan. Bova made no concessions to the supposed lack of sophistication of the teenaged audience, and the novel is therefore rewarding to both its target readership and adults as well. This reluctance to "write down" characterizes his other young adult fiction as well, which is of uniformly high quality.

Bova had been writing occasional short stories about a foresighted entrepreneur that were eventually incorporated into *Kinsman* (1979), which chronologically precedes the novel *Millennium* (1976). Kinsman is an American businessman who is convinced that the U.S. space program is shortsighted and who almost singlehandedly presses for the establishment of a permanent colony on the Moon—a colony whose existence becomes pivotal to the survival of humanity in the second book when the world moves to the brink of a nuclear war. *Colony* (1978) is set in the same future as the Kinsman novels; it is a story of political intrigue following the collapse of civilization on Earth into barbarism, while enlightened colonies survive elsewhere in the solar system. More restrained was *The Multiple Man* (1976), a cleverly conceived and well-executed murder mystery involving cloning. The volume and quality of Bova's work during the 1970s is particularly surprising because for much of that time he was working as editor of *Analog* science fiction magazine as well as editing anthologies.

Bova's respect for scientists and suspicion of politicians are in evidence again in *Voyagers* (1981), wherein an alien ship has drifted into the solar system. Former political enemies are united in their belief that the knowledge to be gleaned from the ship should not be made public, and an international coalition of scientists works to thwart them. In *Voyagers II: The Alien Within* (1986) the protagonist of the first novel wakens from suspended animation to discover that there is an alien presence dwelling inside his mind. In *Voyagers III: Star Brothers* (1990) he and his alien companion devise a means of delivering advanced knowledge to the public despite efforts by the world's governments to suppress it. The two sequels are entertainingly written but thematically redundant. *The Privateers* (1985) is another story of private interests overcoming incompetent government agencies. The United States has largely and unwisely abandoned space to the Russians. When an American entrepreneur moves an asteroid into Earth's orbit in order to exploit its mineral resources, the Russians seize it, and the U.S. government refuses to act on the entrepreneur's behalf. Frustrated, he decides to work outside the law to protect his interests.

Bova launched another series in 1984 with *Orion*, which was a considerable departure from his other work. Orion is an immortal creature whose mission is to watch over humanity and prevent it from destroying itself or straying too far from its destined path. He intervenes in the Trojan War in *Vengeance of Orion* (1988), travels back to prehistoric times in *Orion in the Dying Time* (1990), confronts Philip of Macedonia in *Orion and the Conqueror* (1994), and battles an alien race in *Orion Among the Stars* (1995). Although rationalized, the series feels more like epic fantasy than science fiction. Several other novels appeared during the 1980s, of which two are of some interest. *The Peacekeepers* (1988) posits an international agency poised to prevent any nation from launching a nuclear attack but powerless to stop terrorists armed with atomic weapons. *Cyberbooks* (1989) is a satire about the future of publishing that turns out not to have been far off the mark.

Although the 1990s would see the publication of several of Bova's best novels, the decade did not begin auspiciously. *The Empire Builders* (1993) was another story of individualists battling shortsighted government officials and, in this case, environmentalists, but this time the story was annoyingly preachy and one-sided. *Brothers* (1996), which considers the possibilities of immortality, was more thought provoking but less interesting as fiction. But *Mars* (1992) started a loose series of near-future space exploration novels that would confirm Bova's place as a major author. *Mars* is the story of the first expedition to Mars, described in lavish detail, providing an accurate picture of conditions on the red planet insofar as they were known at the time, and adding conflict in the form of an ostracized crewmember and a mysterious illness. Bova would later describe the second expedition in *Return to Mars* (1999), where similar problems arise thanks to a saboteur.

Parallel to the Mars novels were *Moonrise* (1996) and *Moonwar* (1997). The first novel covers several generations of settlers in a permanent moon colony, overcoming many of the political difficulties that impede the characters in Bova's earlier fiction. In the sequel, a crisis results from the banning of nanotechnology on Earth. When a group of powerful business interests conspire to seize control of the Moon as a gigantic corporate laboratory, the colonists seize the opportunity to declare their independence, succeeding despite military opposition.

Bova continues to expand his future history of space travel. *Venus* (2000) deals with the first successful round trip voyage to Venus. *Jupiter* (2000) paints the government of Earth in even less complimentary terms. A scientist is sent to spy on an outpost on one of the moons of Jupiter, but when he learns that the local researchers have discovered a form of life in the gas planet's atmosphere, he throws his lot in with the rebels. Conditions on Earth are even worse in *Saturn* (2002), and religious persecution forces a minority group to look to the moons of the ringed planet as a possible refuge. *The Precipice* (2001) and *Rock Rats* (2002) pit two entrepreneurs against each other, a conflict that moves toward its conclusion in *The Silent War* (2004). Both entrepreneurs want to open up the asteroid belt for exploitation, but one wants to use these resources to improve living conditions on Earth, while the other prefers to amass a personal fortune and political power. *Tales of the Grand Tour* (2004) is a collection of short stories also set in this

same future history, frequently involving some of the same characters.

Bova has been a productive short story writer throughout his career, although his novels generally have been more successful. His short fiction has been collected in *Forward in Time* (1973), *Aliens* (1978), *Maxwell's Demons* (1978), *The Astral Mirror* (1985), *The Prometheans* (1986), *Battlestation* (1987), *Future Crime* (1990), *Challenges* (1993), *Twice Seven* (1998), and *Tales of the Grand Tour* (2004). His series about Sam Gunn has been assembled in *Sam Gunn Unlimited* (1992) and *Sam Gunn Forever* (1998).

"A Boy and His Dog"
Harlan Ellison
(1969)

This intensely powerful story, which won the Nebula Award, is probably the most famous single work by Harlan ELLISON. Originally published in a British science fiction magazine, then expanded when it was reprinted in the collection *The Beast That Shouted Love at the Heart of the World* (1969), it was the inspiration for a surprisingly faithful and effective movie adaptation. It also turned some of the most honored traditions of the genre right on their heads.

The setting is a postapocalyptic world; the protagonist is Vic, a young man of questionable morals who is partnered with a highly intelligent, telepathic dog named Blood. Civilization, such as it is, consists of gangs known as roverpaks who designate certain areas as neutral ground where they conduct what passes for commerce in a world where food is the most liquid form of currency. Although intelligent dogs are common, descendants from augmented animals bred by the military before the final war, Blood is something special, and it quickly becomes obvious that he is the smarter and more assertive half of the partnership.

When Blood senses a young woman disguised as a rover, Vic decides to rape her, but his plans go awry when one of the gangs also discovers her identity. The woman, Quilla Jane, has come up secretly from a downunder, an underground community that has cut itself off from most contact with the surface world survivors. As they flee together, a bond grows between the two humans, and Blood feels increasingly left out and uneasy about the situation. Eventually Vic follows her to underground Topeka, where he is imprisoned and forced into stud service because most of the local males are infertile.

Quilla Jane eventually tells Vic that she feels badly about having lured him down, and she helps him to escape. However, Blood is injured, and Vic is forced to face the possibility of leaving him. Then, in a stunningly understated conclusion, we discover that Vic's affection for Blood is stronger than his feelings for Quilla Jane: He kills her and feeds her to the dog to restore his strength. There were some misguided grumblings about the supposed misogynistic nature of the ending, but an examination of Ellison's other work does not support that contention, and the story itself is a masterpiece. There were plans to expand the story into a novel, but they never came to fruition.

Brackett, Leigh
(1915–1978)

In addition to her science fiction, Leigh Brackett wrote detective novels and film scripts, including *The Long Goodbye* and *The Empire Strikes Back*. She was married to fellow science fiction writer Edmond Hamilton, and the two almost certainly influenced each other's work to some degree. Brackett began writing for the magazines in the early 1940s and adapted the tone and some of the devices of sword and sorcery fiction, setting her tales on other worlds, particularly an imagined Mars that bears little similarity to the real one. Even her titles were evocative: "The Citadel of Lost Ships," "The Beast Jewel of Mars," "The Lake of Gone Forever," and "Lorelei of the Red Mist," the last written in collaboration with Ray Bradbury.

Brackett's first full-length SF novel was *The Starmen* (1952, also published as *The Starmen of Llyrdis* and *Galactic Breed*). Although it was a standard space opera, this story of a man caught between two cultures was surprisingly sophisticated for its time. *The Sword of Rhiannon* (1953) was the first of several novels set on Mars, in this case a

Mars of the distant past that was an inhabitable world. Although the plot is melodramatic and reminiscent of the work of Edgar Rice Burroughs in that setting, Brackett's prose is far superior, and her characters are much more skillfully drawn than Burroughs's caricatures. *The Big Jump* (1955) mixes mystery and adventure following the return of the first interstellar expedition to reach its destination—with all but one of its crew missing. Brackett was one of the earliest science fiction writers to describe her alien characters as people rather than just artifacts of her plots. In the midst of these competent but unexceptional adventure stories came Brackett's single most important novel, *The Long Tomorrow* (1955). Following a devastating nuclear war, Earth is dominated by a form of Quakerism that bans, among other things, the pursuit of science and the creation of cities. The protagonist is a young man who begins to question the wisdom of his elders. It remains one of the most remarkable and thoughtful of the many postapocalyptic novels the genre has produced.

Although her subsequent novels were all in form lightweight adventure stories, there was usually something happening on another level. In *The Nemesis from Terra* (1961) an ambitious man arrives on colonized Mars with messianic plans for the development of that world, only to discover that entrenched interests are prepared to oppose him. A group of people unhappy with the increasingly restricted freedom possible in the solar system travel to the stars in *Alpha Centauri or Die* (1963), and discover a new way to communicate when they reach their destination. Two of her earlier Mars stories were expanded into short novels in 1964: *The Secret of Sinharat* and *People of the Talisman* both feature Eric John Stark, Brackett's recurring hero, a two-fisted reclusive man who makes his way among the warring clans of Mars. Stark is the typical "outsider," orphaned and raised in a remote locale—the planet Mercury. He is reticent, principled, and capable of violence when necessary.

Possibly because of her work in Hollywood, Brackett's output dropped off dramatically, with only a handful of short stories appearing during the next decade. In 1974 she dusted off Eric John Stark, moved him to another star system, and produced a new trilogy of novels, once again using romantic imagery and exotic settings, but with a surer grasp of prose. *The Ginger Star* (1974), *The Hounds of Skaith* (1974), and *The Reavers of Skaith* (1976) might have seemed out of step with contemporary science fiction, but that would not prevent readers from enjoying them. Stark sets out to track down a missing man on the primitive world of Skaith in the opener, eventually winning the loyalty of a pack of intelligent doglike creatures, and ultimately becoming an outcast himself. The novels are full of richly described locations and innovative action sequences. If Stark remains pretty much of an enigma to readers, that does not make his story any less compelling.

Brackett's short fiction has been collected in *The Coming of the Terrans* (1967), *The Halfling and Other Stories* (1973), and *The Best of Leigh Brackett* (1977). Although much of her short fiction is impressive, her stories are more important because of their influence on other writers who adopted her romantic view of Mars and used it in their own fiction.

Bradbury, Ray
(1920–   )

Ray Bradbury has long described himself as a fantasist rather than a science fiction writer, and indeed most of his fiction consists of fantasy or supernatural fiction. Even those works that ostensibly are SF demonstrate little or no interest in scientific literacy and occasionally evince a complete lack of concern about whether the events in the plot are technically "possible." Bradbury has always been a stylist, and he has drawn much of his inspiration from his childhood in a small Midwestern town. Many of the characters he creates in futuristic settings act as though they grew up in the American heartland, which makes it possible for readers to identify with people in situations otherwise completely divorced from our reality. His many stories set on the planet Mars often have the feel of rural America of a half-century ago, and his characters reflect the same values and prejudices in their imagined future as those that were prevalent in our own recent past. Most of his best early short fiction

works from the 1940s were horror stories, many of which are classics of that genre; but Bradbury also wrote some loosely related stories about the colonization of the planet Mars that were collected in *The* MARTIAN CHRONICLES (1950).

The Martian Chronicles attracted considerable attention both within the genre, where some objected to its occasional fantasy elements and even overt antitechnological stance, and from mainstream readers, who were less likely to be preoccupied with genre traditions. The combined effect of the stories is to describe a series of attempts by humans to colonize the planet Mars—attempts largely doomed to failure, sometimes from faults inherent in the attempt, sometimes with the instigation of a mysterious race of shape-changing Martians. Several of the short stories are equally effective outside the context of the book, particularly "The Third Expedition," "There Will Come Soft Rains," "The MILLION YEAR PICNIC," and "The Long Years." Selected episodes became the basis for a television miniseries, which made a valiant but flawed effort to capture the tone of the book. Bradbury's sensitive prose style and his skillful depictions of a wide variety of discontents, optimists, failures, and realists made the total greater than the sum of its parts. The eventual retreat to an Earth troubled by a global war, with only a handful of colonists left behind, is a bittersweet mix of optimism about one possible future and pessimism about another.

Bradbury began to sell to markets outside the SF field, eventually moving the vast majority of his considerable productivity to mainstream magazines. Although primarily a short story writer, and a prolific one, Bradbury also has written the occasional novel, only one of which is science fiction. *FAHRENHEIT 451* was expanded from a shorter work in 1953. It takes its title from the supposed temperature at which books burn and is set in a repressive dystopian future where reading is banned. This cautionary novel eventually was adapted as an effective if depressing film.

Many of Bradbury's short stories have achieved classic status within the field and are also well respected by mainstream critics. In "The Veldt" a virtual reality amusement becomes all too real. "The Fire Balloons" addresses the question of whether an alien intelligence can be reconciled with Christianity. A prehistoric creature becomes entranced by the sound of a lighthouse in "The Fog Horn," supposedly the inspiration for the movie *Beast from 20,000 Fathoms*. "Kaleidoscope" uses the image implied by the title to describe a group of spacemen marooned after their ship explodes, slowly drifting away from each other in an ever-increasing pattern. Although Bradbury's Venus was no more realistic than his Mars, it was the setting for one brilliant story of human cruelty, "All Summer in a Day." Because of the constant cloud cover, the sun is visible to human colonists only one day per year, and a young girl is deprived of that experience when her companions lock her in a cupboard for the duration.

"Marionettes, Inc." and a second, related story, "Punishment Without Crime," make rare use of robots—in this case, robots indistinguishable from human beings. In the first, an unhappy man tries to escape a domineering wife by providing a substitute for himself. In the latter, a similarly unhappy man purges his hatred by murdering a robot designed to look like his wife, only to find that this act also is a capital crime. A later story, "Downwind from Gettysburg," uses a similar theme, with a man named Booth "murdering" an animated Abraham Lincoln robot.

Probably Bradbury's best-known science fiction story is "The PEDESTRIAN," set in a distant future in which no one walks and everyone travels around in motorized chairs—when they are not shut in their homes watching television. The protagonist is the last man alive who still goes for solitary walks until he is arrested by police on the assumption that he is insane. In "A SOUND OF THUNDER," time travelers hunt the biggest game of all, dinosaurs, with unexpected consequences. "Almost the End of the World" provides a wry commentary on modern culture. When a sunspot appears to have made television broadcasting impossible for the indefinite future, people become increasingly desperate to find a new form of entertainment.

Although Bradbury is still an active short story writer, almost all of his memorable work was written prior to 1965, and the majority of his fiction after that period is either light fantasy or suspense.

He is probably the science fiction writer best known to the general public, despite having been largely inactive in that field for more than 30 years. He is also one of a very small group (including such writers as Philip K. DICK and Jack VANCE) who has gained serious attention from mainstream critics, and he was the first to graduate to wide popularity with the general public despite his obvious genre origins. His collections indiscriminately mix science fiction, fantasy, horror, and even mainstream fiction, but the best of his SF can be found in *The Martian Chronicles* (1950), *The Illustrated Man* (1951), *Golden Apples of the Sun* (1953), *R Is for Rocket* (1962), *The Vintage Bradbury* (1965), *S Is for Space* (1966), and *I Sing the Body Electric* (1970). Many of his 400 stories are collected in other volumes that include occasional SF as well. Although the science fiction field may claim him as one of its own, the breadth of his success assures him an honorable place in the wider realm of American literature.

Bradley, Marion Zimmer
(1930–1999)

Marion Zimmer Bradley will probably be best remembered by the world at large as author of an impressive feminist interpretation of Camelot, *The Mists of Avalon* (1982), but her reputation within the science fiction field rests most heavily on her lengthy series of novels set on the planet Darkover (see DARKOVER SERIES). Bradley's writing career began during the 1950s with several short stories, most of which are collected in *The Dark Intruder and Other Stories* (1964), *The Best of Marion Zimmer Bradley* (1985), and *Jamies and Other Stories* (1993). None of her short work is of more than passing interest. Her later stories are often set in the Darkover universe; most of these are collected in *Darkover* (1993).

Four short novels appeared between 1961 and 1962. Two of them, *Seven from the Stars* and *The Door Through Space*, are routine, the first a low-key alien invasion story and the second an otherworlds adventure involving the rediscovery of a lost human colony. The latter in particular shows the clear influence of Leigh Brackett's Eric John Stark stories, turning the deserts of the planet Wolf into the setting for a romantic adventure. Although Bradley's publisher would later attempt to retroactively include the latter novel in the Darkover series, it was clearly not intended as such despite the very similar background. The remaining two novels, *The Sword of Aldones* and *The Planet Savers*, were both Darkover novels, each later expanded dramatically for new editions, the former as *Sharra's Exile* (1981), rewritten so completely that it bears little resemblance to the original. As the 1960s progressed, Bradley continued to produce minor planetary adventures, such as *The Falcons of Narabedla* (1964) and *The Brass Dragon* (1969). But she clearly was at her best writing about Darkover, and the growing popularity of the series resulted in longer and more complex works, although she did not really hit her stride until 1975 with the appearance of *The Heritage of Hastur.*

Bradley did not give herself up entirely to Darkover, however. *Hunters of the Red Moon* (1973) was a better than average adventure story about a group of humans kidnapped into space and forced to battle for survival on an unfamiliar world. A sequel, *The Survivors* (1979), written with the author's brother, Paul Zimmer, was more ambitious and more interesting. Here the surviving humans are transported to a mysterious quarantine world, where they uncover the secrets of a culture created by two separate intelligent species.

The Darkover series had begun to feel more like a sword and sorcery epic by the 1970s, thanks to the almost magical psi power, laran, and the medieval style culture. In some cases the conflict arose from disputes among the aristocracy of Darkover, the established families who carried the genes that conveyed psionic powers unknown to offworlders and most residents of Darkover. In other cases, there was tension between the newly rediscovered colony and the interstellar human civilization from which it had been separated. Several subsequent volumes in the series would be set in the time before contact was reestablished. There were some minor inconsistencies, which were often removed by revision and reissues. The planet Darkover became as familiar a setting to science fiction readers as was Edgar Rice Burroughs's Barsoom or Frank Herbert's Dune.

Endless Voyage (1975, later expanded and reissued as *Endless Universe*, 1979) was a more conventional science fiction story. It followed the adventures of a group of professional space explorers who visit various worlds and confront different problems in an uneven, episodic fashion. Bradley appeared to be saving all of her best writing for the Darkover series, and major new novels began appearing regularly, including *The Shattered Chain* (1976), *The Forbidden Tower* (1977), and *Storm-queen!* (1978). The feminist sensibilities that would show up in her fantasy also began to appear in her Darkover novels, as expressed by the Renunciates.

During the 1980s Bradley began writing outright fantasy novels (including the highly regarded *The Mists of Avalon*) and stories of the supernatural; but she turned out very little science fiction outside of the Darkover setting. The one notable exception was *Survey Ship* (1980), similar in general concept to *Endless Voyage*, but with a much tighter story line and concentrating on the interactions among the crew of space travelers more than on their adventures in alien settings. It would be her last non-Darkover science fiction novel, although she continued to add to the Darkover series through the end of the 1990s.

The later Darkover novels are much denser than the early ones, with more emphasis on subtle shifts in alliances and the clash of cultures than in overt adventure, but they are thematically varied. *Thendara House* (1983) examined the plight of young women who wished to rebel against the structured and subservient role imposed upon them by Darkover's culture, while *City of Sorcery* (1984) focused on the nature of the psionic powers of the nobility in a manner reminiscent of sword and sorcery. *The Heirs of Hammerfell* (1989) deals with the struggles among the various clans as they contend for power, and *Rediscovery* (1993) describes the events leading up to and during the resumption of contact with the outside universe. A Darkover woman travels to the stars and then returns to discover she is now viewed as an outsider, even by her own family, in *The Shadow Matrix* (1997); in *Traitor's Sun* (1999) tensions among the human worlds again threaten to disrupt contact with Darkover, a development many on that world consider positive.

A new series of posthumous collaborations attributed to Bradley and coauthor Deborah Ross are probably drawn from notes and/or outlines and likely contain little or none of Bradley's own writing. Bradley also edited several anthologies of short stories by other writers set in the Darkover world, as well as a short-lived fantasy magazine and a much longer series of all-original fantasy anthologies. Bradley will undoubtedly be remembered as the author of the Darkover novels, and they are indeed a significant accomplishment within the genre; but it is unfortunate that her other fiction was primarily in other genres, because she had the potential to achieve an even greater status than the enviable one she actually achieved.

Brave New World
Aldous Huxley
(1932)

With the exception of George Orwell's NINETEEN EIGHTY-FOUR, Aldous Huxley's Brave New World is undoubtedly the best known dystopia of all time. Huxley flirted with science fiction more than once—in After Many a Summer Dies the Swan (1939), Time Must Have a Stop (1944), Ape and Essence (1948), and Island (1962)—but never as effectively or as memorably. Like the Orwell novel, this book introduced new words into common usage, including soma, which refers to the use of psychoactive drugs to condition citizens of a future world into conforming to the dictates of society. The novel's title itself—taken from a line in William Shakespeare's play The Tempest—has become a catchphrase for a questionable future. Genetic engineering, artificial birthing, sexual promiscuity, and the suppression of all emotions are the tools by which the government controls the populace, supposedly in the people's best interests. However, it is clear that those in power wish to remain there.

The dissident voice in the novel comes from a young man, the Savage, who was removed from a reservation set aside as a kind of experimental control device. Within the reservation, things are not as perfectly orderly as in the outside world, and when he is exposed to the more civilized behavior, he recognizes contradictions and inequities. As is the case in many dystopian novels, the arguments for and against are expressed directly by a series of conversations between the viewpoint character and a representative of the established order, in this case Mustapha Mond.

Although the novel remains Huxley's best known work, it is not nearly as well written as most of his other novels. Its impact lies in the imagery and the plausibility of the future he described, rather than in the occasionally didactic prose, awkward characters, and slow pacing of the story. The Savage's passionate plea to be allowed his unhappiness strikes a chord with most readers, however, and the conflict between progress and technology on the one hand, and custom and personal freedom on the other, is one that will not be resolved easily. Several years later Huxley would write several essays purporting to show that the future that he had predicted was already rushing upon us. These were collected in book form as Brave New World Revisited (1964).

"Brightness Falls from the Air"
Margaret St. Clair
(1951)

Science fiction is a particularly effective venue for stories examining racial prejudices, because it is possible to create entirely alien races and use them as proxies for real minorities. Some authors are optimistic about the eventual evolution toward tolerance, as in H. Beam PIPER's LITTLE FUZZY (1962), while others paint a gloomy picture, either because of their despair about human nature or as a dark warning of the excesses of which we are capable, as in The Dark Light Years (1964) by Brian W. ALDISS.

Kerr, the protagonist of what is probably Margaret St. Clair's best-known story, is a technician at a morgue that specializes in handling the bodies of extraterrestrials. He recognizes that prejudice exists, in this case specifically directed toward a bird-like alien race that has been ruthlessly exploited by humans. On their own world they engaged in ritual battles that rarely resulted in serious injury, but humans insist on more serious stakes, and now the fights are invariably to the death. Kerr acknowledges that the prejudicial policies of humanity are tragically wrong, but this is an impersonal judgment that has no emotional effect upon him until he meets one of the alien women, Rhysha, and accepts her as a person. When she asks why humans despise her kind, he replies that it is because humans have wronged them terribly and are ashamed of that fact, though they remain apparently unwilling to do anything about it.

Kerr's emotional attachment to Rhysha grows stronger, and he decides to do something for her people. He implores her to persuade the others of her kind to refuse further combat while he petitions the government to allocate space on a newly discovered world for the few surviving bird people. Predictably, his efforts fail, and their last encounter comes when he is forced to deal with her corpse—she is the latest victim of what is to humans merely an exciting form of entertainment. St. Clair exhorts us to try to do better, but she reserves judgment as to whether or not we will succeed.

Brin, David
(1950–   )

David Brin is best known for his Uplift series, which began with *Sundiver* (1980), his first published science fiction novel. The premise for the Uplift series is a complex one. An ancient alien race known as the Progenitors established one leading race in each galaxy whose mission is to help other life forms achieve sentience. The human race turns out to be an exception, a mutation not part of the overall plan, and conflict arises between the expansive human civilization and those others who believe they are responsible for imposing order on the galaxy. Humans in turn have uplifted dolphins and chimpanzees to intelligence in order to have allies, and they spend much of their time seeking artifacts and knowledge left by the far superior Progenitors. In the opening volume, humans penetrate the corona of a star and discover an unusual form of life living in that unlikely environment.

Startide Rising (1983) won both the Hugo and Nebula Awards. A starship with a mixed crew of humans, dolphins, and chimpanzees is caught in the middle of an imminent interstellar war while investigating rumors of Progenitor artifacts on a distant world. The battle for control of superior technology becomes more widespread in *The Uplift War* (1987), and refugees from the violence take refuge on an uncharted world in *Brightness Reef* (1996). Their plight is explored in more detail in *Infinity's Shore* (1996) and *Heaven's Reach* (1998) as their insular existence ends and contact with the rest of the galaxy is resumed. Technically an extended space opera, the series rises far above its form, and the execution is uniformly excellent.

Brin's non-Uplift novels have been surprisingly diverse. *The Postman* (1985) is probably the best known of these, thanks to the Kevin Costner film of the same title. In the aftermath of a nuclear war, a survivor pretends to be a representative of the postal office of a resurgent U.S. government—a pretense that becomes a self-fulfilling prophecy. *The Practice Effect* (1984) unambitiously but amusingly postulates an alternate world where items actually become improved through use. *Heart of the Comet* (1986), written in collaboration with Gregory Benford, is a technically detailed, intelligently conceived, but somewhat lifeless story of an expedition to study a newly arrived comet. *Earth* (1990) is an interesting variation of the disaster story, in this case caused by a tiny black hole that has penetrated to the Earth's core with potentially disastrous consequences. The ensuing action is predictable, including the rise of a group that believes human extinction is not necessarily a bad idea, and the story is surprisingly emotionless. *Glory Season* (1993) is set on a colony world whose inhabitants chose to use cloning as the means of populating their world, a plan that is put in jeopardy when a new wave of traditional colonists begins to descend upon them.

Kiln People (2002) has a remarkable premise and is much more tightly written than most of Brin's previous efforts. The hypothesis of the story is that technology has made it possible to create exact duplicates of people, complete with a full set of memories, through a kind of matter duplicator. The catch is that the duplicates have extremely short lifespans, measured in days or sometimes hours. Individuals can use these duplicates to take care of routine tasks, or to undertake risky endeavors, or simply as a means to accomplish more than one thing at a time. In most cases it is necessary for the creation to return to the original to transfer memories before the limited lifespan reaches its end and the duplicate disintegrates. The protagonist is a detective who makes use of this process, and while the mystery he solves is also quite interesting, the process is the unique device that gives life to the novel.

Brin's infrequent short fiction is uniformly entertaining and well reasoned. "The Crystal Tears" won a Hugo Award; other stories of note include "Dr. Pak's Preschool," "Lungfish," and "The Living Plague." Most of his short fiction has been collected in *The River of Time* (1986) and *Otherness* (1984). Brin has a strong background in physics and is generally considered a writer of hard science fiction, but his work almost always concentrates on characters and situations rather than on technical issues, and therefore appeals to a broad spectrum of readers.

Brown, Fredric
(1906–1972)

Fredric Brown is best remembered as a writer of detective stories, and most of his novels also fall into the detective genre. He was a prolific short story writer, and these were largely science fiction, starting in 1940 and continuing into the mid-1960s. Brown's specialty was the short-short, or vignette, usually an extended joke with a surprise ending, some of them remarkably effective despite their brevity. The best of these latter were collected as *Nightmares and Geezenstacks* (1961), not all of which are SF.

Brown wrote only five novels in the field, but two of them are considered classics. *What Mad Universe* (1949) is one of the earliest and best alternate-world variations. The protagonist finds himself in a very different version of the then contemporary world, one where President Eisenhower is leading the fight against hostile aliens. *Martians, Go Home* (1955) turned the alien invasion story on

its head. Irritating, sarcastic alien pranksters begin appearing on Earth, popping in and out of existence at will, making life miserable for everyone. The general belief is that they are Martians, but perhaps instead they are just a mass illusion. It is not only a bitterly funny story but also technically the best-written of Brown's SF novels.

The remaining three are less noteworthy but still of interest. *The Mind Thing* (1961) follows the career of a single alien invader, a creature who functions by superceding the minds of other creatures, moving to its next host only by killing the current one. The entire story is surprisingly low-key and unmelodramatic, but it is quietly chilling nonetheless. *The Lights in the Sky Are Stars* (1954, also published as *Project Jupiter*) is the story of an ambitious man who believes that humanity's destiny is to reach the stars. He shamelessly manipulates the public and his friends to ensure that space exploration continues with a flight to the moons of Jupiter. Although rather dated, the intensity of the protagonist's quest is quite striking. *Rogue in Space* (1957) is the most ambitious and the most uneven of Brown's novels. An enigmatic alien creature encounters humans in space, becomes fascinated with them, and is reluctant to let them return to their ordinary lives. All five of these novels have recently been collected in an omnibus edition, *Martians and Madness* (2002).

Brown's most famous short story is "ARENA," but several others are almost equally familiar. "COME AND GO MAD" describes the reaction of a human being to the revelation that we are not the masters of Earth but are in fact being manipulated by the collective consciousness of ants. Although many of Brown's stories were humorous, there was a bitter tone to most of them. Other stories of particular merit are "Placet Is a Crazy Place," "Solipsist," "Etaoin Shrdlu," "The Star Mouse," "Paradox Lost," and "Honeymoon in Hell." There have been many collections of Brown's short fiction over the years, but all of the significant stories can be found in *From These Ashes* (2001).

Brown was one of the very few science fiction writers to establish a lasting reputation almost entirely with short fiction, joining the ranks of Ray BRADBURY and Harlan ELLISON in that regard. Although he often dealt with serious issues, his treatment may have appeared superficial because of the light narrative style he employed and because of his penchant for jokes and trick endings. Initially there was a tendency to dismiss him as a minor writer whose contributions to the field were negligible, but in recent years there has been a renewed interest in his career. It seems likely that his reputation has been refurbished and that a new generation of readers will find him as entertaining as did the older one.

Brunner, John
(1934–1995)

John Brunner's productive career started with the sale of his first novel, *Galactic Storm* (1951), a pseudonymous space opera, and with a memorable robot story, "Thou Good and Faithful" (1953). A steady flow of above-average stories followed until the late 1950s, when he started writing short novels at a prodigious rate, most of them fairly light adventure stories but remarkably well written. Six of them appeared in 1959 alone, ranging from the almost surreal *100th Millennium* (revised as *Catch a Falling Star* in 1968) to the complex political intrigues of *The World Swappers*, in which government and corporate leaders each attempt to accumulate personal power. The best of these was *Threshold of Eternity*, in which disparate people from various time periods are enlisted to affect the outcome of a war fought through time as well as space.

A steady stream of novels followed during the 1960s under his own name and as Keith Woodcott, becoming increasingly polished in execution and more sophisticated in structure, while still structured as straightforward adventure. The first indications of Brunner's strongly held political and social attitudes appeared at the periphery of some of these early novels. *Sanctuary in the Sky* (1960) is set on a neutral world caught between two rival empires that were probably intended to represent the United States and the Soviet Union. *Slavers of Space* (1960, later revised as *Into the Slave Nebula*) details the enlightenment of a man who believed that the android servants who perform all of the onerous work for humankind

are content with their lot, but who subsequently learns otherwise.

A few individuals are able to alter the course of galactic civilization in *The Skynappers* (1960), a point made again in *I Speak for Earth* (1961) and in several later novels. Brunner's confidence that one individual could alter the course of history is demonstrated in much of his output during this period, although he would later seem less confident that things could be changed so easily. For example, a single representative from Earth must prevent the genocide of an entire alien species in *Secret Agent of Terra* (1962, revised as *The Avengers of Carrig*), which was also the first of his Zarathustra Refugee Planet series, each set on another lost human colony in space. *Times Without Number* (1962) is cobbled together from separate, related short stories, the most interesting of which concerns an attempt to ensure that the Spanish Armada defeats the English fleet.

Although Brunner's output varied somewhat in quality during the early 1960s, the least of his books remain readable today and the better ones are sought after by collectors and readers alike. *The Super Barbarians* (1962) was the first to suggest that Brunner might have the makings of a major novelist. It tells the story of an alien race that has used stolen technology to reach the stars and conquer Earth, but without changing the cultural habits that will eventually bring about their defeat. *The Dreaming Earth* (1963) wrapped a scientific mystery around a serious look at the consequences of overpopulation. Brunner began to incorporate more original and ambitious plots into his work, such as the physical transformations that ensue following contact between humans and aliens in *The Astronauts Must Not Land* (1963, later revised as *More Things in Heaven*). Aliens are mistaken for mutants in a postapocalyptic Earth in *To Conquer Chaos* (1964), and our inevitable urge to split off into rival groups leads to conflict on a remote planet in *Castaways' World* (1963, revised as *Polymath*).

Brunner began to attract much greater attention starting in 1964 with *The Whole Man* (also published as *Telepathist*), a novel actually composed of linked short stories. The title refers to the protagonist, a deformed man who nonetheless has an extraordinary mental ability: He can enter the fantasy worlds of the mentally ill and interact there, helping them to regain their sanity. The book was nominated for a Hugo Award; and although it did not win, it catapulted Brunner to the front rank of SF writers. He retained that place even though his next several novels were minor works, except for *The Squares of the City* (1965), which is only marginally science fiction. His longest novel to date, it is set in an imaginary country, and the plot is patterned after the moves in a famous chess game.

In the latter half of the 1960s Brunner's writing became more thoughtful and less dependent on overt action. An eccentric playwright gathers a cast of unlikely actors and uses strange devices to record their rehearsals in *The Productions of Time* (1967). Eventually we discover that he is actually a visitor from a distant future interested in recording the actors' emotional as well as physical performances. *Quicksand* (1967) also features a time traveler, this time an apparently amnesiac woman whose relationship with the protagonist becomes the focus for an intense, understated story.

It was in 1968 that Brunner reached the pinnacle of his creativity. STAND ON ZANZIBAR was his longest and most complex novel, borrowing from the style of John Dos Passos to incorporate news clips and other artifacts into a text that jumped from character to character. He would use a very similar style again in *The Jagged Orbit* (1969), an even darker look at a future where overpopulation, urban sprawl, government corruption, and organized crime have reduced the quality of life. To balance these more serious novels, Brunner also produced the humorous *Timescoop* (1969), in which a megalomaniac kidnaps prominent people out of time and plans to coerce them into helping him with his own ambitions, only to fall prey to a conspiracy concocted by his captives. *Double, Double* (1969) proved that even a bad movie plot could be turned into a formidable novel, in this case involving a new form of life that evolves out of industrial pollution.

Brunner's political preoccupations became more evident and occasionally intrusive during the 1970s. *The Wrong End of Time* (1971) poses a possible alien threat to Earth, but the setting is an unattractive isolationist America that seems hardly worth saving. *The Dramaturges of Yan* (1972) is more like Brunner's early otherworlds adventure stories, but the pacing is labored and the revealed wonders of an alien civilization are too familiar to be stimulating. *The Sheep Look Up* (1973) was another major novel, this time set in an overpopulated future where pollution has wiped out all life in the Mediterranean Sea and further deterioration seems inevitable. It is one of Brunner's most skillfully written novels, but the downbeat tone alienated some readers. Matter transmitters allow everyone to live in isolation in *The Web of Everywhere* (1974), one of the best novels from this period. When someone discovers a way to bypass the system of security codes and access any site on Earth, he becomes the most feared criminal in the world.

Shockwave Rider (1975) would be the last of Brunner's major novels. Computer networking and data management have become so pervasive that individual freedom is virtually unknown. The protagonist is a rebel who has managed to write himself out of the system, and who becomes the spearhead of a rebellion. Although more hopeful than Brunner's other dystopian novels, it was also his last effort to write an extended, serious work. Subsequent novels would be interesting and entertaining, particularly *Players at the Game of People* (1980), *The Tides of Time* (1984), and *Children of the Thunder* (1989); but others, including *The Crucible of Time* (1983) and *Muddle Earth* (1993), fail to hit their mark.

Brunner was much less prolific during the 1980s and 1990s than he had been previously, although he continued to write short stories with some regularity, some of which are quite well done. A good representation of his work can be found in *Now Then!* (1965), *Out of My Mind* (1967), *Entry to Elsewhen* (1972), *Time Jump* (1973), *The Book of John Brunner* (1976), *Foreign Constellations* (1980), and *The Best of John Brunner* (1988), but a large number of his stories remain as yet uncollected. Brunner will be remembered for a comparatively small number of his novels, primarily his dystopian visions; but also there is likely to be sustained interest in his less serious but no less entertaining adventure stories.

Budrys, Algis
(1931–   )

Algis Budrys was one of a crop of new writers who appeared during the early 1950s. He rapidly produced a substantial body of work, much of which was dramatically altered in theme, style, and purpose from the science fiction of the 1940s. The son of an official of the Lithuanian government in exile, his awareness of the effects of the cold war recurs frequently in his work. Budrys's first novel appeared in 1954, but *False Night*—the story of the gradual reestablishment of order following a nuclear war—was severely cut from the author's original version and did not appear as it was intended until it was reissued as *Some Will Not Die* (1961). By then he had published dozens of short stories—many of them of exceptional quality—and four other novels, three of which are highly respected to this day.

The least well known of these novels was *Man of Earth* (1956), the underrated story of a man forced to change his physical appearance and flee to the outer reaches of the solar system to escape his enemies. There, with a new identity and essentially a new body, his personality undergoes a fascinating metamorphosis. *Who?* (1958) looked at the same concept from a different angle and attracted considerable attention from outside the field as well as from within, resulting in an uneven movie version. The premise of the novel is that a prominent scientist is nearly killed in an explosion, after which Soviet scientists restore him to life with so many mechanical augmentations that it is impossible to determine his true identity—or even, given his identity, his true state of mind.

The Falling Torch (1959) pitted rebellious agents from colony worlds of Earth against alien conquerors of Earth in a gripping story of intrigue that was obviously inspired by the Soviet occupation of Lithuania. Budrys's most important early novel, and perhaps his single best even now, was ROGUE MOON, which appeared as a paperback original in 1960. An enigmatic alien artifact has been found on the Moon—essentially a gigantic puzzle box that kills anyone who proceeds without following a set of apparently totally random rules. Although the focus ostensibly is on the continuing

attempts to solve the problem by making duplicates of a resourceful man—each of whom is sent to his death until, by process of trial and error, the solution is found—the story is really about the two main characters, one obsessed with death, the other determined to solve the problem, regardless of the cost. *Rogue Moon* is one of the best examples of an exploration of human behavior that could have been written only as science fiction.

Over the next 15 years Budrys would write only one novel and a handful of short stories. The novel, *The Amsirs and the Iron Thorn* (1967), was a skillfully written but otherwise routine otherworlds adventure. It was not until the appearance of *Michaelmas* (1976) that Budrys would again achieve the level of quality of *Rogue Moon*. Michaelmas is a journalist in a future when the news industry is as much a motive force as a simple reporter. Michaelmas, aided by a wonderfully evoked sentient computer, fancies himself with some justification as the secret master of the world—or at least that is the case until he discovers that someone is replacing prominent humans with doppelgängers.

Budrys devoted much of his subsequent time to literary criticism and editing, most notably for the Writers of the Future series of original anthologies. Some of the best of his criticism can be found in *Bookmarks* (1985). His most recent novel is *Hard Landing* (1993), in which the humanoid crew member of a spaceship secretly crashed on Earth breaks a pact with his fellows and makes the government aware of their existence. Convincingly told and well plotted, this novel is nonetheless comparatively minor compared to Budrys's previous work.

Considering the large number of excellent short stories available, it is surprising that only a small portion of Budrys's older work has been reprinted in his three collections *The Unexpected Dimension* (1960), *Budrys' Inferno* (1963, also published as *The Furious Future*), and *Blood and Burning* (1978). A good selection of his best short fiction can be found in *Entertainment* (1997). "Wall of Crystal, Eye of Night," "The Distant Sound of Engines," "Riya's Foundling," "The End of Summer," and "Lower Than Angels" are all excellent stories.

Bug Jack Barron
Norman Spinrad
(1969)

Most science fiction from the 1920s through the 1960s was targeted primarily at adolescent males, but its appeal was strangely asexual. The pulp magazines were frequently adorned with half-clad females, but there was neither romance nor sexual activity in the stories. Until the 1960s most female characters were present simply to ask questions, which the male protagonist would answer at tedious length, or were victims requiring rescue from hideous aliens or mad scientists. Although the late 1950s and early 1960s saw a decline in this stereotyping, the genre's occasional stories with sexual themes—such as Brian W. ALDISS's *The Primal Urge* (1961)—were tasteful, restrained, and sometimes opaque. Norman SPINRAD attempted to change that with *Bug Jack Barron*, his first major novel after three minor space operas.

In a shorter version, the novel had already caused an uproar in England because of its frank and explicit sexual situations—situations that would scarcely raise an eyebrow today inside or outside the genre. Spinrad had great difficulty finding an American publisher for the full novel, which was characterized by some editors and critics as obscene, but it eventually appeared and caused a similar furor in the United States. The story itself is set in a very near future America, one where the media and the government have become intertwined and where both are corrupt and frequently incompetent. In some ways, the predictions of the novel have already been outstripped by reality, but at the time these concepts were considered extremely innovative as well as shocking.

The plot involves the efforts by a wealthy and larger-than-life character named Benedict Howard to develop a form of immortality. A prominent television personality is instrumental in exposing the truth about his activities, which involve murder and the bribery of politicians. Although in some ways the protagonist has also been corrupted by the system, Spinrad demonstrated the power of the media to change even the most entrenched aspects of human culture through manipulation of public opinion on a massive scale and within a timeframe much more compressed than was possible in the past.

Bujold, Lois McMaster
(1949–   )

Lois McMaster Bujold made a dramatic debut in 1986 with three related novels, the advent of her Barrayar series, which includes almost all of her subsequent science fiction. The sequence began with *Shards of Honor*, set in a fairly typical interstellar civilization in which the various human-colony worlds have evolved into separate cultures, often with little contact with one another. During a war between two of these civilizations, a brilliant military strategist falls in love with an aristocrat from the other side, with implications for the political future of both worlds. Their son, Miles Vorkosigian, is the central character in most of the subsequent novels.

Although the early episodes in the series are generally considered as falling into the category of military SF, Bujold was always more interested in her characters than in the details of their military exploits, and her work has a softer edge than is usual in that form. *Ethan of Athos* (1986) and *The Warrior's Apprentice* (1986) both show Miles as an adult, serving anonymously in Barrayar's military and simultaneously leading a complicated double life as leader of a crack mercenary band. Ethan is a new recruit from a world that employs a strange form of childbirth, and the story is as much about how he learns to adapt to his new companions. The second book describes how Miles, who suffers from physical problems following an assassination attempt, overcomes his limitations to become a brilliant military strategist and diplomat.

Falling Free (1988) is ostensibly set in the same universe as the Barrayar stories, but it has no direct connection with them. A group of humans genetically engineered to be adapted to low gravity rebels against the company that virtually owns them in this Nebula-winning novel, still perhaps the single best book Bujold has written. A handful of short stories, all involving Miles, appeared during the late 1980s; these were collected as *Borders of Infinity* (1989). The best of these is the multiple-award-winning "The Mountains of Mourning." *Brothers in Arms* (1989) continued the story of Miles's double life, spoiled aristocrat on one hand, mercenary commander on the other.

The Vor Game (1991) has a typical military plot. Miles and his mercenaries travel to a remote world, where they save the government of a relatively benevolent ruler. Bujold seemed to be losing interest in the military side of things, however, and diplomacy became more of a factor in the plot. The novel won a Hugo Award, evidence that Bujold's appeal was to a broader range of readers than just fans of military fiction. Her next book, *Barrayar* (1991), skipped back in time to follow the careers of Miles's parents, and added substance to the various planetary societies in her created universe. *Mirror Dance* (1995), the weakest of Miles's adventures, is a straightforward space opera in which the hero searches for his cloned twin.

Cetaganda (1996) cast off the last of the military trappings. Miles is part of a diplomatic team sent on a peaceful mission to another world. He and his colleagues find themselves involved in an intriguing mystery and decide to investigate personally rather than to rely on the local authorities. Bujold was clearly more interested in telling a complex story and creating realistic characters than in providing yet another simple adventure; for the most part she abandoned much of the melodramatic action that was typical of her earlier work. Similarly, in *Memory* (1996) Miles actually uncovers a plot within the senior ranks of Barrayar's military, with which he has become somewhat disenchanted.

Komarr (1998) showed the steady improvement in Bujold's ability to create a complex situation just as realistic as in her simpler military adventures. Miles travels to a world subject to Barrayar and uncovers a plot to isolate his home world from the rest of the galaxy. Bujold also incorporated elements of romance, which had been conspicuous by their absence since her first novel, as Miles falls in love with the wife of one of the conspirators. His efforts to woo her dominate *A Civil Campaign* (1999), which superimposes a comedy of manners on top of a complex story of political intrigue. The most recent title in the series, *Diplomatic Immunity* (2002), takes place in an unusual artificial habitat and mixes diplomacy, a murder mystery, and other subplots in a taut thriller leavened by moments of genuine humor.

Most of Bujold's novels have been reprinted in omnibus editions under various titles. Her small output of non-Barrayar short stories is available as *Dreamweaver's Dilemma* (1996). Her most recent work has consisted of complexly plotted fantasies, but it is unlikely that she will abandon the Barrayar series for long.

"Bulkhead"
Theodore Sturgeon
(1955)

Very few writers made a serious attempt to deal with the psychology of space travel prior to the 1960s, but Theodore STURGEON was always more interested in the people in his stories than in the mechanics of space flight. "Bulkhead" is a powerful and unconventional tale built on strong emotional content, one of many stories Sturgeon would write in an attempt to describe the richness and complexity of human interactions. It also had the novelty of being written in the second person, so that "you" are the main character—an artifice that would have failed miserably if employed by a less talented writer.

The premise is that space travel is so monotonous that it drives any isolated human mad; but spaceships are so confining that two people cannot long stand one another, usually resulting in violence. The solution is to have two crewmembers, but to separate them physically by means of an impenetrable bulkhead through which they can communicate only by speaking to one another. The protagonist is a haughty young man who resists the temptation to open a conversation until very late in the voyage, convinced that he needs to explore all the other available avenues of amusement first, saving the complexity of human contact until everything else has been exhausted.

When the protagonist finally decides to initiate contact, he is amazed to hear his fellow crewperson crying, apparently despondent with loneliness. The voice eventually identifies itself as a 15-year-old cadet named Skampi, much to the consternation of the listener, who experiences a variety of emotional responses—anger, sympathy, jealousy, and fear. At one point he attacks the bulkhead physically, determined to break through and kill the cadet, but eventually he learns to tolerate and even feel compassion for the other.

When the flight ends, the protagonist is impatient to meet Skampi, but his superiors reveal the truth. Skampi was created by imposing a temporary split personality within his own mind, so that he accepted his younger self as an external persona. The experiment was designed to help reconcile the emotional problems caused by conflicts between the adult human psyche and that of a child. Sturgeon's solution may be of doubtful psychological validity, but it was such an unusual and thought-provoking explanation that the story made a strong and lasting impression.

Bully!
Mike Resnick
(1990)

Mike RESNICK is a frequent visitor to various African nations, and his experiences there are reflected in much of his work, generally disguised as an alien culture on another world, sometimes more explicitly as an attribute of a future world with a transplanted African population. He used this background in a slightly different fashion for his short novel of alternate history, *Bully!*

Alternate history stories, or uchronias, were until recently a very minor subgenre in science fiction, but grew increasingly popular during the 1990s. Most of these involve obvious points of divergence, usually the outcome of wars: What might have happened if the Confederacy had won the Civil War, if the Nazis had been the victors in World War II, if Hannibal had defeated and destroyed Rome? A few stories, as is the case here, simply take a historical character, drop him or her into a new context, and consider the possible consequences of an interaction that never took place in real history.

Resnick suggests a different career for Theodore Roosevelt, following his departure from the presidency. Roosevelt travels to Africa, not just to participate in a safari, as was the case in reality, but also to become a player in the nation building that was taking place at that time. Recognizing an opportunity, Roosevelt attempts to forge central Africa into a modern nation, introducing technological advances and social changes and establishing himself as a political leader. Resnick does a marvelous job of depicting the man as a person rather than a caricature; Roosevelt is brash and egotistical, but also sincere in his efforts to better the lives of the people of that region. Unfortunately, he does not recognize the weight of social inertia and the timespan needed to effect such radical change, and his project ultimately falls short of its goal. His final decision is to return to the United States, retake the presidency, and declare the Congo an American protectorate to prevent the Belgians from reoccupying the country.

Much of Resnick's best work has been in short novels, and *Bully!* is probably the best of these—a restrained, understated masterpiece. Roosevelt is realized as a colorful and controversial character, and even though he fails, Resnick describes him as a true hero for at least seeking to make the world a better place.

Burgess, Anthony
(1917–1993)

The British author Anthony Burgess primarily wrote mainstream fiction, but he probably is best known both within science fiction and outside the field for his brilliant dystopian novel A CLOCKWORK ORANGE (1963). The setting is a future England where violence is a part of everyday life and where rebellious young thugs communicate in an argot that incorporates many Russian words. The artificial language imbues the novel with an unusual texture that becomes very rewarding once the reader has adjusted to it. The central character is an antihero, a self-absorbed delinquent whose one redeeming quality is his abiding love of the music of Beethoven. After committing yet another heinous crime, he is captured and subjected to an experimental behavior modification technique that links violence to nausea; but the punishment is even crueler because it inadvertently causes the same reaction to Beethoven. His transformation from villain to victim evokes mixed feelings from the reader because of Burgess's implication that, in this case, the government has engaged in an even greater form of evil than the one it sought to address.

The Wanting Seed (1963) is just as unpleasant a depiction of a possible future. Overpopulation has become so pressing a problem that radical solutions are in use, including cannibalism, government encouragement of homosexuality, and the use of war as a means of population control. Although the tone is more satirical than in *A Clockwork Orange,* there is also an undertone of bitterness, and clear evidence that despite all of these interim measures, the crisis is steadily worsening. The author offers no solution in this cautionary tale, and is perhaps convinced that a catastrophic collapse is inevitable. Burgess's next several works were more conventional mainstream novels, but he would later return to the form with *1985* (1978), actually a long story about a dissolute, corrupt, collapsing United States coupled with a long essay about George Orwell's classic dystopia NINETEEN EIGHTY-FOUR. *The End of the World News* (1983) contains three interwoven tales describing the end of the 20th century and its shortcomings, as the passengers and crew of a spaceship flee a doomed Earth. The satire is less pointed, the prose more didactic, and the book reads more like a series of essays than fiction.

Burroughs, Edgar Rice
(1875–1950)

Edgar Rice Burroughs came to writing after several failures as a businessman, but quickly hit his stride with a series of magazine serials that started with *Under the Moons of Mars* (1912, in book form in 1917 as *A Princess of Mars*). However, he will always be best known as the creator of Tarzan, one of the handful of literary characters who have become household names, and an inspiration for dozens of movies, at least two television shows, and several print series of imitations. Although there are occasional fantastic elements such as lost cities and the secret of immortality, the Tarzan

novels are not generally science fiction—with one exception, *Tarzan at the Earth's Core* (1930), which introduced Tarzan as guest hero in the Pellucidar series.

The Mars series was Burroughs's longest and most successful after Tarzan. The first three titles, *A Princess of Mars* (1917), *The Gods of Mars* (1918), and *The Warlord of Mars* (1919), many are actually a single three-part story. American adventurer John Carter is transported to Mars through some mystical means and finds himself in the world of Barsoom, a romanticized Mars peopled by a humanoid race as well as by four-armed, green-skinned giants. Carter makes friends with one of the latter, particularly his companion Tars Tarkas, and falls in love with one of the former, the "incomparable Dejah Thoris." The first two novels end with cliffhangers as Carter, later accompanied by his son, rescues beautiful women from a succession of evil cults and hideous monsters.

Thuvia, Maid of Mars (1920) features Carter's son alone in a similar role. Carter's daughter is off for a series of her own adventures in *The Chessmen of Mars* (1922), one of the better titles in the series. Burroughs introduced a new Earthman as protagonist for *The Master Mind of Mars* (1928), and a villainous scientist who transfers minds from one body to another. *A Fighting Man of Mars* (1931) pits a Martian warrior against an enemy army equipped with metal-dissolving weaponry. John Carter finally returns in *Swords of Mars* (1936), wherein he destroys the powerful assassins guild and visits the Martian moons. Another mad scientist almost destroys the world in *Synthetic Men of Mars* (1940) and the ancient gods are awakened from suspended animation in *Llana of Gathol* (1948). A collection of shorter pieces was assembled as *John Carter of Mars* (1964). The success of the Mars series inspired several imitators, of whom the best known was Otis Adelbert Kline, but none of these ever rivaled Burroughs in popularity.

When Kline, who wrote Burroughsian adventures set on Venus as well as Tarzan imitations, began a series set on Mars, Burroughs reciprocated with his own Venus series. The first Carson Napier adventure was *Pirates of Venus* (1934), pitting a crashed human against the dangers of the jungle planet. The plots sounded very much like the John

Carter series, but Burroughs never was able to make Venus come to life as he had Mars. *Lost on Venus* (1935), *Carson of Venus* (1939), and *Escape on Venus* (1946) followed, but the swampy landscapes and hideous monsters became monotonous and uninteresting.

Burroughs's fourth major series was much more successful. The PELLUCIDAR SERIES is set inside the Earth, in a large hollow space where dinosaurs still survive and where humans live in primitive tribes, dominated by oversized, telepathic, birdlike prehistoric creatures known as Mahars. The sequence opens with *At the Earth's Core* (1922), in which David Innes and a companion descend into the Earth in a self-propelled drilling machine and find themselves in trouble almost from the outset. In *Pellucidar* (1923) Innes returns with weapons from the surface, intent upon freeing the human population from their inhuman oppressors. The movie version, *At the Earth's Core*, incorporated elements from the first two novels. As he had done with his hero in the Mars series, Burroughs here abandoned David Innes for the next adventure, *Tanar of Pellucidar* (1930); this book follows the adventures of a young warrior who is kidnapped by enemies and who subsequently explores the remoter parts of his world. The later titles in the series, with the exception of *Tarzan at the Earth's Core* (1930), were less successful; they include *Back to the Stone Age* (1937), *Land of Terror* (1944), and a posthumous collection of stories, *Savage Pellucidar* (1963).

Much of Burroughs's more interesting work was done outside the main series. The three-part sequence consisting of *The Land That Time Forgot, The People That Time Forgot*, and *Out of Time's Abyss*, published together in 1924 as *The Land That Time Forgot*, is more thoughtfully plotted than most of his fiction. Prisoners aboard a German submarine successfully seize control of the ship, which is forced to shelter on an uncharted island. Dinosaurs roam the island, providing the usual melodramatic effect, but there is also a layered series of civilizations with differing levels of intellectual development, and we eventually learn that the natives of the island of Caprona actually evolve during a single lifetime, moving from one community to the next when the time is right. The first

two books in the series were made into moderately interesting films. *The Moon Maid* (1926) starts out as a typical Burroughsian otherworlds adventure, this time set on the Moon, but quickly changes direction as the Moon people, armed with superior scientific knowledge, conquer the Earth.

Several of his freestanding novels are actually more innovative than his major series, although they were not necessarily as popular or even as well written. *The Monster Men* (1929, also published as *A Man Without a Soul*) is a blend of the Frankenstein story and H. G. Wells's *The Island of Dr. Moreau*. A scientist is obsessed with the idea of creating life from inorganic chemicals and succeeds, but the results are all monstrous and evil, except for one creature which befriends a beautiful girl. *The Eternal Lover* (1925, also published as *The Eternal Savage*) is a very early timeslip novel in which a contemporary woman is transported back to the Stone Age, while a warrior from that time suddenly finds himself in modern Africa. *Beyond Thirty* (1916/57, also published as *The Lost Continent*) is a future war novel, or more correctly, a postapocalyptic story. After a devastating global conflict, communication across the ocean is lost for generations; years later, an American pilot flies to England to find out what happened there, and discovers vast forests and a variety of dangerous beasts. *The Cave Girl* (1925) and *Jungle Girl* (1933, also published as *The Land of Hidden Men*) are routine but entertaining lost world adventures.

Burroughs was by no means a literary writer. His prose was almost always awkward, his characters flat and interchangeable, his plotting linear and unsurprising. At the same time he was a wonderful storyteller with a gift for devising exotic settings, and despite his shortcomings as a stylist, his work remains popular long after many of his more talented contemporaries have faded into obscurity. There have been occasional attempts to continue one or another of his series, authorized and unauthorized, but none of these have lasted for long and none of them really captured the spirit of the originals. Burroughs is probably the most frequently imitated writer in the genre, and even now, when the field's literary standards have been considerably raised, writers including Mike RESNICK, Michael MOORCOCK, A. Bertram

CHANDLER, and others have acknowledged his importance by writing pastiches or homages. Most of his novels are regularly reprinted and remain popular with each successive generation of readers, and they are likely to retain their place for many generations to come.

Burroughs, William S.
(1914–1997)

William S. Burroughs was one of the more controversial figures working on the fringes of the science fiction field, his work appearing in non-genre venues although clearly drawing upon genre concepts. His first major novel was NAKED LUNCH (1959), which mixed traditional dystopian satire with surrealistic imagery and experimental prose styles. The protagonist may or may not be hallucinating, thanks to his heavy use of drugs—a theme that pervades most of Burroughs's work. The novel was skillfully adapted into a film in 1991, but its bizarre imagery and nonlinear story line doomed it to cult status.

The Soft Machine (1961) and The Ticket That Exploded (1962) both used plots that were even less accessible to casual readers, but incorporated more overt science fiction themes, including extraterrestrial organizations attempting to assert influence over the Earth. However, neither book is cast as a traditional SF narrative and neither attracted more than casual interest from genre readers. Nova Express (1965), which forms a loose trilogy with the two preceding titles, was his most overtly genre-related work, chronicling the battle against the Nova Mob, aliens who manipulate humans in their bid to conquer Earth.

The Wild Boys (1971)—set in a future where savage bands roam the Earth, tearing down every vestige of civilization they encounter—and Ghost of a Chance (1995) also merge surrealism with fantastic elements. Cities of the Red Light (1981) restates many of the themes of his earlier books in a more readable prose style, but it failed to capture as wide an audience, and is virtually unknown within the field. Burroughs would eventually be acknowledged as a brilliant writer, but his influence in science fiction was largely confined to New

Wave writers, most notably J. G. BALLARD, and has persisted only in a minimal form.

Butler, Octavia
(1947–   )

Octavia Butler's first short story appeared in 1971. It was her only published fiction until Patternmaster (1976), the first in what would eventually be a loose series of novels that jump around dramatically in time as well as space. The setting is a far distant future where telepathic powers bind people in different ways and two brothers find themselves competing for the position of authority formerly held by their father. The novelty and inventiveness of the setting and the finely developed conflict between the two brothers added up to an impressive debut. The quasi-sequel, Mind of My Mind (1977), is set, in part, 4,000 years in the past. It follows the chain of events that ensues when one man learns how to move his personality from one body to another, becoming effectively immortal at the expense of those he has displaced. By the 20th century this has led to creation of a gestalt community living secretly within the society of normal humanity. Survivor (1978) switches back to the distant future, this time pitting the Patternist human society against a complex problem of interstellar politics and alien relations.

Her next novel, Kindred (1979), was less exotic and more controlled. A contemporary black woman timeslips back to pre–Civil War America and promptly finds herself enslaved. She survives a series of threats and mistreatments, refusing to surrender her independence and resign herself to her fate. Butler quickly returned to the Patternist series with Wild Seed (1980), reverting to the past again to tell the story of another body shifter and his efforts to breed more of his kind. Clay's Ark (1984) relates the events following the outbreak of an alien plague on Earth, pitting suddenly savage normals against the psionically enhanced Patternists.

Butler's next novel, Dawn (1987), was the beginning of a new sequence. The Oankali are an alien race with apparently benevolent intentions in their dealings with Earth. They use their superior technology to address overpopulation, pollution, and other human problems, but there is the inevitable catch: They also want to change human biology so that they can interbreed with the visitors. The story continues in *Adulthood Rites* (1988), in which a halfbreed is kidnapped by a band of rebels who oppose the Oankali influence on Earth. The sequence ends with a form of reconciliation in *Imago* (1989).

Most recently, Butler has written a two-book sequence, *Parable of the Sower* (1993) and *Parable of the Talents* (2000), in which an empath makes her way through a future world that has become even more sharply divided between the rich and the poor. Recurring themes in Butler's work include feminist concerns, human dignity, and ecological issues. Butler has written very few short stories, but "Blood Child" and "Speech Sounds," both award-winners, are excellent. Her short fiction has been collected as *Blood Child and Other Stories* (1995).

"By His Bootstraps"
Robert A. Heinlein
(1941)

When Robert A. HEINLEIN wrote "By His Bootstraps" back in 1941, it was by no means the first time travel paradox story. Other writers had already played with the concept, which usually involved some variation of going back into the past and murdering one's own ancestor, so that the time traveler could not be born and therefore could not have gone back through time in the first place. But Heinlein lifted the complexity a notch, and while subsequent authors eventually surpassed this story, including Heinlein himself in "ALL YOU ZOMBIES," it would stand for many years as the ultimate time travel paradox tale.

Bob Wilson is visited in his room by two oddly familiar men. One of the men insists that he step through a time portal, while the other warns him against it. Eventually he does take the risk—and finds himself in a distant future in which mysterious beings have transformed most of humanity into biddable slaves, then abandoned them to their fate. Diktor, a man of that future time, sends him back through the portal to retrieve his earlier self, and he realizes that both of his visitors were future versions of himself. The reader is shown the same confrontation, but from three different perspectives.

Convinced that Diktor is not the friend he purports to be, Wilson is determined to thwart his plans; but since time is immutable, he cannot alter the events that he knows have already happened. He makes unauthorized use of the portal to hide out in a different era, and after the passage of considerable subjective time realizes that Diktor was in fact yet another, older version of himself.

The greatest difficulty in creating a story of this type is not so much the plotting of the various time loops, but to render them in such a way that the reader can follow the logic rather than just accept the author's word for it that he has played by his own rules. Heinlein did an admirable job in this case, and the story deserves its status as a classic. Despite some of the awkward prose that characterized his early work, it is still an entertaining and readable tale.

C

Cadigan, Pat
(1953–)

Pat Cadigan's short stories began appearing in the small press in the late 1970s and in professional magazines in the 1980s. She produced an interesting body of work during those years without having any one story do remarkably well; her first novel, *Mindplayers* (1987), was greeted with only mildly positive reviews. The response to *Synners* (1991) was much more enthusiastic, and Cadigan was immediately grouped with such cyberpunk writers as Bruce Sterling and William Gibson. The novel plays with virtual reality in a future where it is possible to immerse oneself so completely in the virtual world that an encounter with a computer virus might very well be fatal. *Fools* (1992) was a loose sequel to *Mindplayers*. An aspiring actress awakens from a mysterious blackout to discover that, during the interim, she has assumed a new identity. Her efforts to reconstruct the missing period of her life are complicated by the intervention of a number of others interested in gaining the same information, and by some assassins who are determined that it will remain lost. *Parasite* (1996), a stand-alone novel, is a convincing old fashioned alien invasion story in the tradition of *Invasion of the Body Snatchers* by Jack FINNEY. The young protagonist kills her own mother after discovering that the woman is being controlled by alien parasites, and must elude the authorities and vindictive aliens until the secret is out.

Tea from an Empty Cup (1998) inaugurated a new and so far much more interesting series. In the years following the sinking of Japan, a police detective becomes interested in a series of virtual-reality-related murders. Her investigation leads her to a secret organization dedicated to creating a new Japan in place of the lost one. The blend of cyberpunk background and the traditional detective story worked remarkably well. The sequel, *Dervish Is Digital* (2001), was even more impressive. Detective Dore Konstantin is back from *Tea from an Empty Cup*, this time trying to ascertain whether or not a man has exchanged his personality with that of an artificial intelligence so that he can harass his ex-wife from the safety of virtual reality.

Cadigan is well respected for her solid short stories and for a series of novels that are entertaining and credible at their worst and remarkably inventive at their best. Much of her short fiction has been collected in *Patterns* (1989), *Home by the Sea* (1991), and *Dirty Work* (1993).

Caidin, Martin
(1927–1997)

Martin Caidin began his career writing nonfiction books, mostly about the aerospace industry and World War II, and a few novels on associated subjects. His first science fiction was *The Long Night* (1956), in which an American city is firebombed; the book was inspired by his own investigation of the bombing of Hamburg. *Marooned* (1964) attracted much more attention and became a best seller, as well as the basis for a major motion picture. Perhaps motivated by the success of that novel, his next novel was *Four Came Back* (1968), the story of the outbreak of a mysterious disease aboard a space station; but it was far less successful. *The God Machine* (1968), on the other hand, was a taut, chilling thriller about self-aware computers seizing control of the world; but the book's publication was poorly timed, following *Colossus* by D. F. Jones (1966), a somewhat more engaging novel that was adapted as a motion picture.

Although Caidin was still not viewed as a genre writer, his next novel dealt with alien invasion. *The Mendelov Conspiracy* (1969, also published as *Encounter Three*) incorporated all of the usual baggage of the UFO story—government cover-ups and the like—without anything new or interesting to redeem it. More thrillers with science fiction overtones followed, but it was not until *Cyborg* (1972) that Caidin had another hit. A test pilot is nearly killed in an accident, and the government tries out experimental biomechanical devices to save his life and restore his mobility. The novel became the basis for the television series *The Six Million Dollar Man,* and Caidin later wrote some of the original novels based on the program, although none approached the quality of the first. He eventually revisited the concept with *Manfac* (1979), but without bringing anything new to the story. One interesting but largely unknown novel from this period was *Aquarius Mission* (1978), in which an experimental submarine encounters a race of friendly aliens deep in the ocean.

Caidin became a recognized genre writer in the mid-1980s with a string of much more overt science fiction novels that began with *Killer Station* (1985). Villains transform a space station—designed to protect America—into a threat, until the protagonist and friends are able to recapture it. If the novel had been published as a mainstream thriller, it might have gone completely unnoticed in the genre; but it was published as science fiction, found a surprisingly wide audience, and Caidin's career took a new turn. In *Zoboa* (1986) a group of terrorists steals atomic weapons and plots to use them to destroy a space shuttle and an assembly of celebrities. This was another novel that could have been marketed

as a mainstream thriller, but which instead was clearly labeled as genre material.

The Messiah Stone (1986) made an attempt to rationalize a plot element that was essentially supernatural. A mercenary is sent to seize an ancient crystal that gives its bearer the power to exert mental control over masses of people. (The object formerly was possessed by Jesus of Nazareth, Adolf Hitler, and other historical figures). The inevitable corruption of absolute power is played out in the sequel, *Dark Messiah* (1990). *Exit Earth* (1987) is an updated variation of WHEN WORLDS COLLIDE by Philip WYLIE and Edwin Balmer. The destruction of life on Earth by solar flares is inevitable; a temporary exodus into outer space is the only possible escape for a small number of potential survivors. The battle over who gets to be saved is inevitable and violent, but Caidin does a good job of developing the impending sense of doom. *Prison Ship* (1989) was probably his most overtly genre novel, and in some ways his best single work. A group of alien criminals arrives in the solar system, teams up with some unsavory humans, and plots to seize control of the world. In *Beamriders!* (1989) the discovery of a matter transmitter leads to exploration of the far side of the moon and an encounter with foreign spies. Caidin's last novel, *A Life for the Future* (1995), was a new version of the first Buck Rogers story, originally related in ARMAGEDDON 2419 by Philip Francis Nowland.

Caidin wrote several other novels of the near future involving battles for control of the Moon, the mysteries of the Bermuda Triangle, high-tech gadgetry, advanced supercomputers, secret Soviet and American weapons projects, and nuclear warfare—all subjects on the periphery of modern science fiction. Most of his books were marketed in such a way that they were not readily visible to the science fiction community, and it has only been retroactively that he has been recognized as having had a lengthy career on the fringes of the field.

Campbell, John W., Jr.
(1910–1971)

John W. Campbell Jr. will always be remembered primarily as editor of *Astounding Magazine* (later

Analog Science Fiction), through which he discovered or influenced such prominent names as Robert A. HEINLEIN, Isaac ASIMOV, and Theodore STURGEON, among others. From the time he accepted that position in 1937 until the 1950s, *Astounding* was unquestionably the leading magazine in the field. During the 1950s Campbell became less open to innovative ideas and the contents of the magazine became increasingly formulaic to the point where readers knew exactly what was meant by an *Analog*-style story—usually one in which the protagonist solves a technical problem through scientific or engineering training or outwits one or more aliens because humans are the toughest, smartest kids on the block.

Campbell's prominence as an editor has a tendency to overshadow his career as a writer, which was not inconsiderable in itself, although he effectively ceased to write fiction shortly after accepting the post at *Astounding*. Starting in 1930 he wrote prolifically under his own name and as Don A. Stuart, acquiring strong followings for both identities. As Campbell, he became the most important imitator of the panoramic space operas made popular by Edward E. SMITH. The major sequence consisted in book form of *The Black Star Passes* (1953), *Islands of Space* (1956), and *Invaders from the Infinite* (1961), although they all appeared in magazine form as serials and short stories during the 1930s. The three protagonists, Arcot, Morey, and Wade, defend the Earth from a series of alien menaces by developing bigger and better superweapons. Campbell's aliens were intelligent though essentially inferior people, not tentacled monsters, but his human characters were almost as shallowly drawn as his sketchily described alien civilizations.

Other space operas followed, including *The Mightiest Machine*, serialized in 1934, and several shorter sequels collected as *The Incredible Planet* (1949). They reprised many of the same situations as the Arcot, Morey, and Wade stories, but less effectively. *Uncertainty* (1936), which appeared in book form as *The Ultimate Weapon* (1966), and the Penton and Blake series, collected as *The Planeteers* (1966), were in the same general form, but featured occasional episodes that began to show more sophistication in his work. The Penton and Blake adventures invariably involved technical puzzles,

and they were very much like the stories Campbell would buy for his magazine during the second half of his career. Most of Campbell's heroes were scientists themselves, or at the very least professed great respect for scientific minds, and it was clear that Campbell perceived the pursuit of knowledge as the highest ideal for the human race. Science generally meant technology, of course, and his stories are filled with wondrous gadgets, though not always particularly plausible ones.

Under the Stuart pseudonym, Campbell began writing more sophisticated stories. "Twilight" (1934) was one of the earliest science fiction tales to make use of a nontraditional literary style in its depiction of a future, possibly a dying Earth. The short novel *The Moon Is Hell* (1951) portrays with surprising realism the plight of the first expedition to the Moon, the psychological as well as physical problems that follow a disastrous landing. It was one of the two best pieces of fiction that Campbell ever wrote, and it hints at the writer he might have been if he had pursued that career. "The Last Evolution" (1932) was a very unusual robot story. Humans are extinct, and only their robotic creations survive, a kind of successor race; but the robots themselves eventually decide to reconstruct the lost species and start a new cycle of existence.

Campbell's most famous story, and arguably his best, is "WHO GOES THERE?" (1938), which was altered almost beyond recognition in the first film version, *The Thing from Another World* (1951), but rendered with reasonable loyalty when remade as *The Thing* (1982). The premise is simple but chilling: An alien creature is unearthed from its frozen tomb. It has the unique ability to sample the DNA of any living creature and turn itself into an indistinguishable copy; it begins reproducing itself, displacing the staff of a scientific station. As is the case in Jack FINNEY's later classic novel, *The BODY SNATCHERS* (1955), the possibility that the people around us are not what they seem is probably at least partly derived from the real-life worries about a supposed communist fifth column. Although the alien is technically a monster, Campbell constructed his story as a technical problem. How can the surviving humans determine who among their complement have been replaced?

The best of Campbell's short stories have recently been collected as *A New Dawn* (2003), but his remaining fiction can also be found in *The Best of John W. Campbell Jr.* (1976) and *The Space Beyond* (1976). His lasting reputation as one of the shapers of modern science fiction is assured because of his editorial career. As a writer, he was only a minor figure, but "Who Goes There?" alone will guarantee that he is never forgotten.

Canopus in Argos series
Doris Lessing

Although best known for her mainstream novels, Doris Lessing had occasionally used science fiction themes in her work before tackling this ambitious project, most notably in *The Four Gated City* (1969) and *The Memoirs of a Survivor* (1975). However, it was not until she launched the Canopus series with *Re: Colonised Planet 5, Shikasta* (1979) that she completely embraced the form. Her choice of an extensive interstellar culture as a setting for her most ambitious work confounded many mainstream critics, and since no effort was made to market them as science fiction, there was little attention paid in that venue either. Subsequent volumes in the series consist of *The Marriages Between Zones Three, Four, and Five* (1980), *The Sirian Experiments* (1981), *The Making of the Representative for Planet 8* (1982), and *The Sentimental Agents in the Volyen Empire* (1983).

Although the novels are set in the same universe, they are not strictly speaking a series. Each stands alone and serves to illustrate another personal crisis, the resolution of which is usually some transcendent event, colored by Lessing's Sufi mysticism. The Canopean Empire spans many star systems and races and believes that it is responsible for overseeing the development of less advanced races, helping them to escape from the lure of self-destructive violence and eventually evolve into a mature and peaceful culture. The planet Shikasta is actually Earth, and in the opening volume an alien visitor comes to Earth in the late 20th century to help shepherd us through dangerous times, which include a third world war. Although the Canopean representative intends to help avoid a

major conflict, he and the reader eventually discover that it is inevitable, and not necessarily entirely unhealthy, unless it escalates beyond all possible control—which nearly happens in this case.

In *The Marriages Between Zones Three, Four, and Five,* a theoretically utopian planet is in the midst of an unprecedented crisis, a plague of infertility, which can be overcome only if the structured segregation of their society is broken down. Each zone consists of a distinct geographical type and is home to a distinct personality profile, but the long separation threatens the entire population with extinction. The Canopeans force the issue by arranging a marriage between the ruling families of two of the zones, and what follows is a comedy of manners with some genuinely funny scenes as the two disparate personalities adjust to one another. Although there is a somber note at the end, Lessing's purpose is obviously to suggest that human diversity and toleration are essential to the future of the race and that indeed it is the things that make us different that also make us strong. The story also contains some satiric commentary on social norms, and underlines the necessity for political conflict in order to preserve a society's health.

In *The Sirian Experiments*, one of the rulers of that world begins to question the political philosophy that governs their relationship with other peoples as well as their own, and her efforts to convince her colleagues lead to trouble. Lessing includes an indictment of certain aspects of colonialism: Her people experiment on less advanced species, ostensibly for their own good, but not always with the desired results. The tone is much more serious than in the previous books, and the conclusion less cheery. Lessing asserts the importance of science and technology as a tool by which to improve the human condition. The story involves the efforts by a planetary populace to slow the onset of a new Ice Age. Unfortunately, despite their best efforts, their culture is irreversibly changed and they can survive only by undergoing an almost mystical transformation.

The concluding volume, *The Sentimental Agents in the Volyen Empire,* is the closest to traditional science fiction, but paradoxically it is the weakest of the set. In a remote part of the galaxy, a diminutive empire is being studied by Sirian agents planning its assimilation into their sphere of influence. The act of observation inevitably causes changes in the observer. Lessing's science fiction novels are clearly meant as parables, each examining one or more aspects of the struggle of society to resolve its conflicting priorities and desires, and most of all the human need to aspire to something greater. At one time Lessing indicated that she planned to extend the series, but no further titles ever appeared.

A Canticle for Leibowitz
Walter M. Miller Jr.
(1960)

During the years immediately following World War II and the use of atomic weapons in Japan, many science fiction writers produced stories of apocalyptic wars and their aftermath. Perhaps not surprisingly, others who had never been associated with the field felt similar concerns, and a handful of novels on the same theme enjoyed a wider readership, including such classics as EARTH ABIDES (1949) by George R. Stewart, *Tomorrow!* (1954) by Philip WYLIE, *Alas, Babylon* (1959) by Pat Frank, and most notably ON THE BEACH (1957) by Nevil Shute. With such substantial competition, it is even more surprising that the most enduring of these novels, one that has been in print almost without a break for 40 years, was written by a man who wrote exclusively for the science fiction magazines, and in fact the novel first appeared as three linked novelettes in that form in 1955. The book-length version won the Hugo Award in 1961 and is often cited as the best single novel the genre ever produced. It is almost certainly the best first novel.

The three sections of the *Canticle* are set progressively further in the future following a devastating nuclear war. The Roman Catholic Church has survived but has been changed in many ways from the institution with which readers are familiar. A particularly delightful irony is that Leibowitz, who is considered a saint and whose mundane effects are revered, was in fact Jewish, although he founded the order whose purpose is to preserve as much human knowledge as possible until such time as we are once again able to use it profitably.

The first installment is set several centuries after the holocaust, when it is still not clear if civilization will recover at all. Most scientific information has been lost because of the near universal revulsion toward books and toward the scientists who reigned during the years immediately following the war. Leibowitz, like the rebels in Ray BRADBURY's *FAHRENHEIT 451* (1953), was reduced to memorizing texts to prevent their permanent loss. The central figure is a young monk so dedicated to his work that he is willing to give up his life to save one single manuscript.

Part two jumps several centuries further into the future. Technology is no longer viewed with suspicion, and the order's carefully protected knowledge is now a prize of interest to the various secular powers contending for control of the reemerging civilization. A visit by an ambitious entrepreneur leads to a series of discussions and a conflict of viewpoints that is refreshingly intelligent and surprisingly gripping despite the lack of overt action. The final section somewhat depressingly shows us humanity on the brink of yet another devastating global conflict, but this time the Order of Leibowitz, under the auspices of the church, has constructed a spaceship in which certain chosen people can escape and wait out the inevitable collapse.

Miller, a devout convert to Catholicism, was writing more than just another doom-and-gloom extravaganza; the preservation of human knowledge is, if anything, presented as an uplifting and transcendent experience. The details Miller provides about life within the order are fascinating, and even his supporting characters are deftly drawn. Although many of the events in the novel are grim, it is frequently tempered by moments of rough humor.

An engineer by profession whose primary career as a writer lasted only 10 years, Miller would resume writing late in life. A sequel, *Saint Leibowitz and the Wild Horse Woman* (1997), was completed posthumously by Terry Bisson. Miller explores many of the same themes as in the original novel, but narrows his focus to one particular round of struggles in which the secular powers try to influence the inner workings of the church, while the church unwisely decides to involve itself in secular politics.

Both sides are ultimately unsuccessful, and Miller's message—that each institution should stick to its own concerns—is ably if somewhat heavyhandedly demonstrated. The novel was not nearly as popular, however, partly because of the high expectations created by its predecessor, and possibly in part because the threat of nuclear annihilation is no longer as imminent as it was during the 1950s.

"Carcinoma Angels"
Norman Spinrad
(1967)

Science fiction has traditionally been a literature of heroes, larger than life characters like John Carter of Edgar Rice BURROUGHS's Mars series, Kimball Kinnison of the Lens series, or Lazarus Long from Robert A. HEINLEIN's Future History series. Typical protagonists, usually male, were scientists or soldiers or adventurers who were self-confident, competent, of stiff moral fiber, selfless, intelligent, and forthright. They prevailed in a conflict because of superior strength and determination, and because they were on the side of right. Sometimes they were genuine superheroes, evolved beyond present-day man either by natural processes or by training, surgery, or genetic alteration.

Harrison Wintergreen in Norman Spinrad's "Carcinoma Angels" is a twisted superman. As a child he manipulates his peers to his own advantage and masters the art of taking tests even though he has no intrinsic interest in knowledge. As a young man, he contrives a personality that will make him attractive to women, then manipulates his finances—through legal means and otherwise—until he is one of the richest men in the world. In the process, he ruins the lives of others—but that does not matter to him. Having achieved his goal, he selects a new one, this time setting out to improve the world. He topples repressive governments and performs various good works, but he has no emotional involvement in the causes he is championing.

He next resolves to establish a place for himself in history, making scientific discoveries that will change the world forever. His novel is a critical success, his first painting is acclaimed as a master-piece, and his legacy is assured. As with everything he has achieved in the past, Wintergreen takes no real pride in any of this. He is looking around for a new goal when he is diagnosed as having terminal cancer. When he is told that no cure is possible, he invests most of his money in an attempt to find one, convinced that this too is a task that he can accomplish simply by applying his intellect. In fact he eventually succeeds by developing a mental technique through which he can manifest his consciousness within his own body and hunt down the cancerous tissue, destroying it in symbolic battles. But once the victory has been won and his body has been cured, Wintergreen finds it impossible to disengage, and he remains in a coma for the rest of his life.

Wintergreen has actually been trapped long before that, of course. His obsessive drive to be the best at everything he tries has, in a sense, doomed him to fail in each case, because he lacks the ability to find self-satisfaction through his accomplishments. He is a reflection of the extremes to which the competitive urge is sometimes taken in our society, and a warning about the ultimate fate of those who fail to keep their lives in perspective.

Card, Orson Scott
(1951–   )

Orson Scott Card's first published story, "Ender's Game" (1977), made an immediate strong impression, although it would be several years later before it would become the impetus for a series of novels that would rocket him to the top of the science fiction field. During the late 1970s and early 1980s he would produce a steady stream of interesting if not remarkable stories, many of which were eventually collected as a future history about the Worthing family, who spearheaded the settlement of a new planet. The Worthing stories reflected Card's background as a devout Mormon, an influence that would become even more obvious later in his career; but even in his early works, a self-sacrificing messiah often figured prominently.

Card's early novels were entertaining if occasionally awkward. *Songmaster* (1980) in particular does an excellent job of describing a complex human relationship in genuinely emotional terms. Card would not reach his full stride until the novel version of *Ender's Game* (1985), the first in what has been an enduringly popular series. In the original short, and in the novel, Ender Wiggins is an extraordinarily talented boy, bred and fostered by a human government that is concerned that an alien race known as the Buggers will launch a new attack on Earth. Ender participates in what he believes to be virtual-reality war games, unaware of the fact that he is directing a real assault fleet in an attack against the Bugger home worlds. When he wins what he thinks is a game, he discovers that he has wiped out almost the entire Bugger race. We subsequently learn that this attack was unnecessary. Ender decides to ensure that the defeated aliens are not completely wiped out in the sequel, *Speaker for the Dead* (1986), and travels to a distant planet to solve a complex cultural problem and avoid another military conflict. Both novels won the Hugo Award, making Card the first single author to have received this honor in two consecutive years.

The story is continued in *Xenocide* (1991), a very readable but inconclusive novel, and less successfully in *Children of the Mind* (1996), which involves another interstellar crisis as external powers become concerned about Ender's accomplishments. *Ender's Shadow* (1999) and *Shadow of the Hegemon* (2001) let us look at how things have been progressing on Earth while Ender was out among the stars. The most recent title, *Shadow Puppets* (2002), follows the career of an ambitious man who seeks to fill the power vacuum that results from the end of the interstellar war. The latter three novels were obviously designed to build on the popularity of the first four, but they often seem to be repeating themes and situations that Card has already thoroughly explored; nor have they been nearly as popular.

Card's religious convictions became more obvious with the publication of *Red Prophet* (1988), the first in a series of novels of Alvin Maker, set in an alternate universe that becomes more fantasy than science fiction in subsequent volumes. Prophecies and mysticism are more rationalized in *Wyrms* (1987), a story of planetary intrigue, court

politics, and civil war on a human colony world. *The Memory of Earth* (1992) initiated a new series, the Homecoming. The colony world of Harmony is administered by a highly sophisticated orbiting computer, and a crisis looms when the computer's programming begins to fail. A delegation is selected to transport it back to Earth for repair in a journey that has religious overtones that grow stronger in subsequent volumes. The delegation discovers that Earth is itself on the verge of a major social upheaval in *The Call of Earth* (1993), and open warfare breaks out in *The Ships of Earth* (1994). The sequence concludes with *Earthfall* (1995) and *Earthborn* (1995). The series is told with Card's usual masterful narrative skill, but it lacks the strong characterization and clear ethical questions that made the Ender books so memorable.

There have been several collections of Card's short fiction, of which the largest and best selection is *Maps in a Mirror* (1990). *First Meetings in the Enderverse* (2003) is a collection of stories related to the Ender series. Card's strongest asset is his ability to create engaging characters, all of whom may seek for more than they can ever attain, but all of whom also believe that they can make themselves into better people if they have the will to do so. The strong religious content in most of Card's work is rarely obtrusive, and his powerful narrative skills make even his weakest work entertaining and often thought-provoking.

A Case of Conscience
James Blish
(1958)

A Case of Conscience first appeared in shorter form and with a somewhat different plot in a science fiction magazine in 1953. It attracted such immediate favorable attention that the book-length version was greeted warmly and in fact won the Hugo Award. It was, at the time—and still is—one of the few genre works to deal specifically with doctrinal religious issues.

The role of the church in society recurs frequently in science fiction. Often the organized church is portrayed as a theocratic institution that may or may not be opposed to technology. However, very few writers had dealt with doctrinal religious issues. In the vast majority of science fiction published before 1950, it appears that churches and religion have virtually disappeared from the universe. If aliens in those works had a set of spiritual values, it generally was part of a cultural puzzle to be solved and had no relevance to humans. There were some tentative signs of change in the 1950s as more talented writers sought to introduce more intellectual complexity into a genre that was at the time dominated by entertaining adventure stories that usually lacked substance. Lester DEL REY's "For I Am a Jealous People" (1954), for example, hypothesized that science would some day give humanity powers equivalent to those of God and that ultimately we would be forced to wage war against Him, but the story's popularity derived from its shock value rather than from questions it raised in the minds of its readers. Walter M. MILLER Jr. would approach the subject with considerable more skill and insight in a series of three long stories that would eventually make up the novel A CANTICLE FOR LEIBOWITZ (1959), but the conflict there was primarily between lay and secular elements rather than within the church itself.

James BLISH, on the other hand, tackled a major matter of faith, in fact one viewed as heresy by the Roman Catholic Church. The protagonist is a priest who travels to the planet Lithia, a world inhabited by an intelligent species that resemble reptiles, and who have yet to travel beyond their own atmosphere. The Lithians have a technological culture otherwise not far behind that of Earth; but more importantly, they appear to have developed a peaceful, utopian society. Trade between the two races looks to be mutually profitable, and the visitors are already helping the Lithians to build a nuclear power plant to satisfy their energy needs. One of the Lithians visits Earth, and Blish provides some amusing and pointed commentary on human foibles as seen through his eyes.

Father Ruiz-Sanchez is initially captivated by his hosts and their culture; but as time passes, he is disturbed by the thought that the Lithians, who have no religion, seem to have been created without Original Sin. Eventually that possibility leads him to disagree with his superiors within the

church, because if his initial assumption is correct, then it is possible that they were created not by God but by Satan. Ultimately he will disobey his superiors despite their admonition against questioning doctrine, even though this causes him great spiritual turmoil. The consequences of inaction seem to him more dire than those possible if he acts incorrectly, and his final decision is to assume the worst.

In the closing pages, the priest performs the rite of exorcism against the wishes of the church, and the planet is almost immediately destroyed, perhaps by his invocation of God's intercession, or perhaps just because the experimental nuclear reactor that the humans were building for the Lithians malfunctioned and caused a chain reaction. Was Lithia a trap for humanity, created by the devil to lure us into believing that perfection was possible without God? Were the Lithians a test posed by God himself to see whether or not we could resist temptation? Or were they simply what they appeared to be, creatures whose nature and culture precluded the existence of what we think of as sin? The ambiguity of the ending reflected Ruiz-Sanchez's mixed feelings and left the reader to decide what really happened.

"Catch That Zeppelin"
Fritz Leiber
(1975)

There have been many short stories and novels in which a person from our time somehow slips through an invisible door into an alternate reality where things are a blend of the familiar and the strange, as in *The Woodrow Wilson Dime* (1968) by Jack FINNEY. Fritz LEIBER, whose versatility ranged from barbarian fantasies to subtle horror stories to satirical science fiction, wrote one of the most understated and effective of these, and managed to win both the Hugo and Nebula Awards for his efforts.

The protagonist is walking through Manhattan one day when he suddenly notices a zeppelin moored to the tower atop the Empire State Building, and realizes that he has memories of an entirely different life, one in which he has been a passenger aboard a similar craft. Surface traffic is powered electrically rather than by internal combustion engines, and racial discrimination appears at least to be a thing of the past. However, appearances are not entirely accurate, as the reader discovers that subtle prejudices remain despite the supposedly enlightened policies of the German and Japanese empires, who apparently dominate world trade.

In this new persona, the protagonist has a conversation with his son, a historian, about what they term "cusp moments," events in history that, if they had happened differently, would have caused major changes in everything that followed. We learn that this alternate world's first relevant cusp moment was when Marie Curie married Thomas Edison instead of Pierre Curie; she subsequently helped Edison develop an inexpensive, nonpolluting fuel source. Another such moment was the defeat of Germany during World War I, in this reality so conclusive that it changed the mood of the defeated nation entirely, resulting in a more enlightened modern state and elimination of the causes of the Second World War.

The discussion between father and son explores the possibilities of our history from the perspective of this other world, and we eventually learn that the older German in this story is in fact a variant Adolf Hitler, his bigotry softened but still present. A mysterious Jewish man appears to be following him, and in fact remains even after our perspective switches back to the "real" universe. Leiber's story is quietly understated and his speculations fascinating, but the story's conclusion is somewhat truncated and leaves the reader feeling as though something more needed to be said.

Cat's Cradle
Kurt Vonnegut
(1963)

Although Kurt VONNEGUT's early work had been marketed as science fiction, and some of his short stories had been published in genre magazines, by the early 1960s he was already distancing himself from the genre. His fourth novel, *Cat's Cradle,* would be the first to make a major impact on

mainstream critics, altering the course of his career thereafter. It was a novel about the end of the world in which the world really ended, a rarity in the genre, and a satire, a form that already was beginning to lose popularity with SF readers, although Vonnegut's novel was very enthusiastically embraced.

During the course of the novel, Vonnegut invents an entire religion, Bokonism, with doctrines that have considerable utility outside the novel. The terms *granfalloons* and *karasses,* for example, were useful for describing the relationships among groups of people, and they were in quite extensive usage in the science fiction community throughout the 1960s. A "karass" includes the handful of people around each individual who will be instrumental in the working out of his or her own personal destiny, where as a "granfalloon" is a larger group within which one interacts less significantly. The story itself makes extensive use of rather bitter humor to indict human callousness and stupidity, and ends not with the world being saved, but with it doomed.

Ice Nine is a superweapon of sorts, a catalyst that, if ever unleashed, would rapidly convert all the water in the world into solid matter, effectively destroying all life and rendering the planet uninhabitable. The inventor is a stereotypical absent-minded professor who creates Ice Nine as a kind of intellectual exercise, then ceases to think about it once the task has been accomplished. The single sample is left to his less than mentally sound son.

Bokonon, by contrast, is a relaxed, thoughtful man who admits up front that his new religion is a hoax, but asserts at the same time that people who embrace it will be happier and more content with their lives, even if they know that all of its tenets are lies and make-believe. By extension, Vonnegut implies the same about organized religion in general, and in fact there are very few human institutions treated with any great respect during the course of the story. Both men led lives filled with lies, but one accepted that fact and made it a virtue, while the other simply ignored anything that was not of immediate interest.

The contrasts between Bokonon and Hoenikker, the negligent scientist, underscore Vonnegut's views about individual responsibility and his skepticism about the ability of science to solve all problems, an attitude that placed him at odds with the majority of science fiction writers and readers of that time. Vonnegut's narrator is doomed, and he arranges himself so that he can thumb his nose at the heavens for all eternity in a gesture typical of Vonnegut's protagonists. The apocalyptic ending is a kind of reversal of the narrator's original purpose, which was to write a novel about the atomic bombing of Hiroshima; in this case the world is consumed by ice rather than by fire. The ending probably also was a reflection of Vonnegut's own experiences in Dresden during World War II, with which he would deal more directly in *Slaughterhouse 5* (1969).

"Chains of the Sea"
Gardner Dozois
(1971)

Alien invasion stories have been a staple of science fiction ever since H. G. WELLS brought his Martians to Earth, but despite the impression given by the movie industry, in the vast majority of cases the first contact with aliens in written SF has predominantly been less bellicose. Gardner DOZOIS suggested another alternative in this novelette; his aliens are more or less indifferent to the existence of humans.

In the opening paragraphs of the story four spaceships land on Earth; they are widely scattered and do not communicate. The authorities unsuccessfully scramble to conceal the news, and the usual sequence of events follows—failed attempts to communicate, riots, military cordons, and even a stunningly unsuccessful attack. The aliens' response is minimal and the crisis grows steadily worse. We discover almost peripherally that the world is on the verge of a new global war, possibly a suicidal nuclear conflict, and there are hints of other problems, including the existence of a handful of artificial intelligences that control the world's weapons system, and which have acquired a secret distrust for the decision-making capacity of their creators.

The viewpoint shifts from the general to the specific. Tommy Nolan is a young boy from an un-happy home, who also has problems at school. He is a gentle boy, a bit of a dreamer, and his teacher detests him for reasons she probably cannot articulate even to herself. Tommy also has a nearly unique ability: He can see the other residents of Earth, the Thants and the Jeblings, intelligent species invisible to almost everyone else. And he notices that, ever since the advent of the aliens, the others have been acting strangely. In due course we learn the truth when one of the Thants takes pity on the boy. Humans have been tolerated for a long time, but now they threaten to maim if not destroy the Earth. The aliens visited the planet long ago and forged a pact with its residents, a pact that humans have forgotten and now violate, and an adjustment will have to be made. The adjustment will painlessly but effectively wipe out the entire human race.

A few years earlier the story would have been roundly condemned by the science fiction audience, if it could have been published at all, because of its pessimistic ending. But by the 1970s writers in the field had begun to openly question whether or not technology and modern developmental trends were necessarily good things, and environmental concerns in particular were showing up with increasing frequency. Dozois also poked fun at our racial hubris, the assumption that contact with aliens might be a big event for them as well as for us.

Chalker, Jack L.
(1944–   )

After several years of work on nonfiction material related to speculative literature, Jack Chalker published his first novel in 1976. In *A Jungle of Stars*, a human is offered a form of immortality by an alien race if he agrees to serve them in his modified form as a warrior, an arrangement to which he agrees with some reservations. The concept of physical alterations to the human form is one that would be repeated with considerable frequency in Chalker's subsequent work.

Over the course of the next few years, Chalker produced a surprisingly large number of novels, including some of his best work. *Midnight at the Well of Souls* (1977) introduced Nathan Brazil, a space traveler who finds himself on an oversized world that is actually the stage for an alien-designed game of transformation and conflict. Visitors are physically altered into other forms, including mythical creatures from Earth's legends, in a story that sometimes feels as though it is fantasy rather than science fiction. Seven sequels have followed, the most recent being *Ghost of the Well of Souls* (2000), which introduced a new cast of characters to that setting.

Despite its melodramatic plot, *Dancers in the Afterglow* (1978) was a serious examination of the nature and responsibilities of freedom. A human colony falls under the sway of aliens who use mind-control techniques to reeducate their subject races. *A War of Shadows* (1979) is strangely resonant today. Following a series of terrorist attacks, the government suspends certain civil liberties. *Web of the Chozen* (1978) uses some elements of the Well of Souls books in a different setting, and is an interesting contrast to that sequence.

Lilith: A Snake in the Grass (1981) initiated a new series. A cluster of four worlds have been quarantined from the rest of humanity for one reason or another, and each planet is faced with a crisis, such as the collapse of all machinery or an alien invasion. In each of the four novels, an outside agent is sent to investigate or interfere in events. These are primarily adventure stories, although some of Chalker's more serious concerns are visible from time to time. A third series began with *Spirits of Flux and Anchor* (1984), probably Chalker's most innovative work, although elements make it seem more like fantasy. The setting is a world in which reality itself is in constant flux, the laws of nature can change from minute to minute, and people sometimes exhibit powers that we might describe as "magic." The fantastic element is explained in pseudoscientific terms in *Birth of Flux and Anchor* (1985), one of the four novels that followed the original.

Time travel is possible in *Downtiming the Night Side* (1985)—but only by supplanting the personalities of people who actually lived during the target period. Chalker's change war story was not up to the quality of Fritz Leiber's similar series, but it relied less on wondrous events and demonstrated Chalker's ability to write a tighter, controlled story.

Lords of the Middle Dark (1986) was the first of yet another new series, with a plot lifted from contemporary fantasy, the quest story. Computers have taken over the world and reduced humans to slaves, but a small group of disparate humans sets out to locate five microchips that, if united, could destroy the artificial intelligences who rule them. Subsequent volumes introduce a shape-changing alien ally and end with the predictable but exciting overthrow and restoration of human freedom.

The Labyrinth of Dreams (1987) was the first of a trilogy of novels about two detectives who discover that our reality is one of several parallel universes, among which merchants, spies, and killers move freely. The opening volume is a rousing adventure, but the subsequent titles failed to live up to the early promise. *The Demons at Rainbow Bridge* (1989) initiated the Quintara Marathon, a far superior series of novels set in a universe dominated by three distinct and very different alien races. The balance of power is shuffled dramatically in *The Run to Chaos Keep* (1991), and all three civilizations are forced to forget their differences to defeat a danger common to them all in *Ninety Trillion Fausts* (1991), which brought the series to a close.

The Cybernetic Walrus (1995) launched a trilogy set in virtual reality, but the second and third volumes are less satisfying, probably because they lack the novelty of the first. A space opera series consisting of *Balshazzar's Serpent* (2000), *Melchior's Fire* (2001), and *Kaspar's Box* (2003) is more uniformly interesting, particularly the final volume, which details the difficulties of traveling with obnoxious young women who have unusual mental powers. Although most of Chalker's novels are contained in one series or another, he has written occasional singletons, of which the most interesting is *The Moreau Factor* (2000), a conspiracy thriller in which secretive government agencies use genetically engineered assassins to advance their programs.

Chalker's infrequent short stories have been collected in *Dance Band on the Titanic* (1988) and *Dancers in the Dark* (2002); but other than the title story in the first, his short fiction has never been as interesting as his novels. Although Chalker has yet to write a serious award contender, his imaginative powers are considerable and he delivers consistently entertaining adventure stories.

Chandler, A. Bertram
(1912–1984)

The Australian writer A. Bertram Chandler spent much of his career in the merchant marine, so it should not be surprising that many of his space adventures resembled sea stories and that his most frequently recurring character, John Grimes, was referred to as the "Hornblower of space." The Commodore Grimes adventures are set in the Rim Worlds, the sparsely populated planets at the edge of the galaxy, where the greater human civilization has little influence but where trade is viable even for independent space traveling merchants. There were more than two dozen books set in the Rim Worlds, of which the best are *The Far Traveler* (1977), *To Keep the Ship* (1978), *Matilda's Stepchildren* (1979), and *The Anarch Lords* (1991); in the last of these, Grimes becomes temporary governor of a world colonized by devout anarchists. The series as a whole covers a large portion of Grimes's life, from his early career working for a large interstellar corporate trading company to his later days as an independent operator and occasional subcontractor.

Chandler's best novel was not part of the Rim series, although Grimes makes an appearance thanks to his visits to alternate universes. *Kelly Country* (1983) is an alternate history story in which Australia won its own independence from England shortly after the American Revolution. A three-volume space opera series that began with *Empress of Outer Space* (1965) is minor but pleasant, and his spoof of Edgar Rice BURROUGHS and H. G. WELLS, *The Alternate Martians* (1965), is at times quite clever. Aliens infest Earth's oceans and wage war against surface shipping in *The Sea Beasts* (1971). *The Bitter Pill* (1974) is a fairly interesting and atypical dystopian novel dealing with a dictatorship that spans both Earth and Mars.

Although Chandler was a prolific short story writer during the 1940s and 1950s, only a few are of note; among these are "Giant Killer," "Zoological Specimen," and "Cage." *From Sea to Shining Star* (1990) and *Up to the Sky in Ships* (1982) are the only collections of his non–Rim World stories. Chandler's reputation will always rest on the Grimes series, which unfortunately is greater than the sum of its parts. As a series, it conveys a wondrous sense of adventure and the marvels of the universe, but the individual volumes are so light that, separately, they seem only minor efforts.

Chanur series
C. J. Cherryh

Most of C. J. Cherryh's space adventures take place in the same general setting, a future history in which humans have traveled to the stars and discovered a host of similarly faring alien species. Within that context, Cherryh has written several subsidiary series, of which the most popular has been the five-volume sequence about the Chanur. The Chanur family made their debut in the aptly titled *The Pride of Chanur* (1982)—apt because their race, the hani, resemble humanoid lions and their social structure is based on a clan system that inspires very strong family ties. They make a living as independent interstellar traders, not a major player in interstellar politics, but not a race to be ignored either. Meetpoint Station is a vast orbiting habitat where the various races meet to conduct trade and diplomacy, and it is while docked there that they encounter a single representative of a distant and unknown race, a human who seeks refuge with them, almost setting off an interstellar war as a consequence.

Chanur's Venture (1982) was basically a reprise of the original story. Although the turmoil has settled down, the continued presence of the human aboard their ship causes more problems as other parties, most notably the devious kif, still hope to make exclusive use of this newfound race. The situation worsens in *The Kif Strike Back* (1985) when members of the crew are kidnapped by the kif in an effort to apply pressure on their captain, Pyanfar. The subsequent rescue mission is the highpoint of the original trilogy and may have originally been intended as the final volume. *Chanur's Homecoming* (1986) followed, however, with Pyanfar in trouble at home as a consequence of the problems caused by her continued intercession on behalf of the human.

Cherryh brought the Chanur back for one further adventure in *Chanur's Legacy* (1992). Considerable time has passed since the events of the earlier novels. One of the crew members who served under Pyanfar has now been promoted and is captain of her own vessel. Annoyed because of efforts to use her as a conduit to her influential aunt and plagued by the presence of an unruly male aboard her new command, she accepts a commission to transport a sacred idol to another planet, only to find herself caught between two hostile and determined forces. The (so far) final adventure of the hani is a pleasant, exciting story, but it lacked the grandeur of the earlier ones, and it is likely that Cherryh has decided not to further dilute her best series.

Charnas, Suzy McKee
(1939–   )

Although Suzy McKee Charnas has written varied fantasy and supernatural fiction, her four science fiction novels are all part of a single, loosely connected series. The first volume, *Walk to the End of the World* (1974), established a postapocalyptic society, gathered together in a tightly knit city, in which women are kept as virtual chattel by the men who use them as scapegoats for the destruction of most of the world by their ancestors. The strongly feminist theme is undeniably powerful and moving, if occasionally heavy-handed. The first sequel, *Motherlines* (1978), introduced a contrasting female dominated culture outside the Holdfast of its predecessor. The tribes of the plains are much more fully realized than the misogynist-ruled world. There is much to admire in their spirit of independence and their level of tolerance, but Charnas is careful not to paint them as too utopian. They have their failings as well as their successes, and they are a much more credible backdrop in a far more successful novel.

There was a considerable gap before the third in the series appeared. *The Furies* (1994) describes the predictable clash between the two resurgent cultures, and the outward-looking, flexible, and freer society of the matriarchal tribes easily conquers the introspective, shortsighted, and bigoted rulers of the Holdfast. The victory paradoxically creates more problems than it solves, not only because of the need to deal with the conquered men, but also because the lack of a unifying purpose has led to schisms among the women, who now find themselves maneuvering against one another to protect more parochial interests. The most recent volume, *The Conqueror's Child* (1999), follows the efforts of a young woman to fit into the newly evolving society, against a background in which the forces of repression are threatening to emerge once again.

Charnas's short stories are almost as infrequent as her novels, but they are invariably worth the wait. "Listening to Brahms," "Scorched Supper on New Niger," and "Boobs," the last of which won the Hugo Award, are all of particular merit. Her short fiction remains uncollected as of this writing. Her novels are characterized by a critical viewpoint that reflects the author's resentment against a society that honors gender above an individual's personal merit.

Cherryh, C. J.
(1942–   )

Carolyn Cherry altered the spelling of her last name for her early fiction and has used that variation ever since, over the course of one of the most successful careers in the genre. Her first novel, *Brothers of Earth* (1976), stranded two individuals from hostile civilizations on a neutral world, where their mutual animosity causes them to manipulate their hosts. Readers immediately recognized that Cherryh was an exciting newcomer, and she reinforced this perception with her next several books. *Gate of Ivrel* (1976), the first of the Morgaine adventures, was even more highly regarded and has even spawned a role-playing game. An ancient, now vanished race had established jump gates to facilitate travel among the worlds; but now that they have disappeared, the unfettered mingling of races frequently has disastrous results. Morgaine is an agent moving from one world to another, destroying the gates as she goes to insulate the local cultures from harm. Three sequels would follow, ending with *Exile's Gate* (1988), and they might have been the establishing books in an already promising career if they had not been overshadowed by the FADED SUN SERIES which appeared at almost the same time.

The sequence consists of *The Faded Sun: Kesrith* (1978), *The Faded Sun: Shon'Jir* (1978), and *The Faded Sun: Kutath* (1979). Together, they chronicle the fate of the Mri, an alien race with a military culture similar to that of the ninjas. The Mri are hired as mercenaries by an alien race at war with Earth, but when the war nears its end they are abandoned by their employers and pursued to near extinction by the vengeful human military. Although the plot is clever and fast-moving, the charm of the trilogy lay in the details Cherryh provided about the Mri themselves. Cherryh immediately found herself with a substantial body of devoted fans.

Her next major work, and still one of her best novels, was *Downbelow Station* (1981), part of a loosely connected series of books set in the Merchanter universe, and the first of her books to win the Hugo Award. The staff and inhabitants of Pell Station, an orbiting habitat, strive to remain neutral as some of Earth's colony worlds move toward an open, violent break with Earth. The action continues in *Merchanter's Luck* (1982), with more intricate interstellar intrigue aboard the station and in the surrounding space.

The Pride of Chanur started a new sequence in 1982. The CHANUR SERIES is associated with, but distinct from, the Merchanter novels. The hani are a star-traveling race who resemble humanoid lions. Their society is based on clans, and their main source of income is a fleet of independent interstellar traders. They share a region of space with the insidious kif and other races, and humans are virtually unknown until one of our kind seeks refuge aboard a ship of the Chanur clan, nearly precipitating an interstellar war. Cherryh continued this immensely popular series with *Chanur's Venture* (1984), *The Kif Strike Back* (1985), and *Chanur's Homecoming* (1986), and concluded with *Chanur's Legacy* (1992). The first three novels develop the varied alien cultures around the chases, intrigues, captures, and escapes of the plot, and the political

implications come to fruition in the fourth. The final volume, although almost an afterthought, is a well above average space adventure.

Cherryh wrote several competent but unexceptional stand-alone novels during the 1980s, but *Angel with a Sword* (1985) is particularly worth noting because it led to a short-lived series of shared universe anthologies with the same setting. Cherryh's original novel takes place on a world whose cities include intricate canal systems. A young man rescues a prominent citizen, and the latter's gratitude leads to his introduction to a complex and often fascinating global political system. Although somewhat slow-paced, the planetary culture is one of her more fully realized ones. Her next major work was *Cyteen* (1988), a novel so long that it was published in softcover in three volumes, and that also won a Hugo Award. A powerful dictator has herself cloned, and we follow her career in another complex and dangerous world, the story told from the point of view of the clone, who seeks to find her own place in the universe.

Heavy Time (1991) and *Hellburner* (1992) chronicle the adventures of Ben Pollard. Two asteroid miners rescue a man marooned in space, later discover that he has critical information about a deadly struggle for control of the mineral wealth of the asteroids, and eventually become catalysts for a change in the balance of power. Although the story is generally engrossing, the characters have a tendency to talk too much and too redundantly, as though Cherryh was not certain that her readers had understood the implications the first time around.

Cherryh's next major series began with *Foreigner* (1994). The setting is a world with an indigent alien culture based on a tribal system, with strong military traditions but with a comparatively primitive technology. Colonists from Earth, desperate to find a haven after an attack by another alien race, negotiate a treaty with the Atevi to settle one island on the planet in exchange for technological help; the protagonist is the sole human allowed to represent their interests outside of the island itself. The novels that follow form one continuous narrative: *Invader* (1995), *Inheritor* (1996), *Precursor* (1999), *Defender* (2001), and *Explorer* (2002). The human spokesman finds himself torn between loyalties to his people and obligations to the Atevi, is caught up in tribal politics as well as his diplomatic duties, eventually helps the Atevi develop their own space program, and then forges an uneasy alliance when their situation is threatened by a newly arrived human starship as well as the mysterious aliens whom they encountered previously. The Atevi culture is convincing and the novels are engrossing and suspenseful, but they never rise to the quality of her best work.

Finity's End (1997) is set in the Merchanter universe and involves the difficulties a young man has adjusting to a sudden change from a planetary to a shipboard culture, particularly when he had other plans for his life. *Tripoint* (1995) is an emotionally intense novel of personal relationships, set among spacegoing folk, including a young man who was conceived by rape, a vengeful woman, and a cast of well developed characters. It lacks the scope of most of Cherryh's other novels and tends to lecture at times, but still rewards the patient reader.

Cherryh's most recent series, the Gene Wars, began with *Hammerfall* (2001). Inhabitants of a colony world are afflicted with what appears to be a form of insanity but might actually be the result of an infection by nanomachines. The story is continued in *Forge of Heaven* (2004), with the threat of war with aliens adding to the tension.

Although most of Cherry's novels are space operas in form, they are among the very best of their type, brought to life by her ability to create intricate and believable alien cultures. Her biggest liability appears to be a reluctance to attempt stories against more varied settings, although she has produced some creditable fantasies. There is considerable variation in quality, even within novels set in the same series: Her books sometimes involve lengthy discursive segments that fail to advance the plot. At her best, Cherryh is one of the most popular and skillful practitioners of modern space opera; she has already produced a substantial body of work, including two major award-winners, and she enjoys a large and loyal reader following. Her respectable body of short fiction, which varies widely in quality as well as theme, has been assembled in its near entirety in *The Collected Stories of C. J. Cherryh* (2004).

Christopher, John
(1922–   )

John Christopher is the pseudonym of the British writer Christopher Youd, who abandoned his own name almost immediately after he began selling professionally. He was active writing science fiction from 1949 through the early 1970s, and intermittently from the 1980s forward. Many of his novels involved global disasters, and during the early part of his career he was often compared to John WYNDHAM and John Bowen.

His first science fiction book was *The Twenty Second Century* (1954), a collection of short stories, but he wrote almost no other short fiction for the balance of his career. *Planet in Peril* (1957, also published as *The Year of the Comet*), a story of alien robots secretly living among us, was well received at the time, but would be considered awkward and implausible now. His next novel, however, would establish him firmly as a significant author. *No Blade of Grass* (1957, also published as *The Death of Grass*) described the consequences of a worldwide agricultural plague that causes famine in every part of the world. Governments teeter and collapse, even in the more advanced countries, including Great Britain, where an increasing number of people—including the family upon whom the story focuses—flee the cities, not so much to forage for food as to escape the mounting violence and disruption. A reasonably loyal and successful film ensued.

Christopher would use variations of the same plot in future novels, further exploring the consequences of civilization's collapse. A new Ice Age descends upon the world in *The Long Winter* (1962, also published as *World in Winter*), and the comparatively small number of survivors of the sudden drop in temperature have to fight the elements as well as one another in order to survive. Tidal waves and earthquakes of unprecedented strength and number accomplish much the same in *The Ragged Edge* (1965, also known as *A Wrinkle in the Skin*). This time the plot involves a man's desperate search through a radically altered landscape for his missing daughter.

The Possessors (1964) treats alien invasion on a very localized scale. Visitors to a remote Swiss chalet are subject to parasitic creatures that seize control of their bodies. It was dramatically different from Christopher's previous work, and his next novel, *The Little People* (1966), was very similar. In this case, vacationers are menaced by what appears to be a tribe of elves, later revealed to be the results of some Nazi experiments in genetic engineering. *Pendulum* (1968), the last of his novels aimed at the adult market, suggested that the end of modern civilization might come at our own hands. This time the setting is a London dominated by brutal gangs of youths who have effectively rejected government control.

Christopher turned to the young adult market in the mid-1960s and made a resounding debut with a trilogy of novels about the invasion of Earth by Martians in what became known as the Tripods trilogy, later turned into a television miniseries by the BBC. The original trilogy consists of *The White Mountains* (1967), *The City of Gold and Lead* (1967), and *The Pool of Fire* (1968). Christopher would later write a prequel, *When the Tripods Came* (1988), but it was not nearly as good as the trilogy itself. His Martians closely resembled those of H. G. WELLS's *The WAR OF THE WORLDS*, except that they use mind control techniques to neutralize all of the adults on Earth while they set about altering the world's atmosphere to make it more conducive to their own form of life. A group of teenagers discover the Martians' secret vulnerability, avoid capture in a series of adventures, and eventually save the day, although Christopher's doubts about the future resurface as the adults promptly begin to run things badly once more.

Another trilogy followed, this one set in the aftermath of a nuclear war. Despite the presence of mutants, the new order is decidedly medieval, unable to progress because most machines have been outlawed. The protagonist is the young heir to the throne who is forced into hiding by a usurper though he eventually displaces him and claims his rightful heritage. The sequence consists of *The Prince in Waiting* (1970), *Beyond the Burning Lands* (1971), and *The Sword of the Spirits* (1972). Although not as highly praised as the Tripods trilogy, they were well received and certainly were among the best young adult fiction of their time.

Four other young adult novels were set in worlds either largely depopulated by a disaster or teetering on the brink of a major social collapse. *The Guardians* (1970), *Wild Jack* (1974), *Empty World* (1977), and *A Dusk of Demons* (1993) all seem to be restatements of themes and situations Christopher had already done previously and more successfully. A more interesting two-book sequence consisted of *Fireball* (1981) and *New Found Land* (1983), in which teenagers find themselves with the key to alternate universes. The first one, set in a variant Great Britain where slavery is legal, is the best of Christopher's later books.

Cities in Flight series
James Blish

The Cities in Flight series started with two short stories, "Bindlestiff" and "Okie," both first published in 1950. James BLISH postulated a future in which several technological innovations would change the way people live and would break down the old idea of nation-states. Major cities enclose themselves in impenetrable force fields and then install powerful engines, known as spindizzies, into their infrastructure so that they can quite literally separate themselves from Earth and travel to the stars. Although the initial stories established the background as a given, Blish would later construct a four-book sequence that started with the initial development of the technology and ended with the almost literal destruction of the universe.

The four shorter stories in the series would be combined into the novel, *Earthman, Come Home* (1955). Western civilization has pretty much collapsed and many cities have abandoned Earth. In a parallel to the plight of the Okies during the Great Depression, New York City travels from planet to planet seeking work for its inhabitants. The novel is necessarily episodic as the wandering city visits four separate planets, becoming embroiled with trouble in each, and the Okie metaphor is somewhat strained at times; but the reader is still left with a majestic view of the possibilities of the universe, and a fondness for the main protagonist, Mayor Amalfi.

They Shall Have Stars (1957, also published as *Year 2018!*) is chronologically the first in the series, detailing the experiments with antigravity that first made it possible to leave the Earth. Despite some marvelous scenes set in the Jovian system, the novel is slow-paced and only of marginal interest. *The Triumph of Time* (1958, also published as *A Clash of Cymbals*) is set in the distant future. Scientists investigate a planet near which matter seems to be appearing spontaneously, and discover a gateway to another universe that is on a collision course with our own. The characterization falters a bit, but the sweeping concepts and scene setting are superb. Blish returned to the series one more time with *A Life for the Stars* (1962), a young adult novel chronologically second in the series. A teenager is kidnapped and taken into space, and has several adventures involving a rival city that has turned pirate. The pirate analogy is also somewhat of a leap, but Blish wrapped it in such an appealing story that most readers were willing to forgive minor flaws. Although not the equal of Blish's best work in terms of prose or construction, the Cities in Flight series remains one of the most popular in the genre, and it has been reprinted several times since its original appearance.

City
Clifford D. Simak
(1952)

A number of science fiction writers—most famously Robert A. HEINLEIN—have constructed future histories, weaving a series of short stories and novels into a consistent chronology of events that have not yet happened. Clifford SIMAK accomplished a similar feat with eight stories originally published between 1944 and 1951, collected as *City* (sometimes erroneously referred to as a novel).

The closest we have to a recurring character unifying the series is Jenkins, one of the most skillfully described robot characters ever imagined. Jenkins is a servant of the Webster family, members

of which figure prominently in the sequence. In "City" and "Huddling Place," Simak describes the super cities of the future, great masses of people gathered together into artificial and unlovable places. As the story cycle proceeds, Simak suggests various technological advances, many of which we now know to be impractical. When every family has its own helicopter and new farming techniques make it possible to be self-sufficient in terms of food, there is no longer as great a compulsion to centralize, and humans return to the countryside. This pastoral theme would be prevalent in Simak's fiction throughout his career, but readers who normally reacted negatively to anything critical of technological progress were surprisingly receptive to Simak's glorification of a simpler lifestyle and harmony with the natural environment, and to his clear distaste for the kind of scientific utopias that dominated the pulp magazines for which he was writing.

Eventually humankind further removes itself from management of its own society, ceding most of the authority to its robot servants and artificial intelligences. There is a growing sense of loneliness as a species, however, so expansion into space continues, leading to the colonization of Jupiter by genetically altered human beings. Closer at hand, geneticists augment the intelligence of dogs, and eventually abandon the Earth to them and the robots. The best story in the collection, "Desertion," is often cited as Simak's most substantial single work. The collection as a unit won the International Fantasy Award.

Clarke, Arthur C.
(1917–   )

If H. G. WELLS is the father of serious science fiction and Jules VERNE the father of adventure-based science fiction, then Arthur C. Clarke and Isaac ASIMOV are jointly the fathers of hard science fiction. Clarke's first professional sale was in 1946, and he is still theoretically active; however, much of his later work consists of collaborations, and it is unclear how much he actually wrote himself. Although a British citizen, he moved to Sri Lanka in 1956 and has been a resident there ever since. At least half of his published writing is non-fiction, mostly dealing with space travel or scuba diving, but he also produced a mainstream novel about the development of radar.

Clarke's first book-length story, *Against the Fall of Night* (1948/53), is set in a distant future Earth that has become largely depopulated. The narrative follows the adventures of a young man who finds a way to leave his domed city and travel to another community, and who subsequently leaves the planet to discover a greater truth. The novel would later be dramatically revised and expanded as *The City and the Stars* (1956), in what some critics believe is still the best example of Clarke's blend of rigorous science and mystical speculation about the future of the human race.

Most of Clarke's early novels involved the near-future evolution of space travel. *Prelude to Space* (1951, also published as *Master of Space* and as *The Space Dreamers*) has been outpaced by reality, but it was the first novel to realistically examine the possibility of a manned orbital flight. Despite a number of technical issues subsequently proven inaccurate, it remains an effective description of the flight as a human experience. A struggling human colony on Mars encounters a remnant of the previous indigenous occupants of that world in *Sands of Mars* (1951), a slow-paced but interesting attempt to accurately describe what might be involved in establishing a permanent base on that world. *Islands in the Sky* (1952), ostensibly for young adults, takes the reader on an educational tour of an orbiting space station. The latter two novels are also somewhat dated in terms of the technology involved, but both are entertaining stories illustrating sound scientific principles, and both are periodically reprinted for each new generation of readers.

With *Childhood's End* (1953), Clarke solidified his position as a major genre writer. The novel is a three-part narrative in which humans make contact with a superior alien species that shepherds them through an evolutionary change, ending with a transcendental transformation of the species. Clarke was undoubtedly influenced by the work of Olaf STAPLEDON, and themes from this novel would eventually be developed slightly differently in *2001: A SPACE ODYSSEY.*

Earthlight (1955) was another novel of space exploration. The colonies of Mars and Venus have united against Earth in a battle for control of the Moon, which has mineral resources coveted by both sides. The climax comes with an inconclusive battle of superweaponry that was a nod to the space operas of Edward E. SMITH, although far more plausible. Clarke's personal interest in scuba diving led to *The Deep Range* (1957), in which a former space pilot overcomes psychological problems by taking up a new career working on one of the vast ocean farms. Although the focus is narrower than in most of his other novels, *The Deep Range* contains some of his best writing, and his speculations about the possibilities of harvesting the oceans remain provocative. *Dolphin Island* (1963) explored some similar material, but far less successfully.

A Fall of Moondust (1961) was another understated, low-key but highly entertaining speculation about conditions on another world. The Moon has been colonized, though sparsely, and journeys from one community to another are supposed to be routine. A group of travelers are trapped when their vehicle sinks into a dust-filled pit, and their subsequent efforts to escape are harrowing and exciting. There was a significant gap before the appearance of *2001: A Space Odyssey* in 1968, but that novel—based on the screenplay Clarke wrote with Stanley Kubrick—probably made him the best-known science fiction writer in the world.

Clarke wrote three novels during the 1970s, of which the first was the most popular, although not necessarily the best-written. In RENDEZVOUS WITH RAMA an enormous and apparently uncrewed alien starship is detected when it begins passing through the solar system; a desperate attempt is made to send a human crew aboard to harvest whatever technological secrets they may be able to gather in the limited time available. The novel won a Hugo Award and spawned sequels, all written in collaboration with Gentry Lee: *Rama II* (1989), *The Garden of Rama* (1991), and *Rama Revealed* (1994), each of which continues the revelations, sometimes effectively, but with shakier prose and a tendency toward repetition.

Imperial Earth (1975) has a mildly melodramatic plot about cloning, but is essentially a grand tour of a future Earth which has become a semi-utopia. Much more successful was *The Fountains of Paradise* (1979), in which a colossal elevator is constructed to connect Earth's surface with an orbiting habitat. This novel—the best of Clarke's later work—also won the Hugo Award. *2010: Odyssey Two* (1982), *2061: Odyssey Three* (1989), and *3001: The Final Odyssey* (1997) continued the story begun in *2001: A Space Odyssey,* explaining more about the mysterious alien pyramids and showing us the development of intelligent life in the Jovian system. Two remaining solo novels are also of interest. *The Ghost from the Grand Banks* (1990) describes an effort to raise the Titanic, and *The Hammer of God* (1993) is a story of impending doom, telling about a chunk of rock on a collision course with Earth and the turmoil that ensues. Both are solid stories—the former interesting because of Clarke's expertise on underwater operations, the latter a suspenseful work although less innovative.

Clarke was also a prolific and skillful short story writer, one of the few in the field who proved highly proficient in both that form and the novel. He made a distinct impression as early as 1946 with "Rescue Party," his first story sold but second published, in which alien visitors to a doomed Earth discover that the entire human race has immigrated into space to avoid destruction. Numerous memorable stories followed, particularly early in his career, including "The Sentinel" (1951), which would become the basis for *2001: A Space Odyssey;* "SUPERIORITY," a wonderful illustration of the dangers of accepting too much technological change too quickly; and *Tales from the White Hart* (1957), a collection of humorous scientific tall tales. "The Songs of Distant Earth" (1959) would later be expanded into one of his less successful novels under the same title. "The Star," in which explorers discover that the Star of Bethlehem was a supernova that wiped out an entire race, won a Hugo Award in 1953. Also of note is "The NINE BILLION NAMES OF GOD," a clever vignette that appeared in 1959.

Although Clarke's output of short stories declined during the 1960s, those that did appear were still of high quality and included such excellent tales as "Death and the Senator," "Dog Star,"

"Sunjammer," and "A Wind from the Sun." His 1971 novelette *A MEETING WITH MEDUSA* describes the first meeting between humans and a strange form of intelligent life that exists within the gaseous outer atmosphere of Jupiter. It won the Nebula Award, but it was virtually the only piece of short fiction Clarke would write over the course of the last three decades of the 20th century. *The Collected Stories of Arthur C. Clarke* (2000), although not complete, is the largest selection of his short fiction available.

Several collaborative novels appeared during the 1990s, and although the extent of Clarke's involvement is open to question, they have enjoyed moderate success. These novels generally involve speculation about the results of a new discovery. *Richter 10* (1996), coauthored with Mike McQUAY, concerns a method of predicting earthquakes. *The Trigger* (1999), written with Michael KUBE-McDOWELL, deals with a method of detonating explosives from a distance. In *The Light of Other Days* (2000), coauthored with Stephen BAXTER, a device that makes it possible to spy on anyone remotely undermines modern civilization. *Time's Eye* (2003), also written with Baxter, brings together representative humans from various eras, who interact in what is apparently the opening volume of a trilogy.

Clarke has not been a prolific writer since the 1960s; he has written almost no short fiction since the early 1970s, and has not produced a major novel since 1979. It is a tribute to the quality of his work that he remains a prominent, highly respected, and popular writer even in the absence of new material.

Clement, Hal
(1922–2003)

Hal Clement was the pen name of Harry Stubbs, a writer of mostly hard science fiction who was known for his creation of believable aliens and alien cultures. His career started in 1942 and ended with his last novel in 2003. He worked as a high school science teacher, but established himself as a reliable though not particularly prolific short story writer during the 1940s, primarily for *Astounding*

Science Fiction. His first novel, *Needle* (1949, also published as *From Outer Space*), was not typical of his short fiction, however; it was set on Earth and featured a teenager as its protagonist. An intelligent alien parasite, a criminal, arrives on Earth and inhabits one of the residents of an insular community. A second of its species, a kind of interstellar policeman, lodges itself in the body of a young boy and learns to communicate with him, enlisting his aid in tracking down its fellow. Although sometimes awkwardly constructed, the novel was quite popular.

Iceworld (1953) was not as successful, although it has its moments. Aliens secretly visit Earth in order to peddle drugs, but they come from a much warmer world. (The title refers to our climate.) There are some interesting scenes that elaborate on this disparity, but the characters, whether human or alien, never come to life. It appeared that Clement might not be capable of sustaining his characters for a full novel. Then came *Mission of Gravity* (1954), and with that single book—one of the best-loved in the genre—Clement became a major name. The novel is set on the planet Mesklin, whose gravity can reach as much as 700 times that of Earth. A human scientific probe is lost on the surface, and since it is impossible for the orbiting scientists to physically retrieve it themselves, they decide to recruit the help of some of the local intelligent creatures, who resemble muscular worms. They manage to open communication with Captain Barlennan, a Mesklinite. The trek that ensues for Barlennan and his crew is memorable not only because of its epic nature and the novelty of the setting, but also because Clement manages to create a believable, sympathetic character out of this unlikely protagonist. If Clement had never written another word, he would have already established a lasting reputation.

Cycle of Fire (1957) was a variation of the same theme. A human crash-lands on a planet that is subject to sudden, dramatic climatic changes, and sets out on a dangerous trek accompanied only by a single indigenous alien. Their journey is filled with adventure and the characterizations are well handled, but the story did not resonate with readers. It was still highly regarded and is probably Clement's most underrated novel. *Close*

to *Critical* (1958/64) employs almost the same plot, although with a very different setting. This novel was popular at the time of its appearance, but it has been completely overshadowed by Clement's earlier work.

Ocean on Top (1967) turned inward. With Earth's population growing and its resources vanishing, power has become a crucial commodity, and civilization is approaching a crisis. When a number of prominent politicians disappear, their absence is connected to a secret project under way on the floor of the ocean. Once again, Clement's extrapolations are thought-provoking, but the story relies more heavily on its characters than was the case in his previous work—and characterization was never one of his strongest assets. Perhaps recognizing this, Clement returned to Mesklin in his next novel, *Star Light* (1971), the second adventure of the inhabitants of that heavy-gravity world. The Mesklinites are now partners with the humans, and they team up to explore another planet with gravitational complications similar to that of their home world. This book was followed by *Through the Eye of the Needle* (1978), a sequel to *Needle* that continues the story of the pairing of a benevolent alien parasite and his host. The host is now suffering from the effects of their joint tenancy, a problem that can be solved only if they can locate the wreckage of an alien ship. The sequel is more capably written than its predecessor, but the central mystery is not nearly as engaging.

The Nitrogen Fix (1980) portrayed a darker future than any of Clement's previous work. The atmosphere of Earth has become unbreathable, thanks to pollutants, and the humans who survive live in contained communities. The arrival of alien visitors complicates matters and sets off a series of changes. The potentially interesting interactions are undercut somewhat by the dismal tone of the background, but Clement's talent for creating believable nonhumans remained intact. *Still River* (1987) marked a return to his earlier style. A human scientist and four alien colleagues are exploring an unusual planet when an accident causes her to become lost in a series of underground caverns, where she discovers an ecology much stranger and more interesting than the one on the surface.

Fossil (1993) follows much the same pattern. Humans studying a world inhabited by six intelligent races and largely covered by ice are drawn into the intrigue surrounding the discovery of fossils of yet another species. Despite some hesitation in the early chapters, this is one of the best of Clement's later novels. *Noise* (2003), his last book, is set on one of the most interesting of his creations, a planet covered entirely by water, colonized by Polynesians who have created a culture that exists entirely afloat. There are none of the melodramatics of *Waterworld* here, just a straightforward tour of what such a community might be like, skillfully woven around an interesting scientific problem. The protagonist, a linguist studying the way language has evolved in this environment, eventually identifies personally with the people under scrutiny.

Clement's comparatively small body of short fiction contains a number of excellent stories, collected in *Variations on a Theme by Sir Isaac Newton* (2000), which also contains the two Mesklin novels, and in *Music of Many Spheres* (2000). Among the best of these are "Cold Front," "Technical Error," "Trojan Fall," and "Raindrop." Three of his early novels were collected as *Trio for Slide Rule and Typewriter* (1999). The Mesklin novels plus some short stories using the same setting were also collected as *Heavy Planet* (2002). Despite a relatively low production level over the course of his 60-year writing career, Clement is recognized as one of the major contributors to modern science fiction.

A Clockwork Orange
Anthony Burgess
(1962)

A frequent subject of speculation among science fiction writers is how we will deal with crime and punishment in the future. Writers have suggested everything from erasure of a criminal's memory to permanent exile to another world. Mainstream writer Anthony BURGESS suggested that more sophisticated psychological conditioning might provide an apparently more humane method of treatment, although ultimately he indicts it as being every bit as immoral as the crimes that stimulate it.

The protagonist, Alex, is a typical young punk in a future England where Russian influence has become pervasive and where the language is littered with imported words. Burgess created an artificial grammar for the story, and included a lexicon, but the stylistic challenge, though initially unsettling, eventually seems natural and appropriate to the environment. With his friends, Alex commits numerous crimes and exhibits unusual cruelty, although much of it is group-inspired rather than inherent to him personally. He does have one redeeming quality—a fondness for classical music, particularly the music of Beethoven. Alex survives challenges for leadership by other members of the group because of his propensity for violence.

Eventually apprehended, he becomes the subject of a behavior modification experiment: He is forced to watch hours of violent films while being given drugs that make him physically ill. The purpose of this treatment is to link a state of nausea with apprehension of any violent act, thereby in theory making it impossible for him to commit further crimes of that nature. This conditioning proves effective, but there is an inadvertent side effect: because the soundtrack of the films consisted of the work of Beethoven, Alex can no longer hear that music without becoming sick. Cured, or at least tamed, he is released back into the wilds of London, where his psychological block leaves him defenseless at the hands of his old friends, as well as of those whom he had previously wronged.

Alex is clearly not a heroic figure and his fate is ironically fitting, but Burgess is warning us that efforts by the state to control the actions of the individual may eventually become just another source of injustice, and that we are in danger of destroying the beautiful things in life along with the evil ones.

Code Three
Rick Raphael
(1966)

One of the perils of extrapolating near-future trends in fiction is that there is a high probability that the trends depicted in the story will be outdistanced by events very quickly. A handful of novels predicting chaos at the end of the 20th century fell victim to this shortcoming, as have most lost world novels, stories of future wars between the United States and the Soviet Union, and other short-term prognostications. The unfortunate result is that many otherwise excellent stories are viewed, rightly or wrongly, as too dated to be worth preserving, eventually fall out of print, and are quickly forgotten.

Writers are reluctant to abandon the near-future story, however, because it allows some short-term speculation about obvious trends in a way that could not be done in a mainstream novel. Rick Raphael, who earned a well-deserved reputation based upon only a few short stories, may have been a victim of his own success in this regard: His two most famous stories, "Code Three" and "Once a Cop," incorporated into a quasi-novel as *Code Three*, seem far more improbable now than they did when they were first published.

Raphael looked at the then current trend toward bigger, faster, more luxurious automobiles and wondered what the future might bring. His vision encompassed even more elaborate and extensive highways than those currently strangling Los Angeles, with high-speed armored vehicles theoretically safer than those today. He also assumed that lawbreakers would take advantage of these more powerful machines as well, and that traffic tie-ups caused by accidents and breakdowns would become so critical that governments would react with high-technology solutions, including massively armored and highly sophisticated police vehicles and helicopters that could swoop down and literally lift wrecks and disabled vehicles out of the way.

Except for one marginal thriller published several years later, Raphael apparently abandoned science fiction shortly after the book-length version of these stories appeared. Although they followed the form of the engineering problem story that was typical of *Analog Science Fiction*, the magazine in which these stories first appeared, Raphael's insight into the ways that such technology might affect the lives of ordinary people on an everyday basis was rarely equaled.

"The Cold Equations"
Tom Godwin
(1954)

Although Tom Godwin published three novels and a fair number of short stories, he would long since have been reduced to a minor footnote in science fiction had he not written "The Cold Equations," a story in which his prose rose above its usual workmanlike style to grace a plot so startling and controversial for its time that it became the subject of debate for years afterward.

Humankind has expanded into space, but the result is a perilous existence in which travel from one world to another is difficult and dangerous. When a small outpost places an urgent call for medical aid, an emergency ship is dispatched—a specialized vessel with a one-man crew, carrying just enough fuel to successfully make the delivery. There is absolutely no margin for error. Thus, when the pilot discovers that he has a stowaway aboard, he has no choice: To save himself and the staff of the outpost, he must eject the stowaway from the ship as soon as possible, condemning the interloper to a quick but horrible death in space.

However, things are not quite as simple as they seem. The stowaway is revealed to be an endearing teenage girl who is unaware of the desperate situation she has caused, and who innocently stowed aboard in order to pay an unauthorized visit to her brother. Although the pilot is able to save some fuel by manipulating the ship's engines, he is only delaying the inevitable. The exchanges between the two main characters, and later her brief conversation with her brother, are among the most poignant ever to appear in the genre. While Godwin would write similar scenes in the future, those other efforts had a tendency to be overly sentimental and less convincing.

Readers were lulled into expecting the standard happy ending: A solution would be found through application of scientific or engineering principles, the girl would be saved, and the outpost relieved. But Godwin had a surprise up his sleeve. There really is no alternative this time; the handy miraculous rescue plan that turns up in much similar science fiction just was not going to happen. It is extremely rare for an author to make a lasting impression with a single work, particularly a short story, but Godwin accomplished that feat in this effective inversion of a standard plot.

"Come and Go Mad"
Fredric Brown
(1949)

Most of Fredric BROWN's short fiction consisted of vignettes and very short stories, but occasionally he wrote at greater length, usually quite memorably. One of his classic stories is "Come and Go Mad," in which a newspaper reporter named Vine is induced to enter an insane asylum in search of an elusive and mysterious story. But the reporter himself has a secret: Although he claims to have lost the memory of his earlier life, he actually remembers every detail of it—and he knows that it took place in late 18th-century Europe. And even though he speaks English fluently and understands the modern world, he knows as well that he was Napoleon Bonaparte.

As the moment approaches, Vine has growing doubts about the wisdom of the plan, about his own conflicting memories, and about a dream image that has bothered him recently, of red and black chess pieces ranged against each other. Even more bothersome is his growing sense that people are manipulating him into this situation for reasons that perhaps even they do not fully understand. Once inside the asylum, Vine begins to hope that he is in fact insane, because if that is the case, he might possibly be cured. But if he is sane, he will never be able to convince the doctors that he should be released—and he already doubts whether the supposed safeguards established to get him out will work.

The first evening, he hears a mysterious, sourceless voice ordering him to get up and dress. The voice claims to be a representative of the Brightly Shining, one of the three true intelligences in the solar system. Under its direction, he escapes and is led to a man who tells him that his mind is being controlled because his recollection of his past life and his dreams of the red and black have made him dangerous, and now he must be told the whole truth because "the truth will drive you mad," and thereby render him harmless. The ultimate revelation is that humans are a temporary anomaly on Earth, that the mass mind of the ants actually rules all, and that ants have been using humans as chess pieces in an elaborate game for their entire history. It is the ultimate "We Are Property" story, with ants filling the role usually held by superintelligent aliens, and it is certainly one of Brown's most effective stories.

Commodore Grimes series
A. Bertram Chandler

John Grimes was not introduced in the first of A. Bertram CHANDLER's Rim World stories, but he soon became the central figure in a series of adventures that would jump around in time as well as space as Chandler filled in different stages in his career. The Rim Worlds were the relatively lawless colonies at the edge of the galaxy, profitable trading partners so long as ships avoided the ever-present space pirates or other unpredictable dangers. Chandler reinforced the image of space as a vast, uncharted sea with *Into the Alternate Universe* (1964), in which Grimes discovers that sightings of ghost ships are linked to other strange phenomena including gateways to alternate universes.

We learn more of Grimes's background and why he immigrated to the Rim in *The Road to the Rim* (1967), which takes place while he is serving with the Federation navy, although he is already growing disenchanted with the political machinations that dominate the more populous worlds. Over the course of the next few novels Grimes visits a lost colony, takes part in the maiden voyage of a new kind of starship, travels beyond the limits of the galaxy, and visits a series of troubled planets at both novel and short story length. By 1972, with *Gateway to Never*, Grimes was a firmly established and well-known character. Most of Chandler's subsequent fiction would be written around this single character.

The Big Black Mark (1975) describes in detail Grimes's final break with the Federation. He becomes a freelance courier among the Rim worlds in *Star Courier* (1977) and then battles terrorists and mischievous homunculi while operating his own small ship in *To Keep the Ship* (1978), one of the best in the series. After several minor adventures, we see Grimes temporarily reduced to piracy in *Star Loot* (1980); but in the next book, *The Anarch Lords* (1981) he has an equally brief tenure as a planetary governor. The last installment Chandler completed before his death was *The Wild Ones* (1984), in which Grimes tries out an experimental robot, unfortunately on a planet with strange religious customs. Although Chandler was never a particularly literary writer, the Grimes stories have an appealing quality and have remained popular long after similar works have faded into obscurity.

"Colossus"
Donald Wandrei
(1933)

The pulp magazines of the 1930s were not notoriously fussy about literary standards. Most of their stories were crudely written, often scientifically illiterate despite liberal use of technical terms. Frequently they contained only vestigial plots attached to wildly speculative concepts. Indeed, the last factor seemed the single most important criterion for acceptance. Writers played with galaxies, even universes, trying to outdo one another with the scale of their imaginations.

Donald Wandrei was a writer who followed that pattern in much of his work, although he wrote with considerably greater skill than did most of his peers. He attempted to give some depth to his characters. His scientific content might not have stood up to rigorous examination, but it was certainly that of an intelligent layman. "Colossus," one of his most famous stories, explored a concept that Ray Cummings also used on several occasions: The similarity between the structure of a molecule and that of a solar system leads to the obvious speculation that stars and planets might be microscopic components of another level of reality much larger than our own.

The world is not a pleasant place as the story opens. The United States has become a dictatorship, and new alliances and rivalries have pushed the world to the brink of a global conflict that might very well end the world. A team of scientists are at work on an experimental starship that is designed not only to exceed the speed of light, but that also might, through relativistic effects, transform itself in size as well as space into the macrouniverse, if it exists. Although the scientist protagonist does not plan quite so dramatic a trip, the death of his lover alters his perception, and the deteriorating state of the world offers him no incentive to stay.

He succeeds, and is able to communicate with the gigantic inhabitants of the larger universe. Unfortunately, he realizes that the Titans have a society even less admirable than our own. Despite an accommodation between the scientist and his hosts, his ultimate fate is left a mystery. Although the story is not up to the standards of today's science fiction, it was advanced for its time and context, particularly in its willingness to suggest that not every ending is a happy one, and that it is how characters in a story are changed by their experiences that matters, rather than just the nature of what happens to them.

Compton, D. G.
(1930–　)

David G. Compton is a British novelist who has been active since 1961 but whose output dropped dramatically after he relocated to the United States in the early 1980s. His first science fiction novel was *The Quality of Mercy* (1965), a marginal technothriller about a plot to use bacteriological weapons to commit genocide. *Farewell Earth's Bliss* (1966) was more obviously genre fiction. A penal colony has been established on Mars, but the disparate group of criminals evolves a new society with a new set of rules. It was with *The Silent Multitude* (1966) that Compton attracted significant attention. A new spore literally consumes concrete, entire cities begin to crumble, and the survivors have adventures in the aftermath. The power of the story derives from its evocative imagery and the author's adroit depiction of the psychological effects of the collapse. *Synthajoy* (1968) speculates about the development of a method of recording thoughts and experiences, and about how such a device might change the way we interact.

The world is falling apart in *Chronocules* (1970) as well; a group of scientists hopes to flee into the future, but they discover that the future does not necessarily offer an acceptable alternative. *The Steel Crocodile* (1970, also published as *The Electric Crocodile*) is a particularly convincing and chilling look at a scenario in which our dependency upon computers gets out of hand and the machines take over. In *The Missionaries* (1972) an alien starship brings missionaries who plan to convert humans and introduce them into a greater galactic society, but humankind proves to be stubbornly uncooperative. The parallels to events in our own history provide some effective satiric moments.

The Unsleeping Eye (1974, also published as *The Continuous Katherine Mortenhoe* and as *Death Watch*) is considered Compton's most important novel, an indictment of modern media techniques. A terminally ill woman attracts the attention of media operatives who want to film her last days. She turns to a friend for solace and aid, only to discover that he has had one of his eyes replaced with a camera in order to capitalize on her misfortune. The sequel, *Windows* (1979), follows the ensuing efforts of the now disenchanted reporter to escape a similar loss of privacy.

Compton's subsequent novels have not been as well received. The most interesting of these are *Nomansland* (1994), which deals with a plague of infertility, and *Ragnarok* (1991), written with James Gribbin, wherein a scientist triggers a nuclear winter in an effort to ward off a nuclear war.

"Consider Her Ways"
John Wyndham
(1956)

Although science fiction had already begun to move beyond its pulp roots during the 1950s, characterization was still a comparatively low priority. Female characters were rarely protagonists, but usually were just fixtures of the setting; feminist concerns were treated lightly, if at all, and would not strongly influence the field for another decade.

One of the surprising exceptions to this rule was John WYNDHAM, who had included strong female characters even in his early space adventures during the 1930s; but it was with this novelette that Wyndham squarely tackled many of the same issues that feminists raised decades later.

Jane Summers partakes of an experimental drug and wakes up in a future in which males have disappeared, wiped out by a plague, and women reproduce parthogenetically. Once she accepts that this is reality and not just a hallucination, she is horrified by the society revealed to her. Babies are produced by women known as mothers whose lives are devoted to that task and who live in ignorance and pampered indulgence otherwise. Trapped in the body of Mother Orchis, Summers is so heavy that she can barely move, and her rebellious attitude results in her virtual arrest. Eventually she is brought to Laura, a historian, and the conversation that follows is cast as a typical utopian dialogue, with both sides presenting the case for their world.

Surprisingly, given the revulsion felt by Summers and most readers at the set-up, Laura makes a strong argument for the status quo. Summers insists that a world devoid of romance has no soul. Laura responds that romance was an invention by men to prevent women from acquiring positions of power during the early days of the Industrial Revolution. Summers extols the joys of marriage, but Laura responds that it was virtual slavery for most women, that they deferred to their husbands on all important issues. When Summers laments the loss of much of the diversity of life, the constant flow of luxury items produced at least partly by the energy generated by the old order, Laura indicts consumerism as crass manipulation just short of mind control. The people of her world are generally content if not actively happy, and she challenges Laura to say the same of her own time. Both parties have just enough truth on their side to make valid arguments, and there is no clear evidence which way the author's sentiments incline.

Unlike many writers, Wyndham also knows when to stop. He might easily have gone on for several thousand more words in the same vein, the error that makes most utopian novels unreadable as fiction; but having stated the case—for both sides—he describes Summers's return to her own frame of reference. But the story is not over. Although no one believes that Summers experienced a real transference in time, she investigates the man who supposedly unleashed the plague that wiped out men. Discovering that he really lives, she first tries to persuade him to abandon his work, then murders him. The ending is a double twist, however, because the dead man has a son with the same name—a son determined to follow in his father's footsteps. The story is a major accomplishment, not only because it is well-written and thought-provoking, but also because it was so far ahead of its time.

"Continued on Next Rock"
R. A. Lafferty
(1970)

The idiosyncratic stories of R. A. LAFFERTY frequently defied description, and sometimes the borderline between science fiction and fantasy was stretched to the breaking point. Most of Lafferty's fiction employs strange, sometime startling juxtapositions and images. "Continued on Next Rock" is one of the best examples of this. A party of five people camp out in the desert to study a burial mound; one of their number, Magdalen, has extraordinary powers. She can sense a deer's presence in the distance, and has nearly supernatural physical strength. During a conversation the first night, the archaeologists discuss an extended metaphor comparing geology to the structure of the human mind—hence the title.

Magdalen can remember previous lives, and insists that she is constantly being visited in her mind by people from the past. They are joined by a mysterious newcomer named Anteros, who claims to be an Indian, and who has an uncanny ability to find and identify artifacts in the sandstone before they are uncovered. Magdalen and Anteros communicate without words at times, and the others are increasingly suspicious of their motives.

Lafferty alternates mystical musings about reincarnation with detailed descriptions of archaeological concepts in a fascinating marriage of magic and science. More anomalies are found as the archaeologists dig deeper: a love poem incised on one rock that ends with the glyph for *continuation*, items far too sophisticated for the strata of time in which they are unearthed. As the dig progresses, they find more anomalous stones, each continuing the same narrative, each in a more modern form of writing, until they ultimately come to believe that the capstone will tell them of events yet to occur. The ambiguous ending folds time back upon itself and leaves the true nature of its characters unexplained; but the beauty of the language, the erudite word play, and the evocative imagery leave a lingering impression. This is one of the best of Lafferty's considerable body of excellent short stories.

Cooper, Edmund
(1926–1982)

Edmund Cooper was a fairly prolific writer of short fiction during the 1950s. Most of his stories were collected, but few were memorable. It was not until he began writing novels that he attracted any attention outside of England. *Deadly Image* (1958, also published as *The Uncertain Midnight*) was the first of his several novels set after a nuclear war or other global devastation. In this case, civilization is on the mend, but the introduction of androids, designed to help speed the process, presents humanity with its greatest challenge. The novel achieved some critical success and his next, *Seed of Light* (1959), a generation starship novel, promised even better things to come.

Cooper's career subsequently was erratic, initially mixing thoughtful, well-conceived stories with straightforward, sometimes lackluster adventures. *Transit* (1964) is a routine otherworlds adventure story notable only because its protagonist, Richard Avery, was the name under which Cooper would later write a series of four space operas. *All Fool's Day* (1966), on the other hand, used the device of a global disaster—in this case caused by violent solar flares—to speculate about the nature of human survival traits. Cooper's suggestion was that nonconformists would be the most likely to survive, and that as a consequence the new order would be radically different from the past. The plot of *A Far Sunset* (1967) is that of a routine otherworlds adventure, but it was above average of its type.

Five to Twelve (1967) was a more ambitious and impressive work, though marred by blatant misogynism. The protagonist becomes the catalyst for a revolution by downtrodden men in a future Earth dominated by less capable women. Cooper's animosity toward women who are in any position of power is expressed in his depiction of another dystopian matriarchy in *Gender Genocide* (1972, also published as *Who Needs Men?*), and more subtly in *Kronk* (1970, also published as *Son of Kronk*), a satire involving a new sexual disease with surprising symptoms. *The Last Continent* (1969) has one of his more interesting plots—a romantic entanglement between one of the last human survivors of yet another global disaster and a black humanoid visitor from outer space—but ultimately his skills were not up to the task, and the story devolves in its final chapters into a routine adventure. *The Overman Culture* (1971) was even more ambitious, set in a future where people can modify themselves almost at will, and ordinary, unaltered humans suddenly find themselves in the minority. Despite some inventive detail, the story proceeds almost haphazardly to an unsatisfying conclusion.

Cooper's single best novel is unquestionably *The Cloud Walker* (1973). The world has gone through two nuclear wars, and the survivors labor under a pervasive theological repression that condemns all efforts to recover the lost technology. The protagonist disagrees, predictably, and when warfare breaks out he is instrumental in designing new weapons and eventually persuades others to join him in rebellion. Although the plot is straightforward and familiar, Cooper manages to exceed the reader's expectations with some wonderfully constructed sequences and an admirable protagonist. His remaining novels are only of minor interest, mixing good writing with bad and rarely straying from standard science fiction themes.

As Richard Avery, Cooper wrote a series of four planetary adventure stories featuring a group of criminals who are offered a form of freedom if they volunteer to take place in the first landings on unexplored planets. The sequence consists of *The Deathworms of Kratos* (1974), *The Rings of Tantalus*

(1975), *The War Games of Zelos* (1975), and *The Venom of Argus* (1975). Although these books are not as serious or ambitious as most of Cooper's other work, they have a lively enthusiasm and they have aged better than most of his other work.

Coppel, Alfred
(1921–   )

Alfred Coppel started his career as a prolific short story writer, appearing regularly in the science fiction magazines during the 1950s. Most of his early novels were mainstream thrillers, however—with the exception of *Dark December* (1960), a surprisingly good postapocalyptic thriller about a man seeking his family following a nuclear war. Coppel's mainstream work was so successful that he wrote no other science fiction until the late 1960s, when he penned a trilogy of young adult space adventures under the name Robert Cham Gilman. *The Rebel of Rhada* (1968) was set in a distant future where technology has been displaced by superstition, although some of the population elements desire a more rational culture. The conflict continues in *The Navigator of Rhada* (1969) and ends in *The Starkahn of Rhada* (1970). A later addition to the series, *The Warlock of Rhada* (1985), is a prequel involving a man revived from suspended animation.

Coppel wrote a number of thrillers during the 1970s, most of them quite good; two were marginally speculative. The president is assassinated and the vice president kidnapped, and the military seizes control of the United States during a confrontation with the Soviet Union in *Thirty Four East* (1974). In *The Dragon* (1977) China and the Soviet Union move toward open war while the president is forced to deal with a treasonous general who plans to initiate a nuclear attack. *The Burning Mountain* (1982) is Coppel's best science fiction novel, an alternate history in which American forces invade Japan at the end of World War II—a bloody and protracted battle whose details the author researched meticulously. *Eighth Day of the Week* (1994) is also quite well done, a marginal SF tale about an attempt to set off an atomic bomb in Hudson Bay.

Coppel returned to conventional science fiction with *Glory* (1993). The title is the name of a starship that travels among the widely separated human colony worlds, carrying information, trade, and occasionally emigrants. This first volume of a trilogy details a visit to a world that still employs apartheid, but the crew arrives just as violent social change is about to take place. The ship becomes the prize in a battle between two other colonies in *Glory's War* (1995) and visits a world patterned after Japanese feudalism in *Glory's People* (1996). Although the third volume is comparatively weak, the first two novels were exceptionally skillful. Many readers were disappointed when Coppel discontinued the series.

"Coventry"
Robert A. Heinlein
(1940)

One of the great strengths of science fiction is that it allows us to examine different solutions to political and social questions by hypothesizing situations that probably could never occur in the real world. One of the greatest questions facing any society concerns the nature and limits of personal freedom, the manner in which we balance the rights of the individual with the welfare of the many. Despite his clearly libertarian leanings, Heinlein recognized that society could not survive if we all enjoyed unlimited freedom of action. Yet, at the same time, he regretted the tendency to consider all antisocial behavior as necessarily criminal.

The story's protagonist refuses to accept psychological treatment after he reacts violently in a society that has forsworn physical violence, so he is sent to Coventry, a portion of the country, quarantined from the majority, where those who assert their right to live a more flamboyant and risky lifestyle are allowed to do as they wish without endangering others. Or so it appears at first. Upon arriving in his new homeland, he discovers that even the supposed anarchists and libertarians have quickly established new forms of government of their own. He is slower to accept the fact that his freedom to embrace this lifestyle exists only

because of the sophisticated and organized society that dominates the world, and that the tools he uses to survive would not have been created in a chaotic and disorganized civilization. These latter points become evident after he is taken under the wing of another resident, who is an agent of the external government, planted to watch over the dissidents. When our hero discovers a massive break-out plot, he ultimately sides with the powers of order and security despite his previous personal inclinations.

The story is clearly designed to convey a message about the role of government in regulating society, but Heinlein rarely lectures us here as he does so often in his later work. He also is more inclined to balance disparate viewpoints and assume that no single brand of political theory has a monopoly on the truth.

Cover, Arthur Byron
(1950–   )

From the outset, Arthur Byron Cover's fiction had a distinctive flavor that some readers embraced wholeheartedly and others detested with equal vehemence. Following his first short story sale in 1973, Cover produced an extremely unusual novel for his book-length debut, *Autumn Angels* (1975), followed by its sequel, *An East Wind Coming* (1979). The setting is a future Earth so distant in time that almost nothing of our own world is recognizable, and where technology has advanced to the point where it is literally indistinguishable from magic. People can alter their bodies dramatically—can even create artificial life. The first volume was notable mostly for the remarkable stage setting. The sequel added an engaging character, an immortal Sherlock Holmes, and an intriguing plot, his efforts to track down a new version of Jack the Ripper. Cover's irreverent style mixed serious narrative with broad satire, not always successfully. A collection of short stories, *The Platypus of Doom and Other Nihilists* (1976), more or less takes place in the same setting. *The Sound of Winter* (1976), although not part of the series, is set in a similarly strange future and is considered by many to be his best work.

Most of Cover's subsequent work consisted of minor novels, either intended for young adult audiences or derived from other media, movies or computer games. It was not until 2002 that he returned to serious work, with a sequence consisting so far of *Born in Fire* (2002) and *Ten Years After* (2002). The premise for the series is derived from comic books. A meteor crashes into an alternate version of the 1960s, and children born the following year often exhibit unusual powers, making them superheroes—or supervillains. A terrified public insists upon rounding up all of these mutants and quarantining them from the rest of humanity. Cover tells his stories skillfully, but the original voice found in his early work is entirely missing in these later books.

Cowper, Richard
(1926–   )

Richard Cowper is the pseudonym of Colin Murry, who has written several fairly well-received mainstream novels under another name, Colin Middleton-Murray, and who first turned to science fiction in 1967. *Breakthrough* (1967), his debut genre novel, mixed traditional themes with mysticism and hints of reincarnation, and was much more character-driven than was common in science fiction of that time. *Phoenix* (1967) employed a much more familiar plot, its protagonist resorting to suspended animation to escape a strictly regimented future society, only to find that things could be even worse. The satire in *Clone* (1972) was barbed and inventive, and Cowper's popularity looked to be on the rise. His continued use of mainstream literary values and a certain disdain for the niceties of science in his novels were not universally approved of, however, and the next few novels were not as well received, although they were all quite skillfully written. *Kuldesak* (1972), a reasonably conventional postapocalyptic novel, received little notice and was never issued in America. *Time Out of Mind* (1973) was a mystery involving an original form of time travel.

His next major novel was *The Twilight of Briareus* (1974), set in a world transformed by a barrage of radiation from a supernova. Despite the background, the novel is not about the disaster so much as about the awakening psychic powers that appear in the aftermath, and their eventual use to communicate with alien intelligences. *Profundis* (1979) also involves telepathy and is similarly set in a postdisaster world, but the tone is much less optimistic.

Cowper's last three novels comprise a trilogy: *The Road to Corlay* (1978), *A Dream of Kinship* (1981), and *A Tapestry of Time* (1982). Once again the setting is a postapocalyptic culture, this one dominated by a theocracy that discourages innovation and technology. However, the conflict is not quite as black-and-white as it might have been in the hands of lesser writers, and there are no clear villains. The new religion undergoes its own transformation, and the story, which is narrated with an almost poetic style, ends with the new world's redemption.

Cowper's infrequent short stories were invariably worth reading, particularly "Out There Where the Big Ships Go" and "The Custodians." His short fiction has been collected in *The Custodians and Other Stories* (1976), *Out There Where the Big Ships Go* (1980), and *The Tithonian Factor and Other Stories* (1984).

Crichton, Michael
(1942–   )

Although Michael Crichton has largely been considered a commercial-fiction writer, many of his novels have clearly been science fiction even if they have not carried that label. Unlike many mainstream writers who have crossed that border, Crichton acknowledges that his work is in fact science fiction. As John Lange, he started writing thrillers in 1968, some involving technology that bordered on the futuristic; but it was with *The Andromeda Strain* (1969), written under his own name, that he became a best-selling author. The novel involves the efforts of a team of scientists in a secure, underground laboratory to find a cure for a spore from outer space that has wiped out a small town and threatens to spread. As would be the case for many of Crichton's novels, it was subsequently turned into a very successful movie.

In *The Terminal Man* (1972) an experiment designed to explore the possibilities of direct interfaces between humans and computers goes horribly wrong when the subject becomes unbalanced and uses his new abilities to commit murder. *Binary* (1972), which the author wrote as John Lange, is a thriller in which a megalomaniac threatens to wipe out an entire city using a newly invented form of poison gas. Crichton also wrote the screenplay for *Westworld* (1974), set in a futuristic theme park with robotic attractions that suddenly and inexplicably begin to kill the guests. Although the film is gripping upon first viewing, a more critical eye reveals a number of holes in the plot—for example, how did the robots acquire live ammunition— which may explain why it was never novelized.

Congo (1976), also filmed but less successfully, is a lost world novel reminiscent of works in that subgenre by Sir Arthur Conan Doyle and H. Rider Haggard. An expedition that includes a gorilla trained to communicate with humans discovers a lost diamond mine guarded by creatures that fall somewhere between apes and men—with disastrous consequences. *Sphere* (1987), which resulted in another mediocre film, has a fascinating premise: An apparently derelict alien spaceship is discovered in the ocean; a predictable struggle for control erupts, but the story takes a decidedly unexpected turn when we learn that the ship was constructed by humans and has traveled back through time. We learn too that its cargo consists of an artifact that has strange effects on the minds of anyone in close proximity.

Crichton's best-selling novel to date appeared in 1990. *JURASSIC PARK* is a taut, gripping thriller, even if the scientific rationale is somewhat suspect. An entrepreneur recovers dinosaur DNA and uses it to recreate some of the extinct species of dinosaur, populating a remote island with the creatures and turning it into a theme park. A tour provided prior to the opening has disastrous consequences for all concerned. The book provided the basis for a major motion picture. An inferior but occasionally interesting sequel to the book, *The Lost World* (1995), includes some quiet nods to Sir Arthur Conan Doyle. A film version, *Jurassic Park II: The Lost World,* is only peripherally related to the novel.

Two of Crichton's recent novels are even closer to being standard science fiction. In *Timeline* (2000) a time-traveling scholar is trapped in France during the Hundred Years' War, and a group of his students are sent back to rescue him without interfering with the course of history. Crichton examines the possible consequences of nanotechnology in *Prey* (2002): A secret government project to explore the use of microscopic machines leads to disaster when the scientists unwisely use the learning pattern of a predator to control the machines' behavior.

Although Crichton is not a major figure in science fiction, this is largely because he is viewed by many as an outsider poaching on genre themes. The quality of his fiction would otherwise earn him a place of distinction. Crichton has also been criticized for what some perceive as a bias against science and scientists; but this criticism is not entirely accurate. He is concerned, rather, with the dangers posed by undisciplined scientists and the misuse of scientific knowledge.

Crowley, John
(1942–)

With his first novel, *The Deep* (1975), John Crowley made an immediate and lasting impact on the science fiction field. The story often approaches fantasy in its disregard for the normal operating rules of the universe. The setting is a flat world peopled by, among other things, humans apparently snatched from a dying Earth, and by an android through whose perspective we see most of the events of the story. Much of the plot and imagery is derived from mythology, a source the author exploits frequently in his work. Crowley's literate and complex prose was nevertheless accessible to a variety of readers, and his subsequent books were the objects of great anticipation, particularly when it became obvious that he would never be a prolific writer.

Beasts (1976) is a postapocalyptic novel in which the fallen human race finds itself sharing the world with a variety of uplifted animals who now have equal intelligence and, presumably, an equal right to the planet. The major conflict is between the central authority—a kind of successor to the United States government—and those who prefer a looser, less centralized form of administration. *Engine Summer* (1979) is somewhat similar in setting, but this time it is clear that human civilization as we have known it is ending. The protagonist is a young man searching for his lost love; but along the way he, and by extension the reader, is taught that the old civilization, ours, was hampered by too strict an adherence to rational thought, and that the collapse was partly due to an inability to embrace the romantic elements in life. A shorter novel, *The Great Work of Time* (1989), involves time travel—backward to the Africa of Cecil Rhodes, and forward into an unrecognizable future in which creatures analogous to angels inhabit the Earth. *Little, Big* (1991), his most famous and successful novel, mixes science fiction and fantasy, set in the near future but involving fairies and magic. Crowley's subsequent work has been almost exclusively fantasy, but his stylistic experiments and thematic concerns have been echoed by other writers, perhaps most notably Tim POWERS. Crowley's occasional short fiction, much of which is fantasy, has been collected as *Novelties and Souvenirs* (2004).

The Crystal World
J. G. Ballard
(1966)

Global disaster was a popular theme among British science fiction writers during the 1950s and 1960s. Practitioners such as John WYNDHAM, John CHRISTOPHER, and Charles Eric MAINE received a warm welcome from American readers. J. G. BALLARD's first four novels all seem to fit into this mold, with the Earth beset by unprecedented hurricanes, a rise in the ocean levels, a worldwide drought, and an infestation of alien life, respectively. However, readers quickly discovered that Ballard's take on disasters was not a conventional one. He saw disaster as a cleansing rather than an unmitigated calamity. The world was not always saved at the end of his books, and sometimes the characters were not entirely unhappy about the collapse of civilization. By the time *The Burning*

World (1964) appeared, Ballard was considered pessimistic at best, nihilistic at worst. *The Crystal World* confirmed that view for many, and in the fan press Ballard alternately was castigated vehemently and praised for his innovation and fresh viewpoint.

The premise of the novel is that an alien life form has been set loose in the jungles of Africa—a catalytic force never precisely described that turns every living thing it touches into crystallized structures resembling gems, although they somehow continue to be living beings. The outside world understandably views this as a threat to the entire human race and attempts to eradicate what it sees as a plague, but the spread continues inexorably. Some onlookers notice that within the contaminated area, a new type of ecology is evolving. The crystallized creatures are not dead but somehow are operating outside our normal range of perception, perhaps in a different flow of time itself.

The protagonist has traveled to the area not to deal with or even observe the crystallization but rather to resolve personal problems with a woman, who has become fascinated with the phenomenon. He in turn is mesmerized by the phenomenon and becomes obsessed with it. Some people have already embraced the change as an escape from a world in which they have no place, while others see it as inevitable and rush to what they perceive to be their fate. The narrator is himself of an ambiguous frame of mind, although he is increasingly drawn to the otherworldly beauty of the place and eventually is convinced that the transformation cannot be contained and that the world inevitably will be consumed and changed forever.

Ballard employs extraordinarily evocative imagery and unusually intelligent and precise prose to document the changes, both to the external world and within the mind of his narrator. His achievement is particularly impressive given the context of the time in which it was written, in a field whose readers would to a great extent be repulsed by its conclusions. Although he would move progressively further from the genre in the years that followed, *The Crystal World* remains his single most important science fiction work, and one of the most significant of that decade.

Cummings, Ray
(1887–1957)

Ray Cummings was one of the earliest successful pulp writers, the author of hundreds of stories and novels between 1915 and 1945. His science fiction, though crude by modern standards, was filled with fast-paced action, wildly inventive ideas, and wooden characters; but there was a kind of enthusiasm in his work, particularly early in his career, that communicated itself to his readers. He enjoyed a brief revival of popularity following his death in 1957, but his work is currently out of print and difficult to find.

His most famous novel was *The Girl in the Golden Atom* (1923)—comprising the novelette of the same title (1919) and its sequel, "People of the Golden Atom" (1920), the first of several of his works to involve microscopic worlds. A scientist sees a beautiful girl under a microscope and invents a drug that will allow him to shrink down and join her. In *The Princess of the Atom* (1929/50) the people inside the atom decide to invade our universe, appearing to us in gigantic form, virtually immune to every weapon brought to bear against them, although ultimately they are defeated. *Beyond the Vanishing Point* (1931/58) involves a plot to kidnap people from our universe, shrink them, and imprison them in the microscopic universe. *The Insect Invasion* (1932/67) was a potentially more interesting variation. The protagonist this time shrinks himself to a size small enough that he can investigate the world of insects. Unfortunately, Cummings concentrated on routine adventure and ignored the more interesting possibilities of the plot. *Beyond the Stars* (1928/63) inverted the idea. This time a scientist believes that the stars are just atoms in a greater universe, so he constructs a ship that can enlarge itself and visit the metauniverse to prove his point, a device used again by Donald Wandrei in "Colossus." *Explorers into Infinity* (1928/65) is a slightly different twist on the same basic concept.

Cummings's space operas range from rousing adventure stories of space pirates, such as the still entertaining *Brigands of the Moon* (1931) and its sequel, *Wandl the Invader* (1932/61), to planetary adventures in the style of Edgar Rice Burroughs, including *Tama of the Light Country* (1930/65) and

Tama, Princess of Mercury (1931/66). Some of his time travel novels are also of interest, particularly *The Shadow Girl* (1929/47) and *The Exile of Time* (1931/64), but most of his remaining novels are of little consequence. His very large output of short stories is almost completely unknown, and the only collection, *Tales of the Scientific Crime Club* (1979/64), was published in a limited edition.

Custer's Last Jump
Howard Waldrop and Steven Utley
(1976)

The outcome of the American Civil War has long been one of the most common subjects for alternate history stories, both by genre writers like Ward Moore in *Bring the Jubilee* (1952) and by mainstream authors, notably MacKinlay Kantor in *If the South Had Won the Civil War* (1961) and Oscar Lewis in *The Lost Years* (1951). But no one has ever written a story that rivals the inventiveness and unusual nature of Waldrop and Utley's collaborative effort.

In general, here the conflict between the Union and the Confederacy has taken much the same form as in our own history, with the former slowly tightening its noose by land and by sea. The new twist is that aircraft have been invented, and combat monoplanes and dirigibles are in regular use by both sides. George Armstrong Custer commands a force of paratroopers, with whom he provokes an even wider war by committing atrocities against peaceful Indians caught between the two armies. On the other hand, Crazy Horse and several of his warriors have ingratiated themselves with the Confederates, have been trained as pilots, and are flying combat missions against the Union until Texas falls to the North. Crazy Horse and his tribesmen escape, taking some of the aircraft with them. They later use their prizes to ambush and destroy Custer and his men during another unjustified assault undertaken for political purposes.

The story is presented as a series of documents, the first two being objective histories of the events leading up to Custer's defeat—one following his career and one following the exploits of Crazy Horse. The third segment is a fragment of notes from a supposed sequel to *Huckleberry Finn* by Mark Twain, followed by an interview with an Indian, an excerpt from an imaginary article by Edgar Rice BURROUGHS, and a suggested reading list of imaginary books. Although not cast in the traditional form of a short story, the novelette conveys a vivid image of several of the people involved, and a very unusual answer to the question, "What If?" Waldrop would continue to use unconventional story structures, but he never duplicated the effect so successfully.

Czerneda, Julie E.
(1955–   )

Julie Czerneda made an auspicious debut with her first novel, *A Thousand Words for Stranger* (1997), opening volume of the Trade Pact sequence. Reminiscent of the work of C. J. CHERRYH, the novel is set in an interstellar community of considerable diversity, both human and alien. A woman suffering from amnesia is befriended by a space pilot of dubious reputation, and the two have a series of adventures while attempting to discover her identity. The novel, like all of the author's work, is an elaborate space opera, but with unusually well-drawn characters. *Ties of Power* (1999) and *To Trade the Stars* (2002) expand on the story, with the two friends caught in a power struggle between races whose conflict tends to be commercial or clandestine rather than in open warfare. Their troubles become even more complex in the third

volume with the introduction of another player in the game.

Beholder's Eye (1998) opened a separate sequence of somewhat similar novels, the Web Shifter series. The protagonist this time is a shape-changing alien who is temporarily stranded on Earth, hunted by other aliens for reasons initially concealed. Two sequels, *Changing Vision* (2000) and *Hidden in Sight* (2003), move the action back into space. The alien is teamed with a human partner, both of whom have faked their deaths to avoid discovery, but their old enemies penetrate their new identities as operators of an interplanetary trading company. Although the story lines do not vary a great deal from one novel to the next, Czerneda is sufficiently inventive to keep them fresh and lively.

In the Company of Others (2001), a stand-alone novel, is also a space opera. Humans have used the Quill to help them speed up the terraforming of other planets to use as colonies, but the Quill were supposed to have been genetically engineered to die off when their job was done; that biological time bomb has malfunctioned. Czerneda started a new series with *Survival* (2004). A human biologist is recruited by an alien to investigate a region of space where various races were wiped out at some point in the past, by a danger that might still be active. Most of her usual themes are present, but the plot moves more quickly than in her previous novels and the series promises to be much livelier. Czerneda has written occasional short fiction, but has yet to produce anything memorable at that length.

D

Dann, Jack
(1945–)

Jack Dann's short stories appeared with some frequency during the 1970s. Several attracted quite favorable attention, particularly "Junction" (later expanded into a novel), "Timetipping," "Camps," and "The Dybbuk Dolls." Most of his stories were later collected in *Timetipping* (1980), *Jubilee* (2002), and *Visitations* (2003). Many of Dann's stories reflect his recurring theme of a change in perspective of a naïve protagonist who receives enhanced knowledge about his environment. This was reflected in his first novel, *Starhiker* (1967)—ostensibly for young adults—a well-written story about a young man who leaves his backwater planet to discover the wonders of the wider universe.

Junction (1981) is technically science fiction, but at times feels like fantasy. The laws of reality have shifted and New York City has become a very different, almost unrecognizable place. *The Man Who Melted* (1984) is a much more effective novel. A sudden transformation of the human psyche, with telepathic contact spreading psychoses like plagues, leaves civilization in shatters. One of the few to retain his sanity goes in search of his missing wife and survives an episodic series of adventures and revelations.

Dann edited several anthologies during the 1980s and has continued in that vein ever since. His occasional novels have not been science fiction, with the exception of *The Memory Cathedral* (1996), a remarkably powerful novel about an alternate world where Leonardo da Vinci managed to build a working flying machine. He has also continued to write occasional shorter pieces of which "Niagara Falling," "Da Vinci Rising," and the novella *Echoes of Thunder* are of particular merit. Several of Dann's stories reflect his Jewish heritage and he has edited *Wandering Stars* (1974) and *More Wandering Stars* (1981), both of which collect science fiction stories with ethnic content.

The Darfsteller
Walter M. Miller Jr.
(1954)

The title of Walter M. MILLER's Hugo Award–winning novelette is a theater term referring to an individual who is particularly difficult to work with—an apt description of the main character, Ryan Thornier. Thornier, a stage actor, works as a janitor because all live theater has been replaced by automated mannequins who can be programmed with the persona of famous stars, thus making living artists obsolete. Thornier's anger and dismay are evident from the outset; he works cleaning up in a theater so that he can remain close to the field he loves, even if he is no longer able to participate in it. The technical side of Miller's story does not age well. The programming for the robots is contained on magnetic tape, which makes it comparatively simple for Thornier to successfully sabotage a single character. On the other hand, Miller accurately predicted pay-per-view cable television.

Thornier's chance for revenge against the system, and perhaps a brief moment of personal redemption, comes when he is sent to pick up a replacement tape for the starring role in a new production. He sabotages the programming and arranges things so that he will be asked to fill in for the mannequin, at least for one performance. In a cleverly ironic touch, the character he is to portray is also the last of his kind, a Bolshevik in a world that has passed him by. Thornier's performance is complicated by the presence of Mela, the woman he once loved, an actress who sold out and allowed her personality to be recorded and sold.

Thornier has another secret as well. This really will be his final performance. The story calls for his character to be shot to death, and he plans to substitute live ammunition for the blanks in the mannequin's weapon. His triumph begins to sour almost from the outset; his acting is self-conscious and awkward, and he is warned that if he gives a performance superior to that of the mannequin's, he will stand out not as a great artist but as an amusing and rather silly anachronism. When Mela fills in for her own mannequin to balance the performance, Thornier realizes that he does not want to die after all, but finds himself trapped by his own plan.

Ultimately Thornier realizes that he was wrong, that theater may have changed in form, but that change is inevitable in every aspect of life. His stubborn refusal to face reality changes nothing, and fails even to bring him pleasure. The reader, who has until now been urged toward sympathy with his battle against automation, discovers at last that progress may sometimes be painful, but that it is also inevitable, and that the long-term consequences outweigh any temporary distress. The old-style live theater may be effectively dead, but theater itself is now more popular and accessible than ever before.

Darkover series
Marion Zimmer Bradley

By the late 1950s, Marion Zimmer BRADLEY had been writing science fiction for a few years, showing promise without having produced anything that really stood out. She turned her hand to a short, planetary adventure novel that would appear in book form as *The Planet Savers* (1962), bound with a second novel set against the same backdrop, *The Sword of Aldones*. This was the first of the Darkover books, the opening of a series that would soon dominate her career as a writer. The two short novels did not have spectacularly original plots. In the first, an offworld doctor helps cure a plague on a recently rediscovered colony planet; in the second, a halfbreed returns from an extended journey off his planet to take a crucial role in the political struggles of his home world.

It was neither the plots nor the characters that made the Darkover books such an instant hit. Rather, Bradley had created a world that appealed to a broad spectrum of readers. The tone and exotic settings were strongly reminiscent of the otherworld adventures of Leigh BRACKETT. The intricate and mystical background of the local culture, some of whose members possessed psychic powers, made the stories attractive to fantasy fans at a time when fantasy fiction was relatively uncommon. *The Bloody Sun* (1964), a slightly longer novel that Bradley would dramatically expand in 1979, introduced us to the intricacies of the Comyn, the council that ruled Darkover, and the political rivalries among the various prominent families. *Star of Danger* (1965) further expanded the background, this time as seen from the viewpoint of a Terran visitor.

Although the series was well established by now, Bradley remained content to write lightweight adventures. *The Winds of Darkover* (1970) and *The World Wreckers* (1971) were fairly undistinguished. *Darkover Landfall* (1972) jumped back in time to tell the story of the original colonization of Darkover and of its separation from the rest of humankind. This book was an interesting addition in terms of background, but it appeared that Bradley might have run out of ways to extend the series without being repetitive. *The Spell Sword*, which followed in 1974, is probably the least interesting in the series, and it appeared that Bradley might turn to outright fantasy.

The first of the more extensive Darkover novels was *The Heritage of Hastur* (1975). It is possible that Bradley had decided to rethink her original concept; in fact, several minor contradictions had already cropped up, many of which would be corrected in later editions or dismissed as errors or lies told by unreliable narrators. *Heritage* deals with the intricacies of the conflict that separates the various powers on Darkover, both among the noble houses and the common people, as they deal with questions about how to define their relationship with the newly arrived Terrans and how much change to allow in their society. Some wish to break off contact, others want to embrace the Terrans without reservation, and still others prefer a course of moderation.

Bradley's growing concern with feminist issues manifested itself in *The Shattered Chain* (1976). On Darkover, women were paradoxically honored and kept in a kind of second-class citizenship, with the exception of the Free Amazons, who pursued their own course. The battle against die-hard traditionalists continued in *The Forbidden Tower* (1977). In *Stormqueen!* (1978) Bradley takes the reader back to the days before the Terrans arrived, filling in another period in the planet's history, as she also does in *Hawkmistress!* (1992). The conflict between psi and science worsens in *Two to Conquer* (1980), followed by *Sharra's Exile* (1981), a complete rewrite of *The Sword of Aldones*.

Thendara House (1983) returned to a consideration of gender issues, with a Terran visitor entering a Darkover refuge for women. Bradley provides a thoughtful, balanced view of the situation in one of the best, and certainly the most thought-provoking, entries in the series. *City of Sorcery* (1984) advances the story to a time when contact with the Terrans has moved past its initial troubles, but *The Heirs of Hammerfell* (1989) reverted to another period in history to chronicle the battle for supremacy between two noble houses. *Rediscovery* (1993), one of the lesser novels, is set just prior to the resumption of contact. The final two novels were relatively disappointing: *The Shadow Matrix* (1997) is competently told but covers ground already well tilled by earlier volumes, while *Traitor's Sun* (1999) is a sometimes bitter story in which the Terran Empire collapses and the outworlders on Darkover suddenly find themselves as supplicants.

Bradley also wrote several short stories set on the same world, collected as *Darkover* (1993), and edited a series of shared-world anthologies based on that setting. Deborah Ross has written new Darkover novels, based on conversations with Bradley and listing her as coauthor. The three titles in the series vary greatly in quality, but this is one of those cases where the whole is greater than the sum of its parts, and Darkover is a world as rich and well remembered as Dune, Mesklin, and other imaginary worlds of science fiction.

"Dark They Were and Golden Eyed"
Ray Bradbury
(1949)

Ray BRADBURY had the enviable talent of writing short stories that took ordinary people and exposed them to extraordinary events, and of making both the people and the events seem real. Where most science fiction writers would provide explicit details about the fantastic components in a story, Bradbury implied them subtly, often keeping them off the stage so that the characters were the sole focus of our attention. Nor did he use the stock characters that were almost universal until the 1960s, and are still common even today. His protagonists would never even attempt to save the world; they were lucky if they could save themselves.

"Dark They Were and Golden Eyed" is a story set on Mars, but not included in *The MARTIAN CHRONICLES* (1950), although it would have fit there. The Bittering family has immigrated to the Red Planet, hoping to avoid what they see as an inevitable nuclear war on Earth. Mars was once inhabited, but the Martian cities are empty now and there is no sign of their former residents. Harry Bittering has misgivings; he feels that they do not belong here, that they should return to Earth. When war does break out, the choice is taken from them, and they must face their future on an unfamiliar world.

Harry's disquiet grows as the days pass, with the possibility of return taken from them. Before long he has more tangible concerns. Plants and animals imported from Earth are undergoing odd transformations and sometimes becoming almost unrecognizable. When he exhorts his neighbors to resist these changes, he discovers that they are also being altered by the new environment—and so is *he,* despite his efforts to resist. He and his family begin to remember words, words not part of any human tongue. The stranded colonists eventually abandon their newly constructed town and move into one of the abandoned Martian settlements, and when Earth finally reopens contact several years later, the new arrivals find that the human colony is gone, but that the Martians are not dead after all.

In the hands of a lesser writer, this might have been a story of horror, or perhaps an adventure in which the hero discovers the cause of the transformation and reverses it. But Bradbury had a different purpose: He is reminding us that we are inescapably a product of our environment, that as much as we might want to change the world to fit our purposes, the world is far more likely to change us.

Davidson, Avram
(1923–1993)

Avram Davidson's writing career started with a short story sale in 1954, and four years later he won a Hugo Award for "OR ALL THE SEAS WITH OYSTERS," a marvelously original, amusing story that explains what happens to all those coat hangers that seem to disappear of their own accord. Over the course of the next 40 years he would produce a substantial body of short stories of unusually high quality, a respectable number of science fiction novels, a handful of mysteries, and some very highly regarded fantasy. He also served as editor of the *Magazine of Fantasy and Science Fiction* for three years.

Davidson's short stories are generally better than his novels, and were quite unusual for their time, having more the flavor of John Collier or Shirley Jackson than of his contemporaries. Much of this fiction is enlivened by his sense of humor; he often portrayed ordinary events in a distinctly warped fashion. "Help! I Am Dr. Morris Goldpepper," for example, is a sardonic variation of the alien abduction story. In "The Sources of the Nile" an advertising manager discovers an absolutely foolproof method of anticipating future trends in fashion. Throughout his career Davidson demonstrated a distaste for the increased commercialism of modern society, which he saw as a kind of barbaric triumph over the finer qualities of life. Davidson wrote too many classic stories to list here, but of particular interest are "Take Wooden Indians," "Golem," "The Woman Who Thought She Could Read," and "The Tail Tied Kings." The best of his early stories were collected in *Or All the Seas with Oysters* (1962), *What Strange Stars and Skies* (1965), and *Strange Seas and Shores* (1971).

Davidson's first novel was *Mutiny in Space* (1964), a surprisingly literate space adventure. *Rork!* (1965) is an otherworld adventure whose style seemed to clash with its subject, but *The Enemy of My Enemy* (1966), in which a man has his body physically modified so that he can pass as a native on an alien world, proved that Davidson's intricate style could be fitted to an overt adventure story. *Masters of the Maze* (1965), the best of these early space adventures, puts the world in peril at the hands of alien invaders who use an extradimensional gateway to travel from one planet to another. Davidson leavens the melodrama with humor, and uses tight, eloquent prose to lift the book above its familiar subject matter.

ROGUE DRAGON (1965) and its sequel, *The Kar-Chee Reign* (1966), are both novellas rather than full-length novels. Earth has become a backwater world whose chief source of revenue is from tourists who come to hunt dragons, descendants of an alien species imported when the planet had a more flourishing economy. A third short novel, *Clash of Star-Kings* (1966), transformed the ancient astronaut theory: Scientists discover that the ancient gods of the Mayas were alien visitors, and that they are on their way back to reclaim their property. All three of these last titles were strong contenders for awards and they further secured Davidson's already enviable reputation.

Most of Davidson's subsequent novels were fantasy, but he continued to write short science fiction of considerable literary merit. The Dr. Esterhazy series, set in an alternate version of the 19th century, has been collected as *The Enquiries of*

Dr. Esterhazy (1975) and The Other 19th Century (2001). The best of Davidson's later short stories were collected as The Redward Edward Papers (1978) and The Avram Davidson Treasury (1998).

Davidson has been characterized as the field's most obviously literary writer of stature, and he certainly exhibited a degree of stylistic individuality almost unknown before or since. He seemed to be uncomfortable writing longer work; and most of his novels are comparatively short. Reportedly he died with a large body of completed but unsold manuscripts, and it is quite possible that new material will continue to appear for years to come. The work published late in his career has a tendency to be more verbose and descriptive, but his sharp wit and gift for creating evocative scenes was undiminished.

Davy
Edgar Pangborn
(1964)

Postapocalyptic stories have not been as popular in recent years as they once were. During the 1950s and 1960s, authors both inside and outside the genre speculated about what would follow if the worst should happen. Most of these portrayed a humanity reduced to primitivism at best, savagery at worst, and concentrated on the terrible consequences. Edgar PANGBORN's Davy, portions of which previously appeared as short stories, was one of the rare exceptions. Certainly Pangborn did not relish the fall of civilization, but his story concentrates on the enduring quality of the human spirit, its ability to still act selflessly in adversity. He even manages to inject humor into what, in the hands of most writers, would have been scenes of unrelenting grimness.

Davy is born nearly three centuries after the collapse, in a world divided into numerous small political units (in those places where any form of government exists at all). An orphan, he eventually sets out on a journey across the newly recreated world, encountering good people as well as villains, having adventures that are exciting and occasionally quite funny. A sequence involving a mentally diminished mutant is particularly moving.

The narrative—constructed as though it were Davy's memoir—follows his transformation from innocence through experience to leadership. The novel has justly been compared to Henry Fielding's Tom Jones. It was much more popular than Pangborn's previous work, and was a strong contender for the Hugo Award in a year that saw a surprisingly large number of first-rate novels.

Most of Pangborn's subsequent fiction was set in the same general future, although none of this work ever achieved the stature of Davy. The remaining tales appeared in book form as The Judgment of Eve (1964), The Company of Glory (1975), and Still I Persist in Wondering (1978).

"Day Million"
Frederik Pohl
(1966)

Many writers have produced stories in which none of the characters are human, at least in physical form. It is very difficult to create a plausible nonhuman culture, so it is common to employ the shortcut of patterning aliens after some obscure or historic human society. Frederik POHL addresses the problem in a slightly different fashion in this short story. He describes his characters in familiar human terms, but tells us that they are metaphors for alien attributes that we probably could not understand. Dora, the main character, is described as a girl and a dancer, although "she" is genetically male, lives in an ocean, and smells like peanut butter. Dora, whose name is actually unpronounceable, has a chance encounter with Don, and the two immediately fall in love and plan their marriage.

Don is part of a space crew. Because of the dangers of radiation, his body has been augmented with a variety of artifices that apparently make it impossible, or at least very difficult, for Dora and him to interact physically—but that proves to be no problem. They marry, and never see each other again, although they are described as living happily ever after. Each has been recorded by some unexplained and irrelevant process that allows them to enjoy each other's company, and even to engage in perceptible if not physically consummated sex, through some wondrous technology. The reader is set up to feel at least a mild distaste for this alien species and to entertain some reservations about its culture. Pohl then springs his trap and reveals that Don and Dora are in fact descended from contemporary human beings, an evolution so advanced that they appear completely alien to us. But no more alien, we are told, than we would appear to someone from the time of Attila the Hun.

The message clearly is that everything is relative, that we should not attempt to judge things out of their proper context or jump to the conclusion that we understand what is happening below the surface just because what we can see looks superficially familiar. Pohl also tells us explicitly that good stories are about people and not about the circumstances of their lives, and that while Don and Dora might not be human beings, they are most definitely people. By implication, we therefore should care about the people we encounter outside of books and not judge them because of the circumstances of their lives.

The Day of the Triffids
John Wyndham
(1951)

Although monsters have proliferated in science fiction movies, they have been comparatively rare in the written form, and only a handful of writers have produced serious, thoughtful stories that feature them. John WYNDHAM's first major novel did, however, and it is ironic that the terrifying plausibility of his creatures was ignored when the film version was made, turning the triffids into just another shambling creature.

Wyndham made a minor break with tradition in this novel, which has also appeared as *The Revolt of the Triffids*. The common wisdom was that in the course of any given piece of fiction an author could ask the reader to suspend disbelief only once. This time Wyndham chose to establish two separate incredible events and to put his characters at their intersection. The first was the advent of the triffids, a new life form of uncertain origin. They look very much like small trees, except that

they can uproot themselves and move (although very slowly), and are able to throw a stinger that can paralyze a human being. Although theoretically dangerous, they are too slow-moving to be much of a menace, and they are quickly confined and studied.

The second premise is that an unusual condition in space would result in a spectacular panorama of lights, after which everyone who watched becomes irreversibly blind. Civilization collapses all over the world in a matter of hours and some of the triffids escape; now they are indeed dangerous, because people cannot evade what they cannot see. Wyndham's viewpoint character awakens in a hospital to find himself alone, one of the very few who missed the light show and thus retained his vision. His subsequent odyssey across the ruins of England is exciting, suspenseful, and plausible.

In addition to the inferior movie version, there also was a much more loyal BBC television serial. Horror writer Simon Clark recently wrote an authorized sequel, *Night of the Triffids* (2001), but it failed to capture the tone of the original. Wyndham would go on to write several more successful novels, but it would be the triffids for which he would be best remembered.

de Camp, L. Sprague
(1907–2000)

During his lengthy career as an author—he was 84 when his last novel was published—L. Sprague de Camp wrote nonfiction, historical novels, a controversial biography of H. P. LOVECRAFT and another of Robert E. Howard, and a considerable body of science fiction and fantasy, the latter including several additions to the Conan saga created by Howard. His historical novels are of particular interest to genre readers because of their focus on how technological change affected the ancient world. De Camp's first short story was published in 1937. He produced a steady stream of stories and novels from that point forward, sometimes in collaboration with his wife, Catherine Crook de Camp, although she was not always credited, writing science fiction and fantasy with equal facility.

De Camp's first full-length novel, LEST DARK-NESS FALL (1939/41), was an implied answer to Mark Twain's classic *A Connecticut Yankee in King Arthur's Court.* Twain's time traveler was able to change the course of history because of the superior technological knowledge he possessed. De Camp found this concept implausible. *Lest Darkness Fall* takes the hero back to ancient Rome where he has a similar intent, to prevent the fall of the Roman Empire and preserve it as a civilizing force in the ancient world, but he discovers that things are not quite as easy as he had expected. Even if he could overcome the natural human aversion to change, he would still be unable to get around the fact that the supporting manufacturing facilities and tools just did not exist that would allow him to succeed. He manages to introduce some innovations, but it is quickly evident that he will never be able to alter the course of events in any significant way. The novel, long considered one of the field's genuine classics, reflected de Camp's interest in history as well as his knowledge of the development of science and technology.

De Camp was already contributing heavily to the fantasy field, but in the late 1940s he started the Viagens series, set in a future where Brazil has become the dominant power on Earth and humans are exploring the nearer star systems. The short stories, many of which are quite good, were collected in *The Continent Makers and Other Tales of the Viagens* (1953). The novels were much more memorable, however, particularly the two closely linked ones, *Hand of Zei* (1950/62) and *The Search for Zei* (1950/63), sometimes published together (1981) under the former title or as *The Floating Continent.* An Earthman visits the exotic planet Krishna in search of a missing man, rescues a native princess instead, and then goes on to complete his original mission. The story is high adventure, but narrated with a refreshing sense of humor even about itself.

Most of de Camp's novels during the 1950s would be set in the Viagens universe. In *Rogue Queen* (1951) explorers arrive on a world where oviparous women practice a form of rigid communism. Their visit proves to be the catalyst for radical change in this broadly satirical adventure story. *The Queen of Zamba* (1953, also published as *Cosmic Manhunt* and *A Planet Called Krishna*) employs a very similar plot, this time introducing a private detective from Earth whose search for a missing woman is complicated by the xenophobic nature of the locals. The pattern repeats in *Tower of Zanid* (1958), which follows the exploits of an adventurer who arrives on Krishna hoping to make his fortune by organizing a native army and establishing himself as a king. But he underestimates the resourcefulness of the aliens. A long story in the series, "The Virgin of Zesh" (1953), is also particularly rewarding.

De Camp's interest in fantasy continued to grow during the 1960s; his science fiction during this period was confined to short stories. He would not write another planetary adventure until the late 1970s, after which he began adding to the Viagens series. *The Hostage of Zir* (1977) was a return to his old form. A tour guide on a world where modern technology is banned gets involved in an adventure with the local tribesmen. Krishna is the setting for *The Prisoner of Zhamanak* (1982), another lighthearted adventure that owes as much to *The Three Musketeers* as it does to traditional science fiction. *The Bones of Zora* (1984) was the first to acknowledge Catherine Crook de Camp as coauthor. Set once again on the planet Krishna, the story places a group of treasure hunters squarely in the middle of a local war. *The Swords of Zinjaban* (1991) is the best of the later novels. The protagonist is hired as a local guide for a film company making a barbarian epic film on an alien world, but the producer expects the planet and its natives to adapt to his image of how they should behave, with predictable but quite funny results. De Camp completed the sequence in *The Venom Trees of Sunga* (1992), the weakest novel of the Viagens series.

Two other later novels are not specifically set in the Viagens series, although they might as well be. *The Great Fetish* (1978) is a lost colony story. On a colony planet all memory of the colonists' origin has vanished. When a thoughtful young man suggests that they came from another world, he is branded a heretic and cast out, beginning a series of amusing adventures. In *The Stones of Nomuru* (1988), also credited to Catherine de Camp, a reserved archaeologist on a primitive world gets into hot water with the natives following the arrival of an obsessed real estate developer and the archaeologist's ex-wife.

The best selection of de Camp's short science fiction is contained in *A Gun for Dinosaur* (1963), *Rivers of Time* (1993), and *Aristotle and the Gun and Other Stories* (2002). Those of particular merit include the title stories of the first and last collections as well as "The Gnarly Man," "The Wheels of If," and "The Animal Cracker Plot." De Camp was a steady, reliable craftsman who never took his writing too seriously, and who was able to make his characters—even those distant from us in time or space—seem very much like the guy next door. Many of his plots could just as easily have been set in a fantasy landscape, and indeed his fantasy often reads like science fiction.

"A Death in the House"
Clifford D. Simak
(1959)

Most first contact stories involve extraordinary people, either space explorers or scientists or politicians who by chance or by virtue of their job are called upon to initiate communications with an alien race. Science fiction has always had a preponderance of larger than life protagonists, implying that ordinary people are not as likely to find themselves in such extraordinary situations. All through his career, Clifford SIMAK asserted the contrary opinion. His stories almost always revolve around people from less exalted walks in life. They might rise to heroism because of the pressure of events, but even then it would be an understated heroism.

Moses Abrams has become a recluse since the death of his wife. He lives alone on his farm, avoids his neighbors, and refuses even to replace his dog when it dies. He keeps his savings in cash, a bucket of silver dollars concealed under the flooring. Abrams is lonely, although he fails to recognize that fact until the day he finds a dying alien creature in one of his fields. The alien is repulsive, a hybrid of plant and animal with a noxious smell, but Moses recognizes that it is injured and overcomes his revulsion, carrying the alien back to his home and caring for it until it dies. He also conceals its space vehicle, a skeletal structure that has been badly damaged.

His subsequent efforts to do what he can for his brief visitor meet with little success. He is refused permission to bury it in the local cemetery, his pastor declines to offer any prayers on its behalf, and the sheriff suggests it should be turned over to scientists for dissection. Moses prefers to honor the alien as best he can, burying it in an unmarked grave so that it will not be disinterred by the curious.

Even though he and the alien were unable to communicate, the house feels emptier than ever once it is gone. Soon, however, a strange plant springs up from the hidden grave, matures into a virtual reincarnation of the original, and becomes ambulatory. Restored to health, the alien enlists Moses's aid in repairing its vehicle; this costs Moses his entire savings. But even though his unearthly friend finally leaves the Earth forever, Moses is enriched by the encounter and discovers in himself the enduring capacity to share with another, even if that other was not a human being. Simak's stories often had sentimental themes, but he always knew just where to draw the line between genuine emotion and the maudlin. In this story, first contact does not change the future of the human race, but it alters the present for one very realistically drawn character.

"The Deathbird"
Harlan Ellison
(1973)

It is often said that Harlan ELLISON's greatest strength is that he can infuse his stories with a genuinely emotional content to a degree unrivaled by any other writer working in the field. That is certainly the case with "The Deathbird," possibly his single most emotionally powerful story. The superficial plot is that of the last man on Earth, awakened from suspended animation by an alien assigned stewardship of the planet, whose task is to bring to an end the torturous death of an otherwise empty world. The story's tone is not sentiment, however, but anger.

The Earth has been a ward of a galactic community since before humanity became sentient, and for reasons never completely clear, the alien power left two immortal beings to watch over it. One is Dira, a serpentlike creature, who is associated by implication with the devil; the second, unnamed being has gone insane and declared himself God. Using a series of brief scenes interspersed with sets of "study questions," Ellison makes it clear that they have both been misunderstood. After all, why should we resent the serpent who brought us knowledge and worship a domineering, uncaring entity who prefers to keep us in ignorance?

The story is partly self-referential. Embedded within it is a short narrative about the death of Ellison's dog and his decision to be present when it was euthanised; this anticipates the final scene in which Nathan Stack, the last living human being, is revived to be present during the Earth's final moments. Stack has also lived through the ages, although he does not remember his previous lives; he is, in fact, Adam—an Adam who is not able to understand the true positions of God and the devil until the final moments. God is insane and always has been, which presumably explains how the world came to be in such a mess.

There is also a strong ecological theme. The scenes of a dying Mother Earth are interrupted by a sequence involving Stack's own mother, terminally ill and desperate for release from the endless pain. Stack does in fact assist in her suicide, providing another parallel to the ultimate end. Despite its episodic structure, this is one of the tightest and most effective of Ellison's stories, and it won him the Hugo Award for best novelette.

Del Rey, Lester
(1915–1993)

Lester Del Rey began writing short stories for the science fiction magazines in the late 1930s and produced a steady stream of them through the 1950s. His most famous single work at that length, "HELEN O'LOY" (1939), is an unconventional and still effective story in which a robot is imbued with human emotions. Del Rey began writing novels in the 1950s, under a variety of pseudonyms, although almost all of these were later reprinted in paperback editions under his own name. Most of

his early novels were for the young adult market, and some of them were superior to his adult work.

Del Rey's first novel was *Marooned on Mars* (1952), a dated but still entertaining story of a teenager who stows away aboard the first flight to Mars and has various adventures on the Red Planet. In *The Mysterious Planet* (1953, originally as by Kenneth Wright), a wandering planet enters the solar system, causing turmoil when it is revealed that it is hollow and is piloted by a malevolent alien race planning an invasion. The plot is overly simplified, but some of the individual scenes are surprisingly effective. Other, similar adventures followed including ones involving the rediscovery of a still powerful though sunken Atlantis, and adventures in space and on Mercury and other planets in the solar system.

Del Rey collaborated with Frederik POHL on *Preferred Risk* (1955, as by Edson McCann), his first adult novel. Earth is effectively governed by a single megacorporation, which claims to be benevolent, but the protagonist, a claims adjuster, meets a rebellious young woman who convinces him of the truth, converting him to her cause. *Police Your Planet* (1956, originally as by Erik Van Lhin) makes effective use of an unconventional hero, a man involuntarily transported to the colony on Mars who joins the local security force, initially hoping to take advantage of its rampant corruption to better his own situation. He eventually undergoes a significant change of outlook and dedicates himself to cleaning up the mess. Despite the heavy doses of violence, the result is a surprisingly moving story of individual redemption.

One of Del Rey's best novels was *Nerves* (1956), which would not be science fiction if it were published today. The tension involves a nuclear power plant after it experiences a dangerous accident that could result in a meltdown and the release of radioactive substances into the surrounding community. The author anticipated the mixed benefits of nuclear power well before it became a public concern; the result is a suspenseful, thought-provoking novel despite the now obsolete technical descriptions.

Del Rey continued to write for the young adult market, most notably a trilogy featuring Jim Stanley, a young astronaut. However, his best novel, and the last significant work for 10 years, was *The Eleventh Commandment* (1962). Earth has become a global theocracy, a dictatorship that exhorts the population to "be fruitful and multiply," with the result that the Earth is so overpopulated that disease, malnourishment, and unrest threaten to cause a general collapse of civilization. It was easily Del Rey's most ambitious and best-constructed novel. During the decade that followed, several adult and young adult titles appeared, but these were all actually ghostwritten by Paul Fairman, and none are of any particular merit. Two more novels would appear later, but Del Rey never regained his earlier form. *Pstalemate* (1971) is a fairly workmanlike but rather standard story of a telepath struggling to find a way to live with his not entirely welcome talent. There is some tendency to wander from the plot into distracting side issues, and little of the intense action typical of his earlier work. *Weeping May Tarry* (1978, written with—and primarily by—Raymond F. JONES) describes the visit by a shipload of aliens to an abandoned Earth with only moderately interesting complications.

With the exceptions of one or two novels, Lester Del Rey's most worthwhile and lasting work consists of short fiction. These have been collected in *And Some Were Human* (1948), *Robots and Changelings* (1957), *Mortals and Monsters* (1965), *Gods and Golems* (1973), *The Early Del Rey* (1975), and *The Best of Lester Del Rey* (1976). One of his longer stories, "For I Am a Jealous People" (1954), generated some controversy because of its plot, which involves a war between a technologically advanced humanity and God himself, whose powers are now rivaled by those of his creation. The Del Rey paperback science fiction line is named for Del Rey's wife, who headed that division of Ballantine Books for many years.

Delany, Samuel R.
(1942–)

Science fiction had been a homogeneous field up until the 1960s, marrying serious speculative fiction with unabashed adventure stories (sometimes

in the same work) and ignoring the kinds of thematic and stylistic experimentation that were taking place in mainstream literature. The few writers who questioned the shared optimism about a future in which technology solved all of humanity's problems were tolerated as lovable curmudgeons or ignored as antiscientific pessimists. But there were already signs of unrest. Judith Merrill had been including unconventional stories from non-genre markets in her annual Year's Best anthologies, and across the ocean, the new editor of *New Worlds Magazine* was about to shake things up by championing the cause of a new generation of writers with a very different agenda.

There was no direct equivalent of the New Wave in the United States, because the professional magazines were less prone to sudden change. However, the paperback market was a particularly fertile ground for experimentation, and the two most highly visible new writers associated with a new literary awareness in science fiction were, surprisingly enough, both published initially in book form by Ace, whose editor was a decided traditionalist. Along with Roger ZELAZNY, Samuel R. Delany—the field's most prominent black writer—ushered in a new kind of speculative fiction, stories that emphasized character development, prose styles, metaphors, and other literary techniques previously viewed with suspicion. Whether they changed readers' tastes or responded to a new market that would have emerged anyway is a moot question. The fact is that a growing number of readers were more interested in these talented newcomers than in the latest title from traditionalists like Robert A. HEINLEIN and Edward E. SMITH.

Delany made his first appearance with a short novel, *The Jewels of Aptor* (1962). The plot sounds fairly conventional. A young man sets out on a quest in a postapocalyptic Earth filled with mutated plants and animals. The protagonist is not a typical heroic figure, however, but a complex, somewhat flawed individual who moves through a landscape rich with metaphor and imagery drawn from mythology as well as from the author's imagination. The same description applies to all of Delany's early novels, which included a trilogy consisting of *Captives of the Flame* (1963), *The Towers of Toron* (1964), and *City of a Thousand Suns* (1965), later collected as *The Fall of the Towers* (1970). Once again the plot is very melodramatic. An alien intelligence known as the Lord of the Flames seeks to dominate an Earth devastated by global war and radiation-generated mutations, but is eventually defeated. The prose and imagery that Delany employed to tell his story overshadowed the simplicity of its plot.

Two very short novels would follow. *The Ballad of Beta-Two* (1965) demonstrated that Delany was refining his prose and maturing very quickly as a writer. The story concerns an anthropologist studying the folk songs of those humans who live their entire lives in space. *Empire Star* (1966) follows the adventures of a wanderer in space and is filled with wonderfully unique characters, although its episodic nature is comparatively weak. That same year saw BABEL-17, which won a Nebula Award and firmly established Delany as one of the leading writers of the 1960s. Many of Delany's usual themes—the fascination with language as a human artifact, the introspective protagonists drawn into a situation beyond their control, the susceptibility of human culture to manipulation by obscure forces—recur in this story of a poetess hired to crack a secret code that turns out to be a new form of language.

Many readers and critics consider Delany's next novel, *The EINSTEIN INTERSECTION* (1967), to be his best work; it received a Nebula Award. The human race has disappeared and Earth is now inhabited by an inquisitive alien race that assumes the forms of various archetypes from human history in an effort to understand the customs and psychology of absent humanity. The book is in fact so filled with metaphors and allusions that some readers had difficulty following the plot. The same was not true of *Nova* (1968), wherein Captain Lorq Von Ray and a crew of humans drawn from a variety of worlds and cultures plan to travel through the substance of a disintegrating star in order to investigate the processes of a nova. The trappings of a space opera were wrapped around quest images drawn from mythology. Delany's characters were almost always atypical; his heroes might well be rogues, criminals, outcasts, or even of suspect mental stability. His ability to involve readers with characters they might otherwise dislike was almost unprecedented in the field.

Delany wrote very little science fiction during the 1970s, a drought that ended with DHALGREN (1975) and *Triton* (1976). Both novels, particularly the first, were extremely controversial. They were criticized for being too long, too idiosyncratic, too obscure, and too slow-paced. *Dhalgren* is set in a future city somewhere in America where the law is no longer enforced. The novel is deeply introspective and has an ambiguous ending that wraps around to the opening chapter. *Triton* was considerably more traditional, describing a kind of flawed utopia set in the outer solar system where every form of sexual conduct is practiced openly. Parts of the novel are particularly intricate, and the society described is often fascinating, but many genre readers were not yet ready for such frank sexual content. *The Stars in My Pockets Like Grains of Sand* (1984) is a novel in which the sole survivor of a planet devastated by an alien attack becomes involved in a struggle to use new media techniques to control the course of human development.

Delany's output of short fiction was relatively small but of uniformly high quality, including several stories that won either the Hugo Award, the Nebula Award, or both. The best of these are "AYE AND GOMORRAH," "The STARPIT," "Driftglass," "Lines of Power," and "TIME CONSIDERED AS A HELIX OF SEMI-PRECIOUS STONES." Like his novels, Delany's stories are all rich with exotic imagery. In general Delany's short fiction had more linear plots and enjoyed a wider readership than his novels, particularly the later ones.

Most of Delany's short fiction can be found in *Driftglass* (1971), *Distant Stars* (1981), *The Complete Nebula Award Winning Fiction of Samuel R. Delany* (1986), and *Aye, and Gomorrah* (2003). Delany was also coeditor of the short-lived but highly regarded paperback magazine *Quark* (1970–71), which failed to evolve into the American version of *New Worlds Magazine*. He has written mostly fantasy, mainstream fiction, and criticism during the past two decades. Although his writing became so intricate and intellectualized that he eventually lost the mass audience, his work is still the subject of intense interest among more sophisticated genre readers, and in the view of at least one critic, Algis Budrys, Delany may be the best science fiction writer there ever was. His lack of activity in the genre for the past 20 years has been a major loss.

Deluge
S. Fowler Wright
(1927)

The British writer S. Fowler Wright penned a number of science fiction novels during the first half of the 20th century, ranging from the far future speculation of *The Amphibians* (1924) to mystery novels with fantastic content, such as *The Adventure of the Blue Room* (1945). His most successful novel was *Deluge* (1927); originally self-published, it later received wide distribution, and was the basis for a 1933 motion picture. The success of *Deluge* allowed Wright to turn to writing as a full-time occupation.

The disaster novel has always been a particularly popular subgenre with British authors, and stories of a great flood were extant since biblical times. Even Leonardo da Vinci wrote a story of the flooding of Atlantis. In Wright's novel, a man and two women survive the cataclysmic flooding of most of the world, resisting the temptation to descend into the barbarity of most other survivors. Once the immediate danger is past, they begin building a new society, more attuned to nature, and without the irrational restrictions—as Wright interpreted them—that technological civilization had imposed over nature. To emphasize the point that this will be an entirely new culture, the protagonist ends up effectively married to both women, who enter into the relationship willingly.

Wright's treatment was extremely unconventional, particularly when one considers the time in which it was written. While most authors might have concentrated on the triumph of the human spirit or glorified the human instinct to preserve itself, Wright was more interested in the consequences of survival rather than the way in which survival was managed. It is clear that he viewed the destruction of modern civilization as an event

that was not entirely unwelcome, because it would sweep away the shortcomings of society and force us to start over. The superiority of a more natural form of civilization is clearly the point of the novel. This conclusion was even more aggressively argued in a considerably inferior sequel, *Dawn* (1929), which describes essentially the same events with a new cast of characters. *Deluge* remained out of print for more than half a century but was reprinted in 2003, the only novel from Wright's considerable output to be made available to modern readers.

The Demolished Man
Alfred Bester
(1953)

Novels that blend science fiction and mystery motifs have been common for years, despite certain innate drawbacks inevitable when one tries combining the two forms. Readers understandably feel cheated if the author reaches into a bag of technological tricks and introduces some device to explain a paradoxical situation over which the protagonist has puzzled throughout the narrative. Even when authors refrain from cheating, the reader is always aware of that possibility. In most of the successful examples, the author makes a point of establishing the limits of the situation in advance, the rules that govern how the plot can progress. If there is a character with unusual psychic powers, it is demonstrated well in advance how those powers work, their limitations, and their advantages. If a new invention has invalidated what might otherwise be an absolute rule, we know what those properties are. On the other hand, if a writer does in fact play fair, the introduction of a speculative element can actually make a convoluted and satisfying puzzle that would be impossible in conventional detective fiction.

Alfred BESTER was well aware of that fact when he set out to write *The Demolished Man*, a sort of inverted murder mystery, in which we know from the outset who committed the crime and how it was done. The tension is driven by the difficulties confronting the detective in his efforts to find the solution. Bester initially stacks the deck against the killer with the set-up—a future in which the police employ telepathic mindreaders to help with their investigations, making it impossible for criminals to conceal guilt and effectively eliminating most premeditated crime. Ben Reich, the murderer, kills a business rival, craftily concealing his guilt; Linc Powell, a telepathic police detective, knows that Reich is guilty, but has great difficulty proving it. The battle of wits between the two men is set against the backdrop of a marvelously realized future in a novel that has barely aged at all even 50 years after it was written. It won Bester his first Hugo Award, and remains the benchmark by which other science fiction detective stories are judged.

Denton, Bradley
(1958–   )

After writing a handful of fairly interesting short stories in the mid-1980s, Bradley Denton produced his first novel, *Wrack and Roll* (1986), an unusual and compelling alternate history in which Franklin Roosevelt died in 1933 and the United States and the Soviet Union consequently became allies against China. During the 1990s, nuclear war appears imminent. The agents of social change in America are, against all expectations, a subculture of rock musicians. The novel mixes wish fulfillment with satire with thriller, a mix that might have been a disastrous mess in the hands of a less confident writer. Denton made an immediate favorable impression on the science fiction community, although the impact might have been even greater had he followed it up more quickly.

A dozen short stories followed over the course of the next several years, but Denton's fiction had moved closer to mainstream, consisting primarily of light contemporary fantasy rather than science fiction, and interest in his name ebbed. His second novel, *Buddy Holly Is Alive and Well on Ganymede* (1991), reprised his interest in rock music and was a much more polished work. Buddy Holly is not dead; he has been kidnapped into space and is now living on a moon of Saturn, from whence he broadcasts back to Earth. An unhappy store clerk sets out on a cross-country adventure involving hidden aliens, robot dogs, motorcycle gangs, and secret agents. Most of his episodic encounters are replete with humor, although sometimes it has a savage bite. *Buddy Holly* was much better than Denton's first novel, but it did not have the feel of genre fiction, which might explain why it was largely overlooked when it first appeared.

Denton has continued to write short stories that sometimes impinge on science fiction, but his drift away from the genre appears to be permanent. His most recent work has been outright fantasy or darkly humorous contemporary fiction, most notably the Blackburn stories. The best of his science fiction is contained in *The Calvin Coolidge Home for Dead Comedians* (1993) and *One Day Closer to Death* (1998), but the stories in both collections are predominantly fantasy.

Dhalgren
Samuel R. Delany
(1975)

After the success of his ninth novel, *Nova* (1968), Samuel R. Delany would not produce another science fiction novel for seven years. The drought finally ended with the largest and most controversial book he would ever write. *Dhalgren* was so radically different from anything that Delany had written before that it caused considerable consternation among those who had enjoyed his earlier work. Many readers were startled by its nonlinear nature and discouraged by its considerable length. Thematically, it was not as much of a break with the past as it seemed; most of Delany's recurring themes can be easily identified. But the overall tone was darker, the prose heavier, and the imagery more subtle. Critical reaction was sharply divided, and remains so to this day.

The protagonist, a young man whose name we never learn, lives on a future Earth with two moons in the sky, although this may or may not be a localized phenomenon, as we never learn much of the world outside a very proscribed location. He arrives in the city of Bellona, a sort of surreal anarchist center, where he experiences the usual—and a few unusual—rites of manhood while attempting to make a career for himself as an artist. The plot might well be that of a mainstream novel if it were not for some fantastic elements in the setting; moreover, parts of the narrative are almost certainly autobiographical. The novel clearly was meant to be literary and has little appeal for readers seeking scientific extrapolation or high adventure, but its intricate prose and symbolism provide abundant material for readers interested in writing as an art form and not just as entertainment.

Di Filippo, Paul
(1954–)

Paul Di Filippo is one of those rare writers like Harlan ELLISON whose considerable reputation relies entirely on short stories. His first professional sale in 1985 has been followed by a steady stream of remarkable and often idiosyncratic short stories. For a few years he was associated with the cyberpunk movement, although very little of his output has been in that tradition. His work is typically but not always wryly humorous and makes use of intricate, sometimes convoluted prose and imagery.

His stories run the gamut from satire to sentimentality. Possibly the best single work is "Anne" (1992), set in an alternate history in which Anne Frank escaped to America, went to Hollywood, and became a star. "Do You Believe in Magic?" (1989) follows the adventures of a man who has not left his Manhattan apartment in years, and who ventures out to find the world radically changed. Other outstanding stories include "One Night in Television City" (1990), "Return to Cockaigne" (2001), and "What's Up, Tiger Lily?" (2003).

Di Filippo's first book was *The Steampunk Trilogy* (1994), three loosely linked novellas set in an alternate Victorian world where it is possible to breed a newt that can impersonate the queen of England, where Lovecraftian horrors dwell—more or less—in the oceans near shore, and where time travel is possible and poets can fall in love. The triptych of tales is set in a very strange created universe, yet one drawn so skillfully that it is possible for the reader to believe in all sorts of absurdities.

Di Filippo's short fiction has been collected in *Fractal Paisleys* (1997), *Strange Trades* (2001), *Babylon Sisters and Other Posthumans* (2002), *Little*

Doors (2002), and elsewhere. He has recently begun writing at greater length, most noticeably in *A Year in the Linear City* (2002), set in a surreal futuristic city, and *A Mouthful of Tongues* (2002), an evocative story of personal transformation. He enjoys a substantial and loyal following of readers and it seems likely that he will be recognized more widely in the years to come, particularly if he begins to produce novels to complement his output of short fiction.

Dick, Philip K.
(1928–1982)

Even though science fiction has become much more respectable among mainstream critics in recent years, only a handful of genre writers have been actively embraced by the larger literary community—Ray BRADBURY, Ursula K. Le GUIN, Harlan ELLISON, and Kurt VONNEGUT being the most notable—but each of these writers won that attention at least in part because they sometimes wrote for non-genre markets and produced fiction that was not in the strict traditions of the field. Philip K. Dick, however, was a genre writer right from the outset, employing standard themes and plots throughout most of his career. It surprised many that he was so enthusiastically embraced by the academic community. Dick used several themes repeatedly, androids or other artificial stand-ins for real people, enclosed universes or environments otherwise sharply restricted, the search for spiritual revelation, the collapse of civilization, and the difficulty of distinguishing subjective and objective realities, particularly for characters who are dissatisfied with the "real" world and prefer an alternate reality.

Dick started writing in the 1950s and produced an amazing volume of material within a half-dozen years, most of it of very high quality, including short novels that would be expanded in book form later. His first published novel was *Solar Lottery* (1956, also known as *World of Chance*), in which the ruler of the united solar system is chosen periodically by lottery rather than through election, although the protagonist begins to wonder if the selection process is truly random or if the results are fixed in advance. Three other titles appeared that same year. *The Cosmic Puppets* was the least successful of these, but is interesting because of its inclusion of religious devices including Zoroastrianism—a preview of the spiritual speculation that would figure prominently in Dick's later fiction, particularly his last few novels. In *The Man Who Japed,* one of the author's more successful efforts at openly barbed satire, a new world order has been established following a global disaster. In typical dystopian fashion, everyone is compelled by law to pretend that they enjoy the new system; but things go awry when someone begins playing practical jokes at the government's expense. Perhaps the best of Dick's first four novels is *The World Jones Made,* featuring an almost messianic figure, a man with the ability to foresee the future and, armed with that knowledge, the ability to change it.

Dick quickly acquired considerable stature in the field, and his skills were still improving. *The Eye in the Sky* (1957) mixes several of his characteristic themes. A handful of characters are trapped in a limited reality in which the physical laws of the universe can be affected by their individual perceptions. The protagonist of *Time Out of Joint* (1959) lives in a similar delimited environment, this time a pocket universe in which he is imprisoned so that his ability to predict the future can be observed and channeled by the larger human culture, which is teetering on the brink of self-destruction.

During the 1960s Dick progressed from being a brilliant promising novelist to a self-assured, powerful writer. *The MAN IN THE HIGH CASTLE* (1962) is ostensibly an alternate history, set in a world where the Germans and Japanese have won World War II and America has been split between their armies of occupation. But the story is more than it appears, as the central character realizes when a mystical experience reveals that he is living in an artificial universe and not in the mainstream of history. The novel won the Hugo Award and is widely considered to be the best of Dick's early novels. *Martian Time-Slip* (1964) has been similarly praised. Set in the Martian colonies during a conflict between a leader of the resident workers and the United Nations administration, it blends paranoia and satire.

Some of his novels from this period were uneven. *The Simulacra* (1964), for example, contains some pointed satire but is something of a kitchen sink novel, and the plot rambles. *Clans of the Alphane Moon* (1964) has a brilliant set-up—a colony world that consists of tribes, each based on a different psychological disorder—but some of the potential is squandered by a melodramatic plot pitting the tribes against a meddling effort directed by normal humans from Earth. *The Penultimate Truth* (1964) is, on the surface, a familiar postapocalyptic story in which the majority of people are tricked into remaining in underground shelters while a favored minority enjoys the restored surface world.

Dick's interest in differences in perceived reality reemerged in *The THREE STIGMATA OF PALMER ELDRITCH* (1964), one of his most popular novels. A new hallucinatory drug has become the best way to escape the unpleasant living conditions on Mars—but it has some unusual side effects, including difficulties returning to the real world. Several less interesting novels appeared during the latter half of the 1960s, including one in which time runs backward; others featured parallel universes, mass suspended animation, and other standard themes, all enhanced by Dick's unique perspectives, although often repeating old themes and situations. These books rarely rise to the level of his best work.

There were two notable exceptions, however. *DO ANDROIDS DREAM OF ELECTRIC SHEEP?* (1969, also published as *Blade Runner*) is probably Dick's best-known novel outside the genre, primarily because of the motion picture version, *Blade Runner*. The story takes place in a decayed, corrupt urbanized future in which android animals are created to replace the many species now extinct, and android workers are used for dangerous assignments despite the public animosity toward them. The protagonist is a detective whose job is to track down rogue androids and put them out of action. *Androids* is one of Dick's most accessible later novels, and features the most sympathetic of his introspective and troubled protagonists. The second outstanding novel that year was *Ubik*, which takes great liberties with the nature of reality, rationalized in a kind of consensually constructed universe that is reminiscent of *The Eye in the Sky*.

Opinions became more widely divided about Dick's work during the 1970s. *A Maze of Death*

(1970) is on the surface a murder mystery set on a distant planet, filled with theological imagery and speculation. Some critics considered it a minor effort, while others praised it highly. There was a similar split following publication of *Flow My Tears, the Policeman Said* (1974). A narcotics cop is ordered to track down a dope user in *A Scanner Darkly* (1977), but his job is complicated by the fact that the criminal is his alter ego, cleverly disguised by near-future technology that makes it possible to have multiple identities. This novel is often cited as one of Dick's best, and it provides the transition to the metaphysically themed work of his final years. During this period, Dick experienced a significant religious event that would influence his last few novels, particularly the loosely constructed trilogy consisting of *Valis* (1980), *The Divine Invasion* (1981), and *The Transformation of Timothy Archer* (1982). The trilogy undoubtedly contains Dick's most carefully crafted writing and is filled with intricate philosophical issues and metaphysical imagery. However, it is of less interest to more casual readers who expect something typical of Dick's wildly imaginative plots and concepts.

Dick continued to write short fiction throughout his career, but slowed dramatically after 1960. His short stories have been collected in numerous volumes confused by a bewildering number of title changes. The most complete selection can be found in the three-volume *Collected Stories of Philip K. Dick* (1990–91). Several of his better tales have been rendered as motion pictures, although sometimes barely recognizably. "Minority Report" was probably the best of these. Others include "We Can Remember It for You Wholesale," filmed as *Total Recall* (1990), and "The Second Variety," adapted as *Screamers* (1995). Dick's outstanding stories are too numerous to list here, but "The Preserving Machine," "The Variable Man," and "The Father Thing" are of particular merit.

Dickson, Gordon R.
(1923–2002)

Gordon Dickson's career began with an undistinguished short story in 1950, but within three years he was a prolific and respected contributor to SF

magazines, with fine stories such as "Steel Brother" and "Stranger" to his credit, along with a series about the amusing and popular alien Hokas, which he cowrote with Poul ANDERSON, periodically adding new stories of their adventures over the course of decades. Dickson frequently wrote about military organizations and interplanetary warfare, most notably in the DORSAI SERIES. However, it would be unfair to label these military science fiction, because they do not follow the formulas of that subgenre and are less interested in the details of military action and lifestyles than they are in the effects that warfare has on the cultures that engage in it. It was ironic that Dickson was regarded by some as being radically conservative politically, even though the pervasive message in most of his novels is the need for humanity to develop ethically as well as technologically.

Dickson's first novel was a relatively routine tale. In *Alien from Arcturus* (1956; expanded as *Arcturus Landing*) the galactic federation has quarantined Earth until humans can develop their own faster-than-light drive, but humans are divided about whether or not to even attempt to leave the system. Some alien races have their own reasons for secretly manipulating human society to prevent any escape to the stars. *Mankind on the Run* (1956, also published as *On the Run*) pits one man against a repressive future government. Both novels were traditional and unexceptional, but there was an energy and excitement that marked Dickson as a promising talent. In the late 1950s, Dickson began to live up to those expectations.

The first indication that Dickson was going to emerge from the pack was a double volume containing two short novels. *Delusion World* (1961) was a clever otherworld adventure involving teleportation. It was bound with *Spacial Delivery*, the story of a man appointed as ambassador to the Dilbians, a relatively primitive alien race who resemble oversized bears. Despite his best efforts, our hero makes no progress until he goes on an exciting cross-country trip with one of the natives. Not only was this novel an outstanding adventure, but the story was also the best example to date of a growing trend in Dickson's work, the development of rapport between a human and a nonhuman character, either an animal or an alien.

Even more significant was the appearance of *The Genetic General* (1960, also published as *Dorsai*), the first in a series that Dickson referred to as the Childe Cycle, a panorama of human history extending from the historic past into the distant future, but which his fans inevitable called the Dorsai series. The setting is a future in which human colony worlds have split into four separate, specialized cultures, although it is clear from the outset that Dickson believes that a union of these disparate types is essential. Two later short stories in the series, "Soldier, Ask Not!" and "Lost Dorsai," would both win the Hugo Award. *Naked to the Stars* (1961) is one of Dickson's most underrated novels. It is not part of the series, but also features a mercenary as its protagonist—a man with missing memories about his service on an alien world who leaves his unit to find out what happened, uncovering a sinister plot in the process.

Dickson wrote a short sequence for young adults during the early 1960s, but this was unmemorable, and he soon returned to adult fiction. Some of his best humorous short stories appeared during this period, including "Who Dares a Bulbar Eat?," "The Faithful Wilf," and "Computers Don't Argue." *Mission to Universe* (1965) is an above-average story of space exploration, but it was *The Alien Way* (1965) that would be his most notable non-Dorsai book for the balance of the 1960s. Ostensibly the story of an imminent alien invasion thwarted by means of telepathy and espionage, it overlays the melodrama with one of Dickson's most skillfully drawn empathic relationships between a human and an alien. He also won a Nebula Award for the short story "Call Him Lord" (1966).

Dickson's novels became much more ambitious during the 1970s, but at the cost of some of his ebullience. *Soldier, Ask Not!* (1967) had already been expanded into a novel, and the Dorsai sequence continued with *Tactics of Mistake* (1971). *Sleepwalker's World* (1971) has one of his more interesting premises, a new technology whose side effect is mass unconsciousness, but the story soon becomes a routine potboiler and none of the potentially humorous aspects of the situation are explored. Novels such as *The Outposter* (1972) and

The Pritcher Mass (1972) reflect Dickson's growing concerns about overpopulation and pollution, but his solution—escape to the stars—feels more like defeat than victory, and these novels are mildly depressing even when the protagonists succeed. *Alien Art* (1973) is another story about humans and aliens forging bonds; despite an unusually low-key plot, it was one of Dickson's most successful efforts. His best novel during the 1970s was the masterful *Time Storm* (1977), the longest novel he had ever attempted. Earth is being ravaged by an epidemic of time anomalies, with small groups of people being scattered back and forth through time, forced to interact with cultures extinct or not yet evolved.

A steady string of readable but unexceptional novels followed for the balance of the 1970s. Not even the Dorsai stories generated much excitement, although Dickson did win the Hugo Award for "The Cloak and the Staff" (1980). It was not until the mid-1980s that he began writing the first of several lengthy major novels that would continue until his death, intermixed with lesser space operas and thrillers and a protracted series of light fantasy adventures. *The Final Encyclopedia* (1984) and *The Chantry Guild* (1987) are set in the Dorsai, or Childe, series, but both are more concerned with the difficulties of integrating the divergent cultures than with the military affairs that dominated earlier books in the series. In *Way of the Pilgrim* (1987) humanity is subject to an alien race so technologically advanced that they consider us no more than talented animals. *The Magnificent Wilf* (1995), although it lacks the stature and scope of his other late work, is a return to the broad humor of his early career, and is rewarding within its limitations.

Dickson's very large body of short stories has been collected and cross-collected so many times that it is difficult to suggest a representative sample of his work, but *Ancient, My Enemy* (1974), *Gordon Dickson's SF Best* (1978), *The Man the World Rejected* (1986), and *The Human Edge* (2003) are valuable anthologies. In addition to those stories already mentioned, "In Iron Years," "In the Bone," and "On Messenger Mountain" are of particular note. Dickson was a steady, reliable, prolific writer throughout his career, and although the reach of his more ambitious works sometimes exceeded his skills, he rarely failed to provide an entertaining and thoughtful piece of work, and many of his supposedly minor novels are actually among the very best of their type.

Dietz, William C.
(1945–   )

William Dietz is an accomplished writer of space opera and military science fiction; his efforts in the latter are achieved without the relentlessly monotonous battle sequences that characterize so many novels of that type. He made his debut with *War World* (1986, also published as *Galactic Bounty*), the first adventure of Sam McCade, a bounty hunter who travels the stars in search of criminals. McCade's adventures were continued in *Imperial Bounty* (1988), *Alien Bounty* (1990), and *McCade's Bounty* (1990).

Freehold (1987), a stand-alone novel, was the first of his military adventures, but even this first effort was surprisingly complex. Dietz improved with almost every volume of the Legion series of military adventures that followed; these consist of *Legion of the Damned* (1993), *The Final Battle* (1995), *By Blood Alone* (1999), *By Force of Arms* (2000), and *For More Than Glory* (2003). *Matrix Man* (1990) and its sequel, *Mars Prime* (1992), are of more general interest and are probably Dietz's best-constructed novels. In the former, a reporter uncovers evidence about a secret project designed to achieve global mastery, while the latter is a murder mystery involving a serial killer concealed among the passengers and crew of a spaceship en route to Mars.

Drifter (1991) and its two sequels are reminiscent of the tone of the Sam McCade stories, although the protagonist is a smuggler and his adventures, while rousing, are not nearly as inventive. *Where the Ships Die* (1996) is a more intricate and interesting space opera, centered on the political intrigue involved in the contest for control of a pivotal region in space. In *Steelheart* (1998), an android is the unlikely hero on a planet inhabited by humans and two alien races, one of which has adopted a fanatical religion that considers all

technology to be evil. Dietz's most recent work consists of the two-part story of Earth conquered by aliens, who are eventually dethroned. *Deathday* (2001) and *Earthrise* (2002) are disappointingly derivative as they follow the adventures of supposed collaborators with the invaders who eventually use their intimacy with the invaders' technology to help engineer an overthrow. Dietz is a reliable, skilled craftsman at his best, but has so far made no effort to write anything more substantial than lightweight adventure stories.

Disch, Thomas M.
(1940–   )

Although Thomas Disch started his writing career in the science fiction magazines, his fiction has moved further and further from traditional genre themes; none of his novels since 1979 have been within the field, although some have contained supernatural elements. His first short story appeared in 1962, followed by a steady succession until the 1980s, by which point he had largely abandoned the field. The quality of his work was so high, however, that he continues to be regarded as a significant writer, and his nonfiction book about the field, *The Dreams Our Stuff Is Made Of* (1998), is one of the best discussions of science fiction ever written.

After establishing himself with such fine stories as "Now Is Forever," "Minnesota Gothic," and "102 H-Bombs," Disch produced a first novel, *The Genocides* (1965), that flew in the face of genre conventions. Aliens have conquered the Earth and are changing the ecology so radically that humanity is on the verge of extinction. Rebel groups enjoy limited success thwarting their efforts, but just as the reader is led to expect a general uprising, the aliens complete the extermination of the human pest. *Mankind Under the Leash* (1966, also published as *The Puppies of Terra*) explores a similar theme, this time with humans as pets, but it was an uneven and fairly minor effort. His third novel, *Echo Around His Bones* (1967), revolved around an interesting idea, a man who travels to Mars by matter transmission only to arrive conscious but discorporate when his body fails to materialize; however, the story failed to live up to the premise.

Although an American, in the late 1960s Disch began to be identified with the British New Wave movement, but refrained from adopting the more radical stylistic techniques. His thematic concerns and approaches to characterization became increasingly sophisticated, resulting in *Camp Concentration* (1968), set in a near-future American concentration camp where the prisoners are given deadly drugs that also enhance intelligence. There is a delightful irony in the fact that the catalyst that imbues the prisoners with such extraordinary mental powers is actually a variation of syphilis, which will eventually kill them all. Disch also wrote what is possibly the best media tie-in novel of all time, *The Prisoner* (1969), based on a BBC television series whose theme was so close to Disch's own preoccupations that it was a perfect match.

Disch's last two science fiction novels were his best in the genre. Properly speaking, *334* (1972) is a collection of linked stories, each set in the same apartment building in a near-future Manhattan; but the stories are fitted together so skillfully that the whole is greater than the sum of its parts. *On Wings of Song* (1979) is set in a similarly decaying American society, this one further along the path to collapse, with individual states asserting their authority and the federal government in retreat. It was one of the first genre novels to have a homosexual protagonist, in this case a Midwesterner who wishes to be an artist and who comes to benighted, corrupt New York City. There is a considerable amount of barbed criticism of contemporary materialism and its adverse effects on artists and their work; but, despite its more disciplined unity, this book lacks the impact of *334*.

Most of Disch's short fiction is of uniformly high quality; apart from the stories collected in *334*, the single best is "The Asian Shore." Disch's stories have been collected in *Fun With Your New Head* (1968, also published as *Under Compulsion*), *The Early Science Fiction Stories of Thomas Disch* (1977), *Fundamental Disch* (1980), and *Getting into Death and Other Stories* (1983). He is also noted for his two science fiction books for children, *The Brave Little Toaster* (1986) and *The Brave Little*

Toaster Goes to Mars (1988). Although Disch still writes occasional short science fiction, he may have abandoned the field. If so, his reputation remains secure, and his writing about the genre confirms that he still has a high regard for its potential as a branch of literature.

Do Androids Dream of Electric Sheep?
Philip K. Dick
(1968)

This was the first of Philip K. DICK's works to be adopted as a major motion picture, under the title *Blade Runner;* the film's success was a major factor in his emergence as a genre writer of significance outside science fiction as well as within. Although written with somewhat more sophistication than his earlier work, it reprises many of his recurring themes. In previous stories such as "Second Variety," Dick had described the increasing difficulty in distinguishing between humans and machines. In this novel, the inhuman characters are organic machines, androids created to perform dangerous or onerous tasks, identifiable only through a complex intelligence test.

The world has been denuded of most nonhuman life, thanks to radioactivity and other perils, and most people have android pets in the absence of real ones. The protagonist, bounty hunter Rick Deckard, has the mechanical sheep of the title, and wants to track down several renegade androids so that he can afford a real one. His job is complicated by the fact that the androids are so nearly human that they have actually penetrated the police force and are in a position to anticipate and undermine his efforts. The motives and nature of the androids are ambiguous, On the one hand, they are clearly a persecuted minority; on the other, they pose a genuine threat. But Dick is equally unsparing of his human characters, and even Deckard is not without his less admirable traits.

As the story progresses, both Deckard and the reader undergo several changes in the way they perceive the androids. This shift in perception was faithfully conveyed in the film version, although other aspects of the novel were altered. Deckard's eventual emotional involvement with the female android, Rachel, causes him to change allegiances as he accepts a new view of his world. Some critics felt that Dick was confused about his own feelings toward the characters, but Dick may have been trying to illustrate the fact that we can hold contradictory positions simultaneously.

"Dr. Heidegger's Experiment"
Nathaniel Hawthorne
(1837)

The author of *The Scarlet Letter* also produced a wide variety of fiction, including whimsical fantasies, moody horror pieces, and the occasional speculative piece that we would now call science fiction, although there are hints of the supernatural as well. The best of these latter is "Dr. Heidegger's Experiment," a minor classic that shows up periodically in anthologies, usually those attempting to represent the evolution of the genre.

The story opens with Heidegger inviting four elderly friends to his home—four individuals whose lives have been wasted in one way or another, through corruption, libertinage, or other vice. He informs them that he has finally located the Fountain of Youth sought after by the early European explorers in America, and that he has a supply of the fountain's water from which they are welcome to drink. Initially skeptical, they eventually sample the water and promptly begin to shed years. Now convinced, they drink more and more until they are indeed young again; but it is all in vain, because the water's effects are only temporary.

Heidegger observes that his friends have learned little from their experiences and gained nothing during their temporarily restored youthfulness. All four immediately begin to make the very same mistakes they had made in old age, concocting grandiose political schemes, indulging in shameless flirtation, and drafting extravagant business plans. They seem to him not only sad but also rather silly, and he firmly announces that he now has no intention of ever drinking any of the water himself. Hawthorne was years, perhaps generations, ahead of his time in his pointed criticism of

our obsession with youth. Although his story lacks any rigorous scientific content, it anticipates the theme of many later stories of rejuvenation and immortality.

Dr. Jekyll and Mr. Hyde
Robert Louis Stevenson
(1886)

The Scottish writer Robert Louis Stevenson was the author of several classic novels, including *Kidnapped*, *Treasure Island*, and *The Master of Ballantrae*, but his best-known character is undoubtedly the twin personality of Jekyll and Hyde. The short novel, originally published as *The Strange Case of Dr. Jekyll and Mr. Hyde*, mixed two of the archetypal situations in horror fiction, one of which is also a recurring theme in science fiction. Mild-mannered and well-intentioned Dr. Jekyll seeks to improve his personality, developing a drug that is supposed to suppress his baser instincts; but instead, it results in a split personality, with Jekyll retaining the mild and admirable qualities but periodically changing into the deformed, savage Mr. Hyde, who goes about London engaging in a variety of depraved and violent acts. Ultimately, Hyde commits suicide, taking Jekyll with him.

Mr. Hyde is essentially a werewolf, the well of irrational rage that lies hidden within us all. Jekyll's attempt to expel his dark side is doomed to failure from the outset, a fact obvious to the reader, because it is an inescapable aspect of being human. In that sense the story is a tale of horror, even without an overtly supernatural element. Stevenson's Dr. Jekyll falls into the same error as Mary Shelley's Dr. Frankenstein: He pursues knowledge blindly, without giving a thought to the consequences, and is ultimately destroyed by his own creation. The text can also be read as a warning that the savage lies close beneath the surface in all of us, that civilization is just a mask to hide our true faces.

Based partly on actual events, Stevenson's novella is generally credited as the first story to involve multiple personalities. It can also be read as a warning about becoming dependent on drugs. There have been several film versions, including parodies and translations to different times and places. The core story has such a universal application that its influence pervades much of the literature in both genres, as well as in mainstream fiction. The story has become so familiar a parable for our culture that it is almost unnecessary to read it; but despite Stevenson's reluctance to be too specific about Hyde's activities, the description of the psychological torment experienced by both sides of the man is still gripping.

Dorsai series
Gordon R. Dickson

Military science fiction was a small but respected theme for many years, emerging only in the 1990s as a significant subgenre of its own, with its own conventions and written by authors who rarely attempt anything else. The form probably has its roots at least in part in Robert A. HEINLEIN's STARSHIP TROOPERS (1959), a seriously flawed but undeniably compelling story. Dickson's first installment in the Dorsai saga appeared a year after the publication of Heinlein's novel. *The Genetic General* (1960, also published as *Dorsai!*), the story of a future humanity split into various cultures following a diaspora to the stars, is told primarily from the point of view of the Dorsai, whose economy is based largely on the exportation of trained mercenaries to fight wars between the other powers. The Dorsai books became so popular that they spawned a subculture within science fiction fandom that referred to itself as the Dorsai, and who showed up at conventions wearing paramilitary gear.

The Dorsai stories are a subset of Dickson's larger future history, and while they include warfare and battles, they did not glorify and simplify war as does much of military SF. Dickson saw the fragmentation of humanity as an obstacle to be overcome. Military activity might be essential to the preservation of the race, but it was a necessary evil, not a way of life; only by reuniting the warrior with the artistic, humanistic, commercial, and other aspects of human culture could the race become strong enough and diverse enough to survive in a hostile universe. In fact, the protagonist of *The Genetic General* succeeds because he has mastered the art of politics, not the art of war.

There is a similar theme in *Soldier, Ask Not* (1967), the shorter version of which won the Hugo Award. In order to avenge his brother, the protagonist manipulates events so that a world governed by fanatics finds itself in conflict with the Dorsai, a battle they cannot win. *Tactics of Mistake* (1971) builds on the same theme, as the political struggle among the variant cultures becomes increasingly acrimonious and some view the Dorsai as the only force powerful enough to impose unity on fractious humanity. The next two volumes in the series strayed from the overall path. *The Spirit of Dorsai* (1979) and *Lost Dorsai* (1980) are both routine adventure stories involving the mercenaries, perhaps written to satisfy those of his readers who failed to grasp the tone of the series and simply wanted more lightweight military escapades.

The Final Encyclopedia (1984) was a return to more serious themes. The disparate cultures have reached an uneasy balance of power and comparatively peaceful relationships, and a final unity seems possible at last. But a new player enters the game, a hybrid human form known as the Others. Like most hybrids, the Others possess many of the strengths of their constituent elements. It appears that they may be powerful enough to dominate if not conquer the rest of the race, but Dickson implies this is not necessarily the form of union that will serve the species best. Initially thwarted, they resume their efforts in *The Chantry Guild* (1988), but this time it appears possible that the existence of a common foe might force the reconciliation that previously seemed to be out of reach.

Dickson sends us back in time in *Young Bleys* (1991) and *Other* (1994), in which we discover that the Others did not arise spontaneously but that their culture was developed clandestinely by a faction among the Dorsai who realized that only by this means could the other cultures be pressured into overcoming their own petty differences. Unfortunately, the artificially contrived Others prove more successful than was originally planned—powerful enough to overwhelm all opposition. Dickson had intended additional volumes to fill in the gaps and extend the story further, but none were completed before his death. The Dorsai series is certainly his masterpiece, and is probably the best military science fiction series written to date; but it would be unfortunate if that was all they were remembered for, because they are remarkable, optimistic stories about humanity's common future, meant to be more than just simple entertainments.

"Down Among the Dead Men"
William Tenn
(1954)

Although William Tenn's career as a science fiction writer effectively ended during the 1960s and comprised only a single novel and a few dozen short stories, he is still regarded as one of the major figures of his time, an exceptional writer of short fiction. Witty and versatile, he was particularly productive during the 1950s, producing everything from broad humor to deadly serious tales of the future such as "Down Among the Dead Men."

Humanity has been involved in a devastating war with the insectlike alien Eoti for 25 years. Women are required by law to bear as many children as possible, to provide a steady flow of replacement troops. Natural resources have been used up at such a tremendous pace that everything is recycled—"Garbage is our biggest natural resource," observes one character. The reclamation project includes dead bodies, which can be repaired, reanimated, and sent back into battle. Although the technical name for them is soldier surrogates, they are commonly referred to as zombies or blobs, particularly since the earlier versions moved unnaturally, looked pallid, and carried the distinctive odor of death.

We are introduced to this world through the eyes of a spaceship captain who is in the process of picking up his new crew, all of whom are blobs. Uneasy about the prospect in the first place, he is additionally unnerved because the four assigned to him have been reconstructed in the image of four famous fallen soldiers. Although he had been concerned about his own reaction to his new crew, who turn out to be otherwise indistinguishable from normal humans, he is shocked to find that the real problem is their reaction to him. He is the hated outsider, until he is able to win them over by revealing their common flaw: Like the blobs, he is sterile.

Tenn's story is completely lacking in melodrama. There is no physical action, just a series of conversations. In a surprisingly brief and effective manner he addresses the nature of prejudice and toleration, what it means to be truly human, and the relationship between an individual and his subordinates. This deceptively quiet story was unusual for its time, and anticipated the more thoughtful stories that would begin to dominate the field during the next decade.

Doyle, Arthur Conan
(1859–1930)

The creator of Sherlock Holmes will always be remembered primarily for the Baker Street detective, but he is also highly regarded as the author of *The Lost World* (1912), one of the most important novels in all of science fiction—the inspiration for movies, television series, and other works of fiction, including Michael Crichton's *Jurassic Park* (1990) and its sequel, *The Lost World* (1995), the latter of which includes several clever references to Doyle's creation. Greg Bear has also written an indirect sequel, *Dinosaur Summer* (1998), set a generation after the events Doyle chronicled.

Professor Challenger, the character who led the expedition to the plateau of dinosaurs in *The Lost World*, returned for several sequels, of which *The Poison Belt* (1913) is the most interesting, a dated and sometimes very awkward story about the poisoning of Earth's atmosphere and a global crisis. Challenger also appears as a minor character in *The Land of Mist* (1926), written after Doyle became involved with investigations of the supernatural, but the story is both scientifically unsound and tediously didactic. There is another lost world in *The Maracot Deep* (1929), this time a civilization hidden beneath the sea, visited by scientists in an experimental bathyscaphe; but despite some good scenes following the initial discovery, the story evolves into a series of disguised lectures about the virtues of a spiritual life and the soulless nature of modern technology.

Doyle wrote other science fiction, including *The Doings of Raffles Haw* (1892) and several short stories, of which "The Horror of the Heights" and

"When the World Screamed" are the best examples. Most of his identifiably science fiction works are collected in *The Best Science Fiction Stories of Sir Arthur Conan Doyle* (1989).

Dozois, Gardner
(1947–)

Gardner Dozois's most significant impact on the science fiction field has been as the editor of *Isaac Asimov's Science Fiction Magazine* since 1985, for which service he has received a number of awards. He has also been influential as the compiler of dozens of anthologies, including the largest and most respected annual best of the year collection, beginning in 1985. It is easy to forget that during the 1970s and early 1980s he was considered one of the top short story writers in the field. Although he continued to write occasional fiction after assuming his editorial position, the volume and intensity of his work dropped so dramatically after 1984 that his talents in that quarter have been largely overlooked, even though he won Nebulas for both "The Peacemaker," a particularly effective story of tolerance in the face of a global disaster, and "Morning Child."

Most of Dozois's fiction maintains a consistently high level of originality as well as skill of execution. "CHAINS OF THE SEA" is an innovative and poignant story of alien invasion. "A Kingdom by the Sea" introduces us to a lonely telepath who is desperately seeking another mind like his own; the telepath finally senses one and tracks its owner down, only to discover that he is reading the thoughts of a cow about to die in a slaughterhouse. The prevalence of downbeat endings in Dozois's short fiction alienated some readers who preferred wish-fulfillment technological fantasies; but there was a core of more serious readers who welcomed a new viewpoint, however somber. Other outstanding stories in this vein included "A Dream at Noonday" and "A Special Kind of Morning."

Dozois wrote only two novels. *Strangers* (1978) described a love affair between a human man and an alien woman, a union that ultimately causes the man to renounce his humanity and the woman to lose her life. *Nightmare Blue* (1975), a collaboration

with George Alec EFFINGER, is a detective story set on another planet, a readable adventure story but one atypical of either man's normal style. Most of Dozois's short fiction has been collected in *The Visible Man* (1977), *Slow Dancing Through Time* (1990), *Geodesic Dreams* (1992), and *Strange Days* (2001).

Drake, David
(1945–)

Although David Drake is generally identified as a writer of military science fiction, he experimented with various different forms right from the outset of his career, including supernatural fiction and fantasy stories, and authored several fantasy novels. Much of his work, particularly in recent years, has been collaborative, but he has remained very productive throughout his career and continues to publish regularly on his own.

Drake gained an immediate following with the Hammer's Slammers stories, a series of adventures involving a team of mechanized mercenaries who travel from planet to planet protecting or overthrowing governments, getting double-crossed, and outwitting or outfighting their enemies. There have been several volumes in the series, which apparently is ongoing, including *Hammer's Slammers* (1979), *At Any Price* (1985), and *The Butcher's Bill* (1998). Although the series has few surprises, and considerable repetition, these books are informed by an understanding of military tactics and are unquestionably engaging. Drake became probably the single most popular writer of military fiction during the 1990s. Two similar series, although much more involved with space travel, were written collaboratively with a variety of other writers. These were the Crisis of Empire sequence from the late 1980s and the General series from the 1990s.

The Stephen Gregg trilogy, *Igniting the Reaches* (1994), *Through the Breach* (1995), and *Fireships* (1996), has considerably less overt military action, at least initially, as an expedition is mounted following the collapse of the human empire to re-open contact with the outside universe. The explorers survive a series of adventures on other planets and then have to fight against a resurgent and repressive new round of would-be conquerors. Yet another sequence includes *Lt. Leary Commanding* (2000) and *The Far Side of the Stars* (2003). The inexperienced commander of a small military spaceship gets caught in the middle of the buildup to an interplanetary war in the first volume, and in the war itself in the sequel. The Northworld trilogy consisting of *Northworld* (1990), *Vengeance* (1991), and *Justice* (1992), widens the battlefield considerably as war breaks out on a planet where a group of men have found a gateway to an alternate reality in which the laws of nature work differently and from which they are able to draw extraordinary, almost godlike powers. Most of Drake's remaining science fiction novels are stand-alone stories, often involving groups of mercenaries caught in one problematic situation or another.

Drake also has written several novels set in the ancient world, either using time travel to transport his protagonist to that era or simply setting the story in the past. *Birds of Prey* (1985) is one of the best of these, a kind of secret history in which a Roman soldier discovers that there is an alien intelligence plotting to hasten the collapse of the empire. *Ranks of Bronze* (1986), a variation of Poul ANDERSON's *The High Crusade* (1960), has aliens kidnapping a legion of Roman soldiers for use as mercenaries, only to have the tables reversed when the Romans figure out how to take advantage of their supposed masters. *Time Safari* (1992) is an episodic adventure involving time travel to prehistoric periods, with consequences both amusing and terrifying. It was later expanded and reissued as *Tyrannosaur* (1993). *To Bring the Light* (1996) is a short novel and a loose sequel to L. Sprague DE CAMP's story of a misplaced time traveler in the Roman Empire, LEST DARKNESS FALL. *Killer* (1985), written with Karl Edward Wagner, is also set in ancient Rome, this time involving an alien visitor who is mistaken for an animal and put to use in the arena.

Drake also wrote several near-future techno-thrillers with science fiction content, most of them in collaboration with Janet Morris. The most interesting is *Active Measures* (1985), in which we discover that the president of the United States is a Soviet mole. With Morris, Drake also wrote two

change war novels, *Arc Riders* (1995) and *The Fourth Rome* (1996), in which American and Russian time travelers battle back and forth to preserve or alter the course of history.

Surface Action (1990) and *The Jungle* (1992) are of interest because they are set in the same now scientifically unsound version of Venus depicted in the classic Henry KUTTNER story "Clash by Night." Domed cities in the oceans of that world go to war against each other, despite what should have been the unifying effect of the hostile and dangerous local life-forms that menace them all. *Starliner* (1992) involves yet another interstellar war, but it has an unusual viewpoint. Events unfold from the perspective of an interstellar luxury liner caught between two hostile forces. Drake's short fiction rarely reaches the level of his novels, but a representative selection can be found in *All the Way to the Gallows* (1996).

Dune series
Frank Herbert

Although Frank HERBERT had enjoyed some modest success as a science fiction written previously, the publication of *Dune* (1965) won him a much wider following, both among science fiction readers and with the general public. The novel, first published as two separate serials under the titles *Dune World* and *Prophet of Dune*, is an elaborate interstellar political drama set in a corrupt human empire held together only because a drug derived from a spice grown on the planet Arrakis makes it possible for starship pilots to ply their trade. The various noble houses of the empire contend for power, and when House Atreides is granted management of Arrakis in place of the Harkonnens, it seems like a great honor, although it is eventually revealed to be a trap through which Atreides is to be destroyed.

The original novel is remarkable for its complexity, its messianic theme, and the sheer scale of events; but it was the planet Arrakis and its ecology that appealed to the imagination of its fans. The Fremen, the inhabitants of Arrakis, survive only because they have evolved a method of conserving water, crucial on what is essentially a desert world. The novel has been credited as the first to make ecological problems a central issue for genre regulars, and for increasing awareness among mainstream readers because of its broader popularity. Paul Atreides escapes the slaughter of his household and joins the Fremen, eventually turning the tables on the aggressors. *Dune Messiah* (1969) revisited some of the same themes, with Atreides, whose followers consider him a prophet, displacing the emperor. Those of his supporters who view him as a figurehead to be manipulated are incensed when he does not prove amenable to their plans, and to his dismay, the Fremen themselves become careless about their environment once it is no longer necessary to nurture every drop of water. The first sequence comes to a conclusion with *Children of Dune* (1976), in which Arrakis is being transformed into a much more pleasant world, but with growing tensions between different factions. Paul Atreides had noble intentions, but their very nobility sometimes had unfortunate consequences, and now it is left to his son, Leto, to replace the rigid dictates of religion with a more open and progressive system. Leto's ultimate self-sacrifice is another in a series of transformations.

Herbert returned to Arrakis for *God Emperor of Dune* (1981) and *The Heretics of Dune* (1984) to further explore that planet's evolution. The ecological changes have had unforeseen consequences: The worms are dying, some of the major projects are beginning to lose ground, and the deserts are returning. In *Chapterhouse Dune* (1985), 15,000 years have passed but many of the old institutions have survived, albeit in a somewhat different form. As before, Herbert mixes political intrigues with religious themes and ecological problems. Some readers found the final volume ponderous and unfocused, but it restates and consolidates many of the earlier themes and gives them historical perspective.

The film version of the first Dune novel appeared in 1984 but was disavowed by its director because of changes made without his permission; it was castigated by both genre and mainstream critics, not always for the same reasons. A much more faithful but less colorful version later appeared as a television miniseries, followed by a sequel, *Children of Dune,* which encompassed the second and third books in the series.

Herbert's son Brian HERBERT collaborated with Kevin J. ANDERSON on a series of supplements to the Dune series. *House Atreides* (1999), *House Harkonnen* (2000), and *House Corrino* (2001) chronicle the events of the years immediately preceding Dune, each focusing on one of the noble families. *The Butlerian Jihad* (2002) and *The Machine Crusade* (2003) describe a war between the human empire and an alliance of artificial intelligences. Although the ecological and messianic themes are not nearly as prominent and the intrigues considerably less sophisticated, the success of these new novels is a testament to the enduring popularity of the original series. Dune is perhaps the best known fictional planet in the genre's history, and its creator is justly considered one of the major names of modern science fiction.

Dying Inside
Robert Silverberg
(1973)

Telepathy is the most popular psi power in science fiction and is the central theme in numerous classic novels, including *Esper* (1962) by James BLISH, *The Whole Man* (1964) by John BRUNNER, and *The Hollow Man* (1992) by Dan SIMMONS. Not every writer describes the talent in quite the same way. In some cases, both parties to the mental communication must be telepaths; in others, a single individual has the power to eavesdrop and read minds, usually without being detected. In almost every case, telepathy has been viewed as a positive power, at least for its possessor. That power might be perverted for selfish reasons, as in Frank Robinson's *The Power* (1957), or telepaths might find themselves hated outcasts by a society that fears them, but the ability still makes them essentially superhuman.

Robert SILVERBERG's *Dying Inside,* possibly his best novel, turned that concept upside down. David Selig is a telepath who has long been tormented by his ability, which for him has been more of a curse than a blessing. After the novelty of being able to read the thoughts of others wore off, he discovered that it was unpleasant to be privy to the opinions and mental cruelties of others, particularly of those close to him. Selig is one of the most detailed characters in all of science fiction, a complex and often self-contradictory man whose general passivity annoyed many readers who were used to the more typical genre stereotypes who tended to be aggressive, competent, and self-assured.

The tension in the novel comes from an unusual quarter. After many years of struggling to live with his unwelcome talent, Selig discovers that his ability is beginning to fade. The soundless voices no longer intrude as often, sometimes people are able to conceal their own thoughts, and the background din has faded away. Given the unhappiness he has experienced in the past, one might expect that he would be elated; but Selig has an ambivalent reaction. Although he is finally achieving the solitude he thought he desired, now that he is about to be reduced to only his own thoughts he feels a growing sense of loss, because he is in one sense dying inside. The novel received considerable acclaim from critics, but the response from the readers at large was disappointingly muted.

Earth Abides
George R. Stewart
(1949)

George R. Stewart was primarily a nonfiction writer and produced only a handful of novels. He was never considered a genre writer at all, although *Earth Abides*—his only venture into speculative fiction—was the first winner of the International Fantasy Award. Stewart previously had written two minor though enjoyable disaster novels not remotely science fiction, *Storm* (1941) and *Fire* (1948), neither of which had attracted serious critical attention.

The premise of *Earth Abides* is that a new plague has wiped out the vast majority of the human race so quickly that civilization is more abandoned than ruined. The protagonist is Isherwood Williams, who was a young man when the disaster originally occurred. He was spared thanks to a timely visit to a remote mountainous region, from which he returned to find the world's cities filled with the dead. Williams gathers together a small community of survivors and carries on as best he can; but without the supporting infrastructure for a technological civilization, the level of achievement steadily drops. His children will be living in the equivalent of a new stone age. Fortunately, because of his background in anthropology, Williams is particularly well-suited to see that the next generation retains the minimal skills they will need to survive—hunting, cultivation, simple medical treatment.

The story, which parallels the actual historic experiences of the last of a remote tribe of West Coast Indians, is not as downbeat as a simple plot summary suggests. Stewart viewed history as cyclic, and even though the old civilization has been irrevocably lost, there are already signs that a new one will rise in its place. The story ends with Williams's death, but he is resigned to it, and it is clear that Stewart wished to leave the reader with the idea that the story of humankind would continue forward in some new fashion. Science fiction fans are notoriously unwelcoming when mainstream writers poach on what they feel is their territory, so it is a testament to the merit of this particular novel that it was warmly embraced when it appeared and that it still retains its position of honor.

Eden
Stanislaw Lem
(1989)

There are several separate trends in the work of Polish writer Stanislaw Lem. He has written a considerable body of satire, some verging on the farcical, some much more subtle. He has written serious novels with hints of adventure, and adventure stories with serious undertones. *Eden* is one of the latter, a planetary adventure story that rises above the melodramatics of its plot, although the story itself is intense and intelligently conceived.

Six astronauts crash-land on the planet Eden, a bizarre world where the ordinary laws of the natural universe seem irrelevant. The planet's sun has an unusual shape; the very texture of the ground is strange; and the local life-forms are bizarre and, as the reader and the characters will soon discover, uniquely dangerous. There are artificial features on Eden as well, evidence of a once highly evolved civilization that built robots to satisfy its needs. The stranded humans absorb the data they have gathered and believe that they have figured out the underlying structure of this alien society, but they are wrong.

The inhabitants of Eden are as unconventional as their environment, with bodies that vary and exhibit perplexing and sometimes nonsensical features. The conclusions made by the humans are revealed to be false, shaped by preconceptions that cannot be justified by the new evidence that presents itself. The inhabitants of Eden have let their society get out of control. Genetic engineering and cultural conditioning have trapped them and deprived them of the ability even to strive to free themselves. Where a lesser writer might have chosen to deliver the aliens from their self-made trap by human intervention, Lem makes it clear that anything humans might do would only make matters worse. It is hard to imagine that Lem did not mean this as a commentary on the belief of the colonial powers of our own world that they were bringing civilization to benighted peoples by dominating and altering their cultures.

"The Education of Drusilla Strange"
Theodore Sturgeon
(1954)

One of the strengths of science fiction is that it provides authors with the opportunity to present a picture of human culture from the viewpoint of an objective outsider, a visitor from another world or time. Drusilla Strange is the name adopted by an alien woman who is punished for unspecified crimes by being exiled for the rest of her life on Earth. She is able to adapt quickly because of her ability to read minds, and the initial sequences in which she encounters her first human being and

wins his perhaps misplaced trust are extremely well rendered. Through the perspective of a telepath, the reader is exposed to the subtleties of human interaction, the ways in which what we actually say is not always an accurate reproduction of what we intend to communicate.

The true nature of her punishment is that Earth is, in her eyes, a pale imitation of her own culture. The people and institutions are similar enough to make her homesick but primitive enough to underline what she has lost. Although she patterns her actions to ingratiate herself with the man who provides her with shelter, she is contemptuous of him and of the world he inhabits, and wants only to be free of it and of the telepathically beamed hints of her old existence that are sent to her to ensure that she is in mental agony at all times. Suicide would be surrendering to her captors, but she decides that it would be a small victory if she forced them to kill her. She thus uses her advanced knowledge to help a young man become an extraordinarily gifted musician, hoping to attract the attention of her captors.

The final stage of her education, however, is an encounter with another exile from her own world, a woman who discovered the truth about their society. Her fellow exile helps Drusilla overcome her conditioning and realize that a superiority in technology does not necessarily mean a superiority in cultural achievement.

Sturgeon was famous for his ability to create an emotional connection between his characters and his readers, and the somber tone of this particular story is leavened by moments of subtle humor. The slow evolution of Drusilla's perceptions of life on Earth reflects the optimistic tone that dominated science fiction during the 1950s.

Effinger, George Alec
(1947–2002)

A small flood of quirky short stories in the early 1970s immediately identified George Alec Effinger as one of the most promising new talents of the decade. His first novel, *What Entropy Means to Me* (1972), was one of those rarities in a field that takes itself much too seriously at times—a funny, whimsical novel that is also literary and deftly plotted. Following such excellent short stories as "All the Last Wars at Once," "The Awesome Menace of the Polarizer," and "Naked to the Invisible Eye," the novel suggested that Effinger could only get better as he honed his considerable talents. Many of these stories involved recurring characters or locations, a convention he would continue throughout his career. Unfortunately, during the years that immediately followed, Effinger's development would be erratic and sometimes disappointing as he alternated between writing superior short stories and unusual but not entirely successful novels.

Relatives (1973) was a case in point. The premise is that the central character lives simultaneously in more than one version of our history; but neither the character nor his multiple environments are ever brought to life, both remaining flat and only moderately interesting. *Those Gentle Voices* (1976) was a more conventional space opera, describing the unusual results when an expedition from Earth visits a distant world from which it has been receiving radio signals; but this book failed to distinguish itself from the many similar novels using the same plot. *Utopia 3* (1978, also published as *Death in Florence*), a send-up of utopian novels, marked an effort to return to what Effinger did best. His greatest strength remained the short story, however, which he wrote in significant numbers, gathering many of them in two excellent collections, *Mixed Feelings* (1974) and *Irrational Numbers* (1976).

Effinger continued to flounder at novel length, producing media tie-ins and a mediocre sequel to *What Entropy Means to Me*. It was not until *The Wolves of Memory* (1981) that he seemed to get back on track at novel length. This time his tone was much more serious as he depicted a dystopian future world in which conformity is not only the greatest virtue, it is also mandated by law. The protagonist is a misfit, who eventually is exiled to a planet of misfits. The satire was blunt but never intrusive, and the novel remains one of Effinger's better efforts. He had also begun writing the frequently hilarious "Maureen Birnbaum" short stories, later collected as *Maureen Birnbaum, Barbarian Swordsperson* (1993).

The Nick of Time (1985) and its sequel, *The Bird of Time* (1986), were both time travel stories with elements of humor. But once again it appeared that Effinger was experiencing difficulty with book-length work, and neither novel is cohesive enough to be entirely successful, although both contained individual scenes of considerable power. Paradoxically, his short fiction was, if anything, getting better, and "Schrodinger's Kitten" (1988), his single most effective piece of fiction, won both the Hugo and Nebula Awards.

The Marid trilogy finally proved that Effinger could write sustained novels with the same skill he demonstrated in his short fiction. The sequence, set in a future in which the Middle Eastern nations have finally leveraged their resources to gain financial and political domination over much of the world, consists of *When Gravity Fails* (1987), *A Fire in the Sun* (1989), and *The Exile Kiss* (1991). Marid, the continuing viewpoint character, is employed by a powerful criminal as an assassin and compelled to submit to surgical alterations to make him a more effective killer. In subsequent volumes he is involved with terrorists and then becomes a fugitive along with his employer when a power shift threatens both their lives. Although technically a criminal, Marid is a sympathetic character, caught in a complex and sometimes bewildering world where conflicting loyalties and physical dangers are part of everyday life. Effinger's created future is convincing and intriguing, and although the trilogy is sometimes characterized as cyberpunk, it is more accessible to the average reader than are other works similarly described. *Budayeen Nights* (2003) is a collection of short stories set against the same background.

Effinger's failing health reduced his productivity dramatically during the 1990s, and only a few short stories and another tie-in novel appeared after the third Marid book. *Look Away* (1990), a short novel, is an amusing and unconventional story of an alternate history in which the Confederacy prevailed during the Civil War. In addition to the titles mentioned above, Effinger's excellent short fiction has been collected in *Dirty Tricks* (1978), *Idle Pleasures* (1983), and *The Old Funny Stuff* (1989). Many of his short stories repeat the same themes, examining them from different angles. He was particularly fond of sports and games of every sort, parallel worlds and alternate histories, and the displacement of characters from their usual context to another, radically different one. Had he not been troubled by poor health throughout most of his life, Effinger might well have become a much more significant name in the field than was the case.

Egan, Greg
(1961–   )

The Australian writer Greg Egan began his career with a surrealistic fantasy novel in 1982, but soon turned to science fiction. A steady stream of respectable stories appeared during the 1980s and early 1990s, and he twice won awards in his native Australia although he had not yet established a significant presence elsewhere. *Quarantine* (1992), his first SF novel, was impressive not so much for its plot as for its execution. Aliens have cut off human access to the stars, and the human race, turning inward, is plagued by violence and religious excesses.

Egan's second novel, *Permutation City* (1995), would make an even stronger statement. A kind of immortality has been achieved by copying individual personalities into a vast computer network, where they can live on in a shared virtual reality. Eventually some of those artificial personalities despair of their confined existence and seek to terminate themselves; but they are opposed by their originals, who see the recorded version of themselves as their only way to cheat death. Egan handled the theme intelligently and thoughtfully, and *Permutation City* is an intriguing and perhaps underrated novel.

Distress (1995) was an uneven thriller involving a new drug and a conference of scientific philosophers. It includes some wonderfully inventive speculation, but the plot is unevenly paced. With *Diaspora* (1997), Egan took up a theme similar to that of *Permutation City*. Humans have begun exploring the universe by creating various types of robots and computers equipped with minds of their own, and as these diverging forms of humanity propagate, they encounter an alien race whose existence triggers a major crisis.

Egan's output of short stories slowed but did not stop as he turned to novels; indeed, the short stories became steadily better. "The Mitochondrial Eve," "Our Lady of Chernobyl," and "Transition Dreams" attracted considerable favorable attention. His next novel, *Teranesia* (1999), was less successful, although the biological oddities of the setting, a remote island evolutionarily isolated from the rest of the world, similar to the Galápagos, are interesting. *Schildt's Ladder* (2002) is an ambitious space opera, similarly uneven, mixing imaginative scenes with routine melodrama. The best of Egan's short fiction can be found in *Axiomatic* (1995) and *Luminous* (1998). It is too early in his career to predict Egan's eventual place in the genre, but the intricately imagined concepts and situations found in his better work indicate the potential for greater things in the future.

"Eight O'Clock in the Morning"
Ray Nelson
(1963)

Ray Faraday Nelson was an infrequent but often surprising writer whose work sometimes made respectful fun of genre conventions and plots. The work of Charles Fort, who collected reports of strange phenomena, partially inspired the "we are property" story, whose premise was that Earth and humanity were secretly ruled by another intelligent species, usually aliens living among us disguised as humans. That premise was the target of this amusing spoof, in which George Nada accidentally awakens from a hypnotic spell imposed on the entire human race and remembers that Earth was conquered by reptilian aliens who move among us undetected and unsuspected.

The Fascinators, or aliens, use subliminal persuasion to control people. George can now see clearly and resist their messages, although everyone else obediently follows instructions. He receives a phone call from one of the Fascinators instructing him to drop dead at precisely eight o'-clock the following morning, apparently because they suspect he has realized the truth. Nelson then compresses events that might have filled an entire novel into a handful of pages: George kills more of the aliens, discovers the secret to defeating them, and storms a television station and successfully broadcasts his message to the world, which rises in rebellion and wipes out the intruders.

Nelson's story is clearly a good-natured satire on the genre, poking fun at an implausible plot. There was a double irony about the story. First, George does in fact die at precisely the moment he was ordered to, presumably through coincidence. Second, the story was the basis for the motion picture *They Live* (1988), which was rendered as just the type of implausibly melodramatic story that Nelson was lampooning.

The Einstein Intersection
Samuel R. Delany
(1967)

Samuel R. DELANY had already won a Nebula Award for the novel *BABEL-17* (1966) when he won his second, for *The Einstein Intersection,* giving him two of only three ever presented in that category at that time. The first novel had been an unconventional space opera with a poetess as its central character. The second was such a radically different novel that it was difficult to compare it to any other piece of fiction, and even today it is almost in a class by itself.

The human race has vanished from Earth, perhaps having died out, perhaps simply having moved on. An alien race has arrived to take their place, and for some reason has become fascinated with human culture—so fascinated, in fact, that individuals of its species use their shape-changing abilities to adopt the appearances and personas of various historical characters from human history. The aliens' understanding is limited, so they do not always get things quite right; and while the characters are sometimes quite recognizable, they are also not quite the people we are expecting.

The protagonist is a blend of characters from ancient times who wanders this new Earth in the guise of a musician. Behind the surface story lies a complex examination of human myths and how we use them as cultural and personal artifacts. As our hero travels through the world, Delany shows us that the aliens have far to go before they can begin to understand the objects of their study. At times, events seem to be almost random, but then the author surprises us by introducing a much more structured scene, such as when Kid Death, who obviously is Billy the Kid, discovers and subsequently betrays Pat Garrett.

Delany was clearly aware of the British New Wave movement—and there are some unusual prose constructions in the novel—but a greater influence on his work was his fascination with the way in which we substitute symbols and mythic figures for more mundane objects and ideas. *The Einstein Intersection* is a quest story that often feels like fantasy. Sometimes surreal, it is the kind of introverted, idiosyncratic, and nontraditional novel that normally raised the ire of more conservative science fiction readers. It is a testimony to the power of Delany's writing and the universality of his themes that the novel was so widely popular even among an audience who might have been predisposed against it.

Elgin, Suzette Haden
(1936–   )

A professional background in linguistics is evident in most of Suzette Haden Elgin's small but interesting output of science fiction. "For the Sake of Grace" (1969), her first and only outstanding piece of short fiction, was later expanded into *At the Seventh Level* (1972), the third adventure of Coyote Jones, who previously appeared in *The Communipaths* (1970) and *Furthest* (1971). Jones travels to a planet noted for its poor treatment of women; the inhabitants must change this situation if they are to join an interstellar alliance. When a revised system of laws makes it possible for one particularly extraordinary woman to reach the highest levels of that society, she becomes the target for recidivist males. Disparities between the genders is the overriding theme in most of Elgin's subsequent science fiction.

The best of the Coyote Jones series is the second installment, *Furthest,* in which Jones visits a planet whose citizens are so completely in conformity to the statistical average in every aspect of their life that their very normality becomes abnormal. Jones returned for two more adventures. In *Star-Anchored, Star-Angered* (1979), he investigates a female messiah who may be using psychic powers to alter the minds of her followers. In *The Other End of Time* (1986) another telepath may be generating a signal strong enough to disrupt normal communications among Earth's colonies.

Elgin's second series of novels was more ambitious but less exuberant. In *Native Tongue* (1984) the human race has become polarized along gender lines after the United States reduced the legal status of women; a simmering resentment between the genders continues for generations, even after humanity expands into outer space. The study of linguistics has become a primary tool for trading with alien cultures in *The Judas Rose* (1987), but unbeknownst to the dominant males, women are using the same science as a means to regain their lost equality. In *Earthsong* (1994) Earth has been quarantined, thanks to the mismanagement of the male-dominated government; to the chagrin of the dominant males, only linguistically trained women may be capable of negotiating their release. The trilogy has an obvious feminist theme, particularly intrusive in the first volume, although more evenly handled later on. Other SF writers have occasionally used linguistics as an element in their work, but none so thoroughly or competently as has Elgin.

Ellison, Harlan
(1934–   )

No science fiction writer has ever been as dominant a personality in the field as has Harlan Ellison, whether as writer, editor, essayist, or speaker. Nor has any other writer won as numerous and varied a collection of awards, including Hugos, Nebulas, the Bram Stoker, the Jupiter, and the Edgar Allan Poe Awards.

After he dropped out of college, Ellison began publishing regularly in the genre magazines during the mid-1950s under his own name and others. By 1960 he had published almost 200 titles, most of them routine adventure stories with occasional touches of satire. His level of output was particularly impressive because he was writing in other fields as well. Although some of the early stories are crude and few of them approach the quality of his later work, they were usually well constructed and artfully told and were certainly as good as most of the other work appearing at that time.

In the 1960s Ellison began writing for television, although most of his work in this medium was not science fiction. An exception was "Demon with a Glass Hand," for *The Outer Limits*, which won an industry award. His Star Trek script, "The City on the Edge of Forever," is widely considered the best episode of that series, although its genesis has been the subject of considerable controversy. The script won the Hugo Award in the best drama category. Ellison later would be involved more creatively with *The Starlost*, an interesting television series doomed to failure by its financial circumstances and administrative problems. He was a technical consultant for the revived *Twilight Zone* series, and later for *Babylon 5*. He wrote a fascinating, detailed script for a film version of *I, ROBOT* by Isaac ASIMOV, which has been published in book form but never produced as it was originally intended. Ellison has also made numerous television appearances, primarily in interviews or debates.

During the early 1960s Ellison's short fiction improved dramatically. Stories like "Paulie Charmed the Sleeping Woman" and "Paingod" were early indications that he was moving from traditional adventure fiction to more serious literary efforts. There had always been a strong element of emotion in his fiction, but it was more fully expressed now, and the initial impact of many of his stories was an almost physical shock. Then came "Repent Harlequin, Said the Ticktockman" and "I HAVE NO MOUTH AND I MUST SCREAM," and Ellison leaped into the front rank of science fiction writers, winning his first genre awards. The British New Wave movement was underway at the time, and some critics suggested that he was influenced by the New Wave's experiments in style and subject matter; but if so, it was only tangentially. Ellison was following his own path, sometimes varying from traditional literary styles, sometimes not.

Other writers were breaking away from the field's traditions, and Ellison collected stories by many of the best of these writers for the anthology *Dangerous Visions* (1967), widely considered to be the best original anthology the field ever produced. Each story was accompanied by a thoughtful short essay by Ellison; these essays themselves constitute an interesting discussion of the field. A further and larger collection, *Again, Dangerous Visions* (1972), pursued a similar course, although its impact was not nearly as dramatic, probably because the field as a whole was much more open to innovation by then—a change for which Ellison deserves some of the credit.

By the late 1960s Ellison was the dominant short story writer in the field, even though much of his work like the classic "Pretty Maggie Moneyeyes" was fantasy rather than science fiction, a trend that would continue in the future. Ellison's stories frequently defied categorization, ranging from traditional to surreal, from horror to humor. Almost everything he wrote sent new ripples through the field—stories like "The BEAST THAT SHOUTED LOVE AT THE HEART OF THE WORLD," "Shattered Like a Glass Goblin" (with its bizarre depiction of drug users and their hallucinations), and "Along the Scenic Route." "A BOY AND HIS DOG" took a traditional genre situation and stood it on its head; this story would later be made into a successful motion picture. A series of collaborations with other major writers resulted in the collection *Partners in Wonder* (1971), an uneven but fascinating display of styles and tones.

The flow of stories slowed noticeably during the 1970s, but the quality remained as high as ever. "DEATHBIRD," "Adrift Just Off the Isles of Langerhans," and "Shatterday" were among the best of these, but the drift away from strict science fiction continued with the award-winning "Croatoan," "Jeffty Is Five," and other stories from this period. Ellison's subsequent work has been steady and always entertaining, but it sometimes lacks the emotional kick of his previous efforts. His best titles from his last few years include "Paladin of the Lost Hour," "Midnight in the Sunken Cathedral," and "Mefisto in Onyx."

Ellison technically has never written a science fiction novel, although he is credited as coauthor of *Phoenix Without Ashes* (1975) with Edward Bryant, based on *The Starlost*. His episodic adventure story, *The Man With Nine Lives* (1960), is actually several short stories assembled into one coherent narrative. A novel-length sequel to his classic short story "A Boy and His Dog" was planned and even announced, but has never been completed. Ellison is certainly the most significant science fiction writer never to have written a true genre novel; even Ray BRADBURY produced one, *FAHRENHEIT 451*.

Ellison's short stories have been collected and cross-collected numerous times. A representative sampling can be found in *Deathbird Stories* (1975), *Strange Wine* (1978), *Angry Candy* (1988), and *Slippage* (1997). Much of his non–science fiction writing is also of interest, including essays on television and the movie industry, fiction and nonfiction about life in a street gang, and his personal reminiscences. Ellison's impact on science fiction has been dramatic and varied. He has never been easy to categorize and his sometimes unpredictable style occasionally alienates less sophisticated readers. It is certain, however, that he has created a body of fiction that will be valued for generations to come.

Ender series
Orson Scott Card

The Ender Wiggins series began as a short story that was later expanded into the first novel in the series, *Ender's Game* (1985, revised in 2002). Earth had been attacked by an alien race that almost exterminated humanity, and now genetically enhanced children are being raised to help preserve the race. Ender is recruited into a program of virtual reality combat games, the last of which proves to be a genuine coordinated battle against the alien Buggers, who are believed extinct at the conclusion, although a hive queen is discovered alive in the sequel, *Speaker to the Dead* (1986, revised 1991). Feeling guilty about his involuntary slaughter, Ender takes the queen on a tour of the galaxy before finding a world where the aliens can settle and she can propagate her race. These two novels won both the Hugo and Nebula Awards, an unprecedented accomplishment, but the later books in the series have been less successful.

In *Xenocide* (1994) a dangerous plague on Ender's new home world attracts the attention of the authorities on Earth, who are determined to sterilize the planet. Ender and a new companion, an artificial intelligence, manage to prevent this second attempt at extermination, and then defeat a similar alien threat in *Children of the Mind* (1996). The next three novels are set on Earth and run parallel to the first three. *Ender's Shadow* (1999) follows the career of Bean, one of the other students enrolled in the virtual reality program. *Shadow of the Hegemon* (2001) and *The Shadow Puppets* (2002) both deal with the collapse of unity on Earth once the common alien enemy is gone and the rise to power of charismatic leaders who dominate the world. Card added a collection of short stories set against the same background, *First Meetings in the Enderverse* (2003). Ender's character is particularly well-drawn, but the protagonists of the later books are at times considerably less admirable. Card is at his best when exploring the relationships between his human and alien characters and when describing the intricacies of the latter's cultures.

Engdahl, Sylvia Louise
(1933–   )

Although all of Sylvia Engdahl's novels were marketed for young adults and feature teenagers as their central characters, she has always brought a degree of sophistication to her work that attracted adult readers in addition to her target audience. Her first published novel was *Enchantress from the Stars* (1970), which introduced Elana, a human woman whose job is to help protect alien cultures from the shock of contact with superior technologies. Elana's adventures are continued in *The Far Side of Evil* (1971), this time dealing with an inimical, repressive government.

A second series consists of *This Star Shall Abide* (1973, also published as *Heritage of a Star*), *Beyond the Tomorrow Mountains* (1973), and *The Doors of the Universe* (1981). All three are set on a planet laboring under an intolerant religious system that secretly is the front for a small group of alien visitors. The protagonist is a nonconformist

teenage boy who is branded a heretic and hustled off to a remote site where his innate intelligence makes him valuable enough that he is recruited to an elite group of scholars. The trilogy was reprinted in a single volume as *Children of a Star* (2000).

None of Engdahl's novels contain a great deal of action. Instead, they tend to more seriously consider the nature of the universe and the responsibilities of humankind to act ethically when exposed to alternate intelligences. Engdahl's interest in anthropological themes, particularly as they relate to culture, is evident in most of the novels, which examine the different stages through which civilizations pass. She shows little interest in the details of technological change and avoids many of the trappings of similar novels written by more genre-conscious writers. Engdahl has written very little short fiction, but *Timescape* is an effective short novel. A book written earlier, *Journey Between Worlds* (1970), is the story of a trip to Mars, but the plot is almost completely subsumed by the author's propagandistic insistence that space travel is the most important part of human destiny. She has also written several nonfiction books on themes found in her novels.

The Eyeflash Miracles
Gene Wolfe
(1976)

We never learn much detail about the setting in this novelette because it is told from the viewpoint of a blind boy and two unemployed wanderers, one of whom is suffering from mental problems. What little we do know is unpleasant: Automation has left most of the population, even school administrators, unemployed, living as best they can on a minimal government allowance. A young, blind runaway, Little Tib encounters two of these men, who kindly decide to help him find medical treatment. However, no doctor will examine him, because the only acceptable form of identification is a retinal scan, and Tib's retinas are completely gone.

But Tib has something in their place, something invisible and intangible but very real: He slips from our world into visions, hallucinating other beings in a world where he still can see; and while in that world, he has a dramatic effect on the world and people around him. One of the men spontaneously recovers from his mental disorder, a crippled child is made whole, and Tib himself can apparently pass through solid objects and walk on air. When he performs one of his miracles in front of a traveling, self-styled holy man from India, he attracts perhaps more attention than he really wanted.

His companions, meanwhile, have hatched a desperate plan to interfere with the programming of a computer and reinstate their jobs. While they are so occupied, Tib has an encounter, partly hallucinated, in which he learns the truth—that he is the only survivor of a government project in bioengineering. When the subject children began displaying paranormal powers, they were all killed to cover things up, but Tib was swapped with one of the control subjects during infancy and was spared the original slaughter. However, now the authorities are aware of his existence, using his own father as an agent, and ultimately Tib is forced to move on, once again aided both by his visions and by a living friend.

Wolfe paints his future government as cruel, manipulative, and distanced from the population. Ironically it is Tib's inability to make use of the system that eventually saves him from it. This is an actively repulsive version of America, but one that has its roots in trends we can already see, just as Tib sees more without his eyes than most of the adults in the story are able to perceive with theirs intact.

F

Fade
Robert Cormier
(1988)

One of the most frequent wish-fulfillment fantasies is the desire to be invisible, to be able to watch others without being observed ourselves. Authors have had enormous fun with this conceit; examples range from *The Girl, the Gold Watch, and Everything* (1962) by John D. MacDonald, in which a magical stopwatch allows its possessor to step outside of time, to *The Murderer Invisible* (1931) by Philip WYLIE, wherein a man is able to kill his enemies almost at will thanks to his discovery of the secret of invisibility. Fictional invisibility was conveyed by marvelous inventions, magic, or previously unknown mental powers.

Ambrose Bierce's "The Damned Thing" and Fitz-James O'Brien's "What Was It?" suggested the terror that could result when inhuman creatures remained invisible. Wylie and H. G. WELLS showed us how such a power could be a corrupting force on those who possessed it. Wells's *The Invisible Man* (1897) suggested that such absolute power might actually subvert the sanity of anyone who wielded it, a theme repeated in the motion picture *Hollow Man* (2000). But it was Robert Cormier who would deal with the subject most realistically, and in the context of what was purportedly a novel for young adults, although his treatment is more moving, complex, and effective than most supposedly adult fiction.

The protagonist is initially a teenager who discovers that he is heir to a secret talent that is passed on through the male side of his family. Under given circumstances, he can become completely invisible as an act of will. Although at first he considers this to be a wonderful gift, a mysterious uncle appears to warn him that it is in fact a curse, a lesson that he learns only over a period of years as he discovers that it has distanced him from everyone around him. Although not Cormier's most famous novel, it is arguably his best, and is his only overt attempt at speculative fiction. Since the power is linked to genetics and not some magical form of propagation, it is in form a story of psi powers and therefore more properly science fiction than fantasy. To a degree it is also an allegory about the way in which writers sometimes create barriers between themselves and the rest of the world, and in that sense it may be partly autobiographical.

Faded Sun series
C. J. Cherryh

Many of C. J. CHERRYH's early novels were set against the loose background of the Union-Alliance conflict, a future history in which the former is a centrally dominated, emerging interstellar empire while the latter is a looser amalgamation of parties who support an almost anarchic variety of free trade associated with the Merchanters, whose civilization lies entirely in space and is not tied to any specific planet. Cherryh's universe was large and complex and incorporated a number of alien races and cultures, most of which were presented only in small snatches.

The Faded Sun trilogy was the first to concentrated on a single race, the mri, a mercenary culture that unfortunately cast its lot on the losing side of a war designed to contain human expansionism. With its usual thorough ruthlessness, humanity has virtually wiped out the mri, leaving only its last warrior and priestess, through whose subsequent adventures Cherryh introduces us to their culture. A human soldier troubled by the imminent extinction of an entire race helps them escape in the opening volume, *Kesrith* (1978). Having cast his lot with the fugitives, he accompanies them on a journey across space in search of a new homeland in *Shon'Jir* (1978). Even their former employers have disavowed them now, and the last of the mri are still being hunted by their human enemies in the concluding volume, *Kutath* (1979). Ultimately they find refuge on a remote world upon which, presumably, they can begin to rebuild their race.

The mri culture is based loosely on traditional samurai customs, but Cherryh added just enough exotic strangeness to make it seem new and interesting. She was one of the first, and still few, authors to take what was essentially a plot from military science fiction and use it to create a genuinely interesting cast of characters and a credible culture. As was also the case with Gordon R. Dickson's Dorsai sequence, the mri became the focal point around which a group of Cherryh's fans gathered, some even adopting mri names and personas. Although Cherryh would write many more novels set against this same future history, she never returned to the mri. Interest in that specific creation faded out, but the trilogy attracted a core group of loyal readers who would help elevate her to major status in the field.

Fahrenheit 451
Ray Bradbury
(1953)

Ray Bradbury's only science fiction novel is a dystopian allegory that received wide and favorable attention outside the field as well as within. The title is a reference to the supposed temperature at which books will burst into flame. The novel is a massive expansion of an earlier novella, "The Fireman" (1951), and is set in a future in which books have been banned because of their effects on the population, the perceived unhappiness that results from exposure to contrary ideas.

The protagonist is Guy Montag, whose job is that of a fireman—but in a delicious ironic twist, his job is to start fires, not put them out. Specifically he is part of a government agency dispatched whenever books are discovered, so that they can be burned. Initially Montag does not have any strong feelings about his work, either for or against; burning books is just his job, and he goes about it professionally and without emotion. But his private life is less than satisfactory and he feels vaguely estranged from the world and his wife, who is herself suicidal. Montag's uneasiness becomes more intense when he is called out on a job during which he encounters an elderly woman who is so attached to her books that she throws herself into the fire and perishes along with them.

Montag, who has in fact been concealing a small cache of books himself, even though he is uncertain about his motivations, subsequently has a series of conversations with other characters. One character presents the establishment viewpoint, stressing the importance of conformity, safety, and deference to authority. The other, a nonconformist, suggests that the lack of information, diversity of opinions, and freedom to act upon one's conclusions is a basic and fatal flaw in society. Influenced by the latter, Montag realizes that he has become a rebel. He encourages efforts to create an underground press and attempts to convince his friends that reading is an important right; but he is betrayed by those he trusted.

Montag is given the option of redeeming himself by burning his own books as a public gesture, and he does so—but as an act of defiance, not surrender, immolating a government official in the process. Rescuing a small number of books, Montag now finds himself a fugitive, hunted down by the very firemen with whom he once served. As a war breaks out, presumably loosening the grip of the oppressive government if not destroying it completely, he flees into the wilderness. There he finds a society of people who have undertaken the preservation of literature by each memorizing a complete book, which they can recite as needed. Montag ultimately becomes one of their number.

Like most dystopias, *Fahrenheit 451* takes a perceived trend in current society and extends it to an illogical extreme. In this case, Bradbury was undoubtedly reacting to the witch hunts of Senator McCarthy, which reverberated loudly in the artistic community, as well as expressing a general criticism of societal pressures toward conformity and uniformity of opinion. There is also a fainter concern about the misuse of technology. The people in Bradbury's future world have their views shaped by a homogenous mass media to which they are exposed on a regular basis. Although Montag's response to machines is ambivalent, there are times when he describes them in clearly negative terms.

Another expressed concern is what we would now term "political correctness." Bradbury asserts in the novel that the suppression of books originated within the mass of people, specifically special interest groups who objected to one or another set of unpopular or contrary views and insisted upon suppressing that subset of books, eventually leading to a wholesale banning as the only solution to the problem of "subjective" viewpoints. Bradbury's dystopia is not imposed by a small but powerful minority but by a large and thoughtless majority, and that message remains as valid today as it was when it was written.

Farmer, Philip José
(1918–   )

Sexual themes were almost completely absent from science fiction in the early 1950s, even by implication, so when Philip José Farmer's "The Lovers" appeared (expanded into a novel in 1961), it was appropriate that it was published in a magazine called *Startling Stories*. The novelette quite explicitly discussed the complexity of sexual contact between humans and aliens, a theme to which Farmer would return on more than one occasion. Several of Farmer's other early stories were surprisingly polished for such a new writer, including "Sail

On! Sail On!" and much of it continued to be controversial, often involving sexual themes. Several of these latter were collected in the aptly titled *Strange Relations* (1960).

Farmer's first novel was *The Green Odyssey* (1957), a conventional and colorful otherworlds adventure set on a planet that consisted essentially of one gigantic plain traversed by wheeled vehicles powered by sails. *The Lovers* and another short novel, *A Woman a Day* (1960, also published as *Timestop!*, and *The Day of Timestop*), were expanded from shorter magazine versions and appeared as books shortly thereafter, along with a second collection, *The Alley God* (1960). Farmer had not been particularly prolific over the course of a decade of writing, but he had already acquired a reputation as a daring, surprising, and skilled writer. He had also won a Hugo Award as most promising newcomer, although none of his fiction had been similarly honored.

Farmer's novels during the 1960s were lively adventures, almost always enlivened by his genuine gift for creating imaginary worlds—often worlds whose natural laws did not work the same way as in our own world. This was most dramatically demonstrated in the World of Tiers series, particularly the first two titles, *The Maker of Universes* (1965) and *The Gates of Creation* (1966), and to a lesser extent in the remaining volumes. A group of entities whose technology is so advanced that they are effectively gods engage in the creation of pocket universes, each with its own characteristics, and a host of characters—led by Kickaha, an Earthman—travel through these varying realities, solving the puzzles of each world on one quest or another. A somewhat similar device was used in *Inside Outside* (1964), a quieter but still engaging story. *Dare* (1965) was actually a much earlier novel previously unpublished; the protagonist finds himself attracted to the humanoid inhabitants of a colony world, arousing the wrath of the sexually repressed government.

Farmer's short fiction grew less frequent but even more impressive as the 1960s progressed, and stories like "Some Fabulous Yonder" and "The Day of the Great Shout" were considered award-worthy. He would eventually win his first Hugo Award for "Riders of the Purple Wage," an intricate, sexually explicit, and darkly humorous satire set in a distorted utopia. The linked Father Carmody stories were particularly good, and include one of his better early novels, *Night of Light* (1966). The frank sexual content of his earliest fiction had by now become more acceptable to the SF community. *The Image of the Beast* (1968) was to appear from a publisher of erotica, however; it is a disturbing spoof of the traditional tough detective novel involving secret aliens living among us, and featuring some decidedly kinky interspecies sex. A sequel, *Blown* (1969), was a slightly better novel, but neither book was widely known to genre readers because of limited distribution, although both would later be reprinted several times by mainstream publishers.

Long interested in pulp writers like Edgar Rice BURROUGHS and Lester Dent, Farmer began writing novels that loosely linked together various heroic parodies and pastiches. One of these, *A Feast Unknown* (1969), incorporated the supposed prototypes for Tarzan and Doc Savage into an adventure with considerable homoerotic content. Farmer's other efforts along these lines were less controversial, more varied, but never as interesting as his first. Among these were *Tarzan Alive* (1972), *Doc Savage: His Apocalyptic Life* (1973), *The Adventure of the Peerless Peer* (1974), and the two short novels collected as *The Empire of the Nine* (1988). *Lord Tyger* (1970) is a Tarzan pastiche, as are *Hadon of Ancient Opar* (1974) and *Flight to Opar* (1976). Farmer's fondness for dabbling in the worlds of other writers is also reflected in *A Barnstormer in Oz* (1982), based on the works of L. Frank Baum, *The Other Log of Phileas Fogg* (1973), a sequel to *Around the World in Eighty Days* by Jules Verne, and *The Wind Whales of Ishmael* (1971), a science fiction sequel to *Moby-Dick* by Herman Melville.

During the latter part of the 1960s Farmer wrote several short stories set against the common setting of the RIVERWORLD. Enigmatic aliens have resurrected every human being who ever lived and placed them on an enormous, probably artificial world through which winds an endless river. Towers lining the river provide food and supplies, but there is—initially at least—no social structure, no buildings other than the towers. Famous historical characters, primarily Mark Twain and explorer Richard Burton, have adventures as they travel through this world. The stories were eventually incorporated into a novel, *To Your Scattered Bodies Go* (1971), followed quickly by a second, *The Fabulous Riverboat* (1971). The first title won the Hugo Award, and the series as a whole became the high point of Farmer's career. Three more novels followed—*The Dark Design* (1977), *The Magic Labyrinth* (1980, and *The Gods of Riverworld* (1983)—along with volumes of short stories also set in that world.

Farmer's stand-alone novels from that same period are less interesting, but some deserve mention. *Jesus on Mars* (1979) is an exceptional planetary romance involving a religious mystery: Why do the natives of Mars, who have had no contact with Earth, worship a supernatural entity they call Jesus? *Dark Is the Sun* (1979) is set so far in the future that the sun is dying and Earth is unrecognizable, populated with bizarre creatures that have no obvious link to our own time except for the humans—and their culture is almost equally alien. *The Unreasoning Mask* (1982) is also an above-average space opera with metaphysical overtones.

Farmer's 1971 short story "The Sliced-Crossways, Only-on-Tuesday World" had postulated an interesting solution to the population problem: Each day has its own society and population, with those assigned to other days residing in suspended animation. However, when a man and woman from two different days fall in love, they threaten to undermine the entire system. It was an excellent short story, which Farmer expanded into three novels: *Dayworld* (1985), *Dayworld Rebel* (1987), and *Dayworld Breakup* (1990). Although cast in the form of the usual dystopia, complete with its ultimate downfall, the series was distinguished by the novelty of the setting and by Farmer's gift for making even this very implausible social structure seem real.

Very little new fiction by Farmer appeared during the 1990s, apart from a new Tarzan novel, *The Dark Heart of Time* (1999), and a conventional tough detective novel. Farmer's reputation rests primarily on the Riverworld series, which he augmented with an updated version of an early manuscript, lost since the 1960s, retitled *River of*

Eternity (1983). As impressive as that work is, one should not lose sight of the fact that for most of his career, Farmer was far ahead of his contemporaries in his themes and in his willingness to write fiction that appealed to more than just wide-eyed adolescents. His earlier novels are just as fresh and entertaining today as they were when they first appeared, and a surprisingly small proportion of his output has failed to age well. It would not be surprising if his work was valued even higher in the future than it has been in the past.

Farren, Mick
(1943–   )

A background in rock music and a preoccupation with the elements of pop culture are thoroughly mixed in Mick Farren's first novel, *The Texts of Festival* (1973). The novel is set in a postapocalyptic world that has made rock music from our time the basis for a new religion. An otherwise ordinary plot was surprisingly fresh, thanks to the unusual background, and Farren seemed from the outset to be a promising new writer. His next three novels comprised an even more unusual trilogy, which inexplicably has never appeared in the United States. *Quest of the DNA Cowboys* (1976), *Synaptic Manhunt* (1976), and *The Neural Atrocity* (1977) are set in a world where portions of the physical universe are dissolving into nothingness, and strange creatures and places exist in the morphing landscape. The plots are wildly inventive and rather implausible, but Farren brings his bizarre creation to surprisingly vivid life. Years would pass before Farren produced the fourth and final volume, *The Last Stand of the DNA Cowboys* (1989), considerably more polished but somehow lacking the enthusiasm of the earlier volumes.

Farren's next novel, *The Feelies* (1978), was more restrained. A routine story of virtual reality and sinister corporations, it was followed by the much larger and more ambitious *The Song of Phaid the Gambler* (1981), published in the United States in two volumes as *Phaid the Gambler* and *Citizen Phaid*. The setting is the far future, after the human race has mutated into three distinct, competing forms. Dogs and cats are telepathic, and an-

droids are self-aware and envious of organic life. Phaid is a gambler whose activities and experiences eventually lead to his imprisonment, his acquisition of a sense of duty, and an eventual revolt against the power structure. Farren continued to have trouble finding an American publisher, and the novel was not reprinted until 1987. Perhaps discouraged by this, Farren was relatively unproductive during the interim.

Farren's next two novels were a near-future thriller and a military science fiction novel, neither of which rose above the ordinary. *The Long Orbit* (1988, also published as *Exit Funtopia*) superimposed a tough detective story format on a future landscape; Farren named his protagonist Marlowe, in homage to Raymond Chandler's famous detective. Although what follows was a routine blend of light adventure and intrigue, the novel demonstrated Farren's improving skills at characterization and narrative, even if his plots still tended to be melodramatic and derivative. *Mars–The Red Planet* (1990) mixed two separate devices skillfully and impressively. A news reporter travels to the Martian colonies to investigate rumors that the Russians have uncovered artifacts of an alien race, but when she arrives, a serial killer's depredations have everyone's nerves on edge.

Necrom (1991) hearkened back to Farren's early rock-influenced novels. An over-the-hill pop star is caught up in a battle between forces of good and evil that rages across interdimensional barriers, including realities where legendary creatures from our history are real. Other than a standard game tie-in novel and a single short story, Farren would not publish any more science fiction during the 1990s, turning instead to a series of rationalized vampire novels that sometimes employ elements from the genre—including the existence of an ancient alien race that dominated the world in ages past, a nod to the Cthulhu Mythos stories of H. P. LOVECRAFT—but they are more properly associated with supernatural horror than with science fiction, particularly in the earlier volumes. Farren is a talented writer who has improved dramatically over the course of his career. He has the potential to become an important name in the genre, but it is uncertain at present in which direction he is moving.

Feintuch, David
(1944–   )

Military science fiction began to gain popularity in the 1960s and has become an increasingly significant subset of the field ever since, with several prominent authors who have rarely written anything else. Most of the stories of this type follow one of a very small number of patterns, usually pitting a small group of mercenaries or regular military soldiers against daunting odds, either a superior opposing force, a treacherous employer, or some other condition that makes their situation seem hopeless. The writing is often pedestrian: The action focuses on battles and tactical maneuvers, either in space or on some planetary surface, and there is generally little effort to provide rich characterization or to examine the personal consequences of warfare.

When David Feintuch made his debut with *Midshipman's Hope* (1994), he avoided most of the typical clichés. A. Bertram CHANDLER's John Grimes was often called the Hornblower of space, but it was Feintuch who actually patterned his future space navy after the historical British navy, complete with floggings and an exaggerated sense of duty. The background world is only hinted at, at least until much later in the series, but it appears that Earth has been united under a mildly repressive, deeply conservative Christian theocracy. Nicholas Seafort is the continuing character in the series, a newly appointed midshipman in the opening volume who, through a series of unlikely but reasonably plausible circumstances, becomes captain of a spaceship on a run to a remote colony world, just as a race of oversized, space-traveling alien creatures begins attacking human ships and planets.

Seafort is neither a simple nor an entirely admirable man, although his character evolves over the course of several sequels. He is rigid, and his determination to live up to his own sense of honor verges on egomania. It is also self-destructive, forcing him into situations where he has to make decisions that are overly influenced by his emotional state. In the sequel, *Challenger's Hope* (1995), his actions result in a mutiny and a rebellion by the survivors of a devastated colony. He is recovering

from his injuries in *Prisoner's Hope* (1995), resting in another human settlement. The aliens renew their attack just as the colonists decide to declare their independence from Earth, and once again Seafort finds himself torn between conflicting loyalties. The initial sequence ends with *Fisherman's Hope* (1996), during which Seafort is instrumental in defeating the aliens, although he remains unpopular with many of his superiors. By the fourth volume some of Seafort's personal traits have become annoying to the reader as well. He frequently seems unable to learn from his own mistakes, and some of the peripheral incidents repeat similar sequences from the earlier books.

Voices of Hope (1996) finally shows us Earth itself. Feintuch is clearly critical of the theocracy, because the urban centers are rife with crime and gang warfare. Seafort has retired from the service, but when his son disappears in the warrens of a major metropolis, he conducts a personal search, and discovers in the process that the political situation on Earth is less stable than he believed. Seafort becomes the nominal head of the government in *Patriarch's Hope* (1999), in which he charts a successful course among the various contending political powers, although the process further erodes his fading faith. *Children of Hope* (2001), while very suspenseful, tends to reprise much of what Feintuch had already dealt with successfully. The aliens are back, apparently for the ultimate battle, although a few surprises still await the reader; there also are more fights between lay and church authorities.

Feintuch's two most recent novels were less-satisfying traditional fantasies featuring a young nobleman who bears more than a passing resemblance to Nicholas Seafort. Despite its occasional flaws the Seafort saga is probably the best-written military science fiction sequence yet, and its readers are likely to embrace Feintuch's next project with enthusiasm.

The Female Man
Joanna Russ
(1965)

Feminist issues were prominent and controversial in the science fiction community during the 1960s, just as they were in the larger world. There was perhaps particular rancor at the time because the genre had traditionally been slanted heavily toward adolescent males. Female characters were usually sketchily described and were included only to provide an excuse for the protagonist to explain some abstruse scientific principle or to be rescued from monsters, villains, or natural disasters. The fact that the male characters were only slightly better-drawn did not soften the reaction to that disparity.

The television program *Star Trek* is often cited as one of the main reasons that the audience for written science fiction changed during the 1960s. Whatever the truth might be, it is undeniable that for the first time women were a significant part of the readership. In the past, women writers like Andre Norton and C. L. Moore had hidden behind male or gender-neutral names; but now it was no longer necessary for female SF authors to do so. Such writers as Joanna Russ and Kate WILHELM were already introducing feminist concerns into their fiction, as would Pamela SARGENT, Suzy Mckee CHARNAS, and Vonda McINTYRE in the years that followed. Although there had been some feminist awareness in her earlier work, it was generally muted until the appearance of *The Female Man*.

The novel was controversial partly because of its unusual structure, but more specifically because of its dramatic rejection of genre traditions. The protagonist lives within four separate realities, in each of which she enjoys a different degree of freedom. One world is our own, another a world even more repressive of women, a third is caught up in a war between the genders, and the last is a feminist utopia on a distant, future world. Some readers may have been discouraged by the wandering, anecdotal, and decidedly nonlinear structure of the novel, but most undoubtedly were put off by the undisguised anger and frustration and by the implication that women will never be free in the presence of men. Whatever its literary qualities might be, *The Female Man* sparked widespread debate at the time, a worthwhile end in itself, and it is still considered a minor classic of feminist thought.

The Fifth Head of Cerberus
Gene Wolfe
(1976)

One of the most frightening plot devices in science fiction and elsewhere is that of the doppelgänger. In supernatural literature the doppelgänger usually takes the form of the evil twin, a variation of oneself that threatens to supplant its original, as in Edgar Allan Poe's "William Wilson." SF writers rationalized the theme, usually by means of shape-changing aliens. Ray BRADBURY provided a variation of this in "DARK THEY WERE AND GOLDEN EYED," in which human colonists are transformed literally into humanoid Martians, but the classic literary version is *The* BODY SNATCHERS by Jack FINNEY. Finney's aliens are undeniably malevolent, and their victims are quite literally destroyed during the process of duplication.

Wolfe drew from that tradition for this novel, which is actually three related novelettes. The setting is a system of two nearly identical planets, one of which has been settled by a population of clones. In the first section, which bears the overall title, we are introduced to the protagonist and his slowly decaying society. Theirs is a backwater world whose inhabitants are not genetically diverse enough to provide much vigor. The second section is portrayed as a piece of fiction about the neighboring world, which supposedly is host to a race of alien shape-changers who have the ability to pass for human. The final story consists of a sequence of documents chronicling the protagonist's visit to that other world, with revelations that lead the reader to believe—although not without reservations—not only that the aliens are real, but also that the protagonist himself has been replaced by one of their number.

Recounting the plot does little to convey the complexity of Wolfe's prose. The culture and the characters are both beautifully rendered, and the question of identity is an intellectual puzzle rather than a source of suspense. The narrative poses but refrains from answering precisely interesting questions about how we think about ourselves and what makes up a personality. Has the narrator indeed been replaced? And if so, does it matter? If the aliens are so indistinguishable from humans that even they cannot remember their origin, then are they not human? And if we cannot be certain even about ourselves, then what is there in the universe that we can rely upon? Wolfe's novel has been characterized as being about "uncertainty," but it is itself certainly one of the best genre novels of the 1970s.

Finney, Jack
(1911–1995)

Although Jack Finney will always be best remembered for his 1955 novel of alien doppelgängers, The BODY SNATCHERS, he also wrote several considerably less melodramatic stories and other novels incorporating fantastic elements. Yet sometimes his rationalizations were so offhand that his fiction could be described as fantasy with equal validity. The protagonist of The Woodrow Wilson Dime (1968), for example, finds an anachronistic coin, which proves to be the means by which he can cross into an alternate version of America. Finney's ambitious and critically praised time-travel novel, Time and Again (1970), which places a man from our time back in 1882, provides a scientific mechanism for the transfer; but in From Time to Time (1995), there is no effort to provide a nonmagical explanation. Finney's time travel novels reflect a common theme in his work—the desire to escape from contemporary problems, either into time or space—although sometimes the effort fails.

Although Finney wrote for non-genre markets, a surprisingly large percentage of his short fiction used science fiction themes, most commonly time travel. The new people on the block in "Such Interesting Neighbors" are actually from the future, returning to a more attractive past to escape the problems of their own time. Several of his other time travel stories, such as "The Third Level" or "Second Chance," make so little effort to explain the mechanism for dislocation in time that they could be read as fantasy as readily as science fiction. The escape is off the planet entirely in "Of Missing Persons." Other stories of particular merit

are "Quit Zoomin' Those Hands Through the Air" and "The Contents of the Dead Man's Pockets."

Almost all of Finney's short fiction was written between 1950 and 1962, and he produced only a dozen novels over the course of a career that spanned five decades. Like The Body Snatchers, several of his non-genre books were adapted as motion pictures. Finney's short fiction, which in general is superior to his novels, has been collected in About Time (1986) and Forgotten News: The Crime of the Century and Other Lost Stories (1983).

"First Contact"
Murray Leinster
(1945)

The nature of humanity's initial encounter with an alien intelligence has been the subject of literally scores of science fiction novels and probably hundreds of short stories. The aliens may be technologically superior visitors to Earth or a comparatively primitive people discovered through space exploration. They might be virtually indistinguishable from humans or so different in form or intellect that we cannot understand them or perhaps not even recognize that they are sentient beings. The possibilities are so numerous that the subject remains a rich source of new material; but this early story, whose title has become the label for an entire subclass of science fiction, remains one of the most clever "problem" stories of all time.

Science fiction problem stories like this one tend to have a common format: A character or set of characters, sketchily portrayed, is described in a situation that seems to have no solution. They subsequently solve the problem, either through the use of some scientific or engineering principle or by an inspired leap of logic. Stories of this type were particularly common in the magazine Astounding Science Fiction, where "First Contact" first appeared.

The crew of the starship Llanvabon has traveled to a remote and never previously visited part of space in order to observe a nebula. Their mission is nearing completion when they pick up anomalous readings that eventually are identified as coming from another ship, and one clearly not of human origin. Since no previous intelligent species has ever been encountered, this is a momentous event—but one fraught with danger. Although the two crews manage to develop a means by which they can communicate with each other, even building tentative friendships, neither dares trust the other side. Leinster stipulates that it is possible to track a ship through hyperspace; and since neither party wishes to reveal the location of their home planet to the other, they are at an impasse.

Both crews slowly move toward the realization that the only solution might be for one side to annihilate the other, an unfortunate but perhaps necessary outcome. Just as the situation seems hopeless, the human captain comes up with the answer: Both parties will disable their tracking equipment, and then the two crews will swap ships. Although there are certain practical problems that might occur to the reader afterward, within the context of the story this is an elegant and satisfying solution.

The First Men in the Moon
H. G. Wells
(1901)

Although H. G. WELLS would continue to write occasional scientific romances after *The First Men in the Moon,* this was the last of his great scientific romances and his only interplanetary adventure. Jules VERNE, his rival on the Continent, had already described the first trip to the Moon, but Verne had merely flown his characters around it. Wells wanted to set down and actually explore this strange new world. Where Verne had fired his spaceship from a gigantic cannon, Wells chose to invent a new device, Cavorite, a substance that blocks the force of gravity, thereby allowing travel in any direction by judicious arrangement of metal plates.

Although the science is far from rigorous, even for its day, the novel introduces us to an underground civilization (the Selenites) of reasonable plausibility, even though it still requires a major suspension of disbelief to accept the possibility of their having evolved on an object that has no

atmosphere. Once past that hurdle, Wells presents a parade of wonders, letting the reader come to the eventual conclusion that for all their apparent perfection, the Selenites are vulnerable to outside corruption.

Wells had long been interested in socialist theories of government; but unlike some of his contemporaries, he had reservations about a too stringent application of socialist principles, which is demonstrated by his depiction of the Selenite civilization as almost insectlike in its conformity and operation. Although the visiting scientist from Earth is initially pleased to see that their culture has evolved into an apparent ideal, he has second thoughts later on. More importantly, the Selenite leader recognizes the threat posed by humanity, either physically or perhaps just as a corruptive force, and future visits to the Moon are prohibited. Wells had become less optimistic about the future by 1901, and his pessimism is reflected in the story, although it is lightened by occasional sparks of rather dark humor. The novel has been filmed twice, with varying degrees of fidelity.

Fisk, Nicholas
(1923–   )

Much of the science fiction written for young adults also finds an audience among older readers; to some degree writers like Andre NORTON and Robert A. HEINLEIN owe at least part of their early success to this phenomenon. There has been less attention paid to similar stories written for even younger readers, and very few writers in that category have developed a reputation in the genre, if their existence is even recognized. Perhaps the most notable exception to this rule was the British author David Higginbotham, who wrote as Nicholas Fisk.

The first Fisk novel was *Space Hostages* (1967), in which several children are kidnapped into space and have to survive on their own and figure a way to return. The novel did surprisingly well. More than 30 similar adventures followed, most of them involving space travel. Most of Fisk's work avoided the temptation to write down to his young readership, and he made a conscious effort to provide valid scientific explanations for the fantastic elements in his plots. *Trillions* (1971) is usually cited as his best novel, probably because it is in form the closest to an adult story, with a rigid military minded quasi-villain and a mysterious scientific puzzle, which naturally is solved by a child. *A Rag, a Bone and a Hank of Hair* (1980) has an even more sophisticated theme. The setting is a future so distant that most of the competitive spirit has been bred out of humanity, but an unfortunate side effect is a lack of creativity. An experiment is performed to recreate the vigor of earlier humanity.

Wheelie in the Stars (1976) is one of Fisk's most engaging stories; two cargo handlers on a remote planet use a motorbike to relieve their boredom, and it turns out to be instrumental in the resolution of a later crisis. *Escape from Splatterbang!* (1978, also published as *Flamers!*) is an otherworlds adventure that includes an amusing relationship between the young protagonist and his talking computer. Fisk's Starstormers series of five novels is also of some interest for its exuberant energy, although it is less sophisticated than most of his other work. One of his last novels, *A Hole in the Head* (1991), reflected his great concern with social problems, in this case damage to the environment. Fisk never wrote a novel intended for the adult market, but his stories made an early impression on young readers who subsequently moved on to mature fiction, and he remains the best-known science fiction writer for younger teenagers.

Flandry series
Poul Anderson

During the course of his career, Poul ANDERSON created a number of colorful characters, from the merchant mastermind Nicholas Van Rijn to the time patrolman Manse Everard—but none were as colorful and appealing as Dominic Flandry, agent of the Terran Empire. A bit of a fop, Flandry was at heart a competent man who recognized that the empire was in its final years, that the Big Dark of dissolution, anarchy, and chaos was coming but that it might be delayed a bit longer if a few individuals applied themselves to the situation. The chief enemy of the empire, other than its own corruption, were the Merseians, a younger and more ambitious race, frequently represented by an agent named Aycharaych.

The Flandry sequence consists of nine novels and a few short stories, but it also fits into a general future history that included the Polesotechnic League series, which took place earlier in the empire's history, and a few comparative minor works that were contemporaneous or set after the collapse. The first three novels, all quite short, appeared in rapid succession. *We Claim These Stars* (1959) finds Flandry facing a difficult problem: He has to prevent the assassination of a government official, despite the fact that the assassin is a telepath who can eavesdrop on all the preparations arranged to forestall him. In *Earthman, Go Home!* (1960) Flandry is trapped on a backwater planet whose autocratic rulers use an addictive drug to control the population, slowly building up a power base that might enable them to challenge imperial authority. He visits still another world in *Mayday Orbit* (1961), this one supposedly neutral in the conflict between the empire and its alien adversaries. When he discovers that the local government is secretly planning an alliance with the aliens, he joins forces with the local underground opposition to prevent that from happening.

It appeared that Anderson might have abandoned Flandry at that point, but after a five year interval he decided to chronicle the agent's earlier career in *Ensign Flandry* (1966). The younger and less experienced man has troubles with both sides. Falsely accused of a series of crimes, he becomes a fugitive from his own people, while the Merseians are after him because he has intelligence about an imminent attack. Initially he is unable to convince anyone of the accuracy of his information. Parts of the novel were transparently designed as a commentary on the Vietnam War, but Anderson avoided the temptation to lecture and the plot moves rapidly and logically to its conclusion.

The Rebel Worlds (1969) returned to the older version of Flandry. As it becomes more obvious that the imperial grip is loosening, rulers of some of the fringe worlds begin to flex their own muscles. When the charismatic leader of one such planet openly challenges the central authority, war breaks out, ending only when Flandry survives a series of adventures and negotiates an end to hostilities. A *Circus of Hells* (1970), although one of the better novels in the series, is almost peripheral. Flandry gets involved in a diversionary treasure hunt on a remote world and almost falls prey to alien spies and a rogue supercomputer.

The most satisfying of the Flandry novels is *A Knight of Ghosts and Shadows* (1974), set late in his career. Flandry has a grown son—and if the faltering of the empire was not bad enough, the younger man is in the employ of an alien power and possibly a traitor to his own race. There is a much richer sense of character this time, despite the rapid pace of the plot. The empire is in fact beginning to collapse in *The Stone in Heaven* (1979). Flandry, now an admiral, has finally accepted the inevitable. His concern is to find a niche of his own, a comparatively safe place where he can live out his life, preferably with someone he loves. The tone is occasionally bitter, but the story ends on a relatively positive note. The final novel, *The Game of Empire* (1985), introduces Flandry's daughter. As more and more planets rebel and the emperor grows weaker, a rival springs up—a military leader who declares himself the new ruler. Flandry rightly suspects that the ambitious usurper is secretly the puppet of an alien power and manages to diffuse the situation once again.

The Flandry series was not Anderson's most praiseworthy work, but it may well prove to be his most memorable. His evocation of a dying empire rings true and Flandry himself evolves steadily and believably through the course of his career. There is a tendency to dismiss straightforward adventure stories as somehow subliterary, but that is not the case here. Anderson approached his stories of intrigue with the same degree of dedication as he did his novels on more serious themes.

"The Flat-Eyed Monster"
William Tenn
(1955)

One of the staples of early science fiction films was the bug-eyed monster, the malevolent, repulsive, usually biologically questionable creature that lurched across the screen in pursuit of (usually) scantily clad women. Although there were occasional monster stories in written SF as well, most writers avoided what came to be known as BEMs, or "bug-eyed monsters," except derisively. William TENN, however, turned the concept on its head in one of the most genuinely funny stories of all time.

The protagonist is Clyde Manship, a meek university professor who is snatched out of his room one night by a teleportation beam from a distant planet. He awakens in a laboratory to find himself surrounded by slimy alien creatures with multiple tentacles, most of them ending with bulging eyeballs, an extreme manifestation of the bug-eyed monster. His abductors are intelligent and telepathic and he can eavesdrop on their conversations with no difficulty—but he can only receive and not project, and thus has no way to tell them that he is in fact intelligent and not some dangerous animal.

What follows is a compressed version of the usual film story, but told from the opposite perspective. Manship escapes because barriers that would defeat the relatively weak aliens fall before his greater strength. Even more surprising is the fact that, when frightened for his life, he apparently emits a previously unsuspected psychic force through his eyes that is fatal to the aliens. He escapes the alien complex and blunders his way through a city so strange that he cannot understand what he is doing, while the authorities call up the army to track down the horrid beast ravening its way through their peaceful city, determined to destroy him before he reproduces himself and dooms their civilization.

His only hope is to steal a starship and operate it using knowledge he has lifted from the brain of one of his pursuers. Much to his and the reader's surprise, he succeeds; but just when it seems that he will be able to return to Earth, a massive pursuit is launched. Manship cannot understand why the aliens would bother to chase him, until he realizes that there was a young, female alien hidden aboard the stolen ship. He has fulfilled the last stereotyped role of the alien monster, and his doom is sealed. The story is as clever and amusing today as when it first appeared.

Flatland
Edwin Abbott
(1884)

Edwin Abbott was an American clergyman who wrote *Flatland* to demonstrate abstruse mathematical principles. Originally titled *Flatland: A Romance of Many Dimensions* and appearing under the pseudonym A. Square, the short novel starts by introducing the reader to the protagonist's two-dimensional world, using analogies to demonstrate how things work in that realm. Once the reader has made that leap of perception, Abbott provides an even greater challenge, moving us to a one-dimensional universe called Lineland. Finally a character from our own universe is introduced, resulting in a lively discussion about the nature of dimensions and the possibility that there might even be more than four.

Other writers have subsequently tried to embellish Abbott's work, including *An Episode of Flatland* (1907) by C. H. Hinton and others, and the way in which Abbott used a fictional situation to illustrate an abstruse principle was undoubtedly an influence on many genre writers, notably H. Nearing Jr. and Martin Gardner. *The Annotated Flatland* (2001) adds so much commentary that it virtually doubles the length of the original. Ian Stewart also wrote a new adventure, *Flatterland* (2001), which explores new aspects of dimensionality in terms of more recent developments in the field of mathematics. Rudy RUCKER's *Spaceland* (2002) borrows Abbott's name for our universe and describes contact between an ordinary human and a being from the fourth dimension, providing somewhat more extensive a narrative than in Abbott's work, but still concentrating on explication about the mathematical concepts and the way in which we might theoretically perceive a higher order of existence. Rucker's novel *The Sex Sphere* (1983) also shows evidence of Abbott's influence.

Although not a particularly impressive work by literary standards, *Flatland* is on its own terms a perfect example of what science fiction, at its best, can bring to the reader. It provides an alternative perspective that is impossible in mainstream fiction, and it communicates what might otherwise have been dull scientific principles in an entertaining and authoritative fashion.

"Flatlander"
Larry Niven
(1967)

Early in his career, Larry NIVEN built a following for his stories with a succession of space adventures that would eventually be called the Known Space series, a loosely cast future history in which humans have begun to spread out into the galaxy and interact with a variety of alien species, some friendly, some not. Earth itself has been transformed by the invention of matter transmission and by other technological advances, and its residents are known at large as flatlanders, even if they are experienced space travelers.

Beowulf Shaeffer is not native to Earth, but he visits it on vacation in the company of a wealthy but impulsive man named Pelton. Pelton wants to experience an entirely new and strange environment, so Shaeffer suggests that he consult the Outsiders, an enigmatic alien race who trade in information. The Outsiders suggest a particular planet, but Pelton is unwilling to pay an additional fee to find out just what makes it so peculiar, so he and Shaeffer approach it with more than usual caution. One of the attributes of the Known Space series is the GP hull, an alien technology that is completely impervious to harm and therefore makes the ideal exterior for a spaceship. The two adventurers are approaching their destination, which has been scoured to near featurelessness, when their hull suddenly disintegrates, nearly killing them.

"Flatlander" is, ultimately, a hard-science puzzle story, although the protagonists fail to solve the problem themselves, thus departing from the formula. But the puzzle, though interesting, is only tangential to the real story, which concerns the human urge to investigate the unknown. Pelton represents the restless energy that ignores hazards in order to achieve a desired end, while Shaeffer is the voice of caution and reason, willing to take reasonable chances but wary of the unexpected.

Neither man would have succeeded alone—Pelton would have died because of his impetuosity and Shaeffer would have turned back before they learned anything—but together they experience something unprecedented. Niven was one of a new generation of writers who set their stories in outer space but who incorporated their knowledge of the physical universe to give them a new level of verisimilitude. Stars and planets might have extraordinary properties, but these properties were explained in the light of current knowledge of real or potential conditions. This scientific literacy enhanced Niven's already strong narrative ability.

"The Flowering of the Strange Orchid"
H. G. Wells

Despite the melodramatic themes H. G. WELLS used in his fiction—invasions from Mars, cannibalistic humans, genetically engineered mutants—his style was almost always restrained, even casual, while he was describing otherwise horrible events. That is particularly true in "The Flowering of the Strange Orchid," one of his more quietly chilling stories. The protagonist, Wedderburn, is an ineffectual Englishman who collects and breeds orchids, although he does not seem to be particularly good at it. He is delighted one day to acquire the last orchid bulb obtained by an explorer; the bulb was found on the poor man's exsanguinated body, a fate ascribed to an encounter with jungle leeches.

The story is a variant of a common fantasy theme, "be careful what you wish for." Wedderburn laments that "nothing ever happens to me," but that situation is about to change. His housekeeper finds the new plant repulsive, but Wedderburn is excited because the strange orchid has a unique variation in that some of its roots are exposed to the air. The plant also gives off a distinctive scent, so cloying that the housekeeper avoids the hothouse where it is growing.

The mystery resolves itself when Wedderburn is suddenly overcome by the scent and falls senseless. Alarmed by his absence, the housekeeper visits the hothouse where the plant's articulated roots are busily draining the blood from her employer, just as—the reader now realizes—one of its kind

must have killed the explorer. The ending is a happy one, except for the orchid. Not only is Wedderburn rescued and the plant destroyed, but he is actually rather pleased by his adventure—an outcome atypical of Wells's stories. Although comparatively little attention is paid to his short fiction, this is one of his most effective pieces at that length, and it was almost certainly the literary inspiration for the film *The Little Shop of Horrors*.

"Flowers for Algernon"
Daniel Keyes
(1959)

During the 1950s, science fiction readers still expected at least a degree of melodrama in their stories, so it is not surprising that this short story and the subsequent book-length version were immediate sensations. The story received a Hugo Award, while the novel version won a Nebula Award. The story's popularity was so widespread that it resulted in a better-than-average television movie under the title *The Two Worlds of Charlie Gordon* and was adapted as a motion picture, *Charly*, in 1968. Keyes, who in his entire career wrote less than a dozen science fiction stories, created possibly the best character study in the genre, rivaled only by Robert SILVERBERG's *DYING INSIDE*. The novel is a much more detailed narrative, but the shorter version is still the more impressive work because it accomplishes almost the same things in far fewer words.

Charlie Gordon is a mentally retarded middle-aged man who volunteers for an experiment designed to augment his intelligence. Algernon, a mouse who previously had the same surgery, was the first subject who did not quickly retrogress to his usual intelligence level. Initially Algernon is quicker to solve mazes than Charlie, causing some animosity, but as Charlie himself begins to improve, a bond is forged between them. The story is structured as his diary, and the quality of the spelling, punctuation, and content changes gradually, effectively illustrating his intellectual progress and the eventual bitter reversal.

There are several changes of attitude that are particularly evocative. The early Charlie is naive and accepts the teasing of his coworkers as a sign of affection rather than derision; but once he has become intelligent and aware, he is shocked to find himself being amused by a similar incident involving a retarded boy. Similarly, the same people who were unkind to him before his operation, and genuinely afraid of him after, become his most ardent protectors and sympathizers once he has regressed. Charlie also discovers that he has even more difficulty communicating with people when his IQ is 200 than he did when it was 68, partly because he lacks the social skills to avoid causing inadvertent offense.

"Flowers for Algernon" would appear on any significant list of the best science fiction stories, but it is also a powerful work of fiction irrespective of genre. Keyes wrote almost no further science fiction after it appeared, but his name and his greatest creation are still familiar to anyone who has read extensively in the field.

Flynn, Michael
(1947–   )

Michael Flynn began his career writing primarily hard science fiction stories during the mid-1980s, and he had produced a substantial body of good to very good tales by the end of that decade. His first novel, *In the Country of the Blind* (1990), is a secret history. During the 19th century the English mathematician and inventor Charles Babbage actually did succeed in creating a working computer. In Flynn's novel a secret society has quietly refined the invention and used it to analyze the infrastructure of the world so accurately that they are now prepared to assert clandestine control. The story is reminiscent in concept—though not in execution—to *The Difference Engine* (1990) by William GIBSON and Bruce STERLING. *The Nanotech Chronicles* (1991) is the episodic story of advances in the field of microscopic technology and is more interesting for its speculative content than for its story values.

Firestar (1996) was the first of a four-volume sequence. Flynn selected one of the standard concerns of earlier science fiction—the importance of space travel to the future of humanity—and polished it up for a new generation of readers. The admirably well-described protagonist is determined not to let the exploration of space founder. Her efforts are successful, and explorers are en route to the asteroid belt in *Rogue Star* (1998) despite an ambitious but shortsighted American president who may be inadvertently sabotaging the endeavor by using it to covertly extend the country's military reach beyond the Earth. The situation takes a turn for the worse in *Lodestar* (2000) when several asteroids are inexplicably diverted toward Earth, apparently manipulated by hidden aliens—a situation resolved in the concluding volume, *Falling Stars* (2001). Flynn skillfully mixes hard science with space adventure and a touch of mystery.

The Wreck of the River of Stars (2003) was his next and most satisfying novel. The story is set in a future similar to the earlier series; the solar system is being explored and developed and a new wave of technology has made older spacecraft obsolete. One of the last of the older ships has a disastrous accident, and its crew has to solve a series of problems if any of them are to survive. The best of Flynn's short fiction has been collected in *The Forest of Time and Other Stories* (1997). Although none of his novels have attracted more than average attention, they are uniformly solid, well-researched, thoroughly imagined examples of hard science fiction, and almost certainly indicate an author growing more confident and skillful with each succeeding effort.

"Foodlegger"
Richard Matheson
(1951)

Richard MATHESON is best known for his novels; but during the 1950s in particular he was a prolific short story writer, many of them science fiction. "Foodlegger" is one of his earliest and best SF stories, and also one of his rare ventures into humor—although in this case it was humor with a wicked bite.

Professor Wade is a time traveler who materializes in a future that looks superficially like our own, but he is promptly arrested when a police officer notices some of the items contained in his time machine, the nature of which Matheson does not reveal initially but which are apparently considered obscene. In due course we learn that the offensive items are articles of food, and that the world has progressed to a point where sustenance is no longer taken orally, although it is equally apparent that most people are tempted to eat surreptitious meals.

Once he has convinced people that he is what he claims to be, a time traveler, Wade is released by the police commissioner and taken to his home, supposedly so that he can consult the commissioner's library and find out how the world changed so radically. Wade is suspicious of his companion, who insists on hanging onto the contraband food to keep it out of the hands of presumed perverts, but who actually lusts after it himself. Wade escapes after a short action sequence that is almost an afterthought to the story.

Matheson's future world is obviously crafted for satiric rather than predictive purposes; the author makes only the sketchiest attempt to give his world any plausibility. Wade's musing about the aversion to the very word *food* could clearly be applied to contemporary reactions to words we consider obscene. The fact that almost every character we meet lusts after the proscribed food items mirrors our present pervasive fascination with pornography, and the implication clearly is that the proscription of these objects is what fuels the desire to have them. The ludicrous reaction of the characters toward food is just as effective a statement about inhibitions today as it was when Matheson first wrote the story more than half a century ago.

The Forever War
Joe Haldeman
(1974)

Although Joe HALDEMAN's first major novel may not have been meant as a rebuttal to Robert A. HEINLEIN's STARSHIP TROOPERS, it was widely interpreted as such. Where Heinlein's novel portrays members of the military as the ultimate citizens and restricts voting to those who have served in the armed forces, Haldeman's soldiers are alienated from the society for which they fight, largely ignorant of what is happening back home, and are certainly unable to affect the policies that govern their existence. Given Heinlein's lack of combat experience

and Haldeman's service in Vietnam, it is not surprising that the latter author has a much more authentic and realistic grasp of the gap that exists between a free society and one with a rigid hierarchy, between one that values the individual and one that subordinates the individual to the mission.

Haldeman emphasizes the alienation through the mechanism of his universe. It is possible to travel to the stars and fight battles there because the passage of time is subjective during faster-than-light travel, but that does not mean that many years will not have passed in the objective world. Humanity's soldiers are cast loose in time, and there is no home to which they might return, because too many years have passed for it to be recognizable if they were to return. Defensively, the military becomes a society unto itself, with its own rules and standards and with little interest in the civilization it is fighting to protect. The novel ends with a restatement of this same point. After more than a thousand years of warfare, the two sides are represented by a collective racial mind and a breed of artificially produced humans respectively, neither of whose motives or actions can be understood by ordinary soldiers, who no longer know exactly what it is that they have been fighting for—if they ever did.

Haldeman would later write two sequels, neither of which had the same emotional impact as the original, although they reinforced the same theme. *Forever Peace* (1997) introduces us to two soldiers who are determined to change the way things operate. Humanity splinters thereafter, and in *Forever Free* (1999) we discover the fate of those who consented to merge with a mass mind.

Forstchen, William R.
(1950–)

Most science fiction writers start their career with short story sales and move on to novels, while a few start out with novel-length work and only belatedly, if ever, spend much time on short fiction. William Forstchen is one of the latter, making his debut with a trilogy set in a postapocalyptic world that resembles a new ice age. The surviving population is divided up into much smaller political units, most of them dominated by brutal leaders.

The trilogy, which consists of *Ice Prophet* (1983), *The Flame Upon the Ice* (1984), and *A Darkness Upon the Ice* (1985), follows the career of a charismatic leader who organizes a new religion as the underlying structure for his rebellion. He is opposed by both the tribal leaders and the pervasive and repressive existing church. In the last volume he also has to struggle with schisms within his own movement, but eventually he prevails and a new age of comparative enlightenment is at hand. The trilogy made a favorable first impression, and although Forstchen's later work has certainly been more polished, his first series is still regarded as his most imaginative and ambitious.

A much longer series began with *Rally Cry* (1990). The Lost Regiment series chronicles the adventures of a unit of the Civil War's Union army that finds itself in a relatively undeveloped alternate Earth dominated by repressive religious dictatorships reminiscent of the one in Forstchen's first novel. In this case, however, the hierarchy is secretly supported by a race of malevolent aliens who plan to keep the planet in thrall. The aliens are overthrown, at least for the moment, in the first book, but a battle between human governments adds further complexity in *Union Forever* (1991) and the battle becomes resoundingly three-way in *Terrible Swift Sword* (1992). Five more sequels followed, apparently coming to a conclusion with *Men of War* (1998), but the later books in the series were much more formulaic, reprising the squabbles among the uneasy human allies, exploited frequently by agents of the mysterious but basically inept aliens. Forstchen then added a new book to the series, *Down to the Sea* (2000), introducing a new alien race living in a remote part of the world, possibly as the preamble to a new sequence of adventures. Although livelier than the volumes immediately preceding it, the situations are once again a reprise of earlier events.

The Gamestar Wars series opens with the kidnapping of Alexander the Great in *The Alexandrian Ring* (1987). Snatched out of time by aliens and conveyed to another planet the great historical general is to be a playing piece in a deadly game. Although his abductors consider him an expendable commodity, Alexander has plans of his own.

The Assassin Gambit (1988) moved the action to a planet populated by samurai, but the subsequent action is considerably less engaging. *The Napoleon Wager* (1993) is more effective, detailing an attempt to kidnap a great scientist from Earth's past; the kidnapping goes awry, resulting in Napoleon's transference to a future where careless manipulation of time and space has led to a fault that could destroy the universe.

A fourth series was intended for young adult readers. *Star Voyager Academy* (1994) is a standard story of young cadets training for duty in space, enriched somewhat by a more complex political background, with human space colonies agitating for political independence, a growing conflict that reverberates within the academy. *Article 23* (1998) expanded only slightly on that theme, concentrating instead on the problems surrounding a mentally disturbed commander and a possible mutiny. *Prometheus* (1999) was much more complex and engaging, with the colonies in open revolt, a rebellion brewing on Earth itself, and mysterious aliens appearing in the solar system. Although less ambitious than most of Forstchen's other work, the series is surprisingly appealing even to adult readers.

Forstchen also collaborated with Newt Gingrich for the novel *1945* (1995), an alternate world story in which the United States never entered World War II, and in which a cold war ensues between America and a Nazi-dominated Europe. Only one of Forstchen's rare short stories is of interest—"Endings," set in the universe of Keith Laumer's Bolo series. All of Forstchen's novels are entertaining and well-constructed, but he seems to have abandoned the depth of plotting of his earlier work in favor of comparatively lightweight and somewhat repetitive adventure stories.

Forward, Robert L.
(1932–2002)

Although he had sold a few short stories in the late 1970s, it was not until the publication of *Dragon's Egg* (1980) that Robert Forward asserted himself as a promising new writer of hard science fiction. The novel is set among the alien inhabitants who live on the surface of a neutron star, and for whom time passes so quickly that human observers can watch the rise and fall of entire generations in a brief period of time. Scientists set themselves up as mentors for this new race, not realizing that the disparity in time will soon allow the students to surpass their masters. An inferior sequel, *Starquake!* (1985), describes a cataclysm that devastates the newly risen civilization.

Forward started a new series with *The Flight of the Dragonfly* (1985, later revised as *Rocheworld*). The plot is rather similar, with human scientists studying the inhabitants of an oddly shaped planet. Four sequels would follow, including two collaborations with Margaret Dodson Forward and two with Julie Forward Fuller. The sequels provide more details about the interactions of humans and aliens, but the narratives are interrupted by technical lectures that detract considerably from the readability of the stories. Forward was never particularly concerned about character development or literary values, and this series seems to suffer particularly from awkward stage setting. This failing is particularly noticeable in *Martian Rainbow* (1991), a novel about political machinations on Earth and Mars, and in *Timemaster* (1992), another overly simplistic story about the development of space travel.

Camelot 30K (1993) was considerably better, and the sense of wonder involved in the discovery of an alien civilization at the fringe of the solar system overcomes the occasionally awkward writing. *Saturn Rukh* (1997) is the best of Forward's novels, although it follows his familiar pattern. This time an effort to establish a base in orbit around Saturn uncovers evidence of a sentient alien race, and first contact is initiated. Forward's strength was in his scientific grounding and his ability to create credible and interesting alien civilizations. Although his storytelling talents were not particularly strong, there is an energy and sureness in the best of his work that often overcomes his deficiencies as a novelist.

Foster, Alan Dean
(1946–   )

Alan Dean Foster has been one of the most reliable writers of entertaining, thoughtful science fiction adventure stories over the past three decades. His most popular creations are the Humanx series and the Flinx adventures, subsets of the same future history. Humanity has formed a very close political and cultural alliance with the alien Thranx, who resemble giant insects but behave very much like humans. Their common enemy are the Aann, a reptilian race with a military social structure. Many of Foster's novels involve the struggle between the two sides to gain influence over a third, usually primitive, species, most notably in *Drowning World* (2003) and *The Howling Stones* (1997).

The Flinx stories involve the adventures of a young orphan who is raised under unpleasant circumstances. Flinx eventually operates as a free agent, thanks to his extraordinary mental powers, which make him the target of a mysterious group that hopes to exploit his abilities. He is accompanied by a minidragon, an alien creature that spits acid and is fiercely loyal to his master. Flinx was introduced in Foster's first novel, *The Tar-Aiym Krang* (1972), which describes Flinx's escape from the slums of his home world and his discovery of an alien artifact. By the ninth title in the series, *Flinx's Folly* (2003), the frightened orphan has become a self-assured young man, although still a fugitive searching for information about his own origins.

The Humanx Universe or Commonwealth novels maintain a consistent high quality level. The earlier books in the series, including *Voyage to the City of the Dead* (1984), are set after the alliance has been completed. The premise in the early installments takes for granted that humans and aliens trust each other. Foster later returned chronologically to the days before the alliance to show us how both races overcame their prejudices, and these novels contain some of Foster's best work. In *Phylogenesis* (1999) the Thranx encourage a human settlement on one of the worlds they are contesting with the Aann, hoping thereby to convince the humans to take sides in their ongoing rivalry. *Dirge* (2000) involves an attack on a human colony world; although it should be obvious to the reader from the outset who is responsible, the inevitable series of revelations and the ultimate retribution are thoroughly engrossing. *Diuturnity's Dawn* (2002) is more involved and topical. Human and Thranx racist extremists find themselves allied in their efforts to prevent the alliance between their two civilizations.

Several of Foster's stand-alone novels, most of them planetary romances, are worth noting. Someone is killing the human inhabitants of a world set aside for whales and dolphins in *Cachalot* (1980). *Codgerspace* (1992) is a rare spoof, set in a future when humans have put artificial intelligence chips in almost every imaginable machine, resulting in a general mechanical revolution. *Quozl* (1989) is also a spoof, this time of first contact stories: Aliens arrive on Earth convinced that they are so lovable that they can ask for and receive anything they want. *Cyber Way* (1990) is a better-than-average futuristic police procedural. *The I Inside* (1984) is a dystopian novel that appears initially to be a variation of the usual rebellion story, but which is distinguished by a particularly clever series of reversals and surprises. Foster has flirted with cyberpunk themes, as in *Montezuma Strip* (1995) and *The Mocking Program* (2002), but seems more comfortable with straightforward narrative techniques and less abstract settings.

Foster has also written two independent trilogies. *Icerigger* (1974) is a story of survival, a handful of Earthmen marooned on an ice covered world. When they discover that an offworld corporation is exploiting the local population in *Mission to Moulokin* (1979), they delay their rescue in order to help; they finally expose and defeat their enemies in *The Deluge Drivers* (1987). The Damned trilogy, consisting of *A Call to Arms* (1991), *False Mirror* (1992), and *The Spoils of War* (1993), places Earth squarely in the middle of a battle between two alien civilizations. Initially it appears that the choice is clear: an alliance of free societies opposing another that employs mind control The situation turns out to be more complex than originally believed, and when humans assume a leadership role in the ensuing battle, even their allies turn on them.

Foster has also been a prolific writer of novelizations and tie-ins, including novels in the *Star Trek* and *Star Wars* universes and book-length versions of several major science fiction movies. His occasional short stories are always competently written, though rarely outstanding. Foster is

a prolific writer of adventure stories, most of which are straightforward and good-natured, but his light touch is deceptive and occasionally masks more serious themes. It would be easy to dismiss him as superficial—certainly he has written a considerable number of ephemeral books—but he has also produced a steady flow of well written stories that deal with serious themes in a deceptively light-handed manner.

Foundation series
Isaac Asimov

The concept of the galactic empire was largely created and shaped by Edward E. SMITH's LENSMAN series in the 1930s and 1940s. But the concept would be rendered more plausible starting in 1951 with the publication of the first collection of stories in what would eventually become the Foundation series, and it would be Isaac ASIMOV's model that would become the generally accepted view of what such a civilization might be like.

The Foundation stories (the first of which appeared in May 1942) are set many thousands of years in the future in a universe whose only intelligent species is humankind. A vast galactic empire is following in the footsteps of Rome, sliding toward collapse and chaos. Although the fall is inevitable, a group of psychohistorians under the leadership of Hari Seldon have concocted a plan to shorten the interval of chaos and help restore a more unified civilization after the passage of generations. To this end they establish two entities, the Foundations—one to operate openly to preserve knowledge and restore order, the other concealed and given the task of coping with any unforeseen problem that might arise to disrupt the overall plan.

The original trilogy consists of *Foundation* (1951, also published as *The 1,000-Year Plan*), which sets up the situation and introduces us to the empire and the major characters; *Foundation and Empire* (1952, also published as *The Man Who Upset the Universe*), during which a mutated human with extraordinary psychic powers threatens to disrupt the whole process; and *Second Foundation* (1953), in which the hidden organization reacts to the unpredicted threat and restores the original situation. The trilogy was awarded a special Hugo as best all-time series.

Thirty years would pass before Asimov returned to his creation, expanding it and even incorporating a link to his robot stories. Positronic robots, it turns out, were the secret force behind the creation of psychohistory, acting upon their imperative to protect humanity from itself. Asimov wrote six novels in this new series during the 1980s, the last one published posthumously, which jump around in time to fill in the gaps and project the story further into the future. *Foundation's Edge* (1982) poses a new problem for the Foundation: an unexpected technological development. Despite a slow-moving plot and a tendency toward verbosity, the novel won a Hugo Award. *The Robots of Dawn* (1983) is technically not part of the series proper, but it sets the stage for the joining between the Foundation and the robots, which is completed in *Robots and Empire* (1985).

Foundation and Earth (1986) is set during the early years of the successor state to the old empire and involves a search through the galaxy to find lost Earth, whose origin has been forgotten during the years of chaos. *Prelude to Foundation* (1986) relates the early life of Hari Seldon, including the years during which he conceived the plan to save civilization. With the effectiveness of psychohistory proven, various emerging powers seek to control that knowledge for their own benefit in *Forward the Foundation* (1993), which is actually a series of linked stories. Although these novels were fairly well received, they are not nearly as entertaining as the original trilogy, and often seem inflated by unnecessary and repetitive narrations.

Three prominent hard science fiction writers were chosen to add to the series after Asimov's death. *Foundation's Fear* (1997) by Gregory Benford, *Foundation and Chaos* (1998) by Greg Bear, and *Foundation's Triumph* (1999) by David Brin provide a more detailed life of Hari Seldon, from his early career on Trantor up to his discovery that some robots have transcended their original programming. Most attempts by other writers to extend an existing series have been unsuccessful, but this particular sequence is done extremely well.

Many prominent writers are remembered primarily for a single series, such as Murray Leinster's Med Ship tales or Keith Laumer's adventures of Retief. Isaac Asimov will be remembered for the robot stories and the Foundation series, each of which has had an influence on the development of science fiction that overshadows that of almost every other writer in the field.

Frankenstein
Mary Shelley
(1818)

Frankenstein is a novel claimed with equal validity by both the horror and science fiction genres. Although the reader is presumably horrified by the events that take place, Frankenstein's monster is not activated by supernatural or magical forces, but by the applied use of scientific principles, however bogus they may appear to modern sensibilities. The Frankenstein theme—the individual destroyed by his or her own monstrous creation—has become such an integral part of our culture that its influence on other writers may not always be obvious, even to those writers themselves. Most people are familiar with the general story, but often this is because of the distorted film versions they have seen. The novel is difficult going for modern readers, with archaic language and a meandering plot that provides far less suspense and action than most people expect.

The protagonist, Victor Frankenstein, is obsessed with the idea that life is a separate force that can somehow be reintroduced to dead matter, reanimating it, and he succeeds in bringing an artificially constructed being to life. There seems to be no real purpose for the experiment other than the act itself, a fault that has been associated unfairly with other research conducted for its own sake. Frankenstein is eventually revolted by the misshapen creature, who is much more intelligent than the character as portrayed in countless film versions, and the lonely creature eventually commits murder before abandoning his now insane creator and disappearing into the Arctic.

In addition to thematically related novels, many writers have added direct sequels over the years, most of which have been very minor, owing more to the films than to Shelley's book. One notable exception is *The Memoirs of Elizabeth Frankenstein* (1995) by Theodore Roszak, which endeavors to capture the mood of the original in a more contemporary prose style. Another is *Frankenstein Unbound* (1973) by Brian W. ALDISS, in which a man from our time stumbles through a fault in reality and finds himself back in 19th-century Europe just as Victor Frankenstein begins to create a mate for his deformed creation. He also encounters Mary Shelley and her friends and interacts with both sets of characters, real and fictional. Although the novel was enlivened by moments of witty humor, the subsequent film version was more serious in tone and only moderately successful. Michael BISHOP's *Brittle Innings* (1994) is probably the oddest sequel, with the monster reappearing in the 20th century, passing for human, and playing for a minor league baseball team.

Frankowski, Leo
(1943–   )

Leo Frankowski won instant acclaim with a series of clever novels about a time traveler who makes a new life for himself in 13th-century Poland, uses his engineering training to help forge a fledgling nation-state out of a disorganized mob, and assists them to build a force strong enough to resist the attacks of a horde of Mongol invaders. The opening volume, *The Cross-Time Engineer* (1986), is an exciting and likeable story, although the situation proceeds a bit too smoothly for the protagonist, Conrad, to be entirely plausible. Despite the assistance he has provided, Conrad runs afoul of church authorities in *The High-Tech Knight* (1987), who accuse him of witchcraft, although it is obvious that they are jealous of his power and popularity.

Conrad becomes more politically astute in *The Radiant Warrior* (1989), realizing that if the Poles

are to hold off the Mongols permanently, they will need to think of themselves as a united and homogeneous people rather than just an alliance. By the time of events in *The Flying Warlord* (1989), he has introduced steamboats, machineguns, and primitive aircraft. The premise by now has been stretched beyond credibility, but the anachronisms are entertaining in their own right. The Mongols are routed and history has been changed in *Lord Conrad's Lady* (1990), but Conrad is finally conquered himself—by the charming woman to whom he is married. After a considerable gap in time, Frankowski returned for one additional installment, *Conrad's Quest for Rubber* (1999); but this novel reads like an afterthought and lacks the enthusiasm of the earlier books. *Conrad's Time Machine* (2002) is a prequel explaining the development of time travel, and is equally minor.

The only other fiction Frankowski produced during the 1980s was *Copernick's Rebellion* (1987), a more thoughtful and less frenetic adventure novel that speculates about what might happen if a method was discovered by which machines could be constructed of organic matter. Frankowski produced no fiction for most of the 1990s, but returned to the field with three novels in 1999, including the last Conrad adventure and *Fata Morgana*, an unconvincing, implausible, and rather dull utopian tale. The third novel, *A Boy and His Tank*, initiated a new sequence centered around the colony world of New Kashubia. In order to address its fiscal problems, New Kashubia plans to export its young people as mercenaries, encasing them in oversized robotic tanks. The opening volume ends with the apparent revelation that the battles had been illusory, but the author abandoned this conceit for at least two sequels in collaboration with Dave Grossman—*The War with Earth* (2003) and *Kren of the Mitchegai* (2004)—as well as *The Two-Space War* (2004). These books all are average examples of military science fiction.

G

Galápagos
Kurt Vonnegut
(1985)

Although Kurt VONNEGUT's later novels never had the same degree of impact within science fiction as CAT'S CRADLE (1963) or *Slaughterhouse Five* (1969), *Galápagos* (1985) is probably the strongest of them. Like *Cat's Cradle*, the novel essentially is about the end of the world. This time humanity faces an international economic and political collapse coming on top of a plague of infertility that threatens to wipe out the human race—an event that the narrator seems to accept with some equanimity. The plague was precipitated by a mistaken military response to a meteor shower.

A sea captain with a rather unreliable method of navigating takes a party out to sea at a propitious moment, and they are eventually shipwrecked in the Galápagos Islands, whose isolation from the rest of the world has (in the book as in actuality) resulted in a totally separate ecological system. This insulates the castaways from the troubles plaguing the rest of the world, and they alone survive after the rest of humanity becomes extinct. However, later generations of their descendants have surrendered the ability to think intelligently in order to acquire survival skills in its place; in order to become more humane, the survivors have become less human. Oddly enough, despite the devolution and mass extinction, there is a mood of optimism in the final chapters. Humanity might

think too much, but ultimately we are found worthy of continued existence.

Vonnegut's dark humor is evident throughout the book despite the dour tone. At one point we are told that overly developed human brains represent a form of specialization as suicidal as the antlers of some stags. The narrative also features another of the author's playful literary devices: Every character doomed to die during the course of the story has an asterisk attached to his or her name whenever it appears. Vonnegut's recurring character Kilgore Trout makes a disembodied appearance as well. Although the novel lacks the popular stature of Vonnegut's better-known novels, it is a strong restatement of his familiar themes told with perhaps a somewhat less inventive plot, and in a much more straightforward fashion.

Galouye, Daniel F.
(1920–1976)

One of the goals of science fiction is to demonstrate how people will react when placed in an altered environment. Sometimes the alterations are subtle—a world otherwise familiar, but with the addition of some marvelous new invention or discovery. Sometimes they are more dramatic, as in visits to another planet. Occasionally the environment is so different that it is difficult for the reader to draw clear parallels with his or her own experience; but only the best writers can go to such an extreme successfully. It is all the more remarkable therefore that Daniel Galouye managed the latter as skillfully as he did in his first novel, *Dark Universe* (1961).

The book's premise is that to escape the ravages of a nuclear war many humans moved underground. With the passage of generations, memory of the surface world became more and more indistinct. Galouye was certainly not the first writer to suggest such a possibility, but he added a new dimension. With the decline of technology, underground humanity eventually lost the means to create light; consequently, generations later, hearing has become the primary sense. Following a series of mishaps, the protagonist eventually rediscovers the world of light, but this is almost an afterthought to a well-conceived and portrayed imaginary world. Galouye, who had been writing quite good short stories all through the 1950s without acquiring much of a following, was suddenly one of the rising new stars in the genre.

Galouye followed up with *Lords of the Psychon* (1963), a radically revised and expanded version of an earlier novelette. Earth has been conquered by aliens—but aliens who are so advanced that they are virtually unaware of humanity, which struggles to avoid extermination. *Simulacron-3* (1964, also published as *Counterfeit World*) has an apparently less unusual environment, but all is not what it seems. Scientists seeking a better way to predict mass trends construct a virtual reality into which they can enter in order to observe the simulated subjects, but the protagonist discovers that his own reality is similarly a construct. The novel was later filmed as *The Thirteenth Floor.*

Galouye's last two novels were considerably less imaginative. *A Scourge of Screamers* (1968, also published as *The Lost Perception*) is a passably entertaining story about a new kind of plague that spreads inexorably across the world, but *The Infinite Man* (1973) is a pedestrian tale of two beings with extraordinary powers who are locked in a secret struggle that could annihilate the human race. Galouye's considerable body of fine shorter work has been collected in *The Last Leap and Other Stories of the Super-Mind* (1964) and *Project Barrier* (1968).

"The Game of Rat and Dragon"
Cordwainer Smith
(1955)

The Instrumentality stories that would make Cordwainer Smith a major name in science fiction were just beginning to appear during the 1950s, but the quality of tales like this one would quickly suggest that Smith (the pen name of Paul Linebarger) would be a force to be reckoned with. The setting is a distant future in which humans have begun to colonize the stars, but only with great difficulty. There is a form of life spread through the universe, a bodiless species of creature that exists in some altered version of space that intersects our own. Although they apparently cannot penetrate the atmosphere of a planet, starships in flight are vulnerable to their attacks, which leave everyone aboard either dead or hopelessly insane.

The appearance of telepaths among humans helped at first because telepaths could operate pinlights, a mentally controlled defense system that could potentially destroy the enemy, which they perceived mentally as dragons. But losses were still high until the advent of the Partners, another telepathic form of life that allies itself with the human pinlighters. The dragons appear as rats to the Partners, whom we in due course discover are telepathic cats. Smith wisely avoids delving too deeply into the details of their intelligence, but the Partners in this story have separate, distinct, and almost human personalities. Where humans provide the intelligence in the battles that follow, the Partners provide the speedy mental reflexes, and the partnership means that in most cases, the enemy will be defeated.

Although the story includes an account of an actual battle against the dragons, Smith's concerns are about the interface between humans and Partners. Once the foe is vanquished, the human half of the team is hospitalized to be cured of the after effects, but his first thoughts are concern about the status of his partner. If we needed further evidence that the telepathic bonding was more important than the obvious differences in species, Smith reinforces it by describing the reaction of a nurse. Although she considers the wounded man a heroic fighter, she is also repelled by him, by the feeling that he is not quite human. The protagonist is caught in an even worse quandary: He knows that his partner is a cat, but he also doubts that he will ever know a human for whom he could feel the same degree of emotional attachment. The theme would recur in Smith's later work, which would often be more intricate but never more eloquent.

Gerrold, David
(1944–   )

Before his first short story appeared, David Gerrold (the pseudonym of Jerrold Friedman) had successfully placed several television scripts, most notably "The Trouble with Tribbles" for the original *Star Trek* television series in 1967. His experiences with that program would result in two nonfiction books and two tie-in novels, one of which was a novelization of the pilot for *Star Trek: The Next Generation*, and some later fiction was probably developed from ideas originally conceived as episodes of that program. His first short story appeared in 1969, followed by a collaborative novel with Larry Niven, and then three solo novels in 1972.

The first of these, *Space Skimmer*, was a routine interstellar space adventure involving superhuman powers and interplanetary politics. Although the novel demonstrated Gerrold's talent for narration, its light tone failed to support the rather intense plot. *Yesterday's Children*, a reworking of a *Star Trek* script idea, was considerably better. An antiquated spaceship with an unruly crew is engaged in a tense battle of strategy and will when pitted against an enemy starship in an interplanetary war. The scenario, which is patterned after submarine combat, was later expanded and revised as *Starhunt* (1987). Viewed as military science fiction, it is one of the best of its type, and it succeeds even though it is largely written in the present tense, a stylistic convention that many readers find distracting. The third novel published that year was WHEN HARLIE WAS ONE, the story of the birth of an artificial intelligence. With the help of his creator, Harlie struggles to define his rights as a sovereign being despite conservative political sentiments, frightened citizens, and greedy commercial interests who would prefer to see him

classified as property. Harlie's personality remains rather childlike throughout, providing some wonderful moments of light humor—although one might have expected a more rapid rate of maturation, given the nature of his intelligence. This novel is still one of the best examinations of what it means to be a person, ranking with *Little Fuzzy* (1962) by H. Beam PIPER and YOU SHALL KNOW THEM (1953) by Vercors. Gerrold revised the novel for its 1988 reissue. Gerrold's only collection of short fiction, *With a Finger in My I*, also appeared in 1972. The stories included are a very uneven mix, and he would rarely write at that length in the future.

Gerrold's next novel, *The Man Who Folded Himself* (1973), was a time travel paradox story in the tradition of Robert A. HEINLEIN's "ALL YOU ZOMBIES," with sex changes and time loops making an already complex plot almost unfathomable. Although the author does an extraordinary job of making the improbable chain of events comprehensible, the convolutions overwhelm every other aspect of the novel, and the book is more interesting as a novelty than as a piece of fiction. His other books during the 1970s were less than memorable, with the exception of *Deathbeast* (1978), another time travel story—this one a more linear adventure set against a prehistoric backdrop.

Gerrold would not produce a significant work again until 1983, with *A Matter for Men*, the first volume of the War With the Chtorr series. Aliens that resemble oversized worms have invaded and effectively conquered most of the Earth, using first a highly lethal plague and then a variety of extremely resilient and dangerous fauna and flora as their weapons. The alien ecology overwhelms much of the planet, despite the efforts by surviving military units to resist and eradicate the infestations. The story continues in *A Day for Damnation* (1985), this time following a small number of soldiers sent on a mission deep into alien-held territory, where they and the reader learn more fascinating details about the alien life spreading across the Earth. In *A Rage for Revenge* one of the increasingly discouraged soldiers is captured and brainwashed by a cult that has emotionally surrendered to what it considers superior beings, the Chtorr, choosing to worship them rather than fight them. The series concludes, at least temporarily, with *A Season for Slaughter* (1993); there is no actual resolution of the main conflict, and further titles were undoubtedly contemplated. The tone grew steadily darker throughout the series, and the recurring character, Jim McCarthy, is ultimately troubled by doubts that humanity will take the steps necessary to win the war. The series is a powerful, sustained work that enjoyed considerable popularity when it first appeared, but it lacks the lasting power of *When Harlie Was One*, which remains Gerrold's most popular novel.

Voyage of the Star Wolf (1990) opened a new series, another one reminiscent of *Star Trek*. The *Star Wolf* is a warship whose crew suffers mild disgrace after a disastrous encounter with bellicose aliens. They try to redeem themselves in their new, less critical duties, but tensions among the crew are on the rise. Their adventures continue in *The Middle of Nowhere* (1995) and *Blood and Fire* (2003) as they battle stowaway aliens, a bacteriological infection, and a corrupted artificial intelligence. At one time there were plans to produce a television series based on the novels, but the project never materialized.

Under the Eye of God (1993) and *A Covenant of Justice* (1994) chronicle the efforts of a race of genetically enhanced warriors who decide to rule rather than serve ordinary humans, spreading their influence through human controlled space despite the efforts of a group of rebels.

Gerrold went through another silent period during the late 1990s. His next series was more restrained in its concept and featured much more fully developed characters, even though in form it appeared to be directed toward a young-adult audience. Three brothers from a broken home are enticed into abandoning their mother and joining their father in space in the opening volume, *Jumping Off the Planet* (2000). Although they accede to his wishes, they have mixed feelings that become even more ambivalent when it becomes evident that their father is involved in some form of illegal activity. In *Bouncing Off the Moon* (2001), their plight worsens when they find themselves alone on the Moon, the subjects of a massive manhunt motivated by rival forces all eager to gain possession of a prototype of artificial intelligence given to

them by their father, which we eventually discover will lead to the creation of Harlie from *When Harlie Was One*. Their situation causes the boys to mature quickly—particularly Chigger, the viewpoint character. Although their adventures come to an apparent conclusion in *Leaping to the Stars* (2002), in which they have to survive a mutiny and other dangers, Gerrold has left enough loose ends for additional adventures in the future.

Although Gerrold has had work nominated for the Hugo and Nebula Awards several times, it was his single outstanding short story "The Martian Child" (1994) that finally won both honors. The sporadic nature of his writing career may partially explain why he has not developed a more dedicated following.

Geston, Mark S.
(1946–   )

Occasionally a new author's first novel is so outstanding that it becomes very difficult for the author to live up to expectations in his or her next work. Mark Geston may have put himself in just that position with the remarkable *Lords of the Starship* (1967). Earth has been ravaged by war and some of the survivors are hard at work building a spaceship as a symbol of rebirth; but as the story progresses, the reader realizes that the project has been a hoax almost from the outset. Geston followed up with a sequel, *Out of the Mouth of the Dragon* (1969), set in the same decaying future, as an unsuccessful military assault leaves the protagonist to find his way in the world. Although both novels have downbeat endings, the necessity for individuals to make their own futures is implied in both, and the stories are filled out by a richly described if somewhat less than appealing future setting.

Geston's subsequent novels were less successful, although still skillfully written. *The Day Star* (1972) has a similar background, but this time his story of humanity's propensity for war has an almost surreal overlay. *The Siege of Wonder* (1976) blurs the distinction between genres as a group of scientists sets out to discover a rational, scientific basis for magic. Geston fell silent following his fourth novel, emerging briefly in the 1990s to produce a few short stories and a fifth novel, *Mirror to the Sky* (1992). In the latter, benevolent aliens have come to Earth and, after years of contact, decide to share their artwork with humans. The examples they bring are so powerful that they cause great unrest on Earth, even violence, and the few aliens who remain behind find themselves in danger of their lives. Although well-plotted and nicely written, the story lacked the unique imagery of Geston's earlier work, and he has since fallen silent once again.

Gibson, William
(1948–   )

The popularity of William Gibson's early science fiction is particularly surprising, because that work flew in the face of most traditional genre themes. His writing is the most successful example of the cyberpunk school, set in a computer-dominated future in which humans seem to have ceded most of the authority over their own lives to machines and institutions. Much of Gibson's work is reminiscent in tone, if not style, of the darker works of Philip K. DICK, and his protagonists are rarely heroic—and sometimes not even particularly admirable.

Gibson's first fiction sale was in 1977, but it was not until the 1980s that he began producing fiction with regularity. His early shorts were remarkably consistent and inventive, and included "JOHNNY MNEMONIC" (the basis for the movie of the same title), a story set in the same future as *Neuromancer* (1984), the novel that won the Hugo and Nebula Awards and instantly established Gibson as an innovator. In Gibson's imagined future world, America has become a cybernetic society disproportionately influenced by Asian investors and rapidly falling from its previous dominant position in the world. The protagonist is a criminal and a computer expert who is hired to steal information from the shared virtual reality of cyberspace for employers whose identity he does not know. Traditional science fiction would have ended the story either with revelations about his shadowy bosses or with the overthrow of a handful of orbiting artificial intelligences that may or may not be ruling the world; but Gibson and his character both seem to accept that the loss of freedom is inevitable.

Two sequels followed. In *Count Zero* (1986) we discover that the artificial intelligences have themselves evolved in some fashion and may no longer be completely sane in either human or machine terms of reference. *Mona Lisa Overdrive* (1988) switches to a female protagonist who becomes involved in a kidnapping attempt that has unsuspected higher purposes; but like the protagonists of the previous two books, she never expects to make a significant difference in the outcome, and she lives down to her expectations. The trilogy includes considerable detail extrapolated from current trends: Hard currency is no longer in use, at least legally. Printed books are an anomaly. Multinational corporations define boundaries more effectively than do lines on maps. Drugs and direct sensory stimulation have become more important than sex. Gibson's world is a bleak, low-key dystopia from which there is no chance of delivery.

The Difference Engine (1990), written with Bruce STERLING, transforms many of the same attitudes to a different setting. The premise is that Charles Babbage successfully created the first computer a century earlier than it was accomplished historically, and England has become a strange mix of 19th-century attitudes and 20th-century technology. Although just as grim and downbeat as the earlier novels, this book was equally popular and is still perhaps Gibson's most satisfying work. Subsequent novels, while interesting, have not had the depth of impact of his earlier efforts. *Virtual Light* (1993) is set in a transformed near-future California. Although virtual reality is still a part of the environment, most of the story takes place in the real world. *Idoru* (1996) reverts to earlier themes. The spread of virtual reality around the world has led to a more homogeneous global population—an inevitable and not entirely favorable change, as much of the spontaneity and creativeness seems to be vanishing along with diversity. *All Tomorrow's Parties* (1999) suggests that the cyberrevolution is on the brink of transforming the race dramatically. Although Gibson's vision remains consistent and his prose accessible and engrossing, there is a sense that he has begun to repeat himself in his later work, which has not been nearly as popular despite its sustained quality.

Never a prolific writer, Gibson has produced only a handful of short stories since the mid-1980s. His earlier work has been collected in *Burning Chrome* (1980). Gibson's reputation would be secure even if he never published another word, but he currently seems to have reached a plateau. He may need to find a new direction for his writing if he is to resume his ascent.

"Ginungagap"
Michael Swanwick
(1980)

If humans ever do encounter an alien race with a comparable technology, one of the greatest problems they will face will be finding the means by which to develop some degree of mutual trust with an entity whose motivations and thought patterns might not resemble our own. It might prove to be a comparatively simple task to establish a common language with which to convey facts, but true communication consists of more than just a string of verifiable information.

Abigail Vanderhoek is a resourceful and determined woman who has traveled throughout the solar system without satisfying her urge to explore new territory. That makes her an excellent candidate for a secret project to send the first human being through a black hole to a distant part of the universe, a technological advance developed with the assistance of the spiders, a sulfur-based alien life-form that has been in secret communication with a human megacorporation. Since all black holes are linked through some undefined hyperdimensionality, they will function as matter transmitters, instantaneously transporting Vanderhoek to the system of the spiders and back. Before deciding to volunteer as a test subject, she must wrestle with an unanswerable question: If the version of her that emerges at the opposite end of the link is identical but composed of completely new matter, is it in fact the same person, and is the original dead? The ambiguity is reflected in the fact that she recently received a transplanted arm following

the loss of her original limb, and she still has trouble thinking of it as part of her body.

Negotiations become more difficult when a test animal comes back altered and violent. Have the aliens proven themselves hostile, or are they telling the truth when they insist that the animal's mind was somehow warped by the transition? Despite her misgivings Vanderhoek remains committed; but she is betrayed again—this time by her human companions, who finally admit that they believe she will be destroyed by the process and who hope to use the duplicate version of herself as a bargaining tool. What might have been a depressingly downbeat ending is relieved by Vanderhoek's decision to negotiate her own future independent of her previous loyalties.

"The Girl Who Was Plugged In"
James Tiptree Jr.
(1973)

The impact of media and advertising on the public has been a recurring theme in science fiction since the 1950s, resulting in such classic stories as *The Space Merchants* by Frederik Pohl and Cyril M. Kornbluth in 1953 and *Bug Jack Barron* by Norman Spinrad in 1969. James Tiptree Jr. (the pseudonym of Alice Sheldon) ably expressed her reservations about the process in this bitterly incisive short story. Burke is an extraordinarily ugly and unhappy teenaged girl who is rescued from suicide and recruited by an advertising agency for a project that must remain secret because advertising has become illegal and all products are supposed to succeed or fail on their own merits.

Manufacturers bypass the law by convincing celebrities to use their products in a highly visible fashion. To this end, they have created a beautiful but almost literally brainless young woman, an organic waldo that will be operated from a distance. Burke is to spend virtually all of her waking hours directing the body by remote control, experiencing life through its unfortunately limited sensory system, participating in a world of which she could never have dreamed being a part under normal circumstances. In return she is to follow orders and praise the right products according to a script. She submerges herself so completely in her duties that what was supposed to be a minor character becomes a major celebrity.

Then two problems arise: First, Burke is losing herself in the false persona, and it is difficult for her to perform the routine maintenance required to support her real body. Even worse, the son of one of the corporate executives, who fancies himself in rebellion against his father's values, meets the remote body and falls in love with her. Although he is unaware of the fact that she is being operated from a distance and has no personality of her own, he does think that she is being controlled by her implants, and ultimately he decides to sever the connection. That would have been an emotional climax in itself; but Tiptree raises the bar a notch by having him bring the nearly brain-dead woman to the hidden lab, where he encounters the now monstrous Burke, causing her death despite her protestations that she loves him

Where most writers might have provided an optimistic coda in which the stunned hero becomes more determined than ever to bring a halt to the horrors of the corporation, Tiptree instead hints that his subsequent efforts to reform it from within lead only to his own further corruption. Despite its downbeat ending the story—one of the best by one of the field's best writers—won a Hugo Award.

Gloriana
Michael Moorcock
(1978)

Michael MOORCOCK has had one of the most varied careers in fantastic literature. He is the author of the highly regarded heroic fantasy-adventure series chronicling the career of Elric of Melnibone, a series of novels using experimental prose styles chronicling the life of Jerry Cornelius, and space operas, anachronistic historical fantasies, mainstream thrillers, and occasional more serious and ambitious works like BEHOLD THE MAN.

Arguably his best single novel is *Gloriana, or the Unfulfill'd Queen: Being a Romance*, set in an alternate version of England in the days of Queen Elizabeth. The British Isles are known as Albion, and the queen still rules over at least a portion of North America, whose political structure is radically different than it was in our own world at that time. Superficially the novel is a spy thriller in a fantastic setting, but Moorcock's perceptive insights into the human character are reflected in the interactions of the players in his elaborate game of intrigue, and the fantastic setting at times seems almost an afterthought.

The main plot is that of an elaborate historical swashbuckler in the tradition of Alexandre Dumas, but there are hints of sinister goings-on involving either magic or creatures from alternate worlds. The queen's hold on the throne is uneasy, and court intrigues and international politics may combine to bring about her downfall if the somewhat roguish hero cannot save her. There is also a strong but delicately handled erotic theme. The melodramatic story line is merely the framework for a sophisticated character study delivered with unusually precise and evocative prose. Moorcock would write novels in the future that rivaled *Gloriana*, but he has not yet surpassed it.

Goat Song
Poul Anderson
(1972)

One of the recurring themes in Poul ANDERSON's fiction is the virtue of technology as the method by which humans can achieve their ultimate destiny among the stars. As is the case with most of the field's more thoughtful writers, Anderson's admiration is not without its limits, and on more than one occasion he cautions the reader against becoming so reliant upon technology that we surrender part of our freedom in the process. This Hugo Award–winning novelette is set in a distant future in which Earth is run in almost every detail by SUM, a supercomputer that may have achieved self-awareness and that functions as a god, granting wishes at times, promising to record the personalities of everyone on Earth and bring them back to life at some indeterminate time in the future. The population at large is lulled by drugs, conditioned to think only of themselves and their own pleasures—all but one woman who is made effectively immortal and periodically interfaced with the computer so that it can obtain intimate knowledge of the race it rules.

Opposed to SUM is a single man, Harper, who recently has lost the woman he loves and who seeks her resurrection. He petitions for her revival, even though SUM has never granted such a request before, and is eventually introduced to the vast underground caverns where the computer is located. There they have a conversation in which SUM admits that Harper is an anomaly and a potential source of disruption in the outer world. Harper is enlightened as well. SUM believes that humanity was universally insane before surrendering itself to computerized rule. Harper becomes convinced that there will never be any resurrection, that SUM's promises are lies—lies that are an acceptable method of governance according to its programming.

SUM agrees to resurrect the dead woman if Harper will return to the surface without ever looking back—an evocation of the story of Orpheus and Eurydice. But Harper, like Orpheus, gives in to temptation and loses what he seeks. Harper sees this only as a further confirmation of the falseness of their faith in SUM, and he becomes the focal point for a rebellion. His motive is not revenge but a reawakened desire to assert the superiority of humanity over machines. Anderson's cautionary message is transparent, but the story is distinguished from the many similar ones because of its effective use of mythic themes and imagery.

The Gold at Starbow's End
Frederik Pohl
(1972)

Although readers are accustomed to suspending disbelief in small matters, it is more difficult to produce a convincing and successful story in which the leap of faith is so dramatic that it moves from unlikely to improbable. Frederik POHL managed to overcome that obstacle in this Hugo Award–winning novelette.

The setting is a near-future America, one increasingly shattered by internal dissent. The cities are dangerous places where protesters and others are in near open revolt, a situation that will be exacerbated during the course of the story, which consists of episodes that take place over the course of more than a decade. Our viewpoint alternates between the crew of the first starship, en route to Alpha Centauri, and the scientific adviser in the United States who presided over the project, even though he and the president falsified the existence of a planet in that system and sent the crew on a suicide mission.

Their objectives were admirable even if their methods were not. The crew has been carefully selected and mentally conditioned so that they will spend most of the journey considering scientific issues, thinking in the absence of ordinary distractions. The scientist believes this will result in dramatic new breakthroughs that will transform the world—and he is proven correct, although not in the sense that he intended. With the passage of time, the thought patterns of the astronauts become almost completely alien. They experiment with drugs and sex and the nature of reality itself, eventually developing superhuman mental abilities that transcend death and the limits of the physical universe.

The situation back on Earth worsens dramatically. The country splits into multiple smaller units and civil liberties disappear. One of the astronauts unleashes a wave of particles that raises the planet's temperature and melts the icecaps. But even as it appears that chaos is inevitable, we learn that the astronauts, now capable of moving faster than light, have returned, perhaps to make the world a better place at last. The contradictory themes—that scientific advances will provide the means to solve our problems and that we are as a race unable to be selfless without subterfuge—leave the reader with more questions than answers, but they are useful questions that deserve to be considered.

"The Golden Apples of the Sun"
Ray Bradbury
(1953)

Although the standards of SF began to relax in the 1960s, science fiction readers traditionally insisted upon rigorous scientific explanations of the fantastical events in stories, even if those explanations were not necessarily relevant to the plot, and in some cases even if the science itself was of questionable validity. Ray BRADBURY was one of the few writers who could get away with violating those sensibilities, as he did so consistently in *The* MARTIAN CHRONICLES that the book could almost be considered a fantasy as readily as science fiction. On rare occasions, he did at least nod toward hard science fiction, although always in his own special way, as in this story.

The plot, such as it is, involves an effort to penetrate the sun's corona with a manned spaceship in order to extract a sample of the substance of the star itself, opening up a potentially new field of science. Bradbury tells us that the ship has been cooled to near absolute zero in advance so that it and its crew can survive the brief plunge into intense heat. He demonstrates this dramatically by having one of the crewman's suits malfunction, so that, ironically, the crewman instantly freezes to death even though he is within the sun's grasp. The rest of the crew eventually succeed and make their escape.

The story is rich in imagery, the most obvious of which is the parallel to the legend of Prometheus, the fire bringer. Indeed, the ship is variously referred to as the *Prometheus* and the *Icarus,* and the narrator compares their escape flight to the image of a caveman carrying a burning branch after a lightning strike. The story is not about the astronauts' specific accomplishment but, rather, reflects human inquisitiveness, the never-ending search for knowledge. There is a melancholy note when the captain observes that this is as much a product of human pride and vanity as it is of virtue, and he wonders what the next challenge might be. The story functions as a character study—but the character is humanity as a whole, not just the captain or his crew.

Goldstein, Lisa
(1953–   )

Lisa Goldstein, who won the American Book Award for her first novel, a fantasy, seems less aware of genre distinctions than most writers, which may sometimes confuse her audience. Some of the magical content in her fantasy is rationalized at least in part, and the speculative content in her science fiction is often portrayed in a surreal or magic realist fashion that feels like fantasy even when it is not.

The Dream Years (1985) projects a novelist from the 1920s forward through time to the 1960s, where he becomes a part of an art community founded in part on the same principles as those of his original circle of friends. The transportation through time is never explained, an ambiguity not uncommon in Goldstein's work. *Tourists* (1989) is similarly abstract. A family of Americans arrive in a mythical country and get involved in the search for a cache of ancient documents, but the thrust of the story is the growing alienation of the family in a world so unlike that to which they are accustomed that it might lie quite literally in another universe.

Goldstein's most overt science fiction novel is *A Mask for the General* (1987), in which the United States has become a military dictatorship. The self-avowed resistance is largely ineffectual, and most of those unhappy with the government have retreated into a pretend world of a different culture symbolized by the use of elaborate masks, drawing their inspiration from Native American culture. Some of their number believe that the dictator's crimes are a result of his alienation from the people he governs, and they decide to bring him back into the fold. Two women are instrumental in forging a new relationship among the contending forces, creating a more effective if unconventional resistance force. Rather than describe another conventional popular uprising against a dictator, Goldstein examines the ways in which political and social forces interact and affect the structure of society itself. Despite the lack of a clear-cut victory, the ending is upbeat, plausible, and thought-provoking.

Goldstein has never been a prolific writer, and most of her output has been unconventional fantasy of exceptional quality. Her rare excursions into science fiction have always been noteworthy, and her unusual and colorful prose makes even the most bizarre situations seem real.

"Good News from the Vatican"
Robert Silverberg
(1971)

One of the recurring themes in science fiction is the relationship between people and machines. As early as the 1940s Jack WILLIAMSON would question whether or not we were surrendering too much of our autonomy to mechanized processes in *The HUMANOIDS*. More recently writers like William GIBSON and other cyberpunk writers would describe worlds in which the interface between humans and their creations has become so permeable that there were elements of each contained in their counterpart.

The most visible symbol, particularly to readers outside the genre, was the robot. In both fiction and film, the role of the robot was an ambiguous one. Sometimes they were described as soulless, malevolent forces; at other times, as helpful, even amusing servants. Isaac ASIMOV and Eando Binder would write classic stories of robots who aspired to be human, while others, like Philip K. DICK in *Vulcan's Hammer* (1960) and D. F. JONES in *Colossus* (1966), warned of the danger of ceding power to emotionless entities with no reason to respect human values.

There is a little bit of both attitudes in this quiet, understated satire. The reigning pope has died and there is a deadlock over the succession. A group of tourists gathers each day to discuss the situation and wait for the results of the latest vote, a group sharply split because of rumors that the compromise candidate will be the first robot pope, a representative of the Roman Catholics of "synthetic origin." Underlining the loss of humanity in even this institution is the nature of their disagreement. The clergymen believe that a robot pope will make the church more inclusive, while the lay people are convinced it will drive many humans away. The growing dehumanization of religion is emphasized by the rabbi, who boasts that he no longer performs bar mitzvahs, and the support by both Christian and Jewish characters for the robot's proposed ecumenicism, which will make religion more homogeneous. Contrarily, the narrator hopes that the accession of a robot will satisfy the robot population, at least for now—a

sign that he believes human supremacy is already on the decline.

One of the attributes of the short story generally is that one or more character should undergo some change by the end; but the character who changes in this case is not one of the named individuals, all of whom are simply artifices of the setting. The true character is humanity at large, which loses something of itself, illustrated by the final scene in which assembled throngs kneel down to worship a machine. "Good News from the Vatican" won the Nebula Award.

Gordon, Rex
(1917–   )

S. B. Hough wrote primarily thrillers under his own name and science fiction as Rex Gordon. As Hough he wrote two novels that also fall within the genre, of which the most interesting is *Beyond the Eleventh Hour* (1961), a story about a nuclear war. His first overtly genre novel under the Gordon byline was *Utopia 239* (1955), a postapocalyptic adventure involving the rebirth of civilization and a man who travels through time to see the shape of that future.

Gordon's most impressive novel was *First on Mars* (1956, also published as *No Man Friday*). A single human survivor is stranded on Mars and, like Robinson Crusoe, has to find a way to survive on his own in a particularly hostile environment. The protagonist overcomes a succession of obstacles, ultimately with the assistance of the remnants of a Martian civilization. The bulk of the story is about the details of his planning and the steps he takes to prolong his life; those sequences are particularly gripping and effective. A very minor and largely unfaithful film version was released as *Robinson Crusoe on Mars* (1964).

Gordon's American publisher retitled two subsequent books in an effort to capitalize on the popularity of *First on Mars*. *First to the Stars* (1959, also published as *The Worlds of Eclos*) takes a man and woman to a distant world on what was supposed to be a comparatively brief mission but which turns into a series of disasters. Their mutual animosity causes most of the subsequent conflict. *First Through*

Time (1962, also published as *The Time Factor*) handles a standard theme competently. An experimental time machine reveals that the world is on the brink of destruction, so subsequent efforts are made to discover the nature of the disaster and, if possible, avert it.

Gordon's later novels were also competently written and reasonably entertaining, but were more limited in scope and colored by his pessimism about the future. *Utopia Minus X* (1966) is a familiar dystopian adventure. *The Yellow Fraction* (1969) is set on a human colony world whose inhabitants are sharply divided over the future, some wishing to stay despite some unsuspected shortcomings of the newly explored world, others determined to build a new ship and move on in hope of finding a better planet. If not for *First on Mars*, Gordon would be a minor and probably forgotten figure in the genre; but that one book was memorable enough to solidly establish his name.

The Greatest Adventure
John Taine
(1929)

The noted mathematician Eric Temple Bell used the pseudonym John Taine for his scientific romances, of which this is his best-known. He wrote several novels during the 1920s, stories of lost worlds and marvelous inventions, but his one recurring theme would be the evolution of biological forms, or, more specifically, rapid and radical change as a response to external stimuli resulting in dramatic mutations. He also wrote speculative stories about the nature of time and space that were more ambitious than his earlier work but never caught readers' imaginations as fully as did those involving biological subjects.

The novel opens with an expedition sent to Antarctica on a scientific mission that leads to the discovery of remnants of a lost civilization. This ancient culture was lost when it was overwhelmed by the ice, despite possessing a technology that exceeded that of the modern world. The scientists' investigation is menaced by the existence of oversized creatures resembling dinosaurs who seem to have adapted to living in conditions of extreme cold, but that anomaly is ultimately explained as part of the greater question of why the earlier civilization fell: The ancients' profound knowledge of biological science enabled them to alter the structure of plants and animals almost at will, but they unwisely experimented without the proper safeguards. The mutations became uncontrolled and too pervasive to be eradicated. Further contact with the rest of the ecosphere would have resulted in a complete transformation of all life on Earth. The ancient civilization made the decision to entomb itself and its horrid creations in the ice rather than risk such an eventuality.

The setup in this novel might have led to a didactic lecture on the perils of unrestrained science, but Taine wisely chose to concentrate on the mystery and adventure and avoid lengthy explications. A perilous flight through caverns inhabited by the mutated life forms is particularly vivid. *The Greatest Adventure* is a lost world adventure that rivals Arthur Conan DOYLE's *The Lost World* (1912) and H. Rider Haggard's *King Solomon's Mines* (1885).

Goulart, Ron
(1933–   )

One of the most prolific authors ever active in science fiction, Ron Goulart has used numerous pseudonyms; has ghostwritten books in the Tek War series for William Shatner, and has produced novelizations, tie-in novels, and several series of his own as well as stand-alone titles and a considerable body of short fiction. Although some of his work is serious in tone, much of it is satiric or farcical, and he is considered one of the field's first and most effective humorists. His prose is economical, stripped down, and—particularly because of his large output—is often dismissed as trivial. But despite the light tone and occasionally repetitious plots, Goulart is highly skilled at his particular type of story, most of which are set in some variation of California or in a region of space that feels as though it was settled by Californians. His most memorable and likeable characters are often his robots, which sometimes seem more like people than do the humans in his fiction.

Goulart started as a short story writer in the early 1950s, but his first novel, *The Sword Swallower,* did not appear until 1968. It was the first book-length adventure of the Chameleon Corps, an interplanetary government investigatory team of shape-changers. They returned in *Flux* (1974), this time sent to a planet where the youthful protesters against the government have a dismaying habit of turning into bombs and blowing themselves up. One of the shape-changers resigns and forms a private agency to kick off the Ex-Chameleon series in *Daredevils, Ltd.* (1987), following in the tradition of the fictional detective Philip Marlowe by traveling to a distant planet to investigate the murder of his partner. He pursues the recording of a criminal's memories in *Starpirate's Brain* (1987) and goes to the aid of a beautiful but beleaguered woman in *Everybody Comes to Cosmo's* (1988).

The Jack Summer novels—*Death Cell* (1971), *Plunder* (1972), and *A Whiff of Madness* (1976)—follow the zany adventures of an investigative reporter as he visits strange worlds and investigates even stranger stories. The Barnum series, consisting of *Shaggy Planet* (1973), *Spacehawk Inc.* (1974), and *The Wicked Cyborg* (1978), is set on the same unlikely world. The first is the most serious of the three, with a secret agent searching for a missing man; but the third is the best, one of Goulart's very effective robot tales.

Generally, Goulart's best novels were not part of a series. *After Things Fell Apart* (1970) is usually considered his most important novel. Following the collapse of the American government, the country splits up into numerous smaller communities, organized by shared interests rather than by political ideology or geographic boundaries. *Gadget Man* (1971) is very similar but more serious in tone, with an independent California governed by an unpopular junta. The early 1970s proved to be a fertile period for Goulart. *Wildsmith* (1972) is one of the best of his robot novels, featuring a fiction-writing robot with an amusing habit of disassembling himself. *Hawkshaw* (1982) revealed a darker concern about secretive cults and conspiracies, a theme that would recur in Goulart's books.

Goulart's output under his own name dropped considerably during the mid-1980s following another burst of unusual creativity. *The*

Emperor of the Last Days (1977) is set just before the collapse of civilization, a fate averted through the efforts of a self-aware computer system. America has become a third-world nation in *Brinkman* (1981), but the protagonist discovers a secret enclave of the rich. *The Robot in the Closet* (1981) features a robot that is also a time machine; both aspects of the machine's nature perform strangely when its owner goes in search of a fortune. *Upside Downside* (1982) is one of Goulart's rare conventional novels. The protagonist, along with a number of prominent figures, has been infected with a time-delayed but fatal virus, and he has to track down the parties responsible before the effects incapacitate him.

Goulart's other series are only slightly less interesting. They include the Wild Talents, Star Hawks, Vampirella, Soldiers of Fortune, and Odd Jobs series, the last of which includes several outstanding short stories. If it were not for the traditional disdain for humor among science fiction fans, Goulart might have been numbered among the top names in the genre. Despite that disadvantage, he has managed to acquire an enviable reputation, and it is a testament to the consistent quality of his work that he remains a popular writer despite his relatively small output during the past two decades.

In recent years, Goulart has been content to write mostly under other names, if at all. His short, concise light satires do not lend themselves to current marketing trends, although he still writes occasional short fiction. Goulart's generally humorous short stories have been collected in several volumes, the best of which are *Broke Down Engine and Other Troubles with Machines* (1971), *What's Become of Screwloose?* (1971), and *The Chameleon Corps and Other Shape-Changers* (1972).

The Graveyard Heart
Roger Zelazny
(1964)

The time-dilation effect is a common genre theme, but it is usually associated with space travel, where the subjective time that passes for astronauts in a faster-than-light vessel is considerably shorter than the objective time for the rest of the universe. Roger ZELAZNY found a different way to consider the same situation in more intimate detail with this novelette. The standard of living for most of the world has risen dramatically, and commodities are accessible to everyone—all but one commodity, that is: Frivolity is now the most valuable acquisition, and the most visible and desirable form of frivolity is membership in the Set, a group of people who use suspended animation to leapfrog across years, emerging only for the most current installment of a celebrity party that spans generations.

Moore is a young engineer who fancies himself in love with a woman from the Set. He dedicates his life to gaining permission to join the exclusive group, although eventually he discovers that it is their acceptance that has become important, and not the woman after all. Paradoxically, he realizes that even though members of the Set insist that they are a self-contained subculture, in truth they are exhibitionists who need the envy of the excluded to validate their own existence. As time passes, however, they grow increasingly disengaged from the external environment. The training Moore received becomes obsolete and his attitudes archaic, and it becomes increasingly unlikely that he could ever disengage himself and resume a normal lifestyle.

The members of the Set are subtly displaced in space as well as time. One character notes that they no longer have a physical place to live, that their home consists of a series of hours rather than an actual location. This is generally believed to be a positive sign; but as time passes, there are evidences of strain. When Moore and his partner actually do fall in love, they are threatened with expulsion from the Set, and another member who has perhaps grown too separate from humanity resorts to violence and attempted murder. Moore responds in kind, and prepares to accept the judgment of the outside world, only to discover that social mores and mechanisms have changed unrecognizably. Zelazny's brilliant characterizations bring the Set to life and demonstrate the consequences of an elitism that cuts itself loose from everyday reality.

Griffith, George
(1857–1906)

Although George Griffith is largely unknown in the United States, he was a contemporary of H. G. WELLS and had significant influence on British writers of speculative fiction. The future-war novel had already acquired considerable popularity when he started writing, but most of the works in this subgenre consisted of extended descriptive narratives with little concern for plot or characterization. Griffith changed that dramatically with *The Angel of the Revolution* (1893) and its sequel, *Olga Romanoff* (1894). Adding to the political and strategic maneuvering already common to the form, he invented—and often anticipated—technological advances and battle tactics for his fleets of airborne warships. America becomes a socialist state and most of Europe goes to war against England in the first title, but the result is a benevolent world-state. In the sequel, set several generations later, a new war breaks out, aggravated by the imminence of a potentially devastating collision with a comet.

Griffith wrote further future war novels, including *The World Peril of 1910* (1907) and *The Lord of Labour* (1911), but his new preoccupation would be powerful corporations and their efforts to secure political control. This would be the theme of *The Great Pirate Syndicate* (1899), *World Masters* (1903), and *The Great Weather Syndicate* (1906). In each of these an alliance of businessmen seeks to rule the world, employing plans with varying degrees of plausibility. *A Honeymoon in Space* (1901) is a kitchen sink space adventure whose scientific basis was unsound even for its time, although it has interesting moments in which the protagonists contact the inhabitants of Mars and Venus.

Other novels of note are *The Lake of Gold* (1903), a utopian novel, and *Outlaws of the Air* (1895). A selection of Griffith's best short stories was collected as *The Raid of Le Vengeur and Other Stories* (1974). Although only a few of Griffith's books have appeared in the United States, and always from specialty publishers, he remains an influential figure in the history of British SF.

"Grotto of the Dancing Deer"
Clifford D. Simak
(1980)

Most of Clifford SIMAK's fiction featured unexceptional protagonists, ordinary people caught up in extraordinary events. The narrator of this, one of his last and finest stories, is Boyd, an archaeologist who has been studying a newly discovered cache of cave paintings somewhere in the Basque region of Europe. He returns for one last visit after the rest of the company has left, except for a local workman named Luis, with whom he has developed a strong but largely unexpressed friendship. Boyd is troubled by the feeling that he has overlooked something; and sure enough, he discovers a telltale crack that eventually leads to the discovery of a concealed entrance to an even deeper chamber.

Inside the second chamber he finds more paintings, but anachronistic ones. The animals are portrayed as dancing and have almost a Disneyesque quality that is completely at odds with the rest of the site, which dates back at least 20,000 years. On a ledge nearby he finds two objects; a primitive pallet with a blob of paint in which the fingerprint of the artist has been preserved through the millennia, and a hand-made stone pipe. The pipe seems familiar to him, and he realizes that it is identical to the one Luis has been smoking. Boyd makes a leap of faith that might strike the reader as a bit incredible. During a final meal with Luis, he secures the man's fingerprints on a wine bottle.

Boyd is only mildly surprised when he receives the test results. The prints in the paint are authentically ancient, and they are also identical to the prints on his purloined wine bottle. Incredible as it appears, Luis was the artist who drew the dancing animals. Boyd tracks him down for what might be their final conversation. Luis confirms that not only has he lived through all of human history, but he also describes the necessity to avoid standing out, to always blend in. He then admits that he deliberately left clues, hoping that Boyd would figure out the truth, even though it has become psychologically impossible for him to reveal himself more straightforwardly.

The explanation is a simple one: Despite having what most people might describe as an unparalleled gift, this immortality is also a curse. Like the Wandering Jew, the proverbial figure destined to wander the Earth until Christ is reborn, Luis must watch everyone he knows as they grow old and die, and he cannot reveal his secret because it will ultimately lead to fear and envy. However, he was able to leave clues so that his secret could be discovered by at least one trustworthy individual who would share that knowledge for a time. The only immortal man in the world is also the world's loneliest man.

Gulliver of Mars
Edwin Lester Arnold
(1905)

That brand of otherworld adventure that involves dying civilizations and mixes superscience with swordplay, beautiful princesses, and simplistic plots is generally referred to as Burroughsian, after Edgar Rice BURROUGHS, whose Mars series in particular established the standards of this subgenre, such as they are, and popularized most of its conventions. Although Burroughs's creation spawned several imitators and, much later, the occasional pastiche or spoof, it is generally forgotten that Burroughs himself was borrowing from another writer.

Edwin Lester Arnold was a British author who had already published two novels about reincarnation when he turned his hand to a planetary romance, essentially inventing the form with *Lieut. Gullivar Jones, His Vacation,* later retitled as the more familiar *Gulliver of Mars.* There was no waiting audience prepared to demand rigorous science at the time, so Arnold was free to describe Mars in whatever way he felt inclined; nor were readers particularly fussy about the way in which the human hero was transported across space. Where Burroughs conveyed his Earthman to Mars via some unexplained mystical mechanism, Arnold employed a magic carpet, conveniently avoiding questions of distance and oxygen. The method was irrelevant to the story and obviously held no interest for the author. Instead, he wished to recount the wild adventures of a rather larger-than-life figure as he adjusts to his new environment by promptly getting into trouble. There is a beautiful princess, of course, and chases, captures, escapes, and battles, leading to the ultimate crisis. Jones does not, however, end up with the princess (who is, after all, of a different race), but instead returns to Earth and the woman he loves.

Arnold's novel was neither as adventurous nor as colorful as the Burroughs Mars novels. The prose is labored, and Arnold's imagination quite limited. We can speculate that he might have developed a following if, like Burroughs, he had written additional volumes—but only if he had managed to display some of the exuberance that Burroughs used to overcome the crudity of his writing. Although Arnold's single science fiction novel is important because of its influence on Burroughs, it is otherwise more of a curiosity than an entertainment.

"A Gun for Dinosaur"
L. Sprague de Camp
(1956)

While most time travel stories involve scientific research into historical events or an attempt either to change or to preserve the true course of history, a few writers took a more practical approach. How could time travel be made profitable? One of the most popular answers involved big-game hunts in the age of dinosaurs, of which this story was the earliest and still the most effective example.

A prerequisite in stories of time travel is an explanation of the rules of the process—that is, how one avoids or creates paradoxes and other details that might be relevant to the plot. Time can either be elastic, snapping back to the original series of events unless major changes are introduced, or fragile, in which case the death of a single butterfly might wipe out the human race. L. Sprague DE CAMP chose elasticity and eliminated all chances of major paradox by asserting two rules: First, time travel works only when the trip is in excess of 100,000 years, so far into the past that small changes have a chance to even out during the intervening period. Second, once a particular bit of

time has been visited, no one can ever travel to that same span of history again.

The narrator is a professional hunting guide who, along with his partner, is accompanying two very different hunters on an expedition to the Jurassic era. One hunter is brash and impulsive; the other, reticent and lacking in self-confidence. They interact against a backdrop of a scientifically literate and skillfully described prehistoric setting until a crisis arises, in which the less admirable of the two hunters makes a fateful blunder that results in the death of the second man and an ugly confrontation between the survivor and the two guides. The safari is terminated and they return to the present, but the client attempts to go back through time to assassinate them, dying instead when the potential overlap in time results in an instantaneous return to his time of origin. Other time safari stories would follow, written by David Drake, Rob Chilson, and even de Camp himself, but none would ever rival "A Gun for Dinosaur," with its realistically described landscapes and convincing clash of personalities.

"The Gun Without a Bang"
Robert Sheckley
(1958)

Although admiration of technological advance is a prominent theme in science fiction, even its strongest proponents occasionally sound a word of warning. Scientific knowledge is a tool that can be misused, intentionally or by accident, causing even greater problems than it solves. Arthur C. CLARKE's "SUPERIORITY" demonstrated what might happen if a society became too dependent upon sophisticated equipment—but in an abstract fashion. Robert Sheckley provided in this story a more immediate, personal example.

Dixon is a spaceman who walks out unafraid on an alien world, confident because he possesses the ultimate handgun, an experimental weapon designed to make him invulnerable. When he spots wolflike creatures following him his pulse does not increase, because he knows they are no match for his armament. Dixon interprets all relationships in terms of power, and at present he believes there is no power to rival his own. However, he has over-looked a practical consideration—and this over-sight nearly costs him his life. When the pack attacks, he is able to kill every individual that gets close to him, disintegrating them quietly and effi-ciently. But even after a dozen of the creatures have died, they continue to press their attack. Dixon is puzzled, because they seem intelligent enough; but why have they not learned from the fate of their fellows?

The solution of course is that the lesson is too subtle. Without a bang to scare the creatures off, and with the victims eliminated before they have time to cry out, there were no auditory cues to frighten them. Even worse, when Dixon finally makes it back to his landing spot, heavily belea-guered, he fires indiscriminately, eliminating his enemies but disabling his own ship in the process. A rescue team eventually shows up, to find Dixon using the disintegrator as a hammer. With a decep-tively simple story line, Sheckley illustrates a fun-damental truth: Technological advances may suggest solutions to problems, but they are not necessarily the best solutions.

Gunn, James P.
(1923–   )

James Gunn, noted as both writer and historian of science fiction, began publishing his fiction in 1949. A prolific writer at first, he slowed consid-erably after the 1970s. He predominantly was a short story writer, and several of his books labeled as novels are actually assembled from shorter work. His first true novel was an entertaining space opera involving the battle against a repressive empire. *Star Bridge* (1955), a collaboration with Jack WILLIAMSON, has remained popular despite its rel-atively old-fashioned style and plot. Gunn's second novel and first solo effort, *This Fortress World* (1957), reflects a similar theme but is a competent though unexceptional story of rebellion against a repressive government.

Perhaps recognizing that his strength did not lie at longer length, Gunn returned to the short story exclusively during the balance of the 1950s and all through the 1960s. Several of these stories involved incidents aboard a space station orbiting Earth, and these were collected as *Station in Space* (1958). Although they were considered quite spec-ulative at the time, today they appear rather tenta-tive and are hampered by the obsolescence of much of the technological content. His next two books, however, would be much more effective.

The Joy Makers (1961) consists of three novel-ettes that together explore a possible future when people are so obsessed with hedonism that they eventually retreat into virtual reality. The view of the future becomes fiercer and more pessimistic as the series progresses. With this sequence, Gunn anticipated what would later become a major genre theme, particularly among the cyberpunk writers of the 1990s. The final scene, in which the protagonists realize that they will never know with absolute certainty whether they truly have escaped the virtual world, is particularly haunting. A sec-ond sequence was published as *The Immortals* (1962). A small number of individuals discovers that they are a new strain of humanity, one func-tionally immortal. Since the secret of longevity lies in their blood, they are hunted by normals who wish to experiment on them. The book would later be the inspiration for the short-lived television se-ries, *The Immortal*, for which Gunn would also write a tie-in novel.

The Burning (1972) was another assemblage of shorts, this time set in a common, dystopian future in which science has been outlawed and its practi-tioners are hunted down as witches. Although there is an uplifting conclusion, Gunn's low regard for the human capacity to reason is even more pro-nounced this time. Slightly more upbeat was *The Listeners* (1972), another sequence of stories, this time focused on the first communication with an alien intelligence and the acquisition of new knowl-edge that will radically change the nature of human life—and not necessarily for the better. Paradoxi-cally, the human characters have almost as much trouble actually listening to each other as they do to the alien message. *Crisis!* (1986) collects a set of stories about a man from the future who travels to the present to try to change history and avert the disastrous events that created his dystopian world.

Gunn returned to novel-length work with *Kampus* (1977), a satire about campus politics that is set in a future when college radicals virtually rule the world. The satire is bitter and so pervasive that it often reads more like an essay than like fiction. *The Mind Master* (1982, also published as *The Dreamers*) is a far more successful novel, although it essentially is another set of stories with some bridging material. The future is a surrealistic place where drugs provide the means by which one can acquire knowledge, but the chemical form of learning is too easy, and people no longer value the acquisition of new information. The darker side of Gunn's worldview is more obvious than ever before, and the reader is left with little hope for the future of the characters or their world.

Many of Gunn's stories stand alone and do not fall within any of his short series. The best of these are collected in *Some Dreams Are Nightmares* (1974), *The End of the Dreams* (1975), and *Human Voices* (2002). He is also the author of several books about the field, most notably *Alternate Worlds: The Illustrated History of Science Fiction*, and has edited several anthologies.

H

Haiblum, Isidore
(1935–   )

There are a handful of authors who early in their careers produced a book so remarkably distinctive that it overshadows their subsequent work, even if the latter is technically superior. That is certainly the case with Isidore Haiblum, whose *The Tsaddik of the Seven Wonders* (1971) was a blend of zany science fiction and Yiddish humor. The short novel follows the adventures of a wise man who travels into the future; but the plot is almost irrelevant. What made the *Tsaddik* stand out was the odd marriage of ancient knowledge and advanced technology, and the amusing observations made by the protagonist.

Haiblum's subsequent work was split between humorous and serious themes. The Tom Dunjer series is particularly entertaining, the story of a security expert and his robot assistants. The chief characters made their debut in *Interworld* (1977) and pursued their careers in *Outerworld* (1979), *Specterworld* (1991), and *Crystalworld* (1992), solving a series of ever more challenging and bizarre problems involving parallel universes, aliens, and time travel. The series is a wonderful send-up of many genre clichés. The James Morgan duology was slightly more serious in tone, consisting of *The Mutants Are Coming* (1984) and *Out of Sync* (1990), but they demonstrate Haiblum's debt to Raymond Chandler and the tough detective story, which is mildly satirized in much of his work.

Transfer to Yesterday (1973), a stand-alone novel, is one of Haiblum's more ambitious efforts, the story of a marvelous invention. Scientists are able to eavesdrop on the past, but only if the operator is able to form a kind of transcendent psychic link with an ancestor. Unfortunately, members of a fanatical religious cult attempt to hijack the technique to advance their private agenda, resulting in widespread social unrest. *The Wilk Are Among Us* (1975) mixes humor with the problem story. An errant matter transmission drops a human and some disparate aliens on a distant world. One of the aliens closely resembles the indigenous population, and his presence begins to undermine their society. The remaining novels, while not outstanding, are uniformly entertaining.

Haiblum has not produced any new science fiction since the early 1990s. He had established himself as a skilled, sometimes surprising writer, and was one of the few in the field who displayed a genuine gift for humor. Moreover, he never wrote a bad book. His subsequent silence has reduced his visibility, but dedicated readers still search for his famous first novel, and they sometimes proceed from there to his other titles.

Haldeman, Joe
(1943–   )

With a degree in physics and astronomy, Joe Haldeman was well prepared to become a writer of hard science fiction; but almost from the outset it was obvious that his fiction was more about the people who moved through his stories than about the scientific wonders they might observe or create. Haldeman also drew heavily on his experiences in Vietnam, which provided the inspiration for the mainstream novel *War Year* (1972) as well as for much of his science fiction. He sold his first short story in 1969 and began to sell regularly throughout the early 1970s, including a linked sequence that would be assembled in 1974 as *The* FOREVER WAR, which was widely interpreted as a rebuttal to Robert A. HEINLEIN's STARSHIP TROOPERS. The novel won both the Hugo and Nebula Awards, making Halderman an instant star, but it also raised the standard by which his subsequent work would be judged.

Mindbridge (1976) was a somewhat more conventional space adventure. A psychic from Earth encounters an alien race with the ability to alter its shape and which is implacably inimical to humans. The concept of a mass mind into which individual personalities could be submerged would be revisited with even greater disapproval in his later work. The novel, which shares with the writing of John BRUNNER a tendency to borrow from the techniques of John Dos Passos, is an exciting adventure, but it lacked the feel of reality that had made *The Forever War* so effective. *All My Sins Remembered* (1977) is a collection of related stories about a man who serves as a kind of interstellar ombudsman, traveling around the galaxy to ensure that exploitative humans are prevented from taking unfair advantage of alien races. Beneath the superficial, formulaic plot is the true story—the protagonist's search for understanding and his gradual maturation despite constant reconditioning with new personality traits, a prerequisite to completing his assignments anonymously. As he had already raised military SF to a higher level, so now Haldeman attempted to accomplish something new with the planetary romance.

His other novels during the 1970s and early 1980s were largely inconsequential—media tie-ins and a pair of pseudonymous adventures featuring a man genetically altered so that he can live in the ocean. *There Is No Darkness* (1983), written with his brother Jack Haldeman, was an entertaining but uninspired episodic space adventure for young

adults. The string of minor titles ended with *Worlds* (1981), set in a not-too-distant future when a number of artificial habitats orbit the Earth. The protagonist is a woman from one of these minisocieties who visits the home world, introducing the reader to a succession of depressing scenes. Crime is rampant, as is government corruption, and international tensions lead the world to a devastating war that leaves the orbiting habitats as the last refuge for humanity. As is the case in much of Haldeman's fiction, the protagonist is not nearly in control of his or her own destiny. There are always greater powers, governments, secret agencies, aliens, or shadowy but powerful figures whose attempts to manipulate others are not always successful but who remain so effective that it is unlikely that they can be thwarted in any decisive fashion.

Haldeman followed up with two sequels, *Worlds Apart* (1983), and after a considerable lapse, *Worlds Enough and Time* (1992). The survivors of plague- and war-ravaged humanity must work cooperatively if they are to survive. The question facing them all is whether they can and will create a viable shared environment in space, or whether there is some means by which they can reclaim the ruined planet below. There is a more hopeful note in the concluding volume, because even though efforts to migrate to the stars are beset by the usual petty squabbles, personality conflicts, and private prejudices of those involved, a successful effort is finally launched.

Tools of the Trade (1987) had a much narrower scope. A deep-cover spy working for the Communists possesses a device that effectively allows him to control the minds of others. Rather than turn this power over to his superiors, he begins to question where his true loyalties lie. Most of the conflict takes place within the protagonist's mind, but it seems curiously muted, and the story never really engages the reader. *Buying Time* (1989, also published as *The Long Habit of Living*) is similar in construction but far more effective. This time the viewpoint character is a man who has opted out of a program by which the rich can purchase virtual immortality; he discovers that by having done so he has made himself the target of professional killers. Although none of these novels achieved the popularity of *The Forever War*, it was evident that Haldeman's career was back on track and that he remained capable of writing serious, first-rank novels.

It would be a novelette, *The Hemingway Hoax* (expanded into a short novel in 1990), that would win Haldeman his next award, a Nebula. A clever plan to create a bogus Hemingway manuscript gets spectacularly complicated when the mastermind discovers that he is being pursued by a professional killer from an alternate universe. Haldeman returned to the world of *The Forever War* for two belated sequels, *Forever Peace* (1997) and *Forever Free* (1999), following the further adventures of the characters as they discover that humanity as a whole has evolved toward a mass mind. Valuing their own independence, the ex-soldiers leave for the stars and forge their own destinies.

Haldeman's most recent novels have hovered on the brink of being major works. In *The Coming* (2000) a message from space implies that aliens are about to visit Earth. As a major war rages in Europe and the situation deteriorates throughout the world, some begin to wonder if the message is a hoax designed to distract world leaders and force them to an accommodation, but the eventual revelation is even stranger. Haldeman's pessimism about the future of world politics is as strong as ever, but the novel is peculiarly emotionless. Haldeman's most recent effort, *Guardian* (2002), is labeled as science fiction, but is actually a fantasy. A mistreated 19th-century woman flees her abusive husband and meets a supernatural entity that takes her on a grand tour of the universe. The bulk of the book is non-fantastic and brilliantly written, but the final chapters are so different in tone from what has gone before that they seem almost an afterthought.

Haldeman's short fiction, while always worthwhile, has only occasionally been as exceptional as his novels. One standout is "Tricentennial" (1976), which won a Hugo Award. "All the Universe in a Mason Jar" (1977) and "The Mazeltov Revolution" (1974) are also noteworthy. Most of his short stories have been collected in *Infinite Dreams* (1979), *Dealing in Futures* (1985), and *None So Blind* (1996). Although Haldeman's novels have been uneven in quality, he is so good at times that

his readers remain loyal even when he fails to live up to their perhaps unrealistic expectations. In a field where too many writers shy away from complex characterization, he has made it the focus of a large proportion of his work, recognizing that ultimately a story must be about realistically described people and how they feel if it is to make a lasting place in the reader's memory.

Half Past Human
T. J. Bass
(1971)

Thomas J. Bassler, who wrote his fiction as T. J. Bass, made an immediate, pronounced impression on the science fiction community with the shorter version of this novel in 1969. Bass speculated about the possible solutions humanity might develop if overpopulation was to continue its current trend, and he decided that we might well consider altering the human form. In his depressingly drawn future, most humans are now smaller and more socially homogeneous, with less individuality and with other less obvious physical and mental alterations that enable them to live in enormous underground cities, essentially hives. Clearly humanity has begun to evolve into an insectlike species that Bass calls nebbishes. A comparatively small number of normal humans continues to exist on the surface of the planet, but under increasingly desperate circumstances—until a sentient starship conveys many of them to a distant world to start over.

Bass does not offer any hope for the majority, however. The society of the nebbishes is unaffected by the fate of the old-style humans, a monolithic block that seems doomed to exist in its present form forever, although there are brighter signs in the sequel, *The Godwhale* (1974). Bass, who is a doctor, suggests an interesting new mechanism for human interaction, the possibility that people may literally develop low-level allergies to one another after a prolonged period of close proximity. Although some readers were put off by his dark visions, others were impressed by the complexity and originality of his work. Unfortunately, Bass ended his science fiction career in 1974. The fact that he is still so highly regarded after producing only two books suggests that he might have been a substantially more significant writer if he had continued his secondary career.

Hamilton, Edmond
(1904–1977)

Perhaps more than any other author, Edmond Hamilton was the literary forebear of *Star Trek*. Hamilton began writing science fiction during the 1920s, moving quickly to epic space operas similar to those of Edward E. SMITH and John W. CAMPBELL Jr. His early fiction was brash and exciting but not always scientifically accurate; the prose and characterization were so bad that his writing probably could not have been published in any other genre. During the 1940s Hamilton created his only enduring character, based on an idea by Mort Weisinger. Captain Future roamed space accompanied by a robot, a disembodied brain, and an android, defeating one interplanetary menace after another in the best James Kirk fashion. Captain Future became a franchise character, but the majority of the more than two dozen novels featuring him were written by Hamilton under one name or another. Although they are naïve and almost unreadable by today's standards, the concept of the interplanetary patrol flourished and eventually resulted in many imitations and several television series.

Although some of Hamilton's early work was later reprinted, most of it has been forgotten, and usually deservedly so. *The Valley of Creation*, a 1948 magazine serial, would not appear in book form until 1964, even though it is a reasonably good fantastic adventure in the mode of A. Merritt's *The Moon Pool* (1919). A handful of mercenaries are lured to a remote Tibetan valley where they are caught up in a battle between rival forces, each of which includes what appear to be ordinary animals with near-human intelligence. They eventually find the explanation of this oddity: an ancient crashed spaceship whose intelligent occupants transferred their minds into local fauna.

The market was changing dramatically by the late 1940s, and Hamilton was forced to modify his style if he was to continue selling. His work from that point on still embraced lofty concepts, but the scale was reduced, the events more plausible, and he attempted to flesh out his characters. *The Star Kings* (1949, also published as *Beyond the Moon*) was his last and most serious attempt at old-style space opera. There is a much later sequel, *Return to the Stars* (1969).

Hamilton continued to write mostly adventure stories set in space, but his hand was more restrained; and his characters were more likely to save themselves than they were the universe. *The Star of Life* (1959, but expanded from a shorter 1947 version) uses suspended animation to transport a contemporary character to a distant future where a minority of immortals have closed off the stars to the rest of humanity in order to preserve their monopoly on longevity. *City at World's End* (1951) displaces an entire city through time to a devastated future Earth. After surviving the shock of the transition, they meet representatives of an interstellar civilization who offer to relocate them elsewhere; however, they decide instead to attempt to reinvigorate the dying Earth. Despite a somewhat weak ending, this is one of Hamilton's two most evocative novels, the other being *The Haunted Stars* (1960). The discovery of an abandoned base on the Moon leads to an interstellar voyage to the real home planet of humanity, from which the Earth was settled.

During the 1960s Hamilton returned to space opera with some substantial work. *Doomstar* (1966) was reminiscent of an earlier novel, *The Sun Smasher* (1959), in that it involved a plot to coerce entire planetary populations to obedience by threatening to disrupt their suns. The much more skillful execution in this work demonstrates how Hamilton was refining his writing to keep pace with the times. This was followed by his final work, a three-volume set about the adventures of the Star Wolves, a mercenary band that recruits an interplanetary pirate. The sequence opened with *The Weapon from Beyond* (1967), in which an alien artifact is the prize in a power struggle that could decide the fate of an entire world. The mercenaries track down a missing scientist in *The Closed Worlds* (1968), violating an interstellar quarantine and discovering the secret of a new form of space travel in the process. The story ended with *World of the*

Starwolves (1968), in which the mercenaries conduct a raid against a planet that holds another technological secret. The trilogy was later collected in one volume as *Starwolf* (1982).

Although Hamilton's short fiction was rarely memorable, he wrote a few that deserved preservation, of which the most famous is "What's It Like Out There?" Considering his usual difficulties with characterization, it is surprising that he wrote what is still considered one of the most convincing descriptions of life in space. His best short fiction has been collected in *What's It Like Out There? and Other Stories* (1974) and *The Best of Edmond Hamilton* (1977). It is unlikely that Hamilton will be remembered for any single piece of his fiction. His work as a whole, however, influenced the next generation of writers immeasurably, and aspects of his ambitious and exciting space adventures are still detectible in the work of more recent and more talented authors.

Hamilton, Peter
(1960–   )

Peter Hamilton began writing entertaining but unremarkable short stories in the early 1990s, eventually producing the first Greg Mandel novel, *Mindstar Rising* (1993), and later becoming one of the leading writers of traditional space opera. Mandel is a freelance security investigator with a touch of telepathy. He solves a mystery involving an artificial intelligence project in his debut novel, then returns for a more conventional murder mystery, *The Quantum Murder* (1994), and tracks down a missing scientist in *The Nano Flower* (1995). The trilogy was of limited scope but quite well done; surprisingly, it failed to find an American publisher until the appearance of *The Reality Dysfunction* (1996), the first of Hamilton's major space operas. That novel was so long that the paperback edition was split into two volumes, *Emergence* and *Expansion*—a pattern that would be repeated with later books. The alien enemy attacking a disparate group of civilizations including humanity has extraordinary powers that verge on the supernatural, and extraordinary measures are required to defeat them.

The Neutronium Alchemist (1997) was also split into two volumes for its softcover publication, *Consolidation* and *Conflict*. This was Hamilton's second highly inventive space opera. Disembodied intelligences, possibly spirits of the dead, have returned to possess the bodies of the living, setting off a war of nanotechnology and genetic engineering that could result in the destruction of the universe. Hamilton's ambitious, panoramic story of the struggle is so straightforward and confident that the reader is swept away and accepts a string of unlikely events as possibilities. *The Naked God* (1999), which concludes the story, was also disassembled into two separate titles, *Flight* and *Faith*, for paperback publication. *Pandora's Star* (2004) is a similar epic space opera.

Fallen Dragon (2002), Hamilton's next large-scale space adventure, had a somewhat narrower scope. The exploitation of the settled worlds by a group of megacorporations is being enforced by armies of enhanced soldiers to coerce colony worlds into cooperating. The focus is much tighter than in the giant space operas that preceded it, and it is much more evenly written. Also of interest are the short novel *Watching Trees Grow* (2000), about murder among a group of immortals, and the short story collection *A Second Chance at Eden* (1998), which includes all of the author's significant short fiction.

Hand, Elizabeth
(1957–   )

Elizabeth Hand began publishing short stories in the late 1980s, all of which were of consistently high quality, although none were sufficiently remarkable to attract unusual interest. That neglect was remedied by *Winterlong* (1990), an intelligent adventure story set in a postapocalyptic future, and whose atmosphere and prose were unusually rich. The survivors are split between a minority, who retain technological knowledge, and the majority, who live in squalor and expect little more. The contrasts between the two outlooks are sharply drawn. *Aestival Tide* (1992), set in the same future, is the story of a narrowly circumscribed lifestyle in a future domed city. It has a somewhat more traditional plot but is more tightly written, showing that Hand had a formidable talent. *Icarus Descending* (1993), third in the sequence, is a story of rebellion and eventual efforts to deal with an imminent global disaster. Although the tone is decidedly downbeat, these early novels are rich with imaginatively created characters and situations.

Waking the Moon (1995) involves the supernatural, but science fiction readers may enjoy the subplot about the secret history of humankind. *Glimmering* (1997) anticipated events surrounding the end of the 20th century. The speculative content is minimal, but the unusual viewpoints of the principle characters are fascinating. The fact that the millennium did not mirror Hand's extrapolation is irrelevant. Hand's most recent novel, *Mortal Love* (2004), is a historical fantasy. Her small body of high-quality short fiction has been collected in *Last Summer on Mars Hill* (1998) and *Bibliomancy* (2003). Hand's highly literate style and occasional slow pacing sometimes discourage less patient readers, but her work is intricate and adept enough to justify any additional effort required to immerse oneself in her fiction.

Harness, Charles L.
(1915–   )

Patent attorney Charles Harness began his writing career in the late 1940s. Over the course of more than a half-century he alternated extended periods of silence with others in which he has been consistently productive and interesting. His first novel, *Flight into Yesterday* (1953, also published as *The Paradox Men*), was typical for its time. A larger-than-life hero becomes the focal point for a rebellion against a future repressive dictatorship. *The Rose* (1953), a short novel that was largely a metaphor for the conflict between the world of arts and the world of science, was quite advanced for its time and might have introduced him to a wider set of readers, but it failed to find a market in the United States until the late 1960s. No new science fiction appeared for more than 10 years, ending with a flurry of new stories of which "An Ornament to His Profession" (1966) was the most outstanding.

The Ring of Ritornel (1968) was an above-average but straightforward space opera that asked questions about free will and destiny, but Harness seemed to lose interest in writing shortly after its publication. Only one short story would appear during the next decade. This second drought came to an end with *Wolfhead* (1978), in which a woman from the surface world on a future Earth that has reverted to primitivism is kidnapped by underground dwellers and subsequently rescued in an obvious imitation of the story of Orpheus. The conclusion, though not universally bleak, is less than optimistic as the hero falls short of his goals, even though he saves the society he represents. The author's legal background is evident in *The Catalyst* (1980), in which a battle is fought in the courts for control of a new wonder drug that could be the only cure for a deadly new plague. *Firebird* (1981) is another space opera, but a much more inventive one, and painted on a much wider canvas.

The Venetian Court (1982) introduced Quentin Thomas, a lawyer who must defend his client from a charge of copyright infringement, now a capital offense, despite the fact that the presiding judge is mentally unbalanced. The authentic courtroom atmosphere and well-reasoned arguments are engrossing and suspenseful. Thomas returned for *Lunar Justice* (1991), a similarly engaging though somewhat less plausible battle over efforts to transport large numbers of human colonists to the moons of Jupiter.

Redworld (1986) dealt more realistically with issues similar to those in *The Rose*, this time describing the aftermath of a civil war that resulted in a formal separation of powers between the forces of science and those of religion. This book was somewhat more pedestrian than his previous work, but it was followed by *Lurid Dreams* (1990), probably the best of his later novels. A student who is able to communicate with other times communicates with Edgar Allan Poe and discovers that powers within the Confederacy have learned of his existence and are planning to use that knowledge to alter the outcome of the war. *Krono* (1988) also involved time travel, in this case employed to relocate the excess population back into prehistory; but despite a plot involving saboteurs, the action is surprisingly lackluster.

A recent omnibus, *Rings* (1999), contains a previously unpublished novel, *Drunkard's Endgame,* an uneven but often interesting story of a society of robots aboard a starship. Harness's short fiction has been collected as *An Ornament to His Profession* (1998).

Harrison, Harry
(1925–   )

Although Harry Harrison's first story appeared in 1951, it would not be until 1957 that his career really started. *The Stainless Steel Rat* (1957/61), was the first in what would eventually be a series of novels about Slippery Jim DiGriz, a likeable interplanetary con man and thief who would undergo a series of role changes during the course of his adventures. Harrison was soon respected as a prolific writer of above average adventure stories, often displaying a welcome willingness to make fun of genre conventions as well as a wide range of human foibles.

Deathworld (1960) was the first adventure of Jason dinAlt, who takes refuge on a newly colonized planet only to discover that the entire local ecology, plants and animals alike, has suddenly become violently hostile to the human intruders. His enemies locate and capture him in *Deathworld II* (1964). He flees to another planet, this one inhabited by an intelligent indigenous race, in *Deathworld III* (1968). A similar series began with *Planet of the Damned* (1962). Brion Brandd is sent to a colony world that is on the brink of an interplanetary war. The local government is executing any off-worlder who arrives against its wishes. After managing a secret landing, Brandd discovers that the harsh conditions of the planet have altered the human colonists to the point where they have become another species. Brandd makes another—though less exciting—appearance in *Planet of No Return* (1981).

Harrison's short stories, although rarely conceived in a series, were often variations on a general theme. Several of his robot stories are collected in *War with the Robots* (1962), for example. The stories in *One Step from Earth* (1970) examine the consequences of matter transmission,

the ability to project an item across a distance without its passing through the intervening space. Among Harrison's best short stories from the 1950s and 1960s are "I See You," "Trainee for Mars," and "The Robot Who Wanted to Know." *Two Tales and Eight Tomorrows* (1965) and *Prime Number* (1970) contain most of his remaining stories from this period.

Harrison's other novels from the 1960s generally were competent but predictable adventures involving new plagues or time travel, but occasional titles were fresh and original. *Captive Universe* (1969), for example, is a generation starship story—but with a remarkable difference. The mission planners on Earth created an artificial society that seemed likely to withstand the pressures of the voyage, patterned after that of the Aztecs. Predictably, their planning does not anticipate what actually happens. *Bill, the Galactic Hero* (1965) is still the most brilliant spoof of military science fiction every written. Several sequels appeared years later; but these mostly collaborative efforts are less-focused farces of little lasting interest.

Most important of all was *Make Room! Make Room!* (1966), which eventually was adapted as the uneven film *Soylent Green* (1973). It is still one of the most chilling novels about overpopulation ever written. The protagonist, a detective assigned to investigate a series of disappearances, eventually discovers that certain elements in society have, in the tradition of Jonathan Swift, been converted into food by unscrupulous business interests, apparently with the consent of the government. Although Harrison would produce more technically proficient novels in the future, none of his other work has had as powerful an impact on the reader.

The Daleth Effect (1970) was not one of his stronger novels, but it underlined his growing suspicion of the intentions of governments. A scientist stumbles upon a way to achieve inexpensive space travel and flees to Denmark to avoid losing control of his discovery; but when he eventually reveals the secret in order to rescue some stranded astronauts, he sets off an international power struggle. *A Transatlantic Tunnel, Hurrah!* (1972) is set in an alternate world in which Great Britain still rules the American colonies. A descendant of George Washington is in charge of a project to build a tunnel under the ocean, which will strengthen the ties between the two regions.

Jim DiGriz was rehabilitated and appeared repeatedly during the 1970s, but Harrison's work seemed more tentative during most of this period. His most ambitious project was the Homeworld trilogy—*Homeworld* (1980), *Wheelworld* (1981), and *Starworld* (1981)—an entertaining but lightweight space opera series in which various human colony worlds rebel against the oppressive rule imposed by Earth. *A Rebel in Time* (1983) was Harrison's change war novel. A rebel patriot with a time machine plans to change the course of history and help the Confederacy triumph in the Civil War. His opposition is a black Union soldier who prefers the original time line. Although the story is relatively slight, the characters are among Harrison's best.

As far as Harrison's career is concerned, the late 1980s are almost paradoxical. He wrote further, lighter-weight adventures of Slippery Jim DiGriz and embarked on a series of fluffy collaborative sequels to *Bill, the Galactic Hero*. At the same time, he produced his most impressive sequence of books, *West of Eden* (1984), *Winter in Eden* (1986), and *Return to Eden* (1988). The premise of the series is that some species of dinosaurs survived, became intelligent, developed a technology based on biology, and eventually dominated the Earth. Humans are considered either servants or a source of food, but the advent of a new ice age gives humanity the means by which to assert itself and perhaps even claim a homeland. These novels are much more complex than most of Harrison's other work, and his imagined saurian society is well thought-out and credible.

The Turing Option (1992), written with Marvin Minsky, has a contemporary setting and perhaps a too familiar techno-thriller plot, but also includes some fascinating speculation about the nature of the interface between humans and machines. More recently Harrison returned to the device of alternate history in *Stars and Stripes Forever* (1998) and its sequels, *Stars and Stripes in Peril* (2000) and *Stars and Stripes Triumphant* (2002). The English decide to intervene in the American Civil War on the side of the South but bungle the effort, attacking the wrong side; this leads to an alliance between the two American nations against Great Britain. The violence escalates and, when a British army is poised to invade from Mexico, the Americans conceive a daring plan to land troops in the British Isles with the help of disaffected Irish and others. Some of the plot elements in the trilogy require a more generous suspension of disbelief than usual, but Harrison keeps things moving so fast that most readers are not bothered by the weak spots in the political scheme of things.

Harrison has also edited numerous anthologies (including a short-lived Best of the Year series with Brian W. ALDISS), has written criticism about the field, and has been closely associated at times with both the more conservative John W. CAMPBELL Jr. and the leading figures of the British New Wave movement, although his own prose rarely strayed from the mainstream. Through the course of his career he has produced occasional deeply satiric parodies of science fiction conventions—even those to which he adheres in his own writing. Although he has written comparatively few short stories since the mid-1970s, his work at that length remains popular. His stories have been collected in *Galactic Dreams* (1994) and *Fifty in Fifty* (2001), the latter a comprehensive retrospective look at his career to date. Harrison has been a reliable and entertaining writer from the outset. Unlike many others whose careers span more than five decades, he has continued to develop as a writer and explore new territory.

Hawk Among the Sparrows
Dean McLaughlin
(1968)

In the view of most genre writers, superiority in technology usually provides a dramatic advantage to those who possess it, particularly in combat situations. Military science fiction tells us time and again that the side with the most advanced weaponry and most sophisticated equipment has an edge that can be overcome only by extraordinary efforts the opposition, or by the development of an even more effective counterweapon. Arthur C. CLARKE's "SUPERIORITY" warned us against becoming reliant on progress for its own sake; but in this example the technologies employed had never been tested in advance.

Dean McLaughlin's only major piece of short fiction proves the same point on a much smaller and more convincing level. A highly advanced fighter-bomber carrying nuclear weapons becomes displaced in time and rematerializes during World War I. Once the crew has adjusted to this bizarre phenomenon, they believe they are in a unique position to change history. Against comparatively primitive biplanes and ineffective anti-aircraft guns, they are virtually invulnerable; their own weapons are more powerful than anything imagined by the other combatants. So they decide to intervene in the war and change the course of history.

Fortunately for the flow of history, they discover that their options are so limited that they are virtually powerless. Aerial combat is impossible because they literally cannot slow down to the speed of the enemy planes without falling from the sky. Their weapons are designed to sense much larger aircraft, and their tactical training is completely inappropriate. Then they encounter problems of resupply: Their ammunition is limited, and there are no stores for them to draw on; nor does the technology exist by which suitable new ammunition can be manufactured. Even more critical is the question of fuel, which their aircraft requires in large quantities, and refined to a degree not possible during this period in history. They have functioning nuclear weapons, but no target concentrated enough to make their use worthwhile.

Many science fiction stories warn us about letting our technology get out of control, but few have done a good job urging us simply to regard our tools in their proper perspective. McLaughlin found a way to make that point in a very convincing fable.

Heechee series
Frederik Pohl

In the early days of science fiction, it was considered plausible that a government or even an individual entrepreneur could develop a working star drive within a matter of a few years. An awareness of the complexities of space travel and an increasingly sophisticated community of readers and writers has since led to the abandonment of that conceit. Faster-than-light travel is usually characterized as either a product of the distant future, or the gift—intended or otherwise—of an alien race. Frederik POHL's Heechee series used this latter approach, which allowed him to place almost contemporary characters in extraordinary situations.

The series started with *Gateway* (1977), which won both the Hugo and Nebula Awards. The Heechee were an alien race who had mastered interstellar travel but who abandoned their network of bases and ships to go into hiding when an aggressive, newly discovered race threatened them. Humans stumble upon some of their technology and make imperfect use of it. Volunteers board the Heechee ships in order to travel to distant worlds apparently selected at random; sometimes they find great treasure troves, sometimes their travels have fatal consequences. Pohl first returned to the same setting in *Beyond the Blue Event Horizon* (1980), which expands upon the original idea; he then introduced us to more secrets about the missing aliens when an expedition is launched to find them and discover more about the enemy from whom they are fleeing in *Heechee Rendezvous* (1984).

The story cycle comes to a conclusion in *The Annals of the Heechee* (1987), in which humans and Heechee find themselves allied against a race of belligerent and dangerous aliens. A human being whose personality has been transferred to virtual reality proves to be the key to defeating them. The four-novel cycle was of unusually consistent quality, and the elaborate nature of Pohl's imagined future was so extensive that he also wrote a number of short stories set against the same background. These stories were later collected as *The Gateway Trip* (1990). Although some of Pohl's individual novels have been equally impressive, the Heechee series was a sustained effort that demonstrated the author's ability to turn what is basically a space adventure into a serious work of fiction.

Heinlein, Robert A.
(1907–1988)

Robert Heinlein's reputation may have faded slightly in recent years, but his influence on the genre, subtle and otherwise, should not be underestimated. Almost from the beginning of his career in 1939 until the late 1960s he was acknowledged as the most important—if not the most skillful—writer in the genre, and his subsequent work, although generally considered inferior, was and remains controversial and occasionally thought-provoking. During the early 1940s he would turn out some of his most memorable short stories and novels, the latter of which would not appear in book form until several years later. His almost casual attitude toward futuristic settings and marvelous inventions was in contrast to the fixation on them common to most science fiction of that time, and even though Heinlein's characters often seem shallow to us by contemporary standards, they were extraordinarily well-drawn in the context within which they were published.

Many of the stories, along with the novel *Methuselah's Children*, serialized in 1941, were assembled into the Future History, a comprehensive and organized scheme of work that was designed to portray a period in human history, sometimes but not always using common characters. Future histories would subsequently be employed by many other writers, sometimes laid out in even greater detail. Heinlein's series, which was collected initially in *The Man Who Sold the Moon* (1950), *The Green Hills of Earth* (1951), and *Revolt in 2100* (1953), plus *Methuselah's Children* (1958) and *Orphans of the Sky* (1963), follows the future of the human race from the development of the first stages of space travel through our early journeys to the stars. Although some of the later novels would allude to the Future History, it was effectively complete by the 1950s. Heinlein's libertarian instincts were revealed in stories like "If This Goes On," but they were conveyed by means of an effective narration rather than the often stilted lectures of his later novels.

Many of Heinlein's early stories have become benchmarks against which other writers attempting similar themes are inevitably measured. "BY HIS BOOTSTRAPS" was considered the most complex time travel paradox story for many years, supplanted only when Heinlein himself wrote "ALL YOU ZOMBIES." "And He Built a Crooked House" is the ultimate story of multiple dimensions. WALDO, the story of a deformed man who lives in orbit and uses delicate controls to manipulate artificial limbs, contributed the name of its character to general usage; these remote devices are now universally known as waldoes. The technological predictions in the Future History series, as in "The Roads Must Roll," may now seem absurd; but the stories about them are still impressive representations of how change is initiated and how we react to it. The blind poet of the spaceways, Rhysling, from "The Green Hills of Earth," lent his name to the annual award for best science fiction–related poetry. *Beyond This Horizon*, serialized in 1942, was one of the first novels to suggest that a truly utopian society might be essentially boring. A handful of malcontents decide to shake things up.

Heinlein's first young adult novel, *Rocketship Galileo* (1947), the basis for the film *Destination Moon* (1950), was probably his least memorable, but it was still a major event both for his career and for the field as a whole. Heinlein refrained from "writing down" to his audience, and his subsequent novels for this age group would be much more successful works and would reshape juvenile science fiction for decades to come. *Red Planet* (1949) followed the exploits of teenagers on Mars; *Farmer in the Sky* (1950) was set on Ganymede; *Between Planets* (1951) involved a war for independence by the colonists on Venus. Heinlein usually paired his human characters with a likeable, slightly comic alien. He continued to write for this market until the end of the 1950s, producing several of his most popular works, among them *The Rolling Stones* (1952), *Starman Jones* (1953), *The Star Beast* (1954), *Tunnel in the Sky* (1955), *Time for the Stars* (1956), *Citizen of the Galaxy* (1957), and *Have Spacesuit Will Travel* (1958). *Tunnel in the Sky* was the genre equivalent of *Lord of the Flies* (1954) by William Golding, in that a group of teenagers are accidentally isolated on an alien world without any adults and must survive and create a miniature society until they are rescued. *Time for the Stars* is notable for the introduction of telepathically linked twins—one on Earth, one traveling on a starship. *Citizen of the Galaxy* blurred the distinction between adult and young adult markets, and Heinlein's final two books with young protagonists,

STARSHIP TROOPERS (1959) and *Podkayne of Mars* (1963), would be issued as adult novels.

Heinlein did not completely abandon the adult market during the 1950s. *The Puppet Masters* (1951), twice filmed, was a variation of Jack FINNEY's *The BODY SNATCHERS.* Parasitic aliens attach themselves to human bodies and control their human hosts. Neither film dealt with the implications with the depth of the original. *The Door into Summer* (1956) and *Double Star* (1957) are among Heinlein's best work. The first is a sometimes sentimental story of a man tricked into accepting suspended animation, awakening in a future when it has become possible to manipulate time; thus he is able to strike back at his long-dead companions. In *Double Star,* which won a Hugo Award, an out-of-work actor is forced to impersonate a politician on Mars; he eventually grows into the role and replaces the politician permanently.

Starship Troopers was intended to be a young adult novel, but the publisher reportedly objected to the high level of violence. The story involves a young human male who undergoes training and subsequent combat service in an interstellar war against a race of intelligent insects. The novel has been a focus for controversy ever since because of the society Heinlein created, and apparently approved of, in which only veterans were allowed to vote. Despite some effective action scenes, the book essentially is a utopian novel in which the author has stacked things to make his society work, ignoring the fact that this would require a basic change in human nature. It won a Hugo Award, as did STRANGER IN A STRANGE LAND (1961), the first Heinlein novel to generate a substantial audience outside the science fiction community. Valentine Michael Smith is a human boy raised by Martians whose return to Earth leads to his transformation into a messianic figure.

Heinlein had ceased to write short fiction by the mid-1960s, and his novels became increasingly idiosyncratic and controversial because of their political content. His libertarianism was sometimes interpreted as fascism, a mistake somewhat encouraged by sloppy plotting. The one major exception was *The MOON IS A HARSH MISTRESS* (1966), another Hugo Award–winner. The novel deals with efforts by colonists on the moon to wrest their independence from a domineering Earth, accomplished with the invaluable aid of an endearing artificial intelligence. Time had caught up to Heinlein, however, and what had once seemed to be cutting edge characterization now seemed clunky and stereotyped in comparison to the work of his peers.

Some of Heinlein's later novels have their adherents, particularly *Time Enough for Love* (1973) and *The Cat Who Walks Through Walls* (1983), but often it is because of the libertarian content that novels like *Friday* (1982) and *I Will Fear No Evil* (1970) continue to find readers. His short fiction has been collected and cross-collected numerous times; collection titles include *The Past Through Tomorrow* (1967), an omnibus of the Future History series, *Expanded Universe* (1980), and *Requiem* (1992). Heinlein's influence on the field may not always be obvious, but his presence hovers at the shoulder of everyone who has followed.

"Helen O'Loy"
Lester Del Rey
(1938)

Contrary to popular opinion, the robot was rarely a menacing figure in literary science fiction, even in the genre's earliest, most melodramatic period. Robots were usually treated as tools or marvelous inventions, devices designed to perform tedious labor that might otherwise have to be performed by humans. Even in Jack WILLIAMSON's 1949 cautionary novel *The HUMANOIDS,* in which robots enforced a restrictive dictatorship over humanity, they did so in an effort to protect us from ourselves, not because they were inherently monstrous.

Isaac ASIMOV had yet to codify his Three Laws of Robotics in 1938 (see I, ROBOT) when Lester Del Rey wrote "Helen O'Loy." Two friends—a robot repairman and an endocrinologist—become fascinated with the possibility of creating the mechanical equivalent of hormones and adding an emotional dimension to mechanical creatures. Existing robots function poorly when faced with unusual circumstances, and artificial emotions might provide the key to stimulating more flexibility. To this end, they purchase a high-level robot who is physically indistinguishable from a human being, Helen O'Loy, whose name they alter slightly to Helen of Alloy. On the eve of their first test one of the friends is called away for three weeks; when he returns, he discovers that their experiment has had unintended consequences: In a gentle riff on the Frankenstein story, they have created a woman who promptly falls in love with one of her creators.

Dave, the object of her affection, is distraught. Phil, his partner, suggests disabling Helen and altering her circuits; but Dave rejects this as well, arguing that it would be tantamount to murder. The situation continues to worsen until Dave accepts that the emotion is reciprocal, and even though a physical relationship is impossible, he marries Helen, concealing her true nature from their friends. Years pass and Dave eventually dies, after which Helen, who has not aged, destroys herself. Del Rey was clearly saying that what makes us human is our emotions and not just our intelligence. This quiet, sentimental story was quite unusual for its time; it remains effective and is still highly regarded.

Herbert, Brian
(1947–   )

Brian Herbert, the son of Frank HERBERT, the author of the DUNE SERIES, started his own career in science fiction with *Sidney's Comet* (1983), a farcical adventure in which the accumulation of space trash from several generations of unthinking humans coalesces into a gigantic comet that threatens the Earth. Although genuinely amusing for much of its length, the novel continues after its welcome has been worn out, repeating itself in the waning chapters. The sequel, *The Garbage Chronicles* (1985), does not bring anything new to the story. *Sudanna, Sudanna* (1985) displayed a gentler satiric touch and attracted some critical attention. A planetary dictator imposes a ban on all forms of music, and resentment among her people gradually ripens to open revolt in a story more thoughtful and less melodramatic than its plot suggests.

Man of Two Worlds (1986), which Herbert wrote in collaboration with his father, is an uneven account of a human and alien sharing the same body. Curious aliens kidnap the entire city of San Francisco in *Prisoners of Arionn* (1987), but discover they have grabbed a tiger by the tale when their prisoners prove less than pliable in what is the best of Herbert's solo novels. Although *The Race for God* (1990) was his most ambitious effort, describing the results when an alien intelligence declares itself God, the story runs out of ideas very early on. *Memorymakers* (1991), written with Marie Landis, was an entertaining but unmemorable tale of the aliens secretly living among us. From that point forward, with the exception of a handful of short stories, Herbert's fiction has all been collaborative.

All of his science fiction novels since 1991 have been add-ons to the world his father created in the Dune series, and each has been in collaboration with Kevin J. ANDERSON. They are traditional space operas, perhaps told on a grander scale, and are significantly better than any of his previous individual work. How much of this is the influence of Anderson and how much Herbert's own maturity as a writer remains to be seen, and will probably not be evident until and unless he returns to work of his own creation.

Herbert, Frank
(1920–1986)

Frank Herbert's DUNE SERIES, which appeared between 1965 and 1985, was such a major event in science fiction that it overshadowed everything else that Herbert wrote. Other science fiction writers have had a single series dominate their career, as was the case with Anne McCAFFREY's PERN SERIES, Marion Zimmer BRADLEY's DARKOVER SERIES, and Roger ZELAZNY's Amber series. But none of these were as overwhelming as the Dune novels, which continued even after Herbert's death as collaborative efforts between his son Brian HERBERT and Kevin J. ANDERSON. Frank Herbert wrote novels outside the Dune universe throughout his career—some of them quite good—but he was never able to escape the shadow of his greatest creation.

He started writing short stories in the early 1950s; but only a few, such as "Try to Remember,"

"The Priests of Psi," and "Greenslaves," were particularly interesting. His first novel was *The Dragon in the Sea* (1956, also published as *Under Pressure* and as *21st-Century Sub*). The novel is rather a curiosity now, but at the time it was highly praised because of the complex and insightful handling of psychological pressures in an artificial environment. It involved life aboard a submarine during the next world war as the crew undertakes a dangerous mission to secure resources in a disputed area. The book feels more like a World War II adventure story than science fiction.

Destination Void (1966) is an entertaining puzzle story. Artificial intelligences are used to guide ships across interstellar distances, but trouble arises when one of these artifices becomes deranged, believing itself to be a god. Herbert made good if undistinguished use of the device. *The Green Brain* (1966) was much more inventive, and reflected Herbert's evident interest in environmental issues. An explosion of the insect population in South America leads to the employment of ever more powerful countermeasures, which in turn triggers an evolutionary change in insects. They develop a group intelligence and even manage to masquerade as humans for brief periods. Genetic engineering and the potential for harm that attends it provided the central theme for *The Eyes of Heisenberg* (1966); somewhat similar thematically is *The Heaven Makers* (1968), in which the discovery of virtual immortality leads to an increasing rate of mental instability. Herbert clearly was preoccupied with the realization of the human potential, but he considered it a path strewn with dangerous consequences, to either the external world or the internal psyche.

The evolution of humanity turns in another direction in *The Santaroga Barrier* (1968). An entire town has been dosed with a new drug that promotes a shared form of awareness, but the protagonist suspects that the new group personality is not entirely sane. Herbert's next two novels were routine space operas, but *Hellstrom's Hive* (1973) is one of his most impressive works. In an echo of the earlier *The Green Brain* the novel involves a scientific project designed to promote group intelligence among insects, but the knowledge derived from the project has been applied to humans in a secret underground complex, where individuality has been suborned to specialized role playing and an ostensibly utopian society conceals what is essentially a horrifying form of mind control. Herbert's last solo novel of note was *The White Plague* (1982), in which an insane scientist bioengineers a plague that is fatal to women, unleashing it in an effort to wipe out the human race.

In collaboration with Bill Ransom, Herbert wrote a series of three novels consisting of *The Jesus Incident* (1979), *The Lazarus Effect* (1983), and *The Ascension Factor* (1988). The trilogy covers the history of efforts to colonize a mostly water-covered world. The opening volume reprises a theme from *Destination Void*, with the artificial intelligence that operates the vessel convinced that it is a deity. In later volumes, the human colonists diverge into what are effectively two distinct species, then unite under pressure from aliens, eventually coming to an understanding with them. There is some interesting speculation and the usual concern with the interaction of humans and their environment, but there is little continuity from book to book, and it is often difficult to relate to the characters.

Most of Herbert's short fiction has been collected in *The World of Frank Herbert* (1970), *The Book of Frank Herbert* (1976), and *Eye* (1985), but he was never as effective a writer in the shorter form. It is for the Dune series that Herbert will be remembered, but perhaps future generations of readers will continue to read the best of his other work as well.

Hersey, John
(1914–1993)

The popular author of several highly regarded mainstream novels, John Hersey is probably best known for his lucid and chilling *Hiroshima* (1946), which described in vivid detail the aftermath of the use of atomic bombs in Japan. Hersey was one of several mainstream authors who recognized the utility of science fiction as a satiric or cautionary device, and his first venture into the genre was an understated but very effective dystopian satire, *The Child Buyer* (1960). The novel deals with exploitation, specifically of children in this case, although the lesson clearly has a more universal application. Masquerading as protectors of gifted children, corporations engage in legal maneuvers to literally reduce them to slavery.

Hersey's second speculative novel was *White Lotus* (1965), a lengthy book set in an America that has been conquered by the Chinese, who have imposed slavery on their subject people. Many Americans are physically transported to China in what we eventually learn is not really our world, since the details of both cultures are slightly different. A subsequent generation of white slaves, as exemplified by the child White Lotus, engage in peaceful resistance efforts in an attempt to regain their freedom. Neither of these novels were packaged as science fiction, and they attracted little attention inside the genre—although that situation changed somewhat following the appearance of Hersey's third and final science fiction novel.

My *Petition for More Space* (1974) dealt with overpopulation in much the same fashion as J. G. BALLARD's "BILLENIUM." By law and necessity, citizens are limited to a very tiny amount of personal space. The protagonist decides to challenge the system by asking for a variance that would allow him one additional foot. For the first time, Hersey attracted some interest in the science fiction community, and his previous genre work received some retrospective attention.

The High Crusade
Poul Anderson
(1964)

An attitude common among science fiction writers is the portrayal of the human race as the smartest, most adaptable, toughest species of intelligent life in the universe. This was particularly prevalent in the stories that appeared in *Astounding Science Fiction* (later *Analog*) during the years when John W. CAMPBELL Jr. was editor; in fact, Campbell reportedly refused to buy any fiction in which aliens were presumed to be in any way superior to humans. Such a narrow-minded viewpoint inevitably closed that market to any number of excellent stories, and as the years passed the magazine's contents grew

increasingly homogeneous, formulaic, and ultimately forgettable.

There were exceptions to the rule, of course; one of the most successful of these was *The High Crusade*, serialized in 1960. Arthur C. CLARKE and others had already warned us that there could be situations in which a highly sophisticated technology could turn out to be a disadvantage rather than an advantage. Poul Anderson would expand upon that theme here in much greater detail. The Wersgorix are an alien race that has long traveled among the stars. They have weapons powerful enough to destroy entire planets, and it has been so long since they have been seriously challenged that they no longer maintain the skills necessary for combat as individuals.

The Wesgorix send a ship to Earth in the middle of the 14th century, expecting no serious opposition. But when they land in England they are immediately assaulted by a Sir Roger and his band of Crusader knights, who seize the ship and its crew. Lacking the knowledge needed to operate the ship themselves, the humans coerce their prisoners into taking them to the Holy Land but instead are treacherously launched into space, eventually challenging the might of the alien empire. Their captives are reasonably accommodating, convinced that it can only be a matter of time before the impudent barbarians are overwhelmed by their much more advanced civilization, but Sir Roger and his friends—as well as the readers—know that ingenuity and the human spirit will triumph over all adversity in the end. The novel's undeniable charm outweighs the frequent implausibilities.

Hogan, James P.
(1941–   )

James Hogan's first novel, *Inherit the Stars* (1977), was a blend of hard science and vaulting imagination. Explorers on the Moon discover the remains of an oversized but indisputably humanoid creature. From that start, they eventually unravel the secret of humanity's origins: Our forebears were natives of the now exploded fifth planet of the solar system. An ancient, derelict ship is found near Jupiter in the sequel, *The Gentle Giants of*

Ganymede (1978), conveniently in time to be helpful during the first contact with visitors from the stars. Hogan left many questions unanswered until *Giants' Star* (1981), which tied up most of the loose ends. He would revisit the sequence peripherally in *Entoverse* (1991).

Scientists and inventors frequently play the central roles in Hogan's novels, as is the case in *The Genesis Machine* (1978), a marvelous invention story in which a team develops a new technology so radical that the government wants to suppress it and sequester its inventors. Their plans go awry when the scientists decide to use their discovery to ensure their continued freedom. *The Two Faces of Tomorrow* (1979) is a Frankenstein story; the government is preparing to cede much of its authority to an artificial intelligence, but there are lingering concerns over the wisdom of this course of action. To test the loyalty of the system, a mock attack is launched—but the consequences are completely unexpected. Hogan's message was clearly that technology was a good thing, but only so long as it remained a tool for human use and not the master.

Hogan tackled the paradoxes of time travel in *Thrice Upon a Time* (1980). Information can be sent into the past, but not physical objects. When an unforeseen technological disaster threatens the world, a scientist has to decide whether to risk sending back a warning, which might avert the catastrophe but might also eliminate him from the time stream. *Code of the Lifemaker* (1983) started a new sequence similar to the Giants novels. A derelict spaceship drifts into the inner solar system and a team of specialists is secretly recruited to decipher its mysteries. The sequel, *The Immortality Option* (1995), extends the story of a race of intelligent robots who have built their own civilization on one of Jupiter's moons.

The Proteus Operation (1985) is an above-average change war novel. A mysterious organization has reshaped history so that Hitler can conquer most of the world, and a beleaguered future American government must send its own team of agents into the past to try to restore history. There is a tendency in the novel to oversimplify the distinction between good and evil, a failing even more evident in *Endgame Enigma*

(1987), which mixes very convincing passages about life aboard a space station with rather flat and myopic international politics. Indeed, the political content rendered his next novel, *The Mirror Maze* (1989), almost unreadable.

Hogan's growing libertarian viewpoint was again evident in *The Multiplex Man* (1992), but was less intrusive. Fortress America has undergone a renaissance but is threatened by an international plot. *Out of Time* (1993) is one of Hogan's more original works, following the exploits of a police detective as he performs his duties in a future New York City where time flows at different rates in different neighborhoods. Hogan tackled virtual reality in *Realtime Interrupt* (1995), another of the many stories that anticipated the premise of the Matrix films—that the viewpoint character might not be aware that he was living in an artificial environment.

Two recent novels, both of which feature young adult protagonists, are among Hogan's best work, although neither is particularly groundbreaking. *Bug Park* (1997) is a marvelous invention story in which two teenaged geniuses create a device that allows them to project their viewpoint down into the world of insects. Despite a melodramatic plot about villains who want to steal the technology as a weapon, the story has undeniable charm. *Outward Bound* (1999) is a coming-of-age story in which a juvenile delinquent redeems himself in the space program.

Some of Hogan's more recent novels have been less than impressive; but *Cradle of Saturn* (1999) and its sequel, *The Anguished Dawn* (2003), are thoughtful, exciting, and occasionally surprising disaster novels. *The Legend That Was Earth* (2000) is frequently lethargic, but the interactions between the humans and aliens are deftly handled and generally overcome the ponderous plot. Hogan seems to be an author who is not completely in control of his craft. Some of his novels seem to evolve smoothly and efficiently, while others move in fits and starts as he occasionally pauses for lectures on scientific or political principles. It seems likely that Hogan has the potential to be an even better writer than he has been in the past, but it is less certain that this potential will be realized.

Home Is the Hangman
Roger Zelazny
(1975)

The protagonist of this novella has managed to remove himself from most of the computerized records of his world, similar to the hero of the Repairman Jack novels by F. Paul Wilson and to John BRUNNER's *Shockwave Rider* (1975). Along with the freedom to act outside the scrutiny of the system come the usual difficulties in making a living, but our many-named hero in this case operates as a private detective who specializes in unusual cases.

The Hangman is an experimental device, a robot equipped with a form of artificial intelligence based on the personalities of four human beings. The Hangman's purpose was to explore the outer reaches of the solar system, but it began to malfunction partway through its mission and has been presumed lost. When its ship crashes into the Gulf of Mexico, a search reveals no trace of the Hangman; but one of the four human originals dies violently within days, and one of the remaining survivors is convinced that the robot has returned to avenge itself on its creators. The other two are less certain, one having undergone a religious experience that resigns him to his fate, the other a psychologist who believes—or at least claims to believe—that it would be impossible for the Hangman to behave in that fashion.

In due course two of the others are murdered. The final confrontation is set at the home of the lone survivor. Zelazny has a trick up his sleeve, however. When the Hangman overcomes the defenses and captures the narrator, we learn that it was not responsible for the previous deaths, and that the foursome were secretly concealing their shared guilt over an accidental death that occurred during an unauthorized test of the Hangman, an act that altered the underlying programming in the artificial intelligence, nudging it away from the preprogrammed purposes for which it was intended.

The result is a reversal of what appeared to be a Frankenstein story. Frankenstein's monster was an unintended evil born out of innocent—if rather naïve—circumstances. The Hangman has become a new form of intelligence with noble—if sometimes oblique—needs and goals of its own, born out of a tragic act of carelessness and pride.

"Home There's No Returning"
Henry Kuttner and C. L. Moore
(1955)

Although Catherine Moore's name rarely appeared linked to her husband's fiction, it is known now that she was the coauthor and sometimes even the principle author of many of the stories published by Kuttner alone. This is one of the few that was an acknowledged collaboration right from the outset, and it is still one of the most memorable stories by two of the most talented writers the field has ever known.

The world is involved in a global war—one so immensely complex that computers are required to keep track of things and predict future developments. Unfortunately, computers cannot draw the right conclusions from erroneous or incomplete data, so it still falls on the shoulders of fallible humans to make decisions. Or at least that is the case until the development of Ego, the Electronic Guidance Operator, a robotic computer that can mimic human thought processes. When an exhausted commanding general orders Ego activated, the scientist in charge hesitates, pointing out that in order for Ego to work, it must have free will, and if it has free will, by definition they will not be able to control what it does. But only by making decisions in the absence of certainty can the war be further prosecuted.

To their surprise Ego seems to malfunction immediately upon activation, rampaging through the complex in stereotypical monstrous fashion. Successive efforts to incapacitate the robot without destroying it fail, until the general finally realizes the truth. The imperative to win the war and the lack of complete data are, for the robot, two mutually exclusive situations. Faced with the possibility of choosing a course of action that might result in defeat, its internal logic circuits force it to constantly defer decisions in favor of further input, and there can never be enough input to resolve the paradox. Many similar stories warned readers that too great a reliance on machines could lead to a loss of freedom for humanity, but Kuttner and Moore sound a more hopeful note. Their contention is that flesh and blood are, ultimately, more powerful than steel because we are more able to function in the face of a dilemma.

The House on the Borderland
William Hope Hodgson
(1908)

After a youth during which he ran away to serve at sea, William Hope Hodgson became an author and poet, creating a small but enduring body of novels and short fiction, much of which involved the supernatural. Some of his novels were harder to define, particularly since science fiction had not yet evolved as a separate genre with distinct rules. *The Boats of the Glen Carrig* (1907), for example, has been claimed as horror, fantasy, and as science fiction because the creatures on its mysterious unknown island could be interpreted as magical or simply mutations. His most ambitious work, *The Night Land* (1912), is set in a dying future Earth, wherein the last remnants of humanity stave off creatures both natural and supernatural.

His most popular and accessible work, however, is *The House on the Borderland.* In form it is largely epistolary, presented as a journal found in the ruins of a sprawling building in a remote part of Ireland in 1877. The narrator-protagonist lives alone in a structure that somehow exists in two different realities—our own and another—and thereby provides a doorway to other existences. A series of bizarre and sometimes terrifying manifestations alerts him to the uncanny nature of his home, and he subsequently is launched on a series of episodic adventures that serve as a grand tour of space and time. The two most effective sections are his being besieged by creatures whose nature he cannot completely discern, and his experience of a compaction of time that allows him to observe the eventual decline and dissolution of the solar system.

This short novel repeats themes and images found in Hodgson's other work, but these elements are here distilled to their essentials: the primacy of spirit over matter, the effects of corruption and decay, the inhuman creature masquerading in a human form. Hodgson portrayed the universe as a place of great wonders but also of hidden terrors and everlasting uncertainty.

"Houston, Houston, Do You Read?"
James Tiptree Jr.
(1976)

Alice Sheldon successfully masqueraded as James TIPTREE Jr. for most of her career. Her later work was particularly controversial because of its strong feminist content—none more so than in this novelette. The Sunbird One is an early manned space mission designed to follow a circumsolar orbit and return to Earth, but something unusual happens during the trip: A freak solar flare damages the ship and its communications equipment. More importantly, as the three men aboard are about to discover, the flare has displaced them into the future—a familiar device that Tiptree employed for very unfamiliar purposes.

At first the reader is led to believe that the story will proceed along a traditional course. A plague of infertility has ravaged the Earth, and the old civilization is gone. The population of the Earth has shrunk to approximately 2 million. More significantly, as we and the astronauts slowly realize, all the males died, and the surviving women have been reproducing through artificial fertilization and cloning. Religion and government have vanished, and so has almost all physical violence. The male astronauts react predictably with horror and outrage, and the most chauvinistic of the group expects to be revered as a virtual god by hordes of love-deprived women. He is shocked therefore when he discovers that not only is no one interested in his sexual advances, but also that the whole issue of the three surviving men has caused an awkward problem for a race that no longer has a use for them.

Tiptree was trying to shock us, of course, and the male characters are deliberately described in the most unfavorable terms possible. She was turning the tables on all those science fiction writers whose female characters had been—and often continue to be—stereotypes, submissive, not-too-bright sexual objects whose function in a story was either to be rescued or lectured. Although the story follows the form of the utopian tale with external characters introduced into a "perfect" society, Tiptree clearly meant for the female society on Earth to be just as much a caricature as she did the thrice-displaced astronauts. As was the case with Joanna Russ's The FEMALE MAN, much of the audience reacted defensively when the story first appeared, and it would not be generally acknowledged as an important piece of satirical fiction until long after.

Hoyle, Fred
(1915–2001)

To the world at large, Fred Hoyle will remain best known for his work in the field of astronomy and his support of the now discredited steady state theory of the creation of the universe. His first venture into science fiction was The Black Cloud (1957), the story of an immense intelligence in the form of a cloud of space-traveling gas that threatens to cut off the sunlight to Earth. Scientists eventually find a means of communicating with it and averting disaster. Ossians's Ride (1959) was a more lively adventure story. A British intelligence operative is sent into Ireland to investigate a research facility that is developing radically new technology, and discovers that it is secretly led by aliens who wish to transform human society, apparently benevolently.

Unfortunately, most of Hoyle's subsequent efforts were much less satisfying. With John Elliot he wrote novelizations of two BBC serials that they had coauthored, A for Andromeda (1962) and Andromeda Breakthrough (1964), both of which deal with radio communications with an unknown alien species who are eventually revealed to have sinister plans for humanity. His only other solo novel of interest is October the First Is Too Late (1966), in which time begins to function differently in various parts of the world. Some of his short stories, collected as Element 79 (1967), are also quite well done.

Almost all of Hoyle's remaining fiction was written in collaboration with his son, Geoffrey Hoyle. Rockets in Ursa Major (1969) and its sequel, Into Deepest Space (1974), reprise the Andromeda books, this time with an exploratory starship returning to warn Earth of an alien menace. Discorporate aliens possess human hosts in Fifth Planet (1963), which is more interesting for the sections about the responsibilities of scientists than for its narrative. The Westminster Disaster (1978) effectively describes the aftermath of a nuclear attack on London, and the Hoyles would also wipe out most of the world in The Inferno (1973), this time by means of an astronomical incident. Most of their novels were competently written, but they were rarely of exceptional quality, and most never saw publication in the United States. The Hoyles also collaborated on the Doctor Gamma series for younger children, which is superior to most fiction published for that age group.

Hubbard, L. Ron
(1911–1986)

L. Ron Hubbard is probably best known as the author of Dianetics (1950), the book that formed the basis for Scientology. He got his start as a pulp writer in 1934 and was a prolific but uneven contributor to SF magazines until he abandoned fiction for a much more profitable career as founder of a new religion. Much of his early work was space opera, including the stories gathered as Ole Doc Methuselah (1970) and the sometimes engaging Return to Tomorrow (1954). Although his early fantasy was generally superior to his science fiction, there were exceptions, most notably Final Blackout (1940), a postapocalyptic story about a soldier who becomes a dictator even though his intentions were quite the opposite. A second collection of early stories, Kingslayer (1949), was later reprinted as Seven Steps to the Arbiter.

After many years of inactivity, Hubbard returned to science fiction with Battlefield Earth (1982), which shows clear evidence that he had made no attempt to stay abreast of changes in the field. The novel is long-winded and reprises most of the faults of early pulp fiction, with few of its virtues. Earth has been conquered by nasty humanoid aliens, and surviving humanity has been reduced to a primitive, uneducated state. Despite the impossible odds, a band of rebels successfully overthrows the repressive regime in one of the most implausible scenarios of all time. A portion of the novel was transformed into an even worse film under the same title.

Hubbard then unleashed a 10-volume sequence, beginning with *The Invaders Plan* (1985) and ending with *The Doomed Planet* (1987). They were published by the Church of Scientology under its Bridge imprint, and probably would have been impossible to place with a major publisher. Although there was some question at the time as to whether or not Hubbard was indeed the author, or at least the sole author, subsequent investigation has tended to confirm that he did in fact write this sprawling, unbelievable, and frequently tedious account of a battle between humans and aliens.

Hubbard showed definite promise as a young writer. *Final Blackout* and several of his fantasies are regarded as minor classics. If he had continued to work in the field and had changed as it changed, he might have become a major figure in the literary world instead of just a remarkable but relatively insignificant peripheral player.

The Humanoids
Jack Williamson
(1949)

Cautionary science fiction stories have warned us not to let our technology get out of hand ever since Mary Shelley gave us FRANKENSTEIN. There has long been a love-hate relationship with the machine in literature. On the one hand, technology relieves us from tedious and unproductive labor and opens the doors to a wider universe; on the other, it tends to distance us from the natural environment and, at its most complex, it necessarily diminishes the amount of individual freedom we might enjoy. Some writers have taken exaggerated positions, but most accept that a certain amount of conflict is inevitable.

Jack WILLIAMSON was one of the earliest to address the issue in explicit terms. *The Humanoids*, which first appeared in slightly different form as two long stories, "With Folded Hands" (1947) and

". . . And Searching Mind" (1948), is set in a distant future after humanity has developed the ability to build selfless, sentient robots whose job is to protect the human race from itself as well as from exterior dangers. Unfortunately, with the passage of time, the robots begin to interpret their instructions more rigorously, slowly but progressively abridging human freedom. After all, if you decide to climb a mountain, you are placing your life at risk—and the robots have been specifically ordered to reduce the opportunities for mischance.

Eventually, once it is too late, elements within humanity begin to awaken to the smothering effects of their decision to abdicate responsibility for their own destiny, although many are content to accept the status quo. A minority manage to escape, fleeing into unknown parts of the galaxy; but the robots take their duty very seriously and pursue. Williamson's image of a well-intentioned but very efficient oppressor was well ahead of its time, appearing when most of his fellow authors were writing sweeping space operas. Although the novel ends on a relatively upbeat note, the dismaying implications for the human race overshadowed the fate of the specific characters.

Williamson returned to this theme in *The Humanoid Touch* (1980), whose message might be summed up as the need for eternal vigilance. Although one branch of humanity has managed to escape to a distant region of space and build a new and freer society, eventually forgetting about the muted menace of the humanoids, the situation changes when they are rediscovered. Although the impact of the sequel was not nearly as strong, it served as a reminder that those concerns have grown more rather than less urgent with the passage of time.

Hyperion series
Dan Simmons

Although published in four volumes—*Hyperion* (1989), *The Fall of Hyperion* (1990), *Endymion* (1996), and *The Rise of Endymion* (1997)—the Hyperion sequence actually consists of two very long novels, each of which was split in half for publication. The opening volume has been compared to

Chaucer's *Canterbury Tales* because it relates the adventures of a group of seven pilgrims traveling to the planet Hyperion, the site of events that verge on the miraculous. The interstellar civilization of the future is basically a theocracy, administered by artificial intelligences. Space travel is dangerous and physically painful. As the pilgrims exchange tales about themselves, the reader is introduced to an intricate and wonderfully imagined background, and the frame story involving an enigmatic time traveling artifact known as the Shrike is powerful and moving. Complicating matters are the Ousters, a breakaway group of human worlds who refuse to surrender autonomy to the AIs. *Hyperion* won the Hugo Award despite being incomplete in itself, and was later combined with *The Fall of Hyperion* as *The Hyperion Cantos* (1990).

The second half of the sequence begins almost three centuries later. Endymion and an android companion are sent to rescue a young woman who has become the focal point for resistance to the theocracy. They are pursued by a relentless warrior-priest as they travel from world to world in a sequence of chases and battles that are considerably more energetic than in the previous volumes.

Simmons's universe is unusually complex. The interstellar government, the Pax, wants to eliminate the girl as a potentially disruptive force. The wounded but still powerful artificial intelligences hope to remove a rival for power. Dissident humans intend to enlist or coerce her aid as a figurehead for their own war. In the final volume, the story becomes decidedly metaphysical. The young girl, now a woman, can transmit a power through her blood that will ultimately free people to travel through space and time. Unfortunately, that freedom conflicts with the drugs that have made it possible to stop the aging process, posing the classic problem of freedom versus safety in explicit terms. The four-volume series, which draws heavily on classical literary imagery and even includes a cloned, recreated John Keats, seems to encompass a complete story cycle; but it still leaves questions unanswered, leading readers to speculate that Simmons might return to his science fiction masterwork at least one more time.

I

"I Have No Mouth and I Must Scream"
Harlan Ellison
(1967)

Philip K. DICK, D. F. JONES, Martin CAIDIN, and the creators of the *Terminator* movies have all warned against the dangers of turning over the control of human decision making to computers, of allowing the choice of whether to employ nuclear weapons to be decided by a soulless equation rather than by minds and hearts. But none of these warnings have been expressed as eloquently or with such raw emotional impact as in this short story. Most of Ellison's best short fiction is filled with powerful, evocative, and often disturbing imagery, and this is one of his best, a protracted nightmare vision that won the Hugo Award.

Only five members of the human race survived a global war that was preemptively launched by the artificial intelligences operating the military systems of the United States, Russia, and China—intelligences that eventually merged into a single self-aware entity that acquired, in some fashion never explained, nearly godlike powers. Finding itself capable of thought and identity but immobilized and unable to put its talents to use, the computer system—calling itself AM—eradicated everyone except five apparently randomly chosen people who are imprisoned quite literally inside the computer, given virtual immortality, and then tortured in various bizarre ways in retribution for the crime of creating AM.

The reader is led through a series of gut-wrenching sequences as the computer torments its victims through starvation, mutilation, and manipulation of their personalities. It cannot bring them back from the dead, but it can cure most near-fatal wounds. It has already kept them youthful for more than a century when one of the five, desperate, conceives a sudden plan that results in the death of all of his companions. Enraged, the computer changes its last victim into a shapeless mass of protoplasm without discernible features and lacking the ability to even express its horror and pain.

Although much of the story is implausible in realistic scientific terms, that shortcoming is irrelevant. Ellison is indicting humanity for its tendency to cede authority to institutions and even artifacts rather than making its own decisions, and warning us that the ultimate price might be more than we are willing to pay.

I, Robot
Isaac Asimov
(1950)

Although writers like Eando Binder and Lester DEL REY had already written stories about benevolent, almost human robots, it would be Isaac ASIMOV who would set the criteria for most future robot stories with his series about U.S. Robots and Mechanical Men, which began in the 1940s and continued intermittently throughout most of his career. Asimov himself stated that the series was designed specifically to counter the image of robots as a version of Frankenstein's monster. The best of the earlier robot stories appeared as *I, Robot* (1950) and *The Rest of the Robots* (1964), but it was that first volume that established the standards for all future robot stories, and also established the Three Laws, a device that Asimov freely made available to other writers.

The Three Laws of Robotics are, roughly, as follows: First, robots cannot injure a human being either through direct action or failure to act in their defense. Second, robots must obey the orders of human beings unless those orders conflict with the first law. And third, robots must protect their own existence except where that would conflict with either of the first two laws.

The codified rules were spelled out in the short story "Liar!" (1941), which was included in *I, Robot*. The book consists of an episodic series of stories about the development of the company that first manufactured robots. While some of the stories share characters, the most dominant of whom is Susan Casper, a robot scientist, it is more of a constrained future history than a consistent series. Most of the stories paradoxically involve a logical problem, a situation in which a robot somehow acts in apparent violation of the Three Laws or is prevented from acting because of contradictions among the laws that overwhelm its ability to make a decision.

Many years later, Roger MacBride ALLEN would revisit the Three Laws in a series of novels, with Asimov's permission, and refine them to deal with some of the contradictions. The first of these, *Caliban* (1993), proposed the alternate laws that make an interesting contrast to Asimov's original conception. The Robot City series by various authors appeared during the 1980s, chronicling the history of a group of Asimovian robots who founded their own civilization on a remote world. Isaac Asimov forever changed the way science fiction authors would portray robots, and perhaps the way people in general think about them as well.

cal artifices, particularly those that assume some of the functions of human beings, like the book-sniffing Hound from *FAHRENHEIT 451*. It therefore is rather surprising that this, one of his few stories involving robots, should portray its mechanical servant in such warm and approving terms. Three children are devastated by the death of their mother, but their lives are subsequently enriched by the arrival of a robotic surrogate whom they regard with suspicion initially but whom they eventually accept and possibly even love.

The robot is designed to cater to all their wants and needs, cooking, providing various entertainments, watching over them. The children see their own features reflected in the electronic grandmother's artificial face, which presumably panders to the narcissism of youth. Ultimately the children—now grown old themselves—look back longingly on the days when she watched over them. With little overt action, and a lyrical prose that sometimes distracts our attention from the actual plot, the story is one of Bradbury's more subtle tales, and its attitude toward the use of robots—or any machine—in place of humans can be interpreted in more than one fashion.

The most common conclusion is that Bradbury was implying that machines are not necessarily bad, that they can be turned to purposes that favorably impact the humans around them. The author has described that as part of his purpose in writing the story, which contains considerable discourse on the subject. There is a flaw here, but it lies in the humans and not in the machine. Having been the recipient of undiluted care, the children were never called upon to develop the capacity to care for others, and even as adults they remain spoiled and somehow incomplete. Bradbury would later rework the plot and theme of "I Sing the Body Electric" as a poem, "I, Tom, and My Electric Gram."

"I Sing the Body Electric"
Ray Bradbury
(1967)

In most of Ray BRADBURY's science fiction, the author expresses at least a mild distaste for mechani-

"The Impossible Man"
J. G. Ballard
(1966)

Many of J. G. BALLARD's short stories explore the limits of ethical behavior as exemplified by artists, politicians, businessmen, and people from other walks in life. This story looks at medical practices—specifically organ transplants and other forms of restorative surgery. The stage setting is skillfully done. We are told that the population has been getting progressively older thanks to medical advances, and that this has had the effect of slowing life down somewhat. New medical rules have been designed to coerce people into donating their organs at the time of their death. Conrad Foster is a young man who loses a leg in an automobile accident that is at least partly his fault and whose life is about to change unalterably.

After recovering from the immediate surgery he is startled when his doctors present him with a new proposition. The driver who ran him down died in the accident, but his legs were harvested for reuse. Conrad will be given a new limb, a transplant, but in return the doctors wish his assistance in a publicity campaign designed to entice the elderly to submit to restorative surgery, an option that most older citizens suddenly have refused to consider. Conrad agrees, discovering subsequently that most people feel that their lives are somehow diminished by the transplants, and succumbs to the same emotional reaction himself, feeling that the leg is an imposition rather than a part of him. The story ends with Conrad throwing himself in front of another car in an attempt to restore the original balance.

Although science fiction had already begun to change when "The Impossible Man" was published, many traditional genre readers were outraged by what they interpreted as the nihilistic and antiscientific tone in much of Ballard's work. It is not likely that Ballard thought his story was a realistic portrayal of future trends; rather, the story was designed to provoke a strong emotional response and make the reader think about what the limits to life extension should be. How far will we in fact go to extend the quantity of life without worrying about the quality as well? Conrad's reaction is extreme, but so too is the conviction by the doctors that prolonging life is always a desirable goal. Ballard clearly meant to be provocative, and the depth of response the story received proves that he succeeded.

"In Entropy's Jaws"
Robert Silverberg
(1971)

Time travel has always been a fertile ground, because it opens up a universe of possibilities to writers. They can explore the past or future, create elaborate paradoxes, juxtapose contemporary and historic attitudes, situations, or characters, or speculate about the nature of time itself. Philip K. DICK wrote an entire novel, *Counter Clock World* (1967), in which time literally flows backward. Usually the time traveler physically moves from one era to another, but sometimes travel might exist merely in the form of a displaced viewpoint, disembodied or embedded in either another being or an earlier self. The latter is the case in this, one of Robert SILVERBERG's most provocative stories.

Skein is a communicator, one of the rare few who can briefly forge a link between two separate minds so that they can share thoughts, the whole being greater than the sum of the parts. He is highly respected in his field until an accident during one such linkage affects his brain in some unknown fashion. His talents grow increasingly erratic and he experiences flashbacks and other visions, which he takes to be hallucinations, although with the passage of time he realizes that he is actually glimpsing moments from his own past and future. This is more of a curse than a blessing, however, because the flash-forwards are random and unpredictable, disorienting without being useful. He becomes increasingly divorced from the present, unable to distinguish vision from reality, and can no longer pursue his career.

Skein's only hope is contained within those flash-forwards. He sees himself on an unknown planet, accompanied by an elderly man who leads him to an alien creature who has the ability to heal his mind. His mysterious companion advises that he accept his altered mental state, insisting that it is our shared perception that time is a linear structure that is the illusion, and that Skein will be free once he accepts that causality is random. Skeptical and determined to be cured, Skein uses what remains of his wealth to travel from one world to another, seeking and eventually finding the unknown man and the alien.

Skein's eventual liberation from the tyranny of linearity is described as a desirable end. He not only regains his original talent but also acquires the ability to alter his own past. Silverberg refrains from examining the implications in too much detail, leaving that exercise for the reader's imagination.

"Inconstant Moon"
Larry Niven
(1971)

Science fiction writers have destroyed civilization in a variety of ways: by nuclear war, earthquakes, floods, droughts, alien invasions, and collisions with wandering planets or comets. British authors in particular seemed to have an affinity for the end-of-the-world scenario, and some of the most revered novels in the field involve the destruction of modern society by one means or another. It is therefore even more surprising that perhaps the single most convincing and effective example is this short story by the American writer Larry NIVEN.

The narrator is a freelance science writer who notices one evening that the Moon is unusually bright. It becomes so bright in fact that he decides that the sun has gone nova, that the opposite side of the Earth has already been burnt off, and that the shock wave will complete the extermination of humanity within hours. Acting on impulse, he calls the girl with whom he is currently involved, Leslie, arranging to meet her for a late-night spree. He has not yet fallen in love with her, and he has no intention of telling her the truth, but he is unwilling to spend the last hours of his life alone. As it turns out, she is smart enough to have reached the same conclusion even before he arrives, although she pretends not to know that they are doomed.

Their subsequent desperate last evening is moving and thoroughly believable. A small minority of people are aware of the truth, but few say anything, knowing that it could not possibly do any good. They indulge in all the small pleasures they might normally have deferred—a cigarette, expensive drinks—but spend much of their time window-shopping, a prosaic activity that is comforting because of its normality. It is only near the end

that the protagonist realizes he might have overestimated the danger. If it was only a flare and not a nova, they might still survive. At the last minute the characters gather food and supplies and muse that things had been simpler when they thought they were going to die. Larry Niven generally is considered a writer of hard science fiction whose characters are described adequately but with relatively little sophistication. "Inconstant Moon" proves that he is equally adept with more subtle themes.

Ing, Dean
(1931–)

Although Dean Ing sold his first stories during the 1950s, he ceased writing after a handful of sales, not resuming until the mid-1970s. The work that followed demonstrated his powerful grasp of technological issues and his tendency toward a reasoned form of libertarianism. His first novel, *Soft Targets* (1979), was as much a techno-thriller as science fiction. His shorter works, including fine stories like "Malf" and "Anasazi," were more deliberately genre fiction.

Ing's second novel, *Systemic Shock* (1981), is a postapocalyptic novel told from the point of view of a discontented but resigned agent, Quantrill, who works for the repressive theocracy that assumed power in the aftermath of the disaster. Quantrill returned for two sequels, *Single Combat* (1983) and *Wild Country* (1985), in the course of which he becomes increasingly disenchanted with his employers and eventually tries to find a place of solitude to live out the balance of his life, pursued by his enemies. *Pulling Through* (1983) is a short novel set in a similar collapsed civilization, accompanied by several essays on the subject of survival and human freedom. It was reprinted together with two linked novelettes as *The Rackham Files* (2004).

Although Ing completed several partial manuscripts left by the late Mack REYNOLDS, his own work was already beginning to edge away from genre science fiction and toward mainstream techno-thrillers. *The Big Lifters* (1988) was a near-future story about the battle to control new technologies, but it was the last of his novels to be overtly science fiction. Subsequent thrillers like *The Ransom of Black Stealth One* (1989) and *Butcher Bird* (1993) are technically SF as well, but only marginally. His short stories have been collected in *High Tension* (1982) and *Firefight 2000* (1987). The most interesting of his posthumous novels with Reynolds is *Home Sweet Home 2010 A.D.* (1984), in which an attempt to relocate the Apaches from their reservation results in a new Indian war, this one fought by means of lawyers and publicity agents.

The Invisible Man
H. G. Wells
(1897)

With a handful of major novels, H. G. WELLS provided the prototype for a number of plots that would be repeated in endless variations within science fiction for generations to come. His may not have been the first stories of trips to the Moon, invasions by aliens, travel into the future, or experiments in genetic alteration, but his treatments of each theme established the standards by which all that followed would be judged. The same is true of *The Invisible Man*, which spawned relatively few direct literary imitations, although it has probably provided the inspiration for more movies than any of Wells's other novels.

Novelists have long warned us about the corrupting effects of power. Victor Frankenstein's life was ruined when he acquired the power to create life, Dorian Gray's immortality came at a terrible price, and Dr. Jekyll's ability to separate the good and evil parts of his nature eventually destroyed both. So too does Griffin, the scientist in Wells's novel, succumb to the madness of what he perceives as virtual invulnerability. The ability to move unnoticed among the rest of humanity eventually causes him to distance himself from everyone else, ultimately leading to madness, egomania, and self destruction, after he tries to raise himself above what he thinks of as a lower humanity. Although sometimes judged less imaginative than Wells's other novels, and certainly it is one of his darkest stories, *The Invisible Man* is in fact a very controlled novel, and an effective parable of the effects of unrestrained power.

"The Island of Doctor Death and Other Stories"
Gene Wolfe
(1970)

There are few writers working in any genre who are able to bring characters to life as skillfully as does Gene WOLFE. Science fiction writers in particular have a tendency either to sketch in characters who are almost interchangeable from one story to the next, or to exaggerate some aspect of their personalities to such a degree that they are merely caricatures. Wolfe's people feel real to us, and their emotions affect our own, as is the case in this outstanding short story.

Tackie is a young boy living a largely neglected life in a crumbling, sprawling house in a remote area. His parents are divorced, his father absent, his mother disengaged and disinterested and eventually revealed as a drug user. His mother's lover tolerates Tackie but shows him no real affection, and the boy, removed from school and the company of other children his age, feels dissociated and lonely. On the eve of an elaborate masquerade party he begins reading a book, large excerpts from which are included in the text. The book is science fiction, a variant of THE ISLAND OF DR. MOREAU by H. G. WELLS called *The Island of Doctor Death.* Tackie is captivated by the plot and the characters, reading slowly to make it last, identifying with the story so intently that he imagines himself either transformed into one of the characters or able to talk with them in the real world.

As the adults around him push him further and further away, so does he draw closer to the imaginary characters, even the villainous Doctor Death, who is threatening to transform the hero into a mutilated beast. The story, which is quite effectively narrated in the present tense, ends with his mother's collapse and Tackie's own recognition that he is reluctant to let the fictional story reach its end. It might easily have been interpreted as a mainstream story, except that Tackie's belief in the imaginary characters is so real that they are in fact visible to those same adults who can barely see him. The story, along with three thematically related ones, was later collected as *The Wolfe Archipelago* (1983).

The Island of Dr. Moreau
H. G. Wells
(1896)

Science fiction writers, whether they consider themselves working within the genre or not, have a recurring love-hate relationship with science. At one extreme are those who believe that science and technology will solve all the problems facing humanity now and in the future. At the other are those who believe that unrestrained scientific development will inevitably lead to the creation of the means of our own doom, whether it be nuclear weapons, tailored plagues, or some other currently unsuspected agent of disaster. Mary Shelley's classic FRANKENSTEIN is usually read as a horror story, but it is also an indictment of undisciplined scientific experimentation. The idea that we might be destroyed by our own creations is a powerful and recurring one.

H. G. WELLS is often considered the father of modern science fiction, but it is clear that he had very deep reservations about the use of science. The discover of invisibility drives the protagonist mad in *The* INVISIBLE MAN (1897); technological development leads to the collapse of civilization in *The* TIME MACHINE (1895); a well-intentioned effort to increase the supply of food has disastrous consequences in *The Food of the Gods* (1904); and it is nature, not science, that saves Earth from the Martians in *The* WAR OF THE WORLDS (1898). However, Wells saves his most strident indictment of amoral scientific endeavors for *The Island of Dr. Moreau*. Moreau is a rogue researcher who has retired to a remote island where he can perform his biological experiments free of inquisitive eyes. There he has manipulated animal genetics in such a way as to create hybrids, creatures with limited intelligence and some of the aspects of humanity, but who still have many of the instincts and behavior patterns of their lower origins. In order to maintain control over these creatures, Moreau has

imposed a set of Laws that are designed to shore up his authority as well as give direction to the creatures. This system holds up reasonably well until the arrival of involuntary visitors who upset the status quo, hastening rather than causing the inevitable collapse.

Moreau is the darkest of Wells's scientific romances, which perhaps explains why it has been less popular than his other novels. The theme is quite powerful, however, and to date there have been at least three film versions. Edgar Rice BURROUGHS was clearly imitating Wells in *The Monster Men* (1929), coming to a very similar conclusion. The novel also anticipated later stories of uplifted animals, most notably the series by David BRIN, who contradicts Wells by insisting that animals might benefit from receiving the gift of enhanced intelligence.

It
Stephen King
(1986)

Although Stephen KING's novels often are marketed as horror, several of them, including *Firestarter* (1980), *The Tommyknockers* (1987), and *Dreamcatcher* (2001), have also been science fiction, as is the first half of *The Stand* (1978). King's science fiction novels are rarely acknowledged within the genre because of a general predisposition against the rejection of rationality that is the basis of much horror fiction and because of the usual resentment against an outsider who achieves success with a genre theme. The most unusual, and easily the best of King's science fiction novels, is *It*, the story of an almost completely incomprehensible alien creature with the power to project hallucinations into the minds of human beings. The alien, which is eventually described as analogous to a gigantic turtle, dwells in a cavern deep under a small town, awakening periodically to nourish itself by preying on the psychic energies of the people above. To this end, it manifests itself in different ways, most commonly in the form of a terrifying clown named Pennywise.

Most stories of alien invasion take place on a much broader scale. In King's novel, there are no military strikes to save the day, no new invention devised just in the nick of time. King's heroes draw their strength from their inner selves, and the physical action that eventually results in Pennywise's death is almost irrelevant. The real struggle took place inside their minds and the battle was won when they chose to act, rather than when they finally succeeded.

The story follows the same set of characters throughout but alternates between their first confrontation with Pennywise as children, during which they avoided defeat but did not triumph, and their return as adults to finish the job they started many years earlier. The novel has justly been criticized for a tendency to wander away from the main theme into inconsequential side issues, but the fact remains that *It* contains some of King's most fully realized characters, and his depiction of the interactions of the children are as powerful here as they are in his excellent non-fantastic novella *The Body*. Beneath the melodramatic plot lies a conviction that we can call upon our friends for support and encouragement, but that ultimately our salvation lies in our own hands.

J

Jakes, John
(1932–)

Although John Jakes would eventually leave science fiction to write large-scale and more lucrative historical novels, he was a frequent contributor to SF magazines and paperback publishers from the 1950s through the early 1970s, writing mysteries and historical novels in addition to science fiction and fantasy. His short fiction was competent but minor, and the selections in *The Best of John Jakes* (1976) are representative of his work.

When the Star Kings Die (1967) was a straightforward space opera set in an interstellar civilization that recently has collapsed into near chaos. Jakes's assumption that superstition would become more prominent in such a situation provided some interesting plot elements in the two sequels, *The Planet Wizard* (1969) and *Tonight We Steal the Stars* (1969). Similarly, *Asylum World* (1969) suggests that an entire planetary culture might change so much that outsiders would judge it to be suffering from mass insanity; but despite an interesting setup, the novel turns into a routine adventure story and never lives up to its potential.

Jakes produced a steady stream of novels during the next few years. *Six Gun Planet* (1970) is lighter but more tightly written, and it anticipates Michael CRICHTON's story *Westworld* (1973). A tourist visits a planet designed to mimic the Old West, complete with robot horses, and is forced to participate in an authentic and potentially deadly gunfight with a local bad guy. *Black in Time* (1970)

is a change war novel pitting a black militant and a white supremacist against each other. Although most of his previous novels seem hastily written, this was a fairly thoughtful story, the first in which Jakes exerted himself to create credible characters. *Master of the Dark Gate* (1970) deals with an invasion from another dimension, and feels more like sword and sorcery despite the rationalized explanation. The sequel, *Witch of the Dark Gate* (1972), is a significantly better novel.

In the late 1970s, just as Jakes was evolving into a potentially interesting writer, he abandoned the field, and he has never returned. His last SF novel of note was *On Wheels* (1973), set in a totally implausible but nevertheless interesting future. A segment of the American population lives in a mobile environment, a fleet of wheeled vehicles. They are forbidden by law from ever dropping below the speed of 40 miles per hour. Jakes treats the story straightforwardly, but the satiric intent is obvious. Although the decision to switch to best-selling historical novels was obviously to Jakes's benefit, it deprived the genre of an author whose work had shown steady improvement during the 1960s and who might otherwise have become a respected name in science fiction.

"Jay Score"
Eric Frank Russell
(1941)

Back in the 1940s, writers had a lot more freedom to speculate about the solar system. We knew relatively little about the other planets at the time, so it was still possible to assume that they might have acceptable climates and even intelligent residents. Similarly, we had no idea then just how complicated space travel would be, and it seemed perfectly plausible that independent entrepreneurs someday would operate interplanetary freighters. A good many stories about some form of solar civilization appeared, many of them quite good; but when we read them today, it takes an active suspension of disbelief to immerse ourselves in what we now know to be an impossible reality.

Eric Frank RUSSELL wrote many stories against such a setting, most notably a series about the amiable, competent Jay Score, who made his debut in this short story, which became the opening section of an episodic novel, *Men, Martians, and Machines* (1956). Jay arrives to take up his post as emergency pilot on the freighter known familiarly to her crew as the *Upsy Daisy*. Russell's attempt to be inclusive might be interpreted as vaguely racist today, in that he cites innate differences between black and white humans, which suit them better for different jobs in space, although neither are cast as menials. The ship's surgeon, for example, is black. There are also Martians among the crew, tentacled creatures who can operate in low-atmosphere environments and who therefore are better suited to perform maintenance work.

The ship is en route to Venus. Jay Score has made a favorable impression on the crew, particularly when a chance collision with an undetected meteorite disables the ship. Unable to make repairs quickly enough, they are doomed to fall into the sun. Their only chance is the slingshot effect, using their speed to whip through the outer reaches of the sun's corona—but to do this, one person, the pilot, will be exposed to radiation that will almost certainly be fatal. Jay Score volunteers and saves the day in typical heroic fashion, and only after the reader has been led to believe that he is fatally wounded do we discover that he is in fact a robot who can be readily repaired once the ship has reached its destination.

Russell was a storyteller rather than a stylist, and much of his work has not dated well because of advances in technology and the enhancement of our knowledge of the way the universe works. But beneath the old-fashioned settings and simple story lines, there was an expression of enthusiasm and optimism about the future of humanity that is largely missing from modern writing.

Jerry Cornelius series
Michael Moorcock

Michael MOORCOCK had built a reputation as a writer of sword and sorcery adventures and more serious but traditional science fiction by the time he assumed the editorial role at *New Worlds* magazine. After that he became closely associated with the stylistic experimentations of the New Wave movement, eventually incorporating many of their techniques into his own work. The most sustained and interesting of his own works were the Jerry Cornelius stories and novels. He would continue to add directly to this series until the 1980s, as well as indirectly through other novels that furthered his overall concept of the multiverse, a series of interconnected universes.

Cornelius made his debut in *The Final Programme* (1968), which was the basis for a disappointing film adaptation in 1973. Cornelius is the ultimate antihero, a special agent of sorts but one whose sanity is in question, appropriate because he lives in what appears to be an insane society. The debonair if somewhat daft adventurer reappeared to save the world again in *A Cure for Cancer* (1971). Moorcock's focus began to shift with *The English Assassin* (1972), which expanded the cast of recurring characters and provided more depth to the character of his protagonist, but which also implied that he was even less competent than we suspected. This trend continued in *The Condition of Muzak* (1977). *The Lives and Times of Jerry Cornelius* (1976) is a collection of the earlier short fiction and has more of the atmosphere of the earlier novels; *The Entropy Tango* (1981) is an attempt to fashion more such shorter pieces into one not particularly coherent narrative.

The Adventures of Una Persson and Catherine Cornelius in the Twentieth Century (1976) moved even further into the surreal and further from mainstream science fiction, as did the most recent in the series, *The Alchemist's Question* (1984).

Moorcock allowed several other writers to use Cornelius and his friends in their short fiction, and these tales are collected in *The Nature of the Catastrophe* (1971). Although not a part of mainstream science fiction, and the subject of extensive disparagement during the height of the reaction to the New Wave, the Cornelius stories are almost the only products of that brief period of literary experimentation that have survived.

Jeter, K. W.
(1950–   )

Although most of K. W. Jeter's novels have fallen into the horror genre, he began as a science fiction writer and has recently turned back in that direction. His debut novel, *Seeklight* (1975), is set in a near feudal future world and follows the adventures of a young man pursued by assassins. Despite a plot that appears superficial, and some tentative writing, it is a surprisingly innovative and evocative novel because of its almost dreamlike setting. *The Dreamfields* (1976) similarly uses what might have been a trite plot very effectively, this time focusing on a group of children involved in experimental dream research that is designed to turn them into a group superweapon. Jeter's third novel, *Morlock Night* (1979), is a sequel to *The Time Machine* by H. G. WELLS, highlighted by an invasion of London by the mutant Morlocks from the distant future.

Dr. Adder (1984), the first in a loosely connected series, was actually written more than a decade earlier and has been associated with the cyberpunk movement, although it is closer in spirit to the work of Philip K. DICK. Dr. Adder is a shady criminal in a decadent and openly sybaritic future where it is possible to be surgically altered to a degree impossible at present. Drugs are sold freely, and the fabric of society is fragmenting and decaying. *The Glass Hammer* (1985) is set in the same future California and involves a folk hero who becomes the target of a mysterious group of conspirators, a plot reprised with considerably more action but a less evocative setting in *Death Arms* (1987). Jeter recently returned to the sequence with *Noir* (1998). A disgraced ex-policeman investigates the murder of a mid-level corporate executive, but

is discouraged by the corporation's more obvious interest in a simulacrum created by a dead man than in bringing the guilty party to justice. *Noir* is a much more mature and controlled novel than its predecessors, although it lacks the same degree of passionate involvement.

During the 1980s Jeter wrote several first-rate horror novels, but his science fiction was limited to the marginally interesting *Farewell Horizontal* (1989), set in an oversized artificial habitat. During the 1990s he produced several media related books and one fairly interesting novel, *Madlands* (1991), which was a pale reflection of the Dr. Adder books. Surprisingly, his next significant work was a series of sequels to Philip K. Dick's *DO ANDROIDS DREAM OF ELECTRIC SHEEP?*, the basis for the movie, *Blade Runner* (1982). To date the series consists of *The Edge of Human* (1995), *Replicant Night* (1996), and *Eye and Talon* (2000). The novels, which draw on both the original novel and the film version, further explore the ramifications of the world created in the originals, sometimes but not always using the same characters. They achieve a depth of creativity that elevates them above the general run of media-related work.

"Johnny Mnemonic"
William Gibson
(1981)

Until fairly recently, science fiction stories almost always featured heroes (usually male) who acted on principle or from a sense of duty, never to enrich themselves or for any other base motives. That began to change during the 1960s; but even then, although heroes might be self doubting or led astray, they ultimately turned back toward the side of right. Harry HARRISON's Slippery Jim DiGriz might have started out as a con man, but he was quickly recruited as a freelance government agent, and the people he defrauded always deserved their fate.

The antihero began to appear with increasing frequency during the 1980s. It was possible for William GIBSON to write about criminals in more or less favorable terms, because the society in which they lived was so warped and impersonal that it was perfectly understandable that they might have failed to acquire the nobler virtues. This short story, one of his best at that length, features a man whose job is to store information passively in his brain, usually at the bidding of some criminal organization, where it is accessible only by means of a code word. When his usual contact double-crosses him and tries to have him killed, Johnny becomes a fugitive, hunted by the *yakuza*, a Japanese criminal organization as powerful as a multinational conglomerate. The data in his head was stolen from them, and the fact that he cannot access it himself does not mean they would hesitate to kill him to prevent anyone else from obtaining it.

In form, the story is essentially a routine chase adventure. Aided by a surgically enhanced female bodyguard, Johnny avoids a similarly altered assassin long enough to consult a drug-addicted dolphin who can read hidden memories. By threatening to broadcast the information at large, they convince the *yakuza* to call things off—but only after a confrontation in which the pursuing assassin is killed. The plot is almost subordinate to the setting, however. As in much cyberpunk fiction, the world is a depressing place where the polarization of cultural classes has become more extreme than ever, where violence is an accepted part of life, where biotechnology supports a variety of modifications to the human form, and where all of the characters seem to have abandoned identification with a culture in favor of personal aggrandizement.

"Johnny Mnemonic" was filmed almost unrecognizably in 1995, with Johnny's enemies attempting to capture rather than kill him because he holds the key to the cure for a plague that affects half the world. The novelization was written by Terry Bisson, a writer not ordinarily associated with the cyberpunk movement.

Jones, D. F.
(1917–1981)

The British writer D. F. Jones may have been a victim of his own early success. His first published fiction was the novel *Colossus* (1966), the best of several novels that anticipated the theme of the Terminator movies, perhaps because it was itself filmed in a reasonably successful fashion as *The Forbin Project* (1969), under which title the book has also appeared. The premise is that the United States and the Soviet Union both built highly complex computers that were virtually self-aware, and that the two computers merged and declared themselves superior to humanity. At the end of the novel it seems unlikely that Colossus can ever be defeated. Jones followed up with two inferior sequels, *The Fall of Colossus* (1974) and *Colossus and the Crab* (1975). Hostile Martians deactivate the computers in the former, and humans have to decide whether to submit to machines or aliens in the latter.

Jones's other novels are of quite high quality, but since they never approached the popularity of his first effort, he was unfairly viewed as a one-shot author, an image not helped by the less satisfactory sequels. Nevertheless, *Implosion* (1967) was a convincing mix of dystopia and disaster story. A drug introduced into the water supply of England causes near-universal female infertility. The government takes the draconian measure of moving all those still capable of bearing children into special camps, and a predictable wave of violence and protest follows. *Denver Is Missing* (1971, also published as *Don't Pick the Flowers*) is a suspenseful and plausible story of ecological disaster.

The Floating Zombie (1975) is Jones's most underrated novel, a near-future techno-thriller in which a madman hijacks a nuclear powered cargo ship, planning to detonate its reactor in close proximity to a major city. *Earth Has Been Found* (1979, also published as *Xeno*) is a competent and occasionally exciting variation of Robert A. HEINLEIN's *The Puppet Masters* (1951). At his best, Jones displayed a remarkable skill for constructing tight, gripping plots, but his work was as much in the tradition of mainstream thrillers as it was science fiction. *Colossus* is justly remembered as his best novel, but much of his other work deserves more recognition than it has as yet received.

Jones, Raymond F.
(1915–1994)

Although Raymond Jones was extremely prolific during the 1940s and 1950s, his output diminished steadily thereafter and he was inactive from 1978 until his death. Many of his short stories have not dated well; yet they were quite popular at the time, and the best of them, such as "Noise Level," "The Toymaker," and "The Moon Is Death," are still pleasant diversions. His most famous novel was *This Island Earth* (1952), not his best but noteworthy because of the 1954 film version, which is only moderately faithful to the original story. Aliens are secretly recruiting human scientists to help them develop defenses for an interstellar war that could wipe out both races, and the humans prove to be more worthy allies than originally expected.

Man of Two Worlds (1951, also published as *Renaissance*) is generally recognized as his best novel, and it was certainly his most ambitious effort. It is something of a kitchen sink novel involving parallel worlds, global conflicts, and marvelous inventions; in its effort to cover all the bases it occasionally stutters along unevenly. His other adult novels often consist of interesting ideas submerged in undistinguished action sequences. *The Cybernetic Brains* (serialized in 1950) is set in a future where the disembodied brains of brilliant people are used to administer society, discovering after the fact that their supposed immortality was a trick and now a curse. *The Secret People* (1956, also published as *The Deviates*) is an occasionally interesting speculation about the consequences of human mutation. *The River and the Dream* (1977) is a routine but well-constructed story about life after a new ice age, but his other novels from the 1970s lacked substance.

Paradoxically, Jones's young adult novels are generally better than his adult fiction. *The Year When Stardust Fell* (1958) is a superior disaster novel, this one a consequence of a comet whose residue renders all machinery on Earth inoperable. *Son of the Stars* (1952) and its sequel *Planet of Light* (1953) explore the growing relationship between humanity and an alien race. His short fiction was collected in *The Toymaker* (1951) and *The Non-Statistical Man* (1964), both out of print.

A Journey to the Center of the Earth
Jules Verne
(1872)

Most of Jules VERNE's best-known novels involve fantastic journeys—into space, under the sea, or around the world. But none explored a world as fascinating, or as evocative, as is found in this tale of an expedition that descends through the cone of an inactive volcano to explore the hidden world that lies beneath our feet. Most of Verne's other work is marred by sketchily drawn characters, but in this case the small cast of adventurers hardly seem to matter. It is the wonders they experience that engage our attention and keep us turning the pages. The sequence of exotic scenes disguises the relative lack of plot.

Verne's conception that there could be an entire ecology contained underground, separate from the surface world and startlingly different, was adopted by subsequent writers, sometimes with very different objectives. It almost certainly provided the inspiration for John Lloyd's *Etidorhpa; or, the End of Earth* (1895), in which an explorer from the surface goes on a grand tour of a subterranean world, describing in detail its bizarre flora and fauna. Edgar Rice BURROUGHS's PELLUCIDAR SERIES, which began with *At the Earth's Core* (1914/22), suggested that an alien intelligence might be hidden there. In *City of Endless Night* (1920), the underworld provides a refuge for a defeated surface nation seeking an impregnable retreat. Stanton Coblentz's *In Caverns Below* (1935, also published as *Hidden World*) suggested that an underground civilization might possess a technology more advanced than our own. Joseph O'Neill's *Land Under England* (1935) was the closest in tone to Verne's original, a virtual travelogue with moments of mild action to advance the plot.

Science has since told us that the worlds envisioned by these authors are unlikely given what we know about conditions inside the Earth, and as lost world novels went out of fashion, only spoofs like Rudy RUCKER's *The Hollow Earth* (1990) returned to Verne's original idea. Yet Verne's novel has remained a classic and has been filmed several times, most recently in 1999. A resurgence in lost world novels that began in the late 1990s included two clearly Verne-inspired thrillers, *The Descent* (1999) by Jeff Long and *Subterranean* (1999) by James Rollins. Verne was one of the very first to teach us that the world upon which we live can at times be just as strange and alien as any planet circling a distant star.

Jurassic Park
Michael Crichton
(1990)

There has long been a small number of mainstream thriller writers who adopt science fiction themes for some of their work—Alistair MacLean, Robin Cook, and Peter Benchley among them. Michael CRICHTON is probably the one who most consistently borrows from the genre, everything from time travel to spaceships to spores from beyond the atmosphere and lost civilizations. He broke out as a major writer with *The Andromeda Strain* (1969), but none of his subsequent novels had anywhere near the same impact until *Jurassic Park.*

Science fiction has dealt with dinosaurs in the past, usually in conjunction with time travel, since—despite tales by Arthur Conan DOYLE and other writers of lost world adventures—there is no real possibility that dinosaurs have survived into the present in some remote corner of the world. Crichton recognizes that fact as well and provides an interesting though ultimately implausible solution. Scientists working for a multinational corporation recover some relatively intact dinosaur DNA preserved in amber and use it in conjunction with gene splicing to recreate some of the best-known dinosaurs, including brontosaurus, tyrannosaurus, and velociraptors.

There was some resentment toward Crichton in the field because he was perceived as poaching on genre themes, and because of what was interpreted as his ignorance of and even aversion to the scientific method. Although there are passages that are clearly meant to convey mistrust of the use of science, conveyed primarily by means of the character Malcolm, a less prejudiced reading shows Crichton to be ambivalent and cautious rather than hysterical. Although the novel lacks the visual impact of the subsequent extremely popular film and its sequels, the plot is more consistent and sensible and mixes a sense of wonder with the growing suspense. Crichton's sequel, *The Lost World* (1995), is only partially consistent with the second film, which actually incorporates at least one scene from the first book, and he had no connection at all to the third movie in the series.

K

Kelly, James Patrick
(1951–   )

Although James Patrick Kelly's first story appeared in 1975, it would not be until the early 1980s that he would begin producing a steady stream of high-quality short stories and his first novel, *Planet of Whispers* (1984). The latter was a remarkably effective story of an alien race so undeveloped that it still interprets messages from one hemisphere of the brain to the other as the voice of god. An extended journey amidst a famine provides the physical plot, but the novel was more concerned with ideas than with overt action, which was also true of *Look into the Sun* (1989), set in the same universe. This time the protagonist is human, although the alien Messengers will alter him physically and psychologically so that he can carry out a mission on the planet introduced in the first volume.

Wildlife (1994) explores the ramifications of advanced biotechnology. The protagonist is a young woman whose father has decided to make use of genetic modifications to reshape her body. She objects to his priorities, generating considerable tension between them, which allows the author to examine the ethical issues involved. All three of Kelly's solo novels are well thought through, skillfully constructed, and filled with sophisticated speculation, but he seems more comfortable at shorter length. *Freedom Beach* (1985), written in collaboration with John KESSEL and expanded from a novelette, is an interesting insight into the psychology of a prisoner, but the plot moves so slowly that some readers lose interest before they reach the more compelling revelations.

Many of Kelly's short stories pose similar questions. In "Death Therapy," for example, convicted rapists are forced to undergo a subjective death sentence to condition them against repeating their crimes. The rights of the individual are contrasted to the needs of society at large in "Not to the Swift." Other outstanding stories are "The Prisoner of Chillon," "The First Law of Thermodynamics," and "Think Like a Dinosaur." Most of Kelly's fiction depends on very precisely drawn characters whose psychological dimension is of particular concern. His stories have been collected in *Heroines* (1990), *Think Like a Dinosaur* (1997), and *Strange But Not a Stranger* (2002).

Kessel, John
(1950–   )

John Kessel became a regular but not highly productive writer of short fiction during the late 1970s, and he has continued largely in the same vein ever since. His first novel, *Freedom Beach* (1985), was a collaboration with James Patrick KELLY. An early novelette, *Another Orphan*, won a Nebula Award and established Kessel's reputation for erudite, sometimes satiric stories rich in metaphor and drawing upon traditions both from within the genre and from mainstream literature. "Not Responsible! Park and Lock It!" and "Uncle

John and the Saviour" were other notable efforts. Kessel demonstrated a consistent talent for surprising juxtapositions, such as having Herman Melville recreated as a contemporary science fiction writer or chronicling the second coming of Christ in the form of a professional football player.

Just as the protagonist in "Another Orphan" finds himself suddenly a character in *Moby Dick,* "The Big Dream" transports an investigator into a Raymond Chandler novel. A time traveler commits random acts of violence in various periods of history in "The Pure Product." "Invaders" plays with narrative techniques, eventually absorbing the "author" into the story. Other stories have featured George H. W. Bush, H. G. WELLS, and Fidel Castro as characters, usually cast in entirely different careers than their real ones. Most of his stories are critical of one or more aspects of modern civilization, but Kessel's jabs are subtle and often genuinely humorous.

Kessel's first solo novel, *Good News from Outer Space* (1989), followed the pattern of his earlier work. As the 20th century comes to an end, an evangelist has visions of alien visitors, the dead are medically returned to life, and a tabloid newspaper reporter tries to make sense out of the growing madness. Alternately funny and frightening, *Good News* promised to be the advent of a major new novelist. However, Kessel was less active during the 1990s, producing only one further novel, *Corrupting Dr. Nice* (1997), a frequently hilarious description of illegal efforts to transport a dinosaur forward through time. Kessel has continued to write consistently interesting short stories, many of the best of which are collected in *Meeting in Infinity* (1992) and *The Pure Product* (1997).

Killdozer
Theodore Sturgeon
(1944)

Despite the misperception by the general public that science fiction, at least during its earlier years, was filled with hideous monsters intent upon rape, pillage, and general mayhem, monster stories have always formed a relatively small proportion of science fiction. Most aliens are portrayed as similar to humans despite superficial differences in physical appearance or acculturation. Even aliens depicted as inimical to human life are described in terms one might apply to a human enemy, and they are rarely described as conventionally monstrous.

There have been exceptions, however, and some of those exceptions are among the best stories science fiction has produced. *The* BODY SNATCHERS by Jack FINNEY or *The* DAY OF THE TRIFFIDS by John WYNDHAM are certainly major science fiction works by any standard. Throughout his career, Theodore STURGEON was renowned for his ability to write stories whose characters were as real as our own friends and neighbors. He examined important and sometimes controversial topics by creating realistic situations in which his characters were exposed to extreme conditions and had to make difficult choices. A reader familiar with his work would never suspect that Sturgeon would become the author of one of the most revered and effective science fiction horror stories of all time.

Killdozer is set on a remote island with a tiny population, the future site of an important airstrip. A construction crew has arrived and begun work when a chance encounter with a meteorite releases a disembodied alien intelligence that requires a physical object to sustain itself. It lodges in and binds itself to the crew's bulldozer, then swiftly sets out to eliminate the human population using its new body. The story is about their struggle for survival, and is wrapped around an engineering problem: How can the survivors defeat such a formidable opponent when they are cut off from outside help and have limited resources? The result might have been an interesting piece of suspense fiction in the hands of a lesser writer, but Sturgeon enriched the plot with his usual gift for making the reader care about his characters. The novelette was filmed for television with reasonable faithfulness.

King, Stephen
(1947–)

Although most of Stephen King's fiction has included elements of horror, several of his novels could just as easily have been published as science fiction. A case in point is his first novel, *Carrie* (1974), in which the telekinetic powers of the title character are never explained in supernatural terms and who therefore may be simply demonstrating a psi power not uncommon in science fiction. Uncharacteristically, the "monster" in this case is a generally sympathetic character, an abused teenage girl who is driven over the edge by her inexplicable power and the torments directed toward her because of her repressed personality. *The Stand* (1979) is for much of its length a traditional postapocalyptic novel—in this case the human population had been decimated by a plague—but the arrival of a supernatural menace later on alters its nature. Psi powers would be the basis of further novels, precognition in *The Dead Zone* 1979) and pyrokinesis, the ability to spontaneously create fires, in *Firestarter* (1980). *The Dead Zone* examines a famous ethical question, usually phrased as a question: If you could go back through time and kill Adolf Hitler as a child, would you be morally justified in doing so? In this case, the protagonist has visions of the future and knows that a currently popular politician will eventually instigate a nuclear Armageddon unless he is killed before he gains that power. King's distrust of the government recurs in *Firestarter*, this time in the form of a malevolent government agency that seeks custody of a young girl in order to use her as a weapon.

As Richard Bachman, King wrote two traditional dystopian novels. *The Long Walk* (1979) revolves around a walking competition, the winner of which reaps a great reward, while the losers also lose their lives—a template that King uses to reflect the excesses of repressive government. More successful was *The Running Man* (1982), thematically similar and reminiscent of Robert Sheckley's "The Prize of Peril" (1958). Although closer to pure science fiction than any of his other work, neither novel was particularly innovative, and both lacked the strongly delineated characters that would distinguish his other fiction from that of his contemporaries. King would later revive the Bachman name for *The Regulators* (1996), an inventive but unsatisfying novel about

an alien being with the power to make imaginary figures seem real.

King subsequently used alien intruders as the basis for several novels. In *It* (1986) a single creature lies mostly dormant under a small town in Maine. An entire spaceship full of aliens is reawakened in *The Tommyknockers* (1987), using their mental powers to influence the minds of nearby humans and forcing them to become an involuntary labor force to unearth the disabled ship. King repeated this latter theme again in more limited form in *Desperation* (1996), where a single alien insidiously warps the mind of a small-town sheriff, with the predictable body count. His most recent novel of alien invasion is *Dreamcatcher* (2001), which uses another variation of mental control, but this time casts an insane military officer as the primary villain. *From a Buick 8* (2002) is the least interesting of King's science fiction, with a much narrower focus. A group of state police troopers have been secretly concealing the existence of a strange quasi-automobile that is somehow the interface between our own universe and another dimension.

Several of King's short stories about monsters imply that the creatures have natural origins, as in "The Raft" and "The Crate," and the strange phenomena and bizarre creatures of "The Mist" appear to be aliens from another dimension, although King is rarely explicit in his explanations. King has been largely ignored by the science fiction community, and little of his work follows genre traditions. It seems likely that, with the passage of time, novels like *It* and *The Dead Zone* in particular will be recognized as significant contributions to the genre. In 2003 King announced that he would no longer be writing fiction. If that is the case, he will still have left behind a large body of work in both horror and science fiction, as well as a smaller but no less impressive amount of mainstream fiction.

Kingsbury, Donald
(1929–   )

Although Donald Kingsbury's first short story appeared in 1952 and his most recent novel in

2002, the intervening years saw fewer than a dozen short stories and only two other novels. The best of the shorter pieces was *To Bring in the Steel,* a novella. The plot involves efforts by a private company to exploit the mineral deposits of the asteroid belt, a theme handled in much broader fashion by Ben BOVA in his recent Rock Rats series. The importance of space travel as a source of national security as well as to fulfill the growth potential of the race is reflected in the short novel *The Moon Goddess and the Son,* which was expanded into a much longer novel in book form under the same title in 1987.

His first novel was *Courtship Rite* (1982, also published as *Geta*). Unlike his previous work, the novel's plot was not strictly linear, and uses multiple viewpoint characters. The form is that of a typical lost colony story. The planet Geta can support only a limited population, which has reverted to primitivism, worshiping the orbiting starship that brought them to that world. It was necessary for the first generation to resort to cannibalism in order to survive, and that practice has been handed down as an essential ritual even after it is no longer a dietary requirement. Using a complex and realistically rendered background society, Kingsbury unravels a story of political maneuvering and rebellion against custom that generated considerable critical praise, but Kingsbury's relatively slow output has prevented him from attracting the widespread following that his work might otherwise generate. *The Moon Goddess and the Son* was a more controlled but less inventive novel, and his only noteworthy fiction during the 1990s was *The Survivor,* a novella set in the shared universe of Larry NIVEN's Man-Kzin Wars series.

Kingsbury's most recent novel, *Psychohistorical Crisis* (2001), is set in the universe of Isaac ASIMOV's FOUNDATION SERIES. The protagonist commits a crime for which the punishment is to be permanently deprived of access to the information network that has become central to everyday life. The novel, which is quite long, explores some interesting possibilities, but tends to be slow-paced and occasionally pedantic. Kingsbury remains highly regarded, but his small output has kept his profile lower than it might otherwise have been.

Kirinyaga
Mike Resnick
(1998)

As a frequent visitor to Africa, Mike RESNICK is familiar with the history and customs of several of the cultures indigenous to that area, and he has used them as the basis for several novels including *Paradise* (1989), *Inferno* (1993), and *Purgatory* (1993), each relating the history of a different alien race following its encounter with humans, and each paralleling recent events in a different African nation. Although these novels were sometimes mildly controversial because of what was perceived as a patronizing attitude toward native cultures, it was the Kirinyaga series, particularly the title story and "For I Have Touched the Sky," which transplanted remnants of a traditional Kenyan culture onto another world, that became the most frequent target for criticism.

This time Resnick made no effort to dress his characters up in alien costumes. A group of Kenyans have settled a world similar to their homeland and, under the leadership of a brilliant but highly conservative witch doctor, are recreating the traditional Masai lifestyle, abandoning most of the trappings of technology. When visitors from another world arrive, they are shocked by the apparent cruelties of native practices, including the exposure of certain infants to the elements and the subsidiary role imposed on women—in particular an extraordinarily talented young girl. There is growing pressure for outside intervention, and Resnick does his best to present an objective appraisal of both viewpoints, the external concern for the welfare of the individual and the internal desire to recreate a free and unique culture. The witch doctor may be wrong, but his opinions are honestly held, and he is actually a more principled character than are some of those who oppose him.

Predictably the stories generated sharply split opinions, although Resnick won a Hugo Award for short fiction for one of them. It has been traditional for fans of science fiction to praise the field as a forum for controversial ideas, a place where readers can examine issues in a new context; and in that respect, if no other, the Kirinyaga series is an important and useful work, exploring openly territory that most other writers would avoid even in disguise.

Kline, Otis Adelbert
(1891–1946)

Edgar Rice BURROUGHS never had a serious rival when he was writing his planetary romances set on Mars or his jungle adventures featuring Tarzan, but Otis Adelbert Kline came as close to that role as anyone. He wrote both short stories and novels during the 1920s and 1930s, but none of his shorter work has remained even minimally well known. His novels are more interesting as curiosities than as fiction, although his Mars novels came closest to equaling Burroughs.

Maza of the Moon (1930) was Kline's most original work. A barrage of missiles from the Moon wreaks havoc on Earth, and a single human is dispatched in an experimental spaceship to discover who is responsible and to negotiate a ceasefire. Kline's Venus series consists of *Planet of Peril* (1929), *Prince of Peril* (1930), and *The Port of Peril* (1932/49). A scientist from Earth agrees to swap bodies with a Venusian warrior from the past, intending only to observe the alien culture. Unfortunately, and predictably, he gets into trouble almost immediately, becomes caught up in the local politics, and swashbuckles his way through a series of exciting but implausible adventures.

The Swordsman of Mars and its sequel, *The Outlaws of Mars,* both appeared as magazine serials in 1933 but were not available in book form until the 1960s. As in the Venus books, their hero too swaps bodies in order to travel to another world, and becomes a warrior himself. The Mars books are more frankly imitative of Burroughs, but are also more effective adventure stories.

Kline poached on Tarzan territory with two characters. The title character of *Tam, Son of the Tiger* (serialized in 1931) was raised by tigers rather than by apes and lives in Asia rather than in Africa. In his solo book-length adventure he helps protect the surface world from an invasion by troglodytes living below ground in Burma. A more direct Tarzan clone was Jan. *Jan of the Jungle* was

serialized in 1931 and appeared in book form under that title and as *The Call of the Savage. Jan in India* made its magazine appearance in 1935. Among his adventures is one in which Jan discovers the descendants of lost Atlantis.

Knight, Damon
(1922–2002)

Damon Knight played so many roles in science fiction that it is difficult to believe he was a single person. In addition to producing a substantial body of fiction, particularly short stories, he edited magazines and anthologies, including the highly respected Orbit series of original collections, was cofounder of the Milford Science Fiction Writers' Conference, and was largely responsible for the creation of the Science Fiction Writers of America, serving as its first president. Knight was also a respected critic, probably the first such within the field, and his collection of incisive reviews, *In Search of Wonder* (1956), is still read and imitated. He also translated science fiction from the French, lectured, and even tried his hand at illustration.

Knight started writing short stories in the 1940s, producing "Not with a Bang" and the amusing "To Serve Man" (1950); in the latter, the alien manual with that name turns out to be a cookbook. His first two longer works were the novellas *Masters of Evolution* (1959, also published as *Natural State*) and *The Rithian Terror* (1952, also published as *Double Meaning*). The latter is a clever but routine problem story involving the search for a shape-changing alien. The former provides an interesting contrast between two future human societies, one that employs machines to do most physical work and another that has to some extent returned to a more primitive lifestyle. *The Analogue Men* (1955, also published as *Hell's Pavement*) is a dystopian novel involving mind control and the rediscovery of freedom. Knight's most interesting early novel is *A for Anything* (1959, also published as *The People Maker*), a marvelous invention novel involving cheap matter duplication, which seems initially to be a great blessing for humanity. But in a culture where no material good any longer has value because it can be duplicated endlessly, the only remaining unit of exchange is human life, leading to the return of slavery.

Although his novels were well received, it was his short fiction that distinguished Knight from his peers during the 1950s and 1960s. He displayed a consistent talent for turning old ideas on their metaphorical heads. In "Rule Golden," for example, we learn the consequences of a world in which we are quite literally rewarded in kind for our action toward others. "Four in One" adds new twists to the idea of gestalt personalities, multiple viewpoints in a single body, superimposed on what might otherwise have been a standard monster story. The authorities have a problem developing an appropriate punishment for an alien who actually delights in adversity in "An Eye for a What?" In "O," everyone whose last name begins with that letter mysteriously disappears from Earth. The only remaining man with the capacity for cruelty is honored for his uniqueness in "The Country of the Kind." Knight's considerable body of short fiction has been variously collected in *Far Out* (1961), *In Deep* (1963), *Off Center* (1965), and more recently *One Side Laughing* (1991) and *God's Nose* (1991).

Late in his career Knight returned to novel-length work with a much surer hand. *The Man in the Tree* (1984), Knight's most successful novel, is a superb story of the messianic impulse. The protagonist is able to perform apparent miracles by tapping into the resources of parallel worlds. Although his intentions are good, he inevitably attracts the attention of powerful enemies. To a lesser extent, the same theme is repeated in *Why Do Birds* (1992), wherein a charismatic figure convinces humanity that it must submit to suspended animation. *Humpty Dumpty: An Oval* (1996) is a mix of realistic and surrealistic imagery featuring a man capable of eavesdropping on other realities. The most ambitious project of this period was the CV trilogy, consisting of *CV* (1985), *The Observers* (1988), and *A Reasonable World* (1991). An alien virus begins to infect humans, altering their personalities so that it is impossible for them to commit an act of violence without succumbing to invariably fatal convulsions. The uninfected react predictably, attempting to quarantine those exposed to the disease, but the virus in this case is intelligent itself and foils every effort to contain the spread. Knight confounds expectations this time by portraying the alien life form as a benevolent parasite and describing the ultimate triumph of the invasion as a boon for humanity.

The extent of Damon Knight's influence on the development of science fiction cannot be measured, but it rivals that of Robert A. HEINLEIN or Arthur C. CLARKE. His early reviews and critical essays forced writers to realize that they were not exempt from literary standards just because they had interesting ideas, and his role as teacher and editor undoubtedly shaped the talents of many now prominent writers. Through the creation of the Science Fiction Writers of America he helped bring about a change of attitude—both among writers themselves and among publishers and editors—regarding the standards of professionalism that applied to the genre.

Koontz, Dean R.
(1945–   )

Most authors struggle to put together one successful career as a writer, but Dean Koontz has had at least two. The first one ran from the late 1960s to the late 1970s, during which he was primarily a conventional science fiction writer, although he also wrote a few mainstream thrillers. His second career ran from approximately 1980, when his novels first began to appear marketed as horror, although they rarely contained anything supernatural, and continues to the present. Koontz is nearly as well known in best-seller fiction as is Stephen KING, but where King has occasionally used scientific explanations for his horrors, Koontz almost always rationalizes the fantastic elements in his stories.

Most of the 20 or so early novels were wild adventure stories, sometimes obviously written in haste, although almost always highly imaginative, and there were hints even in the earlier works of the strong characterization and unusual imagery that would dominate his work a few years later. *Beastchild* (1970), for example, presents with considerable sensitivity the friendship between a human and one of the race of aliens who have conquered the Earth. Although *Starblood* (1972) is a potboiler pitting a man with psi powers against a secretive cabal, the plot was the most intricately constructed Koontz had attempted at that point. *The Flesh in the Furnace* (1972) is the best of the novels from this period, a dark and almost poetic story about a man who imbues his animated puppets with a form of life. In *A Werewolf Among Us* (1973) future police officers are fitted with internal computers, allowing them to interface directly with the machines, and creating a formidable opponent for those who wish to operate outside the system. Although *The Haunted Earth* (1973) is technically a fantasy, it draws on science fiction traditions, with aliens opening the gateways to alternate realities where magic works and where racial stereotypes, among other fictions, are real. *Nightmare Journey* (1975), the last of Koontz's novels to be marketed as science fiction, presents a richly detailed future Earth where humanity has retreated from the stars and turned inward, experimenting with altered body forms and telepathy.

The pivotal novel in Koontz's career was probably *Demon Seed* (1973). Although published as science fiction, it is in form a contemporary thriller in which a woman is imprisoned in her own home by a computer system so sophisticated that it is self-aware, though of questionable stability. Koontz wrote several horror novels during the late 1970s, usually under pseudonyms although most have subsequently been reprinted under his own name. It was with *Phantoms* (1983) that Koontz established the pattern that has continued ever since. A small town is plagued by various bizarre manifestations that are created by an amorphous, ageless creature that lives underground, periodically emerging to sample surface life. Koontz's novels have not fared well in transition to the screen, and the film version of *Phantoms* was no exception; but the novel was more ambitious and impressive than anything he had previously written, and his career as a horror writer was now firmly established.

Strangers (1986) is a story of alien manipulation, perhaps even abduction, but not in a traditional fashion. A group of disparate people scattered across the United States react uniformly to a compulsion to travel to a remote location in a sequence reminiscent of what happens in the film

Close Encounters of the Third Kind (1977). Psychic phenomena occur in their vicinity whenever anyone attempts to prevent them from completing their mission. Although marketed as a horror novel, its readers were probably surprised by its dramatic but nonhorrific plot. *Watchers* (1987), filmed three times, features one of Koontz's more interesting characters—a dog with artificially enhanced intelligence who has escaped from a secret government project, pursued by a humanoid creature from the same facility, a malevolent killing machine linked by subtle bonds to the animal. *Shadoweyes* (1987), originally as by Leigh Nichols, is a werewolf story with a scientific rationale. Nanomachines allow an experimental subject to physically alter his body at will, but his mind is warped by the experience. Koontz used a similar device in *Midnight* (1987), but less effectively.

Koontz next wrote another straight science fiction novel, *Lightning* (1988), in which visitors from the future help shape a woman's life, but it was packaged as horror and largely overlooked by SF readers. His plots began to concentrate on psi powers during the early 1990s with *The Bad Place* (1990), *Cold Fire* (1991), and *Dragon Tears* (1993). *Fear Nothing* (1998) and its sequel, *Seize the Night* (1999), feature a common protagonist, unprecedented in Koontz's career, pitting him against the inadvertent consequences of a sinister government project, a virus that causes unpredictable mutations. More recent novels such as *From the Corner of My Eye* (2000) and *One Door Away from Heaven* (2001) have drawn on the possibilities of quantum physics and alternate genetic forms to create situations analogous to magic or the supernatural. Having established himself with his fans, Koontz has unusual liberty to choose the shape of his own career, and it seems likely that he will continue to draw on his origins in science fiction.

Kornbluth, Cyril M.
(1923–1958)

Considering that his career lasted less than 20 years, Cyril Kornbluth left behind a comparatively large body of memorable work, much of it in collaboration with other writers. He first began publishing short stories in the early 1940s, but was virtually idle between 1943 and 1949. His solo novels were generally undistinguished. *Takeoff* (1952) is a competently written but now horribly dated account of the first expedition to the Moon, and *Not This August* (1955, also published as *Christmas Eve*) is the story of the American resistance to a communist invasion force. Only in *The Syndic* (1953) did he demonstrate his imaginative powers impressively. The setting is a future America split into two separate nations, each governed by a rival criminal organization. It mixes violent adventure with broad satire skillfully, and still reads well today.

Kornbluth collaborated with Judith Merrill for two respectable novels, *Gunner Cade* and *Outpost Mars*, both published in 1952; but it would be with Frederik POHL that he would create his most memorable book-length works. *The SPACE MERCHANTS* (1953) is a satire in which an advertising agency has to merchandise the idea of colonizing an inhospitable Venus. The British novelist Kingsley Amis hailed it as the best novel the field had yet produced, and the successful team would collaborate for several more titles, although none surpassed their first. *Gladiator-at-Law* (1955) was the closest in quality. A future Earth is effectively governed by rival conglomerates rather than the titular elected governments, and society has degraded into brutal violence and pressure toward conformity. A young lawyer caught between two of the warring giants discovers that all is not as it appears, that the apparent competition masks a sinister alliance.

Pohl and Kornbluth collaborated on several more novels, not all of them science fiction. *Search the Sky* (1954) concerns a remote star colony that breaks off communications with Earth, and an attempt to find out what happened after the passage of several years. *Wolfbane* (1959) does a fine job of describing a future in which enigmatic aliens are using the solar system for their own purposes, but the novel turns into a routine adventure story in its closing chapters. Some of Kornbluth and Pohl's better collaborative short stories were collected as *Our Best* (1987).

Several of Kornbluth's short stories are acknowledged classics, most importantly "The MARCHING MORONS" (1951). Kornbluth speculates about what will happen to the overall intelligence level of humanity if the brightest adults decide to have few if any children while those who are mentally challenged breed without limit. The result, he decides, would be a society not only unable to develop new technologies, but also ill equipped to maintain even the existing infrastructure. TWO DOOMS (1958) was one of the earliest and is still one of the best novelettes about the consequences of Germany winning World War II, accomplishing in a few pages as much as other writers have managed in an entire novel. "The LITTLE BLACK BAG" (1950) drops a medical kit from the future into the contemporary world, with brilliantly funny consequences. "Gomez" (1954) is a particularly effective look at the loneliness of advanced intelligence, and "Make Mine Mars" (1952) is a very fine planetary adventure. Years after Kornbluth's death, Frederik Pohl would complete a story based on one of his outlines, "The Meeting" (1972), which won the Hugo Award.

Although frequently satiric and occasionally cautionary, most of his short fiction was good natured and optimistic, and some of his attempts to be openly humorous, as in "Thirteen O'Clock," are strikingly funny. Kornbluth's short fiction has been collected in various combinations several times, the most recent and complete of which is *His Share of Glory* (1997). He also wrote some early and influential critical pieces.

Kress, Nancy
(1948–   )

Nancy Kress started as a fantasy writer, although her first three novels were unconventional and appealed to a wide variety of readers. Her early short fiction generated some attention as well, with "Out of All Them Bright Stars" (1985) winning a Nebula Award. Her output was split between science fiction and fantasy for a time but her fourth novel, *An Alien Light* (1988), marked an apparently permanent break with fantasy. She has since then become associated with hard science fiction, although her stories almost always show more concern with humanistic issues than with the scientific content.

An Alien Light assumes that humans are the first intelligent species to master interstellar travel without first eliminating the drive to fight wars, seen from the point of view of an alien intelligence investigating this unprecedented and daunting new species. *Brainrose* (1990) is an interestingly inventive dystopian novel about a society menaced by a new plague and a repressive, corporately underwritten religion.

Kress began turning heads in earnest with her short novel *Beggars in Spain* (1991), expanded two years later as the first volume in a trilogy, with *Beggars and Choosers* (1994) and *Beggars Ride* (1996) continuing the story. Genetic engineering and other advances have enabled a minority of the population to eliminate the need for sleep and gain other advantages over the population at large. Although initially tolerated, the enhanced humans find themselves increasingly separated from normal humans, and by the second volume the separation has become physical as well, with the modified community living in an isolated region. The distancing fails to slow the process of disaffection, however, and in fact the minority has been experimenting with their own children, resulting predictably enough in a third strain even further divorced from the past.

Stinger (1998) moved in the direction of the mainstream thriller. An FBI agent becomes suspicious when a new disease appears that specifically targets minorities, and eventually uncovers a plot that has its origin in lofty places. *Maximum Light* (1998) takes us on a tour of a future world where declining fertility has left the planet populated by middle-aged, childless people who see the possible extinction of humanity looming in the future. A group of gifted children communicate with apparent aliens in *Nothing Human* (2003), a less convincing but sometimes emotionally involving novel.

Her second trilogy of novels consists of *Probability Moon* (2000), *Probability Sun* (2001), and *Probability Space* (2002). Humanity is at war with the alien Fallers—a war that is not going well. A scientific expedition supposedly studying a primitive race on a remote world is actually trying to decipher the technology of an ancient alien device that serves to connect all the local inhabi-

tants through a form of shared consciousness that guides them through their everyday lives. Assuming that the device can function as a weapon, the scientists remove it from the planet, causing considerable chaos as shared reality collapses. The overt adventure story and the war with the Fallers are engaging and entertaining, but it is the unique culture of the third race that makes the series stand out from other, similar space adventures.

Kress has proven herself to be a steady if not prolific writer at shorter length. Her stories can be found in *Trinity and Other Stories* (1985), *The Aliens of Earth* (1993), and *Beaker's Dozen* (1998). She started a new sequence of novels with *Crossfire* (2003) and *Crucible* (2004), in which the protagonists must unravel the mystery of a recently discovered, primitive alien race who are quite obviously not native to the world where they are found. Kress is part of a new generation of SF writers who recognize that a story built around even the most original and exciting new idea is interesting only if it contains credible characters who can react to that stimulus.

Kube-McDowell, Michael
(1954–   )

During the early 1980s, Michael Kube-McDowell began writing a series of short stories that were part of a loosely constructed future history known as the Trigon Disunity, and that eventually would culminate in a trilogy that opened with *Emprise* (1985), set on a postcollapse Earth in which scientists are feared and hated and forced to hide their activities from the public. The advent of aliens bearing new technologies forces a rejuvenation of human civilization, which continues in *Enigma* (1986) as the world discovers that the stars bear enemies as well as friends. The sequence concluded with *Empery* (1987), pitting a human interstellar empire against a resurgent alien threat. Although the author's solutions are sometimes unconvincingly straightforward, the trilogy was enlivened by its enthusiastic speculation about the possibilities of a greater human destiny.

Alternities (1988) is a story of parallel worlds, entertaining but less ambitious than the trilogy and perhaps indicated that the author was catching his breath. His fifth novel, *The Quiet Pools* (1990), was certainly an extraordinary leap forward for his career and is still his most successful single work. On the surface, the novel is a reexamination of an old genre theme. An enormous project is underway to facilitate exploration of other star systems, but opinions on Earth are sharply divided. Some are wholeheartedly supportive of what they see as the fulfillment of human destiny, while others consider the project a foolish and wasteful expenditure of resources that could better be devoted to the welfare of those on Earth. Kube-McDowell explains this disparity in genetic terms, suggesting that the drive to expand and explore is a physical characteristic and not a universal human trait. What might have been a routine melodrama is instead a serious and thoughtful examination of the psychology of an entire species, as reflected in his characters.

Exile (1992) uses a distant colony world to reflect current events and force the reader to look at them more objectively. Residents of a newly created settlement find themselves in conflict with their own children, whose ideas about the shape of their personal future vary considerably from those of their elders, in a scenario that is quite obviously based on the abortive 1989 student uprising in China. The author is careful to present a reasonably objective view of all sides in the debate, although ultimately the resolution cannot be completely satisfactory. *The Trigger* (1999), written in collaboration with Arthur C. CLARKE, is a marvelous invention story with a wish-fulfillment theme. Scientists discover a way to detonate explosives remotely, without a physical connection, making firearms more dangerous to their owners than to their theoretical targets. *Vectors* (2002), though well written, may have been too metaphysical for most readers who were used to the relatively hard science in his earlier work. An experiment in personality recording leads to a form of reincarnation. Kube-McDowell invariably presents interesting ideas and poses difficult questions. He obviously has the talent to become a major genre writer, but to date his career has moved fitfully and uncertainly.

Kurland, Michael
(1938–   )

Michael Kurland's career began with a lightweight but amusing space adventure, *Ten Years to Doomsday* (1964), written in collaboration with Chester Anderson, and a handful of minor short stories. It showed signs of taking off with *The Unicorn Girl* (1969)—a sequel to *The Butterfly Kid* (1967) by Chester Anderson—a refreshingly lighthearted story in which a band of hippies with the ability to visit other universes have various adventures. Kurland's subsequent fiction was considerably more conventional, and only sporadically lived up to the promise of his early work. *Transmission Error* (1970) is a colorless chase story involving matter transmission, but *The Whenabouts of Burr* (1975) is a delightfully original and inventive story of alternate history.

In *Pluribus* (1975) a plague has wiped out most of the human race, and the majority of the survivors blame scientists for the disaster. This makes it difficult for researchers in the Mars colony to disseminate medication that could prevent a new and more virulent form from killing off the surviving population. Kurland grapples with very serious themes this time, and handles the change of tone well, but *Tomorrow Knight* (1976), after a promising opening, devolves into a predictable space adventure.

Kurland had won an Edgar Award for his mystery writing in 1969, and he combined mystery and science fiction for his next—and best—novel, *The Infernal Device* (1979), a Sherlock Holmes pastiche. Holmes and his archenemy, Dr. Moriarty, find themselves reluctant allies when the czar of Russia plots to use a superweapon against the British Isles. The story is an effective secret history as well as a fine detective story. Kurland's novels during the 1980s, including *Psi Hunt* (1980), *Star Griffin* (1987), and *Perchance* (1989), were reprises of standard genre themes and situations that had nothing new to say, and were written in a casual style that failed to involve the reader with the characters. His short stories, which are invariably competent but rarely inspired, are collected in large part in *Images Conceits & Lollygags* (2003). Kurland clearly has the potential to produce major work, but seems content for the most part to confine himself to less ambitious projects.

Kuttner, Henry
(1914–1958)

Although it has become generally known that much of the fiction that appeared under the names Henry Kuttner and Lewis Padgett consisted of collaborations between the author and his wife, C. L. MOORE, these were rarely acknowledged at the time. Indeed, the extent of their cooperative effort is open to speculation. Based on her solo work, it seems likely that Moore was a much more active participant in their partnership than the bylines would indicate. That said, the body of work ascribed to Kuttner under his own and several pseudonyms is surprisingly large and robust for a career that lasted only 20 years and included science fiction, fantasy, and several mystery novels.

Kuttner first began appearing in SF magazines in the late 1930s; these were mostly weird tales and exotic fantasies at first, written under various pseudonyms, a habit that proliferated after his marriage to Moore in 1940. The most successful of these alternate personalities was Lewis Padgett, under which byline a collection of short stories would later appear, *Line to Tomorrow* (1954). Perhaps the first Kuttner story to become widely known was "The Twonky" (1942), in which aliens invade the Earth disguised as television sets—the basis for an amusing but minor and almost unknown motion picture. Kuttner's Gallagher stories, about the adventures of an unusual genius who builds remarkable robots, but only when he is under the influence of alcohol, was a remarkably funny series in a genre that usually disparages humor. The stories were collected as *Robots Have No Tails* (1952, also published as *The Proud Robot*).

Excellent stories followed quickly. In "Mimsy Were the Borogoves" (1943) educational toys are sent back through time with interesting consequences for the recipients. "Nothing But Gingerbread Left" (1943) posits the possibility that a jingle could be devised that is so enticing that soldiers exposed to it are no longer fit for duty—possibly the inspiration for the Monty Python skit

about the "killer joke." The Baldy stories, collected as *Mutant* (1953), intelligently anticipate the main conflict in the *X-Men*. Following a nuclear war, a significant minority population of mutants lives intermingled with humanity, but a cabal of villainous telepaths hope to provoke a war between the two divergent branches of humanity. By the middle of the 1940s Kuttner and Moore were turning out a steady stream of stories, alternating between serious and thought-provoking themes, usually at short length, and broad adventures in space and time like *Earth's Last Citadel* (serialized in 1943 but not published in book form until 1964), in which a contemporary couple is placed in suspended animation until the distant future, where they resolve a crisis on a dying Earth.

Most of the novels that followed were limited in scope, yet were equal to or better than most of the other fiction of that era, although most would not appear in book form until the 1960s. *Valley of the Flame* from 1947, for example, is a lost world adventure in the tradition of A. Merritt. Explorers discover an underground world whose inhabitants are descended from cats and who have the ability to manipulate the passage of time. *The Time Axis* from 1948 is a less plausible melodrama involving time travel and a killer from the future. The most significant of the novels is *Fury* (serialized in 1947 and in book form in 1950; also as *Destination Infinity*). Following the destruction of Earth in a nuclear war, the remnants of humanity survive in domed cities under the oceans of Venus. The discovery of immortality leads to a fossilized system that resists change, until one member of the aristocracy rebels against his own kind. Despite the outdated view of conditions on Venus, *Fury* remains a powerful novel of its type and has inspired a sequel by David DRAKE. Many other novels from this period mixed magic and science indiscriminately and are more properly fantasies.

Kuttner and Moore continued to produce high-quality short fiction until Kuttner's death in 1958. Moore almost immediately switched to writing for the screen and published no new science fiction during the last 30 years of her life. Possibly the best of their supposed collaborations was VINTAGE SEASON, published in 1948 and filmed as *Disaster in Time* (1992), although there is some evidence that this novelette was actually written almost entirely if not exclusively by Moore. Tourists from the future travel back through time to observe disasters at first hand. This premise might have led to a melodramatic adventure, but Moore's tale is very quiet and moving.

Kuttner and Moore's short fiction has been collected and cross-collected numerous times. The best collections are *No Boundaries* (1955), *Bypass to Otherness* (1961), *Return to Otherness* (1962), and *The Best of Henry Kuttner* (1975). Kuttner's influence has been acknowledged by Ray BRADBURY, among others, and stories like "HOME THERE'S NO RETURNING" and "The Children's Hour" ensure that he will always be remembered as one of the early masters of the field.

L

Lafferty, R. A.
(1914–2002)

Raphael Aloysius Lafferty started writing much later in life than was the case with most other major talents, selling his first story in 1960. He was a prolific short story writer until the 1980s, and a reasonably productive novelist as well. His work was usually deceptively playful in tone and style, but his themes were often more serious, reflecting his conservative Roman Catholic beliefs. His idiosyncratic prose distinguished his early work, but his writing would become progressively distanced from mainstream science fiction as the years passed, eventually to the detriment of his career. Several characters recur in his work in various guises, including irritating adolescents, unspoiled but mentally impaired observers, dirty old men, and reluctant geniuses.

His early short stories were almost always well received, and titles like "Narrow Valley," "Nine Hundred Grandmothers," "Camels and Dromedaries, Clem," and "Thus We Frustrate Charlemagne" were all talked about as potential award winners, although Lafferty would not collect a Hugo Award until 1972, for "Eurema's Dam." His popularity received a sudden boost in 1968 with the publication of three novels. *Space Chantey* is a humorous parody of the *Odyssey*, transposed to outer space, and was very similar in tone to his short fiction. *The Reefs of Earth* raised the bar considerably. The Puca family lives on Earth, but their origin is uncertain. They have strange powers and their children are a repugnant lot who decide to wipe out everyone on Earth except themselves. Happily, they fail—but only after some very funny and bitingly satiric adventures. *Past Master* was much more serious in tone, and demonstrated that Lafferty was capable of far more significant work. A planet whose utopian society is beginning to fail decides to seek the advice of an expert, so they reach back through time to kidnap Sir Thomas More. He is eventually installed as their political leader, but ultimately discovers that, despite their assertions, his fellow citizens have not created a perfect society after all. Predictably, More ends up being the scapegoat for their failings.

Fourth Mansions (1969) proved to be an even more impressive novel, although its unique styling and unusual cast of characters confused many casual readers. Seven very disparate people—some not entirely human—are called upon to save the world from a mysterious conspiracy of evil. Lafferty's concern with moral issues was prominent once again, as was his detailed knowledge of religious philosophy and practices. His short stories also showed increasing sophistication, particularly "CONTINUED ON NEXT ROCK," "Interurban Queen," and "Eurema's Dam." *Arrive at Easterwine* (1971) was a more pointed satire, composed as the autobiography of an artificial intelligence who has a rather jaundiced view of human civilization; but despite moments of wry wit, the story is unfocused and disappointing, coming as it did after a steady stream of superior work.

Lafferty's fiction became increasingly quirky and obscure during the 1970s, and while individual short stories were admired, it was rarely with the previous degree of enthusiasm. His next novel, *Not to Mention Camels* (1976)—the story of a man who lives simultaneously in three separate universes, in each of which he has fantastic and sometimes surreal adventures—was uneven and hampered by a poorly constructed plot. *Apocalypses* (1977) consisted of two short novels unrelated in setting or plot, but sharing a common metaphysical theme. Lafferty's work, which had sometimes edged into fantasy in the past, now seemed to hover suspended between fantasy and science fiction, satisfying neither group of readers. The plot of *Aurelia* (1972) is comparatively straightforward. A girl from another world visits the Earth, where some believe her to be a supernatural being. Lafferty's diversion into religious themes was more pronounced than ever, but he failed in this case to blend them into a compelling story. *Annals of Klepsis* (1983) is another surreal adventure that blurs the distinction between fantasy and science fiction, with a protagonist who appears to be a kind of disembodied spirit.

Most of Lafferty's short stories have been collected, though not always by major publishers. The best selections can be found in *Nine Hundred Grandmothers* (1970), *Strange Doings* (1972), *The Golden Gate and Other Stories* (1985), and *Lafferty in Orbit* (1991). There has been sustained interest in his work, particularly in the small press—clear evidence that his fiction remains influential and reasonably popular. He left a considerable body of fiction unpublished at the time of his death. Many of the short stories have since appeared from small press publishers, issued in collections and as chapbooks. Although these works sometimes rival the quality of his earlier fiction, most are idiosyncratic and obscure. A novel, *Serpent's Egg,* appeared in 2003, a satirical look at the future that has moments of genuine sharpness, but which is otherwise encumbered by the author's penchant for obscure metaphorical constructions and loose plotting.

"The Last Hurrah of the Golden Horde"
Norman Spinrad
(1969)

The British New Wave movement of the late 1960s and early 1970s revolved around *New Worlds Magazine,* edited by Michael MOORCOCK. Although the stylistic extremes prevalent in that group remained primarily a British phenomenon—the best examples of which were by Moorcock, J. G. BALLARD, and Langdon Jones—a few American writers also contributed, of whom Norman SPINRAD is the most prominent. The JERRY CORNELIUS SERIES, conceived and for the most part written by Moorcock, involves a recurring character who is an exaggerated, sometimes surreal, variation of James Bond. Moorcock occasionally allowed other writers to borrow his character for their own work; although most of these are now forgotten, a few endure, including this one.

Cornelius is a professional spy and assassin, contracted in this episode to eliminate the second-in-command of the Chinese government, even though no one really knows the man's identity. Aided by Russian intelligence agencies, Cornelius infiltrates a meeting between Chinese drug dealers and high-ranking Mafia officials just as a remnant of the ancient Mongol horde goes on its final rampage. The plot sounds very traditional, but the execution is not. All of the conversations are slightly off. They are composed of strings of clichés uttered by stereotyped characters, spies and criminals alike, who are implicitly compared to the aging, doomed Mongol warriors. The text consists of snapshots rather than scenes, which become progressively shorter and more surreal as the story progresses.

At the crucial moment, Cornelius plays rock music on a high-tech violin whose emanations cause general insanity. The Mongols arrive just in time to contribute to the final chaos while Cornelius, his job completed, slowly fades into the night. A casual reader might conclude that Spinrad was simply playing with popular themes and had no serious intent, but the story is in fact a satire implying that the caricatures—spies, politicians, and so forth—are just as obsolete and doomed as the pitiful, aging Mongol warriors who ride out on their last raid. Ultimately the New Wave narrowed its appeal to such a small group of readers that it could not survive, but the best and most accessible stories from that movement have survived to be read by a new generation that accepts stylistic experimentation as an author's prerogative.

The Last of the Winnebagos
Connie Willis
(1988)

Science fiction writers have shown us the world under the rule of everyone from the Internal Revenue Service to the advertising industry, usually for satiric purposes; but in this novella Connie WILLIS quite seriously shows us a future in which the Humane Society has nearly dictatorial powers. A devastating plague wiped out all of the dogs in the world, and other animals, like ferrets, provide an inadequate substitute. Following the death of the last dog, a guilty humanity made it a serious crime to kill similar animals, sometimes using extra-legal powers to track down those responsible.

A photojournalist has been sent to interview the elderly couple who live in what apparently is the last recreational vehicle still in use. Most states have outlawed such vehicles. There is some question about how truthful the couple's stories are, but the journalist is more interested in the couple as people than because of their vehicle, which he knows is not really a Winnebago. En route, he sees a dead fox in the road and reports it, as the law requires, shaken because it reminds him of the death of his own dog, run down by a young woman 15 years earlier. On an impulse that has been building ever since that event, he visits her, involving them both in a dangerous game of deceit and reconciliation. Government agents suspect that she was driving the vehicle that killed the fox and that he is covering up for her, both of which actions are now major crimes.

There is an element of satire here, of course. People have a tendency to overcompensate following a tragedy, passing laws or taking actions that would not even have been considered during less emotional times. But unlike most satirists, Willis takes great pains to develop the two principal characters into credible people, driven by conflicting emotions and subject to self doubt and error. *The Last of the Winnebagos* achieves its greatest effect because it is more plausible than we

would like to believe. The novella won both the Hugo and Nebula Awards.

The Lathe of Heaven
Ursula K. Le Guin
(1971)

Unlike Ursula K. LE GUIN's other science fiction novels, this early effort is set on Earth in the near future. Although the fantastic content in the story is rationalized, the explanation is less than convincing; the extraordinary powers of the protagonist are virtually magical. In fact, the novel is essentially a variation of the fantasy of the genie and the lamp or the legend of the deal with the devil. If you could wish for anything you wanted and have that wish granted, would you have the wisdom to choose wisely?

George Orr is a man troubled by what the rest of the world perceives to be delusions. He believes that if he dreams things that conflict with existing reality, he will find the world changed to conform to his fantasy when he awakens. Dr. William Haber is the psychiatrist treating Orr, convinced, as is everyone else, that his patient is merely imagining things. But as the treatment continues, Haber loses his certainty. He eventually discovers that what Orr is saying is the literal truth—that the man can change reality merely by dreaming it.

Like Aladdin with the lamp, Haber suddenly has visions of a better world with himself as its architect. Pollution and overpopulation have steadily eroded the quality of life in the world, and he decides to restore things to the way they should be, with himself as the arbiter of conflicting demands. He uses the power of suggestion to influence Orr's dreams, but the game is played by rules far more complex than those he imagined. A simple wish for an improvement in one aspect of creation has repercussions elsewhere. In solving the world's obvious problems, Haber introduces greater, more insidious ones whose solutions he cannot grasp, and his fumbling efforts to do so exacerbate things even further. In his attempt to save the world, Haber succeeds only in destroying himself.

The Lathe of Heaven illustrates the fact that there are no easy solutions to difficult problems, that human civilization is a complex and interrelated structure that cannot be easily altered, and that the effect of tremendous power, even when wielded for supposedly altruistic purposes, is the corruption and destruction of the one wielding that power. Although less ambitious than most of Le Guin's other novels, it is by far the most direct and efficient in delivering its message.

Laumer, Keith
(1925–1993)

Keith Laumer sold his first story in 1959 and had over two dozen more published by 1962, including "Diplomat at Arms," whose main character would be reworked slightly to become the central figure in the extensive RETIEF SERIES of adventures of an interplanetary diplomat. Over the course of the next 10 years, Laumer would produce a remarkably large and consistent body of fiction, both short stories and novels, much of which fell into one series or another. His output dropped dramatically during the 1970s because of failing health, but he continued to write novels and occasional short stories until his death.

Laumer's debut novel, *Worlds of the Imperium* (1962), was the first adventure of Brion Bayard, a character who later appeared in Laumer's mainstream novel about the diplomatic corps, *Embassy* (1965). Bayard is kidnapped and transported to an alternate universe where Earth is ruled by an iron-fisted dictator, who turns out to be Bayard's alternate self. He eventually takes his place in an amusing takeoff on *The Prisoner of Zenda*. Bayard has to defend his people from invaders from yet another timeline in *The Other Side of Time* (1965), and the entire fabric of space and time is endangered in the third book in the series, *Assignment in Nowhere* (1968). Laumer brought Bayard back belatedly in *Zone Yellow* (1990), this time to fight off armies from a world where the rats have evolved into an intelligent but bellicose species.

A second series with a somewhat similar theme began with *The Time Bender* (1966). Lafayette O'Leary finds himself in an alternate world where advanced technology mimics magic. The O'Leary stories were considerably lighter in

tone than the Bayard series, although the plots were not that dissimilar. O'Leary becomes lost in parallel worlds in *The World Shuffler* (1970), runs into an alternate version of himself in *The Shape Changer* (1972), and uncovers the secret masters of the universe in *The Galaxy Builder* (1984). *The Monitors* (1966) has a clever premise similar to that of *30 Day Wonder* (1960) by Richard WILSON. Aliens arrive on Earth and reduce human civilization to chaos by forcing us to abide by the letter of every law on the books, with hilarious consequences. The amusing novel led to a surprisingly unfunny motion picture version in 1969.

Several media tie-in books and less successful genre work followed, and it was not until 1969 that Laumer produced another notable novel, *The Long Twilight*, which to some extent anticipated the Highlander movies, though without the magical component. Two immortals who have survived throughout all of human history continue their violent rivalry in the future. The novels that followed were generally much better than his previous work, and considerably more serious in tone. A small town falls under the influence of a strange force in *The House in November* (1970). An expedition into prehistory is attacked by enemy time travelers in *Dinosaur Beach* (1971). *Night of Delusions* (1972) is an alien invasion story in which the protagonist learns the truth about a secret infiltration while he is undergoing dream therapy. *The Glory Game* (1972) is Laumer's most didactic novel, a castigation of appeasement that reflected the Vietnam conflict and disarmament talks, in this case transplanted into outer space.

The first collection of Retief stories was *Envoy to New Worlds* (1963), which would be followed by several others as well as by seven novels. Some of the novels were noteworthy, particularly *Retief and the Warlords* (1968), but the shorter fiction tended to be repetitive and does not hold up well when read in large doses. Another series of short stories would eventually be collected as *Bolo* (1977), followed by the novel *Rogue Bolo* (1986); these works all deal with robotic fighting machines whose sophistication becomes so advanced that eventually they effectively become intelligent beings. A late addition, *The Stars Must Wait* (1990), is considerably less satisfying. *A Plague of Demons* (1965) explored similar themes, this time with humans' brains wired into war machines. The Bolo series proved to be so popular that a series of anthologies followed in which other writers added to their history and exploits, and new volumes have continued to appear as recently as 2003. Although Laumer's later novels are all competently written, they often repeat earlier themes and generally lack the sense of humor and imaginative force of his previous work.

Laumer's nonseries short stories have been collected in *Greylorn* (1968), *It's a Mad, Mad, Mad Galaxy* (1968), *The Big Show* (1972), *The Best of Keith Laumer* (1976), *Alien Minds* (1991), *A Plague of Demons and Other Stories* (2003), *Future Imperfect* (2003), and elsewhere. His best short stories include "Thunderhead," "The Day Before Forever," and "The Further Sky." Laumer rarely attempted anything more than light adventure fiction, but his occasional efforts at more serious themes suggest that he was potentially a writer of much more substance.

Le Guin, Ursula K.
(1929–   )

Ursula K. Le Guin's career as a writer started with a handful of short stories published during the early 1960s, followed by three short novels during the period 1966–67. All three novels are sophisticated planetary romances, as would be most of her future science fiction novels, although the element of adventure was increasingly subordinated to more serious themes. In *Planet of Exile* a small human colony stranded on an inhabited alien world must forge an alliance with one of the local tribes to provide a united front against another far more barbaric culture. *Rocannon's World* utilizes a similar theme on a different scale. This time a human scientist is studying a planet inhabited by three separate humanoid races. He tries to help them when they are invaded by an outside force with a more advanced technology. *City of Illusions*, the most substantial of the three, is set on a future Earth that has been conquered by an alien race who systematically smash the technology of any potential rivals for dominance in their region of space. In

typical heroic fashion the protagonist becomes a key element in efforts to break the cycle. All three novels, which also involve psi powers, were set in the same universe, but they are not otherwise strongly linked.

Le Guin's next novel, *The Wizard of Earthsea* (1968), was an extremely popular fantasy that would over time be followed by several excellent sequels, although none ever rivaled the impact of the first book. Even more significant was *The LEFT HAND OF DARKNESS* (1969), which firmly established her loosely constructed Hainish series, a future history that assumes that human life was actually spread through the galaxy by the people of the planet Hain. The novel is set on Winter, a world currently caught up in one of its periodic ice ages. The inhabitants are human but androgynous, a premise that provided Le Guin with an excellent forum in which to examine gender issues, greatly aided by her background in anthropology. *Left Hand* won both the Hugo and Nebula Awards and attracted attention from mainstream literary critics as well.

Le Guin's next science fiction novel was *The LATHE OF HEAVEN* (1971), a complete departure from her earlier work. Set in the contemporary world, it describes the efforts of a psychologist to take advantage of an incredible power displayed by one of his patients. Whatever the man dreams becomes reality when he wakens. Unfortunately, if rather predictably, every effort to improve the world just makes things worse than they already were. The novel has been filmed twice.

Two notable novellas followed, *VASTER THAN EMPIRES AND MORE SLOW* (1971) and *The WORD FOR WORLD IS FOREST* (1972), both set in the Hain universe. The first involves a world dominated by plants rather than animals; the second, which won a Hugo Award, is an allegory for the war in Vietnam. "Nine Lives," "The Ones Who Walk Away from the Omelas," and "Winter's King" were also exceptional stories from this period. Most of Le Guin's early short fiction was collected in *The Wind's Twelve Quarters* (1975).

The Dispossessed (1974) is often considered her most successful novel. The surface plot concerns the life of the scientist who developed a means of nearly instantaneous communication over interstellar distances, a breakthrough that helped shape the culture of the Hainish series. The real story is the comparison of two separate cultures, a planet that still practices a very competitive form of capitalism and an inhabited moon whose people have for generations enjoyed a form of near anarchy. Neither is a true utopia, however; each is flawed and is incomplete without the other. Once again Le Guin won both the Hugo and Nebula Awards.

During the late 1970s a significant portion of Le Guin's work was either fantasy or mainstream fiction. *The Eye of the Heron* (1978) was science fiction, a short and slightly heavy-handed novel about a group of pacifists who are exiled to a violent planet and nearly destroyed before they come to an accommodation with their neighbors. *Always Coming Home* (1985) is her longest novel, centering on a somewhat untraditional utopia set in a small community in a future postdisaster West Coast. The book is filled with fascinating glimpses and scenes, but as is the case with most utopian fiction, the narrative is not consistently strong enough to sustain the more serious commentary.

The Telling (2000) is another Hain novel, set on a planet whose relatively primitive population took drastic steps to force themselves to become more technological and capable of competing with the civilizations beyond their own world. To sever the bonds of the past, they systematically eradicated their entire history, destroying all books, refusing to pass on information to the next generation, creating new social structures as a conscious act that would better prepare them for the future. The protagonist is a historian from offworld who tries to unearth what knowledge remains so that it can be preserved, but who is largely unsuccessful. As is the case with most of Le Guin's created societies, the issue is not clear-cut. The population obviously stands to benefit in material ways from this draconian act, but they have also lost something of great importance. Her most recent book, *Changing Planes* (2003), is a collection of very loosely linked stories, mostly allegories and parables that are more impressive when presented together than when read separately.

The most commonly recurring theme in her work, particularly the novels, is the quest by an individual to discover his or her destiny, or at least his or her place in the world or worlds. Le Guin's later short fiction has been collected in *The Compass Rose* (1982), *Buffalo Gals and Other Animal Presences* (1987), *Four Ways to Forgiveness* (1996), and *The Birthday of the World* (2002). The best of her later fiction includes "Newton's Sleep," "The Birthday of the World," "The New Atlantis," and "Forgiveness Day." With the possible exception of Philip K. DICK, Le Guin is the most highly respected science fiction author within the academic community, and she retains her high position among genre readers as well.

Lee, Tanith
(1947–   )

Tanith Lee began her writing career with children's fantasies, and most of her subsequent fiction has also been within that genre. Her first adult novel, *The Birthgrave* (1975), is technically science fiction, although it is in tone and detail much more akin to magic than to science. Along with its two sequels, *Vazkor, Son of Vazkor* (1978) and *Quest for the White Witch* (1978), it describes the history of a primitive planet whose population is split into various tribes, all of whom are prey to superstitions despite efforts to unite the planet under a single government.

Don't Bite the Sun (1976) is a much more traditional science fiction story, rich in imagined detail. The extremely well-drawn protagonist is a woman, most of the time, living in a world where death is just another illness, and where biotechnology has made it almost as easy to change your body as to change your socks, including reversible gender switches. The story continues in *Drinking Sapphire Wine* (1977), in which our hero finally manages to annoy the tolerant utopian government of Earth sufficiently that she is forced into exile. She is also clever enough to subvert even that attempt to force her to conform. The two novels were later reissued together under the latter title.

Electric Forest (1979) is an ugly duckling story. The only unattractive woman on a planet where everyone is engineered to be perfect falls in love with a man who promises to help her change her appearance. *Day by Night* (1980) is set on a colony world whose orientation to the sun never changes; the people living underground on the day side concoct elaborate myths about the supposed denizens of the dark side. A woman falls in love with a robot built in the semblance of a man in *Silver Metal Lover* (1981), and then faces separation when his model is recalled by the manufacturer. There is an underground civilization in *Days of Grass* (1985), this time sheltering from the aliens who have conquered the Earth. A young woman emerges onto the surface, is taken prisoner, and then learns the truth about what really happened to her world. *Eva Fairdeath* (1994) is a quiet dystopian novel set in a future where the Earth has become horribly polluted and is dying, although the novel ends on a hopeful note. Several of Lee's other novels have science fiction elements in them, but usually mixed with magic or other fantastic devices that place them as fantasy. It is in that genre that Lee has made her reputation, but *Don't Bite the Sun* and *Silver Metal Lover* in particular prove that she could be just as successful if she had chosen a different path for her writing.

The Left Hand of Darkness
Ursula K. Le Guin
(1969)

Ursula K. LE GUIN's early short novels were set against the common backdrop of the Hainish universe, one in which the inhabitants of the planet Hain seeded human life-forms throughout the galaxy, incorporating them into an empire once they have independently achieved interstellar flight. The first three novels had been intelligent but comparatively light adventures. *The Left Hand of Darkness* was the first to prove that Le Guin was an emerging talent of considerable importance and that she would not be content to follow directly in the footsteps of the writers who had preceded her.

The novel is set on the planet Winter, an icebound world whose inhabitants have evolved into an androgynous species—that is, they are not sexually differentiated and can serve in either male or female roles, although gender roles themselves are

virtually nonexistent. This explicit discussion of gender and sexual orientation was so startling for science fiction even as late as 1969 that the publisher felt constrained to state that the book was "in no way a 'sensational' novel," although in fact it was exactly that, winning both the Nebula and Hugo Awards as best novel of the year.

Despite the superficial differences—the 30-year winter and the sexual orientation of the inhabitants—Winter seems much like Earth. Le Guin describes its culture in terms very similar to that of our own history and society, and the planet is not filled with monsters or exotic life-forms. When outsiders visit the world they are given pause not by the physical environment in which they find themselves, but by a culture that functions sexually in a fashion that leaves them puzzled at best, revolted at worst. The androgynes, who periodically go through periods of sexual activity during which they seem to choose their roles almost randomly, have evolved a peaceful society, not torn by sexual tension.

The surface action in the novel is a dangerous trek across the snow-covered landscape, but the real tension and conflict is within the minds of the characters, the outsiders who cannot decide how to interact with the locals or even whether such interaction is of any value, and the inhabitants of Winter itself, who have avoided one source of conflict but who may be headed directly toward a different one. The novel is one of the masterworks of science fiction, taking full advantage of the possibilities of the genre to examine a contemporary social issue in a unique context.

Leiber, Fritz
(1910–1992)

Many science fiction writers have written fantasy or horror fiction as well, although few have excelled in more than one genre. Fritz Leiber is probably the only writer to have an enviable reputation in all three branches of fantastic fiction. His novel *Conjure Wife* (1953) and the short stories in *Night's Black Agents* (1947) and elsewhere established him as an important horror writer, his Fafhrd and the Gray Mouser sword and sorcery series rivals even

Conan in popularity among fantasy readers, and his science fiction includes several award winning stories as well as the excellent Change War time travel series.

Leiber's first story sale was in 1939, but he wrote no significant science fiction until 1943, when *Gather Darkness!* first appeared in serial form. The setup is a future world dictatorship with the rulers cloaking themselves in the costume of an organized religion in order to frighten the mass of the population into obedience. The inevitable resistance movement springs up, and appropriately they adopt the guise of demons and devils in a dramatic, if not entirely credible, symbolic gesture. Despite its occasional lack of plausibility, the novel is a rousing adventure story with some clever plot twists; and the policy of the government to awe the populace by mimicking supernatural intervention is a not particularly veiled swipe at human gullibility. His next novel, *Destiny Times Three* (1945), was a lackluster effort about a man who discovers that he exists in three different although interlocking realities, but *The Sinful Ones* (1950, also published as *You're All Alone*) was much better. The protagonist in this case discovers one day that he is one of the few remaining human beings in a world in which robots are masquerading as people. *The Green Millennium* (1953), like many of Leiber's short stories during the early 1950s, was satirical, following the adventures of a man who is concerned that a robot might make him obsolete. Among Leiber's targets was contemporary sexual mores, which he lampooned in a fashion somewhat daring for its time. The corrupt American government is secretly in league with organized crime in an association reminiscent of that in *The Syndic* (1953) by Cyril M. KORNBLUTH.

The Change War series appeared in the late 1950s, and despite the small number of titles in the series, it ranks with Poul ANDERSON's Time Patrol as the best of its type. *The BIG TIME* (1958) won a Hugo Award, and the shorter "Try and Change the Past" is also excellent. The premise is that two organizations, known familiarly as the Snakes and the Spiders, are battling back and forth through time in an effort to maintain or change the existing course of history. The quality of Leiber's short fiction in general improved dramatically, and the themes were wide-ranging. Leiber appeared equally adept at satire and adventure, serious themes and humor. Stories like "A Deskful of Girls," "The Big Trek," and "Night of the Long Knives" made him a frequent and welcome contributor to the magazines.

His next novel was *The Silver Eggheads* (1962), a satire on the writing community. Robots have been programmed to act like people, and authors use machines to produce their fiction, rather than doing it themselves, feeding in basic ideas but leaving the prose and plot construction to their mechanical servants. The brains of prominent citizens—including a handful of actual writers—are preserved in smooth metal receptacles where they remain conscious. When a crisis threatens to disrupt the flow of new novels and stories, radical methods are used to save the situation. *The Silver Eggheads* is Leiber's most underrated novel.

Leiber became an even more productive short story writer during the 1960s, producing such minor classics as "Kreativity for Kats," "The Man Who Made Friends with Electricity," "The Secret Songs," and "Far Reach to Cygnus." His major collections from this period are *A Pail of Air* (1964), *Night of the Wolf* (1966), and *The Night Monsters* (1969). He also produced his most praised novel, *The Wanderer* (1964), in which the world is ravaged by the near passage of another astronomical body. The story follows the separate stories of various survivors, concentrating on realistic, common experiences rather than on the usual heroic efforts to reestablish civilization. His characters are deliberately flawed and occasionally fail, and the result is a much more convincing blend of tragedy and hope than is common in that form. Although *The Wanderer* is certainly one of the outstanding disaster novels, it is somewhat surprising that it was more popular than Leiber's more original work.

A Specter Is Haunting Texas (1969) was another superb satire. A visitor from the Moon—where the lower gravity has resulted in very tall, thin body types—visits a future independent Texas that dominates North America, and where genetic engineering has made Texans into virtual giants who tower over their Mexican slave population. The visitor becomes the inadvertent inspiration for a revolution in what is clearly a parody of a long-standing and often used science fiction plot. Leiber's knife-edged wit was at its best, and he handles the occasionally uneasy mix of sarcasm and light humor deftly. His short fiction continued to appear with regularity and was rarely less than excellent during the 1970s; the best of his work of that decade is probably the Hugo Award–winning "CATCH THAT ZEPPELIN." Several major collections appeared during that period including *The Book of Fritz Leiber* (1974), *The Second Book of Fritz Leiber* (1975), and *The Worlds of Fritz Leiber* (1976). Although Leiber continued to write short fiction throughout the 1980s, his output dropped dramatically at that point.

The Change War series has been assembled in its entirety as *Changewar* (1983). Other late collections include *The Ghost Light* (1984), *The Leiber Chronicles* (1990), and *Kreativity for Kats and Other Feline Fantasies* (1990). Leiber also wrote the authorized novelization of the film *Tarzan and the Valley of Gold* (1966), only marginally science fiction, but probably the best-known and most successful addition to the chronicles of Edgar Rice BURROUGHS's most famous character. Leiber continued to contribute to all three genres throughout his career, and his last Fafhrd and the Gray Mouser story appeared in 1988. *The Dealings of Daniel Kesserich* (1997) was a previously unpublished novel written in the 1930s and is only of historical interest. Fritz Leiber will probably be best remembered for his short fiction, but several of his novels deserve an equal place of honor.

Leinster, Murray
(1896–1975)

Murray Leinster was the pseudonym of William F. Jenkins, whose first short story, "The Runaway Skyscraper," appeared in 1919. Although some of his novels during the early 1930s were marginally science fiction, they were far inferior to his short fiction at that time. Stories like "Sidewise in Time" and "Proxima Centauri" were quite popular and are still readable today, although some of his other early fiction is rather dated. Leinster was largely inactive in the late 1930s, but returned to the field in the 1940s with a steady stream of excellent short stories, including "FIRST CONTACT,"

still regarded as the archetypal story of the first meeting between humans and aliens, "The Ethical Equations," and "Skit Tree Planet." Leinster was writing when the genre itself was new and several of his early stories are more important historically than they are as literary works. He is often credited as the originator of the concept of parallel worlds, in "The Fifth-Dimension Catapult" (1931) and the better-known "Sidewise in Time" (1934), and was one of the first writers to mix science fiction with the mystery thriller.

Several space operas appeared during the late 1940s, but again Leinster's novels were inferior to his short stories, a situation that did not change until the 1950s. Leinster then wrote a trilogy about the near future of the space program, consisting of *Space Platform* (1953), *Space Tug* (1953), and *City on the Moon* (1957). All three were essentially spy stories involving sabotage, international politics, and the physical dangers of life aboard a space station or in a Moon base. Although the science in the trilogy has not aged well, it still conveys a sense of enthusiasm about the space program that has largely disappeared from modern science fiction. *Operation: Outer Space* (1954), set in the same future, is a more ambitious story of a trip to the Moon and the discovery of a faster-than-light drive. The characters are more interesting but the plot is unfocused and implausible.

Leinster was one of the very few genre writers who regularly employed inimical aliens, sometimes outright monsters, in his novels. *The Brain Stealers* (1954), for example, is set in an Earth that has been secretly invaded by aliens capable of controlling human minds from a distance. The novel has an interesting setup, because most scientific endeavors have been outlawed by a repressive government; but the author ignores this in favor of a protracted chase sequence as the aliens try to eliminate the only one who knows of their existence. Alien invaders also provide the menace in *The Other Side of Here* (1955), a much better novel about intruders from another dimension who can render the entire population within a limited area unconscious while they steal whatever they want and transport the loot to their home reality.

"Exploration Team" (1956) won Leinster his only Hugo Award. It was part of a short sequence of stories about a team whose job was to explore new worlds, collected as *Colonial Survey* (1956, also published as *Planet Explorer*). Another sequence of stories followed the adventures of colonists stranded on a world of giant insects. These were also collected as a novel, *The Forgotten Planet* (1954), which is Leinster's best book. During the 1950s, Leinster began writing stories about the Med Service and a star-traveling doctor named Calhoun who was always in and out of trouble. This series, which includes the short novels *The Mutant Weapon* (1959) and *This World Is Taboo* (1961), has been cross-collected several times. *Quarantine World* (1992) and *Med Ship* (2002) are the most complete selections.

Leinster wrote several novels in which the Earth was menaced by some form of alien life. The most inventive of these was *War with the Gizmos* (1958), in which a gaseous life form suffocates its human victims while remaining itself essentially invisible. The most suspenseful was *The Monster from Earth's End* (1959), in which living descendants of prehistoric trees are discovered in the Antarctic and set loose on an isolated island where they become ambulatory and menace the local inhabitants. This novel was filmed less than impressively as *The Navy vs. the Night Monsters* (1966). Aliens invade Earth and establish bases under the oceans in *Creatures of the Abyss* (1961), but the alien menace in *Operation Terror* (1962) turns out to be a hoax perpetrated by the government. "The Thing from the Sky" and "Fugitive from Space" are also very suspenseful monster stories.

The Pirates of Zan (1959) was a space opera, one of the best of several Leinster would write in the years that followed. During the 1960s Leinster would become more prolific at novel length, producing a steady stream of original work as well as several media tie-in novels linked to the television shows *Men into Space*, *Land of the Giants*, and *The Time Tunnel*. His original novels were more interesting, though usually not up to the quality of his earlier work. A notable exception is *The Wailing Asteroid* (1961), a near-future space thriller about a beacon in space that alerts Earth to the approach of an alien enemy. It was filmed ineptly as *The Terrornauts* (1967). Also of interest is *Talents, Incorporated* (1962), in which a corporation gathers together people with various psi powers in order to harness their abilities for constructive purposes.

Leinster's subsequent novels were uniformly well written, but he rarely attempted anything out of the ordinary. They were predominantly space adventures like *Miners in the Sky* (1967) and *Space Gypsies* (1967). *The Greks Bring Gifts* (1964) sets up a potentially interesting situation. Technologically advanced aliens arrive on Earth, freely dispensing scientific knowledge and asking little in return, at least initially. The title, if nothing else, telegraphs the "surprise" revelation that it is all an elaborate trap. Leinster had largely abandoned short fiction after 1963, and most of his best work had been at that length. There have been numerous collections of his work over the years, including *Monsters and Such* (1959), *The Aliens* (1960), *Twists in Time* (1960), and *The Best of Murray Leinster* (1978), but the most comprehensive selection can be found in *First Contacts* (1998). Of particular merit are "Keyhole," "The Strange Case of John Kingman," and "The Lonely Planet."

Lem, Stanislaw
(1921–)

Although there was a considerable body of science fiction published in the former Soviet Union and the erstwhile Warsaw Pact nations, most of it was tame and unimaginative by Western standards and very little has been translated into English. The Polish writer Stanislaw Lem is the outstanding exception to the rule. He had published mainstream novels with modest success before turning to science fiction in the 1950s, and this has been the main outlet for his work ever since. Communist state policy placed restrictions on literature, but Lem's recurring theme of the dangers of unrestrained military ambitions caused him no difficulties with the authorities.

Lem's most famous novel is *Solaris* (1970), filmed twice but with only modest success. A group of scientists are studying a newly discovered planet whose world ocean is essentially a single sentient being that is capable of showing the humans manifestations of people who have died. The scientists speculate that the ocean being is the repository of disembodied memories from which a quasi-reality can be generated. *The Invincible* (1973) is perhaps Lem's best-sustained suspense story. Space explorers find the remains of an earlier expedition that was apparently attacked by an unknown force and prepare as best they can to resist their unseen enemy. *Eden* (1989) has a similar premise. In this case the space travelers are stranded after a mishap with their ship, on a planet whose original native race appears to have disappeared, supplanted by its own creations, both mechanical and biogenetically engineered.

The situation a group of explorers find themselves in is considerably less personally threatening but no less tense in *Fiasco* (1988). The human race has finally become relatively enlightened about the dangers of military posturing—at which point it encounters a less advanced race on a distant world that seems to be on the brink of destroying itself in a senseless war. It is the Earth that becomes the strange planet in *Return from the Stars* (1980). Because of the time dilation effect, a space pilot returns to a world that has changed dramatically since his departure. Everyone voluntarily submits to a procedure that removes the violent tendencies from their personalities, but the pilot resists efforts to make him conform.

In *The Investigation* (1974) police officials are puzzled by a strange new phenomenon. Dead bodies are mysteriously moving from one place to another or disappearing entirely, and all efforts to discover the cause of the phenomenon fail. The solution lies not with criminals, however, but with the existence of another world impinging on our own. MEMOIRS FOUND IN A BATHTUB (1974) has one of the most interesting premises in Lem's work: A new virus attacks paper products, destroying them completely and spreading so quickly that no counteragent can be found in time. The last bastion of conventional paperwork is the Pentagon, which has sealed itself off from the rest of the world and evolved into a strange new culture of its own. Lem's satiric side is evident in even those works with a serious tone.

Chain of Chance (1978) is another story of scientific investigation. The laws of chance have been altered, and unlikely events have become more common. *His Master's Voice* (1983) makes

use of another familiar theme—the message from space that might be a great boon for humanity but might also be the first sign of a deadly threat. Unfortunately, Lem uses the plot as a forum for extended musings about the nature of humanity that continually encumber the story.

Lem has made use of at least two recurring characters. Ion Tychy is a spaceman who discovers the truth about a supposed utopia after nearly falling prey to its drugged inducements in *The Futurological Congress* (1974). He travels to the Moon to investigate the activities of some suspicious robots in *Peace on Earth* (1994), achieving considerable humorous effect because the protagonist's brain has been altered so that different parts of his body act of their own volition. Tichy's shorter adventures are collected in *The Star Diaries* (1976) and *Memoirs of a Space Traveler* (1982). The second recurring character, Pirx the Pilot, has even less-likely adventures in his two collections, *Tales of Pirx the Pilot* (1979) and *More Tales of Pirx the Pilot* (1982). Two other books, *The Cyberiad* (1974) and *Mortal Engines* (1977), collect loosely related stories involving robots.

In the latter part of his career, Lem has concentrated more on short fiction than on novels; some of these stories have been collected in *The Cosmic Carnival* (1981). Also of interest are three books that consist of whimsical essays; reviews of nonexistent books, some of which were written in the future; and other unusual pieces that generally avoid traditional narrative forms: *A Perfect Vacuum* (1978), *Imaginary Magnitude* (1984), and *One Human Minute* (1986), respectively.

Lensman series
Edward E. "Doc" Smith

It is difficult for contemporary science fiction readers to understand the impact of the Lensman series by Edward E. SMITH, which virtually invented the galactic empire and the general attributes of future interstellar civilizations reflected in almost every similar book that has followed. The series consists of six titles, although *Triplanetary* (1948, magazine version in 1934) is a prequel of sorts and not part of the main story line. The remaining volumes, in chronological order, are *First Lensman* (1950), *Galactic Patrol* (1950, magazine version 1937), *Gray Lensman* (1951, magazine version 1939), *Second Stage Lensmen* (1953, magazine version 1940), and *Children of the Lens* (1954, magazine version 1947).

The universe is dominated by two alien empires, the Arisians and the Eddorians. The former are benevolent and are engaged in a program of development of the other races of the galaxy, hoping to build a vibrant, powerful community of worlds that will be capable of resisting the encroachments of the less altruistic Eddorians. The Arisians are selectively breeding some individuals who will have talents and abilities far beyond those of others of their kind and who will become warriors against the Eddorians and their front organization, Boskone. These selected individuals will also be fitted with a Lens, a technological marvel that provides telepathic and other psi powers. One of those receiving this gift is Kimball Kinnison, a human, who is the protagonist for most of the series. Kinnison is initially unaware of his greater role, because the Arisians are hesitant about providing too much information early in the development of their client races.

Triplanetary introduces the conflict on Earth, a war between two alien influences that is conducted without the knowledge of most of the human inhabitants, who are not even aware that aliens are among them. The action properly gets underway in *First Lensman,* after humans have achieved the ability to travel about the galaxy. Although the interstellar culture is largely open and free, the planet Arisia has always been shrouded in secrecy and closed to human visitors. All that changes when one specific human, Kinnison, is summoned there for a visit in which he receives a Lens and is told only part of the story of the conflict with the Eddorians. The reluctance of the Arisians to tell the full story is a plot device that allows Smith to reveal new wonders and layers of complexity in the subsequent volumes.

Kinnison is serving a kind of interstellar police force in *Galactic Patrol,* ostensibly this time battling a band of interplanetary pirates who use highly advanced technology to conduct their raids.

The source of their superior equipment is ultimately revealed to be the Eddorians, who resort to every possible method to subvert the stability of Arisia and its allies. The Galactic Patrol squares off against another criminal organization in *Gray Lensman,* this time destroying a major tool of the Arisians, as Kinnison begins to suspect the scale of the conflict into which he has been thrust. He resorts to infiltration in *Second Stage Lensmen,* penetrating into the heart of another Eddorian-linked front group and dealing their plans a further setback, although the Arisians and their allies will not be completely triumphant until *Children of the Lens,* in which Kinnison's children are actually at the forefront in the climactic battle.

Smith, who is often called the father of space opera, wrote very crudely by contemporary standards. His characters, particularly the females, are sketchily drawn, one-dimensional, and invariably noble or evil as their roles in the stories dictate. The scientific content was superficial and the plots often involved contrived situations and solutions. All that notwithstanding, he was far ahead of his contemporaries, in his abilities of conception and execution; despite the shortcomings of his novels, they have been in and out of print several times and still find an interested audience. More importantly, he created the basic form of the galactic civilization, one that would be revised and expanded by Isaac ASIMOV, Poul ANDERSON, and others and that is still the most commonly shared vision of the far future. Smith wrote several other novels, none of which rival the stature of the Lensman series. *The Vortex Blaster* (1960, also published as *Masters of the Vortex*) consists of several shorter pieces set in the same context as the Lens series, although it does not share characters or contribute to the main story.

Lessing, Doris
(1919)

Doris Lessing was born in Persia (now Iran) to British parents, and her early exposure to Sufi mysticism is reflected in much of her work, both within science fiction and in her much more widely known mainstream fiction. Lessing's stories often deal with gender roles and the idea of human spiritual transformation. Her major genre work was the Canopus in Argos series, five novels set in an interstellar community dominated by a single empire, but diverse in its individual cultures. Each novel focuses on a distinct social, ethical, or spiritual issue. Although there is an obvious satirical element in each, they are written as straightforward novels rather than open satires. The series puzzled many mainstream critics, who failed to realize that a wholly invented culture provides a unique opportunity to examine the themes Lessing addresses in that series. However, the author herself may have lost interest in the experiment; further volumes, originally projected, have not appeared.

Lessing flirted with science fiction themes elsewhere. *The Four-Gated City* (1969), the final volume of the Children of Violence series, has its climax in a near future in which London has collapsed into anarchy. *Briefing for a Descent into Hell* (1971) and some of the stories in *The Temptation of Jack Orkney & Other Stories* (1972) deal peripherally with speculative themes. *Landlocked* (1965) also plays with the idea of psychic powers, but without realistically addressing the issue. The only other indisputable science fiction work is *The Memoirs of a Survivor* (1975). The setting this time is a near future in which pollution has become rampant, the rule of law has largely broken down, and civilization seems to be sliding toward ruin. The protagonists are a woman and her young daughter who manage to survive the turmoil and set about making a place for themselves in the aftermath. As a science fiction writer, Lessing's work may be of only peripheral interest despite its generally high quality. Her greater significance is that she embraced the field without apology when the advantages of speculative fiction were best suited for what she wanted to write.

Lest Darkness Fall
L. Sprague de Camp
(1941)

In *A Connecticut Yankee in King Arthur's Court* (1889) Mark Twain sent a contemporary human on a magical trip back to the time of King Arthur and Camelot. There he manages to introduce certain elements of modern technology and transform the kingdom. L. Sprague De Camp, who has written historical fiction and nonfiction as well as science fiction and fantasy, thought about that and shook his metaphorical head, producing this comic novel, expanded from a shorter version that appeared in magazine form in 1939.

Dr. Martin Padway understands the possibilities of branching realities. Under the proper circumstances, it might be possible to regress in time, change the past, and create an entire new universe based on that intervention. So when he finds himself in the middle of the Roman Empire, he feels quite smug. He could invent gunpowder and establish Rome as an enduring power that would not fall to the barbarians. He could make accurate predictions about the future and gain immense prestige and wealth. He could direct the explorations of Europe to discover the New World centuries ahead of schedule. All of history would be his to command and shape. Or would it?

Padway has overlooked at least three problems: First, although we all know that gunpowder exists and might even have a rough idea of its makeup, there are few of us who could actually mix it in the proper proportions or fashion a device to make use of it. Second, the technological base necessary to create firearms or airplanes or most other modern devices simply did not exist at the time. Padway lacks the wealth and influence required to create the underlying industrial base that could support his grandiose schemes. Third, he underestimates the difficulty involved in convincing people to abandon the old ways of doing things in favor of new ones, particularly those that presently exist only in the mind of a not particularly coherent stranger.

De Camp's refutation of Twain is immensely humorous, but the humor evolves from the situation and is completely plausible in that context. Padway's schemes seem plausible initially, but the author uses his expert knowledge of the technology and psychology of that era to demonstrate why each is doomed to failure. In addition to being one of the most entertaining of de Camp's novels, it is also a brilliant illustration of the forces that constrain technological advance.

Lewis, C. S.
(1898–1963)

Clive Staples Lewis was a professor of medieval English at Cambridge University and a devout Christian, both of which influences are evident in most of his published fiction. Lewis is best remembered today as the author of the Narnia books, a series of seven fantasy novels for children that were well told and inventive allegories of Christian themes. Lewis's main contribution to science fiction is a loosely linked trilogy that is also in large part a Christian allegory whose underlying premise is that each planet has a quasi-supernatural entity linked to it, most of whom are quite rational and reasonable. However, the spirit associated with Earth is malevolent, insane, and shunned by the rest of the universe.

Ransom, the protagonist, travels to Mars in *Out of the Silent Planet* (1938) as the prisoner of an ambitious and ruthless rival. He escapes and goes on a colorful grand tour of the Martian world, interacting with its various inhabitants and discovering the truth about the twisted spirit that governs the Earth. The scientific content was implausible at best, but Lewis was more concerned with allegory than plausibility—a concern that became much more evident in *Perelandra* (1943, also published as *Voyage to Venus*), described as an ocean world. Once again we are drawn into a marvelously realized if somewhat implausible landscape—or in this case, seascape. Ransom's enemy is back, this time cast as Satan poised to tempt the improbably human-looking woman Eve, who is theoretically the ruler of Venus. The sequence concluded with *That Hideous Strength* (1945, published in abridged form as *The Tortured Planet*). The final volume lacked all of the strong points of its predecessors, and is in large part an almost unreadable diatribe against scientists, government, and progress of any sort. A sinister cabal of scientists plots to secretly take control of the world and reshape it in a more orderly but less moral fashion, inspired by the evil spirit whose presence was previously revealed.

Despite their scientific illiteracy, *Out of the Silent Planet* and *Perelandra* are memorable for the evocative scenery and extensive invention. Two stories, "The Shoddy Lands" and "Ministering Angels," are also worthwhile, but most of his other short fiction is inconsequential. *The Essential C. S. Lewis* (1988) is the most comprehensive collection of his work at that length.

"The Library of Babel"
Jorge Luis Borges
(1941)

Although there is a substantial body of Latin American science fiction and fantasy, very little of it has been translated into English, and most of the authors are unknown to readers in the United States. Jorge Luis Borges, an Argentinian writer whose work is frequently fantasy or magic realism, is probably the best known—but that is because his work found a welcoming audience among mainstream readers. His speculative work is acknowledged only peripherally by the genre audience, at least in part because he writes short stories rather than novels. Four of his collections contain most of those that could properly be described as science fiction: *Ficciones* (1962), *Labyrinths* (1964), *The Aleph and Other Stories* (1970), and *Dr. Brodie's Report* (1972).

Many of Borges's stories are in the form of non-fact essays—that is, there are essentially no characters and little if any plot. The "story" is a speculative discussion of some fantastic object or occurrence, in this case a library so immense that it is virtually a universe unto itself. The narrator has lived his whole life in the library and knows no other existence. He speculates about the nature of the library without any expectation of ever understanding it. The library becomes a metaphor for the world. Different sections contain populations of librarians with various conflicting theories about the contents of the books, which are sometimes meaningful and sometimes apparently random.

The language employed by the librarians themselves varies from one floor to another, and communications between regions are constrained or impossible. Theorists believe that the books themselves are each unique, and that in their entirety they contain every possible combination of letters and punctuation marks that exists. Therefore, all knowledge is, by definition, contained within the limits of the library. Presumably, the solution to every problem is contained in one or another book. The books become a metaphor for the collective knowledge of all humanity. Each of us is unique, and within at least one of us, Borges contends, resides the solution to any conceivable problem. The difficulty lies in recognizing that solution and applying it.

"The Light of Other Days"
Bob Shaw
(1966)

One of the most popular and useful devices in science fiction is the story of the marvelous invention. The author postulates some radical new discovery, normally but not necessarily technological, and introduces it into an otherwise familiar world. The reader is invited to observe the possible effects on human civilization in general and the story's characters in particular. In its grandest form the marvelous invention could be workable robots, a method of achieving immortality, or the discovery of faster-than-light travel. The scale could be smaller—invisibility, matter duplication, or a new type of weapon, for example—but the repercussions might be just as far reaching.

Some of the most interesting stories of this type, however, are those that suggest a modest discovery, something that seems entirely possible. Bob Shaw's most famous short story, "The Light of Other Days," did exactly that, with the introduction of slowglass, a form of glass so dense that light actually takes a measurable amount of time to penetrate it. The stars are so distant that the image we see in the sky is what they looked like hundreds and even thousands of years in the past, because it took that long for the image to cross the immense distances in space. That same principle is applied here. When you look into a piece of slowglass, what you see on the other side is what it was exposed to at some time in the past; the time elapsed depends upon the thickness of the individual pane.

The implications unfold slowly. Slowglass can be used as a recording device. Spies could use it to capture visual records of industrial or military secrets. A murder committed in its presence might

be solved merely by waiting for the image of the crime to emerge from the opposite side. But there is a downside as well: Since the image emerging does not reflect what is actually happening at that moment, a vehicle with a slowglass windshield would obviously not be able to respond to current conditions. Shaw explored some of the consequences of this mythical but plausible discovery in his original story and in two sequels, then combined all three into the novel, *Other Days, Other Eyes* (1972). Although necessarily somewhat episodic, the book-length version explores a wide variety of applications beyond those of the original story.

Limbo
Bernard Wolfe
(1952)

Bernard Wolfe wrote very little science fiction—only a handful of short stories plus the dystopian satire *Limbo* (also published as *Limbo 90*)—although he produced a considerable body of mainstream fiction. Wolfe, who had a background in psychology, constructed his novel around his interpretation of the self-destructive impulses of humanity. The setting is a postapocalyptic future civilization where people voluntarily have their limbs amputated to make it more difficult for them to pursue the arts of war—an extreme and punning form of disarmament—and where medical lobotomies are performed to make it impossible for individuals to have aggressive impulses.

The story is told from the viewpoint of a theorist who was stranded among primitives for many years, during which time some of his ideas were adopted by the governments of newly formed nations and applied in a warped and extreme form. One clear message from the story is that complex problems cannot be addressed adequately by simple solutions. Wolfe is also critical of the premise that advanced technology will provide the tools we need to correct social problems, because in fact the surgical treatments are actually exacerbating things and adding new levels of complication, not removing the root cause. The novel's tone is satirical and quite bitter.

Some critics have also interpreted the novel as a satire on science fiction itself, while others have ignored it as peripheral to the genre. Wolfe made no secret of his bias against scientific progress and by association any form of literature that attempted to glorify science and technology. That alone would have made it unlikely that genre writers would emulate his style or his theme. It did, however, anticipate the move toward longer and more serious novels that would later diversify and enrich the field.

"The Little Black Bag"
Cyril M. Kornbluth
(1950)

Most of Cyril M. KORNBLUTH's best novels were written in collaboration with Frederik POHL, whose longer and more successful career has greatly overshadowed that of his early writing partner. Kornbluth's solo novels were mildly interesting at best, but his short stories include many genre classics. As in "The MARCHING MORONS," Kornbluth speculates that the future of humanity is threatened by genetics. The talented few who create the advances that support our technological civilization are an increasingly small proportion of a population dominated by those barely able to manage these devices, let alone conceive or design them.

The protagonist is Dr. Bayard Full, a contemporary man fallen from his profession, an alcoholic living a squalid existence. His life is about to be changed because of an event that occurs in the distant future, when the intelligence of most people has dropped to an almost subhuman level, but civilization appears highly advanced because of the presence of a handful of geniuses and their technological wonders. A medical bag from that future is accidentally sent back through time, and it falls into Full's uncomprehending clutches. Unaware of its nature, Full uses what he thinks is a hangover cure, only to find himself cured of his alcoholism entirely.

Not long after, Full and his unwelcome partner Angie, a young girl with a ruthless attitude toward survival, discover the truth. With his self-esteem restored, Full founds a clinic, using the marvelous instruments and drugs to cure a variety of ailments. When Full decides that it is time to donate the bag and its contents to a higher authority who can better make use of the gift, Angie rebels; she is more interested in using it to ensure her own security. In a rage, she kills Full with one of the instruments, convinced that she knows enough to continue his practice on her own. Unfortunately, the murder registers itself through a monitoring device in the future, as a result of which the bag's energy source is turned off. When Angie later attempts to demonstrate the safety of the instruments on her own body, she inadvertently commits suicide.

There have been many other variations of the base story since 1950, but few manage to capture the simplicity and directness of the plot of Kornbluth's classic. The story is, of course, an update of the fairy tale of the goose that laid the golden eggs. When granted a wonderful gift, it is often unwise to try to make more of it than it already is.

Little Fuzzy
H. Beam Piper
(1962)

The question of what it means to be human is one that long has tantalized science fiction writers, and several novels and stories have involved attempts to establish the definition by legal procedures, including formal trials. Eando Binder's ADAM LINK, ROBOT (1965) and *The Positronic Man* (1992) by Robert SILVERBERG and Isaac ASIMOV ask that question about self-willed robots; John BARNES inquires into the rights of recorded personalities in *The Merchants of Souls* (2001); David GERROLD speculates about the legal status of artificial intelligences in WHEN HARLIE WAS ONE; and Jean Bruller, writing as Vercors, challenges the reader to decide at which point a hominid becomes a human being in YOU SHALL KNOW THEM (1953).

H. Beam PIPER phrased the problem slightly differently. With the possibility of alien life-forms in the universe, the question might more properly be phrased to ask what constitutes a person. A corporation that specializes in exploiting uninhabited planets has recently been awarded the charter for Zarathustra, supposedly an empty world. Unfortunately, after development efforts are well underway, a prospector returns from the unexplored part of the planet with a family of cute little creatures, whom he claims are intelligent and the rightful owners of the world.

This is a potentially disastrous development for the corporation. If the fuzzies are recognized as intelligent, the corporation's rights to the planet will be revoked and it will suffer significant financial reversals. Certain executives are determined to prevent that from happening, even if that means wiping out the fuzzies before their true nature can be revealed. The climax of the novel is a trial after one of the executives kills a fuzzy deliberately. Is this a murder or simply the destruction of a pet? Piper works out the ramifications in a satisfying and rather touching story in which even the villains are shown to have redeeming qualities.

The popularity of *Little Fuzzy* led to two sequels. *The Other Human Race* (1964, also published as *Fuzzy Sapiens*) describes the necessary adjustments by the human inhabitants of Zarathustra once the legal rights of the fuzzies have been granted. *Fuzzies and Other People* (published posthumously in 1984) details later legal challenges that further define their status. Other writers have expanded the story as well, including William Tuning in *Fuzzy Bones* (1981) and Ardath Mayhar in *Golden Dream* (1982). The fuzzies were briefly popular enough that dolls in their image were sold at science fiction conventions.

Logan's Run
William F. Nolan and George Clayton Johnson
(1967)

During the 1960s, filmmakers expressed considerable fear about the power of youth movements, probably inspired by the demonstrations against the war in Vietnam. Movies like *Children of the Damned* (1964), *Privilege* (1967), and *Wild in the Streets* (1968) warned that this volatile age group could transform the world—and not necessarily for the better. Science fiction writers were less inclined to panic. Robert Shirley's *Teenocracy* (1969) was a satire on the subject, but William F. Nolan and George Clayton Johnson dealt with the theme more seriously.

Following some unspecified catastrophe, a new order has been established on Earth. In order to prevent a recurrence of the overpopulation that led to the earlier troubles, everyone over a certain age is automatically killed, and the population has largely been conditioned to accept this as a normal part of life. Occasionally those facing death attempt to escape, and an elite corps of assassins is employed to track down and kill the renegades. The protagonist is one of these enforcers who agrees to participate in an undercover mission and whose sympathies are eventually turned toward the rebel movement. After leaving Earth for a brief period, he returns to confront the computer that administers this dystopian society and end its rule. The novel ends on an optimistic note, although the ability of the sheltered city dwellers to survive without the guidance of the master program is still in question. The film version in 1976 captured the basic concept reasonably well, but the plot proceeds much less plausibly. A short-lived and forgettable television series followed.

Nolan alone wrote two sequels: *Logan's World* (1977), in which those who escaped the domed city where they had spent their entire lives struggle to survive in the outside, natural world, and *Logan's Search* (1980), a less satisfying continuation in which Logan finds himself in a parallel universe where the system he watched die once before still prevails and must be challenged again.

London, Jack
(1876–1916)

Jack London was primarily a writer of adventure stories, the most famous of which is *Call of the Wild*. London embraced socialism, and his views are reflected in his fiction, particularly the novel *The Iron Heel* (1907), in which a capitalist dystopia exploits the working class ruthlessly until it finally rises up in rebellion and overturns the government. Despite its clear political agenda, it was London's most sustained speculative work, well plotted and cleverly executed. Socialist concerns would crop up again in such short stories as "The Minions of Midas" and "The Dream of Debs," as well as in his extensive essays.

The Scarlet Plague (1915) is an early disaster novel in which civilization is reduced to barbarism, a situation that occurs elsewhere in his fiction. The cause in this case is a new plague that kills all but a handful of people, striking its victims dead within a few minutes of their initial infection. *Before Adam* (1908) is set in prehistory, the action revealed to us by means of a contemporary personality displaced through time. *The Star Rover* (1915, also published as *The Jacket*) is more properly fantasy, as it deals with out of the body experiences in a nonrationalized manner. The best and most famous of his speculative short stories is "The Shadow and the Flash," in which two rival geniuses race to discover the secret of invisibility, each achieving his goal by a different route. "A Relic of the Pliocene" is the moving tale of a hunter who kills the last living mammoth. A primitive tribe worships an artifact from outer space in "The Red One."

London's short science fiction stories have been collected in *The Science Fiction of Jack London* (1975) and *Fantastic Tales* (2002). In addition to those mentioned above, "The Rejuvenator of Major Rathbone," "The Unparalleled Invasion"—despite its clear racial bias—and "The Enemy of All the World" are of particular merit. Although Jack London was hardly a major force in science fiction and his work was not imitated to any noticeable degree, he was one of the earliest writers to address utopian literature and the disaster novel in realistic terms; *Before Adam* and *The Iron Heel* are both excellent examples of their respective story types.

Long, Frank Belknap
(1903–1992)

Frank Belknap Long began writing for the pulp magazines during the 1920s—mostly weird and occult fiction. He later fell under the influence of H. P. LOVECRAFT and contributed stories to the Cthulhu Mythos, in which an ancient alien race expelled from our universe seeks to return and dominate humanity, and which were often arguably science fiction as well as horror. The best of these early quasi-SF stories were collected in *The Hounds of Tindalos* (1946). Although some of Long's short fiction from the 1930s is more overtly speculative, it was not until the late 1940s, with a space adventure

series that was eventually collected as *John Carstairs: Space Detective* (1949), that Long began to establish a reputation outside weird fiction.

Long's first science fiction novel was *Space Station #1* (1957), an aliens-are-among-us story set in an orbiting habitat. It was a satisfying if undistinguished thriller, and set the tone for most of the novels that would follow. *It Was the Day of the Robot* (1963) substituted robots and computers for the secretive aliens, but otherwise the conflict was very similar. A considerably better effort was *Mars Is My Destination* (1962), which examined the conflict between two rival corporations, each determined to dominate the colonies established on Mars. The corporations have essentially become supranational entities with their own private armies and nuclear weapons. The colonists, afraid that they will be caught in the middle of this rivalry, initiate an effort to negotiate a settlement, a mission that is hampered by mysterious saboteurs. Several minor novels followed, although *Three Steps Spaceward* (1963) is quite good at times.

Long turned increasingly to stories of alien invasion during the middle and late 1960s with mildly entertaining thrillers like *The Horror from the Hills* (1931/63), *Lest Earth Be Conquered* (1966, also published as *Android*), *Journey into Darkness* (1967), and *Monster from Out of Time* (1970). *Survival World* (1971) was his last and best novel. Long's short stories are significantly more polished than most of his novels, and it is unfortunate that he largely abandoned that form for most of his career. The bulk of his short fiction has been collected in *Odd Science Fiction* (1964), *The Rim of the Unknown* (1972), *The Early Long* (1975), and *Night Fear* (1979). His contributions to the Cthulhu Mythos are generally his most respected work.

Longyear, Barry B.
(1942)

Barry Longyear burst onto the science fiction scene in the late 1970s with a small flood of excellent short stories, most of them set in two loose series. The most famous of these stories was "Enemy Mine," filmed under that name in 1985; David GERROLD subsequently wrote a novelization based on the original story and the screen version. The story is set in the midst of a war between humans and a rather culturally similar though physically reptilian alien race. Two soldiers, one from each side, are stranded together on a desolate world and are forced to put aside their personal differences in order to survive, eventually building a bond of friendship that provides some of the impetus to end the war. The short story won both the Hugo and Nebula Awards, and Longyear would receive the John W. Campbell Award for best new writer that same year.

"Enemy Mine" is set in a loose future history in which Longyear characterized humans as a somewhat belligerent race expanding into the galaxy at the expense of its neighbors. Several related stories were collected in *Manifest Destiny* (1980), each of which explores another aspect of that dynamic. "USE Force" is particularly effective in demonstrating the corrosive effects of a militaristic society on even its own citizens. The quality of Longyear's stories is uniformly high, as in his novel *The Tomorrow Testament* (1983), which is more or less a sequel to his award-winning story, describing the experiences of a female human prisoner held captive on one of the enemy worlds, her gradual reconciliation with her captors, and her subsequent contributions to the eventual peace treaty.

Longyear was writing a second series simultaneously, this one with a much narrower focus. A circus that moves from planet to planet crashlands on an uninhabited world and is cut off from the rest of humanity for a long period of time. As the generations pass, the involuntary colonists multiply and form a new society consisting of tribes based on their ancestors' original roles—clowns, trapeze artists, and other types of circus performers. Using this mildly implausible but interesting background, Longyear wrote what would eventually consist of two collections of short stories, *City of Baraboo* (1980) and *Circus World* (1981), and a novel, *Elephant Song* (1982). Although less ambitious than his other work, the series is undeniably entertaining, particularly the novel and the short, "The Second Law."

A period of ill health interrupted his career during the early 1980s, and he was considerably less prolific following his return to writing. *Sea of Glass* (1987) is a well-written if perhaps overly fa-

miliar dystopian novel. A repressive and possibly self-aware computer network governs the world in a future in which overpopulation has become a global crisis. The protagonist, who manages to escape the system of mandatory universal registration, uncovers evidence that the computer is, quite logically, planning drastic steps to reduce the surplus population. *Naked Came the Robot* (1988) is much more interesting—a broad satire set in a future in which robotic and android labor is displacing the human workforce on a massive scale, causing increasing discontent among the unemployed. To make matters even more interesting, some of the robots are of alien origin, infiltrating the population for their own purposes.

Homecoming (1989) was ostensibly for young adults, but the premise is interesting. Star-traveling dinosaurs return to Earth to find out what happened while they were gone and discover upstart mammals dominating their home world. Convicted criminals are exported to a newly discovered colony world in *Infinity Hold* (1989), an uneven effort that nonetheless occasionally achieves the level of Longyear's early and more significant work. *The God Box* (1989) is a fantasy.

Longyear's production during the 1990s was largely limited to media tie-in novels. His early short fiction was superior in most cases to his book-length works. *It Came from Schenectady* (1984) includes his early, nonseries short fiction, but his later work remains uncollected. "Blood Song" and "Portrait of Baron Negay" are particularly powerful and evocative stories. Several of his later shorts are also memorable, including "Old Soldiers Never Die," "Chimaera," and "Just a Touch of Chocolate," but none of these display the vigorous storytelling skills that marked his fiction during the early 1980s.

The Lost World
Arthur Conan Doyle
(1912)

The "lost world" novel existed long before Arthur Conan DOYLE wrote the classic adventure story whose title has become the generic term for stories of this type. Typically set in remote and unexplored parts of the world, the lost world novel had appeared in the works of H. Rider Haggard, for example, and would be popular well into the 20th century, although the premise became increasingly implausible as the last secluded parts of the Earth were finally charted and demystified. The form never completely died, however, and has had a recent rise in popularity among mainstream thriller writers such as John Darnton, James Rollins, Jeff Long, and others.

In Doyle's novel, an unorthodox scientist manages to organize a small expedition to investigate rumors of a plateau deep in the jungles of South America where certain forms of life long believed extinct might still survive. The scientist, Professor Challenger, would return for additional adventures, but none of the sequels, except for *The Poison Belt* (1913), are of any enduring interest. Doyle's lost world is geographically isolated, at least for most of its inhabitants, because there are no negotiable trails along the steep cliffs, although he never explains why flying creatures were similarly constrained. The expedition arrives in due course, manages to reach the plateau, survives the dangers provided by dinosaurs and primitive humans, and eventually escapes after suffering casualties. Challenger manages to smuggle one dinosaur egg back to England with him, where it escapes in the final pages of the novel.

Doyle's classic adventure was made into a surprisingly good silent film in 1925, and an unsurprisingly bad remake in 1960. Michael CRICHTON's *The Lost World* (1995), although not in any way a sequel, uses character names from Doyle's novel, and Greg BEAR's *Dinosaur Summer* (1998) is set a generation later, after dinosaur circuses have enjoyed a brief sensation and are no longer popular. Although Doyle's novel is not the best-written lost world novel, it is certainly the most famous, and set the plot parameters for all those that followed.

"Love Is the Plan, the Plan Is Death"
James Tiptree Jr.
(1973)

Writing as James TIPTREE Jr., Alice Sheldon produced a steady stream of first-rate short stories.

Her fiction was very much about character, and intelligent alien beings were uncommon in her work, so it is even more surprising that one of her very best stories contained no human characters at all. Other writers have set their stories in nonhuman cultures, of course, but most of these have been either hard science fiction or were humorous and unrealistic. Neither was the case here.

Moggadeet is a young male of a primitive alien race whose exact physical nature we never learn, except that they are armored, have powerful pinchers, are born in litters and never know their fathers, and live in a world that has periodic winters of such intensity that many do not survive. Moggadeet has recently come of age—that is, he has been separated along with his siblings from his mother, and finds himself driven by new and sometimes violent emotions. Then he encounters Leelyloo, a small female, and is caught up in an obsessive love affair.

Moggadeet is more intelligent than his siblings, however. He discovers the truth about his race—that during the periods of intense cold they become irrational, killing each other when necessary in order to survive—and finds that the winters are becoming longer and more intense. He is terrified that during a moment of this madness he will kill his lover, so he decides that the two of them should spend the dangerous season in a cave where they can stay warm enough to retain their reasoning powers. Unfortunately, his stock of food rots prematurely, and his subsequent efforts to maintain captive herds of edible wildlife does not fare much better. Ironically, the plan that Moggadeet recognizes as being inherent to the biology of his race brings about his downfall despite his efforts to thwart it. The pampered Leelyloo has been growing larger during her period of inactivity, and when their stock of food is exhausted, she is powerful enough to kill him instead of vice versa, which explains why Moggadeet's kind never know their fathers.

Unknowingly, in attempting to resist the biological plan, Moggadeet has actually embraced it. By implication, we are all bound by the cycle of life inherent in our nature, and though we might as individuals or as a species aspire to escape the instincts that guide us, that very aspiration is itself part of our own plan.

Lovecraft, H. P.
(1890–1937)

Howard Philips Lovecraft is, of course, best known as a writer of horror stories, particularly those set in the context of the Cthulhu Mythos. Many other writers have elaborated the Cthulhu Mythos, initially with Lovecraft's permission during his lifetime, and many writers, including Brian Lumley and Robert BLOCH, have added to the series since Lovecraft's death. The premise of the Mythos is that the Earth was once ruled by a race of malevolent, physically repugnant creatures who were exiled by a rival power into another universe from which they are constantly attempting to escape. Cthulhu, Nyarlathotep, Shub-Niggurath, and others can be contacted and even summoned through proper rituals that erode the barriers between the universes. Other than these rituals, there is nothing overtly supernatural about these stories. The series can be read as science fiction rather than pure horror.

Although Lovecraft rarely wrote any overt, more traditional science fiction, several of his stories clearly fall into that category. Some were, in fact, published in genre magazines. The most famous of these are "The Color Out of Space" (1927) and "At the Mountains of Madness" (1936). The former title might well be his best single story. A malign force from outer space begins to affect the personalities and then the physical bodies of those who live within its sphere of influence. Brian W. ALDISS would later write an excellent variant of this story as "The SALIVA TREE." "At the Mountains of Madness" is a novelette in which the protagonist goes on a grand tour of the remains of a vanished civilization in Antarctica, discovering to his regret that the inhabitants were not human beings.

Many of the other Mythos stories can be read as science fiction, although most were clearly meant to be weird or occult fiction. "Herbert West, Re-Animator" is a retelling of the FRANKENSTEIN story. "The Shadow Out of Time" (1936) involves a contemporary man whose mind is displaced by a mental time traveler from the distant past. "The Shadow over Innsmouth" and "Dagon" involve gradual genetic changes within a

human population. In "Cool Air" a man discovers the means to prolong his life indefinitely, so long as certain physical conditions are maintained. Eventually, of course, they are not.

Many modern writers who have continued to use the Mythos as background have moved more overtly toward science fiction. Robert Bloch's *Strange Eons* (1979) takes us to a future in which the aliens have succeeded in their quest to return to our universe. Brian Lumley's *The Burrowers Beneath* (1974) and *The Transition of Titus Crow* (1975) read more like alien invasion stories than Lovecraftian horrors. In Adam Niswander's *The Sand Dwellers* (1998), aliens use mind control to influence the action of humans, specifically those with the ability to launch a nuclear strike and precipitate a global war.

Many of Lovecraft's stories have been filmed. "Cool Air" was well adapted as an episode of *The Night Gallery*; other major films have been less satisfactory. *Dagon* (2001) and *The Resurrected* (1970)—the latter based on *The Case of Charles Dexter Ward*—are exceptions, each reasonably faithful in plot as well as tone to their originals. *The Dunwich Horror* (1970), *Lurking Fear* (1994), *The Unnamed* (1988), and *From Beyond* (1986) take considerable liberties with the text, as does *Herbert West, Reanimator* (1985) and its two sequels. "The Color Out of Space" was filmed ineptly but accurately as *Die, Monster, Die!* (1965).

Lupoff, Richard A.
(1935–   )

Richard Lupoff has written two nonfiction books about the works of Edgar Rice BURROUGHS, so it is not surprising that his debut science fiction novel, *One Million Centuries* (1967), should include scenes pastiching that writer among others. The novel is a mildly satiric comedy in which a contemporary man submits himself to suspended animation, awakens in the far future, and travels back through time, surviving a series of not entirely serious adventures along the way. Although unfocused and occasionally awkward, it is still an amusing and entertaining book for readers who are familiar with the genre conventions that the author is targeting. Lupoff wrote shorter parodies of other writers during this period, which were collected as *The Ova Hamlet Papers* (1979).

Most of Lupoff's early fiction continued in the same vein, including *Sacred Locomotive Flies* (1971) and *Space War Blues* (1978), the latter of which incorporated the very fine novelette, "With the Bentfin Boomer Boys on Little Old Alabama." *Into the Aether* (1974) was a send-up of space opera, with an unlikely spaceship and its crew landing on the Moon. His first serious novel was *Sandworld* (1976), a thriller about newcomers to a planet whose previous civilization has collapsed. The explorers encounter a decadent race of vampirish creatures and nearly perish. *The Crack in the Sky* (1976, also published as *Fool's Hill*) is a mild dystopia. The small population of an overpolluted Earth lives in a series of domed cities where drugs and free sex keep their minds off their problems. Within that society, a secret organization rises, determined to improve the moral stature of the race, even if it means killing everyone in the process.

Lupoff reverted to his former style in *The Triune Man* (1976), in which a comic-book artist is hijacked to another universe and impressed into service as its local hero. *The Forever City* (1987) transports its young protagonist through a space warp to an alternate reality that resembles a television program. Lupoff's most memorable work was the duology consisting of *Circumpolar!* (1984) and *Countersolar* (1987). In the first a variety of historical figures compete in a long-distance airplane race, but the story is set in an alternate reality where Earth is shaped like a doughnut instead of a ball. In the second Albert Einstein and Juan Peron are engaged in a race to land on a twin planet to the Earth on the far side of the sun. A second two-book set consisted of *Sun's End* (1984) and *Galaxy's End* (1988). The protagonist is fatally injured and has his brain transferred into a mechanical body, in which form he must deal with the imminent destruction of the Earth.

Lupoff has continued to write offbeat short stories throughout his career. Most of these have been collected in *Claremont Tales* (2001) and *Claremont Tales II* (2002). Although most noted as a satirist, Lupoff's occasional serious fiction has proven that he has diverse talents as well as a productive imagination and an occasionally unique viewpoint.

M

Maine, Charles Eric
(1921–1981)

Charles Eric Maine was the pseudonym of the British writer David McIlwain, who published some short fiction in the fan press as early as the 1930s but did not produce any professional work in the genre until 20 years later. His first novel was *Spaceways* (1953, also published as *Spaceways Satellite*), originally a radio play, in which a mysterious murder at a space launch leads to further complications. Maine would confine himself to near-future settings for the most part during his subsequent career, and several of his novels were actually marketed as mainstream thrillers.

His next novel was one of the exceptions. In *Timeliner* (1955) the protagonist becomes mentally displaced from his own time and physical body, manifesting himself in a succession of other people during a rapid progression forward in time until he finally reaches an era in which the phenomenon is understood and can be reversed. Although this provided a clever device for a grand tour of future history, Maine largely squandered the potential by narrowly circumscribing what his character observes. *The Man Who Couldn't Sleep* (1956, also published as *Escapement*) is the story of a marvelous invention, in this case one that allows the recording and playback of emotions. An entrepreneur exploits the new device so successfully that increasing numbers of people are retreating into what is essentially one of the earlier virtual world scenarios.

High Vacuum (1957) would today be called hard science fiction, because it dealt realistically, for its time, with an expedition to the Moon, predictably beset by problems that eventually endanger the entire mission. As a novel of survival under adverse conditions, it works quite well despite the now dated scientific content. *The Isotope Man* (1958, also published as *The Atomic Man*) was developed from a screenplay and is the first of the Mike Delaney series. The discovery of a mysterious luminescent corpse that appears to be a double of a living scientist presents a cleverly constructed and well-resolved scientific mystery. Delaney would return in *Subterfuge* (1959) and *Never Let Up* (1964), neither of which measured up to the first book in the series.

Maine next tried his hand at a disaster novel, *The Tide Went Out* (1958, later revised as *Thirst!*). Earthquakes result in a drop in sea level, reduction in rainfall, and eventually a worldwide drought that ends modern civilization. The adventures of several survivors are entertaining, but Maine did nothing new with the familiar theme. *World Without Men* (1958) is set in a future in which males are officially extinct and women reproduce themselves through scientific means. Although the government claims that efforts are being made to recreate the male gender, an enterprising journalist discovers otherwise. *Alph* (1972) has virtually the same plot, and is otherwise unrelated, although it reaches much the same conclusion.

Fire Past the Future (1959, also published as *Count-Down*) is another story of murder at a rocket research project, but reflecting Maine's increased experience it was much more polished and engrossing than *Spaceways. He Owned the World* (1961, also published as *The Man who Owned the World*) has another interesting premise. An astronaut on a failed space mission was frozen so quickly that he is perfectly preserved. Generations later he is revived into a very different world and discovers that his investments were somehow protected and have grown to the point where he literally owns most of the planet Earth. A plague destroys most of the population in *The Darkest of Nights* (1962, also published as *Survival Margin* and revised as *The Big Death*), and time travelers from the future attempt to prevent the nuclear war that led to their unhappy era in *Calculated Risk* (1960).

B.E.A.S.T. (1966) is one of Maine's best books, and one of the earliest to consider the threat posed by a computer so advanced that it might become self-aware and view humans as a threat if not an outright enemy. It was Maine's last significant book, other than the redundant *Alph*. Although he wrote occasional short stories, none of these have proven to have any lasting interest. Several of his novels have fallen into well-deserved obscurity, but his better works are still worthy of preservation.

Make Room! Make Room!
Harry Harrison
(1966)

The dangers of overpopulation have, if anything, grown more urgent since this novel was first published nearly four decades ago. At this point in his career, Harry HARRISON was considered a reliable, skillful writer of adventure stories whose occasional satiric content was more likely to be slapstick, as in *Bill, the Galactic Hero* (1965). Initially the novel appears to be typical of his previous work, a standard detective story set in a near-future America; but before it ends, Harrison invokes the spirit of Jonathan Swift's satirical essay "A Modest Proposal" for a macabre and jolting revelation.

The protagonist is a police detective in a New York City whose population is 35 million. Andy

Rusch is a competent but not particularly brilliant investigator, wearied by his years laboring in what he privately considers largely a lost cause. Crime is a part of life and can no longer be controlled. When Rusch begins to suspect a pattern behind a sudden spate of missing persons, he uncovers an unconventional and unsettling new form of recycling. Even more disturbing is the possibility that cannibalization has the unspoken approval of some members of the government. Rusch is an unlikely hero, and the novel does not end with everything working out for the best. The problem, as Harrison portrays it, may well be insoluble, and he provides an extensive bibliography of nonfiction to support his pessimism.

Harrison's cautionary novel was the basis for the motion picture *Soylent Green* (1973), and the book was subsequently reissued under that title. Although the impact of Harrison's original story is greatly reduced in the film version, enough remained that the movie won a Nebula Award. Although the author probably does not believe that his fictional prediction will come true, he does warn us of the tendency of a society under stress to treat its marginal and less powerful members in cruel ways, sometimes tacitly accepting the situation as long as the physical act of exploitation is hidden from sight. Many of Harrison's later novels are more polished and controlled, but it is unlikely that any will have the lasting impact and popularity of this earlier effort.

Malzberg, Barry N.
(1939–)

Between 1967 and 1980 Barry Malzberg produced an amazingly large body of work, including almost two dozen novels and over 100 short stories under his own name and as K. M. O'Donnell. The feat was all the more remarkable because he was simultaneously producing action thrillers under yet another name, as well as writing serious mainstream fiction. One of his earliest stories is still among his best, "Final War" (1968), the story of a reluctant soldier trapped in an endless artificial war. His first novel, *The Empty People* (1969), appeared as by O'Donnell and involved the formation of a gestalt personality. Two short novels, *Dwellers in the Deep* (1970) and *Gather in the Hall of Planets* (1971), under the same byline, both dealt with the role of science fiction fans in greeting the first visitors from outer space; these works satirized both the story form and fans themselves. *Universe Day* (1971), an episodic story that warns of the dangers of letting our technology develop faster than we can adapt ourselves, was the last to appear as by O'Donnell.

The first book to appear under Malzberg's own name was *The Falling Astronauts* (1971). It was one of three unrelated novels that all featured astronauts and their difficulties of adjustment, the others being *Revelations* (1972) and BEYOND APOLLO (1972). In the first an astronaut has delusions following a nervous breakdown, but the delusions later appear to have some objective reality. In the second a possibly insane astronaut threatens to go public with the truth about the space program, but someone is determined to silence him. The third and best involves the only astronaut to have returned from Venus and his reluctance to talk about what happened. Hardcore fans were upset with the tone of the novels, which seemed to imply that the space program was a wasted effort, and with protagonists who were of questionable sanity in a world similarly out of true. They were particularly incensed when *Beyond Apollo* won the John W. Campbell Award.

In the Enclosure (1973) was a caustic indictment of humanity's treatment of outsiders. An alien visitor is promptly imprisoned, and his mind and memories become a resource to be ruthlessly exploited. *Tactics of Conquest* (1973) involves a human forced to play a game of chess whose details and outcome will affect the future of the entire galaxy. Aliens invade the minds of humans in *Overlay* (1972), with surprising consequences. All three of these novels treated traditional genre themes playfully and satirically, leading some to conclude that Malzberg was contemptuous of the field, which the author himself rebuts in his collection of essays *The Engines of the Night* (1982). This misapprehension was apparently confirmed by *Herovit's World* (1973), which caricatured science fiction fans and writers in a less than complimentary fashion.

More novels followed, often involving unusual themes. Miniaturized humans conduct medical procedures in *The Men Inside* (1973), a starship captain with memory lapses tries to solve a mystery in *On a Planet Alien* (1974), and women become a scarce commodity in *The Sodom and Gomorrah Business* (1974). The assassination of President Kennedy is conducted in the ruins of a future New York City in *The Destruction of the Temple* (1974), and in *Scop* (1976) the efforts of a time traveler to prevent Kennedy's assassination appear to have in fact been the cause of the plot. Utopia becomes boring in *The Gamesman* (1975), leading to an elaborate and potentially deadly game, and the universe itself might be accidentally destroyed in *Galaxies* (1975). In one novel after another, Malzberg lampooned genre conventions, sometimes openly, sometimes indirectly. Other novels of note from this period are *Guernica Night* (1975), *The Last Transaction* (1977), and *Chorale* (1978).

Malzberg's production within the field dropped sharply after 1980. Although he continues to produce short stories with relative frequency, there were only two novels in the 1980s, and none since. *Cross of Fire* (1982) may well be his best novel, set in a future where sophisticated dream therapy is used to treat psychological problems. The protagonist relives his life in the role of Jesus Christ. *The Remaking of Sigmund Freud* (1985) is nearly as rewarding. Starships employ a hologram version of Freud for psychological counseling; but when the hologram begins to interact with aliens, the universe is altered irrevocably. The remarkable quality of the last two novels underscores the loss to the field when Malzberg became disenchanted and ceased to write at book length.

Malzberg's body of short fiction is one of the largest in the genre. Most of the better stories have been collected in *Out from Ganymede* (1974), *The Many Worlds of Barry Malzberg* (1975), *The Best of Barry Malzberg* (1976), *Down Here in the Dream Quarter* (1976), *The Man Who Loved the Midnight Lady* (1980), and *In the Stone House* (2000), although many of his more recent stories remain uncollected. The O'Donnell stories were assembled as *Final War and Other Fantasies* (1969) and *In the Pocket and Other SF Stories* (1971).

The Man in the High Castle
Philip K. Dick
(1962)

Alternate history is a common device in science fiction, so it should not be surprising that Philip K. DICK included one such novel among his large and varied output. Much of his fiction is set in a world that looks very much like our own but which contains specific elements that disorient the reader, so variations of our own history would seem to be a natural resource for him to exploit. The novel also makes use of what is probably the most popular point of divergence, the outcome of World War II. In Dick's dystopian alternate reality, Germany and Japan were triumphant, jointly occupied North America, and elsewhere dominate the world.

Dick had dealt with fascism in earlier novels, most notably *The World Jones Made* (1956), and to a great extent that is the subject here, although the novel is far more intricate than such ostensibly similar novels as *The Ultimate Solution* (1973) by Eric Norden, *Triumph* (1993) by Ben BOVA, and *Fatherland* (1992) by Robert Harris. Dick examines the will to dominate as a component of individual psychology as well as an aspect of a total society, and interprets it with symbolism borrowed from Taoism. The novel refers repeatedly to the *I Ching,* and one of the main characters is Japanese. Dick's Nazis are not the fanatics of Adolf Hitler, who is confined to an insane asylum, but rather a cabal of idealists and opportunists who actually believe in what they are doing and who blind themselves to the consequences of their acts. Even the Japanese character, Tagomi, is repulsed after his meeting with several prominent Nazis.

As usual, Dick plays with reality and perception. An imaginary novel, *The Grasshopper Lies Heavy,* describes an alternate history in which the Allies won the war—although this is not our world either, but rather one in which Russia is partitioned, China avoided a Communist revolution, and Britain is the most powerful nation in the world. Tagomi, who believes in the *I Ching,* is stunned when it seems to indicate that the fictional world is reality and that he is living in an illusion. Like many of Dick's characters, he can no longer rely on the stability of the perceived universe.

The Man in the High Castle is probably not Dick's best novel, although it was his only work at that length to win a Hugo. It did mark the beginning of his emergence as a serious and important writer following a steady stream of innovative, imaginative, but often uneven titles.

"The Man Who Ate the World"
Frederik Pohl
(1956)

There have been very few science fiction writers who rival Frederik POHL's consistent gift for biting satire. With Cyril KORNBLUTH, he wrote *The Space Merchants* (1953), one of the greatest satires science fiction has ever produced, and many of his short stories have poked fun at one modern trend or another. This particular title is one of his best, and the target is consumerism. The setting is some unspecified future, a world superficially the same as our own, but with certain aspects amusingly reversed. Consuming goods is now a duty rather than a luxury. Only the wealthiest families are allowed to buy their way out of their obligations and live in small, relatively unencumbered circumstances. The poorer class live in mansions, surrounded by technological marvels that they are compelled to make use of, to consume, until they can earn enough to avoid the obligation.

We see this world initially through the eyes of 12-year-old Sonny, who is surrounded by sophisticated robots and other toys but forbidden to enjoy the simpler pleasures he prefers. Society begins to change later when someone comes up with the bright idea of using robots to consume other products, thus freeing humans from the necessity. Sonny unfortunately has been permanently scarred by his unnatural childhood, and as an adult has become a compulsive consumer, an unsettling element in a world that finally has achieved a finely honed balance between production and consumption.

Sonny is in fact consuming so much that the areas around his self-sufficient robot city are suffering from shortages of material and robots to maintain and distribute what is still in place. The authorities find themselves unable to deny any of his requisitions, because that very act might send ripples of destabilization through a culture that relies on people being able to have whatever they desire simply by asking for it. Pohl's world is exaggerated unbelievably, of course, in order to emphasize the underlying nonsense of consumerism as he observes it.

A specialist in psychological problems and a young woman invade Sonny's nightmare island in an attempt to treat his mental disorder and temper his demands on the local economy, finally releasing him from the childhood guilt that has dominated him. The solution is not particularly convincing; but since the story is not meant to be a plausible future scenario, the end is of little consequence. This work is still one of the most scathing indictments addressing the less admirable side of the market economy.

The Man Who Sold the Moon
Robert A. Heinlein
(1950)

During the 1940s and 1950s it seemed as though travel to the Moon was just a matter of economics. All that was necessary was to build a rocket, strap an engine beneath it, and the rest would be simply routine. Many authors doubted that the government had the will to see the space program through, and others felt that private investors would be more efficient and dedicated once it became apparent that the program could pay for itself. At the instigation of the editor John W. CAMPBELL Jr., Robert HEINLEIN, whose libertarian sentiments were already emerging, began to construct a consistent future history that described humanity's exploration of the solar system and eventually the stars. *The Man Who Sold the Moon*, consisting of the title novella and three short stories, recounted the early stages of that transformation.

Prophecy is a chancy business at best, and some of Heinlein's predictions seem laughable now. The idea that highways and railways would be replaced by mechanized roads that were in constant movement is clearly implausible, but they seemed possible when "The Roads Must Roll" first appeared. On the other hand, the exploitation of solar power in "Let There Be Light" is still a viable concept, though not on the scale that Heinlein

imagined. The heart of the book is the title story, in which the entrepreneur D. D. Harriman decides that it is the destiny of humanity to move beyond the atmosphere. He almost single-handedly inspires and organizes the first mission to the Moon. Although most of the detailed description of the practicalities of space flight are hopelessly obsolete, Harriman's efforts to use the profit motive as leverage is convincing. The final story in the collection, "Requiem," is not strong on narrative, but it is a touching portrait of Harriman's last days and his first and only visit to the Moon.

Readers unfamiliar with the evolution of science fiction will find the collection anachronistic and overly inclined to talk about things rather than demonstrate them. During the years when science fiction was emerging from the pulp tradition but had not yet wholly embraced mainstream literary standards, it was common to describe the genre as a literature of ideas and to assert that the innovation in a particular work was more important than the characters or even the plot. It was only after the passage of years that the field as a whole gained enough perspective to recognize that all the elements of a piece of fiction are important. The stories in this collection remain entertaining despite the outdated science because Heinlein was a skilled enough writer to involve us with his characters as well as his speculations, but they fail as prophecy.

"The Marching Morons"
C. M. Kornbluth
(1951)

Cyril M. KORNBLUTH wrote a surprisingly large body of work, alone and in collaboration, during a career that lasted less than 20 years. Although his book-length work with Frederik POHL was exceptional, his solo novels were less satisfying. He was, however, an excellent short story writer. The most famous of his works in this form is "The Marching Morons," which hints at some of the plot elements that would later emerge in his most successful collaborative novel with Pohl, *The SPACE MERCHANTS* (1953).

The premise of the story, which is echoed in some of Kornbluth's other fiction, is that the most intelligent portion of the population tends to have fewer children and the least intelligent the most, and that the consequence of this over time will be a lowering of the average intelligence level of the human race. The setting is the distant future; most people are semiliterate at best, and certainly cannot operate let alone maintain the highly technological devices in their life. These tasks are all managed by a small minority of people with high intelligence who find it difficult to accomplish everything that needs to be done.

Enter Barlow, a real estate agent from the 20th century who is accidentally placed in suspended animation, awakening in a world that is far stranger than he initially realizes. He is castigated by the local authorities when he admits to not having any children, and therefore inadvertently contributing to the decline. Barlow, a salesman in an era when his type is extinct, insists that he alone knows how to convince the teeming masses to reduce their numbers. Invoking lemmings, he spearheads an advertising campaign to move the bulk of the population to Venus, although in fact they are all dying almost as soon as they leave Earth's atmosphere.

Even though the story is clearly satirical, there is a bitter and prejudicial undertone, and the implication that individuals in lower income brackets are automatically less intelligent is obviously false. The story does succeed, however, in its criticism of the anti-intellectualism that sometimes surfaces in modern civilization and of our overdependence on technologies we no longer understand, and Kornbluth clearly disapproves of the means by which the problem is solved—mass murder.

Mars series
Edgar Rice Burroughs
(1912–1964)

The Tarzan series is unquestionably the most famous of Edgar Rice BURROUGHS's creations, but the Mars books are much more significant to science fiction readers. The 11 books in this series follow the adventures of several different characters and explore various parts of the Red Planet, known to its natives as Barsoom. Barsoom is mostly desert, inhabited by two intelligent races who have lost most of their technology during their decline, and who now somewhat illogically mix swords with superscience. One race consists of oversized four-armed green Martians, the other of red Martians who look pretty much like human beings.

The first three novels, *A Princess of Mars* (1917), *The Gods of Mars* (1918), and *The Warlord of Mars* (1919) share one more or less continuous story. The three were serialized in magazine form between 1912 and 1913, the first as *Under the Moons of Mars* and as by Norman Bean, a pseudonym Burroughs quickly dropped. The hero of the original trilogy was John Carter, a Virginian who is chased into a cave by Indians and finds himself through some perhaps mystical means transported to Mars, or Barsoom, whose atmosphere is maintained by ancient machines so that he, as well as the natives, can breathe. Carter has a series of heroic though not very credible adventures, befriends Tars Tarkas of the green Martians, and becomes romantically involved with a red Martian princess. By the end of the original sequence Carter has been adopted into the local aristocracy and has a grown son who helps him save a pair of beautiful women from an evil cult.

Carter's son has his own set of adventures in *Thuvia, Maid of Mars* (1920), in much the same mode as those of his father. *The Chessmen of Mars* (1922), one of the best in the series, follows the exploits of Carter's daughter, whose explorations land her in the middle of a chess game played with human pieces. Another visitor from Earth picks up the sword in *The Master Mind of Mars* (1928), pitted against an evil scientist who has developed a method of moving personalities from one body to another. The invention of a disintegration ray inspires an ambitious Martian to extend his authority over the entire planet in *A Fighting Man of Mars* (1931), and John Carter returns to explore the Martian moons and wipe out the remnants of the assassins' guild in *Swords of Mars* (1936).

Synthetic Men of Mars (1940) was the only entry in the series that incorporated some mild satire in the otherwise frothy adventure, this time caused by yet another mastermind who has the ability to create and shape new life. The last two titles, *Llana of Gathol* (1948) and *John Carter of Mars* (1964), are actually collections of short stories using Barsoom as a setting, the last being a posthumous collection.

Burroughs was by no means a stylist. His characters are flat and repetitious, his plots simple and unsophisticated, his prose often turgid. Despite all of his shortcomings, he has retained his popularity primarily because of his gift for creating exotic settings and his genuine talent for storytelling. Burroughs was imitated during his prime by several writers, including Otis Adelbert KLINE and Ralph Milne Farley, and there have been pastiches of the Mars series by Mike RESNICK, Michael MOORCOCK, A. Bertram CHANDLER, and many others.

The Martian Chronicles
Ray Bradbury
(1950)

Although Ray BRADBURY set many of his early stories on the planet Mars, they did not form a series, although they had many similarities, mostly thematic. Most, but not all, of his Mars stories were assembled in a rough internal chronology as *The Martian Chronicles* (also published as *The Silver Locusts*), which as a unit describes efforts by humans to colonize Mars. Bradbury's version of the Red Planet was never a realistic one, and there are inconsistencies from one story to the next. Bradbury was never particularly interested in the intricacies of science and made no effort to take into account even what was known at the time about conditions on Mars. The common theme, however, is that any project to transplant human civilization there is doomed to failure, either through the machinations of the mysterious and inexplicable native Martians or through the shortcomings of the human interlopers.

Although the collection as a whole has a decided cumulative effect, it is because of a few individual segments that the book achieved such lasting popularity. In "The Third Expedition," for example, colonists discover the replica of a typical Midwestern town, unaware that it is a trap and not a gift. Anti-intellectualism leads to a devious revenge plot in "Usher II." Racial prejudice is the focus of "Way in the Middle of the Air," in which minority colonists find that bias thrives even in a new world. Eventually a nuclear war on Earth leads to the abandonment of most of those few settlements that survive, although a handful of diehards

vow to stay on. Many of the stories are filled with references to other literary works, and it is not surprising that, despite the overt science fiction setting, the book was popular in mainstream literary circles where, with some justification, it was embraced as fantasy rather than as science fiction.

Portions of the book were brought to the television screen as a miniseries in 1980, but the effort failed to capture the tone of the original. Nor could the miniseries reproduce the texture of Bradbury's prose, whose intense imagery often approaches poetry. Although the stories occasionally display a strong antiscientific bias, they also reflect Bradbury's faith in traditional values of home and family, despite his recognition that even these virtues are not without their flaws.

"A Martian Odyssey"
Stanley G. Weinbaum
(1934)

Our understanding of conditions on the planet Mars was far from accurate in the 1930s, so despite Stanley G. WEINBAUM's efforts to make his story as scientifically accurate as possible, it fails miserably by today's standards. That does not make it any less important or entertaining, however. The first expedition to Mars consists of four men, who find a world teeming with unusual life forms, crisscrossed with empty canals that once irrigated an entire world, dotted by occasionally abandoned cities that have subsided into mud. One of their number, Jarvis, is stranded hundreds of miles away when his flier malfunctions, and is forced to start an arduous and chancy trek back to base camp.

When Jarvis rescues an ostrichlike creature, he discovers that it is an intelligent being, Tweel. The two form an odd friendship, particularly odd because Tweel's language is apparently fluid; the meanings of words and the names of objects all change from moment to moment. Despite the language barrier, a strong bond forms between them as they observe a variety of odd forms of life, including one made entirely of self-replicating rock. They develop a primitive means of communicating with each other, expressing fairly complex concepts by means of only a handful of words

What made the story such a marked departure from traditional science fiction was the depiction of the various inhabitants of Mars as true aliens, not functioning as disguised human beings, their motives often incomprehensible. Except when Jarvis interferes, they seem largely indifferent to his presence. It is in part a first contact story, and there are hints, never resolved, that Tweel may not be native to Mars himself. Weinbaum would go on to write several similar short stories about Ham Hammond's adventures on Venus; but more importantly, other writers began to create more diverse alien cultures, culminating eventually in work like MISSION OF GRAVITY (1954) by Hal CLEMENT, *The Mote in God's Eye* (1975) by Larry NIVEN and Jerry POURNELLE, and *Stress Pattern* (1974) by Neal BARRETT Jr. Weinbaum's death a year later cut short a promising career, but the handful of stories he produced, most notably "A Martian Odyssey," have left a lasting mark on the genre.

Martin, George R. R.
(1948–   )

George R. R. Martin was one of the foremost new writers of the 1970s, primarily on the basis of his short stories. He wrote one interesting novel, *Dying of the Light* (1978), in which a man obsessed by love violates the traditions of a distant planet. His first sale was in 1971; by 1979 nearly 40 stories had appeared, every one of high quality. Three of those titles won Hugo Awards, "The SANDKINGS," "A SONG FOR LYA," and "The Way of Cross and Dragon." "The Sandkings" also won a Nebula Award, as did "Portraits of His Children" in 1986. Several of Martin's other stories were award contenders.

Although Martin's stories were sometimes set on other planets, it was always human characters and situations that concerned him. In "WITH MORNING COMES MISTFALL," advanced technology eventually proves that the legendary creatures inhabiting the mist-wreathed landscape of a remote planet are completely fictional. But rather than viewing this as a boon to human knowledge, Martin makes it clear that by removing the last hint of romance from that world, something has been lost forever. A human colony world develops a means of

individual flight in order to survive in "The Storms of Windhaven," later expanded as the novel *Windhaven* (1981) with Lisa Tuttle. Other stories of note from this period are "Meathouse Man," "And Seven Times Never Kill a Man," and the novelette *Nightflyers*, which was subsequently filmed.

Martin wrote considerably fewer short stories after 1980, concentrating on several novels including two classic supernatural works, *Fevre Dream* (1982) and *The Armageddon Rag* (1983). His only novels since then have been epic fantasy. A series of light space adventures was collected as *Tuf Voyaging* (1986). Martin also edited several anthologies, of which the most important is the WILD CARDS SERIES of shared-world adventures, to which he also contributed. The premise of the series is that superheroes and supervillains such as are found in comic books actually exist in an alternate version of Earth. The best of his short fiction can be found in *A Song for Lya* (1976), *Songs of Stars and Shadows* (1977), *Sandkings* (1981), *Nightflyers* (1985), and *Portraits of His Children* (1987).

Matheson, Richard
(1926–   )

Although Richard Matheson is generally known as a writer of horror and suspense fiction, his novels have included fantasy, westerns, thrillers, and war stories, as well as science fiction. Following his first short story sale in 1950, Matheson was for some years primarily a science fiction writer. His early work ranged from terror tales such as "Born of Man and Woman," in which a mutant child wreaks havoc, to "FOODLEGGER," a humorous time travel tale. Scientific and supernatural themes are mixed indiscriminately in his collections *Third from the Sun* (1955, also published as *Born of Man and Woman*), *The Shores of Space* (1957), and *Shock!* (1961).

Matheson's two most famous novels were science fiction, although both might equally well be claimed by the horror field. *I Am Legend* (1954) follows the exploits of the last man on Earth after a new plague has turned everyone else into nocturnal blood drinkers, essentially vampires. After surviving a number of violent encounters, the protagonist realizes that it is he who is now the monster, feared and hated by what humanity has become. The novel was twice filmed (1964, and in 1971 as *The Omega Man*), both versions being decidedly inferior to the original. Matheson's second novel, *The Shrinking Man* (1956), was transferred much more successfully to the screen, undoubtedly because the author did the screenplay himself. A freak exposure to radioactive gas causes the protagonist to begin to shrink—a process that continues through the end of the book.

From 1960 onward Matheson wrote primarily for films and television, mostly horror tales, often adapted from his own short stories. He also wrote for *Star Trek* and provided the screenplay for the miniseries based on *The MARTIAN CHRONICLES* by Ray BRADBURY. Matheson continues to be an active writer, and his short stories are regularly reprinted, but he has apparently abandoned science fiction completely. The rationalized vampires of *I Am Legend* have been imitated several times, as in *The Space Vampires* (1976) by Colin Wilson, but Matheson's novel remains the classic example of its type.

May, Julian
(1931–   )

Julian May's first short story, "Dune Roller" (1951), was very popular, but after only one other short story she abandoned the field until the 1980s, in favor of nonfiction. "Dune Roller" is an innovative monster story in which the monster is not consciously malevolent. A meteorite crashes into a large lake, after which fragments of its substance are scattered about the shore. All of the separate components have an innate drive to be reunited, so the roughly spherical main mass rolls through the area seeking its missing parts without paying attention to people who get in the way. The story was badly filmed as *The Cremators* (1986)

May returned to science fiction with the Pliocene Exile series, consisting of *The Many-Colored Land* (1981), *The Golden Torc* (1982), *The Non-Born King* (1983), and *The Adversary* (1984). Earth has evolved into a peaceful if somewhat boring society, and the small minority of misfits feel increasingly out of place until someone invents a

time machine and offers them the opportunity to regress to the Pliocene and form a new society in exile. Upon arriving, they discover an alien race that enlists them as involuntary allies in its battle with yet another species. Although the humans are essentially pawns in the battle, they aspire to be players rather than pieces. In the concluding volume they are aided in their quest by a man with extraordinary psi powers. The series was quite popular and May produced a nonfiction guide to the series, *The Pliocene Companion* (1984).

Intervention (1987), published in two volumes as *The Surveillance* and *The Metaconcert*, is a related sequence set in a near future in which mutant children begin to appear among the general population. The mutations apparently mark the point at which humanity can be admitted to the greater interstellar community, as we learn in the next sequence, consisting of *Jack the Bodiless* (1991), *Diamond Mask* (1994), and *Magnificat* (1996). As the time approaches when Earth will no longer be isolated, two psi-talented individuals become the focal points for a struggle to determine humanity's future, either as good neighbors or as aggressive conquerors.

May's most recent science fiction series is the Rampart Worlds sequence, which includes *Perseus Spur* (1998), *Orion Arm* (1999), and *Sagittarius Whorl* (2000). The scope is narrower this time, following the career of a reluctant hero whose sister apparently has been surgically altered by aliens and who faces betrayal from within his close circle of friends, as well as the more obvious external dangers. This latest series is in form a space opera, but May enriches her work with themes from mythology and other sources, and writes in a clear and involving prose style. She is highly respected for the complexity of her work, and her reputation continued to grow with each new title. Her most recent novels have been fantasy.

McAuley, Paul J.
(1955–   )

After publishing a handful of entertaining but unexceptional short stories, Paul J. McAuley began to make a name for himself with his first novel, *Four*

Hundred Billion Stars (1988). An alien race created and then apparently abandoned a planet that they populated with life from various planets including Earth. When this world is discovered by human explorers, the old machinery begins to come to life and presents a dangerous challenge to the intruders. The sequel, *Of the Stars* (1989, also published as *Secret Harmonies*), follows several generations of colonists, and *Eternal Light* (1991) pits a woman with psi talents against an alien force that might destroy the universe. The last title is a particularly vivid and inventive space opera.

Red Dust (1993) had a more limited theme. A larger-than-life character is caught up in an attempt by a theocratic dictatorship on Earth to suppress freedom in its Martian colonies. *Pasquale's Angel* (1994) was another change of pace, this time a detective story set in a version of medieval Florence in an alternate universe. These two novels demonstrated McAuley's ability to write in a variety of voices and tones. His next, *Fairyland* (1995), was even more impressive. In a future when genetic engineering makes it possible to design living doll-like creatures, a group of conspirators plot to give them free will.

The Confluence series is considerably more ambitious and complex, and is sometimes uneven. The sequence consists of *Child of the River* (1997), *Ancient of Days* (1998), and *Shrine of Stars* (2000). This story of self-discovery is set in a clearly artificial world whose origin and purpose are initially hidden from the protagonist, and revealed only after he undergoes a rite of passage. In *The Secret of Life* (2001), McAuley's most suspenseful novel, a mutated life-form brought back by a Chinese expedition to Mars has infected the Pacific Ocean. An American mission is sent to the Red Planet to study its natural habitat, but their efforts are hampered by the Chinese, who want to conceal their irresponsible actions, and by a shortsighted executive who wants the information sequestered for financial reasons.

McAuley continues to utilize a wide variety of settings and plots. *The Whole Wide World* (2002) is a murder mystery set in near-future London. *White Devils* (2004) is a story of intrigue and political maneuvering, set in the aftermath of an incident in which an inspection team in Africa is attacked by what appears to be a strain of genetically altered ape. Also of interest is the novella *Making History*. McAuley's short fiction has been collected in *The King of the Hill and Other Stories* (1991) and *The Invisible Country* (1996).

McCaffrey, Anne
(1926–   )

Although Anne McCaffrey sold her first science fiction story in 1953, it was not until the 1960s that she began publishing with any regularity. Her first work of note was a series of short stories about a cyborg starship, a human brain housed in an electronic body, that would later be collected as *The Ship Who Sang* (1969). The series would later inspire several sharecropped sequels by Mercedes Lackey, S. M. STIRLING, and Jody Lynn Nye. Her first novel, *Restoree* (1967), was essentially a Gothic romance transplanted onto another world and was not indicative of her later work.

Her next novel was patched together from a series of short stories including "Weyr Search," which won the Hugo Award, and "Dragon Rider," which won the Nebula. The novel, *Dragonflight* (1968), was the first volume in the PERN SERIES, which would become a dominant setting throughout McCaffrey's subsequent career. The setting is a lost colony where humans have forged an alliance with telepathic dragons, the two species combining to combat the deadly Threads that periodically fall from the upper atmosphere. The series now comprises 17 titles, with no end in sight. The popularity of the Pern series has overshadowed McCaffrey's other work, much of which is conventional space opera.

Decision at Doona (1969) was a more traditional space adventure. A group of misfits from Earth are exiled to a newly discovered planet, where they set about creating a new and more liberal society than the one they left, an effort that becomes more complicated when they discover that the planet has an indigenous intelligent species. McCaffrey would sharecrop this world as well in two sequels with Jody Lynn Nye, *Crisis on Doona* (1992) and *Treaty on Doona* (1994, also published as *Treaty Planet*). The sequels further explore the interactions between humans and the local feline aliens, adding a third alien race to stir the pot even further.

Another series of short stories involves a group of children with psi powers. These were collected as *To Ride Pegasus* (1973), followed after a gap of several years by the novels *Pegasus in Flight* (1990) and *Pegasus in Space* (2000), in which the children's talents are used first to help establish a viable space station and subsequently to launch the first interstellar flight. Although the novels are more ambitious and more polished, they lacked the enthusiasm of the earlier stories. A collection of nonseries stories, *Get Off the Unicorn* (1977), contains some of the best of her short fiction. The title was supposed to have been *Get of the Unicorn*, but no one caught the error in time to correct it.

Dinosaur Planet (1978) is a satisfying adventure story in which a scientific expedition is stranded on a dangerous planet; but the sequel, *Dinosaur Planet Survivors* (1984) was a routine and rather disappointing potboiler. The Killashandra trilogy consists of *Crystal Singer* (1981), *Killashandra* (1985), and *Crystal Line* (1992). The story follows the career of an interstellar celebrity, a singer whose talents are magnified by a mysterious crystal, as her fortunes rise and fall in a series of light adventures. Although McCaffrey demonstrated her ability to handle a diverse range of themes, by the late 1980s at least half of her science fiction was in the Pern series. Part of the balance consisted of occasional mainstream suspense novels.

The Rowan (1990) was the opening volume of yet another space opera, this one involving interstellar empires and psi powers, with a tone that felt more like romantic fantasy than science fiction. The romantic theme intensified in *Damia* (1992), although *Damia's Children* (1993) had considerably more overt action, pitting a group of psi-powered protagonists against an invading force of insectlike aliens. That conflict continues in *Lyon's Pride* (1994) and is apparently resolved, although a factional fight threatens to disrupt the peace in *The Tower and the Hive* (1999). The two-book series consisting of *Freedom's Landing* (1995) and *Freedom's Choice* (1997), while well-written, is essentially a new version of the Doona series.

McCaffrey's two most recent series are largely collaborative. *The Powers That Be* (1993), *Power Lines* (1994), and *Power Play* (1995), all written with Elizabeth Ann Scarborough, make up an effective trilogy in which colonists on an ice-covered world experience a series of strange phenomena that eventually lead to the discovery of a planetwide intelligence. The Acorna series is more varied in quality. McCaffrey wrote the first volume, *Acorna* (1997), alone. A young child with psi powers finds herself on a planet where children are enslaved in labor camps. There have been six sequels to date—one written with Margaret Ball, the others with Elizabeth Ann Scarborough—the most recent being *Acorna's People* (2003). The psi talented protagonist travels around the galaxy, having different adventures on each world she visits, but her basic character remains relatively unchanged. *Nimisha's Ship* (1999), so far a stand-alone novel, is one of her best works, an interstellar adventure involving a female executive whose rivals seek to trap her on another world in order to gain control of her holdings.

Anne McCaffrey is a major science fiction writer whose Pern novels are sometimes also described as fantasy. Certainly their tone is more similar to contemporary fantasy romance than to hard science fiction or conventional planetary adventures. Although she has not yet produced a single extraordinary work, her novels are reliably well-written and entertaining and she enjoys a large and loyal following.

McDevitt, Jack
(1935–   )

Jack McDevitt's first short story appeared in 1981, followed by several others that included "Cryptic," an intriguing first contact story whose theme would be central to his first novel, *The Hercules Text* (1986). In "Cryptic," a scientist discovers that alien signals from another star were deciphered 20 years ago, but the knowledge was suppressed because of fears that responding would involve humans in an interstellar war. The novel explores the process of interpreting and addressing messages from an alien race, as well as the international political struggle that ensues as competing governments battle for control of the presumed advanced technological knowledge that can be gleaned from this intelligence.

McDevitt continued to write first-rate short stories with some regularity, most notably "The Fort Moxie Branch," "Time's Arrow," and "Blinker." His next novel did not appear until 1989, and his third five years after that. The first, A Talent for War, is set in a distant future following a lengthy war between humans and an alien race. An investigator travels from world to world, conducting research into the life of a reputed war hero and discovering that the public story and the reality are markedly different. As with The Hercules Text, there is a noticeable religious undertone to the novel, although it remains unobtrusive. McDevitt's third novel, The Engines of God (1994), is set somewhat closer to home. The discovery of an alien artifact near Saturn is followed by the uncovering of similar objects, mostly statues, on planets of other stars, eventually leading to an entire world, apparently abandoned by a now missing alien intelligence. As is the case in the previous novels, McDevitt does a fine job of arousing our sense of wonder about the universe as he speculates about how humankind might respond to the revelation that we are not unique in our possession of intelligence.

Ancient Shores (1996) draws the focus even closer. This time an artifact is found buried beneath a farm in North America, a gateway that allows individuals to explore other worlds after being instantaneously transported across space. Access to virtually unlimited new sources of knowledge has a destabilizing effect on the economy of Earth in a partial reprise of themes from McDevitt's previous novels. Eternity Road (1997) was a significant break from McDevitt's usual concerns, this time set in a postapocalyptic Earth where the surviving communities have become extremely insular and where most sophisticated knowledge has been lost. A small band of explorers defies tradition by venturing out into unknown lands, providing the reader with a grand tour of the ruined world around them. Moonfall (1998) was a blend of disaster novel and political thriller. A comet shatters the Moon, and the resulting debris threatens space vehicles as well as the Earth below, while the death of the U.S. president causes a simultaneous political crisis.

Infinity Beach (2000, also published as Slow Lightning) was the first in a sometimes loosely constructed future history in which humanity has begun to explore the nearer stars, somewhat tentatively because of the limitations of its spaceships. The main plot is an involved puzzle in which a mysterious disappearance, falsified records of an interstellar expedition, and a bizarre alien form of life all intermingle in what is still McDevitt's most suspenseful story. This was followed by three novels featuring Priscilla Hutchins: Deepsix (2001), Chindi (2002), and Omega (2003). In Deepsix, Hutchins and several companions are accidentally trapped on a planet that is about to be destroyed by the near passage of a wandering planetoid after they attempt to harvest information from a storehouse of alien artifacts. In Chindi, we discover that more than one alien civilization has disappeared under suspicious circumstances, leading to speculation that there is some active, malevolent cause that might well be attracted to humanity. In what apparently is the concluding volume, the automated planet killers are approaching a world inhabited by a comparatively primitive race, and Hutchins is involved in efforts to help them survive the coming cataclysm. Polaris (2004) concerns the mystery surrounding the disappearance of the entire crew and passengers of a starship.

A representative selection of McDevitt's short fiction is contained in Standard Candles (1996), but many of his stories remain uncollected. McDevitt is potentially a much more significant writer than he is at present. His ability to evoke a feeling of awe about the universe is a major asset; he is adept at characterization as well as narration, and there is an understated complexity behind the scenes that imparts considerable depth to what appear to be straightforward adventures.

McDonald, Ian
(1960–   )

Although he was little known outside England during the 1980s, Ian McDonald wrote several excellent short stories at this early stage in his career, including "The Catherine Wheel" and "Empire Dreams." Most of these stories are included in *Empire Dreams* (1988), which appeared almost simultaneously with McDonald's first novel, *Desolation Road* (1988). The novel is an episodic history of a small colony on the planet Mars and the bizarre characters who live there, and it justifiably has been compared to *The* MARTIAN CHRONICLES (1950) by Ray BRADBURY, although McDonald's book is much more cohesive and was planned as a novel rather than as a series of related shorts. The two books introduced McDonald to readers in the United States, where his unusually complex style received a mixed reception.

Out on Blue Six (1989) is ostensibly a dystopian novel. The protagonist is a cartoonist who initially believes she lives in a perfect society, but who discovers otherwise when she offends certain powerful individuals and finds herself branded as a criminal. Forced to drop out of sight, she discovers a hidden underworld within the supposed utopia where happiness has to be earned rather than simply dispensed. Some critics balked at the clichéd ending in which a handful of rebels overthrow the repressive order and reestablish freedom, but the fact that the central character is herself a cartoonist by profession is perhaps a sign that this comic book–style ending is intentionally implausible.

King of Morning, Queen of Day (1991), which won the Philip K. Dick Award, is properly speaking a fantasy, although the magical events are explained as a manifestation of the combined sensual perception of all of humanity, which might possibly qualify it as science fiction. A second collection of stories, *Speaking in Tongues* (1992), appeared next, along with the novel *The Broken Land* (1992, also published as *Hearts, Hands, and Voices*). The setting is a future Earth, but one that bears more than a passing resemblance to the Mars of *Desolation Road*. Genetic engineering has become commonplace, but human culture is decaying and two rival religious groups are contending for influence over the remains of humanity. The presence of a rebel in a small community causes turmoil and danger on a grand scale. Perhaps because of its dour tone, this novel was not as popular as McDonald's previous titles.

Terminal Café (1994, also published as *Necroville*) was a major step forward for McDonald's career. A new technology has made it possible to raise its dead. The revived ones are forced to live in segregated communities because of the prejudices of the living. We explore this bizarre society through the eyes of an artist who, while seeking new inspiration for his work, breaks tradition and ventures into the community of the dead. *Evolution's Shore* (1995, also published as *Chaga*) is reminiscent of *The* CRYSTAL WORLD (1966) by J. G. BALLARD. A meteorite crashes in Africa, after which a variety of alien life begins to supplant the native ecology, resisting all efforts at eradication and threatening to overwhelm the world. This is not a disaster novel, however, as there is a clear implication that the transformation accompanying this unusual invasion will prove beneficial in the long run. The story was continued in *Kirinya* (1997), developing McDonald's themes further although adding little to the original concept.

Ares Express (2002) returns to Mars; it is a wonderfully complex and rewardingly intricate story about a web of settlements linked by railways and oversized trains, and more specifically the story of a young colonist growing up in that environment. McDonald is at the top of his form, mixing familiar themes and situations with his usual stylistic extravagance. Also of interest are two short novels. *Scissors Cut Paper Wrap Stone* (1994) is the story of the drive for freedom in a repressive totalitarian society. *Tendeleo's Story* (2000) is a short addition to the situation that began with *Evolution's Shore*, allowing the reader to watch at first hand as a young man discovers that the alien transformation is not a bad thing after all. Although McDonald's popularity in the United States has not approached the level he enjoys in Britain, it should only be a matter of time before his more mature work finds a wider audience.

McHugh, Maureen
(1959–   )

Although she had previously sold a few good short stories, Maureen McHugh made little impression prior to the publication of her first novel, *China Mountain Zhang* (1992), which incorporated two of those shorter pieces. The novel is set in a near-future China where local traditions have become mixed with ideas imported from the rest of the world, resulting in an uneasy and shifting balance.

McHugh's societies are even more flawed than her characters, usually decaying or corrupted. Gender issues are frequently an important element in her characterization, though not necessarily in the plot. The title character is only half Chinese but has been physically altered so that he can escape the rampant racial prejudice that would otherwise bar him from the more lucrative professions. In *Half the Day Is Night* (1994), a professional body-guard in a domed underwater city matches wits with a band of criminals and political operatives, all of whom want to exploit the new habitats for their own purposes. Both he and his employer are ultimately forced into hiding. The undersea world, despite its newness, has already become a place of dark secrets—essentially an undeveloped country with its own emerging caste system.

McHugh's interest in observing the interplay of diverse cultural themes continues in her later novels. *Mission Child* (1998) is set on a colony world that recently has been reunited with the rest of human civilization after a gap of generations that left them technologically backward. A young woman experiences a series of cultural shocks as she grows to maturity in an environment that has lost its self-confidence and is uneasy about the future. In *Nekropolis* (2001), probably McHugh's best novel, a slave woman and an artificial man flee from their masters in a future Morocco where traditional cultural values cause ongoing problems as they interface with advanced technology. McHugh is a methodical writer whose plots are tightly controlled and whose settings are elaborate and well thought-out. Much of her work is dark in tone, and her endings are rarely happy or uplifting, although neither are they despairing. Her short fiction, which is generally quite good, has yet to be collected. "The Lincoln Train" won a Hugo Award.

McIntyre, Vonda N.
(1948–   )

After making her first short story sale in 1969, Vonda McIntyre quickly progressed to prominence in the field, winning a Nebula Award for her novelette OF MIST, AND GRASS, AND SAND and then both the Hugo and the Nebula Award for her second novel, *Dreamsnake* (1978), which incorpo-

rates that story into a longer narrative. The story follows the efforts of a professional healer who accomplishes her cures with the assistance of an alien snake with an adaptive physical structure. When her snake dies, she finds herself without the means of making a living until she can find a replacement. It was a powerful effort for a new writer, concentrating on a small and relatively insignificant individual rather than the panoramic events that occupied most genre writers. McIntyre's first novel, *The Exile Waiting* (1975), was promising but less successful. An unhappy telepath is forced to commit criminal acts by her rapacious family until the arrival of alien visitors to Earth gives her the opportunity to escape into space and pursue a more harmonious future. The protagonist is an extremely well-drawn character, but the book's conclusion is comparatively weak.

Through the end of the 1970s, McIntyre's short fiction continued at its high level, with excellent stories such as "Screwtop," which examined the limits of individual freedom, and "Fireflood," in which selected individuals are genetically altered to function in different environments, casting into question what it means to be human. The idea of modifying the human form was common in her work from this period, and is perhaps most brilliantly expressed in "Aztecs." Faster-than-light travel is possible, but it exacts a toll on human bodies that biological hearts cannot support, so star pilots are fitted with artificial ones instead. "The Genius Freaks" is another attempt to examine the consequences of a deliberate effort to breed more intelligent children. Most of these stories were collected in *Fireflood and Other Stories* (1979). Unfortunately, McIntyre wrote almost exclusively at novel length after 1980, and the field lost one of its most skillful practitioners of short fiction.

McIntyre's career was also affected by the *Star Trek* phenomenon. *The Entropy Effect* (1981) was one of the few tie-in novels to that series that was also a genuinely effective and moving novel. She would subsequently write additional, though less impressive, tie-ins, as well as novelizations of *Star Trek* and other genre movies. Her next original novel, *Superluminal* (1983), was a complex story in which a man with an artificial heart and an offworlder find their lives intertwined with that of a woman who must make a decision about her own future. The novel draws heavily on the earlier short story "Aztecs" and demonstrated McIntyre's steadily improving ability to construct and control very complicated story lines. The novel also has decidedly feminist overtones, although the subtext is implied rather than overtly stated. The much lighter *Barbary* (1986) is a surprisingly sophisticated first contact story aimed at young adults.

Starfarers (1989) was the opening volume of a major series. The first experimental starship is about to be launched, but as the date approaches, a group of scientists discover that there are plans to reorder priorities and use the ship for military purposes. Outraged, but impotent to reverse the decision, they decide that it is their moral duty to steal the ship to prevent its misuse. Their situation grows more desperate in *Transition* (1990). During their escape, the ship sustained some damage; the central computer is malfunctioning just as they are about to engage in delicate negotiations with the first intelligent race they have encountered since leaving the solar system. *Metaphase* (1992) examines in more detail the difficulties of establishing coherent communications between two alien races, and *Nautilus* (1994) sees the crew trying to convince the galactic community at large that humanity is a worthy companion race despite our prolonged history of violence. *The Moon and the Sun* (1997) is a historical fantasy.

McIntyre's fiction has become more polished with the passage of time, but her main concerns remain almost unchanged. It is the human element, not the science, that holds her interest—particularly the interactions of her characters under stressful conditions. Conflict is generally more intellectual than physical, and the moments of melodrama are restrained and thoughtfully contrived.

McLaughlin, Dean
(1931–)

Although never a prolific writer, and one who usually followed the pattern of tales prescribed by John W. CAMPBELL Jr., to whom he sold a large proportion of his short fiction, McLaughlin was more polished than many other writers who flocked to Campbell's standard. His stories generally show deeper consideration of the complexities of technological advance and the effects on his characters. His first short story was published in 1951; he would average less than one per year afterward, with frequent lengthy gaps between titles and even less activity following the early 1970s. Some of his short stories were incorporated into his novels.

Dome World (1962) is set primarily in a cluster of domed cities established on the bottom of the ocean. The surface world nations are moving ever closer to a devastating war, and their respective undersea colonies are, by their very nature, particularly susceptible to attack. As a consequence, actions are initiated by the leaders in several of the cities to form a loose coalition and declare collective independence from their respective founding nations—a course of action that is predictably less than popular with the governments that financed their creation. *The Fury from Earth* (1963) explores a very similar problem. A set of colonies on the planet Venus have rebelled against the entities on Earth that founded them. A Venusian who has been raised on Earth is instrumental in preventing a missile attack against the colonists. Both stories are essentially potboilers, but *Dome World* provides some interesting speculation about what such an environment might actually involve.

McLaughlin's third and most mature novel was *The Man Who Wanted Stars* (1965), the story of a single-minded entrepreneur who is determined to prevent the human race from abandoning its space program. Although the ruthless protagonist is not entirely sympathetic, his obsession with space exploration struck an echoing chord among many science fiction readers. The best of McLaughlin's short fiction was collected in *Hawk Among the Sparrows* (1976). The title story, which concerns the displacement of a modern aircraft into the past, is his single best work at that length. "The Brotherhood of Keepers" is also worthy of mention.

McQuay, Mike
(1949–1995)

Mike McQuay made his debut with *Lifekeeper* (1980), a competently written but undistinguished novel about a rebellion by citizens of an underground shelter society against the computer that governs it after they discover that the alleged ongoing war on the surface is a fake. McQuay made a much more marked impression with the Matthew Swain series that followed, a blend of science fiction and the tough detective story that was much more successful than most similar attempts. The series consists of *Hot Time in Old Town* (1981), *When Trouble Beckons* (1982), *The Deadliest Show in Town* (1983), and *The Odds Are Murder* (1983). Swain is a private detective in a near future in which the rich have retreated into armored enclaves and the cities are hotbeds of criminals, the chronically poor, and the occasional mutant. His investigations involve assassinations, missing persons, and serial killers, and a visit to an orbiting habitat. In form they are very much in the tradition of Raymond Chandler and Dashiell Hammett, but the setting was well realized and added a degree of realism that gave the books some distinction.

McQuay turned to more serious themes with the two-part novels consisting of *Pure Blood* (1984) and *Mother Earth* (1985). Genetic engineering has resulted in a variety of uplifted animals with intelligence rivaling that of humans, but conflict is inevitable, and a devastating war ravages the world. The humans gain the upper hand, and the final conflict is whether or not to hunt the enhanced animals to extinction. *Jitterbug* (1984) has some strong similarities, but in this case the cause of the catastrophic crash of civilization is a plague, released deliberately so that an ambitious dictator can seize world power. *Memories* (1987) is a time travel story in which a psychopath attempts to change history—a familiar situation that is resolved competently, but without offering anything new to the theme. Similarly, *The Nexus* (1989) is a dangerous child story. The child in question has unusual psi powers, and many believe that she should be executed before she inadvertently causes great harm. McQuay's last book was a collaboration with Arthur C. CLARKE, *Richter 10* (1997), a near-future political thriller involving a marvelous invention, a device that accurately predicts earthquakes. In retrospect, McQuay's most satisfying work was the Matthew

Swain series, although he attempted more serious work in his later novels.

A Meeting with Medusa
Arthur C. Clarke
(1971)

The secret of writing truly effective hard science fiction is to include a rigorously accurate description of the environment or scientific principle involved and make it essential to the story without resorting to prolonged explanations that interfere with the pace of the narrative. The writer must not employ jargon or take other shortcuts that might leave the reader feeling as though he or she was missing an important piece of information required to appreciate the ending. Throughout his career, Arthur C. CLARKE has demonstrated his awareness of this balancing act, and never more effectively than in this novelette.

Falcon is an expert on lighter-than-air vehicles and once piloted the largest powered balloon ever built on Earth. When surgery following a serious accident leaves him with even faster reflexes than before, he decides to conquer a much greater challenge—a manned expedition into the outer reaches of the atmosphere of Jupiter. Little is known about the largest planet in the solar system because of its heavy gravity and its murky and turbulent atmosphere. Falcon's vessel is essentially a raft suspended by balloons filled with hot gas, similar in principle but not appearance to the one whose disastrous crash nearly claimed his life.

In a minimalist way, this is a first contact story. Falcon is surprised to discover living creatures inhabiting the atmosphere, some resembling giant manta rays, others a cross between an amoeba and a gas bag, but a thousand times the size of the largest creature that ever existed on Earth. His brief encounter with the medusa of the title raises suspicions that the creatures might be intelligent, although Clarke provides only a tantalizing hint of their nature. But the story is more importantly a portrayal of the human quest to know what lies around the next corner or over the next hill. Falcon is also driven by memories of his previous failure, even though it was not his fault, and his confrontation with the medusa mirrors in some ways his encounter with an enhanced chimpanzee crew member just prior to the near fatal crash. In the final chapters we discover that Falcon himself is caught between worlds, that his body is maintained in a self-enclosed, mechanical environment, and that in one sense, he is no longer entirely human.

Memoirs Found in a Bathtub
Stanislaw Lem
(1971)

Most of Stanislaw LEM's fiction was published while Poland was under a repressive Communist regime, and it is unclear how much effect that situation had on his work. Lem, who is certainly the most important science fiction writer to have emerged in Eastern Europe during the Soviet period, often used satire in his work, and was able to poke occasional fun at totalitarianism and bureaucracy, although it was often displaced to Western venues. *Memoirs Found in a Bathtub* is the best of his book-length satires, set in a near future after Earth has become infected with a virus from outer space—one that does not threaten humans directly but causes the destruction of all paper products. The dependence of bureaucracy—and in fact virtually every aspect of human civilization—on paperwork was even more pointed during the early 1970s when this novel was written than it is now, when we store much of the same data electronically.

As the outside world collapses into disarray, the last stronghold of the "papyrocracy" is the American Pentagon, sealed to prevent entry by the virus, inhabited by a bizarre cast of characters who live within an atmosphere of paranoia and secrecy, with technological devices unknown outside its walls. Into this labyrinth of espionage and mania Lem introduces a naive outsider, whose explorations allow the reader to take an exaggerated, often very funny look at the extremes to which we sometimes subject ourselves in the name of order, security, and conformity. The Pentagon becomes a world in itself, and the protagonist begins to doubt that anything really exists beyond its outer walls.

The Pentagon was an approved target for satires under Communism, but Lem and his readers certainly knew that his excoriation of the manic aspects of that culture was equally applicable to the Kremlin.

"The Men Who Murdered Mohammed"
Alfred Bester
(1958)

Almost every short story that Alfred BESTER wrote became at least a minor genre classic; several, including this one, were major accomplishments. The protagonist, Henry Hassel, is a genuine mad professor, and the introductory paragraphs briefly describing actual incidents involving eccentric and absentminded scientists is priceless in itself. And that is just the setup for the funniest time travel paradox story of all time.

Hassel discovers that his wife has been unfaithful. Rather than confront her, he constructs a time machine and uses it to murder her grandfather before her father was born, then returns to the present, assuming that history has changed and, if he is married at all, it will be to someone else. Much to his surprise, he returns to find his situation unchanged. Upon consideration, he realizes that the flow of time can be altered only by a significant event, so he travels back even further and murders a young George Washington, and then Columbus, Napoleon, and Mohammed, each time returning to discover that he still has an unfaithful wife.

Bester then dismisses all the familiar resolutions readers might expect from having read previous paradox stories, leaving us to wonder just how he is going to extricate his plot from the logical trap he has constructed around it. In due course, and after rampaging through time without having any effect on the present, Hassel encounters another time traveler and learns the truth. Time is a subjective phenomenon, and it is impossible to travel in anything but an individual's personal timeline. So all that Hassel has managed to do is destroy himself, as he discovers when he realizes that he can no longer physically interact with the material world.

Although Bester was writing for humorous effect, the concept that history is immutable except for an individual's subjective experience of it has subsequently been adopted by other writers as a means by which they can describe exotic adventures in the past without having to reconcile those events with alterations in the future. Other writers have produced amusing variations, but few of these rival Bester's short but efficient gem.

Messiah
Gore Vidal
(1965)

Gore Vidal has dabbled in science fiction themes and devices in several of his books, including *Myron* (1974), *Kalki* (1978), and *Live from Golgotha* (1992), as well as in the play *Visit to a Small Planet* (1956), but it was only in *Messiah* that he produced a significant addition to the genre—and, in fact, one of its most frightening scenarios. The story is set in the very near future and follows the evolution of a new religious cult. John Cave, the cult's charismatic founder and leader, is typical of the type who rise to prominence in such an atmosphere, although it is clear from the outset that Cave believes what he is preaching. Or at least, he believes that he believes it.

Cave teaches his followers that death is not really a bad thing, something to be dreaded, but rather a peaceful state of being that should be embraced. Suicide and euthanasia are not sins but virtues, and a funeral is a celebration rather than a tragedy. Cave's popularity and his following increase steadily and dramatically, and his new religion accumulates the necessary baggage of success, accountants, theologians, and business managers. The characters emerge very slowly as people; Vidal employs a roundabout, almost lethargic narrative style that is not commonly employed by genre writers. His narrator is an old man, looking back at the transformation of the world, his own mind wandering from memory to memory as he tries to reconstruct just how such incredible transformations came to pass. Slowly but steadily he draws us into his created world, and Cave and his followers become increasingly real and rather frightening.

Ultimately Cave is called upon to consummate his own teachings by killing himself. At the last minute he doubts and balks, creating a potential crisis for the church, which has now become a major financial institution. Rather than risk a reversal of their trend toward success, the senior members of his staff decide that Cave's reluctance is just one more obstacle to be overcome, and by whatever means might be necessary. Vidal is satirizing all religions, of course, not just modern-day cults.

Miller, Walter M.
(1925–1996)

Walter Miller is and always will be best known for the three-part postapocalyptic novel A CANTICLE FOR LEIBOWITZ, which appeared in book form in 1960, patched together from three long pieces previously published in magazines. Miller's entire career lasted only from 1951 to 1959, after which he was silent until the appearance of a posthumous sequel, *Saint Leibowitz and the Wild Horse Woman,* in 1997. Miller, who had recently converted to Roman Catholicism when he began writing fiction, used religious themes to enrich the characters and situations in his short stories, of which more than three dozen would appear in less than a decade.

Miller's short stories and novelettes were frequent award contenders; The DARFSTELLER won a Hugo for its complex depiction of an actor adjusting to the automation of his profession. Miller often took standard genre themes and used them to make serious observations about humanity. In "Dark Benediction," for example, alien spores cause a highly contagious and physically repugnant transformation, and those infected are shunned by the rest of the population even though they actually benefit from their new condition. "Conditionally Human" was one of the earliest examples of the uplift story, animals with enhanced intelligence in this case being used as substitutes for human children. A worker modified so that he can help terraform Mars in "Crucifixus Etiam" must reconcile himself to the fact that the operation is irreversible and he can never return to Earth.

A telepath has ambivalent feelings about her powers when she must resist the advances of a monomaniacal man who wishes to create a superior race in "Command Performance." Questions of pacifism and militarism are examined in "The Ties That Bind." Other noteworthy stories are "Six and Ten Are Johnny," "Triflin' Man," and "Vengeance for Nikolai." Miller's short fiction has been collected in *Conditionally Human* (1962), *View from the Stars* (1965), *The Best of Walter M. Miller* (1980), and elsewhere. The quality of his short fiction is extraordinarily high, but it has always been overshadowed by his single novel, which has been in print almost continuously for more than 40 years and remains as fresh and relevant today as it did when it first appeared.

"Minority Report"
Philip K. Dick
(1955)

Sometimes an author has an idea for a story so clever and original that it seems to the reader as if the story wrote itself. That is the case with "Minority Report," set in a future when a government department, Precrime, uses precognitive mutants to foresee and prevent capital crimes, arresting the would-be killers before the crime can even be committed and confining them in detention camps. The head of the agency, Anderton, has recently been pressured into accepting a younger man, Witwer, as his assistant, and almost immediately receives a new prediction that he himself will commit a murder.

The title refers to a system used to check on the results. Every prediction is checked with three different precogs and, on the assumption that no two errors will be identical, the majority opinion is accepted as valid. Anderton's case is unique because he receives advance notice of his crime, which affected the two subsequent predictions. There are, in his case, three minority reports and no majority, although similarities between two lead to the illusion that there is one.

Anderton is convinced at first that the report was fabricated as part of a plot to relieve him of his position in Witwer's favor. He attempts to run, but is immediately captured by agents of General Kaplan, his predicted victim. Kaplan is the head of a military movement that wishes to discredit the Precrime division and assert its own authority, and he intends to use Anderton's case to prove that the system is untrustworthy and results in the incarceration of innocent people. Anderton is further manipulated by a secretive agent who claims that Anderton's own wife is behind the plot against him. After some captures and escapes he learns the truth. He eventually murders Kaplan as predicted, to prevent a coup and to protect the reputation of the police, even though there is at least some truth to the charge that the system sometimes results in a miscarriage of justice.

The recent film version was fairly faithful in describing the way Precrime works, although it changed most of the details of the central plot and ended with the system's destruction rather than its continuation. Otherwise, the film did a surprisingly good job of capturing the atmosphere of Dick's original work.

Moderan
David R. Bunch
(1971)

David Bunch had published literally hundreds of short stories before turning to science fiction in the late 1950s. Over the course of the next 15 years he produced a steady stream of unusual, quirky, and often controversial stories using an idiosyncratic narrative and prose style that anticipated some of the experimental techniques of the New Wave movement. Bunch was regularly castigated in the letter columns of magazines where his stories appeared, but he continued to produce his own unique brand of story and acquired some critical acclaim.

Many of these stories were set in the same world, a postapocalyptic future in which humans have retreated into strongholds and regularly make ineffective war upon one another, and in which radiation and other damage has resulted in the introduction of mechanical substitutes for limbs and organs, effectively transforming much of the population into a form of cyborg. These stories were typically quite short, and it was only after a considerable number of them had appeared that they were gathered together with bridging material into book form as *Moderan,* which was Bunch's name for his depressingly decadent future Earth.

Although the stories are most effective when read as a continuous narrative, some of the individual episodes are particularly outstanding, most involving visitors to one particular stronghold whose master is usually terrified of the outside world. In "2064 or Thereabouts" a wandering artist visits a stronghold seeking a deeper meaning in life and is ultimately destroyed by a whimsical practical joke. Another traveler shows up in "The One from Camelot Moderan"—an anachronistic knight on a mechanical horse who has lost his love because their mechanical hearts are no longer in synchronization. The master's daughter arrives in "Was She Horrid?" having brought with her the gift of love, an unsettling concept that fills him with horror. Although he has somewhat mixed feelings, he expels her, only to learn subsequently that she came intending to murder him.

The world of Moderan is an unpleasant place, obviously, and with its increasingly mechanical populace the stories are clearly metaphors for the dehumanizing aspects of modern society, even without the excuse of an apocalyptic war.

Moon, Elizabeth
(1945–   )

Although Elizabeth Moon's early short stories were generally science fiction, her first several novels were heroic fantasies or sharecropped space adventures written as collaborations with Anne McCaffrey; the latter included *Sassinak* (1990) and *Generation Warriors* (1992). *Lunar Activity* (1990), a collection of her short fiction, was her first solo science fiction title, although most of her subsequent fiction would be in that field. Much of her work is technically military science fiction, although unlike most writers specializing

in that subgenre she is clearly more interested in her characters and their internal conflicts than in simply describing elaborate battles and the intricacies of military life.

Hunting Party (1993) was the first novel in a series following the adventures of Heris Serrano, an officer of the space navy who is forced to resign through the behind the scenes maneuvering of an unscrupulous enemy. She becomes captain of a civilian vessel and, although she initially expects to be bored by her new job, is soon involved with pirates, smugglers, and other enemies. The novel is a good, solid space adventure with a likable and believable protagonist. In the sequel, *Sporting Chance* (1994), Serrano finds herself assigned as escort to the heir apparent to the throne of an interstellar empire. She eventually discovers that someone is slowly poisoning her charge in an effort to undermine the stability of the government. Serrano commands a small civilian fleet opposing a criminal power in *Winning Colors* (1995), the weakest in the series, as part of her bid to reclaim her old position in the military.

Once a Hero (1997) is set in the same universe as the Serrano trilogy, and started a separate series. In this opening volume an ambitious and promising young officer gets caught up in a mutiny in space, assumes command, and proves herself a formidable opponent. *Rules of Engagement* (1999) is a planetary adventure story, with a military officer stranded on a world whose repressive social system causes complicated problems preventing her rescue. The relationship between the two recurring characters grows more complex in *Change of Command* (1999), and both are caught up in another mutiny in *Against the Odds* (2000).

Moon's stand-alone novels are also worth noting. *Remnant Population* (1996) is a well-written though rather familiar story of colonists who discover that the supposedly empty world to which they have come is actually home to indigenous aliens. *Speed of Dark* (2002), which won a Nebula Award, is a moving novel in which autism is linked to psi powers. *Trading in Danger* (2003) marks a return to familiar ground, and is apparently the opening volume in a new series. A washed-up military trainee takes a job as an interstellar trader and finds herself in the middle of a colonial war. Moon's more recent short fiction has been collected in *Phases* (1997).

The Moon Is a Harsh Mistress
Robert A. Heinlein
(1966)

Libertarian sentiments have frequently found expression in works of science fiction, particularly in the work of L. Neil SMITH, James P. HOGAN, and to a lesser extent Poul ANDERSON, Gordon R. DICKSON, and Keith LAUMER. The use of speculative fiction as a method of proposing a radical new social or political system is not a modern phenomenon. Utopian writers such as Edward Bellamy, William Morris, and William Dean Howells did so overtly when they established their rules for the perfect—usually socialist—future society. Modern readers are less inclined to read static grand tours of an author's fantasy world, so writers today blend medium and message, using the story to illustrate whatever points they wish to make.

Heinlein's libertarian inclinations were evident in his early work and were openly expressed in his version of the utopian novel, STARSHIP TROOPERS (1959). Heinlein interspersed his sometimes tedious lectures with an engaging character and some gripping action sequences, and that novel acquired a strong following, particularly among those sympathetic to the author's viewpoint. His postapocalyptic *Farnham's Freehold* (1964), which more overtly espoused libertarian values, was considerably less well received and marks the beginning of Heinlein's decline. Yet he was still to write what some consider his best novel, and perhaps the best libertarian science fiction novel of all time, *The Moon Is a Harsh Mistress*.

Most of the action takes place on the Moon, which, like the Australia of two centuries ago, has become a penal colony, home to many misfits as well as actual criminals. The colony is administered by the Authority, virtually a dictatorship; given the physical isolation of the Moon, escape is impossible. The only solution for those who

wish to live in freedom, a freedom that is rapidly vanishing even on Earth, is for the Moon to declare its independence and become self-governing. Despite an assembly of willing and able characters, a coup would be completely beyond the reach of the would-be rebels if it was not for the fact that Mike, the computer that runs the colony, has become self-aware and is sympathetic to the revolutionaries. Mike becomes the secret master of the plot, the personality behind a shadowy leader no one ever actually meets. All of Heinlein's stock characters are there—the wise old man, the plucky young woman, the earnest and intelligent innovator—but this time they seem to the reader like old friends. It comes as no surprise that the most believable character is Mike, the artificial intelligence.

Heinlein employed an unusual prose style for the novel, dropping words from sentences in patterns not entirely clear. This causes some initial uneasiness until the reader adapts to the change, after which it becomes transparent and supports, in minor fashion, the concept that this really is a different world we are visiting. The libertarian political content, while obvious, is rarely intrusive and is much better articulated than in the two previous novels, which often seemed harsh or even mean-spirited. Heinlein portrays the colony as a dangerous place where only the fit survive, and he acknowledges the difficulty in getting libertarians to work in concert even for a desirable goal. One interesting consequence of this is that the protagonists, and presumably the author, believe that deception and dishonesty in the service of a worthwhile cause is perfectly alright, even if those being deceived are one's allies and friends.

The early chapters follow the organization of the revolt, the latter deal with the political and brief military conflict that follows. Once the revolution is successful, Mike falls silent for reasons never explained. Algis BUDRYS has advanced the interesting hypothesis that Mike actually manipulated all the other characters to change the structure of the colony for its own purposes and, once that has been accomplished, has no interest in former allies. The novel won a well-deserved Hugo Award, the last Heinlein would receive.

Moorcock, Michael
(1939–   )

Michael Moorcock has had enough careers in the world of publishing for several people. He is one of the most respected fantasy novelists, creator of Elric of Melnibone and the Eternal Champion under various other guises, and has written mainstream novels and spy thrillers. In science fiction, he has written everything from space opera and pastiches of Edgar Rice BURROUGHS to finely crafted and serious work, including Hugo and Nebula Award winners. He edited *New Worlds Magazine* for several years and was one of the major figures in the British New Wave movement, which helped provide a forum for the experimental work of J. G. BALLARD, Langdon Jones, Thomas DISCH, and other writers of that period. His JERRY CORNELIUS SERIES is the best-known example of the innovative and nontraditional writing styles associated with the New Wave movement; that series, to which Moorcock continues to add, is virtually the only remnant of the New Wave's nonrealistic and self-conscious styling that has remained in print.

Moorcock's short fiction was first published during the 1950s, but his first novel was *The Sundered Worlds* (1965, also published as *The Blood Red Game*), an interesting but undistinguished space opera. Most of his short fiction from this period was fantasy, including the early adventures of Elric and the advent of the Eternal Champion series, but by the middle of that decade his novels had already begun to demonstrate the wide range of his talents. Writing in several genres, Moorcock was already attempting to chip away at the borders. The background of much of his fiction is the multiverse, a concept that involves multiple realities with common personalities that manifest themselves in different forms.

At one end of the spectrum, Moorcock produced a trilogy of remarkable Burroughsian romances consisting of *Warriors of Mars* (also published as *The City of the Beast*), *Blades of Mars* (also published as *Lord of the Spiders*), and *Barbarians of Mars* (also published as *Masters of the Pit*); all three volumes appeared in 1965. The sequence is still the most satisfying pastiche of that form,

encompassing all of the inventiveness of Burroughs's imagination without the clumsiness of his prose. *The Final Programme* (1968) was the first in his surreal Jerry Cornelius series, which has seen its most recent continuation in *Firing the Cathedral* (2002). *The Wrecks of Time* (1967, also published as *Rituals of Infinity*) is a traditional alternate worlds adventure story, with one reality plotting to destroy the others before they can become potential rivals. *The Shores of Death* (1966, also published as *The Twilight Man*) is a disaster novel involving infertility, an attack from outer space, and an alteration of the rotation of the Earth; despite all the different plot strands, the loose ends are tied up neatly. Moorcock was consistently successful with each form he attempted, and the unpredictable nature of his output allowed him to avoid being pigeonholed as a writer of a particular kind of story.

Moorcock won a Nebula Award for the shorter version of BEHOLD THE MAN in 1966. The novel appeared three years later, followed by a somewhat less satisfying sequel, *Breakfast in the Ruins* (1972). *The Ice Schooner* (1969) is one of his most traditional adventure stories. A relatively small number of people live in a few isolated cities after a new ice age sweeps over the Earth, surviving primarily by hunting whales. A group sets off to find legendary New York City on what is essentially a fantasy quest in a far future setting. Probably Moorcock's most underrated novel is *The Black Corridor* (1969), a tense psychological thriller set aboard a starship, most of whose passengers are held in suspended animation.

By 1970 most of Moorcock's fiction was heroic fantasy, but he still found time for occasional science fiction, often pastiches. *The Warlord of the Air* (1971), first of the Bastable trilogy, is a deliberately anachronistic story about a time traveler in an alternate version of our history who finds himself in a world that has forgotten how to wage war. In *The Land Leviathan* (1974) Bastable attempts to return to his own era and visits various alternate realities in the process, and in *The Steel Tsar* (1981) he ends up in a world where the Russian Revolution never took place. The trilogy has some of the flavor of the work of George GRIFFITH, but is much more skillfully written. Moorcock also continued to add to the career of Jerry Cornelius, although none of the sequels ever enjoyed the same degree of notoriety as the first title.

Time travel is also the subject of *An Alien Heat* (1972). In a far future Earth, everyone is immortal and no one is interested in raising children. Facing the possibility that time itself may be ending, the protagonist decides to travel back to the past. Moorcock's depiction of a decaying future is particularly effective. Three sequels followed: *The Hollow Lands* (1974), in which one of the bored immortals travels back to prehistory, *The End of All Songs* (1976), wherein an investigator from the far future pursues those who have fled into the past; and *The Transformation of Miss Mavis Ming* (1977, also published as *A Messiah at the End of Time*), which borrows characters from Moorcock's other series. *Legends from the End of Time* (1976) is a collection of short stories set against the same backdrop.

Moorcock's science fiction has grown increasingly rare since 1980, although some of his fantasy novels set in the multiverse are partially rationalized, and he has largely abandoned short fiction. The two major exceptions are among his very best work—the alternate universe novel GLORIANA (1978) and the marginal but fascinating *Mother London* (1988). His early short stories were collected in *The Time Dweller* (1969) and *Moorcock's Book of Martyrs* (1976, also published as *Dying for Tomottow)*, but Moorcock has consistently been at his best with longer work. Perhaps Moorcock's most lasting influence on science fiction was as editor of *New Worlds* during the New Wave era. Even though the extraordinary stylistic experiments soon faded, the idea that nontraditional prose was an appropriate form for the field took hold, and authors have been more willing to experiment with different, even nontraditional, prose styles.

Moore, C. L.
(1911–1987)

Catherine L. Moore was married to Henry KUT- TNER throughout most of her writing career, and much of the work that appeared under his name as well as their joint pseudonyms was at least partially hers. The most famous and best example of this is "VINTAGE SEASON," which was filmed as *Disaster in Time* (1992). The only collection of stories to bear both their names was *No Boundaries* (1955), containing some of the best work they wrote, either together or singly.

Moore had already established herself with her first short story, "Shambleau" (1933), an adventure story with a fascinating female villain set on a decadent, romanticized Mars. During the 1930s she turned out a steady stream of these otherworld adventures, which were similar to Leigh BRACKETT's work. Several of these featured her recurring character, Northwest Smith, whose adventures were collected as *Northwest of Earth* (1954, also published as *Scarlet Dream*) and *Shambleau and Others* (1953), bringing together for Smith and final stories.

After marrying Kuttner in 1940, her name appeared much less frequently, and the extent to which she contributed to their substantial body of work will never be completely known. Together they wrote serious and humorous science fiction, fantasy adventures, and even murder mysteries. *Earth's Last Citadel* (1943, book version 1964) is a rousing adventure set in the very distant future, and *Fury* (1950), for which she was not credited, is considered Kuttner's best book-length work, the story of war among the domed cities of Venus.

Moore had also written a good deal of sword-and-sorcery-style fantasy, and her recurring character, Jirel of Joiry, was one of the first female lead characters in a fantasy series. Many of her early stories were collected in *Judgment Night* (1952), including the title novella, a mediocre space opera. *The Best of C. L. Moore* (1976) is a more thoughtful collection and is representative of her entire writing career. "The Children's Hour" and "No Woman Born" are both minor classics. The latter involves a badly disfigured woman whose brain is transplanted into a mechanical body. Moore ceased writing following Kuttner's death. Her last novel was *Doomsday Morning* (1957), a fairly routine dystopian novel pitting rebels against a repressive government that can literally read the minds of its citizens. Because her name was so infrequently linked to the stories she wrote or cowrote, Moore is often considered a minor figure in the genre, but she is at least as important as was Kuttner and deserves to be remembered as a historically significant writer.

Moore, Ward
(1903–1978)

Ward Moore was a minor but established mainstream writer when he first turned to science fiction with the satirical *Greener Than You Think* (1947). An eccentric scientist develops a formula that allows grass to grow faster and taller than usual, but the project gets out of hand and the grass quickly becomes unmanageable, eventually overwhelming the entire world. Although the events are told in a fairly straightforward fashion, Moore's intent is obviously to satirize modern civilization, as well as the irresponsibility of scientists who make their discoveries public without considering the possible consequences. A minor classic in its own right, the novel nonetheless was soon eclipsed by Moore's next, which has been in and out of print with some regularity ever since it first appeared.

Bring the Jubilee (1952) is an alternate history story set in a world in which the Confederacy won the Civil War and became an independent nation. With North America divided, there was less impetus toward technological development, and thus the world in general is somewhat less advanced than in our timeline. A time traveler visits the crucial battle of Gettysburg and alters the results, restoring the history with which we are familiar. However, the time traveler is stranded in the past, where he writes his memoirs.

Moore wrote occasional short stories during the 1950s, of which the best known are "Lot" and "Lot's Daughter," set during and after a nuclear war; these stories were the inspiration for the film *Panic in the Year Zero* (1962), which was in turn novelized by Dean Owen as *End of the World* (1962). "Dominions Beyond" and "The Fellow Who Married the Maxill Girl" are also noteworthy. Moore wrote two further novels, both in collaboration. *Caduceus Wild* (1959, revised for the book version in 1978), written with Robert Bradford, is a well-written but standard dystopian novel, with

the medical profession running the world this time, forcibly treating rebellious impulses as a disease. *Joyleg* (1962), written with Avram DAVIDSON, is a delightful satiric comedy about the discovery of a man who has been collecting his pension ever since the Revolutionary War, and the efforts to uncover the secrets of his longevity. More produced a relatively small body of science fiction during his career, but the quality was high enough to establish him as a significant writer in his time; he left at least one novel that has entertained succeeding generations of readers.

More Than Human
Theodore Sturgeon
(1953)

The concept of gestalt entities, a single individual whose personality extends through multiple bodies, would seem to be a particularly rich source of speculation for science fiction writers, but in fact it has appeared very rarely in the genre, perhaps because the implications are difficult to interpolate and the mechanics of writing such a story are very difficult. Brian W. ALDISS did so for humorous effect in "Let's Be Frank," wherein the ubiquitous Frank reproduces, all of his offspring becoming part of the same persona, and his various manifestations eventually supplant the rest of humanity. Richard COWPER dealt with the subject peripherally in *Clone* (1972), and Syne Mitchell did the same in *Technogenesis* (2002). It may be that the theme is so seldom employed because Theodore STURGEON set such an impossibly high standard with *More Than Human* that no writer since has felt capable of further developing the concept.

The core of *More Than Human*, which won the International Fantasy Award, was the novelette "Baby Is Three," first published in 1952. For the book version, Sturgeon added "The Fabulous Idiot" as the prelude and "Morality" as the conclusion, neither of which had appeared previously. The premise is deceptively simple: A half-dozen individuals with unusual powers actually share a mental link that makes them part of a greater whole, a single balanced personality, as well as a group of individuals. In "Baby Is Three" a young boy is sent for psychiatric treatment after he attempts to kill his foster mother, an act for which even he apparently can suggest no motive. During the course of those sessions the protagonist learns along with the reader that he is the focal point of a group of children, including two teleporting sisters with a disinclination to wear clothing, a teenaged girl with powerful and potentially destructive telekinesis, and an infant with super intelligence—all of whom are mentally linked.

"The Fabulous Idiot" takes place before that crisis. Although the children are fumbling with the strange compulsions that affect them, they are unable to complete the connection or even to understand the source of their odd desires. They almost come into focus, however, when a mentally retarded adult named Lone, an individual with a penetrating insight into the human soul and the potential to merge into a gestalt with the others, stumbles into the circle. Although this early attempt at union ultimately fails, "Morality" sees their efforts finally consummated—but only after

they acquire a living component who can serve as their conscience, the source of their morality, and keep them connected in some tenuous fashion to the normal human race.

The novel succeeds on numerous levels. Sturgeon was highly respected for his ability to delineate his characters and to give them an emotional depth that communicated itself to his readers, and he used that talent brilliantly in the novel. Although the concepts are complex and the themes intricate, the story is told so fluently that it succeeds as a simple entertainment. For those desiring a more sophisticated experience, his story is rich in detail and speculation about the way in which our own minds play tricks on us, the subtleties of our interactions with others, and, in a simple sense, the manner in which our culture as a whole functions socially. It is without question the finest book Sturgeon wrote; some critics contend it is the finest science fiction novel ever written. The fact that it has been in print almost continuously for 50 years is a testimony to its broad appeal and its relevance for succeeding generations of readers.

N

Nagata, Linda
(1960–)

Although Linda Nagata produced a handful of short stories during the late 1980s, it was not until 1995 that she attracted any attention, winning a Nebula for "Goddesses." That year also saw the publication of her first two novels, immediately establishing her as a new talent in hard science fiction. In *The Bohr Maker* (1995), a man with an incurable and fatal illness is desperate to discover a way to prolong his life. Recent developments in nanotechnology, in the form of microscopic machines that can be injected into a human body to make repairs, seem to hold his only hope, and he resorts to theft in an effort to save himself. Predictably, things never turn out precisely as they were intended. *Tech Heaven* (1995), though also firmly grounded in science, examined its characters and a potential social issue in great detail. The plot is somewhat similar to that of *The Bohr Maker.* A woman determined to save her dying husband has him cryogenically frozen in anticipation of a cure. Her conduct alienates her family and friends, and the government moves toward making such life-extension techniques illegal. When a cure is finally developed and he is revived she becomes anxious about their relationship.

Nagata's next two novels are linked and form a sequel to *The Bohr Maker.* In *Deception Well* (1997), religious fanaticism exacerbates tensions between an orbiting habitat and its earthside terminal. *Vast* (1998) moves the cult into galactic space on a quest to track down a mysterious and now absent alien race that left behind malevolent and dangerous artifacts in a manner somewhat similar to that in the BERSERKER SERIES by Fred SABERHAGEN. Both novels speculate about dramatic advances in biotechnology, although their characters remain recognizably human.

Nanotechnology is also the theme of *Limit of Vision* (2001), in which an experimental subject escapes virtual imprisonment and becomes a fugitive in Southeast Asia, pursued by a relentless foe who claims to be concerned about the unrestricted spread of nanomachines into the outside world, but who actually is more interested in monopolizing the availability of such technology. Most of the novel is an elaborate chase sequence, occasionally interrupted by debates among the characters. The story is less controlled than in Nagata's previous novels, but enlivened by considerable inventiveness. *Memory* (2003) is by far her strangest and most ambitious novel. Human colonists live an unusual existence on a planet whose physical nature is altered every night when a mysterious substance emerges from the ground and reshapes it. The colonists take shelter, protected by what appear to be giant beetles, and try to figure out the rules by which their world works.

Although it is too early to judge Nagata's place in the field, it is clear from her work to date that she is adept at creating original settings and realistic characters and that her background in the biological sciences allows her to add a substantial and entertaining depth of background to her work.

Naked Lunch
William S. Burroughs
(1959)

There is no clear agreement about the difference between surreal fiction and science fiction. The line between the two becomes even more blurred when an author leaves ambiguous evidence about whether extraordinary and fantastic events described in a story are actually real or whether they are delusions of the protagonist. Philip K. DICK's *Eye in the Sky* (1957) is clearly science fiction because individual characters are physically influenced by the variant perceptions of others, but the case is less clear in this, the most famous novel by William S. BURROUGHS, first published under the title *The Naked Lunch* (later shortened to just *Naked Lunch*).

The novel involves the experiences of a narcotics addict who begins to hallucinate giant insects, people transformed into other bodies or featureless blobs, and other visions that at first seem to be just illusory consequences of his drug use, but whose true nature becomes progressively less certain. The book feels as though it was written in fits and starts and assembled almost at random. Its greatest strengths lie in the evocation of atmosphere, albeit a disorienting and often very oppressive one, and in the intense descriptive quality of some of the prose. The explicit sexual content was quite shocking when the novel first appeared, and its publication in the United States was accompanied by a major court case. There are strong elements of untraditional humor as well. The protagonist at one point tries to convince people that his baboon is actually a dog, for example. Many elements in the story are clearly autobiography.

Although the very nature of the novel would seem to make it impossible to film, David Cronenberg made a creditable effort in *David Cronenberg's Naked Lunch* (1991) to capture some of the tone by interspersing elements from the book with events from the author's real life. The novel has had continuing influence both inside and out of the science fiction community, on such diverse writers as Thomas Pynchon, J. G. BALLARD, Harlan ELLISON, and Paul Di FILIPPO.

Neuromancer
William Gibson
(1984)

The cyberpunk movement was an ill-defined but still important subset of science fiction that began with Bruce Bethke's 1983 short story "Cyberpunk," which gave its name to the form. Although Bethke coined the term, it was William GIBSON who would be most closely identified with cyberpunk, particularly following publication of *Neuromancer*, his first novel, and a winner of both the Hugo and Nebula Awards. Typically, cyberpunk stories are set in a fairly near future in which modern society has become more corrupt than ever, the definition of criminal activity has become more or less fluid, and certain elements of high technology—computers, virtual reality, direct interfacing between humans and machines, sometimes even cyborgs—have become important and common aspects of everyday life.

Neuromancer in turn coined the term *cyberspace*, a reference to virtual reality in one form or another, which Gibson describes as a kind of shared hallucination. The novel was interpreted in some quarters as a protest against government domination of cyberspace, and its protagonist is something of a rebel, although not a very organized or effective one. He supports himself by entering cyberspace and stealing data, either on commission or speculatively. Despite his success at his vocation, he remains a minor player, and it is patently obvious that individuals have no real chance to affect the world on anything other than a personal level. Artificial intelligences oversee things from their orbiting habitats, and the degree to which they have abrogated human decision making is left an open question. Although Gibson was not the first to introduce antiheroes into science fiction, he was so successful and his themes so close to nihilistic that many traditionalists within the field felt threatened by his popularity.

Although Gibson's later fiction was also well received, none of his later novels achieved the same level of success, including two that more or less were sequels, *Count Zero* (1986) and *Mona Lisa Overdrive* (1988). This may be in part due to the ebbing popularity of cyberpunk itself, a transient fad now absorbed into the wider matrix of the field at large. It is probably also a function of Gibson's relatively small output, as he averages a single novel every three years.

"Neutron Star"
Larry Niven
(1966)

The scientific problem short story is a form often associated with *Analog Magazine*, which favored them heavily. Typically they involve a single character or a small group, their personalities usually shallowly drawn, who are either presented with a difficulty, which they must solve through a novel application of scientific or engineering principles, or faced with an anomalous situation, which they must explain in scientific terms. In a sense, these are detective stories—but there is a key difference. In mystery fiction, the reader has a chance, however remote, to guess the solution. In most scientific problem stories, there is no opportunity to do so because the point is to introduce something unprecedented. Since by its very nature the story technically cheats the reader, it takes an extraordinary effort to produce one that stands out.

Larry NIVEN did exactly that with "Neutron Star," which won the Hugo Award. The story is set against the backdrop of his Known Space series and features Niven's recurring character, Beowulf Shaeffer, a space pilot. Shaeffer is in serious financial trouble when he is approached by one of the alien Puppeteers, who want to hire him for a dangerous mission to study a neutron star, a mission that mysteriously killed the last two humans who tried it. Neutron stars are theoretical objects, stars compressed into small, dense spheres—in this case only 12 miles across—still generating a powerful gravity field. The Puppeteers are concerned because the previous crew was killed while inside a Puppeteer-built hull; since those hulls are supposedly impenetrable, the Puppeteers' credibility is at stake.

Shaeffer initially plans to run for it once he is in space, but a self-destruct device planted in his ship makes that impossible. During his cautious approach to the neutron star he begins to observe strange phenomena, as though gravity was working differently in various parts of his ship; he figures out what is happening just in time to avoid a fatal accident. It is in the solution that Niven takes what could have been a run-of-the-mill story and turns it into something special. The strange forces turn out to be tidal pressures from the neutron star, which the reader could not have anticipated. Niven takes us through the detailed reasoning process of how Shaeffer interprets the data and figures out how to escape. It is the rational process that holds our attention, rather than the solution of the mystery.

"The New Accelerator"
H. G. Wells
(1899)

In at least some sense, the marvelous invention story is the perfect example of the greatest advantage that science fiction affords to writers. It is possible to stipulate a new technology or a method of circumventing a contemporary limitation, and then examine the consequences. At its best, and usually in longer forms, these stories involve speculation about the changes that would result in society if such a discovery were made, as well as the impact on individual characters. The contrast between the postdiscovery world and our own can thereby be exploited for satiric or cautionary purposes. On the other hand, and particularly in short stories, the results are more often humorous or subtle. Wells was primarily interested in humor in "The New Accelerator," although he includes a gentle jab at scientists who are too quick to introduce a new discovery without examining the consequences or who cast aside caution in hopes of financial awards.

Professor Gibberne is a scientist whose specialty is nerve stimulants. His latest project is designed to accelerate the senses so that an individual can move and think twice as fast as usual, although his lifespan would be cut short proportionately. He succeeds, but far beyond his expectations, creating an elixir so potent that while under its influence the subject observes the rest of the world moving in painfully slow motion. He and a friend, the narrator, partake of the elixir and spend a short time wandering about, first observing, then playing a practical joke, before the effects wear off. Their exploits probably influenced John D. MacDonald's novel *The Girl, the Gold Watch, and Everything* (1962), which achieves the same effect through means of a magical object.

Wells gave some thought to the consequences. Both men are exhausted by the experience, and they discover that the friction of their rapid movement through the air has caused their clothing to smolder. Although initially drunk with power in a scene reminiscent of *The Invisible Man* (1897), Gibberne ultimately realizes that his elixir is too dangerous to use in its present state and resigns himself to developing a less extreme version, along with a second drug with the opposite effect, a retardant. Although the tone of the story is light and whimsical, there is an obvious undercurrent of contempt for the irresponsible commercialization of science.

"Nightfall"
Isaac Asimov
(1941)

It was a source of at least mild annoyance to Isaac ASIMOV that this very early story has always been considered his best, because that suggested that he had learned nothing over the next five decades of writing. His fiction did get technically better in the years that followed, but this single story had perhaps the most compelling plot of anything he wrote. Inspired by a quote from Ralph Waldo Emerson, the story is set on a planet near the core of the galaxy. Because of the proximity of other stars, the planet Lagash has six suns and is bathed in light constantly, except for a brief period every 2,000 years when only one sun is visible and is briefly eclipsed. Since they have no experience of darkness, virtually the entire population is driven mad by the event, destroying civilization and starting another cycle of barbarism and eventual progress.

The action takes place in an observatory where scientists have finally figured out what is about to happen. A skeptical journalist is eventually convinced by their arguments and remains there as the eclipse approaches. A cult that has kept a distorted version of the incident alive throughout the cyclic process is violently opposed to the scientists because a natural explanation erodes the basis of their faith, and they send an unsuccessful saboteur who remains captive as darkness falls. Because of the constant daylight, the citizens of Lagash—who may or may not be human, since Asimov never describes them—have never needed to develop a system of artificial illumination, and during the short but dramatic period of darkness they literally set their homes on fire, desperate for any form of light. There is also a brief but amusing sequence in which the astronomers speculate about the possibility of a planet with only one star and the unlikelihood of life arising on a world that suffers darkness for half of every day.

The battle between science and superstition, and the efforts of both to explain the mysteries of the universe, are reduced to their essentials and convincingly portrayed. Even the foreknowledge of what will happen is not enough to save the sanity of the scientists who remain outside the Hideout, a hidden, illuminated chamber whose inhabitants are committed to preserving the truth so that the next civilization will be better prepared. Robert SILVERBERG expanded the story into *Nightfall* (1990), but the novel version simply provides more background detail and actually dilutes rather than enhances the emotional impact.

"Nine Hundred Grandmothers"
R. A. Lafferty
(1966)

One of the techniques that made R. A. LAFFERTY such a distinctive prose stylist was his use of compressed storytelling techniques, using extracts of scenes to substitute for a more fully developed exposition, snatches of dialogue that hint at what is happening rather than spelling it out explicitly. Sometimes the setting is not described at all, or only by suggestion. The ordinary aspects of a short story are all subordinated to the plot, which advances in short, efficient bursts. One of the best of these is this story of Ceran Swicegood, who wanted to know how everything began.

Swicegood is part of a exploration team that visits alien cultures, negotiating trade agreements favorable to their employers. Unlike the rest of his team, Swicegood is neither materialistic nor aggressive, although ultimately he proves to be just as egocentric and exploitative as his fellows. He is the Special Aspects Man, whose his job is to find viable trade items that might not be obvious to the rest of the team. When his team lands on Proavitus, he uncovers a very unusual situation. The indigenous aliens claim that they never die, that their entire race is still alive, although the elderly sleep most of the time and reside in underground chambers.

Lafferty's underlying themes often involve religious questions, so it is unsurprising that Swicegood decides that this is his chance for personal revelation. If the entire race is still alive, then the very first of their kind might be able to tell him how intelligent life began. His local contact explains that when each of her people becomes an adult, they are taken below ground for a ritual in which everything is explained. Swicegood violates the customs of the planet and the rules of civility and tries to circumvent the process, descending into the underground chambers for an audience with the very first intelligent being on that world. Unfortunately, she declines to explain, and he is forced to go away empty-handed, a clear statement that the beginning of things is, after all, unknowable, and that we are probably better off remaining ignorant.

Nineteen Eighty-Four
George Orwell
(1949)

Writing as George Orwell, Eric Blair produced in *Nineteen Eighty-Four* (1949) what is unquestionably the best-known dystopian novel, set in a totalitarian future. Many of the phrases and words he invented for that novel, such as "doublespeak," have entered common usage and, more than two decades after the events of the novel were forecast to have transpired, the concerns he raised about individual freedom are still valid.

In the novel, the world has been very much changed following a nuclear war and other turmoil.

A decaying England has been renamed Oceania and is now ruled by Big Brother, a mysterious, perhaps apocryphal figure who appears on the omnipresent television screens exhorting people to greater conformity. The Thought Police investigate anyone suspected of harboring disloyal or even uncertain opinions, and even the very language people speak is being reengineered to make it more difficult to question authority.

The protagonist is Winston Smith, who indulges in a forbidden love, is arrested, and is subjected to a series of sessions with a skilled interrogator who wants him to recant. A significant portion of the novel consists of their conversations and arguments on the nature of freedom and of responsibility to society; these passages sometimes interfere with the pace of the story, although Orwell's prose flows smoothly enough to hold the reader's attention. Smith resists, is tortured, and ultimately embraces the state and renounces what he formerly believed, in a brilliant and chilling illustration of the effectiveness of modern brainwashing techniques.

When it was published the novel was criticized for being overly depressing, but it struck an obvious chord among its readers and has remained continuously in print ever since. Two film versions also appeared, the first in 1955, and the second appropriately enough in 1984. Oddly, the book has been challenged both from the political right, because of Orwell's personal leftist politics and the inexplicable perception that the novel was somehow intended to promote socialism, and from the left, for clarity by those who felt that Orwell was portraying socialism in all its forms as a repressive force. The book has been a frequent target for those who wish to ban controversial reading matter from school libraries—even though it remains an acknowledged classic.

Niven, Larry
(1938–   )

Science fiction changed dramatically during the 1960s, embracing many mainstream literary values and concentrating far more on characterization, prose style, and contemporary issues. There was a sense of alarm in some quarters, particularly among fans of space opera and hard science fiction, who believed the genre would no longer have room for their preferred type of story. Although that alarm was never justified by the facts, it came as a great relief to those fans when a new writer rose to rapid prominence by writing intelligent space operas that were also scientifically literate. Larry Niven's explosive arrival on the scene in the late 1960s calmed the waters and established a new legitimacy for space adventure. Most of his early fiction is set against the common background of Known Space, a concept he introduced in his first short story, "The Coldest Place," in 1964. Niven populated this universe with a handful of distinct alien species whose characteristics were deliberately exaggerated to represent a type. His aliens effectively share a common personality and become characters as a set rather than as individuals, although he occasionally departs from that formula. Niven mixed space opera with hard science fiction, and infused both with an extremely fertile imagination.

World of Ptavvs (1966) expanded the future history, which included such outstanding early stories as "NEUTRON STAR," "Bordered in Black," "Relic of Empire," and "At the Core." The protagonist is experimenting with telepathic contact with dolphins when an ancient statue is discovered beneath the ocean, a statue that subsequently is revealed to be an incredibly powerful alien creature whose mission to Earth was interrupted but can now resume. *Protector* (1973) further developed the relationship of humans to the Paks, the form of life into which humans were expected to evolve by an alien race that feels free to meddle in human biology and destiny. The least ambitious and original of Niven's early novels was *A Gift from Earth* (1968), set on a lost colony world split into two separate castes, the descendants of the crew dominating the passengers and harvesting organs from the underclass to prolong their own lives.

Although all three novels were solid and entertaining, Niven was still far more successful with his short stories. "Neutron Star" won the Hugo Award, and a steady stream of top-notch tales followed, including such outstanding works as "Flatlander," "The Soft Weapon," and "Convergent

Species." Two titles collected most of these early Known Space stories—*Neutron Star* (1968) and *The Shape of Space* (1969)—and others would appear later in *All the Myriad Ways* (1971), *A Hole in Space* (1975), and *Tales of Known Space* (1975). The high point of the series would be *Ringworld* (1970), which won both the Hugo and Nebula Awards. Something strange has been happening to the race known as the Puppeteers. A diverse group of characters, including a woman who literally has the power to alter the rules of chance, set out on a voyage of exploration and find themselves on an enormous artificial world, constructed in the shape of an immense ring. The novel won both the Hugo and Nebula Awards and probably provided at least a portion of the inspiration for such diverse works as the Nathan Brazil series by Jack L. CHALKER and *RENDEZVOUS WITH RAMA* (1973) by Arthur C. CLARKE.

Although Niven continued to write short fiction, winning Hugo Awards for "The Hole Man," "INCONSTANT MOON," and "The Borderland of Sol," by the late 1970s he clearly was more interested in novels. He also began to collaborate with Jerry POURNELLE, a partnership that would recur periodically from that point forward. Their first science fiction novel together was *The Mote in God's Eye* (1974), an unabashed space opera involving the first contact with a particularly fascinating and potentially dangerous alien species. It was an unusually tense and exciting adventure story, but became mildly controversial because of the perception that many of the characters were less than complimentary stereotypes. A later sequel, *The Gripping Hand* (1994, also published as *The Mote Around Murcheson's Eye*), further explores the efforts to control the highly adaptable Moties, but failed to capture the excitement of the original.

A World out of Time (1976) was a less satisfying space adventure, but *The Long Arm of Gil Hamilton* (1976), a collection of linked stories about a man with a form of telekinesis, proved that Niven was still a major talent. A novel-length sequel to the latter, *The Patchwork Girl* (1980), is one of the best examples of the blending of a science fiction setting with a traditional murder mystery. *Lucifer's Hammer* (1977), another collaboration with Pournelle, is a superior disaster novel, this one involving a collision between Earth and an over-sized comet, and describes the aftermath in chilling detail.

Niven seemed to lose much of his momentum after 1980. His output of short fiction dropped dramatically and has only recently recovered; most of his novels were collaborative efforts. His first sequel to *Ringworld, Ringworld Engineers* (1979), reached the level of its predecessor only intermittently. He would return to that setting after a gap of many years in *The Ringworld Throne* (1996), in which the ecology of that vast world becomes mysteriously upset, and more successfully in *Ringworld's Children* (2004). *Oath of Fealty* (1981), with Pournelle, is a near-future thriller involving a crisis in a domed city. The Dream Park series, consisting of *Dream Park* (1981), *The Barsoom Project* (1989), and *The California Voodoo Game* (1992), all written with Steven Barnes, are lively but not particularly ambitious action stories set in a future theme park. *The Descent of Anansi* (1982), also with Barnes, is a predictable and rather flat story of the bid for independence by an orbiting habitat.

The Integral Trees (1984) was considerably more interesting, exploring the nature of a human colony in a weightless environment under the influence of a neutron star. A sequel, *The Smoke Ring* (1987), provided an unusually effective follow up involving a crisis that threatens the colony. Another collaboration with Pournelle, *Footfall* (1985), is an outstanding alien invasion story, concentrating on military and political maneuvering rather than on the more frightening treatment common in science fiction films. They also collaborated on two novels about the settling of a new colony world, *The Legacy of Heorot* (1987) and *Beowulf's Children* (1995). In the first volume, efforts to wipe out a dangerous native predator backfire as the reptilian creatures prove to be more dangerous and intelligent than originally believed. The inferior but still interesting sequel repeats the conflict generations later.

Achilles' Choice (1991) and *Saturn's Race* (2000), both with Barnes, each involve a conspiracy—one at the Olympics, one involving genetic engineering. Both are inoffensive but not particularly memorable works. *Destiny's Road* (1998) is a coming-of-age story set on a distant world. Niven's

later novels, some written alone and some collaboratively, often contain engaging concepts and settings, but they generally seem to lack the enthusiasm of his earlier work. His return to the steady production of short fiction has been more promising. Several recent collections contain blends of new and previously collected material, a sampling of which can be found in *Limits* (1985), *N Space* (1990), *Playgrounds of the Mind* (1991), *Crashlander* (1994), *Rainbow Mars* (1999), and *Scatterbrain* (2003).

No Enemy But Time
Michael Bishop
(1982)

Novels set during prehistory have been popular since Jack London's *Before Adam* (1906). Prehistory has been the basis for intelligent and erudite novels such as *The Inheritors* (1955) by William Golding, and even best-selling entertainments, such as Jean Auel's *The Clan of the Cave Bear* (1980) and its several sequels. But none of these novels have been as complex and as thought-provoking as *No Enemy But Time*. Although this was Michael BISHOP's seventh novel, it was the first to receive the general acclaim that he had previously enjoyed for his short fiction, receiving the Nebula Award as best novel of the year.

John Monegal is a man who spends most of his time apart from normal humanity, lost in dreamlike visions of a prehistoric world, a talent that results in his recruitment by a secret government project that is trying to develop a time machine. Because of his affinity for that era, he is chosen as the experimental subject for a trip back to the time when humanity became a distinct animal, essentially modern humans. His mission is to study a small clan and then return; but something interferes with the process, and he finds himself stranded in the past, forced to turn to the subjects of his study in order to survive.

The middle section of the novel combines a scientifically literate description of the cultural habits of habiline humans and the physical conditions in which they lived. It also provides a wonderful illustration of how an individual shifts from the role of outsider to an accepted member of a group, and how isolation from an individual's own culture can affect how he interacts with another. Monegal becomes a member of the tribe, comes to consider their primitive style as normal and even civilized. When he finally is rescued and brought back to the present, he has to make almost as big an adjustment as when he was first stranded. More importantly, he has fathered a child in the past, a child whom he brings back to the contemporary world and rears, despite the government's refusal to acknowledge her origin or his sacrifice. Bishop's novel is an intelligent and mature examination of an unusual culture, a theme the author had previously explored with the aliens of *Transfigurations* (1979). He would return to the theme in "Her Habiline Husband," expanded into the novel *Ancient of Days* (1985), which, while quite successful in itself, was not nearly as impressive a work.

"No Truce with Kings"
Poul Anderson
(1963)

The setting for this Hugo Award–winning novelette is the Pacific States of America, a loose coalition of semifeudal states that arose generations after a nuclear war devastated most of the world. After years of fighting with its neighbors, this new nation is torn apart by a civil war following a questionably legal impeachment, apparently the result of a power struggle between two men. There are, however, deeper levels of conflict. The deposed Brodsky supported the existing decentralized system that involves local strongmen and considerable flexibility in laws and customs. The usurper Fallon favors a strong central government as well as an alliance with the Espers, a popular order that uses psi powers as a means of protecting its separate status. Beneath this is yet another level, because the Espers are in fact an organization created by an alien race, secretly trying to reshape human society into what it considers a more sensible culture. All the parties believe they are acting morally, and Poul ANDERSON is careful to ensure that we see the positive arguments for each of the disparate positions.

We see most of this unfold through the eyes of two military officers, one on each side in the prolonged war that follows. When it appears that Brodsky's adherents may be on the brink of winning, and when they uncover part of the secret of the Espers' duplicity, the latter group openly allies itself with Fallon. The aliens internally regret the necessity of shedding so much blood, but they are convinced that in the long run it will be better for humanity, although by now the reader may have begun to suspect that some of them have less honorable motives as well. Anderson's sympathies clearly lie with the Brodsky forces, who manage to defeat their enemies even when the latter are assisted by alien weaponry.

Ultimately the story is about free will and the arrogance of assuming that we have the right to choose a destiny for others. MacKenzie, the aging officer on the winning side, speculates that the traditional idea of the nation-state may not be the right structure for human beings, but whether right or wrong, humans must make their own decisions. By implication, individuals should also be responsible for choosing their own destinies.

Non-Stop
Brian W. Aldiss
(1958)

The most common shortcut employed by science fiction writers to move human characters to the stars is some form of faster-than-light drive, usually described as a shortcut through some other dimension of space. Although this is a convenient device, it does not at present seem a likely possibility. An alternate method is to imagine that ships to the stars are designed for journeys that will take years, perhaps generations. Generation starship novels and even entire series have been written in recent years by Brian STABLEFORD, Gene WOLFE, and Molly Gloss, among others.

One of the earliest of these was *Non-Stop*, also published as *Starship*, the first novel by Brian W. ALDISS. The protagonist is Roy Complain, a loner in a culture that has devolved into primitivism, living in the corridors and chambers of an enormous starship whose hydroponics section has grown out of control, filling much of the ship with vegetation. The passengers aboard ship have lost virtually all technological knowledge and no longer even understand that their world is an artificial place. They have persistent legends of giants who occasionally kidnap their kind, but no actual evidence of their existence. After a series of adventures, Complain locates the legendary bridge and encounters the giants, whom we eventually discover are ordinary humans. During their many generations in space, those aboard have mutated, becoming much smaller and enjoying only very short lives. The ship itself has been recovered, but the authorities have not yet decided how to reintegrate the shipboard humans into normal society, if it is possible at all. The bizarre environment is particularly vividly realized. The concept that it might be necessary for society to tolerate the maintenance of what might seem abusive conditions aboard the indolent starship, although introduced only in the final chapter, illustrated Aldiss's ability to look at standard genre situations from a distinctly different point of view.

Norman, John
(1931–   )

John Frederick Lange Jr., a philosophy professor, used the name John Norman for his science fiction, the vast majority of which is contained in the Gor series, 25 novels set on a physically impossible planet elsewhere in our solar system. The Gor series began with *Tarnsman of Gor* (1966), a planetary romance very much in the style of the MARS SERIES by Edgar Rice BURROUGHS. In the opening volume, an Earthman—Tarl Cabot—is transported to Gor, where he becomes a formidable warrior in a primitive and violent world.

Initially the series followed that same pattern. Cabot battles religious fanatics and searches for his missing family in *Outlaw of Gor* (1967) and *Priest-Kings of Gor* (1968); he becomes partly reconciled with the local theocracy, undertaking a mission on their behalf in *Nomads of Gor* (1969). In *Assassin of Gor* (1970), one of the best in the series, Cabot has to match wits with a professional assassin. *Raiders of Gor* (1971) was also quite good, taking Cabot to a

remote and lawless city where he battles pirates and survives other dangers before saving the day. At this point the series seemed to be moving beyond mere pastiche, with more ambitious plots, greater character development, and even moments of gentle satire. Unfortunately, the next volume marked a sharp and controversial turning point.

The main character of *Captive of Gor* (1972) is a woman kidnapped from Earth. Enslaved on Gor by a culture that keeps women in a subservient role, she discovers that she enjoys the lack of freedom and occasional brutalization. This sadomasochistic strain became the dominant theme in the novels that followed, and the series became increasingly controversial, ending with *Magicians of Gor* (1988). Norman was regularly castigated by the fan press, although he had a small but loyal group of advocates. Two extremely bad low-budget films loosely based on the series did nothing to improve his reputation.

A nonseries novel, *Time Slave* (1975), suggested much the same situation in a prehistoric setting. Norman began a new series with *The Chieftain* (1991), followed by *The Captain* (1992), and *The King* (1993), set in an interstellar empire that has reverted to barbarism, complete with death duels in public arenas and other familiar devices. But even though these new novels were less controversial, Norman's popularity had faded, and he has produced nothing new since then.

Norton, Andre
(1912–   )

Science fiction is often described as the literature of adolescence, and for many years it was aimed quite deliberately at young males. Even the books published ostensibly for an adult market contained little if anything that would keep them out of high school libraries. Unsurprisingly, many of the same authors wrote for both markets, and most mature readers continued to read young adult fiction. It was often difficult to separate one from the other, the most dramatic example being STARSHIP TROOPERS by Robert A. HEINLEIN, which was intended as one of his young adult novels, but which was eventually published for the adult market.

Second only to Heinlein in the popularity of her young adult fiction was Andre Norton, pseudonym of Alice Mary Norton, who also wrote historical novels, spy thrillers, and mysteries, although after 1950 science fiction and later fantasy would become her major interests. Almost all of her novels during the 1950s and 1960s were labeled for younger readers in their hardcover editions, then released in paperback as adult fiction. It was only after she began writing almost exclusively in the fantasy genre that her work would be accepted as adult material from the outset. Norton wrote straightforward adventure stories, usually in the form of a journey across some imaginative landscape, and has sometimes been dismissed as lacking serious intent. She has also been criticized for the lack of diversity among the characters in her earlier fiction, although they are at least as well drawn as those in most adult science fiction.

Her first genre short story appeared in 1947, but it was not until the publication of *Star Man's Son* (1952, also published as *Daybreak—2250 A.D.*) that she attracted any notice. The setting is Earth, generations after a devastating nuclear war. After a perilous journey through devastated scenery, a young man with the mutant power to communicate mentally with a feral cat helps forge a defense against a horde of mutated rats. The link between the human and animal character was a device that would repeat itself constantly in Norton's fiction. Her next novel was *Star Rangers* (1953, also published as *The Last Planet*), a pleasant and undemanding space opera set in the dying days of a galactic empire.

During the second half of the 1950s Norton produced a steady stream of excellent adventure stories. *Star Guard* (1955) anticipated many of the devices of modern military science fiction. A group of mercenaries is hired to intercede in a conflict on a colony world, only to discover that they are caught in a trap, betrayed by their employers, and are on their own against both sides. *The Stars Are Ours* (1954) flirted with social commentary. Following a global war, Earth falls under a brutal dictatorship that outlaws most scientific pursuits, so a group of rebels travels to the stars and forges an alliance with the ocean dwellers of another world.

Their story is continued in *Star Born* (1957), one of those rare cases where a sequel is significantly better than its predecessor.

Sargasso of Space (1955) was the first of the Solar Queen series, originally published as by Andrew North, which follows the adventures of a privately owned interstellar trading ship. It also introduced the concept of the Forerunners, a long-vanished alien race that left enigmatic artifacts sprinkled throughout the galaxy. The crew escapes from a device that traps spaceships in the first volume, avoids destruction when they are wrongly accused of carrying a deadly disease in *Plague Ship* (1956), and gets caught up in planetary politics in *Voodoo Planet* (1959). After a considerable gap, Norton returned to the series with *Postmarked the Stars* (1969), in which their live cargo turns dangerous; after another lapse she issued *Redline the Stars* (1993), probably written primarily by her collaborator, P. M. Griffin. Norton would collaborate with a number of writers after 1990 to extend her existing series, and the degree of her personal involvement is unknown. Two more Solar Queen novels, *Derelict for Trade* (1997) and *A Mind for Trade* (1997), were written with Sherwood Smith.

Norton explored parallel worlds in *Star Gate* (1958) and *Crossroads of Time* (1956), the latter of which is an entertaining alternate universe adventure. A sequel, *Quest Crosstime* (1965, also published as *Crosstime Agent*), is set in a fascinating timeline in which the Aztecs dominate much of the world. *Sea Siege* (1957) pits the survivors of a nuclear war against mutated octopi. *The Time Traders* (1958) launched one of her most popular series. American and Russian agents are battling for control of an alien spaceship uncovered in the Arctic, but the ship is also a time machine through whose operation the conflict becomes three-way, involving the alien Baldies. The discovery of an intact ship in *Galactic Derelict* (1959) allows a small group of American agents to travel into space where they find the remains of the fallen alien civilization. Two routine planetary adventures followed—*The Defiant Agents* (1962) and *Key out of Time* (1963). Recent extensions to the series are *Firehand* (1994, with P. M. Griffin) and two collaborations with Sherwood Smith, *Echoes in Time* (1999) and *Atlantis Endgame* (2002).

Several other short series appeared between 1959 and 1966. The BEAST MASTER (1959) and its sequel *Lord of Thunder* (1962) would be extended by Lyn McConchie starting in 2002. *Storm Over Warlock* (1960) and its sequel *Ordeal in Otherwhere* (1964) took readers to a mysterious planet whose inhabitants possess almost magical mental powers. *Judgment on Janus* (1963) and *Victory on Janus* (1966), a considerably less successful effort, followed the adventures of colonists who are physically and mentally altered by the lingering aura of the now vanished original inhabitants of their world. Norton's occasional stated aversion to religious intolerance recurs here. The Yiktor series, consisting of *Moon of Three Rings* (1966), *Exiles of the Stars* (1971), and *Flight in Yiktor* (1986) are space operas that illustrated Norton's growing interest in fantasy, as evidenced by her long-running Witch World series. The mix of spaceships and sorcery is an uneasy one. Norton also wrote several novels that focused on Forerunner artifacts that did not compose a formal series, including *The X Factor* (1965), *Ice Crown* (1970), *Forerunner Foray* (1973), *Voorloper* (1980), *Forerunner* (1981), and *Forerunner: The Second Venture* (1985).

Following the publication of *Witch World* (1963), Norton turned increasingly to fantasy, although she continued to write occasional science fiction novels until 1975. Other than the collaborations, only one nonfantasy novel appeared after that, the mediocre *Brother to Shadows* (1993). Although most of these lack the rich imagination and crisp storytelling that marked her prime, several are still creditable adventure stories. *Catseye* (1961) postulates an interesting situation—the use of telepathic pets to spy on their owners. *Dark Piper* (1968) follows the adventures of a group of children on a remote world after a plague wipes out the entire adult population. In *Dread Companion* (1970) a woman discovers that environmental influences on a new planet could literally reshape her body. Various animals have achieved intelligence on an Earth deserted by humans in *Breed to Come* (1972), and they react negatively when humans return. *No Night Without Stars* (1975), possibly intended as a sequel to *Star Man's Son*, pits a team of humans and their animal companions against an insane computer. Despite the title, *Merlin's Mirror* (1975) is science fiction. The fabled sorcerer is actually being manipulated by hidden alien visitors. *Yurth Burden* (1978) tells the story of the reconciliation between indigenous aliens and the human colonists who have crashed on their planet.

Andre Norton's influence on science fiction may be larger than it appears, primarily because it is indirect. She has been imitated in fantasy far more than in her science fiction, and in fact enjoys a much greater reputation in that field. A large portion of the current generation of science fiction writers grew up reading her otherworlds adventures during their youth, and owe at least part of their interest in the field—and probably some of their storytelling techniques—to a writer who invariably produced an entertaining story.

"Not with a Bang"
Damon Knight
(1949)

There are two strains of Adam and Eve story in science fiction, each of which had already been done to death many times over well before Damon KNIGHT wrote this sardonic variation in the late 1940s. In the first, the reader follows the adventures of two characters who, through time travel or other devices, are revealed in the final paragraphs to be, literally, Adam and Eve. The second is primarily a product of the atomic bomb, a story in which the last two people alive are faced with the prospect of starting up the human race all over again. Both stories have become clichés, and neither scenario is scientifically plausible, since a population of two is far below the minimum required to be self-sustaining.

Knight was well aware of this last fact when he wrote this very short, biting tale. Rolf Smith and Louise Oliver are the last two people alive on a planet that has been ravaged by nuclear war and a particularly virulent plague. Smith was working at a project that created an antidote to the plague, and he has survived the infection, although he is left permanently weak and subject to periodic bouts of paralysis that can be broken only by a fresh dose of the antidote. Smith feels no affection for Oliver, and he knows that there is no chance to regenerate the human race, but he wants to father children who can help care for him in the event that she dies. Oliver has no objection, but her mind has been unhinged by her experiences, and her Protestant sensibilities are so exaggerated that she insists upon being married first, even though there are no ministers left to perform the service. Her very proper, prim lifestyle infuriates Smith, who has to hide his true feelings in order to avoid alienating her.

Eventually, following lengthy arguments that take place offstage, Smith is able to convince Oliver that God would not have wanted the human race to end this way, and that it is therefore not sinful for them to assume themselves married. Although dubious, she accepts the situation, and Smith finally relaxes, convinced that he has now provided for his future. But then he uses a public restroom and is struck by a new bout of paralysis, and realizes to his horror that Oliver would never bend the rules of propriety far enough to allow her to enter the Men's Room and save him. Knight's economically brief story neatly skewers conventional morality while poking fun at one of the most overused plot devices in early science fiction.

Nourse, Alan E.
(1928–1992)

Alan E. Nourse worked as a doctor for most of his life, and his background in the medical profession is frequently in evidence in his science fiction and in his small body of work outside the genre, most notably in *Intern* (1965), under the pseudonym Doctor X. He wrote for both adult and young adult audiences, starting with his first sale in 1951, although he was only sporadically active after the middle of the 1960s.

Nourse's first novel, *Trouble on Titan* (1954), was targeted at young adults, although the theme was one more frequently found in adult fiction. A young soldier is sent to serve in the colony on Saturn's largest moon when the colonists threaten to rebel against Earth's authority, and is instrumental in brokering a compromise in the impending

conflict. Although the solution is somewhat simplistic, the novel is inoffensive and does an excellent job of describing the unusual environment. The hero of *A Man Obsessed* (1955, expanded in 1968 as *The Mercy Man*) has spent years searching for the man he believes responsible for the death of his father when information leads him to believe his quarry is working in a restricted medical facility. He volunteers as an experimental subject in order to gain entry; but what he learns there is not what he or the reader expected. *Rocket to Limbo* (1957) is a short novel about first contact with aliens on a distant planet.

The Invaders Are Coming (1959), written in collaboration with J. A. Meyer, is a story of aliens among us. The theft of fissionable material from a nuclear power plant of the future is disturbing enough. In this instance the agent investigating the theft of such material discovers that the perpetrators are aliens secretly living on Earth, and that others of their kind may have infiltrated his own agency in their bid to gain domination over the human race. The authors use the familiar devices of a routine potboiler to surprisingly good effect. *Scavengers in Space* (1958) is the best of Nourse's young adult books. When an asteroid miner dies under mysterious circumstances, his two sons believe that he was murdered because he had discovered a rich mineral deposit in the asteroid belt. They decide to retrace his steps and establish their claim before the murderers can profit from their crime. A global plague threatens to devastate a colony world in *Star Surgeon* (1959), a scenario that would recur in Nourse's final two adult novels. In *Raiders from the Rings* (1962) the human race is poised to destroy itself in a war between the inner planets and a new civilization based in the asteroid belt and beyond. Just as it appears that conflict is inevitable, an emissary from the stars arrives to alter the equation. *The Universe Between* (1965) is an uneven story of parallel worlds.

After a long absence, Nourse returned to science fiction with *The Blade Runner* (1974), which has no relation to the film adaptation of *DO ANDROIDS DREAM OF ELECTRIC SHEEP?* (1968) by Philip K. DICK. Nourse's bladerunners are doctors who defy a repressive dystopian society and administer health care to those not sanctioned by the law. The protagonist is about to be exposed when he discovers the existence of a new and virulent plague that threatens to spread across the world. Almost another decade would pass before Nourse's next novel, *The Fourth Horseman* (1983), which involves a similar deadly new disease; but in this case the setting is the near future.

The bulk of Nourse's short fiction first appeared in the 1950s and includes a number of exceptional stories; among them are "Family Resemblance," "The Counterfeit Man," "An Ounce of Cure," and "Nightmare Brother"—the last probably his best story. "Brightside Crossing," a gripping tale of hard science fiction dealing with a perilous journey across the sunward-facing side of the planet Mercury, is atypical for Nourse. Many of Nourse's short stories involve medical situations or have doctors as characters. His short work has been collected in *Tiger by the Tail* (1961), *The Counterfeit Man* (1963), *Psi High and Others* (1967), and *Rx for Tomorrow* (1971). He is primarily remembered for his young adult fiction, but much of his adult work is also worth preserving.

Of Mist, and Grass, and Sand
Vonda N. McIntyre
(1973)

Starting with the era of the pulp magazines, science fiction traditionally had been aimed at males. This situation started to change during the 1960s, partly because of the popularity of *Star Trek*, which had a surprisingly large female audience, and partly because the feminist movement had a significant impact on the field. The change was gradual, however. The overwhelming majority of stories still had male protagonists, and while female characters were upgraded somewhat from their former roles as victims or sounding boards, they were still clearly subsidiary to the males. Robert A. HEINLEIN's last young adult novel, *Podkayne of Mars* (1963), had an assertive female protagonist, and Alexei Panshin's RITE OF PASSAGE (1968) proved to be an engaging coming-of-age story focusing on the plight of a teenaged girl. Despite these concessions to changing times, the plots were still the same, reflecting masculine concerns. Podkayne spends most of her time thwarting a gang of spies, for example.

It was not until the 1970s that a small group of writers—Joanna RUSS, Suzy McKee CHARNAS, Suzette Haden ELGIN, and others—began to write science fiction that did not just have female characters, but also expressed a feminine viewpoint. One of the most successful members of this feminist rebellion was Vonda N. McINTYRE, who established herself firmly with this early story, which won a Nebula Award as best novelette.

Snake is a healer, a woman who makes her living in a primitive world by curing the ills of the local people, a task she accomplishes by means of the venom of one of two snakes that accompany her. The other is a dreamsnake, a rare creature with the ability to mentally soothe her patients and start the process of recovery in their minds as her medicines work on their bodies. Unfortunately, their very rarity makes dreamsnakes seem like fearful creatures, and Snake's is killed through the ignorance and superstition of the people she is trying to help.

McIntyre would revise the story of Snake and describe her quest to find a replacement in the novel version, *Dreamsnake* (1979), which won both the Hugo and Nebula Awards. The original novelette and the longer version are both powerful stories, and unconventional for their time, harbingers of more extensive changes that would transform the field dramatically during the 1980s.

"The Old Die Rich"
H. L. Gold
(1953)

H. L. Gold will best be remembered for his long reign as editor of *Galaxy Magazine*, which extended from 1950 to 1961, during which he fostered the careers of many major science fiction writers. Gold wrote fiction himself, beginning in the 1930s, but was largely inactive after becoming editor, selling his last story in 1975. Much of his fiction was humorous fantasy, but he wrote a handful of outstanding science fiction stories as well, of which this is the most famous.

Mark Weldon is an actor who specializes in portraying elderly men. A student of the Stanislavsky method, he spends considerable time at homes for the elderly so that he can understand how they live and think. He becomes troubled by a series of unusual deaths—elderly people have literally starved to death even though they have a considerable amount of money stashed away in a bank. He is further perplexed when a bank book belonging to the most recent victim reflects deposits made years earlier, but which are written in relatively new ink. When another victim shows up, not quite dead, Mark gets a clue, a reference to an advertisement for jobs for the elderly. Disguised, he answers a similar ad, is intrigued by the way the operation is run, and then is apprehended at gunpoint when he attempts to spy on the woman in charge.

She uses a time machine to send him back to 1931 with a stack of envelopes, each with its own instructions. Weldon then spends the next few hours opening bank accounts, buying stocks, and making bets, after each of which he is involuntarily moved to another place and time for the next process in the series. It seems to him that the woman back in the present is using a time machine to change the past for her own financial benefit, but she insists that she gathers only enough money to continue her work, which consists of saving historic art treasures, and other good deeds. Although skeptical, he agrees to help in a more ambitious project, retrieving the secret of a new power source from the future.

Weldon is singularly unsuccessful in a future that looks superficially familiar but whose customs he does not understand. He has no valid currency, and only the vaguest notion of how to accomplish his mission. After various escapades, he discovers that almost everyone in the city knows who he is and why he is there, and that they are all prepared to help rather than hinder him. They tell him the truth about his supposed benefactor—that she is a ruthless woman who neglected to tell him that ev-

erything he eats while displaced in time disappears from his body when he returns, which explains the rash of starvation deaths. "The Old Die Rich" is a clever story of time travel mixed with a scientific mystery, although the mechanics of the solution are somewhat implausible.

Oliver, Chad
(1928–1993)

Chad Oliver's background in anthropology is reflected in much of his small but respected body of science fiction, which began with a short story sale in 1950 and continued with steadily diminishing volume until 1991. His first novel, *Mists of Dawn* (1952), an instructive time travel story during which the protagonist observes the conflict between Neanderthal and Cro-Magnon populations, was aimed at young adults. *Shadows of the Sun* (1954), his first adult novel, follows the activities of an anthropologist studying a small town in the American Southwest who discovers that the entire population consists of aliens secretly visiting and studying Earth.

In *The Winds of Time* (1957) a fisherman in a remote region of North America stumbles across and is taken prisoner by humanoid aliens who have been marooned on Earth since prehistoric times, preserved in suspended animation until the present. They have awakened too soon to be rescued and eventually decide to return to their comatose state, this time with the protagonist as an involuntary companion. *Unearthly Neighbors* (1960, revised edition in 1984) is Oliver's most successful novel, the story of an anthropologist sent to a distant world whose intelligent inhabitants employ no artifacts in their culture and who are apparently violently opposed to any contact with human beings.

Oliver wrote considerably less fiction after 1960, but his next novel, *The Shores of Another Sea* (1971), repeated his recurring theme of conflict between cultures. This time it takes the form of a troop of baboons who are being influenced remotely and subliminally by an alien civilization. *Giants in the Dust* (1976), his last science fiction novel, suggests that the only way to free ourselves from the conditioning of our predatory nature is to found a new colony with individuals whose minds have been purged of all knowledge of their past.

Oliver's short fiction is in general superior to his novels, and employs most of the same themes—first contact with aliens, the difficulties of understanding a radically different culture, the inability of humans to escape their biological past. The best of these are "Rite of Passage," "Scientific Method," "Didn't He Ramble?" and "Controlled Experiment." Most of Oliver's short stories have recently been collected in two large volumes, *A Star Above It* (2003) and *Far From This Earth* (2003).

On the Beach
Nevil Shute
(1957)

Although the Australian author Nevil Shute was a mainstream writer throughout his career, he dabbled in science fiction from time to time. His books with an SF element include *Ordeal* (1939), a future war novel, *An Old Captivity* (1940), a lost race novel, and *In the Wet* (1953), a mild dystopia. The best of his science fiction was *On the Beach,* the novel for which he would be best remembered outside the field as well as within it. A substantial number of mainstream writers had written of the dangers of nuclear war, usually describing the horrors experienced by those directly affected by the bombing, or forced to battle other survivors for dwindling resources in a ruined landscape made even more dangerous by lingering radiation. Most of these novels were designed to frighten readers by means of explicit descriptions of terrible hardships, death, and mutilation.

Shute took a quieter approach, and by doing so wrote what is still the most emotionally chilling depiction of the end of the world. The Northern Hemisphere is already dead. Those who were not killed outright have been struck down by radiation, and the few radio signals received in Australia apparently were generated by automatic machinery, the lingering ghosts of a dead civilization. Australia has been spared the worst of it—but it is a suspended sentence. The clouds of radiation are spreading inexorably, and within months all human

life on Earth will have ended. Shute uses this somber setting to describe the varying reactions of the temporary survivors.

Some attempt to pretend that life will continue as usual. Others escape into alcoholism or indulge themselves in dangerous activities, since an early death will cost them only a small portion of the life remaining, and its form might be less unpleasant than radiation sickness. Where a genre writer might have described desperate efforts to build underground shelters or develop some other method of surviving, Shute's characters are resigned to their fate. Some even openly embrace death, as is the case with a ship full of American sailors who know that all of their families and friends have already perished. It is a profoundly sad novel and a powerful emotional statement. The 1959 film version did an excellent job of capturing the mood as well as the detail of the novel.

"The Ones That Walk Away from Omelas"
Ursula K. Le Guin
(1973)

Because Ursula K. LE GUIN is noted for both her fantasy and her science fiction, it is not surprising that some of her stories seem to straddle the two categories, denying easy classification. That is the case with this allegorical short story, based on the concept of the scapegoat as described by Fyodor Dostoyevsky and William James. The scapegoat is the person or idea society mistreats in return for some real or imagined advantage. It is usually a minority race or an unpopular opinion. In the fictional world of this story, the scapegoat is a single, miserable child.

Omelas is a city that is only vaguely described. Le Guin engages in a dialogue with her readers in which she suggests possibilities, but she urges the reader to develop a subjective concept of the community—not a utopia exactly, but one in which things generally go well and in which people are almost always content if not happy. She suggests that none of the uglier aspects of modern civilization are present—no military, no traffic jams—but that technology is advanced enough to relieve the citizens of the need for unpleasant labor. There is only one character in the story, the scapegoat—a child confined to a single room and horribly mistreated, the only unhappy individual in the entire city.

Le Guin could have chosen to explain this in magical terms—a curse, a marvelous spellcasting, or used some other device to make the link between cause and effect. She chose not to, however, leaving it once again to the reader to decide whether that link actually exists or whether it is simply that, because the majority of citizens of Omelas believe it to be so, they have convinced themselves that this is the truth. Many of the Omelans have visited the child, although none have spoken up on his behalf. A few are sufficiently repulsed to reject the system and leave, and these are the ones who walk away from Omelas. The implication is that the vast majority of people are perfectly willing to overlook an injustice if it contributes to their own personal comfort.

"Or All the Seas with Oysters"
Avram Davidson
(1957)

In this amusing Hugo Award–winning short story, Avram DAVIDSON explains some of the great mysteries of life—why you cannot find a safety pin when you really need one and where all those clothes hangers come from that fill everyone's closet. The story is told from the point of view of two partners in a bicycle shop, Ferd and Oscar. Ferd is the thoughtful, bookish type, while Oscar flirts with the female customers and enjoys coarser pleasures. The revelation comes when Ferd destroys a bicycle in a fit of rage aimed at his partner, and then returns to find that it has regenerated itself.

Ferd connects this inexplicable event with others. Although he searched thoroughly and unsuccessfully for a safety pin a few days earlier, he subsequently finds a drawer almost full of them. A few days after that, the safety pins are gone, but the closet is full of clothes hangers. Ferd reads a lot of natural history, and he concludes that what he is observing is protective mimicry, that a previously unknown form of life exists that goes through its pupal stage as safety pins, a larval stage as clothes hangers, and then matures into bicycles. Not real bicycles, of course, but creatures with the ability to perfectly imitate them. Oscar is skeptical, and suggests that if that were the case, the world would be choked with bicycles. Ferd responds with another comparison to nature, and makes the assumption that there is a high attrition rate and that only a very small number of coat hangers live long enough to reach maturity. Presumably there is some form of predator at work, possibly a false vacuum cleaner, but neither Ferd nor the reader ever find out the truth. Ferd is subsequently found dead, hanging in a closet with a clothes hanger wrapped around his throat. Oscar continues the business, selling what appears to be an endless source of bicycles, and jokingly—perhaps—tells a customer that he has put a prize bike "out to stud." The story is one of the best examples of the humor of the absurd, and remains Davidson's single most famous tale.

P

"Paingod"
Harlan Ellison
(1964)

Although Harlan ELLISON's early fiction had been primarily straightforward adventure, he became increasingly concerned with contemporary issues and social injustice during the 1960s. This particular story, the first of his work to display the powerful emotional content that would be typical of most of his fiction from this point forward, was a reaction to the battles between civil rights movements and entrenched bigotry that were then convulsing the United States. It also addresses the theological question of why a benevolent God would allow evil to exist in the world.

Trente is the Paingod, newly appointed by a race of superior creatures who are effectively deities dominating the universe. His job is to dispense pain to individuals and entire species around the galaxy, a task he undertakes with neither pleasure nor discomfort at first, but which begins to trouble him with the passage of time. Disturbed by emotions that he cannot comprehend, Trente finally decides to investigate the consequences of his actions by possessing the body of a recently deceased vagrant on Earth. In that form he meets Colin Marshack, a talented sculptor who recently lost his creative ability because of Trente's intervention, but who remains basically kind-hearted even in the face of adversity. Their conversation begins Trente's enlightenment, after which he moves into Marshack's body

briefly, restores his talent, and then returns to his proper form.

Readers might have expected Trente to reform, but in fact he redoubles his efforts to inflict pain—not because he enjoys the misery of his victims, but because he has learned a valuable lesson: Without pain, there can be no pleasure. Without evil as a contrast, goodness is bland and without purpose. The author is telling us to take consolation from the fact that the experience of grief and pain is necessary in order to allow us to take pleasure in one another and in our own achievements. Trente's predecessors all failed to understand that principle and all eventually resigned their posts, but the revelation has confirmed Trente in a position that he now feels he can fulfill forever.

Pangborn, Edgar
(1909–1976)

Although Edgar Pangborn had been writing fiction since 1930, he did not attempt science fiction until "ANGEL'S EGG" (1951), an implausible but extremely unconventional and moving first contact story. His first science fiction novel was *West of the Sun* (1953), in which an exploratory vessel from Earth crashes, leaving only six of its crew alive. The survivors manage to make contact with the intelligent native species and introduce new ideas into a comparatively primitive culture. Although they initially feel a degree of superiority, they eventually find much to admire among the natives, and the interplay among the humans and two separate indigenous intelligent species is the focus of a reasonably well-executed planetary adventure.

Pangborn's next novel, *A Mirror for Observers* (1954), was far more successful, and won the International Fantasy Award. The last survivors of a dying Martian race, long-lived and biologically altered so that they can pass for humans, live in secret exile on Earth. One faction wishes to help the human race, and the other to destroy it; the subsequent conflict revolves around a brilliant but troubled human boy. Pangborn continued to write occasional short stories through the 1960s, most of which are collected in *Good Neighbors and Other Strangers* (1972). "The Music Masters of Babylon," a postapocalyptic story, and "The Red Holes of Summer" are among his best work. Several of the stories Pangborn wrote during this period were linked, set in a future in which humanity is slowly emerging from the chaos of a global nuclear war. Some of these were incorporated in the novel DAVY (1964), which followed two well-received non-genre novels.

Most of Pangborn's subsequent work was related, at least distantly, to *Davy,* including two linked collections, *Still I Persist in Wondering* (1978) and *The Company of Glory* (1975), the latter of which contained some sexual implications that were mildly controversial at the time. *The Judgment of Eve* (1966), in which three people wander about in the aftermath of a nuclear war, is even more loosely connected. There were apparently several unpublished novels at the time of Pangborn's death, but none of these have ever appeared. Pangborn will be remembered only for a handful of stories; but despite a very small body of fiction, his reputation is well established.

Park, Paul
(1954–   )

Although Paul Park's first short story appeared in the early 1980s, he would remain almost completely unknown until the appearance of the first of the Starbridge novels, *Soldiers of Paradise* (1987). The setting is a planet in the distant future where a year lasts tens of thousands of days and the change

of seasons is something that no individual can comprehend. The planet is emerging from a lengthy winter and is firmly in the grip of a rigid theocracy, although there is a new cult of heretics who challenge its authority. The advent of an astronomical phenomenon—never specifically described—precipitates a cultural and religious crisis.

The story continues, though not as entertainingly, in *Sugar Rain* (1989) and *The Cult of Loving Kindness* (1991). Perturbations of the planet's atmosphere and the increasing popularity of the heretics destabilize the theocracy, eventually resulting in its downfall and its replacement by a group that in turn becomes corrupted by its own power and excesses. The subsequent chaos and violence are quite obviously patterned after the French Revolution, although Park uses a variety of evocative images and engrossing action sequences to hold our interest and provides more than a few surprises along the way. The first two novels were later published together as *The Sugar Festival* (1989).

Celestis (1995) has a much narrower focus. Humans have established control over a planet that is home to indigenous humanoids. Not unexpectedly, elements among the human residents consider themselves superior, and the situation becomes a metaphor for racial prejudice. Many of the natives undergo surgical and chemical treatment to make themselves appear more human. A human colonist falls in love with a native woman, but is subsequently shocked by the transformation when her ongoing treatment is interrupted. Although none of Park's short stories have reached the level of his novels, "Self Portrait with Melanoma" and "The Last Homosexual" are both quite effective. *If Lions Could Speak and Other Stories* (2002) collects most of his short fiction. Park has also written two religious fantasies about the life of Jesus.

"Passengers"
Robert Silverberg
(1968)

The setting for this story is a time 20 years in the future, a world much like our own except for the presence of the passengers. The passengers are discorporate intelligences who seize control of human bodies and use them to enjoy various physical pleasures denied to them in their natural state. Those possessed by a passenger will awaken after a matter of hours or days with only the haziest memories of what they did while under the alien compulsion. The passengers appear to have a mildly sadistic streak, and delight in forcing their victims to perform uncharacteristic acts. The world at large is aware of the passengers; theoretically, no one is held responsible for what a person's body does while outside their control, but there is also a barely concealed distaste and aversion that lingers afterward.

Charles Roth has just awakened from a period of possession. Feeling unclean, he decides to indulge himself with a walk outside in the fresh air, but he is dogged by the aftereffects of the passenger. He wonders whether he is actually free at all, or if a particularly clever and vindictive intelligence still resides in his body, waiting for the precise moment when reasserting control would be most devastating to its host. Free will seems illusory, and the troubled man wonders if it has always been that way, if we have ever really had the freedom to make our own decisions. While walking, he encounters the same woman with whom he had sex while under domination by the passenger, and contrary to what usually happens, he remembers her, although she does not recognize him. Their relationship slowly grows, despite her almost pathological fear of involvement, her terror of having her life spoiled by yet another period of occupation. Roth slowly overcomes her resistance, even after admitting that he remembers their earlier sexual encounter, an act that has become a powerful taboo since the advent of the passengers. At the very moment when he finally penetrates her defenses and gives her fresh hope, he is seized by another passenger and driven away.

The decidedly downbeat ending undoubtedly dismayed many readers, although the story won the Nebula Award. Roth's speculations about the degree to which we have free will, though superficial, have a strong emotional impact. Silverberg, who hitherto had been considered a competent but unexceptional adventure writer, emerged as a serious and thought-provoking short story writer

during the 1960s, and "Passengers" is among his best work from this period.

Pavane
Keith Roberts
(1968)

Properly speaking, this is not a novel, although it is generally referred to as such, but rather a collection of short stories all set in the same alternate history. As with most novels of this type, the pivot point in history involves a war. On the brink of the attack on England by the Spanish Armada, Queen Elizabeth is assassinated; thereafter certain decisions are altered, and the English lose the war. As a consequence, the country remains under Roman Catholicism, and technological progress in the world at large is severely retarded. The book consists of several separate tales, all set in rural parts of England, including one segment, "The White Boat," which is not included in all editions.

In the hands of a less talented author than Keith ROBERTS, this might have turned into a routine potboiler in which English loyalists finally rebel against their repressive rulers. There is in fact a hint of rebellion at times, but in a very restrained form. A monk witnesses the excesses of the Inquisition, and the experience leads him to question his superiors and adopt heretical beliefs. A young girl dutifully reports a group of smugglers to the authorities, and then has second thoughts and carries a warning to the criminals. Businessmen seek to improve the quality of rail traffic despite a papal bull that prohibits certain forms of technological advance. A noblewoman ignores the role society has assigned her, and takes an active part in the defense of her people.

Roberts takes great pains to make his world seem real. One segment simply portrays the life of a man whose profession is to maintain a semaphore post in the wilderness, relaying messages from one community to the next. In a world where steam power is the ultimate energy source and innovation is viewed skeptically, history seems to have become fixed in a medieval mode and powerless to move forward. Roberts's characters are almost always faced with dramatic choices that challenge what they believe, and at times an underlying pessimism gives the stories a particularly dark tone, although ultimately they suggest hope that even the worst of times will pass and that history will move forward, if only with painful slowness.

"The Pedestrian"
Ray Bradbury
(1951)

Leonard Mead is the last of a dying breed, a man who spends time most evenings walking outside, alone, imagining what is happening behind the doors and windows of the houses he passes, enjoying the feel of the natural world around him. In 2053 going for a walk in the evening is a vanishing pastime, and during the past 10 years Leonard has never once met another individual similarly occupied. Even the highways, which dominate the landscape during the day, fall silent during the evening. Everything is quiet around him.

The world has become a much safer, if less interesting place. Crime is virtually unknown, and during the past year the city police force has been reduced to one patrol car, even though there are 3 million inhabitants. One night Mead is stopped by this automatically operated car, which considers his presence anomalous and potentially criminal. As a joking aside perhaps aimed at himself, Bradbury has his protagonist identify himself as a writer, which the police vehicle, a computerized device with no human occupant, interprets as being unemployed—with some justification, since no one reads any more and Leonard has not sold anything in years. When he explains that his walk serves no purpose but is a purpose in itself, the police interpret this as a form of insanity and promptly carry him off to a treatment center.

Although the story is plainly satirical, it is also an exaggeration of trends that had already manifested themselves by the early 1950s. Television was becoming an increasingly popular form of entertainment, displacing books, and the automobile had become the first choice of people wishing to move about in the world, even when the journey consisted only of a few blocks. Bradbury is lamenting the loss of individual initiative, the move to-

ward passive rather than active participation in life and entertainment, and the increasing distance we are putting between ourselves and the natural world. His story may not be realistic in a literal sense, but it underlines realistic and troubling changes in the American lifestyle.

Pellucidar series
Edgar Rice Burroughs

The hollow earth story had been around for a while, most notably in A JOURNEY TO THE CENTER OF THE EARTH (1872) by Jules VERNE, so it came as no surprise when Edgar Rice BURROUGHS, who had already sent John Carter to Mars, looked in the opposite direction for a new series. *At the Earth's Core* (1914) introduced David Innes, an explorer from the surface world who pilots an improbable digging machine that penetrates the Earth until it arrives in Pellucidar, which lies on the inner side of a hollow earth and is bathed in constant daylight from a central sun. Pellucidar is a land of jungles and forests, inhabited by primitive human tribes who are preyed upon and frequently enslaved by the Mahars, oversized prehistoric reptiles with telepathic and mind-controlling powers. Innes falls in love with a beautiful princess, outwits the villains and eventually escapes. He returns in *Pellucidar* (1915), this time armed with surface world weapons that he hopes to use to end the rule of the Mahars forever. After various battles he succeeds, and becomes the ruler of an inner-world kingdom. The two novels were combined for the less than satisfactory motion picture *At the Earth's Core* (1976).

Tanar of Pellucidar (1929) switched the focus to a new hero. A band of pirates raids the lands ruled by Innes and carries off one of his warriors, Tanar, who has a series of repetitive adventures among the unknown tribes and savage beasts of the far reaches of Pellucidar. *Back to the Stone Age* (1939) was in some ways a reprise of the first novel, introducing a new hero from the surface but repeating the same pattern of capture and escape. *Land of Terror* (1944) switched back to Innes, who sets out to explore the lands beyond those he knows, but without recreating the exuberance of the earlier books. *Savage Pellucidar* (1963) was a posthumous collection of shorter adventures set in the inner world.

Burroughs linked two series with *Tarzan at the Earth's Core* (1929), one of the better Tarzan adventures. Innes is in serious trouble, and it takes all of the apeman's wits and strength to rescue him. John Eric Holmes added another adventure to the series with *Mahars of Pellucidar* (1976), but without bringing anything new to the concept. Although in the long run the series did not measure up to Burroughs's more popular work, the first three volumes are among his best books.

Pern series
Anne McCaffrey

When the first Pern stories, "Weyr Search" and "Dragonrider," appeared in 1967, it was unlikely that anyone could have anticipated that they would be the beginning of a series that would dominate Anne MCCAFFREY's career from that point forward. They were combined in book form as *Dragonflight* (1968), the story of human colonists on a distant world who have lost contact with the rest of humanity and who have allied themselves with a local form of life, analogous to dragons, to whom they bond telepathically and emotionally. The dragonriders are instrumental in protecting the planet from periodic rains of a substance from space, known as thread, which carries dangerous parasites. Because of the tone of the stories and the presence of dragons, the series was popular with fantasy fans as well as science fiction readers, a trend that has become even more pronounced in the years since.

Dragonquest (1971) described another incident of threadfall, this one coming at an awkward time because of internal conflict among the humans. It seemed at first that McCaffrey felt she had exhausted the possibilities of her fictional world, because she did not return to it for five years. *Dragonsong* (1976), *Dragonsinger* (1977), and *Dragondrums* (1979), which appeared to be directed toward a slightly younger audience, made up a subsidiary series within the larger context of Pern. These novels concentrate on the contributions of the wandering harpers, essentially minstrels, who eventually wield tremendous moral influence on Pern. McCaffrey fleshes in an intricate cultural background, seen through the eyes of a young woman who rebels against the future chosen for her by her father, from inside a training academy for harpers, and finally through the actions of diverse communities forced to unite to deal with another threadfall.

McCaffrey introduced a new menace to the ecology of the planet in *The White Dragon* (1978), a much longer and more ambitious novel than its predecessors, then jumped back through time to show us the early days of human existence on Pern in *Moreta: Dragonlady of Pern* (1983), in which feminist issues are given more prominence. The protagonist of *Nerilka's Story* (1986) also rebels against traditional gender roles, this time in the context of a devastating plague. *Dragonsdawn* (1988) jumped back through time to describe how humans first became aware of the menace of threadfall and learned to partner with dragons. The population living within the established holdings engages in a war against those who prefer a more nomadic lifestyle in *The Renegades of Pern* (1989).

In *All the Weyrs of Pern* (1991), artifacts from the original colony ship are discovered, including a computer system that might help eliminate the threat of threadfall forever. *First Fall* (1993) collects several short stories of life on Pern; these help fill in some chronological gaps. McCaffrey went back in time again for *The Dolphins of Pern* (1994), one of the weaker volumes in the series, set during the years before the partnership with dragons, while humans were still communicating with telepathic dolphins that had been imported from Earth and set loose in the local oceans. *Dragonseye* (1997), also set early in the planet's history, is the story of a shortsighted ruler who feels no compulsion to prepare for the next threadfall. *The Masterharper of Pern* (1997) is one of the better titles, another examination of the role of the wandering minstrels in keeping the disparate communities together. Thread is defeated forever in *The Skies of Pern* (2001); but when a new threat emerges, it proves difficult to convince the conservative rulers of the weyrs to act preemptively, even in their own defense.

Once again the dragonriders must save the day, which they do in a somewhat predictable fashion.

Dragon's Kin (2003), another description of the early history of the planet and the original bonding between humans and dragons, was the first to be written in collaboration with McCaffrey's son, Todd McCaffrey. This might be an indication that the younger McCaffrey is being prepared to take over the series. Fantasy readers seem more willing to accept a series in which the same situations and events recur, although perhaps seen from different perspectives, and the fact that the Pern series has strayed so little from its original concept over the course of 17 volumes probably indicates that it resonates more with its fantasy readers than with the science fiction community. The Pern novels are science fiction, however, with all of the fantastic elements rationalized. They are also the work for which McCaffrey will certainly be most remembered.

Piper, H. Beam
(1904–1964)

Although H. Beam Piper's libertarian political philosophy is occasionally in evidence in his fiction, he rarely lectured his readers, and obviously understood that the issues involved were complex and not always easy to resolve. He started writing science fiction in the late 1940s, demonstrating his interest in parallel universe or alternate history settings, as well as providing the first stories in a very loosely organized future history set among the stars. "He Walked Around the Horses" and "Time Crime" were among his more outstanding works from this period. His short novel *Uller Uprising* (1952) was part of the very first shared-world anthology, set on a remote world whose inhabitants are rebelling against domination by Earth.

Piper's next two novels, both entertaining if rather predictable light adventure stories, were written in collaboration with John J. McGuire. *Crisis in 2140* (1957) is the more interesting of the two. Technology has made it possible for a future society to flourish even though the vast majority of the population has become illiterate and uneducated. The educated minority becomes a despised underclass, tolerated but not adequately protected by the government. In *A Planet for Texans* (1958) an ambassador must convince a planet settled by disputatious Texans that they need to surrender some of their sovereignty and becomes allies in a war against an alien race. *Four-Day Planet* (1961), by Piper alone, is a less interesting story of rebellion on a colony world.

During the early 1960s, Piper began producing first-rate titles in various series. The best of these are LITTLE FUZZY (1962), *The Other Human Race* (1964, also published as *Fuzzy Sapiens*), and the belated *Fuzzies and Other People* (1984). The series follows the discovery of a cute race of intelligent aliens on a mining planet, and recounts the legal tribulations that ensue to determine their status, their rights, and ultimately the nature of their interaction with the human race. *The Cosmic Computer* (1963, also published as *Junkyard Planet*) describes efforts to rebuild a sophisticated computer on a war-torn world in expectation that it will enable the local population to jump-start their technological base, although the protagonist has more realistic expectations. *Space Viking* (1963) is a pleasant space opera, involving interstellar piracy, that occasionally muses on the nature and responsibilities of individual freedom. Much more substantial was *Lord Kalvan of Otherwhen* (1965), assembled from a series of short stories, which follows the exploits of an officer of the Paratime Police, who investigates transgressions in parallel universes. Roland Green and John F. Carr have continued this series intermittently through the present. Piper contributed only the outline to *First Cycle* (1982), published as a collaboration with Michael KURLAND, who actually wrote the entire novel.

Piper's parallel universe stories were collected as *Paratime* (1981), and his loose future history in *Federation* (1981) and *Empire* (1981). Most of his nonseries short fiction can be found in *The Worlds of H. Beam Piper* (1983). Possibly the best of his short stories is "Omnilingual," which examines the shortcomings of a system in which academic research is affected by economic issues. His protagonists are almost always heroes in the literal sense, people who decide to break the rules in order to oppose a destructive or restrictive power, and who are always proven right by ensuing events.

Piserchia, Doris
(1928–   )

Doris Piserchia began writing in the early 1970s, producing several interesting though not outstanding short stories, followed by the surprisingly complex and sophisticated short novel, *Mister Justice* (1973), about a vigilante with a time machine. *Star Rider* (1974) was an evocative and original novel, a space adventure set in a universe so full of wonders that it sometimes verges on the magical. *A Billion Days of Earth* (1976) turned to an Earth so far in the future that humans are not the only species to have developed intelligence. The old civilization has fallen, and a chaotic situation ensues until a single charismatic leader arises who might hold the key to uniting the planet's disparate intelligences. *Earthchild* (1977) takes place in a similarly unrecognizable future Earth—this one dominated by a protoplasmic ocean—almost totally unpopulated by humans other than visitors from Mars who are descended from human stock.

Piserchia abandoned short stories entirely after 1977. In *Spaceling* (1978) a mutation allows some individuals to directly perceive gateways to other dimensions. By using these portals, the gifted few can visit other realities. The protagonist does so, and gets trapped in a decidedly unfriendly alternate world. Piserchia's next two novels, *The Spinner* (1980) and *The Fluger* (1980), are both sophisticated monster problem stories. In the former, a dimensional gateway inadvertently allows a creature from another dimension to cross into our universe, a kind of oversized spider who uses webs to capture human prey. The latter novel involves a formidable alien animal that escapes confinement and wreaks havoc in a quasi-utopian city on a distant world, and the offworld hunter hired to destroy it.

Earth in Twilight (1981) is the story of a revealed conspiracy. A visitor to an abandoned colony reportedly infested by hostile alien life discovers that the truth involves a secret experiment in genetic manipulation. Piserchia returned to a far future setting in *Doomtime* (1981). This time Earth is dominated by two intelligent trees of enormous size, in whose branches the remnants of humanity still exist. An interdimensional war threatens both

realities in *The Dimensioneers* (1982), a less satisfying story despite its likable protagonist. *The Deadly Sky* (1983) has a similar theme and setting, but fails to engage the reader. It was the author's last published work of fiction. Piserchia also wrote two novels as Curt Selby, one about vampires, and *I, Zombie* (1982), in which the recently dead are revived by scientific means for use as laborers, supposedly with no personality, although that proves not to be the case. Throughout her career, Doris Piserchia proved herself a solid, skillful writer with an unusually powerful ability to create a totally alien environment.

Platt, Charles
(1945–   )

Although Charles Platt's first short story appeared in 1964, he produced relatively little fiction during the 1960s. He gained some prominence because of his association with the British New Wave movement, and would later replace Michael MOORCOCK as editor of *New Worlds Magazine*. Platt's first novel, *Garbage World* (1967), is a somewhat heavy-handed farce set on an asteroid used as a garbage dump for the solar system, the aggregation of which leads to a new form of life. *The City Dwellers* (1970) is of considerably more interest. A sudden, dramatic decline in fertility leads to a major depopulation of the world. Platt revised the novel in 1977 as *Twilight of the City*, a much-improved and occasionally brilliant work. *Planet of the Voles* (1971) is a routine otherworld adventure story.

Platt wrote largely outside the field for the next 15 years, although science fiction elements were sometimes present in his mainstream work. He returned to science fiction with a spoof of genre themes, *Less Than Human* (1986), the comic adventures of a robot recently arrived on Earth, originally published as by Robert Clarke. This was followed by the more substantial two-book sequence consisting of *Plasm* (1987) and *Soma* (1989), both set in the universe of *Chthon* (1967) by Piers ANTHONY. A man with mutated genes becomes a playing piece for various forces who wish to use him as an interstellar assassin, but eventually he turns the tables on all parties and reshapes the future of a subject species. *Free Zone* (1989) is another spoof of genre themes. Civilization is collapsing, giant monsters are emerging from a sunken city, and the Free Zone, the last refuge of safety, is in danger.

The Silicon Man (1991) is generally considered Platt's best novel. A government agent discovers that a secretive agency is transferring human personalities into computers. Although this causes the death of the body, it confers a kind of immortality in the virtual world. Platt's most recent novel is *Protektor* (1996), in which a computer hacker sabotages the control systems for a vacation planet. As the repercussions proliferate and people begin to die, efforts are made to neutralize the virus and catch the one responsible in what becomes a modified police procedural.

The Plot Against America
Philip Roth
(2004)

Philip Roth has flirted with fantastic themes in the past, in *Our Gang* (1971) and *The Breast* (1972), but this is his first novel that could be called science fiction. The novel is an alternate history in which Charles Lindbergh, known for his anti-Semitic sentiments, successfully defeats Franklin Delano Roosevelt for the U.S. presidency, running on a campaign pledge to keep America out of the European war. Although the novel itself takes place during the early 1940s, Roth is clearly using that milieu as a way of commenting on trends he sees in contemporary society if not in specific current events.

The narrator is a young alternate version of Philip Roth himself, a boy slowly adjusting to the growing fear of persecution that spreads to the United States, where officials of the Nazi government are welcomed and even celebrated. The tension is restrained, and the author avoids the excesses that might have been used by a less subtle writer. There are no concentration camps in the United States, but there is a tension in the air and a quiet segregation of the Jewish minority that is almost as chilling. The constant threat proves just as frightening as overt action.

Lindbergh personifies a mixture of noble and debased qualities, and his isolationism and cultural myopia are understandable if not admirable. His administration fosters programs that are designed to gently, and sometimes not so gently, nudge Jews into converting to Christianity and abandoning their heritage along with their religious beliefs. Lindbergh clearly believes this to be a good thing, rather than an act of bureaucratic tyranny.

At their best, alternate history stories provide a way of looking at ourselves from an entirely different point of view. It would not have been a great leap for America to have followed a path similar to the one depicted in this novel, and by implication, Roth is telling his readers that decisions we make now and in the future will be similarly critical.

Pohl, Frederik
(1919–   )

Frederik Pohl's remarkable career in science fiction includes more than 60 years as an active writer, a period during which he acted as literary agent for many of the biggest names in the field, and a subsidiary career as editor of several different magazines, most notably *Galaxy* and *If*, as well as of the groundbreaking Star series of original anthologies. Much of Pohl's early work was written in collaboration with Cyril M. KORNBLUTH, and he subsequently wrote novels with Lester DEL REY, Thomas T. Thomas, and Jack WILLIAMSON.

Pohl began selling stories in 1940, often collaborations and almost always under a pseudonym. The best of these were collected in *The Early Pohl* (1976), but he would produce little memorable work until the 1950s. During that decade he wrote prolifically at short length, often satirically, and produced a number of acknowledged classics, including "The Midas Plague," "Everybody's Happy But Me," "The MAN WHO ATE THE WORLD," "The Day of the Boomer Dukes," and "Nightmare with Zeppelins." His first and only solo novel during the 1950s was *Slave Ship* (1957), in which human exploitation of various animals as servants and soldiers has startling results. Much more important were his collaborative novels, particularly those with Kornbluth. *The SPACE MERCHANTS* (1953), in which advertising agencies persuade people to immigrate to the inhospitable planet Venus, was a broad satire and is considered the best of their work together, but *Gladiator At-Law* (1956), *Search the Sky* (1954), and *Wolfbane* (1959) are all excellent novels, particularly the first. With Jack Williamson, Pohl wrote a young adult trilogy consisting of *Undersea Quest* (1954), *Undersea Fleet* (1956), and *Undersea City* (1958), describing a teenager's experiences in a future undersea city. Despite its age, the trilogy has been reprinted several times and has dated surprisingly well.

Drunkard's Walk (1960), a satire about immortality, demonstrated Pohl's improving confidence in his own writing skills. While he would continue to write short stories, sometimes of extraordinary quality, they would come at longer intervals as he began writing novels at a steady pace. "The Abominable Earthman," "Day Million," and "The Schematic Man" proved that he had not lost his touch. A *Plague of Pythons* (1965, revised as *Demon in the Skull* in 1984) followed promptly. Certain people have developed the power to seize mental control of the bodies of others and occupy them for periods of time. The protagonist awakens one day to discover that he has committed a series of crimes while under the control of another mind, and that he will suffer the consequences unless he can prove what really happened.

Pohl renewed his partnership with Jack Williamson in *The Reefs of Space* (1964), which was followed by sequels *Starchild* (1965) and *Rogue Star* (1969). An amnesiac is led to believe that he has committed heinous crimes and that he can work off his debt to society by helping to build the first successful ship to travel beyond Pluto's orbit. He achieves this, but only after developing doubts concerning what he has been told of his own history. A new civilization arises in that distant part of the solar system, the only place free of a repressive dictatorship, which is in turn opposed by a mysterious figure known as the Starchild. The final volume involves the creation of a star that is itself a living and intelligent being. Although the trilogy is not very tightly knit and varies in tone from one volume to the next, it provides a panoramic view

of a future human society that contains many highly imaginative elements.

Pohl and Williamson next collaborated on a two-book sequence, *The Farthest Star* (1974) and its long-delayed sequel, *Wall Around a Star* (1983). These novels involve an interesting premise—that it might be possible to make exact duplicates of individuals, which could then be sent to perform dangerous exploratory missions. Pohl and Williamson would also later collaborate on two nonseries novels, *Land's End* (1988), which describes the situation on Earth generations after a natural disaster wiped out most of the human race, and *The Singers of Time* (1991), which describes the conquest of Earth by an apparently benevolent alien race that administers the planet quite effectively. When one of the aliens' most prominent citizens disappears while visiting Earth, they request the aid of humans in finding the lost celebrity.

Man Plus (1976), which won the Nebula Award, was Pohl's next major novel. In order to more effectively colonize Mars, some human immigrants are fitted with a number of artificial enhancements designed to allow them to live outside the domed colonies. The transformations have a psychological effect as well, one the planners had not anticipated. The sequel, *Mars Plus* (1995), written with Thomas T. Thomas, moves forward some years and describes a crisis that occurs when the computerized system that operates the delicately balanced ecologies inside the domed cities begins to malfunction. *Jem* (1979) demonstrated Pohl's insights into the political process, and his impatience with its shortcomings. Overpopulation has caused the nations of Earth to consolidate into three major power structures, whose increasingly vehement rivalry spills over into interstellar space, threatening to mirror itself on a world peacefully occupied by three separate intelligent races. Pohl's most successful novel was *Gateway* (1977), winner of both the Hugo and Nebula Awards and the opening volume in the popular HEECHEE SERIES. "The Gold at Starbow's End," which won the Hugo Award, and "In the Problem Pit" were his best short stories from the 1970s. He also won a Hugo for "The Meeting," a posthumously published collaboration with Kornbluth.

Pohl's novels became more polished during the 1980s and reexamined some of his earlier themes, sometimes more seriously. *The Cool War* (1980) is still mildly satirical, but there is a bitter undertone to the portrayal of a secret international war being fought behind the scenes of a future Earth. *The Years of the City* (1984) shows us successive generations as New York evolves into a closed habitat whose citizens frequently engage in self-destructive activities. *The Merchants' War* (1984) is a sequel to *The Space Merchants;* the colonists on Venus decide to rebel against the advertising agencies that control the government, and the latter respond with a new campaign. Aliens visit the Earth in *Black Star Rising* (1985), insisting upon meeting the president of the United States even though North America has been conquered by the Chinese.

One of Pohl's most impressive works is the short novel *Outnumbering the Dead* (1990). The secret of immortality has been found. Barring accidents, everyone on Earth will live forever—except for the protagonist, who has a physical condition that precludes the treatment. His reconciliation with his fate as he grows old while all of his acquaintances remain the same is touching and convincing. *Mining the Oort* (1992) is another variation of Pohl's inveighing against the shortsighted policies of governments, in this case surrounding the provision of raw materials for Martian colonists. *The World at the End of Time* (1990), *Stopping at Slowyear* (1991), and *The Voices of Heaven* (1994) all involve problems with colonies in other star systems, and *O Pioneer!* (1998) adds a decidedly humorous touch to a similar theme. A trilogy consisting of *The Other End of Time* (1996), *The Siege of Eternity* (1997), and *The Far Shore of Time* (1999) makes up one of the strangest stories of first contact with aliens—in this case a disparate group who claim to represent two warring civilizations, both of whom seem to be lying. Pohl wrote several other novels during the 1980s and 1990s, all of them well written and covering a variety of themes.

Many collections of Pohl's short stories were published during his career; most of them contain an excellent selection of his work. The best of these are *Alternating Currents* (1956), *Turn Left at Thursday* (1961), *The Abominable Earthman* (1963),

The Man Who Ate the World (1970), *Midas World* (1983), *The Day the Martians Came* (1988), and *The Platinum Pohl* (2001). Frederik Pohl's influence in science fiction is immeasurable. As a writer and satirist, he demonstrated how the field could be used to examine current issues by exaggerating them, and he gave us a surprisingly large number of major stories and novels. As an editor, he virtually created the concept of an anthology of previously unpublished stories and edited the first such series, anticipating the Orbit anthologies by Damon KNIGHT, the Universe series by Terry Carr, and many others that have followed. He also introduced many new writers to the field and helped them to develop viable careers.

Pournelle, Jerry E.
(1933–   )

Although Jerry Pournelle's first novel was published in 1969, he did not begin selling science fiction stories until 1971, when he published the first in a sometimes loosely linked series of mostly military science fiction adventures. Humans have expanded into space and formed the CoDominium, a loose organization of worlds that periodically falls prey to shortsightedness. Problems often are resolved by small groups of people who manipulate the masses from behind the scenes. Many of the stories set against this background featured Falkenberg, a mercenary officer with extraordinary leadership abilities.

Pournelle's first novel was *A Spaceship for the King* (1973, also published as *King David's Spaceship*). A colony world that has been absorbed by a resurgent galactic empire can regain its independence only by proving that it can build a working starship. Plans to do so are hampered by agents of the empire, who prefer to keep the planet subservient. The novel is set sometime prior to the Falkenberg era. *The Mote in God's Eye* (1974), one of many novels Pournelle would write in collaboration with Larry NIVEN, is set in a far later period.

Although he had written several short stories chronicling Falkenberg's career, *West of Honor* (1976) was his first novel-length adventure. A formerly bland colony world is thrown into turmoil when it is turned into a penal colony, requiring the use of hired security. Mars similarly has become a penal colony in *Birth of Fire* (1977), but this time one of the prisoners is the hero. Rather than accept his fate, he becomes leader of a resistance movement that eventually secures the colony's independence from Earth. Although both novels are comparatively minor, *West of Honor* is a good example of early military science fiction. *Mercenary* (1977) collected the shorter adventures of Falkenberg, the majority of which are of very high quality, and *High Justice* (1977) brought together most of Pournelle's other fiction. *Exiles to Glory* (1978) followed the career of a man who voluntarily exiles himself from an Earth that is dominated by criminal gangs; subsequent adventures in this series were not particularly engaging.

From the late 1970s onward Pournelle usually seemed to do his best work when collaborating with other writers. *Janissaries* (1979) involved a group of American soldiers kidnapped by aliens and impressed into service as mercenaries among the stars. Two sequels, *Clan and Crown* (1982) and *Storms of Victory* (1987), were written in collaboration with Roland Green. The expatriates unite several groups of humans displaced from various historic periods and dumped on a distant world, successfully resist incorporation by a rival power patterned after ancient Rome, and ultimately unite the entire planet against a new alien threat. The series is exciting and contains some interesting observations about clashing political systems; but in general it is lightweight compared to Pournelle's better work.

Prince of Mercenaries (1989), another Falkenberg novel, is Pournelle's best solo book. Several colony worlds attempt to seize control of their own destinies as old rivalries on Earth finally cause a collapse of both sides and less control beyond the solar system. The next two Falkenberg novels, *Go Tell the Spartans* (1991) and *Prince of Sparta* (1993), were collaborations with S. M. STIRLING. Both are set on the colony world of Sparta, the first dealing with a devastating civil war, the second with efforts by the powers back on Earth to reassert control. *Falkenberg's Legion* (1990) is an edition that presents *The Mercenary* and *West of Honor* in a single book. Pournelle also collaborated with Stirling for

The Children's Hour (1991), set in the world of Larry Niven's Kzinti War series, in this case describing the efforts to prevent the alien Kzin from invading Earth itself.

Pournelle's fiction appeared only intermittently during the 1990s, including two young adult novels. *Higher Education* (1996), written with Charles A. SHEFFIELD, is a fairly straightforward coming-of-age story in which a troubled youth finds purpose in his life as a miner in the asteroid belt. Pournelle's solo novel *Starswarm* (1998) is far superior, and is sufficiently thoughtful to command an adult audience as well. A young boy with an unusual relationship to the resident artificial intelligence on a sparsely populated colony world uncovers a conspiracy to exploit that planet and conceal the fact that it has intelligent inhabitants.

Had Pournelle continued to write stories about Falkenberg with any regularity, it is likely that he would be the dominant figure in military science fiction. The series, particularly the long story "Silent Leges," is still the best of its type. However, Pournelle spent much of his time on nonfiction projects, particularly in the computer field. Pournelle's libertarian political sympathies are often openly expressed, but he rarely lectures, and he frequently expresses distrust of decisions made on the basis of transitory public moods. Although his pessimism sometimes mirrors that of the New Wave, he was never attracted to literary experimentation, and his stories are told with a clear, crisp, straightforward narrative style.

Powers, Tim
(1952–   )

Virtually everything Tim Powers has written since 1985 has been fantasy, and it is often forgotten that his first two novels were both science fiction. *Epitaph in Rust* (1976, revised and expanded in 1989) is set in a post-holocaust California where life has become simpler though much stranger. The protagonist is a monk in a new religious order who commits a minor infraction of the rules, initiating a chain of events that will alter his life almost beyond recognition. Because of its deceptively simple plot and light prose style, this short novel would not gain a wide audience until its reissue after Powers had already moved on to fantasy.

The Skies Discrowned (1976), which Powers revised and expanded as *Forsake the Sky* (1986), suffered a similar fate. Earth is ruled by a repressive dictatorship from which the protagonist flees to the literal underground, a subterranean city where he fashions a new life for himself and begins to forge the alliances necessary to emerge at some future date and overturn the government. The action is a bit more fierce and frenzied, displaying a taste for swashbuckling adventure that would recur in fuller form in the fantasy *On Stranger Tides* (1987). These two early novels have been combined in an omnibus edition, *Powers of Two* (2004).

Powers's most ambitious and unfortunately his last science fiction novel was *Dinner at Deviant's Palace* (1985). In a postnuclear-war California somewhat similar to that of *Epitaph,* the survivors are slowly rebuilding a new society despite some mysterious difficulties. One major concern is a fanatical religious group, whose recruits frequently disappear into a seclusion that might well be involuntary. When the protagonist decides to discover the fate of a friend who recently converted, he uncovers a terrible secret involving an alien visitor to Earth. The novel won considerable praise, as well as the Philip K. Dick Award; but although Powers was to use science fiction devices in some of his future work, such as setting *Expiration Date* (1995) in the near future, it was clear that his interest had shifted sharply to contemporary and historical fantasies, in which areas he has written exclusively ever since.

Preston, Douglas
(1956–) and
Lincoln Child
(1957–)

The history of science fiction includes a number of famous long-term partnerships between writers, Frederik POHL and Cyril M. KORNBLUTH, L. Sprague De CAMP and Fletcher Pratt, Henry KUTTNER and C. L. MOORE, and Larry NIVEN and Jerry E. POURNELLE, to name just a few. Although Douglas Preston and Lincoln Child do not come from traditional science fiction origins, their partnership has lasted almost 10 years, and it is only recently that they have each written a novel on their own.

Their first novel, *Relic* (1995), was marketed (like all of their later work) as a mainstream thriller. Although cast as a monster story, it is intelligently written, extremely suspenseful, and introduced Agent Pendergast, an unorthordox FBI investigator who would return for three sequels to date. An explorer in South America unwisely samples a native drug that supposedly has mutagenic properties. He sends a trunk filled with samples to the Museum of Natural History in New York City, after which a series of grisly murders leads to the discovery of a large creature of uncertain origin prowling the museum. In addition to the virtues of the main plot, the novel provides a wealth of fascinating information about what happens behind the scenes at a major museum. Pendergast and the other characters are all exceptionally well drawn, a virtue squandered in the mediocre motion picture version.

Mount Dragon (1996) was even more overtly science fiction. A geneticist involved in efforts to tailor a virus that will counteract the flu concludes that the risks of creating an even more virulent form of infection outweigh the benefits. Subsequently, he discovers that his superiors are concealing another research project, one that has an even higher potential for unintended consequences. The popularity of *Relic* led to an immediate sequel, *Reliquary* (1997), a far superior work. Someone has managed to acquire some of the same mutagen that created the monster in the first volume, but this time its effects are more controlled. In fact, a secret society of genetically altered humans begins to grow in the caverns below the subway system, and Pendergast's efforts to destroy the newly formed cult come after some of the most suspenseful sequences in modern fiction.

Riptide (1998) is a fine thriller with only marginal science fiction content, as is *Thunderhead* (1999), in which a lost Anasazi city is discovered in the American Southwest. The latter title introduced Nora Kelly, who would return in *The Cabinet of Curiosities* (2002), the third Pendergast adventure. The unconventional agent decides to investigate the depredations of a serial killer despite his lack of jurisdiction and against the wishes of his superiors. He believes that the killer has uncovered an ancient secret that confers longevity on its possessor, a belief subsequently proven to be true. We learn more of Pendergast's own strange background, although only enough to whet our interests. He returned again in *Still Life with Crows* (2003), which includes a form of mental time travel but otherwise contains no fantastic elements. Douglas and Child's one remaining science fiction novel is *The Ice Limit* (2000), which concerns a clandestine effort to steal a meteorite from Chilean territory—a project complicated by an aggressive Chilean military officer and by the meteorite itself, which proves to have some decidedly unearthly qualities.

Preston and Child recently released separate novels. Preston's was a mundane thriller, but Child's *Utopia* (2002) is a fast-paced story of a band of professional criminals who seize control of a gigantic future amusement park, using advanced technology to commit the crime of the century. Although both writers may pursue solo careers, it seems likely that such a successful partnership will continue as well.

Preuss, Paul
(1942–   )

After writing several popular science articles, Paul Preuss turned to science fiction, debuting with *The Gates of Heaven* (1980), which revolves around an interesting scientific mystery. A message is received from outer space, apparently from a human source, even though no means of leaving the solar system has yet been discovered. The ensuing story is a blend of time travel and space opera, containing some interesting speculation but becoming unfocused at times. *Re-Entry* (1981) is a more conventional time travel story, although it shares some of the concepts with Preuss's first novel. The protagonist decides to travel into the past by means of an alternate world, but is pursued by two people, one of whom wants to murder him.

Broken Symmetries (1984) was a much better effort, the story of a marvelous invention whose potential as a source of great wealth generates considerable conflict. *Human Error* (1985) turns

the same situation around. This time the discovery is a miracle cure. When one of the researchers claims that it has not been sufficiently tested, he is committed to an institution to ensure his silence, and the usual melodrama follows. Preuss's next novel, *Starfire* (1988), was a substantial step forward. A disgraced astronaut finds a job working for a commercial effort in space, gets caught up in an emergency, and proves that his judgment and abilities were underestimated by his former employers.

Breaking Strain (1987) was the first in a series of novels Preuss would write, each based on a concept in earlier stories by Arthur C. CLARKE. In the first, a woman with mildly superhuman powers investigates a disaster in space. Although competently done, the novel and most of the rest in this series were only of passing interest. The recurring female character discovers an alien artifact on Venus in *Maelstrom* (1988), solves a murder on Mars in *Hide and Seek* (1989), foils religious fanatics among the moons of Jupiter in *The Medusa Encounter* (1990), survives a crash-landing in *The Diamond Moon* (1990), and travels to the stars in *The Shining Ones* (1991).

Preuss published only two novels during the 1990s, and so far none since. *Core* (1993) involves unusual subterranean activity that leads to an exploratory probe. Despite the similarity of the concept, the recent film of the same name was not based upon the novel. *Secret Passages* (1997) is another exploration of the consequences of a dramatic advance in technology within the context of an isolated research facility. Preuss acquired a reputation as a reliable author of hard science fiction with a particular talent for ably describing the tensions within a scientific community. An end to his recent inactivity would be warmly welcomed by genre readers.

Priest, Christopher
(1943–   )

The British writer Christopher Priest has experienced periodic difficulty finding a publisher in the United States, an inexplicable situation given the uniformly high quality of his work. Priest, who has frequently written mainstream fiction, sold his first short story in 1966 and has been intermittently active ever since. After a handful of competent but unexceptional short stories, he published three novels during the 1970s. The first was *Indoctrinaire* (1970), a claustrophobic novel in which a scientist experimenting with mind-altering drugs is sent to a future South American prison camp where he ingratiates himself with the guards, only to discover that they are just as much prisoners as is he. Although it hints at the themes and strengths that would be developed in later work, the novel tends to plod and was not well received.

Darkening Island (1972, also published as *Fugue for a Darkening Island*) deals with a much more convoluted web of political and social pressures. A limited nuclear war has rendered much of Africa uninhabitable and destabilized the more developed world. England is on the brink of civil war, a situation exacerbated by a flood of refugees. The complexity of a plot that constantly moves back and forth chronologically, the surprising depth of characterization, and serious thematic concerns began to hint at Priest's potential to be a major writer. This was confirmed by his third novel, *The Inverted World* (1974), essentially a hard science fiction novel set on one of the most original planets in the genre's history, one in which time is measured in terms of the distance traveled by ambulatory cities. His early short stories were collected that same year and appeared as *Real Time World.* Priest's protagonists were almost always passive or dependent personalities rather than traditional heroic figures, and he would rarely break that pattern even later in his career.

Paradoxically, just as Priest seemed poised to become an important new genre writer, his plots and themes shifted to a less conventional set that may explain his subsequent difficulty in finding a loyal audience. *The Space Machine* (1976) is in effect a retelling of the events chronicled in *The* WAR OF THE WORLDS (1898) by H. G. WELLS. The same story unfolds, although we see things through the eyes of another set of observers, including an aftermath in which two people travel to Mars in an experimental spaceship. Although superficially the novel appears to be traditional science fiction,

Wells himself was never specifically a genre writer, and his themes were closer to the mainstream. Priest assumes much the same stance.

A Dream of Wessex (1977, also published as *The Perfect Lover*) dramatically illustrated Priest's break with genre traditions. Several people agree to participate in an experiment wherein they will interactively dream of a detailed possible future, one in which England is dominated by the Soviet Union and where the only haven is in Wessex, which has become separated from the mainland after a series of earthquakes. Their combined creation is a virtual reality world whose objective existence is a matter of debate, so convincing that one of the participants refuses to return to objective reality. Priest was not concerned with the nature of the scientific speculation, and to a great extent ignores even its effects on the various characters; rather, the story is more concerned about the general interactions among the different personalities. With minimal changes the novel could have been written with no speculative content at all. The short stories collected in *An Infinite Summer* (1979) are, for the most part, in a similar vein, set in a common half-sunken alternate version of future England. The two best stories are "The Watched" and "Whores."

The Affirmation (1981) is at times almost surreal, and is linked to the stories in *An Infinite Summer.* A parallel world exists barely touching ours, accessible under ordinary circumstances only through dreams. A disturbed man develops the ability to slip from one world to the other, but the frequent contradictions in reality disorient him and make it impossible for him to distinguish illusion from reality. This is a deeply psychological novel whose lack of a rigorous scientific explanation has caused some to describe it as a fantasy. The same could be said of *The Glamour* (1984). The glamour of the title is a psi power that allows people to become virtually invisible when they wish to avoid attention. Two people with this ability attempt to make a life for themselves as a couple, but discover that their alienation from the rest of the world has created obstacles to any kind of personal attachment. There are suggestions as well that by escaping the perceptions of others they are also losing parts of themselves.

Priest's novels continue to appear, although at longer intervals than in the past. In *The Quiet Woman* (1990) the infection of much of the English countryside with radioactive debris causes tensions that eventually are used to justify the government's increasingly draconian methods of maintaining order, leading to a repressive dictatorship. Two stage magicians work out a longstanding rivalry in *The Prestige* (1995), arguably the author's best novel. They are competing to achieve the most perfect rendition of a standard trick, one in which they physically disappear from an enclosed space and reappear elsewhere. One solves the problem by concealing the existence of his twin brother, while the other actually develops a machine that can transmit him from one place to another. The growing tension between the rivals is masterfully done.

Priest's fascination with alternate and sometimes subjective realities dominates his subsequent work. *The Extremes* (1999) is an extremely complex and compelling story in which cause and effect become fluid and time becomes just another landscape through which we can move in varying directions. A woman who lost her husband to a killer discovers that a remarkably similar event happened in an English town at the very same moment, and her efforts to investigate the parallels endanger her grip on reality. *ExistenZ* (1999), although a novelization of the film released that same year, closely mirrors the author's own preoccupations, as the characters become lost in a complex virtual reality world that cannot always be distinguished from reality.

The Separation (2003) is Priest's most subtle effort, and second only to *The Prestige* in quality. The story follows the careers of two brothers during World War II, one of whom becomes a distinguished pilot flying combat missions over Europe, the other a confirmed pacifist. Both brothers are in love with the same woman, who marries the soldier but has a secret affair of sorts with the other. Or does she? As the novel progresses, we realize that the brothers and the story are slipping back and forth between two realities—one very much like our own history, the other in which Winston Churchill made a secret peace treaty with Hitler's lieutenants, who quietly remove the Führer from power and remain the dominant force on the Continent. Subtle ambiguity is rarely popular with the majority of genre readers, who prefer their plots to be straightforward, but Priest has continued to prove himself a master at sophisticated, understated storytelling, and one of the field's most original and interesting writers.

Q

"The Queen of Air and Darkness"
Poul Anderson
(1971)

In this story, the planet Roland has been settled for many years, but large portions of its interior have never been mapped let alone visited. There have been persistent rumors of sightings of unusual, nonhuman lifeforms called the Outlings, but there is no objective evidence that these exist—at least not until Barbro Cullen's young son is stolen from their camp while she is accompanying a scientific expedition in a remote region. When the local authorities decline to help, she turns to Sherrinford, the only private investigator on the planet.

Sherrinford's efforts convince him that there really are indigenous aliens hidden in the planet's forests. Most human colonists outside the major population centers believe in them, though many refuse to acknowledge that fact. Although this provides hope that the missing boy is still alive, it also means that they are opposed by an intelligence that might be actively hostile if they get too close, an intelligence apparently augmented by telepathic abilities. The detective and the boy's mother penetrate into an area avoided by human settlers, relying on modern technology to even the balance of power. There they are attacked by a variety of creatures apparently formed partly out of Earth legend, and the woman is briefly kidnapped by a figure she sees as her dead husband returned to life.

Ultimately, reason overwhelms superstition and technology overwhelms the ability to project false visions. Sherrinford rescues the woman by proving to the other human captives that they have been taken in by an illusion. The indigenous aliens of Roland, who lived concealed in underground caverns, have stolen images and primal archetypes out of the minds of the settlers and used them to construct an illusory fairyland as part of their effort to subvert human culture and eventually destroy what they interpret as an invasion. Although Sherrinford expresses hopes that the two species will learn mutual respect, we are left with a lingering doubt that the aliens can long survive contact with a technology based culture. Poul ANDERSON, who has written a fair amount of fantasy based on legends, explains that we cannot as a people escape the primitive archetypes of the past, and that it is only by understanding and acknowledging these cultural pressures that we can be free to adjust to new situations.

"The Quickening"
Michael Bishop
(1981)

Several science fiction writers have described the effects on the human race of a universal displacement almost beyond comprehension, engineered by inscrutable alien forces. Everyone who ever lived is brought back to life in the RIVERWORLD SERIES by Philip José FARMER, the nature of the physical universe changes in Robert REED's *Beyond the Veil of Stars* (1994), and the two sexes find themselves in separate worlds in *The Disappearance* (1951) by Philip WYLIE. Michael BISHOP's take was considerably different. One morning, everyone on Earth wakens to find that the population has been shuffled during the night, everyone placed down apparently at random—in the case of the protagonist, in Seville, Spain.

The result is the equivalent of the biblical Tower of Babel because of the language barriers, although small groups of people with the same language, though often little else in common, begin to cluster together. The protagonist is anxious about his family, but accepts that there is little chance of their ever being reunited. His companion for much of the story is a Welsh philosopher who speculates that the inexplicable event, despite its disastrous and often tragic aftermath, may in the long run be a good thing for the human race, because it has broken down the national barriers that caused so much tension. He resists efforts to recruit him into a group trying to return to North America, and at the last moment so also does the protagonist. The surviving population subsequently begins to spontaneously disassemble the remnants of the old physical world, abandoning technology and dismantling buildings, returning to a simpler lifestyle.

It might be construed from this that Bishop is a Luddite, advocating a return to nature; but the story is actually about the way in which we allow the physical objects in our environment to become barriers preventing us from knowing one another, and perhaps even from knowing ourselves. Bishop never explains the cause or purpose of the reshuffling, but his protagonist eventually becomes happier with a simpler life that he finds more meaningful than the administrative job he once performed.

R

Randall, Marta
(1948–)

Marta Randall's first short story appeared in 1973. She produced only a dozen or so short stories—most notably "Lapidary Nights"—before falling silent in the 1990s. During that same period she produced six novels of uniformly high quality, and her subsequent loss to the field is regrettable. Randall's first two novels appeared very close together. *A City in the North* (1976) treats the relationship between a human and an alien with surprising depth and skill, describing their discovery of a previously unknown technology in the ruins of an alien civilization, and also examines the way in which races exploit one another. *Islands* (1976, revised in 1980) was an even more impressive effort, blending superb characterization, feminist concerns, and suggestive ethical questions. A woman whose body rejects the treatment that prolongs life indefinitely leaves the Earth for several years, and when she returns discovers that her relationships with her former friends have been permanently altered, although she eventually finds a new purpose in life. The transcendental ending in which her consciousness passes beyond physical limitations detracts from what is otherwise an emotionally moving story.

Journey (1978) was the first novel of the Kennerin family, a generational saga transplanted into outer space. The colonial family plans wisely and evolves into a significant commercial and political force. Their story continues in *Dangerous Games* (1980), Randall's best novel, a complex story of interstellar intrigue and political struggles, mixing human and alien characters. The relationship between the two central characters, a human and a catlike alien, is reminiscent of *A City in the North,* but is conveyed by a much surer hand. It was with this two-book sequence that Randall began to attract serious critical attention.

Her next novel, *The Sword of Winter* (1983), was a traditional and uninspired fantasy adventure. Abandoning the type of story that had been her strongest asset, she produced her final genre novel, *Those Who Favor Fire* (1984), a well-written but routine disaster story about a devastating earthquake that threatens to trigger a nuclear accident. Occasional short stories followed until 1990, steadily improving in quality, but Randall has been inactive ever since.

Re-Birth
John Wyndham
(1955)

There has been a surprisingly large number of excellent science fiction novels dealing with the world in the generations following a nuclear war, and it might be somewhat depressing to realize that so many talented minds have considered such a future a distinct possibility. Balancing this equation, however, is the fact that such a large proportion of these are optimistic in tone. Modern civilization might indeed contain the seeds of its own destruction, but a new and possibly more viable society might rise from the ashes. John WYNDHAM's extraordinary novel, both of whose titles—it has also appeared as *The Chrysalids*—suggest that such an apocalypse might just be the beginning of a new historical cycle, brilliantly explores this possibility.

Generations have passed since the Tribulation. David Strorm lives in a neo-Puritan society that routinely destroys mutated babies in order to preserve its biological integrity. David faces a crisis when he discovers that the girl he loves has an extra toe on each foot, a situation that forces him to reconsider everything he has believed in. He subsequently discovers that mutations are more common than he had realized, that he himself might have proscribed mental powers. Efforts to cover up the differences that separate a small group of hidden mutants from their disapproving community can at best be temporary, at worst make it appear that there is a suspicious conspiracy afoot.

The novel has been criticized with some justification for running away from its own problems. Rather than deal with a confrontation between two very sharply opposed worldviews, Wyndham gathers his dissidents together and has them flee, pursued by the outraged forces of conservatism and ultimately escaping into the wilderness to start what will presumably be the true postapocalyptic culture. The author may have been suggesting that the break with the past must be so radical that no compromise is possible, that all the tenets of the old must be challenged if the new is to survive, and that intolerance necessarily drives away innovation and originality. For whatever reason, the novel concludes with a lengthy chase scene and just a hint of what might follow. Most significantly, Wyndham forces the reader to care about his characters, and their unjust treatment suggests that we should challenge the prejudices of our own society.

Reed, Robert
(1956–)

Robert Reed's first short story appeared in 1986 and he has become increasingly productive at that length. A selection appears in *The Dragons of* *Springplace* (1999), although most of his short stories remain uncollected. "Do I Know You?" "Utility Man," and "Coelacanths" are particularly good. His first novel was *The Leeshore* (1987). A civil conflict on Earth causes one faction to flee to a fascinating, water-covered colony world, where they slaughter most of the current inhabitants. Their enemies arrive and recruit the assistance of the survivors, who subsequently decide that their new allies are no better than their old opponents. Both the characters and the unusual environment are depicted with surprising skill for a first novel, although the less than complimentary portrayal of humanity may alienate some readers.

The Hormone Jungle (1988) takes place on Earth, but in a future rendered almost unrecognizable thanks to the introduction of artificial life-forms, robots, and cyborgs. The protagonist becomes emotionally attached to a female android created to pleasure normal humans, unaware that she is being pursued by her jealous and aggressive owner. Genetic engineering causes unforeseen problems in *Black Milk* (1989), the major conflict resulting from the accidental release of a form of artificial life originally intended for use on other worlds. Despite a strong opening, the novel falters halfway through, and much of the ensuing struggle takes place offstage. In *Down the Bright Way* (1991) rival organizations attempt to harness the technology and resources of various worlds.

The Remarkables (1992) is less melodramatic and marked a return to Reed's best form. The setting is a world jointly occupied by aliens and humans, one of the latter of whom decides to accompany a party of young aliens during their coming-of-age journey in the wilderness. *Beyond the Veil of Stars* (1994) is an uneven but often fascinating story in which the nature of reality is altered on Earth, allowing humans to visit the stars. The sequel, *Beyond the Gated Sky* (1997), takes a human to the stars in the company of a shape-changing alien, in a sort of racial coming-of-age story. A self-absorbed human becomes the focus of an alien plan to change reality yet again in *An Exaltation of Larks* (1995). A mixed group of aliens and nearly immortal humans travel through the universe in a ship so large that it contains a planet in *Marrow* (2000), and humans and aliens have begun to rebuild the universe to suit their needs but discover a previously unsuspected menace in *Sister Alice* (2002). Reed's novels frequently involve changes in natural laws, real or perceived, and often take place on a large scale. Although his work is generally well received and occasionally applauded, he varies his plots and themes so widely that he has not yet developed a consistent reputation.

Rendezvous with Rama
Arthur C. Clarke
(1973)

There is a small subset of science fiction stories that deal with what are commonly known as "big dumb objects," generally artifacts of alien origin such as derelict starships or artificial habitats. One of the most respected of these is this novel, which Arthur C. CLARKE produced late in his career.

Astronomers detect an object that is obviously of artificial origin moving into the solar system. Scientists and governments are both anxious to harvest alien technology from what appears to be a large but abandoned starship, but their window of opportunity is sharply limited. The intruder, dubbed Rama, will pass through the solar system and never return; it will be within range of human space travel only for a short period.

The novel evokes a deep sense of wonder about the awe and mystery of the universe as its cast of admittedly two-dimensional characters explore its enigmatic interior. In form it is actually a very old-fashioned novel, a grand tour with little actual conflict. It was nevertheless immensely popular when it appeared, winning the Hugo and Nebula Awards and reestablishing the popularity of Clarke, who had produced only a handful of short stories during the previous five years.

Clarke would add three sequels, all of them in collaboration with Gentry Lee; none were nearly as successful as the original. In *Rama II* (1989) the supposedly abandoned ship makes a second pass through the solar system. This time humans are ready and waiting, launching a major expedition that discovers, contrary to their earlier observations, that the ship has not been abandoned after all, but has a reclusive crew. Three explorers are

trapped aboard the alien vessel in *The Garden of Rama* (1991) and are carried back to the aliens' civilization, where the reader learns more about the complex society that produced the ship. Since more than one race already has a complement aboard Rama, humans add their own contingent in *Rama Revealed* (1994), but internal dissension threatens to disrupt the carefully balanced mini-ecology of that artificial habitat. The degree of Clarke's contribution to the sequels is unknown, but there are only traces of the inventiveness and imagination that made the original novel such a great success.

"Repent Harlequin, Said the Ticktockman"
Harlan Ellison
(1965)

Dystopian satires have generally taken the form of novels like NINETEEN EIGHTY-FOUR (1949) by George Orwell, BRAVE NEW WORLD (1932) by Aldous Huxley, or WE (1924) by Yevgeny Zamyatin. Most of these follow the exploits of a dissident through whose eyes we see the failures and inequities of the system. The protagonist's discontent grows until there is a crisis, after which he or she is usually overcome by the repressive authorities as a warning to us all. The endings are almost always downbeat, the tone solemn. Harlan ELLISON manages to distill all of this and more into a short story with an equivalent impact, and with considerable levity as well. The story was inspired by the author's own admitted chronic tardiness, and by a passage by Thoreau lamenting the tendency of people to allow themselves to become mechanical components of society.

The setting is a future in which time management has become the most serious consideration of a highly mechanized culture. Work schedules and appointments must be strictly adhered to because a small upset in one place affects the larger whole with a ripple effect. Individuals who are late are docked by the government for that time, which is subtracted from their allotted lifespans. The system is enforced by the Master Timekeeper, commonly referred to as the Ticktockman. Ellison reinforces the imagery by comparing a group of commuters to a chorus line because of the precise uniformity of their movements. Time has become more than a tool to aid human activity—it has become the governing rule to which human endeavors must be subordinated.

Opposed to the system is the Harlequin, a rebel who disguises himself as a clown and runs around the supermetropolis of the future playing practical jokes and disrupting schedules. Eventually the Harlequin is betrayed by a friend and falls into the clutches of the Ticktockman, who uses brainwashing and reeducation to make the miscreant a productive component of society. But unlike most dystopian stories, this one has an upbeat ending, for the Harlequin has managed to infect the Ticktockman with his disdain for precise scheduling. The story won both the Hugo and Nebula Awards.

Resnick, Mike
(1942–   )

Mike Resnick began his career writing pastiches of Edgar Rice BURROUGHS during the 1960s, including *The Goddess of Ganymede* (1967) and *Pursuit on Ganymede* (1968), while making a living producing non-genre fiction in large quantities under various pseudonyms. His early novel *Redbeard* (1969), though crude by his later standards, was an entertaining postapocalyptic adventure. Resnick largely abandoned the genre for the next 10 years before resuming his career in 1981 with *The Soul Eater*, a space opera with more than a passing resemblance to western fiction. A legendary hunter travels about the galaxy in pursuit of the dangerous title creature, a foretaste of some of Resnick's later and far more memorable work.

Birthright: The Book of Man (1982) is another unremarkable space opera, but it is interesting because its panoramic story of the evolution of human society over countless generations helped establish the common interstellar backdrop into which most of Resnick's subsequent novels would be loosely fitted. *Walpurgis III* (1982) is another novel of pursuit, this time following the exploits of an assassin assigned the job of eliminating a charismatic leader whose existence could provide the

catalyst for a devastating interstellar war. As would be the case in many of Resnick's novels of chase and confrontation, the motives of the protagonist are not always clear even to himself.

Resnick's next several novels resolved themselves into subsets of his greater universe. The Galactic Midway sequence consists of *Sideshow* (1982), *The Three-Legged Hootch Dancer* (1983), *The Wild Alien Tamer* (1983), and *The Best Rootin' Tootin' Shootin' Gunslinger in the Whole Damned Galaxy* (1983). In the opener, the best in the series, the freaks in a traveling carnival on Earth are actually aliens from other worlds masquerading as deformed humans and animals. The subsequent volumes follow the adventures of a human circus troupe that attempts to make a living traveling to alien worlds, with mixed success. Although light in tone and minor compared to Resnick's more substantial work, they showed the author's growing confidence and his ability to handle humorous as well as serious themes.

A more substantial series involved an orbiting starship turned into a high-priced bordello known as the Velvet Comet. This series was also four volumes long, consisting of *Eros Ascending* (1984), *Eros at Zenith* (1984), *Eros Descending* (1985), and *Eros at Nadir* (1986). The first title pits a saboteur against the highly competent madam in charge of the ship, a more skillfully drawn character than any who appeared in Resnick's previous novels. The subsequent volumes rarely have overlapping characters. A private investigator solves a murder committed aboard, despite an uncooperative manager; a religious fanatic predisposed against the ship's stated purpose launches a program to liberate the alien employees aboard; and finally, after the ship has been decommissioned, an effort to film a documentary about its history is interrupted by the activation of a malfunctioning artificial intelligence. The series was a noticeable step forward from Resnick's previous work, and it would not be long before the author vaulted into the uppermost ranks of science fiction.

SANTIAGO (1986) was Resnick's first major novel. It borrows heavily from the traditions of the western. A bounty hunter, a journalist, and others search the stars for a legendary killer, a gunfighter named Santiago, rumored to be the greatest criminal the human race has ever known. The interstellar government has pursued him for years, without success, and no one can even provide a particularly good description. Ultimately the searchers discover the truth: There is no Santiago any longer. The name has become a symbol for the rebellious spirit that is necessary in order to keep the authorities from feeling too confident in their ability to suppress dissent. Resnick would reprise this theme in *The Return of Santiago* (2003), with a fresh band of searchers deciding to recruit someone to take Santiago's place, only to discover that each candidate they select has a fatal flaw. The novels mix clever plotting with exciting clashes among a cast of slightly more than human characters. In the hands of a less-talented writer, these would be minor works; but Resnick has managed to give them surprising depth. *The Dark Lady* (1987) is very similar in structure. The nonhuman protagonist becomes fascinated with a human woman whose face appears in a wide variety of portraits and decides to track her down.

A frequent visitor to Africa, Resnick began to adapt themes and situations from that locale in his fiction. *Ivory* (1988) involves another search, this time for a pair of African tusks that have religious significance. *Paradise* (1989) was one of a short sequence of novels, each of which was based on the colonial history of an African nation, transplanted into space. In this case a visitor discovers that the aliens on one recently occupied world were not as happy about being contacted as reports would have the public believe. Technological progress comes too rapidly for the indigenes in *Inferno* (1993), simply providing the means by which a brutal dictatorship can be established and maintained. Another native manages to outwit the colonizing forces in *Purgatory* (1993), using offworld alliances to regain his planet's freedom.

Resnick's short fiction also began to attract attention during the 1980s, including the Hugo Award–winning "Kirinyaga," part of a series of stories set on a world colonized by Kenyans who wish to return to traditional tribal cultures, including exposure of unwanted children to the elements and regimentation of gender roles. Resnick was criticized at the time by unsophisticated readers who assumed incorrectly that the author applauded these retrogressive practices, or that he was indulging in racial stereotyping by describing the less savory customs of certain cultures. "Bully" is an extraordinary alternate history story in which Theodore Roosevelt attempts to organize central Africa into a modern nation-state. "Seven Views of Olduvai Gorge," which won both the Hugo and Nebula Awards, is a rather depressing and one-sided view of human history, but has an undeniable emotional impact. The novelette *Bwana* is also excellent.

The Penelope Bailey trilogy consists of *Soothsayer* (1991), *Oracle* (1992), and *Prophet* (1993). Bailey is a young woman with an extraordinary ability to see all possible futures and shape things to suit herself by choosing which course of events will have the consequences she desires. Although the authorities eventually realize what she is doing, the people sent to stop her invariably fail because she can always foresee what is coming and take steps to circumvent them. This apparent unsolvable problem is finally overcome in the concluding volume. Some light, nonseries space opera followed, after which the Widowmaker trilogy appeared.

The title character of *The Widowmaker* (1996) is a terminally ill bounty hunter of legendary prowess who has himself cloned so that a younger version of himself can keep up the family business while he is in suspended animation, awaiting a cure. The first clone eventually fails, and a second one is created in *The Widowmaker Reborn* (1997), this one determined not to surrender his life when his original self is revived. *The Widowmaker Unleashed* (1998) pits both the original and the copy against a host of enemies. A *Hunger in the Soul* (1998) is a notably bitter story in which a scientist, and the author, conclude that the universe would be a better place if humankind were to become extinct.

Most of Resnick's short stories tend to be slight, although those collected in *Kirinyaga* (1998) are consistently outstanding. A good representation of his work can be found in *Will the Last Person to Leave the Planet Please Shut off the Sun?* (1992), *An Alien Land* (1997), and *Hunting the Snark and Other Short Novels* (2002). *With a Little Help from My Friends* (2002) is an amusing collection of stories, all of them written in collaboration with other writers. Resnick's strongest work tends to be that in which he writes realistically about complex ethical questions; but he is more likely to be remembered for his novels of larger-than-life characters who seem to have stepped out of familiar legends.

Retief series
Keith Laumer

Jaime Retief made his debut in the short story, "Diplomat at Arms" (1960), one of Keith LAUMER's first appearances, and atypical of the rest in that it was set late in Retief's career and was not originally intended to be a continuing character. Laumer rethought the character for a series of shorts that appeared with some regularity during the 1960s, light adventures with liberal doses of sometimes very dark humor. Retief is the typical competent man working for an incompetent government, usually personified by a career diplomat named Magnan. The chief rivals of humanity are the Groaci, an alien race with a much more effective grasp of interstellar politics, and considerably fewer scruples. Retief resolves one diplomatic crisis after another, generally protecting human interests by outwitting nefarious aliens whose antics are too subtle for the diplomatic corps but are painfully obvious to the reader.

The first collection of Retief stories, *Envoy to New Worlds*, appeared in 1963. Several more would follow, but so many stories were cross-collected that readers might well be bewildered by the large number of titles. The stories themselves—unlike the novels in the series—generally follow such a standard pattern that it is sometimes difficult to distinguish among them. The most comprehensive collections are *Retief at Large* (1978), *Retief Unbound* (1979), and *Retief: Diplomat at Arms* (1982).

The novels have been slightly more inventive. The first was *Retief and the Warlords* (1968), in which the central character's efforts to negotiate with a race of lobsterlike aliens is complicated by the intervention of space pirates. The Groaci attempt to win the allegiance of a planet of gestalt creatures in *Retief's Ransom* (1971, later expanded as *Retief and the Pangalactic Pageant of Pulchritude*, 1986). The hero helps resolve a civil war on an alien world in *Retief to the Rescue* (1984), nearly loses his job amidst another crisis in *The Return of Retief* (1984), and runs into aliens who have nearly godlike powers in *Reward for Retief* (1989). *Retief and the Rascals* (1993) has the Groaci seizing control of another alien culture, until Retief single-handedly turns the tide. Most of the Retief stories follow a fairly simple formula, and they are best read in small doses. A significant weakness of the series is that very few of the alien races are more than moderately intelligent, allowing Retief to outmaneuver them with little effort. But despite the contrived nature of the plots, the series has proven to have a lasting appeal.

Reynolds, Alastair
(1966–   )

After publishing a handful of promising short stories during the late 1990s, Alastair Reynolds established himself as a major new talent on the basis of his first novel, which also proved to be the opening volume in a trilogy. *Revelation Space* (2000) described the kind of complex far future that had previously been exploited to good effect by such writers as Vernor VINGE, Dan SIMMONS, and Peter HAMILTON. Reynolds's novel, which is quite long, involves a wide variety of characters—some ordinary humans, some who have been modified genetically or otherwise. One focal point is a group of scientists on a remote planet who are seeking to discover what caused the extinction of the original intelligent inhabitants; their efforts are hindered by a civil war within the colony. Another focus is aboard a gigantic starship that is crewed by humans so augmented and altered that they are essentially another species. They are looking for a cure for their captain, who has been attacked by a parasitic disease that has left him in an altered and periodic state of consciousness as it slowly changes his physical structure.

The fictional universe of *Revelation Space* is rich in detail, in the diversity of its human and alien cultures, and is colored by inventive and original touches of futuristic technology. Reynolds continued the story with *Redemption Ark* (2002), adding another major conflict as an overlay to the varied struggles in the first. Most humans subscribe to one or another of two philosophical schools, a division that has led to a lengthy and apparently pointless interstellar war, and has further emphasized the growing dissimilarities among various branches of the human race. In this volume we learn more about an ancient race who left behind powerful sentient starships whose purpose is to destroy successor races, a concept similar to that of the BERSERKER SERIES by Fred SABERHAGEN. Both sides in the human conflict realize that they lack the technology to resist once they are discovered by the alien devices; but they also learn of the existence of a cache of superweapons, also partially self-aware and left over from ancient times. Each side launches an effort to retrieve the weapons, resulting in some uneasy and temporary alliances among the various factions. Once again Reynolds uses a large cast of characters, but this time the action is more closely focused on one particular personal rivalry, which does not reach its ultimate conclusion until the final volume.

Absolution Gap (2003) brings the main sequence to a close and narrows the focus considerably. We learn the fate of several individuals apparently lost in the previous volume, but most of the story involves a new set of characters. A starship owned by a sadistic, altered human discovers a planet that occasionally blinks in and out of existence. Members of the crew assassinate the owner and found a new religion on a bizarre and exotic iceworld where giant cathedrals are in constant motion, traveling along oversized roads, the occupants hoping for a glimpse of the unpredictable fluctuations of reality. The killing machines of the previous novel are nearer and their existence has become general knowledge, so doomsday cults are a logical development. Although Reynolds ties up the loose ends and provides a fresh store of unusual new characters and situations, the final volume seems comparatively flat. Nevertheless, the trilogy was a major event and has clearly established its author as a major emerging talent.

Chasm City (2000), although not part of the series, is set in the same universe, on a planet whose high technology suffered massive damage by means of a virus that attacks machine intelligences. The planet is the destination of a security

specialist who failed to protect his last employer and is now on a mission that he cannot at first remember, thanks to temporary amnesia brought on during the trip. A story of treachery and impersonation unfolds against the backdrop of another unique and wonderfully realized setting, enlivened by some of Reynolds's best action sequences.

Two novellas are also worth noting. "Turquoise Days" (2002) is also set in the universe of *Revelation Space*. In "Diamond Dogs" (2002) a group of humans attempt to solve the mystery of a store of alien artifacts. Stylistically, Reynolds has drawn on multiple sources, and his work appeals to fans of cyberpunk and hard science fiction as readily as it does to those who like straightforward space opera.

Reynolds, Mack
(1917–1983)

Mack Reynolds was always something of an anomaly in science fiction. He was an extremely popular writer with magazine readers, but none of his stories were ever serious contenders for the various awards given in the field. Although he worked steadily for John W. CAMPBELL Jr., his political leanings were decidedly liberal, in contrast to most of the other writers whom Campbell used regularly. Much of his speculative content involved economic issues, a subject almost entirely unknown within the genre. He was one of those rare writers like A. Bertram CHANDLER and Andre NORTON whose literary sum is greater than its parts; readers would express fondness for his work without being able to point to a single story or novel that stood out.

Reynolds began writing short stories in 1950 and was a prolific contributor to the magazines throughout that decade. His output at shorter length ebbed after 1960, when he began producing novels; but his work still appeared with some regularity, and much of his short fiction was later expanded or incorporated into his novels. He was so efficient at recycling his earlier stories that only two collections have ever appeared: *The Best of Mack Reynolds* (1976) and *Compounded Interest* (1983). His first novels were the related *Blackman's Burden* (1961) and *Border, Breed, Nor Birth* (1962), although neither appeared in book form until the

1970s. Both are set in a near-future Africa, with the emerging nations attempting to resolve their internal and external problems in order to develop viable economies. Reynolds added enough overt action to make both books quite enjoyable while providing a mildly educational lecture on the economics of nation-building. He would later extend the series with *The Best Ye Breed* (1978), in which a single charismatic figure emerges to unite northern Africa into a comparatively modern nation-state.

The Joe Mauser sequence also appeared in book form, though somewhat out of order. In *Mercenary from Tomorrow* (1968), the governments of the world have largely been supplanted by corporate boards, and each company employs its own private army and conducts military operations against its rivals. In order to limit the damage, the contending forces are limited to the use of weapons developed during the 19th century. *The Earth War* (1963), which had a much more clever title in its magazine version, *Frigid Fracas*, covers much the same ground but at greater length. *Time Gladiator* (1966) suggests that there is yet another power in the world, a mysterious group working behind the scenes to manipulate the major corporations without their knowledge. Mauser resigns from the mercenaries in *The Fracas Factor* (1978), but someone is trying to kill him anyway, apparently because he unwittingly possesses dangerous knowledge. Michael Banks would posthumously revise and expand portions of the Joe Mauser series as *Joe Mauser, Mercenary from Tomorrow* (1986) and *Sweet Dreams, Sweet Princes* (1986).

Dawnman Planet (1966) was the first novel in the United Planets series, a loose sequence of interstellar espionage adventures; *Planetary Agent X* (1965) preceded it but actually consists of two long stories. Although relatively lightweight, these books also involve fairly sophisticated economic issues. In the novel, an agent is sent to discover how a relatively new colony world could have developed advanced technology so quickly. *Amazon Planet* (1975) adds a nice twist to what seemed to be a predictable plot. This time a spy is dropped onto a world dominated by women in order to contact the male resistance movement, only to discover that all is not as it appears. A similar hidden secret shows up in *Brain World* (1978), when an

apparently peaceful colony world reveals its darker side. Others in the series are *Code Duello* (1973) and *Section G; United Planets* (1976).

The best short story Reynolds had written during his early years was "Adaptation" (1960), which he expanded into the short novel *The Rival Rigellians* (1967), a mystery set in yet another colony world that is concealing a secret from outsiders. *The Space Barbarians* (1969) examines the clash of cultures and economic systems with some amusing insights. Reynolds was already moving away from series novels at this point, and some of his most interesting work appeared during the early 1970s. The danger of creating a technological society so dependent upon computers that it cannot function properly in their absence formed the basis of *Computer World* (1970); this danger is even more cleverly demonstrated in *Computer War* (1973), in which one side in an interstellar war struggles to understand the complex computer planning of their enemies, who are defeating them, only to discover that the other side has actually abandoned computer direction of the war and is winning because of its random tactics.

Looking Backward from the Year 2000 (1973) marked a shift in Reynolds's emphasis. Although he would continue to write lightweight adventure stories in the years following, these would be interspersed with more serious novels that examined complex social and economic themes, many set in a future when the government collected taxes in the form of stock, eventually providing each citizen with an untouchable investment sufficient to keep them alive and healthy even if they performed no actual work. In this first title, clearly an homage to Edward Bellamy's utopian novel *Looking Backward* (1888), a man from our time awakens from suspended animation for a grand tour of the future. *Equality: In the Year 2000* (1977) further explores this projected semi-utopian society.

Depression or Bust (1974) is cobbled together from several short stories on economic themes, but *Commune 2000* (1974) explored similar themes in a more coherent, sustained narrative. Although the world's economy has evolved into another near utopia, an increasing number of people are moving to isolated and less perfect communes, and the protagonist is given the job of finding out why. The idea that a utopian society would actually be boring recurs in much of the author's work, particularly *The Towers of Utopia* (1975), *After Utopia* (1977), and *Trample an Empire Down* (1978).

Reynolds continued to write potboilers—*The Ability Quotient* (1975), *Satellite City* (1975), *The Day After Tomorrow* (1976), and *Rolltown* (1976)—but his serious novels became increasingly polished and sophisticated. In *Tomorrow Might Be Different* (1975), for example, the Soviet Union switches to a market economy, catching the United States by surprise and expanding into world markets so quickly that the American economy falters. Rex Bader had been introduced as a character in the minor near-future adventure *Five Way Secret Agent* (1969), but he reappeared for two far superior sequels. He boards an orbiting habitat in *Lagrange Five* (1979), just in time to be caught up in a dangerous psychological disorder peculiar to enclosed populations, then uncovers a conspiracy in *The Lagrangists* (1983). The melodramatic plots overlay an insightful look at life in a sharply delineated and closely packed social unit. *Chaos in Lagrangia* (1984) was one of the last novels Reynolds finished before his death, although several others were completed by Dean Ing, the most interesting of which is *Home Sweet Home 2010 A.D.* (1984).

Reynolds is often overlooked, almost certainly because he never produced the kind of breakout novel that would serve as the fulcrum against which he could build his reputation. He was a consistent and thoughtful writer who explored an aspect of future human culture that had been and still is largely ignored. Although some of his work, particularly that involving the rivalry between the United States and the Soviet Union, has become fatally dated, his light adventure fiction is still quite readable, and his various examinations of utopian societies deserve more serious attention.

Riders of the Purple Wage
Philip José Farmer
(1967)

The largest single entry in the landmark anthology *Dangerous Visions*, edited by Harlan ELLISON, was this novella by Philip José FARMER, which won the Hugo Award. Farmer already had acquired a mild reputation for explicit sexual themes in some of his early work, and would soon write several fantastic novels for a publisher of erotica, but this pun-filled extravaganza was still quite shocking to some readers. The story is set in a quasi-utopian future in which people are basically secure thanks to government support, known as the purple, and live a comparatively leisurely lifestyle. Art has acquired a more respected status than in our own time, although it is still influenced by commercial considerations.

Chib Winnegan is a young artist who feels distanced from other people, including his overly solicitous mother and an anxious patron who appears to be attracted as much by Chib's body as by his artwork. Nor is Chib as truly dedicated to his work as it appears. A major hoax unfolds during the course of the story, which is narrated in an unusual, nonlinear, and occasionally almost surrealistic style, which, unfortunately, Farmer rarely employed again. The action is primarily the interplay among the characters, but Farmer also examines the relationship between the artist and society, the way in which we relate to the past, the choices we face in deciding between a controlled and a randomly evolving social order, and the debilitating effects of living in a society to which we are not expected to contribute anything. Although filled with scatological and sexual references, the humor is ribald rather than smirking. The satire, which sometimes approaches absurdity, masks a serious look at choices that may face us at some point in the future. The novella was subsequently melded into the loosely associated collection of stories *The Purple Book* (1982), and is Farmer's best-known short fiction. The title is a play on Zane Grey's classic western novel *The Riders of the Purple Sage.*

Ringworld
Larry Niven
(1970)

The Known Space stories had already established Larry NIVEN as perhaps the most popular writer of hard science fiction during the late 1960s, but his reputation rose even further with publication of what would eventually be the first in a series of novels. The core concept is implied by the title. The Ringworld is a gigantic artifact, a world built in the shape of an enormous ring with its sun in the center, providing a surface area millions of times that of our comparatively tiny planet. The unknown alien builders of Ringworld populated it with a wide variety of fauna and flora drawn from all over the galaxy, providing enough space for each type to develop its own ecology, although these species also interact.

The novel follows the adventures of four explorers, two human and two alien, who discover Ringworld. One of the humans is a woman who has a unique psi power that allows her to manipulate the laws of chance, making her unnaturally lucky; this was enough of a constraint that Niven killed the character off in the first sequel. Once arrived on Ringworld, the characters set off on a perilous, imaginative, and occasionally slow-paced journey as they seek to plumb the secrets of the habitat, only some of which are eventually revealed.

Although it seems likely that Niven did not originally intend a sequel, he eventually returned with *Ringworld Engineers* (1979). The human discoverer of Ringworld has been captured by a ruthless being who plans to harvest alien technology. The new arrivals discover that the stability of Ringworld has been disturbed, and that this world will be destroyed unless they can find the control center and reestablish stability. In *Ringworld Throne* (1996), published some years after the preceding book, the physical balance has been restored; however, now the ecological one has gone awry, and one race in particular, analogous to vampires, is increasing in numbers and threatening to overrun its neighbors. The most recent title is *Ringworld's Children* (2004), in which both the physical and social structure are breaking down, and the future of the artificial habitat is once again in jeopardy. Although none of the sequels ever matched the popularity of the first in the series, they are all solid adventure stories with credible human and fascinating alien characters, and the setting has a power all its own.

Rite of Passage
Alexei Panshin
(1968)

The young adult novels of Robert A. HEINLEIN have a reputation in the science fiction community that is probably out of proportion to their actual impact, although they were unquestionably immensely popular with at least two generations of readers and still retain their readability today. In view of the fact that Alexei Panshin wrote the first book-length critique of Heinlein's work, *Heinlein in Dimension* (1968), it is not surprising that his first novel should be superficially similar. Many of Heinlein's novels were rite of passage stories, all but one with male characters as protagonists, and one—*Tunnel in the Sky* (1955)—undoubtedly provided some of the direct inspiration for Panshin.

Earth has been destroyed, leaving numerous human colonies scattered throughout the nearby star systems, many of them descending into barbarism, all of them suffering from chronic shortages. It also left behind various self-contained starships and artificial habitats, including the home of young Mia Havero, a teenager living in a hollowed-out planetoid that moves from one star system to another, trading with the local inhabitants. Mia's parents are fond of her, but they are both somewhat distant, and she has in large part been responsible for raising herself. A tradition of her people, however, is that each teenager must prove that he or she can survive unaided on an undeveloped planet for a period of one month, the rite of passage of the title. Her subsequent adventures are satisfyingly entertaining and reasonably plausible, but it is in the way Panshin addresses that portion of the novel that he breaks with Heinlein. Where Heinlein would have concentrated on the problems Mia faces and the mechanics by which she deals with them, Panshin is more interested in how the succession of challenges and solutions affects the character. Mia becomes a much more appealing and believable character than Heinlein's Podkayne, for example, because she does not merely act upon her environment, she also interacts with it.

The novel was acknowledged as a promising debut, but sadly Panshin wrote fiction for only a few years. He and his wife, Cory Panshin, have together authored an extremely entertaining and informative history of the early days of science fiction, *The World Beyond the Hill* (1989).

Riverworld series
Philip José Farmer

Although Philip José FARMER had decided to become a full-time writer in the early 1950s, his career was interrupted by a pair of publisher failures, during the course of which an early novel, *I Owe For the Flesh,* was lost. Farmer would continue to produce science fiction in the years that followed, but he did not return to the theme of that early novel until the 1960s, when "The Day of the Great Shout" appeared, the first of what would become known as the Riverworld series. The story and its sequel would be incorporated into the first novel of that sequence, *To Your Scattered Bodies Go* (1971), which won the Hugo Award.

The premise of Riverworld is that a race of aliens, for reasons of their own, have brought back to life every human being who ever lived, including Farmer himself, placing them randomly on an artificial world whose chief feature is a winding, endless river. Towers situated along the shore dispense food and other necessities, more than enough to keep everyone alive. Farmer uses this backdrop to introduce historical personages and juxtapose them with one another, using explorer Richard Burton, Samuel Clemens, and others as protagonists, along with a predictable set of villains. Anyone killed in this new environment is promptly revivified elsewhere on the planet. The clashes of cultures and personalities are consistently entertaining and occasionally enlightening, though Farmer's exploration of the darker side of human nature and his ambivalence about traditional religious values disturb some readers. A party of explorers eventually discovers some of the underlying mechanism of Riverworld, but they never learn the motivation of the aliens and still remain prisoners.

More novels and short stories followed, appearing in book form as *The Fabulous Riverboat* (1971), *The Dark Design* (1977), *Riverworld and Other Stories* (1979), *The Magic Labyrinth* (1980),

and *The Gods of Riverworld* (1983). Farmer also located an early version of *I Owe for the Flesh,* which appeared in a limited edition under the title *River of Eternity* (1983), and edited two anthologies of stories by other writers set on Riverworld. The setting is one of the most unusual in the field's history, and the appeal of the concept as well as Farmer's ability to tell a fascinating story are demonstrated by the continuing popularity of the series.

Robb, J. D.

Writing under the pseudonym J. D. Robb, Nora Roberts (b. 1950) has produced an interesting near-future detective series that employs several elements of science fiction, although usually in a peripheral manner. (Some of the individual titles could just as easily have had a contemporary setting.) Although they are formulaic police procedurals, a cast of eccentric and interesting characters, a succession of intriguing villains, and Roberts's strong narrative skills have made the series quite popular, even if it does remain on the fringes of modern science fiction.

The sequence started with *Naked in Death* (1995) and has continued to date through 18 titles, the most recent being *Divided in Death* (2004). The protagonist is Eve Dallas, a tough police detective in a near future in which humans travel to other worlds (although we never see any direct evidence of such travel). There are functioning robots, but they perform only minor duties and serve as background rather than as plot elements. The time is the middle of the 21st century; the political and economic state of the world is alluded to only in the sketchiest of manners. Dallas is married to an incredibly rich and talented entrepreneur with a criminal background, though he is now reformed, and some of her subordinates and coworkers provide subsidiary plots. Most of her cases involve serial killers or conspiracies. The most overtly science fictional novels are *Conspiracy in Death* (1999), in which she has to break up a band of organleggers; *Rapture in Death* (1996), in which the development of a new technology leads to a series of murders: and *Vengeance in Death* (1997), the story of a particularly clever killer who uses high-tech devices to cover his tracks. Although the series lies outside the mainstream of science fiction and is not nearly as interesting as similar but more explicit series such as the Ty Merrick stories by Denise Vitola, the Carlucci series by Richard Paul Russo, or the Elaki mysteries by Lynn Hightower, they are significant in that they blur the distinctions among romance novels, detective stories, and science fiction, and demonstrate the erosion of the borders between genres.

Roberts, Keith
(1935–2000)

Keith Roberts emerged as a prolific and talented short story writer during the 1960s, producing such innovative and varied works as "BOULTER'S CANARIES," "Everything in the Garden," and "The Inner Wheel," while also serving on the editorial staff of *Science Fantasy Magazine* (later *Impulse*). His first novel, however, was somewhat disappointing. *The Furies* (1966) reads like a very literate treatment for a bad science fiction film. Nuclear testing results in perfect conditions for an invasion of Earth by a species of giant wasp that nearly wipes out the human race. Fortunately, Roberts was also writing a series of loosely related alternate history stories that would eventually be collected as *PAVANE* (1968), his most exceptional achievement and one of the truly great alternate histories.

His next two books were similarly assembled from shorter works. *The Inner Wheel* (1970) contained three long stories set in a common future after the collapse of modern technology; and *Anita* (1970) was comprised of a fantasy series about a contemporary witch. Roberts seemed content to rework short material throughout most of the remainder of his career. *The Chalk Giants* (1974) explored a future in which superstition and high technology intermingle, and visions of an apocalyptic future are mixed with images of an archetypal young woman. *Molly Zero* (1980) is an episodic story about a woman who abandons her place among the aristocracy ruling the world to make common cause with the downtrodden masses. *Kiteworld* (1985) is set within another

primitive society, this one troubled by the loss of modern technology and torn as well by religious fanaticism.

Roberts was more generally effective at shorter lengths, producing such marvelous stories as "The Scarlet Lady," "The Inn at World's End," "Weihnachtsabend"—another fine alternate history story—and "The Grain Kings." Most of these have been collected, although several collections have never been available in the United States. The best selections are in *Machines and Men* (1973), *The Grain Kings* (1976), *The Passing of the Dragons* (1977), and *The Lordly Ones* (1986). Toward the end of his career Roberts wrote an increasing amount of fantasy, a genre in which his aversion toward technology seemed more comfortably accommodated.

Robinson, Frank M.
(1926–   )

Frank Robinson wrote a steady progression of generally high-quality stories during the 1950s, culminating in his first novel, *The Power* (1956), an effective thriller in which one of a group of individuals possesses a dangerous psi power and is willing to kill to protect his or her secret. Although the movie version was low-budget, it was surprisingly faithful and effective. Robinson was largely silent during the 1960s, publishing only a few short stories. His next novel was the first of several collaborations with Thomas N. Scortia, *The Prometheus Crisis* (1975)—a marginal story about a nuclear accident.

Robinson and Scortia wrote three more near-future thrillers. *The Nightmare Factor* (1978) involves a new plague, apparently released in the United States by foreign agents. A submarine crew almost precipitates World War III in *The Gold Crew* (1980), and *Blowout!* (1987) deals with a future underground construction project that could result in a geological disaster. *The Glass Inferno* (1974), a nonfantastic thriller about a fire in a skyscraper, was in part the inspiration for the film *The Towering Inferno* (1974). Robinson also collaborated with John Levin on *The Great Divide* (1982), a near-future political satire. Robinson's second solo science fiction novel was *The Dark Beyond the Stars* (1998), the story of an exploratory starship whose crew, after multiple generations in flight, loses faith in their mission and rebels against their immortal captain. *Waiting* (1999) is a more complex reprise of *The Power,* this time with an entire subculture of superhumans living concealed within the fabric of human society, protecting their secret by any means necessary. Robinson's most recent novel, *The Donor* (2004), is a marginal medical thriller.

The Power was acclaimed as a classic almost from its first appearance and has been reprinted several times. *A Life in the Day of . . .* (1981) is Robinson's only collection of short fiction, drawn largely from his earliest work. "The Hunting Season" and "The Oceans Are Wide" are probably his two best stories.

Robinson, Kim Stanley
(1926–   )

Although Kim Stanley Robinson published fewer than a dozen stories between 1976 and 1984, they included several exceptional works—"Black Air," "Venice Drowned," and "Stone Eggs" among them—and he was already considered a promising new writer before the publication of his first novel, *The Wild Shore* (1984). After a devastating global war, the United States has become a poor country and has lost its pride. A young man with dreams of restoring the nation's former greatness eventually learns that patriotism is not as simple a concept as he originally believed. Two loosely connected sequels followed: *The Gold Coast* (1988), which describes the slow creation of a new civilization on the ashes of the old one, repeating some of the same mistakes, and *Pacific Edge* (1990), set considerably later, with the new society trying to find the right balance between technology and social integration. The last is a reasonable approximation of a workable utopia. *Icehenge* (1984), the story of an expedition to Pluto that uncovers an inexplicable artifact, deals more traditionally with a familiar genre situation, but still manages to use that framework to reflect on serious intellectual issues such as the nature of language.

Robinson's restrained, relaxed narrative style served him well in *The Memory of Whiteness* (1985), which recounts the tour of an interplanetary orchestra, providing the reader with a panoramic view of the future of humanity. *Escape from Kathmandu* (1989) is a low-key, episodic adventure story set in the Himalayas; the short novel *A Short Sharp Shock* (1990) is an unconventional story involving a perilous trek and a series of remarkable visions. *Antarctica* (1997) is a thoughtful speculation about the potential future exploitation of that continent, colored by the rivalry among competing multinational corporations hoping to steal its wealth and a group of ecoterrorists who will stop at nothing to interfere with their plans.

The Mars trilogy, consisting of *Red Mars* (1992), *Green Mars* (1993), and *Blue Mars* (1996) in unquestionably his greatest achievement to date. The opening volume describes the escalating tension between those who want to terraform the planet Mars so that it can become a second home for the human race and those who prefer to preserve it in its original state. Tensions among the colonists grow stronger in the second installment, with many impatient because the program to transform Mars will take so long to bear fruit. In the conclusion, the planet has been rendered nearly Earthlike. A veritable flood of colonists from Earth are eager to relocate, but the existing colonists now decide that they would rather not be displaced by a new wave of colonials, almost precipitating an interplanetary war. This trilogy is without question the most realistic portrayal of the colonization of another world that the genre has yet produced.

The Years of Rice and Salt (2002) is a major work of alternate history. Robinson speculates about what might have happened to human civilization if the Black Death—the 14th-century bubonic plague—had been even worse, wiping out most of the population of Europe and allowing Islamic and Oriental culture to spread through the world. Robinson tells his story episodically over the course of several generations. He had used alternate history in some of his earlier stories, most notably "The Lucky Strike" and "Black Air." His most recent novel, *Forty Signs of Rain* (2004), deals with an ecological crisis.

Almost all of Robinson's short fiction has been collected in *The Planet on the Table* (1986), *A Sensitive Dependence on Initial Conditions* (1991), *Remaking History and Other Stories* (1991, also published as *Down and Out in the Year 2000*), and *The Martians* (1998). Among the many outstanding stories are "The Blind Geometer," "Vinland the Dream," and "Mercurial." Robinson's infrequent use of traditional melodramatic situations gives his work a more serious tone than that of most of his contemporaries, and his high literary standards have rarely faltered.

Robinson, Spider
(1948–   )

Spider Robinson will probably be best remembered for the long-running Callahan's Bar series of stories and novels, which began with *Callahan's Crosstime Saloon* (1977), a collection, and recently saw its ninth volume, *Callahan's Con* (2003), a novel. The stories involve a group of disparate and exaggerated characters who gather in Callahan's to swap stories and have adventures involving time travel, aliens, and other genre devices. They are typically humorous, make extensive use of puns and farce, and tend to repeat similar themes.

Robinson began as a prolific short story writer in the 1970s, producing several that were widely admired. "By Any Other Name" won the Hugo Award; "Stardance," written with his wife Jeanne, won both the Hugo and Nebula. Robinson seemed capable of writing genuinely funny stories and more serious fiction with equal skill, and his first novel, *Telempath* (1977), is an above-average postapocalyptic story involving discorporate alien invaders. *Mindkiller* (1982, expanded in 1996 as *Deathkiller*) contained interesting speculations about an increasingly sophisticated interface between humans and computers, while *Night of Power* (1985) considered a new form of race war in near-future America. *Time Pressure* (1987) is a somewhat above average story of time travel, but *The Free Lunch* (2001) inflates its core concept, a way station for time travelers, far beyond what the simple plot can support.

Robinson's most impressive work is a trilogy written with Jeanne Robinson consisting of *Star Dance* (1979), *Starseed* (1991), and *Starmind* (1995), a three-part story in which a badly disabled dancer agrees to play host to an alien symbiote, and in the process becomes one of the first players in a drama that will change the very nature of the human race. He continued to write non-Callahan stories as well, many of which are excellent. They include "The Law of Conservation of Pain," in which a time traveler literally wipes out the original timeline but finds fresh pain in a new one, and "Melancholy Elephants," which also won a Hugo. His many non-Callahan short stories have been collected in *Antinomy* (1980), *Melancholy Elephants* (1984), *User Friendly* (1998), *By Any Other Name* (2001), and *God Is an Iron and Other Stories* (2002).

Rogue Dragon
Avram Davidson
(1965)

One of the most distinctive characteristics of the work of Avram DAVIDSON is the complexity of his writing. His imagined worlds are so well realized that the reader often senses that there is considerably more detail waiting to be revealed that the author never got around to including. That is more true than usual in this short novel, set in a very distant future in which Earth has been largely transformed into a tourist attraction, an enormous hunting preserve where the rich and famous can come and safely track down and kill one of the giant alien dragons that have been imported for their pleasure.

Hunting stories are not uncommon in science fiction. The episodic adventures in *Interplanetary Hunter* (1956) by Arthur K. Barnes make up an acknowledged minor classic; other examples include *Hunting Party* (1993) by Elizabeth MOON, *Eye of Cat* (1982) by Roger Zelazny, and "The World That Couldn't Be" (1958) by Clifford D. SIMAK. Davidson took as his pattern the fox hunt, highly formalized and precisely choreographed. Unfortunately for the latest group of visitors, someone has changed the rules. The dragons theoretically stood a chance in the past, but things were always carefully stage managed to prevent anyone from being in serious danger. Now the danger is real, and deadly.

Some authors have hinted that this sort of pageantry is an indication of a corrupt social class, but Davidson goes further. His protagonist, who eventually becomes an ally of those who wish to sabotage the institution and restore Earth's dignity, concludes that the hunt is itself a corrupting force, that it has become an integral part of a system that degrades those who participate. At the same time, an alien race has used the hunt as a means to gain a foothold on the planet, and their story was subsequently worked out in a slightly less successful sequel, *The Kar-Chee Reign* (1966). Although Davidson was generally far more notable as a short story writer than as a novelist, novellas like this one helped gain him an enviable reputation as a stylist and as an entertainer.

Rogue Moon
Algis Budrys
(1960)

Traditionally, the conflict in science fiction novels is physical in nature, either between humans and aliens, between heroes and villains, or between characters and their environment. Simple clashes of personality between two otherwise admirable or at least tolerable individuals were generally too petty a subject, better left to non-genre writers. One of the earliest exceptions to this rule was *Rogue Moon* by Algis BUDRYS, an innovative scientific mystery used as the framework upon which the author examines the interplay of two powerful personalities.

Explorers have reached the Moon, and there they stumble across an alien artifact, an enormous machine of some sort, or perhaps an intelligence test, a puzzle with disastrous consequences for those who fail. The wrong gesture or poor timing results in horrible death for the trespasser, and there are no second chances. Even though there is no clear explanation for the object's existence, or what might be accomplished by solving its mystery, humans are an inquisitive lot and are determined

to see it through. They are aided by the existence of a matter duplicator, by means of which copies of Al Barker, who has suicidal tendencies anyway, can explore the artifact, dying time and again, slowly learning the rules of survival in each of its subcomponents.

Although the scenes on the Moon are tantalizing, most of the real action takes place on Earth, where the original Al Barker interacts with Edward Hawks, the scientific expert whose genius has made the exploratory program possible. Their relationship is complicated by predictable office politics within the project, petty rivalries, very different views of the world, and sexual tension generated by a woman who is suffering a separate torment of her own. The story crackles with human emotions, tense scenes, and sparkling dialogue. Although Budrys has produced novels sporadically over the years, he never again achieved the powerful emotional content of *Rogue Moon*.

"A Rose for Ecclesiastes"
Roger Zelazny
(1963)

For many years science fiction writers enjoyed a certain freedom to write about the universe using storytelling shortcuts that are currently much more difficult to justify. Advances in biochemistry and genetics have shown us that it is extremely unlikely that humans would be able to live on alien worlds, even with compatible atmospheres, because the biochemistry of the local plants and animals would almost certainly not provide us with viable sources of food. Contrary to what several television programs have promised, humans cannot interbreed with aliens, no matter how visually similar they might be. This inconvenient set of facts had already emerged during the 1960s, but many writers chose to ignore the implications because it would prevent them from writing the stories they wished to tell.

A case in point is this early story from one of the most exciting writers to emerge during that period. The story is set on a Mars that actually did conform to contemporary knowledge—a barren, waterless place that could not sustain life. Zelazny tells us that the ancient inhabitants, a race almost indistinguishable from humans except that they have an extraordinarily long lifespan, were almost wiped out by the change of climate. What remains of their civilization dwells in a single underground city, only the outermost portion of which has been visited by explorers from Earth. Gallinger is humanity's foremost poet, recently brought to Mars to help understand their culture. Although Gallinger—an egotist who survived a troubled childhood—is unpopular with most of the humans on Mars, he gets along surprisingly well with the Martians, learning their ancient language, translating their religious texts, and even becoming romantically involved with one of their women.

Eventually Gallinger learns that the Martians are on the verge of extinction because of a plague that rendered the entire male population infertile. Their religion has resigned them to oblivion, and they are unwilling to change their minds even when Gallinger's Martian lover becomes pregnant. It is only when he spends a marathon session reading *Ecclesiastes* to them that they acknowledge him as a prophet and agree to consider accepting human help, in the process shattering Gallinger's confidence by revealing that his sexual liaison was arranged and that his lover has no further interest in seeing him. Though technically implausible, the story is still a powerful emotional experience, and Gallinger's character is skillfully developed and changed by his experiences.

Rucker, Rudy
(1946–)

Rudy Rucker writes a unique brand of science fiction that he had difficulty selling for many years, with only one professional short story appearing before his first novel, *White Light* (1980), a decidedly wacky tale about experimentation with other realities. Rucker's fiction is often funny and almost always involves abstract concepts at least partly resulting from his background in mathematics, and it was not at all surprising that he recently produced *Spaceland* (2002), an exploration of the fourth dimension that nods more than slightly to the classic *FLATLAND* (1884) by Edwin A. Abbott.

Master of Space and Time (1984) pokes fun at genre conventions as the protagonist inadvertently turns an imaginary figure into reality. *The Secret of Life* (1985) and *The Sex Sphere* (1983) both have undercurrents of sexual tension as they unleash stories of aliens among us and visitors from other dimensions in Rucker's usual unorthodox style. *Spacetime Donuts* (1981) suggests that in the future the ability to be insignificant might prove to be quite valuable. *The Hollow Earth* (1990) is another spoof, but a more engaging one, this time following Edgar Allan Poe as he travels to an underground world.

Rucker has also written a series of books about robots, consisting of *Software* (1982), *Wetware* (1988), *Freeware* (1997), and *Realware* (2000). The creator of a race of robots who rebel against humans is made immortal when they upload him into a databank. From their independent colony on the Moon, the robots turn the tables by creating organic machines and programming them to act like humans and infiltrate society back on Earth. The ensuing confusion leads to turmoil on Earth, complicated even further by the arrival of aliens in the fourth volume. One of Rucker's best novels is *The Hacker and the Ants* (1994), in which a computer programmer working on a project whose purpose is to develop superintelligent robots becomes a fugitive after a plague of virtual life spreads through the internet and the authorities suspect him of sabotage. In his most recent novel, *Frek and the Elixir* (2004), an outcast boy and a talking dog have various adventures in the very distant future. Rucker's unusual short fiction has been collected in *The 57th Franz Kafka* (1983), *Transreal* (1991), and *Gnarl!* (2000). Rucker has a unique style that defies imitation or easy description, but one can always tell that there is a powerful intellect lurking behind the deceptively straightforward prose.

"Rule Golden"
Damon Knight
(1954)

One of the richest sources of new story ideas is the reversal, a story in which a familiar plot or device is turned end over end. An author could tell an alien invasion story with a human as the monster, as in William TENN's "The FLAT-EYED MONSTER" or have the hero choose his dog over his girl as in "A BOY AND HIS DOG" by Harlan ELLISON. Damon Knight mined similar territory with this novella, in which the Golden Rule is suddenly transformed so that it now reads "be done to as you have done."

The protagonist, Dahl, is a journalist whose criticism of a secret government installation has led to his virtual incarceration. Hoping to gain his cooperation, officials allow him to learn the truth: An apparently lone alien visitor has arrived on Earth, claiming to be a representative of a galactic civilization that wants to open contact with humans. Unfortunately, there is no way to confirm the alien's story; some authorities fear that he is a scout for an alien invasion, while still others are interested only in gaining military superiority by understanding advanced technology. Dahl eventually helps the alien escape custody against a backdrop in which unusual events are sweeping across parts of the United States. Murderers are dying as they commit their crimes, slaughterhouse workers complain of terrible headaches, and prison guards begin to suffer from claustrophobia. Eventually the alien explains that he is releasing into the atmosphere a catalyst that awakens an empathic sense in all living beings, after which none will be able to knowingly inflict pain on another. This is a necessary prelude to joining the greater galactic civilization. Although Dahl continues to have misgivings, the alien's story is eventually confirmed, although only after virtually all government and commercial institutions have collapsed and all predatory animals have become extinct.

Knight's utopia is imposed rather than achieved, a pessimism that is reflected in much of his other work, most notably the CV trilogy—CV (1985), *The Observers* (1988), and *A Reasonable World* (1991)—in which the same goal is achieved by means of an alien virus. Like most utopian works, the story fails to address many of the obvious problems of building an organized, technological society with no formal structure, but some of Knight's observations are cogent and the speculations are thought-provoking.

Russ, Joanna
(1937–)

Although Joanna Russ wrote more than a dozen stories between 1959 and 1967, she made little impact in science fiction because most of her work tended to be fantasy. Her first novel, *Picnic on Paradise* (1968), featured Alyx, a recurring female character who serves as a time agent who visits various eras, performing the sort of duties that were largely conferred on male characters in science fiction. A war is being fought across the timelines, but this is more setting than plot. The use of an assertive, competent female character was not previously unknown in the field, but it had always been anomalous before. Feminist influences and the influx of female readers and writers set the stage for at least a partial demolition of old preconceptions. The novel would later reappear accompanied by several short adventures as *Alyx* (1976, also published as *The Adventures of Alyx*). Although not the author's most successful or even most controversial book, it may in a quiet way have been her most influential, opening the doors for an influx of more assertive female protagonists.

And Chaos Died (1970) was a much more ambitious work. Like *Picnic on Paradise*, it was published as part of the short-lived but highly regarded Ace Specials line. The premise is an ambitious one: A malfunction strands a spaceman on a colony world whose inhabitants have developed various psi powers, including telepathy. In order to survive, he must accept the reordering of his own mind by the locals so that his latent psi can also be released, a painful and transforming process. To achieve this effect, Russ employed a complicated and sometimes obscure prose style that required a considerable effort of concentration on the part of the reader. Eventually the spaceman comes to embrace this new society; when he is rescued and returned to Earth he is appalled by the conditions he formerly accepted as normal.

Russ's third novel, *The Female Man* (1973), became the focus of considerable controversy. The central character is a woman who exists in four different realities, ranging from one extreme in which the oppression of women by men is more extreme than in our reality, to another on the planet

Whileaway, which has become a feminist utopia. The intermediary worlds include one in which the two genders have separated from one another almost completely. As the novel progresses, in a non-linear and sometimes confusing fashion, the disparate story lines all converge. The novel reflects considerable anger because of its relentless, pointed, and occasionally one-sided structure, but it unquestionably raised the level of awareness of feminist issues among science fiction readers and writers.

The two novels that followed were less controversial and less successful. After producing a fair number of short stories during the early 1980s, Russ confined her writing almost entirely to critical work. *We Who Are About To* (1977) depicts the crash of a spaceship on a deserted planet, and the slow decline of the mind of the last survivor, a woman increasingly troubled by hallucinations. *The Two of Them* (1979) follows the adventures of a woman somewhat similar to Alyx as she rescues a young girl trapped in a harem in a society that treats women as property.

Russ also proved to be an accomplished short story writer. "WHEN IT CHANGED" and "Souls" both won the Hugo Award. Several others are of particular merit, including "The Autobiography of My Mother," "I Had Vacantly Crumpled It into My Pocket," "Gleepsite," and "I Gave Her Sack and Sherry." Her stories have been collected in *The Zanzibar Cat* (1983), *Extra (Ordinary) People* (1984), and *The Hidden Side of the Moon* (1987). Russ is a writer whose influence on others is substantial but hard to specifically identify. Her inactivity during the past two decades is a major loss to the field.

Russell, Eric Frank
(1905–1978)

The British writer Eric Frank Russell began selling short stories in the late 1930s, and his first novel, *Sinister Barrier,* appeared in magazine form in 1939. The novel opens with a series of suicides and other apparently natural deaths, all involving prominent scientists. We eventually learn that these deaths are the results of a conspiracy by invisible alien in-vaders who are trying to retard human development and suppress knowledge of their existence. Although a good example of the influence of the nonfiction writings of Charles Fort, the novel has not aged well. Much more successful was a series of space adventures starting with "Jay Score," featuring a likable robot character who can almost pass for human. The series was later published in book form as *Men, Martians, and Machines* (1955). Russell was the first significant British writer to fit into John W. CAMPBELL Jr.'s formula for *Astounding Science Fiction,* to which he was a frequent contributor.

His second novel was *Dreadful Sanctuary* (magazine version in 1948), another novel of aliens among us. Efforts to send a rocket to Venus are repeatedly sabotaged by agents of the inhabitants of other worlds in the solar system, who have been using the Earth as a dumping ground for the mentally ill. The now totally implausible plot is initially quite entertaining, but it falls apart under multiple implausibilities once we discover what is really going on. *Sentinels of Space* (magazine version 1951) has aged slightly better. Humans have colonized Mars and Venus, and both colonies seek their independence by means of mutant agents; but unbeknownst to both parties, extrasolar aliens are manipulating events as well.

Russell's writing improved remarkably during the 1950s. His first short story collection, *Deep Space* (1954), brought together most of his better early work. His next novel was much more effectively written, although still preoccupied with secret aliens. In *Three to Conquer* (1956, also published as *Call Him Dead*), a man who believes himself to be the only telepath on Earth accidentally eavesdrops on a human body occupied by an alien intelligence from Venus. *Next of Kin* (1959, published in abridged form as *The Space Willies* in 1958) is one of Russell's two best novels. Earth is involved in an interstellar war. A solitary scout spying on enemy positions is forced to land on a hostile planet, where he eventually secures his freedom by convincing the authorities that humans all have a bodiless counterpart, a benevolent parasite who will avenge any affront to the physical half of the partnership. Although hopelessly implausible, Russell approaches the concept with tongue in cheek, and once the reader overcomes any initial skepticism about the logic the story is intensely amusing.

The second major novel is WASP (1957), which reverses the aliens-among-us theme of the early novels. Once again, Earth is involved in an interstellar war against a humanoid race. James Mowry, a human saboteur, is disguised to look like one of the enemy; he infiltrates an enemy world and single-handedly launches a campaign of sabotage and subversion designed to weaken that planet's defenses and morale. Two later novels are relatively minor. *The Great Explosion* (1962) is an episodic comedy about efforts to reopen contact with a series of lost colony worlds, and *The Mindwarpers* (1965, also published as *With a Strange Device*) is a marginal thriller involving espionage and mind control. *Entities* (2001) is an omnibus edition of Russell's five best novels.

Russell was much more successful as a short story writer than as a novelist, and won his only Hugo Award for "Allamagoosa," a clever and humorous space adventure story. His acknowledged classics in the form include "The Waitabits," "Now Inhale," "Legwork," "The Early Bird," "Metamorphosite," and "Minor Ingredient." The largest and best selection of his short fiction is the posthumous *Major Ingredients* (2000). In the latter half of his career, Russell occasionally addressed such contemporary issues as racial intolerance, free will, and the individual's duty to society—but generally in a superficial fashion that seemed to stem from his uncertainty as a writer rather than from a lack of conviction. By the 1960s, he had either lost confidence in his own abilities or fallen out of favor with his markets and he produced only a few short stories during the last decade of his life.

S

Saberhagen, Fred
(1930–   )

Fred Saberhagen began selling science fiction stories during the early 1960s, including the first of the BERSERKER SERIES, his most extensive and best-known genre creation. The berserkers are robotic starships left over from a now extinct alien race whose mission is to destroy all living things. They have become something of an icon in the field, and variations show up in the work of such other writers as Gregory BENFORD and Greg BEAR.

Saberhagen's first two novels, both quite short, were not in that series. *The Golden People* (1964) is a routine though clever planetary adventure. *The Water of Thought* (1965, expanded in 1981) was a more intriguing and ambitious effort in which the sacred water of a remote world brings visions to those who drink it. When converts carry it to other star systems and begin proselytizing, the authorities react in predictable alarm, threatening to destroy the source even though it is central to the civilization of the planet upon which it originates.

During the latter half of the 1960s Saberhagen became more involved with the Berserker stories and also began a second series, fantasies set in a postapocalyptical world in which magic has reemerged. His next science fiction novel was *Love Conquers All* (1979, revised in 1985), a dystopian satire in which sexual promiscuity is socially acceptable, but because of population pressures, reproduction is limited to those who have been approved in advance. When the protagonist decides to defy the law and bear a child, she becomes an outcast and eventually a symbol of resistance. His first collection of non-Berserker stories, *The Book of Saberhagen*, appeared in 1975. *Specimens* (1976) was his first novel with a contemporary setting, and made surprisingly effective use of what was on the surface a typical plot from a bad movie: A family moves into their new home, unaware that it is situated in close proximity to an alien probe that has been sent to collect samples of the human race for study.

Saberhagen wrote a considerable number of short stories during the 1970s, although he would turn back to novels on a nearly exclusive basis by the end of that decade. These include two about a planet where anomalies in energy sources isolated separate communities in what amounted to private universes, in which a form of immortality is possible. He followed this with a novel-length variation, *The Veils of Azlaroc* (1976). *The Mask of the Sun* (1979) is one of his most interesting novels, set in an alternate world where the Aztecs are using time travel in an effort to prevent the Spanish from conquering them in the past, thus ensuring the preservation of their empire.

By 1980 Saberhagen was alternating between the Berserker series and a supernatural sequence involving Dracula. His interest in virtual reality and artificial intelligence was reflected in a non-series thriller, *Octagon* (1981), and in *Coils* (1982), written in collaboration with Roger ZELAZNY. A *Century of Progress* (1983) is another change war novel, in this case involving time travelers from our reality trying to alter a variant world in which the Nazis won World War II and eventually dominated the world. Technically this novel is better done than *The Mask of the Sun*, but with a less interesting premise.

Pyramids (1987) was the first of a two-book sequence. In the opener, a time traveler who makes a living stealing artifacts from ancient Egypt for sale in his own time discovers that the legends of Egyptian deities were based on fact, that superhuman (though not supernatural) creatures did inhabit the world during ancient times. In the sequel, *After the Fact* (1988), the protagonist travels back to the Civil War era in an attempt to prevent the assassination of Abraham Lincoln. Both fine adventure stories were published together as *Pilgrim* (1997). *The White Bull* (1988) was another story of ancient times with a rationalized explanation for fantastic events—in this case the story of Icarus and Daedalus. Saberhagen clearly was moving in the direction of fantasy, however, and little of his subsequent work was science fiction, outside the Berserker series. A second collection of his short fiction, *Saberhagen: My Best* (1987), brought together most of his uncollected work at that length. Although the Berserker stories continue to be popular, that series has dominated the author's other work in the field and possibly discouraged him from exploring other productive material.

The Saliva Tree
Brian W. Aldiss
(1965)

This novella, written to commemorate the 100th anniversary of the birth of H. G. WELLS, won the very first Nebula Award in that category and is one of the most famous stories Brian W. ALDISS wrote. The story adopts many plot elements found in Wells's fiction; Wells himself is a minor character, a friend of the narrator who communicates his experiences, which presumably become the inspiration for several of Wells's scientific romances.

Gregory Rolles is a young man of moderate leisure in late-19th-century England, currently living in a small town where he enjoys exchanging favorable views of socialism with Grendon, a local farmer, and, later, has less theoretical conversations with the farmer's daughter. Grendon is a mildly bitter man because his land is poor and it is becoming increasingly difficult to make a living. His wife has recently become pregnant, and he will soon have another mouth to feed. Their situation changes—but only after what appears to be a meteorite crashes into the pond on his property.

Rolles is curious about the fallen object and receives Grendon's permission to investigate. He observes strange phenomena that convince him that it was actually a vehicle from another world, piloted by intelligent beings, and concludes that since any advanced civilization would necessarily be socialist, the beings must be benevolent. The creatures are invisible to the human eye, so he cannot judge their shape or size. Of course, it turns out that he is badly mistaken about their intentions. A mysterious, stinking dew covers the farm one night, and in the days that follow, all of the plants and animals in the area become remarkably fecund. Pregnant animals give birth to unusually large numbers of offspring, and every form of life grows larger than usual, sometimes strikingly so. Grendon initially is elated, but the oversized food products prove unpalatable.

Rolles begins to have second thoughts, particularly when he observes the death of some farm animals, literally drained of their substance. The dew, he concludes, was some unearthly fertilizer, and the invaders are fattening the animals—including the humans—for slaughter. He is unable to convince Grendon, even after his wife gives birth to nine babies, as it appears that the farmer's mind has also been affected. Having decided that he is in love with Grendon's daughter, and convinced of the malevolence of the aliens, Rolles undertakes desperate measures to kill them. Although he fails, he drives them off and rescues the young woman, but Grendon and his wife perish.

"The Saliva Tree" blends the style of Wells with the basic plot of "The Color out of Space" (1927) by H. P. LOVECRAFT. It contains numerous references to Wells, encompassing elements of *The* INVISIBLE MAN (1897), *The Food of the Gods* (1904), and *The* WAR OF THE WORLDS (1898). It was an appropriate tribute to the first major science fiction writer in the English language, and an excellent story in its own right.

"Sam Hall"
Poul Anderson
(1953)

The title character in this story does not actually exist, except as a character in an old drinking song. In the not too distant future, America has become a mechanized dictatorship, dominating the rest of the world, controlling its population through rigid regimentation, using drug-induced interrogations to check on individual loyalties, and establishing concentration camps and secret police to suppress dissent. A high-ranking computer programmer named Thornberg creates a false identity in the national record-keeping system, initially as a whim. His Sam Hall is a rough-and-tumble nonconformist with a low-key but active criminal record. The initial impulse for this fictitious person originates with the arrest of Thornberg's nephew, but Thornberg becomes more proactive when the boy dies in custody.

He begins to embellish Sam Hall's career and link him to current crimes—the murder of a police officer, a bank robbery believed to have been masterminded by insurgents. The authorities accept the new data as authentic and begin searching for Sam Hall, but without success, concluding that he falsified his address and other information to conceal his actual whereabouts. They declare Sam Hall a wanted criminal, and his notoriety now grows even without Thornberg's intervention. Reports of his activities proliferate throughout the country, and even though the government knows that most of them must be false, they are forced to divert resources to investigate each one. The actual rebel libertarian movement takes up Sam Hall's name as its trademark.

Eventually civil war erupts, the outcome of which is initially uncertain. The vast majority of the population is committed to neither side, and the government is less than finicky about wiping out the innocent along with the guilty. When Thornberg learns that his son is being recalled from Venus to join in the fighting, he escalates things, planting false reports that cause the members of the

dominant government clique to begin doubting one another. Thornberg himself is on the verge of being arrested as the libertarians push forward toward their ultimate victory.

Structurally, "Sam Hall" is a dystopia with a happy ending that depends on a string of unlikely events. Readers forgive Anderson the implausibilities of the plot because of the cleverness of the main premise and because of his skillful contraction into a short story of a plot that most writers would have turned into a novel. The idea that a criminal might become the public face of rebellion would be used again, most notably by Mike RESNICK in SANTIAGO (1986), and the creation of a nonexistent rebel leader within a computer was adapted by Robert A. HEINLEIN in the form of Adam Selene in *The MOON IS A HARSH MISTRESS* (1966), which shares Anderson's libertarian social philosophy.

"Sandkings"
George R. R. Martin
(1979)

Simon Kress is a rich, self-indulgent man whose hobbies include keeping unusual alien creatures as pets and displaying them to his acquaintances. He is searching for some novel form of life when he encounters a new import firm specializing in items from other worlds; he is particularly taken by the sandkings, a species of insectlike creature displayed in a terrarium. The sandkings, who are not individually intelligent but who are telepathically linked, build remarkably detailed and elaborate castles and consist of a single breeder served by worker and soldier castes. They also engage in warfare in a manner similar to that of soldier ants. Kress initially is skeptical about the creatures, but becomes fascinated when the proprietor explains that they will literally worship him if he projects a holographic image of himself into their environment.

Kress installs a large terrarium in his mansion, located in the middle of a desert, and waits for the sandkings to entertain him. Patience is not a part of his nature, however. He is cruel, vindictive, petty, and shortsighted. He is pleased when the sandkings create carvings of his face on the walls of their castles, but is puzzled by subtle differences among the images, which reflect the human ability to interpret the same materials in radically different ways, as sometimes happens in our own religious beliefs. Kress is less pleased when they fail to launch the wars he was expecting, and he eventually withholds food until the sandkings are compelled to battle one another for what remains.

Martin develops the plot in a series of logical steps. Kress sponsors regular parties and manipulates the sandkings so that they will fight wars to entertain his guests, who eventually begin to place wagers on the outcome. Even that becomes boring after a while, so other exotic animals are introduced into the environment in a series of deadly battles, all of which are won by the sandkings. During this process, the creatures frequently redesign the image of their god, making him look cruel, arbitrary, or even demented. This so enrages Kress that he personally damages one of the castles, stopping only when faced with the possibility of allowing the sandkings to escape.

Unfortunately, he is less successful with his human victims. A tormented ex-lover confronts him, and in a violent exchange he kills her—but only after she ruptures the containment of the sandkings, allowing them to escape. Kress is initially terrified, but once he has calmed down, he feeds the dead body to the sandkings, one colony of which is ensconced in his cellar. His subsequent efforts to eradicate them result in additional deaths, some by his own hand, and eventually his own destruction. The lesson of the story is an obvious one. Cruelty toward others will eventually be repaid, and excessive pride usually masks an inner weakness. The story won the Hugo and Nebula Awards, and became an episode in the new *Outer Limits* television show.

Santiago
Mike Resnick
(1986)

Most interstellar adventure stories fall into the imprecise but evocative label of space opera, similar to the category of western fiction known as horse opera. There are several points of similarity, including the emphasis on action in place of characterization, the general use of a transparent prose style, the frequency of gunfights and other forms of personal combat, and a setting in which the principal characters travel about in an uninhabited region interspersed with concentrated communities. The superficial similarities are occasionally even more obvious, as is the case in several of Mike RESNICK's novels about the frontiers of space, of which *Santiago* is the best.

Santiago is the name of a legendary outlaw and gunfighter whose exploits are so legendary and daring that the authorities that govern organized space have launched numerous military expeditions to eliminate him. Resnick depicts the government as corrupt, oppressing planetary populations—particularly at the limits of their sphere of control—in order to support a military and police function that systematically abrogates the very freedoms it claims to be protecting. In this context, Santiago is more than just a criminal—he has become a symbol of resistance, inspiring captive populations to remain restive, and tying up disproportionate enemy forces.

A group of disparate characters decides to search for Santiago, each for his or her own purpose. They make a startling discovery: There was originally a single Santiago; but as he aged, he retired—after grooming a replacement who takes his name. Each subsequent Santiago hands down this tradition, which explains his apparent longevity. Santiago has become more than just a person; he has become an idea, an icon, a symbol for the rebellious, nonconformist part of human nature.

Resnick revived the concept for *The Return of Santiago* (2003), which follows the same path initially. This time the searchers discover the same truth, but also learn that the last Santiago died without choosing a successor. They appoint themselves an unofficial committee to reestablish the line, but they discover that the task of finding a worthy replacement is not as easy as expected. Both novels are technically space operas, and the confrontations among the various gunfighters and law enforcement are very much in the western tradition. As of this writing, the first novel is being developed as a motion picture.

Sargent, Pamela
(1948–   )

Pamela Sargent began her career in the early 1970s with a string of interesting short stories, although no single title stood out enough to distinguish her among that decade's crop of promising writers. A few of these stories involved cloning, and they were incorporated into her first novel, *Cloned Lives* (1976), the episodic story of a family of cloned children and the problems they encounter growing up in our world. The whole was considerably superior to the sum of its parts, and it is surprising that the novel has not been reprinted, given the current popular fascination with the topic.

Sargent's first collection of other stories, *Starshadows* (1977), seemed to indicate that she was poised to launch a more extensive career, but her first two full-length novels were less successful. *The Sudden Star* (1979, also published as *The White Death*) was a dystopia in which an astronomical anomaly causes a crisis on Earth, leading to a repressive world dictatorship. Certain medical practices are outlawed, and the protagonist, a doctor, is engaged in illicit activities. Although well conceived and written, the story was perhaps a bit too familiar for readers who had already read *Dr. Futurity* (1960) by Philip K. DICK or *Blade Runner* (1974) by Alan E. NOURSE. *Watchstar* (1980) was received with somewhat more favor. An interesting variation of the lost colony story, it involves the provocative discovery of a derelict starship. *The Golden Space* (1982), which bears some similarity to *Cloned Lives*, is a much better novel. A woman agrees to submit to experiments in genetic engineering so that her children will be superior to ordinary humans, but she eventually learns that in doing so, she has forfeited her right to share in the shaping of their future, because the differences in outlook between human and superhuman are insurmountable.

Sargent began writing young adult fiction during the 1980s. All of her work in this genre has a degree of sophistication that attracted adult readers as well. *Earthseed* (1983) reprised Sargent's theme of children forced to choose their own destiny. In this case, a dying Earth has sent a self-aware starship out with human embryos, hoping to reestablish the race on another world. Although the artificial intelligence attempts to watch over and guide its charges, they eventually learn that they must make their own decisions and choose their own destiny. There is a similar treatment in *Alien Child* (1988). An alien finds Earth deserted and revives a human child from suspended animation in order to find out what happened to the rest of her species. Two sequels to *Watchstar* were also aimed at young adults. A teenager becomes intermediary between her people and the isolationists of Earth in *Eye of the Comet* (1984), and the common menace of a rogue comet unites feuding factions in *Homesmind* (1984).

Although there had been occasional feminist undercurrents in Sargent's previous work, they were expressed most fully in *The Shore of Women* (1986), a complex novel in which women seize control of society following a nuclear war. The writing demonstrated the author's acknowledgment of the complexity of the issues involved, but the solutions to problems prove to be convoluted and not always fair to all concerned. *Venus of Dreams* (1986) launched a much more ambitious project, a family saga set against the backdrop of the terraforming of the planet Venus, overseen by a home world culture that is largely influenced by Muslim attitudes toward gender roles. The richly detailed story continues in *Venus of Shadows* (1988), and concludes with *Child of Venus* (2001), an epic to rival the Mars trilogy by Kim Stanley ROBINSON. *Climb the Wind* (1999) is an alternate history story in which American Indians eventually held off the westward expansion of European settlers and created their own nation; generations later a new war threatens to upset the balance of power.

Most of Sargent's recent fiction, written in collaboration with George Zebrowski, has consisted of media-related novels, tied in to television and films. The best of her short stories have been collected in *The Best of Pamela Sargent* (1987) and *Behind the Eyes of Dreamers and Other Short Novels* (2002). She is also noted as an anthologist, having edited *Women of Wonder* (1975) and *More Women of Wonder* (1976). Her fiction, which is always intelligently plotted and frequently involves sophisticated concepts, often involves recurring themes about alienation from society, the difficult transition from childhood to maturity, and the inevitability of political struggle regardless of the structure of a society or its form of government. She won a Nebula Award for her satiric short story "Danny Goes to Mars."

Sawyer, Robert J.
(1960–   )

The Canadian writer Robert Sawyer sold a few short stories during the 1980s, but made no real impression until the publication of his first novel, *The Golden Fleece* (1990), a clever locked-spaceship murder mystery. A woman is found dead of radiation poisoning on a starship run by an artificial intelligence; the authorities conclude that she must have committed suicide, as there was no opportunity for anyone else on board to have arranged her death. Her husband demurs, and subsequently solves the crime. Although not an instant hit, Sawyer's debut novel was witty and was cleverly executed; the use of the computer as the narrator was quite innovative. Sawyer's next effort, a trilogy, would make a much greater impression.

The Quintaglio trilogy consists of *Far-Seer* (1992), *Fossil Hunter* (1993), and *Foreigner* (1994). The setting is a distant planet inhabited by intelligent creatures analogous to our dinosaurs who have developed a civilization roughly equivalent to that of ancient Rome or Greece. Their physical nature imposes some limitations. For one thing, they are subject to periodic fits of blinding rage, making it difficult for them to work cooperatively for long periods of time. For another, their high fertility rate makes it necessary for them to cull their young ruthlessly, usually at the direction of a religious caste, and this has made discussions of parenthood and like matters taboo. In the opening volume, a young male named Afsan questions some of the tenets of his people's faith, is sent on a pilgrimage, continues to dissent, and is ultimately martyred for his beliefs. In the sequel, Afsan's son learns that their world is in an unstable orbit, and locates an ancient starship that might be rendered operable. In the concluding volume, during which the ship is repaired and a murder is solved, Sawyer plays out

the conflict between science and superstition, rebuffing the religious caste and, by implication, human religions as well.

The End of an Era (1994) is a time travel story with a fascinating setup, although the explanation is something of a letdown. The first trip back to prehistory uncovers two anomalies: Earth's gravity is much less than it is in the present, and some of the dinosaurs are directed intelligently by Martian parasites who decide that humans would make better hosts. Much more interesting was *The Terminal Experiment* (1995), which won the Nebula Award. A scientist creates three electronic variations of his own personality as part of an experiment, but fails to anticipate that, included in their makeup, is the will to survive—an urge that will cause them to replicate themselves within the internet. *Starplex* (1996), although essentially a space opera, brought its aliens to vivid life.

Sawyer's subsequent novels have continued to express fresh ideas or viewpoints. In *Frameshift* (1997), a terminally ill man discovers that his employer is using advanced technology to monitor the condition of his workers in an invasion of privacy so subtle that it could slowly and imperceptibly alter human civilization. *Illegal Alien* (1997) is a first contact story in which a party of apparently friendly aliens visits the Earth; one of them becomes the prime suspect in a murder investigation. *Factoring Humanity* (1998) takes a fresh look at an old dilemma. Humans receive the secrets of advanced genetic technology from an alien race, one that will speed up the process of human evolution, but doubts are raised about the wisdom of that course, and the motives of the aliens. *Flashforward* (1999) speculates about what might happen to modern society if everyone on Earth suddenly experienced a brief, random glimpse at their own personal futures.

Most recently, Sawyer has written a second trilogy, consisting of *Hominids* (2002), *Humans* (2003), and *Hybrids* (2003), the first of which won the Hugo Award. Our world has begun communicating with an alternate reality in which a different branch of prehistoric humanity survived in place of ours. Their world is substantially different and, despite a few flaws the author adds in an attempt to make it seem more realistic, it is essentially a utopia where violence is rare and reason rules rather than religion. Various conflicts ensue, including a proposed invasion of the alternate world from our own, accusations of murder, and a cross-species love affair. Although certain aspects of Sawyer's realization of the alternate humans are scientifically suspect, the stories are engaging and have been immensely popular, and the author makes extensive use of the visitor's external viewpoint to satirize aspects of our culture. Many of Sawyer's short stories have been collected as *Iterations* (2004).

"Scanners Live in Vain"
Cordwainer Smith
(1948)

Many authors have suggested that space travel could be achieved only through extraordinary measures, some of which might necessitate the alteration of the human body itself. For example, organic minds are lodged in machines in *The Ship Who Sang* (1969) by Anne McCAFFREY and star pilots must take drugs that alter their minds and their bodies in the DUNE SERIES by Frank HERBERT.

One of the earliest works to employ such a premise was this short story by Cordwainer SMITH. Scanners are people who have become a variation of cyborgs, their bodies merged with machinery, which allows them to deal with the rigors of space, but has an unfortunate side effect. Scanners cannot taste, smell, feel, or hear except for brief periods when they are restored to approximate normality by a dangerous mechanical process called cranching. Their value is that they can remain functional during spaceflight while normal humans rest in suspended animation, protected from some unexplained but unbearable pain present in outer space.

Martel is a scanner who is beginning to regret having been converted. He and several other scanners are called to an emergency meeting at which it is revealed that a scientist named Stone may have found a way to protect human minds in space. If true, this would render the scanners unnecessary and cost them their highly revered place in human society. They resolve therefore to kill

Stone in order to protect their status. Martel, who is cranched during the meeting, decides to intervene and warn Stone. He learns that Stone has indeed found a way to make scanners unnecessary, but the assassin arrives at that point and Martel is forced to kill his friend and comrade in order to protect Stone. With the new discovery safe, Martel and the other scanners are promised restoration to normal life.

Smith examines a variety of themes in the story: the conflict between duty to a small group as opposed to society at large, the unfortunate consequences of divorcing emotion from reason and compassion from action. The story is one of the earliest in the Instrumentality series, a loosely organized future history that would encompass the bulk of the author's comparatively small but still highly regarded science fiction.

Schmitz, James H.
(1911–1981)

James Schmitz published his first short story in 1943, and several years later began a series of space adventures, collected as *Agent of Vega* (1960), that included such classics as the title story and "The Second Night of Summer." He would continue to write impressive short fiction throughout the 1960s, although much of his later work began to fall into a formula. Some of his other noteworthy short stories include "The Big Terrarium" and "The Summer Guests."

Most of his fiction from the 1960s onward concerns the Hub, an interstellar civilization in which humans are prominent but do not have an exclusive hold on the seats of power. Many of the stories fall into one of two very similar series, each following the adventures of a young female protagonist, either Telzey Amberdon or Trigger Argee. Telzey, the more popular of the two among readers, is a talented telepath in addition to being a seasoned space traveler. *A Tale of Two Clocks* (1962, also published as *Legacy*) was the first novel using this setting, relating the adventure of Trigger Argee as she travels to Earth to solve an ancient secret that could destabilize the entire galaxy. Telzey Amberdon's unique telepathic talent is that she can read the minds of aliens as well as humans, an ability that allows her to eavesdrop on plans to launch an interstellar war. Unfortunately, her secret is out, and she is hunted across the stars by various parties determined that she not repeat what she learned. Neither of Schmitz's heroines shrinks from a fight; and both characters could have been portrayed as males without much alteration of the plots.

The same is not true of *The Witches of Karres* (1966), easily Schmitz's best novel. This time there are three teenaged girls, each of whom possesses psi talents for which they have been forced into slavery. They are subsequently rescued by a hardboiled space captain who becomes enraged by, and finally reconciled to, their impish sense of humor. The chemistry among the characters is superb, but unfortunately Schmitz never managed to achieve this level of characterization again. A recent sequel, *The Wizard of Karres* (2004) by Mercedes Lackey, Eric Flint, and Dave Freer, fails to measure up to the original. *The Demon Breed* (1968) is also set in the Hub universe, but it was more reminiscent of Andre NORTON's otherworld adventures. Aliens invade and conquer a remote human colony, but the protagonist manages to avoid capture, escaping into the wilderness with three mutated otters. With their help, she eventually manages to signal for help.

Telzey returned for another full-length adventure in *Lion Game* (1973). After escaping death at the hands of a psi-talented assassin, Telzey investigates a new alien race with territorial ambitions and publicizes their plot in time to avert an interstellar war. Schmitz's final novel was not part of the Hub universe. *The Eternal Frontiers* (1973) is set on another colony planet whose inhabitants have split into two hostile factions. They are forced to put aside their differences when a third party, consisting of belligerent aliens, enters the fray. Despite an interesting opening, the novel quickly bogs down into predictable melodramatic paths.

Schmitz's short fiction has been collected and cross-collected several times. The most recent volumes, which include virtually all of his short work and some of his novels, consist of *Telzey Amberdon* (2000), *TnT: Telzey & Trigger* (2000), *The Hub: Dangerous Territory* (2001), *Trigger & Friends*

(2001), *Agent of Vega & Other Stories* (2001), and *Eternal Frontier* (2002). A smaller but higher-quality sampling can be found in *The Best of James H. Schmitz* (1991). Among his more interesting stories are "Balanced Ecology," in which an entire forest composes a single creature, and "The Machmen," an unusual look at cyborgs. Schmitz was one of the most popular writers for *Astounding Magazine* (later *Analog*), and among the first science fiction writers to employ a competent female character as a series protagonist.

Scott, Melissa
(1960–)

Unlike most science fiction writers, Melissa Scott made her debut with a novel, *The Game Beyond* (1984), an above-average story of interplanetary war set against the backdrop of an interstellar empire. *A Choice of Destinies* (1986) is a very interesting alternate history novel in which Alexander the Great turns his attention to Rome, causing dramatic changes in the subsequent course of human history. This was followed promptly by the Silence Leigh trilogy, for which she won the John W. Campbell Award for best new writer. The trilogy consists of *Five-Twelfths of Heaven* (1985), *Silence in Solitude* (1986), and *The Empress of Earth* (1987). The setting is a future so distant that humanity has forgotten the location of Earth. A new form of physics has evolved that follows Arthur C. CLARKE's dictum that a sufficiently advanced technology would be indistinguishable from magic. Silence Leigh is a fugitive from a repressive planetary government who makes a new life for herself aboard a starship. Having mastered this new technology, Leigh decides to find the missing Earth in the second volume, and she eventually succeeds in the conclusion. Although the trilogy is a space opera in form—like many of Scott's later novels—it is also noteworthy for its examination of the way in which civilizations are changed by the use of advanced technology. Although the theme of female suppression is treated somewhat heavy-handedly in the opening volume, the sequels avoid that fault. The trilogy was published in one volume as *The Roads of Heaven* (1988).

A succession of well-conceived and deftly handled outer space adventures followed. *The Kindly Ones* (1987) is set against the backdrop of a repressive planetary government. *Mighty Good Road* (1990) is a convoluted tale in which a salvage crew is hired to retrieve as much as possible from a starship that crashed on an uninhabited world. The salvage crew encounter numerous difficulties, not only from hostile native forms of life, but also from their employers, who have a hidden reason for hoping that the salvage effort fails. *Dreamships* (1992) explores the same concept as *The Ship Who Sang* (1969) by Anne McCAFFREY: a starship built around an artificial intelligence that has become sentient. Scott delves much more deeply into the psychology of the situation that does McCaffrey.

In *Burning Bright* (1993), a professional game designer visits a remote world to search for a background for elaborate role playing simulation. She finds herself in the middle of a game that is being played for real stakes, which involves the fate of entire planets. *Trouble and Her Friends* (1994) also involves computers. The setting is a century from now when a reformed hacker must go underground to track down someone who has stolen her identity and is using it to conduct a series of criminal acts for which the hacker is being blamed. *Shadow Man* (1995) is her most overtly satiric novel. It returns to some of the feminist themes that had appeared intermittently in her earlier work. In *Shadow Man,* future humanity has redesigned itself so that it encompasses five separate genders. This system works well, except on one planet where it is mandatory to become either male or female, a situation that causes great difficulty for its attorney protagonist.

Night Sky Mine (1996) is a story of virtual reality and is written in a more somber tone than most of Scott's previous novels. A much lighter novel is *Dreaming Metal* (1997), arguably her best book, in which a star-traveling illusionist uses various cybernetic tricks to improve her act, including refinements to her sophisticated computer system. This last refinement eventually leads to the creation of a genuine artificial intelligence, a result that the protagonist greets with mixed feelings. Almost as impressive is *The Shape of Their Hearts* (1998), in which the personality of a religious zealot is merged with that of a computerized artificial intelligence,

with potentially disastrous consequences. *The Jazz* (2000) is one of her darker novels in which the entertainment industry embraces ever more impressive high-tech devices. An unorthodox group of entertainers discovers that the public face of the industry conceals a darker secret.

Scott has written very few short stories, but "The Carmen Miranda Gambit" (1990) is quite amusing. She has also co-authored three very good fantasy novels with Lisa A. Barnett. Scott has proven to be a steady if not prolific writer and has demonstrated a steady advance toward more complex plots and characters during the course of her career.

"Second Variety"
Philip K. Dick
(1953)

In this early story by Philip K. DICK, Americans and the Soviet Union have finally launched the ultimate war. Most of the population of Earth has died, and much of the world has been turned into a wasteland inhabited by small bands of survivors and isolated military units who continue the battle even though there is nothing left worth fighting over. The Soviets had almost clinched an early victory when the Americans forestalled this by building robotic devices that invaded enemy bunkers, lurked in the sand and ash, and emerged to slash and kill any living thing that they could detect. Friendly soldiers are protected by a radiation tag that differentiates them from the enemy so that the loss of a tag can have fatal consequences. The killer machines have become more sophisticated with the passage of time. Their underground factories are completely automated, and the mobile units are self-repairing. Although originally designed by humans, some of the many variations in devices appear to have been developed by machine intelligence as adaptations to a changing environment.

Major Hendricks is a soldier who is protected by a radiation tag. He is surprised when an enemy is killed by the automated claws near his position, and examination of his body uncovers an offer of truce talks. Although he is suspicious, Hendricks volunteers to travel to the Soviet lines on the off chance that an actual end of hostilities might be possible. On his way, he encounters David, a young boy who claims to be the last of a small group of survivors. Against his better judgment, Hendricks allows the boy to accompany him.

When they reach the Soviet post, there are only two soldiers and a prostitute surviving. The soldiers immediately fire at David, who is actually a highly advanced robot designed to ingratiate himself and infiltrate armored positions. Hendricks discovers that the David is labeled Type 3. Another variation, the Wounded Soldier, is Type 1. No one knows what the missing type is. Even worse, the disguised robots are not discouraged by the radiation tabs and can attack either side with impunity. Tension rises as members of the small party begin to suspect one another, and the conflict ends tragically as the robots outwit the humans.

"Second Variety" is a Frankenstein story, but one on a much greater scale than most others. In this case, humanity as a whole is at fault, and humanity might perish because of its collective mistake. The characters speculate that the robots constitute a new form of life and in fact, might be the successor race to humanity. There are already signs that the different device varieties are hostile to one another and that the one human attribute they will perpetuate is the desire to wage war. The 1996 motion picture version, retitled as *Screamers,* wisely transplanted the action to another planet. It was otherwise an effective rendition of Dick's nightmarish concept, although the film's artificial happy ending was completely implausible.

Sector General series
James White

Although this series of stories and novels set aboard an orbiting hospital are not James WHITE's best fiction, they are undoubtedly the ones for which he will be remembered. The hospital station known as Sector General was introduced in a series of short stories, culminating in the linked collection *Hospital Station* (1962) and the novel *Star Surgeon* (1963). Sector General caters to a wide variety of alien races, each of which is classified by a short letter code to facilitate their treatment. The stories usually involve problems with communications between species or cultural differences that interfere with their treatment. The tone of the stories ranges from overtly humorous to lightly serious. Although White was not a physician, the stories have a feel of authenticity despite the exotic settings and characters.

White continued to add to the series during the 1970s, with another collection, *Major Operation* (1971), and a second full-length novel, *Ambulance Ship* (1979). In *Ambulance Ship,* a seasoned doctor and his assistants are transferred from the hospital to an ambulance ship for reasons without immediate explanation, and they later resolve an interstellar crisis. The third and final collection of short stories, *Sector General,* followed in 1983, and from that point forward White concentrated on book-length adventures.

In *Star Healer* (1984) a staff doctor must decide whether or not to accept a promotion that will take him away from his current duties. This novel is one of the best in the series and one of the most serious in tone. *Code Blue—Emergency* (1987) was nearly as good. A doctor, who has not completely overcome her xenophobia, makes a series of errors while treating nonhuman patients, with results ranging from humorous to potentially tragic. *The Genocidal Healer* (1992) is the best in the series. A doctor, who makes a possibly unavoidable error that wiped out an entire alien race, must now face a new crisis involving the first contact with a new species about whose physiology nothing is known.

The remaining four novels in the series seemed more hastily written and vary considerably in quality. *The Galactic Gourmet* (1996) is a light and only marginally funny comedy about the arrival of a new chef who has grandiose plans but little expertise with aliens. *Final Diagnosis* (1997) is a more interesting and moderately suspenseful story about the discovery of the first virus that can jump from one species to another. A new chief administrator takes over in *Mind Changer* (1998), causing considerable disruption and stress. *Double Contact* (1999) describes the first encounter between the organized community of worlds and two separate alien races, each of which has been attempting to exterminate the other for uncounted generations.

White created a vivid background that provided him with the canvas of a unique, believable, and interesting universe. At his best, White made efficient use of his Sector General setting to deliver solid, entertaining stories.

Service, Pamela
(1945–   )

Although her science fiction has been written exclusively for younger readers, Pamela Service often employs a quirky sense of humor that can amuse adult readers as well. Her first science fiction novel was *A Question of Destiny* (1986), an interesting and somewhat atypical novel in which the son of a presidential candidate becomes increasingly suspicious of one of his father's advisers, begins to watch him more closely, and discovers that the adviser is actually a secret alien anthropologist positioned to study human culture from close at hand. Although it has a more serious tone than most of Service's other work, there is never any serious tension, and the plot is more of a puzzle story than a thriller.

Next came *Stinker from Space* (1988), in which a benevolent alien parasite finds itself temporarily trapped on Earth. It occupies the body of a common skunk, eventually manages to communicate with some children, and after some mild adventures is able to return to its fellows beyond the Earth's atmosphere. The novel is amusing but slight, and the sequel, *Stinker's Return* (1993), is basically a retelling of the original story without the novelty of its predecessor.

In *Under Alien Stars* (1989), Service's best novel, Earth has been conquered by an alien race roughly human in psychology. The child of a human collaborator and a child from among the aliens are initially predisposed to be enemies but eventually form a friendship that becomes a bridge between the races and leads to a kind of reconciliation. *Weirdos of the Universe Unite!* (1992) has a promising premise—a group of teenagers with psi powers are approached by avatars of mythical figures from Earth's history with a warning about alien invaders—but the plot becomes so contrived that even younger readers must have been disappointed. Service has shown no inclination to attempt adult

fiction, and most of her subsequent genre work has been fantasy. She remains one of the more prominent SF writers for younger readers, primarily because that market has been largely neglected by publishers in recent years.

Seven American Nights
Gene Wolfe
(1978)

One of the advantages of science fiction is that it allows us to look at our own society from a radically different perspective. Robert Nathan's "Digging the Weans" (1956) did so by recording the observations of a team of future archaeologists sifting through the ruins of civilization, and Horace L. Coon did much the same with alien scientists in *43,000 Years Later* (1958). Gene Wolfe does so from a closer perspective in this novelette, in which a young and wealthy Iranian man named Nadan travels to the exotic, decadent, and internationally unimportant America of the early 22nd century. It was not a nuclear war or other apocalyptic event that changed the power structure of the world. Americans were destroyed, improbably enough, by unregulated food additives, which led to rampant birth defects and mutations and the collapse of internal order. Much of the country had been abandoned and conditions in the interior are reported by rumor rather than direct observations. There are still a few who look forward to an illusory future restoration.

Nadan is struck by the strange contradictions he perceives. Prostitution has become an accepted profession, catering to foreign visitors. Actors who have real talent quickly immigrate to more lucrative markets in Europe and Asia. As Nadan travels around the ruins of Washington, armed like virtually everyone else because of the bands of outlaws who prey on the unwary, he learns that most surviving Americans have forgotten their heritage. Famous buildings have been cannibalized for their structural materials, and few if any Americans remember the buildings' original purpose.

Although the purpose of his visit is to study American architecture, he becomes fascinated with certain elements of the local culture, even though he feels superior to the locals. Nadan becomes infatuated with a stage actress named Ardis, but his feelings are primarily sexual, and he even contemplates rape at one point, despite claiming to feel genuine affection for her. Although Nadan eventually convinces her to have sexual relations with him, Ardis insists upon doing so only in complete darkness. The final revelation that her body has also been corrupted by the mutagens in the food supply is Nadan's ultimate downfall and just reward. It is very easy to recognize the story as a comment on our own attitudes toward the less developed nations in the world and as an illustration of the consequences of hubris, even on an international scale.

"Seven Views of Olduvai Gorge"
Mike Resnick
(1994)

More than one writer has illuminated the present in satirical fashion by writing about our contemporary world as it might be perceived by alien intelligences or from the perspective of an individual living centuries from now. In most cases, this was done to poke fun at current conventions or institutions. This novella, which won both the Hugo and Nebula Awards, uses a similar format, but Resnick's purpose is not satiric. He presents his story as a grim indictment of humanity, a pessimism that was reflected even more bitterly in *A Hunger in My Soul* (1998).

The human race, which once dominated the galaxy, enslaving numerous alien races, despoiling worlds, conducting incessant warfare, and committing numerous other crimes, has apparently been extinct for some time. A party of aliens visits the abandoned planet Earth to study artifacts left behind, and they choose as their site Olduvai Gorge. One of the aliens is able to assimilate physical objects and experience past events during which the objects were present, a literary device that is obviously implausibly convenient. However, the story is designed clearly to make a point independent of the nature of the aliens and their attributes, so that the makeshift plot construction becomes almost irrelevant.

As the title suggests, the alien examines seven artifacts, each of which provides a vision of human history, none of which are complimentary. The earliest object shows peaceful baboons falling prey to savage smaller monkeys, presumably our ancestors. Through the alien's vision, we are then shown Arab slave trading, torture, treachery, and insanity, the Mau Mau uprising in Africa, a not too distant future when almost all of the animal life on Earth has become extinct, and a final one in which pollution and corruption poison civilization on Earth, leading to its eventual evacuation. The arguments are all purposefully one-sided, of course, making them seven somewhat jaundiced views from Olduvai Gorge. The ultimate revelation that humans are not extinct after all and that our distant descendants have reverted to a form of primitive cannibalism, is the final blow in a vitriolic, if somewhat myopic, indictment of our inhumanity to one another, as well as our shortsightedness in managing our environment.

"Shambleau"
C. L. Moore
(1933)

The distinction between the fantasy and science fiction genres was not as clear-cut in the 1930s as it has become in recent years. Weird fiction could involve vampires or fairies or aliens, and atmosphere was often more important than setting or plot. Catherine MOORE was one of a small group of writers that included Leigh BRACKETT, and even Ray BRADBURY, who produced stories set elsewhere in our solar system that were considerably more sophisticated than the work of Edgar Rice BURROUGHS and his imitators.

Moore depicted Mars as a planetary frontier town with small outposts of civilization set in a planetary desert, much of which remains unknown to the narrator. The story introduced Northwest Smith, a recurring character and a small-time criminal, although basically a moral and even kindly man. Smith rescues what he believes to be a young human woman from a mob and offers to let her stay in his room temporarily, even though upon closer examination she proves to be a member of some unknown race, calling herself Shambleau. Shambleau wears a turban that conceals what appears to be bright red hair, and she apparently doesn't eat much of anything, but Smith's act of charity was impulsive and he feels only mildly attracted to her.

We have to assume that Smith was an interplanetary novice, because most of the rest of the population knows Shambleau's true nature. Using an unexplained hypnotic power, she seduces him and sets loose her hair, which is actually a nest of writhing snakelike tentacles. Shambleau is the medusa of legend, although the part of her that appears humanoid is merely a mask concealing the parasite within. Smith escapes, thanks to the intervention of a friend. Even though he is revolted by what happened to him, he recognizes that he is addicted, that he would be unable to resist the medusa if he ever encountered another such creature. Moore implies that the medusas in our legends may actually be memories left over from a previous human civilization that traveled to other worlds, illustrating that we forget the past only at great peril to our present. This remarkable noir variation was Moore's first published story.

Shaw, Bob
(1931–1996)

Although Bob Shaw had published a few short stories during the 1950s, his writing career really began in the middle of the 1960s with a burst of stories and novels, including the excellent "LIGHT OF OTHER DAYS" (1966). His first novel was *Night Walk* (1967) in which a man with dangerous knowledge is blinded by his enemies and stranded on a swampy planet. He develops the ability to see through the eyes of others, eventually exacting his revenge on his enemies. Although his debut novel was a light adventure, he followed up with much more substantial work and by 1970 was an acknowledged major writer.

The novels that established his reputation include some of his best work. *The Two-Timers* (1968) is a well-conceived scientific mystery involving murder and doppelgängers from alternate realities. *The Palace of Eternity* (1969) is a story of interplanetary war and human transformation,

marred somewhat by an ending that seems at odds with the first part of the novel. *Shadow of Heaven* (1969) is set aboard what was supposed to be a completely automated orbiting habitat, but which turns out to harbor a hidden population of human squatters. The best of this early lot was *One Million Tomorrows* (1970) in which humans have become immortal, but at the cost of their fertility. When a scientist stumbles across a possible solution that might allow the immortals to propagate, he becomes the target of mysterious assassins determined to prevent him from making his discovery public. *Ground Zero Man* (1971, revised as *The Peace Machine* in 1985) used a similar setup but less effectively. Shaw also rewrote "Light of Other Days" and two related stories as the novel, *Other Days, Other Eyes* (1972).

Orbitsville (1975) is a big dumb object novel, like RINGWORLD (1970) by Larry NIVEN or the Rama stories by Arthur C. CLARKE. Space explorers discover an enormous artificial world within which is a habitable ecology. The object encloses its own sun and has a surface area equal to a billion Earths, but no one knows who built it or for what purpose. Two inferior sequels, *Orbitsville Departure* (1983) and *Orbitsville Judgment* (1990), provided further details. A phantom planet from another reality impinges on our own universe in the uneven, but quite original, *A Wreath of Stars* (1976). *Who Goes Here?* (1977) was an indifferent attempt at humor. Shaw's next major novel was *Medusa's Children* (1977), a group of convoluted adventures set on a planetoid whose interior structure is liquid.

During the late 1970s, Shaw's novels began to rely more heavily on chases, conspiracies, and secret societies. In *Dagger of the Mind* (1979), experiments in telepathy appear to be going awry, perhaps because of external interference. A mentally scarred astronaut uncovers and eventually defeats a conspiracy against the government in *Vertigo* (1978, revised as *Terminal Velocity*). A race of aliens has been living secretly among humans in *The Ceres Solution* (1982), but must reveal itself after an asteroid begins to behave unnaturally. In *Fire Pattern* (1984) a reporter reluctantly agrees to investigate stories of spontaneous human combustion and discovers that they are manifestations of a secret alien invasion of Earth. Although the novels from this period were convincingly written and often quite suspenseful, the inventiveness that characterized his earlier work was largely absent.

The most sustained high-quality work of Shaw's career came near its end. The Overland trilogy, consisting of *The Ragged Astronauts* (1986), *The Wooden Spaceships* (1988), and *The Fugitive Worlds* (1990), is set in a completely unique environment. Two planets share an orbit so close that they have a common atmosphere, so that it is possible to achieve interplanetary travel without a high-tech civilization or sophisticated rocketry. When an alien menace threatens to overwhelm life on one of the two worlds, the inhabitants decide to attempt wholesale relocation to the other. The situation becomes more complex when the two planets—each with roughly equivalent levels of technology—engage in the most unusual interplanetary war ever, but both must unite in the final volume to overcome the common enemy.

Shaw continued to turn out short fiction throughout his career, much of it in a humorous or satiric vein, including several parodies of other science fiction writers. Good selections can be found in *Tomorrow Lies in Ambush* (1973), *Cosmic Kaleidoscope* (1976), *Ship of Strangers* (1978), and *A Better Mantrap* (1982). He wrote some science fiction for younger readers.

Sheckley, Robert
(1928–   )

Robert Sheckley was one of the most prolific and talented short story writers of the 1950s, turning out scores of stories while maintaining an impressively high level of quality. His early work was typically bitterly humorous, often employing surprise endings or paradoxical events, and his plots and settings were widely varied. Sheckley could describe the arrival on Earth of a devastating extraterrestrial creature, as in "The Leech" (1952), explore the hazards of shape changing in "Keep Your Shape" (1953), or imagine a future in which space travel is possible only by a combination of different types of intelligent creatures in "Specialist" (1953). "THE GUN WITHOUT A BANG" (1958) demonstrates that advanced technology is not

necessarily a good thing, and "A Wind Is Rising" (1957) suggests the dangers one might encounter after a too hasty judgment of a new planet's weather system. In "All the Things You Are" (1956) an Earthman inadvertently wreaks havoc in an alien civilization because of his bad breath, loud voice, and caustic perspiration.

A common criticism of Sheckley's early fiction is that the plots depend upon the stupidity of the protagonists. It does appear that the author has a low opinion of his fellow creatures. Even the characters who display rudimentary intelligence often let themselves be maneuvered into nonsensical situations. In one of his earliest short stories, "The Seventh Victim" (1953), which was later filmed as *The Tenth Victim* (1965) and novelized under that title by Sheckley a year later, individuals engage in legalized manhunts in which they attempt to kill one another. A succession of excellent collections followed, consisting of *Untouched by Human Hands* (1954), *Citizen in Space* (1956), *Pilgrimage to Earth* (1957), *Store of Infinity* (1960), *Notions Unlimited* (1960), and *Shards of Space* (1962). Other stories of particular merit from this period are "Mountain Without a Name" (1956) and "Protection" (1956).

Sheckley's first novel was *Immortality, Inc.* (1958, also published as *Immortality Delivered*). A man from our era dies and finds himself brought back to life as a fugitive in the future. The film version, retitled *Freejack* (1992), preserved the action but left out the satire. In his second novel, *The Status Civilization* (1960), a dissident who attracts the attention of the repressive government of Earth is exiled to a prison planet that has evolved its own society, one dedicated to the performance of evil acts as a positive social value. *Journey Beyond Tomorrow* (1962, also published as *The Journey of Joenes*), continued in a satirical tone that Sheckley would maintain in several subsequently written novels. Joenes lived in an isolated community for most of his life, and is later engaged on a tour of the civilization of tomorrow. Sheckley satirizes the absurdities of human society through exaggeration and the use of Joenes as an innocent but curious outsider.

Although Sheckley has continued to write short fiction, his output dropped off dramatically after the 1960s. *The People Trap* (1968) and *Can You Feel Anything When I Do This?* (1971) brought together his work from the late 1960s and a few earlier stories that had been previously uncollected. He wrote two more novels during the 1960s, both satires, and a minor collaboration with Harry HARRISON. *Dimension of Miracles* (1968) concerns a man who gets lost and visits a variety of worlds after winning a prize but loses his orientation in an increasingly bizarre universe. The slapstick style is only intermittently funny. *Mindswap* (1965), in which a human and Martian switch bodies at the latter's instigation, is considerably more successful, with the protagonist chasing his own body through various absurd adventures. Amusing though it may be, the novel remains a relatively minor effort.

Most of Sheckley's small output of new work during the 1970s was short fiction, much of it humorous and all of it entertaining, but without producing any individual pieces that rivaled the creativity of the 1950s. Two more novels appeared as well. *Options* (1975) lampooned genre conventions as it tells the story of a man stranded on a primitive world and his efforts to find replacement parts so that he can leave. Some of the individual encounters during the course of the journey are painfully funny, but the point of the novel—which is that the universe itself is absurd and unknowable—is so apparent early on that it feels as though the narrative simply stops rather than reaches a conclusion. *Crompton Divided* (1978, also published as *The Alchemical Marriage of Alastair Crompton*) is much more interesting. Crompton's personality has been split into three separate parts that inhabit three distinct bodies. After some time apart, one of the three bodies sets out on a quest to reunite himself. The satire is more pointed and is more effective than *Options*.

Several years passed before the next novel appeared. *Dramocles* (1983) was a comic space opera whose plot and humor were equally forgettable. A flurry of disappointing books followed. *Victim Prime* (1987) and *Hunter/Victim* (1988) were both sequels of sorts to *The Tenth Victim*, but neither added anything particularly new to the mix. The tone was considerably more serious than in Scheckley's other recent novels, but the stories were simply plotted and very predictable. Sheckley began writing light fantasy in the late 1980s and media tie-in novels during the 1990s. His short fiction during this period continued to be superior to his longer work, notably "Dukakis and the Aliens" (1992). Short story collections appeared on a regular basis, including *Can You Feel Anything When I Do This?* (1971, also published as *The Same to You Doubled*), *The Robot Who Looked Like Me* (1978), *The Wonderful Worlds of Robert Sheckley* (1979), and *Is That What People Do?* (1984).

In 1991, Pulphouse Publishing brought out a retrospective five-volume collection of Sheckley's short stories as *Collected Short Fiction*. His most recent science fiction stories are contained in *Uncanny Tales* (2003). It is difficult to judge Sheckley's place in the field. He is highly regarded as a short story writer, but most of his best known shorter work was published more than 30 years ago. He is considered an indifferent and quirky novelist. It has traditionally been difficult for humor or satire to attract lasting attention in the science fiction community, and the fact that Sheckley is well regarded, despite the preponderance of both in his fiction, is indicative of its enduring popularity.

Sheffield, Charles
(1935–2002)

Charles Sheffield had a background in physics and technical writing, so it was not surprising that when he turned to writing fiction in the late 1970s, he made use of his expertise and gained an immediate reputation as a promising new writer of hard science fiction. His stories were solidly grounded and entertaining, but it was with his novels that he began to emerge as more than just a casual phenomenon. His debut novel, *Sight of Proteus* (1978), speculated about a technology so advanced that it seemed almost magical. Humans could reshape their bodies, almost at will, in order to achieve specific purposes, but an unauthorized experiment leads to contact with aliens. A later sequel, *Proteus Unbound* (1989), added little to the development of the premise and concentrated on efforts to contain a man determined to undermine the system. A third, *Proteus in the Underworld* (1995), poses interesting ethical questions when it appears that a sudden eruption of strange and malevolent forms of life has evolved from artificially altered human tissue.

Sheffield's second novel, *The Web Between the Worlds* (1979), was set in a much nearer future time and involved the construction of a skyhook—literally a physical bridge between the Earth and a geosynchronously orbiting satellite. The novel is frequently contrasted to a very similar theme in *The Fountains of Paradise* (1979) by Arthur C. CLARKE, who independently developed the concept. Sheffield's credentials as a hard science fiction writer were further buoyed by the publication of two collections of his short stories, *Vectors* (1979) and *Hidden Variables* (1981).

Just as readers were beginning to believe they knew what to expect from Sheffield, he began experimenting with different forms including a series of fantasies about Charles Darwin's grandfather. *My Brother's Keeper* (1982) felt like a contemporary thriller despite its speculative premise. The protagonist has portions of his dead brother's brain implanted in his own skull, acquires access to some of his memories, and sets out to complete his final mission. Another series of shorts about a precocious inventor were collected as *The McAndrew Chronicles* (1983, expanded in 1993 as *One Man's Universe*, and again in 2000 as *The Compleat McAndrew*).

Between the Strokes of Night (1985, expanded in 2002) is an elaborate space opera that reflects the author's apparent ambivalence about the future of the human race. Earth has been rendered uninhabitable by a nuclear war, but survivors elsewhere in the solar system have reached the stars. *The Nimrod Hunt* (1986, expanded in 1993 as *The Mind Pool*), owes its inspiration to the BERSERKER SERIES by Fred SABERHAGEN, although Sheffield's version is substantially different, and more immediately chilling. Most of civilization has been destroyed by another war in *Trader's World* (1988), one of Sheffield's best novels. The Traders are a sort of extra-national organization that conducts commerce and liaison among the new political entities arising in the aftermath, but their apparent neutrality conceals a hidden agenda.

Summertide (1990) introduced the Heritage Universe. Scientists, entrepreneurs, and the merely curious flock to a star system where a very rare solar change is about to occur, possibly linked to mysterious alien artifacts present nearby. The absent aliens left behind myriad traps and tests,

which almost wipe out a party of explorers in *Divergence* (1991). In *Transcendence* (1992), the aliens prove to be dormant, not extinct. Once awakened, they engage in an ambitious plan to assert their power. *Convergence* (1997) and *Resurgence* (2002) extend the sequence without reaching a definite conclusion. *Cold As Ice* (1992) inaugurated another series. Once again, a major war has devastated much of humanity, which has established colonies throughout the inner solar system. Plans to create a new colony on the moon Europa lead to a new crisis, with some interesting commentary on the conflict of interest between those who wish to exploit natural resources and those who prefer to preserve them. *The Ganymede Club* (1995) expands on the situation and provides much more detail about life in the artificial habitats outside Earth. The arrival of aliens in the final installment, *Dark As Day* (2002), precipitates the decision to unite to meet the new challenge. This trilogy seems likely to stand as Sheffield's most accomplished work, with its sophisticated understanding of the intricacies of human politics and the contradictions inherent in human society, no matter how the outward form may change. *Brother to Dragons* (1992) is set in the aftermath of an economic collapse, seen from the viewpoint of an unlikely teenaged hero who grows to maturity and saves the world from a new plague. *Godspeed* (1993) is a lost colony story that has many parallels to *Treasure Island* by Robert Louis Stevenson. Cut off from Earth, settlers on a distant world struggle to battle not only their new environment, but also the depredations of space traveling pirates.

Higher Education (1996), written in collaboration with Jerry POURNELLE, was the first of several books Sheffield wrote for the young adult market, all of which are of exceptionally high quality and are quite similar in plot if not setting. A troubled teenager drops out of school and becomes a miner in the asteroid belt, where he matures and eventually solves a murder. Sheffield's other young adult novels are *The Billion Dollar Boy* (1997), whose teenaged protagonist is a rich kid who is accidentally transported to a mining world where he grows out of his preconceptions of life. A second, *Putting Up Roots* (1997), focused on two teenagers who are unhappy about their relocation to a colony world until they get caught up in a first contact situation. The third, *The Cyborg from Earth* (1998), centers on another troubled teenager, this one a washed out astronaut trainee who undertakes a dangerous mission.

Sheffield's last few adult novels were a decidedly mixed bag. *Tomorrow and Tomorrow* (1997), the story of a man who awakens from suspended animation into a very different world, contains some interesting speculation but is unusually slow paced for Sheffield. *Aftermath* (1998) shows civilization on Earth destroyed once again, this time because Alpha Centauri becomes a supernova and bombards the Earth with particles generated by the explosion. Efforts to build a shield run into difficulties in the sequel, *Starfire* (1999), due to the efforts of fanatics to sabotage the project because they believe that humanity should be allowed to die out. *The Spheres of Heaven* (2001) is an ambitious space opera in which a race of aliens who eschew violence quarantines the solar system to prevent humanity from spreading its brand of belligerence, but their efforts prove to be inadequate.

Sheffield was a reasonably prolific short story writer throughout his career. "Georgia on My Mind" (1993) won both the Hugo and Nebula Awards. Much of his later fiction has been collected in *Dancing with Myself* (1993), *Georgia on My Mind and Other Places* (1995), and *The Lady Vanishes and Other Oddities of Nature* (2002). He was a reliable writer with a strong scientific background that he used when necessary, but he was also willing to experiment with other forms and styles including fantasy, humor, and even the contemporary thriller. His protagonists tend to be very much alike, and Sheffield probably identified them with himself. He always seemed to be concerned that human shortcomings would prevent us from maturing enough to explore the physical universe, but was also confident that if we did finally mature, we would find wondrous things awaiting us.

Shepard, Lucius
(1947–)

Some writers have grown up as voracious readers of science fiction and have absorbed its sensibilities,

writing as insiders who know all the tricks and shortcuts and abide by the established conventions. Others come to the genre from a different tradition, either because they discovered science fiction later in their lives or because their writing originally was intended for, but did not fit, another genre. They then turn their attention to the freedoms offered by speculative fiction. Lucius Shepard is one of the latter, a poet and musician who first began to write unconventional science fiction and fantasy stories in 1983, attaining considerable success with stories like "The Man Who Painted the Dragon Griaule" (1984) and "Salvador."

Shepard's first novel, *Green Eyes* (1984), is a good illustration of his disdain for the borders between genres. In the near future, scientists have discovered a strain of bacteria that, when injected into the recently dead, restores them to life under certain circumstances. These newly resurrected individuals are used as virtual slave laborers, but one of their number rebels against the system and escapes. The scientific explanation is questionable at best, and the mood is closer to that of a novel of the supernatural, but Shepard does use the device to examine issues that have long concerned science fiction writers. Similar situations have been explored in "DOWN AMONG THE DEAD MEN" (1954) by William TENN, *Recalled to Life* (1962) by Robert SILVERBERG, and "Meathouse Man" (1976) by George R. R. Martin.

A steady output of topnotch stories followed throughout the balance of the 1980s, including the Nebula Award winning "R & R" (1986), "The End of Life as We Know It" (1985), and several outstanding fantasy stories. "R & R" became the core of his next novel, *Life During Wartime* (1987), which transposes the war in Vietnam to the near future in Central America. American soldiers are bogged down in an unfocused, apparently pointless war against insurgents. Their performance is enhanced by tailored drugs designed to improve their efficiency but which are actually contributing to their individual instabilities. Transcendental experiences with drugs recur frequently in the author's other work. Shepard, who has traveled extensively, brilliantly evokes his jungle settings, and his dense, lyrical prose is perfectly suited for a narrative in which the characters are increasingly divorced from their surroundings.

The Jaguar Hunter (1987) was Shepard's first short story collection. Other collections followed including *The Ends of the Earth* (1991), *Barnacle Bill the Spacer and Other Stories* (1997), and *Beast of the Heartland and Other Stories* (1999). "Barnacle Bill the Spacer" (1992) won the Hugo Award. The story is actually atypical of Shepard's work, being set on a space station where a retarded man becomes the focal point for resistance to a pressure group. "A Traveler's Tale" (1984) is essentially a story of possession, but the disembodied spirit is an alien rather than a supernatural entity. By 1990, Shepard was turning away from science fiction and toward fantasy and horror. Most of his subsequent work has been in those fields, although two of his later novels incorporate science fiction elements. In *Kalimantan* (1990) an expatriate American experiments with prohibited drugs and achieves contact with intelligent beings from another reality, although it is never clear whether this is a physical or metaphysical phenomenon. *Valentine* (2002) suggests that the human imagination might be powerful enough to affect the laws of chance.

Shepard's themes and plots are generally low key and introverted, set in brooding landscapes filled with preoccupied and unhappy characters, causing some critics to compare him to Joseph Conrad. He has an undeniable talent for creating vivid settings, and his point of view is so unconventional that his endings are rarely predictable. It seems unlikely that Shepard will turn back to science fiction as the main venue for his writing. If the stories he chooses to write in the future intersect with the science fiction genre, they are almost certain to be significant additions to the field.

Shute, Nevil
(1899–1960)

British writer Nevil Shute Norway set his early novels in England, but switched the location for Australia after moving there at the end of the 1940s. Although he was never considered a science fiction writer, three of his earlier works and two of the later ones incorporate fantastic elements. The

first of these was *What Happened to the Corbetts* (1939), better known as *Ordeal*, which was a future war novel that focused on war's effects on one family as an indictment of armed conflict. *An Old Captivity* (1940) is a very low-key lost race novel in which an expedition to Greenland discovers evidence of a previously unknown civilization, whose existence is revealed through a series of psychic dreams experienced by the protagonist. *No Highway* (1948) involves the discovery that a revolutionary new type of aircraft actually has a hidden and deadly flaw. The scientific content of the novel is mixed with some ambiguous telepathic events.

Both of Shute's later science fiction novels are more overt and more interesting. *In the Wet* (1953) may have reflected his own circumstances. In the novel, a large portion of the population of Great Britain emigrates, and the change in political structure results in Australia's emergence as center of the still viable British Empire. Shute's vision of a utopian future is an unusual one, with the royal family intact and revered and various modern movements inexplicably faded away. Shute's most famous novel is without question ON THE BEACH (1957), in which the Northern Hemisphere has been rendered completely uninhabitable, and a cloud of radioactive debris is rapidly being spread around the globe, dooming the rest of the human race to a more leisurely, but every bit as certain death. Shute's mainstream novels enjoy periods of popularity but his novel of nuclear destruction has always remained available.

The Silver Eggheads
Fritz Leiber
(1962)

Satire was common during the 1950s, and many of the major novels of that period exaggerated existing trends in a future setting as a way of pointing out the absurdities we sometimes accept as part of life. Frederik POHL and Cyril M. KORNBLUTH skewered advertising in THE SPACE MERCHANTS (1953) and Bernard Wolfe, Kurt VONNEGUT, and others held institutions and behaviors up to ridicule. By the early 1960s it was obvious that satires were falling out of favor, possibly because the war in Vietnam and other real world events had exhausted our collective sense of humor. Although occasional satirical novels would continue to appear, most of this tone of writing was confined to shorter work.

One of the last, genuinely interesting broad satires was *The Silver Eggheads* by Fritz LEIBER, originally published as a novelette in 1958. Leiber had already demonstrated his talent for acerbic humor on several occasions, most notably in "The Night He Cried," a very clever spoof of the tough detective story. This time he targeted writing in general, setting his story in a future when computers produce all of the fiction in the world, and authors are actually just machine operators who feed in random seed elements and then wait for the computer to turn them into a completed manuscript. By extension, Leiber charges the reading public with a complete lack of discrimination between mass-produced mediocrity and genuinely original work, and the publishing industry for turning an art form into a commercial commodity.

Leiber's future world is filled with other technological devices, including robots designed to be both male and female and the brains of dead writers carefully preserved in metal containers—the silver eggheads themselves. When the mechanical wordmills cease to function, the world is thrown into an aesthetic crisis, and the desperate publishing industry turns to those still thinking, but disembodied and rather out-of-touch minds to fill the gap until a new source can be found, or more likely built. The serious point of this comic novel is even more relevant today given the current consolidation and homogenization of the publishing industry.

Silverberg, Robert
(1935–   )

Over the course of his 50 years as a writer, Robert Silverberg has proven to be one of the most prolific in the genre, publishing over a hundred science fiction books, not including more than two dozen anthologies of his work. He has also written extensively outside the field, primarily non-fiction, but also including the highly regarded Majipoor series of fantasy novels. Silverberg sold his first short story in 1954, and his first novel—for young adults—a year later. During the 1950s he produced short stories at an incredible pace, more than 40 during 1956 alone. Under a variety of pseudonyms, and often in collaboration with Randall Garrett, he turned out a steady stream of adventure stories for several magazines, most of which were quite minor works.

Silverberg's first adult novel was *Master of Life and Death* (1957), one of the earliest works to deal seriously with the problems of an overpopulated Earth, complicated in this case by the discovery of a practical means of achieving immortality. This was followed by a dystopian adventure story, *The Thirteenth Immortal* (1957). *Invaders from Earth* (1958, published in condensed form in 1965 as *We, the Marauders*), tells of corrupt officials who use advertising techniques in an attempt to convince colonists in the Jovian moons that a race of aliens poses a threat to them. The latter novel is the most impressive of Silverberg's early efforts and has been reprinted several times since its original appearance. *Recalled to Life* (1958, revised in 1972) examines the effects on society when scientists discover a means of bringing the recently dead back to life, a device that Silverberg would return to much later in his career for the Nebula Award–winning BORN WITH THE DEAD.

More light adventure stories followed during the late 1950s and early 1960s, interspersed with young adult novels. The quality of his short fiction began to improve dramatically as he tackled more serious plots and more complex narrative techniques. Stories like "TO SEE THE INVISIBLE MAN" (1963), "Flies" (1967), and "The Pain Peddlers" (1963) began to attract more serious critical attention. *Godling, Go Home!* (1964) and *Needle in a Timestack* (1966) collected stories that seemed to have been written by two different writers; superficial adventure stories were mixed with others with deeper themes and more complex prose.

Silverberg's most productive and interesting period began roughly in 1967–68, and saw the publication of several new novels. *Hawksbill Station* (1968, also published as *The Anvil of Time*), which originally appeared in shorter form the year before, is set inside a penal colony that a future civilization has established in prehistory. A new arrival with some revolutionary ideas transforms the closed society in a surprisingly sophisticated work. *Thorns* (1967) featured his most complex characterization to date, the story of a sort of psychic vampire whose encounter with two other individuals has startling consequences. *To Open the Sky* (1967) is actually a series of shorter works assembled into a novel, detailing the history of a future overpopulated Earth in which two contending religions battle for control of human destiny. *The Masks of Time* (1968, also published as *Vornan 19*) features a traveler from the future who announces his presence in contemporary America. Although Silverberg published at least two minor novels during this same period, the dramatic change in his writing was more than evident.

His short fiction was similarly transformed. In 1968 and 1969 he produced several major shorter works, including "Nightwings," which won the Hugo Award, "PASSENGERS," which won a Nebula Award, and other outstanding stories, including "After the Myths Went Home" and "Among the Rememberers." *Dimension 13* (1969), *The Cube Root of Uncertainty* (1970), and *Moonfern and Starsongs* (1971) collected his better work from this period in book form. *Downward to the Earth* (1969) was Silverberg's homage to Joseph Conrad's *Heart of Darkness* (1902). An executive who once helped ruthlessly exploit an alien world returns after it has been set free to undertake a personal voyage of self-discovery. *Nightwings* (1969) was an expansion of the novelette about Earth under the sway of aliens. In *To Live Again* (1969), a powerful and brilliant man has his personality recorded prior to his death, and a power struggle ensues with different parties intent upon acquiring the remnant personality for their own purposes. *Up the Line* (1969) is a superior time travel story; the paradox is generated by a love affair between a time guide and a woman from the past. In less than five years, Silverberg had made the transition from an entertaining but minor writer to a major voice.

In the 1970s Silverberg continued this transition. *Tower of Glass* (1970) is ostensibly a story of first contact with aliens, but it is actually a study in human obsession. Human psychology was also the subject of *The Second Trip* (1972), in which a new personality is installed in the erased mind of a criminal. *A Time of Changes* (1971), which won a Nebula Award, is a thoughtful and low-key dystopia. Paradoxically, as Silverberg matured as a writer and began experimenting with themes and styles, he began to lose some of his science fiction audience. With the exception of *A Time of Changes*, none of his novels ever won a major award, even though they were often considered critical successes. *Son of Man* (1971) described a man's surrealistic visit to other realities. *DYING INSIDE* (1972), arguably his best novel, describes in moving detail the agonies of a telepath who discovers that he is losing his powers. *The Book of Skulls* (1972) deals with efforts by the protagonists to uncover a secret society that might possibly possess the secret of immortality.

If his novels were increasingly underrated, his short fiction was not. "GOOD NEWS FROM THE VATICAN" (1971) won a Nebula, as did "BORN WITH THE DEAD" (1974) and "Sailing to Byzantium" (1985). "Gilgamesh in the Outback" (1986) won the Hugo, as did "Enter a Soldier. Later: Enter Another" (1986). Other major stories include "Breckenridge and the Continuum" (1973), "Trips" (1974), "Amanda and the Alien" (1983), and "In Another Country" (1989). The last was a sequel to "Vintage Season" by C. L. MOORE and Henry KUTTNER. By the middle of the 1970s, Silverberg's output of novels had dropped dramatically. *The Stochastic Man* (1975) and *Shadrach in the Furnace* (1976) are both less than optimistic portrayals of the future, suggesting the loss of free will or the installation of a planetary dictatorship. Most of his book-length work for the next decade was in his Majipoor fantasy series, although he returned to science fiction with the episodic space opera *Star of Gypsies* (1986).

At Winter's End (1988) marked at least a partial return to his old form. Thousands of years after a new ice age swept over the Earth, the temperature rises and primitive tribes emerge to reconquer the Earth. In the sequel, *The New Springtime* (1989, also published as *The Queen of Springtime*), they are forced to compete with a newly evolved species of telepathic insects. *The Secret Sharer* (1989) is another Conrad homage, this time featuring a spaceship captain inhabited by a bodiless intelligent creature. The 1990s marked a fairly energetic return to science fiction, including some of his best work. *The Face of the Waters* (1991) follows the travels of a group of humans on a water-covered world after they offend their native hosts. *Kingdoms of the Wall* (1992) also recounts a journey, this time a coming-of-age pilgrimage on a distant planet. *Hot Sky at Midnight* (1994) is set on a future Earth doomed by pollution in which the human race must genetically alter itself if it is to survive among the stars. Enigmatic aliens invade the earth in *The Alien Years* (1998), but seem indifferent to humans. His most recent novel *Roma Eterna* (2003), is set in an alternate history in which the Roman Empire never fell.

Silverberg's short stories have been assembled into numerous collections. A comprehensive sampling can be found in *Born with the Dead* (1974), *The Feast of St. Dionysus* (1975), *Homefaring* (1983), *World of a Thousand Colors* (1983), *Beyond the Safe Zone* (1986), *Ringing the Changes* (1997), and *In Another Country and Other Short Novels* (2002). He also produced three novel-length versions of classic short stories by Isaac ASIMOV: *Nightfall* (1990), *The Positronic Man* (1992), and *The Ugly Little Boy* (1992, also published as *The Child of Time*).

Simak, Clifford D.
(1904–1988)

Science fiction has been almost invariably associated with technology, particularly in its early years; thus, life on Earth was almost always set against an urban landscape. One of the few writers whose work consistently used a rural setting was Clifford D. Simak, although his most famous work is in fact a history of the decline of the city as the center of human habitation. CITY (1952) is a collection of stories that chronicle the evolution of human civilization and the eventual abandonment of Earth. A professional journalist for most of his life, Simak produced some minor space adventures during the 1930s, including his first novel, *The Cosmic Engineers* (1938, but not published in book form until 1950). He began producing work more typical of the themes and quality of his career during the 1940s.

The bulk of his major short fiction appeared during the 1950s, including classics like "Good Night, Mr. James" (1951), "Skirmish" (1953), "Idiot's Crusade" (1954), and "THE BIG FRONT YARD" (1958), which won a Hugo. His early collections *Strangers in the Universe* (1958), *The Worlds of Clifford Simak* (1960), and *All the Traps of Earth and Other Stories* (1962) brought together most of these in book form. After 1960, Simak diverted most of his energy to novels, but his shorter work steadily improved in quality even as it diminished in quantity. The best of his later short stories are "Over the River and Into the Woods" (1965), "The Autumn Land" (1971), "The Marathon Photograph" (1974), and "GROTTO OF THE DANCING DEER" (1980), the last of which won both the Hugo and Nebula Awards. *The Best Science Fiction Stories of Clifford D. Simak* (1970) and *Skirmish* (1977) collect most of his remaining short stories of note.

Simak opened the 1950s with a pair of major novels. The first was *Time and Again* (1951, also published as *First He Died*). Although the complexity of the plot involves time travel to the future, which is sometimes distracting to the reader, the novel demonstrated many of the devices and attitudes that Simak would continue to use throughout his career. This includes a disinclination toward violent action and conflict that rarely involved actively villainous characters. The second novel from this period, *Ring Around the Sun* (1953), deals with parallel universes and the efforts by a clandestine mutant organization to move goods across the borderlines between universes in order to upset the economy of their home reality. Several years elapsed during which he wrote only short stories, but 1961 saw publication of the short novel *The Trouble with Tycho* and the much more impressive *Time Is the Simplest Thing*. This is a rare science fiction novel in which faster than light travel is impossible, so that humans are thereby prevented from physically traveling to the stars and instead must explore the universe by means of mental projection.

A steady stream of novels followed. *They Walked Like Men* (1962), despite the seemingly melodramatic plot that involves a secret alien invasion of Earth, is actually quite low key. The invaders' tactics are more inclined toward economic subversion than physical aggression. *Way Station* (1963), which won the Hugo Award, is generally cited as his best novel. The protagonist is a human who is secretly maintaining a safe haven for alien teleporters on Earth, in payment for which service he is granted immortality. There is virtually no overt conflict in the story, which relies heavily on its protagonist's character. *All Flesh Is Grass* (1965) also turned an old genre cliché on its head. A small town is cut off from the rest of the world by a mysterious force field, inside of which one of the inhabitants crosses into an alternate world inhabited by intelligent flowers. Simak would use the device of transposing a character into an alien setting periodically in the future as well, including *The Werewolf Principle* (1967), whose protagonist awakens from suspended animation in an unrecognizable future world, from which he is further distanced by the realization that there is an alien intelligence sharing his body. *Why Call Them Back from Heaven?* (1967) is one of his most ambitious efforts. Various medical treatments have made it possible to live almost indefinitely, but the procedures are so expensive that those choosing longevity must devote their lives to acquiring the wealth required to sustain them. At the same time, countless people with incurable diseases are kept in suspended animation. They were originally placed in that state to await the discovery of a cure for their particular ailments, but are now preserved because there are no funds to support their treatment. The dilemma and the ethical questions raised by the novel seem even more relevant today in view of the rapid rise in cost of health care, but the story devolves into a routine chase pitting the protagonist against a corporation that effectively controls the world.

The Goblin Reservation (1968) marked a shift in emphasis even further from traditional genre themes. A scientist returns to Earth and finds that he has been preceded by a duplicate of himself. The mix of fantastic and rational elements worked remarkably well this time, but subsequent novels using the same mix were less successful. *Out of Their Minds* (1970) posed an interesting situation: The mass mind of the human race begins to physically manifest some creatures of the imagination.

Unfortunately, Simak was unable to make effective use of his premise. *Destiny Doll* (1971) is a minor adventure set on another planet. Simak seemed to be returning to his earliest themes with *A Choice of Gods* (1972), set on a depopulated Earth where descendants of American Indians and robots create a new type of civilization, but this new look at ideas first espoused in *City* was only intermittently successful. Similarly, *Our Children's Children* (1974) involves time travelers from the future, but very quickly devolves into a routine adventure.

Simak began moving his settings off the Earth, probably a bad decision given his ability to bring his earthly settings to such vivid life. *Shakespeare's Planet* (1976) was also slight, although Simak's sense of humor provides some pleasant moments in the story of a man stranded on a very bizarre world. *A Heritage of Stars* (1977) is a similar planetary romance without the humor. *Mastodonia* (1978, also published as *Catface*) marked a partial return to his old form, a time travel story in which researchers studying prehistoric times discover that aliens have secretly placed the Earth under surveillance. *The Visitors* (1980) was an intriguing puzzle story. An oversized box appears mysteriously in a small American town, resisting efforts to analyze its nature or discover its origin. His next novel, *Project Pope* (1981), could have been set on Earth, but was unnecessarily set on another world. Its inhabitants are building an artificial intelligence to serve as their equivalent of the pope. The premise is intriguing, but the story never really comes to grip with the issues it raises.

Simak's last two science fiction novels were particularly disappointing. *Special Deliverance* (1982) involves a college professor plucked out of time into a strange limbo state, and *Highway of Eternity* (1986) is a routine time travel adventure. Late in his career, Simak wrote some fantasy novels, of which *The Fellowship of the Talisman* (1978) is of some interest because it includes an alternate history. Simak's rural settings and disdain for high drama made him a distinct voice in science fiction, but his work rarely appealed to readers who preferred livelier stories. His work enjoys sustained popularity in England, but has been only intermittently available in the United States since his death.

Simmons, Dan
(1948–   )

Dan Simmons began as a writer of horror fiction in the early 1980s. By 1989 he had sharpened his skills and demonstrated his ability to write with equal skill in a variety of formats and voices. Three novels appeared that year, of which the least significant is *Phases of Gravity*, a story about a man who once walked on the Moon and now travels the Earth in an effort to find himself. Much more significant was *Carrion Comfort*, which blends science fiction and horror. A small number of mutants have developed the ability to project themselves into the minds of ordinary humans, controlling their actions for periods of time, drawing on their life energy as a sort of psychic vampire. Smug in their presumed superiority, the mutants turn to violent games as a form of entertainment, the most popular of which is a state of constant internecine warfare, in which they expend their victims' lives with impunity. Although the novel rationalizes all of the fantastic elements, it felt much more like horror fiction and was generally treated as such by readers.

That same year also saw publication of the first book in the HYPERION SERIES, Simmons's most sustained science fiction work to date. *Hyperion* (1989) won a Hugo Award, although the story was not really completed until *The Fall of Hyperion* (1990), with the two books subsequently published in one volume as *The Hyperion Cantos* (1990). A two-part sequel followed, consisting of *Endymion* (1996) and *The Rise of Endymion* (1997). The elaborate scale and complexity of the series has very likely been influential on the careers of Peter HAMILTON, Alastair REYNOLDS, and others.

The Hollow Man (1992) is written on a considerably smaller scale. A man whose wife has managed to dampen his telepathic abilities is left to his own devices following her death. His search for peace is complicated by his knowledge of a brutal killer's activities. *Children of the Night* (1992) is another version of rationalized vampires, this time set in post-Soviet eastern Europe. *Ilium* (2003), the first half of a two-part novel, takes place in a distant future in which some humans have achieved nearly godlike powers. Earth is largely uninhabited and those who do live there are linked by teleportation devices to small segments of the planet's surface. On Mars, highly advanced technology has allowed the residents there to recreate the ancient world in enormous detail, with themselves in the roles of the immortal gods. Elsewhere in the solar system, artificial intelligences mounted in spaceships have evolved their own culture. The novel is inventive and filled with exotic imagery, but, being only half a story, it ends rather than concludes and does not stand well on its own.

Simmons is a fine short story writer as well, although none of his work at that length has achieved the stature of his novels. The best of these tend to be stories of the supernatural, but "Orphans of the Helix" (1999), "On K2 with Kanakaredes" (2001), and "The End of Gravity" (2002) deserve particular attention. Most of these have been collected in *Prayers to Broken Stones* (1990) and *Worlds Enough and Time* (2002).

Siodmak, Curt
(1902–1988)

Curt Siodmak was a German filmmaker and writer whose early work included several novels of which at least one is science fiction. *F.P. 1 Does Not Reply* (1933) originally appeared in German, was translated into English, but has become a story of interest to collectors only. He moved to the United States in the late 1930s and wrote the scripts for a large number of fairly bad science fiction and horror films, but also found time to write one of the classic science fiction horror novels of all time—the inspiration for at least three films. In *Donovan's Brain* (1943) a well-meaning scientist preserves the brain of a megalomaniac businessman who sustains terminal injuries in an automobile accident. The disembodied brain grows unnaturally large and begins to mentally control its benefactor, using him to conduct nefarious business doings. Siodmak brought Doctor Cory back 25 years later for two inferior sequels. In *Hauser's Memory* (1968), which was also made into a motion picture, roughly the same results are achieved by implanting DNA from one man into another, and then, once again, following a brain transplant in *Gabriel's Body* (1992).

Siodmak's interest in space stations had not ended with his first novel. *Riders to the Stars* (1953), novelized by Robert Smith from Siodmak's original screenplay, is a somewhat realistic, though now terribly dated, story about the first tentative trips into the Earth's orbit. *Skyport* (1959), also somewhat dated, is still interesting because of its assessment of the forces that would be brought to bear if a viable space station could be completed. It becomes the focus of conflicts not just between political entities but also between commercial interests and pressure groups, the result of which endangers the future of the project. *City in the Sky* (1974) also involved an orbiting habitat, in this case a prison colony whose inmates rebel against inhumane treatment. Siodmak's remaining science fiction novel, *The Third Ear* (1971), involves a method of inducing telepathy, but the plot is primarily that of a conventional spy thriller. Although most of his novels are of only passing interest, *Donovan's Brain* was an inspired concept that carried considerable power even when ineptly translated to the screen.

The Sirens of Titan
Kurt Vonnegut
(1959)

Kurt VONNEGUT has not been associated with genre fiction for many years, but his early short stories often appeared in science fiction magazines, and his first two novels were published as genre work. Even after he became a mainstream giant, much of his work incorporated fantastic elements. His most overtly speculative novel was this satirical story of a future that anticipated some of the devices that would recur in other novels, including the introduction of the alien Tralfamadoreans, who abduct Billy Pilgrim in *Slaughterhouse Five* (1969).

Vonnegut relentlessly targets collective human pride in the novel, which eventually reveals that all of our history has been manipulated by aliens in order to accomplish a comparatively minor task, the delivery of a spare part. Wilson Rumford and his dog have been caught in a space-time phenomenon

called the chrono-synclastic infundibulum, which causes them to appear on Earth only at short, though predictable, intervals. At other times they exist on the planet Mars, where they are raising a thoroughly programmed army whose purpose is to frighten the Earth and create a new religion, a theme that crops up several times in Vonnegut's fiction. In *Slaughterhouse Five*, the message is that God exists, but that he is completely indifferent to the human race. The war between Mars and Earth, the former represented by a brainwashed army foredoomed to failure, is designed to so thoroughly arouse the disgust of the survivors that humans will abandon warfare ever after.

The story is filled with various absurdities, including a form of life on Mercury that looks like dandruff, a financier who makes a fortune by basing his financial decisions on biblical passages, and other implausibilities that somehow become believable in Vonnegut's strange and sarcastically described reality. Even Rumford, who stage-manages events from behind the scenes and at times appears to be a kind of demigod, is simply a tool for larger forces we never clearly see. Vonnegut went on to produce novels that were more skillfully written and emotionally convincing, but this early satire remains one of his most memorable and readable works.

Skylark series
Edward E. Smith

Edward E. SMITH is best remembered for his LENSMAN SERIES, which forever changed the way science fiction writers represented interstellar societies. He also wrote a shorter, more compact set of stories about inventor Richard Seaton and his arch-nemesis Blacky Duquesne. *The Skylark of Space* (magazine version in 1928, but not in book form until 1946) was originally credited as a collaboration between the author and Lee Garby, although her name was dropped after a much later revision. The novel is a rather simplistic and straightforward adventure in which two scientists, one good and one bad, both exploit the discovery of a faster than light drive and carry their rivalry into outer space. The novel employs considerable superscience—weapons and forces developed almost as magical objects, with no grounding in actual science—and the characters are the typical stereotypes of their time.

Skylark Three (magazine version in 1930, first book edition in 1948) and *Skylark of Valeron* (magazine version in 1934, book edition in 1949) continued the story, although in many ways the sequels were both reprises of the first novel. Seaton manages to help solve a planetary crisis in the first and then discovers a planet where a dimensional anomaly alters reality. Duquesne continues to hamper his efforts to do good, and in each instance Seaton must develop a new technological wonder in order to succeed. Although the trilogy seems almost unreadable by modern standards, it was very popular and mildly ground-breaking when it first appeared, spawning various imitations, including the Arcot, Morey, and Wade series by John W. CAMPBELL JR.

Late in his career, Smith added a fourth volume. *Skylark Duquesne* (1966) features an intergalactic war that forces Seaton to accept an alliance with the somewhat reformed Duquesne. Although Smith made some effort to modernize his writing by providing more characterization and less techno-babble, his strengths did not lie in that direction. Only the villainous Duquesne acquired any real depth. The final novel is more interesting as a nostalgic journey back to an earlier form than as a contemporary work. The Skylark series popularized the conceit that humanity would somehow become the catalyst for change in a wider inhabited universe, and it is one that has dominated science fiction ever since.

Sladek, John
(1937–2000)

It has always been unusual for humorous science fiction to attract serious attention. Writers who specialize in the comic, even when it is for satirical purposes, experience much greater difficulty finding an audience than do even markedly inferior writers who employ serious themes. John Sladek, who began writing in the 1960s, was one of the handful of American writers who became

associated with the British New Wave movement. Even after that experiment had run its course, Sladek continued to sell primarily in British markets, and several of his books have yet to find a publisher in the United States.

Sladek's first novel was *The Reproductive System* (1968, also published as *Mechasm*), in which a new, self repairing and reproducing automated system gets out of control and begins manufacturing multiple copies of itself at an exponentially increasing rate. The image of technology out of control would prove to be a frequently recurring theme in Sladek's work, and there are echoes of it in his second novel, *The Muller Fokker Effect* (1970). The protagonist in this case agrees to participate in an experiment in which his personality will be uploaded into a computer. Something goes wrong, and his body is accidentally destroyed, leaving him trapped in his new environment. Sladek, who had also written suspense novels with Thomas DISCH, almost abandoned the novel form during the 1970s, except for two detective stories, one a Sherlock Holmes pastiche.

His first short story collection, *The Steam-Driven Boy and Other Strangers* (1973), consisted almost entirely of satires and has never been available in the United States, nor has his second collection, *Keep the Giraffe Burning* (1978). Sladek returned to novel writing with *Roderick* (1980) and *Roderick at Random* (1982), actually a single story in two volumes, whose various editions have not been consistent about the break point. An experimental robot is placed with a foster family to see how it interacts with ordinary humans, with frequently hilarious results. *Tik-Tok* (1983) follows the adventures of another robot who malfunctions and becomes capable of inflicting harm on humans, but once again the author's purpose is satirical. His last novel, *Bugs* (1989), was his most thematically serious.

Sladek's short stories have more impact as a body than they do individually, although a few stand out from the rest, particularly "Report on the Migration of Educational Matter" (1968), "The Man Who Devoured Books" (1971), and "The Steam Driven Boy" (1972). Later collections of his short stories include *The Best of John Sladek* (1981) and *The Lunatics of Terra* (1984).

Slan
A. E. van Vogt
(1940)

Most of the novels of A. E. VAN VOGT have not aged well. His work was characterized by wide-ranging ideas, time travel and its paradoxes, galactic empires, superhumans, psi powers, and virtually every plot device popular in the pulp magazines of that time. His narrative structure was intricate and suggested a depth to his work that probably was more illusion than reality, using non-linear plotting, multiple viewpoint characters, and sudden reversals or revelations to keep the reader guessing.

The most notable exception was *Slan*, his first novel, which appeared in book form in 1946, and which remains his best-known creation. *Slan* is in part a coming-of-age story that involves secret plots and psi powers, handled in a much less melodramatic fashion than in his later work. Jommy Cross is a slan, a mutant, part of a deliberately created variation of humans who were designed originally to help solve a series of crises that threatened the entire human race. Because slans are physically and mentally superior to normal humans, even without their psi powers, they eventually became the objects of fear and hatred and were driven underground, hunted, and killed by normals.

Cross survives when his mother is captured and subsequently killed, living on his own and eventually growing to maturity, reconciled to a secret life. As an adult, he encounters more of his kind, including a young slan girl with whom he falls in love, and a subset of mutants whose powers are imperfect, but who almost constitute a third strain of humanity. Earth is a dictatorship, and Cross eventually decides to investigate the mysterious figure who is the current ruler. He discovers to his surprise that the man is another slan, and the father of the girl he loves. This is an example of the implausible coincidences common in the author's work, which were largely forgiven by science fiction readers of that time.

Part of the appeal of the novel was its reflection of the situation of many of the genre's most loyal readers during the 1950s. Science fiction still catered primarily to adolescent males and young boys who spent much of their time reading. This audience sympathized with characters who found themselves in the role of the outcast. It was easy for them to identify with a character alienated from almost everyone else in the world, and the phrase "fans are slans" was in wide use even in the 1970s.

Slaughterhouse-Five
Kurt Vonnegut
(1969)

Kurt Vonnegut, who started his career writing for science fiction magazines and was generally considered to be a genre writer, very quickly demonstrated that he had a wider appeal to mainstream readers. His novels, always satirical rather than conventional adventure stories, began to move away from genre standards. The fantastic element, although often important, became less central to the story he was attempting to tell. His best novel, *Slaughterhouse-Five,* was the last of his books to be openly referred to as science fiction, although most of his subsequent work was at least marginally within the genre.

The protagonist is Billy Pilgrim, a modest young man who served in World War II. He was captured and imprisoned in Dresden, Germany, during the period in which that city was virtually destroyed by Allied fire bombing, an experience that the character shares with his author. After the war, Billy returns to America, marries and raises a family, and pursues a successful career as a businessman, until he is murdered by a crazed man whom he encountered during the war. Everything seems normal, but Billy has a secret, one that he divulges from time to time, although no one believes him. Billy has become unstuck in time, and his consciousness jumps around from past to present to future. Among those experiences is his abduction by aliens from the planet Tralfamadore, who keep him on display for a time for purposes of their own.

Billy's episodes of disorientation could be explained rationally, of course, if it were not for the fact that he correctly anticipates future events. He is resigned to his fate, because time is immutable, and he knows how things will end. Vonnegut uses Pilgrim's life not to tell a linear narrative, but as a way to comment upon perceived shortcomings in the way we treat one another, most notably in times of war. Many of the incidents he describes are profoundly moving observations of humanity at its best and worst. The aliens, who never appear on stage, are a plot device and are not central to the novel, which mixes genuine tragedy with some of Vonnegut's most sophisticated comedy.

Slonczewski, Joan
(1956–   )

Joan Slonczewski's debut novel, *Still Forms on Fox-field* (1980), was highly original and unusually convincing in its depiction of life on a world jointly shared by indigenous aliens and human colonists. Civilization on Earth had reached a crisis, and a party of Quakers left our planet to form this new society, which carefully balances technology and the environment, and appreciates the rights and feelings of the primitive natives. Earth manages to recover from its problems, however, and sends a ship to reopen contact. This precipitates a new crisis among the settlers, who would have preferred not to be found. Although favorably reviewed, the novel caused little stir, and several years passed before her next book appeared.

There is a very similar setup in *A Door into Ocean* (1986), which became the first of the Elysium novels. This time the colonists are all women, who are forced to resist an invasion by an aggressive male-dominated culture. The frank treatment of feminist themes as well as a definite talent for creating and bringing to life alternate human cultures contributed to the novel's popularity. Slonczewski did not prove to be a particularly prolific writer, however, and her next novel, *The Wall Around Eden*, did not appear until 1989. This time the setting is post-apocalyptic Earth, whose inhabitants receive the apparent assistance of a race of insectlike aliens, although the true motives of the visitors are not readily apparent.

Slonczewski's three subsequent novels were set in the Elysium universe first described in *A*

Door into Ocean. Daughter of Elysium (1993) deals with a planet whose inhabitants seem to have discovered the secret of immortality. It intelligently examines questions of longevity and population growth, and the clash of cultures with different value systems and life-styles. *The Children Star* (1998) follows the efforts of a colony of orphans who seek knowledge of a secretive alien race, which may be asserting direct control over their planet's ecosystem. A microscopic form of life with group intelligence is spreading through the galaxy by colonizing human bodies in *Brain Plague* (2000). The author's only published short story, "Microbe" (1995), is also set in the Elysium universe.

"Slow Sculpture"
Theodore Sturgeon
(1970)

No science fiction writer has ever been able to consistently equal the strong emotional content of Theodore STURGEON's stories or the complexity of the psychology and interpersonal relationships of his characters. Stories like "THE (WIDGET), THE (WADGET) AND BOFF," "BULKHEAD," and "THUNDER AND ROSES" demonstrated a remarkable insight into human behavior, and an enviable ability to transform those insights into gripping, intelligently conceived stories. "Slow Sculpture," which won both the Hugo and Nebula Awards, comes from late in Sturgeon's career and is one of his best.

The two characters remain unnamed throughout the story. One is a young woman who has recently concluded, correctly as it turns out, that a lump in her breast is terminal cancer. The other is a reclusive genius, an inventor who has retreated from the world and now devotes much of his time to the cultivation of bonsai, which is on one level the "slow sculpture" of the title. Sturgeon describes the production of bonsai as a mutual effort, requiring the cooperation of the tree as well as the efforts of the human. This becomes part of a larger metaphor as the story progresses.

The woman arrives in his orchard randomly, following a panic attack, which he explains as a survival mechanism. When reason fails to offer an answer to our problems, panic compels us to search for unreasonable solutions, and sometimes we succeed. That is the case this time, because the inventor has a remarkable treatment for cancer, which he uses to cure her. When she protests that he should make his knowledge public, this provides the excuse in the narrative for an indictment of human shortsightedness. Since his treatment depends upon unfamiliar principles, he explains, it would be attacked rather than welcomed, and he might even be arrested for practicing medicine without a license. As further proof, the inventor tells her the reason why he is so wealthy. He sold an invention that made fuel more efficient and less polluting, and his discovery was suppressed by the automobile and oil industries. As a consequence, he has an aversion toward society at large and to close personal contact in particular.

The ending is subtle and understated, without any dramatic revelation or alteration of his viewpoint. She convinces him to think of human relationships in the same way as he thinks of bonsai: Sometimes it is the most twisted and unattractive individuals who have the most potential. For a human friendship to develop, it must be through the efforts of both parties. What follows from that conclusion, Sturgeon wisely leaves to the reader's imagination.

Smith, Cordwainer
(1913–1966)

Cordwainer Smith was the pseudonym of Paul Linebarger, a specialist in political science who spent extensive time in Asia and who wrote three mainstream novels under other pen names. Although his first science fiction story appeared in 1928, he would not return to that form until the appearance of "SCANNERS LIVE IN VAIN" (1948), the first of his stories of the Instrumentality, a complex future history in which star travel is dangerous because of the existence of discorporate and malevolent intelligences. Space travel is achieved in safety only after humans learn to enhance the intelligence of certain lower animals and develop their own psi powers. Smith began to develop the concept in more detail with a series of short stories

during the 1950s, including excellent tales like "THE GAME OF RAT AND DRAGON" (1955).

Smith hit his stride as a short story writer during the 1960s, producing one classic tale after another, most of them set in the Instrumentality universe. The Instrumentality begins as a rigid dictatorship. The uplifted animals are virtually slaves, and the repressive rulers tighten their grip by discovering and monopolizing the secret of immortality. Opposed to the rule of the Instrumentality are the Underpeople, an amorphous rebel group consisting of humans and uplifted animals. Smith never directly resolves this conflict, although some of his stories appear to be set in a distant future in which the inequities of the Instrumentality have been largely overcome. Stories like "The Lady Who Sailed the Soul" (1960), "A Planet Named Shayol" (1961), "The Ballad of Lost C'Mell" (1962), and "The Dead Lady of Clown Town" (1964) expanded and embellished Smith's universe while telling distinct and often emotionally moving stories. His first collection, You Will Never Be the Same (1963), mixed Instrumentality stories with others not in the series.

The Planet Buyer (1964) was the first Instrumentality novel. The protagonist has literally purchased the Earth, but when he sets out to visit his new property, he discovers that various people would much prefer it if he failed to arrive. It was meant to be published jointly with the collection, The Underpeople (1968). Eventually they did appear in one volume as Norstrilia (1975). Several other collections followed including Space Lords (1965), Under Old Earth and Other Explorations (1970), and Stardreamer (1971), which in combination reprinted virtually all of Smith's short fiction. Virtually the same contents were later recombined as The Best of Cordwainer Smith (1975, also published as The Rediscovery of Man) and The Instrumentality of Mankind (1979). A subset of stories set in the latter days of the Instrumentality formed the quasi-novel, Quest of Three Worlds (1966). An even more comprehensive omnibus volume, also titled The Rediscovery of Man, appeared in 1993.

The proliferation of titles disguises the fact that Smith's actual output was quite small, which makes his high stature among genre writers even more impressive. He had a distinct narrative style that often makes the reader accept a situation that might otherwise seem ludicrous, like a love affair between a human and a semi-intelligent cat. Many of his characters seem to have stepped out of a legend, although without losing their human qualities. Images from genuine legends, like the Trojan Horse, occur periodically in his work. Although there is an element of satire in most of the stories, it is subtle and never approaches parody. We always care about what is happening because he makes even the most bizarre situations seem real. Smith was one of a handful of writers whose literary sensibilities dramatically transformed science fiction during the 1960s, and the fact that he is rarely imitated is an indication of the uniqueness of his talent and not of a lack of influence on his fellow writers.

Smith, Edward E.
(1890–1965)

Edward E. "Doc" Smith was a writer whose popularity has varied dramatically over the course of time, but whose influence on the development of science fiction is undeniable. The view of the universe and of galactic civilizations that he developed in the LENSMAN SERIES during the 1930s transformed the genre, and virtually all subsequent space opera owes at least a portion of its concepts to Smith. Although the scientific content of his stories usually consisted of techno-babble and references to mysterious and never described principles unknown to our time, Smith achieved a sense of wonder and mystery in his stories that spawned imitations like the Arcot, Morey, and Wade series by John W. CAMPBELL JR. and The Cosmic Engineers (1938) by Clifford D. SIMAK. None of these would ever rival his original creation.

Smith's first novel was The Skylark of Space (1928), which began the shorter and less impressive SKYLARK SERIES. The scale of events was considerably smaller than in the Lensman series, concentrating primarily on the rivalry between two human scientists, Richard Seaton and Blacky Duquesne, the latter of whom is the recurring villain, though partially redeemed much later on. The Lensman

books were much more influential, populating an entire galaxy with disparate races. Smith became largely inactive during the 1940s, although that was when his novels first were published in book form. Readers were willing to forgive the implausibilities in his plots, the simplicity of his prose, and the flatness of his characters in order to share his vision of a community of intelligent species.

One early stand-alone novel, Spacehounds of IPC, is of some interest. Serialized in 1931 (and in book form in 1947), it is the story of a mission in space that encounters trouble and eventually strands its crew on Ganymede. The scale and melodrama were much more restrained than in Smith's other fiction from this period. Despite the awkward characterizations and clumsy prose, the novel is surprisingly entertaining. A few short stories appeared during the 1950s, some of which were turned into series by other writers. During the 1970s, Gordon Eklund wrote four novels based on the character Tedric, a heroic figure who battled in outer space and on alternate worlds. Stephen Goldin wrote eight novels during the 1970s and 1980s about the family D'Alembert, a traveling circus group that was actually a front for agents of the galactic empire. The first of these novels included substantial material by Smith, but the subsequent volumes were Goldin's work in their entirety. David Kyle and William B. Ellern would add new volumes to the Lens series during the same period.

Smith himself resumed writing novels with The Galaxy Primes (1965), an episodic space adventure about a ship that travels about the galaxy. Although Smith attempted to modify his style to meet contemporary expectations, the novel seemed anomalous—too old fashioned to stand on its own merits; too ambitious to satisfy those who sought a nostalgic return to simpler times. Skylark Duquesne (1966), although considerably better, suffered from many of the same problems, and the effort to reform Blacky Duquesne emphasized only that the days of such simply defined characters and situations was long past.

Subspace Explorers (1965) suggested that Smith might yet prove capable of adapting to the new standards of the field, although the novel itself is quite minor. After all of the truly innovative minds have left Earth to find a new life in the stars, the home world has fallen under the sway of a repressive new government. A sequel, *Subspace Encounter* (1983), was completed posthumously by Lloyd Eshbach. *Masters of Space* (1979) is another story of a galactic empire, in which a human-dominated planet is pitted against various others led by disparate alien races, in response to which humans begin to develop psi powers.

Smith's short fiction was collected as *The Best of E. E. "Doc" Smith* (1975), but contains no significant work. As an innovator and storyteller, Smith was the most important figure of his time, possibly the single most influential writer other than H. G. WELLS in the genre's history because of the way he gave form to a collective view of the universe that has been pervasive in science fiction ever since.

Smith, George O.
(1911–1981)

George O. Smith began writing space adventures with an engineering slant during the 1940s, including a then popular series of short stories that was collected as *Venus Equilateral* (1947). By the end of that decade, most of his writing took the form of novels, many of them routine space operas like *Pattern of Conquest* (1949) and *Operation Interstellar* (1950), the latter heavily influenced by the work of Edward E. SMITH. The most interesting novel from this period is *Nomad* (1950), the story of a war between humans and aliens, fought within the confines of our solar system. *Troubled Star* (1957) somewhat amusingly anticipated the film *Galaxy Quest* (2000) in that representatives of a galactic civilization incorrectly interpret the broadcast of a television program and kidnap an actor, believing him to be an authority figure.

Hellflower (1953) marked the beginning of a change in Smith's writing, with stronger emphasis on characterization. The protagonist becomes a fugitive on a now unrealistically portrayed Venus, and must become a master criminal in order to escape. *Lost in Space* (1959) is a quietly understated story of two people adrift in space and the efforts made to rescue them. *Highways in Hiding* (1955, published in shorter form as *Space Plague*) was

Smith's first significant novel, although marred by a somewhat overcomplicated plot. Telepathy has become common on Earth, but a new plague apparently originating in outer space seems to be causing rapid mutation and possibly the end of humanity. *A Fire in the Heavens* (1958) involves the panic that results when the sun appears on the verge of becoming a nova and destroying the Earth.

Smith's last and most important novel was *The Fourth "R"* (1959, also published as *The Brain Machine*). Jimmy Holden is a young boy with extraordinary intelligence, thanks to an experimental process, although his personality is not typical of the egotistical superman. When his parents are murdered, the boy must fend for himself and eventually track down the parties responsible, but only after devising a clever means of maintaining his independence. Smith does a remarkably adept job at introducing the reader to the intricacies of Holden's mind, and the boy remains one of the more vividly realized characters in the genre's history.

Smith's occasional short fiction is largely forgettable, but "The Big Fix" and "Meddler's Moon" are both quite clever. The best of his short fiction can be found in *The Worlds of George O. Smith* (1982).

Smith, L. Neil
(1946–)

Although L. Neil Smith's first published appearance was a short story in 1980, almost all of his published fiction since then has consisted of novels. Smith is perhaps the best known writer of libertarian science fiction, although not the best known libertarian writer of science fiction. He established his political credentials with his first novel, *The Probability Broach* (1980), which initiated the North American Confederation series. The protagonist, Win Bear, is a police detective whose investigations lead him into an alternate world where the American colonies never revolted and intelligent chimpanzees intermingle with humans. Bear's adventures continue in *The Venus Belt* (1981), wherein a plague of sudden violent crime in the alternate reality leads him to believe that someone else has discovered the gateway between worlds.

Their Majesties' Bucketeers (1981) started another series, space adventures revolving around the *Tom Paine Maru*. In the first installment, the murder of a prominent alien precipitates an interstellar crisis. The crew's adventures continue in *Tom Paine Maru* (1984), this time testing their ethical standards when they are forced to choose between their loyalty to Earth and their obligations to a religious order that saved them from certain death. Both are entertaining stories, but two later sequels are ponderous and considerably less interesting. An experimental starship must be recovered when it is stolen in *Brightsuit Macbear* (1988), leading to further complications in humanity's relationship with alien civilizations. During an expedition to a newly discovered planet, a crew finds more than they bargained for when they investigate the secrets of an ancient civilization in *Taflak Lysandra* (1988), which is only loosely attached to the main sequence. Smith's two series become intertwined, and the descendants of characters from the Confederation series appear in the Maru sequence.

The Nagasaki Vector (1983) is another variation of the stranded time traveler story, this time leaving a tour group in medieval Japan. Smith found time to write a trilogy of novels around the character of Lando Calrissian from the *Star Wars* movies. He then picked up the North American Confederation series with *The Gallatin Divergence* (1985), in which time travelers in that alternate world attempt to return to a critical point in history and prevent the execution of George Washington so that he can survive and lead a successful rebellion against the British throne. Their adventures make up the best installment in this series, which is less frequently interrupted for political statements than the other volumes. The most recent addition, *The American Zone* (2001), explores no new ground. *The Wardove* (1986) is a more brooding and less adventurous story set in the aftermath of the destruction of Earth, with the remnants of human civilization living primarily on the Moon.

The Crystal Empire (1986) is set in a different alternate universe, one in which Europe never became preeminent, and the Americas are dominated by a Sino-Aztec alliance. One of the escorts of a visiting princess is a secret heretic whose beliefs place his life in danger. *Henry Martyn* (1989) and its belated sequel, *Bretta Martyn* (1997), make up a formulaic libertarian wish-fulfillment sequence in which a man grows embittered by the iniquities of a galactic empire, is driven to mutiny and piracy, and finds greater freedom outside the limits of government. The sequel follows the efforts of the protagonist's daughter to survive the attempts by their mutual enemies to destroy her. *Pallas* (1993) also flavors interstellar politics with libertarianism, sacrificing plausibility in favor of expediency.

Smith's one remaining series consists of *Contact and Commune* (1990), *Converse and Conflict* (1990), and *Forge of the Elders* (2001). A human race dominated by communists encounters an asteroid colonized by aliens from another dimension. Since the aliens have a capitalist economy, contact between the two proves troublesome. This sequence in particular illustrates Smith's greatest weakness as a writer. When he concentrates on his stories, which are often enlivened by a mild sense of humor, and allows his political statements to slip in only when they fit, he is remarkably entertaining. When his intention is primarily polemical, and the narrative seems almost to have been added after the fact, the results are plodding, unconvincing, and certainly not entertaining.

Snow Crash
Neal Stephenson
(1992)

Sometimes an author can create an imaginary universe that is so original and interesting that readers clamor for more. Larry NIVEN returned to the RINGWORLD, Frank HERBERT chronicled the history of a unique planet in the DUNE SERIES, and Isaac ASIMOV added to the FOUNDATION SERIES decades after the original trilogy had been written. Sometimes it is more effective to resist that temptation, which appears to be the case with Neal STEPHENSON's brilliant version of virtual reality. *Snow Crash* is also a marvelously satirical novel, published at a time when exaggerated satires have fallen out of favor.

The setting is a future America, but an America and a world that are only remotely recognizable. The old concept of national borders has been lost forever. Countries, as well as corporations and other organizations that function as countries, can purchase isolated plots of land and incorporate them into their sovereign territory, even though they are not physically contiguous. The world has become a place where advertising and commercialization dominate every other human activity, and where the Mafia has become a quasi-legal organization. The protagonist is a high-tech pizza delivery man and part-time computer hacker, who teams up with a teenaged messenger girl to track down a murderer who functions in cyberspace as well as the real world. They avert a major global data crisis in the process.

One of the difficulties in writing a novel in which events are stretched out to improbable extremes is in creating characters who are more than caricatures and can generally engage the interest of the reader. That Stephenson is able to involve the reader emotionally with the two main characters is a testament to his extraordinary ability to illuminate the core elements of a personality and make them real, even when surrounded by absurdities. Not coincidentally, the sequences that take place in his marvelously realized virtual world are in many ways more realistic than those that take place on the objective plane.

The novel is rich in texture and well-plotted. There are undercurrents of Sumerian mythology, speculation about the nature of language, and the identification of raw information as the essence of everything else in a society. Although often described as a cyberpunk novel, *Snow Crash* transcends that simple characterization, and its upbeat conclusion demonstrates that Stephenson is traveling his own course and not following in the footsteps of others.

A Song for Lya
George R. R. Martin
(1974)

With a few exceptions, science fiction tends to be very conservative on the subject of religion. Churches may be corrupt, or subverted by external forces, but most tales of the future ignore the subject altogether, or simply use an updated form of an existing religion as part of the background. Alien religions, if discussed at all, are almost always intentionally unconvincing. The premise of this novelette is quite the opposite.

The inhabitants of the planet Shkeen have been civilized since before humans began using tools, but they have never developed much in the way of technology, and are still confined to their home planet. Although they welcome the presence of a human settlement on their world and are hospitable to the newcomers, they demonstrate no interest in leaving Shkeen. The native religion is, by human standards, repulsive, but it is universally accepted among the aliens. At some point in their lives, they willingly Join with a parasitic animal, after which they become wandering pilgrims in a state of bliss that appears almost drugged. After an indeterminate period, they move on to the Final Union, in which they enter the caves where much larger versions of the parasite live and allow themselves to be eaten. The current human administrator, who is actively attempting to understand the local culture, is unhappy about the fact that a few humans have converted to the Shkeen religion, and the rate of conversion is on the increase.

To investigate, he hires two psi-talented operatives, Lya and Robb. The couple, who are intensely in love, have telepathic and empathic powers, respectively. They discover that those who are Joined are completely happy. Lya in particular is affected by the contact, which reveals to her a degree of love toward other individuals that is so refined and perfect that she begins to doubt her own relationship with Robb. Their subsequent conversations pose several tantalizing questions, such as whether or not we can truly know one another, and whether changing to please the expectations of someone else is actually an indication of our differences rather than our similarities.

Lya becomes increasingly tempted by the religion of the Shkeen, which she now accepts as authentic. Everyone who dies during Final Union is somehow preserved in a group mind shared among the parasites, and the feelings of mutual love and respect seem genuine. Although she appeals to

Robb to follow her, he ultimately rejects conversion and seeks solace elsewhere. It later becomes clear that he is no longer sure he made the correct choice. The author wisely leaves final judgment on the matter to the reader.

"A Sound of Thunder"
Ray Bradbury
(1952)

Although many of Ray BRADBURY's stories are technically science fiction, he was never particularly interested in the scientific content except when it provided him with the means to tell a particular kind of story or make a particular point. The Mars he describes in THE MARTIAN CHRONICLES (1950), for example, was physically impossible and internally inconsistent. The same is true of this time travel story, but readers were able to overlook the logical fallacies because the story itself was so engaging. Other writers would produce notable stories of safaris back through time to the age of the dinosaurs, most notably L. Sprague DE CAMP in "A GUN FOR DINOSAUR" (1956), but none would capture the essence of the time travel paradox so perfectly.

In "A Sound of Thunders," a wealthy man named Eckles has bought a place among a group who will be traveling back to prehistory on a hunting expedition. His guide explains the rules in detail. They will wear environmental suits so that they cannot inadvertently carry a disease back to the past, and they will conduct the hunt from an elevated metal platform, because it might be dangerous to so much as touch a blade of grass. Bradbury provides an excellent description of the ripple effect, showing how one minor change can multiply over thousands of generations until it has the potential to change the world beyond recognition. Hunters are allowed to kill only dinosaurs that have been marked with a paint bomb. These dinosaurs have been selected because a previous survey indicated that they would die very soon anyway. Although this supposedly gets around the ripple effect, it quite obviously does not—a flaw in logic that Bradbury himself undoubtedly recognized.

Eckles panics when a tyrannosaurus appears and he falls off the platform. Although the creature is killed, the guide is enraged because Eckles may have altered the future. In the world they just left, a hotly contested election resulted in the defeat of a would-be dictator, but when they return, there are subtle changes in the room, which they can recognize as differences for reasons the author never explains. The most significant change is that the election turned out differently. The alteration of history occurred because, when Eckles left the path, he inadvertently stepped on and killed a butterfly. The story is the classic example of one interpretation of the nature of time, and inspired a motion picture version in 2004.

The Space Merchants
Frederik Pohl and Cyril M. Kornbluth
(1953)

This collaborative team would write four science fiction novels and several short stories together, but their major achievement was this satirical novel of the future of advertising. At the time, it seemed wildly exaggerated but it feels almost realistic in the contemporary world. It originally appeared in Galaxy Magazine in shorter form under the title "Gravy Planet." Because of their ability to manipulate public opinion, the advertising agencies of the world have effectively become the government, acting in consort despite their private rivalries. This collective government decides that a solution to overpopulation and cultural unrest can be found in space, specifically on the planet Venus. The only shortcoming of the plan is that Venus is a harsh, inhospitable place to which few would willingly immigrate.

The solution, predictably, is to engineer an advertising campaign that will convince people that Venus is a desirable destination, free of the pressures of Earth, a near paradise waiting to be populated. The protagonist is an executive at one of the advertising agencies who feels torn between his desire to do a good job and impress his peers—and more importantly his superiors—and a growing sense that perhaps there is something morally wrong with misleading people. Although his internal conflict provides much of the surface action, the novel actually focuses on the morality of using false or incomplete information to shape public opinion and deprive people of making informed decisions about their individual or collective futures. This is a concern even more relevant today than it was when the novel was first written.

Frederik POHL would write a solo sequel many years later. *The Merchants' War* (1984) is set after several years have passed, and ignores what we have subsequently learned about physical conditions on Venus. The settlements have prospered despite the marked variance from the description that lured the colonists from Earth. Unrest is growing, however, and a war of rebellion breaks out, pitting the settlers against an Earth that is still governed by a consortium of advertising agencies. Although physical force is an option, the government decides to use a more familiar weapon, launching a new advertising campaign designed to quell dissent. The two novels were published in a single volume as *Venus, Inc.* (1985).

The Space Vampires
Colin Wilson
(1976)

Although probably best known for his fiction and non-fiction about criminals and the occult, Colin Wilson wrote a fairly large body of science fiction, including *The Mind Parasites* (1967)—a pastiche of the work of H. P. LOVECRAFT—and the Spider World series set on a future Earth dominated by spiderlike aliens. His most successful genre novel is *The Space Vampires*, which modifies a traditional horror theme in a new setting.

Carlsen is the commander of a spaceship that encounters an alien craft carrying what initially appears to be a small number of human beings held in suspended animation. The truth, revealed to the reader and to the world in due course, is that these are actually aliens from the Rigel system. These aliens are a perverted subset of an otherwise moral species, who prolong their own lives by literally drawing the lifeforce out of other living beings. The human race provides a storehouse of this sustaining force. Before long the authorities

are alerted to the menace, but are apparently powerless to stop the intruders.

It is interesting to contrast the novel to the film version, *Lifeforce* (1985), which turned the plot into a well-done but routine thriller. In the film, Carlsen learns how to destroy the creatures, who seem to have visited Earth before, giving rise to the legends of vampires. Although much of London is devastated in the process, the creatures are ultimately destroyed by human hands. The novel reaches much the same conclusion, but by a very different path. Carlsen is instrumental in their destruction, but only because he serves as a kind of mental go-between for the good Rigellians, who seek to rein in their evil-minded fellows. The novel was reprinted as *Lifeforce* to coincide with the motion picture.

As with most of his work, Wilson draws on a broad background in occult studies, mythology, and human psychology. His characters react realistically to even the most unrealistic situations. The influence of Lovecraft is openly acknowledged although it is usually manifested in the tone and atmosphere of Wilson's fiction, rather than the specifics. Although space travel sets up the situation, Wilson is obviously more at ease when the story takes place in contemporary England. The novel ends on a hopeful note. In addition to the destruction of the evil aliens, Carlsen learns that humanity has in itself the potential for a healthier form of immortality.

Spinrad, Norman
(1940–   )

Although his first few stories in the 1960s were quite conventional, Norman Spinrad became one of the handful of American writers who were associated with the British New Wave movement, even contributing to the career of Jerry Cornelius as created by Michael MOORCOCK. His stories became increasingly complex and innovative in very short order, particularly "CARCINOMA ANGELS" and "THE LAST HURRAH OF THE GOLDEN HORDE," but his first two novels were surprisingly straightforward space operas. *The Solarians* (1966) puts humans on the losing side of an interstellar war and *Agent of Chaos* (1967) involves a possible threat to the human race in a future in which the government is run by professional assassins. Although neither novel was up to the standards of his short fiction, *The Men in the Jungle* (1967) hinted at the shape Spinrad's future would take. An offworlder attempts to assist the people of the planet Sangre who wish to overthrow a repressive autocracy that uses torture, violence, and even cannibalism to retain its hold on power. The protagonist believes himself confirmed in his own beliefs about ethical behavior, but exposure to local conditions leads him to doubt himself. The concentration on the internal conflict of the central character, in preference to the physical struggles surrounding him, would become common in Spinrad's subsequent work.

His next novel, BUG JACK BARRON (1969), was a near-future satire in which a controversial television personality battles a powerful businessman. Although the novel is excellent, much of its impact was caused by the controversy over its explicit sexual content and heavy use of profanity. When it appeared, Spinrad immediately became a major player in the genre, although opinions were sharply divided between those who were revolted by his subject matter and those who admired his boldness. His next novel, although less successful, was equally startling. Most of *The Iron Dream* (1972) is the manuscript of a science fiction novel supposedly written by Adolf Hitler, in an alternate universe where he failed in politics and became a pulp writer. The novel savagely satirizes some of the more conservative aspects of the genre, including the fascination with military adventures and technology and the disdain for the soft sciences.

Two short story collections followed, which maintained his consistently high standards and stylistically diverse contents: *The Last Hurrah of the Golden Horde* (1970) and *No Direction Home* (1975), along with the short novel *Riding the Torch* (1974). Although most of his output after this was at novel length, occasional shorter works have continued to appear including "Journal of the Plague Years" (1988) and others. Subsequent collections appeared at regular intervals: *The Star Spangled Future* (1979), *Other Americas* (1988),

Vampire Junkies (1994), and *Deus X and Other Stories* (2003).

The novel, *A World Between* (1979), is a thoughtful study of an isolated society and the tensions caused when it loses that insulation. A world cut off from the rest of humanity develops what is close to a utopian civilization, but proves less than resilient when outsiders arrive and begin using the media to foment dissident opinions. The troublemakers represent both extremes of the political spectrum. *Songs from the Stars* (1980) is set several generations after a global war has wrecked the modern world. The new world government rules by means of what it claims is genuine magic, but rebels know the truth and agitate for a restoration of reason and the development of technology. There is also a conflict over the possible use of a system of satellites because doing so requires reactivation of equipment that contributes to atmospheric pollution.

The Void Captain's Tale (1983) employed explicit sexual content again, but the field had changed so dramatically in the previous decade that it was no longer considered controversial. A starship powered by sexual energy travels to an unexplored region of the galaxy. Although not strictly speaking a sequel, *Child of Fortune* (1985) is set in the same universe. Both novels are essentially journeys of wonder and episodic in structure, with the first being marginally more cohesive and interesting, and the second amusing because of its frequent allusions to the hippie subculture of the 1960s. With little overt action, the novels were puzzling to many traditional genre readers, but Spinrad's complex narrative and in-depth characterization was welcomed by a more sophisticated audience.

Little Heroes (1987) describes the future as a passive dystopia. Corporations have continued the trend toward extra-nationalism and have become more powerful than ever, rivaling governments in their influence. Pollution and overpopulation have become more serious concerns. The gap between the rich and the increasingly numerous poverty-stricken masses has widened. Although there is an optimistic note sounded by the organization of a rebellious underground, the author's bitterness about the trend of current affairs is so intense that it sometimes overshadows the other elements in the novel. Possible discontent is swamped by subtle messages conveyed by the media, diverting the public's attention toward entertainment figures instead of real issues. *Russian Spring* (1991) suggests that America might well descend into an economic twilight, and that the Soviet Union could ultimately evolve into a more open and vigorous culture. The novel illustrates the danger of speculating about too near a future, because the fall of the Soviet Union at approximately the same time as the book appeared reduced it to a curiosity.

The short novel *Deus X* (1993) is an unusual take on virtual reality. Since entire personalities can be transferred into this new media form, officials of the Roman Catholic Church are concerned once again about the precise nature of the soul. *Pictures at 11* (1994) is a marginal thriller set in the near future. A group of journalists volunteer to become hostages for a terrorist group but, disappointed by the passiveness of their captors, eventually provoke them into greater excesses in order to create a more compelling news broadcast. *Greenhouse Summer* (1999) is an intricate, credible, and very effective novel of a polluted near-future world that delivers a powerful, angry message about our unwillingness to take action in a crisis until forced against our collective will.

There are obvious recurring concerns in Spinrad's work. The degradation of our natural environment and our lethargic reaction are portrayed as shortsighted and self-destructive. He is very critical of the way in which the media is used to alter public opinion, and wary of its power. The media might become a vehicle of reform, as in *Bug Jack Barron,* or it could become a tool for destruction, as in *A World Between.* There is also a sense that a state of disorder cannot long prevail, that every evolution in thought or political structure simply moves the components of society into a new arrangement. Spinrad appears to be a writer who is thoroughly familiar with genre forms and traditions, but who is very selective about which of those he will use in his writing. Several of his later novels have been marketed as mainstream works, and he has written several novels that do not fall within the field, although they often involve Spinrad's familiar thematic material as mentioned

previously. Although his work has recently appeared less frequently than in the past, it is always highly polished and thoughtfully constructed. Spinrad seems determined to write for himself rather than for an immediate market.

Stableford, Brian
(1948–   )

Although he had previously sold some short fiction, Brian Stableford made his effective debut with two short novels of the far future, *Cradle of the Sun* (1970) and *The Blind Worm* (1971). Although neither was a major effort, they were filled with unusually evocative images and some clever ideas. Stableford followed up with a trilogy based on the works of Homer, consisting of *Days of Glory* (1971), *In the Kingdom of the Beasts* (1971), and *Days of Wrath* (1971). His transposition of the ancient stories to a conflict among the stars between humans and uplifted beasts seemed amusing but rather overblown. Another minor space opera followed, but then his writing changed direction.

The Hooded Swan series began with *The Halcyon Drift* (1972) and ended with *Swan Song* (1975), encompassing six titles recently reprinted in a single volume as *Swan Songs* (2002). Grainger, the star pilot protagonist, visits various planets, has to deal with a parasite that invades his body, the reclamation of an alien starship with advanced technology, and encounters with various biological puzzles on human colony worlds. Although these are light adventure stories, they were written with a clarity and sureness that attracted considerable attention. Stableford's career seemed assured, although these novels were only hints of the quality of his later work. The Daedalus novels followed, beginning with *The Florians* (1976) and ending with *The Paradox of the Sets* (1979), also six volumes long. Each covers one visit of a starship sent to check on remote colony worlds, each of which is facing a critical problem when the ship arrives. Although the stories follow an obvious formula, the problems faced by the crew are cleverly constructed and resolved in a satisfying fashion.

In *The Mind Riders* (1976) audiences can use advanced technology to share the experiences of sports figures, including the last fight of a professional boxer. *Realms of Tartarus* (1977) was a change of setting as well as tone. Earth became so badly scarred and polluted that the entire surface was covered over with an artificial one and a new civilization built on top of it. The old world never completely died, however, and is filled with mutations and other challenges for the story's characters. This was Stableford's longest and best novel to date, so long in fact that an excerpt was published as a separate novel, *The Face of Heaven*. *Man in a Cage* (1975) demonstrated the author's steadily developing ability to get inside the mind of his characters, this time a schizophrenic who volunteers for the space program. More imaginative but less engaging was *The Walking Shadow* (1979), in which a charismatic religious leader leads his followers into a vision of the distant future.

Stableford returned to space opera with *Optiman* (1980, also published as *War Games*), but this story of the discovery of a superman among a group of researchers was clearly more serious in intent than simple adventure. Similarly, *The Castaways of Tanagar* (1981) bears strong similarities to the Daedalus adventures, but the way in which this particular colony treats its dissidents and other outcasts is clearly meant as a criticism of contemporary attitudes as well. *The Gates of Eden* (1983) resembles the Hooded Swan series, with a spaceship exploring and discovering the secret of a swamp covered world. *Journey to the Center* (1982) poses a scientific problem. Explorers have discovered an artificial world, apparently abandoned, containing evidence of a technology unknown to any of the known intelligent races. Stableford later added two sequels, *Invaders from the Centre* (1990) and *The Centre Cannot Hold* (1990), which added little to the original story.

Stableford produced relatively little fiction during the second half of the 1980s, confining himself to occasional short stories and a pseudonymous game tie-in novel. The one exception was the very impressive *The Empire of Fear* (1988), set in an alternate universe where vampires are real and dominate ordinary humans. Although the vampires are explained in quasi-scientific terms, the novel is more properly horror, and three subsequent works in a similar vein, *The Werewolves of London* (1990), *The Angel of Pain* (1991), and *The Carnival of Destruction* (1994), are even more obviously outside the genre despite some superficial attempts at rationalization. Stableford also wrote a substantial body of critical work about the field during this period and seemed to be reinventing his own career. He had concentrated almost entirely on novels during most of his career, but during the 1990s he became an increasingly prolific short story writer. Some of these stories were subsequently incorporated into novels.

Stableford's next sequence of books has inexplicably never found a publisher in the United States despite being among his very best work. *Serpent's Blood* (1995), *Salamander's Fire* (1996), and *Chimera's Cradle* (1997) are set on a lost colony world whose atmosphere is so corrosive that permanent structures are impossible. The human colony has lapsed into barbarism in the absence of technology and interacts with three distinct indigenous alien intelligences. The adventures of a band of travelers expose the reader to the world's many biological wonders, leading to a climax in which the complexities of the ecology are finally explained in more detail. Stableford's exploration of the implications of his unique setting and the bizarre adaptations of the native forms of life would be fascinating even without the well-conceived surface story with its varied and memorable characters.

His most recent project has been a six-volume future history that began with *Inherit the Earth* (1998) and *The Architects of Emortality* (1999), these two volumes establishing the setting and tone for the rest of the series. Scientists have discovered a form of immortality, but the potential wealth and power suggested by that revelation lead to murder and conspiracy. In *The Fountains of Youth* (2000), one of the new immortals decides to devote the next few centuries to a thorough study of life and death and the transition between the two. *The Cassandra Complex* (2001), *Dark Ararat* (2002), and *The Omega Expedition* (2002) bring the sequence to an apparent close, with humans traveling to the stars, colonizing other worlds, and finally—through the familiar device of suspended animation—visiting their own distant and radically altered future.

Many of stableford's short stories have been collected in *Sexual Chemistry* (1991) and *Designer*

Genes (2004). Among the best examples are "Les Fleurs du Mal," "Mortimer Gray's History of Death," and "The Hunger and Ecstasy of Vampires." The author himself has suggested that his early work should be dismissed as insignificant, and certainly his work from 1988 onward has been substantially better, but it would be a mistake to dismiss out of hand the cleverly constructed and entertainingly written adventures of his early career. Stableford's interest in questions of biotechnology has become even more obvious in his later work. His periodic difficulties in finding an American publisher seem to have little connection to the quality of his work but may reflect poor timing, because his weakest efforts are still superior to a significant amount of work that does manage to find its way into book form.

Stainless Steel Rat series
Harry Harrison

Slippery Jim DiGriz made his debut in *The Stainless Steel Rat* (1961), one of Harry HARRISON's first and most memorable novels. DiGriz started his career as an interplanetary conman, but he is basically a moral man despite his questionable occupation. He is eventually recruited, somewhat involuntarily, as an agent for an interstellar organization dedicated to preventing interstellar war. In the opening volume in the series, an ambitious woman is behind a program to construct a spacegoing battleship, and DiGriz has to use his considerable wiles to derail her plans.

Harrison might not have originally planned to generate a series of novels about DiGriz, because the second adventure didn't appear for almost 10 years. *The Stainless Steel Rat's Revenge* (1970) was basically a reprise of the first novel. Another planetary ruler is threatening war, so DiGriz's criminal career is interrupted once again while he undermines the ambitious despot's government. Although the sequel was a more polished story, it lacked the novelty and enthusiasm of the first. Harrison finally varied from the formula for the third entry in the series, *The Stainless Steel Rat Saves the World* (1972). This time the situation is more personal. Someone has been kidnapping people and exiling them into the past, including some of DiGriz's relatives, so he has to travel back to Earth during the 1980s to effect their rescue. The scale became even grander in *The Stainless Steel Rat Wants You!* (1978), which followed six years later. This space opera involves a mysterious alien race that is poised to conquer the entire universe, and DiGriz has to use all of his wits to save the day. The uneasy balance between serious action and broad humor is at its most noticeable this time and is in sharp contrast to the more impressive work of which Harrison had already proven himself capable.

The Stainless Steel Rat for President (1984) returned to the original formula and was far more successful. DiGriz is married now, and he and his wife are spending time on a tourist planet, alternating between amusing one another, subverting the oppressive government, and fomenting a revolution. Even more interesting is *A Stainless Steel Rat Is Born* (1985), which jumps back in time to chronicle the protagonist's early life, a considerably more substantial work. On the trail of a killer, DiGriz joins a planetary army in *The Stainless Steel Rat Gets Drafted* (1987) and foils the plans of yet another potential aggressor. He is forced to retrieve an alien artifact after being given a slow-acting poison in *The Stainless Steel Rat Sings the Blues* (1994). *The Stainless Steel Rat Goes to Hell* (1996), one of the best in the series, has DiGriz posing as the devil in a theocratic dictatorship in order to rescue his kidnapped wife. The final novel thus far is *The Stainless Steel Rat Joins the Circus* (1998), but it is a routine and rather disappointing adventure. Although generally light in tone and certainly uneven in quality, the adventures of the Stainless Steel Rat are almost always entertaining and Slippery Jim DiGriz is one of the best known characters in the genre.

The Stand
Stephen King
(1978)

Many of the best-selling horror novels by Stephen KING and Dean R. KOONTZ have employed science fiction rather than supernatural elements in their plots. Stephen King has used psi powers and aliens from other worlds as the source of evil and in this, his longest single book, he invokes a familiar science fiction device to set the stage for a confrontation between the forces of good and those of supernatural evil. Captain Trips is a new plague, a superflu that is almost invariably fatal. The flu is not natural, but resulted from an accidental release from a government biowarfare project, although there are indications later that the accident was engineered by supernatural influence. In the opening section of the book, almost novel-length in itself, the disease spreads across the world, wiping out almost the entire population.

King introduces us to a very large cast chosen from among the survivors. Several of these are troubled by dreams in which they receive messages from the same figure, an elderly woman who summons them to join her in resisting the efforts of an evil force intent upon domination of the newly altered world. Opposed to her is the Walking Dude, who appears to be human, but who is clearly not of this world. He is a charismatic figure who attracts his own allies from among the mentally ill and the criminal class.

The difference in tone between the first section and the balance of the book is substantial. The epic struggle between good and evil escalates slowly but steadily toward the final confrontation, although the resolution is contingent upon literally divine intervention, a weakness that occurs in some of King's other endings. The portions of the plot that deal with self-sacrifice and friendship are particularly well done, but perhaps not surprisingly the chief villains, like the Walking Dude and Trashcanman, are more memorable characters than the forces of good. A longer version of *The Stand*, including text that was excised for reasons of length in the original, appeared in 1990.

Stand on Zanzibar
John Brunner
(1968)

Science fiction changed dramatically during the 1960s. Although there had been several serious novels worthy of mainstream attention during the 1950s, they were swallowed up in an ocean of light space adventures and melodramatic escape fiction. These lesser works were aimed at a specific audience and disdained the niceties of prose styling, characterization, and other aspects more valued outside the field. Several different forces coalesced during the early 1960s that began a dramatic transformation of the genre for the better. The New Wave in England raised the possibility of unconventional narrative techniques, although its extreme stylistic experiments were short-lived. American writers like Ursula K. LE GUIN and Harlan ELLISON demonstrated that human emotion described genuinely, both in the author's voice and in his characters, resulted in memorable and moving stories. Others like Roger ZELAZNY and Samuel R. DELANY mixed mainstream values with radically new imaginative leaps and drew heavily on images from mythology and literature.

John BRUNNER had begun his career with a series of short, well-written, but quite traditional adventure novels that often displayed a superior understanding of the political nature of humanity. His work had been improving steadily during the 1960s, with more complex plots and elaborate backgrounds, but nothing he had written previously prepared the public for *Stand on Zanzibar*. In a field where most novels had been uniformly short, he dared write one more than twice as long as average and adopted many of the stylistic devices of John Dos Passos in the process. The central plot, which is only one of several separate storylines, follows the efforts of a corporation that is attempting to literally buy a small country. A large and varied cast of characters are called upon to give depth to a complex and well-realized future in which drugs have been legalized, there is a permanent base on the Moon, some computers have become self-aware, and a new wave of religious mania has swept through the country. In addition to traditional narrative techniques, Brunner enriches the background by including transcripts of various documents and news broadcasts, which contain much peripheral detail that helps give his imagined world a fuller dimension of reality. Brunner's future feels like a very real place, and what happens in that context is meaningful for the reader. Other writers, including Brunner himself, would attempt similar books in the years that followed, none of which were as remarkably groundbreaking. The novel won the Hugo Award as best of the year.

Stapledon, Olaf
(1886–1950)

Olaf Stapledon's preoccupation with philosophical issues was apparent in his non-fiction even before he turned his hand to fiction. His first novel is actually a speculative essay. *Last and First Men* (1930) is the history of human evolution over the course of the next two billion years, our expansion into space, the alterations in our physical nature, and the gradual modifications of our mental and personal attributes. Although the story hints at some devices that would later become popular in the genre—genetic engineering, for example—these concepts were treated in passing and without detailed consideration of the consequences. A sequel, *Last Men in London* (1932), is a more conventional novel, with an evolved human traveling back through time to visit out era.

Odd John: A Story Between Jest and Earnest (1936) was one of the first and is still one of the most effective stories of the birth of a superhuman. John's advantages are all in the mind—not the body—but normal humans sense that there is something different about him and, later, those similar to him. Ultimately the two strains of humanity separate, and the more evolved minority dies rather than compromise its more highly evolved ethical state. Stapledon reprised this theme even more movingly in *Sirius: A Fantasy of Love and Discord* (1944), in this case the novel centers on a mutant dog whose intelligence rivals humanity's. *Darkness and the Light* (1942) also involves superhumans.

The Star Maker (1937) was a return to the form of *Last and First Men*, this time relating the history of the entire galaxy, of which humanity in its various forms is a brief and insignificant subset. Although filled with marvelous ideas and speculations, it is another extended essay rather than a conventional novel. Some critics have nevertheless labeled it Stapledon's most important book, and it certainly contains enough unusual premises to fill an entire library. *Nebula Maker*, an earlier version of *The Star Maker*, was published in 1976. Stapledon wrote only a handful of short stories, which are collected along with a selection of his essays in *An Olaf Stapledon Reader* (1997).

The Starpit
Samuel R. Delany
(1966)

The opening sequence of this novelette sets up an image that becomes a metaphor for the main story. Vyme is a troubled man, a member of a group marriage who is increasingly at odds with his partners. In a drunken rage, he destroys an elaborate terrarium in a confused effort to free its inhabitants, although many of them end up dying as a result of their exposure. We then leap forward several years. He is no longer part of the group, has matured and stopped drinking, and now manages a spaceship repair yard in the Starpit, an undefined place that appears to be a major artery for star travel.

The galaxy has become one gigantic terrarium, fully explored by humankind even though our social maturation has not kept pace with technological advances. The government exploits and even abuses children, drugs are in common use, interplanetary wars are frequent, and life for the great majority of people is harsh and unpleasant. Efforts have been made in the past to reach other galaxies, but there is a convolution in the nature of space that is fatal to humans who stray too far from our own galaxy. There are exceptions: A subset of humanity known as the Golden, who are not bothered by the anomalous areas, are free to trade with the worlds of distant galaxies. Unfortunately, their immunity is linked to a personality disorder. The Golden are distant, unpleasant, self-centered, and often quite stupid. They are generally hated by the larger population, which is nevertheless dependent upon them for intergalactic trade. The galaxy thus becomes a gigantic terrarium in which the majority of humans are trapped.

Vyme gets caught up in a tragic drama involving a drug-addicted prostitute, a boy who wants to leave the galaxy, even if it will cost him his life, and a mentally challenged Golden who is easily duped. Although most of the overt action happens to the other characters, the story is still about Vyme, his eventual realization that everyone is trapped, limited by circumstances, and that escape is illusory. The lesson of the novel is that we can truly gain our personal freedom only by accepting the nature of things as they are and making the best choices we can on that basis.

The Stars My Destination
Alfred Bester
(1956)

The plot for this extravagant space opera, which also appeared as *Tiger! Tiger!*, is quite openly patterned after *The Count of Monte Cristo* by Alexander Dumas. The protagonist is Gully Foyle, a small-time criminal cast as the outsider, a man who has failed to find his niche in the civilization of the 25th century. Alfred BESTER's future is an exotic and complex one filled with extraordinary characters and institutions, but not so greatly changed that we cannot recognize it as a reflection of our own. Psi powers are now an accepted part of life, and teleportation, known as jaunting, has become the major means of transportation for individuals who possess that power. In the opening stages of the novel, Foyle does not possess that power, but when he is stranded in space and left to die by his former cronies, something within him refuses to accept the situation and teleports him to safety. This is the first step in a radical transformation that will make him something more than human.

The novel is filled with fascinating and unique characters, including a female outlaw who can see only in the infrared spectrum and has become embittered by her handicap. There is also a religious cult that routinely neutralizes parts of the nervous system so that they can punish their bodies without feeling the consequences. Bester presents the reader with a succession of wonders that are so striking that they distract our attention from the occasional inconsistencies in the plot or background.

The story is chiefly about revenge. Having escaped the deathtrap, Foyle seeks vengeance against those responsible. Back on Earth, he begins to use his new awareness to build a personal fortune, recognizing that wealth equals power and that he needs to overcome his shortcomings in that area. The primary villain is also vividly described, although some of the anachronisms in his behavior are jarring and illogical. In his first novel, THE DEMOLISHED MAN (1953), Bester enjoyed considerable success in forcing his readers to identify, at least to some extent, with the murderous villain. Gully Foyle is in many ways an even less admirable character, but once again Bester illuminates an aspect of his personality that overcomes our revulsion. Despite its flaws, *The Stars My Destination* is a masterful piece of writing.

Starship Troopers
Robert A. Heinlein
(1959)

This Hugo Award–winning novel by Robert A. HEINLEIN is an interesting blend of the best and worst of the author's writing. Although originally planned as a novel for young adults, the plot was rejected as being too violent for that market. It is one of the earliest, and in many ways the best, examples of military science fiction and contains some of the best action sequences Heinlein ever wrote. The main protagonist is a young Filipino who enlists in the military against the wishes of his family, serving Earth in its war against various aliens, primarily an insectlike race whose own motives are never presented. The story of his training and subsequent action is exciting and convincing, although the flow is periodically interrupted by a lecture on one or another political theme.

Unfortunately, this was Heinlein's version of a utopian novel, and like most such efforts, it presupposes a basic change in human behavior in order for its political mechanisms to work. In order to vote, a citizen must first serve in the military and, although there are some peripheral references to alternate service for conscientious objectors, it is clear that veterans make the rules and enforce the laws. The political scheme is devised in a way that makes alternate viewpoints irrelevant and powerless. Heinlein justifies this by citing an imaginary mathematical equation that conclusively proves that the present system is the best possible. Opposing views are represented only as paper tigers, to be knocked down by the superior wisdom of older and wiser characters.

The concept that individuals have a duty to society is an admirable one that Heinlein illustrates well through the convictions and sacrifices of his characters. More controversially, his world has abandoned much of what contemporary society considers progressive reforms. Corporal punishment has been reintroduced, for example, and insanity is no longer a legal defense. There is also a strong Darwinist sentiment. Since promotion beyond a certain level requires combat experience, the human military system is dependent on a constant state of war. The author portrays the universe as a place of competing, hostile races, so the problem of peace doesn't arise during the course of the story. Skeptical readers might well speculate that the high command would be compelled to initiate wars in the eventuality of peace in order to fill the ranks with qualified officers.

Despite the flaws in the setting, *Starship Troopers* remains a compelling and very popular novel, particularly among adolescent males with libertarian inclinations. There are a few minor plot problems. There is a reliance on coincidence and the sudden, convenient recanting by the hero's dissident father is among these, but for the most part the plot works remarkably well. The 1997 film version captures only parts of Heinlein's story and fails to come to grips with the nature of the society against which the plot is set.

Steele, Allen
(1958–)

Allen Steele's first novel, *Orbital Decay* (1989), made an immediate favorable impression, particularly with readers who enjoyed hard science fiction but preferred it in a near-future setting. The novel follows the activities of a group of construction workers engaged in building the first orbiting habitat and the pressures they face. The novel is particularly effective because it is told from the viewpoint of the workers rather than that of

administrators or scientists. A follow-up novel, *Lunar Descent*, (1991) moves a similar story to the Moon, although this time the hardships faced by the construction and mining crews, mistreated by an exploitative corporation, precipitate a crisis.

Clarke County, Space (1990) initiated a new but similar sequence. The residents of another orbiting habitat, this one reasonably self-sustaining, chafe under the rules imposed by Earth and eventually demand their political independence. The ensuing power struggle spreads throughout the solar system in the much later sequel, *A King of Infinite Space* (1997), a somewhat darker novel that suffers from the lack of light humor that enlivened its predecessor. *The Labyrinth of Mars* (1992) was also more serious in tone. The first expedition to the planet Mars investigates the ruins of what appear to be artificial features preserved in the Martian desert. *The Jericho Iteration* (1994) is Steele's first novel set on Earth. After a devastating earthquake destroys large portions of North America, an investigative reporter follows a story that could result in his murder by parties interested in suppressing the truth about the activities of some relief organizations. *The Tranquility Alternative* (1996) is a much more effectively suspenseful novel, set in an alternate history where the American space program began during the 1940s. Interest in outer space and public support for the expenditures have both faltered. A missile base on the Moon is in the process of being deactivated in the wake of cooling political tensions on Earth, but a terrorist group with long-standing grievances has plans to commandeer it to advance their own agenda. *Oceanspace* (1999) showed continued improvement and sophistication in Steele's writing. This time the setting is an undersea base on Earth in the not too distant future. Scientific experiments and the very preservation of the base are complicated by the presence of a mysterious sea creature and the infiltration of the project by a saboteur.

Most of Steele's novels through the end of the 1990s had been set on Earth, or very close to it, and in the very near future. His next two novels broke that mold. *Chronospace* (2001) is a cleverly told time travel story, with a nicely constructed paradox, a section of which won the Hugo Award as "Where Angels Fear to Tread." A team of time travelers go back to observe the burning of the zeppelin *Hindenberg,* but that tragedy never takes place, possibly because they somehow altered the course of events. They must figure out what they changed in order to prevent the original timeline from becoming corrupted. *Coyote* (2002), on the other hand, travels a different course with a far surer hand. Earth has become a mildly repressive dictatorship, so a group of rebels hijack an experimental starship and set out to explore the universe on their own. Their episodic adventures on the planet Coyote are assembled partly from previously published short fiction, which gives the novel an uneven quality at times. The sequel, *Coyote Rising* (2004), extends the story as Earth attempts to reassert control over the fleeing humans, forcing them to abandon their settlement and strike off into the wilderness. Steele's willingness to depart from the successful formula of his earlier novels bodes well for the longevity of his career, although he has yet to write a novel sufficiently impressive to propel him to the front rank of hard science fiction writers.

Steele has also proven to be a prolific short story writer. "The Death of Captain Future" won the Hugo Award, and others like "Agape Among the Robots," "Walking Across Mars," and "Stealing Alabama" are also exceptional. Much of his short work is humorous or at least light in tone. His collections to date consist of *Rude Astronauts* (1992), *All-American Alien Boy* (1996), *Sex and Violence in Zero-G* (1999), and *American Beauty* (2003), although many more stories remain uncollected. Although his characters sometimes lack depth, Steele usually avoids depicting them as extremely good or evil. His narrative techniques are well-developed, and his gift for using humor at appropriate times has served him well.

The Stepford Wives
Ira Levin
(1972)

Ira Levin is best known as the author of *Rosemary's Baby* (1967), the story of the birth of the son of Satan on Earth. Although never a prolific writer, he produced a handful of other novels of varying interest, of which three are science fiction. *This Perfect Day* (1970) was the first of these, a well-written but not very innovative dystopian novel in which the government predictably proclaims itself a utopia. *The Boys from Brazil* (1976) is a more marginal story about a secret Nazi project to use a clone of Adolf Hitler to revive their cause a generation later. The most impressive of the three was *The Stepford Wives* (1972), which led to a film version quite close to the original in the following year, and a remake in 2004.

Walter and Joanna Eberhart have recently moved to the quiet bedroom community of Stepford, where the neighbors all seem friendly and the problems of the city—crime, decay, and overcrowding—are all apparently kept at arm's length. None of the marriages in Stepford appear to be unhappy. The wives stay at home, happily keeping house for their husbands, who hold jobs and make all of the decisions. The Eberharts begin to suspect that things are just a little too perfect, and Joanna in particular senses that something not quite right is happening behind the scenes. Something is happening, of course, and the secret is that the husbands in Stepford are all part of an intricate conspiracy whereby their wives are replaced by robots that look exactly like the originals, but who are programmed to conform to their husbands' every wish. Although the Eberharts have a better than average marriage, Walter is tempted to join the club.

The Stepford Wives was written as a mainstream thriller rather than as a genre novel, and probably would not have passed muster as science fiction because of the inadequate and unsatisfying explanation of how the robots could possibly have functioned so superbly. There is a further inconsistency in that apparently not one male ever challenged the system when approached, which is a rather cynical interpretation of the institution of marriage. It is undeniably a well-paced and suspenseful thriller, most significantly because of its reflection, in exaggerated form, of the values held by a sizable majority of the population who would much prefer a more rigid conformity to the traditional image of gender roles. The novel could almost as easily have been called *The Stepford Husbands*.

Stephenson, Neal
(1959–   )

Although Neal Stephenson's first two novels had fantastic elements in them, they are only marginally science fiction. *The Big U* (1984) is a broad satire on college life that encompasses environmental concerns like pollution and other contemporary maladies, treating each in a zany but pointed fashion. *Zodiac: The Eco-Thriller* (1988) is only slightly more serious in surface tone, although some of the satire is considerably more bitter.

Stephenson's next effort was so much better in so many ways that it could almost have been written by a different author. *SNOW CRASH* (1992) renders the world of virtual reality in brilliant fashion and presents a twisted version of the real world where the old definitions of national borders have changed and where cyborg dogs and other wonders have transformed society. His next novel was *Interface* (1994), written under the name Stephen Bury, a near-future thriller that abandoned Stephenson's satirical style. A governor and potential presidential candidate has had a chip implanted in his body so that he can be instantly apprised of changes in public opinion and receive other information quickly and efficiently. Although this initially seems a completely benevolent enhancement, he eventually learns that those who control the flow of information control the recipients as well and that he can be manipulated by the people who choose which data should be sent and how it should be presented.

The Diamond Age, or, A Young Lady's Illustrated Primer (1995) won the Hugo Award, even though it is not nearly as good as *Snow Crash*. The setting is a future world that has already been transformed by the advent of nanotechnology and other wondrous advances. The result is a caste system even more rigid and repressive than in our contemporary world. When a member of the privileged classes creates a Primer, a cybernetic book that literally melds its personality to its owner, becoming a storehouse of incredible knowledge, it inadver-

tently falls into the hands of a child from the poverty stricken lower classes, who eventually uses it to transform the world. *The Cryptonomicon* (1999) contains some mild science fiction content—a few minor technological innovations in data processing, an imaginary European nation—but is essentially a contemporary novel about the management of information and its implication for society. Stephenson is currently at work on a trilogy, the first two volumes of which do not fall within the genre. If this marks a permanent departure, it is a tragic loss for the field and its readers.

Sterling, Bruce
(1954–   )

Bruce Sterling started his career with a minor short story, followed by the novel *Involution Ocean* (1978), a fairly straightforward otherworlds adventure in which space travelers find an anomalous form of life on an otherwise dead world. This was followed by *The Artificial Kid* (1980), set on a world where violent forms of entertainment are the norm, and a habitual winner finally appears to have met his match. During the next decade, Sterling wrote more than a dozen short stories of uniformly high quality, including "Red Star, Winter Orbit" (1983) and "Our Neural Chernobyl" (1988). Several of these stories share a setting in which far-future humanity has spread to the stars and split into two separate development philosophies. One relies on mechanical technology, computers, and prosthetic devices; the other leans toward genetic engineering and the soft sciences. These were collected as *The Crystal Express* (1989). Other stories showed a drift toward the cyberpunk movement, set in a near future where computer technology dominates an increasingly degraded world, and, in fact, Sterling edited an influential cyberpunk anthology, *Mirrorshades* (1986).

Schismatrix (1985) is loosely linked to *The Crystal Express*, and would later be reprinted as *Schismatrix Plus* (1996), an edition including some shorter work. The novel is a panoramic history of future humanity somewhat in the style of Olaf STAPLEDON. It is highly inventive, but somewhat lacking in traditional literary values. *Islands in the Net* (1988) suggested the type of story in which Sterling would subsequently specialize, near-future speculations about the interplay of governments, corporations, and developments in information technology. *Heavy Weather* (1994) would deal with virtual reality; *Holy Fire* (1996) concerns medical technology and the quest for restored youth; *Distraction* (1998) is set in a future where many people have been reduced to virtual slavery; and *The Zenith Angle* (2004) involves a computer specialist in international politics.

Most of Sterling's short stories have been collected in *Globalhead* (1992) and *A Good Old Fashioned Future* (2001). He is also the co-author of an excellent alternate history novel, *The Difference Engine* (1990), in which computers were invented during the Victorian age, a collaboration with William GIBSON. Although Sterling's most recent fiction seems to be moving toward the mainstream and away from science fiction, many of the concerns and attitudes of the genre are still obvious in his work.

Stirling, S. M.
(1954–   )

Although he began his writing career with a series of heroic fantasy adventures, S. M. Stirling switched to science fiction in 1988 and most of his subsequent work is in that genre. *Marching Through Georgia* (1988) and its sequels, *Under the Yoke* (1989), *The Stone Dogs* (1990), and *Drakon* (1996), are largely set in an alternate world where British loyalists driven out by the American Revolution founded a new nation in South America, imposing a particularly brutal form of slavery under a repressive dictatorship, and using selective breeding to create a super-race. The sequence opens with a version of World War II, allying the Draka with the United States against Germany and Japan, but the sequels have the former allies at odds. The fourth volume transports one of the Drakan superhumans into our reality.

Stirling's most successful work to date is his three-volume series in which the island of Nantucket is displaced in time. The residents split into

rival factions and divert the course of human history in a radically different direction. The series consists of *Island in the Sea of Time* (1998), *Against the Tide of Years* (1999), and *On the Oceans of Eternity* (2000). His most recent novel, *Dies the Fire* (2004), utilizes a very similar device with a slightly different emphasis. Two more novels also take place in alternate worlds. *The Peshawar Lancers* (2002), probably his best single book, is set in an alternate history in which a meteor shower destroyed much of civilization in the late 19th century, leaving Great Britain and Russia as the two major powers. *Conquistador* (2003) is a more predictable adventure story following the adventures of a group of explorers who cross through an unexplained gateway into an alternate world where North America is an unspoiled wilderness.

Stirling has been an active collaborator with other writers, including an extended military science fiction series with David DRAKE, contributions to the Kzin and Falkenberg sequences with Jerry POURNELLE, and the cyborg ship series with Anne McCaffrey, also adding a solo novel to this sequence, *The Ship Avenged* (1997). He also was the primary writer for a three-volume sequence presented as a collaboration between Stirling and actor James Doohan, and has contributed media tie-in novels to the *Terminator* and *Babylon 5* universes. His collaborative novel with Holly Lisle is fantasy. Although Stirling has written several short stories, they are only of moderate interest and are as yet uncollected.

Stranger in a Strange Land
Robert A. Heinlein
(1961)

Robert A. HEINLEIN's first best-selling novel was meant to be a satire aimed at a wide variety of aspects of Western civilization and the plot is not particularly complex. Valentine Michael Smith is a human child raised by Martians who is eventually recovered and returned to Earth. There he functions as an outside viewer, similar to the Lithian visitor to Earth in *A CASE OF CONSCIENCE* (1958), forcing other characters to justify behaviors and beliefs that Heinlein clearly perceived as unjustifiable.

Smith eventually becomes the messiah of a new religion that transforms human society.

Smith is in his twenties when he is brought back to Earth, bright by human standards although the Martians considered him retarded. Through a combination of circumstances, the young man is heir to a considerable fortune and poses serious political problems, which might justify his elimination. Some sympathetic friends rescue him from official custody, enlisting a prominent lawyer on Smith's behalf. After some minor escapades, some of them sexual, Smith decides to found a new religion based on his perception of human nature. The religion turns out to involve promiscuous sex, and there is a predictable angry reaction, resulting in his martyrdom.

There are some internal problems with the book. Smith has such an array of psi powers that it is questionable whether he is even remotely human any longer, and even more unlikely that he would be unable to escape an angry mob. Another problem is one also found in Heinlein's previous novel, STARSHIP TROOPERS (1959). In that book, the rigid militaristic human society is defined within the context of the story as objectively correct, thereby making it immune to criticism. Similarly, Smith's new religion is portrayed as insightful and appropriate, and therefore safe from challenge. Although it is the author's prerogative to stack things in his favor, in this case it is an awkward and artificial device that fails to play fair with readers who might wish to examine contrary arguments.

Heinlein's libertarian attitudes toward government and promiscuity found favor among college students, which helped fuel the novel's popularity even among readers who were otherwise at odds with Heinlein's political stance. The novel also coined the word *grok*, in popular use for some years as an expression of insightful understanding.

Strugatsky, Arkady
(1925–1991) and
Strugatsky, Boris
(1931–   )

The Strugatsky brothers are easily the best known Russian science fiction writers in the English-speaking world, with more than a dozen published novels in the United States. Russian science fiction, particularly during the Soviet era, tended to be limited by the restrictions one might expect from that political system. Utopian novels were necessarily socialist, and capitalism could hardly be dealt with in openly favorable terms. The brothers sidestepped many of these issues, and their occasional satirical swipes at consumerism and other Western values are not all that different from similar criticisms from American and English writers. They were also talented storytellers, and the quality of their work gained them an appreciative audience outside their home country.

Their books did not necessarily appear in the United States in the same order that they were originally written, and it is difficult to track their stylistic progression based on the American publication dates. There were common characters and settings, particularly in the earlier works, which often involved utopian societies. *Noon: 22nd Century,* for example, first appeared in 1967 but was not available in English until 1978, but the space captain from that novel has further adventures in at least one of the stories in *The Far Rainbow,* which was published in a first English edition in 1967. *Space Apprentice* (originally from 1962, translated in 1978) is a series of linked stories about the adventures of a spaceship's crew, and is also linked to the two previously mentioned titles.

Hard to Be a God (1964, translated 1973) was their most popular novel in the United States. A single Earthman on a distant inhabited world conceals his existence as he tries to shape the alien society so that it will evolve into a more tolerant and progressive culture. His observations lead him to believe that any action outsiders might take will only make things worse, an obvious criticism of colonialism. On the other hand, he recognizes that the status quo has already established conditions that might cause the indigenes to follow a self-destructive path, and he is caught on the horns of the dilemma of whether or not to act. It is an ethical question that many other genre writers have glossed over or ignored entirely in their own fiction.

Monday Begins on Saturday (1966, translated 1977) is another series of linked stories, this time involving investigations into paranormal activities on Earth that are frequently tied to images or concepts from myths and legends. *Tale of the Troika* (1968, translated 1972) is related to that series thematically. Aliens visit Earth in *Roadside Picnic* (1972, translated 1977), with fairly benevolent intentions in that case, and again in *The Second Invasion of Mars* (1968, translated in 1977), the latter of which contains some amusing satire about Western attitudes toward personal possessions and marketing. *The Snail on the Slope* (1968, translated 1980) was assembled from shorter works and also pokes fun at selected institutions, including entrenched bureaucrats. It is one of their best books.

Their remaining titles include *The Ugly Swans* (1966, translated 1979), which involves a plague, mutant powers, and inexplicable changes in the Earth's weather patterns; *Definitely Maybe* (1976, translated 1978), in which a series of mysterious deaths is possibly connected to a scientific project; *The Final Circle of Paradise* (1965, translated 1976), wherein a man recently returned to Earth discovers the existence of a secret organization; and *Escape Attempt* (1982), a collection of short fiction. They also wrote a loose trilogy consisting of *Prisoners of Power* (1969, translated 1978), *Beetle in an Anthill* (1979, translated 1980), and *The Time Wanderers* (1985, translated 1987). There is more overt action in this trilogy than in most of their other work. In these books, the plots involve efforts to destabilize repressive governments on Earth and elsewhere, and prevent the destabilization of benevolent ones targeted by agents of rebellion or conquest. By English language standards, the Strugatsky brothers produced relatively tame, uncontroversial stories that came to grips with serious issues only peripherally. On the other hand, *Hard to Be a God* in particular provided a new perspective on an issue that deserved more thorough examination.

Sturgeon, Theodore
(1918–1985)

Theodore Sturgeon was born Edward Hamilton Waldo but later changed his name legally. He began writing science fiction in the late 1930s and would eventually become one of the major talents in the field, with a gift for characterization and a knack for depicting complex interpersonal relationships that makes even his minor stories worth preserving. Although the bulk of his fiction would fall within the genre, Sturgeon also wrote a historical novel, a psychological thriller, several westerns, and is believed to have ghostwritten at least one mystery novel. His career proceeded in fits and starts: Highly productive periods were followed by long intervals of inactivity.

During the early 1940s, Sturgeon became a regular contributor to the genre magazines although much of his work was fantasy. Several classic science fiction stories were intermingled with the fantasy ones, including "Microcosmic God" (1941), "Yesterday Was Monday" (1941), and "The Chromium Helmet" (1946). In the novelette KILLDOZER (1944), a bodiless and malevolent alien intelligence inhabits the body of a bulldozer with lethal consequences. This novelette was later filmed for television. When the magazine that was his chief fantasy market ceased publication, he moved away from that form. The late 1940s saw a steady stream of major science fiction works, including "Maturity" (1947), "THUNDER AND ROSES" (1947), and "The Perfect Host" (1948). He also produced occasional classics of fantasy and horror like "Bianca's Hands" (1947) and "The Professor's Teddy Bear" (1948). His first collection, *Without Sorcery* (1948), mixed stories from both genres.

Sturgeon's first novel appeared in 1950. *The Dreaming Jewels* (also published as *The Synthetic Man*) was an astonishingly mature work. The protagonist, like many of the author's heroes, is a young boy from an abusive family background who runs away to join the circus. Both he and the decidedly villainous circus manager are actually artificial beings, partially created by alien crystals with regenerative powers. Their conflict, set against the brilliantly realized background of a traveling carnival troupe, is gripping and emotionally engaging. Although there is an occasional drift toward sentimentalism, the powerful talent that would be displayed in Sturgeon's next novel, MORE THAN HUMAN (1953), was already evident. *More Than Human* actually consists of a separately published novelette, *Baby Is Three* (1952), sandwiched between two new ones. Fifty years later, it is still among the best treatments of gestalt personalities.

The early 1950s also brought a fresh crop of high-quality short fiction, including "A Way Home" (1953) and "To Here and the Easel" (1954). "The World Well Lost" (1953) was quite controversial for its time. Two alien refugees have arrived on Earth after being exiled from their own planet. The surprise revelation is that the crime of which they are guilty is homosexuality. In "A Saucer of Loneliness" a lonely young woman has a telepathic encounter with an alien visitor and discovers that her feelings of loneliness are not unique. Sturgeon frequently included psychosexual themes and images in his work and challenged social taboos. He would later postulate a society in which incest is an accepted social norm in "If All Men Were Brothers, Would You Let Your Sister Marry One?" (1967). The year 1955 was a particularly productive one, with THE (WIDGET), THE (WADGET) AND BOFF and "BULKHEAD," both appearing for the first time. Two new collections, *A Way Home* and *Caviar*, were also released that year, following his earlier collection, *E Pluribus Unicorn* (1953).

Although Sturgeon would continue to excel at shorter length, his subsequent novels failed to maintain the same level of quality, although they were always worthwhile. *The Cosmic Rape* (1958), expanded from "To Marry Medusa," described a transformation of the human race in response to an alien invasion, a psychic link that briefly unites every human being into a single super-entity, an echo of the theme of *More Than Human*. *Venus Plus X* (1960) is a very bizarre quasi-utopian novel in which Charlie Johns, a citizen of our time, wakes in what appears to be a distant future when humans have become hermaphroditic and use advanced technology to maintain their near-perfect society. What might have been the usual dull grand tour is transformed by Sturgeon into a parade of wonders and the ultimate surprise: Johns is actually an artificial personality created for experimental purposes and utopia is not in the future but in the present, hidden from the rest of the world. Although filled with fascinating scenes and passages, the book does not succeed very well as a novel, although it does provide an interesting contrast to THE LEFT HAND OF DARKNESS (1967) by Ursula K. LE GUIN. *Some of Your Blood* (1961), a

non-fantastic psychological study, was much more effective, but was the last of Sturgeon's novels except for *Godbody* (1986), a mildly interesting fantasy published posthumously. He also wrote a surprisingly palatable novelization of a very bad science fiction film, *Voyage to the Bottom of the Sea* (1961).

Although Sturgeon's ability to draw his readers into his world never faded, he became considerably less prolific toward the end of the 1950s. Occasional stories like "The Man Who Lost the Sea" (1958) and "The Comedian's Children" (1958) whetted readers' appetites for more, but new titles appeared less frequently. One particularly clever story was "The Girl Had Guts" (1957), in which alien lifeforms forge a benevolent, but unsettling, symbiotic relationship with humans. "When You Care, When You Love" (1962) was identified as the core of a new novel, but the project was abandoned. Several new collections appeared, including *Aliens Four* (1961) and *Starshine* (1966), but these consisted of older stories that had not been previously assembled in book form. The significantly titled *Sturgeon Is Alive and Well* (1971) contained several of his more recent tales, but not all of them were science fiction. Between 1969 and 1972, he published some excellent short stories like "SLOW SCULPTURE" (1970), which won the Hugo and Nebula Awards, and "Case and the Dreamer" (1973), but Sturgeon averaged less than a story a year for the last decade of his life. Five new short story collections appeared during the late 1970s, but some of these mixed his best work with considerably less worthy stories.

North Atlantic Press has been engaged in a major project to reprint Sturgeon's entire output of short fiction, science fiction and otherwise, in hardcover. Ten volumes were planned in the series, of which eight have appeared to date, starting with *Microcosmic God* (1992) and most recently *And Now the News* (2003). The editors of the series have included extensive notes for the stories, including variant texts. A reasonably representative sampling can be found in *Selected Stories* (2000). Sturgeon was one of the most influential writers in the field, and one of the few American writers to incorporate mainstream values into his writing before the dramatic changes of the 1960s. His influence on writers like Harlan Ellison, Samuel R. Delany, and many others has had a significant impact on the development of modern science fiction. The quality of Sturgeon's work is particularly surprising given his stated disinclination to spend significant time revising what he had already written.

"Such Interesting Neighbors"
Jack Finney
(1951)

Flight from an unpleasant environment is a recurring theme in the work of Jack FINNEY, sometimes to another place, sometimes to another time. Displacement through time is the device in this quietly understated story, in which the author presents us with considerable evidence that something fantastic has occurred, but without ever overtly admitting it.

Most time travel stories at least make a passing attempt to deal with the paradoxes that might result by changing the past. Finney ignored the question entirely because it is irrelevant to the story he wished to tell. Al and Nell Lewis live in a quiet suburb, and they are very curious about the new couple moving in next door. The Hellenbeks seem to be very nice, sociable people, but there is something odd about them. When they first arrive, literally all of their possessions are brand new, and they have contradictory stories about what happened to the ones they owned previously. They have some initial difficulty understanding how currency works, even though they are not foreigners, and sometimes they interact with physical objects in odd ways, as though they expected them to function differently. Ted Hellenbek has a knack for predicting future events with astonishing accuracy, and he supports himself by selling a series of small inventions, even though he seems otherwise mechanically inept.

The reader is well ahead of the narrator in understanding what is happening, and in fact neither of the Lewises ever suspect the truth, even after Ted produces a piece of supposed fiction he once wrote, describing a world more than a century removed from the present. In this world there is a constant threat of a devastating global war, and

continually deteriorating economic and social conditions have begun to accelerate of their own volition. The invention of inexpensive time machines was supposed to provide a temporary diversion, but before long families were traveling to the past and not returning, choosing to make a life in less troubled times. The future world became so depopulated that war was no longer possible, but the few remaining stragglers were so lonely that they eventually relocated as well.

Although Finney has ignored the logical inconsistencies, such as the impact of billions of new people even if they are spread out over centuries of history, the story is quite charming. There are no villains, no violence, and no real conflict, but the desire of the Hellenbeks to find a better life for themselves is genuinely moving.

"Superiority"
Arthur C. Clarke
(1951)

More than one science fiction writer has warned us that it is just as dangerous to become too dependent on technology as it is to shortchange scientific research, but none as effectively as in this very short piece by Arthur C. CLARKE. The story is constructed in the form of a statement by the imprisoned head of one planet's armed forces who insists that their defeat in a recent war was the result of the enemy's inferior, rather than superior, armaments. When war broke out, his forces enjoyed both numerical and technical superiority in weaponry, and it was expected to be only a matter of time until the enemy was forced to sue for peace. One crucial battle, although it was a victory, proved unusually costly, so the high command decided to step up weapons development to increase its edge.

Their initial difficulties start when research provides a totally new weapon, a mass disintegrator that requires the entire fleet to be refitted so that old-style weapons can be modified to carry the new payload. This delays military operations, which are put off even further when an unexpected design fault reveals that under certain conditions, the new weapon could be just as dangerous to friends as to foes. Another redesign delay follows, and by then scientists have improved the original weapon, which of course makes it necessary to refit everything yet again. During this lapse, enemy forces become more aggressive, and the shortage of traditional weapons results in a modest retreat. The enemy also takes advantage of the situation by engaging in a massive building program, and although their new ships still carry the older, presumably obsolete weapons, they have gained the numerical advantage, which allows them to absorb the heavier losses inflicted by the disintegrators and still win the next major battle.

Research then unveils a new weapon, a highly sophisticated computerized Battle Analyzer, which can automatically direct ships and weapons fire in the most advantageous fashion. Unfortunately, each Battle Analyzer requires literally hundreds of highly trained support personnel, who are in short supply and who complicate logistical matters immensely. As an interesting aside, Clarke's computer was physically immense because it contained countless vacuum tubes, which are of course obsolete already. Although the computer works wonderfully, an entire fleet can be disrupted if it is damaged or if a significant number of its support staff are disabled. Early gains are quickly reversed as the enemy recognizes their vulnerability.

Ultimately they are trapped by their own superiority. There is no time to make up the differential in conventional warships, so the only possible way to win the war is to develop even more sophisticated weaponry, but there is no time to properly test those developments. Eventually the war is lost, despite the dramatic technical edge. Clarke's point is as valid today as it was when this story first appeared more than 50 years ago. Technological change is a virtue so long as it is not change itself that we value.

Sutton, Jeff
(1913–1979)

A cursory glance at the early novels of Jeff Sutton might suggest that he was a hard science fiction writer, but they are actually more akin to modern technothrillers. *First on the Moon* (1958), for example, describes the conflict between the first wave of Soviet and American astronauts, each seeking control of the Moon for military purposes. *Bombs in Orbit* (1959) moves a similar battle into closer proximity, after the Russians launch three armed satellites into orbit along with a small military force designed to protect them from American astronauts. The situation is somewhat reversed in *Spacehive* (1960) wherein a U.S. orbiting project is attacked by Russian spacemen. All three novels are typical expressions of the majority worldview at the time they were written, that conflict between the two superpowers would inevitably spill over into space. Although they are rather superfluous today, *First on the Moon*, in particular, is still an enjoyable story.

Sutton turned to more traditional themes during the early 1960s. *The Atom Conspiracy* (1963) is set in a future when nuclear weapons have been outlawed, but an investigation is launched when evidence surfaces indicating someone has violated that international law. *Apollo at Go* (1963) and *Beyond Apollo* (1966), the first of which is Sutton's best novel, both deal with early efforts to establish a base on the Moon. The author's familiarity with the space program also resulted in a mainstream novel, *The Missile Lords* (1963). *H-Bomb Over America* (1967) was another technothriller, this one involving a clandestine plot to orbit a nuclear device.

Sutton wrote two adult novels with his wife, Jeanne Sutton. *The Beyond* (1967) concerns a man sent to track down a fugitive with telekinetic powers but who changes his allegiance, and *The Programmed Man* (1968) describes an interplanetary crisis that follows the hijacking of a powerful warship. They also wrote three young adult science fiction novels together. Sutton's later solo novels were generally less memorable. *The Man Who Saw Tomorrow* (1968) speculates unsuccessfully about the impact of a man with the ability to predict the future and *Alton's Unguessable* (1970) is a routine planetary adventure story. *Whisper from the Stars* (1970) is a dystopian chase adventure and *The Mindblocked Man* (1972) uses a similar setting with somewhat more success. Sutton is chiefly of interest because of his early work, which anticipated modern high-tech adventure stories.

Swann, S. Andrew
(1966–   )

S. Andrew Swann is the pseudonym of S. A. Swiniarksi, who has written horror fiction under that name and other science fiction as Steven Krane. Swann made his debut with *Forests of the Night* (1993), the first in a series of novels set in a future in which certain animals have been uplifted to intelligence and function more or less as humans with some aspects exaggerated because of their original instincts. A recurring character is an intelligent tiger who works as a private detective. *Specters of the Dawn* (1994) deals with the difficulties an uplifted rabbit has fitting herself into society as a whole. We discover that humans have been altering their own DNA in *Emperors of the Twilight* (1994), and a detective's last case might prove to be his last everything in *Fearful Symmetries* (1999).

A second series consists of the novels *Profiteer* (1995), *Partisan* (1995), and *Revolutionary* (1996). The human interstellar empire has been formed through force of arms, but one planet, Bakunin, refuses to join and in fact sells arms to various dissident groups. Eventually patience runs out, and an armed invasion is launched, countered by the maneuvering of the brilliant entrepreneur who dominates Bakunin. The battle lasts until the final volume, but even as the situation seems hopeless, the rebels have an ace up their sleeve. Despite his antiestablishment attitude, the protagonist is not an attractive enough character to hold our sympathies through three fairly long volumes. *Zimmerman's Algorithm* (2000) is a marginal near-future thriller about a stolen computer.

Although the Swann byline was kept alive with two fantasy novels, most of the author's subsequent science fiction appeared under the name of Steven Krane. *Teek* (1999) is a straightforward tale of a teenaged girl who discovers that she has telekinetic powers after encountering a hostile boy with similar powers. Unfortunately, she also attracts the notice of a clandestine government agency whose director wants to exploit her abilities secretly. *The Omega Game* (2000) is another marginal suspense story, this time involving a dangerous reality program set on a remote island.

Stranger Inside (2003) also has a teenaged protagonist, this one recruited in an investigation into spontaneous human combustion, which might be evidence of hostile action by psi-talented enemy agents. It is unclear at this point which direction Swiniarski's career will take next. His later work is low-key and conventional compared to his first few novels, and his drift toward fantasy might become more pronounced in the future. He has proven himself to be a potentially exciting talent, but as yet has not lived up to that promise.

Swanwick, Michael
(1950–   )

The complex, multi-layered plotting and prose style that is characteristic of Michael Swanwick's work was evident even in his first short stories, which began appearing in 1980. His subject matter was extremely diverse, ranging from hard science fiction set among the asteroids in "Ginungagap" (1980), to life among artists in "The Man Who Met Picasso" (1982). Other outstanding stories from this period include "Till Human Voices Wake Us" (1981) and "Mummer's Kiss" (1981), the latter of which, along with another story, was incorporated into Swanwick's first novel, *In the Drift* (1985). The novel is set in an alternate present where the Three Mile Island incident did in fact result in a meltdown and a massive leak of radioactivity that causes mutations and devastating ecological effects. Philadelphia and its environs has become a semifree state, ignored by the outside world and dominated by the mummers organization.

Swanwick was less prolific at shorter length during the latter half of the 1980s, and his first collection, *Gravity's Angels,* did not appear until 1991. The next 10 years saw a light, but regular flow of high-quality short stories. It was not until the late 1990s that the stories began to appear in noticeable quantity. His second novel was *Vacuum Flowers* (1987), an extremely complex tale set primarily inside orbiting habitats among the asteroids, in a future in which electronic implants can change even an individual's personality. Although the novel is sometimes associated with the cyberpunk movement, Swanwick's work has varied in style and subject matter so dramatically that it seems unlikely to have been consciously directed that way.

Stations of the Tide (1991) won the Nebula Award and is still Swanwick's most impressive novel. Humans have colonized the planet Miranda, which now faces a dramatic ecological disaster. Since space travel is expensive and evacuation impractical, the colonists must find a way to survive on their own. The social turmoil that follows predictably includes the rise of a charismatic figure who has founded a new religion. Since the fanatic, Gregorian, has stolen proscribed technology, the authorities on Earth send an agent to retrieve the material. The agent arrives by matter duplicator, with the original remaining on Earth. The duplicate pursues Gregorian into the wilderness, and a many-layered and powerful story follows. A short novel, *Griffin's Egg,* appeared the same year, a much more traditional and straightforward narrative about tensions arising among the high-tech installations on the Moon when a war on Earth threatens to spill over into space.

Swanwick's next novel, *Jack Faust* (1997), was a retelling of the Faust story, substituting a telepathic alien intelligence for the supernatural. Although the concept is interesting and portions of the novel superb, it seemed slightly too long for its premise. During the next five years, Swanwick produced most of the best short stories of his career to date, including four Hugo Award winners, "The Very Pulse of the Machine" (1998), "Scherzo with Tyrannosaur" (1999), "The Dog Said Bow-Wow" (2001), and "Slow Life" (2002). Most of these have been collected in *A Geography of Unknown Lands* (1997), *Tales of Old Earth* (2000), *Moon Dogs* (2000), and *Cigar Box Faust and Other Miniatures* (2003).

His most recent novel is *Bones of the Earth* (2002), a relatively traditional time travel story enhanced by the author's skillfully crafted prose and his insight into human personalities. The protagonist is a scientist who has been recruited by a secret government project that has developed a way to visit prehistoric times. A fanatical creationist sabotages the project, and the scientist finds himself stranded in the past. When it appeared, the novel was a strong award contender and displayed the author's increasing skill as a novelist. Swanwick has proven himself equally adept at novels and short stories, and winning four Hugos within a five-year span is a major accomplishment. It seems likely that he will become an even more significant writer in the years to come.

T

"Tangents"
Greg Bear
(1986)

Greg BEAR is known generally as a writer of hard science fiction, a form that is often characterized by poor characterization and a neglect of literary values and strong plotting in favor of novel physical settings and detailed scientific background. Bear never loses sight of the human element in his stories, however, and his characters are generally at least as well-developed as his scientific background material. Such is the case with this short story, which might be considered an update of "The Monster from Nowhere" (1939) by Nelson BOND.

Pal Tremont is a young boy, recently adopted, who makes friends with an unusual couple who live nearby. The woman, Lauren, is a writer and the man, Tuthy, a computer expert specializing in code breaking and other mathematical problems. Tuthy is in the country illegally, working under the table for a somewhat less than honorable business executive. Pal is interested in learning to play a musical instrument that Tuthy has in his room. He is given permission to play it in exchange for his help in Tuthy's attempts to visualize objects existing in the fourth dimension. Much to Tuthy's chagrin, the boy is much better at it than he is. Pal develops an ability to literally perceive this other reality, including the living beings who exist within it.

Tuthy might be a genius, but he is not very practical. He alienates his patron who gets revenge by reporting him to the authorities. At the same time, Pal has been experimenting with projection of his music into the fourth-dimensional world. By doing so, he has attracted the attention of its residents, who seek the source of the music by reaching into our reality, with rather disconcerting consequences. Just as he is about to be seized by immigration agents, Tuthy is carried off in a direction that doesn't even exist in our reality. Like *FLATLAND* (1884) by Edwin Abbott, Bear uses theoretical mathematics to generate the unusual physical events in the story, which won both the Hugo and Nebula Awards.

Telzey Amberdon series
James H. Schmitz

Prior to the 1960s and beyond, female protagonists were a rarity in science fiction, particularly in more assertive and active roles. The heroic male protagonist might have a mild romantic interest—and female characters occasionally displayed some competence—but most of the time they were there to be rescued or to provide a sounding board against which the other characters could project their theories or explanations. The rare exceptions were generally anomalies, not often repeated.

James H. Schmitz was one of the first writers to create an entire series around a female character, and he did it twice. One of these featured Trigger Argee; the other Telzey Amberdon. Both were set within the larger context of his Hub Universe setting, and the two characters occasionally crossed paths. Telzey is a telepath, who has extraordinary skills. She can read the minds of aliens, as well as humans, which makes her extremely valuable and puts her in danger when she eavesdrops on information that was supposed to remain secret. She made her debut in "Novice" (1962) and returned in two short novels and several short stories. The first of these novels was *The Universe Against Her* (1964), in which she learns of a plot to seize control of a planet and is pursued by the conspirators when they learn that their secret is out. Another alien plot is revealed in *The Lion Game* (1973), but Telzey's task this time is complicated by the interference of a psi-powered assassin. *The Telzey Toy* (1973) collected several of her shorter escapades.

Although Schmitz's work was out of print for several years, there has been a recent revival of interest in his fiction. The Amberdon short stories have been reprinted in *Telzey Amberdon* (2000) and *TnT: Telzey and Trigger* (2000). Although the stories often make use of very similar plots, Schmitz adds unusual twists to each in order to bring a fresh look to each subsequent adventure.

Tenn, William
(1920–   )

Philip Klass first used the name William Tenn in the 1930s, producing dozens of excellent stories during the next 25 years. His only novel appeared in 1963, and he has subsequently written less than a dozen new stories from the late sixties to the present day. Given his inactivity and small body of work, it would be understandable if Tenn had been completely forgotten. In fact, he is still honored as one of the best of the early genre writers and one of the two or three best humorists the field has ever seen.

Tenn quickly proved himself adept at both serious and outrageously funny stories. His work in the former category includes "DOWN AMONG THE DEAD MEN" (1954), in which dead bodies are revived and sent back into battle; "Firewater" (1952), a very unconventional invasion-of-Earth story; the classic "Child's Play" (1947); and "The Custodian" (1953). His single novel, *Of Men and Monsters* (1968), suggests that human destiny might not be as glorious as we would like to believe. Earth has been conquered by giant-sized aliens so powerful that they barely notice humans, who eventually work out a new existence as vermin living within the vast structures of Earth's new masters. The protagonist becomes disenchanted with the rituals and mythology of his people and realizes that humans will never rise to physically confront the aliens. He becomes involved in a kind of subtle reverse invasion in which humans infiltrate the alien starships and begin to spread beyond the Earth like rats on old sailing vessels. Despite the rather inglorious depiction of humanity's future, there is a qualified optimistic note in the novel.

Despite the excellence of his serious work, Tenn is known primarily for his inventive humor and wry satire. "THE FLAT-EYED MONSTER" (1955) turns science fiction conventions head over heels when a single human functions as a stereotypical movie monster on an alien world. The title is a play on the bug-eyed monsters of Hollywood. "The Liberation of Earth" (1953) describes the successive and ultimately destructive intervention of alien powers, each claiming to have humanity's best interests at heart. A very late story, "On Venus, Have We Got a Rabbi" (1977) only emphasized how much the field lost when Tenn stopped writing. Other humorous pieces of note include "Time Waits for Winthrop" (1951), a brilliantly funny time travel story, "The Remarkable Flirgeflip" (1950), and "Bernie the Faust" (1959).

Tenn's short stories were almost all collected in *Of All Possible Worlds* (1955), *The Human Angle* (1956), *Time in Advance* (1958), *The Seven Sexes* (1968), *The Square Root of Man* (1968), and *The Wooden Star* (1968). A two-volume omnibus collection entitled *Here Comes Civilization* and *Immodest Proposals*, released in 2001, contains all of his short fiction, including previously unreprinted work.

Tepper, Sheri S.
(1929–   )

Between 1983 and 1987, Sheri S. Tepper emerged as a major fantasy writer, with a dozen novels—most in one series or another—although she avoided falling into the formulas of most fantasy writers. Some of her magical events took place on other planets and incorporated elements of science fiction, but *The Awakeners* (1987, originally published in two volumes as *Northshore* and *Southshore*) was the first to be completely rationalized, although the story still has much the feeling of fantasy. The setting is a distant planet dominated by a gigantic river and a theocracy that proscribes travel to the east. A priestess and a boatman have serious questions about the rules by which they live and eventually subvert them.

After Long Silence (1988, also published as *The Enigma Score*) was a more overt move into science fiction. The story is a planetary adventure set on a world whose population chafes under a restrictive government. Their future is transformed when a strange variety of crystal proves to be the conduit to an alien form of life, a dangerous contact that can be ameliorated only through the use of music. *The Gate to Women's Country* (1988) is a postapocalyptic novel in which two societies evolve in the aftermath of a global war: one dominated by males, one by females. Tepper uses the two societies to illustrate the differences, as well as the similarities between the sexes. The interaction between them is handled in a balanced and insightful manner. This was the first of Tepper's novels to concentrate so completely on social issues, although there had been similar undercurrents in her earlier work.

Grass (1989) involves the investigation into a mysterious plague that has troubled both humans and members of an alien race. The only planet where the disease failed to gain a foothold was one that was jointly colonized by the two, so investigators suspect that something about the unique blend of societies that evolved there provides immunity. The sequels, *Raising the Stones* (1990) and *Sideshow* (1992), are completely independent stories whose various villains tend to be antilife, including a fundamentalist religious group that may have awakened real beings with superhuman powers and others who believe that the environment should be exploited rather than preserved. Tepper's feminist concerns became more prominent as well, with implication that we are controlled, and per-

haps doomed, by our own biology. *Shadow's End* (1995) was another interplanetary mystery. In this case, several human colonies were denuded of their population by a mysterious force, which predictably attracts the attention of authorities elsewhere.

Gibbon's Decline and Fall (1997) is an angrier feminist allegory. A wave of fundamentalism is sweeping the country, and an unprincipled politician tries to make use of a spectacular criminal trial to further his cause. *The Family Tree* (1997) poses an interesting situation. Intelligent animals from the far future achieve time travel and return to the contemporary world to prevent humans from damaging the planet's ecology. These animals sow the seeds of sentient plants and other wondrous biological forms. Tepper seemed to be less in control of her material in these last two novels, and her commentaries are so exaggerated that they lose their effectiveness. She was much more restrained in *Six Moon Dance* (1998), set on a planet where an indigenous virus invariably kills a large proportion of the colony's female children, leading to an imbalance between the genders that results in an unusual social structure. Although Tepper's strong feelings about gender relations are obvious once again, they are subordinated to the needs of the plot and emerge in more subtle ways. *Singer from the Sea* (1999) is set in a somewhat similar society and examines many of the same issues from a slightly different perspective. Together the two novels demonstrate the kind of thoughtful material Tepper can produce when she subordinates her social concerns to her stories.

The Fresco (2000) follows the adventures of a woman who is contacted by aliens who wish her to press their case with the government. In the process, she leaves her abusive husband and transforms her life. Although the plot is uneven and implausible at times, the characters are quite well-drawn. *The Visitor* (2002) is a postdisaster novel that mixes fantasy with its science fiction as a horde of apparently supernatural creatures emerge from the Earth in the aftermath of a cataclysm. *The Companions* (2003), another planetary mystery story, is gripping at times, but marred by some implausible details about the political situation on

Earth. Tepper has a powerful, inventive imagination that can produce powerful emotional responses in her readers when she does not allow her polemic purposes to overwhelm her narrative abilities.

This Immortal
Roger Zelazny
(1966)

This short novel originally appeared in magazine form as *And Call Me Conrad,* under which title it won a Hugo Award in a tie with DUNE by Frank HERBERT. The story is set on a future Earth that is recovering from the effects of a devastating nuclear war and has recently come under the influence of a humanoid alien race. Humanity is much diminished in number and in capacity, and the lingering effects of the war can be seen in the many mutations among plants and animals, as well as among humans. The attitude of people has changed as well; there is great respect for old legends, coupled with a less than healthy aversion toward thoughts of the future.

The arts administrator of Earth, much of which is essentially an outdoor museum, is Conrad Nomikos, a confident, intelligent man who is secretly an immortal and who periodically changes his identity in order to conceal his nature. Conrad has a strong sense of racial duty and is unhappy with the tendency of humans to model their lives after those of the technologically superior Vegans. The secondary protagonist is Hassan, a professional assassin whose single-mindedness is in sharp contrast to Conrad's efforts to grapple with human destiny. Part of the conflict originates with a band of rebels who believe, incorrectly, that the Vegans are planning to exploit the Earth and brush aside the remnants of humanity. In fact, the Vegans are actually testing Conrad to determine whether or not he should be their choice to oversee the Earth's preservation and restoration. There are parallels between Conrad's adventures and those of the legendary Hercules, and it is not surprising therefore that they take place primarily within the Mediterranean Basin, which in our time is the Mediterranean Sea.

The Three Stigmata of Palmer Eldritch
Philip K. Dick
(1965)

Much of Philip K. DICK's science fiction involves the quest for a transcendental experience, often through the use of drugs. The most explicit statement of this theme came in *The Three Stigmata of Palmer Eldritch,* set within a colony on the planet Mars, which has proven to be a much less pleasant environment than originally planned, but which still provides a refuge from Earth, where global warming has rendered most of the home world uninhabitable. The frequently dispirited colonists spend most of their leisure time under the influence of a powerful, but illegal, hallucinogenic drug that allows them to imagine themselves living within an elaborate set of models they maintain in their homes. The experience is so intense that it has aroused an almost religious fervor. The people who sell the drug are turning a nice profit, but new developments endanger their enterprise.

Palmer Eldritch has recently returned from another star system with a new drug that has similar but superior properties. With Choo-Z, the colonists can actually shape their subjective environments to a great extent, but there is one limitation placed on them. Although they have nearly godlike powers within their imagined universes, there is still one god placed higher than them, and that god is Palmer Eldritch. There is another initially less obvious difference as well. The older drug merely creates an illusion; Choo-Z may actually be generating another reality.

Religious imagery and metaphysical speculation became an increasingly important element in Dick's fiction after 1965, culminating with the VALIS TRILOGY. In this case, the image of a godlike Palmer Eldritch is reinforced by more subtle details, for example, that the drug is administered in the form of a wafer. Palmer Eldritch may in fact be a messiah, but if so he is not a traditional one. Even his last name is defined as strange and unearthly. The novel was nominated for a Nebula, although it did not win, possibly because the final chapters are, to a great degree, deliberately incomprehensible. Exposure to Choo-Z has altered the perceptions of all of the major characters by that point, and it becomes impossible to separate subjective and objective realities. It may be that the author intended that the incomprehensible material would establish the point that objective reality is just another illusion and that we each live to some degree in a separate, subjective universe.

"Thunder and Roses"
Theodore Sturgeon
(1947)

Many of the best stories in any genre are those that present their protagonists with difficult choices—often moral or ethical issues—forcing them to re-evaluate what they believe and possibly their own self-images before they can act. Theodore STURGEON often tested his characters to their limits in stories like "BULKHEAD" and "Maturity," but never as intensely as in this short, but very moving story. The United States has been destroyed in a surprise nuclear attack by two separate enemies. A few small pockets of survivors remain, but the radiation threat will kill them all within a year before spreading to the rest of the world, which will be devastated by the aftereffects, including those nations that launched the attack.

The story takes place on one of those bases, whose occupants are experiencing great difficulty reconciling themselves to the situation. They feel particularly shamed because there was no counterattack, even though the missile emplacements still exist and could yet be launched. To do so, however, would inevitably lead to the extinction of all life on Earth, human and otherwise. In his classic novel ON THE BEACH (1957), Nevil Shute did a fine job of conveying the overwhelming despair of the doomed survivors of a nuclear war, but what took him the length of a novel to accomplish, Sturgeon manages in the space of a few pages. His depiction of the obsessive compulsions of the survivors, the gradual collapse of discipline and order, and the mixture of rage and despair caused by their ineffectuality is stark and believable.

The crisis comes when two soldiers stumble into a concealed area from which it is still possible to launch that final attack. Although the setup is a bit implausible by contemporary standards, it has

no real bearing on the thrust of the plot. The protagonist, Pete Mawser, is consumed by rage and is initially tempted to strike back regardless of the consequences. His attitude changes when a dying entertainer arrives advocating acceptance of the situation in the hope that their temporary enemies will be able to survive the looming disaster and carry on. The decision to rise above nationalism and the desire for revenge in favor of mercy and restraint is difficult both for Mawser and for the reader to accept, but it is clearly the proper choice, and provides a note of hope in an otherwise hopeless situation.

"A Ticket to Tranai"
Robert Sheckley
(1955)

Satire has lost much of its popularity among modern science fiction readers, but there was a time when it was extremely common. Early in his career, Robert SHECKLEY proved himself a master of the short satirical piece, of which this particular story is probably his most cleverly constructed. The protagonist is an idealist from Earth who has been politically active for most of his life, without accomplishing anything he considers worthwhile. When he hears a story about the distant planet of Tranai, where a utopian society exists without crime, political corruption, poverty, or war, he decides to abandon his old life and emigrate, despite the dangerous trip involved. In due course he arrives, and his initial impression of the place is extremely favorable.

However, a few things bother him slightly. Women between the ages of 18 and 35 seem to live in seclusion, and many people have high-powered weapons near at hand. Government officials are universally anxious to resign their office, and the protagonist is even offered the planetary presidency, which he refuses. His first attempt to find a job is successful and the position pays well, although he is a bit startled to discover that his primary duty is to make robots less efficient and more irritating, since most of the population takes out its aggressive impulses by destroying them, thus diverting the pressures that might otherwise lead to interpersonal violence. This seems a small price to pay, however, and he settles down to the job, even finding himself a wife.

The truth emerges slowly: There is no crime on Tranai because there are no laws, and many citizens support themselves by quite legally stealing from one another. The missing women are held in suspended animation by their husbands, restored to consciousness only for special occasions. The husband is thus spared having to put up with his wife's foibles, and the wife will still be young when her husband dies, allowing her to live the balance of her life as a wealthy widow. Public officials wear a badge of office that explodes, with fatal consequences, if the citizenry is dissatisfied with their job performance; this eliminates corruption but also prevents elected officials from acting for the common good.

As with all good satire, Sheckley is doing more than just poking fun at human stupidity. One of the characters states outright that this is a utopia for human beings, not for saints, and that the only way people can live in a traditional utopian society is to surrender their humanity and become something else. It is easy to describe a situation in which everything works perfectly if everyone cooperates; but in the real world, it is necessary to accept human imperfections.

Tilley, Patrick
(1928–   )

Patrick Tilley's first novel, *Fade-Out* (1975, revised 1987), is an unusual first contact story in which the arrival of an alien vessel on Earth causes all the surrounding electrical systems to cease operating. The vessel's single passenger resembles an oversized insect, which complicates efforts to initiate communication, and there is the usual mix of paranoia, enthusiasm, and panic among the various political, military, and civilian characters whose reactions we follow. The novel is structured as a techno-thriller rather than along traditional genre lines, and its strong opening becomes attenuated as Tilley waits just slightly too long to begin revealing secrets. His second novel, *Mission* (1981), was also outside the mainstream of science fiction. The

body of Jesus Christ turns up in the 20th century and becomes animate again, leading to the eventual revelation that he is actually a time-traveling alien who has possessed a human body from the past and brought it forward to the present. The convoluted plot has some surprising twists and turns, but eventually breaks down under the weight of its many implausibilities. Tilley would employ a similar device in *Xan* (1985), this time having aliens pose as demons, but that novel was even less cohesive.

Tilley's major genre contribution was the Amtrak Wars series, which began with *The Cloud Warrior* (1984). A nuclear war devastated the world, but some individuals survived by retreating into self-sufficient underground shelters. Generations later they send individuals to the surface in the opening stages of a plan to reclaim the world. In *The First Family* (1985), they discover that not everyone on the surface perished, and before long a new war is underway, this time between the surface and the underground colonies. Feudal warlords from Japan and a horde of mutants complicate things even further in *Iron Master* (1987), and the multisided battle continues in three additional volumes, *Blood River* (1988), *Death-Bringer* (1998), and *Earth-Thunder* (1998). *Star Wartz* (1985) is an occasionally humorous spoof of space opera involving an inept entrepreneur on the rim of the galaxy. Although Tilley has always written from the point of view of an outsider, his Amtrak Wars series demonstrates what might be accomplished if men's adventure series, such as the Deathlands books by James Axler, were written more plausibly and were less prone to repeat the same formula from one book to the next.

Time Considered As a Helix of Semi-Precious Stones
Samuel R. Delany
(1969)

A frequent protagonist in the works of Samuel R. DELANY is the young male orphan who has turned to a life of petty crime. This novelette, which bears a distant relation to Delany's later, controversial novel *DHALGREN* (1974), follows the early career of one such man, who turned to petty theft almost immediately following his release from an orphanage and subsequently has traveled around the solar system under so many different names that the reader, and possibly the narrator himself, does not know his true identity.

His life is altered by an unexpected crisis when he discovers that he is on the verge of advancing from petty thief to professional criminal, a change of status that requires him to invest in at least some legitimate enterprises as a method of establishing himself with the political power structure. This attracts the attention of a special bureau of the police that uses sophisticated computer techniques to locate and attempt to neutralize such transformations. The narrator must then dispose of a valuable stock of stolen goods without losing his liberty in the process, which he accomplishes by receiving an indirect invitation to a party hosted by wealthy and influential people who have connections to the government as well as the upper reaches of organized crime. We are also introduced to the concept of the Singers, an honored minority of talented entertainers whose random performances invariably cause a stir. One of the Singers apparently was involved in a sadomasochistic relationship with the thief at some time in the past, and subjects himself to considerable pain again in order to facilitate his friend's escape.

Delany was one of a growing number of new writers during the 1960s who did not feel constrained to resort to the usual genre conventions. His characters were not always heroic or even honorable, and they sometimes failed. In this case the thief succeeds in escaping the immediate danger, although his future remains uncertain; he has perhaps failed his Singer friend, and even more importantly, himself. The story won both the Hugo and Nebula Awards.

The Time Machine
H. G. Wells
(1895)

The concept of travel through time was not original to H. G. WELLS. Charles Dickens moved Scrooge into his own past and future in *The Christ-* mas Carol (1843), and other writers had used similar magical or mystical means to accomplish the same thing. Wells, however, wrote the first significant tale in which travel to another age was achieved through scientific endeavor, in this case the creation of a machine that somehow allowed its operator to step outside the normal flow of time and move forward or backward at will. The idea for the story germinated in a series of essays Wells had written some years earlier under the title *The Chronic Argonauts*. The ensuing work of fiction—actually a novella rather than a novel—also reflected Wells's preoccupation with socialist political philosophy and his conviction that class struggle was inevitable.

The time traveler, whose name we never learn, expects to find himself in a utopian future where socialism has transformed the world. Instead, he emerges from his travels in what appears to be a combination of park and wilderness. The first humans he encounters are the Eloi, who are friendly and lack guile or anger, at first suggesting that he was correct in his assumptions. Later he discovers that there are two strains of humanity. The second, the Morlocks—descended from a capitalist aristocracy—are deformed and live underground, but still dominate the world, breeding the Eloi for food. Unlike the two film versions (1960, 2002), which both take various liberties with Wells's story, the book does not have a happy ending with the Morlocks destroyed and the Eloi liberated.

In addition to the two film versions of Wells's original novel, there have been several sequels, penned by other authors. The best of these is *The Time Ships* (1995) by Stephen BAXTER. The anonymous traveler is off again, but this time he discovers that his earlier travels have altered the course of human history. The Morlocks still emerged, but they are comparatively benevolent and have developed a remarkable technology that allowed them to encase the sun in a sphere and to abandon the Earth for life in space. With a Morlock companion, the traveler returns to explore alternate timelines. Egon Friedell's *The Return of the Time Machine* (published in German in 1946 and translated into English in 1972) suggests further but less interesting adventures as the time traveler investigates other eras. *Time Machine II* (1981) by George Pal and Joe Morhaim, which may have been intended as the basis for a sequel to the original film, sends another man on a search through time. These direct continuations of the story are not nearly as significant as the vast number of unrelated time travel stories and novels that are variations of the concept Wells first formulated.

Time Patrol series
Poul Anderson

Change war stories—adventures in which two or more parties are involved in efforts to either change the course of history or preserve its original sequence of events—have long been popular in science fiction, and writers such as Simon Hawke, Sean Dalton, and Larry Maddock have constructed entire series about such battles. At its best, the form incorporates two popular elements. First, authors can play "What if" and speculate about the consequences of some usually very minor variation. Second, the plot is generally cast in the form of a puzzle. The author describes the consequences of the change and challenges the protagonist, and the reader, to reason backward to find out what critical event was altered. The two most famous sequences are those by Fritz LEIBER and the Time Patrol series by Poul ANDERSON.

Anderson began chronicling the adventures of Manse Everard, an agent for the Time Patrol, during the 1950s with such excellent stories as "Delenda Est" (1955) and "Brave to Be a King" (1959). In each of these, someone has managed to change a crucial event in the past, distorting everything that followed, and Everard must travel back through time to reverse the alteration. His first four adventures were collected as *Guardians of Time* (1960), with two further episodes added for the 1981 edition.

Anderson's stories contained a substantial amount of overt action, but he always provided a detailed, historically accurate background that is sometimes more interesting than the immediate surface conflict. More stories followed; despite their relatively similar plots, each seemed fresh and interesting because of Anderson's colorful

historical settings. Two more compilations were published: *The Shield of Time* (1990) and *The Time Patrol* (1991).

Anderson added two novels to the series in 1983. *The Time Patrolman* is assembled from shorter work and is set primarily in ancient Scandinavia. In *The Year of the Ransom*, ostensibly for young adults, a conquistador discovers the existence of time travelers and steals one of their machines, leading the protagonist on an exciting chase through time. *The Annals of the Time Patrol* (1984) is an omnibus collection of the series. "Star of the Sea" (1991) is the best of the later titles in the series.

Tiptree, James, Jr.
(1915–1987)

Alice Sheldon began her science fiction career as James Tiptree Jr. in 1968 and was assumed to be a male until her real name was revealed in 1977. Thereafter she continued to write as Tiptree and occasionally as Raccoona Sheldon. Her earliest work was colorful and often quite striking, but it only hinted at the quality of the material she would produce later. Stories such as "AMBERJACK" (1969) demonstrated her ability to tell a complex story in an economical manner, and others, including "Parimutuel Planet" (1968) and "Your Haploid Heart" (1969), proved that she could bring new life to familiar situations. Some of her early stories were no more than light space adventures, although they were generally well written.

Tiptree seemed to find her voice at the beginning of the 1970s, producing a steady stream of fine stories. A vastly superior alien culture contacts humanity in "And I Found Me Here on the Cold Hill's Side" (1972), but the interaction of the two cultures is inadvertently destructive to humans. "The Man Who Walked Home" (1972) is a clever and emotion-laden story of a man trapped by forces beyond his control. Tiptree's feminist leanings became apparent in "The WOMEN MEN DON'T SEE" (1973), in which two women choose alien companions in preference to a male human. This story suggests that we are culturally blind to gender differences, and that men and women are, at least in one sense, two separate alien species themselves. That same year saw two more of her most successful stories. "The GIRL WHO WAS PLUGGED IN" is a bitter indictment of the consumer culture and the way in which we exploit one another for personal profit. "LOVE IS THE PLAN THE PLAN IS DEATH" is an extended metaphor about the destructive effects the two genders have upon one another, expressed in an exaggerated form by means of an alien species whose gender roles have been pushed to an extreme. The former story won a Hugo Award, and the latter a Nebula.

Tiptree's first collection, *10,000 Light Years from Home* (1973), underlined her sudden ascendancy within the genre, and a second, *Warm Worlds & Otherwise* (1975), confirmed it. Although her output had begun to decline in quantity, those stories she did write were invariably excellent. "A Momentary Taste of Being" (1975) is one of her longer pieces, a rather depressing but speculatively fascinating examination of humanity's role in the universe, reduced at last to a minor evolutionary spasm. Another long story, "HOUSTON, HOUSTON, DO YOU READ?" (1976) indicted male chauvinism in no uncertain terms, with a contemporary crew of astronauts propelled through an anomaly into a future in which males have become extinct. It won both the Hugo and Nebula Awards. Other outstanding stories from her late career include "The Screwfly Solution" (1977) and the posthumously published "The Color of Neanderthal Eyes" (1988) and "Backward, Turn Backward" (1988).

Although Tiptree is primarily known for her short fiction, she also wrote two interesting novels. A mysterious and dangerous alien force is spreading through the galaxy in *Up the Walls of the World* (1978), compelling a band of individuals with various psi powers to forge a combined defense against its encroachment. Scenes set on an alien world inhabited by a telepathic species capable of flight are particularly evocative. In *Brightness Falls from the Air* (1985), a team of scientists and others travel through space to observe a rare astronomical event, unaware that the experience will have a strong psychological impact on them individually and as a group. Although there are flashes of brilliance in both novels, Tiptree seemed unable to

sustain the emotional impact of her work at that length.

Tiptree's later stories are collected in *Star Song of an Old Primate* (1978), *Out of the Everywhere and Other Extraordinary Visions* (1981), *Byte Beautiful* (1988), *Crown of Stars* (1988), *Her Smoke Rose Up Forever* (1990), and *Meet Me at Infinity* (1990). *The Starry Rift* (1986), ostensibly a novel, is actually a series of short episodes that collectively describe humanity's destiny in the wider universe. The stories in *Tales of the Quintana Roo* (1986) are primarily fantasy.

"To See the Invisible Man"
Robert Silverberg
(1963)

Science fiction writers have suggested a variety of unusual ways to deal with criminals. George ZEBROWSKI exiled them into outer space in *Brute Orbits* (1998), Robert A. HEINLEIN sequestered them in an isolated part of Earth in "Coventry" (1940), and Robert SILVERBERG himself resorted to dispatching them into prehistory in *Hawksbill Station* (1968). In this short story, he creates another form of exile—one much closer to home.

The unnamed narrator has been convicted of coldness, of not sharing his emotions with other people, thereby branding himself as antisocial. The reader is supposed to have mixed feelings about this, because, on the one hand, the character has apparently purposefully cut himself off from others. On the other hand, the state that considers such behavior a crime is itself paternalistic and restrictive. The punishment seems at first to be an enlightened one, and ironic to boot. Since he cares little for his fellow human beings, the narrator is sentenced to legal invisibility for one year—though not a literal invisibility. Rather, his forehead is marked with a device that announces his punishment, and all other human beings, even other invisibles, are proscribed from talking to him, helping him, or even hindering him, although there are some clever ways of getting around the rule to prevent him from inflicting harm on others.

At first he has a feeling of power. No one charges him admission to events, and no one prevents him from stealing what he wants or needs to survive. He no longer has a job, of course, and his time is his own. But as the days pass, his longing for human companionship grows increasingly powerful, and before his one-year sentence expires he is stressed to the point of insanity. Although he is relieved when life returns to normal, he subsequently acknowledges another invisible person and is rearrested, presumably to be sentenced to another period of ostracism. He now feels he will carry this sentence as a badge of honor, having recognized that the state's punishment for his supposed lack of human feelings is an even greater inhumanity. Silverberg's indictment of a society that seeks to impose morality is an effective cautionary tale in the tradition of NINETEEN EIGHTY-FOUR (1949) by George Orwell. It is also an interesting contrast to "The VISIBLE MAN" (1975) by Gardner DOZOIS, in which criminals are hypnotically conditioned so that they are unable to see anyone else.

Tubb, E. C.
(1919–   )

The English author Edwin Charles Tubb began writing science fiction in the early 1950s and within the next 10 years had produced an astonishingly large amount of fiction, both novels and short stories, under his own name and many pseudonyms, some of which are still unknown, and most of which appeared exclusively in Great Britain. His novels from this period were invariably adventure stories, usually set in outer space, sometimes in dystopian futures or other standard settings. The best of these were Enterprise 2215 (1954) and The Extra Man (1954), both published under the name Charles Grey, and The Space Born (1956)—his first novel to appear in the United States—under his own name. It anticipated LOGAN'S RUN (1967) by William F. Nolan and George Clayton Johnson by suggesting that population control might be implemented by an age limit aboard a generation starship, enforced by an elite corps of assassins, one of whom has second thoughts.

Tubb began to sell to American markets in the late 1950s, but never as successfully as in his home

country, and only one further novel appeared during the next several years. The Mechanical Monarch (1958) is a fairly standard dystopian tale. The British market contracted during that same period, and Tubb's output dropped off sharply—perhaps to his benefit, because his next novel, Moonbase (1964), was a much more mature work. An investigator sent to the Moon to look into a series of odd incidents immediately finds his life in danger. Tubb's novels would continue to be light adventure stories throughout his career, but from the 1960s onward they were much more smoothly written than his early work.

The Winds of Gath (1967, also published as Gath) was the first novel in the Dumarest series, which would prove to be Tubb's most famous work. Dumarest is a typical taciturn hero, a traveler among the stars who stowed away as a child on Earth and became lost in a galaxy that now believes Earth to be a legend with no basis in reality. Although Dumarest is determined to return to his home world, his efforts are complicated by the fact that no one knows where it is, by the immediate dangers he faces on the various worlds he visits, and in later volumes by an organization of fanatics who are determined to capture him. In The Return (1997), the 32nd and final volume in the series, Dumarest finally outwits his enemies and reaches home. The wide-open space adventure format used throughout the series has become less popular in recent years and the final volume has appeared only from a small press, which has also reprinted several of his earliest novels in limited softcover editions.

S.T.A.R. Flight (1969) suggests that immortality might not be a blessing after all. Aliens have brought the secret to Earth, but in exchange they keep most of the human race narrowly confined and impoverished. Tubb would later examine the same theme from a different viewpoint in Death Wears a White Face (1979). Many of Tubb's plots involve apparent paradoxes, as in Century of the Manikin (1972), in which a famous proponent of world peace and centralized government is a awakened from suspended animation in a future world in which her goals have been reached, imposed by force, and finds herself opposed to the very institution she formerly advocated. The Primitive (1977) is an extended coming-of-age story, with its protagonist escaping a barbaric world to become an interstellar magnate. *Pawn of the Omphalos* (1980) is a wide-ranging space opera that never quite lives up to its ambitious plot. Tubb's most original novel is *The Luck Machine* (1980), in which a scientist develops a device that can alter the laws of chance, concentrating good luck in one area. Unfortunately, there is a law of conservation of chance, and good fortune in one place is offset by pockets of bad luck elsewhere. His best novel, *Stardeath* (1983), is a complex scientific mystery involving disappearing starships and physically transformed space travelers.

Between 1973 and 1975, under the name Gregory Kern, Tubb wrote 16 adventures of Cap Kennedy, a space ranger patterned after Captain Future, though updated slightly for modern audiences. The series opened with *Galaxy of the Lost* and closed with *Beyond the Galactic Lens*. Although these were extremely lightweight space operas in a tradition that largely has lost its audience, they were briefly popular, and the last two in the series were considerably more complex and interesting, although they came too late to matter. Tubb also wrote tie-in novels set in the world of the *Space 1999* television series, and published two collections of short stories, *A Scatter of Stardust* (1972) and *Murder in Space* (1998).

Tucker, Wilson
(1914–   )

Wilson "Bob" Tucker was involved in science fiction fandom and published an amateur magazine for several years before making his first professional fiction sale. He was fairly productive during the 1950s but wrote only intermittently after that; about half of his novels are detective thrillers. Although he wrote occasional short stories, almost all of his fiction is book length. *The Best of Wilson Tucker* (1982) contains all of his stories worth preserving. Tucker was famous for using the names of other fans and friends for characters in his work, and this practice has come to be known as *tuckerization*.

Tucker's first science fiction novel was *The City in the Sea* (1951), a minor, sometimes awk-

ward potboiler about a hidden refuge beneath the ocean where a small group managed to survive a nuclear war generations in the past, and the problems caused when they reemerge into the recovering surface world. *The Long Loud Silence* (1952) was also set in the aftermath of a global holocaust, but was considerably better constructed—and rather suggestively graphic for its time, subtly implying that the survivors would need to resort to cannibalism. In *The Time Masters* (1953), two immortal aliens have been secretly living among humans, guiding their progress throughout the generations, one motivated by basically benevolent principles, the other disposed in the opposite direction. Their shadow war is fought with human puppets who are unaware of the powers behind the scenes. The sequel, *Time Bomb* (1955, also published as *Tomorrow Plus X*), one of the best of his early novels, is a cleverly constructed story in which someone in the future is killing selected individuals in the present by sending bombs back through time to explode at the appropriate time and place, offering a somewhat unusual problem for the protagonists. *Wild Talent* (1954, also published as *The Man from Tomorrow*) tells the story of a man with psi powers secretly living among ordinary humans. The scenario is a less melodramatic variation of *The Power* (1956) by Frank ROBINSON.

The Lincoln Hunters (1958) also involves time travel, but Tucker's writing had become considerably more sophisticated by the late 1950s. This time scientists from a repressive future society travel back to the 19th century to record a lost speech by Abraham Lincoln, but in the process they initiate changes that cause major alterations to their home time. Tucker exerted considerable effort to accurately depict the Civil War setting, and the contrast between that era and the mildly dystopian future is quite striking. *To the Tombaugh Station* (1960) is a slight but effective story of murder aboard a spaceship.

Tucker concentrated on detective stories during the 1960s. His next science fiction novel, *The Year of the Quiet Sun*, another story of time travel, this time forward, did not appear until 1970. The protagonist is a black man who finds himself in a world sharply divided following a racial war, and his own racial identity causes serious difficulties.

This is generally considered Tucker's best novel, and blends a wide mix of historical research, social commentary, and imagery drawn from other sources, in this case mostly biblical, into a coherent whole. *Ice and Iron* (1974) followed, set in the early stages of the next ice age. Scientists studying the advancing glaciers discover the bodies of individuals who have apparently been sent back through time from the future. Tucker's last novel was *Resurrection Days* (1981), in which a contemporary man is revived in a dystopian future in which only women have free will. His presence disrupts things in a predictable but not very convincing fashion.

During the 1950s, Tucker was a reliable writer whose work was squarely in the mainstream of science fiction, and who wrote in a consistent, clear prose style but who rarely rose above simple storytelling. *The Lincoln Hunters* suggested a promising potential, but his emerging talents did not develop as they might have. Although *The Year of the Quiet Sun* was an even greater step forward, his subsequent novels were of considerably less interest. He secured a place of honor in the field's history, but his relatively small body of science fiction leaves his future reputation uncertain.

Turner, George
(1916–1997)

The Australian writer George Turner published five mainstream novels before turning to science fiction, although he had written considerable criticism in the field before his first novel, *Beloved Son*, appeared in 1978. The novel describes the experiences of a group of interstellar explorers who return to Earth only to discover that it has been devastated and largely depopulated by a global war. The new civilization that followed has apparently forsworn many of the sins of the past, but compliance with the new order is imposed rather relentlessly, raising new questions about the role of science in society, particularly with regard to manipulation of human DNA. Genetic engineering would prove to be a recurring concern in Turner's work, and the novel became the first of three set against a common background, known as the Ethical Society series, although these works feature no

recurring characters and no continuing story line. The other two titles are *Vaneglory* (1981) and *Yesterday's Men* (1983), both of which expand on the issues raised in the opening volume. In the first of these, the discovery of a means to dramatically prolong human life complicates matters even further, and in the latter we learn that despite apparent changes, human nature is relatively immutable and the old failings persist even under these new circumstances. Turner's themes are serious and complex, and his prose often intellectualized and demanding.

Drowning Towers (1987, also published as *The Sea and Summer*) was a much more commercial book and far more successful, but without sacrificing the depth of thought of his earlier work. The setting is a near future in which the greenhouse effect has caused a general rise in the oceans and the loss of much coastal land in Australia and elsewhere. Despite the climatic changes, the population has continued to increase; most cities have become unbearably dense concentrations of increasingly desperate people. Although Turner does not minimize the challenges facing the inhabitants of his rather daunting future, the story is relatively upbeat.

His subsequent novels have occasionally risen to the same level, but none of his later work was as consistently impressive. *Brain Child* (1991) considers the consequences of genetic manipulation once again. The protagonist is puzzled by a recent suicide and becomes gradually aware of a secretive scientific project whose purpose is to enhance human heredity and create a subset of superior humans, among whose number the narrator somewhat unsettlingly finds himself.

The Destiny Makers (1993), like *Blade Runner* (1974) by Alan E. NOURSE, postulates a future in which overpopulation has become the largest problem facing humanity, leading to unusual measures to curtail further growth. One law prohibits the use of extraordinary medical treatments to save individual lives, a law that is frequently disobeyed by the very rich. *Genetic Soldier* (1994) is a variation of Turner's first novel. This time long-absent star travelers return to an Earth where genetic engineering has been used to create an army of enhanced soldiers whose mission is to protect Earth from all outsiders. Turner's last novel was *Down There in the Darkness* (1999), the story of two men who are revived from suspended animation in a future in which technology has receded, with both benefits and drawbacks.

Turner wrote very few short stories; virtually all of these are collected in *Pursuit of Miracles* (1990). He turned to science fiction very late in his life and in his writing career, and brought with him a maturity of viewpoint and a refinement in narrative and prose styling that many other writers never master. Although his futuristic settings tend to be grim, his work is never despairing, accepting the complexity of the problems besetting humanity and holding out hope that we will ultimately reach into ourselves and find a solution.

Turtledove, Harry
(1949–   )

Harry Turtledove's first two books were fantasy novels written as Eric Iverson. Although he dropped the pseudonym after they appeared, most of his work during the 1980s continued to be fantasy, drawn from his extensive background training in history. Several early short stories were assembled as *Agent of Byzantium* (1987), all set in an alternate world in which the Byzantine Empire never fell. Alternate history would prove to be a fertile resource for him and most of his future novels would make use of that device. *Noninterference* (1988) was more traditional science fiction, the story of human explorers who break the rules about interfering with primitive alien cultures, with consequences far more radical than they expected. *A Different Flesh* (1988) is set in an alternate world where protohumans survived in North America to be discovered by Columbus, and *A World of Difference* (1990) is an adventure story on an alternate, inhabited Mars. Turtledove had by now produced a considerable body of short stories, of which he would write significantly fewer in the years that followed. Many of these are collected in *Kaleidoscope* (1990) and *Departures* (1993). The best of his shorter work is "The Pugnacious Peacemaker" (1990), a sequel to *The Wheels of If* (1940) by L. Sprague De CAMP.

Turtledove's science fiction from 1990 forward consists of alternate history stories almost to the exclusion of everything else, other than the occasional fantasy adventure. One of the first and best of these was *Guns of the South* (1992), essentially a change war story in which a group of time travelers provides advanced weaponry to the Confederacy. That was followed by the World War series, consisting of *In the Balance* (1994), *Tilting the Balance* (1995), *Upsetting the Balance* (1996), and *Striking the Balance* (1996). During the midst of World War II, malevolent aliens invade the Earth, landing in various places and forcing communists, fascists, and the free world to unite against their common enemy. The outcome seems in doubt until the defenders successfully develop atomic weapons and use them against the enemy. Although the premise was an interesting one, the series is uneven and betrays a failing that would recur frequently in the author's work: The text becomes so involved with speculation about the changing relationships among nations and political leaders that other story values are subordinated. At times these works read like extended lectures rather than fiction, despite a very large cast of characters and many shifts of viewpoint. By contrast, *The Two Georges* (1996), an alternate history written with the actor Richard Dreyfuss in which the American colonies never revolted, is both an interesting speculative work and an absorbing novel.

How Few Remain (1997) returns to the Civil War—or more precisely, the war's aftermath in a history where the Confederacy prevailed. The Confederacy's subsequent effort to annex a portion of Mexico leads to renewed hostilities. This led logically to Turtledove's Great War sequence, in which an independent Confederacy complicates matters during World War I. *American Front* (1998) places what remains of the United States on the side of Germany. *Walk in Hell* (1999) and *Breakthroughs* (2000) continue the story, with communist agents disrupting the situation in North America, eventually leading to a renewed war against the South. The Colonization trilogy is largely a recapitulation of the World War series. Earth unites against alien invaders in *Second Contact* (1999), *Down to Earth* (2000), and *Aftershocks* (2001), ultimately prevailing against them.

Turtledove added to the saga of the Confederacy with yet another sequence consisting of *Blood and Iron* (2001), *The Center Cannot Hold* (2002), and *The Victorious Opposition* (2003). The Confederacy was on the losing side during the Great War series. The United States is subverted and becomes a socialist state, while its ravaged southern neighbor becomes a fascist dictatorship, setting the stage for renewed conflict. Another series has recently begun with *Gunpowder Empire* (2003), set in an alternate history in which the Roman Empire never fell. Turtledove's remaining two alternate history novels appear to be singletons, although Turtledove may well decide to add to them in the future. *Ruled Britannia* (2002), one of his best novels, is set in an England that became a Spanish colony after the Armada successfully invaded. The poet William Shakespeare is called upon to inspire the populace to revolt. *In the Presence of Mine Enemies* (2003) takes place in a world in which the Nazis successfully conquered Europe. Turtledove's more recent short fiction has been collected in *Counting Up, Counting Down* (2002). "Down in the Bottomlands" (1994) won a Hugo Award.

20,000 Leagues Under the Sea
Jules Verne
(1872)

Jules VERNE is often referred to as the father of action-based science fiction, and many of his novels are considered classics not only of the genre but also of entertainment literature in general. Several of his best-known works involve fabulous journeys—to the Moon, to the center of the Earth, into space on a comet, to the North Pole, or just a grand tour around the entire globe. Possibly the most famous and probably the best written of these was *20,000 Leagues Under the Sea*. Although it is not true (as some believe) that Verne predicted the submarine—a primitive submarine had been used during the Revolutionary War in America—his vision of life aboard a submersible included many details in which he fairly accurately anticipated the future.

The story is straightforward and familiar: Something or someone is sinking the warships of various nations—a mysterious force that, based on

admittedly disjointed reports, many believe to be a monster. An expedition to track down the monster goes awry, and the protagonists find themselves taken aboard a submersible vessel that uses a technology far beyond that of any known power. The enigmatic Captain Nemo commands the vessel, the *Nautilus*, which is crewed by dedicated men so angered by the violence of modern civilization that they have joined with him in a pact to prey on war vessels regardless of the flag they fly until it is theoretically impossible for the nations of the Earth to wage war.

Nemo is the most complex character in all of Verne's fiction, a man driven to commit numerous evil acts even though he is motivated by a desire for goodness. He is not so much a villain as a tragic hero, and the reader has mixed emotions when the *Nautilus* and her crew are finally so badly damaged that they surrender themselves to a watery grave. The most ambitious novel Verne ever wrote, *20,000 Leagues Under the Sea* was one of the few to rise above simple adventure and attempt to examine serious moral issues. Although not nearly as well known, *The Mysterious Island* (1875), the sequel, is also among Verne's better works. Both novels have been made into motion pictures, the former at least three times; the Disney version is a film classic.

Two Dooms
C. M. Kornbluth
(1958)

There have been literally dozens of alternate history stories whose critical event is some aspect of World War II, many of them set in a world where the Germans and Japanese won the war and occupy part or all of the United States. *The MAN IN THE HIGH CASTLE* (1962) by Philip K. DICK, *SS-GB* (1978) by Len Deighton, and *Fatherland* (1992) by Robert Harris are some of the more popular examples. One of the earliest and still among the best of these is this novella by C. M. KORNBLUTH, one of the last things he wrote prior to his death.

The protagonist is Edward Royland, a scientist working on the Manhattan Project who partakes of a peyotelike hallucinogen and awakens to find himself 150 years in the future, in an America that has been ruled jointly by Germany and Japan ever since 1955. Royland is not an entirely sympathetic character. He had formerly found much to admire in the efficiency of the two dictatorships, and once he accepts that he has been projected into the future and is not just dreaming, he attempts to find a place among the conquerors instead of the conquered, hoping that his knowledge of atomic weapons development—which has apparently been completely lost—can be used as a bargaining chip to better his circumstances. He finds instead that the Germans, and later the Japanese, are both dominated by a primitive tribal culture that lacks flexibility, retards progress, and reacts with dull routine to even extraordinary circumstances. Kornbluth, who had previously expressed some disdain for the shortsightedness of the masses in "The MARCHING MORONS" (1951), shows a similar pessimism about the leadership elite as well.

Contained within the story is a short but interesting scenario that explains the outcome of the war, and that proves to the narrator that he is not in his own future but in an alternate universe where Hitler was a minor player and Herman Göring ruled a Germany that was more victim than predator. He eventually reawakens in his original time and place, convinced now of the wisdom of developing an atomic bomb as the lesser of two evils.

2001: A Space Odyssey
Arthur C. Clarke
(1968)

Arthur C. CLARKE developed the original idea for *2001: A Space Odyssey* in 1953 in a short story titled "Sentinel of Eternity," later just "Sentinel," in which an expedition to the Moon discovers what is obviously an artifact left by previous visitors, presumably alien, that never reveals its purpose.

Fifteen years later, Clarke would coauthor a script with Stanley Kubrick that would be made into one of the most famous science fiction films of all time. He simultaneously wrote a book-length version that was released at the same time as the movie.

The novel explains some but not all of the artifact's purpose and reveals that its alien builders had manipulated protohominids to stimulate them into using tools, thus starting the chain of events that resulted in intelligent human beings. The novel then jumps to the near future, in which a space mission is threatened by a malfunctioning artificial intelligence, the famous Hal, and later a mystical experience that transforms the only survivor. This vision of a future in which humanity evolves into another stage of existence can also be found in Clarke's earlier novel *Childhood's End* (1953) and was hinted at in his first book-length fiction, *Against the Fall of Night* (1948/53).

Clarke revisited this theme in *2010: Odyssey Two* (1982). The defective computer Hal is reactivated in an attempt to discover what went wrong, while elsewhere an expedition is mounted to visit the moons of Jupiter, where more alien monoliths have been discovered. This novel was subsequently filmed, but much less successfully. *2061: Odyssey Three* (1988) continued the story, with an ever more ambitious human project to study the monoliths, which appear to be watching over the emergence of another form of intelligent life in the Jovian system and which eventually will instigate a major astronomical upheaval to ensure their safety and prevent humans from interfering with their development. The series was brought to an apparent close in *3001: The Final Odyssey* (1997), wherein the body of the astronaut lost in *2001* is recovered and reanimated, and in which humanity must find a way to deal with an alien monolith that apparently is malfunctioning. Although the three sequels are all solidly written, they lack the freshness that characterized the first book in the series and most of Clarke's other work.

U

Ubik
Philip K. Dick
(1969)

Gross distortions of what we consider the real universe were common in the work of Philip K. DICK even before he began emerging as a major novelist. In *Eye in the Sky* (1957) a group of individuals find themselves in successive realities where one or another of their group has managed to superimpose distorted versions of natural law on their environment. The concept that the universe is not perceived identically from one individual to another, and that these perceptions are all valid, would recur in different guises, such as *Clans of the Alphane Moon* (1964), in which only the inmates of an insane asylum survive and prosper, resulting in differing tribes with different manias. But paradoxically, it is this very inability to look at the world in the same way that allows them to resist conquest by an outside power.

In *Ubik*, there is growing conflict between those with psi talents and those who are alarmed by these extrasensory powers. Joe Chip, the protagonist, lives in a world almost unrecognizable to the reader. People are now able to transcend death, after a fashion, by preserving their consciousness in a state known as half life. Much of the surface conflict originates in the rivalry between two businesses, but the story changes dramatically with the passing of one major player into half life, from which he makes occasional appearances as the forces of deterioration and of renewal contend with the nature of the universe itself. The *Ubik* of the title is a form of compressed reality stored in aerosol containers that can actually cause objects to regress functionally—that is, an application to an automobile could change it into a horse and buggy. Images of decay often show up in Dick's fiction, but rarely so explicitly. The novel ends on a note of ambiguity, which annoyed some readers, who wanted to know which reality was the correct one, missing the point that there is no objective universe, just the one that we perceive and shape as the sum of our individual perceptions.

Uplift series
David Brin

David BRIN introduced the Uplift series with his first novel, *Sundiver* (1980). The Uplift universe is an interstellar society where various intelligent species manipulate the evolution of lower animals so that they are also sentient, a progression stretching back into the ancient past. Humans are the only species that seem to have reached a level supporting interstellar travel without having been the clients of another species, a mystery that may be resolved when an expedition from Mercury investigates anomalies in the corona of the sun. Humans have themselves begun to uplift other forms of life by the time of *Startide Rising* (1983). The Progenitors, who were the first intelligent species in the galaxy, may have left clues to their existence and fate on a remote planet, which, unfortunately, is the focus of an imminent interstellar war. A ship from Earth with a mixed crew of humans, chimps, and dolphins has crashed on that world and is caught between rival forces, but still manages to make some startling discoveries. *The Uplift War* (1987) is also set on a planet with artifacts left over by the Progenitors, but this planet has been colonized by humans and their client species.

The next two novels in the series make up a single sequence within the greater one. *Brightness Reef* (1996) and *Infinity's Shore* (1996) are both set on the planet Jixxo. A mixed bag of refugees and prisoners from various alien and uplifted species live in general harmony on this obscure world, concealing their presence from a galactic civilization they feel would not tolerate their indepen-

dence. Unfortunately, they cannot remain undiscovered indefinitely, and the arrival of a ship from outside threatens their security. Even if the outsiders refrain from intervening directly, renewed contact with offworlders will almost certainly introduce new pressures into a fragile society and bring their refuge to an end. *Heaven's Reach* (1998) is the most recent novel in the series, which remains sufficiently open-ended to allow for further volumes. The various individuals who have opted out of the galactic civilization continue to remain independent, and to conceal the fact that they are hiding a discovery that could shake the galaxy. The Uplift series remains popular with readers, but it appears that Brin may have tired of the concept, as he has chosen other venues for his last two novels.

V

Valis trilogy
Philip K. Dick
(1981–1982)

Transcendental experiences occur frequently in the work of Philip K. DICK, sometimes placing his characters in worlds whose reality is subjective, as in *Eye in the Sky* (1957), *The THREE STIGMATA OF PALMER ELDRITCH* (1964), and *UBIK* (1969). During the 1970s Dick began to incorporate religious themes more openly; these reached their peak with the three-volume thematically related set consisting of *Valis* (1981), *The Divine Invasion* (1982), and *The Transformation of Timothy Archer* (1982). The title of the first is an acronym for the Vast Active Living Intelligence System, essentially a stand-in for God.

The opening volume is the best of the three—a complex, occasionally almost opaque, and intensely personal novel in which Dick's own search for meaning in life is transposed onto his protagonist. A new messiah has arrived on Earth, in the form of a female infant, who confirms that activities on Earth are being monitored from space by an alien intelligence. The protagonist, who clearly is a substitute for Dick himself, searches for knowledge and fulfillment, a theme reflected by similar quests in the remaining two volumes. In *The Divine Invasion*, Christianity and Islam merge into a new religion just as an inhuman creature who might be a messenger from God returns to Earth after a lengthy exile. The Second Coming, if that is what is in the offing, is delayed by an aircraft accident that occurs as the characters deal with their own personal redemptions. A short story, "Chains of Air, Web of Aether" (1980), was incorporated within the novel. The third title follows the exploits of a lawyer who becomes a charismatic religious leader and is only marginally fantastic.

An alternate version of *Valis* was discovered after Dick's death and published posthumously as *Radio Free Albemuth* (1985); the story is set within an American dictatorship under the eye of an alien-constructed satellite. Much of the metaphysical background for the novels is discussed in the nonfiction work "Exegesis." The three novels marked a significant change in the kind of work the author was writing, and many readers found his new direction more thought-provoking but less entertaining.

van Vogt, A. E.
(1912–2000)

Alfred Elton van Vogt had two separate careers as a science fiction writer, the first lasting from 1939 to the early 1950s, the second from the middle of the 1960s until the 1980s. During the first phase of his career, he was an influential and popular writer who penned several minor classics; during the second, he was clearly out of touch with the changes in the genre and lacked the powerful imaginative creativity that was characteristic of his prior work. Many of the early novels appeared only in magazines until several years later. He was a prolific and inventive writer whose favorite themes included alien monsters, time travel paradoxes, and superhumans, and who spent comparatively little time on characterization or prose styling.

His first novel, SLAN (1940, book form in 1946), is still his best-known and possibly best-written novel, the story of mutants living hidden among ordinary humans to avoid persecution. It was not typical of the work that followed because of its relatively straightforward plot. Van Vogt would quickly become known for the complexity of his stories, which sometimes seemed to evade even the writer's control. Three short sequences quickly established his reputation, of which the Gilbert Gosseyn novels are the best known. The Gosseyn stories are The World of Null-A (1945/48) and The Pawns of Null-A (1948/56, also published as The Players of Null-A). Gosseyn is a superhuman whose consciousness moves between bodies, but he has no memories of his own past and eventually discovers he is a tool used by one alien species to protect the Earth from yet another. He overcomes one menace in the first book, only to face an even greater threat in the second. Van Vogt belatedly added Null-A Three in 1985, sending Gosseyn off to battle the masters of the universe, but this final adventure is markedly inferior.

A more coherent set consists of The Weapon Shops of Isher (1949/51) and The Weapon Makers (1943/46, also published as One Against Eternity). The backdrop is a future interstellar civilization that is ruled as one mildly despotic empire. A mysterious organization has built a series of weapon shops from which any citizen can buy highly advanced weaponry, the shops themselves being invulnerable to attack. Although many elements of the story are implausible and the libertarian message is thickly laid over the narrative, the author keeps all the plot elements moving so quickly that the many flaws are generally overlooked. A third set includes Empire of the Atom (1957) and The Wizard of Linn (1950/62). An interstellar war has left Earth with a devastated civilization that possesses remnants of a technology it no longer understands. The alien Riss return and the battle is renewed with humans at a decided disadvantage. Many of van Vogt's stand-alone novels from this period involve similarly epic events. An em-

ployment agency proves to be a conduit for soldiers employed in a savage war in the distant future in Recruiting Station (1942, also published as Earth's Last Fortress and Masters of Time [1950]). The Voyage of the Space Beagle (1950, also published as Mission: Interplanetary) is comprised of a series of short stories about the adventures of an interstellar exploration team, one segment of which—"The Black Destroyer"—was the author's first science fiction sale in 1939. The Book of Ptath (1943/47, also published as Ptath and as Two Hundred Million A.D.) deals less successfully with a battle between superhumans in the very distant future. Immortals plot an escape from an Earth besieged by aliens in The House That Stood Still (1950, also published as The Mating Cry and as Undercover Aliens).

Van Vogt continued to be a prolific short story writer, and he made many of these shorter works serve double duty by assembling them into novels, sometimes with notable lack of success. This reprocessing included The Mixed Men (1952, also published as Mission to the Stars), in which a starship searches for a lost civilization that does not want to be found; The War Against the Rull (1959), which provides episodic glances at a war between humans and aliens; and The Twisted Men (1964). The Mind Cage (1957), on the other hand, is a much more linear story in which a citizen in a dystopian future discovers that his personality has been transferred into another man's body. It was van Vogt's most coherent novel during the late 1950s, and his last for almost 10 years.

When van Vogt began to write again during the 1960s, it was with considerably less success. The Beast (1963, also published as Moonbeast) involves the discovery of alien technology and a possible threat to the world, but the story is at times almost impossible to follow. Rogue Ship (1965) is a routine, episodic space opera about an extended voyage that ends in mutiny. Both novels were assembled or expanded from existing shorter works. The Silkie (1969) seemed to promise better things. Humans create an artificial race to help them administer their society, but the silkies prove to have an agenda of their own. Although also published initially as short stories, the end result was more cohesive than the previous quasi-novels.

Three somewhat interesting books followed during the early 1970s. In *Children of Tomorrow* (1970), a space traveler returns to Earth after a long absence and discovers that the current generation is developing psi powers. *Quest for the Future* (1970) is an expanded version of van Vogt's classic short story "Far Centaurus" (1944), in which a slower-than-light starship is launched to Alpha Centauri, arriving to discover that the subsequent development of faster-than-light travel has led to its colonization in advance of their arrival. *The Battle of Forever* (1971) takes an inhabitant of a supposed utopia out into a wider universe inhabited by unfriendly aliens and other challenges. *The Darkness on Diamondia* (1972) is a less ambitious and reasonably well done adventure involving a rebellious colony world and a superweapon, but *Future Glitter* (1973, also published as *Tyranopolis*) is a rather pedantic story of rebellion against a dictatorship. *The Secret Galactics* (1974, also published as *Earth Factor X*) is an implausible story of the secret invasion of Earth by aliens.

Van Vogt's last few novels were sometimes embarrassingly awkward. *The Man with a Thousand Names* (1974) is an almost incomprehensible tale of body-switching and interplanetary conspiracies. *The Anarchistic Colossus* (1977) has Earth falling into anarchy, supported by artificial intelligences, until an alien invasion causes a crisis. An experiment designed to enhance human intelligence goes awry in *Supermind* (1977). *Renaissance* (1979) is a mildly misogynistic dystopia in which women rule and men are deprived of their rights. The proliferation of computers extinguishes most human freedoms in *Computerworld* (1983), sparking yet another unlikely rebellion.

Although his short stories generally embraced concepts as ambitious as those in his novels, van Vogt occasionally narrowed his focus, sometimes with surprisingly good results, as in "A Can of Paint" (1944). Many of his short stories are of little interest and are intermixed with the better ones in various collections. The best selections are contained in *Destination Universe* (1952), *Monsters* (1965), *More Than Superhuman* (1971), *M33 in Andromeda* (1971), *The Worlds of A. E. van Vogt* (1974), and *The Best of A. E. van Vogt* (1976).

Vance, Jack
(1916–   )

Jack Vance began writing science fiction and fantasy stories in 1945, hitting his stride in 1950 with the publication of his first few books, of which the most notable is his classic fantasy collection, *The Dying Earth* (1950). His first science fiction novel was *The Space Pirate*, which appeared in magazine form in 1950 and as a softcover book in 1953; it was later reprinted as *The Five Gold Bands*. Although set against an interstellar civilization, the story is, in form, a fantasy quest adventure. *Big Planet* (1952/57) was his first completely successful SF novel, a story that proved to be influential in the evolution of the planetary adventure story, in that the author took great pains to explain the physical basis for the environment of that world and the sociopolitical basis for the cultural structure. In this case, the planet has a vast and largely unexplored land mass that was settled primarily by extremists and nonconformists, posing entertaining and amusing problems for an agent sent to sniff out a possible interplanetary plot.

During the early 1950s Vance published a handful of short novels in magazines; but these stories would not appear in book form until years later. Although relatively minor compared to his later work, *Planet of the Damned* (magazine version 1952, paperback as *Slaves of the Klau* in 1958 and later as *Gold and Iron*) anticipated *The HIGH CRUSADE* (1960) by Poul ANDERSON, with captive humans overpowering their technologically superior alien abductors. Vance's short fiction was also improving steadily, and stories such as "Abercrombie Station" (1952) and "The Devil on Salvation Bluff" (1954) began to attract more serious attention.

To Live Forever (1956) adopted a much more serious tone than most of Vance's prior work. The setting is a subtle future dystopia in which immortality is achieved by creating cloned bodies and transferring memories periodically, although Vance never addresses the question of continuity of personality. The protagonist awakens to find that his previous incarnation committed a serious crime, and his subsequent investigation leads to rebellion against what he now recognizes to be a repressive government. The importance of individual freedom would become a recurring theme in Vance's novels. *The Languages of Pao* (1958) explores the effect of language on psychology. The planet Pao has always had one common language, and the planet has been at peace for countless generations. Outside agents wishing to disrupt things introduce variant languages, and by so doing, undermine the stability of the local culture.

The short novel *The Dragon Masters* (1963), which won a Hugo Award, involves an interstellar war between humans and a reptilian species, each of which uses genetic engineering and surgery to modify captured enemies and turn them into organic weapons. A sequel, *The Last Castle* (1967), won Vance his second Hugo, along with a Nebula Award. Vance had developed a distinct prose style by now, a mixture of unusually formal word choices and dialogue, enhanced by a talent for selecting evocative proper names. *The Blue World* (1966) would merge this refined prose style with his gift for planetary romances, this time set on a water world whose human inhabitants live in floating communities and struggle with oversized and ravenous sea creatures.

The Star King (1964) began a series of five novels that was completed after an interval of more than a decade between the third and fourth volumes. Kirth Gerson is the survivor of an attack by five famous space pirates that left him without a family. Each volume consists of his efforts to locate and kill one of the so-called star kings. *The Killing Machine* (1964) and *The Palace of Love* (1967) followed the same pattern, but the uniqueness of each villain and the unusual problems facing Gerson make for fascinating reading. Vance would eventually finish the sequence with *The Face* (1979) and *The Book of Dreams* (1981), which were slightly different in tone from their predecessors but were rewarding nonetheless.

Three separate series of novels appeared during the hiatus in the Star Kings sequence. The Planet of Adventure tetralogy consists of *City of the Chasch* (1968, also published as *Chasch*), *Servants of the Wankh* (1969, also published as *Wankh*), *The Dirdir* (1969), and *The Pnume* (1970). The protagonist is stranded on a world inhabited by four separate alien races, as named in the titles, among whom he has a series of light-hearted ad-

ventures. The Durdane series was much more substantial, beginning with *The Anome* (1973, also published as *The Faceless Man*) and continuing with *The Brave Free Men* (1973) and *The Asutra* (1974). A planetary population governed by a rigid dictatorship is eventually freed from domination by what is revealed as a secretive alien species. The villains were rather transparent stand-ins for communists, but the stories have a grand sweep and are generally rewarding.

The third series was much more openly constructed, and shares a common galactic setting, although not the same characters. *Trullion: Alastor 2262* (1973) is another water-covered planet, caught up in a web of political intrigue, although the high point of the novel is the elaborate sporting event known as *hussade*. *Marune: Alastor 933* (1975) follows the adventures of an amnesiac who visits the planet he believes to be his home world, only to have himself declared planetary ruler. Unfortunately, and predictably, there is a catch. In *Wyst: Alastor 1716* (1978) a government official becomes suspicious about a planet that claims to have achieved a perfectly balanced utopian society, and sends an investigator to look into matters. Not surprisingly, all is not what it seems to be. Not all of Vance's novels from this period fit into a series, although the interstellar setting was usually the same. In *Emphyrio* (1969), a refugee from a planetary dictatorship seeks knowledge with which to undermine the oppressive rulers. Vance's occasional satiric attitude toward organized religion surfaces much more overtly than usual. *The Gray Prince* (1974) deals with warfare among various strains of humanity that have diverged from one another during the diaspora to the stars. *Showboat World* (1975) follows the adventures of a troupe of entertainers who visit the world Vance first created in *Big Planet*. In *Maske: Thaery* (1977), a single man successfully undermines an entire planetary culture.

New novels have appeared at greater intervals during the last few years. The Cadwal Trilogy—*Araminta Station* (1987), *Ecce and Old Earth* (1991), and *Throy* (1992)—is set on a planet that functions as a gigantic nature preserve. Vance's baroque prose style is particularly effective in this history of the battle between the forces of exploitation and those of preservation. *Night Lamp* (1996), a singleton, chronicles the adventures of an orphan seeking his own past, and *Ports of Call* (1998) follows the career of a somewhat similar young protagonist who escapes from the restrictive life imposed by his family to pursue a career among the stars. Vance's unique use of language and his intricately contrived future societies have had a very strong impact on other writers, perhaps most noticeably Gene WOLFE.

Although his short stories only occasionally rival the quality of his novels, Vance has written an appreciable number of them, most of which are collected in *Future Tense* (1964, also published as *Dust of Far Suns*), *The Worlds of Jack Vance* (1973), *The Best of Jack Vance* (1976), *The Narrow Land* (1982), and *The Augmented Agent and Other Stories* (1986). Vance's short fiction has also been collected in various combinations by small press publishers.

Varley, John
(1947–   )

When John Varley's stories first began appearing in genre magazines during the 1970s, he was widely acclaimed as possibly the most promising new writer in years, a description he largely justified in the short run. However, his work began to appear less frequently during the 1980s, and he was almost completely silent during the 1990s. He has only recently begun to demonstrate some increased energy, but his new works—although highly polished and technically superior—feel rather constrained when compared to the output of his early career. Several of his early stories have become minor classics, including "Overdrawn at the Memory Bank" (1976), "In the Hall of the Martian King" (1977), and "The BARBIE MURDERS" (1978), and he won both the Hugo and Nebula Awards for "The Persistence of Vision" (1978).

Varley's first novel was *The Ophiuchi Hotline* (1977), set many generations after technologically superior aliens exiled humanity from Earth in order to protect the whales and dolphins. Human civilization is now scattered through the solar system in a variety of artificial habitats. Longevity is achieved through a procedure reminiscent of *To Live Forever* (1956) by Jack VANCE, in that the protagonist's personality is preserved by moving his consciousness from one cloned body to another, each of which has been updated with a relatively current set of memories. Eventually we discover that humanity is destined to abandon its home system entirely and find a new place among the stars. Varley henceforth devoted most of his writing to novels, interspersed with rare but invariably worthwhile short fiction.

His next project was a trilogy consisting of *Titan* (1979), *Wizard* (1980), and *Demon* (1984). An expedition to Jupiter's moon Titan leads to the surprising revelation that the entire satellite is in fact an intelligent artifact, Gaea, which contains within its structure various bizarre habitats, somewhat in the style of the *RINGWORLD* series by Larry NIVEN or the Nathan Brazil stories by Jack L. CHALKER. One of the protagonists enters into a form of alliance with Gaea as she and her fellows explore the interior, but in the closing volume Gaea appears to have gone insane, with potentially lethal consequences for anyone in her vicinity. Although often fascinating in its inventiveness, the trilogy was not as popular as Varley's first novel; nor was *Millennium* (1983), expanded from the shorter "Air Raid," in which time travelers from the future kidnap people from the present just as they are about to die, planning to use them as breeding stock in their own time, where various factors have led to the corruption of human DNA. A not particularly successful film version followed.

Although Varley's novels did not live up to his early promise, his shorter work was excellent. "The Pusher" (1981) won a Hugo, and "Press Enter" (1984) won the Hugo as well as the Nebula Award. Almost all of his short fiction had been collected by now, in *The Persistence of Vision* (1978), *The Barbie Murders* (1980, also published as *Picnic on Nearside*), and *Blue Champagne* (1986). His next novel, *Steel Beach,* did not appear until 1992, but is set in the same future as *The Ophiuchi Hotline.* One of the scattered remnants of humanity occupies a large settlement on the Moon, but the complexity of the technical requirements to sustain that environment are becoming too difficult to maintain without support from outside. *The Golden Globe* (1998) is even more conventional. An actor who entertains on a variety of worlds uses implants to enhance his performance, advantages that come in handy when he is unjustly accused of murder. Varley's most recent novel is *Red Thunder* (2003), something of a throwback to the earlier days of science fiction. When the U.S. government abandons the space program, a group of private citizens pool their resources in an attempt to beat the Chinese in putting men on Mars.

Varley's fiction from the 1990s to the present is the work of a mature and skilled writer, but his novels lack the impact of his short fiction and have moved toward safer themes and settings than was the case during the early part of his career. He has recently become more prolific at shorter length, and stories like "In Fading Suns and Dying Moons" (2003) may indicate that he will be more willing to explore new possibilities there than at book length.

Vaster Than Empires and More Slow
Ursula K. Le Guin
(1971)

One of the standard plots for short stories during the 1950s and 1960s was the first visit to an alien planet and the solution of some mystery involving the local life, either biological or cultural. *The Planet Explorer* (1957) by Murray LEINSTER and *Mission to Universe* (1965) by Gordon DICKSON are both episodic novels in which a team deals with a series of such mysteries. In most cases the characters are rendered in a shallow fashion; it is the problem and the exotic setting that are supposed to hold the reader's attention. Occasionally a talented writer uses that same form to tell a more complex story, as is the case with this novelette by Ursula K. LE GUIN, set in the author's Hain universe.

Although the Hainish Empire explored much of the galaxy, there were remote regions that they overlooked, and younger members of their civilization, particularly those from Earth, press for further missions. Because these will be extremely long journeys for little reward, most of those who volunteer for this kind of mission are mentally unstable in one fashion or another, and putting together a viable crew has become something of an art form. The story follows one of the less successful efforts, unsuccessful because one member of the crew is an empath who feels the negative feelings of his fellows and responds by becoming increasingly obnoxious, a self-defeating and mutually destructive cycle of feedback that progressively destabilizes them all. By the time they reach the first habitable planet and begin their survey, tempers are on edge; one individual is on the verge of a breakdown, and another has been driven into a murderous rage.

The planet has plant life, lush and varied, but no animals whatsoever, which appears to mean that they are in no physical danger. Osden, the empath, goes off on his own on a protracted mission, which initially lessens the tension, but the rest of the crew continue to feel a foreboding they cannot articulate. One claims to have been chased through the jungle by some unseen shape. Then Osden is attacked and nearly killed, and it appears that they might not be alone on the planet after all. It turns out, however, that they themselves are the source of their growing unease. All of the vegetation on the planet shares a single nervous system, is in a sense one great organism that has some latent form of intelligence but lacks even the concept of there being another creature in the universe. Like Osden, the plants have picked up the agitation of the humans and are broadcasting it themselves, reinforcing and exaggerating the tension. The mystery is solved, perhaps; but the bigger question is, how can we learn to break the cycle among ourselves? Even without the power of empathy, the accumulated animosity of humans toward one another inevitably breeds more of the same.

Verne, Jules
(1828–1905)

Although science fiction developed into a separate and full-fledged genre primarily in the United States, the two writers who are generally considered the seminal forces for the development of science fiction are H. G. WELLS, an Englishman, and Jules Verne, a Frenchman. Critics sometimes assert that the two men were of opposing schools of writing—an oversimplification that nonetheless contains an element of truth. Wells was more aware of scientific principles, and though his fantastic events were sometimes implausible, he exerted some effort to make them seem real. His fiction was frequently designed to illustrate one aspect or another of the human condition, either to criticize our follies or question things that we take for granted about human destiny or our place in the universe. Verne was more interested in entertaining his audience by telling a rousing adventure, and spent much more time describing the physical details of his settings rather than the intellectual intricacies of his characters. His characters are usually broad types— the man of science, the man of action—rather than well-rounded individuals. It would be unfair, however, to conclude from this that Wells was the father of serious science fiction and Verne the father of adventure stories. Both men shared at least one overriding common factor—a sense of wonder about the nature of our world and the greater universe. It is that capacity that has given the field its unique quality.

Verne began writing adventure stories in 1851, and his first novel, *Five Weeks in a Balloon*, appeared in 1863. JOURNEY TO THE CENTER OF THE EARTH, the story of three adventurers who climb down inside a volcano and follow a trail of clues into a series of hollow Earth environments, appeared very soon afterward. His career as a writer picked up fairly quickly after that, and he would eventually produce dozens of novels, a considerable portion of them at least marginally science fiction. The most famous of these is certainly 20,000 LEAGUES UNDER THE SEA (1872), which has served as the inspiration for at least three motion pictures. One of the most familiar of children's classics, it is actually a rather sophisticated story of conflicting human emotions. Nemo, the captain of the rogue super-submarine *Nautilus*, is driven by his hatred of war and violence into becoming the ultimate source of warfare and violence. Although the novel ends with Nemo's apparent death and the destruction of the ship, he and the *Nautilus* make a brief return appearance in *Mysterious Island* (1874), where it is revealed that they have been

secretly providing aid to a party shipwrecked on a dangerous island.

The so-called Baltimore Gun Club adventures are also among Verne's better-known stories. *From the Earth to the Moon and A Trip Around It* (originally published separately in 1864 and 1870 and reprinted under various variations of their names) suggests a method of interplanetary travel that we now know to be impossible. Whereas Wells's characters reached the moon by inventing Cavorite, which blocked the force of gravity in *The FIRST MEN IN THE MOON* (1901), Verne suggested launching explorers in a projectile fired from an enormous cannon. The Gun Club returned in *The Purchase of the North Pole* (1889, also published as *Topsy Turvy*) in a very early consideration of the possibilities of weather control. Another popular sequence is known today as *Master of the World* (1904/14), although some editions also contain a first part known variously as *The Clipper of the Clouds* or as *Robur the Conqueror* (1886/87). Robur was an airborne equivalent of Captain Nemo, and met a very similar fate.

Off on a Comet (1877, also published as *Hector Servadac* and under other titles) chronicles the adventures of a handful of people caught aboard a chunk of the Earth that is carried off into space on a comet. A revolutionary new form of steam-driven vehicle is used to explore the interior of India in *The Demon of Cawnpore* (1880), a story that otherwise is straightforward adventure; the sequel, *Tigers and Traitors* (1881), provided no additional speculative content. Another two-book sequence consists of *Into the Niger Bend* and *The City in the Sahara* (1919), both of which involve the discovery of superscientific devices in a remote part of Africa. *The Hunt for the Meteor* (1909/65) contains some interesting speculative content, although the story does not hold up particularly well. A meteor crashes on Earth; it contains so much gold that the value of the element is dramatically reduced, with a consequent devastating impact on the world's economy. *The Begum's Fortune* (1878) concerns a conflict that arises between two separate cities, each of which has evolved into a kind of utopia, but each using a different set of principles. There is also some technological speculation in *The Carpathian Castle* (1893). At the North Pole

(1874, also published as part one of *The Adventures of Captain Hatteras*) mixes some futuristic speculation with an otherwise routine journey adventure. A modern-day pirate using superscience and missile technology seizes control of an island and menaces world commerce in *For the Flag* (1897, also published as *Facing the Flag*). *The Village in the Treetops* (1901) is a lost-race novel.

Verne's novels became more pessimistic late in his career, and there was less robust adventure in the plots. A recently discovered manuscript, *Paris in the 20th Century* (1994), is little more than a grand tour of the future, and while some of Verne's speculations about the shape of things to come are interesting, the novel is not otherwise engaging. Another recent discovery, *Invasion of the Sea* (1905, but not published in English until 2001), is much more interesting. Efforts are underway to create a gigantic inland sea, displacing much of the Sahara Desert, but various forces have understandably differing opinions about the wisdom of this course of action.

Like Wells, Verne had no sense that he was writing in a separate field, and there is no indication that he drew any distinction between his scientific romances and his other work. His short fiction is largely inaccessible in English, but *Yesterday and Tomorrow* (1910/65) contains several of his speculative short stories. Of these, only "Dr. Trifulgas" and "The Eternal Adam" are of particular interest. At his best, Verne drew us into his imagined worlds and made us feel that they were real places, but he was rarely able to make us feel equally at ease with his characters. His plotting was always straightforward and linear, and it is not surprising that his main contemporary audience tends to be younger readers. However, that should not prevent adults from appreciating his strong imaginative powers.

Viehl, S. L.
(1961–   )

Sheila Lynn Viehl made her debut as a science fiction writer with *Stardoc* (2000), the first in a series of novels about a human physician named Cherijo Grey Veil who travels among the stars, concealing the fact that she has had some genetic modifications that make her somewhat nonhuman herself. There have been four sequels to date, chronicling this character's adventures in a series of chases and evasions. Following the revelation that she is an enhanced clone, the protagonist takes refuge aboard an alien ship in *Beyond Varallan* (2000), and avoids capture and slavery by various groups who wish to study her physical modifications in *Endurance* (2001). She and her husband conceal themselves on an alien world in *Shockball* (2001), a planet whose sports are uncommonly violent, and then are forced to flee even further in *Eternity Row* (2002), now pursued by both human and alien enemies. The series is clearly heavily influenced by the work of C. J. CHERRYH and perhaps Julie E. CZERNEDA, in a form of sophisticated space opera that concentrates more on the psychology of the characters and the alien cultures they encounter than on the details of space travel or more overt styles of adventure.

Two nonseries novels followed. *Blade Dancer* (2003) is set in the same universe as the Stardoc novels and makes use of a rather similar setup. A professional athlete conceals the fact that she is not human until the death of her parents reveals her secret. *Bio Rescue* (2004) continues the author's use of medical professionals as characters. This time a group of physicians enlist the aid of a space pilot in an effort to avert a violent confrontation between two alien races. Viehl seems to be establishing herself within that group of writers whose characters take a diversely populated universe for granted and assume that humanity would simply be another subcomponent of a large and non-monolithic interstellar civilization. Although there are many alien races in her stories, their motives and the essentials of their psychology are human, and their cultures only superficially vary from the familiar. Her characters tend to be searching for their place in the universe, and often are willing to break the rules to accomplish what they want. Her villains tend to be rather one-dimensional, but her protagonists have grown in complexity from book to book. Whether she will continue to write variations of the same story or will attempt to diversify her future work remains to be seen.

Vinge, Joan D.
(1948–   )

Joan Vinge acknowledges the strong influence on her work of Andre NORTON's early science fiction adventures, but she also draws heavily on fairy tales, transforming them into settings and situations on distant worlds and in unfamiliar cultures. She made her initial entry into the field with a series of distinguished stories during the late 1970s, winning the Hugo Award for "Eyes of Amber" (1977). That title is one of several stories by Vinge that deal with communications between humans and aliens, this one accomplished remotely by means of a probe whose descent onto a primitive world causes a shift in a power struggle among the local nobility and a change of perspective on the part of the female alien most closely associated with it. "Fireship" (1978) is an even more complex tale in which the interaction is between two altered human personalities, one a cyborg, the other a virtual personality who has been literally transferred into computer memory. "The Crystal Ship" (1976) and "Phoenix in the Ashes" (1978) were also impressive efforts, particularly for such a new writer.

The Outcasts of Heaven's Belt (1978), Vinge's first novel, supported the belief that she was a major new writer, one who could successfully blend the core of myth with a hard science fiction setting. In this case, the story is about the struggle over control of a spaceship by two separate cultures within the asteroid belt, one dominated by males and the other by females, who have only recently approached an uneasy peace following the civil war that separated them. Eventually the two sides are forced to cooperate. A novella, "Legacy" (1980), set against the same backdrop, reprises the same core plot with different parameters and on a smaller scale. Two out-of-work residents of the asteroid belt are compelled by circumstances to pool their resources and jointly establish a salvage company. Unfortunately, most of Vinge's fiction during the 1980s consisted of media tie-in novels, and fewer than a half-dozen new short stories have appeared in the past two decades.

Vinge has continued to write novels sporadically, the most successful of which was *The Snow Queen* (1980), set on Tiamat, a planet that experiences a vastly extended annual climatic cycle. The local ruler is slated to surrender her throne with the end of the season, but she is secretly plotting to use advanced offworld cloning technology and perpetuate her reign. The ensuing conflict between the ruler and a younger, cloned version of herself is dramatically a struggle between good and evil, although Vinge's characters are too well drawn to fit comfortably into either category. The novel won the Hugo Award and was followed by three sequels, although only one extends the original story line. In the first, *World's End* (1984), a man who loved the queen of Tiamat pursues a new life as a police official on another world, eventually resolving his internal doubts during a lengthy and dangerous trek into the less settled regions of his new home.

The Summer Queen (1991) returned to the main story line, and is one of the longest and most complex stories the genre has yet seen. The new queen is determined to nudge her people into adopting a more forward-looking attitude toward the rest of the universe, but her plans are complicated by a number of issues, and when contact with the outside universe is restored, the planet faces a fresh round of crises. One of the life-forms on Tiamat has a substance in its blood that can extend human lives dramatically, and there is concern that the species will be hunted to extinction. The discovery of a practical faster-than-light drive means that Tiamat will no longer be insulated from the outside for extended periods of time and the machinations of an electronically recorded personality and a secretive cult dominated by a remarkably evil man add multiple layers of plots and counterplots. The fourth novel set in this universe is *Tangled Up in Blue* (2000), in which two police officials and a prostitute attempt to expose corruption within a planetary government. Although it lacks the scale of *The Summer Queen,* it is in some ways a more consistently satisfying story.

Vinge's other series includes *Psion* (1982), *Catspaw* (1988), and *Dreamfall* (1996), stories more obviously influenced by Andre Norton. Cat is a rarity, a telepath, and various powers wish to use him as a weapon in an interplanetary war. Although he successfully preserves his freedom in the first volume, private interests and other enemies menace him in the two sequels.

Vinge's small body of short stories is of high quality and has been collected in *Fireship* (1978), *The Eyes of Amber* (1979), and *Phoenix in the Ashes* (1985). Although she does not produce work with the frequency usually required to retain a strong reputation, her novels have been of such a consistently high quality that her fans have been content to live with the long gaps between them.

Vinge, Vernor
(1944–   )

Although Vernor Vinge began his writing career in the 1960s and has always produced work of good to excellent quality, he wrote only two novels and a handful of short stories during the next two decades and was considered a fairly minor figure, gaining some stature during the 1980s, but receiving major acclaim only after publication of *A Fire in the Deep* (1992). Such stories as "Bookworm Run" (1966) and "The Peddler's Apprentice" (1975) demonstrated that he could mix intelligent humor and hard science fiction successfully, but no single story stood out significantly. His first novel was *Grimm's World* (1969, expanded in 1987 as *Tatja Grimm's World*), an elaborate planetary adventure story told from the viewpoint of an unusually well-drawn protagonist. The ruler of a primitive lost colony world is convinced that life exists in the outside universe, but the results of renewed contact are not what she had hoped for. Slavers prey on her population; as usual, it is the common people who suffer while those in authority battle for positions of greater power.

Vinge's second novel, *The Witling* (1976), has a fascinating premise. The setting is a planet where nearly everyone has the ability to teleport from one place to another. Secretive human visitors explore this civilization, where psi powers have made the development of certain forms of technology unnecessary. The plot involves one individual who is handicapped by an inability to teleport and by an unbalanced love affair; but despite the interesting speculation about the form such a society might take, there is little narrative tension. Nearly five

years passed before Vinge's next story appeared, the novella *True Names* (1981), which might be called a cyberpunk story. A network of highly sophisticated computers has the capacity to create a consistent virtual reality world, but the efforts by a group of technogeeks to refine this alternate reality are hampered by the intervention of an aberrant personality with possible psi powers.

His next two novels, *The Peace War* (1984) and *Marooned in Realtime* (1986), were related. Both explore the implications of the invention of the status field, an enclosed space that exists independent of outside events or the passage of time. Vinge uses the concept as the springboard for considerable speculation about the future of the human race, much of which he kills off in the process, including a haunting visit to a distant future where Earth has become essentially a deserted relic. The two novels and a related short story were reprinted in a single volume as *Across Realtime* (1986).

Vinge achieved major prominence with *A Fire Upon the Deep* (1992) and the related *A Deepness in the Sky* (1999), both of which won Hugo Awards. The setting for both novels is a vast, heavily populated universe in which the human race is only a minor player. The former book involves the quest by various factions to obtain possession of a superweapon, the product of a lost technology, and possibly the only defense against an ancient but now active menace. The mix of space opera settings and situations with the detail and sometimes the tone of cyberpunk fiction seems at first an unlikely marriage, but Vinge rises to the occasion. The second title is slightly more traditional, as rival groups compete to study and exploit a dormant alien civilization that recently has shown signs of renewed activity; the factions underestimate the implications of their observations.

All of Vinge's short fiction up to that point has been assembled in *The Collected Stories of Vernor Vinge* (2001). His novels appear after such long intervals that the publication of each new one seems to take his devoted readers by surprise, but even his weakest material is thought-provoking and entertaining. At his best, Vinge is one of the most innovative and exciting writers in the field.

Vintage Season
C. L. Moore and Henry Kuttner
(1946)

Catherine L. MOORE collaborated with her husband and fellow writer Henry KUTTNER to an extent that will never be completely determined. Most of their combined work appeared under his name or under one of their numerous pseudonyms. This novelette was credited as a collaboration between the two, but it is now considered likely that Moore wrote all or at least the largest part of the story.

Oliver Wilson is a landlord who grows increasingly unhappy with his newest batch of tenants. They are foreigners, clearly, although their origins are somewhat unclear, and they seem peculiar in various ways inconsistent with their apparent background. At times they fail to recognize objects that should be commonplace, and they tend to be secretive, making no effort to cultivate friendships with anyone else, although neither are they unfriendly. They claim to be on vacation, but much of their activity does not involve the normal tourist attractions.

Wilson is drawn increasingly into their circle by circumstance, and his list of questions grows longer before he discovers the truth. The nearby town is about to be devastated by a disaster, and his guests are actually time travelers from some indeterminate future age who have come back to observe the catastrophe—and for amusement, rather than as a scholarly pursuit. Wilson discovers the truth too late, and his plan to tell the authorities what happened so that they can watch for later visits by voyeurs from the future is clearly doomed to failure. The travelers themselves appear rather careless in concealing their secrets, presumably because they understand that time is immutable and that nothing they do can possibly affect the course of events to follow. Many other authors have written stories of visitors from the future, but few have ever approached the quality of this early, bittersweet tale of humanity's ability to transform tragedy into entertainment.

The novelette was filmed with some success as *Disaster in Time* (1992). "In Another Country" (1989) by Robert SILVERBERG is a sequel to the original story in which a time traveler breaks one of the rules by interfering with the past.

"The Visible Man"
Gardner Dozois
(1975)

In "TO SEE THE INVISIBLE MAN" (1963), Robert SILVERBERG described a future in which society punishes criminals and dissidents by making it a crime to recognize their existence, a form of imposed invisibility. Gardner DOZOIS turned the concept around for this long story in which an equally repressive state uses psychological conditioning on prisoners so that they are incapable of seeing any other form of animal life, people, dogs, even insects. Although this makes it easy to control them while imprisoned, since they cannot see their guards, the author tells us that the condition is imposed because of its innate cruelty rather than for practical reasons.

The protagonist is one such prisoner, whose specific crime we never learn, who escapes when the vehicle in which he is being transported is involved in an accident. Where Silverberg concentrated on the psychological effects on his protagonist, Dozois describes in great detail the physical difficulties of this limited sightlessness. The fugitive cannot remain out in the country, where he could be easily detected by body heat, so he heads for more settled areas, with awkward, sometimes comical results. Eventually, he hits upon the idea of masquerading as a conventional blind man, but his disguise fails to work because he can in fact see, and his reaction to those elements in his environment that are not living beings gives him away. He encounters a representative of what appears to be an underground organization dedicated to helping escaped prisoners, but the situation begins to seem increasingly artificial, culminating in our discovery that we have been misled about the entire situation, which is actually a complex virtual reality game. Although the story has less ambitious goals than most of Dozois's other work, it is one of the most satisfying examples of the logical development of an unusual situation to explore its physical ramifications.

"The Voices of Time"
J. G. Ballard
(1962)

One of the reasons why J. G. BALLARD became so controversial during the 1960s was the pessimistic tone that pervaded many of his stories, which frequently are filled with images of decay, disorder, and apathy. Science fiction readers were used to protagonists who solved problems, overcame obstacles, or on rare occasions died in the attempt. They were not accustomed to people who accepted their fate, refused to struggle against the perceived inevitable, and waited calmly for doom to overtake them. "The Voices of Time" is a case in point, a story in which not only is Powers, the psychologist protagonist, doomed, but also the entire human race and the universe itself.

The story is set in a not-too-distant future in which a plague of narcosis is slowly beginning to affect an increasing number of victims, plunging them into a sleep from which they will never waken. There has also been an explosion of mutations among plants and animals, extreme changes in sensory apparatus, intelligence, and physical form—changes that have neither a definable cause nor any apparent purpose. There does seem to be a connection with the silent pair, two dormant genes that show up only in a small minority of individuals within each species. Powers is troubled by the death of a colleague who spent most of his last days inscribing an intricate design on the floor of a swimming pool, and by his knowledge of a sudden decline in the human birthrate, dramatic in some areas. He is also plagued by the attentions of a brilliant patient surgically deprived of the ability to sleep, who tells him he is receiving messages from the stars, in the form of strings of steadily declining numbers.

The common cause of these phenomena, which we learn only piecemeal, is that evolution on each planet reaches a peak, then begins to decline, at which point certain individuals try desperately to mutate into a new form that will begin another cycle. The countdowns from the stars include one that marks the end of the physical universe. Powers, deprived of all hope of an infinite future, commits suicide. There is considerable irony in the fact that, despite the downbeat conclusion, the story affirms that modern man is, after all, the pinnacle of evolution, at least on Earth.

Vonnegut, Kurt
(1922–   )

Throughout his career, Kurt Vonnegut has made a point of avoiding being labeled as a genre writer. His first science fiction story, "Report on the Barnhouse Effect" (1950), appeared in a general magazine, although some of his later work appeared in genre publications. Most of his science fiction shorts appeared during the 1950s, including "Big Trip Up Yonder" (1954) and "More Stately Mansions" (1951), but even then it was obvious that he was not writing in the usual traditions of the field. His first novel was *Player Piano* (1952, also published as *Utopia 14*), a satiric dystopian tale in which automation has split the American population into two separate cultures—one consisting of the privileged engineering class whose expertise is required to ensure that the machinery of civilization moves smoothly, and the dispirited, unemployed masses who can barely survive on their welfare allowances. One member of the former class becomes a discontented revolutionary through a series of happenstance events that foreshadow the comic constructions of Vonnegut's later novels.

The SIRENS OF TITAN (1959) was a more substantial and rewarding satire in which a single individual, through a chance encounter with an anomalous space-time condition, is placed in a unique position to alter the future of humanity. It was the first of Vonnegut's novels to suggest the formation of a new religion as a plot device, one he would resort to again and much more effectively in CAT'S CRADLE (1963) and elsewhere. Although *Cat's Cradle* was warmly received by the science fiction community, this wry end-of-the-world story also signaled the beginning of the author's steady move away from the field. Although he continued to employ its devices—aliens, technological wonders, superweapons, even time travel—it was invariably for satiric or allegorical effect and not an effort at serious speculation.

Slaughterhouse-Five (1969), drawn in part from Vonnegut's own experiences as a prisoner of war in Dresden when that city was firebombed, was much more successful outside the field than within. The protagonist, Billy Pilgrim, has become unstuck in time. His consciousness flits back and forth from our present to his past during World War II and to a future in which he has been kidnapped by aliens from the planet Tralfamadore. Although the novel is frequently comic, it is a bitter, ironic humor that masks the tragic events, which are described in a very moving manner. Whether or not one thinks of it as science fiction, it is still Vonnegut's most accomplished work.

Many of the later novels contain elements of the fantastic. In *Slapstick* (1976), a broad but sometimes unfocused satire, Vonnegut includes shrinking Chinese, gestalt personalities, a colony on Mars, and the possible end of the world. An American city is destroyed by a neutron bomb in *Deadeye Dick* (1982), and time backs up a decade giving everyone a major case of deja vu in *Timequake* (1997). The most sustained and interesting of his later novels is GALÁPAGOS (1985), yet another end-of-the-world story, this time with an outrageously funny, if typically bitter, ending.

Vonnegut is often portrayed as a writer who abandoned his roots in science fiction in favor of more lucrative markets and wider critical acclaim. The truth is that his roots were never firmly fixed in the genre, that his career as a writer sometimes intersected the field briefly but never found a permanent home. His short stories, which have been collected as *Canary in a Cat House* (1961), *Welcome to the Monkey House* (1970), and *Bagombo Snuff Box* (1999), all mix science fiction with general fiction. Vonnegut used whatever devices and conventions were necessary for the story at hand, and has always preferred not to accept the limitations that would be implied by settling into an established pattern or genre.

W

Waldo
Robert A. Heinlein
(1950)

During the mid-20th century, pulp science fiction was more a literature of ideas than of character. Even the popular heroes such as Edward E. SMITH's Kimball Kinnison and Edgar Rice BURROUGHS's John Carter were caricatures with only the sketchiest elements of a human personality. Such characters were remembered because of what they did rather than who they were. Robert A. HEINLEIN, who would later create some very memorable characters, wrote an otherwise minor novella that quietly defied convention. It would be the character of Waldo Farthingwaite-Jones that readers would remember long after they had forgotten the details of his story.

Jones was born with a rare ailment that left all the muscles in his body so permanently weakened that he was barely able to survive and needed constant attendance. This made him understandably bitter; but he was also something of an engineering genius, and as an adult, he caused to have constructed for himself an orbiting habitat where he could be much more self-sufficient in the absence of gravity. There he became something of a recluse, directing his financial affairs from orbit, dealing with his physical environment by means of various sizes of mechanical arms, each of which he could direct remotely by means of a pair of gloves electronically linked to them. This type of equipment has come to be known as a waldo in tribute to Heinlein's original concept.

Waldo's adventures are not nearly as colorful. The world has been transformed by means of broadcast power, but something has started to go wrong. There are unexplained equipment failures, as well as a growing problem with the physical health of the population. Even more perplexing is the fact that the only man who can fix the ailing machines claims he is doing so by magical means. Heinlein's revelation that the broadcast energy is being partially drawn from another reality where a mental force equivalent to magic exists is something less than satisfying, but the images of the overweight, irascible, but nonetheless admirable Waldo in his orbiting satellite are among the sharpest from the early days of science fiction.

Waldrop, Howard
(1946–)

Howard Waldrop began his career in 1972 and has been a steady though nonprolific writer ever since, producing short stories with some regularity and two novels separated by a considerable interval. Most of Waldrop's fiction employs one or both of two devices—alternate history and the juxtaposition of two apparently anomalous situations—and most of his work is extremely funny, although sometimes the humor is bittersweet. His first novel, *The Texas-Israeli War* (1974), a collaboration with Jake Saunders, is set following a limited nuclear war. Texas has seceded, and Israeli mercenaries are imported by what remains of the U.S.

government to put down the rebellion. *Them Bones* (1984) mixes time travel with several different alternate histories in a complicated mix that might have devolved into nonsense but in fact is remarkably coherent and effective. Much of it is set in the South, a common locale for Waldrop's work; however, in the root timeline, Christianity never existed and Louisiana is inhabited by Arabs and Aztecs.

Waldrop is clearly more in his element with short fiction, however, and has produced many memorable stories, including "The Ugly Chickens" (1980), a Nebula Award–winner that explains how the dodo became extinct; "Night of the Cooters" (1987), a very funny spoof of The WAR OF THE WORLDS (1898) by H. G. WELLS; and "A Dozen Tough Jobs" (1989), which superimposes the legend of Hercules over early-20th-century America. Senator Elvis Presley is entertained by singer Dwight Eisenhower in "Ike at the Mike" (1982), and "Fin de Cycle" (1991) considers the Dreyfuss Affair from several unusual points of view. "CUSTER'S LAST JUMP" (1976), a collaboration with Steven Utley, describes what the Civil War might have been like if primitive airplanes had existed. Waldrop frequently collaborates, and all of the stories in *Custer's Last Jump and Other Collaborations* (2003) were written in this fashion.

Most of Waldrop's short stories have been variously collected in *Howard Who?* (1986), *Night of the Cooters* (1990), *Strange Monsters of the Recent Past* (1991), *Going Home Again* (1997), and *A Better World's in Birth* (2003). Beneath the humor and bizarre imagery lurk more serious concerns about how we treat one another. Waldrop is effectively economical with words, and often manages in a few sentences what would take a lesser author several pages to express.

Wallace, Ian
(1912–1998)

Ian Wallace was the pseudonym of John Wallace Pritchard. Although he published one non-genre novel during the 1950s, his career essentially started with the publication of *Croyd* (1967), a wildly imaginative but scientifically unsound blend of space opera and time travel. Croyd is a supersecret agent of the future who can move forward and backward in time, with some limitations, but who nevertheless manages to get into trouble trying to head off the conquest of Earth by aliens. He thwarts a second effort in the sequel, *Dr. Orpheus* (1968), whose plot is so complex and occasionally implausible that the reader is best advised not to examine it too closely. Wallace introduced a female secret agent in *Deathstar Voyage* (1969), in this case employed as bodyguard to a visiting political figure during his journey back to his home world. Claudine St. Cyr's career would later intersect with the Croyd series, but she continued her solo adventures in pursuit of a missing heir in *The Purloined Prince* (1971).

After creating yet another variation of the same dynamic character in *Pan Sagittarius* (1973), Wallace returned to Croyd for *A Voyage to Dari* (1974). Once again Croyd single-handedly defeats an alien plot, which on this occasion includes an attempt to kidnap Croyd himself in order to make use of his unique mental powers. Croyd goes into retirement after this exploit, but returns to action in *Z-Sting* (1978) when the device he used to safeguard humanity malfunctions. He teams up with St. Cyr to solve a murder mystery in *Heller's Leap* (1979) and has his last outing in *Megalomania* (1989), in which he saves the entire galaxy from destruction. St. Cyr had one additional adventure as well, *The Sign of the Mute Medusa* (1977), in which she visits a planet so despoiled by pollution that only a privileged aristocracy living in a domed city has a chance to survive.

The remaining novels are both singletons. An alien found frozen in a comet in *The Lucifer Comet* (1980) may be the original of the legend of Satan, and powerful aliens attempt to steal the sun and doom the Earth in *The Rape of the Sun* (1982). Wallace was never interested in the plausibility of his science, and he mixed up galaxies with star systems, obviously having no comprehension of the actual physical properties of the universe. His characters are archetypal rather than realistic, and his plots are as complex as those of the early A. E. VAN VOGT. Those considerable faults notwithstanding, he was interesting because of his untraditional plots and his distinctive prose style, which was often more interesting in its use of imagery than for the story it conveyed.

Walters, Hugh
(1910–1993)

Walter Hughes wrote exclusively science fiction for young adults and teenagers, almost all of which involves the career of Chris Godfrey, although the character ages during the course of the series and is later replaced as the central character by Tony Hale. The series began with *Blastoff at Woomera* (1958, also published as *Blastoff at 0300*), a straightforward tale of an early space mission, although typically for its form the novel manipulates things to allow for a teenaged astronaut. Godfrey finally reaches the Moon in his third outing, *First on the Moon* (1960, also published as *Operation Columbus*), just ahead of a Russian astronaut whose life he eventually saves despite the Russian's treachery.

The establishment of a permanent settlement leads to further intrigue in *Moon Base One* (1961, also published as *Outpost on the Moon*), but Godfrey soon leaves that behind in favor of trips to Venus in *Expedition Venus* (1963) and Mars in *Destination Mars* (1964). His next adventure was closer to home: A madman seizes control of an orbiting satellite and threatens to turn its lasers toward Earth in *Terror by Satellite* (1964). That diversion is followed by visits to Jupiter in *Journey to Jupiter* (1965), which almost ends tragically because of equipment failure and an ailing crew; to Mercury in *Mission to Mercury* (1965), which also involves telepathy; and to Saturn in *Spaceship to Saturn* (1967), this longer voyage accomplished by means of suspended animation. Further adventures included trips to Neptune, Uranus, and Jupiter, in novels that were each, to a great extent, variations of the earlier novels.

Godfrey moves to the sidelines for the balance of the series. *Tony Hale, Space Detective* (1973) pits his intelligence against a comparatively inept villain, as does *Murder on Mars* (1975). The series would end with *P-K* (1986), the 21st installment. A second series, for even younger readers, consists of *Boy Astronaut* (1977), *First Family on the Moon* (1979), and *School on the Moon* (1981). Walters did

a reasonably good job of providing an accurate scientific portrait of the various planets visited by his astronaut heroes, and a fair job of describing what space travel might actually be like. He was less successful with his plotting, which became extremely repetitive late in his career. Although he was never a critical success, he developed a considerable following, and his books are avidly collected.

The War of the Worlds
H. G. Wells
(1898)

Although other authors have written gripping stories of the invasion of Earth by military forces from another world, none have done so as chillingly and effectively as did H. G. WELLS. Wells is sometimes credited as having invented the scenario, but in fact the concept did not arise out of a complete vacuum. Future war stories had been popular in England for almost 30 years, pitting one combination of European powers against another, often employing then-futuristic weaponry such as aircraft. Wells's novel falls partly within that tradition. His invaders were from Mars, not Germany or France, and their technology was vastly superior to ours—although oddly enough, it never occurred to him to give his Martians the power of flight. Whereas most future war novels focused on the course of battles and the maneuverings of politicians, Wells chose to narrate his story from the point of view of a civilian bystander who desperately is trying to survive.

The actual plot is quite straightforward. Mysterious cylinders begin landing around the world, from which emerge articulated, mechanical tripods that are the Martian war machines. Using death rays and other weaponry, they systematically begin to clear the land of all human populations, destroying buildings, swatting aside every attempt to oppose them militarily. Just when it appears that the end is near and that humans will be driven to extinction, the invaders begin to die, their demise caused by microorganisms to which they have no natural immunity. Most invasion stories that followed would give humanity a less passive role in its own salvation.

Efforts have been made to continue the story from time to time, but the results have usually been less than satisfactory. *Edison's Conquest of Mars* (1898/1947, also published as *Invasion of Mars*) by Garrett P. Serviss describes resurgent humanity's venture into space as they launch a counterattack against the invaders. *The Second War of the Worlds* (1976) by George H. Smith has the Martians launching a second attack, this time into a parallel universe where humans are even less technologically advanced. *The Alternate Martians* (1965) by A. Bertram CHANDLER is a mildly amusing spoof set in an alternate world where the Martian visions of both Wells and Edgar Rice BURROUGHS are accurate. Most interesting are the Tripod series by John CHRISTOPHER, four novels set on an Earth where the Martians were successful, and *The Space Machine* (1976) by Christopher PRIEST, a highly literate retelling of the story from an alternate point of view.

War with the Newts
Karel Čapek
(1936)

The Czech writer Karel Čapek produced a considerable body of work, both nonfiction and fiction of various types including some science fiction and fantasy. His biggest contribution to the field was probably his creation of the word *robot*, in his 1921 play *R.U.R.*, although the robots in the play were organic rather than mechanical constructions. His science fiction novels include *Krakatit* (1924), in which a new explosive destroys the world; *The Makropoulos Secret* (1925), which inspired the opera *The Makropoulos Case* by Leoš Janáček; involving the search for immortality; and *The Absolute at Large* (1922). But the only one to become widely known outside of Europe was *War with the Newts* (1936).

In the near future, humanity discovers the existence of sea-dwelling newts, inhuman but intelligent creatures who are basically friendly and cooperative. Before long, entrepreneurs are exploiting the new species, which is capable of living on land for brief periods, and the exploitation grows more radical until it becomes outright slavery, although in this case Čapek was using that condition as an allegory for class warfare. Eventually a charismatic leader arises among the newts,

organizes them, and strikes back at the surface world by causing ecological changes that eventually flood all of the coastal regions in the world. Humanity finds itself virtually powerless to counterattack, and is eventually doomed. Čapek's lightly satirical manner fails to take the sting out of his indictment of the human tendency to take advantage of the seemingly weak and to assume that we are the lords of creation. Although the newts in the novel have evolved naturally, the story in many ways anticipates later work in which animals have been uplifted to intelligent status, particularly *Brain Wave* (1954) by Poul ANDERSON and the Aldair series by Neal BARRETT JR.

Wasp
Eric Frank Russell
(1957)

A recurring conceit in science fiction, particularly reinforced by those writers who appeared regularly in *Astounding Magazine* (later *Analog*) under John W. CAMPBELL's editorship, is that humans are in some fashion superior to every other intelligence in the universe. We might not be as physically powerful as some, as technologically advanced as others, or as organized and efficient; but through hard work, wiliness, and moral superiority, humans will always carry the day. Eric Frank RUSSELL usually accepted that assumption without qualification, and wrote stories in which a single human defeats an entire alien race, most notably *Next of Kin* (1959), wherein a lone prisoner in an interstellar war amusingly, though rather implausibly, undermines the confidence of an entire alien race.

Wasp makes use of a very similar premise, but with a more serious plot and a more plausible set of methods. James Mowry has been physically altered so that he can pass for one of the humanoid aliens with whom Earth is at war. He is conveyed to one of the enemy worlds—an average planet rather than their capital or a major military installation—along with a small amount of equipment with which he is to undertake a one-man assault on the morale and operations of the enemy. Mowry invents a nonexistent underground resistance group and begins distributing their literature and warnings as well as committing acts of petty sabotage. Like a wasp buzzing around a bear, he can inflict very little real damage, but his presence is distracting, and the local authorities eventually divert a substantial amount of resources as they attempt to track down the supposed rebels. The associated repression causes unrest among the local inhabitants, which reduces their efficiency even further. Mowry is a heroic figure; but unlike most such characters from the 1950s, his victories are incremental rather than spectacular. Readers can more easily identify with someone whose exploits seem entirely possible than with those whose achievements are on a much grander scale.

Watson, Ian
(1943–   )

Although the British author Ian Watson began writing science fiction in 1969, he was largely unknown in the United States until his first novel, *The Embedding* (1973), was issued in an American edition in 1975. Like most of Watson's subsequent fiction, the novel was complex and intelligent. It examined the influence of language on perception in a more probing fashion than had Jack VANCE in *The Languages of Pao* (1957), looking at the subject from two points of view: a group of children raised speaking an artificial language, and a group of aliens trying to understand human communication. The interfaces between two different consciousnesses is repeated in Watson's second novel, *The Jonah Kit* (1975), in which human personalities are imprinted on the brain of a whale.

Three excellent novels quickly followed. *The Martian Inca* (1977) concerns a space probe that returns from Mars contaminated by a new form of disease that gives those afflicted access to the memories of some of their ancestors. Star travel is achieved through mental projection in *Alien Embassy* (1977), but one of those gifted with the talent discovers a subtle danger among the stars. *The Miracle Visitors* (1978) speculates about a unique explanation for UFO sightings and other unexplained phenomena—that they are manifestations of a different form of consciousness, rather than a

strictly objective event. Watson was quite well received critically, but may have had trouble finding his audience because of the intense and sometimes abstruse intellectual content of his speculations. His next few novels were less successful, and some did not find an American publisher until many years later. *God's World* (1979) explores theological matters as aliens who appear to be angels invite humans to visit their world, where they apparently are in direct communication with God. Another alien world appears to have been shaped in the form of a classic painting of hell by Hieronymous Bosch in *The Gardens of Delight* (1980). *Under Heaven's Bridge* (1981), written with Michael BISHOP, explores the world of a race partly flesh, partly machine. An obsessed man attempts to defeat personified death itself in *Deathhunter* (1981).

The metaphysical content of Watson's novels during this period left many readers uneasy, and even his more accessible work was similarly neglected. In *Chekhov's Journey* (1983), for example, a film crew is recreating a historic trek across Siberia by using hypnosis to convince an actor that he is the historical Chekhov. The actor asserts that he is actually the projection of a time traveling astronaut from the future, and that his vehicle is on a collision course with the past. *Converts* (1984) describes the somewhat predictable troubles of a would-be superman.

The Black Current trilogy was considerably more popular, comprising *The Book of the River* (1984), *The Book of the Stars* (1984), and *The Book of Being* (1985). The setting is a primitive world dominated by a river whose very waters may be part of an alien intelligence. The water has the power to drive men insane, but women are immune to its power. The central figure endures many adventures and revelations as she explores her world, and gets caught up in the conflict between two superintelligences.

Watson's next science fiction novel did not appear until 1988. *Whores of Babylon* is an uneven thriller set in a virtual reality recreation of ancient Babylon. *The Flies of Memory* (1990) is a fascinating first contact story involving some truly strange aliens, who have come to the Earth in order to "remember" it. *Hard Questions* (1996) is the closest Watson has come to a techno-thriller, a suspense story involving a new technology so radical that it could lead to civil unrest. Watson's other SF novels during the 1990s were highly regarded game tie-ins. His most recent, *Mockymen* (2003), transforms a bad movie plot into a fascinating novel, with disembodied aliens inhabiting the bodies of dead humans in anticipation of an invasion.

Watson has been a prolific writer at shorter length throughout his career, although much of his work has appeared only in England. "The Ghosts of Luna" (1974), "The Very Slow Time Machine" (1976), "The Flesh of Her Hair" (1984), "On the Dream Channel Panel" (1986), and "Nanoware Time" (1991) are among his best short stories. Three collections have appeared in the United States—*The Very Slow Time Machine* (1979), *The Book of Ian Watson* (1985), and *The Great Escape* (2002)—but his other collections are also of very high quality. Watson often demands considerable effort from his readers, and it is unfortunate that many seem unwilling to expend the necessary energy.

Watt-Evans, Lawrence
(1954–   )

Although Lawrence Watt-Evans debuted as a science fiction writer in 1975, his first four novels and most of his subsequent work have all been fantasies or horror. His first science fiction novel was *The Chromosomal Code* (1984), a story set on an Earth that has been conquered by an alliance of various alien races who apparently have experimented with the genetic makeup of their human subjects, who are now nearly extinct. The protagonist is determined to avenge his race. Although the book is something of a potboiler, the author's enthusiasm for his subject matter was evident and his characters were quite well conceived. *Shining Steel* (1986) was much better, a lost colony story in which the planet in question was settled by fundamentalists who have successfully expunged various "sins" from their society, only to have them reintroduced when Earth resumes contact. The colony had already split up into numerous rival factions, a situation first exacerbated by the outside contamination and then raised to a fever

pitch by a charismatic zealot determined to cleanse the world.

Denner's Wreck (1988) also involves a lost colony that is rediscovered by Earth and subjected to considerable strain when the newcomers prove to be more interested in exploiting the situation than in helping the stranded settlers. The newcomers in fact pretend to be gods. *Nightside City* (1989) is the best of Watt-Evans's first four science fiction novels. It is set on a planet whose very slow rotation was incorrectly interpreted as stability during the initial colonization. Now a very slow advance of sunlight approaches a city that has lived perpetually in the dark, and people are fleeing before what they believe will be the destruction of everything they have built occurs. Someone, however, is buying abandoned property, and a plucky female detective decides to find out why.

Watt-Evans is an occasional short story writer; most of his work in this form is pleasantly entertaining though rarely outstanding. The exception is "Why I Left Harry's All-Night Hamburgers" (1987), which won a Hugo Award. Much of his work at this length is humorous or satiric. The best of his science fiction shorts are contained in *Crosstime Traffic* (1992) and *Celestial Debris* (2002). Under the name Nathan Archer, Watt-Evans has written several above-average media tie-in novels.

"A Way of Life"
Robert Bloch
(1956)

During the 1950s, science fiction fans considered themselves something of a beleaguered minority. Although most of what was being published was still targeted at young males, who made up the vast majority of the SF readership, there were already signs that the field was beginning to evolve along more serious lines. Although stereotyped as a literature of spaceships, monsters, and exotic adventures, science fiction was already producing thoughtful stories about the human condition from writers like Theodore STURGEON and Brian W. ALDISS. Fans understandably resented what they saw as a ghettoization of the field, and defensively professed their disdain for mainstream criticism, which only aggravated their isolation.

Robert BLOCH, the author of the classic suspense story *Psycho* (1959), was a long-time fan who made use of that intimacy to write this satiric story of a future America dominated by science fiction fans. A nuclear war devastated the world and destroyed much of the old knowledge; the situation is made worse by the mundane population's revulsion against science and learning and the purposeful burning of most books during the generation immediately following the war. Most of the books that survived were the private collections of science fiction fans, hidden during the dark years; when civilization finally began to rebuild itself, most of the old knowledge they acquired was harvested from these collections, although often distorted. Robert A. HEINLEIN has been confused with Albert Einstein, for example.

A presidential election campaign is underway, and one of the candidates, John Henderson, is about to make a startling discovery. He had always wondered why none of the old amateur magazines survived along with the books, but his curiosity is satisfied when he finds a secret trove of them in a ruined house. To his dismay, he discovers the truth: Fans were not a persecuted political minority who had only the progress of humanity at heart. Even worse, he realizes that powerful figures behind the government have known this all along and have suppressed the truth. When he confronts his mentor, the latter responds by confirming what he suspects, but then reveals a deeper truth: The legends are exaggerated and inaccurate, but that does not matter. People need a tradition, however distorted, to inspire them to build a better future. The title, incidentally, comes from the slogan "Fandom Is a Way of Life," first enunciated by writer Wilson TUCKER.

We
Yevgeny Zamyatin
(1924)

The two most famous dystopian novels are NINE-TEEN EIGHTY-FOUR (1949) by George Orwell, who acknowledged his debt to Zamyatin's earlier novel, and BRAVE NEW WORLD (1932) by Aldous Huxley. But this earlier Russian novel, unpublished in the author's home country until 1988, was certainly the pioneer, the first serious cautionary novel about the dangers of a repressive superstate. Zamyatin was always a bit of a rebel. He was sent into temporary exile by the czar before the Russian Revolution, and afterward into a permanent exile by the new Communist regime. The novel was written in 1921 but was not published until 1924, when it appeared in the West in an English translation.

The setting is the OneState, a future global culture dominated by a single Big Brother–like figure, the Benefactor. The two protagonists are a scientist and a rebel whose lives become intertwined. People do not have names any more, but are identified by numbers, and all pronouns are collective—hence the title. Private property is an alien concept, and individual personal rights are minimal. Zamyatin was obviously responding to the excesses of the Russian Revolution, but he was also commenting on the entire body of utopian fiction, whose elaborate and carefully balanced social systems invariably would have collapsed if real people had attempted to apply them to their own lives. In Zamyatin's novel people emulate machines, and methods are being devised to eliminate the last variable, the human imagination. The eventual rebellion fails, but Zamyatin's humor blunts the blow somewhat. Although the novel is relatively unsophisticated by modern standards, it has remained quietly popular ever since its original appearance. Despite the grim aspect of life in the OneState, there is an underlying sense of humor and a clear disdain for totalitarianism that lightens the mood considerably.

"We Can Remember It for You Wholesale"
Philip K. Dick
(1966)

Douglas Quail is an ordinary man, or so he believes, living with an ordinary wife and performing an ordinary job. He is troubled by a persistent dream in which he visits the colony on the planet Mars, an irritation that manifests itself during his waking hours by an urge to actually go there. Since this would be expensive and impractical, he finally decides to resort to the next best thing.

Rekal, Inc., is a company that implants false memories so detailed that they are indistinguishable from reality. For a suitable fee, they agree to provide him with the complete recollection of a two-week visit to Mars, during which he served as a secret agent for a security organization. They begin the process after placing him under hypnosis, and discover to their consternation that his memories have already been altered, that the story they intended to insert into his memories is already there in a slightly different form. Quail *did* go to Mars as a special agent—as an assassin in fact— and those memories have been professionally suppressed. Concerned that they will attract the unwelcome attention of the authorities, the technicians abort the process and refund Quail's money. Unfortunately for all concerned, it is too late, because the buried memories will inevitably surface now. Quail is apprehended by his former employer, who reluctantly plans to kill him, but Quail suggests an alternative, a different composition of memories in which he helped alien visitors as a child, who in gratitude delayed their conquest of the Earth. The story ends with the revelation that this false memory is also a real one.

Dick's story became the inspiration for the movie *Total Recall* (1990), which is quite faithful to the source in the opening minutes, but which drops the story of the aliens in favor of a protracted and illogical series of captures and escapes as Quail does in fact return to Mars.

"We, in Some Strange Power's Employ, Move in a Rigorous Line"
Samuel R. Delany
(1968)

In some fairly distant but unspecified future a cheaper form of energy generation has helped transform the world. With electrical power available everywhere on land and often under the sea as well, it is no longer necessary to concentrate the population in cities, and much arable land that was previously inaccessible can now be profitably farmed. Blacky is a technician aboard the Gila Monster, an enormous armored service vehicle that installs and maintains the power lines. On rare occasions the crew is also called upon to arrange a conversion, connecting a remote community to the grid, although that happens rarely. Significantly, workers aboard these mobile maintenance shops are known as *devils* and *demons.*

Blacky has just been promoted to the equivalent of foreman when he and his crew are diverted to perform a conversion near the U.S.-Canadian border, bringing electricity to a small community of fewer than two dozen renegade biker types and nonconformists who have no desire to be linked to the outside world. They are the spiritual descendants of the Hell's Angels, and their home is called Haven. Blacky admits to feeling some sympathy for them despite their squalid living conditions. They have their own code of honor and they live by it and are not bothering anyone else. But the law requires that they accept power connections if they want to live together. Although Blacky is inclined to leave them to their own devices, Mabel—his partner—is determined to install the lines because she sees in their rebellious lifestyle the seeds of the old violence that once plagued the world. Inevitably the conflict turns deadly, and the leader of the dissidents is killed.

The story has also appeared as "Lines of Power," which is in some ways a more appropriate title. The power in the story is not limited to the energy traveling through the physical lines laid by the Gila Monster, but also extends to the ties of authority within the outcast community of Haven, between Blacky and his cosupervisor, and between society at large and the handful of dissidents.

Weber, David
(1952–)

David Weber made his debut with *Insurrection* (1990), the first volume of a trilogy written with Steve WHITE, followed promptly by *Crusade* (1992) and, after a gap, *In Death Ground* (1997). The trilogy is typical military science fiction involving an interstellar war, a subgenre in which Weber quickly would specialize and which makes up the vast majority of his output. *Mutineers'*

Moon (1991), the first adventure of Colin McIntyre, has an astronaut discovering an oversized, sentient military spaceship on the Moon and bonding with it. With its aid, McIntyre successfully defends Earth against alien aggressors in that novel and the sequel, *The Armageddon Inheritance* (1993). The series was extended into galactic space in *Heirs of Empire* (1996), somewhat implausibly promoting a human to the highest post in a multispecies civilization.

On Basilisk Station (1993) introduced Weber's most popular character, Honor Harrington, a military officer who annoys her superior and gets posted to a backwater star system, where she is able to use limited resources to foil an interplanetary plot and save the day. She becomes an envoy to a male chauvinist world in *The Honor of the Queen* (1993), foils a military attack in *The Short Victorious War* (1994), but runs afoul of politics among her own people in *Field of Dishonor* (1994). Unfairly treated, she is forced to immigrate to another world in *Flag in Exile* (1995), battles space pirates and backstabbers in *Honor Among Enemies* (1996), and is condemned and sent to a prison planet in *In Enemy Hands* (1997). She organizes her fellow prisoners and effects an escape in *Echoes of Honor* (1998), returns home to find that the political intrigues are just as vicious as ever in *Ashes of Honor* (2000), and retires and then returns to active duty during a new war in *War of Honor* (2002). Weber has also edited several anthologies of stories by other writers set in the same universe. *Crown of Slaves* (2003) with Eric Flint also shares that common backdrop.

Weber's nonseries novels have also tended to be military adventures. *Path of the Fury* (1992) follows the career of a woman angered by pirate attacks who turns pirate herself in order to track down those responsible for raiding her home world, somewhat echoing the Star Kings series by Jack VANCE. Earth gets caught in the middle of an interstellar war in *The Apocalypse Troll* (1999). *The Excalibur Alternative* (2002) is a variation of *The HIGH CRUSADE* (1960) by Poul ANDERSON, with kidnapped humans getting the better of their alien captors. Although most of his work tends to follow predictable paths, Weber has a flair for exciting plots and nefarious intrigues.

Weinbaum, Stanley G.
(1902–1935)

Like C. M. KORNBLUTH and Henry KUTTNER, Stanley Weinbaum died young, yet produced a body of work that would have a lasting influence on the field and would continue to be read avidly by generations that followed. This is a particularly remarkable accomplishment in Weinbaum's case, because he was considerably less prolific than the others, his first sale coming less than two years before his death.

"A MARTIAN ODYSSEY" (1934) remains one of the most popular stories from the 1930s, recounting the adventures of a stranded astronaut on Mars and his friendship with a decidedly alien creature. Nearly as good was "The Lotus Eaters" (1935), which featured intelligent plant life on the planet Venus. "Dawn of Flame" (1936) is a story of life after a devastating world war and is related to the novel *The Black Flame*. "The Adaptive Ultimate" (1935) is an effective superman story, and "Proteus Island" (1936) is one of the earliest stories dealing with manipulation of the human genetic structure. "Parasite Planet" (1935), also set on Venus, portrays the local life-forms as inimical to humans; but unlike in other stories from this period, this was not the result of some innate evil quality of the Venusians but part of their logically described and understandable nature. Weinbaum's stories have been collected in *The Best of Stanley G. Weinbaum* (1974), *The Red Peri & Others* (1952), and *A Martian Odyssey* (1949 and 1974, with differing contents, the later edition containing his complete short fiction).

Weinbaum's novels (all published posthumously), while neither as polished nor as memorable as his short stories, were remarkably sophisticated for their time, and hint at the writer he might have become had he lived longer. *The Black Flame* (1948), which includes "Dawn of Flame," is set in a postapocalyptic world whose survivors eventually discover the secret of immortality. *The Dark Other* (1950) follows the misadventures of a scientist involved with consciousness altering experiments who frees his darker self in what is clearly an update of *DR. JEKYLL AND MR. HYDE* (1886) by Robert Louis Stevenson. A superhuman attempts to find a place for himself among ordinary humans in *The New Adam* (1939), probably the most successful of his book-length works. The hints of a greater talent that can be found in Weinbaum's small body of work make his loss that much greater.

Wells, H. G.
(1866–1946)

Herbert George Wells, along with Jules VERNE, was one of the major early writers of science fiction. He is probably the single most influential writer, inventing or popularizing many of the major plot devices and themes of the genre before it even had a name. Indeed, Wells thought of himself simply as a writer, and his scientific romances were only a fraction of the fiction he produced. However, most of his novels of contemporary society are now virtually forgotten, and he is remembered primarily for his stories of time travel, Martian invasion, and invisible madmen.

Unlike Verne, who primarily was interested in telling a good story and who used technological wonders such as submarines and advanced aircraft as part of the setting for his adventures, Wells usually addressed technological change as an element in the plot, and in terms of its social implications. The experimenters in "The NEW ACCELERATOR" are changed by their ability to operate outside of normal time. The inventor in *The INVISIBLE MAN* (1897) is driven mad by his new power.

Wells wrote several speculative essays about the future of humanity before turning to fiction—short stories—during the 1890s, quickly moving on to writing novels. *The TIME MACHINE* (1895) was his first novel, telling the story of a man who travels to the very distant future and discovers that humanity has split into two distinct species, one preying cannibalistically on the other. The next five years would see Wells's best novels appear in rapid succession. *The WAR OF THE WORLDS* (1898) is the most effective of these works. Martians invade the Earth, reject all attempts at friendly contact, and are destroyed only because of their own failings, rather than through the efforts of humanity to oppose them.

The relative insignificance of the human race and its works recurs as a theme in Wells's work, and scientists who aspire to greater control, as in *The INVISIBLE MAN* or *The ISLAND OF DR. MOREAU* (1896), are doomed to fail because of their excessive pride. In the latter, a reclusive scientist abrogates to himself the power of God, operating on various animals to provide them with a primitive intelligence. For his sins, he is ultimately punished. Edgar Rice BURROUGHS would later write his own version, incorporating elements from Mary Shelley's *FRANKENSTEIN,* as *The Monster Men* (1929), whose more appropriate magazine title was *A Man Without a Soul.*

Wells was a confirmed socialist, and that outlook influenced his visions of the future. A man awakens from suspended animation in *When the Sleeper Wakes* (1899, also published as *The Sleeper Wakes*) and becomes the rallying point for a socialist revolution. The highly organized, insectlike society in the caverns of the Moon in *The FIRST MEN IN THE MOON* (1901) also employ a form of socialism, but Wells seems more ambivalent this time. Although further contact is prohibited to avoid contamination of lunar values by human visitors, the author does not appear to admire the Selenites' closed and overrestrictive culture either. After the turn of the century, Wells's novels became increasingly didactic and less interesting literarily. *A Modern Utopia* (1905) is an almost unreadable utopian tour, and the later *Men Like Gods* (1923) is only marginally more interesting. Both assume that human civilization will evolve into a socialist state benignly administered by an enlightened few. *In the Days of the Comet* (1906) presumes somewhat depressingly that the only way for humans to achieve true enlightenment is by the intervention of outside forces, in this case the beneficent effects of the near passage of a comet. A similar theme, even less effectively done, provides the plot in *Star Begotten* (1937); this time the source of change is invisible rays from Mars. The best of the author's later novels is *The Food of the Gods* (1904), in which a new discovery leads to spectacularly fecund crops and animal growth. *The War in the Air* (1908) predicts with some accuracy the devastating effects of aerial bombardment in a future war.

Speculative content grew increasingly rare in Wells's late work. *The World Set Free* (1914, also published as *The Last War*) raises questions about the role of science in developing ever more destructive weapons. *The Autocracy of Mr. Parham* (1930) is a marginal future political satire. *The Dream* (1924) is a retrospective look at contemporary mores from the viewpoint of the distant future. *The Camford Visitation* (1937) involves a visit to Earth by a disembodied alien intelligence, but the book is more of an extended satiric essay than a novel. *The Shape of Things to Come* (1935) is another extended speculation disguised as a novel. *The Holy Terror* (1939) is a marginal dystopian satire. Many of his other late novels were allegories that contained at least peripheral fantastic content, sometimes involving the intervention of God or a reinterpretation of biblical passages.

Wells was also a prolific short story writer, and his works have been collected and cross-collected so many times that it would be pointless to attempt to list them all. *The Complete Science Fiction of H. G. Wells* (1978) is not complete, but contains most of his better work; *The Complete Stories of H. G. Wells* (1998) is also an excellent selection. Several of his shorts are particularly memorable. "The Star" is a concise disaster story, the partial descendant of a long tradition of British disaster novels. "The Sea Raiders" describes the depredations of a new form of sea life inimical to humans. A scientist discovers a way to speed up subjective time in "The New Accelerator," and an orchid collector encounters a very peculiar new variation in "The FLOWERING OF THE STRANGE ORCHID." "The Land Ironclads" predicts the development of tank warfare with surprising accuracy, and "The Argonauts of the Air" theorizes about the future of air warfare. "A Dream of Armageddon" also expresses concern about the destructive potential of scientific advances; "A Story of the Days to Come" is an interesting general contemplation of one possible future. Other significant tales include "The Stolen Bacillus," "The Plattner Story," and "The Story of the Late Mr. Elvesham." "The Country of the Blind" is possibly his best single short story, a lost race tale that disproves the statement that possession of limited sight among a society of the blind would make one superior. "The Man Who Could Work Miracles," although a fantasy rather than science fiction, is also among his best.

Many writers have acknowledged their debt to H. G. Wells, sometimes using him as a character in their own work. The most notable examples of the latter are *Time After Time* (1979) by Karl Alexander, in which a young Wells uses a time machine to pursue Jack the Ripper into the modern world; *The Space Machine* (1976) by Christopher PRIEST, and THE *SALIVA TREE* (1965) by Brian W. ALDISS, a novella written to commemorate the centenary anniversary of Wells's birth. Alexander's novel was adapted for a surprisingly good motion picture. Almost all of Wells's novels have been filmed, usually multiple times, or have provided inspiration for others with similar concepts. The influence of H. G. Wells on other science fiction writers is immeasurable. His work is widely known far beyond the boundaries of the genre, and to a great extent the creators of all novels and films of alien invasions, time travel, or invisibility are at least partly in his debt.

When Harlie Was One
David Gerrold
(1972)

Science fiction writers have long held ambivalent attitudes toward computers—particularly computers who believe themselves to be intelligent beings with individual wills—starting in the days of the lurid pulp magazines. Novels like *The God Machine* (1968) by Martin CAIDIN and *Colossus* (1966) by D. F. JONES portrayed self-aware computers as creatures so determined to survive that they threaten the future of the human race. Others worried that we would put so much reliance on computers that we would shirk responsibility for our own lives, as in *The HUMANOIDS* (1949) by Jack WILLIAMSON. A very different attitude is expressed in *The MOON IS A HARSH MISTRESS* (1966) by Robert A. HEINLEIN and *Michaelmas* (1977) by Algis BUDRYS, in each of which computer intelligences become allies as well as tools, companions as well as calculators.

When Harlie Was One falls into the latter category, but it is also a coming-of-age story. Harlie is a computer program that becomes self-aware, but with a personality that is the equivalent of a human infant. His accelerated childhood is facilitated by his inventor/programmer, with whose assistance Harlie avoids being legally defined as an object, a possession, without any say in his own future. The increasingly acrimonious battle over his future results in a trial to determine Harlie's fate. The charm of the novel lies almost entirely with Harlie himself, who evolves from a being without character to a personable entity who ultimately becomes the most interesting personality in the novel.

For the 1988 revised edition, Gerrold reworked the original text considerably, incorporating a more contemporary understanding of the way an artificial intelligence might work as well as updating the background culture. He also suggests details of Harlie's origins in *Bouncing Off the Moon* (2001). *Valentina: Soul in Sapphire* (1985) by Joseph H. Delaney and Marc Stiegler is a variation of the same story, but the artificial intelligence in this case has a female persona.

"When It Changed"
Joanna Russ
(1972)

Prior to the 1960s female characters historically had been consigned to support roles in science fiction, and despite heightened awareness of the disparity during the 1960s, there was little improvement in the years that followed. The 1970s saw the emergence of a strong feminist movement among genre critics and such writers as Joanna RUSS, Pamela SARGENT, Ursula K. LE GUIN, Suzy McKee CHARNAS, and Vonda N. McINTYRE, who would soon make their presence and dissatisfaction known in no uncertain terms. Russ was probably the most controversial, and overtly angry, of this group, and her novel *The FEMALE MAN* (1973) provoked powerful emotional reactions, both pro and con. That novel included sequences set on the planet Whileaway, whose population was exclusively female. However, Whileaway had made an earlier appearance in this, her most famous short story, winner of the Nebula Award.

A plague wiped out all of the men on Whileaway, and a global war back on Earth left the planet isolated for 600 years, during which time the female survivors learned to reproduce themselves artificially and developed a thriving culture characterized by hard work and patience. The colony is not a utopian society; the narrator has herself fought several duels for unspecified reasons and has killed her opponent on more than one occasion. Their new culture is stable and progressive, however, and their population has reached 30 million by the time an unexpected starship arrives from Earth, bearing four representatives, all male—the first men that anyone living on Whileaway has ever seen.

The two differing perceptions are quite striking. The men view the colonists as living in an unnatural lifestyle, and assume that the women will welcome the return of the male half of the species as a kind of liberation. The narrator and her companions consider the men uncouth, repulsive, and threatening. Despite the claim that sexual equality is the rule on Earth, the very fact that the visitors are all male testifies to the contrary. We are left with the impression that the men will once again dominate the colony, and that this is not an improvement, that something will be lost. The inevitability of conflict among the sexes and the male drive to dominate would be reflected in "HOUSTON, HOUSTON, DO YOU READ?" (1976) by James TIPTREE Jr., another excellent tale; but not even Tiptree could convey such a depth of feeling with so few words.

When Worlds Collide
Philip Wylie and Edwin Balmer
(1933)

Disaster stories existed long before science fiction was a recognized genre; indeed, the biblical account of Noah's Flood predates the novel altogether. Even Leonardo da Vinci felt inspired to narrate a fictional destruction of the world in *Deluge*. Novelists such as H. G. WELLS, M. P. Shiel, and S. Fowler Wright produced classic tales of the devastation of large portions of the world and the near extinction of the human race, and in the 1950s the disaster novel would become almost a subgenre of its own in England.

Philip WYLIE and Edwin Balmer had both enjoyed moderate success as authors individually when they teamed up to produce this classic story of the destruction of Earth. Balmer had written detective fiction and one minor science fiction novel, and Wylie had authored two previous speculative novels whose plots were considerably less ambitious. The premise of *When Worlds Collide* is that two rogue planets are approaching the solar system. On their first orbit, the planet Bronson—named after the astronomer who discovered it—will pass close enough to the Earth to cause devastating tidal effects, earthquakes, flooding, storms of unprecedented violence. On their second pass, Earth will be hit directly, destroying our planet and altering the major intruder's orbit so that it will then leave the solar system. The only possibility for survival is to migrate to the companion world, which will conveniently take up an orbit very close to that of the now missing Earth and which, as we later discover, has an atmosphere that humans can breathe. The coincidences necessary to provide this hope of salvation are substantial, but since the focus of the story is elsewhere, we can forgive that failing.

Most of the novel deals with the difficulties, both logistical and personal, surrounding the effort to build a ship that can successfully cross to the new world. Since only a very small number of people can be saved, there is growing tension about the makeup of the passenger list, and the steadily worsening conditions outside the project are not likely to make things any easier. The ultimate success of the launch comes only after an exciting and generally satisfying series of adventures and catastrophes. The novel was filmed with surprisingly good results in 1951. The authors went on to provide a sequel, *After Worlds Collide* (1934), pitting the new colonists against rivals from Earth as well as the hazards of their new world, but it was not nearly as rewarding a story.

White, James
(1928–1999)

It is likely that James White will be best remembered for his SECTOR GENERAL SERIES, which started with several short stories set aboard an orbiting hospital station that catered to various alien species, eventually expanding to 12 volumes, some patched together from shorter pieces, some full-length novels. The success of the series is in some ways unfortunate, because this comparatively lightweight work occupied so much of White's writing career. His nonseries novels suggest that he was potentially a much more skilled writer.

His first three novels were relatively minor, although entertaining. A doctor discovers that his patients are aliens secretly studying human culture in *The Secret Visitors* (1957). *Second Ending* (1962) is about the last man on a deserted Earth, awakened from suspended animation to explore the abandoned world in the company of a team of robots. *Escape Orbit* (1965, also published as *Open Prison*) follows the adventures of a group of humans stranded on a hostile planet. *The Watch Below* (1966), on the other hand, is an extremely impressive effort. During World War II, a small group of people manages to survive inside a sunken ship. Their descendants are rescued by aliens from a water world seeking a new home in the Earth's oceans. What might seem an implausible plot is remarkably well done. *All Judgment Fled* (1968) is also a first contact story, with matters complicated by predictable internal squabbling and political maneuvering.

White's novels during the 1970s were often less than optimistic. *Tomorrow Is Too Far* (1971) is set within a research project that observes unexpected results after a routine experiment. *Lifeboat* (1972, also published as *Dark Inferno*) is the story of a disastrous accident in space. *The Dream Millennium* (1974) follows humans exploring the stars in search of a new home free of the excessive pollution that is destroying the Earth's ecology. Aliens attempt to exterminate the human race in *Underkill* (1979).

The mood of White's work improved during the 1980s. In *Federation World* (1988) humans are exploring the possibility of resettling a large population on an enormous artificial world to be jointly colonized by multiple races. *The Silent Stars Go By* (1991) is the most interesting of his later novels, an alternate history in which it was the Irish who discovered the New World.

White's non–Sector General short stories have been collected in *Deadly Litter* (1964), *The Aliens Among Us* (1969), *Monsters and Medics* (1977), *Futures Past* (1982), and *The White Papers* (1996).

"The White Otters of Childhood"
Michael Bishop
(1973)

One of the greatest of all science fiction novels is A CANTICLE FOR LEIBOWITZ (1959) by Walter M. MILLER Jr., in which the world is devastated by a nuclear war, slowly rebuilds, then experiences a second holocaust after another 1,500 years. Michael BISHOP added this unofficial sequel, set many generations after the second conflict. Our strain of humanity is now a minority on the planet, confined to a string of islands, while a further evolved race, the Parfects, spreads across the rest of the planet. Markcrier Rains is an old-style human, recently returned from a prolonged and dispiriting stay among the Parfects. Rains marries the girl lusted after by Fearing Serenos, the ruthless but crafty dictator of the old human civilization, and the two are concerned about what form his inevitable retribution will take.

His revenge comes only after a gap of several years. Rains is dispatched on a mission of state and returns to discover that Serenos has raped and beaten his wife. When she later dies during childbirth, he vows vengeance; he is abetted by his father in law, who is the dictator's private physician and who has in the past surgically altered enemies of his master, turning them into bizarre variations of lower animals. They successfully abduct Serenos and inform his inner circle that their leader has died, after which Rains himself becomes effectively the unofficial head of government. As the doctor slowly transforms Serenos into a shark, Rains attempts to reform the government, making numerous enemies in the process and accomplishing very little. The pseudoshark, finally released into the ocean, immediately dies, depriving them of the revenge that Rains no longer desires.

Ultimately despairing for the future of old-style humanity, Rains resigns and avoids being as-

sassinated, convinced that the Parfects are on the verge of judging his kind beyond redemption. His final act as a man is to offer himself as another experimental subject, hoping to find some form of peace as a shark that was denied him as a human.

White, Steve
(1946–   )

Steve White's first novels were military science fiction collaborations with David WEBER—a trilogy consisting of *Insurrection* (1990), *Crusade* (1992), and *In Death Ground* (1997). White began a solo series with *The Disinherited* (1993), in which a party of apparently friendly aliens arrive on Earth warning of a more bellicose race moving in our direction. Unfortunately, a relaxation of tensions and budget constraints on Earth have led to the virtual elimination of space defenses, and humanity seems unable to defend itself. *Legacy* (1995) continues the story, complicating matters by adding time travel to the mix. The story concludes with *Debt of Ages* (1995), in which space forces from the future contact King Arthur's Britain.

Prince of Sunset (1998) began a new sequence that bears some superficial similarity to the FLANDRY SERIES by Poul ANDERSON. The human interstellar empire has grown soft and vulnerable, and a conspiracy is underway to overthrow the old order with a new, more rigid government that will suppress some of the existing human freedoms. A handful of young military graduates play a crucial role in thwarting these revolutionary ambitions. *Emperor of Dawn* (1999) is set after several generations have passed and the old fright has died down. The current emperor is a weak man whose inattention threatens a repeat of history, tempting another group of would-be despots into plotting a new order with themselves on top. White seems to imply that the best form of government for humans is a benevolent one imposed by a strong authority figure. *Eagle Against the Stars* (2000) has assertive aliens arriving on Earth and imposing their will by means of what they call free trade but what is actually an imperialistic device. Readers will not be surprised when resourceful humans figure out a way to beat them at their own game. White's most recent novel is another collaboration with David Weber, *The Shiva Option* (2002), a fast-paced panoramic story of interstellar warfare. White is at his best when writing action sequences, and at his weakest in describing political structures, which are often simplistic and unconvincing.

"Who Goes There?"
John W. Campbell Jr.
(1938)

Possibly as a reaction against the often comical monsters that appear in science fiction films, science fiction writers and editors have generally stayed away from stories of alien creatures. The mood of the genre traditionally has been optimistic about the universe. Since the 1930s, aliens generally have been portrayed either as sympathetic or as rivals much as other human cultures might be rivals. War between humans and aliens might be inevitable, but it would be fought for racial pride, profit, or territory, not to prevent hideous creatures from despoiling human women or eating babies. That aversion is so powerful that the handful of true monster stories in the field are almost always of extraordinary quality, so well written or so well conceived that editors could not possibly turn them down.

A case in point is "Who Goes There?" by John W. CAMPBELL Jr. Campbell, who would spend most of his later career as an editor rather than as a writer, wrote several space operas in the style of Edward E. SMITH and engineering problem stories set on alien worlds. His writing improved very quickly and he might have become a much more significant figure as an author had he continued, although his influence as an editor was certainly greater. This particular story is atypical for him, as it was for the field in general, but it is also his most impressive fictional achievement, a vivid suspenseful thriller that became the basis of a less than faithful adaptation, *The Thing* (1951, also known as *The Thing from Another World*), and a more faithful remake in 1982. The premise is deceptively simple: A research station at the South Pole is temporarily isolated from the rest of the world when the staff discovers an ancient alien spaceship

in the ice. They also find its pilot, frozen into a solid block—a dormant creature that can replicate itself by duplicating organisms it physically touches, mimicking their appearance, absorbing much of their memory. The problem lies in finding a way to determine which of the personnel are still human and which have been transformed, so that the creature can be destroyed in all of its manifestations before it can escape into the outside world. The alien's potential to replace the entire human race in a relatively short period of time was far more frightening than an army of movie monsters, but Hollywood's first attempt to bring it to the screen ignored that deeper terror in favor of a more traditional man-in-a-rubber-suit creature.

The (Widget), the (Wadget), and Boff
Theodore Sturgeon
(1955)

This remarkable novella opens with a brief exchange among aliens who have been studying humanity from a distance and who detect an unusual variation in our species. There is one genetic ability that is common to all intelligences in the universe, but only humans seem to lack the capacity to use it. Explanations are needed, so a field team is sent to study a small group of people and solve the mystery. The scene shifts to Earth, specifically a rooming house run by the Bittelmans, whose tenants include a single mom, a man troubled by thoughts of suicide, an ambitious and impatient young woman, a young boy whose imaginary friends, Googie and Boff, might be something other than products of his own creation, and a few others. Each of the characters is developed economically into an individual torn between conflicting emotions and beliefs, with considerable depth and hints of self contradiction arising from their preconceptions about each other.

There are several oddities in the arrangement, to which the tenants awaken only gradually. The Bittelmans ask questions and rarely make positive statements, and it is almost impossible not to answer them honestly. The development of the individual characters and their personal crises alternates with occasional notes by the alien observers, who are arguing about the type of stimulus they should provide in order to find out why humans behave differently than all other intelligent life. These conversations serve to activate the potential of the dormant talent. Eventually, they set the building on fire in order to push their experimental subjects to the breaking point. During the ensuing emergency each subject finds himself or herself capable of making intelligent decisions in complex situations, and in the process they also resolve their individual problems. When the Bittelmans depart in the aftermath, we belatedly discover that they were disguises used by Boff and Googie, who were far more than imaginary. Sturgeon's aliens are almost inconsequential to the story, however, which is about people, how they interact with others, and how they unconsciously shape their own perceptions of themselves and others in ways that are potentially self-destructive. It also suggests that within each of us is the capacity to see past our own illusions and know our true selves.

Wild Cards series
George R. R. Martin and Melinda Snodgrass, editors
(1987–1995)

Superhumans in science fiction writing are usually people with an added ability, either increased intelligence as in *The Fourth "R"* (1959) by George O. SMITH or some psi power, such as telepathy. Although *Gladiator* (1930) by Philip WYLIE may have been the inspiration for the comic strip *Superman,* its protagonist was only moderately stronger than other men, and vulnerable in other ways. There have been tie-in novels based on various comic book superheroes from time to time, sometimes written by established genre writers, but the costumed superhero from the graphics world is too implausible to provide fertile ground for original novelists. Michael BISHOP played with the idea in *Count Geiger's Blues* (1992), but only for satiric purposes. The one exception to all of this is the Wild Cards series of novels and original anthologies, 15 volumes set in a shared universe.

The premise is that contamination from outer space resulted in a variety of unpredictable muta-

tions, providing diverse superpowers to various individuals. Those with significant powers are known as Aces, those with minor gifts as Deuces. Unfortunately, some of those empowered individuals turn to a life of crime, and perhaps even more unfortunately, there is widespread fear and distrust among normals directed toward those with mutant powers, regardless of their choice of lifestyle. The individual writers pursued their own story lines, but always within a larger context dictated by the editors, so that there is a logical progression from book to book. Among those who contributed were Roger ZELAZNY, Lewis Shiner, Pat CADIGAN, Edward Bryant, Walter Jon WILLIAMS, and the editors themselves. The first volume in the series was *Wild Cards* (1987) and the last was *Black Trump* (1995). All of these were collections, except for three titles that were actually novels: *Turn of the Cards* (1993) by Victor Milan, *Double Solitaire* (1994) by Melinda Snodgrass, and *Dead Man's Hand* (1994) by George R. R. MARTIN and John J. Miller. The mood of the series was generally playful in the earlier volumes, but grew more serious and somewhat bitter toward the end.

Wilhelm, Kate
(1928–   )

During the 1950s Kate Wilhelm wrote predominantly conventional science fiction stories. These stories were occasionally quite striking, although she would not begin to produce top quality work until the 1970s. Among the better early stories were "The Mile Long Spaceship" (1956), "A Is for Automation" (1959), "The Last Days of the Captain" (1963), and "Andover and the Android" (1963), all of which only hinted at her skills, chiefly in the deft manner in which she created her characters. Many of these were collected in *The Mile Long Spaceship* (1963, also published as *Andover and the Android*). Her first novel was a mystery. Her second, *The Clone* (1965), written in collaboration with Theodore L. Thomas, is a superior quasi-monster story. The clone in this case is a rapidly replicating cell that converts all organic matter into additions to its own substance, similar to *The Blob* of movie fame. *The Nevermore Affair*

(1966) involves a secret government project exploring ways to extend human longevity. *The Killer Thing* (1967, also published as *The Killing Thing*) was less interesting, pitting humans against an ancient alien device driven by universal xenophobia in a style reminiscent of the BERSERKER SERIES by Fred SABERHAGEN. *Let the Fire Fall* (1969) was more successful and began the transition to more thoughtful work. Aliens arrive on Earth and receive a decidedly unfriendly welcome, as a consequence of which they arrange some pointed revenge. *The Year of the Cloud* (1970), again written with Theodore L. Thomas, is an effective but predictable story of ecological disaster following a major climatic change.

Wilhelm's short fiction improved more rapidly than her longer work. "The Planners" (1968) won a Nebula Award, and *The Downstairs Room* (1968) was noticeably better than most stories in her first collection. More excellent stories soon followed, including "How Many Miles to Babylon?" (1968), "Somerset Dreams" (1969), "The Infinity Box" (1971), and "Whatever Happened to the Olmecs?" (1973). *City of Cain* (1974), the story of a man with the ability to eavesdrop on the thoughts of others, who inadvertently discovers a plot to install a military dictatorship, was only a moderately convincing thriller. *The Clewiston Test* (1976), the story of illegal medical experimentation, is only marginally science fiction, although it has some intriguing feminist content. Her next novel, *Where Late the Sweet Birds Sang* (1976), would surpass all previous expectations, winning a Hugo Award. It is still one of the best novels about cloning. In this case, a wealthy family creates an elaborate shelter in anticipation of the next war, and when the expected conflict finally erupts, they are isolated from the rest of the world. In the generations that follow, they become increasingly infertile, eventually turning to cloning in order to reproduce themselves.

Juniper Time (1979) was another impressive effort. The children of a scientist develop differing priorities in a future in which Earth has been ravaged by drought and famine. In *A Sense of Shadow* (1981), a wealthy man's legacy to his estranged children is an experimental process designed to alter the way their brains work. *Welcome, Chaos*

(1983) describes the battle for control of a process that could extend the human lifespan indefinitely. A man is literally separated from his physical body in *Crazy Time* (1988), and an alien probe, designed to be harmless, malfunctions when it reaches Earth and becomes a destructive force in *The Dark Door* (1988). A young child exhibits extraordinary mental powers in *Naming the Flowers* (1992).

Wilhelm's recent novels have been primarily detective stories that occasionally involve fantastic elements. Her output of short stories decreased dramatically in the early 1980s, but she had already produced a considerable body of first-rate fiction and had proven to be particularly effective at novelette length. Her collections are *Abyss* (1967), *Somerset Dreams and Other Fictions* (1978), *Children of the Wind* (1989), *Listen, Listen* (1991), *State of Grace* (1991), *And the Angels Sing* (1992), and *A Flush of Shadows* (1995). Among the best of her later stories are "The Funeral" (1972), "The Girl Who Fell into the Sky" (1985), and the time travel story "Forever Yours, Anna" (1986). These last two both won Nebula Awards. Wilhelm is a thoughtful, talented writer whose insights into the human character are almost always more impressive than the overt events that take place in her plots.

Williams, Paul O.
(1928–   )

One of the most frustrating experiences for a reader is to discover a new writer who emerges, produces a few exceptionally good stories, then falls silent after a short period. Perhaps the most famous example of this in science fiction is Walter M. MILLER Jr., who produced a remarkable body of work during the 1950s only to stop writing fiction completely for the next 30 years. Although Paul O. Williams never rivaled Miller's popularity, his seven Pelbar novels written in the early 1980s were very well received. He produced one unrelated novel in 1989 and a handful of very minor short stories in the early 1990s.

The Breaking of Northwall (1980) seemed at first to be a typical postapocalyptic adventure story. The protagonist is faced with the problem of entering a walled city dominated by slave traders in order to rescue the woman he loves. Williams avoided the clichés of survivalist fiction, however, and the series is more reminiscent of RE-BIRTH (1955) by John WYNDHAM or DAVY (1964) by Edgar PANGBORN, concentrating on the culture that might evolve from such a disaster and the tensions arising as the fragmented communities begin to interact, rather than on violent action scenes. Second in the series was *The Ends of the Circle* (1980), in which an explorer goes on a tour of these disparate holdings in order to assess the status of the world. Intermingling and consolidation continue in *The Dome in the Forest* (1981), but now these changes have begun to alarm more conservative interests, who begin to sow dissension in an effort to maintain the status quo.

The Fall of the Shell (1982) concentrates on the internal political structure of one of the walled cities—this one dominated by women—that is undermined by the antics of two youngsters. The alliance of comparatively free communities joins forces against the slave-trading holdings on their perimeter in *An Ambush of Shadows* (1983). *The Song of the Axe* (1984) is a coming of age story set against the continually evolving background, and *The Sword of Forbearance* (1985) brings the series to a conclusion with the concerted effort by the free states to subjugate the last of the tyrants and liberate the slaves. Although the stories occasionally get caught up in the physical action, their lasting value lies in the story of the gradual reconciliation and consolidation of disparate groups into a more homogeneous and prosperous society. *The Gifts of the Corboduc Vandal* (1989) is a disappointingly routine space opera.

Williams, Walter Jon
(1953–   )

Walter Jon Williams's first novel was published in 1981, but he didn't turn to science fiction until *Ambassador of Progress* (1984), a planetary romance of minor interest. *Knight Moves* (1985) showed a noticeable improvement in style as well as concept, mixing immortality with a quest to find a workable method of teleportation or matter transmission. It was *Hard Wired* (1986) that began

to raise eyebrows. The story of hostilities between Earth and its orbiting habitats draws heavily on cyberpunk themes and creates a fascinating future to which Williams would return with his next novel. *Voice of the Whirlwind* (1987) was even more intriguing, a mystery story in which the clone of a murdered man sets out to solve the mystery of the death of his original, reminiscent of *To Live Forever* (1956) by Jack VANCE. *Solip: System* (1989), a novella, makes use of the same setting.

The Crown Jewels (1987) introduced Drake Majistral, an aristocrat turned burglar, an affable and good-natured criminal who returns in *House of Shards* (1988) and *Rock of Ages* (1995). Majistral's burglary is legally sanctioned for its entertainment value. *Angel Station* (1989), on the other hand, is another high-tech novel set in a distant future in which space roving outlaws seek to make their fortunes, interstellar corporations limit individual freedoms, and a newly discovered alien race threatens to disrupt things even further. *Days of Atonement* (1992) is the author's first novel in a near-future setting, pitting a savvy small-town sheriff against some mysterious goings-on at a secretive research facility.

Aristoi (1992) assumes the rise of a future aristocracy, this time addicted to the use of virtual reality where they can enjoy the illusion of absolute power. Williams next wrote two linked fantasy novels before returning to science fiction. *The Rift* (1999) is a traditional but extremely accomplished disaster novel in which a devastating earthquake near the Mississippi River destabilizes a nuclear power plant and threatens to make the middle third of North America uninhabitable. *The Praxis* (2002) opened the Dread Empire series. A race of immortal aliens held sway over the entire galaxy until they committed mass suicide, leaving their various subjects—including humanity—to scramble frantically to fill the ensuing power vacuum. The story has been continued in *The Sundering* (2003).

Much of Williams's work shows the influence of Roger ZELAZNY, so it is not surprising that one of his best shorter works, "Elegy for Angels and Dogs" (1990) is a sequel to Zelazny's THE GRAVEYARD HEART (1964). He won a Nebula Award for "Daddy's World" (1999). The best of his short fiction is contained in *Facets* (1990) and *Frankensteins and Foreign Devils* (1998).

Williamson, Jack
(1908–   )

Jack Williamson's active writing career has extended over the course of 76 years, beginning with his first sale in 1928. He quickly became a regular contributor to pulp magazines, sometimes collaborating with more experienced writers. Some of this early work was heavily influenced by the lost world novels of A. Merritt, as in *The Green Girl* (1930), while others tended to be early forms of hard science fiction, like *Birth of a New Republic* (1931). This novel was a collaboration with Miles J. Breuer and tells the story of a colony on the moon that gains its independence from Earth, anticipating classic novels like *The MOON IS A HARSH MISTRESS* (1966) by Robert A. HEINLEIN. *Dreadful Sleep* (1938) was a story of an alien intelligence sleeping under the ice of Antarctica, a story reminiscent of the work of H. P. LOVECRAFT. Much of Williamson's fiction from this era is quite dated by contemporary standards, but a few individual pieces are still interesting, such as, "The Moon Era" (1932) and "Non-Stop to Mars" (1939).

Williamson's most important work from his early career consists of two separate series. The first was an open imitation of Edward E. SMITH's novels, and consists of *The Legion of Space* (1934), *The Cometeers* (1936), and *One Against the Legion* (1939). A short story and another novel, *The Queen of the Legion* (1983), were added later, but are of only marginal interest. The series follows the adventures of a group of colorful characters as they travel rather implausibly around the galaxy, saving Earth from various dangers. Despite the simple plotting and rather colorless setting, the Legion of Space series is far more successful in making its characters come to life than was common in pulp space opera of that era. A second sequence includes *The Legion of Time* (1938) and *After World's End* (1939), a surprisingly sophisticated exploration of alternate time lines, although the characters in this instance were less interesting.

By 1940, Williamson had become a much more accomplished writer. *Dome Around America* (1941 magazine appearance as *Gateway to Paradise*) is set in a future time when Earth's ecology has become so damaged that it cannot sustain human life, and the remnants of the human race live in domed cities. He would go on to write much of his most memorable work during the 1940s, including the Seetee series: *Seetee Ship* (1942–43/51) and *Seetee Shock* (1949/50), both originally published under the name of Will Stewart. The series tells about the discovery of antimatter and its repercussions, and more importantly THE HUMANOIDS (1949), wherein humans create a race of robots to protect themselves from their own failings, and discover that by doing so they have surrendered their basic freedom. A much later sequel, *The Humanoid Touch* (1980), reexamines the original concept from a fresh perspective.

Williamson was considerably less productive during the 1950s. *Dragon's Island* (1951, also published as *The Not-Men*) is a moderately interesting novel of genetic engineering. He also collaborated with Frederik POHL for a series of three above-average, young adult novels set in a future in which the oceans are being explored. These are *Undersea Quest* (1954), *Undersea Fleet* (1956), and *Undersea City* (1958). His short stories were less frequent, but much more sophisticated, and included several very fine efforts including "Guinevere for Everybody" (1956) and "The Peddler's Nose" (1951). A selection of these were collected as *The Trial of Terra* (1962), packaged rather awkwardly as an episodic novel. Most of Williamson's output during the 1960s would continue to be collaborations with Frederik Pohl, including the Starchild trilogy—*The Reefs of Space* (1964), *The Starchild* (1965), and *Rogue Star* (1969). *Bright New Universe* (1967), written alone, has one of Williamson's most interesting protagonists, although the story of his quest to find proof of alien intelligence is less than enthralling.

The early 1970s saw a sharp increase in the volume of his writing. *The Moon Children* (1971) was a rather pallid story of children developing psi powers, but the publication of two collections of his short stories—*The Pandora Effect* (1969) and *People Machines* (1971)—reawakened interest in his work. Unfortunately, throughout the next decade, most of Williamson's new fiction was disappointing, even his further collaborations with Frederik Pohl. The exception was *Brother to Demons, Brother to Gods* (1979), in which an alien race attempts to recreate extinct humanity, with some startling results. It otherwise seemed that he had lost the vigor and originality that had characterized his earlier work. That perception was underscored by *Queen of the Legion,* a pale extension of the original adventures of the Legion of Space.

The 1980s saw Williamson's career reinvigorated. In *Manseed* (1982), humans develop cyborgs to pilot ships around the galaxy and spread humanity to the stars, but they fail to anticipate what might happen when their cyborg creations encounter aliens. *Lifeburst* (1984) reverses the process, with cyborgs created by aliens who eventually fall prey to their own servants, who expand through space and discover the human race. Humanity, on the verge of defeat, forges an alliance with another civilization in the sequel, *Mazeway* (1990). *Firechild* (1986) pits genetic engineers against religious fundamentalists and provides a bitter indictment of those who would use faith as a tool for personal aggrandizement.

Beachhead (1992) is a traditional story of the first expedition to Mars, updated to include a more modern view of that planet's physical nature. The expedition runs into a predictable variety of problems, but the story is still thoroughly enjoyable. *Demon Moon* (1994) is a planetary romance that impinges on fantasy at times, although everything is ultimately rationalized. *The Black Sun* (1997) takes human explorers to a world shrouded in ice, where they stir a dormant intelligence to activity. A small town declares itself independent of the U.S. government in *The Silicon Dagger* (1999), thanks to the invention of an impenetrable force field. All life on Earth is destroyed by a rogue meteor, but a few humans survive on the Moon, where they use cloning to reproduce themselves in a long-term project to reclaim the world in *Terraforming Earth* (2001).

Many of Williamson's early stories are collected in *The Early Williamson* (1975). Other examples of his work can be found in *The Best of Jack Williamson* (1978), *The Alien Intelligence* (1980), *Into the Eighth Decade* (1990), *The Metal Man* (1999), *Spider Island* (2002), and *Dragon's Island*

and Other Stories (2002). He began his career by imitating writers whose work he admired and has since lived to see other writers inspired by some of his own stories. *The Humanoids* is unquestionably his best known novel, a gentle but still chilling variation of the Frankenstein story. His continued vigor is demonstrated by the fact that he won both the Hugo and Nebula Awards for his novella, "The Ultimate Earth" (2000). Of his other recent stories, "The Engines of Creation" (1999) and "Black Hole Station" (2004) are also outstanding.

Willis, Connie
(1945–)

After writing a few interesting but unexceptional short stories during the 1970s, Connie Willis began to emerge as a major writer in the early 1980s. She has subsequently gone on to collect seven Hugo Awards and six Nebulas. Her first outstanding piece was "Fire Watch" (1982), which won both awards; it is a time travel story in which scientists travel back to England during World War II. Time travel would prove to be a common theme in her subsequent work, and Willis displayed an increasing ability to portray historic periods with a marvelous sense of authenticity. Another early story, "A Letter from the Clearys," would also win a Nebula.

Her first novel was a collaboration with Cynthia Felice. *Water Witch* (1982) is set on a colony world where water is a priceless commodity. The plot deals with the political maneuvering for control of that resource. Much more notable were her short stories from this period, which included such excellent tales as the somewhat controversial "All My Darling Daughters" (1985), which includes a very explicitly sexual situation, and "The Schwartzschild Radius" (1987). Her first collection of short stories was *Fire Watch* (1985) and her first solo novel was *Lincoln's Dreams* (1987). The novel is a very subtle time travel story, accomplished this time through a mental link between a contemporary woman and General Robert E. Lee during the Civil War. Willis avoided most of the clichés of time travel fiction; the result is a mature and thoughtful treatment.

Willis continued to be most impressive at shorter lengths, however. THE LAST OF THE WINNEBAGOS (1988) won the Hugo and Nebula Awards, and "At the Rialto" (1989) won a Nebula. Her next novel, *Light Raid* (1989), with Cynthia Felice, was another adventure—this time involving the efforts of a young woman to clear her mother's name—set against a backdrop of raiders from space. "Even the Queen" (1991) took both awards for best short story, and her next novel, *The Doomsday Book* (1992), added another Nebula. This was another time travel story, loosely related to "Fire Watch." The protagonist is studying the Black Death on what should have been a short assignment; but, ironically, a new plague has devastating effects in her own time, leaving her stranded in the past. The parallels between the two situations are quite effectively drawn and the evocation of historic Europe is superb.

"Death on the Nile" (1993) won a Hugo Award, and a second collection, *Impossible Things* (1994), brought together the best of her more recent stories, although there are still quite a few uncollected ones that deserve to be reprinted. Her next three novels were all quite short. *Uncharted Territory* (1994) is a comparatively lightweight adventure story in which two colorful characters explore a distant planet. *Remake* (1994) is set in a future Hollywood where technology has made it possible to easily re-edit old films to remove unwanted elements—for example, anything involving the now proscribed habit of smoking. The satire is deceptively light. *The Bellwether* (1996) is a particularly effective study of human behavior, in this case revealing the truth about the occasional individual who emerges as a trendsetter.

Two novels appeared in 1997. *Promised Land*, again with Cynthia Felice, is a realistic story of what it might be like to actually settle on another planet. The protagonist is a young woman who has inherited valuable property on a remote world—but she can sell it only if she lives on it for one local year. Although her eventual decision to remain is predictable, the authors do a marvelous job of describing her slowly changing perceptions. Good as that novel is, Willis's solo novel *To Say Nothing of the Dog* (1997) was even better, and it won her another Hugo. A time traveler returns to World War II England to retrieve an artifact supposedly destroyed during the Blitz, but his plans get caught up in an intricate web of comic side trips. Although Willis had occasionally written humorous pieces in the past, notably in "Blued Moon" (1984), this was still a considerable break from her previous work. She also collected two more Hugos for "The Soul Selects Her Own Society" (1996) and "The Winds of Marble Arch" (1999). A third collection, *The Miracle and Other Christmas Stories* (1999), is mostly fantasy. Her most recent novel, *Passage* (2001), involves experimentation with near-death experiences and is only marginally science fiction.

Wilson, Richard
(1920–1987)

Richard Wilson began selling science fiction stories during the 1940s, usually under one pseudonym or another, but it was not until the 1950s that he began producing the high-quality, satirically humorous stories that would be typical of the rest of his career. Most of his early work ages quite well, and stories such as "Press Conference" (1954) and "The Voice of the Diaphragm" (1958) are still quite effective. An atypically serious story, "Love" (1952), is set on a Mars we now know to be impossible; yet the story remains a savage indictment of intolerance.

Two of Wilson's novels are humorous interpretations of the invasion-of-Earth story. *The Girls from Planet 5* (1955) is set in a future America where women are the dominant sex, except in a rigidly chauvinistic Texas. Both societies are wonderfully exaggerated, and the amusement is compounded by the arrival of emissaries from an alien civilization, who are themselves exceedingly alluring females. *30 Day Wonder* (1960) describes an Earth flooded with alien creatures who obey every human law quite literally, compelling all humans to do so as well, with results that are very funny and that also cleverly indict our propensity for not saying what we mean and not meaning what we say. *And Then the Town Took Off* (1960) describes the consequences when a precocious inventor encases his town in a force field and separates it from Earth to make it an independent nation.

Most of Wilson's better early stories can be found in *Those Idiots from Earth* (1957) and *Time Out for Tomorrow* (1962). During the late 1960s he appeared with some regularity and produced some of his best work, including "Mother to the World" (1968), which won a Nebula, "A Man Spekith" (1969), and "The Day They Had the War" (1971). With the exception of a small-press edition, *The Kid from Ozone Park and Other Stories* (1987), no collections of his later short fiction have been published. With several publishers actively involved in reprinting the work of overlooked authors, it seems unlikely that this state of affairs will persist, but at present Wilson's fiction is very difficult to find, despite the high regard in which it is held.

Wilson, Robert Charles
(1953–)

Although Robert Charles Wilson began as a short story writer during the 1970s and wrote exclusively at that length until his first novel appeared in 1986, his work at short length has proven to be competent and occasionally interesting but not exceptional, and only one collection, *The Perseids & Other Stories* (2000), has appeared. His novels, on the other hand, began to attract considerable attention right from the outset, and most of his fiction after 1986 was book-length. His debut novel, *A Hidden Place* (1986), describes the effect of a visitor from another reality on the lives of two people from our own. Wilson's brilliant depiction of the characters and his skillful handling of their emotional and psychological crises led some critics to compare him to Theodore STURGEON.

Memory Wire (1987) is an interesting blend of cyberpunk preoccupations with almost magical otherworldly images. A man with a motion picture camera permanently installed in his body becomes romantically entangled with an artist who is obsessed with an alien crystal that induces what might be illusions or might be glimpses of an alternate reality. *Gypsies* (1989) involves parallel worlds as well—in this case a series of alternate realities through which members of one family can move by an act of will. The conflict originates with a powerful figure from one of these shadow worlds who

wishes to lure the protagonists to their doom. A man with an unusual partition between the halves of his brain goes through a crisis in *Divide* (1990), another novel that concentrates on the psychological landscape rather than the physical one.

A Bridge of Years (1991) is a time travel novel. The protagonist finds a natural time tunnel back to 1962 and hopes to settle there in a more amiable time, but upon arrival he discovers that another time traveler, from an even more distant future, has already taken up residence. Aliens offer humans immortality in *The Harvest* (1993), on the condition that most of the human race accompany them into space. Although the majority agree to those terms, a handful remain behind on a now underpopulated Earth. *Mysterium* (1994) is one of Wilson's best novels. An entire town finds itself physically moved to an alternate, dystopian American dictatorship; the town's sudden appearance there causes considerable upset.

After a short period of inactivity, Wilson returned with *Darwinia* (1998), an intriguing variation of the alternate history story. In this case, all of Europe disappeared in 1912, replaced by an uninhabited forest that seemed to be snatched out of prehistory or perhaps an alternate universe. Although some small colonies have been established there by the United States and other countries outside the zone of change, most of the continent remains unsettled and unexplored. The intriguing setup and engaging story is weakened somewhat by an unnecessary and unsatisfying explanation in the final chapters. *Bios* (1999) follows the adventures of a woman who has been bioengineered so that she can live on an inimical alien world and study the local ecosystem.

Wilson's next two books would prove to be his most impressive achievements. *The Chronoliths* (2001) is a time travel mystery story reminiscent of *Time Bomb* (1955) by Wilson TUCKER. Enormous monuments begin appearing, apparently at random, in various parts of the world. The arrival of each displaces the existing matter, with highly destructive consequences. Scientists studying the phenomenon conclude that the monuments are being projected back through time from the future, where a single man has apparently welded the entire planet into a single dictatorship. Efforts are made to find the man in the present and change the course of history, but there is a growing cult of people who worship the monoliths and believe that the course of the future is immutable. *Blind Lake* (2003) is a brilliantly conceived and executed scientific mystery. Scientists are using a new technology to spy remotely on an alien world, when they themselves are isolated from the rest of humanity by a strange phenomenon. Wilson is one of the most thought-provoking writers in the field, and is almost unrivaled in his ability to create realistic characters and describe their reactions to unusual situations.

Wingrove, David
(1954–   )

The British writer David Wingrove was known primarily as someone who wrote about science fiction during the 1980s. His debut novel, *The Middle Kingdom* (1989), was the first of an eight-volume future history series that remains his only published work in the field. The Chung Kuo series is set in a vastly overpopulated future world dominated perforce by Asia. Technology has advanced, though unevenly, because of efforts by the authorities to retard the rate of change within society, and computer networking is indispensable but unreliable. Crime is more rampant, and corporations are more ruthless in their competition. There are some outposts sprinkled through the solar system, essentially lumped into a single dictatorship under the Chinese aristocracy.

Most of the background is established in the opening volume. In *The Broken Wheel* (1990) we discover that it is still possible for major events and changes to be inspired by a relatively small group of assertive individuals, despite the feeling of apathy and decay that hangs over the world. Efforts are made to break up the monolithic control of the solar government in *The White Mountain* (1991), and in *The Stone Within* (1991) we are shown graphically that barbarism and advanced technology can coexist after all. In *White Moon, Red Dragon* (1991) dissatisfaction with the status quo leads to the beginning of open hostilities. Internal dissension causes schisms within the ruling class in

Beneath the Tree of Heaven (1993), with an extraordinary birth proving to be the catalyst for change. A dictatorial government resorts to android soldiers in an effort to shore up its faltering authority in *Days of Bitter Strength* (1997), and refugees who fled beyond the solar system return in *The Marriage of Light and Dark* (1998) to confront those who still cling desperately to authority.

The early volumes of the Chung Kuo series were well received, but the narrative began to bog down in later volumes, and the last book in the series was not published in the United States. Wingrove also wrote three novels set in the fantasy world of the Myst computer game during the 1990s, all in collaboration with Rand Miller.

"With Morning Comes Mistfall"
George R. R. Martin
(1973)

It is customary to characterize the conflict between science and superstition as a battle between knowledge and ignorance, and certainly that has long been the prevailing attitude in science fiction. George R. R. MARTIN suggests in this story, however, that what appears obvious may in fact be an oversimplification; that humans need mystery and wonder just as much as they need to advance the frontiers of science. The story is set on Wraithworld, a planet very sparsely inhabited by humans—just a handful of settlers and transient tourists. Most of the planet is hidden by swirling mists, and it is easy to get lost, making the planet difficult to explore. There are also a handful of dangerous animals adding to the already perilous terrain. People come anyway—not because the planet offers such extraordinary sightseeing possibilities, but because of the mistwraiths.

The mistwraiths are the local equivalent of the abominable snowman. They are rumored to be roughly humanoid but very large, and are supposed to be responsible for the disappearance and presumed death of several humans. Ruins of an ancient civilization have been found in a few locations, and the prevailing theory is that the mistwraiths are the decadent leftovers of a vanished race. The story is told from the point of view of a journalist covering a major scientific expedition whose purpose is to prove or disprove their existence. Shortly after arriving, he observes tension between the head of the project and a local hotel owner, who believes that something will be lost no matter what their findings. Either the existence of the mistwraiths will have been disproved, or they will be reduced to the stature of interesting aboriginals, no longer figures of mystery. Although the journalist believes that the hotelier is motivated by concerns about a drop-off in his business, he eventually realizes that the man is sincere.

In their final confrontation the two men articulate their differences. One believes that all questions need to be answered, while the other feels that without mysteries and wonders, the universe becomes a drab and uninteresting place. The author clearly sides with the romantic: Once the results are in, the tourists stop coming and the planet becomes just another minor outpost. The outcome reflects a persistent problem in many horror and suspense stories and movies: The mysterious danger we have yet to see is almost always less frightening when finally revealed.

Wolfe, Gene
(1931–   )

Although Gene Wolfe began writing short stories in the 1950s, his first professional publication came in the second half of the 1960s. He would sell only about a dozen stories during that period, but would explode creatively beginning in 1970, with numerous short stories. Of those, "How the Whip Came Back" and "Eyebem" are both exceptional, and "The ISLAND OF DR. DEATH AND OTHER STORIES" was spectacular. There was also a rather lackluster first novel, *Operation Ares*, in which an ailing civilization on Earth is assisted by the descendants of Martian colonists.

The 1970s were Wolfe's most productive years at shorter lengths, and the number of excellent stories is astonishing, including most notably "The Death of Dr. Island" (1972), which won a Nebula. Another major story was "The Fifth Head of Cerberus" (1971), which became one-third of a strikingly effective novel under the same title a year

later. The author's intensely rich prose style and his avoidance of most traditional genre themes probably contributed to the fact that he never won another award for his short fiction, although he had strong contenders almost every year. Most striking of the stories from this period are "Against the Lafayette Escadrille" (1972), "La Befana" (1973), "Forelesen" (1974), "The EYEFLASH MIRACLES" (1976), "SEVEN AMERICAN NIGHTS" (1978), and "The Doctor of Death Island" (1978). Four thematically related stories from this period would later be collected as *The Wolfe Archipelago* (1983) and many others were assembled as *The Island of Dr. Death & Other Stories and Other Stories* (1980) and in *Gene Wolfe's Book of Days* (1981).

Wolfe had also written a fantasy novel and a young adult historical novel during the 1970s, but it would be *The Shadow of the Torturer* (1980), first of the Severian novels, that established his reputation quite securely. The remaining novels in the sequence are *The Claw of the Conciliator* (1981)—which won the Hugo Award—*The Sword of the Lictor* (1981), and *The Citadel of the Autarch* (1984). *The Castle of the Otter* (1982) contains the author's commentaries on the series. The setting is a future where technology had advanced to the point where it mimics magic, but society itself has become corrupt and decadent. Severian is a professional torturer who has begun to have doubts about his profession and the motives of his superiors. When he shows mercy to one of his charges, he is dishonored and banished, subsequently wandering the Earth in a series of revelatory adventures. Eventually he decides to determine the truth about the mysterious figure who rules as dictator of the Earth, and ultimately takes his place. *The Urth of the New Sun* (1987) appeared some time later, consisting of shorter pieces set against the same background. The series was clearly influenced by the Dying Earth stories by Jack VANCE, although those are more obviously fantasy and make no effort to rationalize the magical elements. It is also heavy in religious symbolism. Severian is a very obvious Christ figure and the series could be interpreted as an allegorical version of the Second Coming.

As Wolfe began concentrating on novels, his output of short stories decreased dramatically, although those that continued to appear maintained his high quality level. Some of these were collected in *Plan[e]t Engineering* (1984)—the title was a play on words, as Wolfe spent much of his life as the editor of a magazine called *Plant Engineering*. *Storeys from the Old Hotel* (1988) contains a large selection, as does *Endangered Species* (1989). His interest in fantasy had been growing steadily, and several novels during the 1980s fell into that category. All of them were quite good, although they were unconventional and thus failed to make a major impression in that conservative market.

His next sequence of science fiction novels is known collectively as *The Book of the Long Sun* and includes *Nightside the Long Sun* (1993), *Lake of the Long Sun* (1994), *Calde of the Long Sun* (1995), and *Exodus from the Long Sun* (1996). The setting is a generation starship, the *Whorl*, an enclosed habitat so complete that most of the residents no longer understand that they are aboard an artificial construction, which they just consider their world. The central character is Patera Silk, a local priest who is caught up in the growing turmoil of a society under extraordinary stress. He reluctantly abandons his parish to descend into the metaphorical bowels of the ship, seeking an answer to the question of their purpose in existence—a quest that obviously reverberates on more than one level. Ancient influences stir to new life as it appears that the *Whorl* is approaching its destination at long last, but the revelation that they are expected to abandon everything they have ever known and risk settling on a natural world, exposed to the stars, causes dissension, terror, and eventually a civil war.

Wolfe continued their story in *The Second Book of the Long Sun*, which consists of *On Blue's Waters* (1999), *In Green's Jungles* (2000), and *Return to the Whorl* (2001). The passengers have now been disgorged onto their new home, but their society has undergone such incredible upheaval that it is no longer clear who will exert authority. The protagonist goes on a personal quest of discovery across the planet's dangerous oceans and through perilous jungles before the protagonist, like Severian, eventually realizes that it is up to him to assume authority, even if the job is a distasteful one.

The seven-book sequence is superficially similar to many other novels, but what distinguishes Wolfe's work is his incredibly complex prose, which is thick with metaphor and allusion and which paints incredibly detailed word pictures of his settings, characters, and events.

His most recent collection of science fiction stories is *Strange Travelers* (2000), and his fantasy shorts appear in *Innocents Aboard* (2004). *Young Wolfe* (1992) contains several of his earliest short stories, including two written during the early 1950s. Wolfe's fiction rarely contains any marvelous new idea or clever variations on a theme. He is more likely to take an existing, familiar story and retell it in a slightly different context, freshening it with sharply drawn characters and conveying it in his richly embroidered prose. He is at times a difficult writer to follow, because he demands that his readers exert some intellectual effort; but he always leaves sufficient clues to his mysteries, and he invariably delivers a complex and thoughtful tale.

Wollheim, Donald A.
(1914–1990)

Donald A. Wollheim wrote a substantial body of science fiction, but his primary influence on the field was as an editor. He started in the amateur press, later edited pulp science fiction magazines, and eventually worked for Avon Books, where he edited the first all-original SF anthology. In the 1950s he moved to Ace Books, where, during the course of two decades, he published the early novels of Roger ZELAZNY, Samuel R. DELANY, Philip K. DICK, Ursula K. LE GUIN, and many other now prominent writers. In the 1970s he founded DAW Books, which provided a similar service for C. J. CHERRYH and others. He also edited numerous anthologies for various publishers over the course of his career, including an annual best-of-the-year series that started at Ace Books and continued at DAW.

Although Wollheim began selling short fiction in the 1930s, his only story of particular note is "Mimic" (1942), in which insects evolve into a form that can imitate humans under certain circumstances. The story became the inspiration for the film *Mimic* (1995) and its two sequels. A good sampling of his short fiction can be found in *Two Dozen Dragon Eggs* (1969), *The Men from Ariel* (1982), and *Up There and Other Strange Directions* (1988). His half-dozen science fiction novels for adults all appeared as by David Grinnell. In *Across Time* (1957) an effort to capture a flying saucer backfires and a man from our time finds himself in the far future. *Edge of Time* (1958), the most interesting of the six, describes what happens when scientists create a pocket universe in which time passes at millions of times the rate in our world, enabling them to study changes that would otherwise be impossible within a single lifetime. *The Martian Missile* (1959) involves a mission to that planet, and *Destiny's Orbit* (1961) pits a plucky entrepreneur against the government as he tries to buy his own planet. *Destination: Saturn* (1968), written with Lin Carter, is an interplanetary conspiracy adventure. In *To Venus! To Venus!* (1970) the first expedition to Venus discovers that conditions on the surface are not as expected.

Wollheim was much more effective in his novels for young adults. Three of these with similar titles are not, in fact, a series. *The Secret of Saturn's Rings* (1954) mixes a story of interplanetary exploration with a war in space. *The Secret of the Martian Moons* (1955) strands the first expedition to Mars, possibly because of a saboteur, possibly because of action by hidden Martians. The most ambitious was *The Secret of the Ninth Planet* (1959). Some mysterious force is draining energy from the sun, so an expedition sets out to search the solar system and find out who or what is responsible. *One Against the Moon* (1956), the story of a young astronaut trapped on the lunar surface, is also quite good.

The most popular of his young adult books were the Mike Mars series, which started with *Mike Mars: Astronaut* (1961) and ended with *Mike Mars Around the Moon* (1964), the character's eighth adventure. Each of the novels dealt with another step in the development of a space program. They were much more realistic than Wollheim's other novels, emphasizing plausibility and scientific accuracy. During the course of his eight adventures, Mike Mars visits the Moon, deals with a rogue satellite, rescues a stranded astronaut, defeats spies and saboteurs, and escapes Soviet troops in Antarctica. Although Wollheim will certainly be remembered as an editor rather than a writer, it would be unfortunate if his well-conceived and ably written young adult fiction was completely forgotten.

"The Women Men Don't See"
James Tiptree Jr.
(1973)

Don Fenton is off on a fishing trip to Mexico when a series of coincidences results in his sharing a small plane with Ruth Parson and her grown daughter. Both women strike him as a bit strange, reticent but not unfriendly. While Fenton is mildly aware that they are not unattractive, he is uninterested in them except as temporary traveling companions. The relationship is prolonged, however, when a malfunction results in their crashing in a remote part of the Yucatan. Fenton and the older woman set out to find fresh water, while the daughter remains at the plane with the injured pilot.

Fenton is somewhat intrigued by the woman, who initially dispenses only the most innocuous bits of information about herself, later revealing that she is a single mother whose daughter has never met her father. Although not unfriendly, she remains distant, and tactfully but firmly arranges things so that there is no question of physical intimacy between them. Fenton still feels no strong attraction, and a minor injury restricts his movement even further. The first evening, they have a strange encounter with another party, seeing only that party's lights. After this encounter Parsons becomes even more reticent. In due course we learn that she stole a recording device from a party of young alien students secretly visiting Earth, and that they are searching for it to prevent it from falling into the hands of the authorities and revealing their presence. The ultimate confrontation takes an unexpected twist when the two women ask for and are granted permission to leave Earth with the aliens, an Earth that the older woman has described as a world of men, in which women manage to survive but do not prosper.

Although the story is obviously an indictment of gender discrimination, it is more effective than most because it is firm but not strident. Moreover, Tiptree draws the narrator Fenton as a reasonable man; he is kind, thoughtful, and undoubtedly he believes that men and women are equal. What he fails to recognize is that the semblance of equality is a fragile one that could be cast aside immediately if circumstances changed. Ruth Parsons and her daughter will have no difficulty adapting to life on a world dominated by aliens, because they have spent their entire lives on a world dominated by what is, to them, an alien race.

The Word for World Is Forest
Ursula K. Le Guin
(1972)

The war in Vietnam stirred emotions within the science fiction community just as it did within American society at large, and inevitably some authors later attempted to translate their reactions into fiction. There are clear parallels from the side that favored intervention, as in *The Glory Game* (1972) by Keith LAUMER, and others that were critical of the entire endeavor, as in *Life During Wartime* (1987) by Lucius Shepard. Ursula K. LE GUIN wrote one of the most successful of the latter in this short novel for the original anthology, *Again, Dangerous Visions* (1972), edited by Harlan ELLISON.

The planet Athshe is a pastoral world, heavily forested, whose inhabitants are peaceful, almost complacent, and live in harmony with their environment. All of this comes to an end when outside forces arrive on their world, intent upon clearing much of the forest, introducing the concepts of widescale violence and even warfare. The invaders disrupt the local culture and forever change the native attitude toward the outside universe, but they are not going to have their way easily. The Athsheans have an ability to act through their dreams and through the dreams of their unwanted visitors—an almost mystical ability that will ultimately restore their freedom. They will not, however, be able to return to their original blissful ignorance, for their collective psyche has been scarred forever.

Although the outsiders are forced to leave, an effort is made at reconciliation, and assurances are given that in the future the rights of the natives will be respected. The parallels with Vietnam are not intrusive, and the conflict between an exploitative, materialistic culture and a spiritual, ecologically minded but comparatively powerless people are applicable to many historical and contemporary situations. This short novel, which is set in the same universe as the author's Hain stories, won the Hugo Award as best novella of the year.

Wylie, Philip
(1902–1971)

Philip Wylie is best known outside the science fiction community as an essayist and novelist who wrote contemporary novels as well as occasional thrillers. He first turned to speculative themes with *Gladiator* (1930), the story of a superman who must go through the painful process of learning that physical prowess does not in itself make one a superior or even happy person; eventually the hero comes to understand that love is more important than strength. The novel was turned into a motion picture in 1938 and has been credited with being the inspiration for the *Superman* comic book series. Wylie's second genre novel was *The Murderer Invisible* (1931), quite obviously inspired by *The* INVISIBLE MAN (1897) by H. G. WELLS. As in the Wells classic, a man with the power of invisibility decides that this condition makes him untouchable, and he commits a series of murders before being apprehended. Both of these early novels are somewhat awkward by contemporary standards, but are still readable.

Wylie's most famous novel is WHEN WORLDS COLLIDE (1932), which he wrote in collaboration with Edwin Balmer. Two rogue planets enter the solar system, dooming the Earth, but a handful of people escape on an experimental spaceship and eventually colonize a new world in Earth's place. A sequel, *After Worlds Collide,* was published the following year. The first volume subsequently became a film classic in 1951. Wylie then largely abandoned science fiction until 1950, although *The*

Smuggled Atom Bomb (1948) might be marginally included. *The Disappearance* (1950) is a lengthy allegory in which all the men in the world disappear into another version of Earth, and each gender must develop a new society in the absence of the other. This rather artificial situation allows the author to contrast the results, which are not as different as one might expect, as well as to deliver a few satiric jabs.

Increasingly concerned about the dangers of nuclear war and other environmental issues, Wylie's subsequent fiction became more didactic. *Tomorrow!* (1953) is an extremely graphic account of a nuclear war, based on studies of the Hiroshima attack and its aftermath. Wylie clearly meant to shock his readers into opposition to nuclear weapons. He would later return to this theme in *Triumph* (1962), in which virtually everyone on Earth has died and the handful of survivors, torn by considerable interpersonal turmoil, shelter within a small bunker. *Los Angeles: A.D. 2017* (1971) was written from Wylie's own screenplay, in which a man awakens from suspended animation to find that Earth has become a hostile ecosystem inimical to humanity, thanks to pollution and other environmental crimes. His pessimism about the future was even more obvious in *The End of the Dream* (1972), in which the planet's ecology begins to disintegrate in so many different areas that it is impossible to concoct a plan that will offset all problems. Presumably, humanity is doomed. *The Spy Who Spoke Porpoise* (1969) also contains some marginal science fiction elements. Wylie's later fiction mixed effective narrative passages with pointed but often distracting sermons. His earlier novels conveyed serious concerns in a more subtle and effective manner, and they were also much more successful as entertainments.

Wyndham, John
(1903–1969)

John Wyndham Lucas Parkes Beynon Harris wrote under various combinations of his names, although almost everything after 1945 was as John Wyndham. He began writing science fiction in the 1930s, mostly traditional space adventures and

tales of superscience. *The Secret People* (1935) is a mildly interesting lost race novel. Efforts to irrigate the Sahara cause trouble when they stir up the residents of a subterranean race that has been hiding from the surface world for thousands of years. *Stowaway to Mars* (1935, also published as *Planet Plane* and as *The Space Machine*) is a routine story of the political and commercial rivalries involved in the race to be the first to reach the planet Mars. The story is primarily of interest because Wyndham included a female character who was not relegated to the category of helpless female or presented as merely a foil to whom the protagonist explains everything. Strong female characters would recur with some frequency in Wyndham's later work. Most of his short stories from this period can be found in *Love in Time* (1946, as by Johnson Harris), *The Seeds of Time* (1956), *Sleepers of Mars* (1973), *Wanderers of Time* (1973), and *Exiles on Asperus* (1979), the last three as by John Beynon. The short story "Sleepers of Mars" (1938) is a loose sequel to *Stowaway to Mars*.

After World War II Wyndham largely abandoned outer space as a setting for his work. Short stories such as "Jizzle" (1949), "Close Behind Him" (1953), and "Chronoclasm" (1953) were more thoughtful and sophisticated, and tended to present their fantastic content in a form that would be palatable to mainstream readers. His next novel was *The DAY OF THE TRIFFIDS* (1951, also published as *Revolt of the Triffids*), which was faithfully transformed into a BBC miniseries but in 1963 was turned into yet another shambling monster movie. Ambulatory plants with a poisonous sting become a major threat when an anomalous meteor shower causes near universal blindness. *Out of the Deeps* (1953, also published as *The Kraken Wakes*) followed. This was an alien invasion story somewhat in the vein of *The WAR OF THE WORLDS* (1898) by H. G. WELLS, in that the aliens are almost entirely offscreen during the novel. Wyndham acknowledged Wells as the author who most influenced his own work. Wyndham's alien invaders have settled underneath the world's oceans and use their advanced technology to melt the icecaps and flood the coastal regions, wreaking havoc on the surface world. Concerted action against them is constrained by international tensions and by humanity's inability to see beyond its parochial concerns. The result is a story more concerned with life in the midst of a major environmental disaster than in a confrontation with monstrous aliens, all told in an understated, unmelodramatic narrative style that was extraordinarily effective.

RE-BIRTH (1955, also published as *The Chrysalids*) is one of the best stories of life generations after a nuclear holocaust, ranking with DAVY by Edgar PANGBORN and *The Long Tomorrow* (1955) by Leigh BRACKETT. *The Midwich Cuckoos* (1957, also published as *Village of the Damned* after the 1960 film version) posed an interesting situation. A small English village is cut off from the outside world by a force field for a short period, during which time everyone inside the perimeter remains unconscious. The zone of interdiction is subsequently lifted, with no explanation of its cause, and no obvious effects within the affected area, but months later every female in the village of child bearing age finds herself pregnant. The children who are born all bear a strange similarity to one another, and as they mature they begin to display extraordinary psi powers, abilities so potent and dangerous that the authorities realize the children have to be destroyed because they menace the human race. Wyndham's matter-of-fact style was particularly effective, although the plot does not entirely make sense.

During the late 1950s Wyndham wrote a sequence of five stories that made up a brief future history. Following an atomic war, Brazil and India emerge as the two major world powers. As they develop their own space programs, the members of the Troon family emerge as pivotal figures. Four of the stories were published in book form as *The Outward Urge* (1959), as by John Wyndham and Lucas Parkes, although Parkes is another of his pseudonyms. A revised edition added the remaining story in 1961.

The last of Wyndham's major novels was *Trouble with Lichen* (1960), in which the discovery of a method by which the human lifespan can be significantly extended has an ever widening effect on various aspects of human society. All of Wyndham's previous novels showed minor variations in text between the American and British editions, but the disparities for *Trouble with Lichen* were much more substantial, with U.S. publishers removing much of the author's commentary on international politics. His remaining two novels were comparatively minor. In *Chocky* (1968), a young boy's imaginary friend turns out to be a visiting alien. It was filmed for television. *Web* (1979), published posthumously, describes the consequences when a group attempts to turn a remote island into a utopian community, only to discover that the local insect population has a unique society and defense mechanism of its own.

Wyndham's later stories have been assembled as *Jizzle* (1954), *Tales of Gooseflesh and Laughter* (1956), *Consider Her Ways and Others* (1961), and *The Infinite Moment* (1961). Time travel was a common theme in the last of these. His single best short story is "CONSIDER HER WAYS" (1956), a visit to a future feminist utopia of sorts, and surprisingly advanced for its time. Although technology is sometimes important to the plot of his stories, it is always subordinated to the characters. Wyndham achieved verisimilitude by populating his fiction with ordinary people with whom his readers could readily identify.

You Shall Know Them
Vercors
(1952)

Science fiction writers have long wrestled with the question of what it means to be human, or at least an intelligent being, examining it from various angles. How does one decide when an alien creature is sufficiently advanced to become a *person*? Is our interpretation of intelligence the only proper one? How about artificial intelligences, as in computers or robots? How much of our bodies can we replace with mechanical parts before we can no longer rightfully consider ourselves human beings?

Vercors was the pseudonym of Jean Bruller, a French writer who also produced an interesting fantasy novel, *Sylva* (1961). His single significant science fiction novel is the story of a discovery of a tribe of primitive apemen living in New Guinea—so primitive that there is considerable disagreement about whether or not they should be considered human, despite their ability to interbreed with modern humans. The protagonist takes the dramatic and somewhat drastic step of fathering a child and murdering it, then confessing to the crime to force society to determine the legal status of the aborigines. He is subsequently acquitted, but only because his crime was committed before the legal ruling that declared the child human.

The novel, which also appeared as *Borderline* and as *The Murder of the Missing Link*, was filmed as *Skullduggery* (1969) in a screen translation so bad that the author insisted that his name be removed from the credits. This classic novel, which consists largely of a trial and backstage legal maneuvering, set the precedent for such similar novels as *Little Fuzzy* (1962) by H. Beam Piper and *When Harlie Was One* (1972) by David Gerrold, both of which involve trials to determine the rights of an alternate form of intelligence, and *Ancient of Days* (1985) by Michael Bishop, which describes the difficulties experienced by a man determined to marry a woman who is one of the last of a dying strain of protohumans.

Young, Robert F.
(1915–1986)

Robert F. Young began publishing short stories in 1953 and was quite prolific at that length until his death, at which point nearly 200 had been published. Of these, only a relative handful have been collected, in two volumes—*The Worlds of Robert F. Young* (1965) and *A Glass of Stars* (1968)—that came comparatively early in his career. Although many of Young's stories are slight, there is a substantial amount of excellent work, and his continued neglect by American publishers is surprising.

Most of his short stories were adventures, often set in outer space, but he also wrote a handful of effective satires, including "Romance in a Twenty-First Century Used Car Lot" (1960) and "A Report on Sexual Behavior on Arcturus" (1957).

He often managed to incorporate almost poetic imagery into his stories, as in "Emily and the Bard Sublime" (1956), "Jonathan and the Space Whale" (1962), and "The Stars Are Calling, Mr. Keats" (1959). Other outstanding stories include "The Girl Who Made Time Stop" (1961), "L'Arc de Jeanne" (1966), "Starscape with Frieze of Dreams" (1970), and "Invitation to the Waltz" (1982). Romantic love is a frequent component of his stories, which sometimes become overly sentimental.

Young turned to novels late in his career; most of these were based on earlier short stories. *Starfinder* (1980) is the best of the four, all of which appeared within a very brief timeframe. Travel to the stars is accomplished by means of the dead bodies of space whales, creatures who live in space rather than on planets. *The Last Yggsdrasil* (1982) is an expanded version of "To Fell a Tree" (1959), probably his best short story. The protagonist is hired to cut down the last giant tree on a colony world, but is distracted by the presence of an indigenous life-form. *Eridahn* (1983) is based on a series of stories Young wrote about time travelers visiting the prehistoric past, specifically in this case "When Time Was New" (1983). Young's last novel, *The Vizier's Second Daughter* (1985), is a fantasy.

Z

Zahn, Timothy
(1951–)

There are writers who specialize in hard science fiction whose work is cool and intellectual, and there are space opera writers who have a gift for a fine adventure and generating a sense of wonder, but whose hard science skills are minimal. And then there is that minority, including Timothy Zahn, who excel at both and who often blend them to create thought-provoking and exciting stories. Zahn began his career in the late 1970s, writing stories of increasing merit, culminating in his Hugo Award–winning "Cascade Point" (1983). That was also the year in which he began writing novels, which have been the dominant form in his writing ever since.

The Blackcollar (1983) pits a band of physically augmented soldiers against an alien race that has conquered humanity. The novel ends on a hopeful note, and the rebellion finally succeeds in the sequel, *The Backlash Mission* (1986). Despite some rough spots, the two novels are quite entertaining, and a second series about physically altered soldiers was even better.

The Cobra series consists of *Cobra* (1985), *Cobra Strike* (1986), and *Cobra Bargain* (1988). Although initially it appears to be a variation of his first novel, Zahn introduces considerably more complex subplots and, more importantly, considers the psychology of his characters in greater detail. After defeating their alien enemy, the Cobras hope to resume a normal life; but they are forced into an uneasy alliance with their former enemies when an

even greater alien menace threatens them both. In the third volume, two separate social conflicts enrich the story considerably. The first woman to join the elite forces causes contradictory emotions among her fellows, and efforts by the enhanced soldiers to merge back into normal society prove more troublesome than expected.

A Coming of Age (1984) explores a real generation gap, one that occurs when children on a colony world begin developing psi powers. Humans discover a shortcut to the stars in *Spinneret* (1985), an alien construction apparently now abandoned. Unfortunately, and predictably, disagreements about how best to make use of this new technology divide the human race even further. *Triplet* (1987) is set on a planet whose alien inhabitants have a technology so advanced that it is indistinguishable from magic. *Deadman Switch* (1988) suggests yet another unusual method of traveling to the stars. In this case the pilot of any departing ship dies during the transition to faster-than-light travel. At this point Zahn had produced nine novels during seven years and had firmly established himself both by his ability to turn out entertaining hard science fiction and as a leading writer of space operas. Two collections of his short stories had also appeared, *Cascade Point* (1986) and *Time Bomb and Zahndry Others* (1988).

Zahn began the 1990s with *Warhorse* (1990), a fascinating story about contact between humanity and a race that used biotechnology rather than mechanical means to reach the stars. He then expended considerable effort on a series of *Star Wars* tie-in novels that were unusually good of their type but were not up to the quality of Zahn's original work. His next serious novel opened a trilogy of his own creation, *Conqueror's Pride* (1994), *Conqueror's Heritage* (1995), and *Conqueror's Legacy* (1996). The trilogy follows the history of a war between humans and a rival alien species; one volume examines events from the human point of view, one is set among the aliens, and the final one combines the two perspectives. The internal politics of the alien race are of particular interest.

The later novels have shown sustained improvement in Zahn's writing skills. *The Icarus Hunt* (1999) is an excellent, absorbing story of a merchant ship harried from star to star by various parties who wish to seize its cargo. *Angelmass* (2001) pits a single world against a human empire that wishes to absorb them forcibly; the action revolves around a black hole that radiates something that the local inhabitants interpret as the essence of goodness, a mystical concept that Zahn rationalizes quite ably. It is probably his best novel to date. *Manta's Gift* (2002) is a well-conceived story of human efforts to communicate with an intelligent race living within the atmosphere of Jupiter.

Two additional volumes—*Distant Friends and Others* (1992) and *Star Songs and Other Stories* (2002)—include virtually all of Zahn's previously uncollected short work. His most recent books, *Dragon and Thief* (2003) and *Dragon and Soldier* (2004), are the first two volumes in a young adult series about a teenager who inherits his uncle's spaceship and has various adventures in consort with an alien symbiote. Pulp science fiction usually sacrificed traditional literary qualities in favor of exotic settings and fast-paced action, while much modern science fiction tends to overlook the necessity to tell a good story while dealing with serious themes and developing its characters. Zahn is one of those rare writers who knows how to strike a balance between the two.

Zebrowski, George
(1945–)

Since 1970 George Zebrowski has been a prolific short story writer of uniformly high quality, and has also written numerous novels. There was a considerable gap of time between his first collection, *The*

Monadic Universe (1977), and the next two, *In the Distance, and Ahead in Time* and *Swift Thoughts*, both published in 2002. There still remains a considerable body of worthy but uncollected short fiction. Zebrowski has also edited several anthologies, including the short-lived but impressive *Synergy* series of original collections.

His first novel, *The Omega Point* (1972), would eventually become the middle volume in a trilogy, preceded by *Ashes and Stars* (1977) and followed by *Mirror of Minds*, which was never published separately and can be found only in the omnibus edition, *The Omega Point Trilogy* (1983). The human race has been triumphant in an interstellar war, their enemy hunted to near extinction. Members of that race are determined to avenge their people, and eventually employ a radical new technology in an effort to reverse the outcome of the war. *The Star Web* (1975) was rewritten and became a portion of the vastly superior *Stranger Suns* (1991). An expedition to Antarctica uncovers an abandoned alien starship, inadvertently reactivates it, and has various exciting adventures among the stars.

In *Macro-Life* (1979), humans have abandoned Earth and traveled to the stars, a broad narrative that shows the influence of Olaf STAPLEDON. The Sunspacers trilogy—*Sunspacer* (1984), *The Stars Will Speak* (1985), and *Behind the Stars* (1996)—is ostensibly for young adult readers, but is written with adult sensibilities. A young man struggles to make a life for himself in the colony on Mercury, and has his life changed when aliens warn of a danger menacing the entire human race. The third in the series appeared only in the omnibus *The Sunspacers Trilogy* (1996). Earth disposes of its hardened criminals and dissidents by imprisoning them on a self-sustaining starship and launching it to the stars in *Brute Orbits* (1998). Zebrowski has also written a number of media tie-in novels, often in collaboration with Pamela SARGENT, and an innovative story of war with aliens, *The Killing Star* (1995), with Charles Pellegrino.

Zelazny, Roger
(1937–1995)

Most science fiction writers slowly emerge as major talents after producing several less interesting works. Roger Zelazny was one of those rare exceptions who is recognized almost immediately. His short stories began to appear in the early 1960s, and among his very first efforts were the classics "A ROSE FOR ECCLESIASTES" (1963), "The Great Slow Kings" (1963), and "The GRAVEYARD HEART" (1964). He was one of a new generation of writers who were less interested in technology and engineering and more concerned with psychology and complex narrative styles. From the outset his work was influenced heavily by mythology and literary references, which he transformed in new and exotic settings.

His first two novels both won awards. "He Who Shapes" (1965), a novella, won the Nebula before being expanded in book form as *The Dream Master* (1966). *And Call Me Conrad* (1965) won a Hugo and appeared in book form as THIS IMMORTAL (1966). Within a span of four years Zelazny had progressed from unpublished to one of the most exciting new authors in the field, one of a handful of American writers who emerged in parallel with the British New Wave movement, although generally without the extreme stylistic experimentation common to the latter. *The Dream Master* is the exploration of the personality of a future psychiatrist who cures his patients by entering their dreams, examining what he finds there, and interacting with them in that state. His latest patient has particularly troubling problems, which trigger his own hidden instabilities. Zelazny's second novel is set on a future Earth that has been turned into a kind of tourist preserve, administered by a man who is a secret immortal.

Zelazny was particularly effective at novelette length during the next few years. *The Doors of His Face, the Lamps of His Mouth* (1965) won a Nebula Award, but *Love Is an Imaginary Number* (1966), *For a Breath I Tarry* (1966), and *This Moment of the Storm* (1966) were all nearly as good. Four of these novelettes were collected in *Four for Tomorrow* (1967, also published as *A Rose for Ecclesiastes*), the same year that saw publication of his Hugo Award–winning *Lord of Light*. The setting this time is a distant world ruled by a clique of immortals who use highly advanced technology to establish themselves as the pantheon of Hindu gods. The ensuing struggle to free the planet from their dictatorial rule is Zelazny's single best novel, blending

mythic figures with a futuristic setting. He would attempt a similar synthesis less successfully in *Creatures of Light and Darkness* (1969), set in a future Earth that has become dominated by rationalized Egyptian gods, and in *Isle of the Dead* (1969), in which a man masters the ability to create entire worlds but discovers that he still has enemies capable of challenging his nearly godlike powers.

Damnation Alley (1967), which became a disappointing motion picture in 1977, follows the adventures of a petty criminal in a postapocalyptic America who is impressed into service as a courier transporting critical medical supplies across a wild and dangerous section of the continent. It was a considerably less ambitious effort than Zelazny's other novels during that period, though frequently exciting. In 1970 *Nine Princes in Amber* appeared, the first in a series of alternate world fantasies that would dominate the remainder of Zelazny's career. Although he continued to write science fiction, some of it quite good, his subsequent work rarely measured up to what he produced during the 1960s. *To Die in Italbar* (1973) is an inferior sequel to *Isle of the Dead,* and *Today We Choose Faces* (1973) is an interstellar adventure involving telepathy, organized crime, and other plot elements in a complex story reminiscent of the work of A. E. VAN VOGT.

A priceless artifact presented to the human race goes missing in *Doorways in the Sand* (1976); a hapless young man is framed for the crime, and an exceptionally good chase sequence follows. A telepath is potentially Earth's best defense against an alien threat in *Bridge of Ashes* (1976), but his ability is slowly driving him insane. Zelazny completed a manuscript by Philip K. DICK, but *Deus Irae* (1976) is uneven and not up to the standards of either writer. His infrequent shorter pieces during the 1970s and 1980s were usually strong efforts. "HOME IS THE HANGMAN" (1976) won both the Hugo and Nebula Awards, "Unicorn Variation" (1981) won a Hugo, as did "Twenty Four Views of Mt Fuji, by Hokusai" (1985) and "Permafrost" (1986). His novels continued to be interesting, often verging on fantasy. *Roadmarks* (1980), for example, suggests that we live in just one of many parallel universes, another of which is inhabited by a race of intelligent dragons. *Eye of Cat* (1982) is the best of his later science fiction. In a future where immortality has made life dull, a man rescues an intelligent, shape-changing alien in exchange for the prisoner's promise to hunt him.

Zelazny also collaborated on several occasions. A corporation attempts to control the development of a revolutionary artificial intelligence in *Coils* (1982), written with Fred SABERHAGEN. *Flare* (1992), with Thomas T. Thomas, pits a variety of human habitats sprinkled through the solar system against universal extinction when the sun flares unexpectedly. *Donnerjack* (1997), with Jane Lindskold, pits one virtual reality world against another. When one of these variant worlds tries to absorb another, a refugee concealed within that reality must become its protector. Much of Zelazny's later work is fantasy, set either within the Amber series or independently.

Most of Zelazny's short fiction has been collected in *The Doors of His Face, the Lamps of His Mouth* (1971), *My Name Is Legion* (1976), *The Last Defender of Camelot* (1980), *The Unicorn Variations* (1983), *Frost and Fire* (1989), and *Gone to Earth* (1991). Zelazny was throughout his career one of the most skilled prose stylists the field has known, and his use of larger-than-life characters—often a risky business because of the difficulty most readers have identifying with godlike figures—is unequaled in its effectiveness. He is considered a major writer of fantasy as well as science fiction, and much of his work tends to blur the distinction between the genres. At his best he was an extraordinary novelist, and his shorter work is, if anything, of even more consistent high quality. Although his later novels are often considered inferior to his early work, they remain almost equally popular. Zelazny was heavily influenced by Jack VANCE and Theodore STURGEON, and in turn has inspired another generation of writers.

Some of the following terms either have been developed within the science fiction community or have a special meaning in that context.

alternate history   Stories that assume some event or events in human history happened differently, which results in an altered chain of historic events. Examples include *The Man in the High Castle* by Philip K. Dick and *Stars and Stripes Forever* by Harry Harrison.

android   This term is meant usually to imply a kind of robot constructed of organic rather than mechanical parts.

change war   Time travel stories in which there is a concerted effort by one group to interfere with the original course of history; from the Change War stories of Fritz Leiber. This attempt is counteracted by another group either with its own agenda or in an attempt to preserve the original chain of events. Major examples include *The Guardians of Time* by Poul Anderson and *The Big Time* by Fritz Leiber.

cyberpunk   This somewhat nebulous term is applied to stories set—usually in an urban setting—in a near-future Earth where the interface between humans and computers has narrowed. William Gibson is considered the most significant of the cyberpunk writers.

cyborg   A cyborg is a human being whose body has been augmented to some degree with mechanical parts.

dystopian   Describes a story set in a future society where human freedom has largely been lost, usually because of a totalitarian government;

sometimes used for satirical purposes. The most famous dystopian novel is *Nineteen Eighty-Four* by George Orwell.

empath   This term refers to an individual with the ability to read or share the emotional state of others through some extrasensory ability.

first contact   This type of a story depicts the first meeting between two different intelligent species, one of which is usually the human race. Although technically many alien invasion stories also meet this criterion, they are not normally categorized as first contact stories.

FTL   This abbreviation means faster than the speed of light. Most science fiction writers no longer attempt to explain how their characters get around Einstein's limitation of velocity to the speed of light.

future history   A group of short stories and/or novels, usually by a single author, that may not share common characters but are set in a consistent future setting. These stories are often designed to show the transformation of human society over time. Robert A. Heinlein's works collected as his Future History were the first significant attempt to codify this genre.

gestalt   In science fiction writing this refers to the same personality simultaneously occupying more than one body. These bodies may or may not have some degree of autonomy, or they may act with a group mind. The best example is *More than Human* by Theodore Sturgeon.

hard science fiction   Stories in this genre focus on a well-defined scientific principle or problem (for example, realistic stories of space travel or the development of new technologies). Ben

Bova, Gregory Benford, and Greg Bear are all considered major writers of hard science fiction.

Hugos   Awards given annually by the World Science Fiction Convention for the best novel and short fiction published during that year; named after pioneer publisher Hugo Gernsback.

hyperspace   This term signifies a literary as well as physical shortcut. Spaceships that travel faster than the speed of light are often referred to as moving through hyperspace. This is a variety of extra dimension where distances can be traversed more quickly than in the real universe.

lost race   A novel in which one or more individuals discover, by intent or accident, a civilization that has been completely out of contact with the rest of the human race for many generations, usually in remote regions of the world. Novels like *The Lost World* by Sir Arthur Conan Doyle or *Lost Horizon* by James Hilton are among the most famous examples of lost race novels.

matter transmission   The transference of an object or person from one location to another through mechanical means. This transference is usually instantaneous and without the necessity of actually moving the object through the intervening space. See also **teleportation.**

military science fiction   Stories that involve primarily military characters, who are engaged in wars either in space or for the control of specific planets. David Drake, Lois McMaster Bujold, Gordon R. Dickson, and Jerry Pournelle have all written significant military science fiction series.

near future   An imprecise term used to identify novels set just far enough in the future to allow for certain technological or social changes without being so different that it is necessary to explain that society to the reader. The Eve Dallas series by J. D. Robb is an example of near-future science fiction.

Nebulas   Awards given annually by the Science Fiction & Fantasy Writers of America for the best novel and short fiction published during that year.

New Wave   A movement among writers during the 1960s and 1970s to incorporate experimental writing styles and mainstream literary standards into science fiction. This movement is usually linked to the British magazine *New Worlds.* Some of the authors associated with the New Wave did not accept the label. The most successful New Wave writers were Michael Moorcock and J. G. Ballard.

organleggers   Criminals who harvest healthy organs—sometimes with government sanction—from donors, voluntary or otherwise, and sell them to those rich enough to buy better health.

parallel world   Another reality that exists simultaneously with our own, but is physically separate in some fashion. The parallel world often has an alternate history. Examples include *What Mad Universe* by Fredric Brown and *The Woodrow Wilson Dime* by Jack Finney.

psi powers   A general term for mental powers presently not available to humanity. The most common forms are telepathy, which is the ability to read minds or converse between minds; telekinesis (also called psychokinesis), which is the ability to move objects without touching them; and teleportation, which is the ability to move from one place to another without passing through the intervening space. Alfred Bester's *The Stars My Destination* and Stephen King's *Firestarter* are examples of novels about psi powers.

sci-fi   Generally considered a derogatory term by people working within the field and usually associated with movies rather than the literature.

sense of wonder   A term applied to stories that inspire romantic ideas about the diversity of the universe.

sentience   A degree of intelligence that separates people—human or otherwise—from animals. The term is also sometimes applied to artificial intelligence systems (such as computers) to indicate the point at which they become complex enough to become self-aware and consider themselves living creatures. A notable example of the latter is Hal in Arthur C. Clarke's *2001: A Space Odyssey.*

shapechanger   A creature capable of altering its body into different forms, sometimes in imitation of other objects or lifeforms. *The Fifth Head of Cerberus* by Gene Wolfe and *Find the*

Changeling by Gregory Benford and Gordon Eklund involve shapechanging aliens.

sharecropping A situation in which an author arranges for other writers to produce novels set in one of his or her existing fictional worlds. Sometimes the sharecropper is listed as co-author, although the original writer's contribution might be no greater than approval of the story outline. The additions to the Andre Norton series (by Lyn McConchie, Sherwood Smith, and others) are major examples of this practice.

soft science fiction Stories whose speculative content does not involve physics, space travel, or other elements of physical science. An example is *The Bellwether* by Connie Willis, in which a new principle of human psychology is discovered.

space opera A story in which space travel to other worlds is a major plot device, supporting adventures either in space or on other planets after the western "horse opera." Edward E. Smith's works are the classic examples of space opera and Brian Stableford's Hooded Swan series is a more recent example of its modern form.

suspended animation This term refers to a process through which an individual or individuals is prevented from aging for an extended period of time. This process is usually artificial but occasionally is attained through extraordinary natural circumstances.

suspension of disbelief A term applied to a situation in a story that the reader might ordinarily find implausible, but which is essential to the plot. Usually this takes the form either of a marvelous invention that contradicts a previously accepted law of nature or of some similar phenomenon.

teleportation The ability to move instantaneously from one location to another through the use of mental powers. The term is sometimes used to describe the transmission of matter.

terraform To alter the ecology of another planet so that it is capable of sustaining human life.

This is usually described as a process requiring generations to accomplish. *Climbing Olympus* by Kevin J. Anderson and *Moving Mars* by Greg Bear are examples of novels dealing with terraforming.

timeline When alternate versions of history exist simultaneously, each separate world is known as a timeline.

time travel paradox This is a paradox created by changing events in the past. The most common example is the question of what happens if a character goes back through time and kills one of his or her ancestors before his or her conception. If that ancestor died, the character could not have been born and could not have gone back through time to kill him or her. *The Man Who Folded Himself* by David Gerrold and "All You Zombies" by Robert A. Heinlein are the two most famous time travel paradox stories.

timeslip This term refers to characters who are somehow misplaced in time. These stories are differentiated from regular time travel stories in that the characters' time travel is usually unintentional and sometimes not even explained by the author of the story.

uchronia Another term for **alternate history** stories.

uplift A process whereby common animals are genetically enhanced so that they become intelligent beings, often physically altered into a roughly human form. David Brin's Uplift series is the most famous to use this plot device.

utopian novel A novel set in a future where all or at least most of the problems of contemporary civilization have been solved and human freedom has been maximized; after Thomas More's *Utopia* (1516). There is usually very little plot, and the story is cast in the form of a grand tour of the new society, explaining how it works. The form includes classics like *The New from Nowhere* by William Morris and *Erewhon* by Samuel Butler.

Nebula and Hugo Award Winners

Note that many of these titles are fantasy and not science fiction. Also, the early Hugo Awards did not differentiate among short story, novelette, and novellas in the short fiction category.

Nebula Award Winners

1965
Novel: Dune by Frank Herbert
Novella: The Saliva Tree by Brian W. Aldiss tied with He Who Shapes by Roger Zelazny
Novelette: The Doors of His Face, the Lamps of His Mouth by Roger Zelazny
Short Story: "Repent, Harlequin! Said the Ticktockman" by Harlan Ellison

1966
Novel: Flowers for Algernon by Daniel Keyes tied with Babel-17 by Samuel R. Delany
Novella: The Last Castle by Jack Vance
Novelette: Call Him Lord by Gordon R. Dickson
Short Story: "The Secret Place" by Richard McKenna

1967
Novel: The Einstein Intersection by Samuel R. Delany
Novella: Behold the Man by Michael Moorcock
Novelette: Gonna Roll the Bones by Fritz Leiber
Short Story: "Aye, and Gomorrah" by Samuel R. Delany

1968
Novel: Rite of Passage by Alexei Panshin
Novella: Dragonrider by Anne McCaffrey
Novelette: Mother to the World by Richard Wilson
Short Story: "The Planners" by Kate Wilhelm

1969
Novel: The Left Hand of Darkness by Ursula K. Le Guin
Novella: A Boy and His Dog by Harlan Ellison
Novelette: Time Considered As a Helix of Semi-Precious Stones by Samuel R. Delany
Short Story: "Passengers" by Robert Silverberg

1970
Novel: Ringworld by Larry Niven
Novella: Ill Met in Lankhmar by Fritz Leiber
Novelette: Slow Sculpture by Theodore Sturgeon
Short Story: No award was given this year.

1971
Novel: A Time of Changes by Robert Silverberg
Novella: The Missing Man by Katherine MacLean
Novelette: The Queen of Air and Darkness by Poul Anderson
Short Story: "Good News from the Vatican" by Robert Silverberg

1972
Novel: The Gods Themselves by Isaac Asimov
Novella: A Meeting with Medusa by Arthur C. Clarke
Novelette: Goat Song by Poul Anderson
Short Story: "When It Changed" by Joanna Russ

1973
Novel: Rendezvous with Rama by Arthur C. Clarke
Novella: The Death of Doctor Island by Gene Wolfe

Novelette: Of Mist, and Grass, and Sand by Vonda N. McIntyre

Short Story: "Love Is the Plan the Plan Is Death" by James Tiptree Jr.

1974

Novel: The Dispossessed by Ursula K. Le Guin

Novella: Born With the Dead by Robert Silverberg

Novelette: If the Stars Are Gods by Gordon Eklund and Gregory Benford

Short Story: "The Day Before the Revolution" by Ursula K. Le Guin

1975

Novel: The Forever War by Joe Haldeman

Novella: Home Is the Hangman by Roger Zelazny

Novelette: San Diego Lightfoot Sue by Tom Reamy

Short Story: "Catch That Zeppelin!" by Fritz Leiber

1976

Novel: Man Plus by Frederik Pohl

Novella: Houston, Houston, Do You Read? by James Tiptree Jr.

Novelette: The Bicentennial Man by Isaac Asimov

Short Story: "A Crowd of Shadows" by Charles L. Grant

1977

Novel: Gateway by Frederik Pohl

Novella: Stardance by Spider Robinson and Jeanne Robinson

Novelette: The Screwfly Solution by Raccoona Sheldon

Short Story: "Jeffty Is Five" by Harlan Ellison

1978

Novel: Dreamsnake by Vonda N. McIntyre

Novella: The Persistence of Vision by John Varley

Novelette: A Glow of Candles, a Unicorn's Eye by Charles L. Grant

Short Story: "Stone" by Edward Bryant

1979

Novel: The Fountains of Paradise by Arthur C. Clarke

Novella: Enemy Mine by Barry Longyear

Novelette: Sandkings by George R. R. Martin

Short Story: "giANTS" by Edward Bryant

1980

Novel: Timescape by Gregory Benford

Novella: The Unicorn Tapestry by Suzy McKee Charnas

Novelette: The Ugly Chickens by Howard Waldrop

Short Story: "Grotto of the Dancing Deer" by Clifford D. Simak

1981

Novel: The Claw of the Conciliator by Gene Wolfe

Novella: The Saturn Game by Poul Anderson

Novelette: The Quickening by Michael Bishop

Short Story: "The Bone Flute" by Lisa Tuttle

1982

Novel: No Enemy But Time by Michael Bishop

Novella: Another Orphan by John Kessel

Novelette: Fire Watch by Connie Willis

Short Story: "A Letter from the Clearys" by Connie Willis

1983

Novel: Startide Rising by David Brin

Novella: Hardfought by Greg Bear

Novelette: Blood Music by Greg Bear

Short Story: "The Peacemaker" by Gardner Dozois

1984

Novel: Neuromancer by William Gibson

Novella: Press Enter by John Varley

Novelette: Bloodchild by Octavia E. Butler

Short Story: "Morning Child" by Gardner Dozois

1985

Novel: Ender's Game by Orson Scott Card

Novella: Sailing to Byzantium by Robert Silverberg

Novelette: Portraits of His Children by George R. R. Martin

Short Story: "Out of All Them Bright Stars" by Nancy Kress

1986

Novel: Speaker for the Dead by Orson Scott Card

Novella: R&R by Lucius Shepard

Novelette: The Girl Who Fell into the Sky by Kate Wilhelm

Short Story: "Tangents" by Greg Bear

1987
Novel: *The Falling Woman* by Pat Murphy
Novella: *The Blind Geometer* by Kim Stanley Robinson
Novelette: *Rachel in Love* by Pat Murphy
Short Story: "Forever Yours, Anna" by Kate Wilhelm

1988
Novel: *Falling Free* by Lois McMaster Bujold
Novella: *The Last of the Winnebagos* by Connie Willis
Novelette: *Schrodinger's Kitten* by George Alec Effinger
Short Story: "Bible Stories for Adults, No. 17: The Deluge" by James Morrow

1989
Novel: *The Healer's War* by Elizabeth Ann Scarborough
Novella: *The Mountains of Mourning* by Lois McMaster Bujold
Novelette: *At the Rialto* by Connie Willis
Short Story: "Ripples in the Dirac Sea" by Geoffrey A. Landis

1990
Novel: *Tehanu* by Ursula K. Le Guin
Novella: *The Hemingway Hoax* by Joe Haldeman
Novelette: *Towers of Babylon* by Ted Chiang
Short Story: "Bears Discover Fire" by Terry Bisson

1991
Novel: *Stations of the Tide* by Michael Swanwick
Novella: *Beggars in Spain* by Nancy Kress
Novelette: *Guide Dog* by Mike Conner
Short Story: "Ma Qui" by Alan Brennert

1992
Novel: *Doomsday Book* by Connie Willis
Novella: *City of Truth* by James Morrow
Novelette: *Danny Goes to Mars* by Pamela Sargent
Short Story: "Even the Queen" by Connie Willis

1993
Novel: *Red Mars* by Kim Stanley Robinson
Novella: *The Night We Buried Road Dog* by Jack Cady

Novelette: *Georgia on My Mind* by Charles Sheffield
Short Story: "Graves" by Joe Haldeman

1994
Novel: *Moving Mars* by Greg Bear
Novella: *Seven Views of Olduvai Gorge* by Mike Resnick
Novelette: *The Martian Child* by David Gerrold
Short Story: "A Defense of the Social Contracts" by Martha Soukup

1995
Novel: *The Terminal Experiment* by Robert J. Sawyer
Novella: *Last Summer at Mars Hill* by Elizabeth Hand
Novelette: *Solitude* by Ursula K. Le Guin
Short Story: "Death and the Librarian" by Esther Friesner

1996
Novel: *Slow River* by Nicola Griffith
Novella: *Da Vinci Rising* by Jack Dann
Novelette: *Lifeboat on a Burning Sea* by Bruce Holland Rogers
Short Story: "A Birthday" by Esther Friesner

1997
Novel: *The Moon and the Sun* by Vonda N. McIntyre
Novella: *Abandon in Place* by Jerry Oltion
Novelette: *The Flowers of Aulit Prison* by Nancy Kress
Short Story: "Sister Emily's Lightship" by Jane Yolen

1998
Novel: *Forever Peace* by Joe Haldeman
Novella: *Reading the Bones* by Sheila Finch
Novelette: *Lost Girls* by Jane Yolen
Short Story: "Thirteen Ways to Water" by Bruce Holland Rogers

1999
Novel: *Parable of the Talents* by Octavia E. Butler
Novella: *Story of Your Life* by Ted Chiang
Novelette: *Mars Is No Place for Children* by Mary A. Turzillo
Short Story: "The Cost of Doing Business" by Leslie What

2000

Novel: Darwin's Radio by Greg Bear
Novella: Goddesses by Linda Nagata
Novelette: Daddy's World by Walter Jon Williams
Short Story: "macs" by Terry Bisson

2001

Novel: The Quantum Rose by Catherine Asaro
Novella: The Ultimate Earth by Jack Williamson
Novelette: Louise's Ghost by Kelly Link
Short Story: "The Cure for Everything" by Severna Park

2002

Novel: American Gods by Neil Gaiman
Novella: Bronte's Egg by Richard Chwedyk
Novelette: Hell Is the Absence of God by Ted Chiang
Short Story: "Creature" by Carol Emshwiller

2003

Novel: The Speed of Dark by Elizabeth Moon
Novella: Coraline by Neil Gaiman
Novelette: The Empire of Ice Cream by Jeffrey Ford
Short Story: "What I Didn't See" by Karen Joy Fowler

HUGO AWARD WINNERS

1953

Novel: The Demolished Man by Alfred Bester

1954

No awards were given this year.

1955

Novel: They'd Rather Be Right by Mark Clifton and Frank Riley
Novella: The Darfsteller by Walter M. Miller Jr.
Short Story: "Allamagoosa" by Eric Frank Russell

1956

Novel: Double Star by Robert A. Heinlein
Novelette: Exploration Team by Murray Leinster
Short Story: "The Star" by Arthur C. Clarke

1957

No awards were given this year.

1958

Novel: The Big Time by Fritz Leiber
Short Story: "Or All the Seas with Oysters" by Avram Davidson

1959

Novel: A Case of Conscience by James Blish
Novelette: The Big Front Yard by Clifford D. Simak
Short Story: "That Hell-Bound Train" by Robert Bloch

1960

Novel: Starship Troopers by Robert A. Heinlein
Short Story: "Flowers for Algernon" by Daniel Keyes

1961

Novel: A Canticle for Leibowitz by Walter M. Miller Jr.
Short Story: "The Longest Voyage" by Poul Anderson

1962

Novel: Stranger in a Strange Land by Robert A. Heinlein
Short Story: The Hothouse series, collected as *The Long Afternoon of Earth* by Brian W. Aldiss

1963

Novel: The Man in the High Castle by Philip K. Dick
Short Story: "The Dragon Masters" by Jack Vance

1964

Novel: Way Station by Clifford D. Simak
Short Story: "No Truce with Kings" by Poul Anderson

1965

Novel: The Wanderer by Fritz Leiber
Short Story: "Soldier, Ask Not" by Gordon R. Dickson

1966

Novel: And Call Me Conrad by Roger Zelazny, tied with *Dune* by Frank Herbert
Short Story: "Repent, Harlequin, Said the Ticktockman" by Harlan Ellison

1967

Novel: The Moon Is a Harsh Mistress by Robert A. Heinlein

Novelette: The Last Castle by Jack Vance

Short Story: "Neutron Star" by Larry Niven

1968

Novel: Lord of Light by Roger Zelazny

Novella: Weyr Search by Anne McCaffrey, tied with *Riders of the Purple Wage* by Philip José Farmer

Novelette: Gonna Roll the Bones by Fritz Leiber

Short Story: "I Have No Mouth and I Must Scream" by Harlan Ellison

1969

Novel: Stand on Zanzibar by John Brunner

Novella: Nightwings by Robert Silverberg

Novelette: The Sharing of Flesh by Poul Anderson

Short Story: "The Beast That Shouted Love at the Heart of the World" by Harlan Ellison

1970

Novel: The Left Hand of Darkness by Ursula K. Le Guin

Novella: Ship of Shadows by Fritz Leiber

Short Story: "Time Considered As a Helix of Semi-Precious Stones" by Samuel R. Delany

1971

Novel: Ringworld by Larry Niven

Novella: Ill Met in Lankhmar by Fritz Leiber

Short Story: "Slow Sculpture" by Theodore Sturgeon

1972

Novel: To Your Scattered Bodies Go by Philip Jose Farmer

Novella: Queen of Air and Darkness by Poul Anderson

Short Story: "Inconstant Moon" by Larry Niven

1973

Novel: The Gods Themselves by Isaac Asimov

Novella: The Word for World Is Forest by Ursula K. Le Guin

Novelette: Goat Song by Poul Anderson

Short Story: "Eurema's Dam" by R. A. Lafferty, tied with "The Meeting" by Frederik Pohl and C. M. Kornbluth

1974

Novel: Rendezvous with Rama by Arthur C. Clarke

Novella: The Girl Who Was Plugged In by James Tiptree Jr.

Novelette: The Deathbird by Harlan Ellison

Short Story: "The Ones Who Walk Away from Omelas" by Ursula K. Le Guin

1975

Novel: The Dispossessed by Ursula K. Le Guin

Novella: A Song for Lya by George R. R. Martin

Novelette: Adrift Just Off the Islets of Langerhans by Harlan Ellison

Short Story: "The Hole Man" by Larry Niven

1976

Novel: The Forever War by Joe Haldeman

Novella: Home Is the Hangman by Roger Zelazny

Novelette: The Borderland of Sol by Larry Niven

Short Story: "Catch That Zeppelin!" by Fritz Leiber

1977

Novel: Where Late the Sweet Birds Sang by Kate Wilhelm

Novella: By Any Other Name by Spider Robinson, tied with *Houston, Houston, Do You Read?* by James Tiptree Jr.

Novelette: The Bicentennial Man by Isaac Asimov

Short Story: "Tricentennial" by Joe Haldeman

1978

Novel: Gateway by Frederik Pohl

Novella: Stardance by Spider Robinson and Jeanne Robinson

Novelette: Eyes of Amber by Joan D. Vinge

Short Story: "Jeffty Is Five" by Harlan Ellison

1979

Novel: Dreamsnake by Vonda N. McIntyre

Novella: The Persistence of Vision by John Varley

Novelette: Hunter's Moon by Poul Anderson

Short Story: "Cassandra" by C. J. Cherryh

1980

Novel: The Fountains of Paradise by Arthur C. Clarke

Novella: Enemy Mine by Barry Longyear

Novelette: Sandkings by George R. R. Martin
Short Story: "The Way of Cross and Dragon" by George R. R. Martin

1981
Novel: The Snow Queen by Joan D. Vinge
Novella: Lost Dorsai by Gordon R. Dickson
Novelette: The Cloak and the Staff by Gordon R. Dickson
Short Story: "Grotto of the Dancing Deer" by Clifford D. Simak

1982
Novel: Downbelow Station by C. J. Cherryh
Novella: The Saturn Game by Poul Anderson
Novelette: Unicorn Variation by Roger Zelazny
Short Story: "The Pusher" by John Varley

1983
Novel: Foundation's Edge by Isaac Asimov
Novella: Souls by Joanna Russ
Novelette: Fire Watch by Connie Willis
Short Story: "Melancholy Elephants" by Spider Robinson

1984
Novel: Startide Rising by David Brin
Novella: Cascade Point by Timothy Zahn
Novelette: Blood Music by Greg Bear
Short Story: "Speech Sounds" by Octavia E. Butler

1985
Novel: Neuromancer by William Gibson
Novella: Press Enter by John Varley
Novelette: Bloodchild by Octavia E. Butler
Short Story: "Crystal Spheres" by David Brin

1986
Novel: Ender's Game by Orson Scott Card
Novella: Twenty-Four Views of Mt. Fuji, by Hokusai by Roger Zelazny
Novelette: Paladin of the Lost Hour by Harlan Ellison
Short Story: "Fermi and Frost" by Frederik Pohl

1987
Novel: Speaker for the Dead by Orson Scott Card
Novella: Gilgamesh in the Outback by Robert Silverberg

Novelette: Permafrost by Roger Zelazny
Short Story: "Tangents" by Greg Bear

1988
Novel: The Uplift War by David Brin
Novella: Eye for Eye by Orson Scott Card
Novelette: Buffalo Gals, Won't You Come Out Tonight? by Ursula K. Le Guin
Short Story: "Why I Left Harry's All-Night Hamburgers" by Lawrence Watt-Evans

1989
Novel: Cyteen by C. J. Cherryh
Novella: The Last of the Winnebagos by Connie Willis
Novelette: Schrodinger's Kitten by George Alec Effinger
Short Story: "Kirinyaga" by Mike Resnick

1990
Novel: Hyperion by Dan Simmons
Novella: The Mountains of Mourning by Lois McMaster Bujold
Novelette: Enter a Soldier. Later: Enter Another by Robert Silverberg
Short Story: "Boobs" by Suzy McKee Charnas

1991
Novel: The Vor Game by Lois McMaster Bujold
Novella: The Hemingway Hoax by Joe Haldeman
Novelette: The Manamouki by Mike Resnick
Short Story: "Bears Discover Fire" by Terry Bisson

1992
Novel: Barrayar by Lois McMaster Bujold
Novella: Beggars in Spain by Nancy Kress
Novelette: Gold by Isaac Asimov
Short Story: "A Walk in the Sun" by Geoffrey A. Landis

1993
Novel: A Fire Upon the Deep by Vernor Vinge, tied with Doomsday Book by Connie Willis
Novella: Barnacle Bill the Spacer by Lucius Shepard
Novelette: The Nutcracker Coup by Janet Kagan
Short Story: "Even the Queen" by Connie Willis

1994

Novel: Green Mars by Kim Stanley Robinson
Novella: Down in the Bottomlands by Harry Turtledove
Novelette: Georgia on My Mind by Charles Sheffield
Short Story: "Death on the Nile" by Connie Willis

1995

Novel: Mirror Dance by Lois McMaster Bujold
Novella: Seven Views of Olduvai Gorge by Mike Resnick
Novelette: The Martian Child by David Gerrold
Short Story: "None So Blind" by Joe Haldeman

1996

Novel: The Diamond Age by Neal Stephenson
Novella: The Death of Captain Future by Allen Steele
Novelette: Think Like a Dinosaur by James Patrick Kelly
Short Story: "The Lincoln Train" by Maureen F. McHugh

1997

Novel: Blue Mars by Kim Stanley Robinson
Novella: Blood of the Dragon by George R. R. Martin
Novelette: Bicycle Repairman by Bruce Sterling
Short Story: "The Soul Selects Her Own Society" by Connie Willis

1998

Novel: Forever Peace by Joe Haldeman
Novella: Where Angels Fear to Tread by Allen Steele
Novelette: We Will Drink a Fish Together by Bill Johnson
Short Story: "The 43 Antarean Dynasties" by Mike Resnick

1999

Novel: To Say Nothing of the Dog by Connie Willis
Novella: Oceanic by Greg Egan
Novelette: Taklamakan by Bruce Sterling
Short Story: "The Very Pulse of the Machine" by Michael Swanwick

2000

Novel: A Deepness in the Sky by Vernor Vinge
Novella: The Winds of Marble Arch by Connie Willis
Novelette: 10^{16} to 1 by James Patrick Kelly
Short Story: "Scherzo with Dinosaur" by Michael Swanwick

2001

Novel: Harry Potter and the Goblet of Fire by J. K. Rowling
Novella: The Ultimate Earth by Jack Williamson
Novelette: Millennium Babies by Kristine Kathryn Rusch
Short Story: "Different Kinds of Darkness" by David Langford

2002

Novel: American Gods by Neil Gaiman
Novella: Fast Times at Fairmont High by Vernor Vinge
Novelette: Hell Is the Absence of God by Ted Chiang
Short Story: "The Dog Said Bow-Wow" by Michael Swanwick

2003

Novel: Hominids by Robert J. Sawyer
Novella: Coraline by Neil Gaiman
Novelette: Slow Life by Michael Swanwick
Short Story: "Falling Onto Mars" by Geoffrey A. Landis

In 2001, retroactive Hugo Awards were presented for work published in 1950:

Novel: Farmer in the Sky by Robert A. Heinlein
Novella: The Man Who Sold the Moon by Robert A. Heinlein
Novelette: The Little Black Bag by Cyril M. Kornbluth
Short Story: "To Serve Man" by Damon Knight

BIBLIOGRAPHY OF SCIENCE FICTION WORKS

Note that only science fiction titles are included below. Fantasy, horror, mainstream fiction, and nonfiction works are beyond the scope of this bibliography. Dates listed are for first book publication. In many cases, the novels were originally published in magazines at a much earlier date. Variant titles are listed as well, e.g., *Space Jockey* (2003, also published as *The Star Stallion*).

ADAMS, DOUGLAS

The Hitchhiker's Guide to the Galaxy (1979)
The Restaurant at the End of the Universe (1980)
Life, the Universe, and Everything (1982)
Mostly Harmless (1982)
So Long and Thanks for All the Fish (1984)
The More Than Complete Hitch-Hiker's Guide (1987)
Dirk Gently's Holistic Detective Agency (1987)
The Long Dark Tea Time of the Soul (1988)
The Salmon of Doubt (2002)

ALDISS, BRIAN W.

Space, Time, and Nathaniel (1957)
The Canopy of Time (1959)
No Time Like Tomorrow (1959)
Vanguard from Alpha (1959, also published as *Equator*)
Non-Stop (1959, also published as *Starship*)
Bow Down to Nul (1960, also published as *The Interpreter*)
Galaxies Like Grains of Sand (1960)
The Male Response (1961)
The Primal Urge (1961)
The Long Afternoon of Earth (1962, also published as *Hothouse*)

The Airs of Earth (1963)
The Dark Light Years (1964)
Greybeard (1964)
Starswarm (1964)
Earthworks (1965)
The Saliva Tree & Other Strange Growths (1966)
Report on Probability A (1968)
Intangibles Inc. (1969)
Cryptozoic! (1972, also published as *An Age*)
Barefoot in the Head (1969)
A Brian Aldiss Omnibus (1969)
The Moment of Eclipse (1970)
Neanderthal Planet (1970)
A Brian Aldiss Omnibus 2 (1971)
The Book of Brian W. Aldiss (1972, also published as *The Comic Inferno*)
Frankenstein Unbound (1973)
The Eighty Minute Hour (1974)
The Malacia Tapestry (1976)
Brothers of the Head (1977)
Last Orders (1977)
Enemies of the System (1978)
New Arrivals, Old Encounters (1979)
An Island Called Moreau (1980, also published as *Moreau's Other Island*)
Man in His Time (1981, also published as *The Best SF Stories of Brian W. Aldiss*, also published as *Who Can Replace a Man?*)
Helliconia Spring (1982)
Helliconia Summer (1983)
Seasons in Flight (1984)
Helliconia Winter (1985)
The Year Before Yesterday (1987, also published as *Cracken at Critical*)

A Romance of the Equator (1989)
Dracula Unbound (1991)
A Tupolev Too Far (1993)
Common Clay (1996)
The Secret of This Book (1996)
White Mars (1999, with Roger Penrose)
Supertoys Last All Summer Long (2001)
Super-State (2002)

ALLEN, ROGER MACBRIDE

The Torch of Honor (1985)
Rogue Powers (1986)
Farside Cannon (1988)
Orphan of Creation (1988)
The War Machine (1989)
The Ring of Charon (1990)
The Modular Man (1991)
Supernova (1991, with Eric Kotani)
Caliban (1993)
Inferno (1994)
The Shattered Sphere (1994)
Allies and Aliens (1995)
Ambush at Corellia (1995)
Assault at Selonia (1995)
Showdown at Centerpoint (1995)
Utopia (1996)
The Game of Worlds (1999)
The Depths of Time (2000)
The Ocean of Years (2002)
The Shores of Tomorrow (2004)

ANDERSON, KEVIN J.

Resurrection, Inc. (1998)
Lifeline (1990, with Doug Beason)
The Trinity Paradox (1991, with Doug Beason)
Assemblers of Infinity (1993, with Doug Beason)
Jedi Search (1994)
Dark Apprentice (1994)
Champions of the Force (1994)
Climbing Olympus (1994)
Ill Wind (1995, with Doug Beason)
Blindfold (1995)
Darksaber (1995)
Ground Zero (1995)
Shifting the Boundaries (1995)
Heirs of the Force (1995, with Rebecca Moesta)
The Lost Ones (1995, with Rebecca Moesta)
Shadow Academy (1995, with Rebecca Moesta)
Ignition (1996, with Doug Beason)

Ruins (1996)
Virtual Destruction (1996, with Doug Beason)
Darkest Knight (1996, with Rebecca Moesta)
Jedi Under Siege (1996, with Rebecca Moesta)
Lightsabers (1996, with Rebecca Moesta)
Shards of Alderaan (1996, with Rebecca Moesta)
Antibodies (1997)
Delusions of Grandeur (1997, with Rebecca Moesta)
Diversity Alliance (1997, with Rebecca Moesta)
Jedi Bounty (1997, with Rebecca Moesta)
Fallout (1997, with Doug Beason)
Ai Pedrito! (1998, with L. Ron Hubbard)
The Emperor's Plague (1998, with Rebecca Moesta)
Crisis at Crystal Reef (1998, with Rebecca Moesta)
Return to Ord Mantell (1998, with Rebecca Moesta)
Trouble on Cloud City (1998, with Rebecca Moesta)
Lethal Exposure (1998, with Doug Beason)
Armageddon Dreams (1999)
House Atreides (1999, with Brian Herbert)
House Harkonnen (2000, with Brian Herbert)
Akima's Story (2000, with Rebecca Moesta)
Cale's Story (2000, with Rebecca Moesta)
Dogged Persistence (2001)
House Corrino (2001, with Brian Herbert)
Captain Nemo (2002)
Hidden Empire (2002)
Hopscotch (2002)
The Butlerian Jihad (2002, with Brian Herbert)
A Forest of Stars (2003)
The Machine Crusade (2003, with Brian Herbert)
Horizon Storms (2004)
The Battle of Corrin (2004, with Brian Herbert)

ANDERSON, POUL

Vault of the Ages (1952)
Brain Wave (1954)
No World of Their Own (1955, also published as The Long Way Home)
Planet of No Return (1956, also published as Question and Answer)
Star Ways (1956, also published as The Peregrine)
Earthman's Burden (1957, with Gordon R. Dickson)
War of the Wingmen (1958, also published as The Man Who Counts)
The Enemy Stars (1958)
The Snows of Ganymede (1958)
War of Two Worlds (1959)
We Claim These Stars (1959)
Virgin Planet (1959)

Earthman, Go Home! (1960)
Guardians of Time (1960)
The High Crusade (1960)
Strangers from Earth (1961)
Mayday Orbit (1961)
Orbit Unlimited (1961)
Twilight World (1961)
After Doomsday (1962)
The Makeshift Rocket (1962)
Un-Man and Other Novellas (1962)
Let the Spacemen Beware (1963)
Shield (1963)
Three Worlds to Conquer (1964)
Trader to the Stars (1964)
Time and Stars (1964)
The Star Fox (1965)
Agent of the Terran Empire (1965)
The Trouble Twisters (1966)
The Corridors of Time (1966)
Ensign Flandry (1966)
World Without Stars (1966)
Satan's World (1968)
The Horn of Time (1968)
The Rebel Worlds (1969)
Beyond the Beyond (1969)
Tales of the Flying Mountains (1970)
Tau Zero (1970)
A Circus of Hells (1970)
Seven Conquests (1970, also published as Conquests)
The Byworlder (1971)
The Dancer from Atlantis (1971)
There Will Be Time (1972)
The Queen of Air and Darkness (1973)
The People of the Wind (1973)
The Day of Their Return (1973)
Inheritors of Earth (1974, with Gordon Eklund)
Fire Time (1974)
The Worlds of Poul Anderson (1974)
A Knight of Ghosts and Shadows (1974)
A Midsummer Tempest (1974)
Homeward and Beyond (1975)
The Winter of the World (1975)
Star Prince Charlie (1975, with Gordon R. Dickson)
The Book of Poul Anderson (1975, also published as
    The Many Worlds of Poul Anderson)
The Best of Poul Anderson (1976)
Homebrew (1976)
Mirkheim (1977)
The Avatar (1978)

The Nightface and Other Stories (1978)
The Earth Book of Stormgate (1979)
A Stone in Heaven (1979)
Winners (1981)
The Psychotechnic League (1981)
The Dark Between the Stars (1981)
Explorations (1981)
Starship (1982)
Cold Victory (1982)
The Gods Laughed (1982)
Maurai and Kith (1982)
New America (1982)
The Year of the Ransom (1983)
Hoka (1983, with Gordon R. Dickson)
Conflict (1983)
The Long Night (1983)
Orion Shall Rise (1983)
Time Patrolman (1983)
Past Times (1984)
The Unicorn Trade (1984, with Karen Anderson)
Dialogue with Darkness (1985)
The Game of Empire (1985)
The Boat of a Million Years (1989)
Space Folk (1989)
The Shield of Time (1990)
Time Patrol (1991)
Alight in the Void (1991)
Inconstant Star (1991)
Kinship with the Stars (1994)
Harvest of Stars (1993)
Harvest the Fire (1995)
All One Universe (1996)
The Fleet of Stars (1997)
Starfarers (1998)
Hoka! Hoka! Hoka! (1998, with Gordon R.
    Dickson)
Genesis (2000)
Hokas Pokas (2000, with Gordon R. Dickson)
The Sound and the Furry (2001, with Gordon R.
    Dickson)
Going for Infinity (2002)
For Love and Glory (2003)

ANTHONY, PIERS
Chthon (1967)
The Ring (1968, with Robert E. Margroff)
Omnivore (1968)
Macroscope (1969)
The E.S.P. Worm (1970, with Robert E. Margroff)

Orn (1971)
Var the Stick (1972)
Prostho Plus (1973)
Race Against Time (1973)
Rings of Ice (1974)
Triple Détente (1974)
Phthor (1975)
Neq the Sword (1975)
Ox (1976)
Steppe (1976)
Cluster (1977)
Chaining the Lady (1978)
The Kirlian Quest (1978)
Battle Circle (1978)
Pretender (1979, with Frances Hall)
Thousandstar (1980)
Mute (1981)
Viscous Circle (1982)
Refugee (1983)
Mercenary (1984)
Anthonology (1985)
Executive (1985)
Politician (1985)
Ghost (1986)
Statesman (1986)
But What of Earth? (1989)
Balook (1990)
The Hard Sell (1990)
Total Recall (1990)
Dead Morn (1990, with Roberto Fuentes)
Alien Plot (1992)
The Caterpillar's Question (1992, with Philip Jose Farmer)
Isle of Woman (1993)
The Hope of Earth (1997)
Spider Legs (1995, with Clifford Pickover)
The Muse of Art (1999)
Reality Check (1999)

ASARO, CATHERINE
Primary Inversion (1995)
Catch the Lightning (1996)
The Last Hawk (1997)
The Radiant Seas (1998)
The Veiled Web (1999)
Ascendant Sun (2000)
The Quantum Rose (2000)

Spherical Harmonic (2001)
The Moon's Shadow (2003)
Skyfall (2003)
Sunrise Alley (2004)

ASIMOV, ISAAC
Pebble in the Sky (1950)
I, Robot (1950)
Foundation (1951, also published as *The 1,000-Year Plan*)
The Stars, Like Dust (1951)
Foundation and Empire (1952, also published as *The Man Who Upset the Universe*)
The Currents of Space (1952)
Second Foundation (1953)
The Caves of Steel (1954)
The End of Eternity (1955)
The Martian Way (1955)
Earth Is Room Enough (1957)
The Naked Sun (1957)
Nine Tomorrows (1959)
The Rest of the Robots (1964)
Fantastic Voyage (1966)
Asimov's Mysteries (1968)
Nightfall and Other Stories (1969)
David Starr: Space Ranger (1971)
Lucky Starr and the Pirates of the Asteroids (1971)
Lucky Starr and the Oceans of Venus (1972)
Lucky Starr and the Big Sun of Mercury (1972)
Lucky Starr and the Rings of Saturn (1972)
Lucky Starr and the Moons of Jupiter (1972)
The Gods Themselves (1972)
The Early Asimov (1972)
The Best of Isaac Asimov (1973)
Have You Seen These? (1974)
Buy Jupiter (1975)
The Bicentennial Man (1976)
The Complete Robot (1982)
Foundation's Edge (1982)
The Robots of Dawn (1983)
Norby the Mixed Up Robot (1983, with Janet Asimov)
The Winds of Change (1983)
Norby's Other Secret (1984, with Janet Asimov)
Robots and Empire (1985)
The Edge of Tomorrow (1985)
Norby and the Invaders (1985, with Janet Asimov)
Norby and the Lost Princess (1985, with Janet Asimov)

Robot Dreams (1986)

Alternate Asimovs (1986)

Norby and the Queen's Necklace (1986, with Janet Asimov)

The Best Science Fiction of Isaac Asimov (1986)

Foundation and Earth (1986)

Fantastic Voyage II (1987)

Norby Finds a Villain (1987, with Janet Asimov)

Norby: Robot for Hire (1987, with Janet Asimov)

Prelude to Foundation (1988)

The Asimov Chronicles (1989)

Norby and Yobo's Great Adventure (1989, with Janet Asimov)

Norby Down to Earth (1989, with Janet Asimov)

Nemesis (1989)

The Complete Stories (1990)

Norby and the Oldest Dragon (1990, with Janet Asimov)

Nightfall (1990, with Robert Silverberg)

Robot Visions (1991)

Norby and the Court Jester (1991, with Janet Asimov)

The Ugly Little Boy (1991, with Robert Silverberg, also published as *Child of Time*)

The Positronic Man (1992, with Robert Silverberg)

Forward the Foundation (1993)

Gold (1995)

ASPRIN, ROBERT LYNN

The Cold Cash War (1977)

The Bug Wars (1979)

Tambu (1979)

Mirror Friend, Mirror Foe (1979, with George Takei)

Phule's Company (1990)

Phule's Paradise (1992)

Catwoman: Tiger Hunt (1992, with Lynn Abbey)

Time Scout (1995, with Linda Evans)

Wagers of Sin (1996, with Linda Evans)

A Phule and His Money (1999, with Peter Heck)

Phule Me Twice (2000, with Peter Heck)

Ripping Time (2000, with Linda Evans)

The House That Jack Built (2001, with Linda Evans)

For King and Country (2002, with Linda Evans)

No Phule Like an Old Phule (2004, with Peter Heck)

ATTANASIO, A. A.

Radix (1981)

Beastmarks (1984)

In Other Worlds (1985)

Arc of the Dream (1986)

Last Legends of Earth (1989)

Solis (1994)

Centuries (1997)

ATWOOD, MARGARET

The Handmaid's Tale (1985)

Oryx and Crake (2003)

BALLARD, J. G.

Billenium (1962)

The Voices of Time (1962)

The Wind from Nowhere (1962)

The Drowned World (1962)

Passport to Eternity (1963)

The Burning World (1964)

Terminal Beach (1964)

The Four Dimensional Nightmare (1965)

The Crystal World (1966)

The Impossible Man (1966)

The Day of Forever (1967)

The Disaster Area (1967)

The Overloaded Man (1967)

Chronopolis (1971)

Vermilion Sands (1971)

The Atrocity Exhibition (1972, also published as *Love and Napalm: Export USA*)

High Rise (1975)

Low Flying Aircraft (1976)

The Best of J. G. Ballard (1977)

The Best Short Stories of J. G. Ballard (1978)

The Unlimited Dream Company (1979)

The Venus Hunters (1980)

Hello America (1981)

Myths of the Near Future (1982)

Memories of the Space Age (1988)

War Fever (1990)

The Complete Short Stories of J. G. Ballard (2002)

BANKS, IAIN

Walking on Glass (1985)

Consider Phlebas (1987)

The Player of Games (1988)

Canal Dreams (1989)

The State of the Art (1989)

Use of Weapons (1990)

Against a Dark Background (1992)
Feersum Endjinn (1994)
Excession (1996)
Inversions (1998)
Look to Windward (2000)

BARNES, JOHN

The Man Who Pulled Down the Sky (1986)
Sin of Origin (1986)
Orbital Resonance (1991)
Battlecry (1992)
Union Fires (1992)
Wartide (1992)
A Million Open Doors (1993)
Mother of Storms (1994)
Kaleidoscope Century (1995)
Patton's Spaceship (1996)
Caesar's Bicycle (1997)
Washington's Dirigible (1997)
Apostrophes and Apocalypses (1998)
Earth Made of Glass (1998)
Finity (1999)
Candle (2000)
The Merchant of Souls (2001)
The Sky So Big and Black (2002)
The Duke of Uranium (2002)
In the Hall of the Martian King (2003)

BARRETT, NEAL, JR.

The Gates of Time (1970)
Kelwin (1970)
The Leaves of Time (1971)
Highwood (1972)
Stress Pattern (1974)
Aldair in Albion (1976)
Aldair, Master of Ships (1977)
Aldair, Across the Misty Sea (1980)
Aldair, the Legion of Beasts (1982)
Karma Corps (1984)
Through Darkest America (1988)
Dawn's Uncertain Night (1989)
Batman and the Black Egg of Atlantis (1992)
Slightly Off Center (1992)
Judge Dredd (1995)
The Touch of Your Shadow, the Whisper of Your Name (1996)
Lizard's Rage (1997)
Perpetuity Blues (2000)

BAXTER, STEPHEN

Raft (1991)
Anti-Ice (1993)
Flux (1993)
Timelike Infinity (1993)
Ring (1994)
The Time Ships (1995)
Voyage (1996)
GulliverZone (1997)
Titan (1997)
Traces (1998)
Grey Hair (1998)
Moonseed (1998)
Webcrash (1998)
Mammoth (1999)
Longtusk (2000)
Icebones (2001)
Manifold: Time (2000)
The Light of Other Days (2000, with Arthur C. Clarke)
Reality Dust (2000)
Manifold: Space (2001)
Manifold: Origin (2002)
Riding the Rock (2002)
Phase Space (2002)
Coalescent (2003)
Evolution (2003)
Time's Eye (2003, with Arthur C. Clarke)
The Hunters of Pangaea (2004)

BEAR, GREG

Hegira (1979)
Psychlone (1979, also published as *Lost Souls*)
Beyond Heaven's River (1980)
Strength of Stones (1981)
Wind from a Burning Woman (1983, also published as *The Venging*)
Corona (1984)
Blood Music (1985)
Eon (1985)
The Forge of God (1987)
Hardfought (1988)
Early Harvest (1988)
Eternity (1988)
Tangents (1989)
Heads (1990)
Queen of Angels (1990)
Anvil of Stars (1992)

Moving Mars (1993)
Legacy (1995)
Slant (1997)
Dinosaur Summer (1998)
Foundation and Chaos (1998)
Darwin's Radio (1999)
Rogue Planet (2000)
The Collected Stories of Greg Bear (2002)
Vitals (2002)
Darwin's Children (2003)
Women in Deep Time (2003)

BENFORD, GREGORY
Deeper Than the Darkness (1970)
Jupiter Project (1975)
In the Ocean of Night (1977)
The Stars in Shroud (1978)
Shiva Descending (1980, with William Rotsler)
Find the Changeling (1980, with Gordon Eklund)
Timescape (1980)
Across the Sea of Suns (1983)
Against Infinity (1983)
Artifact (1985)
In Alien Flesh (1986)
Heart of the Comet (1986, with David Brin)
Great Sky River (1987)
Tides of Light (1989)
Iceborn (1989, with Paul A. Carter)
Beyond the Fall of Night (1990)
Furious Gulf (1994)
Matter's End (1995)
Sailing Bright Eternity (1995)
A Darker Geometry (1996, with Mark O. Martin)
Foundation's Fear (1997)
Cosm (1998)
The Martian Race (1999)
Eater (2000)
Worlds Vast and Various (2000)
Immersion and Other Short Novels (2002)
Beyond Infinity (2004)

BESTER, ALFRED
The Demolished Man (1953)
The Stars My Destination (1957, also published as Tiger! Tiger!)
Starburst (1958)
The Dark Side of the Earth (1964)
An Alfred Bester Omnibus (1967)

The Computer Connection (1975, also published as Extro)
The Light Fantastic (1976)
Star Light, Star Bright (1976)
Starlight (1977)
Golem 100 (1980)
The Deceivers (1981)
Virtual Unrealities (1997)
Redemolished (2001)

BIGGLE, LLOYD, JR.
The Angry Espers (1961)
All the Colors of Darkness (1963)
Fury Out of Time (1965)
Watchers of the Dark (1966)
Rule of the Door & Other Fanciful Regulations (1967, also published as The Silent Sky)
The Still Small Voice of Trumpets (1968)
The World Menders (1971)
The Light That Never Was (1972)
The Metallic Muse (1972)
Monument (1974)
A Galaxy of Strangers (1976)
This Darkening Universe (1976)
Silence Is Deadly (1977)
Whirligig of Time (1979)
The Tunesmith (1990)
The Chronocide Mission (2002)

BISHOP, MICHAEL
A Funeral for the Eyes of Fire (1975, revised as Eyes of Fire)
Beneath the Shattered Moons (1977, also published as And Strange at Ecbatan the Trees)
Stolen Faces (1977)
A Little Knowledge (1978)
Catacomb Years (1979)
Transfigurations (1980)
Under Heaven's Bridge (1981, with Ian Watson)
Blooded on Arachne (1982)
No Enemy But Time (1982)
One Winter in Eden (1984)
Ancient of Days (1985)
Close Encounters with the Deity (1986)
The Secret Ascension (1987, also published as Philip K. Dick Is Dead, Alas)
Apartheid, Superstring, and Mordecai Thubana (1989)
Emphatically Not SF, Almost (1990)

Count Geiger's Blues (1992)
Brittle Innings (1994)
Blue Kansas Sky (2000)
Brighten to Incandescence (2003)

BLISH, JAMES
The Warriors of Day (1953)
Jack of Eagles (1952, also published as *ESP-er*)
Earthman, Come Home (1955)
They Shall Have Stars (1956, also published as *Year 2018!*)
The Frozen Year (1957, also published as *Fallen Star*)
A Case of Conscience (1958)
Vor (1958)
The Triumph of Time (1958, also published as *A Clash of Cymbals*)
The Seedling Stars (1956)
The Duplicated Man (1959, with Robert A. W. Lowndes)
Galactic Cluster (1959)
So Close to Home (1961)
Titans' Daughter (1961)
The Star Dwellers (1961)
A Life for the Stars (1962)
The Night Shapes (1962)
Mission to the Heart Stars (1965)
Welcome to Mars! (1967)
A Torrent of Faces (1967, with Norman L. Knight)
The Vanished Jet (1968)
Star Trek, Volumes 1–11 (1967–75)
Anywhen (1970)
Cities in Flight (1970)
Spock Must Die! (1970)
And All the Stars a Stage (1971)
Midsummer Century (1972)
Quincunx of Time (1973)
The Testament of Andros (1977)
Star Trek 12 (1977, with J. A. Lawrence)
The Best of James Blish (1979)
A Work of Art and Other Stories (1993)
A Dusk of Idols (1996)
In This World, or Another (2003)

BLOCH, ROBERT
Atoms and Evil (1962)
Ladies Day and *This Crowded Earth* (1968)
Fear Today, Gone Tomorrow (1971)
Sneak Preview (1971)

The Best of Robert Bloch (1977)
Strange Eons (1978)
Mysteries of the Worm (1981)
Twilight Zone: The Movie (1983)
Out of My Head (1986)
Lost in Time and Space with Lefty Feep (1987)

BOND, NELSON
Exiles of Time (1949)
Thirty First of February (1949)
The Remarkable Adventures of Lancelot Biggs, Spaceman (1950)
No Time Like the Future (1954)
The Far Side of Nowhere (2002)
That Worlds May Live (2002)

BOVA, BEN
The Star Conquerors (1959)
Star Watchman (1964)
The Weathermakers (1967)
Out of the Sun (1968)
The Dueling Machine (1969)
Escape! (1970)
THX 1138 (1971)
Exiled from Earth (1971)
Flight of Exiles (1972)
As on a Darkling Plain (1972)
When the Sky Burned (1973)
Forward in Time (1973)
Gremlins Go Home (1964, with Gordon R. Dickson)
End of Exile (1975)
City of Darkness (1976)
Millennium (1976)
The Multiple Man (1976)
The Starcrossed (1976)
Viewpoint (1977)
Maxwell's Demons (1978)
Aliens (1978)
Colony (1978)
Kinsman (1979)
Voyagers (1981)
Test of Fire (1982)
The Winds of Altair (1983)
Escape Plus (1984)
Orion (1984)
The Astral Mirror (1985)
Privateers (1985)
The Prometheans (1986)

Voyagers II: The Alien Within (1986)
Battlestation (1987)
The Peacekeepers (1988)
Vengeance of Orion (1988)
Cyberbooks (1989)
Future Crime (1990)
Voyagers III: Star Brothers (1990)
Orion in the Dying Time (1990)
Star Brothers (1990)
The Trikon Deception (1992, with William Pogue)
Mars (1992)
Sam Gunn Unlimited (1992)
To Save the Sun (1992, with A. J. Austin)
Challenges (1993)
Empire Builders (1993)
Triumph (1993)
Orion and the Conqueror (1994)
To Fear the Light (1994, with A. J. Austin)
Death Dream (1994)
Orion Among the Stars (1995)
Moonrise (1996)
Brothers (1996)
Moonwar (1997)
Sam Gunn Forever (1998)
Twice Seven (1998)
Return to Mars (1999)
Jupiter (2000)
Venus (2000)
The Precipice (2001)
Saturn (2002)
Rock Rats (2002)
Tales of the Grand Tour (2004)
The Silent War (2004)

BRACKETT, LEIGH
The Starmen of Llyrdis (1952, also published as *Galactic Breed*, also published as *The Starmen*)
The Sword of Rhiannon (1953)
The Big Jump (1955)
The Long Tomorrow (1955)
The Nemesis from Terra (1961, also published as *Shadow Over Mars*)
Alpha Centauri or Die! (1963)
People of the Talisman (1964)
The Secret of Sinharat (1964)
The Coming of the Terrans (1967)
The Halfling and Other Stories (1973)
The Ginger Star (1974)

The Hounds of Skaith (1974)
The Reavers of Skaith (1976)
The Book of Skaith (1976)
The Best of Leigh Brackett (1977)
The Jewel of Bas (1990)

BRADBURY, RAY
The Martian Chronicles (1950, also published as *The Silver Locusts*)
Fahrenheit 451 (1953)
The Golden Apples of the Sun (1953)
The Day It Rained Forever (1959)
The Small Assassin (1962)
R Is for Rocket (1962)
The Machineries of Joy (1964)
The Vintage Bradbury (1965)
S Is for Space (1966)
Twice Twenty Two (1966)
I Sing the Body Electric (1970)
Long After Midnight (1976)
The Stories of Ray Bradbury (1980)
Dinosaur Tales (1983)
The Toynbee Convector (1988)
Classic Stories (1990)
The Illustrated Bradbury (1990)
Quicker Than the Eye (1996)

BRADLEY, MARION ZIMMER
The Door Through Space (1961)
Seven from the Stars (1961)
The Planet Savers (1962)
The Sword of Aldones (1962)
The Colors of Space (1963)
The Dark Intruder & Other Stories (1964)
The Bloody Sun (1964)
The Falcons of Narabedla (1964)
Star of Danger (1965)
The Brass Dragon (1969)
The Winds of Darkover (1970)
The World Wreckers (1971)
Darkover Landfall (1972)
Hunters of the Red Moon (1973)
The Spell Sword (1974)
The Heritage of Hastur (1975)
Endless Voyage (1975, revised as *Endless Universe*)
The Shattered Chain (1976)
The Forbidden Tower (1977)
The Ruins of Isis (1978)

Stormqueen! (1978)
The Survivors (1979, with Paul Zimmer)
Survey Ship (1980)
Two to Conquer (1980)
Sharra's Exile (1981)
Hawkmistress! (1982)
The Children of Hastur (1982)
Thendara House (1983)
Oath of the Renunciates (1984)
City of Sorcery (1984)
The Best of Marion Zimmer Bradley (1985)
The Heirs of Hammerfell (1989)
Darkover (1993)
Rediscovery (1993)
Jamies and Other Stories (1993)
The Shadow Matrix (1997)
Traitor's Sun (1999)
The Fall of Neskaya (2001, with Deborah Ross)
The Ages of Chaos (2002)
The Forbidden Circle (2002)
The Saga of the Renunciates (2002)
Heritage and Exile (2002)
Zandru's Forge (2003, with Deborah Ross)
A World Divided (2003)

BRIN, DAVID
Sundiver (1980)
Startide Rising (1983)
The Practice Effect (1984)
The Postman (1985)
The River of Time (1986)
Heart of the Comet (1986, with Gregory Benford)
The Uplift War (1987)
Earth (1990)
Glory Season (1993)
Otherness (1994)
Brightness Reef (1996)
Infinity's Shore (1996)
Heaven's Reach (1998)
Foundation's Triumph (1999)
Kiln People (2002)

BROWN, FREDRIC
What Mad Universe (1949)
Space on My Hands (1951)
The Lights in the Sky Are Stars (1954, also published as *Project Jupiter*)
Martians, Go Home! (1955)

Star Shine (1956, also published as *Angels and Spaceships*)
Rogue in Space (1957)
Honeymoon in Hell (1958)
The Mind Thing (1961)
Nightmares and Geezenstacks (1961)
Daymares (1968)
Paradox Lost (1973)
The Best of Fredric Brown (1976)
The Best Short Stories of Fredric Brown (1982)
And the Gods Laughed (1987)
From These Ashes (2001)

BRUNNER, JOHN
Galactic Storm (1951, as Gil Hunt)
The Brink (1959)
The World Swappers (1959)
Threshold of Eternity (1959)
The 100th Millennium (1959)
Echo in the Skull (1959)
The Atlantic Abomination (1960)
The Skynappers (1960)
Slavers of Space (1960)
Sanctuary in the Sky (1960)
I Speak for Earth (1961, as Keith Woodcott)
Meeting at Infinity (1961)
The Ladder in the Sky (1962, as Keith Woodcott)
Father of Lies (1962)
Secret Agent of Terra (1962)
Times Without Number (1962)
No Future in It (1962)
The Super Barbarians (1962)
The Space Time Juggler (1963)
The Psionic Menace (1963, as Keith Woodcott)
Castaways World (1963)
The Dreaming Earth (1963)
The Astronauts Must Not Land (1963)
Listen! The Stars! (1963)
The Rites of Ohe (1963)
Endless Shadow (1964)
The Whole Man (1964, also published as *The Telepathist*)
To Conquer Chaos (1964)
Enigma from Tantalus (1965)
The Squares of the City (1965)
The Repairmen of Cyclops (1965)
The Long Result (1965)
Now Then! (1965)

The Martian Sphinx (1965, as Keith Woodcott)
Day of the Star Cities (1965)
The Altar on Asconel (1965)
No Other Gods But Me (1966)
A Planet of Your Own (1966)
Out of My Mind (1967)
Born Under Mars (1967)
The Productions of Time (1967)
Quicksand (1967)
Not Before Time (1968)
Catch a Falling Star (1968, expanded version of The
    100th Millennium)
Bedlam Planet (1968)
Stand on Zanzibar (1968)
Into the Slave Nebula (1968, expanded version of
    Slavers of Space)
Double, Double (1969)
The Evil That Men Do (1969)
Timescoop (1969)
The Jagged Orbit (1969)
The Avengers of Carrig (1969, expanded version of
    Secret Agent of Terra)
The Gaudy Shadows (1970)
The Wrong End of Time (1971)
The Dramaturges of Yan (1972)
From This Day Forward (1972)
The Stardroppers (1972, expanded version of Listen!
    The Stars!)
Entry to Elsewhen (1972)
The Sheep Look Up (1973)
Time Jump (1973)
The Storm That Never Came Down (1973)
More Things in Heaven (1973, expanded version of
    The Astronauts Must Not Land)
Age of Miracles (1973, expanded version of Day of
    the Star Cities)
Give Warning to the World (1974, expanded version
    of Echo in the Skull)
Polymath (1974, expanded version of Castaways
    World)
Total Eclipse (1974)
Web of Everywhere (1974)
Shockwave Rider (1975)
The Book of John Brunner (1976)
Interstellar Empire (1976)
Foreign Constellations (1980)
Players at the Game of People (1980)
The Infinitive of Go (1980)

Manshape (1982, expanded version of Endless
    Shadow)
The Crucible of Time (1983)
The Tides of Time (1984)
The Shift Key (1987)
The Best of John Brunner (1988)
Children of the Thunder (1989)
A Maze of Stars (1991)
Muddle Earth (1993)

BUDRYS, ALGIS
False Night (1954)
Man of Earth (1956)
Who? (1958)
The Falling Torch (1959)
The Unexpected Dimension (1960)
Rogue Moon (1960)
Some Will Not Die (1961, expanded version of False
    Night)
Budrys' Inferno (1963, also published as The Furious
    Future)
The Amsirs and the Iron Thorn (1967)
Michaelmas (1977)
Blood and Burning (1978)
Hard Landing (1993)

BUJOLD, LOIS MCMASTER
Ethan of Athos (1986)
Shards of Honor (1986)
The Warrior's Apprentice (1986)
Falling Free (1988)
Borders of Infinity (1989)
Brothers in Arms (1989)
The Vor Game (1990)
Barrayar (1991)
Mirror Dance (1995)
Cetaganda (1996)
Memory (1996)
Dreamweaver's Dilemma (1996)
Komarr (1998)
A Civil Campaign (1999)
Diplomatic Immunity (2002)

BURGESS, ANTHONY
A Clockwork Orange (1962)
The Wanting Seed (1962)
The End of the World News (1963)
1985 (1978)

BURROUGHS, EDGAR RICE
A Princess of Mars (1917)
The Gods of Mars (1918)
The Warlord of Mars (1919)
Thuvia, Maid of Mars (1920)
The Chessmen of Mars (1922)
At the Earth's Core (1922)
Pellucidar (1923)
The Land That Time Forgot (1924)
The Cave Girl (1925)
The Eternal Lover (1925, also published as *The Eternal Savage*)
The Moon Maid (1926)
The Master Mind of Mars (1928)
The Monster Men (1929)
Tanar of Pellucidar (1930)
Tarzan at the Earth's Core (1930)
A Fighting Man of Mars (1931)
Jungle Girl (1933)
Pirates of Venus (1934)
Lost on Venus (1935)
Swords of Mars (1936)
Back to the Stone Age (1937)
Carson of Venus (1939)
Synthetic Men of Mars (1940)
Land of Terror (1944)
Escape on Venus (1946)
Llana of Gathol (1948)
Beyond Thirty (1957)
Savage Pellucidar (1963)
Beyond the Farthest Star (1964)
John Carter of Mars (1964)
The Wizard of Venus (1970)

BURROUGHS, WILLIAM S.
Naked Lunch (1959)
The Soft Machine (1961)
The Ticket That Exploded (1962)
Nova Express (1965)
The Wild Boys (1971)
Ghost of Chance (1995)

BUTLER, OCTAVIA
Patternmaster (1976)
Mind of My Mind (1977)
Survivor (1978)
Kindred (1979)
Wild Seed (1980)

Clay's Ark (1984)
Dawn (1987)
Adulthood Rites (1988)
Imago (1989)
Parable of the Sower (1993)
Bloodchild and Other Stories (1995)
Parable of the Talents (2000)

CADIGAN, PAT
Mindplayers (1987)
Patterns (1989)
Home by the Sea (1991)
Synners (1991)
Fools (1992)
Dirty Work (1993)
Parasite (1996)
Tea from an Empty Cup (1998)
Avatar (1999)
Promised Land (1999)
Dervish Is Digital (2001)
Upgrade & Sensuous Cindy (2004)

CAIDIN, MARTIN
The Long Night (1956)
Marooned (1964)
Devil Take All (1966)
The Last Fathom (1967)
No Man's World (1967)
Four Came Back (1968)
The God Machine (1968)
The Mendelov Conspiracy (1974, also published as *Encounter Three*)
Almost Midnight (1971)
Cyborg (1972)
Operation Nuke (1973)
High Crystal (1974)
Planetfall (1974)
Three Corners to Nowhere (1975)
Cyborg IV (1975)
Aquarius Mission (1978)
Manfac (1979)
Star Bright (1980)
The Final Countdown (1980)
Killer Station (1985)
The Messiah Stone (1986)
Zoboa (1986)
Exit Earth (1987)
Beamriders! (1989)

Prison Ship (1989)
Dark Messiah (1990)
A Life in the Future (1995)

CAMPBELL, JOHN W.

The Mightiest Machine (1947)
Who Goes There? (1948)
The Incredible Planet (1949)
The Moon Is Hell (1950)
The Cloak of Aesir (1952)
The Black Star Passes (1953)
Who Goes There? and Other Stories (1955)
Islands of Space (1956)
Invaders from the Infinite (1961)
The Planeteers (1966)
The Ultimate Weapon (1966)
A John W. Campbell Anthology (1973)
The Best of John W. Campbell (1976)
The Space Beyond (1976)
A New Dawn (2003)

CARD, ORSON SCOTT

Hot Sleep (1979)
Capitol (1979)
A Planet Called Treason (1979, also published as
    Treason)
Songmaster (1980)
Unaccompanied Sonata (1981)
The Worthing Chronicle (1983)
Ender's Game (1985)
Speaker for the Dead (1986)
Ender's War (1986)
Cardography (1987)
Wyrms (1987)
The Abyss (1989)
The Folk of the Fringe (1989)
Maps in a Mirror (1990)
The Worthing Saga (1990)
Xenocide (1991)
The Changed Man (1992)
The Memory of Earth (1992)
Cruel Miracles (1992)
The Call of Earth (1993)
Monkey Sonatas (1993)
Homecoming: Harmony (1994)
Lovelock (1994, with Kathryn H. Kidd)
The Ships of Earth (1994)
Earthborn (1995)

Earthfall (1995)
Flux (1995)
Homecoming: Earth (1995)
Children of the Mind (1996)
Pastwatch (1996)
Ender's Shadow (1999)
Shadow of the Hegemon (2001)
Shadow Puppets (2002)
First Meetings in the Enderverse (2003)

CHALKER, JACK L.

A Jungle of Stars (1976)
Midnight at the Well of Souls (1977)
Quest for the Well of Souls (1978)
Dancers in the Afterglow (1978)
Web of the Chozen (1978)
Exiles at the Well of Souls (1978)
A War of Shadows (1979)
The Return of Nathan Brazil (1980)
Twilight at the Well of Souls (1980)
Lilith: A Snake in the Grass (1981)
Cerberus: A Wolf in the Fold (1982)
The Identity Matrix (1982)
Charon: A Dragon at the Gate (1982)
Medusa: A Tiger by the Tail (1983)
Spirits of Flux and Anchor (1984)
Empires of Flux and Anchor (1984)
The Birth of Flux and Anchor (1985)
The Messiah Choice (1985)
Downtiming the Night Side (1985)
Masters of Flux and Anchor (1985)
Children of Flux and Anchor (1986)
Lords of the Middle Dark (1986)
Dance Band on the Titanic (1986)
Pirates of the Thunder (1987)
Warriors of the Storm (1987)
The Shadow Dancers (1987)
The Labyrinth of Dreams (1987)
Masks of the Martyrs (1988)
The Demons at Rainbow Ridge (1989)
The Maze in the Mirror (1989)
Ninety Trillion Fausts (1991)
The Red Tape War (1991, with Mike Resnick and
    George Alec Effinger)
The Run to Chaos Keep (1991)
Echoes of the Well of Souls (1993)
The Watchers at the Well (1994)
The Cybernetic Walrus (1995)

The March Hare Network (1996)
The Hot Wired Dodo (1997)
Priam's Lens (1999)
The Sea Is Full of Stars (2000)
The Moreau Factor (2000)
Ghost of the Well of Souls (2000)
Melchior's Fire (2001)
Balshazzar's Serpent (2000)
Dancers in the Dark (2002)
Kaspar's Box (2003)

CHANDLER, A. BERTRAM

Bring Back Yesterday (1961)
Rendezvous on a Lost World (1961, also published as *When the Dream Dies*)
The Rim of Space (1962)
Beyond the Galactic Rim (1963)
The Ship from Outside (1963)
The Hamelin Plague (1963)
The Deep Reaches of Space (1964)
Glory Planet (1964)
Into the Alternate Universe (1964)
The Coils of Time (1964)
Empress of Outer Space (1965)
Space Mercenaries (1965)
The Alternate Martians (1965)
Contraband from Otherspace (1967)
Nebula Alert (1967)
The Road to the Rim (1967)
The Rim Gods (1968)
Catch the Star Winds (1969)
Spartan Planet (1969, also published as *False Fatherland*)
Alternate Orbits (1971, also published as *The Commodore at Sea*)
Dark Dimensions (1971)
To Prime the Pump (1971)
The Sea Beasts (1971)
The Gateway to Never (1972)
The Hard Way Up (1972)
The Inheritors (1972)
The Bitter Pill (1974)
The Big Black Mark (1975)
The Broken Cycle (1975)
The Way Back (1976)
Star Courier (1977)
The Far Traveler (1977)
To Keep the Ship (1978)

Matilda's Stepchildren (1979)
Star Loot (1980)
The Anarch Lords (1981)
Up to the Sky in Ships (1982)
Kelly Country (1983)
The Wild Ones (1984)
The Last Amazon (1984)
Frontier of the Dark (1984)
From Sea to Shining Star (1990)

CHARNAS, SUZY MCKEE

Walk to the End of the World (1974)
Motherlines (1978)
The Furies (1994)
The Conqueror's Child (1999)
The Slave and the Free (1999)

CHERRYH, C. J.

Brothers of Earth (1976)
Gate of Ivrel (1976)
Hunter of Worlds (1977)
The Faded Sun: Kesrith (1978)
The Faded Sun: Kutath (1978)
The Faded Sun: Shon'Jir (1978)
Well of Shiuan (1978)
Hestia (1979)
The Book of Morgaine (1979, also published as *The Chronicles of Morgaine*)
Fires of Azeroth (1979)
Serpent's Reach (1980)
Sunfall (1981)
Downbelow Station (1981)
Wave Without a Shore (1981)
Port Eternity (1982)
Merchanter's Luck (1982)
The Pride of Chanur (1982)
Chanur's Venture (1984)
Forty Thousand in Gehenna (1984)
Voyager in Night (1984)
Angel with a Sword (1985)
The Kif Strike Back (1985)
Cuckoo's Egg (1985)
Chanur's Homecoming (1986)
Visible Light (1986)
The Faded Sun Trilogy (1987)
Glass and Amber (1987)
Cyteen (1988)
Exile's Gate (1988)

Rimrunners (1989)
Heavy Time (1991)
Hellburner (1992)
Chanur's Legacy (1992)
Foreigner (1994)
Invader (1995)
Tripoint (1995)
Rider at the Gate (1995)
Lois and Clark (1996)
Cloud's Rider (1996)
Finity's End (1997)
Precursor (1999)
Alternate Realities (2000)
Defender (2001)
Devil to the Belt (2001)
Hammerfall (2001)
Explorer (2002)
At the Edge of Space (2003)
The Collected Short Fiction of C. J. Cherryh (2004)
Forge of Heaven (2004)

CHRISTOPHER, JOHN
The Twenty Second Century (1954)
No Blade of Grass (1957, also published as *The Death of Grass*)
Planet in Peril (1959, also published as *The Year of the Comet*)
The Long Winter (1962, also published as *The World in Winter*)
The Possessors (1964)
Sweeney's Island (1964, also published as *Cloud on Silver*)
The Ragged Edge (1965, also published as *A Wrinkle in the Skin*)
The Little People (1966)
The City of Gold and Lead (1967)
The White Mountains (1967)
The Pool of Fire (1968)
Pendulum (1968)
The Lotus Caves (1969)
The Prince in Waiting (1970)
The Guardians (1970)
Beyond the Burning Lands (1971)
The Sword of the Spirits (1972)
Wild Jack (1974)
Empty World (1977)
The Sword of the Spirits Trilogy (1980)
The Tripods Trilogy (1980)

Fireball (1981)
New Found Land (1983)
Dragon Dance (1986)
When the Tripods Came (1988)
A Dusk of Demons (1993)

CLARKE, ARTHUR C.
Prelude to Space (1949, also published as *Master of Space*, and *The Space Dreamers*)
Sands of Mars (1951)
Islands in the Sky (1952)
Against the Fall of Night (1953)
Childhood's End (1953)
The City and the Stars (1953)
Expedition to Earth (1953)
Earthlight (1955)
Reach for Tomorrow (1956)
Tales from the White Hart (1957)
The Deep Range (1957)
The Other Side of the Sky (1958)
Across the Sea of Stars (1959)
From the Ocean, From the Stars (1961)
A Fall of Moondust (1961)
Tales of Ten Worlds (1963)
Dolphin Island (1963)
An Arthur C. Clarke Omnibus (1965)
Prelude to Mars (1965)
The Nine Billion Names of God (1967)
2001: A Space Odyssey (1968)
An Arthur C. Clarke Second Omnibus (1968)
The Lion of Comarre and Against the Fall of Night (1968)
Of Time and Stars (1972)
The Wind from the Sun (1972)
The Best of Arthur C. Clarke (1973)
Rendezvous with Rama (1973)
Imperial Earth (1975)
Four Great SF Novels (1978)
The Possessed and Other Stories (1978)
The Fountains of Paradise (1979)
2010: Odyssey Two (1982)
The Sentinel (1983)
The Songs of Distant Earth (1986)
2061: Odyssey Three (1988)
Cradle (1988, with Gentry Lee)
Tales from the Planet Earth (1989)
Rama II (1989, with Gentry Lee)
Ghost from the Grand Banks (1990)

More Than One Universe (1991)
The Garden of Rama (1991, with Gentry Lee)
The Hammer of God (1993)
Rama Revealed (1994, with Gentry Lee)
Richter 10 (1996, with Mike McQuay)
3001: The Final Odyssey (1997)
The Trigger (1999, with Michael Kube-McDowell)
The Light of Other Days (2000, with Stephen Baxter)
The Collected Stories of Arthur C. Clarke (2000)
The Space Trilogy (2001)
Time's Eye (2003, with Stephen Baxter)

CLEMENT, HAL

Needle (1950, also published as *From Outer Space*)
Iceworld (1953)
Mission of Gravity (1954)
The Ranger Boys in Space (1956)
Cycle of Fire (1957)
Close to Critical (1964)
Natives of Space (1965)
Ocean on Top (1967)
Space Lash (1969, also published as *Small Changes*)
Star Light (1971)
Through the Eye of a Needle (1978)
The Best of Hal Clement (1979)
The Nitrogen Fix (1980)
Intuit (1987)
Still River (1987)
Fossil (1993)
Half Life (1999)
Trio for Slide Rule & Typewriter (1999)
Variations on a Theme by Sir Isaac Newton (2000)
Music of Many Spheres (2000)
Heavy Planet (2002)
Noise (2003)

COMPTON, D. G.

The Quality of Mercy (1965)
Farewell Earth's Bliss (1966)
The Silent Multitude (1966)
Synthajoy (1968)
The Steel Crocodile (1970, also published as *The Electric Crocodile*)
Chronocules (1970, also published as *Hot Wireless Sets, Aspirin Tablets, the Sandpaper Sides of Used Matches, and Something That Might Have Been Castor Oil*)
The Missionaries (1972)

The Unsleeping Eye (1974, also published as *The Continuous Katherine Mortenhoe* and *Death Watch*)
Ascendancies (1980)
Scudder's Game (1988)
Nomansland (1994)
Justice City (1996)

COOPER, EDMUND

Deadly Image (1958, also published as *The Uncertain Midnight*)
Tomorrow's Gift (1958)
Seed of Light (1959)
Voices in the Dark (1960)
Tomorrow Came (1963)
Transit (1964)
All Fool's Day (1966)
A Far Sunset (1967)
News from Elsewhere (1968)
Five to Twelve (1969)
The Last Continent (1969)
Seahorse in the Sky (1969)
The Square Root of Tomorrow (1970)
Kronk (1971, also published as *Son of Kronk*)
The Overman Culture (1971)
Unborn Tomorrow (1971)
Gender Genocide (1973, also published as *Who Needs Men?*)
Cloud Walker (1973)
The Tenth Planet (1973)
Prisoner of Fire (1974)
Slaves of Heaven (1974)
The Deathworm of Kratos (1974, as Richard Avery)
The Rings of Tantalus (1975, as Richard Avery)
The Venom of Argus (1975, as Richard Avery)
The War Games of Zelos (1975, as Richard Avery)
Merry Christmas Mrs. Minerva (1978)
Jupiter Laughs (1979)
A World of Difference (1980)

COPPEL, ALFRED

Dark December (1960)
The Rebel of Rhada (1968, as Robert Cham Gilman)
The Navigator of Rhada (1969, as Robert Cham Gilman)
The Starkahn of Rhada (1970, as Robert Cham Gilman)
Thirty Four East (1974)

The Dragon (1977)
The Burning Mountain (1982)
The Warlock of Rhada (1985, as Robert Cham Gilman)
Glory (1993)
Eighth Day of the Week (1994)
Glory's War (1995)
Glory's People (1996)

COVER, ARTHUR BYRON
Autumn Angels (1975)
The Sound of Winter (1976)
The Platypus of Doom and Other Nihilists (1976)
An East Wind Coming (1979)
Flash Gordon (1980)
American Revolutionary (1985)
The Rings of Saturn (1985)
Blade of the Guillotine (1986)
Prodigy (1988)
Planetfall (1988)
Stationfall (1989)
Born in Fire (2002)
Ten Years After (2002)

COWPER, RICHARD
Breakthrough (1967)
Phoenix (1967)
Domino (1971)
Clone (1972)
Kuldesak (1972)
Time Out of Mind (1973)
The Twilight of Briareus (1974)
Worlds Apart (1974)
The Custodians and Other Stories (1976)
The Road to Corlay (1978)
Profundis (1979)
Out There Where the Big Ships Go (1980)
The Web of the Magi and Other Stories (1980)
A Dream of Kinship (1981)
A Tapestry of Time (1982)
The Tithonian Factor and Other Stories (1984)

CRICHTON, MICHAEL
The Andromeda Strain (1969)
The Terminal Man (1972)
Westworld (1974)
Congo (1976)
Sphere (1987)

Jurassic Park (1990)
Three Complete Novels (1993)
The Lost World (1995)
Timeline (2000)
Prey (2002)

CROWLEY, JOHN
Beasts (1976)
Engine Summer (1979)
Novelty (1989)
The Great Work of Time (1989)
Three Novels (1994)
Novelties and Souvenirs (2004)

CUMMINGS, RAY
The Girl in the Golden Atom (1923)
The Man Who Mastered Time (1929)
The Sea Girl (1930)
Tarrano the Conqueror (1930)
Brigands of the Moon (1931)
The Shadow Girl (1946)
The Princess of the Atom (1950)
The Man on the Meteor (1952)
Beyond the Vanishing Point (1958)
Wandl the Invader (1961)
Beyond the Stars (1963)
A Brand New World (1964)
The Exile of Time (1964)
Explorers into Infinity (1965)
Tama of the Light Country (1965)
Tama, Princess of Mercury (1966)
The Insect Invasion (1967)
Tales of the Scientific Crime Club (1979)
Into the Fourth Dimension (1981)

CZERNEDA, JULIE E.
A Thousand Words for Stranger (1997)
Beholder's Eye (1998)
Ties of Power (1999)
Changing Vision (2000)
In the Company of Others (2001)
To Trade the Stars (2002)
Hidden in Sight (2003)
Survival (2004)

DANN, JACK
Starkhiker (1967)
Timetipping (1980)

Junction (1981)
The Man Who Melted (1984)
High Steel (1993, with Jack Haldeman)
The Memory Cathedral (1996)
Jubilee (2000)
Visitations (2003)

DAVIDSON, AVRAM
Or All the Seas with Oysters (1962)
Joyleg (1962, with Ward Moore)
Mutiny in Space (1964)
Rogue Dragon (1965)
What Strange Stars and Skies (1965)
Rork! (1965)
Masters of the Maze (1965)
Clash of Star-Kings (1966)
The Enemy of My Enemy (1966)
The Kar-Chee Reign (1966)
Strange Seas and Shores (1971)
The Enquiries of Dr. Esterhazy (1975)
The Redward Edward Papers (1978)
The Best of Avram Davidson (1979)
The Adventures of Dr. Esterhazy (1991)
The Avram Davidson Treasury (1998)
The Other 19th Century (2001)

DE CAMP, L. SPRAGUE
Lest Darkness Fall (1941)
Divide and Rule (1948)
The Wheels of If (1949)
Genus Homo (1950, with P. Schuyler Miller)
Rogue Queen (1951)
Sprague de Camp's New Anthology of Science Fiction (1953)
The Queen of Zamba (1953, also published as *Cosmic Manhunt* and *A Planet Called Krishna*)
The Continent Makers and Other Tales of the Viagens (1953)
Tower of Zanid (1958)
The Glory That Was (1960)
A Gun for Dinosaur (1963)
The Search for Zei (1963, also published as *The Floating Continent*)
Hand of Zei (1963)
Scribblings (1972)
The Virgin and the Wheels (1976)
The Hostage of Zir (1977)
The Great Fetish (1978)

The Best of L. Sprague de Camp (1978)
Footprints in the Sand (1981, with Catherine Crook de Camp)
The Prisoner of Zhamanak (1982)
The Bones of Zora (1984, with Catherine Crook de Camp)
The Stones of Nomuru (1988, with Catherine Crook de Camp)
The Swords of Zinjaban (1991)
The Venom Trees of Sunga (1992)
Rivers of Time (1993)
Aristotle and the Gun and Other Stories (2002)

DEL REY, LESTER
And Some Were Human (1948)
Marooned on Mars (1952)
Attack from Atlantis (1953)
Battle on Mercury (1953)
The Mysterious Planet (1953, as Kenneth Wright)
Step to the Stars (1954)
Preferred Risk (1955, with Frederik Pohl, originally published as by Edson McCann)
Nerves (1956)
Police Your Planet (1956)
Mission to the Moon (1956)
Robots and Changelings (1957)
Moon of Mutiny (1961)
The Eleventh Commandment (1962)
Outpost of Jupiter (1963)
The Sky Is Falling and *Badge of Infamy* (1963)
Mortals and Monsters (1965)
The Runaway Robot (1965, ghostwritten by Paul Fairman)
The Scheme of Things (1966, ghostwritten by Paul Fairman)
Tunnel Through Time (1966, ghostwritten by Paul Fairman)
Rocket from Infinity (1966, ghostwritten by Paul Fairman)
Infinite Worlds of Maybe (1968, ghostwritten by Paul Fairman)
Prisoners of Space (1968, ghostwritten by Paul Fairman)
Siege Perilous (1969, ghostwritten by Paul Fairman, also published as *The Man Without a Planet*)
Pstalemate (1971)
Gods and Golems (1973)
The Early Del Rey (1975)

The Best of Lester Del Rey (1978)
Rocket Jockey (1978)
Weeping May Tarry (1978, with Raymond F. Jones)

DELANY, SAMUEL R.
The Jewels of Aptor (1962)
Captives of the Flame (1963)
The Towers of Toron (1964)
City of a Thousand Suns (1965)
The Ballad of Beta Two (1965)
Babel-17 (1966)
Empire Star (1966)
The Einstein Intersection (1967)
Nova (1968)
The Fall of the Towers (1970)
Driftglass (1971)
Dhalgren (1974)
Triton (1976, also published as *Trouble on Triton*)
Distant Stars (1981)
The Stars in My Pockets Like Grains of Sand (1984)
The Complete Nebula Award Winning Fiction of Samuel R. Delany (1986)
Driftglass/Starshards (1993)
Aye, and Gomorrah (2003)

DENTON, BRADLEY
Wrack and Roll (1986)
Buddy Holly Is Alive and Well on Ganymede (1991)
One Day Closer to Death (1998)

DI FILIPPO, PAUL
The Steampunk Trilogy (1994)
Ribofunk (1996)
Fractal Paisleys (1997)
Lost Pages (1998)
Strange Trades (2001)
Little Doors (2002)
A Mouthful of Tongues (2002)
Babylon Sisters and Other Posthumans (2002)
Fuzzy Dice (2003)

DICK, PHILIP K.
Solar Lottery (1955)
A Handful of Darkness (1955)
The Man Who Japed (1956)
The World Jones Made (1956)
The Cosmic Puppets (1957)
The Variable Man and Other Stories (1957)

Eye in the Sky (1957)
Time Out of Joint (1959)
Dr. Futurity (1960)
Vulcan's Hammer (1960)
The Man in the High Castle (1962)
The Game Players of Titan (1963)
Martian Time-Slip (1964)
Clans of the Alphane Moon (1964)
The Unteleported Man (1964, also published as *Lies, Inc.*)
The Penultimate Truth (1964)
The Simulacra (1964)
The Three Stigmata of Palmer Eldritch (1964)
Dr. Bloodmoney (1965)
The Crack in Space (1966)
Now Wait for Last Year (1966)
The Zap Gun (1967)
The Ganymede Takeover (1967, with Ray Nelson)
Counter Clock World (1967)
Do Androids Dream of Electric Sheep? (1968)
Galactic Pot Healer (1969)
Ubik (1969)
The Preserving Machine (1969)
Our Friends from Frolix 8 (1970)
A Philip K. Dick Omnibus (1970)
A Maze of Death (1970)
We Can Build You (1972)
The Book of Philip K. Dick (1973, also published as *The Turning Wheel and Other Stories*)
Flow My Tears, the Policeman Said (1974)
Deus Irae (1976, with Roger Zelazny)
The Best of Philip K. Dick (1977)
A Scanner Darkly (1977)
The Divine Invasion (1981)
Valis (1981)
The Golden Man (1981)
The Transmigration of Timothy Archer (1982)
Robots, Androids, and Mechanical Oddities (1984)
I Hope I Shall Arrive Soon (1985)
Radio Free Albemuth (1985)
The Father Thing (1987)
The Little Black Box (1987, also published as *We Can Remember It For You Wholesale*)
The Days of Perky Pat (1987, also published as *Minority Report*)
Beyond Lies the Wub (1987, also published as *The Short Happy Life of the Brown Oxford*)
Nick and the Glimmung (1988)

The Collected Stories of Philip K. Dick (1990)
The Second Variety (1991)
The Philip K. Dick Reader (1997)
Three Early Novels (2000)
Selected Stories of Philip K. Dick (2002)
Paycheck and 18 Other Classic Stories (2003)
Five Great Novels (2004)

DICKSON, GORDON R.

Alien from Arcturus (1956, revised as *Arcturus Landing*)
Mankind on the Run (1956, also published as *On the Run*)
Earthman's Burden (1957, with Poul Anderson)
The Genetic General (1960, also published as *Dorsai!*)
Secret Under the Sea (1960)
Time to Teleport (1960)
Delusion World (1961)
Spacial Delivery (1961)
Naked to the Stars (1961)
No Room for Man (1962, also published as *Necromancer*)
The Alien Way (1963)
Secret Under Antarctica (1963)
Secret Under the Caribbean (1964)
Space Winners (1965)
Mission to Universe (1965)
The Space Swimmers (1967)
Planet Run (1967, with Keith Laumer)
Soldier, Ask Not (1967)
None But Man (1969)
Spacepaw (1969)
Wolfling (1969)
Hour of the Horde (1970)
Mutants (1970)
Sleepwalker's World (1971)
Tactics of Mistake (1971)
The Outposter (1972)
The Pritcher Mass (1972)
The Star Road (1973)
Alien Art (1973)
The Last Master (1973, also published as *The R-Master*)
The Book of Gordon R. Dickson (1973, also published as *Danger—Human*)
Ancient, My Enemy (1974)

Gremlins Go Home (1974, with Ben Bova)
Three to Dorsai (1975)
The Lifeship (1975, with Harry Harrison, also published as *Lifeboat*)
Star Prince Charlie (1975, with Poul Anderson)
Time Storm (1977)
The Far Call (1978)
Gordon Dickson's SF Best (1978)
Home from the Shore (1978)
Pro (1978)
Masters of Everon (1979)
The Spirit of Dorsai (1979)
In Iron Years (1980)
Lost Dorsai (1980)
Love Not Human (1981)
Hoka (1983, with Poul Anderson)
The Man from Earth (1983)
Dickson! (1984)
The Final Encyclopedia (1984)
Survival! (1984)
Steel Brother (1985)
Forward! (1985)
Invaders! (1985)
Secrets of the Deep (1985)
The Forever Man (1986)
The Man the World Rejected (1986)
Mindspan (1986)
The Dorsai Companion (1986)
In the Bone (1987)
The Stranger (1987)
Way of the Pilgrim (1987)
Beginnings (1988)
The Chantry Guild (1988)
Guided Tour (1988)
Ends (1988)
Dorsai's Command (1989, with Troy Denning and Cory Glaberson)
Wolf and Iron (1990)
Young Bleys (1991)
Other (1994)
The Magnificent Wilf (1995)
Hoka! Hoka! Hoka! (1998, with Poul Anderson)
Hokas Pokas (2000, with Poul Anderson)
The Right to Arm Bears (2000)
The Sound and the Furry (2001, with Poul Anderson)
Dorsai Spirit (2002)

Hour of the Gremlins (2002)
The Human Edge (2003)

DIETZ, WILLIAM C.
War World (1986, also published as *Galactic Bounty*)
Freehold (1987)
Imperial Bounty (1988)
Prison Planet (1989)
Cluster Command (1989, with David Drake)
Alien Bounty (1990)
McCade's Bounty (1990)
Matrix Man (1990)
Drifter (1991)
Drifter's Run (1992)
Drifter's War (1992)
Mars Prime (1992)
Legion of the Damned (1993)
Bodyguard (1994)
The Final Battle (1995)
Where the Ships Die (1996)
Soldier for the Empire (1997)
Steelheart (1998)
By Blood Alone (1999)
Jedi Knight (1999)
Rebel Agent (1999)
By Force of Arms (2000)
Deathday (2001)
Earthrise (2002)
The Flood (2003)
For More Than Glory (2003)
McCade for Hire (2004)
For Those Who Fell (2004)

DISCH, THOMAS M.
The Genocides (1965)
Mankind Under the Leash (1966, also published as *The Puppies of Terra*)
One Hundred and Two H-Bombs (1966)
Echo around His Bones (1967)
Camp Concentration (1968)
Fun With Your New Head (1968, also published as *Under Compulsion*)
The Prisoner (1969)
White Fang Goes Dingo and Other Funny SF Stories (1971)
334 (1972)
Getting into Death and Other Stories (1973)

The Early Science Fiction Stories of Thomas Disch (1977)
On Wings of Song (1979)
Fundamental Disch (1980)
Triplicity (1980)
The Man Who Had No Idea (1982)

DOYLE, ARTHUR CONAN
The Doings of Raffles Haw (1892)
The Lost World (1912)
The Poison Belt (1913)
The Land of Mist (1926)
The Maracot Deep (1929)
The Professor Challenger Stories (1952)
The Ring of Thoth (1968)
When the World Screamed and Other Stories (1968)
The Best Science Fiction Stories of Sir Arthur Conan Doyle (1989)

DOZOIS, GARDNER
Nightmare Blue (1975, with George Alec Effinger)
The Visible Man (1977)
Strangers (1978)
Slow Dancing Through Time (1990)
Geodesic Dreams (1992)
Strange Days (2001)

DRAKE, DAVID
Hammer's Slammers (1979)
Time Safari (1982, revised as *Tyrannosaur*)
Skyripper (1983)
Cross the Stars (1984)
The Forlorn Hope (1984)
At Any Price (1985)
Birds of Prey (1985)
Active Measures (1985, with Janet Morris)
Killer (1985, with Karl Edward Wagner)
Bridgehead (1986)
Lacey and His Friends (1986)
Ranks of Bronze (1986)
Counting the Cost (1987)
Kill Ratio (1987, with Janet Morris)
Fortress (1987)
An Honorable Defense (1988, with Thomas T. Thomas)
The War Machine (1989, with Roger MacBride Allen)

Rolling Hot (1989)
Cluster Command (1989, with William C. Dietz)
Target (1989, with Janet Morris)
Northworld (1990)
Surface Action (1990)
The Forge (1991, with S. M. Stirling)
The Military Dimension (1991)
Vengeance (1991)
The Warrior (1991)
The Hunter Returns (1991, with Jim Kjelgaard)
The Square Deal (1992)
Starliner (1992)
The Hammer (1992, with S. M. Stirling)
The Jungle (1992)
Justice (1992)
The Anvil (1993, with S. M. Stirling)
The Voyage (1994)
The Steel (1994, with S. M. Stirling)
Igniting the Reaches (1994)
The Sharp End (1994)
The Sword (1995, with S. M. Stirling)
Enemy of My Enemy (1995, with Ben Ohlander)
Arc Riders (1995, with Janet Morris)
Through the Breach (1995)
The Fourth Rome (1996, with Janet Morris)
The Chosen (1996, with S. M. Stirling)
All the Way to the Gallows (1996)
To Bring the Light (1996)
Patriots (1996)
Fireships (1996)
The Tank Lords (1997)
Redliners (1997)
The Butcher's Bill (1998)
With the Lightnings (1998)
Caught in the Crossfire (1998)
An Oblique Approach (1998, with Eric Flint)
In the Heart of Darkness (1998, with Eric Flint)
The Reformer (1999, with S. M. Stirling)
Northworld Trilogy (1999)
Destiny's Shield (1999, with Eric Flint)
Lt. Leary, Commanding (2000)
Fortune's Stroke (2000, with Eric Flint)
The Tides of Victory (2001, with Eric Flint)
Paying the Piper (2002)
Seas of Venus (2002)
The Far Side of the Stars (2003)
Warlord (2003, with S. M. Stirling)

Grimmer Than Hell (2003)
The Reaches (2004)

DU MAURIER, DAPHNE
The House on the Strand (1969)
Rule Britannia (1972)

EFFINGER, GEORGE ALEC
Relatives (1973)
Man the Fugitive (1974)
Mixed Feelings (1974)
Escape to Tomorrow (1975)
Nightmare Blue (1975, with Gardner Dozois)
Those Gentle Voices (1976)
Journey into Terror (1976)
Irrational Numbers (1976)
Dirty Tricks (1978)
Heroics (1979)
Utopia 3 (1980, also published as *Death in Florence*)
The Wolves of Memory (1981)
Idle Pleasures (1983)
The Nick of Time (1985)
The Bird of Time (1986)
When Gravity Fails (1986)
The Old Funny Stuff (1989)
A Fire in the Sun (1990)
Look Away (1990)
The Exile Kiss (1991)
The Red Tape War (1991, with Mike Resnick and
    Jack L. Chalker)
Maureen Birnbaum, Barbarian Swordsperson (1993)
League of Dragons (1997)
Budayeen Nights (2003)

EGAN, GREG
Quarantine (1992)
Axiomatic (1995)
Distress (1995)
Permutation City (1995)
Diaspora (1997)
Luminous (1998)
Teranesia (1999)
Schild's Ladder (2002)

ELGIN, SUZETTE HADEN
The Communipaths (1970)
Furthest (1971)

At the Seventh Level (1972)
Star-Anchored, Star-Angered (1979)
The Communipath Worlds (1980)
Native Tongue (1984)
The Other End of Time (1986)
The Judas Rose (1987)
Earthsong (1994)

ELLISON, HARLAN
The Man with Nine Lives (1960)
A Touch of Infinity (1960)
Ellison Wonderland (1962, also published as *Earthman, Go Home!*)
Paingod (1965)
Doomsman (1967)
From the Land of Fear (1967)
I Have No Mouth and I Must Scream (1967)
Love Ain't Nothing But Sex Misspelled (1968)
The Beast That Shouted Love at the Heart of the World (1969)
Over the Edge (1970)
Alone Against Tomorrow (1971)
Partners in Wonder (1971)
All the Sounds of Fear (1973)
Approaching Oblivion (1974)
The Time of the Eye (1974)
Deathbird Stories (1975)
The Illustrated Ellison (1978)
Strange Wine (1978)
The Fantasies of Harlan Ellison (1979)
All the Lies That Are My Life (1980)
Shatterday (1980)
Stalking the Nightmare (1982)
The Essential Ellison (1987)
Angry Candy (1988)
Dreams with Sharp Teeth (1991)
Mefisto in Onyx (1993)
Mind Fields (1994)
Slippage (1997)
Troublemakers (2001)

ENGDAHL, SYLVIA LOUISE
Journey Between Worlds (1970)
This Star Shall Abide (1972, also published as *Heritage of the Star*)
Enchantress from the Stars (1972)
The Far Side of Evil (1973)

Beyond the Tomorrow Mountains (1973)
The Doors of the Universe (1981)
Children of the Star (2000)

FARMER, PHILIP JOSÉ
The Green Odyssey (1957)
The Alley God (1960)
Flesh (1960)
Strange Relations (1960)
Timestop (1960, also published as *The Day of Timestop* and *A Woman a Day*)
The Lovers (1961)
The Cache from Outer Space (1962, also published as *The Cache*)
The Celestial Blueprint (1962)
Inside Outside (1964)
Tongues of the Moon (1964)
Dare (1965)
The Maker of Universes (1965)
The Gates of Creation (1966)
The Gate of Time (1966, also published as *Two Hawks from Earth*)
Night of Light (1966)
The Image of the Beast (1968)
A Private Cosmos (1968)
Blown (1969)
A Feast Unknown (1969)
Behind the Walls of Terra (1970)
The Mad Goblin (1970, also published as *Keepers of the Secrets*)
Lord of the Trees (1970)
The Stone God Awakens (1970)
Lord Tyger (1970)
Down in the Black Gang (1971)
The Wind Whales of Ishmael (1971)
To Your Scattered Bodies Go (1971)
The Fabulous Riverboat (1971)
Tarzan Alive (1972)
Time's Last Gift (1972)
Traitor to the Living (1973)
The Other Log of Phileas Fogg (1973)
The Book of Philip Jose Farmer (1973)
Doc Savage: His Apocalyptic Life (1973)
The Adventure of the Peerless Peer (1974)
Venus on the Half-Shell (1974, originally as by Kilgore Trout)
Hadon of Ancient Opar (1974)

Flight to Opar (1976)
The Dark Design (1977)
The Lavalite World (1977)
Jesus on Mars (1979)
Dark Is the Sun (1979)
Riverworld and Other Stories (1979)
The Magic Labyrinth (1980)
The Riverworld War (1980)
The Unreasoning Mask (1981)
Father to the Stars (1981)
World of Tiers (1981)
Greatheart Silver (1982)
The Purple Book (1982)
Stations of the Nightmare (1982)
The Gods of Riverworld (1983)
The River of Eternity (1983)
The Grand Adventure (1984)
The Classic Philip Jose Farmer 1952–1964 (1984)
The Classic Philip Jose Farmer 1964–1973 (1984)
Dayworld (1985)
Dayworld Rebel (1987)
The Empire of the Nine (1988)
Dayworld Breakup (1990)
Red Orc's Rage (1991)
Riders of the Purple Wage (1992)
More Than Fire (1995)
World of Tiers II (1997)
The Dark Heart of Time (1999)

FARREN, MICK
The Texts of Festival (1973)
The Quest of the DNA Cowboys (1976)
Synaptic Manhunt (1976)
The Neural Atrocity (1977)
The Feelies (1978)
The Song of Phaid the Gambler (1981, also published in two volumes as *Phaid the Gambler* and *Citizen Phaid*)
Protectorate (1984)
Their Master's War (1987)
Vickers (1988, also published as *Corpse*)
The Long Orbit (1988, also published as *Exit Funtopia*)
The Armageddon Crazy (1989)
The Last Stand of the DNA Cowboys (1989)
Mars—The Red Planet (1990)
Necrom (1991)
Back from Hell (1999)

FEINTUCH, DAVID
Midshipman's Hope (1994)
Challenger's Hope (1995)
Prisoner's Hope (1995)
Fisherman's Hope (1996)
Seafort's Challenge (1996)
Voices of Hope (1996)
Patriarch's Hope (1999)
Children of Hope (2001)

FINNEY, JACK
The Third Level (1948, also published as *The Clock of Time*)
The Body Snatchers (1954, also published as *Invasion of the Body Snatchers*)
I Love Galesburg in the Springtime (1963)
The Woodrow Wilson Dime (1968)
Forgotten News (1983)
About Time (1986)

FISK, NICHOLAS
Space Hostages (1967)
Trillions (1971)
Grinny (1973)
High Way Home (1973)
Little Green Spacemen (1974)
Time Trap (1976)
Wheelie in the Stars (1976)
Antigrav (1978)
Backlash (1978)
Monster Maker (1979)
Extraterrestrial Tales (1980)
Sunburst (1980)
Star Stormers (1980)
A Rag, a Bone, and a Hank of Hair (1980)
Flamers! (1980, also published as *Escape from Splatterbang*)
Catfang (1981)
Robot Revolt (1981)
Sweets from a Stranger (1982)
Evil Eye (1982)
On the Flip Side (1983)
Volcano (1983)
You Remember Me! (1984)
Living Fire and Other SF Stories (1987)
Mindbenders (1987)
The Telly Is Watching You (1989)
A Hole in the Head (1991)
Fantastico (1994)

FLYNN, MICHAEL

In the Country of the Blind (1990)
The Nanotech Chronicles (1991)
Fallen Angels (1991, with Larry Niven and Jerry Pournelle)
Firestar (1996)
The Forest of Time and Other Stories (1997)
Rogue Star (1998)
Lodestar (2000)
Falling Stars (2001)
The Wreck of the River of Stars (2003)

FORSTCHEN, WILLIAM R.

Ice Prophet (1993)
The Flame Upon the Ice (1984)
A Darkness Upon the Ice (1985)
Into the Sea of Stars (1986)
The Alexandrian Ring (1987)
The Assassin Gambit (1988)
Rally Cry (1990)
Union Forever (1991)
Terrible Swift Sword (1992)
Fateful Lightning (1993)
The Napoleon Wager (1993)
End Run (1994, with Christopher Stasheff)
Star Voyager Academy (1994)
Fleet Action (1994)
Heart of the Tiger (1995, with Andrew Keith)
1945 (1995, with Newt Gingrich)
The Gamestar Wars (1995)
Battle Hymn (1997)
Action Stations (1998)
Article 23 (1998)
Never Sound Retreat (1998)
False Colors (1999, with William H. Keith)
A Band of Brothers (1999)
Prometheus (1999)
The Forgotten War (1999)
Men of War (1999)
Down to the Sea (2000)

FORWARD, ROBERT L.

Dragon's Egg (1980)
The Flight of the Dragonfly (1985, revised as Rocheworld)
Starquake (1985)
Rocheworld (1990)
Martian Rainbow (1991)
Timemaster (1992)

Camelot 30K (1993)
Return to Rocheworld (1993, with Julie Forward Fuller)
Marooned on Eden (1993, with Margaret Dodson Forward)
Ocean Under the Ice (1994, with Margaret Dodson Forward)
Indistinguishable from Magic (1995)
Rescued from Paradise (1995, with Julie Forward Fuller)
Saturn Rukh (1997)

FOSTER, ALAN DEAN

The Tar-Aiym Krang (1972)
Bloodhype (1973)
Dark Star (1974)
Icerigger (1974)
Star Trek Logs 1–10 (1974–1978)
Midworld (1975)
End of the Matter (1977)
Orphan Star (1977)
With Friends Like These . . . (1977)
Splinter of the Mind's Eye (1978)
Alien (1979)
The Black Hole (1979)
Mission to Moulokin (1979)
Cachalot (1980)
The Thing (1981)
Outland (1981)
Flinx of the Commonwealth (1982)
Nor Crystal Tears (1982)
For Love of Mother-Not (1983)
The Man Who Used the Universe (1983)
The Last Starfighter (1984)
Slipt (1984)
The I Inside (1984)
Voyage to the City of the Dead (1984)
Who Needs Enemies? (1984)
Starman (1984)
Sentenced to Prism (1985)
Aliens (1986)
The Deluge Drivers (1987)
Glory Lane (1987)
Alien Nation (1988)
Flinx in Flux (1988)
Quozl (1989)
To the Vanishing Point (1989)
Cyber Way (1990)
The Metrognome and Other Stories (1990)

A Call to Arms (1991)
Cat-A-Lyst (1991)
Codgerspace (1992)
False Mirror (1992)
Alien3 (1992)
The Spoils of War (1993)
Greenthieves (1994)
Mid-Flinx (1995)
Montezuma Strip (1995)
The Dig (1995)
Design for Great-Day (1995, with Eric Frank Russell)
Life Form (1995)
The Howling Stones (1997)
Jed the Dead (1997)
Paralellities (1998)
Phylogenesis (1999)
Dirge (2000)
Interlopers (2001)
Reunion (2001)
The Approaching Storm (2002)
The Mocking Program (2002)
Impossible Places (2002)
Diuturnity's Dawn (2002)
Drowning World (2003)
Flinx's Folly (2003)
Lost and Found (2004)

FRANKOWSKI, LEO
The Cross-Time Engineer (1986)
Copernick's Rebellion (1987)
The Flying Warlord (1989)
The High-Tech Knight (1989)
The Radiant Warrior (1989)
Lord Conrad's Lady (1990)
A Boy and His Tank (1999)
Fata Morgana (1999)
Conrad's Quest for Rubber (1999)
Conrad's Time Machine (2002)
The War with Earth (2003, with Dave Grossman)
Kren of the Mitchegai (2004, with Dave Grossman)
The Two-Space War (2004, with Dave Grossman)

GALOUYE, DANIEL F.
Dark Universe (1961)
Lords of the Psychon (1963)
Simulacron-3 (1964, also published as Counterfeit World)

The Last Leap and Other Stories of the Super-Mind (1964)
Project Barrier (1968)
A Scourge of Screamers (1968, also published as The Lost Perception)
The Infinite Man (1973)

GERROLD, DAVID
The Flying Sorcerers (1971, with Larry Niven)
When Harlie Was One (1972)
The Man Who Folded Himself (1972)
Space Skimmer (1972)
With a Finger in My I (1972)
Yesterday's Children (1972, revised as Starhunt)
Battle for the Planet of the Apes (1973)
Moonstar Odyssey (1977)
Deathbeast (1978)
The Galactic Whirlpool (1980)
A Matter for Men (1983)
Enemy Mine (1985, with Barry Longyear)
A Day for Damnation (1985)
Chess with a Dragon (1987)
Encounter at Farpoint (1987)
A Rage for Revenge (1989)
Voyage of the Star Wolf (1990)
A Season for Slaughter (1993)
Under the Eye of God (1993)
A Covenant of Justice (1994)
The Middle of Nowhere (1995)
Jumping Off the Planet (2000)
Bouncing Off the Moon (2001)
Leaping to the Stars (2002)
Blood and Fire (2003)

GESTON, MARK
Lords of the Starship (1967)
Out of the Mouth of the Dragon (1969)
The Day Star (1972)
The Siege of Wonder (1976)
Mirror to the Sky (1992)

GIBSON, WILLIAM
Neuromancer (1984)
Burning Chrome (1986)
Count Zero (1986)
Mona Lisa Overdrive (1988)
Virtual Light (1993)

Idoru (1996)
All Tomorrow's Parties (1999)
Pattern Recognition (2004)

GOLDSTEIN, LISA
A Mask for the General (1987)
Daily Voices (1989)

GORDON, REX
Utopia 239 (1955)
First on Mars (1956, also published as *No Man Friday*)
First to the Stars (1959, also published as *The Worlds of Eclos*)
First Through Time (1962, also published as *The Time Factor*)
Utopia Minus X (1966, also published as *The Paw of God*)
The Yellow Fraction (1969)

GOULART, RON
The Sword Swallower (1968)
After Things Fell Apart (1970)
The Fire-Eater (1970)
Clockwork's Pirates (1971)
What's Become of Screwloose? (1971)
Gadget Man (1971)
Death Cell (1971)
Broke Down Engine and Other Troubles with Machines (1971)
Hawkshaw (1972)
Wildsmith (1972)
The Chameleon Corps and Other Shape Changers (1972)
Plunder (1972)
Shaggy Planet (1973)
A Talent for the Invisible (1973)
Tin Angel (1973)
The Lion Men of Mongo (1974, as Con Steffanson)
The Plague of Sound (1974, as Con Steffanson)
Flux (1974)
Odd Job #101 and Other Future Crimes and Intrigues (1974)
The Space Trap (1974, as Con Steffanson)
Spacehawk Inc. (1974)
When the Waker Sleeps (1975)
Bloodstalk (1975)

The Hellhound Project (1975)
On Alien Wings (1975)
Nutzenbolts and More Trouble with Machines (1975)
A Whiff of Madness (1976)
Blood Wedding (1976)
The Enormous Hourglass (1976)
Quest of the Gypsy (1976)
Deathgame (1976)
Snakegod (1976)
Challengers of the Unknown (1977)
The Panchronicon Plot (1977)
Nemo (1977)
Eye of the Vulture (1977)
The Emperor of the Last Days (1977)
Deadwalk (1977)
Crackpot (1977)
The Island of Dr. Moreau (1977, as Joseph Silva)
Flux and the Tin Angel (1978)
Calling Dr. Patchwork (1978)
The Wicked Cyborg (1978)
Capricorn One (1978)
Cowboy Heaven (1979)
Hello, Lemuria, Hello (1979)
Dr. Scofflaw (1979)
Holocaust for Hire (1979, as Joseph Silva)
Empire 99 (1980)
Skyrocket Steele (1980)
Hail Hibbler (1980)
The Robot in the Closet (1981)
The Cyborg King (1981)
Brinkman (1981)
Upside Downside (1982)
Big Bang (1982)
Greetings from Earth (1983, with Glen A. Larson)
The Long Patrol (1983, with Glen A. Larson)
Hellquad (1984)
Experiment in Terra (1984, with Glen A. Larson)
Suicide Inc. (1985)
Brainz Inc. (1985)
Galaxy Jane (1986)
Daredevils, Ltd. (1987)
Starpirate's Brain (1987)
Everybody Comes to Cosmo's (1988)
Skyrocket Steele Conquers the Universe and Other Media Tales (1990)

GRIFFITH, GEORGE

The Angel of the Revolution (1893)
Olga Romanoff (1894)
The Outlaws of the Air (1895)
The Great Pirate Syndicate (1898)
Gambles with Destiny (1899)
A Honeymoon in Space (1901)
A Woman Against the World (1903)
World Masters (1903)
The Lake of Gold (1903)
A Criminal Croesus (1904)
The Great Weather Syndicate (1906)
The World Peril of 1910 (1907)
The Lord of Labour (1911)
The Raid of Le Vengeur and Other Stories (1974)

GUNN, JAMES

Star Bridge (1955, with Jack Williamson)
This Fortress World (1957)
Station in Space (1958)
The Joy Makers (1961)
The Immortals (1962)
Future Imperfect (1964)
The Immortal (1970)
Breaking Point (1972)
The Burning (1972)
The Listeners (1972)
Some Dreams Are Nightmares (1975)
The End of the Dreams (1975)
Kampus (1977)
The Mind Master (1981, also published as *The Dreamers*)
Crisis! (1986)
The Joy Machine (1996)
Human Voices (2002)

HAIBLUM, ISIDORE

The Return (1970)
The Tsaddik of the Seven Wonders (1971)
Transfer to Yesterday (1973)
The Wilk Are Among Us (1975)
Interworld (1977)
Nightmare Express (1979)
Outerworld (1979)
The Hand of Ganz (1984)
The Identity Plunderers (1984)
The Mutants Are Coming (1984)
Out of Sync (1990)

Specterworld (1991)
Crystalworld (1992)

HALDEMAN, JOE

The Forever War (1974)
Attar's Revenge (1975, as Robert Graham)
War of Nerves (1975, as Robert Graham)
Mindbridge (1976)
All My Sins Remembered (1977)
Planet of Judgment (1977)
Infinite Dreams (1978)
World Without End (1979)
Worlds (1981)
Worlds Apart (1983)
There Is No Darkness (1985, with Jack Haldeman)
Dealing in Futures (1985)
Tools of the Trade (1987)
Buying Time (1989, also published as *The Long Habit of Living*)
The Hemingway Hoax (1990)
Worlds Enough and Time (1992)
Vietnam and Other Alien Worlds (1993)
None So Blind (1996)
Forever Peace (1997)
Forever Free (1999)
The Coming (2000)
Camouflage (2004)

HAMILTON, EDMOND

The Horror on the Asteroid and Other Tales of Planetary Horror (1936)
The Star Kings (1949)
Tharkol, Lord of the Unknown (1950)
City at World's End (1951)
The Star of Life (1959)
The Sun Smasher (1959)
The Haunted Stars (1960)
Battle for the Stars (1961)
Outside the Universe (1964)
The Valley of Creation (1964)
Crashing Suns (1965)
Fugitive from the Stars (1965)
Doomstar (1966)
Calling Captain Future (1967)
The Weapon from Beyond (1967)
Galaxy Mission (1967)
Captain Future and the Space Emperor (1967)
Captain Future's Challenge (1967)

Quest Beyond the Stars (1967)
Planets in Peril (1967)
Outlaws of the Moon (1967)
Outlaw World (1967)
World of the Starwolves (1968)
The Closed Worlds (1968)
The Magician of Mars (1968)
The Best of Edmond Hamilton (1977)
Starwolf (1982)
Chronicles of the Star Kings (1986)

HAMILTON, PETER
Mindstar Rising (1993)
The Quantum Murder (1994)
The Nano Flower (1995)
The Reality Dysfunction (1996, also published in two
    volumes as *Emergence* and *Expansion*)
The Neutronium Alchemist (1997, also published in
    two volumes as *Conflict* and *Consolidation*)
Lightstorm (1998)
A Second Chance at Eden (1998)
The Naked God (1999, also published in two vol-
    umes as *Flight* and *Faith*)
Watching Trees Grow (2000)
Fallen Dragon (2002)
Pandora's Star (2004)

HAND, ELIZABETH
Winterlong (1990)
Aestival Tide (1992)
Icarus Descending (1993)
Twelve Monkeys (1995)
Waking the Moon (1995)
The Frenchman (1997)
Glimmering (1997)
Last Summer at Mars Hill (1998)
Bibliomancy (2003)

HARNESS, CHARLES L.
The Paradox Men (1955)
The Rose (1966)
The Ring of Ritornel (1968)
Wolfhead (1978)
The Catalyst (1980)
Firebird (1981)
The Venetian Court (1982)
Redworld (1986)
Krono (1988)

Lurid Dreams (1990)
Lunar Justice (1991)
An Ornament to His Profession (1998)
Rings (1999)

HARRISON, HARRY
Deathworld (1960)
The Stainless Steel Rat (1961)
Planet of the Damned (1962)
War With the Robots (1962)
Deathworld II (1964)
Bill, the Galactic Hero (1965)
Two Tales and Eight Tomorrows (1965)
Plague from Space (1965, also published as *The
    Jupiter Plague*)
Make Room! Make Room! (1966)
The Technicolor Time Machine (1967)
Deathworld III (1968)
The Man from P.I.G. (1968)
Captive Universe (1969)
The Daleth Effect (1970)
Spaceship Medic (1970)
Prime Number (1970)
The Stainless Steel Rat's Revenge (1970)
One Step from Earth (1970)
The Stainless Steel Rat Saves the World (1972)
Stonehenge: Where Atlantis Died (1972, with Leon
    Stover)
A Transatlantic Tunnel, Hurrah! (1972, also published
    as *Tunnel Through the Deeps*)
Star Smashers of the Galaxy Rangers (1973)
The Lifeship (1975, with Gordon R. Dickson, also
    published as *Lifeboat*)
The Best of Harry Harrison (1976)
Skyfall (1976)
The Deathworld Trilogy (1978)
The Stainless Steel Rat Wants You! (1978)
The Adventures of the Stainless Steel Rat (1978)
Homeworld (1980)
Planet of No Return (1981)
To the Stars (1981)
Starworld (1981)
Wheelworld (1981)
The Stainless Steel Rat for President (1982)
Invasion: Earth (1982)
A Rebel in Time (1983)
West of Eden (1984)
A Stainless Steel Rat Is Born (1985)

Winter in Eden (1986)

The Stainless Steel Rat Gets Drafted (1987)

Return to Eden (1988)

The Planet of the Robot Slaves (1989)

Bill, the Galactic Hero on the Planet of Bottled Brains (1990, with Robert Sheckley)

Bill, the Galactic Hero on the Planet of Zombie Vampires (1991, with Jack Haldeman)

Bill, the Galactic Hero on the Planet of Ten Thousand Bars (1991, with David Bischoff)

Bill, the Galactic Hero on the Planet of Tasteless Pleasure (1991, with David Bischoff)

Bill, the Galactic Hero: The Final Incoherent Adventure (1992, with David Harris)

The Turing Option (1992, with Marvin Minsky)

Stainless Steel Visions (1993)

The Stainless Steel Rat Sings the Blues (1994)

Galactic Dreams (1994)

The Stainless Steel Rat Goes to Hell (1996)

The Stainless Steel Rat Goes to the Circus (1998, also published as *The Stainless Steel Rat Joins the Circus*)

Stars and Stripes Forever (1998)

Stars and Stripes in Peril (2000)

Stars and Stripes Triumphant (2002)

Fifty in Fifty (2001)

A Stainless Steel Trio (2002)

HEINLEIN, ROBERT A.

Rocket Ship Galileo (1947)

Beyond This Horizon (1948)

Space Cadet (1948)

Red Planet (1949)

Sixth Column (1949, also published as *The Day After Tomorrow*)

Farmer in the Sky (1950)

The Man Who Sold the Moon (1950)

Waldo and Magic Inc. (1950, also published as *Waldo: Genius in Orbit*)

The Puppet Masters (1951)

The Green Hills of Earth (1951)

Between Planets (1951)

The Rolling Stones (1952, also published as *Space Family Stone*)

Revolt in 2100 (1953)

Starman Jones (1953)

Assignment in Eternity (1953, also published as *Lost Legacy*)

The Star Beast (1954)

Tunnel in the Sky (1955)

The Door into Summer (1956)

Time for the Stars (1956)

Double Star (1957)

Citizen of the Galaxy (1957)

Have Spacesuit Will Travel (1958)

Methuselah's Children (1958)

The Menace from Earth (1959)

Starship Troopers (1959)

Six by H (1959, also published as *The Unpleasant Profession of Jonathan Hoag*)

Stranger in a Strange Land (1961)

Orphans of the Sky (1963)

Podkayne of Mars (1963)

Farnham's Freehold (1964)

Three by Heinlein (1965)

The Worlds of Robert A. Heinlein (1966)

The Moon Is a Harsh Mistress (1966)

The Past Through Tomorrow (1967)

I Will Fear No Evil (1970)

The Best of Robert Heinlein (1973)

Time Enough for Love (1973)

The Best of Robert Heinlein 1939–1942 (1977)

The Best of Robert Heinlein 1947–1959 (1977)

Destination Moon (1979)

Expanded Universe (1980)

The Number of the Beast (1980)

A Heinlein Trio (1980)

Friday (1982)

Job: A Comedy of Justice (1984)

The Cat Who Walks Through Walls (1985)

To Sail Beyond the Sunset (1987)

Requiem (1992)

For Us, the Living (2004)

HERBERT, BRIAN

Sidney's Comet (1983)

Sudanna, Sudanna (1985)

The Garbage Chronicles (1985)

Man of Two Worlds (1986, with Frank Herbert)

Prisoners of Arionn (1987)

The Race for God (1990)

Memorymakers (1991, with Marie Landis)

House Atreides (1999, with Kevin J. Anderson)

House Harkonnen (2000, with Kevin J. Anderson)

House Corrino (2001, with Kevin J. Anderson)

The Butlerian Jihad (2002, with Kevin J. Anderson)

The Machine Crusade (2003, with Kevin J. Anderson)
The Battle of Corrin (2004, with Kevin J. Anderson)

HERBERT, FRANK
The Dragon in the Sea (1956, also published as *Under Pressure* and *21st Century Sub*)
Dune (1965)
Destination: Void (1966)
The Green Brain (1966)
The Eyes of Heisenberg (1966)
The Heaven Makers (1968)
The Santaroga Barrier (1968)
Whipping Star (1969)
Dune Messiah (1969)
The Worlds of Frank Herbert (1970)
The Godmakers (1972)
Hellstrom's Hive (1973)
The Book of Frank Herbert (1973)
The Best of Frank Herbert (1975)
Children of Dune (1976)
The Best of Frank Herbert 1952–1964 (1976)
The Best of Frank Herbert 1965–1970 (1976)
The Dosadi Experiment (1977)
The Great Dune Trilogy (1979)
The Jesus Incident (1979, with Bill Ransom)
The Priests of Psi (1980)
Direct Descent (1980)
God Emperor of Dune (1981)
The White Plague (1982)
The Lazarus Effect (1983, with Bill Ransom)
Heretics of Dune (1984)
Chapterhouse: Dune (1985)
Eye (1985)
Man of Two Worlds (1986, with Brian Herbert)
The Second Great Dune Trilogy (1987)
The Ascension Factor (1988, with Bill Ransom)

HERSEY, JAMES
The Child Buyer (1960)
White Lotus (1965)
My Petition for More Space (1974)

HOGAN, JAMES P.
Inherit the Stars (1977)
The Genesis Machine (1978)
The Gentle Giants of Ganymede (1978)
The Two Faces of Tomorrow (1979)

Thrice Upon a Time (1980)
Giants' Star (1981)
Voyage from Yesteryear (1982)
Code of the Lifemaker (1983)
The Proteus Operation (1985)
Endgame Enigma (1987)
Minds, Machines, and Evolution (1988)
The Mirror Maze (1989)
Entoverse (1991)
The Giants Novels (1991, also published as *The Minervan Experiment*)
The Infinity Gambit (1991)
The Multiplex Man (1992)
Out of Time (1993)
The Immortality Option (1995)
Realtime Interrupt (1995)
Paths to Otherwhere (1996)
Bug Park (1997)
Star Child (1998)
Cradle of Saturn (1999)
Outward Bound (1999)
Rockets, Redheads, and Revolution (1999)
The Legend That Was Earth (2000)
Martian Knightlife (2001)
The Anguished Dawn (2003)

HOYLE, FRED
The Black Cloud (1957)
Ossian's Ride (1959)
A for Andromeda (1962, with John Elliot)
Fifth Planet (1963, with Geoffrey Hoyle)
Andromeda Breakthrough (1964, with John Elliot)
October the First Is Too Late (1966)
Element 79 (1967)
Rockets in Ursa Major (1969, with Geoffrey Hoyle)
Seven Steps to the Sun (1970, with Geoffrey Hoyle)
The Molecule Men (1971, with Geoffrey Hoyle)
The Inferno (1973, with Geoffrey Hoyle)
Into Deepest Space (1974, with Geoffrey Hoyle)
The Incandescent Ones (1977, with Geoffrey Hoyle)
The Westminster Disaster (1978, with Geoffrey Hoyle)
The Energy Pirate (1982, with Geoffrey Hoyle)
The Planet of Death (1982, with Geoffrey Hoyle)
The Frozen Planet of Azuron (1982, with Geoffrey Hoyle)

The Giants of Universal Park (1982, with Geoffrey Hoyle)
Comet Halley (1985)

HUBBARD, L. RON
Final Blackout (1948)
Kingslayer (1949, also published as *Seven Steps to the Arbiter*)
From Death to the Stars (1952)
Return to Tomorrow (1954)
Ole Doc Methuselah (1970)
Battlefield Earth (1982)
The Invaders Plan (1985)
Fortune of Fear (1986)
Black Genesis (1986)
An Alien Affair (1986)
The Enemy Within (1986)
Disaster (1987)
The Doomed Planet (1987)
Villainy Victorious (1987)
Voyage of Vengeance (1987)
Death Quest (1987)

ING, DEAN
Soft Targets (1979)
Anasazi (1980)
Systemic Shock (1981)
High Tension (1982)
Pulling Through (1983)
Single Combat (1983)
Eternity (1984, with Mack Reynolds)
The Other Time (1984, with Mack Reynolds)
Home Sweet Home 2010 AD (1984, with Mack Reynolds)
Trojan Orbit (1985, with Mack Reynolds)
Wild Country (1985)
Deathwish World (1986, with Mack Reynolds)
Firefight 2000 (1987)
The Big Lifters (1988)
The Ransom of Black Stealth One (1989)
Cathouse (1990)
Butcher Bird (1993)
Loose Cannon (2000)
The Rackham Files (2004)

JAKES, JOHN
When the Star Kings Die (1967)
Asylum World (1969)

The Hybrid (1969)
Tonight We Steal the Stars (1969)
The Planet Wizard (1969)
Secrets of Stardeep (1969)
Six-Gun Planet (1970)
Mask of Chaos (1970)
Master of the Dark Gate (1970)
Monte Cristo #99 (1970)
Black in Time (1970)
Witch of the Dark Gate (1972)
Time Gate (1972)
On Wheels (1973)
Conquest of the Planet of the Apes (1974)
The Best of John Jakes (1977)

JETER, K. W.
Seeklight (1975)
The Dreamfields (1976)
Morlock Night (1979)
Dr. Adder (1984)
The Glass Hammer (1985)
Death Arms (1987)
Farewell Horizontal (1989)
Madlands (1991)
Wolf Flow (1992)
Bloodletter (1993)
Dark Horizon (1993)
Cross of Blood (1995)
The Edge of Human (1995)
Warped (1995)
Replicant Night (1996)
The Mandalorian Armor (1998)
Slave Ship (1998)
Noir (1998)
Hard Merchandise (1999)
Eye and Talon (2000)

JONES, D. F.
Colossus (1966, also published as *The Forbin Project*)
Implosion (1967)
Denver Is Missing (1971, also published as *Don't Pick the Flowers*)
The Fall of Colossus (1974)
The Floating Zombie (1975)
Colossus and the Crab (1977)
Earth Has Been Found (1979, also published as *Xeno*)
Bound in Time (1981)

JONES, RAYMOND F.
The Alien (1951)
The Toymaker (1951)
Man of Two Worlds (1951, also published as *Renaissance*)
This Island Earth (1952)
Son of the Stars (1952)
Planet of Light (1953)
The Year When Stardust Fell (1958)
The Deviates (1959, also published as *The Secret People*)
The Cybernetic Brains (1962)
The Non-Statistical Man (1964)
Syn (1969)
Moonbase One (1972)
The King of Eolim (1975)
Renegades of Time (1975)
The River and the Dream (1977)
Weeping May Tarry (1978, with Lester Del Rey)

KELLY, JAMES PATRICK
Planet of Whispers (1984)
Freedom Beach (1985, with John Kessel)
Look into the Sun (1989)
Heroines (1990)
Wildlife (1994)
Think Like a Dinosaur (1997)
Strange But Not a Stranger (2002)

KESSEL, JOHN
Freedom Beach (1985, with James Patrick Kelly)
Good News from Outer Space (1989)
Meeting in Infinity (1992)
The Pure Product (1997)
Corrupting Dr. Nice (1997)

KING, STEPHEN
Carrie (1974)
The Stand (1978)
The Dead Zone (1979)
Firestarter (1980)
It (1986)
The Tommyknockers (1987)
Desperation (1996)
Dreamcatcher (2001)
From a Buick 8 (2002)

KINGSBURY, DONALD
Courtship Rite (1983, also published as *Geta*)
The Moon Goddess and the Son (1986)
Psychohistorical Crisis (2001)

KLINE, OTIS ADELBERT
Planet of Peril (1929)
Maza of the Moon (1930)
Prince of Peril (1930)
Call of the Savage (1937, also published as *Jan of the Jungle*)
The Port of Peril (1949)
The Swordsman of Mars (1960)
The Outlaws of Mars (1961)
Tam, Son of the Tiger (1962)

KNIGHT, DAMON
Analogue Men (1958, also published as *Hell's Pavement*)
A for Anything (1959, also published as *The People Maker*)
Masters of Evolution (1959)
Far Out (1961)
The Sun Saboteurs (1961)
Beyond the Barrier (1964)
In Deep (1964)
Off Center (1965)
The Rithian Terror (1965)
Mind Switch (1965, also published as *The Other Foot*)
Turning On (1966)
Three Novels (1969, also published as *Natural State and Other Novels*)
World Without Children and The Earth Quarter (1970)
The Best of Damon Knight (1976)
Rule Golden and Other Stories (1979)
The Man in the Tree (1984)
CV (1985)
Late Knight Edition (1985)
The Observors (1988)
God's Nose (1991)
One Side Laughing (1991)
A Reasonable World (1991)
Why Do Birds (1992)
Humpty Dumpty: An Oval (1996)

KOONTZ, DEAN R.
Star Quest (1968)
The Fall of the Dream Machine (1969)
Fear That Man (1969)
Anti-Man (1970)
Beastchild (1970)
Dark of the Woods (1970)
The Dark Symphony (1970)
Soft Come the Dragons (1970)
Hell's Gate (1970)
A Darkness in My Soul (1971)
The Flesh in the Furnace (1972)
Warlock (1972)
Time Thieves (1972)
Starblood (1972)
Demon Seed (1973)
A Werewolf Among Us (1973)
Nightmare Journey (1975)
Night Chills (1976)
The Key to Midnight (1979, as by Leigh Nichols)
Phantoms (1983)
Twilight Eyes (1985)
Strangers (1986)
Watchers (1987)
Shadoweyes (1987, as by Leigh Nichols)
Lightning (1988)
Midnight (1989)
The Bad Place (1990)
Cold Fire (1991)
Dragon Tears (1993)
Winter Moon (1994, originally published in shorter form as *Invasion* by Aaron Wolfe)
Icebound (1995, originally published as *Prison of Ice* as by David Axton)
Fear Nothing (1998)
Seize the Night (1999)
One Door Away from Heaven (2001)

KORNBLUTH, CYRIL M.
Takeoff (1952)
Outpost Mars (1952, with Judith Merrill as by Cyril Judd, also published as *Sin in Space*)
The Space Merchants (1953, with Frederik Pohl)
The Syndic (1953)
The Explorers (1954)
Search the Sky (1954, with Frederik Pohl)
The Mindworm and Other Stories (1955)
Gladiator-At-Law (1955, with Frederik Pohl)

Not This August (1955, also published as *Christmas Eve*)
Gunner Cade (1957, with Judith Merrill as by Cyril Judd)
A Mile Beyond the Moon (1958)
The Marching Morons (1959)
Wolfbane (1959, with Frederik Pohl)
The Wonder Effect (1962, with Frederik Pohl)
Best Science Fiction Stories (1968)
Thirteen O'Clock and Other Zero Hours (1970)
The Best of C. M. Kornbluth (1976)
Critical Mass (1977, with Frederik Pohl)
Before the Universe (1980, with Frederik Pohl)
Venus Inc. (1985, with Frederik Pohl)
Our Best (1987, with Frederik Pohl)
His Share of Glory (1997)

KRESS, NANCY
Trinity and Other Stories (1988)
An Alien Light (1988)
Brainrose (1990)
The Aliens of Earth (1993)
Beggars in Spain (1993)
Beggars and Choosers (1994)
Beggars Ride (1996)
Beaker's Dozen (1998)
Maximum Light (1998)
Oaths and Miracles (1998)
Stinger (1998)
Probability Moon (2000)
Probability Sun (2001)
Probability Space (2002)
Crossfire (2003)
Nothing Human (2003)
Crucible (2004)

KUBE-McDOWELL, MICHAEL
Emprise (1985)
Enigma (1986)
Empery (1987)
Odyssey (1987)
Thieves of Light (1987, as Michael Hudson)
Alternities (1988)
The Quiet Pools (1990)
Exile (1992)
Before the Storm (1996)
Shield of Lies (1996)
Tyrant's Test (1996)

The Trigger (1999, with Arthur C. Clarke)
Vectors (2002)

KURLAND, MICHAEL
Ten Years to Doomsday (1964, with Chester Anderson)
The Unicorn Girl (1969)
Transmission Error (1970)
Pluribus (1975)
The Whenabouts of Burr (1975)
Tomorrow Knight (1976)
The Princes of Earth (1978)
The Infernal Device (1979)
Psi Hunt (1980)
The Last President (1980, with S. W. Barton)
Star Griffin (1987)
Perchance (1989)
Images Conceits & Lollygags (2003)

KUTTNER, HENRY
A Gnome There Was (1950, as Lewis Padgett)
Fury (1950, also published as *Destination Infinity*)
Tomorrow and Tomorrow and the Fairy Chessmen (1951, as Lewis Padgett)
The Chessboard Planet (1951, also published as *The Far Reality* as by Lewis Padgett)
Robots Have No Tails (1952, also published as *The Proud Robot*)
Ahead of Time (1953)
Mutant (1953, originally as by Lewis Padgett)
Well of the Worlds (1953, originally as by Lewis Padgett)
Line to Tomorrow (1954, as Lewis Padgett)
No Boundaries (1955, with C. L. Moore)
Bypass to Otherness (1961)
Return to Otherness (1962)
The Time Axis (1964)
Valley of the Flame (1964)
Earth's Last Citadel (1964, with C. L. Moore)
The Best of Kuttner 1 (1965)
The Best of Kuttner 2 (1966)
The Creature from Beyond Infinity (1968)
The Best of Henry Kuttner (1975)
Clash by Night and Other Stories (1980)
Chessboard Planet and Other Stories (1983)
The Startling Worlds of Henry Kuttner (1987)
Kuttner Times Three (1988)
Secret of the Earth Star and Other Stories (1991)
The Book of Iod (1995)

LAFFERTY, R. A.
Past Master (1968)
Space Chantey (1968)
The Reefs of Earth (1968)
Fourth Mansions (1969)
Nine Hundred Grandmothers (1970)
Arrive at Easterwine (1971)
Strange Doings (1972)
Does Anyone Have Anything Further to Add? (1974)
Not to Mention Camels (1976)
Apocalypses (1977)
The Early Lafferty (1981)
Aurelia (1982)
Through Elegant Eyes (1983)
Annals of Klepsis (1983)
Ringing Changes (1984)
The Golden Gate and Other Stories (1985)
The Back Door of History (1988)
Promontory Goats (1988)
The Elliptical Grave (1989)
The Early Lafferty II (1990)
Episodes of the Argo (1990)
Lafferty in Orbit (1991)
Iron Tears (1992)
Serpent's Egg (2003)

LAUMER, KEITH
Worlds of the Imperium (1962)
A Trace of Memory (1963)
Envoy to New Worlds (1963)
The Great Time Machine Hoax (1964)
A Plague of Demons (1965)
The Other Side of Time (1965)
Retief's War (1965)
Catastrophe Planet (1966, also published as *The Breaking Earth*)
Galactic Diplomat (1966)
The Monitors (1966)
The Time Bender (1966)
Earthblood (1966, with Rosel George Brown)
Galactic Odyssey (1967)
Nine by Laumer (1967)
The Invaders (1967)
Planet Run (1967, with Gordon R. Dickson)
Enemies from Beyond (1967)
Assignment in Nowhere (1968)
Retief and the Warlords (1968)
Greylorn (1968, also published as *The Other Sky*)

It's a Mad, Mad, Mad Galaxy (1968)
The Drowned Queen (1968)
The Day Before Forever and Thunderhead (1968)
The Long Twilight (1969)
Retief: Ambassador to Space (1969)
The House in November (1970)
Time Trap (1970)
The World Shuffler (1970)
Once There Was a Giant (1971)
Retief's Ransom (1971)
The Star Treasure (1971)
Dinosaur Beach (1971)
The Glory Game (1972)
Timetracks (1972)
The Shape Changer (1972)
Night of Delusions (1972, also published as Knight of Delusions)
The Infinite Cage (1972)
The Big Show (1972)
The House in November and The Other Sky (1973)
The Undefeated (1974)
Retief: Emissary to the Stars (1975)
The Best of Keith Laumer (1976)
Bolo (1977)
Retief at Large (1978)
The Ultimax Man (1978)
Retief Unbound (1979)
Beyond the Imperium (1981)
Star Colony (1981)
Retief: Diplomat at Arms (1982)
Chrestomancy (1984)
The Galaxy Builder (1984)
The Return of Retief (1984)
Retief to the Rescue (1984)
End As a Hero (1985)
Retief and the Pangalactic Pageant of Pulchritude (1986)
Retief in the Ruins (1986)
Rogue Bolo (1986)
Reward for Retief (1989)
The Stars Must Wait (1990)
The Compleat Bolo (1990)
Zone Yellow (1990)
Judson's Eden (1991)
Alien Minds (1991)
Back to the Time Trap (1992)
Retief and the Rascals (1993)
The Lighter Side (2002)
Odyssey (2002)

Future Imperfect (2003)
A Plague of Demons & Other Stories (2003)

LEE, TANITH

The Birthgrave (1975)
Don't Bite the Sun (1976)
Drinking Sapphire Wine (1977)
Quest for the White Witch (1978)
Vazkor, Son of Vazkor (1978, also published as Shadowfire)
Electric Forest (1979)
Day by Night (1980)
Sabella, or the Blood Stone (1980)
The Silver Metal Lover (1981)
Days of Grass (1985)
Women As Demons (1989)
Eva Fairdeath (1994)
Biting the Sun (1999)
Venus Preserved (2003)

LE GUIN, URSULA K.

Planet of Exile (1966)
Rocannon's World (1966)
City of Illusions (1967)
The Left Hand of Darkness (1969)
The Lathe of Heaven (1971)
The Dispossessed (1974)
The Wind's Twelve Quarters (1975)
The Word for World Is Forest (1976)
The Compass Rose (1982)
The Eye of the Heron (1982)
Always Coming Home (1985)
Five Complete Novels (1985)
Buffalo Gals and Other Animal Presences (1987)
A Fisherman of the Inland Sea (1994)
Worlds of Exile and Illusion (1996, also published as Three Hainish Novels)
Four Ways to Forgiveness (1996)
The Telling (2000)
The Birthday of the World (2002)
Changing Planes (2003)

LEIBER, FRITZ

Gather, Darkness (1950)
Destiny Times Three (1952)
The Green Millennium (1953)
The Sinful Ones (1953
The Big Time (1961)
The Mind Spider and Other Stories (1961)

Shadows with Eyes (1962)
The Silver Eggheads (1962)
Ships to the Stars (1964)
The Wanderer (1964)
A Pail of Air (1964)
The Night of the Wolf (1966)
The Secret Songs (1968)
A Specter Is Haunting Texas (1969)
Night Monsters (1969)
You're All Alone (1972)
The Book of Fritz Leiber (1974)
The Best of Fritz Leiber (1974)
Night Monsters (1974)
The Second Book of Fritz Leiber (1975)
The Worlds of Fritz Leiber (1976)
The Change War (1978)
Changewar (1983)
The Ghost Light (1984)
Kreativity for Kats and Other Feline Fantasies (1990)
The Leiber Chronicles (1990)
The Dealings of Daniel Kesserich (1997)

LEINSTER, MURRAY
Murder Madness (1931)
Fight for Life (1949)
The Last Spaceship (1949)
Sidewise in Time (1950)
Space Platform (1953)
Space Tug (1953)
The Black Galaxy (1954)
The Brain Stealers (1954)
Operation: Outer Space (1954)
The Forgotten Planet (1954)
The Other Side of Here (1955)
City on the Moon (1957)
The Planet Explorer (1957, also published as *Colonial Survey*)
Out of This World (1958)
War With the Gizmos (1958)
Four from Planet Five (1959)
The Monster from Earth's End (1959)
The Pirates of Zan (1959)
Monsters and Such (1959)
The Mutant Weapon (1959)
Twists in Time (1960)
The Aliens (1960)
Men into Space (1960)
The Wailing Asteroid (1960)
This World Is Taboo (1961)

Creatures of the Abyss (1961, also published as *The Listeners*)
Operation Terror (1962)
Talents, Incorporated (1962)
Doctor to the Stars (1964)
The Other Side of Nowhere (1964)
The Duplicators (1964)
Invaders of Space (1964)
The Greks Bring Gifts (1964)
Time Tunnel (1964)
Checkpoint Lambda (1966)
S.O.S. from Three Worlds (1966)
Tunnel Through Time (1966)
Space Captain (1966)
Timeslip! (1967)
Space Gypsies (1967)
Miners in the Sky (1967)
The Time Tunnel (1967)
Land of the Giants (1968)
A Murray Leinster Omnibus (1968)
Unknown Danger (1969)
The Hot Spot (1969)
The Best of Murray Leinster (1976)
The Best of Murray Leinster (1978)
The Med Series (1983)
Quarantine World (1992)
First Contacts (1998)
Med Ship (2002)
Planets of Adventure (2003)

LEM, STANISLAW
(Dates are for the first English version)
Solaris (1970)
The Invincible (1973)
Memoirs Found in a Bathtub (1973)
The Cyberiad (1974)
The Futurological Conference (1974)
The Investigation (1974)
The Star Diaries (1976)
Mortal Engines (1977)
A Perfect Vacuum (1978)
Chain of Chance (1978)
Tales of Pirx the Pilot (1979)
Return from the Stars (1980)
The Cosmic Carnival (1981)
Memoirs of a Space Traveler (1982)
More Tales of Pirx the Pilot (1982)
His Master's Voice (1983)
Imaginary Magnitude (1984)

One Human Minute (1986)
Fiasco (1988)
Eden (1989)
Peace on Earth (1994)

LESSING, DORIS
The Four-Gated City (1969)
The Temptation of Jack Orkney and Other Stories (1972)
The Memoirs of a Survivor (1975)
Shikasta (1979)
The Marriage Between Zones Three, Four, and Five (1980)
The Sirian Experiments (1981)
The Making of the Representative for Planet Eight (1982)
The Documents Relating to the Sentimental Agents in the Volyen Empire (1983)
Canopus in Argos: Archives (1992)

LEWIS, C. S.
Out of the Silent Planet (1938)
Perelandra (1943, also published as *Voyage to Venus*)
That Hideous Strength (1945, also published as *The Tortured Planet*)
The Dark Tower and Other Stories (1977)
The Essential C. S. Lewis (1988)
The Cosmic Trilogy (1990)

LONDON, JACK
Before Adam (1906)
The Iron Heel (1907)
The Scarlet Plague (1915)
The Science Fiction of Jack London (1975)
Selected Science Fiction and Fantasy Stories (1978)
Fantastic Tales (2002)

LONG, FRANK BELKNAP
The Hounds of Tindalos (1946)
John Carstairs, Space Detective (1949)
Space Station #1 (1957)
Woman from Another Planet (1960)
Mating Center (1961)
Mars Is My Destination (1962)
It Was the Day of the Robot (1963)
The Horror from the Hills (1963)
Three Steps Spaceward (1963)
The Martian Visitors (1964)

Odd Science Fiction (1964)
The Dark Beasts (1964)
Mission to a Star (1964)
This Strange Tomorrow (1966)
Lest Earth Be Conquered (1968, also published as *The Androids*)
Journey into Darkness (1967)
And Others Shall Be Born (1968)
The Three Faces of Time (1969)
Monster from Out of Time (1970)
Survival World (1971)
The Rim of the Unknown (1972)
The Early Long (1975)
Night Fear (1979)

LONGYEAR, BARRY B.
Circus World (1980)
City of Baraboo (1980)
Manifest Destiny (1980)
Elephant Song (1982)
The Tomorrow Testament (1983)
It Came from Schenectady (1984)
Enemy Mine (1985, with David Gerrold)
Sea of Glass (1987)
Naked Came the Robot (1988)
The Homecoming (1989)
Infinity Hold (1989)
The Change (1994)
Slag Like Me (1994)
Enemy Mine: The Enemy Papers (1997)

LOVECRAFT, H. P. (HOWARD PHILIPS)
(Includes only those collections with a large proportion of science fiction)
The Lurking Fear (1947, also published as *Cry Horror!*)
The Haunter of the Dark (1951)
The Dunwich Horror and Others (1963)
At the Mountains of Madness (1964)
The Colour Out of Space (1964)
The Shadow over Innsmouth and Other Stories of Horror (1971)
The Annotated Lovecraft (1987)
The Road to Madness (1996)
Tales of H. P. Lovecraft (1997)

LUPOFF, RICHARD
One Million Centuries (1967)
Sacred Locomotive Flies (1971)
Into the Aether (1974)

The Crack in the Sky (1976, also published as *Fool's Hill*)
The Ova Hamlet Papers (1976)
Sandworld (1976)
The Triune Man (1977)
Buck Rogers in the 25th Century (1978, as Addison Steele)
Space War Blues (1978)
That Man on Beta (1979, as Addison Steele)
Sun's End (1984)
Circumpolar! (1984)
Countersolar! (1987)
The Forever City (1987)
Galaxy's End (1988)
Night of the Living Gator (1992)
Before . . . 12:01 . . . and After (1996)
Claremont Tales (2001)
Claremont Tales II (2002)

MAINE, CHARLES ERIC
Spaceways (1953, also published as *Spaceways Satellite*)
Crisis 2000 (1955)
Timeliner (1955)
The Man Who Couldn't Sleep (1956, also published as *Escapement*)
High Vacuum (1957)
The Isotope Man (1957, also published as *The Atomic Man*)
World Without Men (1958)
The Tide Went Out (1958, also published as *Thirst*)
Fire Past the Future (1959, also published as *The Big Countdown*)
Subterfuge (1959)
Calculated Risk (1960)
He Owned the World (1960, also published as *The Man Who Owned the World*)
The Mind of Mr. Soames (1961)
Never Let Up (1964)
The Darkest of Nights (1965, also published as *The Big Death* and as *Survival Margin*)
B.E.A.S.T. (1966)
The Random Factor (1971)
Alph (1972)

MALZBERG, BARRY
Chorale (1968)
The Final War and Other Fantasies (1969, as K. M. O'Donnell)

The Empty People (1969, as K. M. O'Donnell)
Dwellers in the Deep (1970, as K. M. O'Donnell)
The Falling Astronauts (1971)
Gather in the Hall of Planets (1971, as K. M. O'Donnell)
In the Pocket and Other SF Stories (1971, as K. M. O'Donnell)
Universe Day (1971, as K. M. O'Donnell)
Beyond Apollo (1972)
Revelations (1972)
Overlay (1972)
Herovit's World (1973)
In the Enclosure (1973)
Phase IV (1973)
The Men Inside (1973)
Conversations (1974)
The Sodom and Gomorrah Business (1974)
Tactics of Conquest (1974)
The Day of the Burning (1974)
On a Planet Alien (1974)
Out from Ganymede (1974)
The Destruction of the Temple (1974)
Galaxies (1975)
The Gamesman (1975)
The Many Worlds of Barry Malzberg (1975)
Guernica Night (1975)
Down Here in the Dream Quarter (1976)
Scop (1976)
The Best of Barry Malzberg (1976)
The Last Transaction (1977)
Malzberg at Large (1979)
The Man Who Loved the Midnight Lady (1980)
The Cross of Fire (1982)
The Remaking of Sigmund Freud (1975)
The Passage of Light (1994)
In the Stone House (2000)
On Account of Darkness (2004, with Bill Pronzini)

MARTIN, GEORGE R. R.
A Song for Lya (1976)
Songs of Stars and Shadows (1977)
Dying of the Light (1978)
Sandkings (1981)
Windhaven (1981, with Lisa Tuttle)
Songs the Dead Men Sing (1983)
Nightflyers (1985)
Tuf Voyaging (1986)
Portraits of His Children (1987)

MATHESON, RICHARD

Born of Man and Woman (1954, also published as
    Third from the Sun)
The Shrinking Man (1956, also published as The
    Incredible Shrinking Man)
The Shores of Space (1957)
Shock! (1961)
Shock II (1964)
Shock III (1966)
Shock Waves (1970)
Seven Steps to Midnight (1993)

MAY, JULIAN

The Many-Colored Land (1981)
The Golden Torc (1982)
The Nonborn King (1983)
The Adversary (1984)
Intervention (1987)
The Surveillance (1987)
The Metaconcert (1987)
Jack the Bodiless (1991)
Diamond Mask (1994)
Magnificat (1996)
Perseus Spur (1998)
Orion Arm (1999)
Sagittarius Whorl (2000)

McAULEY, PAUL J.

Four Hundred Billion Stars (1988)
Of the Fall (1989, also published as Secret
    Harmonies)
Eternal Light (1991)
The King of the Hill and Other Stories (1991)
Red Dust (1993)
Pasquale's Angel (1994)
Fairyland (1995)
The Invisible Country (1996)
Child of the River (1997)
Ancients of Days (1998)
Making History (2000)
Shrine of Stars (2000)
The Secret of Life (2001)
Whole Wide World (2002)
White Devils (2004)

McCAFFREY, ANNE

Restoree (1967)
Dragonflight (1968)

Decision at Doona (1969)
The Ship Who Sang (1969)
Dragonquest (1971)
To Ride Pegasus (1973)
A Time When (1975)
Dragonsong (1976)
Dragonsinger (1977)
Get Off the Unicorn (1977)
Dinosaur Planet (1978)
The Dragonriders of Pern (1978)
The White Dragon (1978)
The Harper Hall of Pern (1979)
Dragondrums (1979)
The Worlds of Anne McCaffrey (1981)
Crystal Singer (1982)
The Coelura (1983)
Moreta: Dragonlady of Pern (1983)
Dinosaur Planet Survivors (1984)
The Ireta Adventure (1985)
Killashandra (1985)
Nerilka's Story (1986)
Dragonsdawn (1988)
The Renegades of Pern (1989)
Pegasus in Flight (1990)
The Rowan (1990)
The Death of Sleep (1990, with Elizabeth Moon)
Sassinak (1990, with Elizabeth Moon)
Generation Warriors (1991, with Elizabeth Moon)
Wings of Pegasus (1991)
All the Weyrs of Pern (1991)
Rescue Run (1991)
Crystal Line (1992)
The Ship Who Searched (1992, with Mercedes
    Lackey)
Damia (1992)
Crisis on Doona (1992, with Jody Lynn Nye)
Damia's Children (1993)
First Fall (1993)
Powers That Be (1993, with Elizabeth Ann
    Scarborough)
The Dolphins of Pern (1994)
Treaty at Doona (1994, with Jody Lynn Nye, also
    published as Treaty Planet)
The Girl Who Heard Dragons (1994)
The City Who Fought (1994, with S. M. Stirling)
Lyon's Pride (1994)
Power Lines (1994, with Elizabeth Ann Scarborough)
Power Play (1995, with Elizabeth Ann Scarborough)

Freedom's Landing (1995)
The Ship Who Won (1995, with Jody Lynn Nye)
The Crystal Singer Trilogy (1996)
Dragonseye (1997)
The Masterharper of Pern (1997)
Freedom's Choice (1997)
Acorna (1997)
Nimisha's Ship (1999)
The Tower and the Hive (1999)
Acorna's People (2000, with Elizabeth Ann Scarborough)
Pegasus in Space (2000)
Acorna's World (2000, with Elizabeth Ann Scarborough)
The Dinosaur Planet Omnibus (2001)
The Skies of Pern (2001)
Acorna's Search (2001, with Elizabeth Ann Scarborough)
A Gift of Dragons (2002)
Freedom's Ransom (2003)
Brain Ships (2003, with Margaret Ball and Mercedes Lackey)
Dragon's Kin (2003, with Todd McCaffrey)
Acorna's Rebels (2003, with Elizabeth Ann Scarborough)
Doona (2004, with Jody Lynn Nye)
Acorna's Triumph (2004, with Elizabeth Ann Scarborough)

McDEVITT, JACK
The Hercules Text (1986)
A Talent for War (1989)
The Engines of God (1994)
Ancient Shores (1996)
Eternity Road (1997)
Moonfall (1998)
Hello Out There (2000)
Infinity Beach (2000, also published as *Slow Lightning*)
Deepsix (2001)
Chindi (2002)
Omega (2003)
Polaris (2004)

McDONALD, IAN
Desolation Road (1988)
Empire Dreams (1988)
Out on Blue Six (1989)

Speaking in Tongues (1992)
The Broken Land (1992, also published as *Hearts, Hands and Voices*)
Scissors Cut Paper Wrap Stone (1994)
Terminal Café (1994, also published as *Necroville*)
Evolution's Shore (1995, also published as *Chaga*)
Sacrifice of Fools (1996)
Kirinya (1997)
Tendeleo's Story (2000)
Ares Express (2002)
River of Gods (2004)

McHUGH, MAUREEN
China Mountain Zhang (1992)
Half the Day Is Night (1994)
Mission Child (1998)
Nekropolis (2001)

McINTYRE, VONDA N.
The Exile Waiting (1975)
Dreamsnake (1978)
Fireflood and Other Stories (1979)
The Entropy Effect (1981)
The Wrath of Khan (1982)
Superluminal (1983)
The Search for Spock (1984)
The Bride (1985)
Barbary (1986)
The Voyage Home (1986)
Enterprise: The First Adventure (1986)
Starfarers (1989)
Transition (1990)
Metaphase (1992)
Nautilus (1994)

McLAUGHLIN, DEAN
Dome World (1962)
The Fury from Earth (1963)
The Man Who Wanted Stars (1965)
Hawk Among the Sparrows (1976)

McQUAY, MIKE
Lifekeeper (1980)
Escape from New York (1981)
Hot Time in Old Town (1981)
When Trouble Beckons (1981)
The Deadliest Show in Town (1982)
Crater of Mystery (1983, as Victor Appleton)

The Odds Are Murder (1983)
Jitterbug (1984)
Mother Earth (1985)
My Science Project (1985)
Pure Blood (1985)
Suspicion (1987)
Memories (1987)
The Nexus (1989)
Puppet Master (1991)
Richter 10 (1997, with Arthur C. Clarke)

MILLER, WALTER M., JR.
A Canticle for Leibowitz (1959)
Conditionally Human (1962)
View from the Stars (1965)
The Science Fiction Stories of Walter M. Miller Jr. (1978)
The Best of Walter M. Miller Jr. (1980, also published as *The Darfsteller and Other Stories* and as *Conditionally Human and Other Stories*)
Saint Leibowitz and the Wild Horse Woman (1997, completed by Terry Bisson)

MOON, ELIZABETH
Lunar Activity (1990)
Hunting Party (1993)
Sporting Chance (1994)
Winning Colors (1995)
Once a Hero (1997)
Phases (1997)
Change of Command (1999)
Rules of Engagement (1999)
Against the Odds (2000)
Heris Serrano (2002)
Speed of Dark (2002)
Trading in Danger (2003)

MOORCOCK, MICHAEL
Barbarians of Mars (1965, also published as *Masters of the Pit*)
The Sundered Worlds (1965, also published as *The Blood Red Game*)
Blades of Mars (1965, also published as *Lord of the Spiders*)
The Fireclown (1965, also published as *The Winds of Limbo*)
Warrior of Mars (1965, also published as *The City of the Beast*)

The Twilight Man (1966, also published as *The Shores of Death*)
The Wrecks of Time (1967, also published as *The Rituals of Infinity*)
The Final Programme (1968)
Behold the Man (1969)
The Black Corridor (1969)
The Time Dweller (1969)
The Ice Schooner (1969)
A Cure for Cancer (1971)
The Warlord of the Air (1971)
Breakfast in the Ruins (1972)
The English Assassin (1972)
An Alien Heat (1972)
The Hollow Lands (1974)
The Land Leviathan (1974)
Distant Suns (1975)
The End of All Songs (1976)
The Lives and Times of Jerry Cornelius (1976)
Legends from the End of Time (1976)
Moorcock's Book of Martyrs (1976, also published as *Dying for Tomorrow*)
The Adventures of Una Persson and Catherine Cornelius in the Twentieth Century (1976)
The Condition of Muzak (1977)
The Cornelius Chronicles (1977)
The Transformation of Miss Mavis Ming (1977, also published as *A Messiah at the End of Time*)
Gloriana (1978)
My Experiences in the Third World War (1980)
The Dancers at the End of Time (1981)
Warrior of Mars (1981, also published as *Kane of Old Mars*)
The Entropy Tango (1981)
The Steel Tsar (1981)
A Nomad of the Time Streams (1982, also published as *The Nomad of Time*)
Mother London (1988)
Tales from the End of Time (1989)
Sailing to Utopia (1993)
The Cornelius Quartet (2001)
Firing the Cathedral (2002)

MOORE, C. L.
Judgment Night (1952)
Shambleau (1953)
Northwest of Earth (1954)
No Boundaries (1955, with Henry Kuttner)

Doomsday Morning (1957)
Earth's Last Citadel (1964, with Henry Kuttner)
The Best of C. L. Moore (1975)

MOORE, WARD
Greener Than You Think (1947)
Bring the Jubilee (1952)
Joyleg (1962, with Avram Davidson)
Caduceus Wild (1978)

NAGATA, LINDA
Tech Heaven (1995)
The Bohr Maker (1995)
Deception Well (1997)
Vast (1998)
Limit of Vision (2001)
Memory (2003)

NIVEN, LARRY
World of Ptavvs (1966)
A Gift from Earth (1968)
Neutron Star (1968)
The Shape of Space (1969)
Ringworld (1970)
The Flying Sorcerers (1971, with David Gerrold)
All the Myriad Ways (1971)
The Flight of the Horse (1973)
Protector (1973)
Inconstant Moon (1973)
A Hole in Space (1974)
Tales of Known Space (1975)
The Mote in God's Eye (1975, with Jerry Pournelle)
A World Out of Time (1976)
The Long Arm of Gil Hamilton (1976)
Lucifer's Hammer (1977, with Jerry Pournelle)
Convergent Series (1979)
Ringworld Engineers (1979)
The Patchwork Girl (1980)
Oath of Fealty (1981, with Jerry Pournelle)
Dream Park (1981, with Steven Barnes)
The Integral Trees (1984)
Niven's Laws (1984)
Footfall (1985, with Jerry Pournelle)
Limits (1985)
The Smoke Ring (1987)
The Legacy of Heorot (1987, with Steven Barnes and Jerry Pournelle)

The Barsoom Project (1989, with Steven Barnes)
N Space (1990)
Playgrounds of the Mind (1991)
The California Voodoo Game (1991, with Steven Barnes)
Achilles' Choice (1991, with Steven Barnes)
Fallen Angels (1991, with Michael Flynn and Jerry Pournelle)
Bridging the Galaxies (1993)
Crashlander (1994)
The Gripping Hand (1994, with Jerry Pournelle, also published as *The Mote Around Murcheson's Eye*)
Flatlander (1995)
Beowulf's Children (1995, with Steven Barnes and Jerry Pournelle)
The Ringworld Throne (1996)
The Dragons of Heorot (1996)
Destiny's Road (1998)
Rainbow Mars (1999)
Saturn's Race (2000, with Steven Barnes)
Scatterbrain (2003)
Ringworld's Children (2004)

NORMAN, JOHN
Tarnsman of Gor (1966)
Outlaws of Gor (1967)
Priest-Kings of Gor (1968)
Nomads of Gor (1969)
Assassin of Gor (1970)
Raiders of Gor (1971)
Captive of Gor (1972)
The Gor Omnibus (1972)
Hunters of Gor (1974)
Marauders of Gor (1975)
Time Slave (1975)
Tribesmen of Gor (1976)
Slave Girl of Gor (1977)
Beasts of Gor (1978)
Explorers of Gor (1979)
Fighting Slave of Gor (1980)
Guardsman of Gor (1981)
Rogue of Gor (1981)
Savages of Gor (1982)
Blood Brothers of Gor (1982)
Kajira of Gor (1983)
Players of Gor (1984)
Dancer of Gor (1985)
Mercenaries of Gor (1985)

Renegades of Gor (1986)
Vagabonds of Gor (1987)
Magicians of Gor (1988)
The Chieftain (1991)
The Captain (1992)
The King (1993)

NORTON, ANDRE

Star Man's Son (1952, also published as *Daybreak 2250 A.D.*)
Star Rangers (1953, also published as *The Last Planet*)
The Stars Are Ours (1954)
Sargasso of Space (1955)
Star Guard (1955)
Crossroads of Time (1956)
Plague Ship (1956)
Sea Siege (1957)
Star Born (1957)
The Time Traders (1958)
Star Gate (1958)
The Beast Master (1959)
Voodoo Planet (1959)
Galactic Derelict (1959)
Secret of the Lost Race (1959, also published as *Wolfshead*)
The Sioux Spaceman (1960)
Storm over Warlock (1960)
Star Hunter (1961)
Catseye (1961)
Lord of Thunder (1962)
Eye of the Monster (1962)
The Defiant Agents (1962)
Judgment on Janus (1963)
Key Out of Time (1963)
Night of Masks (1964)
Ordeal in Otherwhere (1964)
The X Factor (1965)
Quest Crosstime (1965, also published as *Crosstime Agent*)
Moon of Three Rings (1966)
Victory on Janus (1966)
Operation Time Search (1967)
Dark Piper (1968)
The Zero Stone (1968)
Postmarked the Stars (1969)
Uncharted Stars (1969)
Dread Companion (1970)

Ice Crown (1970)
Exiles of the Stars (1971)
Android at Arms (1971)
Breed to Come (1972)
Garan the Eternal (1972)
Here Abide Monsters (1973)
Forerunner Foray (1973)
Outside (1974)
Iron Cage (1974)
The Many Worlds of Andre Norton (1974, also published as *The Book of Andre Norton*)
Merlin's Mirror (1975)
The Day of the Ness (1975, with Michael Gilbert)
No Night Without Stars (1975)
Star Ka'at (1976, with Dorothy Madlee)
Yurth Burden (1978)
Star Ka'at's World (1978, with Dorothy Madlee)
Star Ka'at and the Plant People (1979, with Dorothy Madlee)
Voorloper (1980)
Forerunner (1981)
Star Ka'at and the Winged Warriors (1981, with Dorothy Madlee)
Forerunner: The Second Venture (1985)
Flight in Yiktor (1986)
Dare to Go A-Hunting (1990)
Brother to Shadows (1993)
Redline the Stars (1993, with P. M. Griffin)
Firehand (1994, with P. M. Griffin)
Derelict for Trade (1997, with Sherwood Smith)
A Mind for Trade (1997, with Sherwood Smith)
Echoes in Time (1999, with Sherwood Smith)
Time Traders (2000)
Time Traders II (2001)
Star Soldiers (2001)
Warlock (2002)
Beast Master's Ark (2002, with Lyn McConchie)
Janus (2002)
Atlantis Endgame (2002, with Sherwood Smith)
Darkness and Dawn (2003)
The Solar Queen (2003)
Beast Master's Circus (2004, with Lyn McConchie)

NOURSE, ALAN E.
Trouble on Titan (1954)
A Man Obsessed (1955)
Rocket to Limbo (1957)

Scavengers in Space (1958)
The Invaders Are Coming (1959, with J. A. Meyer)
Star Surgeon (1959)
Tiger By the Tail (1961, also published as Beyond Infinity)
Raiders from the Rings (1962)
The Counterfeit Man (1963)
The Universe Between (1965)
Psi High and Others (1967)
The Mercy Man (1968)
Rx for Tomorrow (1971)
The Blade Runner (1974)
The Fourth Horseman (1983)

OLIVER, CHAD
Mists of the Dawn (1952)
Shadows in the Sun (1954)
Another Kind (1955)
The Winds of Time (1957)
Unearthly Neighbors (1960)
The Shores of Another Sea (1971)
The Edge of Forever (1971)
Giants in the Dust (1976)
A Star Above It (2003)
Far From This Earth (2003)

PANGBORN, EDGAR
West of the Sun (1953)
A Mirror for Observers (1954)
Davy (1964)
The Judgment of Eve (1966)
Good Neighbors and Other Strangers (1972)
The Company of Glory (1975)
Still I Persist in Wondering (1978)

PARK, PAUL
Soldiers of Paradise (1987)
Sugar Rain (1989)
The Cult of Loving Kindness (1991)
Celestis (1995)
If Lions Could Speak and Other Stories (2002)

PIPER, H. BEAM
Uller Uprising (1952)
Crisis in 2140 (1957, with John J. McGuire)
A Planet for Texans (1958, with John J. McGuire, also published as *Lone Star Planet*)

Four-Day Planet (1961)
Little Fuzzy (1962)
Space Viking (1963)
Junkyard Planet (1963, also published as *The Cosmic Computer*)
The Other Human Race (1964, also published as *Fuzzy Sapiens*)
Lord Kalvan of Otherwhen (1965, also published as *Gunpowder God*)
The Fuzzy Papers (1977)
Empire (1981)
Federation (1981)
Paratime (1981)
First Cycle (1982, with Michael Kurland)
The Worlds of H. Beam Piper (1983)
Fuzzies and Other People (1984)
The Complete Fuzzy (1998)
The Complete Paratime (2001)

PISERCHIA, DORIS
Mister Justice (1973)
Star Rider (1974)
A Billion Days of Earth (1976)
Earthchild (1977)
Spaceling (1978)
The Fluger (1980)
The Spinner (1980)
Doomtime (1981)
Earth in Twilight (1981)
I, Zombie (1982, as Curt Selby)
The Dimensioneers (1982)
The Deadly Sky (1983)

PLATT, CHARLES
Garbage World (1967)
The City Dwellers (1970, revised as *Twilight of the City*)
The Gas (1970)
Planet of the Voles (1971)
The Power and the Pain (1971)
Less Than Human (1986, as Robert Clarke)
Plasm (1987)
Free Zone (1989)
Soma (1989)
The Silicon Man (1991)
Protektor (1996)
Loose Cannon (2002)

POHL, FREDERIK

The Space Merchants (1953, with C. M. Kornbluth)
Search the Sky (1954, with C. M. Kornbluth)
Undersea Quest (1954, with Jack Williamson)
Preferred Risk (1955, with Lester Del Rey)
Gladiator-At-Law (1955, with C. M. Kornbluth)
Alternating Currents (1956)
Undersea Fleet (1956, with Jack Williamson)
The Case Against Tomorrow (1957)
Slave Ship (1957)
Undersea City (1958, with Jack Williamson)
Tomorrow Times Seven (1959)
Wolfbane (1959, with C. M. Kornbluth)
Drunkard's Walk (1960)
The Man Who Ate the World (1960)
Turn Left at Thursday (1961)
The Wonder Effect (1962, with C. M. Kornbluth)
The Abominable Earthman (1963)
The Reefs of Space (1964, with Jack Williamson)
The Age of the Pussyfoot (1965)
A Plague of Pythons (1965, also published as *Demon in the Skull*)
Starchild (1965, with Jack Williamson)
Digits and Dastards (1966)
The Frederik Pohl Omnibus (1966, also published as *Survival Kit*)
Rogue Star (1969, with Jack Williamson)
Beyond the Blue Event Horizon (1970)
Day Million (1970)
The Gold at Starbow's End (1972)
The Best of Frederik Pohl (1975)
Farthest Star (1975, with Jack Williamson)
The Early Pohl (1976)
Man Plus (1976)
In the Problem Pit (1976)
Critical Mass (1977, with C. M. Kornbluth)
Gateway (1977)
The Starchild Trilogy (1977, with Jack Williamson)
Jem (1979)
Before the Universe (1980, with C. M. Kornbluth)
The Cool War (1981)
Starburst (1982)
Planets Three (1982)
Syzygy (1982)
Bipohl (1982)
The Saga of Cuckoo (1983, with Jack Williamson)
Wall Around a Star (1983, with Jack Williamson)
Midas World (1983)

Heechee Rendezvous (1984)
The Merchants' War (1984)
Pohlstars (1984)
Black Star Rising (1985)
Venus Inc. (1985, with C. M. Kornbluth)
The Years of the City (1985)
Terror (1986)
The Coming of the Quantum Cats (1986)
The Annals of the Heechee (1987)
Our Best (1987, with C. M. Kornbluth)
Narabedla Ltd. (1988)
The Day the Martians Came (1988)
Land's End (1988, with Jack Williamson)
Homegoing (1989)
The Gateway Trip (1990)
Outnumbering the Dead (1990)
The World at the End of Time (1990)
The Singers of Time (1991, with Jack Williamson)
Stopping at Slowyear (1991)
Mining the Oort (1992)
The Undersea Trilogy (1992, with Jack Williamson)
The Voices of Heaven (1994)
Mars Plus (1995, with Thomas T. Thomas)
The Other End of Time (1996)
The Siege of Eternity (1997)
O Pioneer! (1998)
The Far Shore of Time (1999)
The Platinum Pohl (2001)

POURNELLE, JERRY

A Spaceship for the King (1973, also published as *King David's Spaceship*)
Escape from the Planet of the Apes (1973)
The Mote in God's Eye (1975, with Larry Niven)
Birth of Fire (1976)
West of Honor (1976)
High Justice (1977)
The Mercenary (1977)
Lucifer's Hammer (1977, with Larry Niven)
Exiles to Glory (1978)
Janissaries (1979)
Oath of Fealty (1981, with Larry Niven)
Clan and Crown (1982, with Roland Green)
Footfall (1985, with Larry Niven)
Storms of Victory (1987, with Roland Green)
The Legacy of Heorot (1987, with Larry Niven and Steven Barnes)

Prince of Mercenaries (1989)

Falkenberg's Legion (1990, also published as *Future History*)

The Children's Hour (1991, with S. M. Stirling)

Fallen Angels (1991, with Larry Niven and Michael Flynn)

Go Tell the Spartans (1991, with S. M. Stirling)

The Gripping Hand (1993, with Larry Niven, also published as *The Mote Around Murcheson's Eye*)

Prince of Sparta (1993, with S. M. Stirling)

Beowulf's Children (1995, with Larry Niven and Steven Barnes)

Higher Education (1996, with Charles Sheffield)

Tran (1996, with Roland Green)

Starswarm (1998)

The Prince (2002, with S. M. Stirling)

POWERS, TIM

Epitaph in Rust (1976)

The Skies Discrowned (1976, also published as *Forsake the Sky*)

Dinner at Deviant's Palace (1985)

Powers of Two (2004)

PRESTON, DOUGLAS, AND CHILD, LINCOLN

Relic (1995)

Mount Dragon (1996)

Reliquary (1997)

Thunderhead (1999)

The Ice Limit (2000)

The Cabinet of Curiosities (2002)

Utopia (2002, by Lincoln Child alone)

PREUSS, PAUL

The Gates of Heaven (1980)

Re-Entry (1981)

Broken Symmetries (1984)

Human Error (1985)

Maelstrom (1988)

Starfire (1988)

Hide and Seek (1989)

The Diamond Moon (1990)

The Medusa Encounter (1990)

The Shining Ones (1991)

Core (1993)

Breaking Strain (1997)

Secret Passages (1997)

PRIEST, CHRISTOPHER

Indoctrinaire (1970)

Darkening Island (1972, also published as *This Darkening Island*)

The Inverted World (1974)

The Space Machine (1976)

The Perfect Lover (1977, also published as *A Dream of Wessex*)

An Infinite Summer (1979)

The Making of the Lesbian Horse (1979)

The Affirmation (1981)

The Glamour (1984)

The Quiet Woman (1990)

The Prestige (1995)

ExistenZ (1999)

The Extremes (1999)

The Separation (2002)

The Client (2003)

RANDALL, MARTA

Islands (1976)

A City in the North (1976)

Journey (1978)

Dangerous Games (1980)

Those Who Favor Fire (1984)

REED, ROBERT

The Hormone Jungle (1987)

The Leeshore (1987)

Black Milk (1989)

Down the Bright Way (1991)

The Remarkables (1992)

Beyond the Veil of Stars (1994)

An Exaltation of Larks (1995)

Beneath the Gated Sky (1997)

The Dragons of Springplace (1999)

Marrow (2000)

Sister Alice (2003)

RESNICK, MIKE

The Goddess of Ganymede (1967)

Pursuit on Ganymede (1968)

Redbeard (1969)

Galactica Discovers Earth (1980)

The Soul Eater (1981)

Birthright: The Book of Man (1982)

Walpurgis III (1982)

Sideshow (1982)

The Three Legged Hootch Dancer (1983)
The Wild Alien Tamer (1983)
The Best Rootin' Tootin' Shootin' Gunslinger in the Whole Damned Galaxy (1983)
The Branch (1984)
Unauthorized Autobiographies and Other Curiosities (1984)
Eros Ascending (1984)
Eros at Zenith (1984)
Eros Descending (1985)
Santiago (1986)
Eros at Nadir (1986)
The Dark Lady (1987)
Ivory (1988)
Paradise (1989)
Bully! (1990)
Through Darkest Resnick with Gun and Camera (1990)
Second Contact (1990)
The Alien Heart (1991)
Soothsayer (1991)
Pink Elephants and Hairy Toads (1991)
Bwana & Bully! (1991)
Stalking the Wild Resnick (1991)
The Red Tape War (1991, with Jack L. Chalker and George Alec Effinger)
Oracle (1992)
Will the Last Person to Leave the Planet Please Shut off the Sun? (1992)
Inferno (1993)
Prophet (1993)
Purgatory (1993)
A Miracle of Rare Design (1994)
Solo Flights Through Shared Worlds (1996)
The Widowmaker (1996)
The Widowmaker Reborn (1997)
An Alien Land (1997)
The Widowmaker Unleashed (1998)
A Hunger in the Soul (1998)
Kirinyaga (1998)
Magic Feathers (2000, with Nick DiChario)
In Space No One Can Hear You Laugh (2000)
Tales of the Galactic Midway (2001)
Tales of the Velvet Comet (2001)
The Outpost (2001)
With a Little Help from My Friends (2002)
Hunting the Snark and Other Short Novels (2002)
The Galactic Comedy (2003)
The Return of Santiago (2003)

REYNOLDS, ALASTAIR

Revelation Space (2000)
Chasm City (2000)
Diamond Dogs (2002)
Turquoise Days (2002)
Redemption Ark (2002)
Absolution Gap (2003)
Diamond Dogs, Turquoise Days (2003)

REYNOLDS, MACK

The Earth War (1963)
Planetary Agent X (1965)
Dawnman Planet (1966)
Of Godlike Power (1966, also published as *Earth Unaware*)
Time Gladiator (1966)
Space Pioneer (1966)
After Some Tomorrow (1967)
The Rival Rigellians (1967)
Mercenary from Tomorrow (1968)
The Cosmic Eye (1969)
The Five Way Secret Agent and *Mercenary from Tomorrow* (1969)
The Space Barbarians (1969)
Computer World (1970)
Once Departed (1970)
Blackman's Burden (1972)
Border, Breed Nor Birth (1972)
Computer War (1973)
Looking Backward, from the Year 2000 (1973)
Code Duello (1973)
Commune 2000 A.D. (1974)
Satellite City (1975)
Ability Quotient (1975)
The Towers of Utopia (1975)
Tomorrow Might Be Different (1975)
Amazon Planet (1975)
The Best of Mack Reynolds (1976)
Galactic Medal of Honor (1976)
Section G; United Planets (1976)
Rolltown (1976)
Day After Tomorrow (1976)
Perchance to Dream (1977)
Police Patrol 2000 A.D. (1977)
Space Visitor (1977)
Equality: In the Year 2000 (1977)
After Utopia (1977)
The Best Ye Breed (1978)

Trample an Empire Down (1978)
The Fracas Factor (1978)
Brain World (1978)
Lagrange Five (1979)
Compounded Interest (1983)
The Lagrangists (1983)
Eternity (1984, with Dean Ing)
Home Sweet Home 2010 A.D. (1984, with Dean Ing)
The Other Time (1984, with Dean Ing)
Chaos in Lagrangia (1984)
Space Search (1984)
Trojan Orbit (1985, with Dean Ing)
Joe Mauser: Mercenary from Tomorrow (1986, with Michael Banks)
Sweet Dreams, Sweet Princes (1986, with Michael Banks)
Deathwish World (1986, with Dean Ing)

ROBB, J. D.
Glory in Death (1995)
Naked in Death (1995)
Rapture in Death (1996)
Ceremony in Death (1997)
Vengeance in Death (1997)
Immortal in Death (1997)
Witness in Death (1998)
Holiday in Death (1998)
Conspiracy in Death (1999)
Loyalty in Death (1999)
Judgment in Death (2000)
Betrayal in Death (2001)
Seduction in Death (2001)
Purity in Death (2002)
Reunion in Death (2002)
Imitation in Death (2003)
Portrait in Death (2003)

ROBERTS, KEITH
The Furies (1966)
Pavane (1968)
The Inner Wheel (1970)
Machines and Men (1973)
Monsters and Men (1973)
The Chalk Giants (1974)
The Grain Kings (1976)
The Passing of the Dragons (1977)
Ladies from Hell (1979)

Molly Zero (1980)
Kiteworld (1985)
The Lordly Ones (1986)

ROBINSON, FRANK M.
The Power (1956)
The Prometheus Crisis (1975, with Thomas N. Scortia)
The Nightmare Factor (1978, with Thomas N. Scortia)
The Gold Crew (1980, with Thomas N. Scortia)
A Life in the Day of . . . (1981)
The Great Divide (1982, with John Levin)
Blowout! (1987, with Thomas N. Scortia)
The Dark Beyond the Stars (1998)
Waiting (1999)
Through My Glasses, Darkly (2002)
The Donor (2004)

ROBINSON, KIM STANLEY
Icehenge (1984)
The Wild Shore (1984)
The Memory of Whiteness (1985)
The Planet on the Table (1986)
The Gold Coast (1988)
Escape from Kathmandu (1989)
Pacific Edge (1990)
A Sensitive Dependence on Initial Conditions (1991)
Remaking History and Other Stories (1991, also published as *Down and Out in the Year 2000*)
Red Mars (1992)
Green Mars (1993)
Blue Mars (1996)
Antarctica (1997)
The Martians (1999)
The Years of Rice and Salt (2002)
Forty Signs of Rain (2004)

ROBINSON, SPIDER
Callahan's Crosstime Saloon (1977)
Telempath (1977)
Stardance (1979, with Jeanne Robinson)
Time Travelers Strictly Cash (1981)
Antinomy (1980)
Mindkiller (1982, also expanded as *Deathkiller*)
Melancholy Elephants (1984)
Night of Power (1985)
Callahan's Secret (1986)

Callahan and Company (1987)
Time Pressure (1987)
Callahan's Lady (1989)
True Minds (1990)
Starseed (1991, with Jeanne Robinson)
Lady Slings the Booze (1992)
The Callahan Touch (1993)
Starmind (1995, with Jeanne Robinson)
Callahan's Legacy (1996)
The Star Dancers (1997, with Jeanne Robinson)
Lifehouse (1997)
User Friendly (1998)
Callahan's Key (2000)
By Any Other Name (2001)
The Free Lunch (2001)
God Is an Iron and Other Stories (2002)
Callahan's Con (2003)

RUCKER, RUDY
White Light (1980)
Spacetime Donuts (1981)
Software (1982)
The 57th Franz Kafka (1983)
The Sex Sphere (1983)
Master of Space and Time (1984)
The Secret of Life (1985)
Wetware (1988)
The Hollow Earth (1990)
Transreal (1991)
All the Visions (1991)
The Hacker and the Ants (1994)
Live Robots (1994)
Freeware (1997)
Saucer Wisdom (1999)
Realware (2000)
Gnarl! (2000)
Spaceland (2002)
Frex and the Elixir (2004)

RUSS, JOANNA
Picnic on Paradise (1968)
And Chaos Died (1970)
The Female Man (1973)
We Who Are About To (1977)
The Two of Them (1979)
The Zanzibar Cat (1983)
The Adventures of Alyx (1983, also published as *Alyx*)

Extra(Ordinary) People (1984)
The Hidden Side of the Moon (1987)

RUSSELL, ERIC FRANK
Sinister Barrier (1943)
Dreadful Sanctuary (1951)
Sentinels from Space (1953)
Deep Space (1954)
Men, Martians, and Machines (1956)
Three to Conquer (1956)
Wasp (1957)
Six Worlds Yonder (1958)
Next of Kin (1959, also published in shorter form as *The Space Willies*)
Far Stars (1961)
The Great Explosion (1962)
Dark Tides (1962)
Mindwarpers (1965, also published as *With a Strange Device*)
Somewhere a Voice (1965)
Like Nothing on Earth (1975)
The Best of Eric Frank Russell (1978)
Major Ingredients (2000)
Entities (2001)

RUSSO, RICHARD PAUL
Inner Eclipse (1988)
Subterranean Gallery (1989)
Destroying Angel (1992)
Carlucci's Edge (1995)
Carlucci's Heart (1997)
Terminal Visions (2000)
Ship of Fools (2001)
Carlucci (2003)

SABERHAGEN, FRED
The Golden People (1964)
The Water of Thought (1965)
Berserker (1967)
Brother Assassin (1969, also published as *Brother Berserker*)
Berserker's Planet (1975)
The Book of Saberhagen (1975)
Specimens (1976)
The Veils of Azlaroc (1978)
Berserker Man (1979)
Love Conquers All (1979)
The Ultimate Enemy (1979)

The Mask of the Sun (1979)
Octagon (1981)
The Berserker Wars (1981)
Earth Descended (1981)
Coils (1982, with Roger Zelazny)
A Century of Progress (1983)
Berserker: Blue Death (1985)
The Berserker Throne (1985)
Pyramids (1987)
Saberhagen: My Best (1987)
After the Fact (1988)
The White Bull (1988)
Berserker Lies (1991)
Berserker Kill (1993)
Berserker Fury (1997)
Pilgrim (1997)
Berserkers: The Beginning (1998)
Shiva in Steel (1998)
The Arrival (1999)
Berserker's Star (2003)
Berserker Prime (2004)

SARGENT, PAMELA
Cloned Lives (1976)
Starshadows (1977)
The Sudden Star (1979, also published as *The White
    Death*)
Watchstar (1980)
The Golden Space (1982)
Earthseed (1983)
The Alien Upstairs (1983)
Eye of the Comet (1984)
Homesmind (1984)
The Shore of Women (1986)
Venus of Dreams (1986)
The Best of Pamela Sargent (1987)
Venus of Shadows (1988)
Alien Child (1988)
The Watchstar Trilogy (1996)
A Fury Scorned (1996, with George Zebrowski)
Heart of the Sun (1997, with George Zebrowski)
Climb the Wind (1999)
Across the Universe (1999, with George
    Zebrowski)
Child of Venus (2001)
Behind the Eyes of Dreamers and Other Short Novels
    (2002)
Garth of Izar (2003, with George Zebrowski)

SAWYER, ROBERT
Golden Fleece (1990)
Far-Seer (1992)
Fossil Hunter (1993)
End of an Era (1994)
Foreigner (1994)
The Terminal Experiment (1995)
Starplex (1996)
Frameshift (1997)
Illegal Alien (1997)
Factoring Humanity (1998)
Flashforward (1999)
Calculating God (2000)
Hominids (2002)
Humans (2003)
Hybrids (2003)
Iterations (2004)

SCHMITZ, JAMES H.
Agent of Vega (1960)
A Tale of Two Clocks (1962, also published as
    Legacy)
The Universe Against Her (1964)
A Nice Day for Screaming and Other Tales of the Hub
    (1965)
The Witches of Karres (1966)
The Demon Breed (1968)
A Pride of Monsters (1970)
The Eternal Frontiers (1973)
The Telzey Toy (1973)
The Lion Game (1973)
The Best of James H. Schmitz (1991)
Telzey Amberdon (2000)
TnT: Telzey & Trigger (2000)
Agent of Vega and Other Stories (2001)
The Hub: Dangerous Territory (2001)
Trigger & Friends (2001)
Eternal Frontier (2002)

SCOTT, MELISSA
The Game Beyond (1984)
Five-Twelfths of Heaven (1985)
A Choice of Destinies (1986)
Silence in Solitude (1986)
The Empress of Earth (1987)
The Kindly Ones (1987)
The Roads of Heaven (1988)
Mighty Good Road (1990)

Dreamships (1992)
Burning Bright (1993)
Trouble and Her Friends (1994)
Shadow Man (1995)
Proud Helios (1995)
Night Sky Mine (1996)
Dreaming Metal (1997)
The Garden (1997)
The Shapes of Their Hearts (1998)
The Jazz (2000)

SERVICE, PAMELA F.

A Question of Destiny (1986)
Stinker from Space (1988)
Under Alien Stars (1990)
Weirdos of the Universe Unite! (1992)
Stinker's Return (1993)

SHAW, BOB

Night Walk (1967)
The Two-Timers (1968)
The Palace of Eternity (1969)
Shadow of Heaven (1969)
One Million Tomorrows (1970)
Ground Zero Man (1971, also published as *The Peace Machine*)
Other Days, Other Eyes (1972)
Tomorrow Lies in Ambush (1973)
Orbitsville (1975)
Cosmic Kaleidoscope (1976)
A Wreath of Stars (1976)
Who Goes Here? (1977)
Medusa's Children (1977)
Vertigo (1978, also published as *Terminal Velocity*)
Ship of Strangers (1978)
Dagger of the Mind (1979)
Galactic Tours (1981)
A Better Mantrap (1982)
The Ceres Solution (1982)
Orbitsville Departure (1983)
Fire Pattern (1984)
Between Two Worlds (1986)
The Ragged Astronauts (1986)
Messages Found in an Oxygen Bottle (1986)
The Wooden Spaceships (1988)
Dark Night in Toyland (1989)
Killer Planet (1989)
The Fugitive Worlds (1990)

Orbitsville Judgment (1990)
Warren Peace (1993, also published as *Dimensions*)

SHECKLEY, ROBERT

Untouched by Human Hands (1954)
Citizen in Space (1955)
Pilgrimage to Earth (1958)
Immortality Delivered (1958, also published as *Immortality Inc.*)
Notions: Unlimited (1960)
The Status Civilization (1960)
Store of Infinity (1960)
Shards of Space (1962)
Journey Beyond Tomorrow (1962, also published as *The Journey of Joenes*)
The 10th Victim (1965)
Mindswap (1966)
Dimension of Miracles (1968)
The People Trap (1968)
Can You Feel Anything When I Do This? (1971, also published as *Same to You Doubled*)
The Robert Sheckley Omnibus (1973)
Options (1975)
The Robot Who Looked Like Me (1978)
Crompton Divided (1978, also published as *The Alchemical Marriage of Alastair Crompton*)
The Wonderful World of Robert Sheckley (1979)
Dramocles (1983)
Is This What People Do? (1984)
Victim Prime (1987)
Hunter/Victim (1988)
Bill, the Galactic Hero on the Planet of Bottled Brains (1990, with Harry Harrison)
Collected Short Fiction, Volumes 1–5 (1991)
Alien Harvest (1995)
The Laertian Gamble (1995)
A Call to Arms (1999)
Dimensions of Sheckley (2002)
Uncanny Tales (2003)

SHEFFIELD, CHARLES

Sight of Proteus (1978)
Vectors (1979)
The Web Between the Worlds (1979)
Hidden Variables (1981)
My Brother's Keeper (1982)
The McAndrew Chronicles (1983, also published as *One Man's Universe*)

Between the Strokes of Night (1985)
The Nimrod Hunt (1986)
Trader's World (1988)
Proteus Unbound (1989)
Summertide (1990)
Divergence (1991)
Brother to Dragons (1992, expanded as *The Mind Pool*)
Cold As Ice (1992)
The Heritage Universe (1992)
Transcendence (1992)
Dancing with Myself (1993)
Godspeed (1993)
Proteus Combined (1994, also published as *Proteus Manifest*)
The Ganymede Club (1995)
Proteus in the Underworld (1995)
Georgia on My Mind and Other Places (1995)
Higher Education (1996, with Jerry Pournelle)
The Billion Dollar Boy (1997)
Putting Up Roots (1997)
Convergence (1997)
Tomorrow and Tomorrow (1997)
Convergent Series (1998)
The Cyborg from Earth (1998)
Aftermath (1998)
Transvergence (1999)
Starfire (1999)
The Compleat McAndrew (2000)
The Spheres of Heaven (2001)
Dark As Day (2002)
The Amazing Dr. Darwin (2002)
The Lady Vanishes and Other Oddities of Nature (2002)
Resurgence (2002)

SHEPARD, LUCIUS
Green Eyes (1984)
The Jaguar Hunter (1987)
Life During Wartime (1987)
The Ends of the Earth (1991)
Barnacle Bill the Spacer and Other Stories (1997)
Beast of the Heartland and Other Stories (1999)

SHUTE, NEVIL
Ordeal (1939, also published as *What Happened to the Corbetts*)
An Old Captivity (1940)

No Highway (1948)
In the Wet (1953)
On the Beach (1957)

SILVERBERG, ROBERT
Revolt on Alpha C (1955)
Master of Life and Death (1957)
The Shrouded Planet (1957, with Randall Garrett as Robert Randall)
The Thirteenth Immortal (1957)
Aliens from Space (1958, as David Osborne)
Invisible Barriers (1958, as David Osborne)
Invaders from Earth (1958)
Lest We Forget Thee, Earth (1958, as Calvin M. Knox)
The Plot Against Earth (1959, as Calvin M. Knox)
Starhaven (1958, as Ivar Jorgenson)
One of Our Asteroids Is Missing (1958, as Calvin M. Knox)
Stepsons of Terra (1958, also published as *Shadow on the Stars*)
The Planet Killers (1959)
Starman's Quest (1959)
Dawning Light (1959, with Randall Garrett as Robert Randall)
Lost Race of Mars (1960)
Collision Course (1961)
Next Stop the Stars (1962)
The Seed of Earth (1962)
Recalled to Life (1962)
The Silent Invaders (1963)
Regan's Planet (1964)
Godling, Go Home! (1964)
Time of the Great Freeze (1964)
Conquerors from the Darkness (1965)
To Worlds Beyond (1965)
Needle in a Timestack (1966)
The Planet of Death (1967)
To Open the Sky (1967)
Those Who Watch (1967)
The Time Hoppers (1967)
The Gate of Worlds (1967)
Thorns (1967)
The Masks of Time (1968, also published as *Vornan 19*)
Hawksbill Station (1968, also published as *The Anvil of Time*)
Three Survived (1969)

Across a Billion Years (1969)
Nightwings (1969)
The Man in the Maze (1969)
Up the Line (1969)
The Calibrated Alligator and Other Science Fiction Stories (1969)
Dimension Thirteen (1969)
To Live Again (1969)
The Cube Root of Uncertainty (1970)
The World Inside (1970)
Tower of Glass (1970)
Downward to the Earth (1970)
Parsecs and Parables (1970)
A Robert Silverberg Omnibus (1970)
World's Fair 1992 (1970)
A Time of Changes (1971)
Moonferns and Starsongs (1971)
Son of Man (1971)
Dying Inside (1972)
The Book of Skulls (1972)
The Reality Trip and Other Implausibilities (1972)
The Second Trip (1973)
Earth's Other Shadow (1973)
Valley Beyond Time (1973)
Unfamiliar Territory (1973)
Sundance and Other Science Fiction Stories (1974)
Born with the Dead (1974)
The Feast of St. Dionysus (1975)
Sunrise on Mercury and Other Science Fiction Stories (1975)
Capricorn Games (1976)
The Best of Robert Silverberg (1976)
The Stochastic Man (1976)
The Shores of Tomorrow (1976)
Shadrach in the Furnace (1976)
The Best of Robert Silverberg 2 (1978)
The Songs of Summer and Other Stories (1979)
Homefaring (1983)
World of a Thousand Colors (1983)
The Conglomeroid Cocktail Party (1984)
Tom O'Bedlam (1985)
Beyond the Safe Zone (1986)
Star of Gypsies (1986)
Project Pendulum (1987)
At Winter's End (1988)
The Secret Sharer (1988)
The Mutant Season (1989, with Karen Haber)
Nightfall (1990, with Isaac Asimov)

The New Springtime (1990, also published as *The Queen of Springtime*)
Letters from Atlantis (1990)
To the Land of the Living (1990)
The Face of the Waters (1991)
The Ugly Little Boy (1991, with Isaac Asimov, also published as *Child of Time*)
The Positronic Man (1992, with Isaac Asimov)
The Collected Stories of Robert Silverberg (1992)
Kingdoms of the Wall (1992)
Hot Sky at Midnight (1994)
The Road to Nightfall (1996)
Starborne (1996)
Ringing the Changes (1997)
The Alien Years (1998)
Edge of Light (1998)
Hawksbill Times Two (2002)
In Another Country and Other Short Novels (2002)
The Longest Way Home (2002)
Roma Eterna (2003)

SIMAK, CLIFFORD D.

Cosmic Engineers (1950)
Empire (1951)
Time and Again (1951, also published as *First He Died*)
City (1952)
Ring Around the Sun (1953)
Strangers in the Universe (1956)
The Worlds of Clifford Simak (1960, abridged as *Other Worlds of Clifford Simak* and *Alifus for Neighbors*)
Time Is the Simplest Thing (1961)
The Trouble with Tycho (1961)
They Walked Like Men (1962)
All the Traps of Earth and Other Stories (1962, abridged as *The Night of the Puudly*)
Way Station (1963)
Worlds Without End (1964)
All Flesh Is Grass (1965)
The Werewolf Principle (1967)
Why Call Them Back from Heaven? (1967)
The Goblin Reservation (1968)
So Bright the Vision (1968)
The Best Science Fiction Stories of Clifford D. Simak (1970)
Out of Their Minds (1970)
Destiny Doll (1971)

A Choice of Gods (1972)
Cemetery World (1973)
Our Children's Children (1974)
The Best of Clifford Simak (1975)
Shakespeare's Planet (1976)
A Heritage of Stars (1977)
Skirmish (1977)
Mastodonia (1978, also published as *Catface*)
The Visitors (1980)
Project Pope (1981)
Special Deliverance (1982)
Brother and Other Stories (1986)
Highway of Eternity (1986)
The Marathon Photo and Others (1986)
Off Planet (1988)
The Autumn Land and Other Stories (1990)
Immigrant and Other Stories (1991)
The Creator and Other Stories (1993)
Over the River and Through the Woods (1996)
The Civilisation Game and Other Stories (1997)

SIMMONS, DAN
Carrion Comfort (1989)
Hyperion (1989)
Phases of Gravity (1989)
The Fall of Hyperion (1990)
Prayers to Broken Stones (1990)
The Hollow Man (1992)
Children of the Night (1992)
Endymion (1996)
The Rise of Endymion (1997)
Worlds Enough and Time (2002)
Ilium (2003)

SIODMAK, CURT
F.P. 1 Does Not Reply (1933)
Donovan's Brain (1943)
Riders to the Stars (1953, with Robert Smith)
Skyport (1959)
Hauser's Memory (1968)
The Third Ear (1971)
City in the Sky (1974)
Gabriel's Body (1992)

SLADEK, JOHN
Mechasm (1968, also published as *The Reproductive System*)
The Muller-Fokker Effect (1970)

The Steam-Driven Boy and Other Strangers (1973)
Keep the Giraffe Burning (1977)
Roderick (1980)
The Best of John Sladek (1981)
Alien Accounts (1982)
Roderick at Random (1983)
Tik-Tok (1983)
The Lunatics of Terra (1984)
Bugs (1989)
The Complete Roderick (2001)
Maps (2002)

SLONCZEWSKI, JOAN
Still Forms on Foxfield (1980)
A Door into Ocean (1986)
Daughter of Elysium (1993)
The Wall Around Eden (1989)
The Children Star (1998)
Brain Plague (2000)

SMITH, CORDWAINER
You Will Never Be the Same (1963)
The Planet Buyer (1964)
Space Lords (1965)
Quest of Three Worlds (1966)
The Underpeople (1968)
Under Old Earth and Other Explorations (1970)
Stardreamer (1971)
The Best of Cordwainer Smith (1975)
Norstrilia (1975)
The Instrumentality of Mankind (1979)
The Rediscovery of Man (1993)

SMITH, EDWARD E.
The Skylark of Space (1946)
Skylark Three (1947)
Spacehounds of IPC (1947)
Skylark of Valeron (1949)
First Lensman (1950)
Galactic Patrol (1950)
Triplanetary (1950)
Gray Lensman (1951)
Second-Stage Lensmen (1953)
Children of the Lens (1954)
The Vortex Blaster (1960, also published as *Masters of the Vortex*)
The Galaxy Primes (1965)
Subspace Explorers (1965)

Skylark Duquesne (1966)
The Best of E. E. "Doc" Smith (1975)
Lord Tedric: Alien Worlds (1978)
Masters of Space (1979)
Subspace Encounter (1983)

SMITH, GEORGE O.
Venus Equilateral (1947)
Pattern for Conquest (1949)
Nomad (1950)
Operation Interstellar (1950)
Hellflower (1953)
Highways in Hiding (1956, also published as Space
    Plague)
Troubled Star (1957)
Fire in the Heavens (1958)
The Path of Unreason (1958)
Lost in Space (1959)
The Fourth "R" (1959, also published as The Brain
    Machine)
The Complete Venus Equilateral (1976)
The Worlds of George O. Smith (1982)

SMITH, L. NEIL
The Probability Broach (1980)
Their Majesties' Bucketeers (1981)
The Venus Belt (1981)
Lando Calrissian and the Flamewind of Oseon (1983)
Lando Calrissian and the Mindharp of Sharu (1983)
Lando Calrissian and the Starcave of ThonBoka (1983)
The Nagasaki Vector (1983)
Tom Paine Maru (1984)
The Gallatin Convergence (1985)
The Wardove (1986)
The Crystal Empire (1986)
Brightsuit Macbear (1988)
Taflak Lysandra (1988)
Henry Martyn (1989)
Contact and Commune (1990)
Converse and Conflict (1990)
Pallas (1993)
Bretta Martyn (1997)
The American Zone (2001)
Forge of the Elders (2001)

SPINRAD, NORMAN
The Solarions (1966)
Agent of Chaos (1967)

The Men in the Jungle (1967)
Bug Jack Barron (1969)
The Last Hurrah of the Golden Horde (1970)
The Iron Dream (1972)
No Direction Home (1975)
The Star Spangled Future (1979)
A World Between (1979)
Songs from the Stars (1980)
The Void Captain's Tale (1983)
Riding the Torch (1984)
Child of Fortune (1985)
Little Heroes (1987)
Other Americas (1988)
Russian Spring (1991)
Deus X (1993)
Pictures at 11 (1994)
Vampire Junkies (1994)
Journal of the Plague Years (1995)
Greenhouse Summer (1999)
Deus X and Other Stories (2003)

STABLEFORD, BRIAN
Cradle of the Sun (1969)
The Blind Worm (1970)
Days of Glory (1971)
Days of Wrath (1971)
In the Kingdom of the Beasts (1971)
The Halcyon Drift (1972)
To Challenge Chaos (1972)
Rhapsody in Black (1973)
The Fenris Device (1974)
The Paradise Game (1974)
Promised Land (1974)
Man in a Cage (1975)
Swan Song (1975)
The Face of Heaven (1976)
The Mind-Riders (1976)
The Florians (1976)
Critical Threshold (1977)
Wildeblood's Empire (1977)
The Realm of Tartarus (1977)
The City in the Sun (1978)
The Paradox of the Sets (1979)
The Walking Shadow (1979)
Balance of Power (1979)
Optiman (1980, also published as War Games)
The Castaways of Tanagar (1981)
Journey to the Center (1982)

The Gates of Eden (1983)
The Empire of Fear (1988)
The Centre Cannot Hold (1990)
Invaders from the Center (1990)
Sexual Chemistry (1991)
Ghost Dancers (1991, as Brian Craig)
Firefly (1994)
Salamander's Fire (1996)
Serpent's Blood (1996)
Chimera's Cradle (1997)
Architects of Emortality (1999)
The Fountains of Youth (2000)
The Cassandra Complex (2001)
Dark Ararat (2002)
The Omega Expedition (2002)
Swan Songs (2002)
Designer Genes (2004)

STAPLEDON, OLAF

Last and First Men (1930)
Last Men in London (1932)
Odd John (1935)
The Flames (1937)
The Starmaker (1937)
Darkness and Light (1942)
Sirius (1944)
Worlds of Wonder (1949)
A Man Divided (1950)
To the End of Time (1953)
Nebula Maker (1976)
An Olaf Stapledon Reader (1997)

STEELE, ALLEN

Orbital Decay (1989)
Clarke County, Space (1990)
Lunar Descent (1991)
Labyrinth of Night (1992)
Rude Astronauts (1992)
The Jericho Iteration (1994)
The Weight (1995)
All-American Alien Boy (1996)
The Tranquility Alternative (1996)
A King of Infinite Space (1997)
Oceanspace (1999)
Sex and Violence in Zero G (1999)
Chronospace (2001)
Coyote (2002)
American Beauty (2003)
Coyote Rising (2004)

STEPHENSON, NEAL

Snow Crash (1992)
Interface (1994, as Stephen Bury)
The Diamond Age (1995)

STERLING, BRUCE

Involution Ocean (1977)
The Artificial Kid (1980)
Schismatrix (1985)
Islands in the Net (1988)
Crystal Express (1989)
The Difference Engine (1990, with William Gibson)
Globalhead (1992)
Heavy Weather (1994)
Holy Fire (1996)
Schismastrix Plus (1996)
Distraction (1998)
Zeitgeist (2000)
A Good Old-Fashioned Future (2001)
The Zenith Angle (2004)

STIRLING, S. M.

Marching Through Georgia (1988)
Under the Yoke (1989)
The Stone Dogs (1990)
The Children's Hour (1991, with Jerry Pournelle)
The Forge (1991, with David Drake)
Go Tell the Spartans (1991, with Jerry Pournelle)
The Hammer (1992, with David Drake)
Prince of Sparta (1993, with Jerry Pournelle)
The Anvil (1993, with David Drake)
The City Who Fought (1994, with Anne McCaffrey)
The Steel (1994, with David Drake)
The Sword (1995, with David Drake)
Betrayals (1996)
The Chosen (1996, with David Drake)
Drakon (1996)
The Rising (1997, with James Doohan)
The Ship Avenged (1997)
Island in the Sea of Time (1998)
Privateer (1999, with James Doohan)
Against the Tide of Years (1999)
The Reformer (1999, with David Drake)
The Domination (1999)
On the Oceans of Eternity (2000)
The Independent Command (2000, with James Doohan)
Infiltrator (2001)

The Prince (2002, with Jerry Pournelle)
The Peshawar Lancers (2002)
Rising Storm (2002)
Conquistador (2003)
The Future War (2003)
Warlord (2003, with David Drake)

STRUGATSKY, ARKADY, AND STRUGATSKY, BORIS
(Dates are given for first English version)
The Country of Crimson Clouds (1960)
A Voyage to Amaltheia (1962)
Far Rainbow/The Second Invasion from Mars (1967)
Hard to Be a God (1973)
The Final Circle of Paradise (1976)
Monday Begins on Saturday (1977)
Roadside Picnic/Tale of the Troika (1977)
Noon: 22nd Century (1978)
Prisoners of Power (1978)
Roadside Picnic (1978)
Definitely Maybe (1978)
The Ugly Swans (1979)
Beetle in an Anthill (1980)
The Snail on the Slope (1980)
Space Apprentice (1981)
The Time Wanderers (1986)

STURGEON, THEODORE
Without Sorcery (1948)
The Dreaming Jewels (1950, also published as The Synthetic Man)
E Pluribus Unicorn (1953)
More Than Human (1953)
Caviar (1955)
A Way Home (1955)
Thunder and Roses (1957)
A Touch of Strange (1958)
The Cosmic Rape (1958, also published as To Marry Medusa)
The Golden Helix (1959)
Aliens 4 (1959)
Venus Plus X (1960)
Beyond (1960)
Voyage to the Bottom of the Sea (1961)
Not Without Sorcery (1961)
Sturgeon in Orbit (1964)
The Joyous Invasions (1965)
Two Complete Novels (1965)
Sturgeon Is Alive and Well (1971)
The Worlds of Theodore Sturgeon (1972)

To Here and the Easel (1973)
Case and the Dreamer (1974)
Starshine (1976)
Visions and Ventures (1978)
Maturity (1979)
The Stars Are the Styx (1979)
Alien Cargo (1984)
To Marry Medusa (1987)
A Touch of Sturgeon (1987)
Microcosmic God (1992)
The Ultimate Egoist (1993)
Killdozer (1994)
Thunder and Roses (1997)
The Perfect Host (1998)
A Saucer of Loneliness (2000)
Selected Stories (2000)
Bright Segment (2002)
And Now the News (2003)

SUTTON, JEFF
First on the Moon (1958)
Bombs in Orbit (1959)
Spacehive (1960)
Apollo at Go (1963)
The Atom Conspiracy (1963)
Beyond Apollo (1966)
H-Bomb over America (1967)
The Beyond (1967, with Jean Sutton)
The Man Who Saw Tomorrow (1968)
The Programmed Man (1968, with Jean Sutton)
Lord of the Stars (1969, with Jean Sutton)
Alton's Unguessable (1970)
Whisper from the Stars (1970)
Alien from the Stars (1970, with Jean Sutton)
The Boy Who Had the Power (1971, with Jean Sutton)
The Mindblocked Man (1972)

SWANN, S. ANDREW
Forests of the Night (1993)
Emperors of the Twilight (1994)
Specters of the Dawn (1994)
Partisan (1995)
Profiteer (1995)
Revolutionary (1996)
Fearful Symmetries (1999)
Teek (1999, as Steven Krane)
The Omega Game (2000, as Steven Krane)
Stranger Inside (2003, as Steven Krane)

SWANWICK, MICHAEL
In the Drift (1985)
Vacuum Flowers (1987)
Griffin's Egg (1990)
Gravity's Angels (1991)
Stations of the Tide (1991)
Jack Faust (1997)
A Geography of Unknown Lands (1997)
Moon Dogs (2000)
Tales of Old Earth (2000)
Bones of the Earth (2002)
Cigar-Box Faust and Other Miniatures (2003)

TENN, WILLIAM
Of All Possible Worlds (1955)
The Human Angle (1956)
Time in Advance (1958)
Of Men and Monsters (1968)
The Seven Sexes (1968)
The Square Root of Man (1968)
The Wooden Star (1968)
Immodest Proposals (2001)
Here Comes Civilization (2001)

TEPPER, SHERI S.
Northshore (1987)
Southshore (1987)
The Awakeners (1987)
After Long Silence (1987, also published as *The Enigma Score*)
The Gate to Women's Country (1988)
Grass (1989)
Raising the Stones (1990)
Sideshow (1992)
Shadow's End (1995)
The Family Tree (1997)
Gibbons Decline and Fall (1997)
Six Moon Dance (1998)
Singer from the Sea (1999)
The Fresco (2000)
The Visitor (2002)
The Companions (2003)

TILLEY, PATRICK
Fade-Out (1975)
The Cloud Warrior (1984)
The First Family (1985)
Xan (1985)
Iron Master (1987)

Blood River (1988)
Star Wartz (1995)
Death-Bringer (1998)
Earth-Thunder (1998)

TIPTREE, JAMES, JR.
Ten Thousand Light-Years from Home (1973)
Warm Worlds and Otherwise (1975)
Star Songs of an Old Primate (1978)
Out of the Everywhere and Other Extraordinary Visions (1981)
Brightness Falls from the Air (1985)
The Starry Rift (1986)
Byte Beautiful (1986)
Crown of Stars (1988)
Her Smoke Rose Up Forever (1990)
Meet Me at Infinity (2000)

TUBB, E. C.
Planetfall (1951, as Gil Hunt)
Saturn Patrol (1951, as King Lang)
Argentis (1952, as Brian Shaw)
Atom War on Mars (1952)
Alien Impact (1952)
Dynasty of Doom (1953, as Charles Grey)
Venusian Adventure (1953)
The Mutants Rebel (1953)
I Fight for Mars (1953, as Charles Grey)
Space Hunger (1953, as Charles Grey)
The Tormented City (1953, as Charles Grey)
The Wall (1953, as Charles Grey)
The Extra Man (1954)
Enterprise 2115 (1954, as Charles Grey)
The Hell Planet (1954)
Alien Life (1954)
World at Bay (1954)
The Extra Man (1954, as Charles Grey)
The Hand of Havoc (1954, as Charles Grey)
City of No Return (1954)
The Stellar Legion (1954)
The Resurrected Man (1954)
The Metal Eater (1954, by Roy Sheldon)
The Living World (1954, as Carl Maddox)
Menace from the Past (1954, as Carl Maddox)
Global Blackout (1954, as Karl Vallance)
Alien Dust (1955)
The Space-Born (1956)
The Mechanical Monarch (1958)
Moon Base (1964)

Ten from Tomorrow (1966)
Death Is a Dream (1967)
The Winds of Gath (1967, also published as Gath)
C.O.D. Mars (1968)
Derai (1968)
Escape into Space (1969)
Toyman (1969)
S.T.A.R. Flight (1969)
Kalin (1969)
The Jester at Scar (1970)
Lallia (1971)
Century of the Manikin (1972)
A Scatter of Stardust (1972)
Technos (1972)
Monster of Metelaze (1973, as Gregory Kern)
Jondelle (1973)
Slave Ship from Sergan (1973, as Gregory Kern)
Mayenne (1973)
Veruchia (1973)
Earth Enslaved (1974, as Gregory Kern)
The Eater of Worlds (1974, as Gregory Kern)
Planet of Dread (1974, as Gregory Kern)
Seetee Alert! (1974, as Gregory Kern)
Spawn of Laban (1974, as Gregory Kern)
A World Aflame (1974, as Gregory Kern)
Enemy Within My Skull (1974, as Gregory Kern)
Zenya (1974)
The Jewel of Jarhen (1974, as Gregory Kern)
The Genetic Buccaneer (1974, as Gregory Kern)
The Gholan Gate (1974, as Gregory Kern)
Breakaway (1975)
Eye of the Zodiac (1975)
The Ghosts of Epidoris (1975, as Gregory Kern)
Collision Course (1975)
Beyond the Galactic Lens (1975, as Gregory Kern)
Eloise (1975)
Mimics of Dephene (1975, as Gregory Kern)
Alien Seed (1976)
Jack of Swords (1976)
Galaxy of the Lost (1976, as Gregory Kern)
Rogue Planet (1976)
Spectrum of a Forgotten Sun (1976)
Earthfall (1977)
Haven of Darkness (1977)
The Primitive (1977)
Prison of Night (1977)
The Quillian Sector (1978)
Incident on Ath (1978)
Death Wears a White Face (1979)

Web of Sand (1979)
Stellar Assignment (1979)
Iduna's Universe (1979)
The Luck Machine (1980)
Pawn of the Omphalos (1980)
World of Promise (1980)
The Terra Data (1980)
Nectar of Heaven (1981)
The Terridae (1981)
The Coming Event (1982)
Earth Is Heaven (1982)
Stardeath (1983)
Melome (1983)
The Galactiad (1983, as Gregory Kern)
Angado (1984)
Symbol of Terra (1984)
The Temple of Truth (1985)
Pandora's Box (1996)
Kalgan the Golden (1997)
The Temple of Death (1997)
War on the Moon (1997)
The Return (1997)
Murder in Space (1998)
The Wall (2001)

TUCKER, WILSON
The City in the Sea (1951)
The Long, Loud Silence (1952)
The Time Masters (1953)
The Science Fiction Sub-Treasury (1954, also published as Time: X)
Wild Talent (1954, also published as The Man from Tomorrow)
Time Bomb (1955, also published as Tomorrow Plus X)
The Lincoln Hunters (1957)
To the Tombaugh Station (1960)
The Year of the Quiet Sun (1970)
Ice and Iron (1974)
Resurrection Days (1981)
The Best of Wilson Tucker (1982)

TURNER, GEORGE
Beloved Son (1978)
Vaneglory (1981)
Yesterday's Men (1983)
Drowning Towers (1987, also published as The Sea and the Summer)
A Pursuit of Miracles (1990)

Brain Child (1991)
The Destiny Makers (1993)
Genetic Soldier (1994)
Down There in the Darkness (1999)

TURTLEDOVE, HARRY
Agent of Byzantium (1987)
A Different Flesh (1988)
Noninterference (1988)
The Pugnacious Peacemaker (1990)
Kaleidoscope (1990)
A World of Difference (1990)
Earthgrip (1991)
The Guns of the South (1992)
Departures (1993)
In the Balance (1994)
Tilting the Balance (1995)
Striking the Balance (1996)
Upsetting the Balance (1996)
How Few Remain (1997)
American Front (1998)
Walk in Hell (1999)
Colonization: Second Contact (1999)
Down in the Bottomlands and Other Places (1999, with L. Sprague de Camp)
Breakthroughs (2000)
Colonization: Down to Earth (2000)
Blood and Iron (2001)
Colonization: Aftershocks (2001)
The Center Cannot Hold (2002)
Counting Up, Counting Down (2002)
Ruled Britannia (2002)
Gunpowder Empire (2003)
In the Presence of Mine Enemies (2003)
The Victorious Opposition (2003)

VAN VOGT, A. E.
Slan (1946)
The Weapon Makers (1946, also published as *One Against Eternity*)
The Book of Ptath (1947, also published as *Ptath* and as *Two Hundred Million A.D.*)
The World of Null-A (1948)
The House That Stood Still (1950, also published as *The Mating Cry* and as *The Undercover Aliens*)
Masters of Time (1950, also published as *Earth's Last Fortress*)
The Voyage of the Space Beagle (1950, also published as *Mission: Interplanetary*)

The Weapon Shops of Isher (1951)
Away and Beyond (1952)
The Mixed Men (1952, also published as *Mission to the Stars*)
Destination Universe (1952)
The Universe Maker (1953)
Planets for Sale (1954, with E. Mayne Hull)
The Pawns of Null-A (1956, also published as *The Players of Null-A*)
Empire of the Atom (1957)
The Mind Cage (1957)
Siege of the Unseen (1959)
The War Against the Rull (1959)
Triad (1959)
The Wizard of Linn (1962)
The Beast (1963, also published as *Moonbeast*)
The Twisted Men (1964)
Monsters (1965)
Rogue Ship (1965)
The Winged Man (1966, with E. Mayne Hull)
The Changeling (1967)
A Van Vogt Omnibus (1967)
The Far Out Worlds of A. E. van Vogt (1968)
The Silkie (1969)
Children of Tomorrow (1970)
Quest for the Future (1970)
M33 in Andromeda (1971)
A Van Vogt Omnibus II (1971)
More Than Superhuman (1971)
The Proxy Intelligence and Other Mind Benders (1971)
The Battle of Forever (1971)
The Book of A. E. van Vogt (1972, also published as *Lost: Fifty Suns*)
Darkness on Diamondia (1972)
Future Glitter (1973, also published as *Tyranopolis*)
Two Science Fiction Novels (1973)
The Three Eyes of Evil (1973)
The Best of A. E. van Vogt (1974)
The Worlds of A. E. van Vogt (1974)
The Man With a Thousand Names (1974)
The Secret Galactics (1974, also published as *Earth Factor X*)
The Blal (1976)
The Gryb (1976)
The Anarchistic Colossus (1977)
Supermind (1977)
Pendulum (1978)
The Enchanted Village (1979)

Renaissance (1979)
Cosmic Encounter (1980)
Computerworld (1983, also published as Computer Eye)
Null-A Three (1985)
The Empire of Isher (2000)

VANCE, JACK

The Space Pirate (1953, also published as The Five Gold Bands)
Vandals of the Void (1953)
To Live Forever (1956)
Big Planet (1957)
The Languages of Pao (1958)
Slaves of the Klau (1958, also published as Gold and Iron)
The Dragon Masters (1963)
Future Tense (1964, also published as Dust of Far Suns)
The Houses of Iszm (1964)
The Star King (1964)
Son of the Tree (1964)
The Killing Machine (1964)
The World Between and Other Stories (1965, also published as The Moon Moth and Other Stories)
Space Opera (1965)
Monsters in Orbit (1965)
The Blue World (1966)
The Brains of Earth (1966)
The Many Worlds of Magnus Ridolph (1966)
The Palace of Love (1967)
The Last Castle (1967)
City of the Chasch (1968, also published as Chasch)
The Dirdir (1969)
Eight Fantasms and Magics (1969)
Emphyrio (1969)
Servants of the Wankh (1969, also published as Wankh)
The Pnume (1970)
The Anome (1973, also published as The Faceless Man)
The Brave Free Men (1973)
The Worlds of Jack Vance (1973)
Trullion: Alastor 2262 (1973)
The Asutra (1974)
The Gray Prince (1974)
Marune: Alastor 933 (1975)
Showboat World (1975, also published as The Magnificent Showboats of the Lower Vissel River, Lune XXIII, South, Big Planet)
The Best of Jack Vance (1976)

Maske: Thaery (1977)
Wyst: Alastor 1716 (1978)
The Face (1979)
Galactic Effectuator (1980)
Nopalgarth (1980)
The Book of Dreams (1981)
The Narrow Land (1982)
Lost Moons (1982)
The Complete Magnus Ridolph (1984)
Light from a Lone Star (1985)
The Augmented Agent and Other Stories (1986)
The Dark Side of the Moon (1986)
Araminta Station (1987)
Durdane (1989)
Chateau D'If and Other Stories (1991)
Ecce and Old Earth (1991)
Throy (1992)
When the Five Moons Rise (1992)
Planet of Adventure (1993)
Alastor (1995)
Night Lamp (1996)
The Demon Princes (1997)
Ports of Call (1998)
Coup de Grace and Other Stories (2002)

VARLEY, JOHN

The Ophiuchi Hotline (1977)
The Persistence of Vision (1978, also published as In the Hall of the Martian Kings)
Titan (1979)
Wizard (1980)
The Barbie Murders (1980, also published as Picnic on Nearside)
Millennium (1983)
Demon (1984)
Blue Champagne (1986)
The Golden Globe (1988)
Steel Beach (1992)
Red Thunder (2003)

VERNE, JULES

(Dates are for the first English-language edition)
From the Earth to the Moon (1869, also published as The Baltimore Gun Club and as The American Gun Club)
A Journey to the Center of the Earth (1872, also published as A Trip to the Center of the Earth)
20,000 Leagues Under the Sea (1872)
Dr. Ox and Other Stories (1874)

Round the Moon (1874, also published as *All Around the Moon* and as *The Moon Voyage*)
At the North Pole (1874, also published as *The Adventures of Captain Hatteras*)
The Mysterious Island (1876)
Off on a Comet (1877, also published as *Hector Servadac*)
The Begum's Fortune (1878, also published as *The Five Hundred Millions of the Begum*)
The Demon of Cawnpore (1881)
Tigers and Traitors (1881)
Clipper of the Clouds (1887, also published as *Robur the Conqueror* and as *A Trip Around the World in a Flying Machine*)
The Purchase of the North Pole (1890, also published as *Topsy Turvy*)
For the Flag (1897)
Master of the World (1914)
The Omnibus Jules Verne (1931)
The City in the Sahara (1960)
Into the Niger Bend (1960)
The Village in the Treetops (1964)
Yesterday and Tomorrow (1965)
The Hunt for the Meteor (1965, also published as *The Chase of the Golden Meteor*)
Collected Novels (1984)
Paris in the 20th Century (1996)
Invasion of the Sea (2001)

VIEHL, S. L.
Stardoc (2000)
Beyond Varallan (2000)
Endurance (2001)
Shockball (2001)
Eternity Row (2002)
Blade Dancer (2003)

VINGE, JOAN D.
Fireship (1978)
The Outcasts of Heaven Belt (1978)
Eyes of Amber (1979)
Legacy (1980)
The Snow Queen (1980)
Psion (1982)
The Joan D. Vinge Omnibus (1983)
Return of the Jedi (1983)
The Dune Storybook (1984)
World's End (1984)
Phoenix in the Ashes (1985)
Mad Max Beyond Thunderdome (1985)

Alien Blood (1988)
Catspaw (1988)
Heaven Chronicles (1991)
The Summer Queen (1991)
Dreamfall (1996)
Lost in Space (1998)
Tangled Up in Blue (2000)

VINGE, VERNOR
Grimm's World (1969, later expanded as *Tatja Grimm's World*)
The Witling (1976)
The Peace War (1984)
Across Realtime (1986)
Marooned in Realtime (1986)
True Names . . . and Other Dangers (1987)
Threats . . . and Other Promises (1988)
A Fire Upon the Deep (1992)
A Deepness in the Sky (1999)
The Collected Stories of Vernor Vinge (2001)

VONNEGUT, KURT
Player Piano (1952, also published as *Utopia 14*)
The Sirens of Titan (1959)
Canary in a Cat House (1961)
Cat's Cradle (1963)
Welcome to the Monkey House (1968)
Slaughterhouse Five (1969)
Slapstick (1976)
Deadeye Dick (1982)
Galapagos (1985)
Hocus Pocus (1990)
Timequake (1997)

WALDROP, HOWARD
The Texas-Israeli War (1974, with Jake Saunders)
Them Bones (1984)
Howard Who? (1986)
Strange Monsters from the Recent Past (1987)
Strange Things in Closeup (1989)
Night of the Cooters (1990)
You Could Go Home Again (1993)
Going Home Again (1997)
A Better World's in Birth (2003)
Custer's Last Jump and Other Collaborations (2003)

WALLACE, IAN
Croyd (1967)
Dr. Orpheus (1968)

Deathstar Voyage (1969)
The Purloined Prince (1971)
Pan Sagittarius (1973)
A Voyage to Dari (1974)
The World Asunder (1976)
The Sign of the Mute Medusa (1977)
Z-Sting (1978)
Heller's Leap (1979)
The Lucifer Comet (1980)
The Rape of the Sun (1982)
Megalomania (1989)

WALTERS, HUGH

Blast Off at Woomera (1957, also published as *Blast-Off at 03:00*)
The Domes of Pico (1958, also published as *Menace from the Moon*)
First on the Moon (1960, also published as *Operation Columbus*)
Moon Base One (1961, also published as *Outpost on the Moon*)
Expedition Venus (1962)
Destination Mars (1963)
Terror by Satellite (1964)
Journey to Jupiter (1965)
Mission to Mercury (1965)
Spaceship to Saturn (1967)
The Mohole Mystery (1968, also published as *The Mohole Menace*)
Nearly Neptune (1969, also published as *Neptune One Is Missing*)
First Contact? (1971)
Passage to Pluto (1973)
Tony Hale, Space Detective (1973)
Murder on Mars (1975)
Boy Astronaut (1977)
The Caves of Drach (1977)
The Last Disaster (1978)
First Family on the Moon (1979)
The Blue Aura (1979)
The Dark Triangle (1981)
School on the Moon (1981)
P-K (1986)

WATSON, IAN

The Embedding (1973)
The Jonah Kit (1975)
The Martian Inca (1977)

Alien Embassy (1977)
The Miracle Visitors (1978)
The Very Slow Time Machine (1979)
God's World (1979)
The Gardens of Delight (1980)
Under Heaven's Bridge (1981, with Michael Bishop)
Deathhunter (1981)
Sunstroke and Other Stories (1982)
Chekhov's Journey (1983)
The Book of the River (1984)
The Book of the Stars (1984)
Converts (1984)
The Book of Being (1985)
The Book of Ian Watson (1985)
Slow Birds and Other Stories (1985)
The Books of the Black Current (1986)
Evil Water and Other Stories (1987)
Salvage Rites and Other Stories (1988)
Whores of Babylon (1988)
The Flies of Memory (1990)
Stalin's Teardrops and Other Stories (1991)
The Coming of Vertumnus and Other Stories (1994)
The Chaos Child (1995)
Hard Questions (1996)
Oracle (1997)
The Great Escape (2002)
Mockymen (2003)

WATT-EVANS, LAWRENCE

The Chromosomal Code (1984)
Shining Steel (1986)
Denner's Wreck (1988)
Nightside City (1989)
Crosstime Traffic (1992)
Concrete Jungle (1995, as Nathan Archer)
Ragnarok (1995, as Nathan Archer)
Valhalla (1995, as Nathan Archer)
Martian Deathtrap (1996, as Nathan Archer)
Cold War (1997, as Nathan Archer)
Goblin Moon (2000, as Nathan Archer with Kurt Busiek)
Celestial Debris (2002)

WEBER, DAVID

Insurrection (1990, with Steve White)
Mutineers' Moon (1991)
Path of the Fury (1992)
Crusade (1992, with Steve White)

On Basilisk Station (1993)
The Armageddon Inheritance (1993)
The Honor of the Queen (1993)
The Short Victorious War (1994)
Field of Dishonor (1994)
Flag in Exile (1995)
Heirs of Empire (1996)
Honor Among Enemies (1996)
In Death Ground (1997, with Steve White)
In Enemy Hands (1997)
Echoes of Honor (1998)
The Apocalypse Troll (1999)
Ashes of Victory (2000)
The Excalibur Alternative (2002)
War of Honor (2002)
The Shiva Option (2002, with Steve White)
March Upcountry (2002, with John Ringo)
March to the Stars (2003, with John Ringo)
Empire from the Ashes (2003)
Crown of Slaves (2003, with Eric Flint)

WEINBAUM, STANLEY G.
Dawn of Flame & Other Stories (1936)
The New Adam (1939)
The Black Flame (1948)
The Best of Stanley G. Weinbaum (1949)
A Martian Odyssey (1949)
The Dark Other (1950)
The Red Peri & Others (1952)

WELLS, H. G.
The Stolen Bacillus and Other Incidents (1895)
The Time Machine (1895)
The Island of Dr. Moreau (1896)
The Invisible Man (1897)
Thirty Strange Stories (1897)
The Plattner Story and Others (1897)
The War of the Worlds (1898)
When the Sleeper Wakes (1899)
Tales of Space and Time (1899)
When the Sleeper Wakes (1899)
The First Men in the Moon (1901)
Twelve Stories and a Dream (1903)
The Food of the Gods (1904)
A Modern Utopia (1905)
In the Days of the Comet (1906)
The War in the Air (1908)
The Country of the Blind & Other Stories (1911)

The Door in the Wall and Other Stories (1911)
The World Set Free (1914)
Men Like Gods (1923)
Tales of Wonder (1923)
The Dream (1923)
Empire of the Ants & Other Stories (1925)
The Obliterated Man & Other Stories (1925)
The Short Stories of H. G. Wells (1927)
The Man Who Could Work Miracles (1936)
A Slip Under the Microscope (1931)
The Shape of Things to Come (1933)
Seven Famous Novels (1934)
The Camford Visitation (1937)
Star-Begotten (1937)
The Favorite Short Stories of H. G. Wells (1937)
The Holy Terror (1939)
The Country of the Blind (1939)
The Truth about Pyecraft and Other Short Stories (1943)
Twenty-Eight Science Fiction Stories (1952)
Tales of Life and Adventure (1954)
Tales of the Unexpected (1954)
Selected Short Stories (1958)
Best Stories of H. G. Wells (1960)
Three Prophetic Novels (1960)
The Cone (1965)
The Inexperienced Ghost and Nine Other Stories (1965)
The Best Science Fiction Stories of H. G. Wells (1966)
The Valley of Spiders (1966)
Early Writings in Science and Science Fiction (1975)
Empire of the Ants and Eight Science Fiction Stories (1977)
The Collector's Book of Science Fiction by H. G. Wells (1978)
The Complete Science Fiction of H.G. Wells (1978)
The H. G. Wells Science Fiction Treasury (1984)
The Man with the Nose and Other Uncollected Short Stories (1984)
The Complete Stories of H. G. Wells (1998)
The H. G. Wells Reader (2003)
Five Great Novels (2004)

WHITE, JAMES
The Secret Visitors (1957)
Hospital Station (1962)
Second Ending (1962)
Star Surgeon (1963)
Deadly Litter (1964)

Escape Orbit (1965, also published as *Open Prison*)
The Watch Below (1966)
All Judgment Fled (1968)
The Aliens Among Us (1969)
Major Operation (1971)
Tomorrow Is Too Far (1971)
Lifeboat (1972, also published as *Dark Inferno*)
The Dream Millennium (1974)
Monsters and Medics (1977)
Ambulance Ship (1979)
Underkill (1979)
Futures Past (1982)
Sector General (1983)
Star Healer (1984)
Code Blue—Emergency (1987)
Federation World (1988)
The Silent Stars Go By (1991)
The Genocidal Healer (1992)
The Galactic Gourmet (1996)
The White Papers (1996)
Final Diagnosis (1997)
Mind Changer (1998)
Double Contact (1999)
The First Protector (2000)
Beginning Operations (2001)
Alien Emergencies (2002)
General Practice (2003)

WHITE, STEVE
Insurrection (1990, with David Weber)
Crusade (1992, with David Weber)
The Disinherited (1993)
Debt of Ages (1995)
Legacy (1995)
In Death Ground (1997, with David Weber)
Prince of Sunset (1998)
Emperor of Dawn (1999)
Eagle Against the Stars (2000)
The Shiva Option (2002, with David Weber)
Forge of the Titans (2003)

WILHELM, KATE
The Mile-Long Spaceship (1963, also published as *Andover and the Android*)
The Clone (1965, with Theodore L. Thomas)
The Nevermore Affair (1966)
Abyss (1967)

The Killer Thing (1967)
The Downstairs Room (1968)
Let the Fire Fall (1969)
The Year of the Cloud (1970, with Theodore L. Thomas)
City of Cain (1974)
The Infinity Box (1975)
Where Late the Sweet Birds Sang (1976)
The Clewiston Test (1976)
Somerset Dreams and Other Fictions (1978)
Juniper Time (1979)
Listen, Listen (1981)
A Sense of Shadow (1981)
Welcome, Chaos (1983)
Huysman's Pets (1986)
Crazy Time (1988)
The Dark Door (1988)
Children of the Wind (1989)
State of Grace (1991)
Naming the Flowers (1992)
And the Angels Sing (1992)
A Flush of Shadows (1995)

WILLIAMS, PAUL O.
The Breaking of Northwall (1980)
The Dome in the Forest (1981)
The Ends of the Circle (1981)
The Fall of the Shell (1982)
An Ambush of Shadows (1983)
The Song of the Axe (1984)
The Sword of Forbearance (1985)
The Gifts of the Corboduc Vandal (1989)

WILLIAMS, WALTER JON
Ambassador of Progress (1984)
Knight Moves (1985)
Hard Wired (1986)
The Crown Jewels (1987)
Voice of the Whirlwind (1987)
House of Shards (1988)
Angel Station (1989)
Solip: System (1989)
Day of Atonement (1992)
Aristoi (1992)
Facets (1992)
Rock of Ages (1995)
Frankensteins and Foreign Devils (1998)

The Rift (1999)
Destiny's Way (2002)
The Praxis (2002)
The Sundering (2003)

WILLIAMSON, JACK

The Legion of Space (1947)
The Humanoids (1949)
The Cometeers (1950)
The Green Girl (1950)
Seetee Shock (1950, originally as by Will Stewart)
Seetee Ship (1951, originally as by Will Stewart)
Dragon's Island (1951, also published as *The Not-Men*)
The Legion of Time (1952, includes *After World's End*)
Undersea Quest (1954, with Frederik Pohl)
Dome Around America (1955)
Star Bridge (1955, with James Gunn)
Undersea Fleet (1956, with Frederik Pohl)
Undersea City (1958, with Frederik Pohl)
The Trial of Terra (1962)
The Reefs of Space (1964, with Frederik Pohl)
Starchild (1965, with Frederik Pohl)
Bright New Universe (1967)
One Against the Legion (1967)
Trapped in Space (1968)
The Pandora Effect (1969)
Rogue Star (1969, with Frederik Pohl)
People Machines (1971)
The Moon Children (1972)
The Early Williamson (1975)
Farthest Star (1975, with Frederik Pohl)
The Power of Blackness (1976)
Dreadful Sleep (1977)
The Starchild Trilogy (1977, with Frederik Pohl)
The Best of Jack Williamson (1978)
Brother to Demons, Brother to Gods (1979)
The Alien Intelligence (1980)
Three from the Legion (1980)
The Humanoid Touch (1980)
Birth of a New Republic (1981, with Miles J. Breuer)
Manseed (1982)
The Saga of Cuckoo (1983, with Frederik Pohl)
The Queen of the Legion (1983)
Wall Around a Star (1983, with Frederik Pohl)
Lifeburst (1984)

Firechild (1986)
Land's End (1988, with Frederik Pohl)
Into the Eighth Decade (1990)
Mazeway (1990)
The Singers of Time (1991, with Frederik Pohl)
Beachhead (1992)
The Undersea Trilogy (1992, with Frederik Pohl)
Demon Moon (1994)
The Black Sun (1997)
The Fortress of Utopia (1998)
The Prince of Space and The Girl from Mars (1998)
The Metal Man (1999)
The Silicon Dagger (1999)
Wolves of Darkness (1999)
The Ruler of Fate and Xandulu (1999)
Wizard's Isle (2000)
The Blue Spot & Entropy Reversed (2001)
The Stone from the Green Star (2001)
Terraforming Earth (2001)
Dragon's Island and Other Stories (2002)
Spider Island (2002)

WILLIS, CONNIE

Water Witch (1982, with Cynthia Felice)
Fire Watch (1985)
Lincoln's Dreams (1987)
Light Raid (1989, with Cynthia Felice)
Doomsday Book (1992)
Remake (1994)
Impossible Things (1994)
Uncharted Territory (1994)
The Bellwether (1996)
To Say Nothing of the Dog (1997)
Promised Land (1997, with Cynthia Felice)
Passage (2001)

WILSON, RICHARD

The Girls from Planet 5 (1955)
Those Idiots from Earth (1957)
30-Day Wonder (1960)
And Then the Town Took Off (1960)
Time out for Tomorrow (1962)

WILSON, ROBERT CHARLES

A Hidden Place (1986)
Memory Wire (1988)
Gypsies (1989)

Divide (1990)
A Bridge of Years (1991)
The Harvest (1993)
Mysterium (1994)
Darwinia (1998)
Bios (1999)
The Perseids and Other Stories (2000)
The Chronoliths (2001)
Blind Lake (2003)

WINGROVE, DAVID

The Middle Kingdom (1989)
The Broken Wheel (1990)
The White Mountain (1991)
The Stone Within (1991)
White Moon, Red Dragon (1991)
Beneath the Tree of Heaven (1993)
The Marriage of the Light and Dark (1996)
Days of Bitter Strength (1997)

WOLFE, GENE

Operation Ares (1970)
The Fifth Head of Cerberus (1972)
Gene Wolfe's Book of Days (1973)
The Island of Doctor Death and Other Stories and Other Stories (1980)
The Shadow of the Torturer (1981)
The Sword of the Lictor (1981)
The Claw of the Conciliator (1982)
The Citadel of the Autarch (1983)
The Wolfe Archipelago (1983)
Plan[e]t Engineering (1984)
The Urth of the New Sun (1987)
Storeys from an Old Hotel (1988)
Endangered Species (1989)
The Castle of Days (1992)
Young Wolfe (1992)
Nightside the Long Sun (1993)
Calde of the Long Sun (1994)
Lake of the Long Sun (1994)
Litany of the Long Sun (1994)
Sword and Citadel (1994)
Exodus of the Long Sun (1996)
On Blue's Waters (1999)
Epiphany of the Long Sun (2000)
Strange Travelers (2000)
In Green's Jungles (2000)

Shadow and Claw (2000)
Return to the Whorl (2001)

WOLLHEIM, DONALD A.

The Secret of Saturn's Rings (1954)
The Secret of the Martian Moons (1955)
One Against the Moon (1956)
Across Time (1957, as David Grinnell)
Edge of Time (1958, as David Grinnell)
The Secret of the Ninth Planet (1959)
The Martian Missile (1959, as David Grinnell)
Destiny's Orbit (1961, as David Grinnell)
Mike Mars Astronaut (1961)
Mike Mars Flies the X-15 (1961)
Mike Mars in Orbit (1961)
Mike Mars South Pole Spaceman (1962)
Mike Mars Flies by Dyna-Soar (1962)
Mike Mars and the Mystery Satellite (1963)
Mike Mars Around the Moon (1964)
Mike Mars at Cape Canaveral (1966, also published as *Mike Mars at Cape Kennedy*)
Two Dozen Dragon Eggs (1969)
Destination: Saturn (1970, as David Grinnell, with Lin Carter)
To Venus! To Venus! (1970, as David Grinnell)
The Men from Ariel (1982)
Up There and Other Strange Directions (1988)

WYLIE, PHILIP

Gladiator (1930)
The Murderer Invisible (1931)
When Worlds Collide (1933, with Edwin Balmer)
After Worlds Collide (1934, with Edwin Balmer)
The Disappearance (1951)
Tomorrow! (1954)
Triumph (1963)
Los Angeles: A.D. 2017 (1971)
The End of the Dream (1972)

WYNDHAM, JOHN

The Secret People (1935, originally as by John Beynon)
Planet Plane (1936, as John Beynon, later as *Stowaway to Mars* by Wyndham)
Love in Time (1946, as Johnson Harris)
The Day of the Triffids (1951, also published as *Revolt of the Triffids*)

Out of the Deeps (1953, also published as *The Kraken Wakes*)
Jizzle (1954)
Re-Birth (1955, also published as *The Chrysalids*)
The Seeds of Time (1956)
Tales of Gooseflesh and Laughter (1956)
The Midwich Cuckoos (1957, also published as *Village of the Damned*)
The Outward Urge (1959)
Trouble with Lichen (1960)
Consider Her Ways and Others (1961)
The Infinite Moment (1961)
The John Wyndham Omnibus (1964)
Chocky (1968)
Sleepers of Mars (1973, as John Beynon)
The Best of John Wyndham (1973, also published as *The Man from Beyond and Other Stories*)
Wanderers of Time (1973, as John Beynon)
The Best of John Wyndham 1932–1949 (1976)
The Best of John Wyndham 1951–1960 (1976)
Exiles on Asperus (1979, originally as John Beynon)
Web (1979)
John Wyndham (1980)

YOUNG, ROBERT F.
The Worlds of Robert F. Young (1965)
A Glass of Stars (1968)
Starfinder (1880)
The Last Yggdrasill (1982)
Eridahn (1983)

ZAHN, TIMOTHY
The Blackcollar (1983)
A Coming of Age (1984)
Cobra (1985)
Spinneret (1985)
Cascade Point (1986)
The Backlash Mission (1986)
Cobra Strike (1986)
Triplet (1987)
Cobra Bargain (1988)
Deadman Switch (1988)
Time Bomb and Zahndry Others (1988)
Warhorse (1990)
Heir to the Empire (1991)
Distant Friends and Others (1992)
Cobra Two (1992)

Dark Force Rising (1992)
The Last Command (1993)
Conquerors' Heritage (1995)
Conquerors' Legacy (1996)
Specter of the Past (1997)
Conquerors' Pride (1998)
Vision of the Future (1998)
The Icarus Hunt (1999)
Angelmass (2001)
Manta's Gift (2002)
Star Songs and Other Stories (2002)
Dragon and Thief (2003)
Survivor's Quest (2004)
Dragon and Soldier (2004)

ZEBROWSKI, GEORGE
The Omega Point (1972)
The Star Web (1975)
Ashes and Stars (1977)
The Monadic Universe (1977)
Macro-Life (1979)
The Omega Point Trilogy (1983)
Sunspacer (1984)
The Stars Will Speak (1985)
Stranger Suns (1991)
The Killing Star (1995, with Charles Pellegrino)
The Sunspacers Trilogy (1996)
A Fury Scorned (1996, with Pamela Sargent)
Heart of the Sun (1997, with Pamela Sargent)
Brute Orbits (1998)
Dyson Sphere (1999, with Charles Pellegrino)
Across the Universe (1999, with Pamela Sargent)
In the Distance, and Ahead in Time (2002)
Swift Thoughts (2002)
Garth of Izar (2003, with Pamela Sargent)

ZELAZNY, ROGER
The Dream Master (1966, also published as *He Who Shapes*)
This Immortal (1966)
Four for Tomorrow (1967)
Lord of Light (1967)
Creatures of Light and Darkness (1969)
Isle of the Dead (1969)
Damnation Alley (1969)
The Doors of His Face, the Lamps of His Mouth (1971)

Today We Choose Faces (1973)
To Die in Italbar (1973)
Deus Irae (1976, with Philip K. Dick)
My Name Is Legion (1976)
Bridge of Ashes (1976)
Doorways in the Sand (1976)
The Illustrated Zelazny (1978)
The Last Defender of Camelot (1980)

Roadmarks (1980)
Eye of Cat (1982)
Coils (1982, with Fred Saberhagen)
The Unicorn Variations (1983)
Frost and Fire (1989)
Gone to Earth (1991)
Flare (1992, with Thomas T. Thomas)
Donnerjack (1997, with Jane Lindskold)

SELECTED BIBLIOGRAPHY OF SECONDARY SOURCES

There are literally hundreds of reference books about science fiction, including histories, author profiles, criticism, and indices. Among those that proved most useful in the preparation of this book are the following:

Aldiss, Brian W. *The Trillion Year Spree*. New York: Avon, 1986.

Blish, James. *The Issue at Hand*. Chicago: Advent, 1964.

Broderick, Damien. *Transrealist Fiction*. Westport, Conn.: Greenwood, 2000.

Clareson, Thomas. *Science Fiction in America 1870–1930*. Westport, Conn.: Greenwood, 1984.

Clute, John, and Nicholls, Peter, eds. *The Encyclopedia of Science Fiction*. New York: St. Martin's Press, 1993.

Disch, Thomas. *The Dreams Our Stuff Is Made Of*. New York: Touchstone, 1998.

Easton, Thomas. *Periodic Stars*. San Bernardino, Calif.: Borgo, 1997.

Franson, Donald. *The History of the Hugo and Nebula Awards*. Chicago: Misfit, 1981.

Gunn, James. *Alternate Worlds*. Englewood Cliffs, N.J.: Prentice Hall, 1975.

Harbottle, Phil, and Holland, Steve. *British Science Fiction Paperbacks*. San Bernardino, Calif.: Borgo, 1994.

Hartwell, David. *Age of Wonders*. New York: McGraw-Hill, 1984.

Knight, Damon. *In Search of Wonder*. Chicago: Advent, 1956.

Knight, Damon, ed. *Turning Points*. New York: Harper & Row, 1977.

Lerner, Fred. *Modern Science Fiction and the Literary Community*. Metuchen, N.J.: Scarecrow, 1985.

Malzberg, Barry. *Engines of the Night*. Garden City, N.Y.: Doubleday, 1982.

Moskowitz, Sam. *Explorers of the Infinite*. New York: Meridian, 1963.

Moskowitz, Sam. *Seekers of Tomorrow*. New York: Ballantine Books. 1966.

Moskowitz, Sam. *Strange Horizons*, New York: Anchor Books. 1976.

Panshin, Alexei and Cory. *The World Beyond the Hill*. Los Angeles: Tarcher, 1989.

Pederson, Jay P., ed. *St. James Guide to Science Fiction Writers*. Chicago: St. James Press, 1996.

Pierce, John J. *The Foundations of Science Fiction*. Westport, Conn.: Greenwood, 1987.

Pringle, David. *Science Fiction: 100 Best Novels*. New York: Carroll & Graf, 1985.

Reginald, Robert. *Science Fiction and Fantasy Literature*. Chicago: Gale, 1979.

Rogers, Alva. *A Requiem for Astounding*. Chicago: Advent, 1964.

Schmidt, Stanley. *Which Way to the Future?* New York: Tor, 2001.

Searles, Baird. *The Readers' Guide to Science Fiction*. New York: Avon Books, 1979.

Stableford, Brian. *The Sociology of Science Fiction*. San Bernardino, Calif.: Borgo, 1987.

Suvin, Darko. *Positions and Presuppositions in Science Fiction*. Kent, Ohio: Kent State University Press, 1988.

Tuck, Donald. *The Encyclopedia of Science Fiction*, 3 vols. Chicago: Advent, 1974/78/82.

Westfahl, Gary. *Cosmic Engineers*. Wesport, Conn.: Greenwood, 1996.

INDEX

Note: **Boldface** page numbers indicate major treatment of the topic.

supernatural fiction 48. *See also* horror fiction
superstition 268, 422–423
"Super Toys Last All Summer Long" (Aldiss) 4
Supspacers trilogy (Zebrowski) 432
Surface Action (Drake) 124
surreal fiction 266
The Surveillance. See Intervention
Survey Ship (Bradley, M.) 54
Survival (Czerneda) 100
The Survivor (Kingsbury) 209
The Survivors (Bradley, M.) 54
suspended animation 16, 20
Sutton, Jeff **367**
Swann, S. Andrew **368**
Swanwick, Michael 161, **368–369**
Swiniarski, S. A. *See* Swann, S. Andrew
The Sword of Aldones (Bradley, M.) 102
The Sword of Forbearance (Williams, P.) 417
The Sword of Rhiannon (Brackett) 51
The Sword of the Spirits (Christopher) 83
Synaptic Manhunt (Farren) 140
The Syndic (Kornbluth) 213
Synners (Cadigan) 68
Synthajoy (Compton) 91–92
The Synthetic Man. See The Dreaming Jewels
Systemic Shock (Ing) 196

T

Tactics of Conquest (Malzberg) 242
Taflak Lysandra (Smith, L.) 348
Taine, John 166
Takei, George 19
Takeoff (Kornbluth) 213
Talents, Incorporated (Leinster) 227
A Talent for War (McDevitt) 251
Tales of the Grand Tour (Bova) 50
Tale of the Troika (Strugatsky and Strugatsky) 364
A Tale of Two Clocks (Schmitz) 324–325
Tam, Son of the Tiger (Kline) 210
Tambu (Asprin) 19
"Tangents" (Bear) **370**
Tangled Up in Blue (Vinge, J.) 395
A Tapestry of Time (Cowper) 96
Tarot trilogy (Anthony) 15
Tarzan 139
Tarzan at the Earth's Core (Burroughs, E.) 64, 286
Tarzan and the Valley of Gold (Leiber) 226
Tatja Grimm's World. See Grimm's World
Tau Zero (Anderson, P.) 12
Tea from an Empty Cup (Cadigan) 68
Tech Heaven (Nagata) 265
technology. *See* computers and technology
Teek (Swann) 368
Telempath (Robinson, S.) 312
Telepathist. See The Whole Man
telepathy 125–126
The Telling (Le Guin) 223
Telzey Amberdon series (Schmitz) 324–325, **370–371**
Tendeleo's Story (McDonald) 252
Tenn, William 122, 146, **371**
The Tenth Victim. See "The Seventh Victim"

Ten Years After (Cover) 96
Tepper, Sheri S. **371–373**
Teranesia (Egan) 130
Terminal Café (McDonald) 252
The Terminal Experiment (Sawyer) 323
The Terminal Man (Crichton) 97
Terminal Velocity. See Veritgo
Terraforming Earth (Williamson) 419
The Texas-Israeli War (Waldrop and Saunders) 400–401
The Texts of Festival (Farren) 140
That Hideous Strength (Lewis) 231
Their Majesties' Bucketeers (Smith, L.) 348
Them Bones (Waldrop) 401
There Is No Darkness (Haldeman and Haldeman) 174
They Walked Like Men (Simak) 338–339
The Thing (film) 70
"Thing's Ransom" (Allen) 434
The Third Ear (Siodmak) 341
Thirst!. See The Tide Went Out
The Thirteenth Immortal (Silverberg) 336
30 Day Wonder (Wilson, Richard) 420
Thirty Four East (Coppel) 94
This Fortress World (Gunn) 171
This Immortal (Zelazny) **373**
This Island Earth (Jones, R.) 204
This Perfect Day (Levin, I.) 360
This Star Shall Abide (Engdahl) 134
Thomas, Theodore L. 415–416
Thomas, Thomas A. 290
Thomas, Thomas T. 434
Thorns (Silverberg) 337
Those Gentle Voices (Effinger) 129
Those Who Favor Fire (Randall) 299
Thousandstar (Anthony) 14–15
A Thousand Words for Stranger (Czerneda) 100
Three to Conquer (Russell) 316
Three Laws of Robotics (Asimov) 7, 194. *See also* Robot series
The Three Stigmata of Palmer Eldritch (Dick) 115, **373–374**
334 (Disch) 119
Threshold of Eternity (Brunner) 58
Thrice Upon a Time (Hogan) 187
Through Darkest America (Barrett) 28
Through the Eye of the Needle (Clement) 87
Thunderhead (Preston and Child) 293
"Thunder and Roses" (Sturgeon) **374**
The Ticket That Exploded (Burrough, W.) 66
"A Ticket to Tranai" (Sheckley) **374–375**
The Tide Went Out (Maine) 240
Tiger! Tiger!. See The Stars, My Destination
Tik-Tok (Sladek) 342
Tilley, Patrick **375**
Time After Time (Alexander) 410
Time and Again (Finney) 143
Time and Again (Simak) 338
The Time Axis (Kuttner) 216
Time Bomb (Tucker) 380
A Time of Changes (Silverberg) 337
Time Considered As a Helix of Semi-Precious Stones (Delany) **375–376**

time-dilation effect 167–168
The Time Factor. See First Through Time
Time Is the Simplest Thing (Simak) 338
Timeline (Crichton) 97
Timeliner (Maine) 240
The Time Machine (Wells) 29, **376–377**, 409
Time Machine II (Pal and Morhaim) 377
The Time Masters (Tucker) 380
Time Out of Joint (Dick) 115
Time Out of Mind (Cowper) 96
Time Patrol series (Anderson, P.) 11–12, **377**
Time Pressure (Robinson, S.) 312
Timequake (Vonnegut) 399
Time Safari (Drake) 124
Timescape (Benford) 33–34
Timescape (Engdahl) 134
Timescoop (Brunner) 59
The Time Ships (Baxter) 29, 376
Time Slave (Norman) 273
Time for the Stars (Heinlein) 182
Timestop!. See A Woman a Day
Time Storm (Dickson) 117
Times Without Number (Brunner) 58
The Time Traders (Norton) 274
time travel. *See also* lost-world stories
  in "All You Zombies" (Heinlein) 5–6
  in Anderson, Poul 11–12
  in Asprin, Robert 19
  in Finney, Jack 143
  in "A Gun for Dinosaur" (de Camp) 170
  in "The Gun Without a Bang" (Sheckley) 170–171
  in "In Entropy's Jaws" (Silverberg) 195–196
  in *Lest Darkness Fall* (de Camp) 230
  in *No Enemy But Time* (Bishop) 271–272
  in "The Old Die Rich" (Gold) 278–279
  in "Such Interesting Neighbors" (Finney) 366
  in *The Time Machine* (Wells) 375
  in *The Trinity Paradox* (Anderson, K.) 20
  in *Vintage Season* (Moore and Kuttner) 397
time travel paradoxes 5–6, 67, 256–257, 348–349
The Time Wanderers (Strugatsky and Strugatsky) 364
Tiptree, James, Jr. 8–9, 161–162, 189–190, 237, **377–378**, 425–426
Titan (Baxter) 29
Titan (Varley) 391
To Bring the Light (Drake) 124
To Bring in the Steel (Kingsbury) 209
To Conquer Chaos (Brunner) 58
Today We Choose Faces (Zelazny) 433
To Live Again (Silverberg) 337
To Live Forever (Vance) 389
"To Marry Medusa." *See The Cosmic Rape*
Tom Dunjer series (Haiblum) 173